Official 1988 National Football League Record & Fact Book

A National Football League Book.
Workman Publishing Co., New York.

National Football League, 1988

410 Park Avenue, New York, N.Y. 10022 (212) 758-1500

Commissioner: Pete Rozelle
Executive Vice President & League Counsel: Jay Moyer
Treasurer: John Schoemer
Executive Director: Don Weiss
Director of Administration: Joe Rhein
Director of Communications: Joe Browne
Director of Operations: Jan Van Duser
Director of Broadcasting: Val Pinchbeck, Jr.
Assistant Director of Broadcasting: Nancy Behar
Director of Public Relations: Jim Heffernan
Director of Security: Warren Welsh
Assistant Director of Security: Charles R. Jackson
Director of Player Personnel: Joel Bussert
Supervisor of Officials: Art McNally
Assistant Supervisors of Officials: Jack Reader, Joe Gardi, Tony Veteri
Director of Special Events: Jim Steeg
Assistant Director of Special Events: Susan McCann Minogue
Director of Equal Employment & Assistant Counsel: David Cornwell
Director of Personnel: John Buzzeo
Controller: Tom Sullivan
Special Projects Manager: Bill Granholm
Director of Player Relations: Mel Blount
Operations Assistant: Frank Cuce

American Football Conference

President: Lamar Hunt, Kansas City Chiefs
Assistant to President: Roger Goodell
Director of Information: Pete Abitante

National Football Conference

President: Wellington Mara, New York Giants
Assistant to President: Jim Noel
Director of Information: Dick Maxwell

Cover Photograph by Rob Brown.

Printed in the United States of America.

A National Football League Book.
Compiled by the NFL Public Relations Department and Seymour Siwoff, Elias Sports Bureau.
Edited by Pete Abitante, NFL Public Relations and Chuck Garrity, Jr., NFLP Creative Services.
Statistics by Elias Sports Bureau.
Produced by NFL Properties, Inc., Creative Services Division.

Workman Publishing Co.
708 Broadway, New York, N.Y. 10003
Manufactured in the United States of America.
First printing, July 1988.
10 9 8 7 6 5 4 3 2 1

Contents

A
Active List 12
AFC vs. NFC, 1970-87 287
All-Pro Teams, 1987 166
Atlanta Falcons 84
Attendance, NFL's 10 Biggest Weekends 296
Attendance, 1987 209
Attendance, Paid 296
Awards, 1987 165

B
Buffalo Bills 26

C
Calendar, 1988-1991 11
Chicago All-Star Game 295
Chicago Bears 88
Chronology of Professional Football 230
Cincinnati Bengals 30
Cleveland Browns 34
Coaches, Active, Career Victories 22
Coaches, 100 Career Victories 22

D
Dallas Cowboys 92
Denver Broncos 38
Detroit Lions 96
Draft, All-Time Number-One Choices 297
Draft, 1988 20

F
First-Round Selections 298

G
Green Bay Packers 100

H
Houston Oilers 42

I
Indianapolis Colts 46
Instant Replay 16
International Games 295

K
Kansas City Chiefs 50

L
Los Angeles Raiders 54
Los Angeles Rams 104

M
Miami Dolphins 58
Minnesota Vikings 108
Monday Night Football 288

N
New England Patriots 62
New Orleans Saints 112
New York Giants 116
New York Jets 66
1987 Season Recap
- 1987 Preseason Standings and Results 143
- 1987 Regular-Season Standings and Results 144
- 1987 Ten Best Passing Performances 169
- 1987 Ten Best Pass Receiving Performances 170
- 1987 Ten Best Rushing Performances 168
- 1987 Week by Week 146

O
Official Signals 358
Officials, 1988 Roster of 356
Overtime, History of 291

P
Passer Rating System 17
Philadelphia Eagles 120
Phoenix Cardinals 124
Pittsburgh Steelers 70
Playoff Bowl 295
Playoff Games
- AFC Championship Games 275
- AFC Divisional Playoff Games 278
- AFC First-Round Playoff Games 280
- NFC Championship Games 276
- NFC Divisional Playoff Games 279
- NFC First-Round Playoff Games 281

Pro Bowl, Game Summaries 282
Pro Bowl, Records 351
Pro Football Hall of Fame 226
Pro Football Hall of Fame Games 295

R
Records, All-Time 304
Records, Postseason 342
Reserve Lists 12
Roster Limits 12
Rules, Digest of 362

S
San Diego Chargers 74
San Francisco 49ers 128
Schedule, Figuring 1989 14
Schedule, 1988 Season 4
Scoring, Top 10 Weekends 296
Seattle Seahawks 78
Standings, 1920-87 238
Statistics
- AFC Active Leaders 18
- Inside the Numbers, Statistical Highlights 212
- NFC Active Leaders 19
- Outstanding Performers 324
- What to Look for in 1988 23
- Yearly Leaders 329

Statistics, 1987
- AFC, NFC, and NFL Summary 176
- American Football Conference Team Defense 173
- American Football Conference Team Offense 172
- Club Leaders 177
- Club Rankings by Yards 177
- Individual Field Goals 181
- Individual Fumbles 201
- Individual Interceptions 193
- Individual Kickoff Returns 198
- Individual Passing 187
- Individual Pass Receiving 190
- Individual Punting 196
- Individual Punt Returns 197
- Individual Rushing 183
- Individual Sacks 206
- Individual Scoring 178
- National Football Conference Team Defense 175
- National Football Conference Team Offense 174
- Takeaway-Giveaway Table 177

Super Bowl, Game Summaries 269
Super Bowl, Records 335

T
Tampa Bay Buccaneers 132
Team vs. Team Results 245
Television, 10 Most Watched Programs in TV History 296
Television, Top 10 Televised Sports Events 296
Tie-Breaking Procedures 13
Trades, 1987-88 142
Trading Period 12

W
Waivers 12
Washington Redskins 136

1988 SCHEDULE AND NOTE CALENDAR

All times P.M. local daylight.
Nationally televised games in parentheses. CBS and NBC television doubleheader games in the regular season to be announced.

Preseason/First Week

Saturday, July 30	Hall of Fame Game at Canton, Ohio Cincinnati ___ vs. Los Angeles Rams ___	(ABC) 2:30
Sunday, July 31	American Bowl '88 at London, England Miami ___ vs. San Francisco ___	(NBC) 6:00
Wednesday, August 3	Denver ___ at Los Angeles Rams ___	7:00
Thursday, August 4	Buffalo ___ at Houston ___	7:00
	Phoenix ___ at Seattle ___	7:30
Friday, August 5	Pittsburgh ___ at Washington ___	8:00
Saturday, August 6	Atlanta ___ at New England ___	7:00
	Cincinnati ___ at Kansas City ___	7:30
	Dallas ___ at San Diego ___	6:00
	Detroit ___ at Cleveland ___	7:00
	Indianapolis ___ at Tampa Bay ___	7:00
	Los Angeles Raiders ___ at San Francisco ___	(CBS) 6:00
	Miami ___ at Chicago ___	6:00
	New York Giants ___ at Green Bay ___	7:00
	New York Jets ___ at Philadelphia ___	7:30
Sunday, August 7	New Orleans ___ at Minnesota ___	(ESPN) 7:00

Preseason/Second Week

Thursday, August 11	Seattle ___ at Detroit ___	7:30
Friday, August 12	New Orleans ___ at Phoenix ___	7:30
Saturday, August 13	Cincinnati ___ at Buffalo ___	7:30
	Cleveland ___ at Tampa Bay ___	7:00
	Dallas ___ at Los Angeles Raiders ___	1:00
	Green Bay ___ at Indianapolis ___	7:30
	Houston ___ vs. New England ___ at Memphis, Tenn.	7:00
	Kansas City ___ at Atlanta ___	7:30
	New York Jets ___ at New York Giants ___	8:00
	San Diego ___ at Los Angeles Rams ___	8:00
	San Francisco ___ at Denver ___	7:00
	Washington ___ at Miami ___	(ABC) 8:00
Sunday, August 14	Chicago ___ vs. Minnesota ___ at Gothenburg, Sweden	(CBS) 7:00
	Philadelphia ___ at Pittsburgh ___	(ESPN) 8:00

Preseason/Third Week

Thursday, August 18	Cleveland ___ vs. New York Jets ___ at Montreal, Canada	7:30
Friday, August 19	Buffalo ___ at Seattle ___	7:30
	Denver ___ at Miami ___	(NBC) 9:00
	Kansas City ___ vs. Green Bay ___ at Milwaukee	7:00
Saturday, August 20	Detroit ___ at Cincinnati ___	7:30
	Houston ___ at Los Angeles Rams ___	7:00
	New England ___ at Philadelphia ___	7:30
	New Orleans ___ at Indianapolis ___	7:30
	Pittsburgh ___ at New York Giants ___	8:00
	San Francisco ___ at San Diego ___	6:00
	Tampa Bay ___ at Atlanta ___	7:30
	Washington ___ at Los Angeles Raiders ___	(CBS) 7:00
Sunday, August 21	Minnesota ___ at Phoenix ___	(ESPN) 5:00
Monday, August 22	Chicago ___ at Dallas ___	(ABC) 7:00

Preseason/Fourth Week

Thursday, August 25	Buffalo ___ vs. Tampa Bay ___ at Nashville, Tenn.	7:00
	Indianapolis ___ at Denver ___	(ESPN) 6:00
	Philadelphia ___ at Detroit ___	7:30
	Phoenix ___ at Kansas City ___	7:30
Friday, August 26	Cincinnati ___ at New England ___	7:00
	Los Angeles Raiders ___ at Chicago ___	8:00
	Los Angeles Rams ___ at San Diego ___	8:00
	Miami ___ at Minnesota ___	7:00
	New York Giants ___ at Cleveland ___	(NBC) 9:00
	Seattle ___ at San Francisco ___	6:00
Saturday, August 27	Atlanta ___ vs. Washington ___ at Birmingham, Ala.	7:00
	Houston ___ at Dallas ___	8:00
	New York Jets ___ vs. Green Bay ___ at Madison, Wis.	1:00
	Pittsburgh ___ at New Orleans ___	(ABC) 11:30 A.M.

First Week

Sunday, September 4 (NBC-TV doubleheader)	Atlanta ___ at Detroit ___	1:00
	Cleveland ___ at Kansas City ___	3:00
	Dallas ___ at Pittsburgh ___	1:00
	Houston ___ at Indianapolis ___	3:00
	Los Angeles Rams ___ at Green Bay ___	12:00
	Miami ___ at Chicago ___	12:00
	Minnesota ___ at Buffalo ___	1:00
	New York Jets ___ at New England ___	4:00
	Philadelphia ___ at Tampa Bay ___	1:00
	Phoenix ___ at Cincinnati ___	1:00
	San Diego ___ at Los Angeles Raiders ___	1:00
	San Francisco ___ at New Orleans ___	12:00
	Seattle ___ at Denver ___	2:00
Monday, September 5	Washington ___ at New York Giants ___	(ABC) 9:00

Second Week

Sunday, September 11 (NBC-TV doubleheader)	Chicago ___ at Indianapolis ___	12:00
	Cincinnati ___ at Philadelphia ___	4:00
	Detroit ___ at Los Angeles Rams ___	1:00
	Kansas City ___ at Seattle ___	1:00
	Los Angeles Raiders ___ at Houston ___	3:00
	Miami ___ at Buffalo ___	1:00
	New England ___ at Minnesota ___	3:00
	New Orleans ___ at Atlanta ___	1:00
	New York Jets ___ at Cleveland ___	4:00
	Pittsburgh ___ at Washington ___	1:00
	San Diego ___ at Denver ___	2:00
	San Francisco ___ at New York Giants ___	1:00
	Tampa Bay ___ at Green Bay ___	12:00
Monday, September 12	Dallas ___ at Phoenix ___	(ABC) 6:00

Third Week

Sunday, September 18 (CBS-TV doubleheader)	Atlanta ___ at San Francisco ___	1:00
	Buffalo ___ at New England ___	1:00
	Cincinnati ___ at Pittsburgh ___	1:00
	Denver ___ at Kansas City ___	12:00
	Green Bay ___ at Miami ___	1:00
	Houston ___ at New York Jets ___	1:00
	Los Angeles Rams ___ at Los Angeles Raiders ___	1:00
	Minnesota ___ at Chicago ___	12:00
	New Orleans ___ at Detroit ___	1:00
	New York Giants ___ at Dallas ___	3:00
	Philadelphia ___ at Washington ___	1:00
	Phoenix ___ at Tampa Bay ___	1:00
	Seattle ___ at San Diego ___	1:00
Monday, September 19	Indianapolis ___ at Cleveland ___	(ABC) 8:00

Fourth Week

Sunday, September 25 (CBS-TV doubleheader)	Atlanta ___ at Dallas ___		12:00
	Chicago ___ at Green Bay ___		12:00
	Cleveland ___ at Cincinnati ___		1:00
	Los Angeles Rams ___ at New York Giants ___		4:00
	Miami ___ at Indianapolis ___		12:00
	New England ___ at Houston ___		12:00
	New York Jets ___ at Detroit ___		1:00
	Philadelphia ___ at Minnesota ___		12:00
	Pittsburgh ___ at Buffalo ___		1:00
	San Diego ___ at Kansas City ___		3:00
	San Francisco ___ at Seattle ___		1:00
	Tampa Bay ___ at New Orleans ___		12:00
	Washington ___ at Phoenix ___		1:00
Monday, September 26	Los Angeles Raiders ___ at Denver ___	(ABC)	6:00

Fifth Week

Sunday, October 2 (CBS-TV doubleheader)	Buffalo ___ at Chicago ___		12:00
	Cincinnati ___ at Los Angeles Raiders ___		1:00
	Cleveland ___ at Pittsburgh ___		1:00
	Denver ___ at San Diego ___		1:00
	Detroit ___ at San Francisco ___		1:00
	Green Bay ___ at Tampa Bay ___		1:00
	Houston ___ at Philadelphia ___		1:00
	Indianapolis ___ at New England ___		1:00
	Kansas City ___ at New York Jets ___		4:00
	Minnesota ___ at Miami ___		4:00
	New York Giants ___ at Washington ___		1:00
	Phoenix ___ at Los Angeles Rams ___		1:00
	Seattle ___ at Atlanta ___		1:00
Monday, October 3	Dallas ___ at New Orleans ___	(ABC)	8:00

Sixth Week

Sunday, October 9 (NBC-TV doubleheader)	Chicago ___ at Detroit ___		1:00
	Denver ___ at San Francisco ___		1:00
	Indianapolis ___ at Buffalo ___		1:00
	Kansas City ___ at Houston ___		12:00
	Los Angeles Rams ___ at Atlanta ___		1:00
	Miami ___ at Los Angeles Raiders ___		1:00
	New England ___ vs. Green Bay ___ at Milwaukee		12:00
	New Orleans ___ at San Diego ___		1:00
	New York Jets ___ at Cincinnati ___		1:00
	Pittsburgh ___ at Phoenix ___		1:00
	Seattle ___ at Cleveland ___		1:00
	Tampa Bay ___ at Minnesota ___		12:00
	Washington ___ at Dallas ___		12:00
Monday, October 10	New York Giants ___ at Philadelphia ___	(ABC)	9:00

Seventh Week

Sunday, October 16 (CBS-TV doubleheader)	Atlanta ___ at Denver ___		2:00
	Cincinnati ___ at New England ___		1:00
	Dallas ___ at Chicago ___		12:00
	Detroit ___ at New York Giants ___		1:00
	Green Bay ___ at Minnesota ___		12:00
	Houston ___ at Pittsburgh ___		1:00
	Los Angeles Raiders ___ at Kansas City ___		12:00
	New Orleans ___ at Seattle ___		1:00
	Philadelphia ___ at Cleveland ___		1:00
	Phoenix ___ at Washington ___		1:00
	San Diego ___ at Miami ___		1:00
	San Francisco ___ at Los Angeles Rams ___		1:00
	Tampa Bay ___ at Indianapolis ___		12:00
Monday, October 17	Buffalo ___ at New York Jets ___	(ABC)	9:00

Eighth Week

Sunday, October 23 (NBC-TV doubleheader)	Cleveland ___ at Phoenix ___		1:00
	Dallas ___ at Philadelphia ___		1:00
	Denver ___ at Pittsburgh ___		1:00
	Detroit ___ at Kansas City ___		12:00
	Houston ___ at Cincinnati ___		1:00
	Indianapolis ___ at San Diego ___		1:00
	Los Angeles Raiders ___ at New Orleans ___		12:00
	Minnesota ___ at Tampa Bay ___		1:00
	New England ___ at Buffalo ___		1:00
	New York Giants ___ at Atlanta ___		1:00
	New York Jets ___ at Miami ___		4:00
	Seattle ___ at Los Angeles Rams ___		1:00
	Washington ___ vs. Green Bay ___ at Milwaukee		12:00
Monday, October 24	San Francisco ___ at Chicago ___	(ABC)	8:00

Ninth Week

Sunday, October 30 (CBS-TV doubleheader)	Atlanta ___ at Philadelphia ___		1:00
	Chicago ___ at New England ___		1:00
	Cincinnati ___ at Cleveland ___		1:00
	Green Bay ___ at Buffalo ___		1:00
	Kansas City ___ at Los Angeles Raiders ___		1:00
	Los Angeles Rams ___ at New Orleans ___		12:00
	Miami ___ at Tampa Bay ___		1:00
	Minnesota ___ at San Francisco ___		1:00
	New York Giants ___ at Detroit ___		4:00
	Phoenix ___ at Dallas ___		12:00
	Pittsburgh ___ at New York Jets ___		1:00
	San Diego ___ at Seattle ___		1:00
Sunday Night	Washington ___ at Houston ___	(ESPN)	7:00
Monday, October 31	Denver ___ at Indianapolis ___	(ABC)	9:00

Tenth Week

Sunday, November 6 (CBS-TV doubleheader)	Buffalo ___ at Seattle ___		1:00
	Dallas ___ at New York Giants ___		1:00
	Detroit ___ at Minnesota ___		12:00
	Green Bay ___ at Atlanta ___		1:00
	Kansas City ___ at Denver ___		2:00
	Los Angeles Rams ___ at Philadelphia ___		1:00
	Miami ___ at New England ___		1:00
	New Orleans ___ at Washington ___		4:00
	New York Jets ___ at Indianapolis ___		4:00
	Pittsburgh ___ at Cincinnati ___		1:00
	San Francisco ___ at Phoenix ___		2:00
	Tampa Bay ___ at Chicago ___		12:00
Sunday Night	Los Angeles Raiders ___ at San Diego ___	(ESPN)	5:00
Monday, November 7	Cleveland ___ at Houston ___	(ABC)	8:00

Eleventh Week

Sunday, November 13 (NBC-TV doubleheader)	Chicago ___ at Washington ___		1:00
	Cincinnati ___ at Kansas City ___		12:00
	Cleveland ___ at Denver ___		2:00
	Houston ___ at Seattle ___		1:00
	Indianapolis ___ at Green Bay ___		12:00
	Los Angeles Raiders ___ at San Francisco ___		1:00
	New England ___ at New York Jets ___		1:00
	New Orleans ___ at Los Angeles Rams ___		1:00
	New York Giants ___ at Phoenix ___		2:00
	Philadelphia ___ at Pittsburgh ___		1:00
	San Diego ___ at Atlanta ___		1:00
	Tampa Bay ___ at Detroit ___		1:00
Sunday Night	Minnesota ___ at Dallas ___	(ESPN)	7:00
Monday, November 14	Buffalo ___ at Miami ___	(ABC)	9:00

Twelfth Week

Date	Game	Network	Time
Sunday, November 20 (NBC-TV doubleheader)	Atlanta ___ at Los Angeles Raiders ___		1:00
	Chicago ___ at Tampa Bay ___		1:00
	Cincinnati ___ at Dallas ___		12:00
	Denver ___ at New Orleans ___		12:00
	Detroit ___ vs. Green Bay ___ at Milwaukee		12:00
	Indianapolis ___ at Minnesota ___		12:00
	New York Jets ___ at Buffalo ___		1:00
	Philadelphia ___ at New York Giants ___		4:00
	Phoenix ___ at Houston ___		12:00
	Pittsburgh ___ at Cleveland ___		1:00
	San Diego ___ at Los Angeles Rams ___		1:00
	Seattle ___ at Kansas City ___		12:00
Sunday Night	New England ___ at Miami ___	(ESPN)	8:00
Monday, November 21	Washington ___ at San Francisco ___	(ABC)	6:00

Thirteenth Week

Date	Game	Network	Time
Thursday, November 24 Thanksgiving Day	Houston ___ at Dallas ___	(NBC)	3:00
	Minnesota ___ at Detroit ___	(CBS)	12:30
Sunday, November 27 (CBS-TV doubleheader)	Buffalo ___ at Cincinnati ___		1:00
	Cleveland ___ at Washington ___		1:00
	Green Bay ___ at Chicago ___		12:00
	Kansas City ___ at Pittsburgh ___		1:00
	Los Angeles Rams ___ at Denver ___		2:00
	Miami ___ at New York Jets ___		1:00
	New England ___ at Indianapolis ___		4:00
	Phoenix ___ at Philadelphia ___		1:00
	San Francisco ___ at San Diego ___		1:00
	Tampa Bay ___ at Atlanta ___		1:00
Sunday Night	New York Giants ___ at New Orleans ___	(ESPN)	7:00
Monday, November 28	Los Angeles Raiders ___ at Seattle ___	(ABC)	6:00

Fourteenth Week

Date	Game	Network	Time
Sunday, December 4 (NBC-TV doubleheader)	Buffalo ___ at Tampa Bay ___		1:00
	Dallas ___ at Cleveland ___		1:00
	Denver ___ at Los Angeles Raiders ___		1:00
	Green Bay ___ at Detroit ___		1:00
	Indianapolis ___ at Miami ___		1:00
	New Orleans ___ at Minnesota ___		12:00
	New York Jets ___ at Kansas City ___		3:00
	Phoenix ___ at New York Giants ___		1:00
	San Diego ___ at Cincinnati ___		1:00
	San Francisco ___ at Atlanta ___		1:00
	Seattle ___ at New England ___		1:00
	Washington ___ at Philadelphia ___		1:00
Sunday Night	Pittsburgh ___ at Houston ___	(ESPN)	7:00
Monday, December 5	Chicago ___ at Los Angeles Rams ___	(ABC)	6:00

Fifteenth Week

Date	Game	Network	Time
Saturday, December 10	Indianapolis ___ at New York Jets ___	(NBC)	12:30
	Philadelphia ___ at Phoenix ___	(CBS)	2:00
Sunday, December 11 (CBS-TV doubleheader)	Atlanta ___ at Los Angeles Rams ___		1:00
	Cincinnati ___ at Houston ___		12:00
	Dallas ___ at Washington ___		1:00
	Detroit ___ at Chicago ___		12:00
	Kansas City ___ at New York Giants ___		1:00
	Los Angeles Raiders ___ at Buffalo ___		1:00
	Minnesota ___ at Green Bay ___		12:00
	New Orleans ___ at San Francisco ___		1:00
	Pittsburgh ___ at San Diego ___		1:00
	Tampa Bay ___ at New England ___		1:00
Sunday Night	Denver ___ at Seattle ___	(ESPN)	5:00
Monday, December 12	Cleveland ___ at Miami ___	(ABC)	9:00

Sixteenth Week

Saturday, December 17	New England ___ at Denver ___	(NBC)	2:00
	Washington ___ at Cincinnati ___	(CBS)	12:30
Sunday, December 18 (NBC-TV doubleheader)	Atlanta ___ at New Orleans ___		12:00
	Buffalo ___ at Indianapolis ___		1:00
	Detroit ___ at Tampa Bay ___		1:00
	Green Bay ___ at Phoenix ___		2:00
	Houston ___ at Cleveland ___		1:00
	Kansas City ___ at San Diego ___		1:00
	Miami ___ at Pittsburgh ___		1:00
	New York Giants ___ at New York Jets ___		1:00
	Philadelphia ___ at Dallas ___		12:00
	Seattle ___ at Los Angeles Raiders ___		1:00
Sunday Night	Los Angeles Rams ___ at San Francisco ___	(ESPN)	5:00
Monday, December 19	Chicago ___ at Minnesota ___	(ABC)	8:00

First-Round Playoff Games

Site Priorities
Two wild card teams (fourth- and fifth-best records) from each conference will enter the first round of the playoffs. The wild cards from the same conference will play each other. Home clubs will be the clubs with the best won-lost-tied percentage in the regular season. If tied in record, the tie will be broken by the tie-breaking procedures already in effect.

Saturday, December 24, 1988
American Football Conference

___ at ___ (NBC)

Monday, December 26, 1988
National Football Conference

___ at ___ (CBS)

Divisional Playoff Games

Site Priorities
In each conference, the two division winners with the highest won-lost-tied percentage during the regular season will be the home teams. The division winner with the best percentage will be host to the wild card winner from the first-round playoff, and the division winner with the second-best percentage will be host to the third division winner, unless the wild card team is from the same division as the winner with the highest percentage. In that case, the division winner with the best percentage will be host to the third division winner and the second highest division winner will be host to the wild card.

Saturday, December 31, 1988
American Football Conference

___ at ___ (NBC)

National Football Conference

___ at ___ (CBS)

Sunday, January 1, 1989
American Football Conference

___ at ___ (NBC)

National Football Conference

___ at ___ (CBS)

Conference Championship Games, Super Bowl XXIII, and AFC-NFC Pro Bowl

Site Priorities for Championship Games
The home teams will be the surviving divisional playoff winners with the best won-lost-tied percentage during the regular season. The wild card team will never be the home team, in either the divisional playoffs or the championship games. Any ties in won-lost-tied percentage will be broken by the tie-breaking procedures already in effect.

Sunday, January 8, 1989
American Football Conference Championship Game

___ at ___ (NBC)

National Football Conference Championship Game

___ at ___ (CBS)

Sunday, January 22, 1989
Super Bowl XXIII at Joe Robbie Stadium, Miami, Florida

___ vs. ___ (NBC)

Sunday, January 29, 1989
AFC-NFC Pro Bowl at Honolulu, Hawaii

AFC ___ vs. NFC ___ (ESPN)

Postseason Games

Saturday, December 24	AFC First-Round Playoff (NBC)
Monday, December 26	NFC First-Round Playoff (CBS)
Saturday, December 31	AFC and NFC Divisional Playoffs (NBC and CBS)
Sunday, January 1	AFC and NFC Divisional Playoffs (NBC and CBS)
Sunday, January 8	AFC and NFC Championship Games (NBC and CBS)
Sunday, January 22	Super Bowl XXIII at Joe Robbie Stadium, Miami, Florida (NBC)
Sunday, January 29	AFC-NFC Pro Bowl at Honolulu, Hawaii (ESPN)

1988 Nationally Televised Games

(All games carried on CBS Radio Network.)

Regular Season

Monday, September 5	Washington at New York Giants (night, ABC)
Monday, September 12	Dallas at Phoenix (night, ABC)
Monday, September 19	Indianapolis at Cleveland (night, ABC)
Monday, September 26	Los Angeles Raiders at Denver (night, ABC)
Monday, October 3	Dallas at New Orleans (night, ABC)
Monday, October 10	New York Giants at Philadelphia (night, ABC)
Monday, October 17	Buffalo at New York Jets (night, ABC)
Monday, October 24	San Francisco at Chicago (night, ABC)
Sunday, October 30	Washington at Houston (night, ESPN)
Monday, October 31	Denver at Indianapolis (night, ABC)
Sunday, November 6	Los Angeles Raiders at San Diego (night, ESPN)
Monday, November 7	Cleveland at Houston (night, ABC)
Sunday, November 13	Minnesota at Dallas (night, ESPN)
Monday, November 14	Buffalo at Miami (night, ABC)
Sunday, November 20	New England at Miami (night, ESPN)
Monday, November 21	Washington at San Francisco (night, ABC)
Thursday, November 24	Houston at Dallas (day, NBC)
(Thanksgiving)	Minnesota at Detroit (day, CBS)
Sunday, November 27	New York Giants at New Orleans (night, ESPN)
Monday, November 28	Los Angeles Raiders at Seattle (night, ABC)
Sunday, December 4	Pittsburgh at Houston (night, ESPN)
Monday, December 5	Chicago at Los Angeles Rams (night, ABC)
Saturday, December 10	Indianapolis at New York Jets (day, NBC)
	Philadelphia at Phoenix (day, CBS)
Sunday, December 11	Denver at Seattle (night, ESPN)
Monday, December 12	Cleveland at Miami (night, ABC)
Saturday, December 17	New England at Denver (day, NBC)
	Washington at Cincinnati (day, CBS)
Sunday, December 18	Los Angeles Rams at San Francisco (night, ESPN)
Monday, December 19	Chicago at Minnesota (night, ABC)

1988 AFC-NFC Interconference Games

(Sunday unless noted; all times local.)

September 4	Dallas at Pittsburgh	1:00
	Miami at Chicago	12:00
	Minnesota at Buffalo	1:00
	Phoenix at Cincinnati	1:00
September 11	Chicago at Indianapolis	12:00
	Cincinnati at Philadelphia	4:00
	New England at Minnesota	3:00
	Pittsburgh at Washington	1:00
September 18	Green Bay at Miami	1:00
	L.A. Rams at L.A. Raiders	1:00
September 25	New York Jets at Detroit	1:00
	San Francisco at Seattle	1:00
October 2	Buffalo at Chicago	12:00
	Houston at Philadelphia	1:00
	Minnesota at Miami	4:00
	Seattle at Atlanta	1:00
October 9	Denver at San Francisco	1:00
	New England at Green Bay	12:00
	New Orleans at San Diego	1:00
	Pittsburgh at Phoenix	1:00
October 16	Atlanta at Denver	2:00
	New Orleans at Seattle	1:00
	Philadelphia at Cleveland	1:00
	Tampa Bay at Indianapolis	12:00
October 23	Cleveland at Phoenix	1:00
	Detroit at Kansas City	12:00
	L.A. Raiders at New Orleans	12:00
	Seattle at Los Angeles Rams	1:00
October 30	Chicago at New England	1:00
	Green Bay at Buffalo	1:00
	Miami at Tampa Bay	1:00
	Washington at Houston (night)	7:00
November 13	Indianapolis at Green Bay	12:00
	L.A. Raiders at San Francisco	1:00
	Philadelphia at Pittsburgh	1:00
	San Diego at Atlanta	1:00
November 20	Atlanta at Los Angeles Raiders	1:00
	Cincinnati at Dallas	12:00
	Denver at New Orleans	12:00
	Indianapolis at Minnesota	12:00
	Phoenix at Houston	12:00
	San Diego at Los Angeles Rams	1:00
November 24	Houston at Dallas (Thanksgiving)	3:00
November 27	Cleveland at Washington	1:00
	Los Angeles Rams at Denver	2:00
	San Francisco at San Diego	1:00
December 4	Buffalo at Tampa Bay	1:00
	Dallas at Cleveland	1:00
December 11	Kansas City at New York Giants	1:00
	Tampa Bay at New England	1:00
December 17	Washington at Cincinnati (Saturday)	12:30
December 18	New York Giants at New York Jets	1:00

Sunday and Monday Night Games at a Glance

(All times local; Sunday on ESPN; Monday on ABC-TV; all on CBS Radio Network.)

Monday, September 5	Washington at New York Giants (ABC)	9:00
Monday, September 12	Dallas at Phoenix (ABC)	6:00
Monday, September 19	Indianapolis at Cleveland (ABC)	8:00
Monday, September 26	Los Angeles Raiders at Denver (ABC)	6:00
Monday, October 3	Dallas at New Orleans (ABC)	8:00
Monday, October 10	New York Giants at Philadelphia (ABC)	9:00
Monday, October 17	Buffalo at New York Jets (ABC)	9:00
Monday, October 24	San Francisco at Chicago (ABC)	8:00
Sunday, October 30	Washington at Houston (ESPN)	7:00
Monday, October 31	Denver at Indianapolis (ABC)	9:00
Sunday, November 6	L.A. Raiders at San Diego (ESPN)	5:00
Monday, November 7	Cleveland at Houston (ABC)	8:00
Sunday, November 13	Minnesota at Dallas (ESPN)	7:00
Monday, November 14	Buffalo at Miami (ABC)	9:00
Sunday, November 20	New England at Miami (ESPN)	8:00
Monday, November 21	Washington at San Francisco (ABC)	6:00
Sunday, November 27	N.Y. Giants at New Orleans (ESPN)	7:00
Monday, November 28	Los Angeles Raiders at Seattle (ABC)	6:00
Sunday, December 4	Pittsburgh at Houston (ESPN)	7:00
Monday, December 5	Chicago at Los Angeles Rams (ABC)	6:00
Sunday, December 11	Denver at Seattle (ESPN)	5:00
Monday, December 12	Cleveland at Miami (ABC)	9:00
Sunday, December 18	L.A. Rams at San Francisco (ESPN)	5:00
Monday, December 19	Chicago at Minnesota (ABC)	8:00

Important Dates

1988

July 5	Claiming period of 24 hours begins in waiver system. All waivers for the year are no-recall and no-withdrawal.
Mid-July	Team training camps open.
July 30	Hall of Fame Game, Canton, Ohio: Cincinnati vs. Los Angeles Rams.
July 31	American Bowl '88, London, England: Miami vs. San Francisco.
August 3-7	First preseason weekend.
August 11-14	Second preseason weekend.
August 18-22	Third preseason weekend.
August 23	Roster cutdown to maximum of 60 players.
August 25-27	Fourth preseason weekend.
August 29	Roster cutdown to maximum of 45 players.
September 4-5	Regular season opens.
September 20	Priority on multiple waiver claims is now based on the current season's standings.
October 11	Clubs may begin signing free agents for the 1989 season.
October 11	Trading of player contracts/rights ends at 4:00 P.M., New York Time.
October 25-26	NFL Meeting, Chicago, Illinois.
November 19	Deadline for reinstatement of players in Reserve List categories of Retired, Did Not Report, and Veteran Free Agents Asked to Re-Sign.
December 12-13	Balloting for AFC-NFC Pro Bowl.
December 16	Deadline for waiver requests in 1988.
December 21	Deadline for postseason participants to sign free agents for playoffs, except punters or kickers.
December 24	AFC First-Round Playoff Game.
December 26	NFC First-Round Playoff Game.
December 31	AFC and NFC Divisional Playoff Games.

1989

January 1	AFC and NFC Divisional Playoff Games.
January 8	AFC and NFC Championship Games.
January 22	Super Bowl XXIII at Joe Robbie Stadium, Miami, Florida.
January 29	AFC-NFC Pro Bowl at Aloha Stadium, Honolulu, Hawaii.
January 30	Waiver system begins for 1989.
January 30	Trading period begins.
March 20-24	NFL Annual Meeting, Palm Springs, California.
April-May	54th annual NFL Selection Meeting, New York, New York.
August 5	Hall of Fame Game, Canton, Ohio: Buffalo vs. Washington.
August 11-13	First preseason weekend.
September 10-11	Regular season opens.
December 25	Regular season closes.
December 31	AFC and NFC First-Round Playoff Games.

1990

January 6-7	AFC and NFC Divisional Playoff Games.
January 14	AFC and NFC Championship Games.
January 28	Super Bowl XXIV at Louisiana Superdome, New Orleans, Louisiana.
February 4	AFC-NFC Pro Bowl.
March 12-16	NFL Annual Meeting, Orlando, Florida.
August 4	Hall of Fame Game, Canton, Ohio: Denver vs. Chicago
August 10-12	First preseason weekend.
September 9-10	Regular season opens.
December 24	Regular season closes.
December 30	AFC and NFC First-Round Playoff Games.

1991

January 5-6	AFC and NFC Divisional Playoff Games.
January 13	AFC and NFC Championship Games.
January 27	Super Bowl XXV at Tampa Stadium, Tampa, Florida.
February 3	AFC-NFC Pro Bowl.
March 14-18	NFL Annual Meeting, Kona, Hawaii.

Future Super Bowl Dates and Sites

Super Bowl XXIII	January 22, 1989	Joe Robbie Stadium, Miami, Florida
Super Bowl XXIV	January 28, 1990	Louisiana Superdome, New Orleans, Louisiana
Super Bowl XXV	January 27, 1991	Tampa Stadium, Tampa, Florida

Future Pro Football Hall of Fame Games

1991	Miami Dolphins (AFC) vs. Detroit Lions (NFC)
1992	New York Jets (AFC) vs. Philadelphia Eagles (NFC)
1993	Los Angeles Raiders (AFC) vs. Green Bay Packers (NFC)
1994	Cleveland Browns (AFC) vs. Dallas Cowboys (NFC)
1995	San Diego Chargers (AFC) vs. Atlanta Falcons (NFC)
1996	Indianapolis Colts (AFC) vs. New Orleans Saints (NFC)
1997	Seattle Seahawks (AFC) vs. Minnesota Vikings (NFC)
1998	Pittsburgh Steelers (AFC) vs. Tampa Bay Buccaneers (NFC)

Waivers

The waiver system is a procedure by which player contracts or NFL rights to players are made available by a club to other clubs in the League. During the procedure the 27 other clubs either file claims to obtain the players or waive the opportunity to do so—thus the term "waiver." Claiming clubs are assigned players on a priority based on the inverse of won-and-lost standing. The claiming period normally is 10 days during the offseason and 24 hours from early July through December. In some circumstances another 24 hours is added on to allow the original club to rescind its action (known as a recall of a waiver request) and/or the claiming club to do the same (known as withdrawal of a claim). If a player passes through waivers unclaimed and is not recalled by the original club, he becomes a free agent. All waivers from July through December are no recall and no withdrawal. Under the Collective Bargaining Agreement, from February 1 through October 11, any veteran who has acquired four years of pension credit may, if about to be assigned to another club through the waiver system, reject such assignment and become a free agent.

Active List

The Active List is the principal status for players participating for a club. It consists of all players under contract, including option, who are eligible for preseason, regular season, and postseason games. Clubs are allowed to open training camp with an unlimited number of players but thereafter must meet a series of mandatory roster reductions prior to the season opener. Teams will be permitted to dress up to 45 players for each regular season and postseason game during the 1988 season; in addition, each club will have an Inactive List of two players. The Active List maximums and dates for 1988 are:

August 23 . . . . 60 players
August 29 . . . . 45 players (plus two-player Inactive List)

Reserve List

The Reserve List is a status for players who, for reasons of injury, retirement, military service, or other circumstances, are not immediately available for participation with a club. Those players in the category of Reserve/Injured who were physically unable to play football for a minimum of four weeks from the date of going onto Reserve may be re-activated by their clubs upon clearing procedural recall waivers; in addition, each club will have five free re-activations for players meeting the four-week requirement, but no more than two can be used for players who were placed on Reserve/Injured prior to or concurrent with the final cutdown on August 29. Clubs participating in postseason competition will be granted an additional re-activation. Players not meeting the four-week requirement may return to their club if they are released, re-signed, and subsequently clear procedural recall waivers. Players in the category of Reserve/Retired, Reserve/Did Not Report, or Reserve/Veteran Free Agent Asked to Re-sign, may not be reinstated during the period from 30 days before the end of the regular season on through the postseason.

Trades

Unrestricted trading between the AFC and NFC is allowed in 1988 through October 11, after which trading of player contracts/rights will end until January 30, 1989.

Annual Active Player Limits

NFL

Year(s)	Limit
1985-88	45
1983-84	49
1982	45†–49
1978–81	45
1975–77	43
1974	47
1964–73	40
1963	37
1961–62	36
1960	38
1959	36
1957–58	35
1951–56	33
1949–50	32
1948	35
1947	35*–34
1945–46	33
1943–44	28
1940–42	33
1938–39	30
1936–37	25
1935	24
1930–34	20
1926–29	18
1925	16

†45 for first two games
*35 for first three games

AFL

Year(s)	Limit
1966–69	40
1965	38
1964	34
1962–63	33
1960–61	35

Tie-Breaking Procedures

The following procedures will be used to break standings ties for postseason playoffs and to determine regular season schedules.

To Break a Tie Within a Division

If, at the end of the regular season, two or more clubs in the same division finish with identical won-lost-tied percentages, the following steps will be taken until a champion is determined.

Two Clubs

1. Head-to-head (best won-lost-tied percentage in games between the clubs).
2. Best won-lost-tied percentage in games played within the division.
3. Best won-lost-tied percentage in games played within the conference.
4. Best won-lost-tied percentage in common games, if applicable.
5. Best net points in division games.
6. Best net points in all games.
7. Strength of schedule.
8. Best net touchdowns in all games.
9. Coin toss.

Three or More Clubs

(Note: If one team wins multiple-team tiebreaker to advance to playoff round, remaining teams revert to step 1 of applicable two-club format, i.e., either in division tiebreaker or Wild Card tiebreaker. If two teams in a multiple-team tie possess superior marks in a tiebreaking step, this pair of teams revert to top of applicable two-club format to break tie. One team advances to playoff round, while other returns to original group and step 1 of applicable tiebreaker).

1. Head-to-head (best won-lost-tied percentage in games among the clubs).
2. Best won-lost-tied percentage in games played within the division.
3. Best won-lost-tied percentage in games played within the conference.
4. Best won-lost-tied percentage in common games.
5. Best net points in division games.
6. Best net points in all games.
7. Strength of schedule.
8. Best net touchdowns in all games.
9. Coin toss.

To Break a Tie for the Wild Card Team

If it is necessary to break ties to determine the two Wild Card clubs from each conference, the following steps will be taken.

1. If the tied clubs are from the same division, apply division tie-breaker.
2. If the tied clubs are from different divisions, apply the following steps.

Two Clubs

1. Head-to-head, if applicable.
2. Best won-lost-tied percentage in games played within the conference.
3. Best won-lost-tied percentage in common games, minimum of four.
4. Best average net points in conference games.
5. Best net points in all games.
6. Strength of schedule.
7. Best net touchdowns in all games.
8. Coin toss.

Three or More Clubs

(Note: If one team wins multiple-team tiebreaker to advance to playoff round, remaining teams revert to step 1 of applicable two-club format, i.e., either in division tiebreaker or Wild Card tiebreaker. If two teams in a multiple-team tie possess superior marks in a tiebreaking step, this pair of teams revert to the top of the applicable two-club format to break tie. One team advances to playoff round, while other returns to original group and step 1 of applicable tiebreaker.)

1. Head-to-head sweep. (Applicable only if one club has defeated each of the others, or if one club has lost to each of the others.)
2. Best won-lost-tied percentage in games played within the conference.
3. Best won-lost-tied percentage in common games, minimum of four.
4. Best average net points in conference games.
5. Best net points in all games.
6. Strength of schedule.
7. Best net touchdowns in all games.
8. Coin toss.

Tie-Breaking Procedure for Selection Meeting

If two or more clubs are tied for selection order, the conventional strength of schedule tiebreaker will be applied, subject to the following exceptions for playoff teams.

1. The Super Bowl winner will be last and the Super Bowl loser will be next-to-last.
2. Any non-Super Bowl playoff team involved in a tie moves down in drafting priority as follows:
   A. Participation by a club in the playoffs without a victory adds one-half victory to the club's regular season won-lost-tied record.
   B. For each victory in the playoffs, one full victory will be added to the club's regular season won-lost-tied record.
3. Clubs with the best won-lost-tied records after these steps are applied will drop to their appropriate spots at the bottom of the tied segment. In no case will the above process move a club lower than the segment in which it was initially tied.
4. Tied clubs will alternate priority throughout the 12 rounds of the draft. In case of a tie involving three or more teams, the club with priority in the first round will drop to the bottom of the tied segment in the second round and move its way back to the top of the segment in each succeeding round.

Figuring the 1989 NFL Schedule

As soon as the final game of the 1988 NFL regular season (Chicago at Minnesota, December 19) has been completed, it will be possible to determine the 1989 opponents of the 28 teams.

Each 1989 team schedule is based on a "common opponent" formula initiated for the 1978 season and most recently modified in 1987. Under the common opponent format, the first- through fourth-place teams in a division play at least 12 of their 16 games the following season against common opponents, and the fifth-place team in the division plays at least 10 common opponent games. It is not a position scheduling format in which the strong play the strong and the weak play the weak.

For years the NFL had been seeking a more easily understood and balanced schedule that would provide both competitive equality and a variety of opponents. Under the old rotation scheduling system in effect from 1970–77, non-division opponents were determined by a pre-set formula. This often resulted in competitive imbalances.

With "common opponents" the basis for scheduling, a more competitive and equitable method of determining division champions and postseason playoff representatives has developed. Teams battling for a division title are playing at least 75 percent of their games against common opponents.

In 1987, NFL owners passed two by-law proposals designed to modify the common opponent scheduling format in the hopes of creating even more equity. The first concerns pairings with non-division opponents:

Prior Year's Finish in Division	Pairings in Non-Division Games Within Conference	Previous Pairings 1978-86
1	1-1-2-3	1-1-4-4
2	1-2-2-4	2-2-3-3
3	1-3-3-4	2-2-3-3
4	2-3-4-4	1-1-4-4

The second change, recommended by the NFL's Competition Committee, states: "For the 1987, 1988, and 1989 seasons, site locations for the interconference games of teams which finish 1 through 4 in a division and fifth-place teams where possible, will be assigned so that, where possible by formula, teams do not play a second consecutive regular-season home or road game with an opponent."

Under the common opponent format, schedules of any NFL team are figured according to one of the following three formulas. (The reference point for the figuring is the team's final division standing. Ties for a position in divisions are broken according to the tie-breaking procedures outlined on page 13. The chart on the following page is included for use as you go through each step.)

A. First- through fourth-place teams in a five-team division (AFC East, AFC West, NFC East, NFC Central).

1. Home-and-home round-robin within the division (8 games).
2. One game each with the first- through fourth-place teams in a division of the other conference (4 games). In 1989, the AFC East will play the NFC West, the AFC Central will play the NFC Central, and the AFC West will play the NFC East.
3. The first-place team plays the first-place teams in the other divisions within the conference plus a second- and third-place team within the conference. The second-place team plays the second-place teams in the other divisions within the conference plus a first- and fourth-place team within the conference. The third-place team plays the third-place teams in the other divisions within the conference plus a first- and fourth-place team within the conference. The fourth-place team plays the fourth-place teams in the other divisions within the conference plus a second- and third-place team within the conference (4 games).

This completes the 16-game schedule.

B. First- through fourth-place teams in a four-team division (AFC Central, NFC West).

1. Home-and-home round-robin within the division (6 games).
2. One game with each of the fifth-place teams in the conference (2 games).
3. The same procedure that is listed in step A2 (4 games).
4. The same procedure that is listed in step A3 (4 games).

This completes the 16-game schedule.

C. The fifth-place teams in a division (AFC East, AFC West, NFC East, NFC Central).

1. Home-and-home round-robin within the division (8 games).
2. One game with each team in the four-team division of the conference (4 games).
3. A home-and-home with the other fifth-place team in the conference (2 games).
4. One game each with the fifth-place teams in the other conference (2 games).

This completes the 16-game schedule.

The 1989 Opponent Breakdown chart on the following page does not include the round-robin games within the division. Those are automatically on a home-and-away basis.

1988 NFL Standings

AFC

EAST AE

1
2
3
4
5

CENTRAL AC

1
2
3
4

WEST AW

1
2
3
4
5

NFC

EAST NE

1
2
3
4
5

WEST NW

1
2
3
4

CENTRAL NC

1
2
3
4
5

A Team's 1989 Schedule

Team Name

1989 Opponent Breakdown

*Game Site to be Determined by Rotational Formula

AE AFC East Home Away	AC AFC Central Home Away	AW AFC West Home Away	NE NFC East Home Away	NC NFC Central Home Away	NW NFC West Home Away
AE-1 AC-1 AC-3 AW-2 AW-1 *NW-1 *NW-3 *NW-2 *NW-4	**AC-1** AE-2 AE-1 AW-1 AW-3 AE-5 AW-5 *NC-1 *NC-3 *NC-2 *NC-4	**AW-1** AE-1 AE-3 AC-2 AC-1 *NE-1 *NE-3 *NE-2 *NE-4	**NE-1** NW-1 NW-3 NC-2 NC-1 *AW-1 *AW-3 *AW-2 *AW-4	**NC-1** NE-1 NE-3 NW-2 NW-1 *AC-1 *AC-3 *AC-2 *AC-4	**NW-1** NE-2 NE-1 NC-1 NC-3 NE-5 NC-5 *AE-1 *AE-3 *AE-2 *AE-4
AE-2 AC-2 AC-1 AW-4 AW-2 *NW-1 *NW-3 *NW-2 *NW-4	**AC-2** AE-4 AE-2 AW-2 AW-1 AW-5 AE-5 *NC-1 *NC-3 *NC-2 *NC-4	**AW-2** AE-2 AE-1 AC-4 AC-2 *NE-1 *NE-3 *NE-2 *NE-4	**NE-2** NW-2 NW-1 NC-4 NC-2 *AW-1 *AW-3 *AW-2 *AW-4	**NC-2** NE-2 NE-1 NW-4 NW-2 *AC-1 *AC-3 *AC-2 *AC-4	**NW-2** NE-4 NE-2 NC-2 NC-1 NC-5 NE-5 *AE-1 *AE-3 *AE-2 *AE-4
AE-3 AC-3 AC-4 AW-1 AW-3 *NW-1 *NW-3 *NW-2 *NW-4	**AC-3** AE-1 AE-3 AW-3 AW-4 AE-5 AW-5 *NC-1 *NC-3 *NC-2 *NC-4	**AW-3** AE-3 AE-4 AC-1 AC-3 *NE-1 *NE-3 *NE-2 *NE-4	**NE-3** NW-3 NW-4 NC-1 NC-3 *AW-1 *AW-3 *AW-2 *AW-4	**NC-3** NE-3 NE-4 NW-1 NW-3 *AC-1 *AC-3 *AC-2 *AC-4	**NW-3** NE-1 NE-3 NC-3 NC-4 NE-5 NC-5 *AE-1 *AE-3 *AE-2 *AE-4
AE-4 AC-4 AC-2 AW-3 AW-4 *NW-1 *NW-3 *NW-2 *NW-4	**AC-4** AE-3 AE-4 AW-4 AW-2 AW-5 AE-5 *NC-1 *NC-3 *NC-2 *NC-4	**AW-4** AE-4 AE-2 AC-3 AC-4 *NE-1 *NE-3 *NE-2 *NE-4	**NE-4** NW-4 NW-2 NC-3 NC-4 *AW-1 *AW-3 *AW-2 *AW-4	**NC-4** NE-4 NE-2 NW-3 NW-4 *AC-1 *AC-3 *AC-2 *AC-4	**NW-4** NE-3 NE-4 NC-4 NC-2 NC-5 NE-5 *AE-1 *AE-3 *AE-2 *AE-4
AE-5 AW-5 AW-5 *AC-2 *AC-1 *AC-4 *AC-3 *NC-5 *NE-5		**AW-5** AE-5 AE-5 *AC-1 *AC-2 *AC-3 *AC-4 *NE-5 *NC-5	**NE-5** NC-5 NC-5 *NW-2 *NW-1 *NW-4 *NW-3 *AE-5 *AW-5	**NC-5** NE-5 NE-5 *NW-1 *NW-2 *NW-3 *NW-4 *AW-5 *AE-5	

Instant Replay Approved for 1988

For the third consecutive season, NFL clubs have approved a limited system of Instant Replay on a one-year basis.

The system basically stays the same as in 1987 with the exception that the Replay Official will now be assigned a regular officiating crew and will attend crew meetings the day before each game. League office personnel will no longer be used as Replay Officials.

In 1987, there were 490 plays closely reviewed (defined as a contact to the field, but not necessarily stoppage of play). There were 57 reversals in 210 games for an average of one reversal in each four games. In 1986, there were 374 plays closely reviewed resulting in 38 reversals in 224 games.

In 1986, the system was approved by a 23-4-1 vote. In 1987, the vote was 21-7. In 1988, replay was cleared by a 23-5 margin.

The NFL has discussed Instant Replay in some degree or other since the early 1970s. The League experimented in 1976 and 1978 using two basic frameworks—an independent system using cameras, replay machines, and technicians separate from the network covering the games, and a "no-frills" approach using existing TV coverage.

In 1985 the NFL used the network feed of the nine nationally-televised preseason games to experiment with the basic system which later was adopted for 1986, 1987, and 1988. A total of 28 plays (17 confirmed call, 4 inconclusive, 1 reversed, and 6 no replay shown) were closely examined in the 1985 experiment.

Q—What is the objective of this system?

A—The clubs feel that on certain plays the telecast viewed by the general public should be used to correct an indisputable error. The system will be used to reverse an on-field decision only when the Replay Official has **indisputable visual evidence** available to him that warrants the change.

Q—Who will be involved?

A—The Replay Official (a veteran former NFL or collegiate official) will be positioned in a sideline Replay Booth, which will house two TV monitors and two high-speed VCRs plus radio communications to the on-field officials. The Replay Official makes the decision although a Communicator (normally a member of the League Office staff) and a Technician also will be there to lend logistical help.

Q—Why is the system referred to as "limited" Instant Replay?

A—This system will concentrate on plays of **possession** or **touching** (e.g. fumbles, receptions, interceptions, muffs) and most plays governed by the **sidelines, goal lines, end lines,** and **line of scrimmage** (e.g. receiver or runner in or out of bounds, forward or backward passes, breaking the plane of the goal line). It also will be used to determine whether there are more than 11 men on the field.

Q—Why aren't most fouls included in this system?

A—It is recognized that in most circumstances the on-field officials have the best vantage points involving fouls. It is for this reason that Instant Replay **will not review** a list of the following 26 fouls:

1. Clipping
2. Encroachment and offsides
3. Grasp of facemask
4. False start
5. Defensive pass interference
6. Offensive pass interference
7. Offensive holding and illegal use of hands
8. Illegal batting or punching ball
9. Illegal block on free kick or scrimmage kick
10. Illegal crackback
11. Illegal motion
12. Illegal use of forearm or elbow
13. Illegal use of hands by defense
14. Illegally kicking ball
15. Illegally snapping ball
16. Intentional grounding
17. Member of punting team downfield early
18. Illegal formation
19. Palpably unfair act
20. Piling on
21. Roughing the passer
22. Running into/roughing kicker
23. Striking, kicking, or kneeing
24. Unnecessary roughness
25. Unsportsmanlike conduct
26. Use of helmet as a weapon

Q—Is the television network carrying the game part of the review process?

A—No. Although the Replay Official will be viewing the live network feed, there is no communication to television personnel as to which plays to show or not to show.

Q—What is the step-by-step procedure of a play review?

A—The Replay Official will view game action and a play will be replayed immediately on one of the two monitors, while the other one continues to record the live feed.

The Replay Official makes a determination if further study of the play is needed. If not, there is no contact with the field and play continues without interruption.

If the Replay Official believes an error may have been made the Umpire will be contacted via a headset.

The Replay Official will watch replay(s) on one or both monitors and complete his review within a reasonable period after the play is over.

The Replay Official will inform the Umpire of his decision, and the Referee will make the appropriate announcement on the wireless microphone.

NFL Passer Rating System

The NFL rates its forward passers for statistical purposes against a pre-fixed performance standard based on statistical achievements of all qualified pro passers since 1960. The system now being used replaced one that rated passers in relation to their position in a total group based on various criteria. The current system, which was adopted in 1973, removes inequities that existed in the former method and, at the same time, provides a means of comparing passing performances from one season to the next.

It is important to remember that the system is used to rate **passers,** not **quarterbacks.** Statistics do not reflect leadership, play-calling, and other intangible factors that go into making a successful professional quarterback. Four categories are used as a basis for compiling a rating:

—Percentage of touchdown passes per attempt
—Percentage of completions per attempt
—Percentage of interceptions per attempt
—Average yards gained per attempt

The base, or **average** standard, is 1.000. The bottom is .000. To earn a 2.000 rating a passer must perform at exceptional levels, i.e., 70 percent in completions, 10 percent in touchdowns, 1.5 percent in interceptions, and 11 yards average gain per pass attempt. The **maximum** a passer can receive in any category is 2.375.

For example, to gain a 2.375 in completion percentage, a passer would have to complete 77.5 percent of his passes. The NFL record is 70.55 by Ken Anderson (Cincinnati, 1982). To gain 2.375 in percentage of interceptions, a passer would have to go the entire season without an interception. The 2.375 figure in average yards is 12.50, compared with the NFL record of 11.17 by Tommy O'Connell (Cleveland, 1957). To earn a 2.375 in percentage of touchdowns, a passer would have to achieve an 11.9. The record is 13.9 by Sid Luckman (Chicago, 1943).

In order to make the rating more understandable, the point rating is then converted into a scale of 100. For instance, if a passer completes 11 of 23 passes for 114 yards, with one touchdown and no interceptions, the four components would be:

—**Percentage of Completions**—11 of 23 is 47.8 percent. The point rating is 0.890.

—**Percentage of Touchdown Passes**—1 touchdown in 23 attempts works out to 4.3 percent for a rating of 0.860.

—**Percentage of Interceptions**—You can't do better than zero, so the passer receives a maximum rating of 2.375.

—**Average Yards Gained Per Attempt**—23 attempts divided into 114 yards equals 4.96 yards per attempt for a corresponding rating of 0.490.

The sum of the four components is 4.615, which converts to a rating of 76.9. In order for a passer to achieve 100, his points would have to total 6.000. In rare cases, where statistical performance has been superior, it is possible for a passer to go over 100. However, such an instance is rare. The leading passers each year were checked from 1932 when the NFL began keeping official statistics, and only nine passers in history have scored over 100 in the year they led the league in passing. The most recent passer to lead the league and score over 100 was Miami quarterback Dan Marino, who achieved a 108.9 rating in 1984. The highest-rated passer in a single season was Milt Plum, who had a 110.4 rating with Cleveland in 1960.

AFC ACTIVE STATISTICAL LEADERS

LEADING ACTIVE PASSERS, AMERICAN FOOTBALL CONFERENCE
1,000 or more attempts

	Yrs.	Att.	Comp.	Pct. Comp.	Yards	Avg. Gain	TD	Pct. TD	Had Int.	Pct. Int.	Rate Pts.
Dan Marino, Mia.	5	2494	1512	60.6	19422	7.79	168	6.7	80	3.2	94.1
Ken O'Brien, N.Y.J.	4	1566	947	60.5	11676	7.46	69	4.4	43	2.7	86.8
Bernie Kosar, Clev.	3	1168	675	57.8	8465	7.25	47	4.0	26	2.2	84.6
Dave Krieg, Sea.	8	2116	1224	57.8	15808	7.47	130	6.1	88	4.2	84.6
Boomer Esiason, Cin.	4	1442	815	56.5	11253	7.80	70	4.9	51	3.5	83.1
Tony Eason, N.E.	5	1352	791	58.5	9722	7.19	57	4.2	42	3.1	81.9
Bill Kenney, K.C.	8	2316	1272	54.9	16728	7.22	105	4.5	81	3.5	78.3
Gary Danielson, Clev.	10	1880	1074	57.1	13440	7.15	81	4.3	77	4.1	76.8
John Elway, Den.	5	2158	1168	54.1	14835	6.87	85	3.9	77	3.6	74.1
Ron Jaworski, Mia.	13	4042	2142	53.0	27682	6.85	176	4.4	159	3.9	72.9
Steve Grogan, N.E.	13	3100	1629	52.5	23740	7.66	165	5.3	178	5.7	71.6
Warren Moon, Hou.	4	1683	899	53.4	12342	7.33	61	3.6	77	4.6	70.2
Steve DeBerg, K.C.	10	2997	1698	56.7	19582	6.53	116	3.9	139	4.6	70.1
Marc Wilson, Raiders	8	1666	871	52.3	11760	7.06	77	4.6	86	5.2	69.0
Jim Plunkett, Raiders	15	3701	1943	52.5	25882	6.99	164	4.4	198	5.3	67.5
Mike Pagel, Clev.	6	1157	589	50.9	7527	6.51	39	3.4	47	4.1	65.9
Mark Malone, S.D.	7	1374	690	50.2	8582	6.25	54	3.9	68	4.9	62.4
Vince Evans, Raiders	8	1036	503	48.6	6802	6.57	36	3.5	57	5.5	58.6

TOP 10 ACTIVE RUSHERS, AFC
2,000 or more yards

	Yrs.	Att.	Yards	TD
1. Eric Dickerson, Ind.	5	1748	8256	61
2. Marcus Allen, Raiders	6	1489	6151	54
3. Freeman McNeil, N.Y.J.	7	1306	5850	22
4. Curt Warner, Sea.	5	1189	5049	42
5. Sammy Winder, Den.	6	1194	4413	31
6. James Brooks, Cin.	7	917	4173	27
7. Frank Pollard, Pitt.	8	922	3896	20
8. Randy McMillan, Ind.	6	990	3876	24
9. Earnest Jackson, Pitt.	5	985	3852	19
10. Walter Abercrombie, Pitt.	6	842	3343	22

Other Leading Rushers

	Yrs.	Att.	Yards	TD
Larry Kinnebrew, Cin.	5	639	2582	37
Kevin Mack, Clev.	3	597	2504	22
Craig James, N.E.	4	581	2454	10
Mosi Tatupu, N.E.	10	563	2246	16
Johnny Hector, N.Y.J.	5	560	2228	26
Steve Grogan, N.E.	13	426	2150	34
Earnest Byner, Clev.	4	515	2137	20
Mike Rozier, Hou.	3	561	2081	15
Herman Heard, K.C.	4	482	2040	13

TOP 10 ACTIVE PASS RECEIVERS, AFC
200 or more receptions

	Yrs.	No.	Yards	TD
1. Steve Largent, Sea.	12	752	12041	95
2. Ozzie Newsome, Clev.	10	575	7073	42
3. James Lofton, Raiders	10	571	10536	54
4. Wes Chandler, S.D.	10	555	8933	56
5. Kellen Winslow, S.D.	9	541	6741	45
6. Stanley Morgan, N.E.	11	475	9364	60
7. Todd Christensen, Raiders	9	446	5682	41
8. Henry Marshall, K.C.	12	416	6545	33
9. Wesley Walker, N.Y.J.	11	404	7666	64
Cris Collinsworth, Cin.	7	404	6471	35

Other Leading Receivers

	Yrs.	No.	Yards	TD
Russ Francis, N.E.	12	382	5101	40
Steve Watson, Den.	9	353	6112	36
Mickey Shuler, N.Y.J.	10	339	3692	32
Billy Johnson, Ind.	13	337	4211	25
Marcus Allen, Raiders	6	334	3167	15
Carlos Carson, K.C.	8	299	5554	29
Jerry Butler, Buff.	7	278	4301	29
Mark Duper, Mia.	6	257	4869	40
Mark Clayton, Mia.	5	255	4425	40
Bruce Hardy, Mia.	10	251	2407	25
James Brooks, Cin.	7	249	2412	16
Drew Hill, Hou.	8	238	4617	30
Ray Butler, Sea.	8	221	3706	33
Charlie Brown, Ind.	6	220	3548	25
Matt Bouza, Ind.	7	209	2722	13

TOP 10 ACTIVE SCORERS, AFC
250 or more points

	Yrs.	TD	FG	PAT	TP
1. Pat Leahy, N.Y.J.	14	0	218	424	1078
2. Chris Bahr, Raiders	12	0	206	424	1042
3. Tony Franklin, N.E.	9	0	173	335	854
4. Jim Breech, Cin.	9	0	161	325	808
5. Nick Lowery, K.C.	9	0	174	281	803
6. Matt Bahr, Clev.	9	0	142	277	703
7. Gary Anderson, Pitt.	6	0	137	198	609
8. Steve Largent, Sea.	12	96	0	1	577
9. Rich Karlis, Den.	6	0	114	208	550
10. Norm Johnson, Sea.	6	0	99	234	531

Other Leading Scorers

	Yrs.	TD	FG	PAT	TP
Marcus Allen, Raiders	6	70	0	0	420
Wesley Walker, N.Y.J.	11	64	0	0	386*
Eric Dickerson, Ind.	5	63	0	0	378
Stanley Morgan, N.E.	11	61	0	0	366
Wes Chandler, S.D.	10	56	0	0	336
James Lofton, Raiders	10	55	0	0	330
Tony Zendejas, Hou.	3	0	63	89	278
Curt Warner, Sea.	5	46	0	0	276
Kellen Winslow, S.D.	9	45	0	0	270
Fuad Reveiz, Mia.	3	0	45	130	265
Ozzie Newsome, Clev.	10	44	0	0	264
James Brooks, Cin.	7	43	0	0	258
Todd Christensen, Raiders	9	42	0	0	252

**total includes safety*

TOP 10 ACTIVE INTERCEPTORS, AFC
20 or more interceptions

	Yrs.	No.	Yards	TD
1. Mike Haynes, Raiders	12	43	658	2
2. Deron Cherry, K.C.	7	34	539	1
3. Raymond Clayborn, N.E.	11	31	490	1
4. Mike Harden, Den.	8	29	607	4
Glenn Blackwood, Mia.	9	29	398	1
6. Charles Romes, Sea.	11	28	493	1
7. Dwayne Woodruff, Pitt.	8	26	413	2
Vann McElroy, Raiders	6	26	279	1
9. Roland James, N.E.	8	23	303	0
Hanford Dixon, Clev.	7	23	199	0

Other Leading Interceptors

	Yrs.	No.	Yards	TD
Steve Wilson, Den.	9	21	257	0
Albert Lewis, K.C.	5	21	176	0

TOP 10 ACTIVE QUARTERBACK SACKERS, AFC
Official statistic since 1982

	No.
1. Mark Gastineau, N.Y.J.	67
Jacob Green, Sea.	67
3. Andre Tippett, N.E.	65.5
4. Howie Long, Raiders	52
5. Al Baker, Clev.	49.5
6. Rulon Jones, Den.	47.5
Greg Townsend, Raiders	47.5
8. Eddie Edwards, Cin.	47
9. Doug Betters, Mia.	43.5
Bill Pickel, Raiders	43.5

TOP 10 ACTIVE PUNT RETURNERS, AFC
40 or more punt returns

	Yrs.	No.	Yards	Avg.	TD
1. Bobby Joe Edmonds, Sea.	2	54	670	12.4	1
2. JoJo Townsell, N.Y.J.	3	42	498	11.9	1
3. Billy Johnson, Ind.	13	279	3291	11.8	6
4. Louis Lipps, Pitt.	4	99	1155	11.7	3
5. Irving Fryar, N.E.	4	126	1407	11.2	3
6. James Brooks, Cin.	7	52	565	10.9	0
7. Gerald Willhite, Den.	6	88	922	10.5	1
8. Mike Martin, Cin.	5	120	1244	10.4	0
Mike Haynes, Raiders	12	112	1168	10.4	2
Stanley Morgan, N.E.	11	92	960	10.4	1

Other Leading Punt Returners

	Yrs.	No.	Yards	Avg.	TD
Gerald McNeil, Clev.	2	74	734	9.9	1
Lionel James, S.D.	4	96	915	9.5	2
Roland James, N.E.	8	42	400	9.5	1
Mark Clayton, Mia.	5	52	485	9.3	1
Kenny Johnson, Hou.	8	61	562	9.2	0
Paul Skansi, Sea.	5	95	858	9.0	0
Ron Pitts, Buff.	2	41	343	8.4	1
Nesby Glasgow, Ind.	9	79	651	8.2	1
Willie Drewrey, Hou.	3	61	488	8.0	0
Brian Brennan, Clev.	4	44	352	8.0	1
Kurt Sohn, N.Y.J.	6	65	510	7.8	0
Billy Brooks, Ind.	2	40	277	6.9	0
Ron Fellows, Raiders	7	48	327	6.8	0
Wes Chandler, S.D.	10	61	400	6.6	0
Robb Riddick, Buff.	5	46	289	6.3	0

TOP 10 ACTIVE KICKOFF RETURNERS, AFC
40 or more kickoff returns

	Yrs.	No.	Yards	Avg.	TD
1. Raymond Clayborn, N.E.	11	57	1538	27.0	3
2. Bobby Humphery, N.Y.J.	4	85	2050	24.1	2
3. Billy Johnson, Ind.	13	123	2941	23.9	2
4. Glen Young, Clev.	4	84	1991	23.7	0
5. Albert Bentley, Ind.	3	81	1861	23.0	0
6. Nesby Glasgow, Ind.	9	84	1904	22.7	0
Carlos Carson, K.C.	8	57	1296	22.7	0
8. Willie Tullis, Ind.	7	63	1384	22.0	1
9. Mike Martin, Cin.	5	75	1643	21.9	0
10. Bobby Joe Edmonds, Sea.	2	61	1328	21.8	0

Other Leading Kickoff Returners

	Yrs.	No.	Yards	Avg.	TD
Barry Redden, S.D.	6	64	1390	21.7	0
Gene Lang, Den.	4	61	1323	21.7	0
Willie Drewrey, Hou.	3	59	1278	21.7	0
James Brooks, Cin.	7	117	2529	21.6	0
Lorenzo Hampton, Mia.	3	70	1506	21.5	0
Tim McGee, Cin.	2	58	1249	21.5	0
Wes Chandler, S.D.	10	48	1032	21.5	0
Steve Tasker, Buff.	3	40	857	21.4	0
Lionel James, S.D.	4	99	2094	21.2	0
Stephen Starring, N.E.	5	107	2259	21.1	0
Gerald McNeil, Clev.	2	58	1202	20.7	1
Gary Anderson, S.D.	3	59	1217	20.6	1
Robb Riddick, Buff.	5	57	1176	20.6	0
Ron Fellows, Raiders	7	73	1478	20.2	0
Drew Hill, Hou.	8	172	3460	20.1	1
Randall Morris, Sea.	4	71	1403	19.8	0
Stanford Jennings, Cin.	4	49	959	19.6	0
Allen Pinkett, Hou.	2	43	841	19.6	0
Steve Wilson, Den.	9	58	1107	19.1	0
Kurt Sohn, N.Y.J.	6	54	1005	18.6	0

TOP 10 ACTIVE PUNTERS, AFC
50 or more punts

	Yrs.	No.	Avg.	LG
1. Rohn Stark, Ind.	6	450	44.5	72
2. Reggie Roby, Mia.	5	272	43.7	77
3. Rich Camarillo, N.E.	7	468	42.6	76
4. Ralf Mojsiejenko, S.D.	3	207	42.4	67
5. Scott Fulhage, Cin.	1	52	41.7	58
6. Mike Horan, Den.	4	248	41.6	75
7. Lee Johnson, Clev.	3	221	41.0	66
Ralph Giacomarro, Raid.	4	185	41.0	58
9. John Kidd, Buff.	4	319	40.9	67
Kelly Goodburn, K.C.	1	59	40.9	55

Other Leading Punters

	Yrs.	No.	Avg.	LG
Jeff Gossett, Hou.	6	340	40.7	64
Stan Talley, Raiders	1	56	40.7	63
Lewis Colbert, K.C.	2	109	40.5	56
Harry Newsome, Pitt.	3	228	40.4	64

NFC ACTIVE STATISTICAL LEADERS

LEADING ACTIVE PASSERS, NATIONAL FOOTBALL CONFERENCE

1,000 or more attempts

	Yrs.	Att.	Comp.	Pct. Comp.	Yards	Avg. Gain	TD	Pct. TD	Had Int.	Pct. Int.	Rate Pts.
Joe Montana, S.F.	9	3276	2084	63.6	24552	7.49	172	5.3	89	2.7	92.5
Neil Lomax, Phx.	7	2710	1562	57.6	19376	7.15	116	4.3	79	2.9	82.0
Danny White, Dall.	12	2908	1732	59.6	21685	7.46	154	5.3	129	4.4	82.0
Jim McMahon, Chi.	6	1321	760	57.5	9857	7.46	61	4.6	49	3.7	81.1
Phil Simms, N.Y.G.	8	2774	1489	53.7	19815	7.14	121	4.4	112	4.0	74.3
Tommy Kramer, Minn.	11	3339	1851	55.4	22605	6.77	147	4.4	141	4.2	73.6
Jay Schroeder, Wash.	3	1017	517	50.8	7445	7.32	39	3.8	37	3.6	72.6
Eric Hipple, Det.	7	1501	811	54.0	10463	6.97	55	3.7	67	4.5	69.8
Doug Williams, Wash.	7	2034	976	48.0	13804	6.79	84	4.1	78	3.8	68.1
Dave Wilson, N.O.	6	1023	546	53.4	6914	6.76	36	3.5	54	5.3	64.5

TOP 10 ACTIVE RUSHERS, NFC

2,000 or more yards

	Yrs.	Att.	Yards	TD
1. Tony Dorsett, Dall.	11	2755	12036	72
2. Ottis Anderson, N.Y.G.	9	1884	8086	47
3. Gerald Riggs, Atl.	6	1474	6143	47
4. James Wilder, T.B.	7	1419	5370	36
5. Joe Cribbs, S.F.	7	1304	5335	27
6. Joe Morris, N.Y.G.	6	1011	4213	43
7. Tony Galbreath, N.Y.G.	12	1031	4072	34
8. Roger Craig, S.F.	5	964	4069	34
9. Stump Mitchell, Phx.	7	779	3758	28
10. Darrin Nelson, Minn.	6	800	3512	15

Other Leading Rushers

James Jones, Det.	5	864	3138	23
Charles White, Rams	7	692	2752	23
Matt Suhey, Chi.	8	721	2642	17
Wayne Wilson, Wash.	9	684	2531	18
Greg Bell, Rams	4	597	2446	19
Rueben Mayes, N.O.	2	529	2270	13

TOP 10 ACTIVE PASS RECEIVERS, NFC

200 or more receptions

	Yrs.	No.	Yards	TD
1. Art Monk, Wash.	8	504	7033	34
2. Tony Galbreath, N.Y.G.	12	490	4066	9
3. Tony Dorsett, Dall.	11	382	3432	13
4. J.T. Smith, Phx.	10	381	4985	23
5. James Wilder, T.B.	7	379	3033	6
6. David Hill, Det.	12	358	4212	28
Roger Craig, S.F.	5	358	3234	14
8. Roy Green, Phx.	9	357	5899	48
9. Jimmie Giles, Phil.	11	328	4802	38
10. Mike Renfro, Dall.	10	323	4708	28

Other Leading Receivers

Mike Quick, Phil.	6	319	5593	54
Ottis Anderson, N.Y.G.	9	310	2557	5
Kevin House, Rams	8	299	5169	34
Doug Cosbie, Dall.	9	288	3616	30
John Spagnola, Phil.	8	256	2833	14
James Jones, Det.	5	256	2059	10
Gerald Carter, T.B.	8	239	3443	17
Matt Suhey, Chi.	8	231	1886	4
Joe Cribbs, S.F.	7	224	2199	15
Steve Jordan, Minn.	6	217	2812	12
Emery Moorehead, Chi.	11	210	2847	13
Darrin Nelson, Minn.	6	209	1903	5
Gary Clark, Wash.	3	202	3257	19
Jerry Rice, S.F.	3	200	3575	40

TOP 10 ACTIVE SCORERS, NFC

250 or more points

	Yrs.	TD	FG	PAT	TP
1. Ray Wersching, S.F.	15	0	222	456	1122
2. Eddie Murray, Det.	8	0	172	249	765
3. Mick Luckhurst, Atl.	7	0	115	213	558
4. Morten Andersen, N.O.	6	0	125	171	546
5. Tony Dorsett, Dall.	11	86	0	0	516
6. Mike Lansford, Rams	6	0	96	177	465
7. Raul Allegre, N.Y.G.	5	0	98	130	424
8. Paul McFadden, Phil.	4	0	91	117	390
9. Kevin Butler, Chi.	3	0	78	115	349
10. Mike Quick, Phil.	6	54	0	0	324

Other Leading Scorers

Ali Haji-Sheikh, Wash.	5	0	76	95	323
Ottis Anderson, N.Y.G.	9	52	0	0	312
Roy Green, Phx.	9	51	0	0	306
Roger Craig, S.F.	5	48	0	0	288
Al Del Greco, Phx.	4	0	54	120	282
Gerald Riggs, Atl.	6	47	0	0	282
Joe Morris, N.Y.G.	6	45	0	0	270
Tony Galbreath, N.Y.G.	12	43	2	1	265
Joe Cribbs, S.F.	7	43	0	0	258
Jerry Rice, S.F.	3	43	0	0	258
Chuck Nelson, Minn.	4	0	43	127	256
James Wilder, T.B.	7	42	0	0	252

TOP 10 ACTIVE INTERCEPTORS, NFC

20 or more interceptions

	Yrs.	No.	Yards	TD
1. Dave Brown, G.B.	13	53	659	5
2. John Harris, Minn.	10	47	514	2
3. Everson Walls, Dall.	7	42	391	0
4. Ronnie Lott, S.F.	7	38	524	5
5. Nolan Cromwell, Rams	11	37	671	4
6. Michael Downs, Dall.	7	32	430	1
7. LeRoy Irvin, Rams	8	28	586	5
Dave Waymer, N.O.	8	28	238	0
9. Mark Lee, G.B.	8	25	202	0
10. John Anderson, G.B.	10	24	166	1

Other Leading Interceptors

Steve Freeman, Minn.	13	23	329	3
Bobby Butler, Atl.	7	23	200	1
Vernon Dean, Phx.	6	21	243	2
Roynell Young, Phil.	8	21	101	0
Bobby Watkins, Det.	6	20	85	0

TOP 10 ACTIVE QUARTERBACK SACKERS, NFC

Official statistic since 1982

	No.
1. Lawrence Taylor, N.Y.G.	73.5
2. Dexter Manley, Wash.	73
3. Richard Dent, Chi.	61.5
4. Rickey Jackson, N.O.	58
5. Greg Brown, Atl.	52.5
6. Reggie White, Phil.	52
7. Curtis Greer, Phx.	50.5
Randy White, Dall.	50.5
9. Ed Jones, Dall.	49.5
10. Doug Martin, Minn.	48

TOP 10 ACTIVE PUNT RETURNERS, NFC

40 or more punt returns

	Yrs.	No.	Yards	Avg.	TD
1. Vai Sikahema, Phx.	2	87	1072	12.3	3
2. Henry Ellard, Rams	5	112	1355	12.1	4
3. J.T. Smith, Phx.	10	247	2611	10.6	4
4. Dana McLemore, S.F.	6	152	1598	10.5	4
5. Pete Mandley, Det.	4	106	1073	10.1	2
6. LeRoy Irvin, Rams	8	145	1448	10.0	4
Dennis McKinnon, Chi.	4	83	827	10.0	3
8. Ricky Smith, Det.	4	54	537	9.9	0
9. Don Griffin, S.F.	2	47	456	9.7	1
10. Eric Yarber, Wash.	2	46	416	9.0	0

Other Leading Punt Returners

Walter Stanley, G.B.	3	75	668	8.9	1
Stump Mitchell, Phx.	7	156	1377	8.8	1
Lew Barnes, Chi.	1	57	482	8.5	0
Phillip Epps, G.B.	6	100	819	8.2	1
Phil McConkey, N.Y.G.	4	173	1395	8.1	0
Eric Martin, N.O.	3	46	368	8.0	0
Evan Cooper, Phil.	4	99	753	7.6	0

TOP 10 ACTIVE KICKOFF RETURNERS, NFC

40 or more kickoff returns

	Yrs.	No.	Yards	Avg.	TD
1. Mel Gray, N.O.	2	61	1502	24.6	1
2. Sylvester Stamps, Atl.	4	71	1715	24.2	1
3. Dennis Gentry, Chi.	6	90	2163	24.0	3
4. Darrin Nelson, Minn.	6	76	1788	23.5	0
5. Roy Green, Phx.	9	83	1917	23.1	1
6. Stump Mitchell, Phx.	7	167	3836	23.0	0
7. Wayne Wilson, Wash.	9	72	1630	22.6	0
Vai Sikahema, Phx.	2	71	1608	22.6	0
9. Ricky Smith, Det.	4	67	1505	22.5	1
10. Darryl Clack, Dall.	2	48	1056	22.0	0

Other Leading Kickoff Returners

Dokie Williams, S.F.	5	44	949	21.6	0
Del Rodgers, S.F.	3	76	1637	21.5	1
Phil Freeman, T.B.	3	79	1667	21.1	0
Dana McLemore, S.F.	6	56	1147	20.5	0
Walter Stanley, G.B.	3	40	818	20.5	0
Cliff Austin, T.B.	5	57	1147	20.1	1
Robert Lavette, Atl.	3	76	1490	19.6	0
Jeff Smith, T.B.	3	67	1295	19.3	0
Phil McConkey, N.Y.G.	4	65	1254	19.3	0
Keith Griffin, Wash.	4	49	940	19.2	0
Mark Lee, G.B.	8	45	859	19.1	0
Butch Woolfolk, Det.	6	49	930	19.0	0
Charles White, Rams	7	50	932	18.6	0
Thomas Sanders, Chi.	3	43	758	17.6	0

TOP 10 ACTIVE PUNTERS, NFC

50 or more punts

	Yrs.	No.	Avg.	LG
1. Rick Donnelly, Atl.	3	198	43.8	71
2. Sean Landeta, N.Y.G.	3	225	43.5	68
3. Brian Hansen, N.O.	4	291	42.4	66
4. Jim Arnold, Det.	5	366	42.3	64
5. Steve Cox, Wash.	7	380	42.1	77
6. Bucky Scribner, Minn.	3	174	41.9	70
7. Dale Hatcher, Rams	3	260	40.9	67
8. Mike Saxon, Dall.	3	235	40.8	63
9. Greg Coleman, Minn.	11	781	40.7	73
10. Don Bracken, G.B.	3	153	40.5	65

Other Leading Punters

Max Runager, S.F.	9	595	40.4	64
Danny White, Dall.	12	610	40.2	73
John Teltschik, Phil.	2	190	40.1	62
Vince Gamache, S.F.	2	92	38.8	55

DRAFT LIST FOR 1988

53rd Annual NFL Draft, April 24-25, 1988

Atlanta Falcons

1. Aundray Bruce—1, LB, Auburn
2. Marcus Cotton—28, LB, Southern California
3. Alex Higdon—56, TE, Ohio State
4. Choice to Tampa Bay through Philadelphia
5. Charles Dimry—110, DB, Nevada-Las Vegas
6. George Thomas—138, WR, Nevada-Las Vegas
   Houston Hoover—140, G, Jackson State, from Tampa Bay
7. Michael Haynes—166, WR, Northern Arizona
8. Phillip Brown—194, LB, Alabama
9. James Primus—222, RB, UCLA
10. Stan Clayton—250, T, Penn State
11. James Milling—278, WR, Maryland
12. Carter Wiley—306, DB, Virginia Tech

Buffalo Bills

1. Choice to L.A. Rams
2. Thurman Thomas—40, RB, Oklahoma State
3. Bernard Ford—65, WR, Central Florida
4. Choice to San Diego
5. Ezekial Gadson—123, DB, Pittsburgh
   Kirk Roach—135, K, Western Carolina, from San Francisco
6. Dan Murray—150, LB, E. Stroudsburg
7. Tim Borcky—177, T, Memphis State
   Bo Wright—184, RB, Alabama, from San Diego
8. John Hagy—204, DB, Texas
   Jeff Wright—213, NT, Central Missouri, from Indianapolis
9. Carlton Bailey—235, NT, North Carolina
10. Martin Mayhew—262, DB, Florida State
11. Pete Curkendall—289, NT, Penn State
12. John Driscoll—309, T, New Hampshire, from Kansas City
    Tom Erlandson—316, LB, Washington

Chicago Bears

1. Brad Muster—23, RB, Stanford
   Wendell Davis—27, WR, Louisiana State, from Washington
2. Dante Jones—51, LB, Oklahoma
3. Ralph Jarvis—78, DE, Temple
4. Jim Thornton—105, TE, Cal State-Fullerton
5. Troy Johnson—133, LB, Oklahoma
6. Lemuel Stinson—161, DB, Texas Tech
7. Caesar Rentie—189, T, Oklahoma
8. David Tate—208, DB, Colorado, from New England
   Harvey Reed—217, RB, Howard
9. Rogie Magee—245, WR, Louisiana State
10. Joel Porter—273, G, Baylor
11. Steve Forch—301, LB, Nebraska
12. Greg Clark—329, LB, Arizona State

Cincinnati Bengals

1. Rickey Dixon—5, DB, Oklahoma
2. Ickey Woods—31, RB, Nevada-Las Vegas
3. Kevin Walker—57, LB, Maryland
4. David Grant—84, NT, West Virginia
5. Herb Wester—114, T, Iowa
6. Paul Jetton—141, G, Texas
7. Rich Romer—168, LB, Union, N.Y.
8. Curtis Maxey—195, NT, Grambling
9. Brandy Wells—226, DB, Notre Dame
10. Ellis Dillahunt—253, DB, East Carolina
11. Paul Hickert—280, K, Murray State
12. Carl Parker—307, WR, Vanderbilt

Cleveland Browns

1. Clifford Charlton—21, LB, Florida
2. Michael Dean Perry—50, DT, Clemson
3. Van Waiters—77, LB, Indiana
4. Anthony Blaylock—103, DB, Winston-Salem State
5. Choice to Phoenix
6. Choice to Philadelphia
7. Thane Gash—188, DB, East Tennessee State
8. J.J. Birden—216, WR, Oregon
9. Danny Copeland—244, DB, Eastern Kentucky
10. Brian Washington—272, DB, Nebraska
11. Hendley Hawkins—300, WR, Nebraska
12. Steve Slayden—328, QB, Duke

Dallas Cowboys

1. Michael Irvin—11, WR, Miami
2. Ken Norton, Jr.—41, LB, UCLA
3. Mark Hutson—67, G, Oklahoma
4. Dave Widell—94, T, Boston College,
5. Choice to Phoenix through Seattle
6. Scott Secules—151, QB, Virginia
7. Owen Hooven—178, T, Oregon State
8. Mark Higgs—205, RB, Kentucky
9. Brian Bedford—232, WR, California
10. Billy Owens—263, DB, Pittsburgh
11. Chad Hennings—290, DE, Air Force
12. Ben Hummel—317, LB, UCLA

Denver Broncos

1. Ted Gregory—26, NT, Syracuse
2. Gerald Perry—45, T, Southern U., from Minnesota
   Choice to Minnesota
3. Kevin Guidry—79, DB, Louisiana State, from New Orleans
   Choice to New Orleans
4. Choice to Minnesota
5. Corris Ervin—136, DB, Central Florida
6. Choice to Minnesota
7. Pat Kelly—174, TE, Syracuse, from L.A. Rams
   Garry Frank—192, G, Mississippi State
8. Choice to Miami
9. Mel Farr, Jr.—248, RB, UCLA
10. Channing Williams—268, RB, Arizona State, from Pittsburgh
    Choice to New Orleans
11. Richard Calvin—304, RB, Washington State
12. Johnny Carter—332, NT, Grambling

Detroit Lions

1. Choice to Kansas City
   Bennie Blades—3, DB, Miami, from Kansas City
2. Chris Spielman—29, LB, Ohio State, from Kansas City
   Pat Carter—32, TE, Florida State
3. Ray Roundtree—58, WR, Penn State
4. William White—85, DB, Ohio State
5. Eric Andolsek—111, G, Louisiana State
6. Carl Painter—142, RB, Hampton Institute
7. Jeff James—169, WR, Stanford
8. Gary Hadd—196, DE, Minnesota
9. Kip Corrington—223, DB, Texas A&M
   Todd Irvin—234, T, Mississippi, from Philadelphia
10. Paco Craig—254, WR, UCLA
11. Danny McCoin—281, QB, Cincinnati
12. Choice to Indianapolis

Green Bay Packers

1. Sterling Sharpe—7, WR, South Carolina
2. Shawn Patterson—34, DT, Arizona State
3. Keith Woodside—61, RB, Texas A&M
4. Rollin Putzier—88, DT, Oregon, from L.A. Raiders
   Chuck Cecil—89, DB, Arizona
5. Darrell Reed—116, LB, Oklahoma
6. Nate Hill—144, DE, Auburn
7. Gary Richard—173, DB, Pittsburgh
8. Patrick Collins—200, RB, Oklahoma
9. Neal Wilkinson—228, TE, James Madison
10. Bud Keyes—256, QB, Wisconsin
11. Choice to Seattle
12. Scott Bolton—312, WR, Auburn

Houston Oilers

1. Lorenzo White—22, RB, Michigan State
2. Quintin Jones—48, DB, Pittsburgh
3. Greg Montgomery—72, P, Michigan State, from San Diego
   Choice to N.Y. Jets through L.A. Raiders
4. Choice to San Francisco through L.A. Raiders
5. Cris Dishman—125, DB, Purdue, from San Diego
   Chris Verhulst—130, TE, Cal State-Chico
6. Kurt Crain—157, LB, Auburn
7. Tracey Eaton—187, DB, Portland State
8. Dave Viaene—214, C, Minnesota-Duluth
9. David Spradlin—241, LB, Texas Christian
10. Marco Johnson—271, WR, Hawaii
11. Jethro Franklin—298, DE, Fresno State
12. John Brantley—325, LB, Georgia

Indianapolis Colts

1. Choice to L.A. Rams
2. Choice to L.A. Rams
3. Chris Chandler—76, QB, Washington
4. Michael Ball—104, DB, Southern U.
5. John Baylor—129, DB, Southern Mississippi
6. Choice to Washington
7. Choice to N.Y. Giants
8. Choice to Buffalo
9. Jeff Herrod—243, LB, Mississippi
10. O'Brien Alston—270, LB, Maryland
11. Donnie Dee—297, TE, Tulsa
12. Aatron Kenney—308, WR, Wisconsin-Stevens Point, from Detroit
    Tim Vesling—327, K, Syracuse

Kansas City Chiefs

1. Neil Smith—2, DE, Nebraska, from Detroit
   Choice to Detroit
2. Choice to Detroit
3. Kevin Porter—59, DB, Auburn
4. Choice to Tampa Bay
   J.R. Ambrose—96, WR, Mississippi, from Pittsburgh
5. Choice to New Orleans
6. James Saxon—139, RB, San Jose State
7. Troy Stedman—170, LB, Washburn
8. Alfredo Roberts—197, TE, Miami
9. Azizuddin Abdur-Ra'Oof—224, WR, Maryland
10. Kenny Gamble—251, RB, Colgate
11. Danny McManus—282, QB, Florida State
12. Choice to Buffalo

Los Angeles Raiders

1. Tim Brown—6, WR, Notre Dame
   Terry McDaniel—9, DB, Tennessee, from L.A. Rams through Houston
   Scott Davis—25, DE, Illinois, from San Francisco
2. Choice to San Francisco
3. Choice to San Diego through Houston
4. Choice to Green Bay
   Tim Rother—90, DT, Nebraska, from N.Y. Jets
5. Choice to New England
   Dennis Price—131, DB, UCLA, from Seattle through San Francisco and N.Y. Jets
6. Erwin Grabisna—143, LB, Case Western
7. Derrick Crudup—171, DB, Oklahoma
8. Mike Alexander—199, WR, Penn State
9. Reggie Ware—227, RB, Auburn
   Scott Tabor—229, P, California, from N.Y. Giants
10. Newt Harrell—255, T, West Texas State
11. David Weber—283, QB, Carroll, Wis.
12. Greg Kunkel—311, G, Kentucky

Los Angeles Rams

1. Choice to L.A. Raiders through Houston
   Gaston Green—14, RB, UCLA, from Buffalo
   Aaron Cox—20, WR, Arizona State, from Indianapolis
2. Anthony Newman—35, DB, Oregon
   Willie Anderson—46, WR, UCLA, from San Diego
   Fred Strickland—47, LB, Purdue, from Indianapolis
3. Choice to Washington
   Mike Piel—82, DT, Illinois, from Washington
4. Choice to San Diego
5. Robert Delpino—117, RB, Missouri
   James Washington—137, DB, UCLA, from Washington
6. Keith Jones—147, RB, Nebraska
   Jeff Knapton—165, DT, Wyoming, from Washington
7. Choice to Denver
8. Darryl Franklin—201, WR, Washington
9. Pat Foster—231, DT, Montana
10. R.C. Mullin—258, T, Southwestern Louisiana
11. Choice to San Diego
12. Choice to Washington
    Jeff Beathard—333, WR, Southern Oregon, from Washington

Miami Dolphins

1. Eric Kumerow—16, DE, Ohio State
2. Jarvis Williams—42, DB, Florida
3. Ferrell Edmunds—73, TE, Maryland
4. Greg Johnson—99, T, Oklahoma
5. Rodney Thomas—126, DB, Brigham Young
6. Melvin Bratton—153, RB, Miami
   George Cooper—156, RB, Ohio State, from Minnesota
7. Kerwin Bell—180, QB, Florida
8. Harry Galbreath—212, G, Tennessee
   Louis Cheek—220, T, Texas A&M, from Denver
9. Jeff Cross—239, DE, Missouri
10. Artis Jackson—266, NT, Texas Tech
11. Tom Kelleher—292, RB, Holy Cross
12. Brian Kinchen—320, TE, Louisiana State

Minnesota Vikings

1. Randall McDaniel—19, G, Arizona State
2. Choice to Denver
   Brad Edwards—54, DB, South Carolina, from Denver
3. Al Noga—71, DT, Hawaii
4. Choice to New England
   Todd Kalis—108, G, Arizona State, from Denver
5. Darrell Fullington—124, DB, Miami
6. Choice to Miami
   Derrick White—164, DB, Oklahoma, from Denver
7. Brad Beckman—183, TE, Nebraska-Omaha
8. Joe Cain—210, LB, Oregon Tech
9. Paul McGowan—237, LB, Florida State
10. Brian Habib—264, DT, Washington
11. Norman Floyd—296, DB, South Carolina
12. Choice to N.Y. Giants

New England Patriots

1. John Stephens—17, RB, Northwestern State, La.
2. Vincent Brown—43, LB, Mississippi Valley State
3. Tom Rehder—69, T, Notre Dame
4. Tim Goad—87, NT, North Carolina, from Tampa Bay
   Sammy Martin—97, WR, Louisiana State, from Minnesota
   Teddy Garcia—100, K, Northeastern Louisiana
5. Troy Wolkow—115, G, Minnesota, from L.A. Raiders
   Choice to Washington
6. Steve Johnson—154, TE, Virginia Tech
7. Darryl Usher—181, WR, Illinois
8. Choice to Chicago
9. Neil Galbraith—240, DB, Central State, Okla.
10. Rodney Lossow—267, C, Wisconsin
11. Marvin Allen—294, RB, Tulane
12. Dave Nugent—321, NT, Boston College

New Orleans Saints

1. Craig Heyward—24, RB, Pittsburgh
2. Brett Perriman—52, WR, Miami
3. Choice to Denver
   Tony Stephens—81, NT, Clemson, from Denver
4. Lydell Carr—106, RB, Oklahoma
5. Greg Scales—112, TE, Wake Forest, from Kansas City
   Keith Taylor—134, DB, Illinois
6. Bob Sims—162, G, Florida
7. Brian Forde—190, LB, Washington State
8. Glenn Derby—218, T, Wisconsin
9. Clarence Nunn—246, DB, San Diego State
10. Todd Santos—274, QB, San Diego State
    Vincent Fizer—276, LB, Southern U., from Denver
11. Gary Couch—302, WR, Minnesota
12. Paul Jurgensen—330, DE, Georgia Tech

New York Giants

1. Eric Moore—10, T, Indiana
2. John Elliott—36, T, Michigan
3. Sheldon White—62, DB, Miami, Ohio
4. Ricky Shaw—92, LB, Oklahoma State
5. Jon Carter—118, DE, Pittsburgh
6. David Houle—145, G, Michigan State
7. Mike Perez—175, QB, San Jose State
   Danta Whitaker—186, TE, Mississippi Valley State, from Indianapolis
8. Sammy Lilly—202, DB, Georgia Tech
9. Choice to L.A. Raiders
10. Eric Hickerson—259, DB, Indiana
    Steve Wilkes—265, TE, Appalachian State, from San Diego
11. Greg Harris—286, WR, Troy State
12. David Futrell—313, NT, Brigham Young
    Brendan McCormack—323, DT, South Carolina, from Minnesota

New York Jets

1. Dave Cadigan—8, T, Southern California
2. Terry Williams—37, DB, Bethune-Cookman
3. Erik McMillan—63, DB, Missouri
   James Hasty—74, DB, Washington State, from Houston through L.A. Raiders
4. Choice to L.A. Raiders
5. Mike Withycombe—119, T, Fresno State
6. Paul Frase—146, DE, Syracuse
7. Gary Patton—172, RB, Eastern Michigan
8. Keith Neubert—203, TE, Nebraska
9. Ralph Tamm—230, G, West Chester University
10. John Booty—257, DB, Texas Christian
11. John Galvin—287, LB, Boston College
12. Albert Goss—314, NT, Jackson State

Philadelphia Eagles

1. Keith Jackson—13, TE, Oklahoma
2. Eric Allen—30, DB, Arizona State, from Tampa Bay
   Choice to San Francisco through Tampa Bay
3. Matt Patchan—64, T, Miami
4. Choice exercised in 1987 Supplemental Draft for Cris Carter, WR, Ohio State
5. Eric Everett—122, DB, Texas Tech
6. Don McPherson—149, QB, Syracuse
   Rob Sterling—160, DB, Maine, from Cleveland
7. Todd White—176, WR, Cal State-Fullerton
8. David Smith—207, RB, Western Kentucky
9. Choice to Detroit
10. Joe Schuster—261, DT, Iowa
11. Izel Jenkins—288, DB, North Carolina State
12. Steve Kaufusi—319, DE, Brigham Young

Phoenix Cardinals

1. Ken Harvey—12, LB, California
2. Tony Jeffery—38, RB, Texas Christian
3. Tom Tupa—68, P, Ohio State
4. Michael Brim—95, DB, Virginia Union
5. Chris Gaines—120, LB, Vanderbilt, from Dallas through Seattle
   Choice to Pittsburgh
   Tony Jordan—132, RB, Kansas State, from Cleveland
6. Jon Phillips—148, G, Oklahoma
7. Ernie Jones—179, WR, Indiana
8. Tim Moore—206, LB, Michigan State
9. Scott Dill—233, G, Memphis State
10. Andy Schillinger—260, WR, Miami, Ohio
11. Keith McCoy—291, DB, Fresno State
12. Chris Carrier—318, DB, Louisiana State

Pittsburgh Steelers

1. Aaron Jones—18, DE, Eastern Kentucky
2. Dermontti Dawson—44, G, Kentucky
3. Chuck Lanza—70, C, Notre Dame
4. Choice to Kansas City
5. Darin Jordan—121, LB, Northeastern, from Phoenix
   Jerry Reese—128, NT, Kentucky
6. Warren Williams—155, RB, Miami
7. Marc Zeno—182, WR, Tulane
8. Mark Nichols—209, NT, Michigan State
   Mike Hinnant—211, TE, Temple, from San Diego
9. Gordie Lockbaum—236, RB, Holy Cross
10. John Jackson—252, T, Eastern Kentucky, from Tampa Bay
    Choice to Denver
11. Bobby Dawson—295, DB, Illinois
12. James Earle—322, LB, Clemson

San Diego Chargers

1. Anthony Miller—15, WR, Tennessee
2. Choice to L.A. Rams
3. Quinn Early—60, WR, Iowa, from L.A. Raiders through Houston
   Choice to Houston
4. Joe Campbell—91, DE, New Mexico State, from L.A. Rams
   Stacy Searels—93, T, Auburn, from Buffalo
   David Richards—98, T, UCLA
5. Choice to Houston
6. Cedric Figaro—152, LB, Notre Dame
7. Choice to Buffalo
8. Choice to Pittsburgh
9. Joey Howard—238, T, Tennessee
10. Choice to N.Y. Giants
11. Ed Miller—285, C, Pittsburgh, from L.A. Rams
    George Hinkle—293, NT, Arizona
12. Wendell Phillips—324, DB, North Alabama

San Francisco 49ers

1. Choice to L.A. Raiders
2. Danny Stubbs—33, DE, Miami, from L.A. Raiders
   Pierce Holt—39, DT, Angelo State, from Philadelphia through Tampa Bay
   Choice to Tampa Bay
3. Bill Romanowski—80, LB, Boston College
4. Barry Helton—102, P, Colorado, from Houston through L.A. Raiders
   Choice to Tampa Bay
5. Choice to Buffalo
6. Choice to Tampa Bay
7. Kevin Bryant—191, LB, Delaware State
8. Larry Clarkson—219, T, Montana
9. Brian Bonner—247, LB, Minnesota
10. Tim Foley—275, K, Georgia Southern
11. Chet Brooks—303, DB, Texas A&M
12. George Mira, Jr.—331, LB, Miami

Seattle Seahawks

1. Choice exercised in 1987 Supplemental Draft for Brian Bosworth, LB, Oklahoma
2. Brian Blades—49, WR, Miami
3. Tommy Kane—75, WR, Syracuse
4. Kevin Harmon—101, RB, Iowa
5. Choice to L.A. Raiders through San Francisco and N.Y. Jets
6. Roy Hart—158, NT, South Carolina
7. Ray Jackson—185, DB, Ohio State
8. Robert Tyler—215, TE, South Carolina State
9. Deatrich Wise—242, NT, Jackson State
10. Derwin Jones—269, DE, Miami
11. Rick McLeod—284, T, Washington, from Green Bay
    Dwayne Harper—299, DB, South Carolina State
12. Dave Des Rochers—326, T, San Diego State

Tampa Bay Buccaneers

1. Paul Gruber—4, T, Wisconsin
2. Choice to Philadelphia
   Lars Tate—53, RB, Georgia, from San Francisco
3. Choice exercised in 1987 Supplemental Draft for Dan Sileo, DT, Miami
4. Robert Goff—83, DT, Auburn, from Atlanta through Philadelphia
   John Bruhin—86, G, Tennessee, from Kansas City
   Choice to New England
   Monte Robbins—107, P, Michigan, from San Francisco
5. William Howard—113, RB, Tennessee
6. Choice to Atlanta
   Shawn Lee—163, DT, North Alabama, from San Francisco
7. Kerry Goode—167, RB, Alabama
8. Anthony Simpson—198, RB, East Carolina
9. Reuben Davis—225, DT, North Carolina
10. Choice to Pittsburgh
11. Frank Pillow—279, WR, Tennessee State
12. Victor Jones—310, LB, Virginia Tech

Washington Redskins

1. Choice to Chicago
2. Chip Lohmiller—55, K, Minnesota
3. Mike Oliphant—66, KR, Puget Sound, from L.A. Rams
   Choice to L.A. Rams
4. Jamie Morris—109, RB, Michigan
5. Carl Mims—127, DB, Sam Houston State, from New England
   Choice to L.A. Rams
6. Stan Humphries—159, QB, Northeastern Louisiana, from Indianapolis
   Choice to L.A. Rams
7. Harold Hicks—193, DB, San Diego State
8. Darryl McGill—221, RB, Wake Forest
9. Blake Peterson—249, LB, Mesa College, Colo.
10. Henry Brown—277, T, Ohio State
11. Curt Koch—305, DE, Colorado
12. Wayne Ross—315, P, San Diego State, from L.A. Rams
    Choice to L.A. Rams

Active Coaches' Career Records

Start of 1988 Season

Coach	Team(s)	Regular Season					Postseason				Career			
		Yrs.	Won	Lost	Tied	Pct.	Won	Lost	Tied	Pct.	Won	Lost	Tied	Pct.
Don Shula	Baltimore Colts, Miami Dolphins	25	255	101	6	.713	16	13	0	.552	271	114	6	.701
Tom Landry	Dallas Cowboys	28	247	149	6	.622	20	16	0	.556	267	165	6	.616
Chuck Noll	Pittsburgh Steelers	19	163	114	1	.588	15	7	0	.682	178	121	1	.595
Chuck Knox	Los Angeles Rams, Buffalo Bills, Seattle Seahawks	15	139	82	1	.628	7	10	0	.412	146	92	1	.609
Bill Walsh	San Francisco 49ers	9	82	53	1	.607	7	4	0	.636	89	57	1	.609
Joe Gibbs	Washington Redskins	7	74	30	0	.712	11	3	0	.786	85	33	0	.720
Dan Reeves	Denver Broncos	7	66	37	1	.639	4	4	0	.500	70	41	1	.629
Mike Ditka	Chicago Bears	6	61	27	0	.693	4	3	0	.667	65	30	0	.684
John Robinson	Los Angeles Rams	5	46	33	0	.582	2	4	0	.333	48	37	0	.565
Bill Parcells	New York Giants	5	42	36	1	.538	5	2	0	.714	47	38	1	.552
Joe Walton	New York Jets	5	41	38	0	.519	1	2	0	.333	42	40	0	.525
Marv Levy	Kansas City Chiefs, Buffalo Bills	7	40	55	0	.421	0	0	0	.000	40	55	0	.421
Raymond Berry	New England Patriots	4	34	21	0	.618	3	2	0	.600	37	23	0	.617
Marty Schottenheimer	Cleveland Browns	4	34	21	0	.618	2	3	0	.400	36	24	0	.600
Ron Meyer	New England Patriots, Indianapolis Colts	5	30	21	0	.588	0	2	0	.000	30	23	0	.566
Sam Wyche	Cincinnati Bengals	4	29	34	0	.460	0	0	0	.000	29	34	0	.460
Ray Perkins	New York Giants, Tampa Bay Buccaneers	5	27	45	0	.375	1	1	0	.500	28	46	0	.378
Marion Campbell	Atlanta Falcons, Philadelphia Eagles	7	26	60	1	.305	0	0	0	.000	26	60	1	.305
Jerry Burns	Minnesota Vikings	2	17	14	0	.548	2	1	0	.667	19	15	0	.559
Jim Mora	New Orleans Saints	2	19	12	0	.613	0	1	0	.000	19	13	0	.594
Darryl Rogers	Detroit Lions	3	16	31	0	.340	0	0	0	.000	16	31	0	.340
Jerry Glanville	Houston Oilers	3	14	19	0	.424	1	1	0	.500	15	20	0	.429
Buddy Ryan	Philadelphia Eagles	2	12	18	1	.403	0	0	0	.000	12	18	1	.403
Al Saunders	San Diego Chargers	2	11	12	0	.478	0	0	0	.000	11	12	0	.478
Gene Stallings	Phoenix Cardinals	2	11	19	1	.371	0	0	0	.000	11	19	1	.371
Frank Gansz	Kansas City Chiefs	1	4	11	0	.267	0	0	0	.000	4	11	0	.267
Lindy Infante	Green Bay Packers	0	0	0	0	.000	0	0	0	.000	0	0	0	.000
Mike Shanahan	Los Angeles Raiders	0	0	0	0	.000	0	0	0	.000	0	0	0	.000

Coaches With 100 Career Victories

Start of 1988 Season

Coach	Team(s)	Regular Season					Postseason				Career			
		Yrs.	Won	Lost	Tied	Pct.	Won	Lost	Tied	Pct.	Won	Lost	Tied	Pct.
George Halas	Chicago Bears	40	319	148	31	.672	6	3	0	.667	325	151	31	.672
Don Shula	Baltimore Colts, Miami Dolphins	25	255	101	6	.713	16	13	0	.552	271	114	6	.701
Tom Landry	Dallas Cowboys	28	247	149	6	.622	20	16	0	.556	267	165	6	.616
Earl (Curly) Lambeau	Green Bay Packers, Chicago Cardinals, Washington Redskins	33	226	132	22	.624	3	2	0	.600	229	134	22	.623
Paul Brown	Cleveland Browns, Cincinnati Bengals	21	166	100	6	.621	4	8	0	.333	170	108	6	.609
Chuck Noll	Pittsburgh Steelers	18	155	107	1	.591	15	7	0	.682	170	114	1	.598
Bud Grant	Minnesota Vikings	18	158	96	5	.620	10	12	0	.455	168	108	5	.607
Steve Owen	New York Giants	23	151	100	17	.595	2	8	0	.200	153	108	17	.581
Chuck Knox	Los Angeles Rams, Buffalo Bills, Seattle Seahawks	15	139	82	1	.628	7	10	0	.412	146	92	1	.613
Hank Stram	Kansas City Chiefs, New Orleans Saints	17	131	97	10	.571	5	3	0	.625	136	100	10	.573
Weeb Ewbank	Baltimore Colts, New York Jets	20	130	129	7	.502	4	1	0	.800	134	130	7	.507
Sid Gillman	Los Angeles Rams, San Diego Chargers, Houston Oilers	18	122	99	7	.550	1	5	0	.167	123	104	7	.541
George Allen	Los Angeles Rams, Washington Redskins	12	116	47	5	.705	2	7	0	.222	118	54	5	.681
Don Coryell	St. Louis Cardinals, San Diego Chargers	14	111	83	1	.572	3	6	0	.333	114	89	1	.561
John Madden	Oakland Raiders	10	103	32	7	.750	9	7	0	.563	112	39	7	.731
Ray (Buddy) Parker	Chicago Cardinals, Detroit Lions, Pittsburgh Steelers	15	104	75	9	.577	3	1	0	.750	107	76	9	.581
Vince Lombardi	Green Bay Packers, Washington Redskins	10	96	34	6	.728	9	1	0	.900	105	35	6	.740

Look for in 1988

Things that could happen in 1988:

• **Steve Largent,** Seattle, starts 1988 with 12,041 receiving yards and needs 106 yards to supplant Charlie Joiner (12,146) as the NFL record holder in that category. (Largent comes into 1988 with 752 receptions, having broken Joiner's NFL mark of 750 last season.)

• Largent enters 1988 with 95 touchdown receptions, only four short of Don Hutson's NFL record. Largent, who also has one rushing touchdown in his career, needs four more touchdowns to become only the seventh player to score 100 touchdowns in an NFL career.

• Largent's next 100-yard receiving game will be the forty-first of his career, and will tie him with Lance Alworth for second place on the all-time list. Don Maynard holds the NFL record of 50 100-yard receiving games.

• **Jerry Rice,** San Francisco, has caught a touchdown pass in 13 consecutive games, already an NFL record. He is five games short of Lenny Moore's NFL record of 18 consecutive games scoring touchdowns (by any means).

• **Eric Dickerson,** Indianapolis, starts the season with 8,256 yards rushing, and needs 1,744 to become the first player to accumulate 10,000 yards rushing in his first six seasons in the NFL.

• Dickerson has had five consecutive 1,000-yard rushing seasons, one short of the NFL record shared by Franco Harris and Walter Payton.

• Dickerson has 44 career 100-yard games, three shy of Franco Harris in third place on the all-time list with 47. Jim Brown is second with 58 behind Walter Payton's NFL record 77.

• **Tony Dorsett,** Dallas, has 12,036 yards rushing, and needs 85 yards to pass Franco Harris (12,120) into third place on the all-time list; he needs 277 yards rushing to pass Jim Brown (12,312) into second place.

• **Joe Montana,** San Francisco, has passed for 3,000-or-more yards in five seasons, one short of the NFL record held by Dan Fouts.

• **Dan Marino,** Miami, has had 26 300-yard passing games in his career. His next such game will break a tie with Johnny Unitas and boost him into second place behind Dan Fouts's 51 300-yard games.

• Marino has had 14 games in his five-year career in which he has thrown at least four touchdown passes. He is three short of the NFL record held by Johnny Unitas, who played for 18 seasons.

• There have been only 12 quarterbacks in NFL history to have passed for 200-or-more touchdowns. Montana (172) and Marino (168) start 1988 within striking distance of that total.

• Three players start 1988 less than 50 receptions short of 600 for their respective careers, a mark reached by only five players in NFL history: **Ozzie Newsome,** Cleveland (575); **James Lofton,** Los Angeles Raiders (571); and **Wes Chandler,** San Diego (555).

• Lofton has accumulated 10,536 receiving yards during his 10-year career, 464 yards from becoming the fourth player in league history to reach the 11,000-yard plateau.

• **Stanley Morgan,** New England, needs 636 yards on receptions to become only the seventh player in NFL history to reach 10,000 career yards on receptions.

• Morgan needs 25 receptions to become the twenty-second player in NFL history to reach the 500 career mark. Morgan also has 38 career 100-yard receiving games to place fourth in NFL annals behind Don Maynard (50), Lance Alworth (41), and Steve Largent (40).

• **Dave Brown,** Green Bay, needs three interceptions to tie Lem Barney and Pat Fischer, who had 56 apiece, for tenth place in NFL history.

• **Reggie Williams,** Cincinnati, needs one recovery of an opponent's fumble to move past Carl Eller into third place in NFL history in that category. Williams and Eller had 23 apiece, and trail only record-holder Jim Marshall (29) and Dick Butkus (25).

• If **Rulon Jones,** Denver, scores a safety, he will tie the NFL record of four in a career. That record is shared by Ted Hendricks and Doug English.

• **Vai Sikahema,** Phoenix, has led the NFL in punt-return yardage in each of the past two seasons. No player has ever led the NFL in that category three consecutive seasons.

• **Pat Leahy,** New York Jets, needs three points to break into the NFL's all-time top 10 scorers. Leahy starts the 1988 season with 1,078 points; the current tenth-place scorer is Don Cockroft (1,080).

• **Gary Anderson,** Pittsburgh, carries a streak of 174 consecutive extra points into the 1988 season. He needs to convert his next 26 attempts to become only the fourth NFL player to fashion a streak of 200 consecutive extra points. Tommy Davis (234), Jim Turner (221), and George Blanda (201) are the others.

• **Nick Lowery,** Kansas City, has kicked 14 field goals of 50-or-more yards in his nine-year career. He needs three more to tie the record of 17, set by Jan Stenerud over 19 seasons.

• When **Tom Landry,** Dallas, coaches his first 1988 game, he will tie the NFL record for consecutive seasons coaching one NFL team; that mark of 29 years is held by former Green Bay coach Earl (Curly) Lambeau.

• The Cowboys will try to extend their NFL-best opening-day record of 22-5-1 (.804). Dallas holds the NFL record of 17 consecutive opening-game victories from 1965-81.

• **Earnest Jackson,** Pittsburgh, needs a 1,000-yard rushing season to become the first player in NFL history to gain 1,000 yards in a single season with three different teams. Jackson rushed for 1,179 yards with the Chargers in 1984 and gained 1,028 with the Eagles in 1985.

• **Henry Ellard,** Los Angeles Rams, needs to average 15.88 yards for at least 25 punt returns to lift his career average to 12.79 and become the NFL's all-time punt-return leader. George McAfee is the current leader at 12.78.

• **Kevin Butler,** Chicago, needs to convert 22 field-goal attempts to become only the second kicker in NFL history to kick 108 field goals in his first four seasons. Jan Stenerud kicked 108 field goals his first four seasons with Kansas City.

• **Marcus Allen,** Los Angeles Raiders, needs eight touchdowns to become the Raiders' all-time scoring leader. Fred Biletnikoff is the team's current career leader with 77. Allen has scored 70 touchdowns in six seasons.

• **John Robinson** will become the first person to coach the Rams for more than five seasons as he begins his sixth campaign in 1988. Robinson needs seven victories to pass Chuck Knox (54 wins) as the winningest coach in Rams history. Robinson has a 46-33-0 record in his five seasons with the Rams.

• **Everson Walls,** Dallas, needs 11 interceptions to become the Cowboys' all-time interception leader, surpassing Mel Renfro's 14-year total of 52. Walls has 42 interceptions in seven seasons.

• **Mike Webster,** Pittsburgh, by suiting up for the 1988 season, will become the first player in Steelers history to play in 15 seasons with the team.

• **Kellen Winslow,** San Diego, needs 46 receptions to become the Chargers' all-time receiving leader. Winslow begins the season with 541 catches, second in club history to Charlie Joiner's 586.

THE AFC

Buffalo Bills....................26
Cincinnati Bengals....................30
Cleveland Browns....................34
Denver Broncos....................38
Houston Oilers....................42
Indianapolis Colts....................46
Kansas City Chiefs....................50
Los Angeles Raiders....................54
Miami Dolphins....................58
New England Patriots....................62
New York Jets....................66
Pittsburgh Steelers....................70
San Diego Chargers....................74
Seattle Seahawks....................78

American Football Conference Eastern Division

Team Colors: Royal Blue, Scarlet Red, and White

One Bills Drive
Orchard Park, New York 14127
Telephone: (716) 648-1800

Club Officials

President: Ralph C. Wilson, Jr.
Executive Vice President: David N. Olsen
General Manager and Vice President-Administration: Bill Polian
Vice President-Head Coach: Marv Levy
Treasurer: Jeff Littmann
Assistant General Manager: Bill Munson
Administrative Assistant: Jim Overdorf
Director of Administration: Ed Stillwell
Director of College Scouting: John Butler
Director of Pro Personnel: Bob Ferguson
Director of Media Relations: Dave Senko
Director of Public and Community Relations: Denny Lynch
Director of Marketing and Sales: Jerry Foran
Box Office Comptroller: June Foran
Director of Stadium Operations: Steve Champlin
Trainers: Ed Abramoski, Bud Carpenter
Equipment Manager: Dave Hojnowski
Assistant Equipment Manager: Randy Ribbeck
Strength and Conditioning Coordinator: Rusty Jones
Video Director: Henry Kunttu

Stadium: Rich Stadium • **Capacity:** 80,290
One Bills Drive
Orchard Park, New York 14127

Playing Surface: AstroTurf

Training Camp: Fredonia State University
Fredonia, New York 14063

1988 Schedule

Preseason

Aug. 4	at Houston	7:00
Aug. 13	**Cincinnati**	7:30
Aug. 19	at Seattle	7:30
Aug. 25	vs. T.B. at Nashville, Tenn.	7:00

Regular Season

Sept. 4	**Minnesota**	1:00
Sept. 11	**Miami**	1:00
Sept. 18	at New England	1:00
Sept. 25	**Pittsburgh**	1:00
Oct. 2	at Chicago	12:00
Oct. 9	**Indianapolis**	1:00
Oct. 17	at New York Jets (Monday)	9:00
Oct. 23	**New England**	1:00
Oct. 30	**Green Bay**	1:00
Nov. 6	at Seattle	1:00
Nov. 14	at Miami (Monday)	9:00
Nov. 20	**New York Jets**	1:00
Nov. 27	at Cincinnati	1:00
Dec. 4	at Tampa Bay	1:00
Dec. 11	**Los Angeles Raiders**	1:00
Dec. 18	at Indianapolis	1:00

Bills Coaching History

(167-237-8)

1960-61	Buster Ramsey	11-16-1
1962-65	Lou Saban	38-18-3
1966-68	Joe Collier*	13-17-1
1968	Harvey Johnson	1-10-1
1969-70	John Rauch	7-20-1
1971	Harvey Johnson	1-13-0
1972-76	Lou Saban**	32-29-1
1976-77	Jim Ringo	3-20-0
1978-82	Chuck Knox	38-38-0
1983-84	Kay Stephenson***	10-26-0
1985-86	Hank Bullough****	4-17-0
1986-87	Marv Levy	9-13-0

*Released after two games in 1968
**Resigned after five games in 1976
***Released after four games in 1985
****Released after nine games in 1986

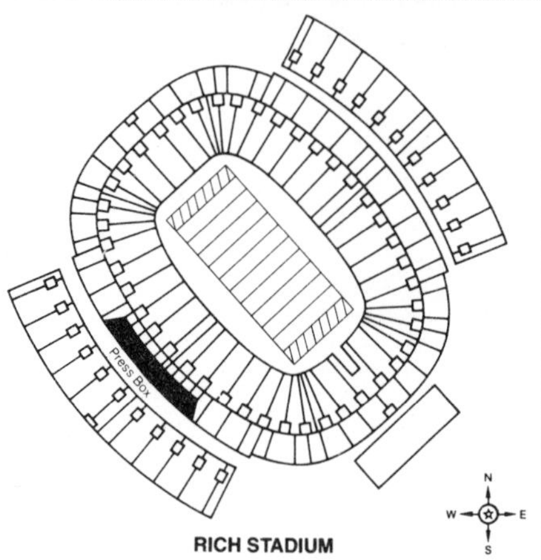

RICH STADIUM

Record Holders

Individual Records—Career

Category	Name	Performance
Rushing (Yds.)	O.J. Simpson, 1969-1977	10,183
Passing (Yds.)	Joe Ferguson, 1973-1984	27,590
Passing (TDs)	Joe Ferguson, 1973-1984	181
Receiving (No.)	Elbert Dubenion, 1960-67	296
Receiving (Yds.)	Elbert Dubenion, 1960-67	5,304
Interceptions	George (Butch) Byrd, 1964-1970	40
Punting (Avg.)	Paul Maguire, 1964-1970	42.1
Punt Return (Avg.)	Keith Moody, 1976-79	10.5
Kickoff Return (Avg.)	Wallace Francis, 1973-74	27.2
Field Goals	John Leypoldt, 1971-76	74
Touchdowns (Tot.)	O.J. Simpson, 1969-1977	70
Points	O.J. Simpson, 1969-1977	420

Individual Records—Single Season

Category	Name	Performance
Rushing (Yds.)	O.J. Simpson, 1973	2,003
Passing (Yds.)	Joe Ferguson, 1981	3,652
Passing (TDs)	Joe Ferguson, 1983	26
Receiving (No.)	Frank Lewis, 1981	70
Receiving (Yds.)	Frank Lewis, 1981	1,244
Interceptions	Billy Atkins, 1961	10
	Tom Janik, 1967	10
Punting (Avg.)	Billy Atkins, 1961	44.5
Punt Return (Avg.)	Keith Moody, 1977	13.1
Kickoff Return (Avg.)	Ed Rutkowski, 1963	30.2
Field Goals	Pete Gogolak, 1965	28
Touchdowns (Tot.)	O.J. Simpson, 1975	23
Points	O.J. Simpson, 1975	138

Individual Records—Single Game

Category	Name	Performance
Rushing (Yds.)	O.J. Simpson, 11-25-76	273
Passing (Yds.)	Joe Ferguson, 10-9-83	419
Passing (TDs)	Joe Ferguson, 9-23-79	5
	Joe Ferguson, 10-9-83	5
Receiving (No.)	Greg Bell, 9-8-85	13
Receiving (Yds.)	Jerry Butler, 9-23-79	255
Interceptions	Many times	3
	Last time by Jeff Nixon, 9-7-80	
Field Goals	Pete Gogolak, 12-5-65	5
Touchdowns (Tot.)	Cookie Gilchrist, 12-8-63	5
Points	Cookie Gilchrist, 12-8-63	30

1987 Team Record

Preseason (1-3)

Date	Result		Opponents
8/15	L	14-19	at Atlanta
8/22	W	7- 3	at L.A. Raiders
8/29	L	14-34	at Kansas City
9/4	L	20-34	at Miami
		55-90	

Regular Season (7-8)

Date	Result		Opponents	Att.
9/13	L	28-31	N.Y. Jets	76,718
9/20	W	34-30	Houston	56,534
9/27	C		at Dallas	
10/4	L	6-47	Indianapolis	9,860
10/11	L	7-14	at New England	11,878
10/18	W	6- 3	N.Y. Giants (OT)	15,737
10/25	W	34-31	at Miami (OT)	61,295
11/1	L	7-27	Washington	71,640
11/8	W	21-14	Denver	63,698
11/15	L	21-27	at Cleveland	78,409
11/22	W	17-14	at N.Y. Jets	58,407
11/29	W	27- 0	Miami	68,055
12/6	L	21-34	at L.A. Raiders	43,143
12/13	W	27- 3	at Indianapolis	60,253
12/20	L	7-13	New England	74,945
12/27	L	7-17	at Philadelphia	57,547

(OT) Overtime
C (Cancelled due to players' strike.)

Score by Periods

Bills	17	86	51	110	6	—	270
Opponents	54	113	77	61	0	—	305

Attendance

Home 437,187 Away 370,932 Total 808,119
Single-game home record, 79,951 (9-7-86)
Single-season home record, 601,712 (1981)

1987 Team Statistics

	Bills	Opp.
Total First Downs	294	297
Rushing	111	114
Passing	151	162
Penalty	32	21
Third Down: Made/Att.	77/208	82/220
Fourth Down: Made/Att.	8/19	10/18
Total Net Yards	4741	4906
Avg. Per Game	316.1	327.1
Total Plays	1018	1022
Avg. Per Play	4.7	4.8
Net Yards Rushing	1840	2052
Avg. Per Game	122.7	136.8
Total Rushes	465	541
Net Yards Passing	2901	2854
Avg. Per Game	193.4	190.3
Sacked/Yards Lost	37/345	34/267
Gross Yards	3246	3121
Att./Completions	516/292	447/249
Completion Pct.	56.6	55.7
Had Intercepted	19	17
Punts/Avg.	83/38.2	88/36.7
Net Punting Avg.	33.9	31.8
Penalties/Yards Lost	94/762	103/840
Fumbles/Ball Lost	41/24	37/14
Touchdowns	33	37
Rushing	9	11
Passing	21	25
Returns	3	1
Avg. Time of Possession	28:41	31:19

1987 Individual Statistics

Scoring	TD R	TD P	TD Rt	PAT	FG	Saf	TP
Norwood	0	0	0	31/31	10/15	0	61
Riddick	5	3	0	0/0	0/0	1	50
Reed	0	5	0	0/0	0/0	0	30
Burkett	0	4	0	0/0	0/0	0	24
Harmon	2	2	0	0/0	0/0	0	24
T. Johnson	0	2	0	0/0	0/0	0	12
Mueller	2	0	0	0/0	0/0	0	12
Rolle	0	2	0	0/0	0/0	0	12
Schlopy	0	0	0	1/2	2/5	0	7
Broughton	0	1	0	0/0	0/0	0	6
M. Brown	0	1	0	0/0	0/0	0	6
Kelso	0	0	1	0/0	0/0	0	6
McFadden	0	1	0	0/0	0/0	0	6
McNanie	0	0	1	0/0	0/0	0	6
Smith	0	0	1	0/0	0/0	0	6
Tasker	0	0	0	0/0	0/0	1	2
Bills	9	21	3	32/33	12/20	2	270
Opponents	11	25	1	36/37	15/20	1	305

Passing	Att.	Comp.	Yds.	Pct.	TD	Int.	Tkld.	Rate
Kelly	419	250	2798	59.7	19	11	27/239	83.8
McClure	38	20	181	52.6	0	3	2/17	32.9
Totten	33	13	155	39.4	2	2	5/62	49.4
Manucci	21	7	68	33.3	0	2	3/27	3.8
Miller	3	1	9	33.3	0	1	0/0	2.8
Kidd	1	0	0	0.0	0	0	0/0	39.6
Riddick	1	1	35	100.0	0	0	0/0	118.8
Bills	516	292	3246	56.6	21	19	37/345	73.7
Opponents	447	249	3121	55.7	25	17	34/267	80.4

Rushing	Att.	Yds.	Avg.	LG	TD
Harmon	116	485	4.2	21	2
Mueller	82	354	4.3	20	2
Byrum	66	280	4.2	30	0
Riddick	59	221	3.7	25	5
R. Porter	47	177	3.8	13	0
Kelly	29	133	4.6	24	0
Bell	14	60	4.3	11	0
Shepherd	12	42	3.5	19	0
King	9	28	3.1	8	0
Williams	9	25	2.8	9	0
Partridge	1	13	13.0	13	0
Totten	12	11	0.9	7	0
Manucci	4	6	1.5	9	0
McClure	2	4	2.0	3	0
Reed	1	1	1.0	1	0
K. Porter	2	0	0.0	1	0
Bills	465	1840	4.0	30	9
Opponents	541	2052	3.8	42	11

Receiving	No.	Yds.	Avg.	LG	TD
Reed	57	752	13.2	40	5
Burkett	56	765	13.7	47	4
Harmon	56	477	8.5	42	2
Metzelaars	28	290	10.4	34	0
T. Johnson	15	186	12.4	26t	2
Riddick	15	96	6.4	17t	3
M. Brown	9	120	13.3	30	1
Gaines	9	115	12.8	37	0
McKeller	9	80	8.9	22	0
R. Porter	9	70	7.8	26	0
Broughton	5	90	18.0	39	1
McFadden	4	41	10.3	13t	1
Bell	4	37	9.3	12	0
Byrum	3	23	7.7	20	0
Mueller	3	13	4.3	11	0
Bynum	2	24	12.0	17	0
Rolle	2	6	3.0	3t	2
Kelly	1	35	35.0	35	0
Chetti	1	9	9.0	9	0
Belk	1	7	7.0	7	0
Williams	1	5	5.0	5	0
King	1	3	3.0	3	0
Shepherd	1	2	2.0	2	0
Bills	292	3246	11.1	47	21
Opponents	249	3121	12.5	55t	25

Interceptions	No.	Yds.	Avg.	LG	TD
Kelso	6	25	4.2	12	0
Pitts	3	19	6.3	12	0
Burroughs	2	11	5.5	14	0
Radecic	2	4	2.0	4	0
Clark	1	23	23.0	23	0
Schankweiler	1	7	7.0	7	0
Cokeley	1	4	4.0	4	0
Davis	1	0	0.0	0	0
Bills	17	93	5.5	23	0
Opponents	19	177	9.3	28	0

Punting	No.	Yds.	Avg.	In 20	LG
Kidd	64	2495	39.0	20	67
Partridge	18	678	37.7	3	52
Bills	83	3173	38.2	23	67
Opponents	88	3229	36.7	13	77

Punt Returns	No.	FC	Yds.	Avg.	LG	TD
Pitts	23	12	149	6.5	19	0
McFadden	8	3	83	10.4	23	0
Bills	31	15	232	7.5	23	0
Opponents	35	13	179	5.1	17	0

Kickoff Returns	No.	Yds.	Avg.	LG	TD
Tasker	11	197	17.9	39	0
R. Porter	8	219	27.4	40	0
McFadden	7	121	17.3	26	0
Riddick	7	151	21.6	31	0
Mueller	5	74	14.8	20	0
Armstrong	2	25	12.5	18	0
M. Brown	2	35	17.5	18	0
Harmon	1	30	30.0	30	0
Radecic	1	14	14.0	14	0
Rolle	1	6	6.0	6	0
Bills	45	872	19.4	40	0
Opponents	43	679	15.8	34	0

Sacks	No.
Smith	12.0
Bennett	8.5
Seals	3.5
McNanie	2.5
Armstrong	2.0
Bentley	1.0
Drane	1.0
Martin	1.0
Smerlas	1.0
Talley	1.0
Conlan	0.5
Bills	34.0
Opponents	37.0

Buffalo Bills 1988 Veteran Roster

No.	Name	Pos.	Ht.	Wt.	Birth-date	NFL Exp.	College	Hometown	How Acq.	'87 Games/ Starts
2	Beecher, Willie	K	5-10	170	4/14/63	2	Utah State	Logan, Utah	FA-'87	3/0*
55	Bennett, Cornelius	LB	6-2	235	8/25/66	2	Alabama	Birmingham, Ala.	T(Ind)-'87	8/7
50	Bentley, Ray	LB	6-2	245	11/25/60	3	Central Michigan	Grand Rapids, Mich.	FA-'86	9/4
81	Broughton, Walter	WR	5-10	180	10/20/62	3	Jacksonville State	Weaver, Ala.	FA-'86	9/0
85	Burkett, Chris	WR	6-4	210	8/21/62	4	Jackson State	Collins, Miss.	D2b-'85	12/12
29	Burroughs, Derrick	CB	6-1	180	5/18/62	4	Memphis State	Mobile, Ala.	D1b-'85	12/12
61	Burton, Leonard	T	6-3	275	6/18/64	3	South Carolina	Memphis, Tenn.	D3-'86	12/3
80	Butler, Jerry	WR	6-0	178	10/12/57	8	Clemson	Ware Shoals, S.C.	D1b-'79	0*
35	Byrum, Carl	RB	6-0	235	6/29/63	3	Mississippi Valley State	Southaven, Miss.	D5-'86	13/8
69	Christy, Greg	G	6-4	285	4/29/62	2	Pittsburgh	Freeport, Pa.	FA-'85	0*
58	Conlan, Shane	LB	6-3	230	4/3/64	2	Penn State	Frewsburg, N.Y.	D1-'87	12/12
21	Davis, Wayne	CB	5-11	175	7/17/63	4	Indiana State	Mt. Healthy, Ohio	T(SD)-'87	10/0
70	†Devlin, Joe	T	6-5	280	2/23/54	12	Iowa	Frazer, Pa.	D2b-'76	12/12
45	Drane, Dwight	S	6-2	205	5/6/62	3	Oklahoma	Miami, Fla.	SD1-'84	11/6
46	†Fox, Chas	WR-KR	5-11	190	10/3/63	2	Furman	Rapid City, S.D.	FA-'87	0*
59	Frerotte, Mitch	G	6-3	280	3/30/65	2	Penn State	Kittanning, Pa.	FA-'87	12/0
53	Furjanic, Tony	LB	6-1	228	2/26/64	3	Notre Dame	Chicago, Ill.	FA-'87	8/0
99	Garner, Hal	LB	6-4	235	1/18/62	3	Utah State	Logan, Utah	D3b-'85	0*
8	Gelbaugh, Stan	QB	6-3	207	12/4/62	2	Maryland	Carlisle, Pa.	FA-'86	0*
75	Hamby, Mike	DE	6-4	270	11/2/62	2	Utah State	Lehi, Utah	D6-'85	0*
33	Harmon, Ronnie	RB	5-11	192	5/7/64	3	Iowa	Queens, N.Y.	D1a-'86	12/10
71	Hellestrae, Dale	T	6-5	275	7/11/62	3	Southern Methodist	Scottsdale, Ariz.	D4b-'85	0*
67	Hull, Kent	C	6-4	275	1/13/61	3	Mississippi State	Greenwood, Miss.	FA-'86	12/12
47	Jackson, Kirby	CB	5-10	180	2/2/65	2	Mississippi State	Sturgis, Miss.	FA-'87	5/3*
48	Johnson, Lawrence	S	5-11	202	9/11/57	8	Wisconsin	Gary, Ind.	T(Clev)-'84	6/3
86	Johnson, Trumaine	WR	6-1	196	1/16/60	4	Grambling	Baker, La.	T(SD)-'87	12/0
52	†Kaiser, John	LB	6-3	227	6/6/62	5	Arizona	Hartland, Wis.	W(Sea)-'87	12/0
12	Kelly, Jim	QB	6-3	218	2/14/60	3	Miami	East Brady, Pa.	D1b-'83	12/12
38	Kelso, Mark	S	5-11	177	7/23/63	3	William & Mary	Pittsburgh, Pa.	FA-'86	12/12
4	Kidd, John	P	6-3	208	8/22/61	5	Northwestern	Findlay, Ohio	D5-'84	12/0
63	Lingner, Adam	C	6-4	260	11/2/60	6	Illinois	Rock Island, Ill.	W(Den)-'87	12/0
95	McNanie, Sean	DE	6-5	270	9/9/61	5	San Diego State	Mundelein, Ill.	D3b-'84	12/12
54	Marve, Eugene	LB	6-2	240	8/14/60	7	Saginaw Valley State	Flint, Mich.	D3-'82	5/4
74	Mesner, Bruce	NT	6-5	280	3/21/64	2	Maryland	Harrison, N.Y.	D8b-'87	11/0
88	Metzelaars, Pete	TE	6-7	243	5/24/60	7	Wabash	Portage, Mich.	T(Sea)-'85	12/12
25	Mitchell, Roland	CB-KR	5-11	180	3/15/64	2	Texas Tech	Bay City, Tex.	D2b-'87	11/0
39	Mueller, Jamie	RB	6-1	225	10/4/64	2	Benedictine College	Fairview Park, Ohio	D3b-'87	12/6
11	Norwood, Scott	K	6-0	207	7/17/60	4	James Madison	Alexandria, Va.	FA-'85	12/0
37	Odomes, Nate	CB-KR	5-9	188	8/25/65	2	Wisconsin	Columbus, Ga.	D2a-'87	12/12
57	Pike, Mark	LB	6-4	257	12/27/63	2	Georgia Tech	Villa Hills, Ky.	D7b-'86	3/0
27	Pitts, Ron	CB-S	5-10	175	10/14/62	3	UCLA	Orchard Park, N.Y.	D7-'85	12/3
30	Porter, Kerry	RB	6-1	210	9/23/64	2	Washington State	Great Falls, Mont.	D7-'87	6/0
26	†Porter, Ricky	RB	5-10	210	1/14/60	4	Slippery Rock State	Baltimore, Md.	FA-'87	9/0
79	†Prater, Dean	DE	6-4	260	9/28/58	7	Oklahoma State	Wichita Falls, Tex.	FA-'85	10/0
97	Radecic, Scott	LB	6-3	242	6/14/62	5	Penn State	Pittsburgh, Pa.	W(KC)-'87	12/9
83	Reed, Andre	WR	6-0	190	1/29/64	4	Kutztown State	Allentown, Pa.	D4a-'85	12/12
14	Reich, Frank	QB	6-3	208	12/4/61	4	Maryland	Lebanon, Pa.	D3a-'85	0*
40	Riddick, Robb	RB	6-0	195	4/26/57	7	Millersville State	Perkasie, Pa.	D9-'81	6/1
51	†Ritcher, Jim	G	6-3	265	5/21/58	9	North Carolina State	Medina, Ohio	D1-'80	12/12
87	†Rolle, Butch	TE	6-3	242	8/19/64	3	Michigan State	Hallandale, Fla.	D7c-'86	12/0
42	Roquemore, Durwood	S	6-1	190	1/19/60	4	Texas A&I	Dallas, Tex.	FA-'87	5/2
45	†Sampson, Clint	WR	5-11	183	1/4/61	5	San Diego State	Los Angeles, Calif.	T(Den)-'87	0*
96	Seals, Leon	DE	6-4	265	1/30/64	2	Jackson State	Baton Rouge, La.	D4b-'87	13/1
76	†Smerlas, Fred	NT	6-3	280	4/8/57	10	Boston College	Waltham, Mass.	D2a-'79	12/12
78	Smith, Bruce	DE	6-4	285	6/18/63	4	Virginia Tech	Norfolk, Va.	D1a-'85	12/12
56	Talley, Darryl	LB	6-4	227	7/10/60	6	West Virginia	Cleveland, Ohio	D2-'83	12/12
89	†Tasker, Steve	WR-KR	5-9	185	4/10/62	4	Northwestern	Leoti, Kan.	W(Hou)-'86	12/0
62	Traynowicz, Mark	G	6-5	280	11/20/62	4	Nebraska	Omaha, Neb.	D2-'85	11/0
24	Vital, Lionel	RB	5-9	195	7/15/63	2	Nicholls State	Loreauville, La.	FA-'87	3/3*
65	Vogler, Tim	G	6-3	285	10/2/56	10	Ohio State	Covington, Ohio	FA-'79	12/12
73	Wolford, Will	T	6-5	276	5/18/64	3	Vanderbilt	Louisville, Ky.	D1b-'86	12/12

* Beecher played 3 games with Miami in '87; Butler, Christy, Garner, Gelbaugh, Hamby, Hellestrae, and Sampson missed '87 season due to injury; Fox last active with Kansas City in '86; Jackson played 5 games with Rams; Reich active for 12 games but did not play; Vital played 3 games with Washington.

†Option playout; subject to developments.

Also played with Bills in '87—NT-RB Ira Albright (3 games), CB John Armstrong (3), TE Veno Belk (2), RB Greg Bell (2), CB Gerald Bess (2), C Joe Bock (1), DE Jack Brayvak (1), WR Marc Brown (3), T Tony Brown (2), WR Reggie Bynum (1), S Bill Callahan (1), DE Arnold Campbell (3), RB Joe Chetti (2), S Steve Clark (3), LB Will Cokeley (3), T Sean Dowling (3), G Mike Estep (2), S Larry Friday (1), WR Sheldon Gaines (3), DE Scott Garnett (3), C Will Grant (1), WR Kris Haines (1), NT Scott Hernandez (2), LB Mike Jones (1), RB Bruce King (3), G Kevin Lamar (1), LB Bob LeBlanc (3), CB John Lewis (3), RB Warren Loving (2), LB Steve Maidlow (2), QB Dan Manucci (3), CB Dave Martin (3), QB Brian McClure (1), WR Thad McFadden (3), NT Joe McGrail (2), TE Keith McKeller (1), QB Mark Miller (1), S Chip Nuzzo (3), RB Mike Panepinto (1), CB Kerry Parker (2), P Rick Partridge (3), C Erik Rosenmeier (1), LB Scott Schankweiler (3), K Todd Schlopy (3), G Rick Schulte (3), RB Johnny Shepherd (2), C Mark Shupe (2), C Joe Silipo (1), T Don Sommer (3), DE Richard Tharpe (3), QB Willie Totten (2), TE Mark Walczak (2), LB Craig Walls (3), LB Scott Watters (3), LB Al Wenglikowski (1), TE Gary Wilkins (1), RB Leonard Williams (2), DE Billy Witt (2).

Coaching Staff

Head Coach, Marv Levy

Pro Career: Begins second full season as Bills head coach. In first full year in 1987, he led Bills to 7-8 record. Replaced Hank Bullough on November 3, 1986, and compiled a 2-5 record over final seven weeks of season. Previously served as head coach of the Kansas City Chiefs from 1978-82, producing a 31-42 mark. Levy began pro coaching career in 1969 as an assistant with the Philadelphia Eagles. He joined George Allen and the Los Angeles Rams as an assistant one year later and followed Allen to Washington, where he remained with the Redskins through the 1972 season when the Redskins played in Super Bowl VII. He was named head coach of the Montreal Alouettes (CFL) in 1973 and posted a 50-34-4 record and two Grey Cup victories (1974, 1977) in five seasons in Canada. After two seasons away from football, he became head coach of the Chicago Blitz of the USFL in 1984, the team's only year in existence. No pro playing experience. Career record: 40-55.

Background: Running back Coe College 1948-50. Coached high school for two years before returning to alma mater from 1953-55. Joined New Mexico staff in 1956 where he served as head coach in 1958-59. Head coach at California from 1960-63 before becoming head coach at William & Mary from 1964-68.

Personal: Born August 3, 1928, Chicago, Ill. Levy was Phi Beta Kappa at Coe College and earned master's degree in English history from Harvard. Marv and his wife, Dorothy, live in Orchard Park, N.Y.

Assistant Coaches

Walt Corey, defensive coordinator, linebackers; born May 9, 1938, Latrobe, Pa., lives in West Seneca, N.Y. Defensive end Miami 1957-59. Pro linebacker Kansas City Chiefs 1960-66. College coach: Utah State 1967-69, Miami 1970-71. Pro coach: Kansas City Chiefs 1971-74, 1978-86, Cleveland Browns 1975-77, joined Bills in 1987.

Ted Cottrell, defensive line; born June 13, 1947, Chester, Pa., lives in Getzville, N.Y. Linebacker Delaware Valley College 1966-68. Pro linebacker Atlanta Falcons 1969-70, Winnipeg Blue Bombers (CFL) 1971. College coach: Rutgers 1973-80, 1983. Pro coach: Kansas City Chiefs 1981-82, New Jersey Generals (USFL) 1983-84, joined Bills in 1986.

Bruce DeHaven, special teams; born September 6, 1948, Trousdale, Kan., lives in Orchard Park, N.Y. No college or pro playing experience. College coach: Kansas 1979-81, New Mexico State 1982. Pro coach: New Jersey Generals (USFL) 1983, Pittsburgh Maulers (USFL) 1984, Orlando Renegades (USFL) 1985, joined Bills in 1987.

Chuck Dickerson, special assistant to head coach; born August 1, 1937, Hammond, Ind., lives in Buffalo, N.Y. Defensive tackle Florida 1955-56, Illinois 1961. Pro defensive lineman Montreal Alouettes (CFL) 1962-64. College coach: Eastern Illinois 1967-70, 1981-82, Minnesota 1983. Pro coach: Toronto Rifles (Continental League) 1964-66, Chicago Fire (WFL) 1974-75, Toronto Argonauts (CFL) 1976-79, Memphis Showboats (USFL) 1984-86, joined Bills in 1987.

Rusty Jones, strength and conditioning; born August 14, 1953, Berwick, Maine, lives in Hamburg, N.Y. No college or pro playing experience. College coach: Springfield 1978-79. Pro coach: Pittsburgh Maulers (USFL) 1983-84, joined Bills in 1985.

Chuck Lester, defensive assistant; born May 18, 1955, lives in Orchard Park, N.Y. Linebacker Oklahoma 1974. No pro playing experience. College coach: Iowa State 1980-81, Oklahoma 1982-84. Pro coach: Joined Bills in 1987.

Buffalo Bills 1988 First-Year Roster

Name	Pos.	Ht.	Wt.	Birth-date	College	Hometown	How Acq.
Amoia, Vince (1)	RB	5-11	218	3/30/63	Arizona State	Buffalo, N.Y.	FA
Bailey, Carlton	LB	6-2	240	12/15/64	North Carolina	Baltimore, Md.	D9
Ballard, Howard	T	6-6	300	11/3/63	Alabama A&M	Ashland, Ala.	D11-'87
Borcky, Tim	T	6-7	295	12/10/65	Memphis State	Trainer, Pa.	D7a
Brown, Tony (1)	T	6-5	285	7/11/64	Pittsburgh	Stamford, Conn.	FA-'87
Brady, Kerry (1)	K	6-2	195	8/27/63	Hawaii	Vancouver, Wash.	FA
Bynum, Reggie (1)	WR	6-1	185	2/10/64	Oregon State	San Jose, Calif.	FA-'87
Curkendall, Pete	NT	6-2	280	3/8/66	Penn State	Elmira, N.Y.	D11
Driscoll, John	T	6-5	285	9/4/64	New Hampshire	Fitchburg, Mass.	D12a
Erlandson, Tom	LB	6-1	220	6/19/66	Washington	Denver, Colo.	D12b
Ford, Bernard	WR	5-9	168	2/27/66	Central Florida	Cordele, Ga.	D3
Gadson, Ezekial	S	6-0	205	5/13/66	Pittsburgh	Frogmore, S.C.	D5a
Hagy, John	S	5-11	190	12/9/65	Texas	San Antonio, Tex.	D8a
Hammond, Steve (1)	LB	6-4	225	2/25/60	Wake Forest	Merrick, N.Y.	FA-'87
Howard, Joe (1)	WR	5-9	165	12/21/62	Notre Dame	Clinton, Md.	FA-'87
Johnson, Flip (1)	WR-KR	5-10	185	7/13/63	McNeese State	Beaumont, Tex.	FA-'87
Loving, Warren (1)	RB	6-1	230	11/12/61	William Penn	Jersey City, N.J.	FA
Mayhew, Martin	CB	5-8	172	10/8/65	Florida State	Tallahassee, Fla.	D10
McClure, Brian (1)	QB	6-6	222	12/28/63	Bowling Green	Rootstown, Ohio	FA-'87
McKeller, Keith (1)	TE	6-6	230	7/9/64	Jacksonville State	Fairfield, Ala.	D9-'87
Murray, Dan	LB	6-1	240	10/20/66	East Stroudsburg	Vernon, N.J.	D6
Roach, Kirk	K	6-1	217	11/8/66	Western Carolina	Doraville, Ga.	D5b
Starks, Kevin (1)	TE	6-4	226	9/14/63	Minnesota	Blue Island, Ill.	FA
Thomas, Thurman	RB	5-10	198	5/16/66	Oklahoma State	Missouri City, Tex.	D2
Tucker, Erroll (1)	CB-S-KR	5-8	170	7/6/64	Utah	Lynwood, Calif.	FA
Wright, Bo	RB	5-10	210	9/16/65	Alabama	Prichard, Ala.	D7b
Wright, Jeff	NT	6-2	270	6/13/63	Central Missouri St.	Lawrence, Kan.	D8b

The term NFL Rookie is defined as a player who is in his first season of professional football and has not been on the roster of another professional football team for any regular-season or postseason games. A Rookie is designated by an "R" on NFL rosters. Players who have been active in another professional football league or players who have NFL experience, including either preseason training camp or being on an active roster for fewer than three regular-season or postseason games, are termed NFL First-Year Players. An NFL First-Year Player is designated by a "1" on NFL rosters. Thereafter, a player on an NFL active roster for at least three regular-season or postseason games is credited with an additional year of NFL playing experience.

NOTES

Ted Marchibroda, quarterbacks, passing-game coordinator; born March 15, 1931, Franklin, Pa., lives in East Aurora, N.Y. Quarterback St. Bonaventure 1950-51, Detroit 1952. Pro quarterback Pittsburgh Steelers 1953, 1955-56, Chicago Cardinals 1957. Pro coach: Washington Redskins 1961-65, 1971-74, Los Angeles Rams 1966-70, Baltimore Colts 1975-79 (head coach), Chicago Bears 1981, Detroit Lions 1982-83, Philadelphia Eagles 1984-85, joined Bills in 1987.

Elijah Pitts, running backs; born February 3, 1938, Mayflower, Ark., lives in Orchard Park, N.Y. Running back Philander Smith 1957-60. Pro running back Green Bay Packers 1961-69, 1971, Los Angeles Rams 1970, Chicago Bears 1970, New Orleans Saints 1970. Pro coach: Los Angeles Rams 1974-77, Buffalo Bills 1978-80, Houston Oilers 1981-83, Hamilton Tiger-Cats (CFL) 1984, rejoined Bills in 1985.

Jim Ringo, offensive coordinator, running-game coordinator, offensive line; born November 21, 1932, Orange, N.J., lives in Orchard Park, N.Y. Center Syracuse 1950-52. Pro center Green Bay Packers 1953-63, Philadelphia Eagles 1964-66. Pro coach: Chicago Bears 1969-71, Buffalo Bills 1972-77 (head coach 1976-77), New England Patriots 1978-81, Los Angeles Rams 1982, New York Jets 1983-84, rejoined Bills in 1985. Member of Pro Football Hall of Fame.

Dick Roach, defensive backs; born August 23, 1937, Rapid City, S.D., lives in West Seneca, N.Y. Defensive back Black Hills State 1952-55. No pro playing experience. College coach: Montana State 1966-69, Oregon State 1970, Wyoming 1971-72, Fresno State 1973, Washington State 1974-75. Pro coach: Montreal Alouettes (CFL) 1976-77, Kansas City Chiefs 1978-80, New England Patriots 1981, Michigan Panthers (USFL) 1983-84, Tampa Bay Buccaneers 1985-86, joined Bills in 1987.

Ted Tollner, receivers; born May 29, 1940, San Francisco, Calif., lives in Orchard Park, N.Y. Quarterback Cal Poly-SLO 1959-61. No pro playing experience. College coach: College of San Mateo 1971-72 (head coach), San Diego State 1973-80, Brigham Young 1981, Southern California 1982-86 (head coach 1983-86). Pro coach: Joined Bills in 1987.

American Football Conference Central Division

Team Colors: Black, Orange, and White

200 Riverfront Stadium
Cincinnati, Ohio 45202
Telephone: (513) 621-3550

Club Officials

President: John Sawyer
General Manager: Paul E. Brown
Assistant General Manager: Michael Brown
Business Manager: Bill Connelly
Director of Public Relations: Allan Heim
Director of Player Personnel: Pete Brown
Accountant: Jay Reis
Ticket Manager: Paul Kelly
Consultant: John Murdough
Trainer: Marv Pollins
Equipment Manager: Tom Gray
Video Director: Al Davis

Stadium: Riverfront Stadium • **Capacity:** 59,754
200 Riverfront Stadium
Cincinnati, Ohio 45202

Playing Surface: AstroTurf-8

Training Camp: Wilmington College
Wilmington, Ohio 45177

1988 Schedule

Preseason

July 30	vs. Rams at Canton, Ohio	2:30
Aug. 6	at Kansas City	7:30
Aug. 13	at Buffalo	7:30
Aug. 20	**Detroit**	7:30
Aug. 26	at New England	7:00

Regular Season

Sept. 4	**Phoenix**	1:00
Sept. 11	at Philadelphia	4:00
Sept. 18	at Pittsburgh	1:00
Sept. 25	**Cleveland**	1:00
Oct. 2	at Los Angeles Raiders	1:00
Oct. 9	**New York Jets**	1:00
Oct. 16	at New England	1:00
Oct. 23	**Houston**	1:00
Oct. 30	at Cleveland	1:00
Nov. 6	**Pittsburgh**	1:00
Nov. 13	at Kansas City	12:00
Nov. 20	at Dallas	12:00
Nov. 27	**Buffalo**	1:00
Dec. 4	**San Diego**	1:00
Dec. 11	at Houston	12:00
Dec. 17	**Washington** (Saturday)	12:30

Bengals Coaching History

(144-154-1)

1968-75	Paul Brown	55-59-1
1976-78	Bill Johnson*	18-15-0
1978-79	Homer Rice	8-19-0
1980-83	Forrest Gregg	34-27-0
1984-87	Sam Wyche	29-34-0

*Resigned after five games in 1978

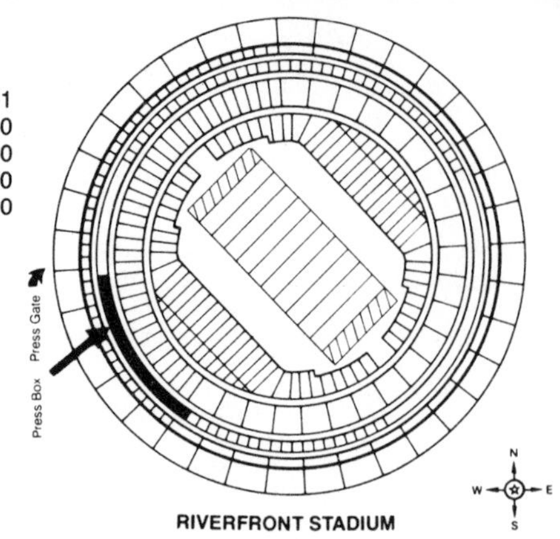

RIVERFRONT STADIUM

Record Holders

Individual Records—Career

Category	Name	Performance
Rushing (Yds.)	Pete Johnson, 1977-1983	5,421
Passing (Yds.)	Ken Anderson, 1971-1986	32,838
Passing (TDs)	Ken Anderson, 1971-1986	197
Receiving (No.)	Isaac Curtis, 1973-1984	420
Receiving (Yds.)	Isaac Curtis, 1973-1984	7,106
Interceptions (No.)	Ken Riley, 1969-1983	63
Punting (Avg.)	Dave Lewis, 1970-73	43.9
Punt Return (Avg.)	Mike Martin, 1983-87	10.4
Kickoff Return (Avg.)	Lemar Parrish, 1970-78	24.7
Field Goals	Jim Breech, 1980-87	143
Touchdowns (Tot.)	Pete Johnson, 1977-1983	70
Points	Jim Breech, 1981-87	713

Individual Records—Single Season

Category	Name	Performance
Rushing (Yds.)	James Brooks, 1986	1,087
Passing (Yds.)	Boomer Esiason, 1986	3,959
Passing (TDs)	Ken Anderson, 1981	29
Receiving (No.)	Dan Ross, 1981	71
Receiving (Yds.)	Cris Collinsworth, 1983	1,130
Interceptions	Ken Riley, 1976	9
Punting (Avg.)	Dave Lewis, 1970	46.2
Punt Return (Avg.)	Mike Martin, 1984	15.7
Kickoff Return (Avg.)	Lemar Parrish, 1980	30.2
Field Goals	Horst Muhlmann, 1972	27
Touchdowns (Tot.)	Pete Johnson, 1981	16
Points	Jim Breech, 1985	120

Individual Records—Single Game

Category	Name	Performance
Rushing (Yds.)	James Brooks, 12-7-86	163
Passing (Yds.)	Ken Anderson, 11-17-75	447
Passing (TDs)	Boomer Esiason, 12-21-86	5
Receiving (No.)	Many times	10
	Last time by Cris Collinsworth, 9-22-85	
Receiving (Yds.)	Cris Collinsworth, 10-2-83	216
Interceptions	Many times	3
	Last time by Ken Riley, 11-28-83	
Field Goals	Horst Muhlmann, 11-8-70	5
	Horst Muhlmann, 9-24-72	5
Touchdowns (Tot.)	Larry Kinnebrew, 10-28-84	4
Points	Larry Kinnebrew, 10-28-84	24

1987 Team Record

Preseason (2-2)

Date	Result		Opponents
8/15	W	31-30	at Tampa Bay
8/22	L	9-23	at Detroit
8/29	W	28-20	at Green Bay
9/4	L	14-26	New Orleans
		82-99	

Regular Season (4-11)

Date	Result		Opponents	Att.
9/13	W	23-21	at Indianapolis	59,387
9/20	L	26-27	San Francisco	53,498
9/27	C		at L.A. Rams	
10/4	L	9-10	San Diego	26,209
10/11	W	17-10	at Seattle	31,739
10/18	L	0-34	Cleveland	40,179
10/25	L	20-23	at Pittsburgh	53,692
11/1	L	29-31	Houston	52,700
11/8	L	14-20	Miami	53,840
11/15	W	16-10	at Atlanta	25,758
11/22	L	16-30	Pittsburgh	59,910
11/29	L	20-27	at N.Y. Jets	41,135
12/6	W	30-27	Kansas City (OT)	46,489
12/13	L	24-38	at Cleveland	77,331
12/20	L	24-41	New Orleans	43,424
12/27	L	17-21	at Houston	49,775

(OT) Overtime
C (Cancelled due to players' strike.)

Score by Periods

Bengals	87	72	40	83	3	—	285
Opponents	44	106	96	124	0	—	370

Attendance

Home 376,249 Away 338,817 Total 715,066
Single-game home record, 60,284 (10-17-71)
Single-season home record, 433,081 (1986)

1987 Team Statistics

	Bengals	Opp.
Total First Downs	319	286
Rushing	130	99
Passing	159	169
Penalty	30	18
Third Down: Made/Att.	81/216	79/194
Fourth Down: Made/Att.	8/18	4/8
Total Net Yards	5377	4697
Avg. Per Game	358.5	313.1
Total Plays	1045	937
Avg. Per Play	5.1	5.0
Net Yards Rushing	2164	1641
Avg. Per Game	144.3	109.4
Total Rushes	538	441
Net Yards Passing	3213	3056
Avg. Per Game	214.2	203.7
Sacked/Yards Lost	32/255	40/303
Gross Yards	3468	3359
Att./Completions	475/255	456/267
Completion Pct.	53.7	58.6
Had Intercepted	20	14
Punts/Avg.	73/41.0	75/40.2
Net Punting Avg.	34.5	33.4
Penalties/Yards Lost	99/791	79/669
Fumbles/Ball Lost	29/12	26/12
Touchdowns	30	43
Rushing	13	15
Passing	17	24
Returns	0	4
Avg. Time of Possession	30:24	29:36

1987 Individual Statistics

Scoring

Scoring	TD R	TD P	TD Rt	PAT	FG	Saf	TP
Breech	0	0	0	25/27	24/30	0	97
Kinnebrew	8	0	0	0/0	0/0	0	48
Brooks	1	2	0	0/0	0/0	0	18
E. Brown	0	3	0	0/0	0/0	0	18
Jennings	1	2	0	0/0	0/0	0	18
Martin	0	3	0	0/0	0/0	0	18
Holman	0	2	0	0/0	0/0	0	12
Kattus	0	2	0	0/0	0/0	0	12
B. Johnson	1	0	0	0/0	0/0	0	6
Logan	1	0	0	0/0	0/0	0	6
Manca	0	0	0	3/3	1/2	0	6
McCluskey	1	0	0	0/0	0/0	0	6
McGee	0	1	0	0/0	0/0	0	6
Muñoz	0	1	0	0/0	0/0	0	6
Russell	0	1	0	0/0	0/0	0	6
Schutt	0	0	0	0/0	0/0	1	2
Bengals	13	17	0	28/30	25/32	1	285
Opponents	15	24	4	43/43	23/26	0	370

Passing

Passing	Att.	Comp.	Yds.	Pct.	TD	Int.	Tkld.	Rate
Esiason	440	240	3321	54.5	16	19	26/209	73.1
D. Walter	21	10	113	47.6	0	0	2/15	64.2
Breen	8	3	9	37.5	1	0	3/18	85.4
Bennett	6	2	25	33.3	0	1	0/0	7.6
Hillary	0	0	0	—	0	0	1/13	0.0
Bengals	475	255	3468	53.7	17	20	32/255	71.6
Opponents	456	267	3359	58.6	24	14	40/303	86.3

Rushing

Rushing	Att.	Yds.	Avg.	LG	TD
Kinnebrew	145	570	3.9	52	8
Jennings	70	314	4.5	18	1
Brooks	94	290	3.1	18	1
Esiason	52	241	4.6	19	0
B. Johnson	39	205	5.3	20	1
Logan	37	203	5.5	51	1
McCluskey	29	94	3.2	12	1
Wright	24	74	3.1	10	0
D. Walter	16	70	4.4	16	0
Rice	18	59	3.3	8	0
Meehan	4	19	4.8	17	0
Breen	6	18	3.0	9	0
Bennett	2	17	8.5	9	0
E. Brown	1	0	0.0	0	0
McGee	1	−10	−10.0	−10	0
Bengals	538	2164	4.0	52	13
Opponents	441	1641	3.7	42t	15

Receiving

Receiving	No.	Yds.	Avg.	LG	TD
E. Brown	44	608	13.8	47t	3
Jennings	35	277	7.9	24	2
Collinsworth	31	494	15.9	53	0
Holman	28	438	15.6	61t	2
McGee	23	408	17.7	49	1
Brooks	22	272	12.4	46	2
Martin	20	394	19.7	54t	3
Kattus	18	217	12.1	57	2
Kinnebrew	9	114	12.7	25	0
Hillary	5	65	13.0	23	0
Wright	4	28	7.0	11	0
Meehan	3	25	8.3	12	0
B. Johnson	3	19	6.3	9	0
Logan	3	14	4.7	18	0
Pleasant	2	45	22.5	35	0
Russell	2	27	13.5	23	1
Muñoz	2	15	7.5	12	1
McCluskey	1	8	8.0	8	0
Bengals	255	3468	13.6	61t	17
Opponents	267	3359	12.6	53	24

Interceptions

Interceptions	No.	Yds.	Avg.	LG	TD
Jackson	3	49	16.3	29	0
Fulcher	3	30	10.0	28	0
Breeden	2	49	24.5	44	0
D. Smith	2	0	0.0	0	0
Wilcots	1	37	37.0	37	0
Niehoff	1	19	19.0	19	0
Thomas	1	3	3.0	3	0
Bussey	1	0	0.0	0	0
Bengals	14	187	13.4	44	0
Opponents	20	336	16.8	76	2

Punting

Punting	No.	Yds.	Avg.	In 20	LG
Fulhage	52	2168	41.7	10	58
Horne	19	759	39.9	2	57
Esiason	2	68	34.0	1	41
Bengals	73	2995	41.0	13	58
Opponents	75	3017	40.2	15	66

Punt Returns

Punt Returns	No.	FC	Yds.	Avg.	LG	TD
Martin	28	5	277	9.9	21	0
K. Brown	5	3	16	3.2	10	0
Horton	1	0	0	0.0	0	0
Jackson	0	1	0	—	0	0
Bengals	34	9	293	8.6	21	0
Opponents	42	8	299	7.1	26	0

Kickoff Returns

Kickoff Returns	No.	Yds.	Avg.	LG	TD
Bussey	21	406	19.3	34	0
McGee	15	242	16.1	24	0
Wright	13	266	20.5	30	0
K. Brown	3	45	15.0	20	0
Logan	3	31	10.3	16	0
Martin	3	51	17.0	20	0
Brooks	2	42	21.0	23	0
Jennings	2	32	16.0	18	0
Kattus	2	22	11.0	13	0
Fulcher	1	0	0.0	0	0
Hillary	1	15	15.0	15	0
Meehan	1	9	9.0	9	0
Bengals	67	1161	17.3	34	0
Opponents	62	1145	18.5	62	0

Sacks

Sacks	No.
Williams	6.0
Skow	4.5
Edwards	4.0
King	4.0
Krumrie	3.5
Fulcher	3.0
Berthusen	2.5
Catchings	2.5
Buck	2.0
Bussey	2.0
Hammerstein	1.0
Kelly	1.0
Schutt	1.0
Thomas	1.0
Ward	1.0
Zander	1.0
Bengals	40.0
Opponents	32.0

Cincinnati Bengals 1988 Veteran Roster

No.	Name	Pos.	Ht.	Wt.	Birth-date	NFL Exp.	College	Hometown	How Acq.	'87 Games/Starts
35	Barber, Chris	S	6-0	187	1/15/64	2	North Carolina A&T	Winston-Salem, N.C.	FA-'87	3/3
53	Barker, Leo	LB	6-2	227	11/7/59	5	New Mexico State	Cristobal, Panama	D7-'84	12/0
24	Billups, Lewis	CB	5-11	190	10/10/63	3	North Alabama	Ft. Walton Beach, Fla.	D2-'86	11/11
74	Blados, Brian	G	6-5	295	1/11/62	5	North Carolina	Arlington, Va.	D1b-'84	11/4
55	†Brady, Ed	LB	6-2	235	6/17/60	5	Illinois	Morris, Ill.	D8-'84	12/0
3	Breech, Jim	K	5-6	161	4/11/56	10	California	Sacramento, Calif.	FA-'80	12/0
21	Brooks, James	RB	5-10	182	12/28/58	8	Auburn	Warner Robins, Ga.	T(SD)-'84	9/7
81	Brown, Eddie	WR	6-0	185	12/17/62	4	Miami	Miami, Fla.	D1-'85	12/12
99	Buck, Jason	DE	6-5	264	7/27/63	2	Brigham Young	St. Anthony, Idaho	D1-'87	12/0
27	†Bussey, Barney	S	6-0	195	5/20/62	3	South Carolina	Lincolnton, Ga.	D5-'84	12/1
80	Collinsworth, Cris	WR	6-6	192	1/27/59	8	Florida	Titusville, Fla.	D2-'81	8/6
93	†DeAyala, Kiki	LB	6-1	225	10/23/61	3	Texas	Miami, Fla.	D6-'83	12/2
67	Douglas, David	T	6-4	280	3/20/63	3	Tennessee	Evansville, Tenn.	D8-'86	12/4
73	Edwards, Eddie	DE	6-5	256	4/25/54	12	Miami	Sumter, S.C.	D1-'77	14/14
7	Esiason, Boomer	QB	6-4	220	4/17/61	5	Maryland	East Islip, N.Y.	D2-'84	12/12
33	†Fulcher, David	S	6-3	228	9/28/64	3	Arizona State	Los Angeles, Calif.	D3b-'86	11/11
17	Fulhage, Scott	P	5-11	191	11/17/61	2	Kansas State	Beloit, Kan.	FA-'87	11/0
71	Hammerstein, Mike	DE	6-4	270	3/29/63	3	Michigan	Wapakoneta, Ohio	D3a-'86	11/0
89	Hillary, Ira	WR	5-11	190	11/13/62	2	South Carolina	Edgefield, S.C.	FA-'86	11/0
82	Holman, Rodney	TE	6-3	238	4/20/60	7	Tulane	Ypsilanti, Mich.	D3-'82	12/12
20	Horton, Ray	CB	5-11	190	4/12/60	6	Washington	Tacoma, Wash.	D2-'83	12/8
92	Inglis, Tim	LB	6-3	232	3/10/64	2	Toledo	Toledo, Ohio	FA-'87	8/3
37	†Jackson, Robert	S	5-10	186	10/10/58	7	Central Michigan	Allendale, Mich.	D11-'81	12/12
36	Jennings, Stanford	RB	6-1	205	3/12/62	5	Furman	Summerville, S.C.	D3-'84	12/5
30	Johnson, Bill	RB	6-2	230	10/31/60	4	Arkansas State	Millerton, N.Y.	SD2-'85	11/4
84	Kattus, Eric	TE	6-5	235	3/4/63	3	Michigan	Cincinnati, Ohio	D4-'86	11/0
58	Kelly, Joe	LB	6-2	227	12/11/64	3	Washington	Los Angeles, Calif.	D1-'86	10/10
90	King, Emanuel	LB	6-4	251	8/15/63	4	Alabama	Leroy, Ala.	D1a-'85	12/12
28	†Kinnebrew, Larry	RB	6-1	258	6/11/59	6	Tennessee State	Rome, Ga.	D6a-'83	11/8
64	Kozerski, Bruce	G	6-4	275	4/2/62	5	Holy Cross	Plains, Pa.	D9-'84	8/4
69	Krumrie, Tim	NT	6-2	262	5/20/60	6	Wisconsin	Eau Claire, Wis.	D10-'83	12/12
52	Manos, Sam	C	6-3	265	10/2/63	2	Marshall	New Castle, Pa.	FA-'87	3/3
88	Martin, Mike	WR	5-10	186	11/18/60	6	Illinois	Washington, D.C.	D8-'83	12/0
72	McClendon, Skip	DE	6-6	270	4/9/64	2	Arizona State	Detroit, Mich.	D3a-'87	12/0
85	McGee, Tim	WR	5-10	175	8/7/64	3	Tennessee	Cleveland, Ohio	D1a-'86	11/5
47	Meehan, Greg	WR	6-0	191	4/27/63	2	Bowling Green	Lincoln Park, Mich.	FA-'87	3/3
65	Montoya, Max	G	6-5	275	5/12/56	10	UCLA	La Puente, Calif.	D7-'79	10/9
78	Muñoz, Anthony	T	6-6	278	8/19/58	9	Southern California	Ontario, Calif.	D1-'80	11/11
12	†Norseth, Mike	QB	6-2	200	8/22/64	2	Kansas	Lawrence, Kan.	FA-'87	0/0
75	Reimers, Bruce	T	6-7	280	9/18/60	5	Iowa State	Humboldt, Iowa	D8-'84	10/8
46	Rice, Dan	RB	6-1	241	11/9/63	2	Michigan	Dorchester, Mass.	FA-'87	3/0
87	Riggs, Jim	TE	6-5	245	9/29/63	2	Clemson	Laurinburg, N.C.	D4-'87	9/0
50	†Rimington, Dave	C	6-3	288	5/22/60	6	Nebraska	Omaha, Neb.	D1-'83	8/8
15	Schonert, Turk	QB	6-1	196	1/15/57	9	Stanford	Placentia, Calif.	FA-'87	11/0
70	Skow, Jim	DE	6-3	250	6/29/63	3	Nebraska	Omaha, Neb.	D3-'86	12/12
25	Smith, Daryl	CB	5-9	185	5/8/63	2	North Alabama	Opelika, Ala.	FA-'87	3/3
22	Thomas, Eric	CB	5-11	175	9/11/64	2	Tulane	Sacramento, Calif.	D2-'87	12/3
63	Walter, Joe	T	6-6	290	6/18/63	4	Texas Tech	Dallas, Tex.	D7a-'85	12/12
51	White, Leon	LB	6-2	236	10/4/63	3	Brigham Young	La Mesa, Calif.	D5-'86	12/0
41	Wilcots, Solomon	CB	5-11	180	10/9/64	2	Colorado	Rubidoux, Calif.	D8-'87	12/0
57	Williams, Reggie	LB	6-0	228	9/19/54	13	Dartmouth	Flint, Mich.	D3a-'76	15/15
32	Wilson, Stanley	RB	5-10	210	8/23/61	3	Oklahoma	Carson, Calif.	D9-'83	0*
49	Wright, Dana	RB	6-1	219	6/2/63	2	Findlay College	Ravenna, Ohio	FA-'87	5/0
91	Zander, Carl	LB	6-2	235	3/23/63	4	Tennessee	Mendham, N.J.	D2-'85	12/12

* Wilson missed '87 season due to suspension.

†Option playout; subject to developments.

Also played with Bengals in '87—QB Ben Bennett (1 game), NT Bill Berthusen (3), S Nate Borders (3), CB Louis Breeden (8), WR Kenneth Brown (3), WR Tom Brown (2), LB Toney Catchings (3), T Keith Cupp (3), NT James Eaddy (2), DE Willie Fears (3), LB Tom Flaherty (3), G John Fletcher (3), RB Pat Franklin (2), P Greg Horne (4), CB Gary Hunt (3), TE Curtis Jeffries (3), S Mark Johnson (3), RB Marc Logan (3), K Massimo Manca (3), CB Aaron Manning (3), RB David McCluskey (3), S Rob Niehoff (3), WR Marquis Pleasant (3), G Bill Poe (3), G Tom Richey (3), T Bob Riley (3), TE Dave Romasko (3), T Wade Russell (3), LB Scott Schutt (3), LB Lance Sellers (3), TE Reginald Sims (1), DE Jeff Smith (3), G Ken Smith (3), T Mark Tigges (3), WR Rodney Tweet (2), QB Dave Walter (3), LB David Ward (3).

COACHING STAFF

Head Coach, Sam Wyche

Pro Career: Became the fifth head coach in Cincinnati history when he was named to lead the Bengals on December 28, 1983. Played quarterback with Bengals 1968-70, Washington Redskins 1971-73, Detroit Lions 1974-75, St. Louis Cardinals 1976, and Buffalo Bills 1977. Quarterback coach with the San Francisco 49ers 1979-82. Career record: 29-34.

Background: Attended North Fulton High School in Atlanta and Furman University where he was the quarterback from 1962-66. Assistant coach at South Carolina in 1967. Head coach at Indiana University in 1983.

Personal: Born January 5, 1945, in Atlanta, Ga. Sam and his wife, Jane, have two children—Zak and Kerry. They live in Cincinnati.

Assistant Coaches

Jim Anderson, running backs; born March 27, 1948, Harrisburg, Pa., lives in Cincinnati. Linebacker-defensive end Cal Western (U.S. International) 1969-70. No pro playing experience. College coach: Cal Western 1970-71, Scottsdale Community College 1973, Nevada-Las Vegas 1974-75, Southern Methodist 1977-80, Stanford 1981-83. Pro coach: Joined Bengals in 1984.

Bruce Coslet, offensive coordinator; born August 5, 1946, Oakdale, Calif., lives in Cincinnati. Tight end University of the Pacific 1965-67. Pro tight end Cincinnati Bengals 1969-76. Pro coach: San Francisco 49ers 1980, joined Bengals in 1981.

Bill Johnson, tight ends; born July 14, 1926, Tyler, Tex., lives in Cincinnati. Center Texas A&M 1944-46. Pro center San Francisco 49ers 1948-55. Pro coach: San Francisco 49ers 1956-67, Cincinnati Bengals 1968-78 (head coach 1976-78), Tampa Bay Buccaneers 1979-82, Detroit Lions 1983-84, rejoined Bengals in 1985.

Dick LeBeau, defensive coordinator-defensive backs; born September 9, 1937, London, Ohio, lives in Cincinnati. Halfback Ohio State 1957-59. Pro defensive back Detroit Lions 1959-72. Pro coach: Philadelphia Eagles 1973-75, Green Bay Packers 1976-79, joined Bengals in 1980.

Jim McNally, offensive line-running game; born December 13, 1943, Buffalo, N.Y., lives in Cincinnati. Guard Buffalo 1961-65. No pro playing experience. College coach: Buffalo 1966-69, Marshall 1973-75, Boston College 1976-78, Wake Forest 1979. Pro coach: Joined Bengals in 1980.

Dick Selcer, linebackers; born August 22, 1937, Cincinnati, Ohio, lives in Cincinnati. Running back Notre Dame 1955-58. No pro playing experience. College coach: Xavier, Ohio 1962-64, 1970-71 (head coach), Cincinnati 1965-66, Brown 1967-69, Wisconsin 1972-74, Kansas State 1975-77, Southwestern Louisiana 1978-80. Pro coach: Houston Oilers 1981-83, joined Bengals in 1984.

Mike Stock, special teams; born September 29, 1939, Barberton, Ohio, lives in Cincinnati. Fullback Northwestern 1958-60. No pro playing experience. College coach: Northwestern 1961, Buffalo 1966-67, Navy 1968, Notre Dame 1969-75, Wisconsin 1976-77, Eastern Michigan 1978-82 (head coach), Notre Dame 1983-86. Pro coach: Joined Bengals in 1987.

Bill Urbanik, defensive line; born December 27, 1946, Donora, Pa., lives in Cincinnati. Lineman Ohio State 1965-68. No pro playing experience. College coach: Marshall 1971-73, 1975, Northern Illinois 1976-78, Wake Forest 1979-83. Pro coach: Joined Bengals in 1984.

Kim Wood, strength; born July 12, 1945, Barrington, Ill., lives in Cincinnati. Running back Wisconsin 1965-68. No pro playing experience. Pro coach: Joined Bengals in 1975.

Cincinnati Bengals 1988 First-Year Roster

Name	Pos.	Ht.	Wt.	Birth-date	College	Hometown	How Acq.
Aronson, Doug (1)	G	6-3	290	8/14/64	San Diego State	San Francisco, Calif.	FA-'87
Dillahunt, Ellis	S	5-11	200	11/25/64	East Carolina	Jacksonville, N.C.	D10
Dixon, Rickey	CB	5-11	177	12/26/66	Oklahoma	Dallas, Tex.	D1
Gaffney, John	K	6-2	200	10/22/64	Virginia	Bethesda, Md.	FA
Grant, David	NT	6-4	277	9/17/65	West Virginia	Belleville, N.J.	D4
Hickert, Paul	K	6-3	186	3/30/66	Murray State	Clearwater, Fla.	D11
Holifield, Jon (1)	RB	6-0	202	7/14/64	West Virginia	Romulus, Mich.	FA
Jetton, Paul	G	6-4	288	10/6/64	Texas	Houston, Tex.	D6
Lee, Darryl (1)	NT	6-3	270	10/12/63	Ohio State	Columbus, Ohio	FA
Maxey, Curtis	NT	6-3	285	6/28/65	Grambling	Indianapolis, Ind.	D8
McConnell, Andrew (1)	NT	6-3	300	12/17/64	St. Francis Xavier	Toronto, Canada	FA
Parker, Carl	WR	6-2	201	2/5/65	Vanderbilt	Valdosta, Ga.	D12
Romer, Rich	LB	6-3	214	2/27/66	Union College	East Greenbush, N.Y.	D7
Smith, Dave	T	6-6	290	12/12/64	Southern Illinois	Lansing, Ill.	FA
Stewart, Vernon (1)	WR	6-2	192	3/1/64	Akron	Farrell, Pa.	FA
Thompson, Robert	WR	5-9	175	9/9/63	Youngstown State	Hollywood, Fla.	FA
Tiefenthaler, Jeff (1)	WR	6-1	185	6/6/63	South Dakota State	Brookings, S.D.	FA
Walker, Kevin	LB	6-2	238	12/24/65	Maryland	West Milford, N.J.	D3
Wells, Brandy	CB	5-10	184	6/12/65	Notre Dame	Milwaukee, Wis.	D9
Wester, Herb	T	6-7	300	5/7/65	Iowa	Nashua, N.H.	D5
Willis, Steve (1)	K	6-3	200	4/28/62	Kansas State	Shawnee, Kan.	FA
Woods, Ickey	RB	6-0	231	2/28/66	Nevada-Las Vegas	Fresno, Calif.	D2

The term NFL Rookie is defined as a player who is in his first season of professional football and has not been on the roster of another professional football team for any regular-season or postseason games. A Rookie is designated by an "R" on NFL rosters. Players who have been active in another professional football league or players who have NFL experience, including either preseason training camp or being on an active roster for fewer than three regular-season or postseason games, are termed NFL First-Year Players. An NFL First-Year Player is designated by a "1" on NFL rosters. Thereafter, a player on an NFL active roster for at least three regular-season or postseason games is credited with an additional year of NFL playing experience.

NOTES

CLEVELAND BROWNS

American Football Conference Central Division

Team Colors: Seal Brown, Orange, and White

Tower B
Cleveland Stadium
Cleveland, Ohio 44114
Telephone: (216) 696-5555

Club Officials

President and Owner: Arthur B. Modell
Executive Vice President/Legal and Administrative: Jim Bailey
Executive Vice President/Football Operations: Ernie Accorsi
Vice President/Public Relations: Kevin Byrne
Vice President/Finance: Mike Poplar
Director of Player Relations: Ricky Feacher
Director of Marketing: David Modell
Operations Manager: John Lemmo
Director of Security: Ted Chappelle
Treasurer: Mike Susen
Assistant Directors of Public Relations: Bob Eller, Francine Lubera
Player Personnel: Dom Anile, Tom Dimitroff, Chip Falivene, Gary Horton, Mike Lombardi
Head Trainer: Bill Tessendorf
Equipment Manager: Charley Cusick

Stadium: Cleveland Stadium • **Capacity:** 80,098
West 3rd Street
Cleveland, Ohio 44114

Playing Surface: Grass

Training Camp: Lakeland Community College
Mentor, Ohio 44060

1988 Schedule

Preseason

Aug. 6	**Detroit**	7:00
Aug. 13	at Tampa Bay	7:00
Aug. 18	vs. Jets at Montreal, Can.	7:30
Aug. 26	**New York Giants**	9:00

Regular Season

Sept. 4	at Kansas City	3:00
Sept. 11	**New York Jets**	4:00
Sept. 19	**Indianapolis** (Monday)	8:00
Sept. 25	at Cincinnati	1:00
Oct. 2	at Pittsburgh	1:00
Oct. 9	**Seattle**	1:00
Oct. 16	**Philadelphia**	1:00
Oct. 23	at Phoenix	1:00
Oct. 30	**Cincinnati**	1:00
Nov. 7	at Houston (Monday)	8:00
Nov. 13	at Denver	2:00
Nov. 20	**Pittsburgh**	1:00
Nov. 27	at Washington	1:00
Dec. 4	**Dallas**	1:00
Dec. 12	at Miami (Monday)	9:00
Dec. 18	**Houston**	1:00

Browns Coaching History

(325-213-9)

1950-62	Paul Brown	115-49-5
1963-70	Blanton Collier	79-38-2
1971-74	Nick Skorich	30-26-2
1975-77	Forrest Gregg*	18-23-0
1977	Dick Modzelewski	0-1-0
1978-84	Sam Rutigliano**	47-52-0
1984-87	Marty Schottenheimer	36-24-0

*Resigned after 13 games in 1977
**Released after eight games in 1984

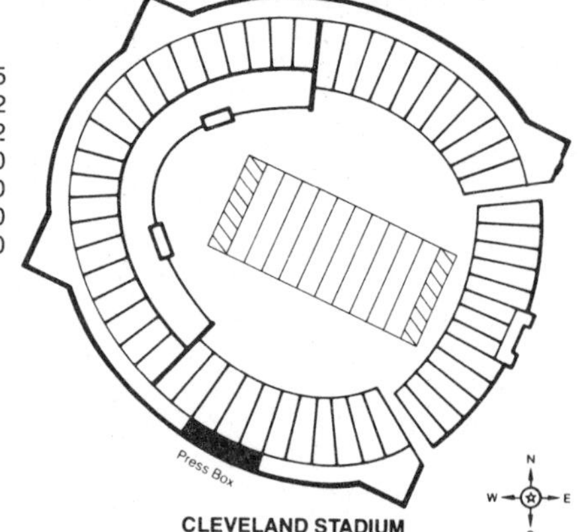

CLEVELAND STADIUM

Record Holders

Individual Records—Career

Category	Name	Performance
Rushing (Yds.)	Jim Brown, 1957-1965	12,312
Passing (Yds.)	Brian Sipe, 1974-1983	23,713
Passing (TDs)	Brian Sipe, 1974-1983	154
Receiving (No.)	Ozzie Newsome, 1978-1987	575
Receiving (Yds.)	Ozzie Newsome, 1978-1987	7,073
Interceptions	Thom Darden, 1972-74, 1976-1981	45
Punting (Avg.)	Horace Gillom, 1950-56	43.8
Punt Return (Avg.)	Greg Pruitt, 1973-1981	11.8
Kickoff Return (Avg.)	Greg Pruitt, 1973-1981	26.3
Field Goals	Lou Groza, 1950-59, 1961-67	234
Touchdowns (Tot.)	Jim Brown, 1957-1965	*126
Points	Lou Groza, 1950-59, 1961-67	1,349

Individual Records—Single Season

Category	Name	Performance
Rushing (Yds.)	Jim Brown, 1963	1,863
Passing (Yds.)	Brian Sipe, 1980	4,132
Passing (TDs)	Brian Sipe, 1980	30
Receiving (No.)	Ozzie Newsome, 1983	89
	Ozzie Newsome, 1984	89
Receiving (Yds.)	Paul Warfield, 1968	1,067
Interceptions	Thom Darden, 1978	10
Punting (Avg.)	Gary Collins, 1965	46.7
Punt Return (Avg.)	Leroy Kelly, 1965	15.6
Kickoff Return (Avg.)	Billy Reynolds, 1954	29.5
Field Goals	Matt Bahr, 1984	24
Touchdowns (Tot.)	Jim Brown, 1965	21
Points	Jim Brown, 1965	126

Individual Records—Single Game

Category	Name	Performance
Rushing (Yds.)	Jim Brown, 11-24-57	237
	Jim Brown, 11-19-61	237
Passing (Yds.)	Bernie Kosar, 1-3-87	489
Passing (TDs)	Frank Ryan, 12-12-64	5
	Bill Nelsen, 11-2-69	5
	Brian Sipe, 10-7-79	5
Receiving (No.)	Ozzie Newsome, 10-14-84	14
Receiving (Yds.)	Ozzie Newsome, 10-14-84	191
Interceptions	Many times	3
	Last time by Frank Minnifield, 11-22-87	
Field Goals	Don Cockroft, 10-19-75	5
Touchdowns (Tot.)	Dub Jones, 11-25-51	*6
Points	Dub Jones, 11-25-51	36

*NFL Record

1987 Team Record

Preseason (3-1)

Date	Result		Opponents
8/15	W	31-16	St. Louis
8/22	L	10-24	at N.Y. Giants
8/29	W	23- 3	at Atlanta
9/5	W	30-24	vs. Green Bay at Milw. (OT)
		94-67	

Regular Season (10-5)

Date	Result		Opponents	Att.
9/13	L	21-28	at New Orleans	59,900
9/20	W	34-10	Pittsburgh	79,543
9/28	C		Denver	
10/4	W	20-10	at New England	14,830
10/11	L	10-15	Houston	38,927
10/18	W	34- 0	at Cincinnati	40,179
10/26	W	30-17	L.A. Rams	76,933
11/1	L	24-27	at San Diego (OT)	55,381
11/8	W	38- 3	Atlanta	71,135
11/15	W	27-21	Buffalo	78,409
11/22	W	40- 7	at Houston	51,161
11/29	L	24-38	at San Francisco	60,248
12/6	L	7- 9	Indianapolis	70,661
12/13	W	38-24	Cincinnati	77,331
12/20	W	24-17	at L.A. Raiders	40,275
12/26	W	19-13	at Pittsburgh	56,394

(OT) Overtime
C (Cancelled due to players' strike.)

Postseason (1-1)

Date	Result		Opponents	Att.
1/9	W	38-21	Indianapolis	78,586
1/17	L	33-38	at Denver	75,993

Score by Periods

Browns	49	160	106	75	0	—	390
Opponents	41	56	54	85	3	—	239

Attendance

Home 492,939 Away 378,368 Total 871,307
Single-game home record, 85,073 (9-21-70)
Single-season home record, 620,496 (1980)

1987 Team Statistics

	Browns	Opp.
Total First Downs	310	251
Rushing	110	86
Passing	171	134
Penalty	29	31
Third Down: Made/Att.	82/197	71/200
Fourth Down: Made/Att.	5/12	6/14
Total Net Yards	5200	4264
Avg. Per Game	346.7	284.3
Total Plays	985	902
Avg. Per Play	5.3	4.7
Net Yards Rushing	1745	1433
Avg. Per Game	116.3	95.5
Total Rushes	474	401
Net Yards Passing	3455	2831
Avg. Per Game	230.3	188.7
Sacked/Yards Lost	29/170	34/257
Gross Yards	3625	3088
Att./Completions	482/291	467/246
Completion Pct.	60.4	52.7
Had Intercepted	12	23
Punts/Avg.	57/36.9	81/37.5
Net Punting Avg.	32.4	29.5
Penalties/Yards Lost	100/857	120/1008
Fumbles/Ball Lost	33/17	26/13
Touchdowns	47	26
Rushing	16	7
Passing	27	15
Returns	4	4
Avg. Time of Possession	31:44	28:16

1987 Individual Statistics

Scoring	TD R	TD P	TD Rt	PAT	FG	Saf	TP
Jaeger	0	0	0	33/33	14/22	0	75
Byner	8	2	0	0/0	0/0	0	60
Slaughter	0	7	0	0/0	0/0	0	42
Brennan	0	6	0	0/0	0/0	0	36
Mack	5	1	0	0/0	0/0	0	36
Bahr	0	0	0	9/10	4/5	0	21
Mason	2	1	0	0/0	0/0	0	18
Tennell	0	3	0	0/0	0/0	0	18
Kemp	0	2	0	0/0	0/0	0	12
McNeil	0	2	0	0/0	0/0	0	12
Weathers	0	2	0	0/0	0/0	0	12
Franco	0	0	0	2/2	3/4	0	11
Ellis	0	0	1	0/0	0/0	0	6
Grayson	0	0	1	0/0	0/0	0	6
Kosar	1	0	0	0/0	0/0	0	6
Langhorne	0	1	0	0/0	0/0	0	6
Matthews	0	0	1	0/0	0/0	0	6
Wright	0	0	1	0/0	0/0	0	6
Kelley	0	0	0	1/1	0/0	0	1
Browns	16	27	4	45/47	21/31	0	390
Opponents	7	15	4	26/26	17/25	3	239

Passing	Att.	Comp.	Yds.	Pct.	TD	Int.	Tkld.	Rate
Kosar	389	241	3033	62.0	22	9	22/129	95.4
Christensen	58	24	297	41.4	1	3	5/37	42.1
Danielson	33	25	281	75.8	4	0	2/4	140.3
Fontenot	1	1	14	100.0	0	0	0/0	118.8
Jaeger	1	0	0	0.0	0	0	0/0	39.6
Browns	482	291	3625	60.4	27	12	29/170	92.0
Opponents	467	246	3088	52.7	15	23	34/257	63.7

Rushing	Att.	Yds.	Avg.	LG	TD
Mack	201	735	3.7	22t	5
Byner	105	432	4.1	21	8
Mason	56	207	3.7	22	2
Manoa	23	116	5.0	35	0
Everett	34	95	2.8	16	0
Christensen	11	41	3.7	15	0
Fontenot	15	33	2.2	14	0
Driver	9	31	3.4	16	0
Kosar	15	22	1.5	7	1
McNeil	1	17	17.0	17	0
Verser	1	9	9.0	9	0
Davis	1	7	7.0	7	0
Danielson	1	0	0.0	0	0
Katolin	1	0	0.0	0	0
Browns	474	1745	3.7	35	16
Opponents	401	1433	3.6	27t	7

Receiving	No.	Yds.	Avg.	LG	TD
Byner	52	552	10.6	37	2
Slaughter	47	806	17.1	54t	7
Brennan	43	607	14.1	53t	6
Newsome	34	375	11.0	25	0
Mack	32	223	7.0	17	1
Langhorne	20	288	14.4	25	1
Kemp	12	224	18.7	34	2
Weathers	11	153	13.9	37t	2
Tennell	9	102	11.3	24	3
McNeil	8	120	15.0	39t	2
Everett	8	41	5.1	10	0
Mason	5	26	5.2	15	1
Fontenot	4	40	10.0	25	0
Pierce	2	21	10.5	13	0
Tinsley	1	17	17.0	17	0
R. Watson	1	13	13.0	13	0
L. Watson	1	9	9.0	9	0
Manoa	1	8	8.0	8	0
Browns	291	3625	12.5	54t	27
Opponents	246	3088	12.6	83t	15

Interceptions	No.	Yds.	Avg.	LG	TD
Wright	4	152	38.0	68	1
Minnifield	4	24	6.0	27	0
Matthews	3	62	20.7	36	1
Dixon	3	5	1.7	6	0
Rockins	2	25	12.5	15	0
Harper	2	16	8.0	16	0
Horn	1	28	28.0	28	0
E. Johnson	1	11	11.0	11	0
M. Johnson	1	3	3.0	3	0
D. Robinson	1	0	0.0	0	0
Wilson	1	0	0.0	0	0
Hairston	0	40	—	40	0
Browns	23	366	15.9	76	2
Opponents	12	173	14.4	48t	2

Punting	No.	Yds.	Avg.	In 20	LG
Gossett	19	769	40.5	4	55
L. Johnson, Hou.-Clev.	50	1969	39.4	8	66
L. Johnson, Clev.	9	317	35.2	3	66
Walters	11	400	36.4	2	56
Winslow	18	616	34.2	5	45
Browns	57	2102	36.9	14	66
Opponents	81	3035	37.5	13	57

Punt Returns	No.	FC	Yds.	Avg.	LG	TD
McNeil	34	9	386	11.4	40	0
Wilson	10	3	101	10.1	17	0
Browns	44	12	487	11.1	40	0
Opponents	17	9	93	5.5	21	0

Kickoff Returns	No.	Yds.	Avg.	LG	TD
Young	18	412	22.9	44	0
McNeil	11	205	18.6	33	0
Fontenot	9	130	14.4	24	0
Manoa	2	14	7.0	13	0
Tinsley	2	31	15.5	18	0
Beauford	1	22	22.0	22	0
Byner	1	2	2.0	2	0
Driver	1	16	16.0	16	0
Grayson	1	6	6.0	6	0
Langhorne	1	8	8.0	8	0
Mason	1	0	0.0	0	0
Browns	48	846	17.6	44	0
Opponents	72	1343	18.7	39	0

Sacks	No.
Hairston	8.0
Puzzuoli	5.5
Baker	3.5
T. Crawford	3.0
Matthews	2.5
Clancy	2.0
M. Johnson	2.0
Golic	1.5
Camp	1.0
Carter	1.0
Grayson	1.0
Harper	1.0
E. Johnson	1.0
Rusinek	1.0
Browns	34.0
Opponents	29.0

Cleveland Browns 1988 Veteran Roster

No.	Name	Pos.	Ht.	Wt.	Birth-date	NFL Exp.	College	Hometown	How Acq.	'87 Games/ Starts
61	Baab, Mike	C	6-4	270	12/6/59	7	Texas	Euless, Tex.	D5-'82	12/12
9	Bahr, Matt	K	5-10	175	7/6/56	10	Penn State	Neshaminy, Pa.	T(SF)-'81	3/0
60	†Baker, Al	DE	6-6	270	12/9/56	11	Colorado State	Newark, N.J.	T(StL)-'87	12/1
43	Baker, Tony	RB	5-10	175	6/11/64	2	East Carolina	High Point, N.C.	FA-'87	0*
77	Bolden, Rickey	T	6-6	280	9/8/61	5	Southern Methodist	Dallas, Tex.	D4a-'84	5/5
75	Bosley, Keith	T	6-5	320	6/19/63	2	Eastern Kentucky	Richmond, Ky.	FA-'88	3/2
36	Braggs, Stephen	CB-S	5-9	173	8/29/65	2	Texas	Houston, Tex.	D6-'87	12/0
86	Brennan, Brian	WR	5-9	178	2/15/62	5	Boston College	Bloomfield, Mich.	D4b-'84	13/1
44	Byner, Earnest	RB	5-10	215	9/15/62	5	East Carolina	Milledgeville, Ga.	D10-'84	12/12
96	†Camp, Reggie	DE	6-4	280	2/28/61	6	California	San Francisco, Calif.	D3-'83	6/5
91	†Clancy, Sam	DE	6-7	260	5/29/58	5	Pittsburgh	Pittsburgh, Pa.	T(Sea)-'85	13/8
47	Crawford, Mike	RB	5-10	215	1/3/64	2	Arizona State	Thousand Oaks, Calif.	FA-'88	3/0
18	Danielson, Gary	QB	6-2	196	9/10/51	11	Purdue	Dearborn, Mich.	T(Det)-'85	6/1
29	Dixon, Hanford	CB	5-11	186	12/25/58	8	Southern Mississippi	Theodore, Ala.	D1-'81	12/12
26	Dudley, Brian	S	6-1	180	8/30/60	2	Bethune-Cookman	Los Angeles, Calif.	FA-'88	3/3
74	†Farren, Paul	T-G	6-5	280	12/24/60	6	Boston University	Cohasset, Mass.	D12-'83	12/12
69	Fike, Dan	G	6-7	280	6/16/61	4	Florida	Pensacola, Fla.	FA-'85	12/12
28	Fontenot, Herman	RB	6-0	206	9/12/63	4	Louisiana State	Beaumont, Tex.	FA-'85	12/0
79	Golic, Bob	NT	6-2	270	10/26/57	9	Notre Dame	Cleveland, Ohio	W(NE)-'82	12/12
56	Grayson, David	LB	6-2	229	2/27/64	2	Fresno State	San Diego, Calif.	FA-'87	11/5
53	Griggs, Anthony	LB	6-3	230	2/12/60	7	Ohio State	Somerville, N.J.	T(Phil)-'86	12/2
27	†Gross, Al	S	6-3	195	1/4/61	6	Arizona	Stockton, Calif.	W(Dall)-'83	6/5
94	Guilbeau, Rusty	LB	6-4	235	11/20/58	6	McNeese State	Sunset, La.	FA-'87	1/0
78	Hairston, Carl	DE	6-4	260	12/15/52	13	Maryland-Eastern Shore	Martinsville, Va.	T(Phil)-'84	14/14
65	†Haley, Darryl	T-G	6-4	265	2/16/61	6	Utah	Los Angeles, Calif.	FA-'87	9/1
23	†Harper, Mark	CB	5-9	174	11/5/61	3	Alcorn State	Memphis, Tenn.	FA-'86	12/0
48	Hoggard, D. D.	CB	6-0	188	5/7/65	3	North Carolina State	Falls Church, Va.	FA-'86	1/0
38	Horn, Alvin	S	5-11	185	3/7/65	2	Nevada-Las Vegas	Hanford, Calif.	FA-'88	3/3
8	Jaeger, Jeff	K	5-11	189	11/26/64	2	Washington	Kent, Wash.	D3b-'87	10/0
51	†Johnson, Eddie	LB	6-1	225	2/3/59	8	Louisville	Albany, Ga.	D7-'81	12/11
11	†Johnson, Lee	P	6-2	198	11/27/61	4	Brigham Young	Conroe, Tex.	FA-'87	3/0
59	†Johnson, Mike	LB	6-1	228	11/26/62	3	Virginia Tech	Hyattsville, Md.	SD1b-'84	11/10
54	Junkin, Mike	LB	6-3	238	11/21/64	2	Duke	Belvidere, Ill.	D1-'87	4/0
19	Kosar, Bernie	QB	6-5	210	11/25/63	4	Miami	Boardman, Ohio	SD1-'85	12/12
88	Langhorne, Reggie	WR	6-2	195	4/7/63	4	Elizabeth City State	Smithfield, Va.	D7-'85	12/12
34	Mack, Kevin	RB	6-0	225	8/9/62	4	Clemson	King Mountain, N.C.	SD1a-'84	12/12
42	Manoa, Tim	RB	6-1	227	9/9/64	2	Penn State	Pittsburgh, Pa.	D3a-'87	12/0
57	†Matthews, Clay	LB	6-2	235	3/15/56	11	Southern California	Los Angeles, Calif.	D1a-'78	12/12
89	McNeil, Gerald	WR-KR	5-7	147	3/27/62	3	Baylor	Killeen, Tex.	SD2a-'84	12/0
52	†Miller, Nick	LB	6-2	238	10/26/63	2	Arkansas	Fayetteville, Ark.	D5-'86	9/1
31	Minnifield, Frank	CB	5-9	180	1/1/60	5	Louisville	Lexington, Ky.	FA-'84	12/12
82	Newsome, Ozzie	TE	6-2	232	3/16/56	11	Alabama	Muscle Shoals, Ala.	D1b-'78	13/13
10	Pagel, Mike	QB	6-2	206	9/13/60	7	Arizona State	Phoenix, Ariz.	T(Ind)-'86	4/0
72	†Puzzuoli, Dave	NT	6-3	260	1/12/61	6	Pittsburgh	Stamford, Conn.	D6b-'83	12/1
73	Rakoczy, Gregg	T	6-6	290	5/18/65	2	Miami	Medford, N.J.	D2-'87	12/0
63	Risien, Cody	T	6-7	280	3/22/57	9	Texas A&M	Cypress, Tex.	D7-'79	13/13
37	†Rockins, Chris	S	6-0	195	5/18/62	5	Oklahoma State	Sherman, Tex.	D2a-'84	12/1
98	Rusinek, Mike	NT	6-3	250	5/1/63	2	California	Phoenix, Ariz.	FA-'88	3/3
50	†Sanford, Lucius	LB	6-2	216	2/14/56	11	Georgia Tech	Atlanta, Ga.	FA-'87	11/8
99	Sims, Darryl	DE	6-3	282	7/23/61	4	Wisconsin	Bridgeport, Conn.	FA-'87	10/4
84	Slaughter, Webster	WR	6-0	170	10/19/64	3	San Diego State	El Cajon, Calif.	D2-'86	12/12
50	Teifke, Mike	C	6-4	255	12/29/63	2	Akron	Toledo, Ohio	FA-'88	3/3
81	Tennell, Derek	TE	6-5	245	2/12/64	2	UCLA	West Covina, Calif.	FA-'87	11/2
87	Tucker, Travis	TE	6-3	240	9/19/63	4	So. Connecticut State	Brooklyn, N.Y.	D11-'85	4/0
85	Weathers, Clarence	WR	5-9	170	1/10/62	6	Delaware State	Fort Pierce, Fla.	W(NE)-'85	12/0
70	Williams, Larry	G	6-5	290	7/3/63	3	Notre Dame	Santa Ana, Calif.	D10-'85	12/8
64	Winters, Frank	C	6-3	290	1/23/64	2	Western Illinois	Union City, N.J.	D10-'87	12/0
22	†Wright, Felix	S	6-2	190	6/22/59	4	Drake	Carthage, Mo.	FA-'85	12/7
83	Young, Glen	WR-KR	6-2	205	10/11/60	5	Mississippi State	Greenwood, Miss.	FA-'87	10/0

* T. Baker missed '87 season due to injury.

†Option playout; subject to developments.

Also played with Browns in '87—S-CB Vincent Barnett (3 games), WR Clayton Beauford (1), DE Robert Brannon (1), LB Dave Butler (1), DE-LB James Capers (3), S-CB Vincent Carrecker (2), DE Alex Carter (3), QB Jeff Christensen (3), NT Scott Cooper (active for 1 game but did not play), LB Tim Crawford (3), RB Johnny Davis (1), RB Stacey Driver (2), TE Don Echols (3), S Ray Ellis (12), RB Major Everett (4), K Brian Franco (2), P Jeff Gossett (5), LB Cliff Hannemann (3), CB-S Enis Jackson (1), RB Kirk Jones (1), QB Homer Jordan (active for 2 games but did not play), C Mike Katolin (3), TE Chris Kelley (2), WR Perry Kemp (3), LB Mike Kovaleski (1), G Mark Krerowicz (3), K Goran Lingmerth (1), RB Larry Mason (3), DE Aaron Moog (3), LB Steve Nave (2), LB Jerry Parker (2), WR Steve Pierce (2), LB Tom Polley (2), CB DeJuan Robinson (3), S-CB Billy Robinson (3), G Dave Sparenberg (1), WR Keith Tinsley (3), T Ralph Van Dyke (2), WR David Verser (2), P Dale Walters (2), CB Troy Wilson (3), G Blake Wingle (3), P George Winslow (5).

COACHING STAFF

Head Coach, Marty Schottenheimer

Pro Career: Begins his fourth full season as head coach. Became sixth head coach in Cleveland history on October 22, 1984. After Browns' 1-7 start in 1984 under Sam Rutigliano, he led Browns to 4-4 finish. In first three full seasons, has guided Browns to three consecutive AFC Central championships. In the last two years, the Browns' 22-9 record is the AFC's best. Joined the Cleveland staff in 1980 as defensive coordinator. Served as an assistant coach with the Portland Storm (WFL) in 1974. Was linebackers' coach and defensive coordinator with New York Giants from 1975-77. Served as linebackers coach with the Detroit Lions from 1978-79. Selected in the seventh round of the 1965 draft by the Buffalo Bills. Played linebacker for the Bills from 1965-68 and for the Boston Patriots in 1969-70. Career record: 36-24.

Background: All-America linebacker at University of Pittsburgh 1962-64. Following retirement from pro football, worked as a real estate developer in both Miami and Denver from 1971-74.

Personal: Born September 23, 1943, Canonsburg, Pa. Marty and his wife, Patricia, live in Strongsville, Ohio, and have two children—Kristen and Brian.

Assistant Coaches

Dave Adolph, defensive coordinator; born June 6, 1937, Akron, Ohio, lives in Berea, Ohio. Guard-linebacker Akron 1955-58. No pro playing experience. College coach: Akron 1963-64, Connecticut 1965-68, Kentucky 1969-72, Illinois 1973-76, Ohio State 1977-78. Pro coach: Cleveland Browns 1979-84, San Diego Chargers 1985, rejoined Browns in 1986.

Ray Braun, special assistant-offense; born March 6, 1939, Killdeer, N.D., lives in Strongsville, Ohio. College coach: Washington State 1972-74, Oregon State 1975-78, 1981-83, Colorado 1979-80. Pro coach: Seattle Seahawks 1984, joined Browns part-time in 1985, first full year with Browns.

Bill Cowher, secondary; born May 8, 1957, Pittsburgh, Pa., lives in Strongsville, Ohio. Linebacker North Carolina State 1975-78. Pro linebacker Cleveland Browns 1980-82, Philadelphia Eagles 1983-84. Pro coach: Joined Browns in 1985 (special team's coach 1985-86).

Richard Mann, receivers; born April 20, 1947, Aliquippa, Pa., lives in Strongsville, Ohio. Wide receiver Arizona State 1966-68. No pro playing experience. College coach: Arizona State 1974-79, Louisville 1980-81. Pro coach: Indianapolis Colts 1982-84, joined Browns in 1985.

Howard Mudd, offensive line; born February 10, 1942, Midland, Mich., lives in Medina, Ohio. Guard Hillsdale 1961-63. Pro guard San Francisco 49ers 1964-69, Chicago Bears 1970-71. College coach: California 1972-73. Pro coach: San Diego Chargers 1974-76, San Francisco 49ers 1977, Seattle Seahawks 1978-82, joined Browns in 1983.

Joe Pendry, running backs; born August 5, 1947, Matheny, W. Va., lives in Strongsville, Ohio. Tight end West Virginia 1966-67. No pro playing experience. College coach: West Virginia 1967-74, 1976-77, Kansas State 1975, Pittsburgh 1978-79, Michigan State 1980-81. Pro coach: Philadelphia Stars (USFL) 1983, Pittsburgh Maulers (USFL, head coach) 1984, joined Browns in 1985.

Tom Pratt, defensive line; born June 21, 1935, Edgerton, Wis., lives in Medina, Ohio. Linebacker Miami 1954-56. No pro playing experience. College coach: Miami 1957-59, Southern Mississippi 1960-62. Pro coach: Kansas City Chiefs 1963-77, New Orleans Saints 1978-80, joined Browns in 1981.

Dave Redding, strength and conditioning; born June 14, 1952, North Platte, Neb., lives in Medina, Ohio. Defensive end Nebraska 1972-75. No pro playing experience. College coach: Nebraska 1976, Washington State 1977, Missouri 1978-81. Pro coach: Joined Browns in 1982.

Cleveland Browns 1988 First-Year Roster

Name	Pos.	Ht.	Wt.	Birth-date	College	Hometown	How Acq.
Bauer, Trey	LB	6-1	215	11/28/64	Penn State	Paramus, N.J.	FA
Bell, Albert (1)	WR	6-0	170	4/23/64	Alabama	Los Angeles, Calif.	FA-'87
Birden, J.J.	WR	5-9	160	5/16/65	Oregon	Portland, Ore.	D8
Blaylock, Anthony	CB	5-11	190	2/21/65	Winston-Salem State	Raleigh, N.C.	D4
Buchanan, Charles (1)	DE	6-3	245	9/20/64	Tennessee State	Memphis, Tenn.	FA
Bullitt, Steve (1)	LB	6-2	228	4/21/65	Texas A&M	El Paso, Tex.	D8-'87
Burdick, Shaun (1)	P	6-4	185	5/28/63	Cincinnati	Cincinnati, Ohio	FA
Caston, Willie	RB	5-10	191	6/3/66	Idaho State	Pocatello, Idaho	FA
Charlton, Clifford	LB	6-2	238	2/16/65	Florida	Gainesville, Fla.	D1
Conyers, Lorne	RB	5-10	185	3/1/66	Baldwin-Wallace	Masury, Ohio	FA
Copeland, Danny	S	6-2	210	1/24/66	Eastern Kentucky	Richmond, Ky.	D9
Cullity, Dave (1)	T-G-C	6-7	275	6/15/64	Utah	La Mirada, Calif.	FA-'87
Gash, Thane	S	6-0	200	9/9/65	East Tennessee State	Johnson City, Tenn.	D7
Grooms, Greg (1)	RB	6-2	198	10/16/64	Richmond	Richmond, Va.	FA
Hawkins, Hendley	WR	5-9	190	1/3/65	Nebraska	Los Angeles, Calif.	D11
Hill, Will (1)	CB-S	6-0	197	3/5/63	Bishop College	Vero Beach, Fla.	FA-'87
Holmes, Bruce (1)	LB	6-3	235	10/24/64	Minnesota	New Brighton, Minn.	FA
Incollingo, John	C	6-2	280	5/2/65	Temple	Philadelphia, Pa.	FA
Jackson, David (1)	WR	5-9	175	1/7/65	Southeast Missouri St.	Bradshaw, Md.	FA
Jones, Marlon (1)	DE	6-4	260	7/1/64	Central State, Ohio	Baltimore, Md.	FA-'87
Knox, Darryl (1)	LB	6-3	230	9/3/62	Nevada-Las Vegas	Las Vegas, Nev.	FA
Logan, Marc (1)	RB	5-11	204	5/9/65	Kentucky	Lexington, Ky.	FA
McKee, Eric (1)	TE	6-4	243	4/2/65	Southern California	Carson, Calif.	FA
Meech, Pat	T	6-3	270	12/10/64	Northern Arizona	Rialto, Calif.	FA
Negrin, Rich	G	6-3	275	5/29/66	Wagner	Edison, N.J.	FA
Patterson, Reno (1)	NT	6-2	255	4/22/61	Bethune-Cookman	Chicago, Ill.	FA
Perry, Michael Dean	DE-NT	6-1	280	8/27/65	Clemson	Clemson, S.C.	D2
Pike, Chris	DE-NT	6-7	291	1/13/64	Tulsa	Washington, D.C.	FA
Price, Mitchell (1)	DE	6-3	260	7/29/61	Livingston	Stony Creek, Ontario	FA
Redick, Corn (1)	WR	5-11	187	1/7/64	Cal State-Fullerton	Fullerton, Calif.	FA
Sam, Aaron (1)	RB	5-9	196	1/17/66	Central Florida	Glen Mills, Pa.	FA-'87
Shelley, Jonathan (1)	CB-S	5-11	180	8/6/64	Mississippi	University, Miss.	FA
Slayden, Steve	QB	6-1	185	1/22/66	Duke	Durham, N.C.	D12
Sorrells, Tyrone (1)	G	6-3	280	5/10/63	Georgia Tech	Buford, Ga.	FA
Stephens, Tony	LB	6-1	226	9/7/65	Kent State	Newton Falls, Ohio	FA
Swarn, George (1)	RB	5-10	205	2/15/64	Miami, Ohio	Mansfield, Ohio	FA-'87
Taylor, Greg	WR	5-10	180	1/23/66	Bethune-Cookman	Quincy, Fla.	FA
Waiters, Van	LB	6-4	240	2/27/65	Indiana	Miami, Fla.	D3
Wall, Jerry	LB	6-3	220	8/5/66	Pittsburgh	Ingomar, Pa.	FA
Washington, Brian	S	6-0	225	9/10/65	Nebraska	Richmond, Va.	D10
Watson, Louis (1)	WR	5-11	173	1/11/63	Mississippi Valley St.	Mobile, Ala.	FA
Watson, Remi (1)	WR	6-0	174	8/11/64	Bethune-Cookman	Plantation, Fla.	FA-'87
Watson, Troy	WR	6-0	172	7/27/63	East Tennessee State	Arlington, Tenn.	FA
White, Bobby (1)	LB	6-2	242	1/7/64	Penn State	State College, Pa.	FA
Wisnosky, John	T	6-4	280	5/16/65	Western Illinois	Springfield, Ill.	FA

The term NFL Rookie is defined as a player who is in his first season of professional football and has not been on the roster of another professional football team for any regular-season or postseason games. A Rookie is designated by an "R" on NFL rosters. Players who have been active in another professional football league or players who have NFL experience, including either preseason training camp or being on an active roster for fewer than three regular-season or postseason games, are termed NFL First-Year Players. An NFL First-Year Player is designated by a "1" on NFL rosters. Thereafter, a player on an NFL active roster for at least three regular-season or postseason games is credited with an additional year of NFL playing experience.

NOTES

Kurt Schottenheimer, special teams; born October 1, 1949, McDonald, Pa., lives in Medina, Ohio. Defensive back Miami 1969-70. No pro playing experience. College coach: William Patterson 1974, Michigan State 1978-82, Tulane 1983, Louisiana State 1984-85, Notre Dame 1986. Pro coach: Joined Browns in 1987.

Marc Trestman, quarterbacks; born January 15, 1956, Minneapolis, Minn., lives in Strongsville, Ohio. Quarterback Minnesota 1975-77, Moorhead (Minn.) State 1978. No pro playing experience. College coach: Miami 1981-84. Pro coach: Minnesota Vikings 1985-86, Tampa Bay Buccaneers 1987, joined Browns in 1988.

Darvin Wallis, special assistant-defense; born February 14, 1949, Ft. Branch, Ind., lives in Middleburg Heights, Ohio. Defensive end Arizona 1970-71. No pro playing experience. College coach: Adams State 1976-77, Tulane 1978-79, Mississippi 1980-81. Pro coach: Joined Browns in 1982.

DENVER BRONCOS

American Football Conference Western Division

Team Colors: Orange, Royal Blue, and White

5700 Logan Street
Denver, Colorado 80216
Telephone: (303) 296-1982

Club Officials

President-Chief Executive Officer: Pat Bowlen
Vice President-Head Coach: Dan Reeves
General Manager: John Beake
Chief Financial Officer-Treasurer: Robert M. Hurley
Director of Administration: Sandy Waters
Director of Player Personnel: Reed Johnson
Director of Pro Personnel: Lide Huggins
Director of Media Relations: Jim Saccomano
Ticket Manager: Gail Stuckey
Director of Marketing: Bill Harpole
Video Director: Rusty Nail
Director of Player and Community Relations: Charlie Lee
Equipment Manager: Dan Bill
Trainer: Steve Antonopulos

Stadium: Denver Mile High Stadium • **Capacity:** 76,273
1900 West Eliot
Denver, Colorado 80204

Playing Surface: Grass (PAT)

Training Camp: University of Northern Colorado
Greeley, Colorado 80639

1988 Schedule

Preseason

Aug. 3	at Los Angeles Rams	7:00
Aug. 13	**San Francisco**	7:00
Aug. 19	at Miami	9:00
Aug. 25	**Indianapolis**	6:00

Regular Season

Sept. 4	**Seattle**	2:00
Sept. 11	**San Diego**	2:00
Sept. 18	at Kansas City	12:00
Sept. 26	**L.A. Raiders** (Monday)	6:00
Oct. 2	at San Diego	1:00
Oct. 9	at San Francisco	1:00
Oct. 16	**Atlanta**	2:00
Oct. 23	at Pittsburgh	1:00
Oct. 31	at Indianapolis (Monday)	9:00
Nov. 6	**Kansas City**	2:00
Nov. 13	**Cleveland**	2:00
Nov. 20	at New Orleans	12:00
Nov. 27	**Los Angeles Rams**	2:00
Dec. 4	at Los Angeles Raiders	1:00
Dec. 11	at Seattle	5:00
Dec. 17	**New England** (Saturday)	2:00

Broncos Coaching History

(194-213-10)

1960-61	Frank Filchock	7-20-1
1962-64	Jack Faulkner*	9-22-1
1964-66	Mac Speedie**	6-19-1
1966	Ray Malavasi	4-8-0
1967-71	Lou Saban***	20-42-3
1971	Jerry Smith	2-3-0
1972-76	John Ralston	34-33-3
1977-80	Robert (Red) Miller	42-25-0
1981-87	Dan Reeves	70-41-1

*Released after four games in 1964
**Resigned after two games in 1966
***Resigned after nine games in 1971

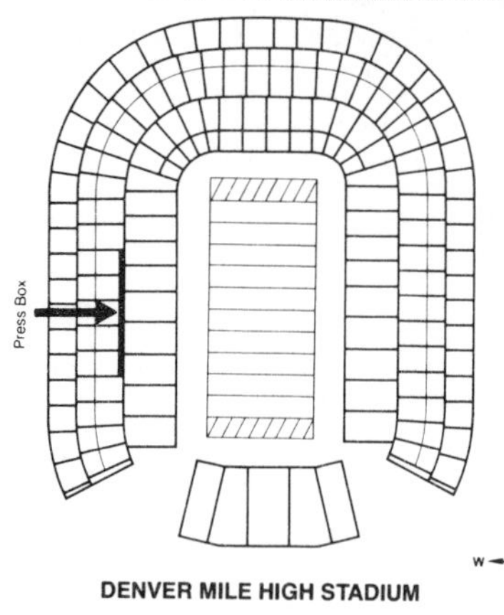

DENVER MILE HIGH STADIUM

Record Holders

Individual Records—Career

Category	Name	Performance
Rushing (Yds.)	Floyd Little, 1967-1975	6,323
Passing (Yds.)	John Elway, 1983-87	14,835
Passing (TDs)	John Elway, 1983-1987	85
Receiving (No.)	Lionel Taylor, 1960-66	543
Receiving (Yds.)	Lionel Taylor, 1960-66	6,872
Interceptions	Steve Foley, 1976-1986	44
Punting (Avg.)	Jim Fraser, 1962-64	45.2
Punt Return (Avg.)	Rick Upchurch, 1975-1983	12.1
Kickoff Return (Avg.)	Abner Haynes, 1965-66	26.3
Field Goals	Jim Turner, 1971-79	151
Touchdowns (Tot.)	Floyd Little, 1967-1975	54
Points	Jim Turner, 1971-79	742

Individual Records—Single Season

Category	Name	Performance
Rushing (Yds.)	Otis Armstrong, 1974	1,407
Passing (Yds.)	John Elway, 1985	3,891
Passing (TDs)	Frank Tripucka, 1960	24
Receiving (No.)	Lionel Taylor, 1961	100
Receiving (Yds.)	Steve Watson, 1981	1,244
Interceptions	Goose Gonsoulin, 1960	11
Punting (Avg.)	Jim Fraser, 1963	46.1
Punt Return (Avg.)	Floyd Little, 1967	16.9
Kickoff Return (Avg.)	Bill Thompson, 1969	28.5
Field Goals	Gene Mingo, 1962	27
Touchdowns (Tot.)	Sammy Winder, 1986	14
Points	Gene Mingo, 1962	137

Individual Records—Single Game

Category	Name	Performance
Rushing (Yds.)	Otis Armstrong, 12-8-74	183
Passing (Yds.)	Frank Tripucka, 9-15-62	447
Passing (TDs)	Frank Tripucka, 10-28-62	5
	John Elway, 11-18-84	5
Receiving (No.)	Lionel Taylor, 11-29-64	13
	Bobby Anderson, 9-30-73	13
Receiving (Yds.)	Lionel Taylor, 11-27-60	199
Interceptions	Goose Gonsoulin, 9-18-60	*4
	Willie Brown, 11-15-64	*4
Field Goals	Gene Mingo, 10-6-63	5
	Rich Karlis, 11-20-83	5
Touchdowns (Tot.)	Many times	3
	Last time by Gerald Willhite, 11-16-86	
Points	Gene Mingo, 12-10-60	21

*NFL Record

1987 Team Record

Preseason (3-2)

Date	Result		Opponents
8/9	L	27-28	vs. L.A. Rams at London, England
8/15	W	20-14	vs. Green Bay at Tempe, Arizona
8/24	W	31-28	Miami
8/29	W	24-20	at L.A. Rams
9/3	L	17-27	Minnesota
		119-117	

Regular Season (10-4-1)

Date	Result		Opponents	Att.
9/13	W	40-17	Seattle	75,999
9/20	T	17-17	at Green Bay (OT)	50,624
9/28	C		at Cleveland	
10/4	L	10-40	Houston	38,494
10/12	W	30-14	L.A. Raiders	61,230
10/18	W	26-17	at Kansas City	20,296
10/26	L	27-34	at Minnesota	51,011
11/1	W	34- 0	Detroit	75,172
11/8	L	14-21	at Buffalo	63,698
11/16	W	31-29	Chicago	75,783
11/22	W	23-17	at L.A. Raiders	61,318
11/29	W	31-17	at San Diego	61,880
12/6	W	31-20	New England	75,795
12/13	L	21-28	at Seattle	61,759
12/19	W	20-17	Kansas City	75,053
12/27	W	24- 0	San Diego	21,189

(OT) Overtime
C (Cancelled due to players' strike.)

Postseason (2-1)

Date	Result		Opponents	Att.
1/10	W	34-10	Houston	75,968
1/17	W	38-33	Cleveland	75,993
1/31	L	10-42	Washington	73,302

Score by Periods

Broncos	92	110	79	98	0	—	379
Opponents	70	110	64	44	0	—	288

Attendance

Home 498,715 Away 370,586 Total 869,301
Single-game home record, 76,105 (1-4-87)
Single-season home record, 598,224 (1981)

1987 Team Statistics

	Broncos	Opp.
Total First Downs	331	277
Rushing	132	103
Passing	173	148
Penalty	26	26
Third Down: Made/Att.	105/223	64/183
Fourth Down: Made/Att.	6/13	5/12
Total Net Yards	5624	4813
Avg. Per Game	374.9	320.9
Total Plays	1070	941
Avg. Per Play	5.3	5.1
Net Yards Rushing	1970	2017
Avg. Per Game	131.3	134.5
Total Rushes	510	454
Net Yards Passing	3654	2796
Avg. Per Game	243.6	186.4
Sacked/Yards Lost	30/220	31/244
Gross Yards	3874	3040
Att./Completions	530/285	456/261
Completion Pct.	53.8	57.2
Had Intercepted	19	28
Punts/Avg.	65/39.9	75/42.1
Net Punting Avg.	31.6	33.5
Penalties/Yards Lost	95/812	96/785
Fumbles/Ball Lost	29/17	35/19
Touchdowns	45	35
Rushing	18	16
Passing	24	15
Returns	3	4
Avg. Time of Possession	31:55	28:09

1987 Individual Statistics

Scoring	TD R	TD P	TD Rt	PAT	FG	Saf	TP
Karlis	0	0	0	37/37	18/25	0	91
V. Johnson	0	7	0	0/0	0/0	0	42
Winder	6	1	0	0/0	0/0	0	42
Elway	4	0	0	0/0	0/0	0	24
Lang	2	2	0	0/0	0/0	0	24
Massie	0	4	0	0/0	0/0	0	24
Sewell	2	1	0	0/0	0/0	0	18
Clendenen	0	0	0	7/7	3/4	0	16
Dudek	2	0	0	0/0	0/0	0	12
M. Jackson	0	2	0	0/0	0/0	0	12
Micho	0	2	0	0/0	0/0	0	12
Nattiel	0	2	0	0/0	0/0	0	12
Boddie	1	0	0	0/0	0/0	0	6
Clark	0	0	1	0/0	0/0	0	6
Haynes	0	0	1	0/0	0/0	0	6
Hunley	0	0	1	0/0	0/0	0	6
Mobley	0	1	0	0/0	0/0	0	6
Poole	1	0	0	0/0	0/0	0	6
Swanson	0	1	0	0/0	0/0	0	6
Watson	0	1	0	0/0	0/0	0	6
Ryan	0	0	0	0/0	0/0	1	2
Broncos	18	24	3	44/45	21/29	1	379
Opponents	16	15	4	32/35	14/21	2	288

Passing	Att.	Comp.	Yds.	Pct.	TD	Int.	Tkld.	Rate
Elway	410	224	3198	54.6	19	12	20/138	83.4
Karcher	102	56	628	54.9	5	4	5/45	73.5
Kubiak	7	3	25	42.9	0	2	2/14	13.1
May	5	0	0	0.0	0	1	1/7	0.0
McGuire	3	2	23	66.7	0	0	0/0	89.6
V. Johnson	1	0	0	0.0	0	0	0/0	39.6
Lang	1	0	0	0.0	0	0	1/7	39.6
Willhite	1	0	0	0.0	0	0	0/0	39.6
Sewell	0	0	0	—	0	0	1/9	0.0
Broncos	530	285	3874	53.8	24	19	30/220	77.5
Opponents	456	261	3040	57.2	15	28	31/244	62.9

Rushing	Att.	Yds.	Avg.	LG	TD
Winder	196	741	3.8	19	6
Elway	66	304	4.6	29	4
Lang	89	303	3.4	28	2
Dudek	35	154	4.4	16	2
Willhite	26	141	5.4	29	0
Poole	28	126	4.5	15	1
Sewell	19	83	4.4	17	2
Caldwell	16	53	3.3	7	0
Bell	13	43	3.3	11	0
Nattiel	2	13	6.5	10	0
Micho	4	8	2.0	5	0
Boddie	3	7	2.3	4	1
Karcher	9	3	0.3	8	0
Kubiak	1	3	3.0	3	0
May	2	−4	−2.0	−2	0
V. Johnson	1	−8	−8.0	−8	0
Broncos	510	1970	3.9	29	18
Opponents	454	2017	4.4	72	16

Receiving	No.	Yds.	Avg.	LG	TD
V. Johnson	42	684	16.3	59t	7
Nattiel	31	630	20.3	54	2
Kay	31	440	14.2	30	0
M. Jackson	26	436	16.8	52	2
Micho	25	242	9.7	26t	2
Lang	17	130	7.6	29	2
Mobley	16	228	14.3	28	1
Winder	14	74	5.3	13	1
Massie	13	244	18.8	39t	4
Sewell	13	209	16.1	72t	1
Watson	11	167	15.2	49	1
Boddie	9	85	9.4	26	0
Willhite	9	25	2.8	6	0
Dudek	7	41	5.9	19	0
Swanson	6	87	14.5	35t	1
Andrews	4	53	13.3	20	0
Brown	4	40	10.0	18	0
Caldwell	4	34	8.5	14	0
Poole	1	9	9.0	9	0
Bell	1	8	8.0	8	0
Payne	1	8	8.0	8	0
Broncos	285	3874	13.6	72t	24
Opponents	261	3040	11.6	51t	15

Interceptions	No.	Yds.	Avg.	LG	TD
Harden	4	85	21.3	32	0
Clark	3	105	35.0	50	0
Haynes	3	39	13.0	25	1
Lilly	3	29	9.7	24	0
Mecklenburg	3	23	7.7	16	0
Robbins	3	9	3.0	9	0
Ryan	3	7	2.3	5	0
Hunley	2	64	32.0	52t	1
D. Smith	2	21	10.5	15	0
Lucas	1	11	11.0	11	0
Dennison	1	10	10.0	10	0
Broncos	28	403	14.4	52t	2
Opponents	19	362	19.1	103t	2

Punting	No.	Yds.	Avg.	In 20	LG
Giacomarro	18	757	42.1	4	50
Horan	44	1807	41.1	11	61
Elway	1	31	31.0	1	31
Broncos	65	2595	39.9	16	61
Opponents	75	3158	42.1	15	62

Punt Returns	No.	FC	Yds.	Avg.	LG	TD
Clark	18	1	233	12.9	71t	1
Nattiel	12	1	73	6.1	14	0
Swanson	9	1	132	14.7	33	0
Willhite	4	1	22	5.5	9	0
Harden	2	0	11	5.5	7	0
Lilly	2	0	6	3.0	4	0
V. Johnson	1	0	9	9.0	9	0
Broncos	48	4	486	10.1	71t	1
Opponents	34	7	424	12.5	85t	2

Kickoff Returns	No.	Yds.	Avg.	LG	TD
Bell	15	323	21.5	42	0
Swanson	9	234	26.0	50	0
V. Johnson	7	140	20.0	34	0
Lang	4	78	19.5	25	0
Nattiel	4	78	19.5	25	0
Brown	3	57	19.0	28	0
Clark	2	33	16.5	25	0
Ryan	2	9	4.5	9	0
Broncos	46	952	20.7	50	0
Opponents	61	1168	19.1	50	0

Sacks	No.
R. Jones	7.0
Mecklenburg	7.0
Fletcher	4.0
Kragen	2.0
Lucas	2.0
Ryan	1.5
Tupper	1.5
Brooks	1.0
Hunley	1.0
Robbins	1.0
Townsend	1.0
Wilson	1.0
Bowyer	0.5
Woodard	0.5
Broncos	31.0
Opponents	30.0

Denver Broncos 1988 Veteran Roster

No.	Name	Pos.	Ht.	Wt.	Birth-date	NFL Exp.	College	Hometown	How Acq.	'87 Games/ Starts
86	Andrews, Mitch	TE	6-2	239	3/4/64	2	Louisiana State	Houma, La.	FA-'87	8/3
35	†Bell, Ken	RB	5-10	190	11/16/64	3	Boston College	Greenwich, Conn.	FA-'86	12/1
54	Bishop, Keith	C-G	6-3	265	3/10/57	8	Baylor	La Jolla, Calif.	D6-'80	12/12
24	Boddie, Tony	RB	5-11	198	11/11/60	2	Montana State	Portsmith, Wash.	FA-'86	5/0
65	Bowyer, Walt	DE	6-4	260	9/8/60	4	Arizona State	Wilkinsburg, Pa.	FA-'87	15/3
56	Brooks, Michael	LB	6-1	235	10/2/64	2	Louisiana State	Rustin, La.	D3-'87	12/0
64	†Bryan, Billy	C	6-2	255	9/21/55	12	Duke	Burlington, N.C.	D4-'77	4/4
95	Bryan, Steve	NT	6-2	256	5/6/64	2	Oklahoma	Wagoner, Okla.	FA-'87	4/3
28	†Castille, Jeremiah	CB-S	5-10	175	1/15/61	6	Alabama	Columbus, Ga.	W(TB)-'87	11/0
27	Clark, Kevin	S	5-10	185	6/8/64	2	San Jose State	Salto, Calif.	FA-'87	11/3
69	†Colorito, Tony	NT	6-5	260	9/8/64	2	Southern California	Brooklyn, N.Y.	D5-'86	0*
55	Dennison, Rick	LB	6-3	220	6/22/58	7	Colorado State	Kalispel, Mont.	FA-'82	12/0
	t-Dorsett, Tony	RB	5-11	188	4/7/54	12	Pittsburgh	Aliquippa, Pa.	T(Dall)-'88	12/6
7	Elway, John	QB	6-3	210	6/28/60	6	Stanford	Port Angeles, Wash.	T(Balt)-'83	12/12
73	Fletcher, Simon	LB-DE	6-5	240	2/18/62	4	Houston	Bay City, Tex.	D2b-'85	12/12
62	Freeman, Mike	G	6-3	256	10/13/61	4	Arizona	Mt. Holly, N.J.	FA-'84	13/9
90	†Gilbert, Freddie	DE	6-4	275	4/8/62	3	Georgia	Griffin, Ga.	SD1-'84	7/3
31	Harden, Mike	CB-S	6-1	192	2/16/59	9	Michigan	Memphis, Tenn.	D5a-'80	12/12
36	Haynes, Mark	CB	5-11	195	11/6/58	9	Colorado	Kansas City, Kan.	T(NYG)-'86	12/12
78	Hood, Winford	G	6-3	265	3/29/62	5	Georgia	Atlanta, Ga.	FA-'87	3/2
2	†Horan, Mike	P	5-11	190	2/1/59	5	Long Beach State	Orange, Calif.	FA-'86	12/0
79	†Humphries, Stefan	G	6-3	268	1/20/62	5	Michigan	Broward, Fla.	T(Chi)-'87	7/7
98	†Hunley, Ricky	LB	6-2	238	11/11/61	5	Arizona	Petersburg, Va.	T(Cin)-'84	12/12
80	Jackson, Mark	WR	5-9	174	7/23/63	3	Purdue	Chicago, Ill.	D6b-'86	12/9
82	Johnson, Vance	WR	5-11	174	3/13/63	4	Arizona	Trenton, N.J.	D2a-'85	11/9
20	Jones, Daryll	S	6-0	193	3/23/62	3	Georgia	Decatur, Ga.	FA-'87	1/1
75	Jones, Rulon	DE	6-6	260	3/25/58	9	Utah State	Salt Lake City, Utah	D2-'80	12/12
12	Karcher, Ken	QB	6-3	205	7/1/63	2	Tulane	Pittsburgh, Pa.	FA-'87	3/3
3	†Karlis, Rich	K	6-0	180	5/23/59	7	Cincinnati	Salem, Ohio	FA-'82	12/0
72	Kartz, Keith	T	6-4	270	5/5/63	2	California	Las Vegas, Nev.	FA-'87	12/3
88	Kay, Clarence	TE	6-2	237	7/30/61	5	Georgia	Seneca, S.C.	D7-'84	12/12
97	Klostermann, Bruce	LB	6-4	225	4/17/63	2	South Dakota State	Dubuque, Iowa	D8-'86	9/0
71	Kragen, Greg	NT	6-3	245	3/4/62	4	Utah State	Chicago, Ill.	FA-'85	12/9
8	Kubiak, Gary	QB	6-0	192	8/15/61	6	Texas A&M	Houston, Tex.	D8-'83	12/0
33	Lang, Gene	RB	5-10	196	3/15/62	5	Louisiana State	Pass Christian, Miss.	D11-'84	12/6
76	Lanier, Ken	T	6-3	269	7/8/59	8	Florida State	Columbus, Ohio	D5-'81	12/12
68	†Lee, Larry	G-C	6-2	263	9/10/59	8	UCLA	Dayton, Ohio	T(Mia)-'87	9/5
22	†Lilly, Tony	S	6-0	199	2/16/62	5	Florida	Alexandria, Va.	D3-'84	13/9
59	Lucas, Tim	LB	6-3	230	4/3/61	2	California	Stockton, Calif.	FA-'87	11/3
85	Massie, Rick	WR	6-1	190	1/16/60	2	Kentucky	Paris, Ky.	FA-'87	9/4
77	Mecklenburg, Karl	LB-DE	6-3	230	9/1/60	6	Minnesota	Edina, Minn.	D12-'83	12/12
46	Micho, Bobby	RB	6-3	235	3/7/62	4	Texas	Omaha, Neb.	W(SD)-'86	15/3
89	Mobley, Orson	TE	6-5	256	3/4/63	3	Salem College	Brooksville, Fla.	D6a-'86	10/6
51	Munford, Marc	LB	6-2	231	2/14/65	2	Nebraska	Lincoln, Neb.	D4-'87	12/0
84	Nattiel, Ricky	WR	5-9	180	1/25/66	2	Florida	Gainesville, Fla.	D1-'87	12/3
38	Plummer, Bruce	CB	6-1	197	9/1/64	2	Mississippi State	Bogalusa, La.	D9-'87	11/0
74	Remsberg, Dan	T	6-6	275	4/7/62	3	Abilene Christian	Temple, Tex.	FA-'86	5/0
48	†Robbins, Randy	S	6-2	189	9/14/62	5	Arizona	Casa Grande, Ariz.	D4-'84	10/4
50	Ryan, Jim	LB	6-1	225	5/18/57	10	William & Mary	Bellmawr, N.J.	FA-'79	14/14
30	Sewell, Steve	RB	6-3	210	4/2/63	4	Oklahoma	San Francisco, Calif.	D1-'85	7/0
49	†Smith, Dennis	S	6-3	200	2/3/59	8	Southern California	Santa Monica, Calif.	D1-'81	6/6
70	Studdard, Dave	T	6-4	260	11/22/55	10	Texas	San Antonio, Tex.	FA-'79	14/14
61	Townsend, Andre	DE-NT	6-3	265	10/8/62	5	Mississippi	Chicago, Ill.	D2-'84	12/11
81	Watson, Steve	WR	6-4	195	5/28/57	10	Temple	Baltimore, Md.	FA-'79	5/1
47	Willhite, Gerald	RB	5-10	200	5/30/59	7	San Jose State	Sacramento, Calif.	D1-'82	3/1
45	†Wilson, Steve	CB	5-10	195	8/25/57	10	Howard	Los Angeles, Calif.	FA-'82	11/5
23	Winder, Sammy	RB	5-11	203	7/15/59	7	Southern Mississippi	Madison, Miss.	D5-'82	12/10

* Colorito missed '87 season due to injury.

†Option playout; subject to developments.

t-Broncos traded for Dorsett (Dallas).

Also played with Broncos in '87—G John Ayers (9 games), T Kevin Belcher (1), S Tyrone Braxton (2), WR Laron Brown (3), RB Scott Caldwell (3), K Mike Clendenen (3), G Mark Cooper (5), LB Stan David (active for 1 game but did not play), LB Kirk Dodge (3), RB Joe Dudek (2), S Steve Fitzhugh (3), P Ralph Giacomarro (3), WR Sam Graddy (1), G-T Archie Harris (3), S Roger Jackson (3), S Earl Johnson (3), LB Tim Joiner (3), G David Jones (3), S Leonard Jones (2), LB Mike Knox (3), RB Zeph Lee (1), DE-NT Bill Lobenstein (3), TE Kerry Locklin (3), LB Dan MacDonald (3), RB Warren Marshall (1), QB Dean May (3), QB Monte McGuire (2), RB Bruce McIntyre (active for 1 game but did not play), DE-NT Ron McLean (3), TE Russell Payne (1), C Jack Peavey (3), CB Lyle Pickens (1), RB Nathan Poole (2), CB Martin Rudolph (3), CB-S Darryl Russell (3), C Carlos Scott (active for 1 game but did not play), LB Matt Smith (3), WR Shane Swanson (3), WR Robert Thompson (2), NT Jeff Tupper (4), LB Bryant Winn (3), DE Ray Woodard (3).

Coaching Staff

Head Coach, Dan Reeves

Pro Career: Became ninth head coach in Broncos history on February 28, 1981, after spending entire pro career as both player and coach with Dallas Cowboys. Reeves's Broncos won the AFC Western Division title and AFC championship in 1986 and 1987, the first AFC team to repeat as conference champion since 1978-79. Denver posted regular-season records of 10-4-1 (1987) and 11-5 (1986). Led Denver to an 11-5 record in 1985, barely missing a playoff berth. Guided Broncos to AFC West championship with a 13-3 record in 1984, and a 9-7 mark and playoff berth in 1983. His teams were 10-6 in 1981 and 2-7 in 1982. He joined the Cowboys as a free agent running back in 1965 and became a member of the coaching staff in 1970 when he undertook the dual role of player-coach for two seasons. Was Cowboys offensive backfield coach from 1972-76 and became offensive coordinator in 1977. Was an all-purpose running back during his eight seasons as a player, rushing for 1,990 yards and catching 129 passes for 1,693. Career record: 70-41-1.

Background: Quarterback at South Carolina from 1962-64. He was inducted into the school's Hall of Fame in 1978.

Personal: Born January 19, 1944, Rome, Ga. Dan and his wife, Pam, live in Denver and have three children—Dana, Laura, and Lee.

Assistant Coaches

Marvin Bass, special assistant; born August 28, 1919, Norfolk, Va., lives in Denver. Tackle William & Mary 1940-42. No pro playing experience. College coach: William & Mary 1944-48, 1950-51 (head coach), North Carolina 1949, 1953-55, South Carolina 1956-59, 1961-65, Georgia Tech 1960, Richmond 1973. Pro coach: Washington Redskins 1952, Montreal Beavers (Continental League) 1966-67, Montreal Alouettes (CFL) 1968, Buffalo Bills 1969-71, Birmingham Americans (WFL) 1974-75, joined Broncos in 1982.

Rubin Carter, assistant defensive line; born December 12, 1952, Pompano Beach, Fla., lives in Aurora, Colo. Nose tackle Miami 1972-74. Pro nose tackle Denver Broncos 1975-86. Pro coach: Joined Broncos in 1987.

Joe Collier, assistant head coach, defense; born June 7, 1932, Rock Island, Ill., lives in Denver. End Northwestern 1950-53. No pro playing experience. College coach: Western Illinois 1957-59. Pro coach: Boston Patriots 1960-62, Buffalo Bills 1963-68 (head coach 1966-68), joined Broncos in 1969.

Mo Forte, running backs; born March 1, 1947, Hannibal, Mo., lives in Denver. Running back Minnesota 1965-69. No pro playing experience. College coach: Minnesota 1970-75, Duke 1976-77, Michigan State 1978-79, Arizona State 1980-81, North Carolina A & T 1982-87 (head coach). Pro coach: Joined Broncos in 1988.

Chan Gailey, quarterbacks; born January 5, 1952, Americus, Ga., lives in Denver. Quarterback Florida 1971-74. No pro playing experience. College coach: Troy State 1976-77, 1983-84 (head coach), Air Force 1978-82. Pro coach: Joined Broncos in 1985.

George Henshaw, offensive line; born January 22, 1948, Richmond, Va., lives in Denver. Defensive tackle West Virginia 1967-69. No pro playing experience. College coach: West Virginia 1970-75, Florida State 1976-82, Alabama 1983-86, Tulsa 1987 (head coach). Pro coach: Joined Broncos in 1988.

Stan Jones, defensive line; born November 24, 1931, Altoona, Pa., lives in Denver. Tackle Maryland 1950-53. Pro lineman Chicago Bears 1954-65, Washington Redskins 1966. Pro coach: Denver Broncos 1967-71, Buffalo Bills 1972-75, rejoined Broncos in 1976.

Larry Kennan, wide receivers; born June 13, 1944, Pomona, Calif., lives in Denver. Quarterback La-Verne College 1962-65. College coach: Colorado 1969-72, Nevada-Las Vegas 1973-75, Southern Methodist 1976-78, Lamar 1979-81. Pro coach: Los Angeles Raiders 1982-87, joined Broncos in 1988.

Denver Broncos 1988 First-Year Roster

Name	Pos.	Ht.	Wt.	Birth-date	College	Hometown	How Acq.
Baran, Dave (1)	C	6-5	280	6/28/63	UCLA	Vineland, N.J.	FA-'87
Braxton, Tyrone (1)	S	5-11	174	12/17/64	North Dakota State	Madison, Wis.	D12-'87
Calvin, Richard	RB	6-0	198	9/1/65	Washington State	Dallas, Tex.	D11
Carter, Johnny	NT	6-3	295	4/23/65	Grambling	New Orleans, La.	D12
Demerritt, James (1)	RB	6-0	225	5/31/63	Jackson State	Miami, Fla.	FA-'87
Dudek, Joe (1)	RB	6-0	181	1/22/64	Plymouth State	Worcester, Mass.	FA-'86
Ervin, Corris	CB	5-11	173	8/30/66	Central Florida	Vine, N.J.	D5
Farr, Mel	RB	6-0	223	8/12/66	UCLA	Santa Monica, Calif.	D9
Frank, Garry	G	6-2	289	12/20/64	Mississippi State	Berlin, Wis.	D7a
Graddy, Sam (1)	WR	5-10	165	2/10/64	Tennessee	Gaffney, S.C.	FA-'87
Gregory, Ted	NT	6-1	265	2/11/65	Syracuse	East Islip, N.Y.	D1
Guidry, Kevin	CB	6-0	176	5/16/64	Louisiana State	Lake Charles, La.	D3
Juriga, Jim (1)	G-T	6-6	269	9/12/64	Illinois	Fort Wayne, Ind.	D4-'86
Kelly, Pat	TE	6-6	239	10/29/65	Syracuse	Rochester, N.Y.	D7b
Marshall, Warren (1)	RB	6-0	216	7/24/64	James Madison	High Point, N.C.	D6-'87
Perry, Gerald	T	6-6	311	11/12/64	Southern University	Columbia, S.C.	D2
Reed, Richard (1)	NT-DE	6-4	260	11/18/63	Oklahoma	Ft. Worth, Tex.	FA-'87
Wilkinson, Rafe (1)	LB	6-3	235	12/28/65	Richmond	Redwood City, Calif.	D10-'87
Williams, Channing	RB	5-10	227	2/22/64	Arizona State	Amarillo, Tex.	D10

The term NFL Rookie is defined as a player who is in his first season of professional football and has not been on the roster of another professional football team for any regular-season or postseason games. A Rookie is designated by an "R" on NFL rosters. Players who have been active in another professional football league or players who have NFL experience, including either preseason training camp or being on an active roster for fewer than three regular-season or postseason games, are termed NFL First-Year Players. An NFL First-Year Player is designated by a "1" on NFL rosters. Thereafter, a player on an NFL active roster for at least three regular-season or postseason games is credited with an additional year of NFL playing experience.

NOTES

Pete Mangurian, tight ends/assistant offensive line; born June 17, 1955, Los Angeles, Calif., lives in Denver. Defensive lineman Louisiana State 1975-78. No pro playing experience. College coach: Southern Methodist 1979-80, New Mexico State 1981, Stanford 1982-83, Louisiana State 1984-87. Pro coach: Joined Broncos in 1988.

Al Miller, strength and conditioning; born August 29, 1947, El Dorado, Ark., lives in Denver. Wide receiver Northeast Louisiana 1966-69. No pro playing experience. College coach: Northwestern Louisiana 1974-78, Mississippi State 1980, Northeast Louisiana 1981, Alabama 1982-84. Pro coach: Joined Broncos in 1985.

Myrel Moore, linebackers; born March 9, 1934, Sebastopol, Calif., lives in Denver. Receiver California-Davis 1955-57. Pro defensive back Washington Redskins 1958. College coach: Santa Ana, Calif., J.C. 1959-62, California 1963-71. Pro coach: Denver Broncos 1972-77, Oakland Raiders 1978-79, rejoined Broncos in 1982.

Mike Nolan, special teams/assistant linebackers; born March 7, 1959, Baltimore, Md., lives in Denver. Safety Oregon 1977-80. No pro playing experience. College coach: Stanford 1982-83, Rice 1984-85, Louisiana State 1986. Pro coach: Joined Broncos in 1987.

Charlie Waters, special teams/assistant defensive backs; born September 10, 1948, Miami, Fla., lives in Denver. Safety Clemson 1967-69. Pro safety Dallas Cowboys 1970-81. Pro coach: Joined Broncos in 1988.

Charlie West, defensive backs; born August 31, 1946, Big Spring, Tex., lives in Denver. Defensive back Texas-El Paso 1963-67. Pro defensive back Minnesota Vikings 1968-73, Detroit Lions 1974-77, Denver Broncos 1978-79. College coach: MacAlister 1981, California 1982. Pro coach: Joined Broncos in 1983.

American Football Conference Central Division

Team Colors: Columbia Blue, Scarlet, and White

6910 Fannin Street
Houston, Texas 77030
Telephone: (713) 797-9111

Club Officials

President: K. S. (Bud) Adams, Jr.
Executive Vice President-General Manager: Ladd K. Herzeg
Assistant to the General Manager: Mike Holovak
Director of Administration: Rick Nichols
Director of Media Relations: Chip Namias
Director of Public Relations: Gregg Stengel
Ticket Manager: Mike Mullis
Head Trainer: Brad Brown
Assistant Trainer: Don Moseley
Equipment Manager: Gordon Batty

Stadium: Astrodome • **Capacity:** 50,594
Loop 610, Kirby and Fannin Streets
Houston, Texas 77054

Playing Surface: AstroTurf-8

Training Camp: Blanco Hall
Southwest Texas State University
San Marcos, Texas 78666-4616

1988 Schedule

Preseason

Aug. 4	**Buffalo**	7:00
Aug. 13	vs. N.E. at Memphis, Tenn.	7:00
Aug. 20	at Los Angeles Rams	7:00
Aug. 27	at Dallas	8:00

Regular Season

Sept. 4	at Indianapolis	3:00
Sept. 11	**Los Angeles Raiders**	3:00
Sept. 18	at New York Jets	1:00
Sept. 25	**New England**	12:00
Oct. 2	at Philadelphia	1:00
Oct. 9	**Kansas City**	12:00
Oct. 16	at Pittsburgh	1:00
Oct. 23	at Cincinnati	1:00
Oct. 30	**Washington**	7:00
Nov. 7	**Cleveland** (Monday)	8:00
Nov. 13	at Seattle	1:00
Nov. 20	**Phoenix**	12:00
Nov. 24	at Dallas (Thanksgiving)	3:00
Dec. 4	**Pittsburgh**	7:00
Dec. 11	**Cincinnati**	12:00
Dec. 18	at Cleveland	1:00

Oilers Coaching History

(180-232-6)

1960-61	Lou Rymkus*	12-7-1
1961	Wally Lemm	10-0-0
1962-63	Frank (Pop) Ivy	17-12-0
1964	Sammy Baugh	4-10-0
1965	Hugh Taylor	4-10-0
1966-70	Wally Lemm	28-40-4
1971	Ed Hughes	4-9-1
1972-73	Bill Peterson**	1-18-0
1973-74	Sid Gillman	8-15-0
1975-80	O.A. (Bum) Phillips	59-38-0
1981-83	Ed Biles***	8-23-0
1983	Chuck Studley	2-8-0
1984-85	Hugh Campbell****	8-22-0
1985-87	Jerry Glanville	15-20-0

*Released after five games in 1961
**Released after five games in 1973
***Resigned after six games in 1983
****Released after 14 games in 1985

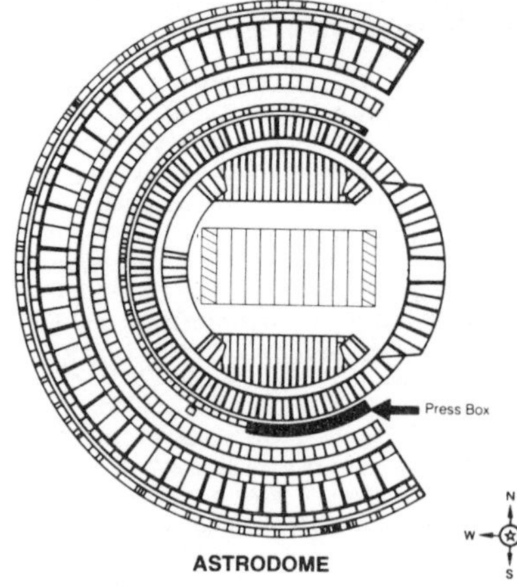

ASTRODOME

Record Holders

Individual Records—Career

Category	Name	Performance
Rushing (Yds.)	Earl Campbell, 1978-1984	8,574
Passing (Yds.)	George Blanda, 1960-66	19,149
Passing (TDs)	George Blanda, 1960-66	165
Receiving (No.)	Charley Hennigan, 1960-66	410
Receiving (Yds.)	Ken Burrough, 1971-1981	6,907
Interceptions	Jim Norton, 1960-68	45
Punting (Avg.)	Jim Norton, 1960-68	42.3
Punt Return (Avg.)	Billy Johnson, 1974-1980	13.2
Kickoff Return (Avg.)	Bobby Jancik, 1962-67	26.4
Field Goals	George Blanda, 1960-66	91
Touchdowns (Tot.)	Earl Campbell, 1978-1984	73
Points	George Blanda, 1960-66	596

Individual Records—Single Season

Category	Name	Performance
Rushing (Yds.)	Earl Campbell, 1980	1,934
Passing (Yds.)	Warren Moon, 1986	3,489
Passing (TDs)	George Blanda, 1961	36
Receiving (No.)	Charley Hennigan, 1964	101
Receiving (Yds.)	Charley Hennigan, 1961	*1,746
Interceptions	Fred Glick, 1963	12
	Mike Reinfeldt, 1979	12
Punting (Avg.)	Jim Norton, 1965	44.2
Punt Return (Avg.)	Billy Johnson, 1977	15.4
Kickoff Return (Avg.)	Ken Hall, 1960	31.2
Field Goals	Tony Zendejas, 1986	22
Touchdowns (Tot.)	Earl Campbell, 1979	19
Points	George Blanda, 1960	115

Individual Records—Single Game

Category	Name	Performance
Rushing (Yds.)	Billy Cannon, 12-10-61	216
Passing (Yds.)	George Blanda, 10-29-61	464
Passing (TDs)	George Blanda, 11-19-61	*7
Receiving (No.)	Charley Hennigan, 10-13-61	13
Receiving (Yds.)	Charley Hennigan, 10-13-61	272
Interceptions	Many times Last time by Willie Alexander, 11-14-71	3
Field Goals	Skip Butler, 10-12-75	6
Touchdowns (Tot.)	Billy Cannon, 12-10-61	5
Points	Billy Cannon, 12-10-61	30

*NFL Record

1987 Team Record

Preseason (2-2)

Date	Result		Opponents
8/13	L	20-32	Kansas City
8/22	W	16-13	at New Orleans
8/29	L	6-17	at Indianapolis
9/5	W	18-13	at Dallas
		60-75	

Regular Season (9-6)

Date	Result		Opponents	Att.
9/13	W	20-16	L.A. Rams	33,186
9/20	L	30-34	at Buffalo	56,534
9/27	C		L.A. Raiders	
10/4	W	40-10	at Denver	38,494
10/11	W	15-10	at Cleveland	38,927
10/18	L	7-21	New England	26,294
10/25	W	37-33	Atlanta	29,062
11/1	W	31-29	at Cincinnati	52,700
11/8	L	20-27	at San Francisco	59,740
11/15	W	23- 3	at Pittsburgh	56,177
11/22	L	7-40	Cleveland	51,161
11/29	L	27-51	at Indianapolis	54,999
12/6	W	33-18	San Diego	31,714
12/13	L	10-24	at New Orleans	68,257
12/20	W	24-16	Pittsburgh	38,683
12/27	W	21-17	Cincinnati	49,775

C (Cancelled due to players' strike.)

Postseason (1-1)

Date	Result		Opponents	Att.
1/3	W	23-20	Seattle (OT)	49,622
1/10	L	10-34	at Denver	75,968

(OT) Overtime

Score by Periods

Oilers	47	97	89	112	0	—	345
Opponents	75	117	71	86	0	—	349

Attendance

Home 259,875 Away 425,828 Total 685,703
Single-game home record, 55,452 (12-4-80)
Single-season home record, 400,156 (1980)

1987 Team Statistics

	Oilers	Opp.
Total First Downs	294	287
Rushing	118	98
Passing	150	153
Penalty	26	36
Third Down: Made/Att.	73/208	65/201
Fourth Down: Made/Att.	9/16	5/11
Total Net Yards	5223	4993
Avg. Per Game	348.2	332.9
Total Plays	998	976
Avg. Per Play	5.2	5.1
Net Yards Rushing	1923	1848
Avg. Per Game	128.2	123.2
Total Rushes	486	446
Net Yards Passing	3300	3145
Avg. Per Game	220.0	209.7
Sacked/Yards Lost	30/234	35/271
Gross Yards	3534	3416
Att./Completions	482/240	495/266
Completion Pct.	49.8	53.7
Had Intercepted	23	23
Punts/Avg.	75/39.1	77/39.4
Net Punting Avg.	31.4	34.6
Penalties/Yards Lost	114/1029	101/874
Fumbles/Ball Lost	32/14	37/14
Touchdowns	38	37
Rushing	12	10
Passing	24	25
Returns	2	2
Avg. Time of Possession	30:17	29:43

1987 Individual Statistics

Scoring	TD R	TD P	TD Rt	PAT	FG	Saf	TP
Zendejas	0	0	0	32/33	20/26	0	92
Givins	0	6	0	0/0	0/0	0	36
D. Hill	0	6	0	0/0	0/0	0	36
Duncan	0	5	0	0/0	0/0	0	30
Diettrich	0	0	0	5/5	6/6	0	23
Moon	3	0	0	0/0	0/0	0	18
Rozier	3	0	0	0/0	0/0	0	18
J. Williams	0	3	0	0/0	0/0	0	18
Highsmith	1	1	0	0/0	0/0	0	12
Pinkett	2	0	0	0/0	0/0	0	12
Gehring	0	1	0	0/0	0/0	0	6
Jackson	1	0	0	0/0	0/0	0	6
Lyles	0	0	1	0/0	0/0	0	6
McDonald	0	1	0	0/0	0/0	0	6
Pease	1	0	0	0/0	0/0	0	6
Seale	0	0	1	0/0	0/0	0	6
Tillman	1	0	0	0/0	0/0	0	6
O. Williams	0	1	0	0/0	0/0	0	6
Baker	0	0	0	0/0	0/0	1	2
Oilers	12	24	2	37/38	26/32	1	345
Opponents	10	25	2	35/37	30/36	1	349

Passing	Att.	Comp.	Yds.	Pct.	TD	Int.	Tkld.	Rate
Moon	368	184	2806	50.0	21	18	25/198	74.2
Pease	113	56	728	49.6	3	5	5/36	60.6
D. Hill	1	0	0	0.0	0	0	0/0	39.6
Oilers	482	240	3534	49.8	24	23	30/234	70.8
Opponents	495	266	3416	53.7	25	23	35/271	73.1

Rushing	Att.	Yds.	Avg.	LG	TD
Rozier	229	957	4.2	41	3
Jackson	60	232	3.9	16t	1
Pinkett	31	149	4.8	22	2
Hunter	34	144	4.2	21	0
Moon	34	112	3.3	20	3
Highsmith	29	106	3.7	25	1
Wallace	19	102	5.4	19	0
Pease	15	33	2.2	8	1
Tillman	12	29	2.4	13	1
Cobble	9	23	2.6	12	0
Moore	7	22	3.1	11	0
Harris	1	17	17.0	17	0
Valentine	5	10	2.0	4	0
Givins	1	−13	−13.0	−13	0
Oilers	486	1923	4.0	41	12
Opponents	446	1848	4.1	57	10

Receiving	No.	Yds.	Avg.	LG	TD
Givins	53	933	17.6	83t	6
D. Hill	49	989	20.2	52t	6
Rozier	27	192	7.1	27	0
Duncan	13	237	18.2	48	5
J. Williams	13	158	12.2	25	3
O. Williams	11	165	15.0	36t	1
Drewrey	11	148	13.5	35	0
Harris	10	164	16.4	39	0
Jackson	10	44	4.4	16	0
Jeffires	7	89	12.7	23	0
Wallace	7	34	4.9	7	0
Walters	5	99	19.8	51	0
Gehring	5	64	12.8	31t	1
McDonald	4	56	14.0	24	1
Highsmith	4	55	13.8	33t	1
Moore	3	21	7.0	10	0
Hunter	3	17	5.7	11	0
Valentine	2	10	5.0	7	0
Darrington	1	38	38.0	38	0
James	1	14	14.0	14	0
Pinkett	1	7	7.0	7	0
Oilers	240	3534	14.7	83t	24
Opponents	266	3416	12.8	72t	25

Interceptions	No.	Yds.	Avg.	LG	TD
Bostic	6	−14	−2.3	7	0
Bryant	4	75	18.8	29	0
Donaldson	4	16	4.0	9	0
St. Brown	2	45	22.5	35	0
Lyles	2	42	21.0	27	0
Seale	1	73	73.0	73t	1
P. Allen	1	37	37.0	24	0
Small	1	3	3.0	3	0
R. Johnson	1	0	0.0	0	0
Newsom	1	−3	−3.0	−3	0
Oilers	23	274	11.9	73t	1
Opponents	23	225	9.8	37	1

Punting	No.	Yds.	Avg.	In 20	LG
Gossett, Clev.-Hou.	44	1777	40.4	4	55
Gossett, Hou.	25	1008	40.3	0	53
L. Johnson	41	1652	40.3	5	59
Superick	8	269	33.6	2	45
Oilers	75	2929	39.1	7	59
Opponents	77	3033	39.4	22	62

Punt Returns	No.	FC	Yds.	Avg.	LG	TD
K. Johnson	24	5	196	8.2	26	0
Duncan	8	2	23	2.9	9	0
Drewrey	3	1	11	3.7	5	0
Walters	2	6	19	9.5	12	0
Oilers	37	14	249	6.7	26	0
Opponents	43	10	454	10.6	45	0

Kickoff Returns	No.	Yds.	Avg.	LG	TD
Duncan	28	546	19.5	62	0
Pinkett	17	322	18.9	30	0
Drewrey	8	136	17.0	27	0
Hunter	4	79	19.8	28	0
Harris	3	87	29.0	43	0
K. Johnson	2	24	12.0	18	0
J. Davis	1	0	0.0	0	0
Fuller	1	0	0.0	0	0
Tillman	1	0	0.0	0	0
Valentine	1	13	13.0	13	0
Walters	1	18	18.0	18	0
Wallace*	0	0	—	0	0
Oilers	67	1225	18.3	62	0
Opponents	57	1177	20.6	74	0

*One Fair Catch.

Sacks	No.
Childress	6.0
Martin, G.B.-Hou.	4.0
Martin, Hou.	3.0
Meads	4.0
D. Smith	3.5
Bostic	3.0
Baker	2.5
Cooks	2.0
Fuller	2.0
B. Johnson	2.0
Lyles	2.0
Byrd	1.0
Donaldson	1.0
Fox	1.0
Newsom	1.0
Seale	1.0
Oilers	35.0
Opponents	30.0

Houston Oilers 1988 Veteran Roster

No.	Name	Pos.	Ht.	Wt.	Birth-date	NFL Exp.	College	Hometown	How Acq.	'87 Games/ Starts
29	†Allen, Patrick	CB	5-10	180	8/26/61	5	Utah State	Seattle, Wash.	D4b-'84	11/11
36	Birdsong, Craig	S	6-2	217	8/16/64	2	North Texas State	Kaufman, Tex.	FA-'87	8/0
25	Bostic, Keith	S	6-1	223	1/17/61	6	Michigan	Ann Arbor, Mich.	D2b-'83	12/12
24	†Brown, Steve	CB	5-11	187	3/20/60	6	Oregon	Sacramento, Calif.	D3c-'83	10/10
38	Bryant, Domingo	S	6-4	175	12/8/63	2	Texas A&M	Garrison, Tex.	FA-'87	13/3
71	Byrd, Richard	DE	6-4	265	3/20/62	4	Southern Mississippi	Jackson, Miss.	D2b-'85	12/11
56	Caston, Toby	LB	6-1	235	7/17/65	2	Louisiana State	Monroe, La.	D6b-'87	6/0
79	Childress, Ray	DE	6-6	276	10/20/62	4	Texas A&M	Richardson, Tex.	D1a-'85	13/13
98	Cooks, Rayford	DE	6-3	245	8/25/62	2	North Texas State	Dallas, Tex.	FA-'87	10/1
77	Davis, Bruce	T	6-6	280	6/21/56	10	UCLA	Indian Head, Md.	T(Raid)-'87	11/11*
73	Davis, John	T-G	6-4	304	8/22/65	2	Georgia Tech	Ellijay, Ga.	D11-'87	6/0
31	Donaldson, Jeff	S	6-0	194	4/19/62	5	Colorado	Ft. Collins, Colo.	D9a-'84	12/12
82	Drewrey, Willie	WR-KR	5-7	164	4/28/63	4	West Virginia	Columbus, N.J.	D11b-'85	12/0
80	Duncan, Curtis	WR-KR	5-11	184	1/26/65	2	Northwestern	Detroit, Mich.	D10-'87	10/0
51	†Fairs, Eric	LB	6-3	238	2/17/64	3	Memphis State	Memphis, Tenn.	FA-'86	12/0
95	†Fuller, William	DE	6-3	260	3/8/62	3	North Carolina	Chesapeake, Va.	T(Rams)-'86	12/1
81	Givins, Ernest	WR	5-9	172	9/3/64	3	Louisville	St. Petersburg, Fla.	D2-'86	12/12
8	Gossett, Jeff	P	6-2	200	1/25/57	7	Eastern Illinois	Charleston, Ill.	FA-'87	9/0*
59	Grimsley, John	LB	6-2	236	2/25/62	5	Kentucky	Canton, Ohio	D6a-'83	12/12
83	Harris, Leonard	WR	5-8	165	11/27/60	3	Texas Tech	McKinney, Tex.	FA-'87	3/3
32	Highsmith, Alonzo	RB	6-1	235	2/26/65	2	Miami	Miami, Fla.	D1a-'87	8/3
85	Hill, Drew	WR	5-9	170	2/5/56	9	Georgia Tech	Newnan, Ga.	T(Rams)-'85	12/12
88	James, Arrike	TE	6-4	238	12/31/64	2	Delta State	Dumas, Ark.	FA-'87	3/1
84	Jeffires, Haywood	WR	6-2	198	12/12/64	2	North Carolina State	Greensboro, N.C.	D1b-'87	9/1
22	Johnson, Kenny	S	5-10	175	1/7/58	9	Mississippi State	Moss Point, Miss.	FA-'87	12/3
23	Johnson, Richard	CB	6-1	190	9/16/63	4	Wisconsin	Dixmoor, Ill.	D1b-'85	5/1
57	Johnson, Walter	LB	6-0	241	11/13/63	2	Louisiana Tech	Ferriday, La.	D2-'87	10/0
93	Lyles, Robert	LB	6-1	223	3/21/61	5	Texas Christian	Los Angeles, Calif.	D5-'84	12/12
78	Maggs, Don	T-G	6-5	277	11/1/61	2	Tulane	Youngstown, Ohio	SD2-'84	0*
94	Martin, Charles	NT	6-4	280	8/31/59	5	Livingston	Canton, Ga.	W(GB)-'87	14/5*
74	Matthews, Bruce	T-G	6-5	280	8/8/61	6	Southern California	Arcadia, Calif.	D1-'83	8/6
26	†McMillian, Audrey	CB	6-0	190	8/13/62	4	Houston	Carthage, Tex.	W(NE)-'85	12/2
91	†Meads, Johnny	LB	6-2	230	6/25/61	5	Nicholls State	Napoleonville, La.	D3-'84	12/12
1	Moon, Warren	QB	6-3	210	11/18/56	5	Washington	Los Angeles, Calif.	FA-'84	12/12
63	Munchak, Mike	G	6-3	280	3/5/60	7	Penn State	Scranton, Pa.	D1-'82	12/12
89	Parks, Jeff	TE	6-4	240	9/14/64	3	Auburn	Gardendale, Ala.	D5-'86	7/0
10	Pease, Brent	QB	6-2	200	10/8/64	2	Montana	Mountain Home, Idaho	FA-'87	6/3
52	†Pennison, Jay	C	6-1	275	9/9/61	3	Nicholls State	Houma, La.	FA-'86	12/12
20	Pinkett, Allen	RB	5-9	185	1/25/64	3	Notre Dame	Sterling, Va.	D3-'86	8/0
30	Rozier, Mike	RB	5-10	211	3/1/61	4	Nebraska	Camden, N.J.	SD1-'84	11/11
53	Seale, Eugene	LB	5-10	250	6/3/64	2	Lamar	Jasper, Tex.	FA-'87	9/4
54	Smith, Al	LB	6-1	230	11/26/64	2	Utah State	Los Angeles, Calif.	D6a-'87	12/11
99	†Smith, Doug	NT	6-5	282	6/13/60	4	Auburn	Bayboro, N.C.	D2a-'84	14/13
70	†Steinkuhler, Dean	T-G	6-3	278	1/27/61	5	Nebraska	Burr, Neb.	D1-'84	11/11
33	Tillman, Spencer	RB	5-11	206	4/21/64	2	Oklahoma	Tulsa, Okla.	D5-'87	5/1
45	Valentine, Ira	RB	6-0	212	6/4/63	2	Texas A&M	Marshall, Tex.	D12-'87	7/0
35	Wallace, Ray	RB	6-0	220	12/3/63	3	Purdue	Indianapolis, Ind.	D6-'86	12/9
69	Williams, Doug	T-G	6-5	288	10/1/62	3	Texas A&M	Cincinnati, Ohio	W(NYJ)-'86	7/7
87	†Williams, Jamie	TE	6-4	245	2/25/60	6	Nebraska	Davenport, Iowa	W(TB)-'84	12/12
7	Zendejas, Tony	K	5-8	165	5/15/60	4	Nevada-Reno	Chino, Calif.	T(Wash)-'85	13/0

* B. Davis played 4 games with L.A. Raiders in '87, 7 with Houston; Gossett played 5 games with Cleveland, 4 with Houston; Maggs was active for 1 game but did not play; Martin played 2 games with Green Bay, 12 with Houston.

†Option playout; subject to developments.

Traded—Safety Bo Eason to San Francisco.

Also played with Oilers in '87—LB Robert Abraham (2 games), CB Earl Allen (1), DE Jesse Baker (9), T Scott Boucher (2), LB Tom Briehl (3), S Sonny Brown (2), CB Charles Clinton (2), RB Eric Cobble (3), WR Chris Darrington (3), TE Mitch Daum (2), K John Diettrich (2), NT Joe Dixon (2), TE Scott Eccles (1), LB Scott Fox (2), T Jerrell Franklin (3), TE Mark Gehring (6), NT Mike Golic (2), G Kent Hill (12), RB Herman Hunter (3), RB Andrew Jackson (7), LB Thad Jefferson (3), LB Byron Johnson (3), P Lee Johnson (9), S Larry Joyner (1), S Kurt Kafentzis (2), T Doug Kellermeyer (3), G Mike Kelley (1), C Billy Kidd (7), DE Eric Larkin (1), S Allan Lyday (7), WR Keith McDonald (3), T Clay Miller (3), RB Ricky Moore (3), DE Kenny Neil (1), CB Tony Newsom (5), DE Bob Otto (3), G Brett Petersmark (3), T Barry Pettyjohn (2), S Donovan Small (1), LB Larry Smith (3), T Scott Stroughton (active for one game but did not play), G Vince Stroth (9), P Steve Superick (2), CB Emmuel Thompson (3), NT Dwain Turner (1), LB Paul Vogel (1), WR Joey Walters (5), CB Robert White (3), WR Oliver Williams (3), QB John Witkowski (active for 3 games but did not play), G Almon Young (3).

COACHING STAFF

Head Coach, Jerry Glanville

Pro Career: Named Houston's head coach on January 20, 1986, after serving as interim coach for last two games of 1985 season. Glanville was the Oilers' defensive coordinator in 1984-85, and has 24 years of coaching experience. He initially coached in the NFL for the Detroit Lions from 1974-76 as the special teams/defense coach. His next NFL position was with the Atlanta Falcons from 1977-82, first serving as defensive backfield/special teams coach before being elevated to defensive coordinator. In 1983, Glanville joined the Buffalo Bills as defensive backfield coach before assuming his duties with the Oilers. Career record: 15-20.

Background: Attended Montana State in 1960 before transferring to Northern Michigan, where he played linebacker from 1961-63. He coached in the Ohio high school system from 1964-66 before accepting an assistant coaching post at Western Kentucky in 1967. From 1968-73, he was an assistant at Georgia Tech, helping the Yellow Jackets to three bowl games.

Personal: Born October 14, 1941, in Detroit, Mich. Jerry and his wife, Brenda, live in Sugar Land, Tex., with their son, Justin.

Assistant Coaches

Kim Helton, offensive line; born July 28, 1948, Pensacola, Fla., lives in Sugar Land, Tex. Center Florida 1967-69. No pro playing experience. College coach: Florida 1972-78, Miami 1979-82. Pro coach: Tampa Bay Buccaneers 1983-86, joined Oilers in 1987.

Milt Jackson, receivers; born October 16, 1943, Groesbeck, Tex., lives in Missouri City, Tex. Defensive back Tulsa 1965-66. Pro defensive back San Francisco 49ers 1967. College coach: Oregon State 1973, Rice 1974, California 1975-76, Oregon 1977-78, UCLA 1979. Pro coach: San Francisco 49ers 1980-82, Buffalo Bills 1983-84, Philadelphia Eagles 1985, joined Oilers in 1986.

June Jones, quarterbacks; born February 19, 1953, Portland, Ore., lives in Missouri City, Tex. Quarterback Hawaii 1973-74, Portland State 1975-76. Pro quarterback Atlanta Falcons 1977-81, Toronto Argonauts (CFL) 1982. College coach: Hawaii 1983. Pro coach: Toronto Argonauts (CFL) 1982, Houston Gamblers (USFL) 1984, Denver Gold (USFL) 1985, joined Oilers in 1987.

Floyd Reese, linebackers; born August 8, 1948, Springfield, Mo., lives in Sugar Land, Tex. Linebacker UCLA 1967-69. Pro defensive lineman Montreal Alouettes (CFL) 1970. College coach: UCLA 1971-73, Georgia Tech 1974. Pro coach: Detroit Lions 1975-77, San Francisco 49ers 1978, Minnesota Vikings 1979-85, joined Oilers in 1986.

Nick Saban, defensive backs; born October 31, 1951, Fairmont, W. Va., lives in Sugar Land, Tex. Defensive back Kent State 1970-72. No pro playing experience. College coach: Kent State 1973-76, Syracuse 1977, West Virginia 1978-79, Ohio State 1980-81, Navy 1982, Michigan State 1983-87. Pro coach: Joined Oilers in 1988.

Ray Sherman, running backs; born November 27, 1951, Berkeley, Calif., lives in Missouri City, Tex. Wide receiver Laney, Calif., J.C. 1969-70, Fresno State 1971-72. Pro defensive back Green Bay Packers 1973. College coach: San Jose State 1974, California 1975, Michigan State 1976-77, Wake Forest 1978-80, California 1981, Purdue 1982-85, Georgia 1986-87. Pro coach: Joined Oilers in 1988.

Doug Shively, defensive line; born March 18, 1938, Lexington, Ky., lives in Sugar Land, Tex. End Kentucky 1955-58. No pro playing experience. College coach: Virginia Tech 1960-66, Kentucky 1967-70, Clemson 1971-72, North Carolina 1973. Pro coach: New Orleans Saints 1974-76, Atlanta Falcons 1977-82, Arizona Wranglers (USFL, head coach) 1983, San Diego Chargers 1984, Tampa Bay Buccaneers 1985, joined Oilers in 1986.

Houston Oilers 1988 First-Year Roster

Name	Pos.	Ht.	Wt.	Birth-date	College	Hometown	How Acq.
Brantley, John	LB	6-2	229	10/23/65	Georgia	Wildwood, Fla.	D12
Burt, Kerry	S	6-1	207	12/17/64	Iowa	Waterloo, Iowa	FA
Clinton, Charles	CB	5-8	170	1/29/62	San Jose State	Long Beach, Calif.	FA
Crain, Kurt	LB	6-2	228	12/31/64	Auburn	Birmingham, Ala.	D6
Dishman, Cris	CB	6-0	173	8/13/65	Purdue	Louisville, Ky.	D5a
Eaton, Tracey	S	6-1	190	7/19/65	Portland State	Medford, Ore.	D7
Endre, Pete	T	6-5	265	9/7/66	Indiana State	Mt. Prospect, Ill.	FA
Franklin, Jethro	DE	6-1	260	10/25/65	Fresno State	San Jose, Calif.	D11
Johnson, Marco	WR-KR	5-9	170	9/4/65	Hawaii	Lancaster, Calif.	D10
Jones, Quintin	CB	5-11	193	7/28/66	Pittsburgh	Pompano Beach, Fla.	D2
Lee, Ivery	NT	6-1	271	3/5/64	Georgia Tech	Statesboro, Ga.	FA
Montgomery, Greg	P	6-3	210	10/29/64	Michigan State	Red Bank, N.J.	D3
Rhone, Mike	CB	6-0	200	9/24/65	North Texas State	Austin, Tex.	FA
Spradlin, David	LB	6-3	239	9/23/64	Texas Christian	Seminole, Tex.	D9
Verhulst, Chris	TE	6-2	239	5/16/66	Chico State	San Ramon, Calif.	D5b
Viaene, David	C	6-5	291	7/14/65	Minnesota-Duluth	Appleton, Wis.	D8
White, Lorenzo	RB	5-11	207	4/12/66	Michigan State	Ft. Lauderdale, Fla.	D1
Willis, Keith	WR	5-8	170	6/14/65	Sam Houston State	Waco, Tex.	FA

The term NFL Rookie is defined as a player who is in his first season of professional football and has not been on the roster of another professional football team for any regular-season or postseason games. A Rookie is designated by an "R" on NFL rosters. Players who have been active in another professional football league or players who have NFL experience, including either preseason training camp or being on an active roster for fewer than three regular-season or postseason games, are termed NFL First-Year Players. An NFL First-Year Player is designated by a "1" on NFL rosters. Thereafter, a player on an NFL active roster for at least three regular-season or postseason games is credited with an additional year of NFL playing experience.

NOTES

Richard Smith, special teams-tight ends; born October 17, 1955, Los Angeles, Calif., lives in Sugar Land, Tex. Offensive lineman Rio Hondo, Calif., J.C. 1975-76, Fresno State 1977-78. No pro playing experience. College coach: Rio Hondo, Calif., J.C. 1979-80, Cal State-Fullerton 1981-83, California 1984-86, Arizona 1987. Pro coach: Joined Oilers in 1988.

Steve Waterson, strength and rehabilitation; born November 27, 1956, Newport, R.I., lives in Sugar Land, Tex. University of Rhode Island. No college or pro playing experience. Pro coach: Philadelphia Eagles 1984-85 (assistant trainer), joined Oilers in 1986 (elevated to assistant coach in 1988).

INDIANAPOLIS COLTS

American Football Conference Eastern Division

Team Colors: Royal Blue and White

P.O. Box 535000
Indianapolis, Indiana 46253
Telephone: (317) 297-2658

Club Officials

President-Treasurer: Robert Irsay
Vice President-General Manager: James Irsay
Vice President-General Counsel: Michael G. Chernoff
Assistant General Manager: Bob Terpening
Director of Player Personnel: Jack Bushofsky
Controller: Kurt Humphrey
Director of Operations: Pete Ward
Director of Public Relations: Craig Kelley
Ticket Manager: Larry Hall
Assistant Director of Public Relations: Keith Newton
Purchasing Administrator: David Filar
Equipment Manager: Jon Scott
Assistant Equipment Manager: Chris Matlock
Video Director: Marty Heckscher
Assistant Video Director: John Starliper
Head Trainer: Hunter Smith
Assistant Trainer: Dave Hammer
Team Physician and Orthopedic Surgeon: K. Donald Shelbourne
Orthopedic Surgeon: Arthur C. Rettig

Stadium: Hoosier Dome • **Capacity:** 60,127
100 South Capitol Avenue
Indianapolis, Indiana 46225

Playing Surface: AstroTurf

Training Camp: Anderson University
Anderson, Indiana 46011

1988 Schedule

Preseason

Aug. 6	at Tampa Bay	7:00
Aug. 13	**Green Bay**	7:30
Aug. 20	**New Orleans**	7:30
Aug. 25	at Denver	6:00

Regular Season

Sept. 4	**Houston**	3:00
Sept. 11	**Chicago**	12:00
Sept. 19	at Cleveland (Monday)	8:00
Sept. 25	**Miami**	12:00
Oct. 2	at New England	1:00
Oct. 9	at Buffalo	1:00
Oct. 16	**Tampa Bay**	12:00
Oct. 23	at San Diego	1:00
Oct. 31	**Denver** (Monday)	9:00
Nov. 6	**New York Jets**	4:00
Nov. 13	at Green Bay	12:00
Nov. 20	at Minnesota	12:00
Nov. 27	**New England**	4:00
Dec. 4	at Miami	1:00
Dec. 10	at N.Y. Jets (Saturday)	12:30
Dec. 18	**Buffalo**	1:00

Colts Coaching History

Baltimore 1953-83
(251-244-7)

1953	Keith Molesworth	3-9-0
1954-62	Weeb Ewbank	61-52-1
1963-69	Don Shula	73-26-4
1970-72	Don McCafferty*	26-11-1
1972	John Sandusky	4-5-0
1973-74	Howard Schnellenberger**	4-13-0
1974	Joe Thomas	2-9-0
1975-79	Ted Marchibroda	41-36-0
1980-81	Mike McCormack	9-23-0
1982-84	Frank Kush***	11-28-1
1984	Hal Hunter	0-1-0
1985-86	Rod Dowhower****	5-24-0
1986-87	Ron Meyer	12-7-0

*Released after five games in 1972
**Released after three games in 1974
***Resigned after 15 games in 1984
****Released after 13 games in 1986

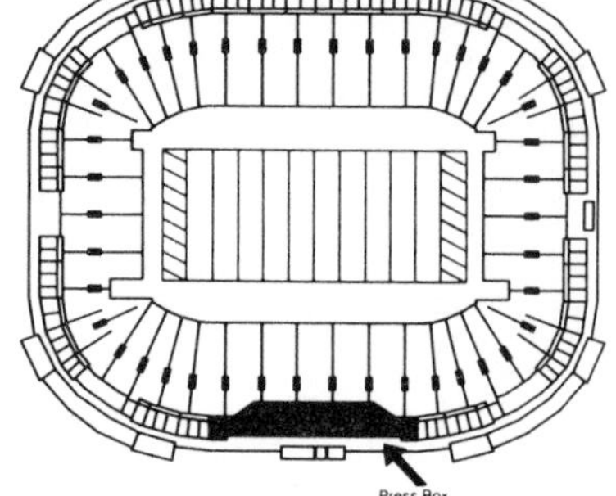

HOOSIER DOME

Record Holders

Individual Records—Career

Category	Name	Performance
Rushing (Yds.)	Lydell Mitchell, 1972-77	5,487
Passing (Yds.)	Johnny Unitas, 1956-1972	39,768
Passing (TDs)	Johnny Unitas, 1956-1972	287
Receiving (No.)	Raymond Berry, 1955-1967	631
Receiving (Yds.)	Raymond Berry, 1955-1967	9,275
Interceptions	Bob Boyd, 1960-68	57
Punting (Avg.)	Rohn Stark, 1982-87	44.5
Punt Return (Avg.)	Wendell Harris, 1964	12.6
Kickoff Return (Avg.)	Jim Duncan, 1969-1971	32.5
Field Goals	Lou Michaels, 1964-69	107
Touchdowns (Tot.)	Lenny Moore, 1956-1967	113
Points	Lenny Moore, 1956-1967	678

Individual Records—Single Season

Category	Name	Performance
Rushing (Yds.)	Lydell Mitchell, 1976	1,200
Passing (Yds.)	Johnny Unitas, 1963	3,481
Passing (TDs)	Johnny Unitas, 1959	32
Receiving (No.)	Joe Washington, 1979	82
Receiving (Yds.)	Raymond Berry, 1960	1,298
Interceptions	Tom Keane, 1953	11
Punting (Avg.)	Rohn Stark, 1985	45.9
Punt Return (Avg.)	Wendell Harris, 1964	12.6
Kickoff Return (Avg.)	Jim Duncan, 1970	35.4
Field Goals	Raul Allegre, 1983	30
Touchdowns (Tot.)	Lenny Moore, 1964	20
Points	Lenny Moore, 1964	120

Individual Records—Single Game

Category	Name	Performance
Rushing (Yds.)	Norm Bulaich, 9-19-71	198
Passing (Yds.)	Johnny Unitas, 9-17-67	401
Passing (TDs)	Gary Cuozzo, 11-14-65	5
	Gary Hogeboom, 10-4-87	5
Receiving (No.)	Lydell Mitchell, 12-15-74	13
	Joe Washington, 9-2-79	13
Receiving (Yds.)	Raymond Berry, 11-10-57	224
Interceptions	Many times	3
	Last time by Leonard Coleman, 10-12-86	
Field Goals	Many times	5
	Last time by Raul Allegre, 10-30-83	
Touchdowns (Tot.)	Many times	4
	Last time by Lydell Mitchell, 10-12-75	
Points	Many times	24
	Last time by Lydell Mitchell, 10-12-75	

1987 Team Record

Preseason (3-1)

Date	Result		Opponents
8/15	W	22-19	at Detroit
8/22	L	19-37	at Minnesota
8/29	W	17- 6	Houston
9/5	W	23- 6	Tampa Bay
		81-68	

Regular Season (9-6)

Date	Result		Opponents	Att.
9/13	L	21-23	Cincinnati	59,387
9/20	L	10-23	Miami	57,524
9/27	C		at St. Louis	
10/4	W	47- 6	at Buffalo	9,860
10/11	W	6- 0	N.Y. Jets	34,927
10/18	L	7-21	at Pittsburgh	34,627
10/25	W	30-16	New England	48,850
11/1	W	19-14	at N.Y. Jets	60,863
11/8	L	13-16	San Diego	60,459
11/15	W	40-21	at Miami	65,433
11/22	L	0-24	at New England	56,906
11/29	W	51-27	Houston	54,999
12/6	W	9- 7	at Cleveland	70,661
12/13	L	3-27	Buffalo	60,253
12/20	W	20- 7	at San Diego	46,211
12/27	W	24- 6	Tampa Bay	60,468

C (Cancelled due to players' strike.)

Postseason (0-1)

Date	Result		Opponent	Att.
1/9	L	21-38	at Cleveland	78,586

Score by Periods

Colts	48	120	61	71	0	—	300
Opponents	61	52	48	77	0	—	238

Attendance

Home 436,867 Away 344,561 Total 781,428
Single-game home record, 61,479 (11-13-83)
Single-season home record, 481,305 (1984)

1987 Team Statistics

	Colts	Opp.
Total First Downs	285	276
Rushing	122	97
Passing	138	161
Penalty	25	18
Third Down: Made/Att.	70/201	85/218
Fourth Down: Made/Att.	7/16	5/13
Total Net Yards	4995	4550
Avg. Per Game	333.0	303.3
Total Plays	968	1003
Avg. Per Play	5.2	4.5
Net Yards Rushing	2143	1790
Avg. Per Game	142.9	119.3
Total Rushes	497	463
Net Yards Passing	2852	2760
Avg. Per Game	190.1	184.0
Sacked/Yards Lost	24/190	39/313
Gross Yards	3042	3073
Att./Completions	447/255	501/250
Completion Pct.	57.0	49.9
Had Intercepted	16	20
Punts/Avg.	78/37.7	82/37.2
Net Punting Avg.	30.8	31.0
Penalties/Yards Lost	90/742	85/689
Fumbles/Ball Lost	36/18	43/25
Touchdowns	31	28
Rushing	14	6
Passing	16	19
Returns	1	3
Avg. Time of Possession	30:10	29:50

1987 Individual Statistics

Scoring

Scoring	TD R	TD P	TD Rt	PAT	FG	Saf	TP
Biasucci	0	0	0	24/24	24/27	0	96
Bentley	7	2	0	0/0	0/0	0	54
Dickerson, Rams-Ind.	6	0	0	0/0	0/0	0	36
Dickerson, Ind.	5	0	0	0/0	0/0	0	30
Bouza	0	4	0	0/0	0/0	0	24
Brooks	0	3	0	0/0	0/0	0	18
Murray	0	3	0	0/0	0/0	0	18
Jordan	0	0	0	7/7	3/5	0	16
Noble	0	2	0	0/0	0/0	0	12
Brown	1	0	0	0/0	0/0	0	6
J. Jones	0	1	0	0/0	0/0	0	6
Sherwin	0	1	0	0/0	0/0	0	6
Thompson	0	0	1	0/0	0/0	0	6
Wonsley	1	0	0	0/0	0/0	0	6
Leiding	0	0	0	0/0	0/0	1	2
Colts	14	16	1	31/31	27/32	1	300
Opponents	6	19	3	25/28	15/26	0	238

Passing

Passing	Att.	Comp.	Yds.	Pct.	TD	Int.	Tkld.	Rate
Trudeau	229	128	1587	55.9	6	6	13/100	75.4
Hogeboom	168	99	1145	58.9	9	5	8/63	85.0
Kiel	33	17	195	51.5	1	3	0/0	41.9
Salisbury	12	8	68	66.7	0	2	2/18	41.7
Nugent	5	3	47	60.0	0	0	1/9	91.3
Colts	447	255	3042	57.0	16	16	24/190	75.0
Opponents	501	250	3073	49.9	19	20	39/313	65.2

Rushing

Rushing	Att.	Yds.	Avg.	LG	TD
Dickerson, Rams-Ind.	283	1288	4.6	57	6
Dickerson, Ind.	223	1011	4.5	53	5
Bentley	142	631	4.4	17t	7
Banks	50	245	4.9	35	0
Brown	19	85	4.5	18t	1
Wonsley	18	71	3.9	12	1
McLemore	17	58	3.4	9	0
Kiel	4	30	7.5	16	0
Trudeau	15	7	0.5	9	0
Carver	2	3	1.5	3	0
Hogeboom	3	3	1.0	2	0
Nugent	2	1	0.5	3	0
Brooks	2	−2	−1.0	1	0
Colts	497	2143	4.3	53	14
Opponents	463	1790	3.9	51	6

Receiving

Receiving	No.	Yds.	Avg.	LG	TD
Brooks	51	722	14.2	52t	3
Bouza	42	569	13.5	44t	4
Bentley	34	447	13.1	72t	2
Beach	28	239	8.5	16	0
Murray	20	339	17.0	43	3
Dickerson, Rams-Ind.	18	171	9.5	28	0
Dickerson, Ind.	13	133	10.2	28	0
Noble	10	78	7.8	18t	2
Boyer	10	73	7.3	15	0
Sherwin	9	86	9.6	32	1
Banks	9	50	5.6	18	0
Bellini	5	69	13.8	19	0
Wonsley	5	48	9.6	16	0
Brandes	5	35	7.0	13	0
Kearse	3	56	18.7	21	0
Hawthorne	3	41	13.7	21	0
J. Jones	3	25	8.3	13	1
McLemore	2	9	4.5	5	0
Johnson	1	15	15.0	15	0
Bryant	1	12	12.0	12	0
Utt	1	−4	−4.0	−4	0
Colts	255	3042	11.9	72t	16
Opponents	250	3073	12.3	61t	19

Interceptions

Interceptions	No.	Yds.	Avg.	LG	TD
Prior	6	57	9.5	38	0
Tullis	3	0	0.0	0	0
Robinson	2	86	43.0	68	0
E. Daniel	2	34	17.0	34	0
B. Jones	2	26	13.0	23	0
Davis	1	7	7.0	7	0
Cooks	1	2	2.0	2	0
Curry	1	0	0.0	0	0
Glasgow	1	0	0.0	0	0
Perryman	1	0	0.0	0	0
Colts	20	212	10.6	68	0
Opponents	16	181	11.3	45t	1

Punting

Punting	No.	Yds.	Avg.	In 20	LG
Stark	61	2440	40.0	12	63
Kiel	12	440	36.7	3	50
Colquitt	2	61	30.5	0	33
Colts	78	2941	37.7	15	63
Opponents	82	3048	37.2	15	57

Punt Returns

Punt Returns	No.	FC	Yds.	Avg.	LG	TD
Brooks	22	9	136	6.2	17	0
Johnson	9	2	42	4.7	12	0
Tullis	4	1	27	6.8	10	0
Simmons	2	0	5	2.5	5	0
Ahrens	1	0	0	0.0	0	0
Colts	38	12	210	5.5	17	0
Opponents	39	9	376	9.6	28	0

Kickoff Returns

Kickoff Returns	No.	Yds.	Avg.	LG	TD
Bentley	22	500	22.7	45	0
K. Daniel	10	225	22.5	29	0
Wright	10	187	18.7	27	0
Johnson	6	98	16.3	28	0
Prior	3	47	15.7	22	0
Noble	2	35	17.5	18	0
Perryman	1	4	4.0	4	0
Wonsley	1	19	19.0	19	0
Colts	55	1115	20.3	45	0
Opponents	60	1068	17.8	40	0

Sacks

Sacks	No.
Bickett	8.0
Thompson	5.5
Cooks	5.0
Darby	3.0
Thorp	3.0
Krauss	2.0
Benjamin	1.0
Bulluck	1.0
Chatman	1.0
Elko	1.0
Grimsley	1.0
Hand	1.0
Leiding	1.0
Mattiace	1.0
Perryman	1.0
Prior	1.0
Sally	1.0
Wright	1.0
Glasgow	0.5
Colts	39.0
Opponents	24.0

Indianapolis Colts 1988 Veteran Roster

No.	Name	Pos.	Ht.	Wt.	Birth-date	NFL Exp.	College	Hometown	How Acq.	'87 Games/ Starts
57	Ahrens, Dave	LB	6-4	249	12/6/58	8	Wisconsin	Oregon, Wis.	T(StL)-'85	12/2
78	†Armstrong, Harvey	NT	6-3	268	12/29/59	6	Southern Methodist	Houston, Tex.	FA-'86	11/1
35	Banks, Chuck	RB	6-1	227	1/4/64	3	West Virginia Tech	Baltimore, Md.	FA-'87	3/1
81	Beach, Pat	TE	6-4	252	12/28/59	6	Washington State	Pullman, Wash.	D6-'82	12/12
87	Bellini, Mark	WR	5-11	185	1/19/64	2	Brigham Young	San Leandro, Calif.	D7-'87	10/1
20	Bentley, Albert	RB	5-11	214	8/15/60	4	Miami	Immokalee, Fla.	SD2-'84	12/4
4	†Biasucci, Dean	K	6-0	191	7/25/62	4	Western Carolina	Niagara Falls, N.Y.	FA-'86	12/12
50	Bickett, Duane	LB	6-5	243	12/1/62	4	Southern California	Los Angeles, Calif.	D1-'85	12/12
85	†Bouza, Matt	WR	6-3	212	4/8/59	7	California	Sacramento, Calif.	FA-'82	12/12
84	†Boyer, Mark	TE	6-4	242	9/16/62	4	Southern California	Huntington Beach, Calif.	D9-'85	7/6
88	Brandes, John	TE	6-2	237	4/2/64	2	Cameron University	Fort Riley, Kan.	FA-'87	12/2
80	Brooks, Bill	WR	6-0	191	4/6/64	3	Boston University	Milton, Mass.	D4-'86	12/12
74	†Brotzki, Bob	T	6-5	293	12/24/62	3	Syracuse	Sandusky, Ohio	D9-'86	11/0
68	†Broughton, Willie	DE	6-5	281	9/9/64	3	Miami	Fort Pierce, Fla.	D4-'85	0*
43	t-Brown, Charlie	WR	5-10	184	10/29/58	7	South Carolina State	St. John's Island, S.C.	T(Atl)-'88	6/0
72	†Call, Kevin	T	6-7	302	11/13/61	5	Colorado State	Boulder, Colo.	D5b-'84	12/12
31	Coleman, Leonard	S	6-2	202	1/30/62	4	Vanderbilt	Boynton Beach, Fla.	D1-'84	4/0
98	Cooks, Johnie	LB	6-4	252	11/23/58	7	Mississippi State	Leland, Miss.	D1a-'82	10/10
38	Daniel, Eugene	CB	5-11	178	5/4/61	5	Louisiana State	Baton Rouge, La.	D8-'84	12/11
72	†Darby, Byron	DE	6-4	260	6/4/60	6	Southern California	Los Angeles, Calif.	FA-'87	12/4
29	Dickerson, Eric	RB	6-3	217	9/2/60	6	Southern Methodist	Sealy, Tex.	T(Rams)-'87	9/8
69	Dixon, Randy	T	6-3	293	3/12/65	2	Pittsburgh	Clewiston, Fla.	D4-'87	3/0
53	Donaldson, Ray	C	6-3	288	5/17/58	9	Georgia	Rome, Ga.	D2a-'80	12/12
48	Ellis, Ray	S	6-1	196	4/27/59	9	Ohio State	Canton, Ohio	FA-'88	12/10*
25	Glasgow, Nesby	S	5-10	187	4/15/57	10	Washington	Los Angeles, Calif.	D6a-'79	11/11
37	Goode, Chris	CB-S	6-0	193	9/17/63	2	Alabama	Town Creek, Ala.	D10-'87	8/0
78	Hand, Jon	DE	6-7	298	11/13/63	3	Alabama	Sylacauga, Ala.	D1-'86	12/11
9	t-Herrmann, Mark	QB	6-4	207	1/8/59	8	Purdue	Carmel, Ind.	T(SD)-'88	3/2
75	Hinton, Chris	G	6-4	295	7/31/61	6	Northwestern	Chicago, Ill.	T(Den)-'83	12/12
7	Hogeboom, Gary	QB	6-4	208	8/21/58	9	Central Michigan	Grand Rapids, Mich.	T(Dall)-'86	6/6
21	†Holt, John	CB	5-10	179	6/14/59	8	West Texas State	Lawton, Okla.	T(TB)-'86	12/1
58	James, June	LB	6-1	236	12/2/62	3	Texas	Jennings, La.	FA-'87	11/0
42	Johnson, Billy	WR-KR	5-9	170	1/27/52	13	Widener	Chichester, Pa.	FA-'88	12/1*
90	Johnson, Ezra	DE	6-4	264	10/2/55	12	Morris Brown	Shreveport, La.	FA-'88	6/0*
94	Kellar, Scott	NT	6-3	279	12/31/63	3	Northern Illinois	Elgin, Ill.	D5a-'86	3/2
63	Klecko, Joe	NT-DE	6-3	263	10/15/53	12	Temple	Chester, Pa.	W(NYJ)-'88	7/7*
55	Krauss, Barry	LB	6-3	269	3/17/57	10	Alabama	Pompano Beach, Fla.	D1-'79	12/11
59	Lowry, Orlando	LB	6-4	236	8/14/61	4	Ohio State	Shaker Heights, Ohio	FA-'85	8/1
44	Marsh, Doug	TE	6-3	238	6/18/58	9	Michigan	Akron, Ohio	FA-'88	0*
49	McCloskey, Mike	TE	6-5	246	2/2/61	4	Penn State	Philadelphia, Pa.	FA-'87	0*
32	McMillan, Randy	RB	6-0	220	12/17/58	7	Pittsburgh	Jarrettsville, Md.	D1a-'81	0*
86	Murray, Walter	WR	6-4	202	12/13/62	3	Hawaii	Berkeley, Calif.	T(Wash)-'86	14/3
93	Odom, Cliff	LB	6-2	245	9/15/58	8	Texas-Arlington	Beaumont, Tex.	W(Raid)-'82	12/12
65	Patten, Joel	T	6-7	307	2/7/58	3	Duke	Augsburg, Germany	FA-'87	12/0
43	Perryman, Jim	CB-S	6-0	187	12/23/60	3	Millikin	Walnut Creek, Calif.	FA-'87	14/3
39	†Prior, Mike	CB-S	6-0	200	11/14/63	3	Illinois State	Chicago Heights, Ill.	FA-'87	12/7
47	Robinson, Freddie	CB-S	6-1	191	2/1/64	2	Alabama	Mobile, Ala.	D6-'87	9/9
13	†Salisbury, Sean	QB	6-5	215	3/9/63	3	Southern California	Escondido, Calif.	FA-'87	2/0
76	†Sally, Jerome	NT	6-3	270	2/24/59	7	Missouri	Chicago, Ill.	T(NYG)-'87	12/8
83	Sherwin, Tim	TE	6-5	252	5/4/58	8	Boston College	Watervliet, N.Y.	D4-'81	8/5
66	†Solt, Ron	G	6-3	285	5/19/62	5	Maryland	Wilkes-Barre, Pa.	D1b-'84	12/12
3	Stark, Rohn	P	6-3	204	5/4/59	7	Florida State	Minneapolis, Minn.	D2b-'82	12/0
26	Swoope, Craig	CB-S	6-1	200	2/3/64	3	Illinois	Fort Pierce, Fla.	W(TB)-'87	3/0
99	Thompson, Donnell	DE	6-4	275	10/27/58	8	North Carolina	Lumberton, N.C.	D1b-'81	12/12
62	Thorp, Don	NT-DE	6-4	260	7/10/62	3	Illinois	Chicago, Ill.	FA-'87	6/3
10	Trudeau, Jack	QB	6-3	213	9/9/62	3	Illinois	Livermore, Calif.	D2-'86	10/8
42	†Tullis, Willie	CB	5-11	195	4/5/58	8	Troy State	Stafford, Tex.	FA-'87	12/12
64	Utt, Ben	G	6-6	286	6/13/59	7	Georgia Tech	Visalia, Calif.	FA-'82	12/12
39	Verdin, Clarence	WR	5-8	160	6/14/63	3	Southwestern Louisiana	New Orleans, La.	T(Wash)-'88	3/1*
48	Walczak, Mark	TE	6-6	246	4/26/62	2	Arizona	Rochester, N.Y.	FA-'87	8/0
34	Wonsley, George	RB	5-10	219	11/23/60	5	Mississippi State	Moss Point, Miss.	D4b-'84	11/0
27	Wright, Terry	CB-S	6-0	195	7/17/65	2	Temple	Phoenix, Ariz.	FA-'87	13/2

* Broughton and McMillan missed '87 season due to injury; Ellis played 12 games with Cleveland in '87; B. Johnson played 12 games with Atlanta; E. Johnson played 6 games with Green Bay; Klecko played 7 games with N.Y. Jets; Marsh last active with St. Louis in '86; McCloskey on inactive list for 6 games; Verdin played 3 games with Washington.

†Option playout; subject to developments.

t-Colts traded for Brown (Atlanta), Herrmann (San Diego).

Also played with Colts in '87—T Sid Abramowitz (3 games), CB-S Pat Ballage (3), WR Roy Banks (1), T Mark Boggs (1), RB Gordon Brown (3), WR Steve Bryant (1), LB Brian Bulluck (2), T Milt Carthens (1), RB Mel Carver (1), LB Ricky Chatman (3), G Jeff Criswell (3), CB-S Craig Curry (3), CB Kenny Daniel (2), S-CB Lee Davis (3), NT Bill Elko (3), CB Jitter Fields (1), T Marsharne Graves (3), DE Bob Hamm (3), LB Kevin Hancock (1), WR Greg Hawthorne (3), NT Marcus Jackson (1), WR Kelley Johnson (3), CB Bryant Jones (3), TE Joe Jones (3), K Steve Jordan (3), WR Tim Kearse (3), QB Blair Kiel (4), G Steve Knight (3), TE Keith Lester (1), NT Frank Mattiace (3), RB Chris McLemore (2), NT Jim Merritts (1), WR James Noble (3), LB Bob Ontko (3), LB Gary Padjen (1), C-G Ron Plantz (3), LB Roger Remo (3), LB Brad Saar (1), S John Simmons (2), RB John Williams (2).

COACHING STAFF

Head Coach, Ron Meyer

Pro Career: Named Colts' twelfth head coach on December 1, 1986. Led Colts to AFC Eastern Division championship in 1987 with a 9-6 record. Served as head coach with New England Patriots from 1982-84. Compiled 18-15 regular-season record with one playoff game following the 1982 season. Career record: 30-23.

Background: Entered coaching ranks at Penn High School in Mishawauka, Indiana, in 1964. Joined staff at Purdue (where he played defensive back 1959-62) in 1965 in charge of the offensive backfield, receivers, and overall passing game. Remained at Purdue until becoming a scout with Dallas Cowboys for the 1971-72 seasons. Named head coach at Nevada-Las Vegas in 1973, directing the Rebels to a three-year 27-8 mark, including an undefeated (11-0) regular season in 1974 before losing in the national semifinals in the NCAA Division II playoffs. Named head coach at Southern Methodist in 1976, where he coached until 1981. The Mustangs had a 34-31-1 record during Meyer's tenure and won the Southwestern Conference championship his final year.

Personal: Born February 17, 1941, in Westerville, Ohio. Ron and his wife, Cindy, live in Indianapolis with their daughters Kathryn and Elizabeth. Ron's sons, Ron, Jr., and Ralph, reside in Dallas.

Assistant Coaches

John Becker, offensive coordinator; born February 16, 1943, Alexandria, Va., lives in Indianapolis. Cal State-Northridge 1965. No college or pro playing experience. College coach: UCLA 1970, New Mexico State 1971, New Mexico 1972-73, Los Angeles Valley J.C. 1974-76 (head coach), Oregon 1977-79. Pro coach: Philadelphia Eagles 1980-83, Buffalo Bills 1984, joined Colts in 1985.

Leon Burtnett, running backs; born May 30, 1943, Fresno, Calif., lives in Indianapolis. Fullback Southwestern (Kan.) University 1961-65. No pro playing experience. College coach: Montana State 1970, Washington State 1971, Wyoming 1972-73, San Jose State 1974-75, Michigan State 1976, Purdue 1977-86 (head coach 1982-86). Pro coach: Joined Colts in 1987.

George Catavolos, secondary; born May 8, 1945, Chicago, Ill., lives in Indianapolis. Defensive back Purdue 1964-66. No pro playing experience. College coach: Purdue 1967-68, 1971-76, Middle Tennessee State 1969, Louisville 1970, Kentucky 1977-81, Tennessee 1982-83. Pro coach: Joined Colts in 1984.

George Hill, defensive coordinator; born April 28, 1933, Bay Village, Ohio, lives in Indianapolis. Tackle-fullback Denison 1954-57. No pro playing experience. College coach: Findlay 1959, Denison 1960-64, Cornell 1965, Duke 1966-70, Ohio State 1971-78. Pro coach: Philadelphia Eagles 1979-84, joined Colts in 1985.

Tom Lovat, assistant head coach-offensive line; born December 28, 1938, Bingham, Utah, lives in Indianapolis. Guard-linebacker Utah 1958-60. No pro playing experience. College coach: Utah 1967, 1972-76 (head coach 1974-76), Idaho State 1968-70, Stanford 1977-79. Pro coach: Saskatchewan Roughriders (CFL) 1971, Green Bay Packers 1980, St. Louis Cardinals 1981-84, joined Colts in 1985.

John Marshall, defensive line; born October 2, 1945, Arroyo Grande, Calif., lives in Indianapolis. Linebacker Washington State 1964. No pro playing experience. College coach: Oregon 1970-76, Southern California 1977-79. Pro coach: Green Bay Packers 1980-82, Atlanta Falcons 1983-85, joined Colts in 1986.

Chip Myers, receivers; born July 9, 1945, Panama City, Fla., lives in Indianapolis. Receiver Northwest Oklahoma 1964-66. Pro receiver San Francisco 49ers 1967, Cincinnati Bengals 1969-76. College coach: Illinois 1980-82. Pro coach: Tampa Bay Buccaneers 1983-84, joined Colts in 1985.

Keith Rowen, special teams-assistant offensive line; born September 2, 1952, New York, N.Y., lives in Indianapolis. Offensive tackle Stanford 1972-74. No pro playing experience. College coach: Stanford 1975-76, Long Beach State 1977-78, Arizona 1979-82. Pro coach: Boston/New Orleans Breakers (USFL) 1983-84, Cleveland Browns 1984, joined Colts in 1985.

Rick Venturi, linebackers; born February 23, 1946, Taylorville, Ill., lives in Indianapolis. Quarterback Northwestern 1965-67. No pro playing experience. College coach: Northwestern 1968-72, 1978-80 (head coach), Purdue 1973-76, Illinois 1977. Pro coach: Joined Colts in 1982.

Tom Zupancic, strength and conditioning; born September 14, 1955, Indianapolis, Ind., lives in Indianapolis. Defensive tackle-offensive tackle Indiana Central 1975-78. No pro playing experience. Pro coach: Joined Colts in 1984.

Indianapolis Colts 1988 First-Year Roster

Name	Pos.	Ht.	Wt.	Birth-date	College	Hometown	How Acq.
Alexander, Rogers (1)	LB	6-3	231	8/11/64	Penn State	Washington, D.C.	FA
Allen, Douglas (1)	WR	5-10	180	4/22/63	Arizona State	Columbus, Ohio	FA
Alston, O'Brien	LB	6-6	241	12/21/65	Maryland	New Haven, Conn.	D10
Atkinson, Ricky (1)	CB-S	6-0	180	8/28/65	So. Connecticut St.	Middletown, Conn.	FA
Ayres, Marvin (1)	DE	6-5	265	9/12/63	Grambling	Dallas, Tex.	FA
Ball, Michael	CB-S	6-0	211	8/5/64	Southern University	New Orleans, La.	D4
Baylor, John	CB-S	6-0	192	3/5/65	Southern Mississippi	Meridian, Miss.	D5
Bulluck, Brian	LB	6-2	236	10/29/65	North Carolina State	Roanoke Rapids, N.C.	FA
Chandler, Chris	QB	6-4	215	10/12/65	Washington	Everett, Wash.	D3
Crawford, Tim (1)	LB	6-4	250	12/17/62	Texas Tech	Houston, Tex.	FA
Cunningham, Tim (1)	LB	6-4	235	7/21/64	Indiana State	Charleroy, Pa.	FA
Davis, Bruce (1)	WR	5-8	170	2/25/63	Baylor	Dallas, Tex.	FA
Dee, Donnie	TE	6-4	235	3/17/65	Tulsa	Kansas City, Mo.	D11
Garza, Louis (1)	T	6-5	290	11/17/62	New Mexico State	San Antonio, Tex.	FA
Hancock, Kevin (1)	LB	6-2	225	1/6/62	Baylor	Texas City, Tex.	FA-'87
Herrod, Jeff	LB	6-0	237	7/29/66	Mississippi	Birmingham, Ala.	D9
Kenney, Aatron	WR	5-11	171	9/6/63	Wis.-Stevens Point	Dallas, Tex.	D12a
Knox, Mike (1)	LB	6-2	240	11/21/62	Nebraska	Boulder, Colo.	FA
Modesitt, Jeff (1)	TE	6-5	246	1/1/64	Delaware	Terre Haute, Ind.	FA
Pickens, Lyle (1)	CB-S	5-11	185	9/5/64	Colorado	New Orleans, La.	FA
Pizzo, Joe (1)	QB	6-3	215	6/25/64	Mars Hill College	Los Altos, Calif.	FA
Snyder, Patrick (1)	C	6-1	218	11/23/63	Purdue	Paulding, Ohio	FA
Thomas, Ricky (1)	CB-S	6-1	205	3/29/65	Alabama	London, England	FA
Vesling, Tim	K	5-11	178	11/20/64	Syracuse	Rochester, N.Y.	D12b

The term NFL Rookie is defined as a player who is in his first season of professional football and has not been on the roster of another professional football team for any regular-season or postseason games. A Rookie is designated by an "R" on NFL rosters. Players who have been active in another professional football league or players who have NFL experience, including either preseason training camp or being on an active roster for fewer than three regular-season or postseason games, are termed NFL First-Year Players. An NFL First-Year Player is designated by a "1" on NFL rosters. Thereafter, a player on an NFL active roster for at least three regular-season or postseason games is credited with an additional year of NFL playing experience.

NOTES

American Football Conference Western Division

Team Colors: Red, Gold, and White

One Arrowhead Drive
Kansas City, Missouri 64129
Telephone: (816) 924-9300

Club Officials

Owner: Lamar Hunt
President: Jack Steadman
Vice President-General Manager: Jim Schaaf
Assistant to General Manager: Dennis Thum
Vice President-Administration: Don Steadman
Treasurer: Bob Tamasi
Secretary: Jim Seigfreid
Player Personnel Director: Whitey Dovell
Director of Public Relations and Community Relations: Gary Heise
Assistant Director of Public Relations: Jim Carr
Public Relations Assistant: Theotis Brown
Community Relations Manager: Brenda Boatright
Director of Sales and Promotions: Mitch Wheeler
Director of Marketing: Ken Blume
Manager of Ticket Operations: Phil Youtsey
Stadium Operations: Bob Wachter
Trainer: Dave Kendall
Equipment Coordinator: Jon Phillips
Video Coordinator: Mike Dennis

Stadium: Arrowhead Stadium • **Capacity:** 78,067
One Arrowhead Drive
Kansas City, Missouri 64129

Playing Surface: AstroTurf-8

Training Camp: William Jewell College
Liberty, Missouri 64068

1988 Schedule

Preseason

Aug. 6	**Cincinnati**	7:30
Aug. 13	at Atlanta	7:30
Aug. 19	vs. Green Bay at Milw.	7:00
Aug. 25	**Phoenix**	7:30

Regular Season

Sept. 4	**Cleveland**	3:00
Sept. 11	at Seattle	1:00
Sept. 18	**Denver**	12:00
Sept. 25	**San Diego**	3:00
Oct. 2	at New York Jets	4:00
Oct. 9	at Houston	12:00
Oct. 16	**Los Angeles Raiders**	12:00
Oct. 23	**Detroit**	12:00
Oct. 30	at Los Angeles Raiders	1:00
Nov. 6	at Denver	2:00
Nov. 13	**Cincinnati**	12:00
Nov. 20	**Seattle**	12:00
Nov. 27	at Pittsburgh	1:00
Dec. 4	**New York Jets**	3:00
Dec. 11	at New York Giants	1:00
Dec. 18	at San Diego	1:00

Chiefs Coaching History

Dallas Texans 1960-62
(206-197-10)

1960-74	Hank Stram	129-79-10
1975-77	Paul Wiggin*	11-24-0
1977	Tom Bettis	1-6-0
1978-82	Marv Levy	31-42-0
1983-86	John Mackovic	30-35-0
1987	Frank Gansz	4-11-0

*Released after seven games in 1977

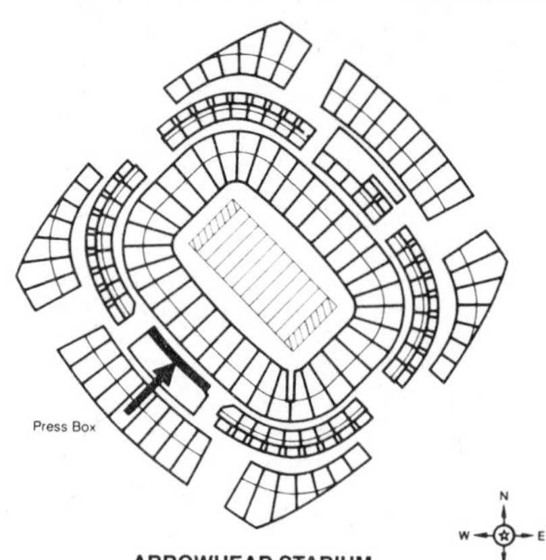

ARROWHEAD STADIUM

Record Holders

Individual Records—Career

Category	Name	Performance
Rushing (Yds.)	Ed Podolak, 1969-1977	4,451
Passing (Yds.)	Len Dawson, 1962-1975	28,507
Passing (TDs)	Len Dawson, 1962-1975	237
Receiving (No.)	Henry Marshall, 1976-1987	416
Receiving (Yds.)	Otis Taylor, 1965-1975	7,306
Interceptions	Emmitt Thomas, 1966-1978	58
Punting (Avg.)	Jerrel Wilson, 1963-1977	43.5
Punt Return (Avg.)	J.T. Smith, 1979-1984	10.6
Kickoff Return (Avg.)	Noland Smith, 1967-69	26.8
Field Goals	Jan Stenerud, 1967-1979	279
Touchdowns (Tot.)	Otis Taylor, 1965-1975	60
Points	Jan Stenerud, 1967-1979	1,231

Individual Records—Single Season

Category	Name	Performance
Rushing (Yds.)	Joe Delaney, 1981	1,121
Passing (Yds.)	Bill Kenney, 1983	4,348
Passing (TDs)	Len Dawson, 1964	30
Receiving (No.)	Carlos Carson, 1983	80
Receiving (Yds.)	Carlos Carson, 1983	1,351
Interceptions	Emmitt Thomas, 1974	12
Punting (Avg.)	Jerrel Wilson, 1965	46.0
Punt Return (Avg.)	Abner Haynes, 1960	15.4
Kickoff Return (Avg.)	Dave Grayson, 1962	29.7
Field Goals	Jan Stenerud, 1968	30
	Jan Stenerud, 1970	30
Touchdowns (Tot.)	Abner Haynes, 1962	19
Points	Jan Stenerud, 1968	129

Individual Records—Single Game

Category	Name	Performance
Rushing (Yds.)	Joe Delaney, 11-15-81	193
Passing (Yds.)	Len Dawson, 11-1-64	435
Passing (TDs)	Len Dawson, 11-1-64	6
Receiving (No.)	Ed Podolak, 10-7-73	12
Receiving (Yds.)	Stephone Paige, 12-22-85	*309
Interceptions	Bobby Ply, 12-16-62	*4
	Bobby Hunt, 12-4-64	*4
	Deron Cherry, 9-29-85	*4
Field Goals	Jan Stenerud, 11-2-69	5
	Jan Stenerud, 12-7-69	5
	Jan Stenerud, 12-19-71	5
Touchdowns (Tot.)	Abner Haynes, 11-26-61	5
Points	Abner Haynes, 11-26-61	30

*NFL Record

1987 Team Record

Preseason (4-1)

Date	Result		Opponents
8/8	L	7-20	vs. San Francisco at Canton, Ohio
8/13	W	32-20	at Houston
8/22	W	13-10	Atlanta
8/29	W	34-14	Buffalo
9/4	W	13-10	vs. St. Louis at Memphis, Tenn. (OT)
		99-74	

Regular Season (4-11)

Date	Result		Opponents	Att.
9/13	W	20-13	San Diego	56,940
9/20	L	14-43	at Seattle	61,667
9/27	C		Minnesota	
10/4	L	17-35	at L.A. Raiders	10,708
10/11	L	0-42	at Miami	25,867
10/18	L	17-26	Denver	20,296
10/25	L	21-42	at San Diego	47,972
11/1	L	28-31	at Chicago	63,498
11/8	L	16-17	Pittsburgh	45,249
11/15	L	9-16	N.Y. Jets	40,718
11/22	L	3-23	Green Bay	34,611
11/26	W	27-20	at Detroit	43,820
12/6	L	27-30	at Cincinnati (OT)	46,489
12/13	W	16-10	L.A. Raiders	63,834
12/19	L	17-20	at Denver	75,053
12/27	W	41-20	Seattle	20,370

(OT) Overtime
C (Cancelled due to players' strike.)

Score by Periods

Chiefs	55	88	74	56	0	—	273
Opponents	88	116	93	88	3	—	388

Attendance

Home 282,018 Away 375,074 Total 657,092
Single-game home record, 82,094 (11-5-72)
Single-season home record, 509,291 (1972)

1987 Team Statistics

	Chiefs	Opp.
Total First Downs	265	344
Rushing	97	139
Passing	141	172
Penalty	27	33
Third Down: Made/Att.	77/192	92/206
Fourth Down: Made/Att.	4/10	5/15
Total Net Yards	4418	5639
Avg. Per Game	294.5	375.9
Total Plays	899	1045
Avg. Per Play	4.9	5.4
Net Yards Rushing	1799	2333
Avg. Per Game	119.9	155.5
Total Rushes	419	535
Net Yards Passing	2619	3306
Avg. Per Game	174.6	220.4
Sacked/Yards Lost	48/366	26/167
Gross Yards	2985	3473
Att./Completions	432/236	484/279
Completion Pct.	54.6	57.6
Had Intercepted	17	11
Punts/Avg.	69/40.4	56/40.4
Net Punting Avg.	32.3	31.7
Penalties/Yards Lost	108/861	112/936
Fumbles/Ball Lost	41/24	24/17
Touchdowns	30	45
Rushing	7	16
Passing	17	25
Returns	6	4
Avg. Time of Possession	27:11	32:49

1987 Individual Statistics

Scoring	TD R	TD P	TD Rt	PAT	FG	Saf	TP
Lowery	0	0	0	26/26	19/23	0	83
Carson	0	7	0	0/0	0/0	0	42
Paige	0	4	0	0/0	0/0	0	24
Heard	3	0	0	0/0	0/0	0	18
Okoye	3	0	0	0/0	0/0	0	18
Hayes	0	2	0	0/0	0/0	0	12
Palmer	0	0	2	0/0	0/0	0	12
Hamrick	0	0	0	4/4	2/2	0	10
Adickes	0	1	0	0/0	0/0	0	6
Coffman	0	1	0	0/0	0/0	0	6
Fields	0	0	1	0/0	0/0	0	6
Harris	0	0	1	0/0	0/0	0	6
R. Jones	0	1	0	0/0	0/0	0	6
Keel, Sea.-K.C.	0	1	0	0/0	0/0	0	6
Maas	0	0	1	0/0	0/0	0	6
Moriarty	0	1	0	0/0	0/0	0	6
Parker	1	0	0	0/0	0/0	0	6
Ross	0	0	1	0/0	0/0	0	6
Chiefs	7	17	6	30/30	21/25	0	273
Opponents	16	25	4	44/45	24/35	1	388

Passing	Att.	Comp.	Yds.	Pct.	TD	Int.	Tkld.	Rate
Kenney	273	154	2107	56.4	15	9	22/161	85.8
Stevens	57	32	315	56.1	1	1	6/53	70.4
Seurer	55	26	340	47.3	0	4	10/82	36.9
Blackledge	31	15	154	48.4	1	1	7/43	60.4
Espinoza	14	9	69	64.3	0	2	2/17	36.6
Hudson	1	0	0	0.0	0	0	1/10	39.6
Palmer	1	0	0	0.0	0	0	0/0	39.6
Chiefs	432	236	2985	54.6	17	17	48/366	73.1
Opponents	484	279	3473	57.6	25	11	26/167	87.8

Rushing	Att.	Yds.	Avg.	LG	TD
Okoye	157	660	4.2	43t	3
Heard	82	466	5.7	64t	3
Palmer	24	155	6.5	35	0
Parker	47	150	3.2	10	1
C. Smith	26	114	4.4	11	0
Moriarty	30	107	3.6	11	0
Lacy	14	49	3.5	17	0
Seurer	9	33	3.7	11	0
Blackledge	5	21	4.2	11	0
Goodburn	1	16	16.0	16	0
Pippens	3	16	5.3	11	0
Clemons	2	7	3.5	7	0
Stevens	3	7	2.3	6	0
Espinoza	1	5	5.0	5	0
Stockemer	1	2	2.0	2	0
Hudson	1	0	0.0	0	0
Kenney	12	−2	−0.2	6	0
Carson	1	−7	−7.0	−7	0
Chiefs	419	1799	4.3	64t	7
Opponents	535	2333	4.4	48	16

Receiving	No.	Yds.	Avg.	LG	TD
Carson	55	1044	19.0	81t	7
Paige	43	707	16.4	51	4
Okoye	24	169	7.0	22	0
Hayes	21	272	13.0	33	2
Heard	14	118	8.4	15	0
Marshall	10	126	12.6	19	0
Moriarty	10	37	3.7	8	1
Keel, Sea.-K.C.	8	97	12.1	24t	1
Keel, K.C.	2	9	4.5	7	0
R. Jones	8	76	9.5	16	1
Parker	7	44	6.3	14	0
Brown	5	69	13.8	23	0
Montagne	5	47	9.4	16	0
Coffman	5	42	8.4	13t	1
Trahan	4	40	10.0	14	0
Palmer	4	27	6.8	10	0
Arnold	3	26	8.7	10	0
Estell	3	24	8.0	11	0
D. Colbert	3	21	7.0	9	0
Koss	2	25	12.5	14	0
Nash	2	22	11.0	14	0
C. Smith	2	21	10.5	16	0
Pippens	2	12	6.0	7	0
Stockemer	1	4	4.0	4	0
Adickes	1	3	3.0	3t	1
Chiefs	236	2985	12.6	81t	17
Opponents	279	3473	12.4	44	25

Interceptions	No.	Yds.	Avg.	LG	TD
Cherry	3	58	19.3	30	0
Ross	3	40	13.3	40	0
Robinson	2	42	21.0	25	0
Bryant	1	0	0.0	0	0
Cooper	1	0	0.0	0	0
Lewis	1	0	0.0	0	0
Chiefs	11	140	12.7	40	0
Opponents	17	141	8.3	35	0

Punting	No.	Yds.	Avg.	In 20	LG
Goodburn	59	2412	40.9	13	55
L. Colbert	10	377	37.7	0	47
Chiefs	69	2789	40.4	13	55
Opponents	56	2260	40.4	14	61

Punt Returns	No.	FC	Yds.	Avg.	LG	TD
Clemons	19	4	162	8.5	44	0
Fields	8	3	161	20.1	85t	1
Wyatt	2	0	4	2.0	4	0
Cocroft	1	0	0	0.0	0	0
D. Colbert	1	0	11	11.0	11	0
Montagne	1	1	8	8.0	8	0
Chiefs	32	8	346	10.8	85t	1
Opponents	43	6	442	10.3	33	0

Kickoff Returns	No.	Yds.	Avg.	LG	TD
Palmer	38	923	24.3	95t	2
Moriarty	6	102	17.0	24	0
Robinson	5	97	19.4	25	0
Wyatt	5	121	24.2	29	0
Lacy	4	44	11.0	20	0
Parker	3	49	16.3	25	0
Lane	2	37	18.5	21	0
A. Pearson	2	4	2.0	4	0
Clemons	1	3	3.0	3	0
D. Colbert	1	18	18.0	18	0
Fields	1	13	13.0	13	0
S. Griffin	1	16	16.0	16	0
B. Smith	1	10	10.0	10	0
Chiefs	70	1437	20.5	95t	2
Opponents	55	1263	23.0	88t	1

Sacks	No.
Bell	6.5
Maas	6.0
Still	5.5
Del Rio	3.0
Hackett	2.0
Snipes, S.D.-K.C.	2.0
Snipes, K.C.	1.0
Ross	1.0
Holle	0.5
Koch	0.5
Woodard, Den.-K.C.	0.5
Chiefs	26.0
Opponents	48.0

Kansas City Chiefs 1988 Veteran Roster

No.	Name	Pos.	Ht.	Wt.	Birth-date	NFL Exp.	College	Hometown	How Acq.	'87 Games/ Starts
61	Adickes, Mark	G	6-4	270	4/22/61	3	Baylor	Waco, Tex.	SD1-'84	12/12
76	†Alt, John	T	6-7	290	5/30/62	5	Iowa	Columbia Heights, Minn.	D1b-'84	9/9
91	Baldinger, Gary	NT-DE	6-3	265	10/4/63	3	Wake Forest	Long Island, N.Y.	D9-'86	7/0
77	Baldinger, Rich	G-T	6-4	285	12/31/59	7	Wake Forest	Long Island, N.Y.	FA-'83	12/11
58	Baugh, Tom	C	6-3	274	12/1/63	3	Southern Illinois	North Riverside, Ill.	D4a-'86	12/6
99	Bell, Mike	DE	6-4	260	8/30/57	8	Colorado State	Wichita, Kan.	D1a-'79	12/12
34	Burruss, Lloyd	S	6-0	209	10/31/57	8	Maryland	Charlottesville, N.C.	D3c-'81	11/11
88	†Carson, Carlos	WR	5-11	180	12/28/58	9	Louisiana State	Lake Worth, Fla.	D5a-80	12/12
20	Cherry, Deron	S	5-11	193	9/12/59	8	Rutgers	Palmyra, N.J.	FA-'81	8/8
46	Clemons, Michael	RB-KR	5-5	166	1/15/65	2	William & Mary	Clearwater, Fla.	D8-'87	8/0
22	Cocroft, Sherman	S-CB	6-1	192	8/29/61	4	San Jose State	Mobile, Ala.	FA-'85	12/1
54	Cofield, Tim	LB	6-2	245	5/18/63	3	Elizabeth City State	Murfreesboro, N.C.	FA-'86	12/5
81	Colbert, Darrell	WR	5-10	174	11/16/64	2	Texas Southern	Beaumont, Tex.	FA-'87	12/0
5	Colbert, Lewis	P	5-11	179	8/23/63	2	Auburn	Phenix City, Ala.	D8-'86	2/0
55	†Cooper, Louis	LB	6-2	240	8/5/63	4	Western Carolina	Marion, S.C.	FA-'85	12/6
17	t-DeBerg, Steve	QB	6-3	210	1/19/54	12	San Jose State	Anaheim, Calif.	T(TB)-'88	12/8
50	†Del Rio, Jack	LB	6-4	238	4/4/63	4	Southern California	Castro Valley, Calif.	T(NO)-'87	10/7
51	†Donnalley, Rick	C	6-2	260	12/11/58	7	North Carolina	Wilmington, Del.	T(Wash)-'86	6/6
75	Eatman, Irv	T	6-7	293	1/1/61	3	UCLA	Dayton, Ohio	D8-'83	12/8
40	†Fields, Jitter	CB-S-KR	5-9	180	8/16/62	3	Texas	Dallas, Tex.	FA-'87	6/0*
2	Goodburn, Kelly	P	6-2	195	4/14/62	2	Emporia State	Cherokee, Iowa	FA-'87	13/0
98	Griffin, Leonard	DE	6-4	258	9/22/62	3	Grambling	Lake Providence, La.	D3-'86	12/2
56	Hackett, Dino	LB	6-3	228	6/28/64	3	Appalachian State	Greensboro, N.C.	D2-'86	11/11
57	Harrell, James	LB	6-2	240	7/19/57	9	Florida	Tampa, Fla.	FA-'87	11/4
86	†Harry, Emile	WR	5-11	175	4/5/63	2	Stanford	Los Angeles, Calif.	FA-'86	0*
64	Harvey, James	G	6-3	265	11/27/65	2	Jackson State	New Orleans, La.	FA-'87	3/3
59	Hawkins, Andy	LB	6-2	230	3/31/58	7	Texas A&I	Bay City, Tex.	FA-'87	2/0*
85	Hayes, Jonathan	TE	6-5	240	8/11/62	4	Iowa	Pittsburgh, Pa.	D2-'85	12/7
44	†Heard, Herman	RB	5-10	182	11/24/61	5	Southern Colorado	Denver, Colo.	D3-'84	12/6
23	†Hill, Greg	CB	6-1	197	2/12/61	6	Oklahoma State	Orange, Tex.	W(Hou)-'87	6/0*
93	†Holle, Eric	NT	6-5	265	9/5/60	5	Texas	Austin, Tex.	D5a-'84	8/1
53	Howard, Todd	LB	6-2	235	2/18/65	2	Texas A&M	Bryan, Tex.	D3-'87	12/0
81	Jones, Rod	TE	6-4	242	3/3/64	2	Washington	Richmond, Calif.	FA-'87	3/1
73	Jozwiak, Brian	G	6-5	310	6/20/63	3	West Virginia	Baltimore, Md.	D1-'86	10/1
80	Keel, Mark	TE	6-4	228	10/1/62	2	Arizona	Fort Worth, Tex.	FA-'87	10/3*
9	Kenney, Bill	QB	6-4	207	1/20/55	10	Northern Colorado	San Clemente, Calif.	FA-'79	11/8
74	Koch, Pete	DE	6-6	265	1/23/62	5	Maryland	Manhasset, N.Y.	FA-'85	6/6
29	Lewis, Albert	CB	6-2	192	10/6/60	6	Grambling	Mansfield, La.	D3-'83	12/12
8	Lowery, Nick	K	6-4	189	5/27/56	9	Dartmouth	Washington, D.C.	FA-'80	12/0
72	Lutz, David	T	6-6	290	12/30/59	6	Georgia Tech	Peachland, N.C.	D2-'83	12/7
63	†Maas, Bill	NT	6-5	268	3/2/62	5	Pittsburgh	Newtown Square, Pa.	D1-'84	11/11
89	†Marshall, Henry	WR	6-2	216	8/9/54	13	Missouri	Dalzell, S.C.	D3d-'76	12/0
32	†Moriarty, Larry	RB	6-1	237	4/24/58	6	Notre Dame	Santa Barbara, Calif.	T(Hou)-'86	12/4
35	Okoye, Christian	RB	6-1	253	8/16/61	2	Azusa Pacific	Enugu, Nigeria	D2-'87	12/12
83	Paige, Stephone	WR	6-2	185	10/15/61	6	Fresno State	Long Beach, Calif.	FA-'83	12/11
26	Palmer, Paul	RB-KR	5-9	184	10/14/64	2	Temple	Potomac, Md.	D1-'87	12/1
43	Parker, Robert	RB	6-1	190	1/7/63	2	Brigham Young	Alexander City, Ala.	FA-'87	3/2
96	Pearson, Aaron	LB	6-0	240	8/22/64	3	Mississippi State	Gadsden, Ala.	D11-'86	12/9
24	Pearson, J.C.	CB	5-11	183	8/17/63	3	Washington	Oceanside, Calif.	FA-'86	12/2
31	Ross, Kevin	CB	5-9	182	1/16/62	5	Temple	Paulsboro, N.J.	D7-'84	12/11
10	Seurer, Frank	QB	6-1	195	8/16/62	3	Kansas	Huntington Beach, Calif.	FA-'86	8/2
97	Snipes, Angelo	LB	6-0	215	1/11/63	3	West Georgia	Atlanta, Ga.	FA-'87	6/0*
67	Still, Art	DE	6-7	255	12/5/55	11	Kentucky	Camden, N.J.	D1-'78	12/12
38	Thomas, Carlton	CB	6-0	195	11/25/63	2	Elizabeth City State	Portsmouth, Va.	FA-'87	4/2
62	Tupper, Jeff	NT	6-5	269	12/26/62	3	Oklahoma	Joplin, Mo.	FA-'87	4/2*
98	Walker, John	DE-NT	6-6	270	9/12/61	2	Nebraska-Omaha	Omaha, Neb.	FA-'87	3/2
70	Woodard, Ray	DE	6-6	290	1/22/60	2	Texas	Detroit, Mich.	FA-'87	8/1*

* Fields played 1 game with Indianapolis in '87, 5 with Kansas City; Harry missed '87 season due to injury; Hawkins played 2 games with San Diego in '87; Hill played 2 games with L.A. Raiders, 4 with Kansas City; Keel played 3 games with Seattle, 7 with Kansas City; Snipes played 2 games with San Diego, 4 with Kansas City; Tupper played 4 games with Denver, active for 1 game with Kansas City but did not play; Woodard played 3 games with Denver, 5 with Kansas City.

†Option playout; subject to developments.

t-Chiefs traded for DeBerg (Tampa Bay).

Traded—Quarterback Todd Blackledge to Pittsburgh, safety Mark Robinson to Tampa Bay.

Also played with Chiefs in '87—NT Bill Acker (2 games), C Kevin Adkins (2), G John Aimonetti (active for 1 game but did not play), TE Walt Arnold (5), T James Black (1), WR Eric Brown (2), CB Trent Bryant (3), TE Paul Coffman (12), CB Jeff Colter (1), T Dan Doubiago (3), S Cornelius Dozier (2), S Jack Epps (3), QB Alex Espinoza (1), WR Richard Estell (2), RB James Evans (2), NT Jeff Faulkner (3), LB Randy Frazier (3), G Lee Getz (3), RB Stephen Griffin (1), K James Hamrick (3), LB Bob Harris (3), WR Eric Hodges (1), DE Tony Holloway (1), LB Bruce Holmes (3), T Doug Hoppock (3), QB Doug Hudson (1), C Glenn Hyde (7), C-G Byron Ingram (1), DE Ken Johnson (3), LB Fred Jones (2), TE Stein Koss (2), RB Ken Lacy (3), CB Garcia Lane (1), DE Chris Lindstrom (3), LB Ken McAlister (1), WR David Montagne (3), DE Mitchell Morris (active for 1 game but did not play), LB Gary Moten (1), NT Lloyd Mumphrey (3), WR Kenny Nash (1), T Mark Nelson (1), S Ted Nelson (3), C Jim Pietrzak (2), RB Woodie Pippins (2), T Steve Rogers (3), S Blane Smith (3), RB Chris Smith (3), LB Gary Spann (2), QB Matt Stevens (3), RB Ralph Stockemer (2), T Terry Summers (active for 1 game but did not play), G Arland Thompson (3), WR John Trahan (3), TE Riley Walton (2), K Paul Woodside (active for 1 game but did not play), CB Kevin Wyatt (2).

COACHING STAFF

Head Coach, Frank Gansz

Pro Career: Begins his second season as Chiefs head coach. Was named sixth head coach in Chiefs history on January 10, 1987. Had been NFL assistant coach previous nine years, including two different stints in Kansas City. Coached Chiefs special teams and tight ends in 1981-82 under Marv Levy, then rejoined club in 1986 under John Mackovic as assistant head coach and special teams coach. Led special teams to NFL-high and team-record 10 blocked kicks and five touchdowns. Entered NFL in 1978 as special teams coach for San Francisco 49ers. Also, held special teams and tight ends coaching duties with Cincinnati Bengals (1979-80) and Philadelphia Eagles (1983-85). No pro playing experience. Career record: 4-11.

Background: Began coaching career in 1964 as general assistant coach at the Air Force Academy while serving as a military officer. Spent three years at Air Force, then was commercial airline pilot for two years. Returned to coaching in 1968 as head freshman coach at Colgate. Spent three years as assistant at U.S. Naval Academy (1969-72), then became receivers coach at Oklahoma State (1973, 1975), offensive coordinator at Army (1974), and offensive assistant at UCLA (1976-77). Played center and linebacker for Naval Academy, graduating in 1960.

Personal: Born November 22, 1938, Altoona, Pa. Frank and wife, Barbara, live in Kansas City, and have two children—Frank, Jr., and Jennifer Anne.

Assistant Coaches

Ed Beckman, special teams; born January 2, 1955, Key West, Fla., lives in Kansas City. Tight end Florida State 1970-73. Pro tight end Kansas City Chiefs 1977-84. Pro coach: Joined Chiefs in 1987.

Tom Bettis, defensive backfield; born March 17, 1933, Chicago, Ill., lives in Kansas City. Linebacker-offensive guard Purdue 1951-54. Pro linebacker Green Bay Packers 1955-61, Pittsburgh Steelers 1962, Chicago Bears 1963. Pro coach: Kansas City Chiefs 1966-77 (head coach for final seven games, 1977), St. Louis Cardinals 1978-84, Cleveland Browns 1985, Houston Oilers 1986-87, rejoined Chiefs in 1988.

David Brazil, linebackers; born March 25, 1936, Detroit, Mich., lives in Kansas City. No college or pro playing experience. College coach: Holy Cross 1968-69, Tulsa 1970-71, Eastern Michigan 1972-74, Boston College 1978-79. Pro coach: Detroit Wheels (WFL) 1975, Chicago Fire (WFL) 1976, joined Chiefs in 1984.

J.D. Helm, offensive quality control, tight ends; born December 27, 1940, El Dorado Springs, Mo., lives in Overland Park, Kan. Running back Kansas 1959-60. No pro playing experience. College coach: Brigham Young 1969-75. Pro coach: Joined Chiefs in 1976.

C.T. Hewgley, strength and conditioning coordinator, linemen; born August 22, 1925, Nashville, Tenn., lives in Kansas City. Tackle Wyoming 1947-50. No pro playing experience. College coach: Miami 1968-70, Wyoming 1971-73, Nebraska-Omaha 1974 (head coach), Michigan State 1976-79, Arizona State 1980-82. Pro coach: Joined Chiefs in 1983.

Don Lawrence, defensive line; born June 4, 1937, Cleveland, Ohio, lives in Kansas City. Tackle Notre Dame 1953-55. Pro tackle Washington Redskins 1956-61. College coach: Notre Dame 1963-67, Kansas State 1968-69, Cincinnati 1970, Virginia 1971-73 (head coach), Texas Christian 1974-75, Missouri 1976-77. Pro coach: British Columbia Lions (CFL) 1978-79, Kansas City Chiefs 1980-82, Buffalo Bills 1983-84, Tampa Bay Buccaneers 1985-86, rejoined Chiefs in 1987.

Billie Matthews, running backs; born March 15, 1930, Houston, Tex., lives in Kansas City. Quarterback Southern University 1948-51. No pro playing experience. College coach: Kansas 1970, UCLA 1971-78. Pro coach: San Francisco 49ers 1979-82, Philadelphia Eagles 1983-84, Indianapolis Colts 1985-86, joined Chiefs in 1987.

Kansas City Chiefs 1988 First-Year Roster

Name	Pos.	Ht.	Wt.	Birth-date	College	Hometown	How Acq.
Abdur-Ra'oof, Azizuddin	WR	6-0	200	4/8/65	Maryland	Annapolis, Md.	D9
Ambrose, J.R.	WR	6-0	188	4/19/64	Mississippi	Monroe, La.	D4
Brock, Ray (1)	C	6-3	270	8/30/63	Louisiana State	Portland, Ore.	FA
Collier, Willie	CB	5-10	190	8/31/64	Fort Valley State	Montezuma, Ga.	FA
DeLine, Dave	K	5-10	167	1/12/65	Colorado	Denver, Colo.	FA
Espinoza, Alex (1)	QB	6-1	193	5/31/64	Iowa State	Los Angeles, Calif.	FA
Freeman, Tom	G	6-4	275	3/9/65	Notre Dame	Shawnee Mission, Kan.	FA
Gaines, Darryl	CB-S	5-11	197	11/9/64	Miss. Valley State	Mobile, Ala.	FA
Gamble, Kenny	RB	5-10	197	3/8/65	Colgate	Holyoke, Mass.	D10
Hobbs, Stephen	WR	5-11	190	11/14/65	North Alabama	Mendenhall, Miss.	FA
Holt, Daryl	C	6-2	257	8/30/64	Vanderbilt	Gallatin, Tenn.	FA
Hudson, Doug (1)	QB	6-2	201	9/11/64	Nicholls State	Gulf Breeze, Fla.	D7-'87
Ingram, Byron (1)	G	6-2	295	11/17/64	Eastern Kentucky	Lexington, Ky.	FA
Jenkins, Keyvan (1)	RB	5-10	192	1/6/61	Nevada-Las Vegas	Stockton, Calif.	FA
Johnson, Sidney (1)	CB	5-9	170	3/7/65	California	Cerritos, Calif.	FA
Kantner, Craig	C	6-3	272	4/23/65	Ball State	Mentone, Ind.	FA
Leonard, Thomas	RB	6-0	219	3/17/64	Miss. Valley State	Jackson, Miss.	FA
Lowery, Thomas	G	6-4	276	2/5/62	Jackson State	Prairie Point, Miss.	FA
MacDonald, Dan (1)	LB	6-3	240	9/2/63	Idaho State	San Bernardino, Calif.	FA
McManus, Danny	QB	6-0	205	6/17/65	Florida State	Dania, Fla.	D11
Montoya, Mark	P	5-9	175	4/17/64	Eastern New Mexico	Morton, Tex.	FA
Norman, Kurt (1)	LB	6-2	230	8/12/63	Hillsdale	Pontiac, Mich.	FA
Porter, Kevin	CB-S	5-10	210	4/11/66	Auburn	Bronx, N.Y.	D3
Randolph, Paul	LB	6-0	234	6/22/66	Tennessee-Martin	Gainesville, Ga.	FA
Ray, Mickey	LB	6-2	230	11/2/65	Appalachian State	Asheville, N.C.	FA
Roberts, Alfredo	TE	6-3	246	3/1/65	Miami	Hollywood, Fla.	D8
Saxon, James	RB	5-11	195	3/23/66	San Jose State	Burton, S.C.	D6
Schnitzius, Brett	T	6-6	282	10/6/63	Utah State	San Diego, Calif.	FA
Smith, Neil	DE	6-4	260	4/10/66	Nebraska	New Orleans, La.	D1
Standifer, Bob (1)	NT	6-5	265	6/3/63	Tenn.-Chattanooga	Chattanooga, Tenn.	FA
Stedman, Troy	LB	6-3	235	5/19/65	Washburn	Cedar Falls, Iowa	D7
Stewart, Michael	CB-S	6-0	191	7/30/65	Yale	Manchester, N.H.	FA
Taylor, Kitrick (1)	WR	5-10	183	7/22/64	Washington State	Claremont, Calif.	D5-'87
Thetford, Pat (1)	TE	6-3	245	9/2/63	Missouri	Kansas City, Mo.	FA
Van Drutten, Richard	T	6-5	270	9/23/62	Abilene Christian	Johannesburg, So. Africa	FA
White, Terry	CB	5-8	170	12/20/64	West Virginia	Cambridge, Ohio	FA
Williams, Cecil (1)	TE	6-4	235	2/4/62	Cal State-Sacramento	Sacramento, Calif.	FA

The term NFL Rookie is defined as a player who is in his first season of professional football and has not been on the roster of another professional football team for any regular-season or postseason games. A Rookie is designated by an "R" on NFL rosters. Players who have been active in another professional football league or players who have NFL experience, including either preseason training camp or being on an active roster for fewer than three regular-season or postseason games, are termed NFL First-Year Players. An NFL First-Year Player is designated by a "1" on NFL rosters. Thereafter, a player on an NFL active roster for at least three regular-season or postseason games is credited with an additional year of NFL playing experience.

NOTES

Carl Mauck, offensive line; born July 7, 1947, McLeansboro, Ill., lives in Kansas City. Center Southern Illinois 1965-68. Pro center San Diego Chargers 1969-74, Houston Oilers 1975-80. Pro coach: New Orleans Saints 1982-85, joined Chiefs in 1986.

Rod Rust, defensive coordinator; born August 2, 1928, Webster City, Iowa, lives in Kansas City. Center-linebacker Iowa State 1947-49. No pro playing experience. College coach: New Mexico 1960-62, Stanford 1963-66, North Texas State 1967-72 (head coach). Pro coach: Montreal Alouettes (CFL) 1973-75, Philadelphia Eagles 1976-77, Kansas City Chiefs 1978-82, New England Patriots 1983-87, rejoined Chiefs in 1988.

George Sefcik, offensive coordinator; born December 27, 1939, Cleveland, Ohio, lives in Kansas City. Halfback Notre Dame 1959-61. No pro playing experience. College coach: Notre Dame 1963-68, Kentucky 1969-72. Pro coach: Baltimore Colts 1973-74, Cleveland Browns 1975-77, Cincinnati Bengals 1978-83, Green Bay Packers 1984-87, joined Chiefs in 1988.

Richard Wood, receivers; born February 2, 1936, Lanett, Ala., lives in Kansas City. Quarterback Auburn 1956-59. Pro quarterback Baltimore Colts 1960-61, San Diego Chargers 1962, Denver Broncos 1962, New York Jets 1963-64, Oakland Raiders 1965, Miami Dolphins 1966. College coach: Georgia 1967-68, Mississippi 1971-73, Auburn 1986. Pro coach: Oakland Raiders 1969-70, Cleveland Browns 1974, New Orleans Saints 1976-77, Atlanta Falcons 1978-82, Philadelphia Eagles 1983, joined Chiefs in 1987.

LOS ANGELES RAIDERS

American Football Conference Western Division

Team Colors: Silver and Black

332 Center Street
El Segundo, California 90245
Telephone: (213) 322-3451

Club Officials

Managing General Partner: Al Davis
Executive Assistant: Al LoCasale
Player Personnel: Ron Wolf
Pro Football Scout: George Karras
Finance: Gary Huff
Senior Executive: John Herrera
Senior Administrators: Irv Kaze, Mike Ornstein
Community Relations: Gil Lafferty-Hernandez
Publications: Steve Hartman
Ticket Operations: Peter Eiges
Trainers: George Anderson, H. Rod Martin
Equipment Manager: Richard Romanski

Stadium: Los Angeles Memorial Coliseum •
Capacity: 92,488
3911 South Figueroa Street
Los Angeles, California 90037

Playing Surface: Grass

Training Camp: Radisson Hotel
Oxnard, California 93030

1988 Schedule

Preseason

Aug. 6	at San Francisco	6:00
Aug. 13	**Dallas**	1:00
Aug. 20	**Washington**	7:00
Aug. 26	at Chicago	8:00

Regular Season

Sept. 4	**San Diego**	1:00
Sept. 11	at Houston	3:00
Sept. 18	**Los Angeles Rams**	1:00
Sept. 26	at Denver (Monday)	6:00
Oct. 2	**Cincinnati**	1:00
Oct. 9	**Miami**	1:00
Oct. 16	at Kansas City	12:00
Oct. 23	at New Orleans	12:00
Oct. 30	**Kansas City**	1:00
Nov. 6	at San Diego	5:00
Nov. 13	at San Francisco	1:00
Nov. 20	**Atlanta**	1:00
Nov. 28	at Seattle (Monday)	6:00
Dec. 4	**Denver**	1:00
Dec. 11	at Buffalo	1:00
Dec. 18	**Seattle**	1:00

Raiders Coaching History

Oakland 1960-81
(270-154-11)

1960-61	Eddie Erdelatz*	6-10-0
1961-62	Marty Feldman**	2-15-0
1962	Red Conkright	1-8-0
1963-65	Al Davis	23-16-3
1966-68	John Rauch	35-10-1
1969-78	John Madden	112-39-7
1979-87	Tom Flores	91-56-0

*Released after two games in 1961
**Released after five games in 1962

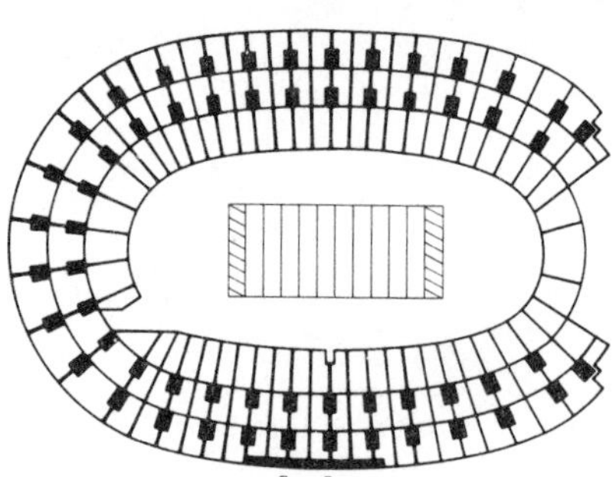

MEMORIAL COLISEUM

Record Holders

Individual Records—Career

Category	Name	Performance
Rushing (Yds.)	Marcus Allen, 1982-1987	6,151
Passing (Yds.)	Ken Stabler, 1970-79	19,078
Passing (TDs)	Ken Stabler, 1970-79	150
Receiving (No.)	Fred Biletnikoff, 1965-1978	589
Receiving (Yds.)	Fred Biletnikoff, 1965-1978	8,974
Interceptions	Willie Brown, 1967-1978	39
	Lester Hayes, 1977-1986	39
Punting (Avg.)	Ray Guy, 1973-1986	42.5
Punt Return (Avg.)	Claude Gibson, 1963-65	12.6
Kickoff Return (Avg.)	Jack Larscheid, 1960-61	28.4
Field Goals	George Blanda, 1967-1975	156
Touchdowns (Tot.)	Fred Biletnikoff, 1965-1978	77
Points	George Blanda, 1967-1975	863

Individual Records—Single Season

Category	Name	Performance
Rushing (Yds.)	Marcus Allen, 1985	1,759
Passing (Yds.)	Ken Stabler, 1979	3,615
Passing (TDs)	Daryle Lamonica, 1969	34
Receiving (No.)	Todd Christensen, 1986	95
Receiving (Yds.)	Art Powell, 1964	1,361
Interceptions	Lester Hayes, 1980	13
Punting (Avg.)	Ray Guy, 1973	45.3
Punt Return (Avg.)	Claude Gibson, 1964	14.4
Kickoff Return (Avg.)	Harold Hart, 1975	30.5
Field Goals	George Blanda, 1973	23
Touchdowns (Tot.)	Marcus Allen, 1984	18
Points	George Blanda, 1968	117

Individual Records—Single Game

Category	Name	Performance
Rushing (Yds.)	Bo Jackson, 11-30-87	221
Passing (Yds.)	Cotton Davidson, 10-25-64	427
Passing (TDs)	Tom Flores, 12-22-63	6
	Daryle Lamonica, 10-19-69	6
Receiving (No.)	Dave Casper, 10-3-76	12
Receiving (Yds.)	Art Powell, 12-22-63	247
Interceptions	Many times	3
	Last time by Charles Phillips, 12-8-75	
Field Goals	Many times	4
	Last time by Chris Bahr, 10-6-85	
Touchdowns (Tot.)	Art Powell, 12-22-63	4
	Marcus Allen, 9-24-84	4
Points	Art Powell, 12-22-63	24
	Marcus Allen, 9-24-84	24

1987 Team Record

Preseason (1-3)

Date	Result		Opponents
8/15	L	16-42	San Francisco
8/22	L	3- 7	Buffalo
8/30	W	34-10	at Dallas
9/5	L	17-20	Chicago
		70-79	

Regular Season (5-10)

Date	Result		Opponents	Att.
9/13	W	20- 0	at Green Bay	54,983
9/20	W	27- 7	Detroit	50,300
9/27	C		at Houston	
10/4	W	35-17	Kansas City	10,708
10/12	L	14-30	at Denver	61,230
10/18	L	17-23	San Diego	23,541
10/25	L	13-35	Seattle	52,735
11/1	L	23-26	at New England	60,664
11/8	L	20-31	at Minnesota	57,150
11/15	L	14-16	at San Diego	60,639
11/22	L	17-23	Denver	61,318
11/30	W	37-14	at Seattle	62,802
12/6	W	34-21	Buffalo	43,143
12/13	L	10-16	at Kansas City	63,834
12/20	L	17-24	Cleveland	40,275
12/27	L	3- 6	Chicago	78,019

C (Cancelled due to players' strike.)

Score by Periods

	1	2	3	4	OT		Total
Raiders	49	85	72	95	0	—	301
Opponents	62	98	64	65	0	—	289

Attendance

Home 350,409 Away 421,302 Total 771,711
Single-game home record, 90,334 (1-1-84)
Single-season home record, 516,205 (1986)

1987 Team Statistics

	Raiders	Opp.
Total First Downs	300	267
Rushing	107	98
Passing	158	135
Penalty	35	34
Third Down: Made/Att.	75/200	81/207
Fourth Down: Made/Att.	3/9	7/14
Total Net Yards	5267	4364
Avg. Per Game	351.1	290.9
Total Plays	985	938
Avg. Per Play	5.3	4.7
Net Yards Rushing	2197	1637
Avg. Per Game	146.5	109.1
Total Rushes	475	469
Net Yards Passing	3070	2727
Avg. Per Game	204.7	181.8
Sacked/Yards Lost	53/359	44/361
Gross Yards	3429	3088
Att./Completions	457/247	425/224
Completion Pct.	54.0	52.7
Had Intercepted	18	13
Punts/Avg.	71/39.4	78/42.6
Net Punting Avg.	34.4	36.2
Penalties/Yards Lost	114/1048	95/652
Fumbles/Ball Lost	24/13	28/15
Touchdowns	35	33
Rushing	13	12
Passing	19	18
Returns	3	3
Avg. Time of Possession	30:45	29:15

1987 Individual Statistics

Scoring

	TD R	TD P	TD Rt	PAT	FG	Saf	TP
Bahr	0	0	0	27/28	19/29	0	84
B. Jackson	4	2	0	0/0	0/0	0	36
Allen	5	0	0	0/0	0/0	0	30
Lofton	0	5	0	0/0	0/0	0	30
Do. Williams	0	5	0	0/0	0/0	0	30
Aikens	0	3	0	0/0	0/0	0	18
Christensen	0	2	0	0/0	0/0	0	12
C. Ellis	2	0	0	0/0	0/0	0	12
Hardy	0	0	0	7/7	0/1	0	7
Calhoun	0	0	1	0/0	0/0	0	6
Evans	1	0	0	0/0	0/0	0	6
Horton	0	1	0	0/0	0/0	0	6
McElroy	0	0	1	0/0	0/0	0	6
Mueller	1	0	0	0/0	0/0	0	6
Perry	0	1	0	0/0	0/0	0	6
Toran	0	0	1	0/0	0/0	0	6
Raiders	13	19	3	34/35	19/30	0	301
Opponents	12	18	3	31/33	20/29	0	289

Passing

	Att.	Comp.	Yds.	Pct.	TD	Int.	Tkld.	Rate
Wilson	266	152	2070	57.1	12	8	33/238	84.6
Hilger	106	55	706	51.9	2	6	12/80	55.8
Evans	83	39	630	47.0	5	4	7/38	72.9
Allen	2	1	23	50.0	0	0	1/3	91.7
Raiders	457	247	3429	54.0	19	18	53/359	75.8
Opponents	425	224	3088	52.7	18	13	44/361	77.7

Rushing

	Att.	Yds.	Avg.	LG	TD
Allen	200	754	3.8	44	5
B. Jackson	81	554	6.8	91t	4
Mueller	37	175	4.7	35	1
Evans	11	144	13.1	24	1
C. Ellis	33	138	4.2	14	2
Strachan	28	108	3.9	20	0
Horton	31	95	3.1	14	0
Wilson	17	91	5.4	16	0
McLemore, Ind.-Raiders	17	58	3.4	9	0
Harrison	9	49	5.4	13	0
Calhoun	7	36	5.1	18	0
Hawkins	4	24	6.0	7	0
Smith	5	18	3.6	15	0
Hilger	8	8	1.0	6	0
Aikens	1	1	1.0	1	0
Browne	2	1	0.5	2	0
Lofton	1	1	1.0	1	0
Raiders	475	2197	4.6	91t	13
Opponents	469	1637	3.5	28	12

Receiving

	No.	Yds.	Avg.	LG	TD
Allen	51	410	8.0	39	0
Christensen	47	663	14.1	33	2
Lofton	41	880	21.5	49	5
Do. Williams	21	330	15.7	33	5
B. Jackson	16	136	8.5	23	2
Fernandez	14	236	16.9	47	0
Mueller	11	95	8.6	14	0
Aikens	8	134	16.8	32t	3
Lathan	5	98	19.6	33	0
C. Ellis	5	39	7.8	15	0
Da. Williams	4	104	26.0	44	0
Strachan	4	42	10.5	14	0
R. Wheeler	3	61	20.3	29	0
Smith	3	46	15.3	32	0
Horton	3	44	14.7	32t	1
Harrison	2	18	9.0	15	0
Junkin	2	15	7.5	8	0
McLemore, Ind.-Raiders	2	9	4.5	5	0
Browne	2	8	4.0	5	0
Hester	1	30	30.0	30	0
Calhoun	1	17	17.0	17	0
Woods	1	14	14.0	14	0
Hawkins	1	6	6.0	6	0
Perry	1	3	3.0	3t	1
Raiders	247	3429	13.9	49	19
Opponents	224	3088	13.8	67t	18

Interceptions

	No.	Yds.	Avg.	LG	TD
McElroy	4	41	10.3	35t	1
Toran	3	48	16.0	48t	1
Haynes	2	9	4.5	7	0
Anderson	1	58	58.0	58	0
Adams	1	8	8.0	8	0
King	1	8	8.0	8	0
Millen	1	6	6.0	6	0
Raiders	13	178	13.7	58	2
Opponents	18	371	20.6	75t	2

Punting

	No.	Yds.	Avg.	In 20	LG
Talley	56	2277	40.7	13	63
Gamache	13	519	39.9	2	53
Raiders	71	2796	39.4	15	63
Opponents	78	3321	42.6	19	65

Punt Returns

	No.	FC	Yds.	Avg.	LG	TD
Woods	26	4	189	7.3	34	0
Calhoun	8	1	92	11.5	55t	1
Adams	5	2	39	7.8	12	0
Fellows	2	0	19	9.5	18	0
Harkey	2	0	17	8.5	9	0
J. Davis	1	0	0	0.0	0	0
Raiders	44	7	356	8.1	55t	1
Opponents	34	8	256	7.5	27	0

Kickoff Returns

	No.	Yds.	Avg.	LG	TD
Mueller	27	588	21.8	46	0
Do. Williams	14	221	15.8	27	0
Calhoun	9	217	24.1	50	0
Adams	3	61	20.3	25	0
Woods	3	55	18.3	22	0
Foster	1	12	12.0	12	0
Harkey	1	20	20.0	20	0
Millen	1	0	0.0	0	0
R. Washington	1	0	0.0	0	0
Raiders	60	1174	19.6	50	0
Opponents	59	1136	19.3	42	0

Sacks

	No.
Townsend	8.5
Jones	6.0
King	4.5
Robinson	4.5
Long	4.0
Martin	3.5
Taylor	3.0
Brown	2.0
Ackerman	1.0
Buczkowski	1.0
Cormier	1.0
McMillen	1.0
Millen	1.0
Pickel	1.0
R. Washington	1.0
Browner, S.F.-Raiders	0.5
Raiders	44.0
Opponents	53.0

Los Angeles Raiders 1988 Veteran Roster

No.	Name	Pos.	Ht.	Wt.	Birth-date	NFL Exp.	College	Hometown	How Acq.	'87 Games/ Starts
44	Adams, Stefon	S	5-10	185	8/11/63	3	East Carolina	High Point, N.C.	D3-'85	9/0
32	Allen, Marcus	RB	6-2	205	3/26/60	7	Southern California	San Diego, Calif.	D1-'82	12/12
33	Anderson, Eddie	S	6-1	200	7/22/63	3	Fort Valley State	Warner Robins, Ga.	FA-'87	13/3
10	Bahr, Chris	K	5-10	170	2/3/53	13	Penn State	Feasterville, Pa.	FA-'80	13/0
56	Barnes, Jeff	LB	6-2	230	3/1/55	12	California	Hayward, Calif.	D5-'77	7/0
91	t-Bennett, Barry	DE	6-4	260	12/10/55	11	Concordia	St. Paul, Minn.	T(NYJ)-'88	13/11
	t-Carter, Russell	CB-S	6-2	195	2/10/62	5	Southern Methodist	Ardmore, Pa.	T(NYJ)-'88	8/6
46	Christensen, Todd	TE	6-3	230	8/3/56	10	Brigham Young	Eugene, Ore.	FA-'79	12/12
78	Clay, John	T	6-5	295	5/1/64	2	Missouri	St. Louis, Mo.	D1-'87	10/9
45	†Davis, James	S	6-0	195	6/12/57	7	Southern	Los Angeles, Calif.	D5-'81	12/1
11	Evans, Vince	QB	6-2	200	6/14/55	9	Southern California	Greensboro, N.C.	FA-'87	3/3
21	Fellows, Ron	CB	6-0	175	11/7/58	8	Missouri	South Bend, Ind.	T(Dall)-'87	12/2
86	Fernandez, Mervyn	WR	6-3	200	12/29/59	2	San Jose State	San Jose, Calif.	D10-'83	7/7
63	Gesek, John	C-G	6-5	275	2/18/63	2	Cal State-Sacramento	Danville, Calif.	D10-'87	3/1
73	Hannah, Charley	G	6-5	265	7/26/55	12	Alabama	Chattanooga, Tenn.	T(TB)-'83	5/5
22	†Haynes, Mike	CB	6-2	190	7/1/53	13	Arizona State	Los Angeles, Calif.	T(NE)-'83	8/7
84	Hester, Jessie	WR	5-11	170	1/21/63	4	Florida State	Belle Glade, Fla.	D1-'85	10/0
12	Hilger, Rusty	QB	6-4	205	5/9/62	4	Oklahoma State	Oklahoma City, Okla.	D6-'85	5/5
76	†Holloway, Brian	T	6-7	285	7/25/59	8	Stanford	Potomac, Md.	T(NE)-'87	12/8
34	Jackson, Bo	RB	6-1	230	11/30/62	2	Auburn	Bessemer, Ala.	D7-'87	7/5
74	Jordan, Shelby	T	6-7	285	1/23/52	12	Washington, Mo.	East St. Louis, Ill.	T(NE)-'83	0*
87	Junkin, Trey	TE	6-2	230	1/23/61	6	Louisiana Tech	Winfield, La.	FA-'85	12/1
59	Kimmel, Jamie	LB	6-3	235	3/28/62	3	Syracuse	Conklin, N.Y.	D4-'85	15/0
52	King, Linden	LB	6-4	250	6/28/55	11	Colorado State	Colorado Springs, Colo.	FA-'86	12/8
40	†Lee, Zeph	RB	6-3	210	6/17/63	2	Southern California	San Francisco, Calif.	D9-'86	3/0*
51	Lewis, Bill	G-C	6-7	275	7/12/63	3	Nebraska	Sioux City, Iowa	D7-'86	8/6
80	Lofton, James	WR	6-3	190	7/5/56	11	Stanford	Los Angeles, Calif.	T(GB)-'87	12/12
75	Long, Howie	DE	6-5	265	1/6/60	8	Villanova	Charlestown, Mass.	D2-'81	14/14
53	Martin, Rod	LB	6-2	225	4/7/54	12	Southern California	Los Angeles, Calif.	D12-'77	12/12
65	Marvin, Mickey	G	6-4	270	10/5/55	11	Tennessee	Hendersonville, N.C.	D4-'77	1/0
26	McElroy, Vann	S	6-2	195	1/13/60	7	Baylor	Uvalde, Tex.	D3-'82	12/12
54	McKenzie, Reggie	LB	6-1	235	2/8/63	4	Tennessee	Knoxville, Tenn.	D10-'85	10/5
20	McLemore, Chris	RB	6-1	230	12/31/63	2	Arizona	Las Vegas, Nev.	D11-'87	5/0*
55	†Millen, Matt	LB	6-2	245	3/12/58	9	Penn State	Hokendauqua, Pa.	D2-'80	12/12
72	Mosebar, Don	C	6-6	275	9/11/61	6	Southern California	Visalia, Calif.	D1-'83	12/12
42	Mueller, Vance	RB	6-0	210	5/5/64	3	Occidental	Jackson, Calif.	D4-'86	12/0
81	Parker, Andy	TE	6-5	245	9/8/61	5	Utah	Ramona, Calif.	D5-'84	12/0
71	Pickel, Bill	DT	6-5	260	11/5/59	6	Rutgers	Brooklyn, N.Y.	D2-'83	12/11
16	Plunkett, Jim	QB	6-2	225	12/5/47	17	Stanford	San Jose, Calif.	FA-'78	0*
77	†Riehm, Chris	G	6-6	275	4/4/61	2	Ohio State	Toledo, Ohio	FA-'86	1/0
57	Robinson, Jerry	LB	6-2	225	12/18/56	10	UCLA	Santa Rosa, Calif.	T(Phil)-'85	12/12
43	Seale, Sam	CB	5-9	185	10/6/62	5	Western State, Colo.	East Orange, N.J.	D8-'84	12/5
35	Smith, Steve	RB	6-1	235	8/30/64	2	Penn State	Clinton, Md.	D3-'87	7/3
39	†Strachan, Steve	RB	6-1	220	3/22/63	4	Boston College	Burlington, Mass.	D11-'85	11/3
5	Talley, Stan	P	6-5	220	9/5/58	2	Texas Christian	Dana Point, Calif.	FA-'87	12/0
96	†Taylor, Malcolm	DT	6-6	280	6/20/60	5	Tennessee State	Crystal Springs, Miss.	FA-'87	12/3
30	†Toran, Stacey	S	6-3	200	10/11/61	5	Notre Dame	Indianapolis, Ind.	D6-'84	12/12
93	Townsend, Greg	DE	6-3	250	11/3/61	6	Texas Christian	Compton, Calif.	D4-'83	13/1
48	Washington, Lionel	CB	6-0	185	10/21/60	6	Tulane	New Orleans, La.	T(StL)-'87	11/10
67	Wheeler, Dwight	G-C	6-3	280	1/3/55	8	Tennessee State	Memphis, Tenn.	FA-'87	7/4*
68	Wilkerson, Bruce	G	6-5	280	7/28/64	2	Tennessee	Philadelphia, Tenn.	D2-'87	11/5
98	†Willis, Mitch	DT	6-8	275	3/16/62	4	Southern Methodist	Arlington, Tex.	D7-'84	10/0
6	†Wilson, Marc	QB	6-6	205	2/15/57	9	Brigham Young	Seattle, Wash.	D1-'80	15/7
90	Wise, Mike	DE	6-7	265	6/5/64	2	California-Davis	Novato, Calif.	D4-'86	0*
88	Woods, Chris	WR	5-11	190	7/19/62	2	Auburn	Birmingham, Ala.	SD1-'84	9/1
66	Wright, Steve	T	6-6	270	4/8/59	6	Northern Iowa	Wayzata, Minn.	FA-'87	9/6

* Jordan and Plunkett missed '87 season due to injury; Lee played 1 game with Denver, 2 with L.A. Raiders in '87; McLemore played 2 games with Indianapolis, 3 with L.A. Raiders; Wheeler played 3 games with San Diego, 4 with L.A. Raiders; Wise active for 1 game but did not play.

†Option playout; subject to developments.

t-Raiders traded for Bennett (N.Y. Jets), Carter (N.Y. Jets).

Traded—Defensive end Sean Jones to Houston, wide receiver Dokie Williams to San Francisco.

Retired—Curt Marsh, 7-year guard, missed '87 with injury; Dean Miraldi, 6-year guard, 10 games in '87.

Also played with Raiders in '87—DT Rick Ackerman (3 games), WR Carl Aikens (3), DE Brian Belway (1), G Barry Black (3), DE-LB Ron Brown (3), RB Jim Browne (2), LB Keith Browner (1), LB Darryl Byrd (3), RB Rick Calhoun (3), CB Chetti Carr (2), DE Ted Chapura (2), LB Joe Cormier (2), T Bruce Davis (4), G Andy Dickerson (1), C Paul Dufault (1), RB Craig Ellis (3), LB Jim Ellis (3), S Ron Foster (3), P Vince Gamache (3), DE Rick Goltz (1), LB Darryl Goodlow (2), DE Paul Grimes (2), K David Hardy (2), CB-S Lance Harkey (2), CB-S Rob Harrison (2), CB Greg Hill (2), CB Rod Hill (4), RB Ethan Horton (4), LB Leonard Jackson (1), S Victor Jackson (2), WR Greg Lathan (3), WR Wade Lockett (2), LB Dan McMillen (1), LB Mike Noble (1), TE Mario Perry (3), T David Pyles (2), C Shawn Regent (3), DT Mike Rodriguez (1), CB Willie Teal (1), CB Tony Tillmon (3), LB Ronnie Washington (2), TE Ron Wheeler (3), WR David Williams (3), S Demise Williams (1), CB Ricky Williams (1), QB Scott Woolf (1), G Jon Zogg (1).

COACHING STAFF

Head Coach, Mike Shanahan

Pro Career: Named eighth head coach in Raiders history on February 29, 1988. Had been NFL assistant coach previous four years with the Denver Broncos. Offensive coordinator with Broncos AFC championship teams in 1986-87. Denver had 49-20-1 record during his four seasons there, winning three division titles and two conference championships. No pro playing experience.

Background: Entered coaching ranks in 1973 as graduate assistant at Eastern Illinois University (where he had played quarterback). Joined staff at Oklahoma in 1975, working with running backs and receivers as Sooners won NCAA national championship. Served as offensive backfield coach at Northern Arizona in 1977. In 1978, was offensive coordinator at Eastern Illinois, helping guide them to NCAA Division II national championship. Offensive coordinator at Minnesota in 1979. Offensive coordinator at Florida 1980-83 as Gators built 32-15-1 record and played in bowl games in each of those four seasons. Served as assistant head coach at Florida in 1983 at age of 31. Had 77-29-3 record as college assistant coach.

Personal: Born August 24, 1952, in Oak Park, Ill. Mike and wife Peggy live in El Segundo, Calif., with their son Kyle and daughter Krystal.

Assistant Coaches

Willie Brown, defensive backfield; born December 2, 1940, Yazoo City, Miss., lives in Rancho Palos Verdes, Calif. Defensive back Grambling 1959-62. Pro cornerback Denver Broncos 1963-66, Oakland Raiders 1967-78. Pro coach: Joined Raiders in 1979.

John Dunn, strength and conditioning; born July 22, 1956, Great Barrington, Mass., lives in El Segundo, Calif. Guard Penn State 1975-77. No pro playing experience. College coach Penn State 1978. Pro coach: Washington Redskins 1984-86, joined Raiders in 1987.

Alex Gibbs, special assistant to head coach; born February 11, 1941, Morganton, N.C., lives in El Segundo, Calif. Running back-defensive back Davidson 1959-63. No pro playing experience. College coach: Duke 1969-70, Kentucky 1971-72, West Virginia 1973-74, Ohio State 1975-78, Auburn 1979-81, Georgia 1982-83. Pro coach: Denver Broncos 1984-87, joined Raiders in 1988.

Sam Gruneisen, linebackers; born January 16, 1941, Louisville, Ky., lives in El Segundo, Calif. Tight end-linebacker-kicker Villanova 1959-61. Pro center San Diego Chargers 1962-72, Houston Oilers 1973. College coach: Grossmont, Calif., J.C. 1981, California 1982-83, San Jose State 1986. Pro coach: Los Angeles Express (USFL) 1984-85, joined Raiders in 1987.

Earl Leggett, defensive line; born May 5, 1933, Jacksonville, Fla., lives in Fountain Valley, Calif. Tackle Hinds J.C. 1953-54, Louisiana State 1955-56. Pro defensive tackle Chicago Bears 1957-65, Los Angeles Rams 1966, New Orleans Saints 1967-68. College coach: Nicholls State 1971, Texas Christian 1972-73. Pro coach: Southern California Sun (WFL) 1974-75, Seattle Seahawks 1976-77, San Francisco 49ers 1978, joined Raiders in 1980.

Nick Nicolau, receivers; born May 5, 1933, New York, N.Y., lives in El Segundo, Calif. Running back Southern Connecticut 1957-59. No pro playing experience. College coach: Southern Connecticut 1960, Springfield 1961, Bridgeport 1962-69 (head coach 1965-69), Massachusetts 1970, Connecticut 1971-72, Kentucky 1973-75, Kent State 1976. Pro coach: Hamilton Tiger-Cats (CFL) 1977, Montreal Alouettes (CFL) 1978-79, New Orleans Saints 1980, Denver Broncos 1981-87, joined Raiders in 1988.

Terry Robiskie, coaches assistant; born November 12, 1954, New Orleans, La., lives in Beverly Hills, Calif. Running back Louisiana State 1973-76. Pro running back Oakland Raiders 1977-79, Miami Dolphins 1980-81. Pro coach: Joined Raiders in 1982.

Los Angeles Raiders 1988 First-Year Roster

Name	Pos.	Ht.	Wt.	Birth-date	College	Hometown	How Acq.
Alexander, Mike	WR-TE	6-3	215	3/19/65	Penn State	Piscataway, N.J.	D8
Beuerlein, Steve (1)	QB	6-2	205	3/7/65	Notre Dame	Fullerton, Calif.	D4-'87
Brown, Tim	WR	6-0	190	7/22/66	Notre Dame	Dallas, Tex.	D1a
Buczkowski, Bob (1)	DE	6-5	270	5/5/64	Pittsburgh	Monroeville, Pa.	D1-'86
Cooper, Scott (1)	DE	6-5	275	6/20/64	Kearney State	Oshkosh, Neb.	FA
Cormier, Joe (1)	LB	6-6	235	5/3/63	Southern California	Gardena, Calif.	FA-'87
Crudup, Derrick	CB	6-2	210	2/15/65	Oklahoma	Delray Beach, Fla.	D7
Davis, Scott	DE	6-7	270	8/7/65	Illinois	Plainfield, Ill.	D1c
Grabisna, Erwin	LB	6-3	250	8/28/66	Case Western	Parma, Ohio	D6
Grimes, Phil (1)	DE	6-5	255	2/26/65	Central Missouri	Birmingham, Ala.	FA
Harrell, Newt	G	6-5	295	9/7/64	West Texas State	Canyon, Tex.	D10
Hutson, Brian (1)	S	6-1	195	2/20/65	Mississippi State	Brandon, Miss.	FA-'87
Johnson, Matt (1)	S	6-2	205	9/10/62	Southern California	San Jose, Calif.	FA
Knapp, Gregg (1)	QB	6-4	200	3/15/63	Cal State-Sacramento	Seal Beach, Calif.	FA
Kunkel, Greg	G	6-5	285	2/9/64	Kentucky	Elsmere, Ky.	D12
McDaniel, Terence	CB	5-10	170	2/8/65	Tennessee	Saginaw, Mich.	D1b
Price, Dennis	CB	6-1	170	6/14/65	UCLA	Long Beach, Calif.	D5
Reynosa, Jim (1)	LB	6-5	255	5/19/64	Arizona State	Glendale, Calif.	FA
Rother, Tim	DT	6-7	265	9/28/65	Nebraska	Bellevue, Neb.	D4
Short, Stanley (1)	G	6-4	270	9/20/63	Penn State	Fort Riley, Kan.	FA
Stone, Tim (1)	T	6-5	290	11/24/60	Kansas State	Elmira, N.Y.	FA
Tabor, Scott	P	6-3	195	6/15/65	California	Lakeport, Calif.	D9b
Ware, Reggie	RB	6-1	240	2/8/65	Auburn	Huntsville, Ala.	D9a
Weber, David	QB	6-3	215	6/23/65	Carroll, Wis.	Menomonee Falls, Wis.	D11

The term NFL Rookie is defined as a player who is in his first season of professional football and has not been on the roster of another professional football team for any regular-season or postseason games. A Rookie is designated by an "R" on NFL rosters. Players who have been active in another professional football league or players who have NFL experience, including either preseason training camp or being on an active roster for fewer than three regular-season or postseason games, are termed NFL First-Year Players. An NFL First-Year Player is designated by a "1" on NFL rosters. Thereafter, a player on an NFL active roster for at least three regular-season or postseason games is credited with an additional year of NFL playing experience.

NOTES

Pete Rodriguez, special teams; born July 25, 1940, Chicago, Ill., lives in El Segundo, Calif. Guard-linebacker Denver University 1959-60, Western State (Colo.) 1961-63. No pro playing experience. College coach: Western State (Colo.) 1964, Arizona 1968-69, Western Illinois 1970-73, 1979-82 (head coach), Florida State 1974-75, Iowa State 1976-78, Northern Iowa 1986. Pro coach: Michigan Panthers (USFL) 1983-84, Denver Gold (USFL) 1985, Jacksonville Bulls (USFL) 1986, Ottawa Rough Riders (CFL) 1987, joined Raiders in 1988.

Joe Scannella, offensive backfield; born May 22, 1932, Passaic, N.J., lives in El Segundo, Calif. Quarterback Lehigh 1947-50. Pro safety Saskatchewan Roughriders (CFL) 1951-52. College coach: Cornell 1960, C.W. Post 1963-68 (head coach 1964-68), Vermont 1970-71. Pro coach: Montreal Alouettes (CFL) 1969, Oakland Raiders 1972-77, Montreal Alouettes (CFL) 1978-81 (head coach), Cleveland Browns 1982-84, rejoined Raiders in 1987.

Art Shell, offensive line; born November 26, 1946, Charleston, S.C., lives in Rancho Palos Verdes, Calif. Tackle Maryland State 1965-67. Pro offensive tackle Oakland-Los Angeles Raiders 1968-82. Pro coach: Joined Raiders in 1983.

Charley Sumner, linebackers; born October 19, 1930, Radford, Va., lives in El Segundo, Calif. Back William & Mary 1952-54. Pro defensive back Chicago Bears 1955-60, Minnesota Vikings 1961-62. Pro coach: Oakland-Los Angeles Raiders 1963-68, 1979-83, Pittsburgh Steelers 1969-72, New England Patriots 1973-78, Oakland Invaders (USFL) 1985 (head coach), rejoined Raiders in 1987.

Tom Walsh, quarterbacks; born April 16, 1949, Vallejo, Calif., lives in Manhattan Beach, Calif. UC-Santa Barbara 1971. No college or pro playing experience. College coach: University of San Diego 1972-76, U.S. International 1979, Murray State 1980, Cincinnati 1981. Pro coach: Joined Raiders in 1982.

Jimmy Warren, defensive backs; born July 20, 1939, Ferriday, La., lives in Torrance, Calif. Running back-defensive back Illinois 1961-63. Pro defensive back San Diego Chargers 1964-65, Miami Dolphins 1966-69, Oakland Raiders 1970-74, 1977. College coach: Bethune-Cookman 1983-84. Pro coach: Orlando Renegades (USFL) 1985, joined Raiders in 1987.

MIAMI DOLPHINS

American Football Conference Eastern Division

Team Colors: Aqua, Coral, and White

Joe Robbie Stadium
2269 N.W. 199th Street
Miami, Florida 33056
Telephone: (305) 620-5000/625-6491

Club Officials

President: Joseph Robbie
Executive V.P./General Manager: J. Michael Robbie
V.P./Administration: Eddie J. Jones
V.P./Public Affairs: Tim Robbie
Head Coach: Don Shula
Director of Pro Scouting: Charley Winner
Director of Player Personnel: Chuck Connor
Director of Publicity: Eddie White
Publicity Assistant: Jeff Blumb
Director of Finance: William T. Duffy
Traveling Secretary: Bryan Wiedmeier
Trainer: Bob Lundy
Equipment Manager: Bob Monica

Stadium: Joe Robbie Stadium • **Capacity:** 74,930
2269 N.W. 199th Street
Miami, Florida 33056

Playing Surface: Grass (PAT)

Training Camp: St. Thomas University
16400-D N.W. 32nd Avenue
Miami, Florida 33054

1988 Schedule

Preseason

July 31	vs. S.F. at London, Eng.	6:00
Aug. 6	at Chicago	6:00
Aug. 13	**Washington**	8:00
Aug. 19	**Denver**	9:00
Aug. 26	at Minnesota	7:00

Regular Season

Sept. 4	at Chicago	12:00
Sept. 11	at Buffalo	1:00
Sept. 18	**Green Bay**	1:00
Sept. 25	at Indianapolis	12:00
Oct. 2	**Minnesota**	4:00
Oct. 9	at Los Angeles Raiders	1:00
Oct. 16	**San Diego**	1:00
Oct. 23	**New York Jets**	4:00
Oct. 30	at Tampa Bay	1:00
Nov. 6	at New England	1:00
Nov. 14	**Buffalo** (Monday)	9:00
Nov. 20	**New England**	8:00
Nov. 27	at New York Jets	1:00
Dec. 4	**Indianapolis**	1:00
Dec. 12	**Cleveland** (Monday)	9:00
Dec. 18	at Pittsburgh	1:00

Dolphins Coaching History

(213-127-4)

1966-69	George Wilson	15-39-2
1970-87	Don Shula	198-88-2

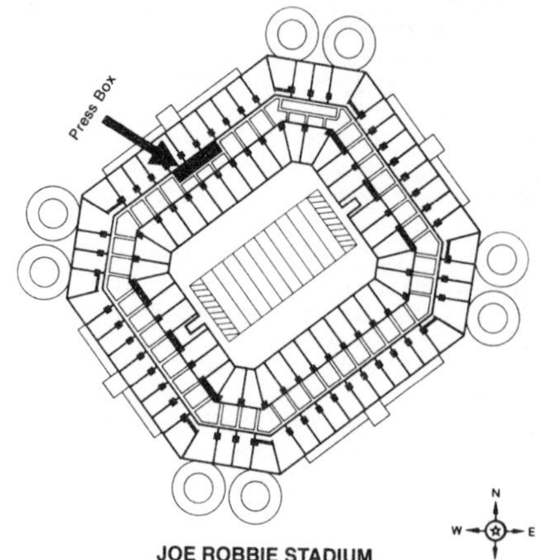

JOE ROBBIE STADIUM

Record Holders

Individual Records—Career

Category	Name	Performance
Rushing (Yds.)	Larry Csonka, 1968-1974, 1979	6,737
Passing (Yds.)	Bob Griese, 1967-1980	25,092
Passing (TDs)	Bob Griese, 1967-1980	192
Receiving (No.)	Nat Moore, 1974-1986	510
Receiving (Yds.)	Nat Moore, 1974-1986	7,547
Interceptions	Jake Scott, 1970-75	35
Punting (Avg.)	Reggie Roby, 1983-87	43.7
Punt Return (Avg.)	Freddie Solomon, 1975-77	11.4
Kickoff Return (Avg.)	Mercury Morris, 1969-1975	26.5
Field Goals	Garo Yepremian, 1970-78	165
Touchdowns (Tot.)	Nat Moore, 1974-1986	75
Points	Garo Yepremian, 1970-78	830

Individual Records—Single Season

Category	Name	Performance
Rushing (Yds.)	Delvin Williams, 1978	1,258
Passing (Yds.)	Dan Marino, 1984	*5,084
Passing (TDs)	Dan Marino, 1984	*48
Receiving (No.)	Mark Clayton, 1984	73
Receiving (Yds.)	Mark Clayton, 1984	1,389
Interceptions	Dick Westmoreland, 1967	10
Punting (Avg.)	Reggie Roby, 1984	44.7
Punt Return (Avg.)	Freddie Solomon, 1975	12.3
Kickoff Return (Avg.)	Duriel Harris, 1976	32.9
Field Goals	Garo Yepremian, 1971	28
Touchdowns (Tot.)	Mark Clayton, 1984	18
Points	Garo Yepremian, 1971	117

Individual Records—Single Game

Category	Name	Performance
Rushing (Yds.)	Mercury Morris, 9-30-73	197
Passing (Yds.)	Dan Marino, 12-2-84	470
Passing (TDs)	Bob Griese, 11-24-77	6
	Dan Marino, 9-21-86	6
Receiving (No.)	Many Times	10
	Last time by Ron Davenport, 12-7-87	
Receiving (Yds.)	Mark Duper, 11-10-85	217
Interceptions	Dick Anderson, 12-3-73	*4
Field Goals	Garo Yepremian, 9-26-71	5
Touchdowns (Tot.)	Paul Warfield, 12-15-73	4
Points	Paul Warfield, 12-15-73	24

*NFL Record

1987 Team Record

Preseason (2-2)

Date	Result		Opponents
8/16	L	3-10	Chicago
8/24	L	28-31	at Denver
8/29	W	35- 3	at Philadelphia
9/4	W	34-20	Buffalo
		100-64	

Regular Season (8-7)

Date	Result		Opponents	Att.
9/13	L	21-28	at New England	54,642
9/20	W	23-10	at Indianapolis	57,524
9/27	C		N.Y. Giants	
10/4	L	20-24	at Seattle	19,448
10/11	W	42- 0	Kansas City	25,867
10/18	L	31-37	at N.Y. Jets (OT)	18,249
10/25	L	31-34	Buffalo (OT)	61,295
11/1	W	35-24	Pittsburgh	52,578
11/8	W	20-14	at Cincinnati	53,840
11/15	L	21-40	Indianapolis	65,433
11/22	W	20-14	at Dallas	56,519
11/29	L	0-27	at Buffalo	68,055
12/7	W	37-28	N.Y. Jets	62,592
12/13	W	28-10	at Philadelphia	63,841
12/20	W	23-21	Washington	65,715
12/28	L	10-24	New England	61,192

(OT) Overtime
C (Cancelled due to players' strike.)

Score by Periods

Dolphins	90	100	89	83	0	—	362
Opponents	63	105	61	97	9	—	335

Attendance

Home 394,672 Away 392,118 Total 786,790
Single-game home record, 78,939 (1-2-72; Orange Bowl), 65,715 (12-20-87; Joe Robbie Stadium)
Single-season home record, 542,951 (1985; Orange Bowl), 394,672 (1987; Joe Robbie Stadium)

1987 Team Statistics

	Dolphins	Opp.
Total First Downs	331	314
Rushing	109	115
Passing	197	176
Penalty	25	23
Third Down: Made/Att.	96/202	95/209
Fourth Down: Made/Att.	9/18	5/13
Total Net Yards	5538	5445
Avg. Per Game	369.2	363.0
Total Plays	1005	1013
Avg. Per Play	5.5	5.4
Net Yards Rushing	1662	2198
Avg. Per Game	110.8	146.5
Total Rushes	408	498
Net Yards Passing	3876	3247
Avg. Per Game	258.4	216.5
Sacked/Yards Lost	13/101	21/183
Gross Yards	3977	3430
Att./Completions	584/338	494/295
Completion Pct.	57.9	59.7
Had Intercepted	20	16
Punts/Avg.	63/38.5	71/38.8
Net Punting Avg.	35.3	32.7
Penalties/Yards Lost	76/634	103/850
Fumbles/Ball Lost	37/17	32/16
Touchdowns	47	42
Rushing	16	18
Passing	29	21
Returns	2	3
Avg. Time of Possession	29:43	30:17

1987 Individual Statistics

Scoring	TD R	TD P	TD Rt	PAT	FG	Saf	TP
Reveiz	0	0	0	28/30	9/11	0	55
Duper	0	8	0	0/0	0/0	0	48
Clayton	0	7	0	0/0	0/0	0	42
Stradford	6	1	0	0/0	0/0	0	42
Tiffin, T.B.-Mia.	0	0	0	11/11	5/7	0	26
Tiffin, Mia.	0	0	0	4/4	0/1	0	4
Beecher	0	0	0	12/12	3/4	0	21
Pruitt	0	3	0	0/0	0/0	0	18
R. Scott	3	0	0	0/0	0/0	0	18
Davenport	1	1	0	0/0	0/0	0	12
Hardy	0	2	0	0/0	0/0	0	12
Da. Johnson	0	2	0	0/0	0/0	0	12
Mackey	2	0	0	0/0	0/0	0	12
Banks	0	1	0	0/0	0/0	0	6
Douglas	0	1	0	0/0	0/0	0	6
Hampton	1	0	0	0/0	0/0	0	6
Hobley	0	0	1	0/0	0/0	0	6
Hooper	0	0	1	0/0	0/0	0	6
Isom	1	0	0	0/0	0/0	0	6
Jensen	0	1	0	0/0	0/0	0	6
Lewis	0	1	0	0/0	0/0	0	6
Marino	1	0	0	0/0	0/0	0	6
W. Smith	0	1	0	0/0	0/0	0	6
Tagliaferri	1	0	0	0/0	0/0	0	6
Dolphins	16	29	2	44/47	12/16	0	362
Opponents	18	21	3	41/41	14/22	0	335

Passing	Att.	Comp.	Yds.	Pct.	TD	Int.	Tkld.	Rate
Marino	444	263	3245	59.2	26	13	9/77	89.2
Mackey	109	57	604	52.3	3	5	4/24	58.8
Strock	23	13	114	56.5	0	1	0/0	51.7
Stankavage	7	4	8	57.1	0	1	0/0	22.6
Stradford	1	1	6	100.0	0	0	0/0	91.7
Dolphins	584	338	3977	57.9	29	20	13/101	81.0
Opponents	494	295	3430	59.7	21	16	21/183	81.5

Rushing	Att.	Yds.	Avg.	LG	TD
Stradford	145	619	4.3	51	6
Hampton	75	289	3.9	34	1
R. Scott	47	199	4.2	24	3
Davenport	32	114	3.6	27	1
W. Bennett	25	102	4.1	18	0
Mackey	17	98	5.8	17	2
Bailey	10	55	5.5	13	0
Konecny	6	46	7.7	19	0
Tagliaferri	13	45	3.5	7	1
Isom	9	41	4.6	8	1
Nathan	4	20	5.0	8	0
Jensen	4	18	4.5	9	0
Roth	3	10	3.3	9	0
Clayton	2	8	4.0	4	0
T. Brown	3	3	1.0	3	0
Roby	1	0	0.0	0	0
Marino	12	−5	−0.4	5t	1
Dolphins	408	1662	4.1	51	16
Opponents	498	2198	4.4	31	18

Receiving	No.	Yds.	Avg.	LG	TD
Stradford	48	457	9.5	34	1
Clayton	46	776	16.9	43	7
Duper	33	597	18.1	59t	8
Hardy	28	292	10.4	31	2
Davenport	27	249	9.2	29	1
Pruitt	26	404	15.5	37	3
Jensen	26	221	8.5	20	1
Hampton	23	223	9.7	24	0
Tagliaferri	12	117	9.8	27	0
Nathan	10	77	7.7	14	0
Douglas	9	92	10.2	17	1
Sampleton	8	64	8.0	19	0
Chavis	7	108	15.4	27	0
Lewis	6	53	8.8	22	1
Konecny	6	26	4.3	10	0
Reilly	5	70	14.0	20	0
Da. Johnson	4	35	8.8	22	2
W. Bennett	4	18	4.5	6	0
Caterbone	2	46	23.0	30	0
W. Smith	2	13	6.5	8	1
R. Scott	2	7	3.5	5	0
Isom	1	11	11.0	11	0
Banks	1	10	10.0	10t	1
T. Brown	1	6	6.0	6	0
Farmer	1	5	5.0	5	0
Dolphins	338	3977	11.8	59t	29
Opponents	295	3430	11.6	55	21

Interceptions	No.	Yds.	Avg.	LG	TD
Lankford	3	44	14.7	44	0
Blackwood	3	17	5.7	17	0
Randle	2	16	8.0	11	0
Hooper	2	11	5.5	11	0
Judson	2	11	5.5	10	0
Hobley	2	7	3.5	7	0
Sowell	1	29	29.0	29	0
B. Brown	1	0	0.0	0	0
Dolphins	16	135	8.4	44	0
Opponents	20	298	14.9	68	2

Punting	No.	Yds.	Avg.	In 20	LG
Roby	32	1371	42.8	8	77
Hayes	7	274	39.1	1	51
Gore	14	502	35.9	6	60
Strock	9	277	30.8	5	44
Dolphins	63	2424	38.5	20	77
Opponents	71	2753	38.8	21	73

Punt Returns	No.	FC	Yds.	Avg.	LG	TD
Schwedes	24	6	203	8.5	31	0
Caterbone	9	4	78	8.7	21	0
B. Brown	2	1	8	4.0	8	0
Blackwood	1	1	1	1.0	1	0
Hooper	1	0	0	0.0	0	0
Stradford	0	1	0	—	0	0
Dolphins	37	13	290	7.8	31	0
Opponents	26	12	141	5.4	15	0

Kickoff Returns	No.	Yds.	Avg.	LG	TD
Hampton	16	304	19.0	32	0
Stradford	14	258	18.4	32	0
Schwedes	9	177	19.7	34	0
Hardy	5	62	12.4	18	0
Farmer	3	56	18.7	23	0
Da. Johnson	2	13	6.5	10	0
Roth	2	49	24.5	26	0
Isom	1	11	11.0	11	0
Lewis	1	0	0.0	0	0
R. Scott	1	22	22.0	22	0
Dolphins	54	952	17.6	34	0
Opponents	67	1222	18.2	47	0

Sacks	No.
Turner	4.0
Sochia	3.5
Bosa	3.0
Readon	2.0
Lambrecht	1.5
Offerdahl	1.5
Brudzinski	1.0
M. Brown	1.0
Frye	1.0
Graf	1.0
S. Scott	1.0
Wimberly	0.5
Dolphins	21.0
Opponents	13.0

Miami Dolphins 1988 Veteran Roster

No.	Name	Pos.	Ht.	Wt.	Birth-date	NFL Exp.	College	Hometown	How Acq.	'87 Games/ Starts
86	Banks, Fred	WR	5-10	180	5/26/62	3	Liberty	Columbus, Ga.	FA-'87	3/0
93	Bennett, Charles	DE	6-5	255	2/9/63	2	Southwestern Louisiana	Clarksdale, Miss.	FA-'88	3/3
34	Bennett, Woody	RB	6-2	244	3/24/56	10	Miami	York, Pa.	W(NYJ)-'80	12/11
75	†Betters, Doug	DE	6-7	265	6/11/56	11	Nevada-Reno	Arlington Heights, Ill.	D6-'78	12/0
47	†Blackwood, Glenn	S	6-0	190	2/23/57	10	Texas	San Antonio, Tex.	D8b-'79	10/10
97	Bosa, John	DE	6-4	263	1/10/64	2	Boston College	Keene, N.H.	D1-'87	12/12
43	Brown, Bud	S	6-0	194	4/19/61	5	Southern Mississippi	DeKalb, Miss.	D11-'84	9/7
51	Brown, Mark	LB	6-2	235	7/18/61	6	Purdue	Inglewood, Calif.	D9-'83	12/12
59	†Brudzinski, Bob	LB	6-4	223	1/1/55	12	Ohio State	Fremont, Ohio	T(Rams)-'81	12/8
19	Caterbone, Mike	WR-KR	5-11	180	2/17/62	2	Franklin and Marshall	Lancaster, Pa.	FA-'88	3/1
68	Cesario, Sal	T-G	6-4	255	7/4/63	2	Cal Poly-SLO	San Jose, Calif.	FA-'88	3/3*
83	Clayton, Mark	WR	5-9	175	4/8/61	6	Louisville	Indianapolis, Ind.	D8b-'83	12/12
98	Cline, Jackie	NT	6-5	276	3/13/60	2	Alabama	McCalla, Ala.	W(Pitt)-'87	8/0*
67	Conlin, Chris	G-C	6-4	290	6/7/65	2	Penn State	Glenside, Pa.	D5-'87	3/0
30	†Davenport, Ron	RB	6-2	230	12/22/62	4	Louisville	Atlanta, Ga.	D6b-'85	10/1
65	†Dellenbach, Jeff	T-C	6-6	280	2/14/63	4	Wisconsin	Wausau, Wis.	D4b-'85	11/6
74	Dennis, Mark	T	6-6	291	4/15/65	2	Illinois	Washington, Ill.	D8b-'87	5/2
85	†Duper, Mark	WR	5-9	187	1/25/59	7	Northwestern State, La.	Moreauville, La.	D2-'82	11/11
61	Foster, Roy	G	6-4	275	5/24/60	7	Southern California	Shawnee Mission, Kan.	D1-'82	12/12
53	†Frye, David	LB	6-2	227	6/21/61	6	Purdue	Cincinnati, Ohio	FA-'86	12/1
79	†Giesler, Jon	T	6-5	265	12/23/56	10	Michigan	Woodville, Ohio	D1-'79	10/9
66	Gilmore, Jim	G	6-5	275	12/19/62	3	Ohio State	Philadelphia, Pa.	FA-'87	3/2
58	Graf, Rick	LB	6-5	239	8/29/63	2	Wisconsin	Madison, Wis.	D2a-'87	12/5
55	Green, Hugh	LB	6-2	225	7/27/59	8	Pittsburgh	Natchez, Miss.	T(TB)-'85	9/1
9	Halloran, Shawn	QB	6-4	215	4/23/64	2	Boston College	South Ashburnham, Mass.	FA-'88	3/2*
27	Hampton, Lorenzo	RB	6-0	203	3/12/62	4	Florida	Lake Wales, Fla.	D1-'85	12/6
84	Hardy, Bruce	TE	6-5	234	6/1/56	11	Arizona State	Bingham, Utah	D9-'78	12/12
29	Hobley, Liffort	S	6-0	199	5/12/62	3	Louisiana State	Shreveport, La.	FA-'87	14/6
94	Hunley, Lamonte	LB	6-1	240	1/31/63	3	Arizona	Petersburg, Va.	FA-'88	0*
17	Jaworski, Ron	QB	6-1	195	3/23/51	14	Youngstown State	Lackawanna, N.Y.	FA-'87	0*
11	Jensen, Jim	WR-RB	6-4	215	11/14/58	8	Boston University	Doylestown, Pa.	D11-'81	12/0
87	†Johnson, Dan	TE	6-3	245	5/17/60	6	Iowa State	New Hope, Minn.	D7a-'82	7/0
49	Judson, William	CB	6-2	190	3/26/59	7	South Carolina State	Atlanta, Ga.	D8-'81	12/12
	Kehoe, Scott	T	6-4	282	9/20/64	2	Illinois	Oak Lawn, Ill.	FA-'87	3/3
54	Kolic, Larry	LB	6-1	238	8/31/63	2	Ohio State	Smithville, Ohio	D7-'86	7/0
69	Lambrecht, Mike	NT	6-1	271	5/2/63	2	St. Cloud State	Watertown, Minn.	FA-'87	5/3
44	†Lankford, Paul	CB	6-2	184	6/15/58	7	Penn State	Farmingdale, N.Y.	D3-'82	12/12
72	Lee, Ronnie	T	6-4	265	12/24/56	10	Baylor	Tyler, Tex.	T(Atl)-'84	9/9
99	†Little, George	DE-NT	6-4	270	6/27/63	4	Iowa	Duquesne, Pa.	D3a-'85	9/0
13	Marino, Dan	QB	6-4	214	9/15/61	6	Pittsburgh	Pittsburgh, Pa.	D1-'83	12/12
78	Marrone, Doug	G-C	6-5	269	7/25/64	2	Syracuse	New York, N.Y.	FA-'87	4/0
28	McNeal, Don	CB	5-11	192	5/6/58	8	Alabama	Atmore, Ala.	D1-'80	12/0
52	†Nicolas, Scott	LB	6-3	226	8/7/60	7	Miami	Clearwater, Fla.	FA-'87	12/0
56	Offerdahl, John	LB	6-2	232	8/17/64	3	Western Michigan	Fort Atkinson, Wis.	D2-'86	9/9
82	Pruitt, James	WR	6-2	199	1/29/64	3	Cal State-Fullerton	Los Angeles, Calif.	D4-'86	12/1
7	Reveiz, Fuad	K	5-11	217	2/24/63	4	Tennessee	Miami, Fla.	D7-'85	11/0
4	Roby, Reggie	P	6-2	242	7/30/61	6	Iowa	East Waterloo, Iowa	D6-'83	10/0
81	Schwedes, Scott	WR-KR	6-0	174	6/30/65	2	Syracuse	DeWitt, N.Y.	D2b-'87	12/0
68	Scott, Chris	DE	6-4	250	12/11/61	4	Purdue	Berea, Ohio	FA-'88	3/3*
50	†Shipp, Jackie	LB	6-2	236	3/19/62	5	Oklahoma	Stillwater, Okla.	D1-'84	12/12
64	Simpson, Travis	C-G	6-2	265	11/19/63	2	Oklahoma	Norman, Okla.	FA-'88	3/0*
25	Smith, Mike	CB	6-0	175	10/24/62	4	Texas-El Paso	Houston, Tex.	D4a-'85	8/0
70	†Sochia, Brian	NT	6-3	274	7/21/61	6	N.W. Oklahoma State	Brasher Falls, N.Y.	FA-'86	12/12
57	Stephenson, Dwight	C	6-2	258	11/20/57	9	Alabama	Hampton, Va.	D2-'80	9/9
23	Stradford, Troy	RB	5-9	191	9/11/64	2	Boston College	Linden, N.J.	D4-'87	12/5
10	†Strock, Don	QB	6-5	225	11/27/50	15	Virginia Tech	Pottstown, Pa.	D5-'73	12/0
24	Thompson, Reyna	CB	5-11	194	8/28/63	3	Baylor	Dallas, Tex.	D9-'86	9/1
76	Toth, Tom	G	6-5	275	5/23/62	3	Western Michigan	Orland Park, Ill.	FA-'86	12/12
95	Turner, T.J.	DE	6-4	275	5/16/63	3	Houston	Lufkin, Tex.	D3-'86	12/12
1	Warren, Vince	WR	6-0	180	2/18/63	2	San Diego State	Albuquerque, N.M.	FA-'88	0*
64	Wimberly, Derek	DE	6-4	265	1/4/64	2	Purdue	Miami, Fla.	FA-'88	3/3

* Cesario played 3 games with Dallas in '87; Cline played 1 game with Pittsburgh, 7 games with Miami; Halloran played 3 games with St. Louis; Hunley last active with Indianapolis in '86; Jaworski active for 2 games but did not play; Scott played 3 games with Indianapolis; Simpson played 3 games with Green Bay; Warren last active with N.Y. Giants in '86.

†Option playout; subject to developments.

Also played with Dolphins in '87—RB Clarence Bailey (3 games), T Bill Bealles (3), K Willie Beecher (3), RB Tom Brown (1), S Marvell Burgess (1), LB Laz Chavez (3), WR Eddie Chavis (3), T Greg Cleveland (2), WR Leland Douglas (3), WR George Farmer (1), WR Todd Feldman (1), LB Dennis Fowlkes (3), C Guy Goar (active for 1 game but did not play), P Stacy Gore (3), P Jeff Hayes (2), CB Trell Hooper (3), G Jim Huddleston (active for 2 games but did not play), S Mark Irvin (3), FB Rickey Isom (3), G Steve Jacobson (3), S Demetrious Johnson (3), T Greg Koch (1), RB Mark Konecny (3), TE David Lewis (5), LB Steve Lubischer (1), QB Kyle Mackey (3), LB David Marshall (2), LB Victor Morris (3), RB Tony Nathan (6), G Louis Oubre (3), C Greg Ours (3), LB Tim Pidgeon (3), CB Floyd Raglin (2), S Tate Randle (3), NT Ike Readon (3), WR Dameon Reilly (3), S Donovan Rose (12), RB Pete Roth (3), TE Lawrence Sampleton (3),LB Duke Schamel (3), RB Ronald Scott (3), DE Stanley Scott (3), TE Rich Siler (1), TE Willie Smith (3), CB Robert Sowell (3), QB Scott Stankavage (3), LB Greg Storr (3), CB John Swain (1), RB John Tagliaferri (3), K Van Tiffin (1), TE Joel Williams (3), G Jeff Wiska (3).

COACHING STAFF

Head Coach, Don Shula

Pro Career: Begins his twenty-sixth season as an NFL head coach, and nineteenth with the Dolphins. Miami has won or shared first place in the AFC East in 13 of his 18 years. Has highest regular-season winning percentage (.713) among active NFL coaches. Captured back-to-back NFL championships, defeating Washington 14-7 in Super Bowl VII and Minnesota 24-7 in Super Bowl VIII. Lost to Dallas 24-3 in Super Bowl VI, to Washington 27-17 in Super Bowl XVII, and to San Francisco 38-16 in Super Bowl XIX. His 1972 17-0 club is the only team in NFL history to go undefeated throughout the regular season and postseason. Started his pro playing career with Cleveland Browns as defensive back in 1951. After two seasons with Browns, spent 1953-56 with Baltimore Colts and 1957 with Washington Redskins. Joined Detroit Lions as defensive coach in 1960 and was named head coach of the Colts in 1963. Baltimore had a 13-1 record in 1968 and captured NFL championship before losing to New York Jets in Super Bowl III. Career record: 271-114-6.

Background: Outstanding offensive player at John Carroll University in Cleveland before becoming defensive specialist as a pro. His alma mater gave him doctorate in humanities in May, 1973. Served as assistant coach at Virginia in 1958 and at Kentucky in 1959.

Personal: Born January 4, 1930, in Painesville, Ohio. Don and his wife, Dorothy, live in Miami Lakes, Fla., and have five children—David, Donna, Sharon, Annie, and Mike. David is a Dolphins' assistant coach and Mike is an assistant coach for Tampa Bay.

Assistant Coaches

Tom Olivadotti, defense; born September 22, 1945, Long Branch, N.J., lives in Cooper City, Fla. Defensive end-wide receiver Upsala 1963-66. No pro playing experience. College coach: Princeton 1975-77, Boston College 1978-79, Miami 1980-83. Pro coach: Cleveland Browns 1985-86, joined Dolphins in 1987.

Mel Phillips, defensive backfield; born January 6, 1942, Shelby, N.C., lives in Miami Lakes, Fla. Defensive back-running back North Carolina A&T 1964-65. Pro defensive back San Francisco 49ers 1966-77. Pro coach: Detroit Lions 1980-84, joined Dolphins in 1985.

John Sandusky, offense-offensive line; born December 28, 1925, Philadelphia, Pa., lives in Hollywood, Fla. Tackle Villanova 1946-49. Pro tackle Cleveland Browns 1950-55, Green Bay Packers 1956. College coach: Villanova 1957-58. Pro coach: Baltimore Colts 1959-72 (head coach 1972), Philadelphia Eagles 1973-75, joined Dolphins in 1976.

Larry Seiple, receivers; born February 14, 1945, Allentown, Pa., lives in Miami. Running back-receiver-punter Kentucky 1964-66. Pro punter-tight end-receiver-running back Miami Dolphins 1967-77. Pro coach: Detroit Lions 1980-84, Tampa Bay Buccaneers 1985-86, joined Dolphins in 1988.

Dan Sekanovich, defensive line; born July 27, 1933, West Hazleton, Pa., lives in Cooper City, Fla. End Tennessee 1951-53. Pro defensive end Montreal Alouettes (CFL) 1954. College coach: Susquehanna 1961-63, Connecticut 1964-67, Pittsburgh 1968, Navy 1969-70, Kentucky 1971-72. Pro coach: Montreal Alouettes (CFL) 1973-76, New York Jets 1977-82, Atlanta Falcons 1983-85, joined Dolphins in 1986.

David Shula, assistant head coach-quarterbacks-passing game; born May 28, 1959, Lexington, Ky., lives in Miami Lakes, Fla. Wide receiver Dartmouth 1978-80. Pro wide receiver Baltimore Colts 1981. Pro coach: Joined Dolphins in 1982.

Miami Dolphins 1988 First-Year Roster

Name	Pos.	Ht.	Wt.	Birth-date	College	Hometown	How Acq.
Andrade, Eric	WR	6-1	194	9/28/65	Boise State	Anaheim, Calif.	FA
Banks, Robert	WR	6-2	185	12/13/63	Adrian College	Ann Arbor, Mich.	FA
Beasley, Jerry	LB	6-1	220	2/13/65	Arizona	Tucson, Ariz.	FA
Bell, Kerwin	QB	6-2	200	6/15/65	Florida	Day, Fla.	D7
Bratton, Melvin	RB	6-1	225	2/2/65	Miami	Miami, Fla.	D6a
Brown, Jeff	QB	6-3	205	3/5/66	Southeast Missouri St.	Milwaukee, Wis.	FA
Brown, Selwyn	S	5-11	200	9/28/65	Miami	St. Petersburg, Fla.	FA
Brown, Tom (1)	RB	6-1	225	11/20/64	Pittsburgh	Lower Burrell, Pa.	D7-'87
Burgess, Marvell (1)	S	6-3	195	10/7/65	Henderson State	Hialeah, Fla.	FA
Burton, Steve	RB	6-3	230	8/11/61	Northwestern	Framingham, Mass.	FA
Cannon, Willie	RB	6-1	206	9/28/64	Murray State	Sarasota, Fla.	FA
Cheek, Louis	T	6-6	288	10/6/64	Texas A&M	Fairfield, Tex.	D8b
Clayton, McCarthon	CB	5-11	190	5/24/64	Nebraska	Orlando, Fla.	FA
Cooper, George	RB	6-1	245	12/8/65	Ohio State	Wyandanch, N.Y.	D6b
Cross, Jeff	DE	6-4	261	3/25/66	Missouri	Blythe, Calif.	D9
Edmunds, Ferrell	TE	6-6	241	4/16/65	Maryland	Danville, Va.	D3
Galbreath, Harry	G	6-1	271	1/1/65	Tennessee	Clarksville, Tenn.	D8a
Gruber, Bob (1)	T	6-5	280	6/7/58	Pittsburgh	Greenville, Pa.	FA-'87
Hansen, James (1)	T	6-5	265	9/17/64	Utah	Salt Lake City, Utah	FA
Harris, Gerald (1)	RB	5-9	200	4/11/64	Georgia Southern	Swainsboro, Ga.	FA
Jackson, Artis	NT	6-5	309	8/9/65	Texas Tech	Dallas, Tex.	D10
Jackson, Chris	RB	5-9	179	9/25/64	Boise State	Dallas, Tex.	FA
James, Michel (1)	WR	6-0	180	11/19/63	Washington State	Tacoma, Wash.	FA
Jenkins, DeShon (1)	S	6-1	198	12/19/64	Northwestern St., La.	Jena, La.	FA-'87
Johnson, Greg	T	6-4	311	12/19/64	Oklahoma	Moore, Okla.	D4
Karsatos, Jim (1)	QB	6-4	225	5/26/63	Ohio State	Fullerton, Calif.	D12-'87
Kelleher, Tom	RB	6-1	230	8/24/65	Holy Cross	Rockville, Conn.	D11
Kinchen, Brian	TE	6-2	227	8/6/65	Louisiana State	Baton Rouge, La.	D12
Kumerow, Eric	DE	6-7	264	4/17/65	Ohio State	Oak Park, Ill.	D1
Kwiatkowski, Pete	DE	6-2	250	8/29/66	Boise State	Santa Barbara, Calif.	FA
Manu, Tika	DE	6-3	250	12/5/64	Utah	Salt Lake City, Utah	FA
Mathis, Mark (1)	CB	5-8	183	8/23/65	Liberty	Marietta, Ga.	FA
McCormick, John	G	6-1	274	1/28/65	Nebraska	Omaha, Neb.	FA
McNeil, Mark (1)	CB	6-0	198	8/25/62	Houston	San Antonio, Tex.	FA
Reherman, Leo	C	6-3	274	7/4/66	Cornell	Louisville, Ky.	FA
Rose, Shawn	LB	6-0	240	10/16/63	Washburn University	Keokuk, Iowa	FA
Slater, Elton (1)	CB	5-10	193	3/10/64	S.W. Louisiana	Port Arthur, Tex.	FA
Smith, Harvey	WR	5-10	165	11/5/64	West Virginia	Monroeville, Pa.	FA
Smith, Quint	WR	6-1	190	5/11/65	North Carolina	Alexandria, Va.	FA
Stark, Chad (1)	RB	6-1	225	4/4/65	North Dakota State	Brookings, S.D.	FA
Thomas, Derrick (1)	RB	6-0	224	3/8/65	Arkansas	Paducah, Ky.	FA
Thomas, Rodney	CB	5-10	196	12/21/65	Brigham Young	Ontario, Calif.	D5
Vlatas, Tony	TE	6-7	235	5/24/65	Princeton	Annandale, Va.	FA
Williams, Eric	CB	5-9	177	11/27/65	Florida State	Safety Harbor, Fla.	FA
Williams, Jarvis	S	6-0	195	5/16/65	Florida	Palatka, Fla.	D2

The term NFL Rookie is defined as a player who is in his first season of professional football and has not been on the roster of another professional football team for any regular-season or postseason games. A Rookie is designated by an "R" on NFL rosters. Players who have been active in another professional football league or players who have NFL experience, including either preseason training camp or being on an active roster for fewer than three regular-season or postseason games, are termed NFL First-Year Players. An NFL First-Year Player is designated by a "1" on NFL rosters. Thereafter, a player on an NFL active roster for at least three regular-season or postseason games is credited with an additional year of NFL playing experience.

NOTES

Chuck Studley, linebackers; born January 17, 1929, Maywood, Ill., lives in Miami Lakes, Fla. Guard Illinois 1949-51. No pro playing experience. College coach: Illinois 1955-59, Massachusetts 1960 (head coach), Cincinnati 1961-68 (head coach). Pro coach: Cincinnati Bengals 1969-78, San Francisco 49ers 1979-82, Houston Oilers 1983 (interim head coach for last 10 games), joined Dolphins in 1984.

Carl Taseff, offensive backfield; born September 28, 1928, Cleveland, Ohio, lives in Miami. Back John Carroll 1947-50. Pro defensive back Cleveland Browns 1951, Baltimore Colts 1953-61, Philadelphia Eagles 1961, Buffalo Bills 1962. Pro coach: Boston Patriots 1964, Detroit Lions 1965-66, joined Dolphins in 1970.

Junior Wade, strength-conditioning; born February 2, 1947, Bath, S.C., lives in Miami. South Carolina State 1969. No college or pro playing experience. Pro coach: Joined Dolphins in 1975, coach since 1983.

Mike Westhoff, special teams-tight ends; born January 10, 1948, Pittsburgh, Pa., lives in Ft. Lauderdale, Fla. Center-linebacker Wichita State 1967-69. No pro playing experience. College coach: Indiana 1974-75, Dayton 1976, Indiana State 1977, Northwestern 1978-80, Texas Christian 1981. Pro coach: Baltimore/Indianapolis Colts 1982-84, Arizona Outlaws (USFL) 1985, joined Dolphins in 1986.

NEW ENGLAND PATRIOTS

American Football Conference Eastern Division

Team Colors: Red, White, and Blue

Sullivan Stadium
Route 1
Foxboro, Massachusetts 02035
Telephone: (508) 543-7911

Club Officials

President: William H. Sullivan, Jr.
Executive Vice President: Charles W. Sullivan
Vice President: Francis J. (Bucko) Kilroy
General Manager: Patrick J. Sullivan
Vice President, Finance: Richard M. Regan, Jr.
Director of Player Development: Dick Steinberg
Director of Pro Scouting: Bill McPeak
Director of College Scouting: Joe Mendes
Executive Director of Player Personnel: Darryl Stingley
Personnel Scouts: Larry Cook, Charles Garcia, Mike Pollom, Pat Naughton, Ken Sternfeld, Bob Teahan
Director of Public Relations and Sales: Dave Wintergrass
Director of Publicity: Jim Greenidge
Assistant Publicity Director: Jimmy Oldham
Box Office Manager: Frank Napoli
Trainer: Ron O'Neil
Equipment Manager: George Luongo
Video Manager: Ken Deininger

Stadium: Sullivan Stadium • **Capacity:** 60,794
Route 1
Foxboro, Massachusetts 02035

Playing Surface: SuperTurf

Training Camp: Bryant College
Smithfield, Rhode Island 02917

1988 Schedule

Preseason

Aug. 6	**Atlanta**	7:00
Aug. 13	vs. Hou. at Memphis, Tenn.	7:00
Aug. 20	at Philadelphia	7:30
Aug. 26	**Cincinnati**	7:00

Regular Season

Sept. 4	**New York Jets**	4:00
Sept. 11	at Minnesota	3:00
Sept. 18	**Buffalo**	1:00
Sept. 25	at Houston	12:00
Oct. 2	**Indianapolis**	1:00
Oct. 9	vs. Green Bay at Milw.	12:00
Oct. 16	**Cincinnati**	1:00
Oct. 23	at Buffalo	1:00
Oct. 30	**Chicago**	1:00
Nov. 6	**Miami**	1:00
Nov. 13	at New York Jets	1:00
Nov. 20	at Miami	8:00
Nov. 27	at Indianapolis	4:00
Dec. 4	**Seattle**	1:00
Dec. 11	**Tampa Bay**	1:00
Dec. 17	at Denver (Saturday)	2:00

Patriots Coaching History

Boston 1960-70
(197-208-9)

1960-61	Lou Saban*	7-12-0
1961-68	Mike Holovak	53-47-9
1969-70	Clive Rush**	5-16-0
1970-72	John Mazur***	9-21-0
1972	Phil Bengtson	1-4-0
1973-78	Chuck Fairbanks****	46-41-0
1978	Hank Bullough-Ron Erhardt#	0-1-0
1979-81	Ron Erhardt	21-27-0
1982-84	Ron Meyer##	18-16-0
1984-87	Raymond Berry	37-23-0

*Released after five games in 1961
**Released after seven games in 1970
***Resigned after nine games in 1972
****Resigned after 15 games in 1978
#Co-coaches
##Released after eight games in 1984

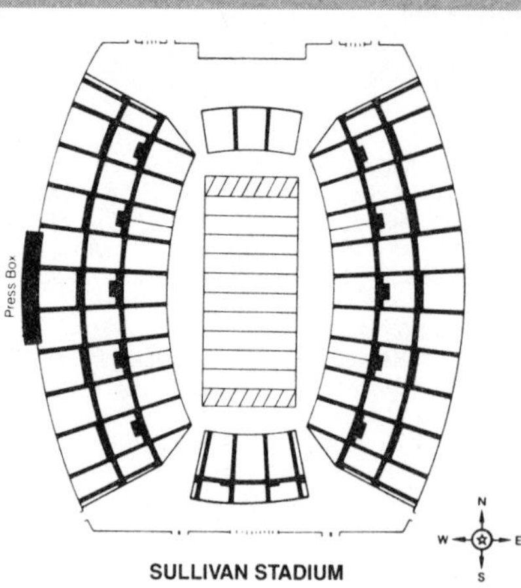

SULLIVAN STADIUM

Record Holders

Individual Records—Career

Category	Name	Performance
Rushing (Yds.)	Sam Cunningham, 1973-79, 1981-82	5,453
Passing (Yds.)	Steve Grogan, 1975-1987	23,740
Passing (TDs)	Steve Grogan, 1975-1987	165
Receiving (No.)	Stanley Morgan, 1977-1987	475
Receiving (Yds.)	Stanley Morgan, 1977-1987	9,364
Interceptions	Raymond Clayborn, 1977-1987	31
Punting (Avg.)	Rich Camarillo, 1981-87	42.6
Punt Return (Avg.)	Mack Herron, 1973-75	12.0
Kickoff Return (Avg.)	Horace Ivory, 1977-1981	27.6
Field Goals	Gino Cappelletti, 1960-1970	176
Touchdowns (Tot.)	Stanley Morgan, 1977-1987	61
Points	Gino Cappelletti, 1960-1970	1,130

Individual Records—Single Season

Category	Name	Performance
Rushing (Yds.)	Jim Nance, 1966	1,458
Passing (Yds.)	Vito (Babe) Parilli, 1964	3,465
Passing (TDs)	Vito (Babe) Parilli, 1964	31
Receiving (No.)	Stanley Morgan, 1986	84
Receiving (Yds.)	Stanley Morgan, 1986	1,491
Interceptions	Ron Hall, 1964	11
Punting (Avg.)	Rich Camarillo, 1983	44.6
Punt Return (Avg.)	Mack Herron, 1974	14.8
Kickoff Return (Avg.)	Raymond Clayborn, 1977	31.0
Field Goals	Tony Franklin, 1986	32
Touchdowns (Tot.)	Steve Grogan, 1976	13
	Stanley Morgan, 1979	13
Points	Gino Cappelletti, 1964	155

Individual Records—Single Game

Category	Name	Performance
Rushing (Yds.)	Tony Collins, 9-18-83	212
Passing (Yds.)	Tony Eason, 9-21-86	414
Passing (TDs)	Vito (Babe) Parilli, 11-15-64	5
	Vito (Babe) Parilli, 10-15-67	5
	Steve Grogan, 9-9-79	5
Receiving (No.)	Art Graham, 11-20-66	11
Receiving (Yds.)	Stanley Morgan, 11-8-81	182
Interceptions	Many times	3
	Last time by Roland James, 10-23-83	
Field Goals	Gino Cappelletti, 10-4-64	6
Touchdowns (Tot.)	Many times	3
	Last time by Stanley Morgan, 9-21-86	
Points	Gino Cappelletti, 12-18-65	28

1987 Team Record

Preseason (2-2)

Date	Result		Opponents
8/16	L	17-19	N.Y. Giants
8/23	L	13-19	Philadelphia (OT)
8/29	W	38-27	at Minnesota
9/4	W	14-13	vs. Atlanta at Jacksonville, Fla.
		82-78	

Regular Season (8-7)

Date	Result		Opponents	Att.
9/13	W	28-21	Miami	54,642
9/21	L	24-43	at N.Y. Jets	70,847
9/27	C		at Washington	
10/4	L	10-20	Cleveland	14,830
10/11	W	14- 7	Buffalo	11,878
10/18	W	21- 7	at Houston	26,294
10/25	L	16-30	at Indianapolis	48,850
11/1	W	26-23	L.A. Raiders	60,664
11/8	L	10-17	at N.Y. Giants	73,817
11/15	L	17-23	Dallas (OT)	60,567
11/22	W	24- 0	Indianapolis	56,906
11/29	L	31-34	Philadelphia (OT)	54,198
12/6	L	20-31	at Denver	75,795
12/13	W	42-20	N.Y. Jets	60,617
12/20	W	13- 7	at Buffalo	74,945
12/28	W	24-10	at Miami	61,192

(OT) Overtime
C (Cancelled due to players' strike.)

Score by Periods

Patriots	76	111	72	61	0	—	320
Opponents	39	68	71	106	9	—	293

Attendance

Home 374,302 Away 431,740 Total 806,042
Single-game home record, 61,457 (12-5-71)
Single-season home record, 482,572 (1986)

1987 Team Statistics

	Patriots	Opp.
Total First Downs	266	293
Rushing	84	112
Passing	158	159
Penalty	24	22
Third Down: Made/Att.	82/220	84/228
Fourth Down: Made/Att.	9/14	11/23
Total Net Yards	4454	4877
Avg. Per Game	296.9	325.1
Total Plays	986	1053
Avg. Per Play	4.5	4.6
Net Yards Rushing	1771	1778
Avg. Per Game	118.1	118.5
Total Rushes	513	490
Net Yards Passing	2683	3099
Avg. Per Game	178.9	206.6
Sacked/Yards Lost	33/246	43/339
Gross Yards	2929	3438
Att./Completions	440/236	520/273
Completion Pct.	53.6	52.5
Had Intercepted	18	21
Punts/Avg.	89/37.6	77/38.1
Net Punting Avg.	30.5	33.8
Penalties/Yards Lost	64/506	110/846
Fumbles/Ball Lost	36/13	42/21
Touchdowns	39	34
Rushing	12	13
Passing	22	17
Returns	5	4
Avg. Time of Possession	29:37	30:23

1987 Individual Statistics

Scoring	TD R	TD P	TD Rt	PAT	FG	Saf	TP
T. Franklin	0	0	0	37/38	15/26	0	82
Collins	3	3	0	0/0	0/0	0	36
Fryar	0	5	0	0/0	0/0	0	30
Dupard	3	0	0	0/0	0/0	0	18
Jones	0	3	0	0/0	0/0	0	18
Morgan	0	3	0	0/0	0/0	0	18
Starring	0	3	0	0/0	0/0	0	18
Baty	0	2	0	0/0	0/0	0	12
Grogan	2	0	0	0/0	0/0	0	12
Linne	0	2	0	0/0	0/0	0	12
Lippett	0	0	2	0/0	0/0	0	12
Scott	0	1	1	0/0	0/0	0	12
Bleier	1	0	0	0/0	0/0	0	6
Clayborn	0	0	1	0/0	0/0	0	6
LeBlanc	1	0	0	0/0	0/0	0	6
Ramsey	1	0	0	0/0	0/0	0	6
Tippett	0	0	1	0/0	0/0	0	6
Woods	1	0	0	0/0	0/0	0	6
Schubert	0	0	0	1/1	1/2	0	4
Patriots	12	22	5	38/39	16/28	0	320
Opponents	13	17	4	33/33	18/27	1	293

Passing	Att.	Comp.	Yds.	Pct.	TD	Int.	Tkld.	Rate
Grogan	161	93	1183	57.8	10	9	7/55	78.2
Ramsey	134	71	898	53.0	6	6	14/90	70.4
Eason	79	42	453	53.2	3	2	8/70	72.4
Bleier	39	14	181	35.9	1	1	3/28	49.2
Flutie	25	15	199	60.0	1	0	1/3	98.6
Jones	1	0	0	0.0	0	0	0/0	39.6
Tatupu	1	1	15	100.0	1	0	0/0	158.3
Patriots	440	236	2929	53.6	22	18	33/246	74.1
Opponents	520	273	3438	52.5	17	21	43/339	67.5

Rushing	Att.	Yds.	Avg.	LG	TD
Collins	147	474	3.2	19	3
Dupard	94	318	3.4	49	3
Tatupu	79	248	3.1	19	0
Perryman	41	187	4.6	48	0
LeBlanc	49	170	3.5	42	1
Ramsey	13	75	5.8	19	1
Fryar	9	52	5.8	16	0
Hansen	16	44	2.8	7	0
Davis	9	43	4.8	27	0
Flutie	6	43	7.2	13	0
Grogan	20	37	1.9	8	2
Eason	3	25	8.3	13	0
C. McSwain	9	23	2.6	9	0
Woods	4	20	5.0	13	1
Starring	2	13	6.5	10	0
C. James	4	10	2.5	5	0
Camarillo	1	0	0.0	0	0
Bleier	5	−5	−1.0	1t	1
Whitten	2	−6	−3.0	−2	0
Patriots	513	1771	3.5	49	12
Opponents	490	1778	3.6	60t	13

Receiving	No.	Yds.	Avg.	LG	TD
Collins	44	347	7.9	29	3
Morgan	40	672	16.8	45	3
Fryar	31	467	15.1	40	5
Jones	25	388	15.5	29	3
Francis, S.F.-N.E.	22	202	9.2	19	0
Starring	17	289	17.0	34t	3
Baty	15	138	9.2	22	2
Tatupu	15	136	9.1	23	0
Dawson	12	81	6.8	14	0
Linne	11	158	14.4	30	2
Scott	5	35	7.0	15	1
Coffey	3	66	22.0	35	0
Gadbois	3	51	17.0	20	0
D. Williams	3	30	10.0	12	0
Perryman	3	13	4.3	7	0
Dupard	3	1	0.3	2	0
Frain	2	22	11.0	11	0
LeBlanc	2	3	1.5	3	0
Hansen	1	22	22.0	22	0
Pickering	1	10	10.0	10	0
Patriots	236	2929	12.4	45	22
Opponents	273	3438	12.6	61t	17

Interceptions	No.	Yds.	Avg.	LG	TD
Marion	4	53	13.3	25	0
Lippett	3	103	34.3	45t	2
Clayborn	2	24	12.0	24	0
Gibson	2	17	8.5	17	0
Bowman	2	3	1.5	3	0
E. Williams	1	51	51.0	51	0
R. James	1	27	27.0	27	0
R. McSwain	1	17	17.0	17	0
Shegog	1	7	7.0	7	0
Holmes	1	4	4.0	4	0
Rembert	1	1	1.0	1	0
P. Williams	1	0	0.0	0	0
Peterson	1	0	0.0	0	0
Patriots	21	307	14.6	51	2
Opponents	18	160	8.9	38	2

Punting	No.	Yds.	Avg.	In 20	LG
Camarillo	62	2489	40.1	14	73
Herline	25	861	34.4	1	50
Patriots	89	3350	37.6	15	73
Opponents	77	2937	38.1	25	62

Punt Returns	No.	FC	Yds.	Avg.	LG	TD
Fryar	18	12	174	9.7	36	0
Linne	5	2	22	4.4	16	0
Marion	1	2	0	0.0	0	0
Starring	1	1	17	17.0	17	0
Patriots	25	17	213	8.5	36	0
Opponents	41	11	397	9.7	34	0

Kickoff Returns	No.	Yds.	Avg.	LG	TD
Starring	23	445	19.3	43	0
Fryar	6	119	19.8	31	0
Davis	5	134	26.8	43	0
Dupard	4	61	15.3	21	0
Perryman	3	43	14.3	16	0
LeBlanc	2	31	15.5	24	0
C. McSwain	2	32	16.0	24	0
Alexander	1	4	4.0	4	0
Collins	1	18	18.0	18	0
Hansen	1	14	14.0	14	0
Patriots	48	901	18.8	43	0
Opponents	63	1130	17.9	60	0

Sacks	No.
Tippett	12.5
Veris	7.0
B. Williams	5.0
T. Williams	4.5
Rembert	2.0
Reynolds	2.0
Sims	1.5
Blackmon	1.0
Hodge	1.0
Lippett	1.0
Mangiero	1.0
McCabe	1.0
McGrew	1.0
Wichard	1.0
Wilburn	1.0
Bowman	0.5
Patriots	43.0
Opponents	33.0

New England Patriots 1988 Veteran Roster

No.	Name	Pos.	Ht.	Wt.	Birth-date	NFL Exp.	College	Hometown	How Acq.	'87 Games/ Starts
78	Armstrong, Bruce	T	6-4	284	9/7/65	2	Louisville	Miami, Fla.	D1-'87	12/12
28	Bowman, Jim	S	6-2	210	10/26/63	4	Central Michigan	Cadillac, Mich.	D2b-'85	12/8
58	Brock, Pete	C	6-5	275	7/14/54	13	Colorado	Portland, Ore.	D1b-'76	4/3
3	Camarillo, Rich	P	5-11	185	11/29/59	8	Washington	Pico Rivera, Calif.	FA-'81	12/0
26	Clayborn, Raymond	CB	6-0	186	1/2/55	12	Texas	Ft. Worth, Tex.	D1a-'77	10/10
40	Davis, Elgin	RB	5-10	192	10/23/65	2	Central Florida	Jacksonville, Fla.	D12-'87	4/0
87	Dawson, Lin	TE	6-3	240	6/24/59	7	North Carolina State	Kinston, N.C.	D8b-'81	12/11
21	Dupard, Reggie	RB	5-11	205	10/30/63	3	Southern Methodist	New Orleans, La.	D1-'86	8/3
11	†Eason, Tony	QB	6-4	212	10/8/59	6	Illinois	Walnut Grove, Calif.	D1-'83	4/3
66	Fairchild, Paul	G-C	6-4	270	9/14/61	5	Kansas	Glidden, Iowa	D5-'84	11/2
62	Farrell, Sean	G	6-3	260	5/25/60	7	Penn State	Westhampton, N.Y.	T(TB)-'87	14/14
2	Flutie, Doug	QB	5-10	175	10/23/62	3	Boston College	Natick, Mass.	T(Chi)-'87	2/1*
49	Francis, Russ	TE	6-6	242	4/3/53	13	Oregon	Pleasant Hill, Ore.	FA-'87	9/7*
1	Franklin, Tony	K	5-8	182	11/18/56	10	Texas A&M	Big Spring, Tex.	T(Phil)-'84	14/0
80	†Fryar, Irving	WR	6-0	200	9/28/62	5	Nebraska	Mt. Holly, N.J.	D1-'84	12/12
48	Gadbois, Dennis	WR	6-1	183	9/18/63	2	Boston University	Biddeford, Maine	FA-'87	3/1
43	Gibson, Ernest	CB	5-10	185	10/3/61	5	Furman	Jacksonville, Fla.	D6-'84	12/5
14	Grogan, Steve	QB	6-4	210	7/24/53	14	Kansas State	Ottawa, Kan.	D5a-'75	7/6
35	Hansen, Bruce	RB	6-1	225	9/18/61	2	Brigham Young	American Fork, Utah	FA-'87	6/2
97	†Hodge, Milford	NT	6-3	278	3/11/61	3	Washington State	San Francisco, Calif.	FA-'86	12/0
41	Holmes, Darryl	S	6-2	190	9/6/64	2	Fort Valley State	Warner Robins, Ga.	FA-'87	15/3
32	James, Craig	RB	6-0	215	1/2/61	4	Southern Methodist	Houston, Tex.	D7-'83	2/0
38	James, Roland	S	6-2	191	2/18/58	9	Tennessee	Xenia, Ohio	D1a-'80	9/4
83	†Jones, Cedric	WR	6-1	184	6/1/60	7	Duke	Weldon, N.C.	D3a-'82	12/4
93	Jordan, Tim	LB	6-3	226	4/26/64	2	Wisconsin	Madison, Wis.	D4c-'87	5/0
42	†Lippett, Ronnie	CB	5-11	180	12/10/60	6	Miami	Sebring, Fla.	D8-'83	12/12
31	Marion, Fred	S	6-2	191	8/2/59	7	Miami	Gainesville, Fla.	D5-'82	12/12
64	Matich, Trevor	C	6-4	270	10/9/61	4	Brigham Young	Sacramento, Calif.	D1-'85	6/4
48	McCabe, Jerry	LB	6-1	225	1/25/65	2	Holy Cross	Detroit, Mich.	FA-'87	3/3
50	†McGrew, Lawrence	LB	6-5	233	7/23/57	8	Southern California	Berkeley, Calif.	D2-'80	12/12
23	†McSwain, Rod	CB	6-1	198	1/28/62	5	Clemson	Caroleen, N.C.	T(Atl)-'84	12/0
67	Moore, Steve	T	6-5	305	10/1/60	6	Tennessee State	Memphis, Tenn.	D3b-'83	5/4
86	Morgan, Stanley	WR	5-11	181	2/17/55	12	Tennessee	Easley, S.C.	D1b-'77	9/9
75	Morriss, Guy	C-G	6-4	260	5/13/51	16	Texas Christian	Arlington, Tex.	FA-'84	11/7
34	Perryman, Bob	RB	6-1	233	10/16/64	2	Michigan	Bourne, Mass.	D3-'87	9/1
70	Plunkett, Art	T	6-8	282	3/8/59	7	Nevada-Las Vegas	Salt Lake City, Utah	FA-'85	7/1
22	Profit, Eugene	CB	5-10	175	11/11/64	3	Yale	Gardena, Calif.	FA-'86	7/0
12	†Ramsey, Tom	QB	6-1	189	7/9/61	4	UCLA	Granada Hills, Calif.	D10c-'83	9/3
52	†Rembert, Johnny	LB	6-3	234	1/19/61	6	Clemson	Arcadia, Fla.	D4-'83	11/1
95	Reynolds, Ed	LB	6-5	242	9/23/61	6	Virginia	Ridgeway, Va.	FA-'83	12/1
65	Ruth, Mike	NT	6-1	266	2/25/64	2	Boston College	Norristown, Pa.	D2a-'86	2/0
88	†Scott, Willie	TE	6-4	245	2/13/59	8	South Carolina	Newberry, S.C.	T(KC)-'86	9/1
77	†Sims, Kenneth	DE	6-5	271	10/31/59	7	Texas	Kosse, Tex.	D1a-'82	12/8
81	†Starring, Stephen	WR	5-10	172	7/30/61	6	McNeese State	Vinton, La.	D3a-'83	11/1
30	Tatupu, Mosi	RB	6-0	227	4/26/55	11	Southern California	Honolulu, Hawaii	D8b-'78	12/9
56	Tippett, Andre	LB	6-3	241	12/27/59	7	Iowa	Newark, N.J.	D2b-'82	13/13
60	Veris, Garin	DE	6-4	255	2/27/63	4	Stanford	Chillicothe, Ohio	D2a-'85	12/12
73	Villa, Danny	T	6-5	305	9/21/64	2	Arizona State	Nogales, Ariz.	D5a-'87	11/7
24	Weathers, Robert	RB	6-2	225	9/13/60	6	Arizona State	Ft. Pierce, Fla.	D2a-'82	0*
98	Wilburn, Steve	DE	6-4	266	2/25/61	2	Illinois State	Chicago, Ill.	FA-'87	3/3
96	Williams, Brent	DE	6-3	278	10/23/64	3	Toledo	Flint, Mich.	D7b-'86	12/4
54	†Williams, Ed	LB	6-4	244	9/8/61	5	Texas	Ector, Tex.	D2-'84	12/7
90	†Williams, Toby	NT	6-4	270	11/19/59	6	Nebraska	Washington, D.C.	D10b-'83	12/12
61	†Wooten, Ron	G	6-4	273	6/28/59	7	North Carolina	Kinston, N.C.	D6-'81	13/13

* Flutie played 1 game with Chicago, 1 with New England in '87; Francis played 8 games with San Francisco, 1 game with New England; Weathers missed '87 season due to injury.

†Option playout; subject to developments.

Retired—Don Blackmon, 7-year linebacker, 4 games in '87; Steve Nelson, 14-year linebacker, 11 games in '87.

Also played with Patriots in '87—DE Julius Adams (10 games), LB Rogers Alexander (3), CB Ricky Atkinson (1), TE Greg Baty (5), WR Mike Benson (active for 1 game but did not play), RB Frank Bianchini (1), LB Mel Black (3), QB Bob Bleier (3), WR Brian Carey (2), S Duffy Cobbs (3), WR Wayne Coffey (3), RB Tony Collins (13), T George Colton (3), LB Rico Corsetti (2), LB Steve Doig (1), TE Todd Frain (3), TE Arnold Franklin (3), NT John Guzik (3), CB David Hendley (2), P Alan Herline (3), WR Harold Jackson (active for 1 game but did not play), WR Bill LaFreniere (active for 1 game but did not play), RB Michael LeBlanc (4), WR Larry Linne (3), NT Dino Mangiero (2), LB Joe McHale (3), RB Chuck McSwain (3), LB Greg Moore (3), CB Joe Peterson (3), WR Clay Pickering (1), NT Tom Porell (1), DE Benton Reed (3), T Greg Robinson (3), LB Frank Sacco (2), G Todd Sandham (2), G Brian Saranovitz (active for 2 games but did not play), CB Jon Sawyer (2), K Eric Schubert (1), LB Randy Sealby (2), S Ron Shegog (3), G Eric Stokes (1), DE Bill Turner (2), C Darren Twombly (1), QB Todd Whitten (1), DE Murray Wichard (3), WR Derwin Williams (10), CB Perry Williams (3), RB Carl Woods (2).

COACHING STAFF

Head Coach, Raymond Berry

Pro Career: Has led the Patriots to two playoff appearances in three full seasons as the team's head coach (came to club midway through 1984). New England went 8-7 last year, and 11-5 in each of the prior two seasons. In 1986, the Patriots won the AFC East title and then lost to the host Denver Broncos in divisional playoff game. The previous season, 1985, saw the Patriots reach Super Bowl XX after gaining entry into the playoffs as a wild-card team. New England reached the Super Bowl by winning three straight road games, the only time it has been done in NFL history. Became the ninth head coach in Patriots history when he was named to replace Ron Meyer on October 25, 1984, after the eighth game of the season. Played receiver for the Baltimore Colts 1955-67. Made 631 catches for 9,275 yards and 68 touchdowns in his playing career. His number of career catches is presently fifth-best ever in the NFL, while his receiving yardage is eighth-best and his career touchdown catches fifteenth. Helped Colts to two world championships (1958 and 1959) and to NFL Championship Game (1964). Named all-pro three times (1958-60) and played in five Pro Bowl games. Led NFL in receiving 1958-60. Holds NFL Championship Game records for yardage (178) and receptions (12), set in 1958 sudden-death title game vs. New York Giants. Was inducted into Pro Football Hall of Fame on July 29, 1973, five years after his retirement. Was receivers coach with Dallas Cowboys in 1968-69, Detroit Lions 1973-75, Cleveland Browns 1976-77, and New England Patriots 1978-81. Career record: 37-23.

Background: Attended Paris (Tex.) High School, Schreiner (Tex.) Institute, and Southern Methodist 1951-54, where he played receiver. Receivers coach at Arkansas 1970-72.

Personal: Born February 27, 1933, in Corpus Christi, Tex. Raymond and his wife, Sally, live in Medfield, Mass., with their children—Mark, Suzanne, and Ashley.

Assistant Coaches

Don Blackmon, staff assistant; born March 14, 1958, Pompano Beach, Fla., lives in Norfolk, Mass. Linebacker Tulsa 1976-80. Pro linebacker New England Patriots 1981-87. Pro coach: Joined Patriots in 1988.

Jimmy Carr, defensive backs; born March 25, 1933, Kayford, W. Va., lives in North Attleboro, Mass. Running back-defensive back-linebacker Morris Harvey (now Univ. of Charleston, W. Va.) 1951-54. Pro running back-defensive back-linebacker Chicago Cardinals 1955-57, Montreal Alouettes (CFL) 1958, Philadelphia Eagles 1959-63, Washington Redskins 1964-65. Pro coach: Minnesota Vikings 1966-68, 1979-81, Chicago Bears 1969, 1973-74, Philadelphia Eagles 1970-72, Detroit Lions 1975-76, Buffalo Bills 1977, San Francisco 49ers 1978, Denver Gold (USFL) 1983-84, joined Patriots in 1985.

Bobby Grier, offensive backs, running game coordinator; born November 10, 1942, Detroit, Mich., lives in Holliston, Mass. Running back Iowa 1961-64. No pro playing experience. College coach: Eastern Michigan 1974-77, Boston College 1978-80. Pro coach: New England Patriots 1981. Moved to team's scouting department 1982-84. Rejoined Patriots coaching staff in 1985.

Ray Hamilton, assistant defensive line; born January 20, 1951, Omaha, Neb., lives in Sharon, Mass. Defensive tackle Oklahoma 1970-72. Nose tackle New England Patriots 1973-81. Pro coach: Joined Patriots in 1985.

Rod Humenuik, assistant head coach-offense, offensive coordinator; born June 17, 1938, Detroit, Mich., lives in Mansfield, Mass. Guard Southern California 1956-58. Pro guard Winnipeg Blue Bombers (CFL) 1960-62. College coach: Fullerton, Calif., J.C. 1964-65, Southern California 1966-70, Cal State-Northridge 1971-72 (head coach). Pro coach: Toronto Argonauts (CFL) 1973-74, Cleveland Browns 1975-82, Kansas City Chiefs 1983-84, joined Patriots in 1985.

New England Patriots 1988 First-Year Roster

Name	Pos.	Ht.	Wt.	Birth-date	College	Hometown	How Acq.
Allen, Marvin	RB	5-10	215	11/26/65	Tulane	Wichita Falls, Tex.	D11
Beasley, Derrick (1)	S	6-1	205	7/13/65	Winston-Salem State	Detroit, Mich.	D4b-'87
Brantley, LaRoy	LB	6-5	237	5/17/66	Amherst	Dorchester, Mass.	FA
Brown, Vincent	LB	6-2	245	1/9/65	Mississippi Valley St.	Decatur, Ga.	D2
Crumpler, Bobby	RB	5-11	200	4/22/65	North Carolina State	Newton Grove, N.C.	FA
Dickens, Gerold	LB	6-2	230	11/19/64	Florida	Plant City, Fla.	FA
Feagles, Jeff	P	6-0	198	3/7/66	Miami	Scottsdale, Ariz.	FA
Feggins, Howard	CB	5-9	198	5/6/65	North Carolina	South Hill, Va.	FA
Flynn, Chris	RB	5-9	185	10/15/65	Pennsylvania	Springfield, Pa.	FA
Galbraith, Neil	CB	6-0	170	10/25/65	Central State, Okla.	Guthrie, Okla.	D9
Garcia, Teddy	K	5-10	190	6/4/64	Northeast Louisiana	Lewisville, Tex.	D4c
Gibson, Tom (1)	DE	6-7	250	12/20/63	Northern Arizona	Saugus, Calif.	D5b-'87
Goad, Tim	NT	6-3	280	2/6/66	North Carolina	Claudville, Va.	D4a
Goldammer, Duane	G	6-4	268	2/19/65	Mankato State	St. Paul, Minn.	FA
Henning, Dan	QB	6-0	188	6/22/65	Maryland	Annandale, Va.	FA
Heren, Dieter (1)	LB	6-3	230	8/9/64	Michigan	Ft. Wayne, Ind.	FA
Hull, Lee	WR	6-0	185	12/31/65	Holy Cross	Vineland, N.J.	FA
Johnson, Steve	TE	6-6	245	6/22/65	Virginia Tech	Huntsville, Ala.	D6
Knizner, Matt	QB	6-3	203	1/17/65	Penn State	Greensbury, Pa.	FA
Lewis, Walter (1)	QB	6-0	198	4/26/62	Alabama	Brewton, Ala.	SD3-'84
Lloyd, Andre	LB	6-2	240	6/29/65	Jackson State	Brookhaven, Miss.	FA
Lossow, Rodney	C	6-3	275	8/28/65	Wisconsin	Minneapolis, Minn.	D10
Martin, Sammy	WR-KR	5-11	175	8/21/65	Louisiana State	New Orleans, La.	D4b
McPhearson, Gerrick	CB	5-9	173	5/31/66	Boston College	Towson, Md.	FA
Naposki, Eric	LB	6-2	230	12/20/66	Connecticut	Eastchester, N.Y.	FA
Nugent, David	NT	6-3	275	7/19/65	Boston College	Reading, Mass.	D12
Parker, Barry	WR	5-9	160	6/26/65	Texas-El Paso	LaMarque, Tex.	FA
Rehder, Tom	T	6-7	280	1/27/65	Notre Dame	Santa Maria, Calif.	D3
Richardson, Bruce	S	6-1	195	5/24/66	Stanford	Mahwah, N.J.	FA
Riley, Eric (1)	TE	6-3	240	10/10/64	Eastern Washington	Snoqualmie, Wash.	FA
Rundle, Todd	LB	6-3	240	3/21/66	Massachusetts	Essex Junction, Vt.	FA
Sealby, Randall (1)	LB	6-2	225	5/16/60	Missouri	Evergreen, Colo.	FA
Smith, David	CB	5-11	186	2/12/65	North Alabama	Opelika, Ala.	FA
Stephens, John	RB	6-1	220	2/23/66	Northwestern St., La.	Springhill, La.	D1
Stokes, Dan	C	6-4	255	7/9/65	Northeastern	Ansonia, Conn.	FA
Thompson, Bill	LB	6-3	230	3/7/66	Boston College	Trenton, N.J.	FA
Tumey, Terry	LB	6-2	230	10/29/65	UCLA	Tulsa, Okla.	FA
Usher, Darryl	WR-KR	5-8	170	1/3/65	Illinois	San Mateo, Calif.	D7
Vercheval, Pierre	C	6-1	275	11/22/64	Western Ontario	Trois-Rivieres, Canada	FA
Walker, Mike	DE	6-3	260	1/7/62	Fresno State	Richmond, Calif.	FA
Ward, David (1)	LB	6-2	232	3/10/64	Southern Arkansas	West Helena, Ark.	FA
White, Kevin	WR	5-11	203	6/30/65	South Carolina	Charlotte, N.C.	FA
Wilkins, Peter	LB	6-4	225	9/27/65	Idaho	Spokane, Wash.	FA
Wolkow, Troy	G	6-4	280	6/25/66	Minnesota	Lakeville, Minn.	D5
Yahn, Tom	RB	5-10	205	9/9/64	Penn State	Bronx, N.Y.	FA

The term NFL Rookie is defined as a player who is in his first season of professional football and has not been on the roster of another professional football team for any regular-season or postseason games. A Rookie is designated by an "R" on NFL rosters. Players who have been active in another professional football league or players who have NFL experience, including either preseason training camp or being on an active roster for fewer than three regular-season or postseason games, are termed NFL First-Year Players. An NFL First-Year Player is designated by a "1" on NFL rosters. Thereafter, a player on an NFL active roster for at least three regular-season or postseason games is credited with an additional year of NFL playing experience.

NOTES

Harold Jackson, receivers; born January 6, 1946, Quincy, Miss., lives in Milford, Mass. Wide receiver Jackson State 1964-67. Pro wide receiver Los Angeles Rams 1968, 1973-77, Philadelphia Eagles 1969-72, New England Patriots 1978-81, Seattle Seahawks 1983. Pro coach: Joined Patriots in 1985.

Eddie Khayat, defensive line; born September 14, 1935, Moss Point, Miss., lives in Milford, Mass. Offensive-defensive end Millsaps 1953, Perkinston J.C. 1954, Tulane 1955-56. Pro defensive end-defensive tackle Washington Redskins 1957, 1962-63, Philadelphia Eagles 1958-61, 1964-65, Boston Patriots 1966. Pro coach: New Orleans Saints 1967-70, Philadelphia Eagles 1971-72 (head coach), Detroit Lions 1973-74, 1982-84, Atlanta Falcons 1975-76, Baltimore Colts 1977-81, joined Patriots in 1985.

John Polonchek, special assistant to head coach; born January 1, 1928, in Granastrov, Czechoslovakia, lives in Norton, Mass. Running back-defensive back Michigan State 1947-49. No pro playing experience. College coach: Michigan State 1950, 1955-57, Colorado 1959-61. Pro coach: Oakland Raiders 1967-71, Green Bay Packers 1972-74, New England Patriots 1975-81, New Jersey Generals (USFL) 1982-83, Los Angeles Raiders 1984 (scout), rejoined Patriots in 1985.

Dante Scarnecchia, special teams, tight ends; born February 15, 1948, Los Angeles, Calif., lives in Wrentham, Mass. Center Taft, Calif., J.C. 1966-67, California Western 1968-69. No pro playing experience. College coach: California Western 1970-72, Iowa State 1973-74, Southern Methodist 1975-76, 1980-81, Pacific 1977-78, Northern Arizona 1979. Pro coach: Joined Patriots in 1982.

Don Shinnick, linebackers; born May 15, 1935, Kansas City, Mo., lives in Walpole, Mass. Guard-defensive back-running back-linebacker UCLA 1954-56. Pro linebacker Baltimore Colts 1957-69. College coach: Central Methodist College (head coach) 1979-81. Pro coach: Chicago Bears 1970-71, St. Louis Cardinals 1972, Oakland Raiders 1973-77, joined Patriots in 1985.

Les Steckel, quarterbacks, passing-game coordinator; born July 1, 1946, Whitehall, Pa., lives in Foxboro, Mass. Running back Kansas 1964-68. No pro playing experience. College coach: Colorado 1972-76, Navy 1977. Pro coach: San Francisco 49ers 1978, Minnesota Vikings 1979-84 (head coach 1984), joined Patriots in 1985.

NEW YORK JETS

American Football Conference Eastern Division

Team Colors: Kelly Green and White

598 Madison Avenue
New York, New York 10022
Telephone: (212) 421-6600

Club Officials

Chairman of the Board: Leon Hess
President: Steve Gutman
Director of Player Personnel: Mike Hickey
Pro Personnel Director: Jim Royer
Talent Scouts: Joe Collins, Don Grammer, Sid Hall, Ron Nay, Marv Sunderland
Director of Public Relations: Frank Ramos
Assistant Director of Public Relations: Ron Cohen
Director of Operations: Mike Kensil
Ticket Manager: Bob Parente
Video Director: Jim Pons
Trainer: Bob Reese
Assistant Trainers: Pepper Burruss, Joe Patten
Equipment Manager: Bill Hampton

Stadium: Giants Stadium • **Capacity:** 76,891
East Rutherford, New Jersey 07073

Playing Surface: AstroTurf

Training Center: 1000 Fulton Avenue
Hempstead, New York 11550
(516) 538-6600

1988 Schedule

Preseason

Aug. 6	at Philadelphia	7:30
Aug. 13	at New York Giants	8:00
Aug. 18	vs. Clev. at Montreal, Can.	7:30
Aug. 27	vs. G.B. at Madison, Wis.	1:00

Regular Season

Sept. 4	at New England	4:00
Sept. 11	at Cleveland	4:00
Sept. 18	**Houston**	1:00
Sept. 25	at Detroit	1:00
Oct. 2	**Kansas City**	4:00
Oct. 9	at Cincinnati	1:00
Oct. 17	**Buffalo** (Monday)	9:00
Oct. 23	at Miami	4:00
Oct. 30	**Pittsburgh**	1:00
Nov. 6	at Indianapolis	4:00
Nov. 13	**New England**	1:00
Nov. 20	at Buffalo	1:00
Nov. 27	**Miami**	1:00
Dec. 4	at Kansas City	3:00
Dec. 10	**Indianapolis** (Saturday)	12:30
Dec. 18	**New York Giants**	1:00

Jets Coaching History

New York Titans 1960-62
(188-219-7)

1960-61	Sammy Baugh	14-14-0
1962	Clyde (Bulldog) Turner	5-9-0
1963-73	Weeb Ewbank	73-78-6
1974-75	Charley Winner*	9-14-0
1975	Ken Shipp	1-4-0
1976	Lou Holtz**	3-10-0
1976	Mike Holovak	0-1-0
1977-82	Walt Michaels	41-49-1
1983-87	Joe Walton	42-40-0

*Released after nine games in 1975
**Resigned after 13 games in 1976

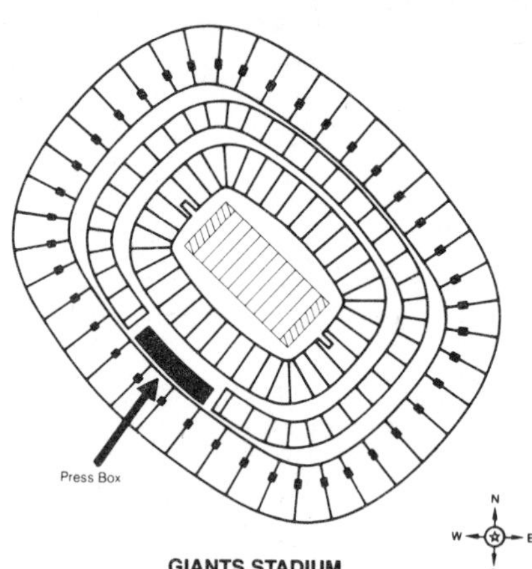

GIANTS STADIUM

Record Holders

Individual Records—Career

Category	Name	Performance
Rushing (Yds.)	Freeman McNeil, 1981-87	5,850
Passing (Yds.)	Joe Namath, 1965-1976	27,057
Passing (TDs)	Joe Namath, 1965-1976	170
Receiving (No.)	Don Maynard, 1960-1972	627
Receiving (Yds.)	Don Maynard, 1960-1972	11,732
Interceptions	Bill Baird, 1963-69	34
Punting (Avg.)	Curley Johnson, 1961-68	42.8
Punt Return (Avg.)	Dick Christy, 1961-63	16.2
Kickoff Return (Avg.)	Bobby Humphery, 1984-87	24.1
Field Goals	Pat Leahy, 1974-1987	218
Touchdowns (Tot.)	Don Maynard, 1960-1972	88
Points	Pat Leahy, 1974-1987	1,078

Individual Records—Single Season

Category	Name	Performance
Rushing (Yds.)	Freeman McNeil, 1985	1,331
Passing (Yds.)	Joe Namath, 1967	4,007
Passing (TDs)	Al Dorow, 1960	26
	Joe Namath, 1967	26
Receiving (No.)	Al Toon, 1986	85
Receiving (Yds.)	Don Maynard, 1967	1,434
Interceptions	Dainard Paulson, 1964	12
Punting (Avg.)	Curley Johnson, 1965	45.3
Punt Return (Avg.)	Dick Christy, 1961	21.3
Kickoff Return (Avg.)	Bobby Humphery, 1984	30.7
Field Goals	Jim Turner, 1968	34
Touchdowns (Tot.)	Art Powell, 1960	14
	Don Maynard, 1965	14
	Emerson Boozer, 1972	14
Points	Jim Turner, 1968	145

Individual Records—Single Game

Category	Name	Performance
Rushing (Yds.)	Freeman McNeil, 9-15-85	192
Passing (Yds.)	Joe Namath, 9-24-72	496
Passing (TDs)	Joe Namath, 9-24-72	6
Receiving (No.)	Clark Gaines, 9-21-80	17
Receiving (Yds.)	Don Maynard, 11-17-68	228
Interceptions	Dainard Paulson, 9-28-63	3
	Bill Baird, 10-31-64	3
	Rich Sowells, 9-23-73	3
Field Goals	Jim Turner, 11-3-68	6
	Bobby Howfield, 12-3-72	6
Touchdowns (Tot.)	Wesley Walker, 9-21-86	4
Points	Jim Turner, 11-3-68	19
	Pat Leahy, 9-16-84	19

1987 Team Record

Preseason (2-2)

Date	Result		Opponents
8/15	W	13-10	Philadelphia
8/22	L	27-29	at Tampa Bay
8/29	W	30-23	at N.Y. Giants
9/4	L	6-30	at San Diego
		76-92	

Regular Season (6-9)

Date	Result		Opponents	Att.
9/13	W	31-28	at Buffalo	76,718
9/21	W	43-24	New England	70,847
9/27	C		at Pittsburgh	
10/4	L	24-38	Dallas	12,370
10/11	L	0- 6	at Indianapolis	34,927
10/18	W	37-31	Miami (OT)	18,249
10/25	L	16-17	at Washington	53,497
11/1	L	14-19	Indianapolis	60,863
11/9	W	30-14	Seattle	60,452
11/15	W	16- 9	at Kansas City	40,718
11/22	L	14-17	Buffalo	58,407
11/29	W	27-20	Cincinnati	41,135
12/7	L	28-37	at Miami	62,592
12/13	L	20-42	at New England	60,617
12/20	L	27-38	Philadelphia	30,572
12/27	L	7-20	at N.Y. Giants	68,318

(OT) Overtime
C (Cancelled due to players' strike.)

Score by Periods

Jets	32	95	68	133	6	—	334
Opponents	58	129	105	68	0	—	360

Attendance

Home 352,895 Away 397,387 Total 750,282
Single-game home record, 74,975 (12-2-84)
Single-season home record, 541,832 (1985)

1987 Team Statistics

	Jets	Opp.
Total First Downs	292	300
Rushing	97	117
Passing	169	153
Penalty	26	30
Third Down: Made/Att.	95/234	81/210
Fourth Down: Made/Att.	10/21	4/8
Total Net Yards	4630	5041
Avg. Per Game	308.7	336.1
Total Plays	1041	993
Avg. Per Play	4.4	5.1
Net Yards Rushing	1671	1835
Avg. Per Game	111.4	122.3
Total Rushes	458	476
Net Yards Passing	2959	3206
Avg. Per Game	197.3	213.7
Sacked/Yards Lost	66/443	29/206
Gross Yards	3402	3412
Att./Completions	517/302	488/260
Completion Pct.	58.4	53.3
Had Intercepted	15	18
Punts/Avg.	82/37.1	80/38.4
Net Punting Avg.	33.5	31.0
Penalties/Yards Lost	135/1055	96/881
Fumbles/Ball Lost	33/19	23/11
Touchdowns	39	43
Rushing	17	15
Passing	18	27
Returns	4	1
Avg. Time of Possession	30:28	29:32

1987 Individual Statistics

Scoring	TD R	TD P	TD Rt	PAT	FG	Saf	TP
Leahy	0	0	0	31/31	18/22	0	85
Hector	11	0	0	0/0	0/0	0	66
Toon	0	5	0	0/0	0/0	0	30
Shuler	0	3	0	0/0	0/0	0	18
Ragusa	0	0	0	7/7	2/4	0	13
Faaola	2	0	0	0/0	0/0	0	12
Harper	0	1	1	0/0	0/0	0	12
E. Hunter	0	2	0	0/0	0/0	0	12
Sohn	0	2	0	0/0	0/0	0	12
Bligen	1	0	0	0/0	0/0	0	6
Chirico	1	0	0	0/0	0/0	0	6
Griggs	0	1	0	0/0	0/0	0	6
Humphery	0	0	1	0/0	0/0	0	6
S. Hunter	0	1	0	0/0	0/0	0	6
Kurisko	0	1	0	0/0	0/0	0	6
McNeil	0	1	0	0/0	0/0	0	6
Miano	0	0	1	0/0	0/0	0	6
Ryan	1	0	0	0/0	0/0	0	6
Townsell	0	0	1	0/0	0/0	0	6
Vick	1	0	0	0/0	0/0	0	6
Walker	0	1	0	0/0	0/0	0	6
Lyons	0	0	0	0/0	0/0	1	2
Jets	17	18	4	38/38	20/26	1	334
Opponents	15	27	1	42/43	20/29	0	360

Passing	Att.	Comp.	Yds.	Pct.	TD	Int.	Tkld.	Rate
O'Brien	393	234	2696	59.5	13	8	50/364	82.8
Norrie	68	35	376	51.5	1	4	15/72	48.4
Ryan	53	32	314	60.4	4	2	1/7	86.5
Briggs	2	0	0	0.0	0	1	0/0	0.0
Jennings	1	1	16	100.0	0	0	0/0	118.8
Jets	517	302	3402	58.4	18	15	66/443	77.7
Opponents	488	260	3412	53.3	27	18	29/206	78.7

Rushing	Att.	Yds.	Avg.	LG	TD
McNeil	121	530	4.4	30	0
Hector	111	435	3.9	20t	11
Vick	77	257	3.3	14	1
E. Hunter	48	169	3.5	23	0
Bligen	31	128	4.1	15	1
O'Brien	30	61	2.0	11	0
Faaola	14	43	3.1	18	2
Chirico	12	22	1.8	4	1
D. Foster	1	9	9.0	9	0
Jennings	2	5	2.5	4	0
Norrie	5	5	1.0	2	0
Ryan	4	5	1.3	8t	1
Briggs	1	4	4.0	4	0
Townsell	1	−2	−2.0	−2	0
Jets	458	1671	3.6	32	17
Opponents	476	1835	3.9	35	15

Receiving	No.	Yds.	Avg.	LG	TD
Toon	68	976	14.4	58t	5
Shuler	43	434	10.1	32t	3
Hector	32	249	7.8	27	0
McNeil	24	262	10.9	57	1
Sohn	23	261	11.3	31	2
Harper	18	225	12.5	35t	1
Holman	15	155	10.3	30	0
Klever	14	152	10.9	30	0
Vick	13	108	8.3	23	0
Bligen	11	81	7.4	19	0
Walker	9	190	21.1	59	1
S. Hunter	6	50	8.3	12	1
E. Hunter	5	24	4.8	8t	2
E. Riley	4	42	10.5	16	0
Townsell	4	37	9.3	11	0
Chirico	4	18	4.5	8	0
Sweet	3	45	15.0	22	0
Griggs	2	17	8.5	13	1
Kurisko	1	41	41.0	41t	1
Faaola	1	16	16.0	16	0
Gaffney	1	10	10.0	10	0
D. Foster	1	9	9.0	9	0
Jets	302	3402	11.3	59	18
Opponents	260	3412	13.1	57	27

Interceptions	No.	Yds.	Avg.	LG	TD
Howard	3	29	9.7	29	0
Hamilton	3	25	8.3	25	0
Miano	3	24	8.0	21	0
Radachowsky	2	45	22.5	45	0
Robinson	1	38	38.0	38	0
Heath	1	35	35.0	35	0
Holmes	1	20	20.0	20	0
Haslett	1	9	9.0	9	0
Crable	1	8	8.0	8	0
Hogan	1	5	5.0	5	0
Rose	1	1	1.0	1	0
Jets	18	239	13.3	45	0
Opponents	15	210	14.0	44	0

Punting	No.	Yds.	Avg.	In 20	LG
Jennings	64	2444	38.2	12	58
O'Connor	18	602	33.4	2	47
Jets	82	3046	37.1	14	58
Opponents	80	3073	38.4	17	67

Punt Returns	No.	FC	Yds.	Avg.	LG	TD
Townsell	32	11	381	11.9	91t	1
Harper	4	1	93	23.3	78t	1
D. Foster	2	0	8	4.0	4	0
R. Smith	2	0	9	4.5	7	0
Collins	1	0	0	0.0	0	0
Sohn	1	0	6	6.0	6	0
Jets	42	12	497	11.8	91t	2
Opponents	33	22	162	4.9	15	0

Kickoff Returns	No.	Yds.	Avg.	LG	TD
Humphery	18	357	19.8	47	0
Townsell	11	272	24.7	60	0
E. Hunter	8	123	15.4	27	0
Martin	8	180	22.5	47	0
Klever	5	85	17.0	29	0
Harper	4	75	18.8	22	0
R. Smith	4	60	15.0	20	0
Sohn	3	47	15.7	18	0
Barber	2	5	2.5	5	0
Faaola	1	4	4.0	4	0
Griggs	1	13	13.0	13	0
Jets	65	1221	18.8	60	0
Opponents	54	1013	18.8	43	0

Sacks	No.
Gordon	5.0
Gastineau	4.5
Lyons	3.5
Crable	2.5
Nichols	2.5
Howard	2.0
Bennett	1.5
Mersereau	1.5
Rose	1.5
Brophy	1.0
Holmes	1.0
Klecko	1.0
Zordich	1.0
Glenn	0.5
Jets	29.0
Opponents	66.0

New York Jets 1988 Veteran Roster

No.	Name	Pos.	Ht.	Wt.	Birth-date	NFL Exp.	College	Hometown	How Acq.	'87 Games/ Starts
60	Alexander, Dan	G-T	6-4	274	6/17/55	12	Louisiana State	Houston, Tex.	D8a-'77	12/12
97	Baldwin, Don	DE	6-3	263	7/9/64	2	Purdue	St. Charles, Mo.	FA-'87	8/0
95	Baldwin, Tom	DT	6-4	270	5/13/61	4	Tulsa	Lansing, Ill.	D9-'84	0*
63	Banker, Ted	G-C	6-2	275	2/17/61	5	Southeast Missouri	Belleville, Ill.	FA-'83	13/9
31	Barber, Marion	RB	6-3	228	12/6/59	7	Minnesota	Detroit, Mich.	D2-'81	12/0
54	†Benson, Troy	LB	6-2	235	7/30/63	3	Pittsburgh	Altoona, Pa.	D5a-'85	11/11
64	Bingham, Guy	C-G	6-3	260	2/25/58	9	Montana	Aberdeen, Wash.	D10-'80	12/11
23	Bligen, Dennis	RB	5-11	215	3/3/62	5	St. John's	Queens Village, N.Y.	FA-'87	6/2
59	†Clifton, Kyle	LB	6-4	236	8/23/62	5	Texas Christian	Bridgeport, Tex.	D3-'84	12/8
50	Crable, Bob	LB	6-3	230	9/22/59	7	Notre Dame	Cincinnati, Ohio	D1-'82	12/11
22	Dykes, Sean	CB	5-10	170	8/8/64	2	Bowling Green	New Orleans, La.	FA-'87	6/2
52	Elam, Onzy	LB	6-2	225	12/1/64	2	Tennessee State	Miami, Fla.	D3-'87	5/0
30	†Faaola, Nuu	RB	5-11	210	1/15/64	3	Hawaii	Honolulu, Hawaii	D9-'86	12/0
8	Flick, Tom	QB	6-2	190	9/30/58	5	Washington	Bellevue, Wash.	FA-'87	0*
98	Foster, Jerome	DE-DT	6-2	275	7/25/60	4	Ohio State	Detroit, Mich.	FA-'86	4/0
99	Gastineau, Mark	DE	6-5	255	11/20/56	10	East Central Oklahoma	Springerville, Ariz.	D2-'79	15/7
35	Glenn, Kerry	CB	5-9	175	3/31/62	3	Minnesota	East St. Louis, Ill.	D10-'85	8/2
55	Gordon, Alex	LB	6-5	246	9/14/64	2	Cincinnati	Jacksonville, Fla.	D2-'87	12/12
81	Griggs, Billy	TE	6-3	230	8/4/62	4	Virginia	Pennsauken, N.J.	D8a-'84	12/1
79	Haight, Mike	G-T	6-4	270	10/6/62	3	Iowa	Dyersville, Iowa	D1-'86	6/1
39	†Hamilton, Harry	S	6-0	195	11/29/62	5	Penn State	Wilkes-Barre, Pa.	D7-'84	12/12
84	Harper, Michael	WR	5-10	180	5/11/61	3	Southern California	Kansas City, Mo.	FA-'86	3/2
51	Haslett, Jim	LB	6-3	236	12/9/56	9	Indiana, Pa.	Pittsburgh, Pa.	FA-'87	3/2
34	Hector, Johnny	RB	5-11	200	11/26/60	6	Texas A&M	New Iberia, La.	D2-'83	11/6
47	†Holmes, Jerry	CB	6-2	175	12/22/57	7	West Virginia	Hampton, Va.	FA-'86	8/7
28	†Howard, Carl	CB-S	6-2	190	9/20/61	5	Rutgers	Irvington, N.J.	FA-'85	12/7
48	†Humphery, Bobby	CB-KR	5-10	180	8/23/61	5	New Mexico State	Lubbock, Tex.	D9-'83	12/2
89	†Klever, Rocky	TE	6-3	230	7/10/59	6	Montana	Anchorage, Alaska	D9-'82	12/6
5	Leahy, Pat	K	6-0	193	3/19/51	15	St. Louis	St. Louis, Mo.	FA-'74	12/0
26	Lyles, Lester	S	6-3	218	12/27/62	4	Virginia	Washington, D.C.	D2-'84	4/1
93	Lyons, Marty	DE-DT	6-5	269	1/15/57	10	Alabama	St. Petersburg, Fla.	D1-'79	13/13
86	Martin, Tracy	WR-KR	6-3	205	12/4/64	2	North Dakota	Minneapolis, Minn.	D6-'87	12/0
57	McArthur, Kevin	LB	6-2	245	5/11/63	3	Lamar	Lake Charles, La.	FA-'86	12/3
68	McElroy, Reggie	T	6-6	275	3/4/60	6	West Texas State	Beaumont, Tex.	D2-'82	8/5
24	McNeil, Freeman	RB	5-11	214	4/22/59	8	UCLA	Carson, Calif.	D1-'81	9/8
56	Mehl, Lance	LB	6-3	233	2/14/58	9	Penn State	Bellaire, Ohio	D3-'80	3/2
94	Mersereau, Scott	DE	6-3	278	4/8/65	2	Southern Connecticut	Riverhead, N.Y.	FA-'87	13/4
36	†Miano, Rich	S	6-0	200	9/3/62	4	Hawaii	Honolulu, Hawaii	D6b-'85	12/11
58	Monger, Matt	LB	6-1	238	11/15/61	4	Oklahoma State	Miami, Okla.	D8-'85	12/0
77	Nichols, Gerald	DT	6-2	261	2/10/64	2	Florida State	St. Louis, Mo.	D7-'87	13/5
7	O'Brien, Ken	QB	6-4	208	11/27/60	6	California-Davis	Sacramento, Calif.	D1-'83	12/12
25	Radachowsky, George	S	5-11	190	9/7/62	4	Boston College	Danbury, Conn.	FA-'87	8/3
92	Rose, Ken	LB	6-1	215	6/9/61	2	Nevada-Las Vegas	Sacramento, Calif.	FA-'87	10/3
10	Ryan, Pat	QB	6-3	210	9/16/55	11	Tennessee	Oklahoma City, Okla.	D11-'78	13/1
82	Shuler, Mickey	TE	6-3	231	8/21/56	11	Penn State	Enola, Pa.	D3-'78	11/10
87	†Sohn, Kurt	WR-KR	5-11	180	6/26/57	7	Fordham	Huntington, N.Y.	FA-'81	12/4
53	†Sweeney, Jim	T-G	6-4	275	8/8/62	5	Pittsburgh	Pittsburgh, Pa.	D2a-'84	12/12
88	Toon, Al	WR	6-4	205	4/30/63	4	Wisconsin	Newport News, Va.	D1-'85	12/11
83	†Townsell, JoJo	WR-KR	5-9	180	11/4/60	4	UCLA	Reno, Nev.	D3-'83	12/0
43	Vick, Roger	RB	6-3	232	8/11/64	2	Texas A&M	Tomball, Tex.	D1-'87	12/10
85	Walker, Wesley	WR	6-0	182	5/26/55	12	California	Carson, Calif.	D2-'77	5/4
38	Zordich, Mike	S	5-11	207	10/12/63	2	Penn State	Youngstown, Ohio	FA-'87	10/0

* T. Baldwin missed '87 season due to injury; Flick was active for 1 game but did not play.

†Option playout; subject to developments.

Traded—Defensive end Barry Bennett to Los Angeles Raiders, cornerback Russell Carter to Los Angeles Raiders.

Also played with Jets in '87—LB Lynwood Alford (1 game), DT Adam Bethea (active for 1 game but did not play), QB Walter Briggs (1), LB Jay Brophy (3), T Chris Brown (1), RB Joe Burke (2), DE Tony Chickillo (2), RB John Chirico (3), S Trent Collins (3), C Martin Cornelson (3), G-T Anthony Corvino (2), G-C Eric Coss (3), C-G Joe Fields (10), RB Derrick Foster (3), WR Derrick Gaffney (2), DE Tony Garbarczyk (2), G-T Mitch Geier (active for 1 game but did not play), CB-S Jo Jo Heath (2), CB Marc Hogan (3), WR Scott Holman (3), G Tom Humphery (3), RB Eddie Hunter (3), WR Stan Hunter (3), G Vince Jasper (3), P Dave Jennings (12), T Ken Jones (3), T Gordon King (2), NT Joe Klecko (7), TE Jamie Kurisko (3), G Pete McCartney (3), RB Tim Newman (1), QB David Norrie (2), P Tom O'Connor (3), K Pat Ragusa (3), TE Eric Riley (2), CB Larry Robinson (3), DE Don Smith (3), WR-KR Reggie Smith (1), CB Treg Songy (2), TE Tony Sweet (3), T John Thomas (3), RB Maurice Turner (1), C Vinny Tuzeo (active for 1 game but did not play), LB Henry Walls (3), LB Ladell Wills (3), LB Mike Witteck (3).

COACHING STAFF

Head Coach, Joe Walton

Pro Career: Begins sixth year as head coach of the Jets. Entered pro coaching ranks as an assistant with the New York Giants in 1969-73. Joined the Washington Redskins' staff in 1974 and became the Redskins' offensive coordinator in 1978. Originally came to the Jets as the offensive coordinator in 1981. He played professionally for the Washington Redskins 1957-60 and the New York Giants 1961-63. Walton did some radio work before joining the Giants' staff as a scout in 1967-68. Career record: 42-40.

Background: Played tight end for the University of Pittsburgh 1953-56.

Personal: Born December 15, 1935, in Beaver Falls, Pa. Joe and his wife, Ginger, have three children—Jodi, Stacy, and Joseph, Jr. They live in Long Island.

Assistant Coaches

Zeke Bratkowski, quarterbacks; born October 20, 1931, Danville, Ill., lives in Long Island. Quarterback Georgia 1951-53. Pro quarterback Chicago Bears 1954, 1957-60, Los Angeles Rams 1961-63, Green Bay Packers 1963-68, 1971. Pro coach: Green Bay Packers 1969-70, 1975-81, Chicago Bears 1972-74, Baltimore-Indianapolis Colts 1982-84, joined Jets in 1985.

Ray Callahan, quality control; born April 28, 1933, Lebanon, Ky., lives in Long Island. Guard-linebacker Kentucky 1952-56. No pro playing experience. College coach: Kentucky 1963-67, Cincinnati 1968-72 (head coach 1969-72). Pro coach: Baltimore Colts 1973, Florida Blazers (WFL) 1974, Chicago Bears 1975-77, Washington Redskins 1978-80, Houston Oilers 1981-82, joined Jets in 1983.

Bud Carson, defensive coordinator; born April 28, 1931, Brackenridge, Pa., lives in Connecticut. Defensive back North Carolina 1948-52. No pro playing experience. College coach: North Carolina 1957-64, South Carolina 1965, Georgia Tech 1966-71 (head coach). Pro coach: Pittsburgh Steelers 1972-77, Los Angeles Rams 1978-81, Baltimore Colts 1982, Kansas City Chiefs 1983-84, joined Jets in 1985.

Wally Chambers, defensive line; born May 15, 1951, Phenix City, Ala., lives in Long Island. Defensive lineman Eastern Kentucky 1969-72. Pro defensive lineman Chicago Bears 1973-77, Tampa Bay Buccaneers 1978-79. College coach: Northern Iowa 1983-84, East Carolina 1985-86, Temple 1987. Pro coach: Joined Jets in 1988.

Mike Faulkiner, secondary; born March 27, 1947, Cameron, W. Va., lives in Long Island. Quarterback-defensive back West Virginia Tech 1967-70. No pro playing experience. College coach: Eastern Illinois 1981. Pro coach: Toronto Argonauts (CFL) 1979, New York Giants 1980, Montreal Alouettes (CFL) 1982, joined Jets in 1983.

Bobby Hammond, running backs; born February 20, 1952, Orangeburg, S.C., lives in New York. Running back Morgan State 1973-75. Pro running back New York Giants 1976-79, Washington Redskins 1979-80. Pro coach: Joined Jets in 1983.

Rich Kotite, offensive coordinator, receivers; born October 13, 1942, Brooklyn, N.Y., lives in Staten Island. End Wagner 1963-65. Pro tight end New York Giants 1967, 1969-72, Pittsburgh Steelers 1968. College coach: Tennessee-Chattanooga 1973-76. Pro coach: New Orleans Saints 1977, Cleveland Browns 1978-82, joined Jets in 1983.

Larry Pasquale, special teams; born April 21, 1941, Brooklyn, N.Y., lives in Long Island. Quarterback Bridgeport 1961-63. No pro playing experience. College coach: Slippery Rock State 1967, Boston University 1968, Navy 1969-70, Massachusetts 1971-75, Idaho State 1976. Pro coach: Montreal Alouettes (CFL) 1977-78, Detroit Lions 1979, joined Jets in 1980.

New York Jets 1988 First-Year Roster

Name	Pos.	Ht.	Wt.	Birth-date	College	Hometown	How Acq.
Booty, John	CB	6-1	180	10/9/65	Texas Christian	Carthage, Tex.	D10
Brown, Orlando (1)	RB	5-10	195	12/31/62	Indiana	Memphis, Tenn.	FA
Brown, Dave (1)	LB	6-2	215	1/17/64	Miami, Ohio	Dayton, Ohio	FA
Cadigan, Dave	T	6-4	280	4/6/65	Southern California	Newport Beach, Calif.	D1
Davis, Kelvin (1)	G	6-3	265	2/7/63	J.C. Smith	East Orange, N.J.	FA
Farris, Ray (1)	CB	5-8	161	1/14/65	Utah State	Belmont, Calif.	FA
Frase, Paul	DE	6-5	270	5/5/65	Syracuse	Barrington, N.H.	D6
Galimore, Jeff (1)	TE	6-2	232	6/14/64	Arizona State	Oxnard, Calif.	FA
Galvin, John	LB	6-2	226	7/9/65	Boston College	Lowell, Mass.	D11
Goss, Albert	NT	6-7	355	11/15/64	Jackson State	Miami, Fla.	D12
Hampton, Kwante (1)	WR	6-0	183	12/11/63	Long Beach State	Van Nuys, Calif.	FA
Hasty, James	CB	6-0	200	5/23/65	Washington State	Seattle, Wash.	D3b
Harris, Jamie (1)	WR	5-7	156	3/23/63	Oklahoma State	McKinney, Tex.	FA
Lewis, Sid (1)	CB	5-11	180	5/30/64	Penn State	Canton, Ohio	D10-'87
Lott, John (1)	G	6-2	258	5/9/64	North Texas State	Denton, Tex.	FA
Makins, Mike (1)	DE	6-4	260	10/19/65	Tenn.-Chattanooga	Atlanta, Ga.	FA
McCarthy, Tom (1)	P	6-2	200	6/25/62	Hawaii	Honolulu, Hawaii	FA
McMillan, Erik	S	6-2	200	5/3/65	Missouri	Silver Spring, Md.	D3a
Metcalf, Major (1)	WR	6-4	215	11/20/63	Central Michigan	Muskegon, Mich.	FA
Miller, Jeff (1)	QB	6-2	216	3/14/63	Indiana State	Ossian, Ind.	FA
Neubert, Keith	TE	6-5	250	9/13/64	Nebraska	Fort Atkinson, Wis.	D8
O'Malley, Chris (1)	LB	6-3	225	9/14/64	Hofstra	Norcross, Ga.	FA
O'Brien, Chris (1)	P-K	5-10	187	8/5/64	San Diego State	Woodside, Calif.	FA
Oliver, Darryl (1)	RB	5-10	198	7/13/64	Miami	Palatka, Fla.	FA
Patton, Gary	RB	5-9	195	1/20/66	Eastern Michigan	Lorain, Ohio	D7
Quick, Greg (1)	T	6-5	290	4/26/64	Catawba	Laurinburg, N.C.	FA
Reilly, Dameon (1)	WR	5-11	175	5/10/63	Rhode Island	New York, N.Y.	FA
Riley, Bobby (1)	WR	5-8	168	10/17/64	Oklahoma State	Stroud, Okla.	FA
Ross, Alvin (1)	RB	5-10	233	5/3/63	Central State, Okla.	Aurora, Ill.	FA
Sanders, Bill (1)	TE	6-3	229	9/25/64	Cal State-Sacramento	Martinez, Calif.	FA
Sawyer, Jon (1)	CB	5-8	167	4/6/65	Cincinnati	Miami, Fla.	FA
Stepanek, Joe (1)	DE	6-4	259	11/6/63	Minnesota	Cedar Rapids, Iowa	FA
Tamm, Ralph	G-DE	6-3	275	3/11/66	West Chester State	Bensalem, Pa.	D9
Thomas, Curtland (1)	WR	5-11	189	2/19/62	Missouri	St. Louis, Mo.	FA
Tilton, Ron (1)	G	6-4	270	8/9/63	Tulane	Tampa, Fla.	FA
Walker, Gary (1)	G	6-4	266	12/15/63	Boston University	Portsmouth, N.H.	FA
Walton, Riley (1)	TE	6-3	230	8/6/62	Tennessee State	Nashville, Tenn.	FA
Williams, Albert (1)	LB	6-2	231	9/7/64	Texas-El Paso	San Antonio, Tex.	FA
Williams, Maurice (1)	RB	5-11	212	11/16/64	VPI	Virginia Beach, Va.	FA
Williams, Terry	CB	5-11	205	10/14/65	Bethune-Cookman	Homestead, Fla.	D2
Withycombe, Mike	T	6-5	310	11/18/64	Fresno State	Lemoore, Calif.	D5
Woods, Carl (1)	RB	5-11	197	10/22/64	Vanderbilt	Gallitin, Tenn.	FA

The term NFL Rookie is defined as a player who is in his first season of professional football and has not been on the roster of another professional football team for any regular-season or postseason games. A Rookie is designated by an "R" on NFL rosters. Players who have been active in another professional football league or players who have NFL experience, including either preseason training camp or being on an active roster for fewer than three regular-season or postseason games, are termed NFL First-Year Players. An NFL First-Year Player is designated by a "1" on NFL rosters. Thereafter, a player on an NFL active roster for at least three regular-season or postseason games is credited with an additional year of NFL playing experience.

NOTES

Dan Radakovich, offensive line; born November 27, 1935, Duquesne, Pa., lives in Long Island. Center-linebacker Penn State 1954-56. No pro playing experience. College coach: Penn State 1960-69, Cincinnati 1970, Colorado 1972-73, North Carolina State 1982. Pro coach: Pittsburgh Steelers 1971, 1974-77, San Francisco 49ers 1978, Los Angeles Rams 1979-81, Denver Broncos 1983, Minnesota Vikings 1984, joined Jets in 1985.

Jim Vechiarella, linebackers; born February 20, 1937, Youngstown, Ohio, lives in Long Island. Linebacker Youngstown State 1955-57. No pro playing experience. College coach: Youngstown State 1964-74, Southern Illinois 1976-77, Tulane 1978-80. Pro coach: Charlotte Hornets (WFL) 1975, Los Angeles Rams 1981-82, Kansas City Chiefs 1983-85, joined Jets in 1986.

PITTSBURGH STEELERS

American Football Conference Central Division

Team Colors: Black and Gold

Three Rivers Stadium
300 Stadium Circle
Pittsburgh, Pennsylvania 15212
Telephone: (412) 323-1200

Club Officials

Chairman of the Board: Arthur J. Rooney, Sr.
President: Daniel M. Rooney
Vice President: John R. McGinley
Vice President: Arthur J. Rooney, Jr.
Business Manager: Joe Gordon
Chief Negotiator: James A. Boston
Office Manager-Stadium: Dan Ferens
Publicity Director: Dan Edwards
Assistant Publicity Director: Pat Hanlon
Director of Player Personnel: Dick Haley
Director of Pro Scouting: Tom Modrak
Talent Scout-West: Bob Schmitz
Talent Scout-East: Tom Donahoe
Talent Scout-Midwest: Jesse Kaye
Director of Ticket Sales: Geraldine R. Glenn
Computer Director-Accounting: Jim Ellenberger
Trainers: Ralph Berlin, Francis Feld
Equipment Manager: Anthony Parisi

Stadium: Three Rivers Stadium •
Capacity: 59,000
300 Stadium Circle
Pittsburgh, Pennsylvania 15212

Playing Surface: AstroTurf

Training Camp: St. Vincent College
Latrobe, Pennsylvania 15650

1988 Schedule

Preseason

Aug. 5	at Washington	8:00
Aug. 14	**Philadelphia**	8:00
Aug. 20	at New York Giants	8:00
Aug. 27	at New Orleans	11:30 A.M.

Regular Season

Sept. 4	**Dallas**	1:00
Sept. 11	at Washington	1:00
Sept. 18	**Cincinnati**	1:00
Sept. 25	at Buffalo	1:00
Oct. 2	**Cleveland**	1:00
Oct. 9	at Phoenix	1:00
Oct. 16	**Houston**	1:00
Oct. 23	**Denver**	1:00
Oct. 30	at New York Jets	1:00
Nov. 6	at Cincinnati	1:00
Nov. 13	**Philadelphia**	1:00
Nov. 20	at Cleveland	1:00
Nov. 27	**Kansas City**	1:00
Dec. 4	at Houston	7:00
Dec. 11	at San Diego	1:00
Dec. 18	**Miami**	1:00

Steelers Coaching History

Pittsburgh Pirates 1933-40
(339-376-20)

1933	Forrest (Jap) Douds	3-6-2
1934	Luby DiMelio	2-10-0
1935-36	Joe Bach	10-14-0
1937-39	Johnny Blood (McNally)*	6-19-0
1939-40	Walt Kiesling	3-13-3
1941	Bert Bell**	0-2-0
	Aldo (Buff) Donelli***	0-5-0
1941-44	Walt Kiesling****	13-20-2
1945	Jim Leonard	2-8-0
1946-47	Jock Sutherland	13-10-1
1948-51	Johnny Michelosen	20-26-2
1952-53	Joe Bach	11-13-0
1954-56	Walt Kiesling	14-22-0
1957-64	Raymond (Buddy) Parker	51-47-6
1965	Mike Nixon	2-12-0
1966-68	Bill Austin	11-28-3
1969-87	Chuck Noll	178-121-1

*Released after three games in 1939
**Resigned after two games in 1941
***Released after five games in 1941
****Co-coach with Earle (Greasy) Neale in Philadelphia-Pittsburgh merger in 1943 and with Phil Handler in Chicago Cardinals-Pittsburgh merger in 1944

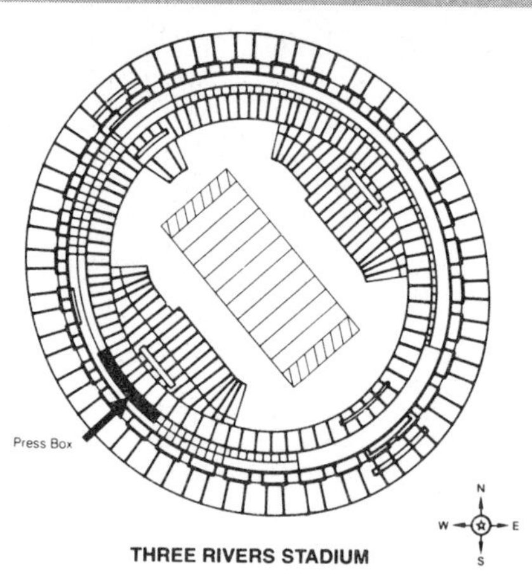

THREE RIVERS STADIUM

Record Holders

Individual Records—Career

Category	Name	Performance
Rushing (Yds.)	Franco Harris, 1972-1983	11,950
Passing (Yds.)	Terry Bradshaw, 1970-1983	27,989
Passing (TDs)	Terry Bradshaw, 1970-1983	212
Receiving (No.)	John Stallworth, 1974-1987	537
Receiving (Yds.)	John Stallworth, 1974-1987	8,723
Interceptions	Mel Blount, 1970-1983	57
Punting (Avg.)	Bobby Joe Green, 1960-61	45.7
Punt Return (Avg.)	Bobby Gage, 1949-1950	14.9
Kickoff Return (Avg.)	Lynn Chandnois, 1950-56	29.6
Field Goals	Roy Gerela, 1971-78	146
Touchdowns (Tot.)	Franco Harris, 1972-1983	100
Points	Roy Gerela, 1971-78	731

Individual Records—Single Season

Category	Name	Performance
Rushing (Yds.)	Franco Harris, 1975	1,246
Passing (Yds.)	Terry Bradshaw, 1979	3,724
Passing (TDs)	Terry Bradshaw, 1978	28
Receiving (No.)	John Stallworth, 1984	80
Receiving (Yds.)	John Stallworth, 1984	1,395
Interceptions	Mel Blount, 1975	11
Punting (Avg.)	Bobby Joe Green, 1961	47.0
Punt Return (Avg.)	Bobby Gage, 1949	16.0
Kickoff Return (Avg.)	Lynn Chandnois, 1952	35.2
Field Goals	Gary Anderson, 1985	33
Touchdowns (Tot.)	Louis Lipps, 1985	15
Points	Gary Anderson, 1985	139

Individual Records—Single Game

Category	Name	Performance
Rushing (Yds.)	John Fuqua, 12-20-70	218
Passing (Yds.)	Bobby Layne, 12-3-58	409
Passing (TDs)	Terry Bradshaw, 11-15-81	5
	Mark Malone, 9-8-85	5
Receiving (No.)	J.R. Wilburn, 10-22-67	12
Receiving (Yds.)	Buddy Dial, 10-22-61	235
Interceptions	Jack Butler, 12-13-53	*4
Field Goals	Gary Anderson, 11-10-85	5
Touchdowns (Tot.)	Ray Mathews, 10-17-54	4
	Roy Jefferson, 11-3-68	4
Points	Ray Mathews, 10-17-54	24
	Roy Jefferson, 11-3-68	24

*NFL Record

1987 Team Record

Preseason (0-4)

Date	Result		Opponents
8/14	L	17-23	at Washington
8/22	L	14-50	at Chicago
8/29	L	28-31	at New Orleans
9/5	L	20-26	N.Y. Giants
		79-130	

Regular Season (8-7)

Date	Result		Opponents	Att.
9/13	W	30-17	San Francisco	55,735
9/20	L	10-34	at Cleveland	79,543
9/27	C		N.Y. Jets	
10/4	W	28-12	at Atlanta	16,667
10/11	L	21-31	at L.A. Rams	20,219
10/18	W	21- 7	Indianapolis	34,627
10/25	W	23-20	Cincinnati	53,692
11/1	L	24-35	at Miami	52,578
11/8	W	17-16	at Kansas City	45,249
11/15	L	3-23	Houston	56,177
11/22	W	30-16	at Cincinnati	59,910
11/29	L	16-20	New Orleans	47,896
12/6	W	13- 9	Seattle	48,881
12/13	W	20-16	at San Diego	51,605
12/20	L	16-24	at Houston	38,683
12/26	L	13-19	Cleveland	56,394

C (Cancelled due to players' strike.)

Score by Periods

Steelers	50	88	51	96	0	—	285
Opponents	45	79	77	98	0	—	299

Attendance

Home 353,402 Away 364,454 Total 717,856
Single-game home record, 59,541 (9-30-85)
Single-season home record, 462,567 (1983)

1987 Team Statistics

	Steelers	Opp.
Total First Downs	263	289
Rushing	114	94
Passing	126	170
Penalty	23	25
Third Down: Made/Att.	85/214	65/189
Fourth Down: Made/Att.	3/7	6/15
Total Net Yards	4410	4920
Avg. Per Game	294.0	328.0
Total Plays	973	962
Avg. Per Play	4.5	5.1
Net Yards Rushing	2144	1610
Avg. Per Game	142.9	107.3
Total Rushes	517	455
Net Yards Passing	2266	3310
Avg. Per Game	151.1	220.7
Sacked/Yards Lost	27/198	26/196
Gross Yards	2464	3506
Att./Completions	429/198	481/290
Completion Pct.	46.2	60.3
Had Intercepted	25	27
Punts/Avg.	82/40.2	70/39.2
Net Punting Avg.	31.2	33.4
Penalties/Yards Lost	105/801	95/771
Fumbles/Ball Lost	37/8	41/17
Touchdowns	31	34
Rushing	11	8
Passing	13	22
Returns	7	4
Avg. Time of Possession	29:45	30:15

1987 Individual Statistics

Scoring	TD R	TD P	TD Rt	PAT	FG	Saf	TP
G. Anderson	0	0	0	21/21	22/27	0	87
Carter	0	3	0	0/0	0/0	0	18
Malone	3	0	0	0/0	0/0	0	18
Pollard	3	0	0	0/0	0/0	0	18
Abercrombie	2	0	0	0/0	0/0	0	12
Alston	0	2	0	0/0	0/0	0	12
Hall	0	0	2	0/0	0/0	0	12
Shell	0	0	2	0/0	0/0	0	12
Stallworth	0	2	0	0/0	0/0	0	12
Trout	0	0	0	10/10	0/2	0	10
Bono	1	0	0	0/0	0/0	0	6
Clinkscales	0	1	0	0/0	0/0	0	6
Gothard	0	1	0	0/0	0/0	0	6
Gowdy	0	0	1	0/0	0/0	0	6
Hairston	0	1	0	0/0	0/0	0	6
Hoge	0	1	0	0/0	0/0	0	6
Jackson	1	0	0	0/0	0/0	0	6
Lockett	0	1	0	0/0	0/0	0	6
Sanders	1	0	0	0/0	0/0	0	6
Thompson	0	1	0	0/0	0/0	0	6
Woodruff	0	0	1	0/0	0/0	0	6
Woodson	0	0	1	0/0	0/0	0	6
Carr	0	0	0	0/0	0/0	1	2
Steelers	11	13	7	31/31	22/29	1	285
Opponents	8	22	4	31/34	20/26	2	299

Passing	Att.	Comp.	Yds.	Pct.	TD	Int.	Tkld.	Rate
Malone	336	156	1896	46.4	6	19	18/151	46.7
Bono	74	34	438	45.9	5	2	6/30	76.3
Brister	12	4	20	33.3	0	3	2/14	2.8
Collier	7	4	110	57.1	2	1	1/3	101.8
Steelers	429	198	2464	46.2	13	25	27/198	50.3
Opponents	481	290	3506	60.3	22	27	26/196	74.6

Rushing	Att.	Yds.	Avg.	LG	TD
Jackson	180	696	3.9	39	1
Pollard	128	536	4.2	33	3
Abercrombie	123	459	3.7	28t	2
Malone	34	162	4.8	42t	3
Stone	17	135	7.9	51	0
Sanders	11	65	5.9	14	1
Bono	8	27	3.4	23	1
Collier	4	20	5.0	12	0
Newsome	2	16	8.0	16	0
Carter	5	12	2.4	4	0
Hoge	3	8	2.7	5	0
Reeder	2	8	4.0	4	0
Steelers	517	2144	4.1	51	11
Opponents	455	1610	3.5	58	8

Receiving	No.	Yds.	Avg.	LG	TD
Stallworth	41	521	12.7	45	2
Abercrombie	24	209	8.7	24	0
Thompson	17	313	18.4	63	1
Sweeney	16	217	13.6	34	0
Carter	16	180	11.3	26t	3
Pollard	14	77	5.5	17	0
Clinkscales	13	240	18.5	57	1
Lee	12	124	10.3	24	0
Lipps	11	164	14.9	27	0
Lockett	7	116	16.6	25	1
Hoge	7	97	13.9	27	1
Jackson	7	52	7.4	23	0
Alston	3	84	28.0	42t	2
Hairston	2	16	8.0	11	1
Young	2	10	5.0	6	0
Gothard	2	9	4.5	7	1
Stone	1	22	22.0	22	0
Sanders	1	11	11.0	11	0
Bono	1	2	2.0	2	0
Boyle	1	0	0.0	0	0
Steelers	198	2464	12.4	63	13
Opponents	290	3506	12.1	52t	22

Interceptions	No.	Yds.	Avg.	LG	TD
Woodruff	5	91	18.2	33t	1
Hall	3	29	9.7	25t	1
Everett	3	22	7.3	21	0
Hinkle	3	15	5.0	8	0
Gowdy	2	50	25.0	45t	1
Merriweather	2	26	13.0	15	0
Griffin	2	2	1.0	2	0
Shell	1	50	50.0	50t	1
Woodson	1	45	45.0	45t	1
A. Riley	1	4	4.0	4	0
Sheffield	1	2	2.0	2	0
Cole	1	0	0.0	0	0
Edwards	1	0	0.0	0	0
R. Williams	1	0	0.0	0	0
Steelers	27	336	12.4	50t	5
Opponents	25	330	13.2	49	1

Punting	No.	Yds.	Avg.	In 20	LG
Newsome	64	2678	41.8	8	57
Bruno	16	619	38.7	5	56
Steelers	82	3297	40.2	13	57
Opponents	70	2741	39.2	17	55

Punt Returns	No.	FC	Yds.	Avg.	LG	TD
Woodson	16	1	135	8.4	20	0
M. Anderson	7	1	38	5.4	10	0
Lipps	7	1	46	6.6	12	0
Everett	4	2	22	5.5	11	0
Lockett	2	0	3	1.5	5	0
Steelers	36	5	244	6.8	20	0
Opponents	46	7	395	8.6	44	0

Kickoff Returns	No.	Yds.	Avg.	LG	TD
Stone	28	568	20.3	34	0
Woodson	13	290	22.3	36	0
Sanchez	6	116	19.3	27	0
Britt	2	9	4.5	5	0
Jones	2	38	19.0	22	0
M. Anderson	1	8	8.0	8	0
Clark	1	18	18.0	18	0
Gowdy	1	0	0.0	0	0
Hoge	1	13	13.0	13	0
A. Riley	1	0	0.0	0	0
Steelers	56	1060	18.9	36	0
Opponents	65	1083	16.7	33	0

Sacks	No.
Merriweather	5.5
Gary	4.0
Carr	3.0
Willis	3.0
Hinkle	2.0
Little	1.5
Cole	1.0
Dawkins	1.0
Warren	1.0
G. Williams	1.0
J. Williams	1.0
Steelers	26.0
Opponents	27.0

Pittsburgh Steelers 1988 Veteran Roster

No.	Name	Pos.	Ht.	Wt.	Birth-date	NFL Exp.	College	Hometown	How Acq.	'87 Games/ Starts
34	Abercrombie, Walter	RB	6-0	210	9/26/59	7	Baylor	Waco, Tex.	D1-'82	12/12
81	Alston, Lyneal	WR	6-1	205	7/23/64	2	Southern Mississippi	Mobile, Ala.	FA-'87	3/1
1	Anderson, Gary	K	5-11	170	7/16/59	7	Syracuse	Durban, South Africa	W(Buff)-'82	12/0
72	Aydelette, Buddy	T-C	6-4	262	8/19/56	3	Alabama	Mobile, Ala.	W(Minn)-'87	12/5
66	Behning, Mark	T	6-6	277	9/26/61	2	Nebraska	Denton, Tex.	D2-'85	0*
14	t-Blackledge, Todd	QB	6-3	223	2/25/61	6	Penn State	Canton, Ohio	T(KC)-'88	3/2
60	Blankenship, Brian	G-C	6-1	281	4/7/63	2	Nebraska	Omaha, Neb.	FA-'87	13/3
15	Bono, Steve	QB	6-4	215	5/11/62	4	UCLA	Norristown, Pa.	FA-'87	3/3
65	Boyle, Jim	T	6-5	270	7/27/62	2	Tulane	Cincinnati, Ohio	FA-'87	3/3
6	Brister, Bubby	QB	6-3	195	8/15/62	3	Northeast Louisiana	Monroe, La.	D3-'86	2/0
10	Bruno, John	P	6-2	190	9/10/64	2	Penn State	Pittsburgh, Pa.	FA-'87	3/0
91	Carr, Gregg	LB	6-2	224	3/31/62	4	Auburn	Birmingham, Ala.	D6-'85	12/0
24	Carter, Rodney	RB	6-0	212	10/30/64	2	Purdue	Elizabeth, N.J.	D7-'86	11/2
88	Clinkscales, Joey	WR	6-0	204	5/21/64	2	Tennessee	Knoxville, Tenn.	D9-'87	7/3
56	Cole, Robin	LB	6-2	225	9/11/55	12	New Mexico	Compton, Calif.	D1-'77	12/12
67	Dunn, Gary	NT	6-3	278	8/24/53	12	Miami	Coral Gables, Fla.	D6-'76	13/13
27	Everett, Thomas	S	5-9	179	11/21/64	2	Baylor	Daingerfield, Tex.	D4-'87	12/9
68	Freeman, Lorenzo	NT	6-5	270	5/23/64	2	Pittsburgh	East Camden, N.J.	FA-'87	6/0
92	Gary, Keith	DE	6-3	260	9/14/59	6	Oklahoma	Fairfax, Va.	D1-'81	11/6
86	Gothard, Preston	TE	6-4	242	2/23/62	4	Alabama	Montgomery, Ala.	FA-'85	2/2
29	Gowdy, Cornell	S-CB	6-1	197	10/2/63	3	Morgan State	Seat Pleasant, Md.	FA-'87	13/3
22	Griffin, Larry	S-CB	6-0	199	1/11/63	3	North Carolina	Chesapeake, Va.	FA-'87	7/3
35	Hall, Delton	CB	6-1	205	1/16/65	2	Clemson	Greensboro, N.C.	D2-'87	12/12
96	Henton, Anthony	LB	6-1	234	7/27/63	2	Troy State	Bessemer, Ala.	D9-'86	0*
53	Hinkle, Bryan	LB	6-2	215	6/4/59	7	Oregon	Silverdale, Wash.	D6-'81	12/12
33	Hoge, Merril	RB	6-2	212	1/26/65	2	Idaho State	Pocatello, Idaho	D10-'87	13/0
62	Ilkin, Tunch	T	6-3	265	9/23/57	9	Indiana State	Highland Park, Ill.	D6-'80	11/11
43	Jackson, Earnest	RB	5-9	219	12/18/59	6	Texas A&M	Rosenberg, Tex.	FA-'86	12/9
78	Johnson, Tim	DE-NT	6-3	260	1/29/65	2	Penn State	Sarasota, Fla.	D6-'87	12/0
84	Lee, Danzell	TE	6-2	229	3/16/63	2	Lamar	Corsicana, Tex.	FA-'87	13/13
83	Lipps, Louis	WR	5-10	190	8/9/62	5	Southern Mississippi	Reserve, La.	D1-'84	4/2
50	Little, David	LB	6-1	230	1/3/59	8	Florida	Miami, Fla.	D7-'81	12/12
89	Lockett, Charles	WR	6-0	179	10/1/65	2	Long Beach State	Los Angeles, Calif.	D3-'87	11/1
74	Long, Terry	G	5-11	275	7/21/59	5	East Carolina	Columbia, S.C.	D4-'84	13/13
71	Lucas, Jeff	T	6-7	288	5/30/64	2	West Virginia	Hackensack, N.J.	FA-'87	3/3
57	Merriweather, Mike	LB	6-2	221	11/26/60	7	Pacific	Vallejo, Calif.	D3-'82	12/12
99	Minter, Michael	NT	6-3	275	8/13/65	2	North Texas State	Mt. Pleasant, Tex.	FA-'87	3/2
18	Newsome, Harry	P	6-0	189	1/25/63	4	Wake Forest	Cheraw, S.C.	D8-'85	12/0
54	Nickerson, Hardy	LB	6-2	224	9/1/65	2	California	Los Angeles, Calif.	D5-'87	12/0
30	Pollard, Frank	RB	5-10	230	6/15/57	9	Baylor	Meridian, Tex.	D11-'80	12/7
79	Rienstra, John	G	6-5	269	3/22/63	3	Temple	Colorado Springs, Colo.	D1-'86	12/2
28	Sanchez, Lupe	S-KR	5-10	195	10/28/61	3	UCLA	Visalia, Calif.	FA-'86	12/3
20	Stone, Dwight	RB-KR	6-0	188	1/28/64	2	Middle Tennessee State	Florala, Ala.	FA-'87	14/0
90	Stowe, Tyronne	LB	6-1	232	5/30/65	2	Rutgers	Passaic, N.J.	FA-'87	13/3
87	Thompson, Weegie	WR	6-6	210	3/21/61	5	Florida State	Midlothian, Va.	D4-'84	12/3
52	Webster, Mike	C	6-2	254	3/18/52	15	Wisconsin	Tomahawk, Wis.	D5-'74	15/15
98	Williams, Gerald	DE-NT	6-3	270	9/3/63	3	Auburn	Lanett, Ala.	D2-'86	9/1
93	Willis, Keith	DE	6-1	260	7/29/59	7	Northeastern	Newark, N.J.	FA-'82	11/10
73	Wolfley, Craig	G	6-1	272	5/19/58	9	Syracuse	Orchard Park, N.Y.	D5-'80	12/12
49	Woodruff, Dwayne	CB	6-0	198	2/18/57	9	Louisville	New Richmond, Ohio	D6-'79	12/12
26	Woodson, Rod	CB-S-KR	6-0	202	3/10/65	2	Purdue	Ft. Wayne, Ind.	D1-'87	8/0
80	Young, Theo	TE	6-2	237	4/25/65	2	Arkansas	Newport, Ark.	D12-'87	12/1

* Behning and Henton missed '87 season due to injury.

t-Steelers traded for Blackledge (Kansas City).

Traded—QB Mark Malone to San Diego.

Retired—Rich Erenberg, 3-year running back, missed '87 season due to injury; Donnie Shell, 14-year safety, 13 games in '87; John Stallworth, 14-year wide receiver, 12 games in '87.

Also played with Steelers in '87—WR Mel Anderson (2 games), LB Steve Apke (3), LB Craig Bingham (3), TE Ralph Britt (3), RB Mike Clark (1), DE Jackie Cline (1), QB Reggie Collier (2), DE Tommy Dawkins (2), G Charlie Dickey (1), S Dave Edwards (3), WR Moses Ford (1), WR Russell Hairston (3), NT Alan Huff (2), CB-S Bruce Jones (2), LB Darryl Knox (3), G Ben Lawrence (1), C John Lott (1), S Kelvin Middleton (2), NT-DE Edmund Nelson (10), NT David Opfar (3), C Paul Oswald (2), G Ted Petersen (2), T Ray Pinney (12), RB Dan Reeder (2), CB Rock Richmond (2), LB Avon Riley (3), RB Chuck Sanders (5), CB Chris Sheffield (5), DE Bret Shugarts (2), WR Calvin Sweeney (9), K David Trout (3), CB Anthony Tuggle (2), DE Xavier Warren (2), T Robert Washington (3), LB Albert Williams (3), LB Joe Williams (3), CB-S Ray Williams (1), LB Ken Woodard (7).

COACHING STAFF

Head Coach, Chuck Noll

Pro Career: Became only NFL coach to win four Super Bowls when Steelers defeated Los Angeles Rams 31-19 in Super Bowl XIV. Put together 13 consecutive non-losing seasons and has guided Steelers into postseason play 11 of last 16 years. Led Pittsburgh to consecutive NFL championships twice (1974-75, 1978-79). With 178 career wins, is third among active NFL coaches behind Don Shula (271) and Tom Landry (267). Has tenth-highest winning percentage (.595) among active coaches and is fifth among the NFL's all-time winningest coaches with a 178-121-1 career record. Noll is one of only four coaches in NFL history to lead a team for 20 consecutive seasons—Curly Lambeau (29), Landry (27), and Steve Owen (23) are the others. Played pro ball as guard-linebacker for Cleveland Browns from 1953-59. At age 28, he started coaching career as defensive coach with Los Angeles (San Diego) Chargers in 1960. Left after 1965 season to become Don Shula's defensive backfield coach in Baltimore. Remained with Colts until taking over Pittsburgh reins as head coach in 1969. Career record: 178-121-1.

Background: Was an all-state star at Benedictine High in Cleveland. Captained the University of Dayton team, playing both tackle and linebacker. He was drafted by the Browns in 1953.

Personal: Born in Cleveland on January 5, 1932. He and his wife, Marianne, live in Pittsburgh and have one son—Chris.

Assistant Coaches

Ron Blackledge, offensive line-tackles/tight ends; born April 15, 1938, Canton, Ohio, lives in Pittsburgh. Tight end-defensive end Bowling Green 1957-59. No pro playing experience. College coach: Ashland 1968-69, Cincinnati 1970-72, Kentucky 1973-75, Princeton 1976, Kent State 1977-81 (head coach 1979-81). Pro coach: Joined Steelers in 1982.

Tony Dungy, defensive coordinator; born October 6, 1955, Jackson, Mich., lives in Pittsburgh. Quarterback Minnesota 1973-76. Pro safety Pittsburgh Steelers 1977-78, San Francisco 49ers 1979. College coach: Minnesota 1980. Pro coach: Joined Steelers in 1981.

Walt Evans, conditioning and training; born May 15, 1951, Pittsburgh, Pa., lives in Pittsburgh. Marietta College 1974. No college or pro playing experience. Pro coach: Joined Steelers in 1983.

Dennis Fitzgerald, special teams/defensive assistant; born March 13, 1936, Ann Arbor, Mich., lives in Pittsburgh. Running back Michigan 1958-60. No pro playing experience. College coach: Michigan 1961-68, Kentucky 1969-70, Kent State 1971-77 (head coach 1975-77), Syracuse 1978-80, Tulane 1981. Pro coach: Joined Steelers in 1982.

Joe Greene, defensive line; born September 24, 1946, Temple, Tex., lives in Pittsburgh. Defensive tackle North Texas State 1966-68. Pro defensive tackle Pittsburgh Steelers 1969-81. Pro coach: Joined Steelers in 1987.

Dick Hoak, offensive backfield; born December 8, 1939, Jeannette, Pa., lives in Greensburg, Pa. Halfback-quarterback Penn State 1958-60. Pro running back Pittsburgh Steelers 1961-70. Pro coach: Joined Steelers in 1972.

Jed Hughes, linebackers; born November 14, 1947, New York, N.Y., lives in Pittsburgh. Linebacker Springfield 1966-68, tight end Gettysburg 1969-70. No pro playing experience. College coach: Stanford 1971-72, Michigan 1973-75, UCLA 1976-81. Pro coach: Minnesota Vikings 1982-83, joined Steelers in 1984.

Hal Hunter, offensive line-guards/centers; born June 3, 1934, Canonsburg, Pa., lives in Pittsburgh. Linebacker-guard Pittsburgh 1955-57. No pro playing experience. College coach: Richmond 1958-61, West Virginia 1962-63, Maryland 1964-65, Duke 1966-70, Kentucky 1971-72, Indiana 1973-76, California State (Pa.) 1977-80 (head coach). Pro coach: Hamilton Tiger-Cats (CFL) 1981, Indianapolis Colts 1982-84, joined Steelers in 1985.

Jon Kolb, special teams/offensive assistant; born August 30, 1947, Ponca City, Okla., lives in Pittsburgh. Center-linebacker Oklahoma State 1966-68. Pro tackle Pittsburgh Steelers 1969-81. Pro coach: Joined Steelers in 1982.

Tom Moore, offensive coordinator; born November 7, 1938, Owatonna, Minn., lives in Pittsburgh. Quarterback Iowa 1957-60. No pro playing experience. College coach: Iowa 1961-62, Dayton 1965-68, Wake Forest 1969, Georgia Tech 1970-71, Minnesota 1972-73, 1975-76. Pro coach: New York Stars (WFL) 1974, joined Steelers in 1977.

Dwain Painter, receivers; born February 13, 1942, Monroeville, Pa., lives in Pittsburgh. Quarterback-defensive back Rutgers 1961-64. No pro playing experience. College coach: San Jose State 1971-72, College of San Mateo 1973, Brigham Young 1974-75, UCLA 1976-78, Northern Arizona 1979-81 (head coach), Georgia Tech 1982-85, Texas 1986, Illinois 1987. Pro coach: Joined Steelers in 1988.

Pittsburgh Steelers 1988 First-Year Roster

Name	Pos.	Ht.	Wt.	Birth-date	College	Hometown	How Acq.
Bain, Tolbert	S	6-2	207	7/29/64	Miami	Miami, Fla.	FA
Boulay, Paul	NT	6-1	265	4/24/66	New Hampshire	Farmington, N.H.	FA
Clark, David (1)	RB	6-0	205	10/7/62	Penn State	Woodbury Heights, N.J.	FA
Cobb, Brian	WR	6-0	183	2/12/66	Rutgers	Steelton, Pa.	FA
Dawson, Bobby	S	5-11	211	2/18/66	Illinois	Sacramento, Calif.	D11
Dawson, Dermontti	C-G	6-2	272	6/17/65	Kentucky	Lexington, Ky.	D2
Earle, James	LB	6-4	224	3/26/66	Clemson	Easley, S.C.	D12
Gainer, Herb	WR	6-2	195	8/25/65	Florida State	Sarasota, Fla.	FA
Garczynski, Andy	WR	6-0	205	6/2/66	Temple	Philadelphia, Pa.	FA
Hinnant, Mike	TE	6-3	254	9/8/66	Temple	Washington, D.C.	D8b
Jackson, John	T	6-6	287	1/4/65	Eastern Kentucky	Cincinnati, Ohio	D10
Jones, Aaron	DE	6-5	258	12/18/66	Eastern Kentucky	Richmond, Ky.	D1
Jordan, Darin	LB	6-1	245	12/4/64	Northeastern	Stoughton, Mass.	D5a
Lanza, Chuck	C	6-2	270	9/20/64	Notre Dame	Germantown, Tenn.	D3
Lee, Greg	CB-S	6-1	204	1/15/65	Arkansas State	Pine Bluff, Ark.	FA
Lloyd, Greg (1)	LB	6-2	224	5/26/65	Fort Valley State	Fort Valley, Ga.	D6-'87
Lockbaum, Gordie	RB	5-11	195	11/16/65	Holy Cross	Glassboro, N.J.	D9
Markland, Jeff	TE	6-3	245	11/16/65	Illinois	Gresham, Ore.	FA
Nichols, Mark	NT	6-2	262	8/29/64	Michigan State	Bloomfield Hills, Mich.	D8a
Osborn, Cassius	WR	6-0	192	8/26/66	Georgia	Athens, Ga.	FA
Quick, Jerry (1)	T-G	6-5	273	12/30/63	Wichita State	Anthony, Kan.	FA-'86
Reese, Jerry	NT-DE	6-2	270	7/11/64	Kentucky	Hopkinsville, Ky.	D5b
Riley, Cameron (1)	S	6-1	195	5/13/64	Missouri	Metropolis, Ill.	FA-'87
Strom, Rick	QB	6-3	206	3/11/65	Georgia Tech	Pittsburgh, Pa.	FA
Walker, Chad	LB	6-2	223	8/11/66	Arkansas Tech	Jacksonville, Ark.	FA
Williams, Al	LB	6-5	237	6/17/65	James Madison	South Boston, Va.	FA
Williams, Warren	RB	6-0	203	7/29/65	Miami	Fort Myers, Fla.	D6
Zeno, Marc	WR	6-3	202	5/21/65	Tulane	Lutcher, La.	D7

The term NFL Rookie is defined as a player who is in his first season of professional football and has not been on the roster of another professional football team for any regular-season or postseason games. A Rookie is designated by an "R" on NFL rosters. Players who have been active in another professional football league or players who have NFL experience, including either preseason training camp or being on an active roster for fewer than three regular-season or postseason games, are termed NFL First-Year Players. An NFL First-Year Player is designated by a "1" on NFL rosters. Thereafter, a player on an NFL active roster for at least three regular-season or postseason games is credited with an additional year of NFL playing experience.

NOTES

American Football Conference Western Division

Team Colors: Navy Blue, White, and Gold

San Diego Jack Murphy Stadium
P.O. Box 20666
San Diego, California 92120
Telephone: (619) 280-2111

Club Officials

Chairman of the Board/President: Alex G. Spanos
Vice Chairman: Dean A. Spanos
Director of Football Operations: Steve Ortmayer
Director of Administration: Jack E. Teele
Special Assistant to Chairman of the Board: Warren B. Jones, Jr.
Director of Player Personnel: Chet Franklin
Pro Scouting: Rudy Feldman
Director of Public Relations: Rick Smith
Business Manager: Pat Curran
Director of Marketing: Rich Israel
Director of Ticket Operations: Joe Scott
Director of Community Relations: Bill Johnston
Public Relations Assistant: Rob Boulware
Chief Financial Officer: Jeremiah T. Murphy
Financial Officer: James T. Kesaris
Head Trainer: Larry Roberts
Equipment Manager: Sid Brooks

Stadium: San Diego Jack Murphy Stadium •
Capacity: 60,750
9449 Friars Road
San Diego, California 92108

Playing Surface: Grass

Training Camp: University of California-San Diego
Third College
La Jolla, California 92037

1988 Schedule

Preseason

Aug. 6	**Dallas**	6:00
Aug. 13	at Los Angeles Rams	8:00
Aug. 20	**San Francisco**	6:00
Aug. 26	**Los Angeles Rams**	8:00

Regular Season

Sept. 4	at Los Angeles Raiders	1:00
Sept. 11	at Denver	2:00
Sept. 18	**Seattle**	1:00
Sept. 25	at Kansas City	3:00
Oct. 2	**Denver**	1:00
Oct. 9	**New Orleans**	1:00
Oct. 16	at Miami	1:00
Oct. 23	**Indianapolis**	1:00
Oct. 30	at Seattle	1:00
Nov. 6	**Los Angeles Raiders**	5:00
Nov. 13	at Atlanta	1:00
Nov. 20	at Los Angeles Rams	1:00
Nov. 27	**San Francisco**	1:00
Dec. 4	at Cincinnati	1:00
Dec. 11	**Pittsburgh**	1:00
Dec. 18	**Kansas City**	1:00

Chargers Coaching History

Los Angeles 1960
(208-197-11)

1960-69	Sid Gillman*	83-51-6
1969-70	Charlie Waller	9-7-3
1971	Sid Gillman**	4-6-0
1971-73	Harland Svare***	7-17-2
1973	Ron Waller	1-5-0
1974-78	Tommy Prothro****	21-39-0
1978-86	Don Coryell#	72-60-0
1986-87	Al Saunders	11-12-0

*Retired after nine games in 1969
**Resigned after 10 games in 1971
***Resigned after eight games in 1973
****Resigned after four games in 1978
#Resigned after eight games in 1986

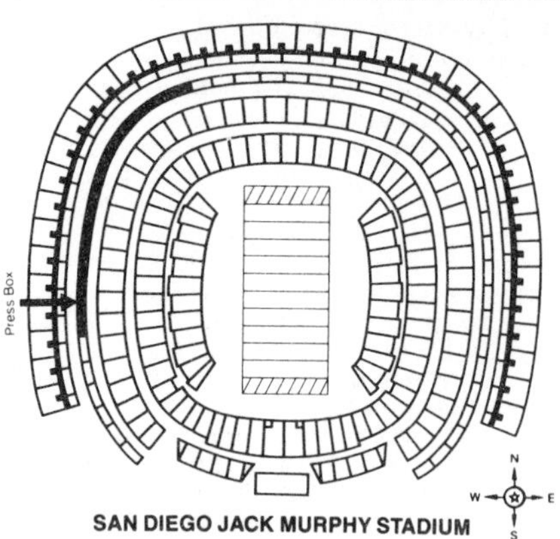

SAN DIEGO JACK MURPHY STADIUM

Record Holders

Individual Records—Career

Category	Name	Performance
Rushing (Yds.)	Paul Lowe, 1960-67	4,963
Passing (Yds.)	Dan Fouts, 1973-1987	43,040
Passing (TDs)	Dan Fouts, 1973-1987	254
Receiving (No.)	Charlie Joiner, 1976-1986	586
Receiving (Yds.)	Lance Alworth, 1962-1970	9,585
Interceptions	Dick Harris, 1960-65	29
Punting (Avg.)	Maury Buford, 1982-84	42.7
Punt Return (Avg.)	Leslie (Speedy) Duncan, 1964-1970	12.3
Kickoff Return (Avg.)	Leslie (Speedy) Duncan, 1964-1970	25.2
Field Goals	Rolf Benirschke, 1977-1986	146
Touchdowns	Lance Alworth, 1962-1970	83
Points	Rolf Benirschke, 1977-1986	766

Individual Records—Single Season

Category	Name	Performance
Rushing (Yds.)	Earnest Jackson, 1984	1,179
Passing (Yds.)	Dan Fouts, 1981	4,802
Passing (TDs)	Dan Fouts, 1981	33
Receiving (No.)	Kellen Winslow, 1980	89
Receiving (Yds.)	Lance Alworth, 1965	1,602
Interceptions	Charlie McNeil, 1961	9
Punting (Avg.)	Dennis Partee, 1969	44.6
Punt Return (Avg.)	Leslie (Speedy) Duncan, 1965	15.5
Kickoff Return (Avg.)	Keith Lincoln, 1962	28.4
Field Goals	Rolf Benirschke, 1980	24
Touchdowns	Chuck Muncie, 1981	19
Points	Rolf Benirschke, 1980	118

Individual Records—Single Game

Category	Name	Performance
Rushing (Yds.)	Keith Lincoln, 1-5-64	206
Passing (Yds.)	Dan Fouts, 10-19-80	444
	Dan Fouts, 12-11-82	444
Passing (TDs)	Dan Fouts, 11-22-81	6
Receiving (No.)	Kellen Winslow, 10-7-84	15
Receiving (Yds.)	Wes Chandler, 12-20-82	260
Interceptions	Many times Last time by Pete Shaw, 11-2-80	3
Field Goals	Many times Last time by Rolf Benirschke, 12-22-80	4
Touchdowns (Tot.)	Kellen Winslow, 11-22-81	5
Points	Kellen Winslow, 11-22-81	30

1987 Team Record

Preseason (2-2)

Date	Result		Opponents
8/15	W	29- 0	Dallas
8/23	L	21-23	L.A. Rams
8/27	L	3-17	at San Francisco
9/4	W	30- 6	N.Y. Jets
		83-46	

Regular Season (8-7)

Date	Result		Opponents	Att.
9/13	L	13-20	at Kansas City	56,940
9/20	W	28-24	St. Louis	47,988
9/27	C		Seattle	
10/4	W	10- 9	at Cincinnati	26,209
10/11	W	17-13	at Tampa Bay	23,873
10/18	W	23-17	at L.A. Raiders	23,541
10/25	W	42-21	Kansas City	47,972
11/1	W	27-24	Cleveland (OT)	55,381
11/8	W	16-13	at Indianapolis	60,459
11/15	W	16-14	L.A. Raiders	60,639
11/22	L	3-34	at Seattle	62,444
11/29	L	17-31	Denver	61,880
12/6	L	18-33	at Houston	31,714
12/13	L	16-20	Pittsburgh	51,605
12/20	L	7-20	Indianapolis	46,211
12/27	L	0-24	at Denver	21,189

(OT) Overtime
C (Cancelled due to players' strike.)

Score by Periods

Chargers	79	55	25	91	3	—	253
Opponents	68	104	68	77	0	—	317

Attendance

Home 371,676 Away 306,369 Total 678,045
Single-game home record, 61,880 (11-29-87)
Single-season home record, 415,626 (1985)

1987 Team Statistics

	Chargers	Opp.
Total First Downs	264	280
Rushing	68	120
Passing	175	136
Penalty	21	24
Third Down: Made/Att.	58/193	75/215
Fourth Down: Made/Att.	5/15	6/10
Total Net Yards	4588	4953
Avg. Per Game	305.9	330.2
Total Plays	951	1008
Avg. Per Play	4.8	4.9
Net Yards Rushing	1308	2171
Avg. Per Game	87.2	144.7
Total Rushes	396	522
Net Yards Passing	3280	2782
Avg. Per Game	218.7	185.5
Sacked/Yards Lost	39/322	45/298
Gross Yards	3602	3080
Att./Completions	516/303	441/227
Completion Pct.	58.7	51.5
Had Intercepted	23	13
Punts/Avg.	84/42.0	89/41.5
Net Punting Avg.	33.8	33.6
Penalties/Yards Lost	98/743	107/869
Fumbles/Ball Lost	38/20	26/15
Touchdowns	29	37
Rushing	11	14
Passing	13	19
Returns	5	4
Avg. Time of Possession	28:08	31:52

1987 Individual Statistics

Scoring

Scoring	TD R	TD P	TD Rt	PAT	FG	Saf	TP
Abbott	0	0	0	22/23	13/22	0	61
James	2	3	1	0/0	0/0	0	36
G. Anderson	3	2	0	0/0	0/0	0	30
Winslow	0	3	0	0/0	0/0	0	18
Gaffney	0	0	0	4/5	3/6	0	13
Chandler	0	2	0	0/0	0/0	0	12
Fouts	2	0	0	0/0	0/0	0	12
Neuheisel	1	0	0	1/1	0/0	0	7
Adams	1	0	0	0/0	0/0	0	6
Bernstine	0	1	0	0/0	0/0	0	6
Brandon	0	0	1	0/0	0/0	0	6
Glenn	0	0	1	0/0	0/0	0	6
L. Miller	0	0	1	0/0	0/0	0	6
Middleton	1	0	0	0/0	0/0	0	6
Moffett	0	1	0	0/0	0/0	0	6
Patterson	0	0	1	0/0	0/0	0	6
Sartin	1	0	0	0/0	0/0	0	6
A. Williams	0	1	0	0/0	0/0	0	6
L. Williams	0	0	0	0/0	0/0	1	2
Chargers	11	13	5	27/29	16/28	2	253
Opponents	14	19	4	36/37	19/29	1	317

Passing

Passing	Att.	Comp.	Yds.	Pct.	TD	Int.	Tkld.	Rate
Fouts	364	206	2517	56.6	10	15	24/176	70.0
Neuheisel	59	40	367	67.8	1	1	10/89	83.1
Herrmann	57	37	405	64.9	1	5	3/37	55.1
Kelley	29	17	305	58.6	1	0	1/7	106.3
Vlasic	6	3	8	50.0	0	1	1/13	16.7
Smith	1	0	0	0.0	0	1	0/0	0.0
Chargers	516	303	3602	58.7	13	23	39/322	69.9
Opponents	441	227	3080	51.5	19	13	45/298	76.2

Rushing

Rushing	Att.	Yds.	Avg.	LG	TD
Adams	90	343	3.8	24	1
G. Anderson	80	260	3.3	25	3
Ti. Spencer	73	228	3.1	16	0
James	27	102	3.8	15t	2
Jenkins	22	88	4.0	9	0
Middleton	28	74	2.6	21	1
Sartin	19	52	2.7	10	1
Neuheisel	6	41	6.8	18	1
Redden	11	36	3.3	7	0
To. Spencer	14	24	1.7	5	0
Holland	1	17	17.0	17	0
Kelley	4	17	4.3	10	0
A. Williams	1	11	11.0	11	0
Bernstine	1	9	9.0	9	0
Steels	1	3	3.0	3	0
Zachary	1	3	3.0	3	0
Moffett	1	1	1.0	1	0
Fouts	12	0	0.0	2	2
Herrmann	4	−1	−0.3	0	0
Chargers	396	1308	3.3	25	11
Opponents	522	2171	4.2	53	14

Receiving

Receiving	No.	Yds.	Avg.	LG	TD
Winslow	53	519	9.8	30	3
G. Anderson	47	503	10.7	38	2
James	41	593	14.5	46	3
Chandler	39	617	15.8	27	2
Holohan	20	239	12.0	18	0
Ti. Spencer	17	123	7.2	18	0
A. Williams	12	247	20.6	57	1
Bernstine	10	76	7.6	15	1
Middleton	8	43	5.4	17	0
Jenkins	8	40	5.0	7	0
Holt	7	56	8.0	17	0
Redden	7	46	6.6	13	0
Holland	6	138	23.0	45	0
Rome	6	49	8.2	13	0
Sartin	6	19	3.2	8	0
Moffett	5	80	16.0	25	1
Adams	4	38	9.5	21	0
Muhammad	2	87	43.5	67	0
To. Spencer	2	47	23.5	45	0
Ware	2	38	19.0	23	0
Steels	1	4	4.0	4	0
Chargers	303	3602	11.9	67	13
Opponents	227	3080	13.6	63t	19

Interceptions

Interceptions	No.	Yds.	Avg.	LG	TD
Smith	5	28	5.6	12	0
Glenn	4	166	41.5	103t	1
Patterson	1	75	75.0	75t	1
Banks	1	20	20.0	20	0
Plummer	1	2	2.0	2	0
Brazley	1	0	0.0	0	0
Chargers	13	291	22.4	103t	2
Opponents	23	266	11.6	58	1

Punting

Punting	No.	Yds.	Avg.	In 20	LG
Mojsiejenko	67	2875	42.9	15	57
Prokop	17	654	38.5	1	50
Chargers	84	3529	42.0	16	57
Opponents	89	3694	41.5	18	61

Punt Returns

Punt Returns	No.	FC	Yds.	Avg.	LG	TD
James	32	7	400	12.5	81t	1
A. Williams	10	1	96	9.6	25	0
Rome	3	1	12	4.0	6	0
Chargers	45	9	508	11.3	81t	1
Opponents	43	9	429	10.0	71t	1

Kickoff Returns

Kickoff Returns	No.	Yds.	Avg.	LG	TD
Holland	19	410	21.6	46	0
G. Anderson	22	433	19.7	31	0
Sartin	5	117	23.4	28	0
Adams	4	32	8.0	11	0
Kirk	3	15	5.0	10	0
James	2	41	20.5	21	0
Jenkins	2	46	23.0	25	0
Rome	2	28	14.0	17	0
Bernstine	1	13	13.0	13	0
Hunter	1	0	0.0	0	0
Zachary	1	2	2.0	2	0
Chargers	62	1137	18.3	46	0
Opponents	50	985	19.7	95t	1

Sacks

Sacks	No.
L. Williams	8.0
Phillips	5.0
Winter	4.0
Ehin	3.5
Banks	3.0
L. Miller	3.0
Smith	3.0
Bayless	2.5
Unrein	2.5
K. Simmons	1.5
Benson	1.0
Charles	1.0
Hunter	1.0
Jackson	1.0
Kirk	1.0
T. Simmons	1.0
Snipes	1.0
K. Wilson	1.0
A. Anderson	0.5
Glenn	0.5
Chargers	45.0
Opponents	39.0

San Diego Chargers 1988 Veteran Roster

No.	Name	Pos.	Ht.	Wt.	Birth-date	NFL Exp.	College	Hometown	How Acq.	'87 Games/ Starts
10	Abbott, Vince	K	5-11	206	5/31/59	2	Cal State-Fullerton	Santa Ana, Calif.	FA-'87	12/0
42	†Adams, Curtis	RB	5-11	194	4/30/62	3	Central Michigan	Muskegon, Ill.	D8-'85	12/4
40	Anderson, Gary	RB	6-0	181	4/18/61	4	Arkansas	Columbia, Mo.	D1b-'83	12/7
96	†Baldwin, Keith	DE	6-4	270	10/13/60	6	Texas A&M	Smiley, Tex.	FA-'87	6/1
56	†Banks, Chip	LB	6-4	236	9/18/59	7	Southern California	Augusta, Ga.	T(Clev)-'86	12/12
44	Bayless, Martin	S	6-2	200	11/11/62	5	Bowling Green	Dayton, Ohio	T(Buff)-'87	12/11
57	†Benson, Thomas	LB	6-2	235	9/6/61	5	Oklahoma	Ardmore, Tex.	T(Atl)-'86	11/8
82	Bernstine, Rod	TE	6-3	235	2/8/65	2	Texas A&M	Bryan, Tex.	D1-'87	10/2
58	Brandon, David	LB	6-4	225	2/9/65	2	Memphis State	Memphis, Tenn.	T(Buff)-'87	8/1
15	Brookins, Mitchell	WR	5-11	192	12/10/60	3	Illinois	Chicago, Ill.	FA-'88	0*
55	Busick, Steve	LB	6-4	227	12/10/58	8	Southern California	Temple City, Calif.	FA-'87	1/0
22	Byrd, Gill	CB-S	5-11	196	2/20/61	6	San Jose State	San Francisco, Calif.	D1c-'83	12/12
71	†Charles, Mike	NT	6-4	287	9/23/62	6	Syracuse	Newark, N.J.	W(TB)-'87	11/10
77	Claphan, Sam	G-T	6-6	288	10/10/56	8	Oklahoma	Stillwell, Okla.	FA-'81	9/4
37	Dale, Jeff	S	6-3	213	10/6/62	3	Louisiana State	Winnfield, La.	D2b-'85	0*
61	Dallafior, Ken	G	6-4	278	8/26/59	4	Minnesota	Madison Heights, Mich.	D2a-'85	9/0
36	†Davis, Mike	S	6-3	205	4/15/56	10	Colorado	Los Angeles, Calif.	FA-'87	8/0
78	†Ehin, Chuck	NT	6-4	266	7/1/61	6	Brigham Young	Leyton, Utah	D12b-'83	12/4
70	FitzPatrick, James	G-T	6-7	286	2/1/64	3	Southern California	Beaverton, Ore.	D1b-'86	10/9
25	Glenn, Vencie	S	6-0	187	10/26/64	3	Indiana State	Terre Haute, Ind.	T(NE)-'86	12/12
92	Hardison, Dee	DE	6-4	291	5/2/56	11	North Carolina	Fayetteville, N.C.	W(NYG)-'86	3/0
86	Holland, Jamie	WR	6-1	186	2/1/64	2	Ohio State	Wake Forest, N.C.	D7-'87	12/0
27	Hunter, Daniel	CB	5-11	178	9/1/62	4	Henderson State	Arkadelphia, Ark.	FA-'86	12/0
52	Jackson, Jeffery	LB	6-1	230	10/9/61	4	Auburn	Griffin, Ga.	FA-'87	11/6
26	James, Lionel	WR	5-6	170	5/25/62	5	Auburn	Albany, Ga.	D5-'84	12/11
29	Johnson, Demetrious	S	6-0	196	7/21/61	6	Missouri	St. Louis, Mo.	FA-'88	3/2
10	Kelly, Mike	QB	6-3	195	12/31/59	2	Georgia Tech	Augusta, Ga.	FA-'87	3/1
94	Kirk, Randy	LB	6-2	235	12/27/64	2	San Diego State	San Jose, Calif.	FA-'87	13/1
68	Kowalski, Gary	G-T	6-6	273	7/2/60	5	Boston College	Clinton, Conn.	T(Rams)-'85	12/9
74	Lachey, Jim	T	6-6	289	6/4/63	4	Ohio State	St. Henry, Ohio	D1-'85	12/12
62	Macek, Don	C	6-2	270	7/2/54	13	Boston College	Manchester, N.H.	D2-'76	11/11
16	t-Malone, Mark	QB	6-4	224	11/22/58	9	Arizona State	El Cajon, Calif.	T(Pitt)-'88	12/12
60	McKnight, Dennis	C-G	6-3	270	9/12/59	7	Drake	Staten Island, N.Y.	FA-'82	12/12
69	Miller, Les	DE	6-7	285	3/1/65	2	Fort Hays State	Arkansas City, Kan.	FA-'87	9/4
17	Moffett, Tim	WR	6-2	190	2/8/62	4	Mississippi	Taylorville, Miss.	FA-'87	2/1
2	Mojsiejenko, Ralf	P	6-3	212	1/28/63	4	Michigan State	Bridgman, Mich.	D4-'85	12/0
91	O'Neal, Leslie	DE	6-4	255	5/7/64	2	Oklahoma State	Little Rock, Ark.	D1a-'86	0*
34	Patterson, Elvis	CB	5-11	198	10/21/60	5	Kansas	Houston, Tex.	FA-'87	14/12*
93	Pettitt, Duane	DE	6-4	265	11/2/64	2	San Diego State	Tehachapi, Calif.	FA-'87	3/0
75	†Phillips, Joe	DE	6-5	275	7/15/63	3	Southern Methodist	Vancouver, Wash.	FA-'87	13/7
50	Plummer, Gary	LB	6-2	240	1/26/60	3	California	Fremont, Calif.	FA-'86	8/7
53	Price, Stacey	LB	6-2	194	3/3/62	2	Arkansas State	Texarkana, Ark.	FA-'87	3/0
	t-Quillan, Fred	C	6-5	266	1/27/56	11	Oregon	Portland, Ore.	T(SF)-'88	11/4
20	Redden, Barry	RB	5-10	219	7/21/60	7	Richmond	Sarasota, Fla.	T(Rams)-'87	12/0
66	Rosado, Dan	G-T	6-3	280	7/6/59	2	Northern Illinois	Canton, Ga.	FA-'87	4/3
79	Rouse, Curtis	G-T	6-3	340	7/13/60	7	Tennessee-Chattanooga	Augusta, Ga.	FA-'87	10/3
85	Sievers, Eric	TE	6-4	230	11/9/58	8	Maryland	Arlington, Va.	D4b-'81	12/1
54	Smith, Billy Ray	LB	6-3	236	8/10/61	6	Arkansas	Plano, Tex.	D1a-'83	12/12
43	†Spencer, Tim	RB	6-1	227	12/10/60	4	Ohio State	St. Clairsville, Ohio	D11b-'83	12/7
72	Stadnik, John	C-G	6-4	265	2/18/60	2	Western Illinois	Blue Island, Ill.	FA-'88	3/3
59	Taylor, John	LB	6-4	235	6/21/61	4	Hawaii	Seattle, Wash.	FA-'87	7/3
76	Thompson, Broderick	G-T	6-4	290	8/14/60	3	Kansas	Cerritos, Calif.	FA-'87	8/3
98	Unrein, Terry	NT-DE	6-5	280	10/24/62	3	Colorado State	Ft. Lupton, Colo.	D3a-'86	9/2
13	Vlasic, Mark	QB	6-3	206	10/25/63	2	Iowa	Monaca, Pa.	D4-'87	1/0
23	†Walters, Danny	CB	6-1	200	11/4/60	5	Arkansas	Chicago, Ill.	D4-'83	12/5
81	Ware, Timmie	WR	5-10	170	4/2/63	3	Southern California	Compton, Calif.	FA-'86	12/1
84	Williams, Al	WR	5-10	180	2/4/62	2	Nevada-Reno	Long Beach, Calif.	FA-'87	3/3
99	†Williams, Lee	DE	6-5	263	10/15/62	5	Bethune-Cookman	Ft. Lauderdale, Fla.	SD1-'84	12/12
72	Wilson, Karl	DE	6-4	268	9/10/64	2	Louisiana State	Baton Rouge, La.	D3-'87	7/0
80	Winslow, Kellen	TE	6-5	251	11/5/57	10	Missouri	St. Louis, Mo.	D1-'79	12/12

* Brookins last active with Buffalo in '85; Dale and O'Neal missed '87 season due to injury; Patterson played 1 game with N.Y. Giants, 13 with San Diego in '87.

†Option playout; subject to developments.

t-Chargers traded for Malone (Pittsburgh), Quillan (San Francisco).

Traded—Wide receiver Wes Chandler to San Francisco; quarterback Mark Herrmann to Pittsburgh; tight end Pete Holohan to Los Angeles Rams; nose tackle Blaise Winter to Green Bay.

Retired—Dan Fouts, 15-year quarterback, 11 games in '87.

Also played with Chargers in '87—LB Ty Allert (3), S Anthony Anderson (3), DE Monte Bennett (3), CB Ed Berry (2), CB Carl Brazley (2), WR Bruce Davis (active for 1 game but did not play), C-G David Diaz-Infante (3), LB Chuck Faucette (2), T Greg Feasel (3), TE Kevin Ferguson (2), K Jeff Gaffney (3), C Joe Goebel (2), DE Willard Goff (1), S Walt Harris (3), LB Andy Hawkins (2), TE Harry Holt (3), CB-S Darrel Hopper (4), S Mike Hudson (3), LB Mike Humiston (7), LB Brian Ingram (1), RB Keyvan Jenkins (3), LB James Johnson (1), RB Frank Middleton (3), LB Pat Miller (1), WR Calvin Muhammad (2), QB Rick Neuheisel (3), RB Jeff Powell (1), P-K Joe Prokop (3), WR Tag Rome (3), CB Charles Romes (5), RB Martin Sartin (3), T Gary Schippang (active for 1 game but did not play), DE Tony Simmons (3), S King Simmons (3), T Emil Slovacek (2), LB Angelo Snipes (2), RB Todd Spencer (3), RB Anthony Steels (2), S Ted Watts (1), G-T Dwight Wheeler (3), DE Earl Wilson (1).

COACHING STAFF

Head Coach, Al Saunders

Pro Career: Begins second full season as San Diego's head coach. Named seventh head coach in Chargers history on October 29, 1986. Led team to 8-7 record in 1987, best since 1982. Came to Chargers and the NFL in 1983 as receivers coach and was named assistant head coach/receivers at the start of the 1986 season. Career record: 11-12.

Background: Academic All-America defensive back and team captain at San Jose State 1969. Graduate assistant at Southern California 1970-71. Receivers coach at Missouri 1972. Offensive backfield coach at Utah State 1973-75. Assistant head coach and offensive coordinator at California 1976-81. Offensive coordinator and quarterbacks coach at Tennessee 1982.

Personal: Born February 1, 1947, in London, England. Attended St. Ignatius High School in San Francisco. Graduated with honors from San Jose State 1969. Received masters degree in education and physical education from Stanford in 1970 before moving to Southern California, where he is completing his doctorate in sports administration. Saunders and his wife, Karen, live in Scripps Ranch, Calif., and have three children—Robert, William, and Korrin.

Assistant Coaches

Gunther Cunningham, defensive line; born June 19, 1946, Munich, Germany, lives in San Diego. Linebacker Oregon 1965-67. No pro playing experience. College coach: Oregon 1969-71, Arkansas 1972, Stanford 1973-76, California 1977-80. Pro coach: Hamilton Tiger-Cats (CFL) 1981, Indianapolis Colts 1982-84, joined Chargers in 1985.

Mike Haluchak, linebackers; born November 28, 1949, Concord, Calif., lives in San Diego. Linebacker Southern California 1967-70. No pro playing experience. College coach: Southern California 1976-77, Cal State-Fullerton 1978, Pacific 1979-80, California 1981, North Carolina State 1982. Pro coach: Oakland Invaders (USFL) 1983-85, joined Chargers in 1986.

Bobby Jackson, running backs; born February 16, 1940, Forsyth, Ga., lives in San Diego. Linebacker-running back Samford (Ga.) 1959-62. No pro playing experience. College coach: Florida State 1965-69, Kansas State 1970-74, Louisville 1975-76, Tennessee 1977-82. Pro coach: Atlanta Falcons 1983-86, joined Chargers in 1987.

Charlie Joiner, receivers; born October 14, 1947, Many, La., lives in San Diego. Wide receiver Grambling 1965-68. Defensive back-wide receiver Houston Oilers 1969-72, wide receiver Cincinnati Bengals 1972-75, San Diego Chargers 1976-86. Pro coach: Joined Chargers in 1987.

Dave Levy, tight ends; born October 25, 1932, Carrollton, Mo., lives in Solana Beach, Calif. Guard UCLA 1952-53. No pro playing experience. College coach: UCLA 1954, Long Beach City College 1955, Southern California 1960-75. Pro coach: Joined Chargers in 1980.

Ron Lynn, defensive coordinator; born December 6, 1944, Youngstown, Ohio, lives in San Diego. Quarterback-defensive back Mount Union (Ohio) 1963-65. College coach: Toledo 1966, Mount Union 1967-73, Kent State 1974-76, San Jose State 1977-78, Pacific 1979, California 1980-82. Pro coach: Oakland Invaders (USFL) 1983-85, joined Chargers in 1986.

Jerry Rhome, offensive coordinator; born March 6, 1942, Dallas, Tex., lives in San Diego. Quarterback Southern Methodist 1960-61, Tulsa 1963-64. Pro quarterback Dallas Cowboys 1965-68, Cleveland Browns 1969, Houston Oilers 1970, Los Angeles Rams 1971-72. College coach: Tulsa 1973-75. Pro coach: Seattle Seahawks 1976-82, Washington Redskins 1983-87, joined Chargers in 1988.

San Diego Chargers 1988 First-Year Roster

Name	Pos.	Ht.	Wt.	Birth-date	College	Hometown	How Acq.
Bennett, Roy (1)	CB-S	6-2	200	7/5/61	Jackson State	Birmingham, Ala.	FA-'87
Brock, Lou (1)	CB	5-10	175	5/8/64	Southern California	St. Louis, Mo.	D2-'87
Campbell, Joe	DE-NT	6-3	242	12/28/66	New Mexico State	Tempe, Ariz.	D4a
Deline, Steve (1)	K	5-11	185	8/19/61	Colorado State	Englewood, Colo.	FA
Early, Quinn	WR	6-0	190	4/13/65	Iowa	Great Neck, N.Y.	D2
Faucette, Chuck (1)	LB	6-3	238	10/17/63	Maryland	Willingboro, N.J.	FA-'87
Figaro, Cedric	LB	6-2	250	8/17/66	Notre Dame	Lafayette, La.	D6
Fletcher, John (1)	DE	6-3	285	8/22/65	Texas A&I	Corpus Christi, Tex.	FA
Foster, Ron (1)	CB-S	6-0	205	11/25/63	Cal State-Northridge	Woodland Hills, Calif.	FA
Goebel, Joe (1)	C	6-5	264	12/12/63	UCLA	Midland, Tex.	FA-'87
Hinkle, George	DE-NT	6-5	269	3/17/65	Arizona	Pacific, Mo.	D11b
Howard, Joey	T	6-5	285	9/14/65	Tennessee	Springfield, Ohio	D9
Hudson, Robert	TE	6-4	256	1/6/64	Nevada-Reno	Bakersfield, Calif.	FA
Jackson, Enis (1)	CB	5-9	175	5/16/63	Memphis State	Helena, Ark.	FA
Jones, Nelson (1)	CB-S	6-1	190	2/13/64	North Carolina State	Woodbury, N.J.	D5-'87
Mac Esker, Joe (1)	T	6-7	305	9/21/65	Texas-El Paso	Mahopac, N.Y.	D8a-'87
Miller, Anthony	WR	5-11	180	4/15/65	Tennessee	Pasadena, Calif.	D1
Miller, Ed	T-G-C	6-3	275	8/4/65	Pittsburgh	Kenilworth, N.J.	D11a
Miller, Pat (1)	LB	6-1	220	6/24/64	Florida	Panama City, Fla.	FA-'87
Phillips, Wendell	CB-S	5-11	195	4/3/66	North Alabama	Leighton, Ala.	D12
Richards, David	T	6-5	305	4/11/66	UCLA	Dallas, Tex.	D4c
Scott, Kevin (1)	RB	5-9	181	10/24/63	Stanford	Puyallup, Wash.	FA-'87
Searels, Stacy	T-G-C	6-5	281	5/19/65	Auburn	Trion, Ga.	D4b
Williams, Kevin (1)	CB-S	5-10	175	11/28/61	Washington	San Diego, Calif.	FA
Zachary, Ken (1)	RB	6-0	222	11/19/63	Oklahoma State	Sapulpa, Okla.	FA

The term NFL Rookie is defined as a player who is in his first season of professional football and has not been on the roster of another professional football team for any regular-season or postseason games. A Rookie is designated by an "R" on NFL rosters. Players who have been active in another professional football league or players who have NFL experience, including either preseason training camp or being on an active roster for fewer than three regular-season or postseason games, are termed NFL First-Year Players. An NFL First-Year Player is designated by a "1" on NFL rosters. Thereafter, a player on an NFL active roster for at least three regular-season or postseason games is credited with an additional year of NFL playing experience.

NOTES

Wayne Sevier, special teams; born July 3, 1941, San Diego, Calif., lives in San Diego. Quarterback Chaffey, Calif., J.C. 1960, San Diego State 1961-62. No pro playing experience. College coach: California Western 1968-69. Pro coach: St. Louis Cardinals 1974-75, Atlanta Falcons 1976, San Diego Chargers 1979-80, Washington Redskins 1981-86, rejoined Chargers in 1987.

Jerry Wampfler, offensive line; born August 6, 1932, New Philadelphia, Ohio, lives in San Diego. Tackle Miami, Ohio 1951-54. No pro playing experience. College coach: Presbyterian 1955, Miami, Ohio 1963-65, Notre Dame 1966-69, Colorado State 1970-72 (head coach). Pro coach: Philadelphia Eagles 1973-75, 1979-83, Buffalo Bills 1976-77, New York Giants 1978, Green Bay Packers 1984-87, joined Chargers in 1988.

SEATTLE SEAHAWKS

American Football Conference Western Division

Team Colors: Blue, Green, and Silver

11220 N.E. 53rd Street
Kirkland, Washington 98033
Telephone: (206) 827-9777

Club Officials

President-General Manager: Mike McCormack
Vice President/Assistant General Manager: Chuck Allen
Player Personnel Director: Mike Allman
Vice President/Public Relations: Gary Wright
Assistant Public Relations Director: Dave Neubert
Administrative Assistant: Sandy Gregory
Sales and Marketing Coordinator: Lowell Perry
Sales and Marketing Assistant: Reggie McKenzie
Business Manager: Mickey Loomis
Data Processing Director: Tom Monroe
Ticket Manager: James Nagaoka
Trainer: Jim Whitesel
Equipment Manager: Walt Loeffler

Stadium: Kingdome • **Capacity:** 64,984
201 South King Street
Seattle, Washington 98104

Playing Surface: AstroTurf

Training Camp: 11220 N.E. 53rd Street
Kirkland, Washington 98033

1988 Schedule

Preseason

Aug. 4	**Phoenix**	7:30
Aug. 11	at Detroit	7:30
Aug. 19	**Buffalo**	7:30
Aug. 26	at San Francisco	6:00

Regular Season

Sept. 4	at Denver	2:00
Sept. 11	**Kansas City**	1:00
Sept. 18	at San Diego	1:00
Sept. 25	**San Francisco**	1:00
Oct. 2	at Atlanta	1:00
Oct. 9	at Cleveland	1:00
Oct. 16	**New Orleans**	1:00
Oct. 23	at Los Angeles Rams	1:00
Oct. 30	**San Diego**	1:00
Nov. 6	**Buffalo**	1:00
Nov. 13	**Houston**	1:00
Nov. 20	at Kansas City	12:00
Nov. 28	**L.A. Raiders** (Monday)	6:00
Dec. 4	at New England	1:00
Dec. 11	**Denver**	5:00
Dec. 18	at Los Angeles Raiders	1:00

Seahawks Coaching History

(90-96-0)

1976-82	Jack Patera*	35-59-0
1982	Mike McCormack	4-3-0
1983-87	Chuck Knox	51-34-0

*Released after two games in 1982

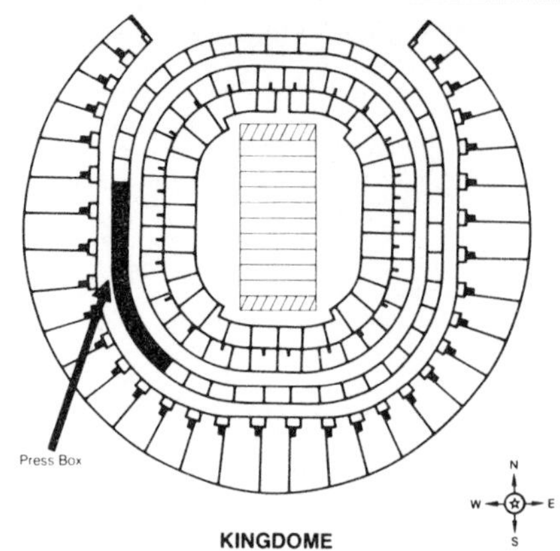

Record Holders

Individual Records—Career

Category	Name	Performance
Rushing (Yds.)	Curt Warner, 1983-87	5,049
Passing (Yds.)	Jim Zorn, 1976-1984	20,042
Passing (TDs)	Dave Krieg, 1980-87	130
Receiving (No.)	Steve Largent, 1976-1987	*752
Receiving (Yds.)	Steve Largent, 1976-1987	12,041
Interceptions	Dave Brown, 1976-1986	50
Punting (Avg.)	Herman Weaver, 1977-1980	40.0
Punt Return (Avg.)	Bobby Joe Edmonds, 1986-87	12.4
Kickoff Return (Avg.)	Zachary Dixon, 1983-84	23.4
Field Goals	Norm Johnson, 1982-87	99
Touchdowns (Tot.)	Steve Largent, 1976-1987	96
Points	Steve Largent, 1976-1987	577

Individual Records—Single Season

Category	Name	Performance
Rushing (Yds.)	Curt Warner, 1986	1,481
Passing (Yds.)	Dave Krieg, 1984	3,671
Passing (TDs)	Dave Krieg, 1984	32
Receiving (No.)	Steve Largent, 1985	79
Receiving (Yds.)	Steve Largent, 1985	1,287
Interceptions	John Harris, 1981	10
	Kenny Easley, 1984	10
Punting (Avg.)	Herman Weaver, 1980	41.8
Punt Return (Avg.)	Bobby Joe Edmonds, 1987	12.6
Kickoff Return (Avg.)	Al Hunter, 1978	24.1
Field Goals	Norm Johnson, 1986	22
Touchdowns (Tot.)	David Sims, 1978	15
	Sherman Smith, 1979	15
Points	Norm Johnson, 1984	110

Individual Records—Single Game

Category	Name	Performance
Rushing (Yds.)	Curt Warner, 11-27-83	207
Passing (Yds.)	Dave Krieg, 11-20-83	418
Passing (TDs)	Dave Krieg, 12-2-84	5
	Dave Krieg, 9-15-85	5
Receiving (No.)	Steve Largent, 10-18-87	15
Receiving (Yds.)	Steve Largent, 10-18-87	261
Interceptions	Kenny Easley, 9-3-84	3
Field Goals	Norm Johnson, 9-20-87	5
Touchdowns (Tot.)	Daryl Turner, 9-15-85	4
Points	Daryl Turner, 9-15-85	24

*NFL Record

1987 Team Record

Preseason (2-2)

Date	Result		Opponents
8/13	L	14-23	at L.A. Rams
8/22	L	21-28	at St. Louis
8/28	W	38-10	Detroit
9/4	W	34-10	San Francisco
		107-71	

Regular Season (9-6)

Date	Result		Opponents	Att.
9/13	L	17-40	at Denver	75,999
9/20	W	43-14	Kansas City	61,667
9/27	C		at San Diego	
10/4	W	24-20	Miami	19,448
10/11	L	10-17	Cincinnati	31,739
10/18	W	37-14	at Detroit	8,310
10/25	W	35-13	at L.A. Raiders	52,735
11/1	W	28-17	Minnesota	61,134
11/9	L	14-30	at N.Y. Jets	60,452
11/15	W	24-13	Green Bay	60,963
11/22	W	34- 3	San Diego	62,444
11/30	L	14-37	L.A. Raiders	62,802
12/6	L	9-13	at Pittsburgh	48,881
12/13	W	28-21	Denver	61,759
12/20	W	34-21	at Chicago	62,518
12/27	L	20-41	at Kansas City	20,370

C (Cancelled due to players' strike.)

Postseason (0-1)

Date	Result		Opponent	Att.
1/3	L	20-23	at Houston (OT)	49,622

(OT) Overtime

Score by Periods

Seahawks	79	132	95	65	0	—	371
Opponents	51	110	75	78	0	—	314

Attendance

Home 421,956 Away 329,265 Total 751,221
Single-game home record, 64,411 (12-15-84)
Single-season home record, 493,657 (1985)

1987 Team Statistics

	Seahawks	Opp.
Total First Downs	301	297
Rushing	120	133
Passing	154	148
Penalty	27	16
Third Down: Made/Att.	92/189	85/196
Fourth Down: Made/Att.	4/9	4/10
Total Net Yards	4735	5159
Avg. Per Game	315.7	343.9
Total Plays	937	954
Avg. Per Play	5.1	5.4
Net Yards Rushing	2023	2201
Avg. Per Game	134.9	146.7
Total Rushes	496	472
Net Yards Passing	2712	2958
Avg. Per Game	180.8	197.2
Sacked/Yards Lost	36/316	37/238
Gross Yards	3028	3196
Att./Completions	405/237	445/255
Completion Pct.	58.5	57.3
Had Intercepted	21	17
Punts/Avg.	61/38.9	63/39.1
Net Punting Avg.	33.1	32.7
Penalties/Yards Lost	79/668	104/890
Fumbles/Ball Lost	31/15	38/21
Touchdowns	46	36
Rushing	13	14
Passing	31	20
Returns	2	2
Avg. Time of Possession	30:35	29:25

1987 Individual Statistics

Scoring	TD R	TD P	TD Rt	PAT	FG	Saf	TP
N. Johnson	0	0	0	40/40	15/20	0	85
Warner	8	2	0	0/0	0/0	0	60
Largent	0	8	0	0/0	0/0	0	48
Turner	0	6	0	0/0	0/0	0	36
R. Butler	0	5	0	0/0	0/0	0	30
Jo. Williams	1	3	0	0/0	0/0	0	24
Krieg	2	0	0	0/0	0/0	0	12
Teal	0	2	0	0/0	0/0	0	12
Tice	0	2	0	0/0	0/0	0	12
Hagler	0	0	0	4/4	2/2	0	10
Keel	0	1	0	0/0	0/0	0	6
Morton	1	0	0	0/0	0/0	0	6
Pardridge	0	1	0	0/0	0/0	0	6
Parros	1	0	0	0/0	0/0	0	6
Robinson	0	0	1	0/0	0/0	0	6
Skansi	0	1	0	0/0	0/0	0	6
F. Young	0	0	1	0/0	0/0	0	6
Seahawks	13	31	2	44/46	17/22	0	371
Opponents	14	20	2	35/36	21/26	0	314

Passing	Att.	Comp.	Yds.	Pct.	TD	Int.	Tkld.	Rate
Krieg	294	178	2131	60.5	23	15	27/247	87.6
Mathison	76	36	501	47.4	3	5	6/49	54.8
Kemp	33	23	396	69.7	5	1	3/20	137.1
Largent	2	0	0	0.0	0	0	0/0	39.6
Seahawks	405	237	3028	58.5	31	21	36/316	85.9
Opponents	445	255	3196	57.3	20	17	37/238	78.8

Rushing	Att.	Yds.	Avg.	LG	TD
Warner	234	985	4.2	57t	8
Jo. Williams	113	500	4.4	48	1
Krieg	36	155	4.3	17	2
B. Green	21	77	3.7	17	0
Morris	21	71	3.4	13	0
Morton	19	52	2.7	10	1
Lane	13	40	3.1	7	0
Burse	7	36	5.1	16	0
Largent	2	33	16.5	21	0
Parros	13	32	2.5	7	1
A. Moore	3	15	5.0	13	0
Mathison	5	15	3.0	10	0
Kemp	5	9	1.8	12	0
Hagen	2	3	1.5	4	0
Griffith	1	0	0.0	0	0
Rodriguez	1	0	0.0	0	0
Seahawks	496	2023	4.1	57t	13
Opponents	472	2201	4.7	91t	14

Receiving	No.	Yds.	Avg.	LG	TD
Largent	58	912	15.7	55	8
Jo. Williams	38	420	11.1	75t	3
R. Butler	33	465	14.1	40t	5
Skansi	19	207	10.9	25	1
Warner	17	167	9.8	30t	2
Teal	14	198	14.1	47	2
Turner	14	153	10.9	20t	6
Tice	14	106	7.6	27	2
Pardridge	8	145	18.1	47	1
Juma	7	95	13.6	26	0
Keel	6	88	14.7	24t	1
Lane	4	30	7.5	12	0
Bengen	2	33	16.5	24	0
Franklin	1	7	7.0	7	0
Parros	1	7	7.0	7	0
Millard	1	−5	−5.0	−5	0
Seahawks	237	3028	12.8	75t	31
Opponents	255	3196	12.5	81t	20

Interceptions	No.	Yds.	Avg.	LG	TD
Easley	4	47	11.8	22	0
Robinson	3	75	25.0	44	0
Jenkins	3	46	15.3	34	0
Glaze	2	53	26.5	53	0
F. Young	1	50	50.0	50t	1
Taylor	1	11	11.0	9	0
Caldwell	1	4	4.0	4	0
Hunter	1	3	3.0	3	0
Moyer	1	0	0.0	0	0
Seahawks	17	289	17.0	53	1
Opponents	21	146	7.0	32	0

Punting	No.	Yds.	Avg.	In 20	LG
Rodriguez	47	1880	40.0	17	63
Griffith	11	386	35.1	1	51
Bowman	3	104	34.7	0	36
Seahawks	61	2370	38.9	18	63
Opponents	63	2465	39.1	13	60

Punt Returns	No.	FC	Yds.	Avg.	LG	TD
Edmonds	20	4	251	12.6	40	0
Hollis	6	0	33	5.5	15	0
Teal	6	4	38	6.3	13	0
Seahawks	32	8	322	10.1	40	0
Opponents	32	12	251	7.8	91t	1

Kickoff Returns	No.	Yds.	Avg.	LG	TD
Edmonds	27	564	20.9	43	0
Hollis	10	263	26.3	41	0
Morris	9	149	16.6	20	0
Teal	6	95	15.8	23	0
Powell	3	23	7.7	14	0
Bengen	2	47	23.5	36	0
Lane	2	34	17.0	22	0
Pardridge	2	29	14.5	16	0
Burse	1	1	1.0	1	0
B. Green	1	20	20.0	20	0
Scholtz	1	11	11.0	11	0
Seahawks	64	1236	19.3	43	0
Opponents	67	1379	20.6	92t	1

Sacks	No.
J. Green	9.5
F. Young	9.0
Bosworth	4.0
Bryant	4.0
Nash	3.5
Glaze	2.0
Dorning	1.5
Moyer	1.0
Wiley	1.0
L. Williams	1.0
Scholtz	0.5
Seahawks	37.0
Opponents	36.0

Seattle Seahawks 1988 Veteran Roster

No.	Name	Pos.	Ht.	Wt.	Birth-date	NFL Exp.	College	Hometown	How Acq.	'87 Games/ Starts
65	Bailey, Edwin	G	6-4	276	5/15/59	8	South Carolina State	Savannah, Ga.	D5-'81	12/12
62	Barbay, Roland	NT	6-4	260	10/1/64	2	Louisiana State	New Orleans, La.	D7a-'87	5/0
76	†Borchardt, Jon	T	6-5	272	8/13/57	10	Montana State	Minneapolis, Minn.	FA-'86	12/0
55	Bosworth, Brian	LB	6-2	248	3/9/65	2	Oklahoma	Irving, Tex.	D1-'88	12/12
77	†Bryant, Jeff	DE	6-5	272	5/22/60	7	Clemson	Decatur, Ga.	D1-'82	12/12
97	Burnham, Tim	T	6-5	280	5/6/63	2	Washington	Anderson, Calif.	FA-'88	3/3
34	Burse, Tony	RB	6-0	220	4/4/65	2	Middle Tennessee State	Lafayette, Ga.	D12b-'87	12/0
59	†Bush, Blair	C	6-3	272	11/25/56	11	Washington	Palos Verdes, Calif.	T(Cin)-'83	11/11
53	†Butler, Keith	LB	6-4	239	5/16/56	11	Memphis State	Huntsville, Ala.	D2-'78	12/0
83	†Butler, Ray	WR	6-3	206	6/28/56	9	Southern California	Sweeny, Tex.	FA-'85	12/3
45	Easley, Kenny	S	6-3	198	1/15/59	8	UCLA	Chesapeake, Va.	D1-'81	12/11
30	Edmonds, Bobby Joe	RB	5-11	186	9/26/64	3	Arkansas	St. Louis, Mo.	D5-'86	11/0
54	Feasel, Grant	C	6-7	280	6/28/60	4	Abilene Christian	Barstow, Calif.	FA-'87	12/2
88	†Franklin, Byron	WR	6-1	183	9/3/58	7	Auburn	Sheffield, Ala.	T(Buff)-'85	6/0
56	†Gaines, Greg	LB	6-3	222	10/16/58	7	Tennessee	Hermitage, Tenn.	FA-'81	11/10
79	Green, Jacob	DE	6-3	252	1/21/57	9	Texas A&M	Houston, Tex.	D1-'80	12/12
47	Hardy, Andre	RB	6-1	233	11/28/61	3	St. Mary's, Calif.	San Diego, Calif.	FA-'87	1/0*
78	t-Heller, Ron	T	6-6	280	8/25/62	5	Penn State	Farmingdale, N.Y.	T(TB)-'88	12/10
25	Hollis, David	CB	5-11	175	7/4/65	2	Nevada-Las Vegas	Gardena, Calif.	FA-'87	11/0
29	Holloway, Johnny	CB	5-11	182	11/8/63	3	Kansas	Houston, Tex.	FA-'88	3/1*
23	Hunter, Patrick	CB	5-11	185	10/24/64	3	Nevada-Reno	San Francisco, Calif.	D3-'86	11/11
24	Jenkins, Melvin	CB	5-10	170	3/16/62	2	Cincinnati	Jackson, Miss.	FA-'87	12/1
52	Johnson, M.L.	LB	6-3	225	1/24/64	2	Hawaii	Los Angeles, Calif.	D9-'87	8/0
9	†Johnson, Norm	K	6-2	198	5/31/60	7	UCLA	Garden Grove, Calif.	FA-'82	13/0
26	Justin, Kerry	CB	5-11	185	5/3/55	9	Oregon State	Los Angeles, Calif.	FA-'86	7/0
15	Kemp, Jeff	QB	6-0	201	7/11/59	8	Dartmouth	Bethesda, Md.	T(SF)-'87	13/1
17	Krieg, Dave	QB	6-1	196	10/20/58	9	Milton	Schofield, Wis.	FA-'80	12/12
37	†Lane, Eric	RB	6-0	201	1/6/59	8	Brigham Young	Hayward, Calif.	FA-'87	12/2
80	Largent, Steve	WR	5-11	184	9/28/54	13	Tulsa	Oklahoma City, Okla.	T(Hou)-'76	13/13
13	†Mathison, Bruce	QB	6-3	205	4/25/59	5	Nebraska	Superior, Wis.	FA-'87	3/2
70	†Mattes, Ron	T	6-6	306	8/8/63	3	Virginia	Shenandoah, Va.	D7-'85	12/12
51	†Merriman, Sam	LB	6-3	232	5/5/61	6	Idaho	Tucson, Ariz.	D7-'83	9/0
71	Millard, Bryan	G	6-5	284	12/2/60	5	Texas	Dumas, Tex.	FA-'84	12/12
61	Mitz, Alonzo	DE	6-3	273	6/5/63	3	Florida	Ft. Pierce, Fla.	D8-'86	6/0
35	Moore, Mark	S	6-0	194	9/3/64	2	Oklahoma State	Nacogdoches, Tex.	D4-'87	5/0
43	†Morris, Randall	RB	6-0	200	4/22/62	5	Tennessee	Long Beach, Calif.	D10-'84	10/0
21	†Moyer, Paul	S	6-1	201	7/26/61	6	Arizona State	Villa Park, Calif.	FA-'83	12/1
72	†Nash, Joe	NT	6-2	257	10/11/60	7	Boston College	Dorchester, Mass.	FA-'82	12/12
73	†Powell, Alvin	G	6-5	296	11/19/59	2	Winston-Salem State	Fayetteville, N.C.	SD2-'84	12/0
41	Robinson, Eugene	S	6-0	186	5/28/63	4	Colgate	Hartford, Conn.	FA-'85	12/12
5	Rodriguez, Ruben	P	6-2	220	3/3/65	2	Arizona	Woodlake, Calif.	D5b-'87	12/0
27	†Romes, Charles	CB	6-1	190	12/16/53	12	North Carolina Central	Durham, N.C.	FA-'87	5/0*
58	Scholtz, Bruce	LB	6-6	242	9/26/58	7	Texas	Austin, Tex.	D2-'82	8/7
74	Singer, Curt	T	6-5	279	11/4/61	2	Tennessee	Aliquippa, Pa.	FA-'86	0*
82	†Skansi, Paul	WR	5-11	183	1/11/61	6	Washington	Gig Harbor, Wash.	FA-'85	12/0
87	Strozier, Wilbur	TE	6-4	255	11/12/64	2	Georgia	LaGrange, Ga.	FA-'87	12/3
20	†Taylor, Terry	CB	5-10	191	7/18/61	5	Southern Illinois	Youngstown, Ohio	D1-'84	12/12
85	†Teal, Jimmy	WR	5-11	175	8/18/62	4	Texas A&M	Diboll, Tex.	FA-'87	4/2
86	†Tice, Mike	TE	6-7	247	2/2/59	8	Maryland	Central Islip, N.Y.	FA-'81	12/12
90	Tipton, Rico	LB	6-2	240	7/31/61	2	Washington State	Pittsburg, Calif.	FA-'88	3/2
81	†Turner, Daryl	WR	6-3	194	12/15/61	5	Michigan State	Flint, Mich.	D2-'84	12/8
28	Warner, Curt	RB	5-11	205	3/18/61	5	Penn State	Pineville, W.Va.	D1-'83	12/12
32	Williams, John L.	RB	5-11	226	11/23/64	3	Florida	Palatka, Fla.	D1-'86	12/10
91	Williams, Lester	NT	6-3	290	1/19/59	6	Miami	Carol City, Fla.	FA-'88	2/0
75	Wilson, Mike	T	6-5	280	5/28/55	11	Georgia	Gainesville, Ga.	T(Cin)-'86	12/12
57	Woods, Tony	LB	6-4	244	9/11/65	2	Pittsburgh	Newark, N.J.	D1-'87	12/7
92	Wyman, David	LB	6-2	229	3/31/64	2	Stanford	Reno, Nev.	D2-'87	4/0
50	Young, Fredd	LB	6-1	233	11/14/61	5	New Mexico State	Dallas, Tex.	D3-'84	13/13

* Hardy played 1 game with San Francisco in '87; Holloway played 3 games with St. Louis; Romes played 5 games with San Diego; Singer missed '87 season due to injury.

†Option playout; subject to developments.

t-Seahawks traded for Heller (Tampa Bay).

Traded—Defensive end Randy Edwards to Tampa Bay.

Also played with Seahawks in '87—S Harvey Allen (2 games), C Tom Andrews (2), CB Curtis Baham (3), WR Brant Benge (3), CB Anthony Blue (3), P Barry Bowman (1), CB Arnold Brown (2), LB Tony Caldwell (1), TE Cris Corley (1), LB Julio Cortes (3), CB Fred Davis (1), LB Ron DeVita (1), DE Dale Dorning (3), NT John Eisenhooth (1), WR Russell Evans (1), DE Don Fairbanks (3), CB Charles Glaze (3), NT David Graham (3), RB Boyce Green (2), P Russell Griffith (2), RB Mike Hagen (2), K Scott Hagler (2), G Matt Hanousek (3), C Doug Hire (3), DE Van Hughes (1), LB Joe Jackson (3), WR Kevin Juma (3), TE Mark Keel (3), LB Paul Lavine (3), S Kim Mack (1), LB John McVeigh (3), RB Alvin Moore (1), RB Michael Morton (2), TE John O'Callaghan (1), LB Fred Orns (2), WR Curtis Pardridge (3), RB Rick Parros (1), C Dean Perryman (1), DE Greg Ramsey (2), T Howard Richards (2), TE Ken Sager (3), T Ron Scoggins (3), G Jack Sims (3), S Dallis Smith (3), WR Donald Snell (1), RB Chad Stark (2), LB Joe Terry (2), G Garth Thomas (1), S Ricky Thomas (1), S Chris White (1), NT Charles Wiley (1), RB James Williams (1), CB Renard Young (3).

COACHING STAFF

Head Coach, Chuck Knox

Pro Career: Named head coach of Seahawks on January 26, 1983, after five seasons as head coach at Buffalo, where he led Bills to AFC East title in 1980. Led Los Angeles Rams to five straight NFC West titles before taking over Bills in 1978. Pro assistant with New York Jets 1963-66, coaching offensive line, before moving to Detroit in 1967. Served Lions in same capacity until named head coach of Rams in 1973. No pro playing experience. Career record: 146-92-1.

Background: Played tackle for Juniata College in Huntingdon, Pa., 1950-53. Was assistant coach at his alma mater in 1954, then spent 1955 season as line coach at Ellwood City High School in Pennsylvania. Moved to Wake Forest as an assistant coach in 1959-60, then Kentucky in 1961-62.

Personal: Born April 27, 1932, Sewickley, Pa. Chuck and his wife, Shirley, live in Bellevue, Wash., and have four children—Chris, Kathy, Colleen, and Chuck.

Assistant Coaches

Tom Catlin, assistant head coach-defensive coordinator; born September 8, 1931, Ponca City, Okla., lives in Redmond, Wash. Center-linebacker Oklahoma 1950-52. Pro linebacker Cleveland Browns 1953-54, 1957-58, Philadelphia Eagles 1959. College coach: Army 1956. Pro coach: Dallas Texans-Kansas City Chiefs 1960-65, Los Angeles Rams 1966-77, Buffalo Bills 1978-82, joined Seahawks in 1983.

George Dyer, defensive line; born May 4, 1940, Alhambra, Calif., lives in Redmond, Wash. Center-linebacker U.C. Santa Barbara 1961-63. No pro playing experience. College coach: Humboldt State 1964-66, Coalinga, Calif., J.C. 1967 (head coach), Portland State 1968-71, Idaho 1972, San Jose State 1973, Michigan State 1977-79, Arizona State 1980-81. Pro coach: Winnipeg Blue Bombers (CFL) 1974-76, Buffalo Bills 1982, joined Seahawks in 1983.

Chick Harris, offensive backfield; born September 21, 1945, Durham, N.C., lives in Redmond, Wash. Running back Northern Arizona 1966-69. No pro playing experience. College coach: Colorado State 1970-72, Long Beach State 1973-74, Washington 1975-80. Pro coach: Buffalo Bills 1981-82, joined Seahawks in 1983.

Ralph Hawkins, defensive backfield; born May 4, 1935, Washington, D.C., lives in Redmond, Wash. Quarterback-defensive back Maryland 1953-55. Pro defensive back New York Titans (AFL) 1960. College coach: Maryland 1959, 1967, Southern Methodist 1961, Kentucky 1962-65, Army 1966, Cincinnati 1968. Pro coach: Buffalo Bills 1969-71, 1981-82, Washington Redskins 1973-77, Baltimore Colts 1978, New York Giants 1979-80, joined Seahawks in 1983.

Ken Meyer, quarterbacks; born July 14, 1926, Erie, Pa., lives in Bellevue, Wash. Quarterback Denison 1947-50. No pro playing experience. College coach: Denison 1952-57, Wake Forest 1958-59, Florida State 1960-62, Alabama 1963-67, Tulane 1981-82. Pro coach: San Francisco 49ers 1968, 1977 (head coach), New York Jets 1969-72, Los Angeles Rams 1973-76, Chicago Bears 1978-80, joined Seahawks in 1983.

Steve Moore, offensive coordinator-receivers; born August 19, 1947, Los Angeles, Calif., lives in Bellevue, Wash. Wide receiver U.C. Santa Barbara 1968-69. No pro playing experience. College coach: U.C. Santa Barbara 1970-71, Army 1975, Rice 1976-77. Pro coach: Buffalo Bills 1978-82, joined Seahawks in 1983.

Russ Purnell, tight ends-assistant special teams; born June 12, 1948, Chicago, Ill., lives in Bellevue, Wash. Center Orange Coast, Calif., J.C. and Whittier College 1966-70. No pro playing experience. College coach: Whittier 1970-71, Southern California 1982-85. Pro coach: Joined Seahawks in 1986.

Seattle Seahawks 1988 First-Year Roster

Name	Pos.	Ht.	Wt.	Birth-date	College	Hometown	How Acq.
Agee, Tommie (1)	RB	6-0	220	2/22/64	Auburn	Maplesville, Ala.	D5a-'87
Blades, Brian	WR	5-11	182	7/24/65	Miami	Ft. Lauderdale, Fla.	D2
Clark, Louis (1)	WR	6-0	206	7/3/64	Mississippi State	Shannon, Miss.	D10-'87
DesRochers, Dave	T	6-7	290	12/1/64	San Diego State	Glendora, Calif.	D12
Dove, Wes (1)	DE	6-7	270	2/9/64	Syracuse	Tonawanda, N.Y.	D12a-'87
Eisenhooth, Stan (1)	C	6-6	300	7/8/63	Towson State	Wingate, Md.	FA-'86
Hairston, Ray (1)	LB	6-2	235	7/6/63	Illinois	Colorado Spgs., Colo.	FA-'87
Harmon, Kevin	RB	6-0	190	10/26/65	Iowa	New York, N.Y.	D4
Harper, Dwayne	CB	5-11	165	3/29/66	South Carolina State	Orangeburg, S.C.	D11b
Hart, Roy	NT	6-1	280	7/10/65	South Carolina	Tift, Ga.	D6
Hollie, Doug (1)	DE	6-4	265	12/15/60	Southern Methodist	Highland Park, Mich.	FA
Hood, James (1)	WR	6-1	175	9/9/61	Arizona State	Westchester, Calif.	FA-'87
Jackson, Ray	CB	5-11	190	1/11/65	Ohio State	Akron, Ohio	D7
Jones, Derwin	DE	6-3	270	9/4/64	Miami	Miami, Fla.	D10
Kane, Tommy	WR	5-11	180	1/14/64	Syracuse	Montreal, Canada	D3
McLeod, Rick	T	6-6	280	8/29/64	Washington	Bakersfield, Calif.	D11a
Mokofisi, Filipo (1)	LB	6-1	230	10/22/62	Utah	Salt Lake City, Utah	FA-'87
Stouffer, Kelly	QB	6-3	210	7/6/64	Colorado State	Rushville, Neb.	T(Phx)-'88
Tyler, Robert	TE	6-5	259	10/12/65	South Carolina State	Salley, N.C.	D8
Williams, Bob (1)	TE	6-3	235	9/22/63	Penn State	Easton, Pa.	FA-'87
Wise, Deatrich	NT	6-4	280	5/6/65	Jackson State	Evergreen, Ala.	D9

The term NFL Rookie is defined as a player who is in his first season of professional football and has not been on the roster of another professional football team for any regular-season or postseason games. A Rookie is designated by an "R" on NFL rosters. Players who have been active in another professional football league or players who have NFL experience, including either preseason training camp or being on an active roster for fewer than three regular-season or postseason games, are termed NFL First-Year Players. An NFL First-Year Player is designated by a "1" on NFL rosters. Thereafter, a player on an NFL active roster for at least three regular-season or postseason games is credited with an additional year of NFL playing experience.

NOTES

Kent Stephenson, offensive line; born February 4, 1942, Anita, Iowa, lives in Redmond, Wash. Guard-nose tackle Northern Iowa 1962-64. No pro playing experience. College coach: Wayne State 1965-68, North Dakota 1969-71, Southern Methodist 1972-73, Iowa 1974-76, Oklahoma State 1977-78, Kansas 1979-82. Pro coach: Michigan Panthers (USFL) 1983-84, joined Seahawks in 1985.

Rusty Tillman, special teams, assistant linebackers; born February 27, 1948, Beloit, Wis., lives in Bellevue, Wash. Linebacker Northern Arizona 1967-69. Pro linebacker Washington Redskins 1970-77. Pro coach: Joined Seahawks in 1979.

Joe Vitt, special assignments; born August 23, 1954, Camden, N.J., lives in Redmond, Wash. Linebacker Towson State 1973-75. No pro playing experience. Pro coach: Baltimore Colts 1979-81, joined Seahawks in 1982.

THE NFC

Atlanta Falcons 84
Chicago Bears. 88
Dallas Cowboys 92
Detroit Lions 96
Green Bay Packers 100
Los Angeles Rams 104
Minnesota Vikings 108
New Orleans Saints. 112
New York Giants 116
Philadelphia Eagles 120
Phoenix Cardinals 124
San Francisco 49ers 128
Tampa Bay Buccaneers. 132
Washington Redskins. 136

National Football Conference Western Division

Team Colors: Red, Black, White, and Silver

Suwanee Road at I-85
Suwanee, Georgia 30174
Telephone: (404) 945-1111

Club Officials

Chairman of the Board: Rankin M. Smith, Sr.
President: Rankin Smith, Jr.
Executive Vice President: Taylor Smith
Vice President & Chief Financial Officer: Jim Hay
Administrative Assistant: Wallace Norman
Director of College Player Personnel: Ken Herock
Administrative Assistant: Danny Mock
Director of Pro Personnel: Bill Jobko
Scouts: Elbert Dubenion, Bill Groman, Joe Mack
Director of Marketing: Tommy Nobis
Assistant Director of Marketing: Carol Breeding
Director of Public Relations: Charlie Taylor
Assistant Director of Public Relations: Frank Kleha
Ticket Manager: Jack Ragsdale
Assistant Ticket Manager: Luci Bailey
Director of Video Operations: Tom Atcheson
Assistant Director of Video Operations: Andy Commer
Head Trainer: Jerry Rhea
Assistant Trainer: Billy Brooks
Equipment Manager: Whitey Zimmerman
Assistant Equipment Manager: Horace Daniel

Stadium: Atlanta-Fulton County Stadium • **Capacity:** 59,643
521 Capitol Avenue, S.W.
Atlanta, Georgia 30312

Playing Surface: Grass (PAT)

Training Camp: Suwanee Road at I-85
Suwanee, Georgia 30174

1988 Schedule

Preseason

Aug. 6	at New England	7:00
Aug. 13	**Kansas City**	7:30
Aug. 20	**Tampa Bay**	7:30
Aug. 27	vs. Wash. at Birmingham, Ala.	7:00

Regular Season

Sept. 4	at Detroit	1:00
Sept. 11	**New Orleans**	1:00
Sept. 18	at San Francisco	1:00
Sept. 25	at Dallas	12:00
Oct. 2	**Seattle**	1:00
Oct. 9	**Los Angeles Rams**	1:00
Oct. 16	at Denver	2:00
Oct. 23	**New York Giants**	1:00
Oct. 30	at Philadelphia	1:00
Nov. 6	**Green Bay**	1:00
Nov. 13	**San Diego**	1:00
Nov. 20	at Los Angeles Raiders	1:00
Nov. 27	**Tampa Bay**	1:00
Dec. 4	**San Francisco**	1:00
Dec. 11	at Los Angeles Rams	1:00
Dec. 18	at New Orleans	12:00

Falcons Coaching History

(122-197-5)

1966-68	Norb Hecker*	4-26-1
1968-74	Norm Van Brocklin**	37-49-3
1974-76	Marion Campbell***	6-19-0
1976	Pat Peppler	3-6-0
1977-82	Leeman Bennett	47-44-0
1983-86	Dan Henning	22-41-1
1987	Marion Campbell	3-12-0

*Released after three games in 1968
**Released after eight games in 1974
***Released after five games in 1976

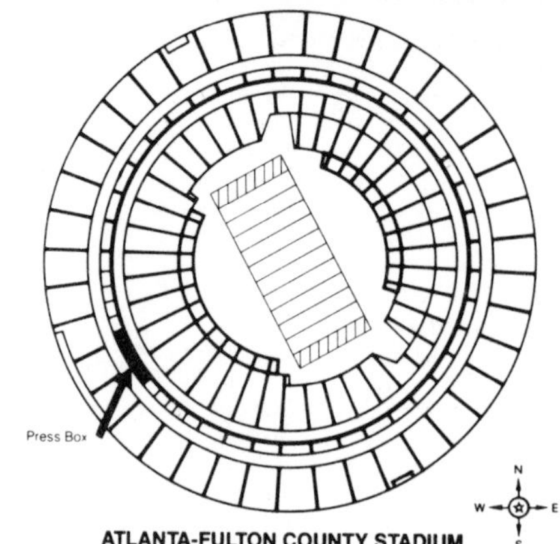

ATLANTA-FULTON COUNTY STADIUM

Record Holders

Individual Records—Career

Category	Name	Performance
Rushing (Yds.)	Gerald Riggs, 1982-87	6,143
Passing (Yds.)	Steve Bartkowski, 1975-1985	23,468
Passing (TDs)	Steve Bartkowski, 1975-1985	154
Receiving (No.)	Alfred Jenkins, 1975-1983	359
Receiving (Yds.)	Alfred Jenkins, 1975-1983	6,257
Interceptions	Rolland Lawrence, 1973-1980	39
Punting (Avg.)	Rick Donnelly, 1985-87	43.8
Punt Return (Avg.)	Al Dodd, 1973-74	11.8
Kickoff Return (Avg.)	Ron Smith, 1966-67	24.3
Field Goals	Mick Luckhurst, 1981-87	115
Touchdowns (Tot.)	Gerald Riggs, 1982-87	47
Points	Mick Luckhurst, 1981-87	558

Individual Records—Single Season

Category	Name	Performance
Rushing (Yds.)	Gerald Riggs, 1985	1,719
Passing (Yds.)	Steve Bartkowski, 1981	3,830
Passing (TDs)	Steve Bartkowski, 1980	31
Receiving (No.)	William Andrews, 1981	81
Receiving (Yds.)	Alfred Jenkins, 1981	1,358
Interceptions	Rolland Lawrence, 1975	9
Punting (Avg.)	Billy Lothridge, 1968	44.3
Punt Return (Avg.)	Gerald Tinker, 1974	13.9
Kickoff Return (Avg.)	Sylvester Stamps, 1987	27.5
Field Goals	Nick Mike-Mayer, 1973	26
Touchdowns (Tot.)	Alfred Jenkins, 1981	13
	Gerald Riggs, 1984	13
Points	Mick Luckhurst, 1981	114

Individual Records—Single Game

Category	Name	Performance
Rushing (Yds.)	Gerald Riggs, 9-2-84	202
Passing (Yds.)	Steve Bartkowski, 11-15-81	416
Passing (TDs)	Randy Johnson, 11-16-69	4
	Steve Bartkowski, 10-19-80	4
	Steve Bartkowski, 10-18-81	4
Receiving (No.)	William Andrews, 11-15-81	15
Receiving (Yds.)	Alfred Jackson, 12-2-84	193
Interceptions	Many times	2
	Last time by Dennis Woodberry, 11-30-86	
Field Goals	Nick Mike-Mayer, 11-4-73	5
	Tim Mazzetti, 10-30-78	5
Touchdowns (Tot.)	Many times	3
	Last time by Gerald Riggs, 11-17-85	
Points	Many times	18
	Last time by Gerald Riggs, 11-17-85	

1987 Team Record

Preseason (1-3)

Date	Result		Opponents
8/15	W	19-14	Buffalo
8/22	L	10-13	at Kansas City
8/29	L	3-23	Cleveland
9/4	L	13-14	vs. New England at Jacksonville, Fla.
		45-64	

Regular Season (3-12)

Date	Result		Opponents	Att.
9/13	L	10-48	at Tampa Bay	51,250
9/20	W	21-20	Washington	50,882
9/27	C		at New Orleans	
10/4	L	12-28	Pittsburgh	16,667
10/11	L	17-25	San Francisco	8,684
10/18	W	24-20	L.A. Rams	15,813
10/25	L	33-37	at Houston	29,062
11/1	L	0-38	New Orleans	42,196
11/8	L	3-38	at Cleveland	71,135
11/15	L	10-16	Cincinnati	25,758
11/22	L	13-24	at Minnesota	53,866
11/29	L	21-34	St. Louis	15,909
12/6	W	21-10	at Dallas	40,103
12/13	L	0-33	at L.A. Rams	43,310
12/20	L	7-35	at San Francisco	54,698
12/27	L	13-30	Detroit	13,906

C (Cancelled due to players' strike.)

Score by Periods

Falcons	34	43	67	61	0	—	205
Opponents	87	136	95	118	0	—	436

Attendance

Home 189,815 Away 343,424 Total 533,239
Single-game home record, 59,257 (10-30-77)
Single-season home record, 442,457 (1980)

1987 Team Statistics

	Falcons	Opp.
Total First Downs	230	354
Rushing	73	162
Passing	139	164
Penalty	18	28
Third Down: Made/Att.	57/187	114/224
Fourth Down: Made/Att.	5/15	9/16
Total Net Yards	4066	5907
Avg. Per Game	271.1	393.8
Total Plays	880	1070
Avg. Per Play	4.6	5.5
Net Yards Rushing	1298	2734
Avg. Per Game	86.5	182.3
Total Rushes	333	600
Net Yards Passing	2768	3173
Avg. Per Game	184.5	211.5
Sacked/Yards Lost	46/340	17/118
Gross Yards	3108	3291
Att./Completions	501/247	453/243
Completion Pct.	49.3	53.6
Had Intercepted	32	15
Punts/Avg.	83/40.7	60/39.7
Net Punting Avg.	31.5	33.4
Penalties/Yards Lost	98/807	92/729
Fumbles/Ball Lost	27/17	18/12
Touchdowns	24	54
Rushing	5	24
Passing	17	26
Returns	2	4
Avg. Time of Possession	26:01	33:59

1987 Individual Statistics

Scoring	TD R	TD P	TD Rt	PAT	FG	Saf	TP
Luckhurst	0	0	0	17/17	9/13	0	44
Dixon	0	5	0	0/0	0/0	0	30
Bailey	0	3	0	0/0	0/0	0	18
Matthews	0	3	0	0/0	0/0	0	18
Davis	0	0	0	6/6	3/4	0	15
Barney	0	2	0	0/0	0/0	0	12
Campbell	2	0	0	0/0	0/0	0	12
Riggs	2	0	0	0/0	0/0	0	12
Badanjek	1	0	0	0/0	0/0	0	6
Kamana	0	1	0	0/0	0/0	0	6
McIntosh	0	1	0	0/0	0/0	0	6
Moore	0	0	1	0/0	0/0	0	6
Stamps	0	0	1	0/0	0/0	0	6
Taylor	0	1	0	0/0	0/0	0	6
Whisenhunt	0	1	0	0/0	0/0	0	6
Falcons	5	17	2	23/24	12/17	1	205
Opponents	24	26	4	51/54	19/30	2	436

Passing	Att.	Comp.	Yds.	Pct.	TD	Int.	Tkld.	Rate
Campbell	260	136	1728	52.3	11	14	25/178	65.0
Kramer	92	45	559	48.9	4	5	10/82	60.0
C. Miller	92	39	552	42.4	1	9	5/37	26.4
Van Raaph'st	34	18	174	52.9	1	2	3/19	52.8
Archer	23	9	95	39.1	0	2	3/24	15.7
Falcons	501	247	3108	49.3	17	32	46/340	53.7
Opponents	453	243	3291	53.6	26	15	17/118	82.4

Rushing	Att.	Yds.	Avg.	LG	TD
Riggs	203	875	4.3	44	2
Campbell	21	102	4.9	24	2
Everett, Clev.-Atl.	34	95	2.8	16	0
Badanjek	29	87	3.0	31	1
Settle	19	72	3.8	12	0
Flowers	14	61	4.4	14	0
M. Williams	14	49	3.5	9	0
C. Miller	4	21	5.3	11	0
Granger	6	12	2.0	6	0
McIntosh	5	11	2.2	5	0
Kramer	2	10	5.0	11	0
Archer	2	8	4.0	7	0
Stamps	1	6	6.0	6	0
Van Raaphorst	1	6	6.0	6	0
Emery	1	5	5.0	5	0
J. Butler	1	1	1.0	1	0
Oliver	1	0	0.0	0	0
Steve B. Griffin	1	−2	−2.0	−2	0
Dixon	3	−3	−1.0	7	0
Matthews	1	−4	−4.0	−4	0
Donnelly	3	−6	−2.0	0	0
Taylor	1	−13	−13.0	−13	0
Falcons	333	1298	3.9	44	5
Opponents	600	2734	4.6	35	24

Receiving	No.	Yds.	Avg.	LG	TD
Dixon	36	600	16.7	51t	5
Matthews	32	537	16.8	57	3
Riggs	25	199	8.0	48	0
Bailey	20	325	16.3	35	3
Whisenhunt	17	145	8.5	26	1
Taylor	12	171	14.3	28	1
Settle	11	153	13.9	36	0
Cox	11	101	9.2	19	0
Barney	10	175	17.5	32	2
M. Williams	9	70	7.8	15	0
Johnson	8	84	10.5	19	0
Everett, Clev.-Atl.	8	41	5.1	10	0
Byrd	7	125	17.9	33	0
Kamana	7	51	7.3	15	1
Flowers	7	50	7.1	24	0
Badanjek	6	35	5.8	16	0
C. Brown	5	103	20.6	23	0
Emery	5	31	6.2	13	0
Stamps	4	40	10.0	19	0
Gonzalez	3	40	13.3	22	0
McIntosh	3	15	5.0	9	1
Granger	2	34	17.0	26	0
J. Butler	2	7	3.5	4	0
Sharp	2	6	3.0	5	0
Evans	1	8	8.0	8	0
Oliver	1	2	2.0	2	0
Middleton	1	1	1.0	1	0
Falcons	247	3108	12.6	57	17
Opponents	243	3291	13.5	57	26

Interceptions	No.	Yds.	Avg.	LG	TD
B. Butler	4	48	12.0	31	0
Croudip	2	40	20.0	40	0
Gordon	2	28	14.0	27	0
Moore	2	23	11.5	18	0
Huff	2	14	7.0	14	0
Moss	1	18	18.0	18	0
Case	1	12	12.0	12	0
Britt	1	−1	−1.0	4	0
Falcons	15	182	12.1	40	0
Opponents	32	342	10.7	47t	2

Punting	No.	Yds.	Avg.	In 20	LG
Donnelly	61	2686	44.0	9	62
Luckhurst	1	37	37.0	0	37
Berry	7	258	36.9	0	51
Starnes	6	203	33.8	2	49
Davis	6	191	31.8	0	55
Falcons	83	3375	40.7	11	62
Opponents	60	2383	39.7	16	60

Punt Returns	No.	FC	Yds.	Avg.	LG	TD
Johnson	21	6	168	8.0	45	0
Barney	5	0	28	5.6	11	0
Moss	3	1	15	5.0	11	0
J. Butler	2	0	10	5.0	9	0
Falcons	31	7	221	7.1	45	0
Opponents	48	7	541	11.3	78t	1

Kickoff Returns	No.	Yds.	Avg.	LG	TD
Stamps	24	660	27.5	97t	1
Emery	21	440	21.0	66	0
Settle	10	158	15.8	22	0
Oliver	5	90	18.0	28	0
Flowers	4	72	18.0	20	0
McIntosh	3	108	36.0	71	0
Badanjek	2	27	13.5	16	0
Everett	2	33	16.5	18	0
M. Williams	2	15	7.5	15	0
J. Butler	1	13	13.0	13	0
Cox	1	11	11.0	11	0
Croudip	1	18	18.0	18	0
Steve B. Griffin	1	21	21.0	21	0
Moss	1	23	23.0	23	0
Sharp	1	11	11.0	11	0
Falcons	79	1700	21.5	97t	1
Opponents	44	915	20.8	92t	1

Sacks	No.
Moor	4.0
Bryan	2.5
G. Brown	2.0
Casillas	2.0
Harrison	1.5
Gann	1.0
Green	1.0
Rade	1.0
Tuggle	1.0
Morris	0.5
Studaway	0.5
Falcons	17.0
Opponents	46.0

Atlanta Falcons 1988 Veteran Roster

No.	Name	Pos.	Ht.	Wt.	Birth-date	NFL Exp.	College	Hometown	How Acq.	'87 Games/ Starts
47	Badanjek, Rick	RB	5-8	217	4/25/62	2	Maryland	Trumbull, Ohio	FA-'88	2/2
82	Bailey, Stacey	WR	6-0	157	2/10/60	7	San Jose State	San Rafael, Calif.	D3-'82	7/6
93	Bohm, Ron	DE	6-3	253	9/3/64	2	Illinois	Walnut, Ill.	FA-'88	3/3*
98	Brown, Greg	DE	6-5	265	1/5/57	8	Kansas State	Washington, D.C.	T(Phil)-'87	12/5
77	†Bryan, Rick	DE	6-4	265	3/20/62	5	Oklahoma	Coweta, Okla.	D1-'84	9/9
23	†Butler, Bobby	CB	5-11	182	5/28/59	8	Florida State	Delray Beach, Fla.	D1-'81	12/12
10	Campbell, Scott	QB	6-0	195	4/15/62	5	Purdue	Hershey, Pa.	FA-'86	12/9
25	†Case, Scott	CB	6-0	178	5/17/62	5	Oklahoma	Edmond, Okla.	D2a-'84	11/10
75	Casillas, Tony	NT	6-3	280	10/26/63	3	Oklahoma	Norman, Okla.	D1a-'86	9/9
28	Clark, Bret	S	6-3	198	2/24/61	2	Nebraska	Nebraska City, Neb.	T(Raid)-'86	1/1
56	†Costello, Joe	LB	6-3	244	6/1/60	3	Central Connecticut State	New York, N.Y.	FA-'86	9/4
88	†Cox, Arthur	TE	6-2	262	2/5/61	6	Texas Southern	Plant City, Fla.	FA-'83	12/10
30	†Croudip, David	CB	5-8	183	1/25/59	5	San Diego State	Compton, Calif.	FA-'85	12/2
86	Dixon, Floyd	WR	5-9	170	4/9/64	3	Stephen F. Austin	Beaumont, Tex.	D6a-'86	12/12
3	†Donnelly, Rick	P	6-0	190	5/17/62	4	Wyoming	Long Island, N.Y.	FA-'85	12/0
64	†Dukes, Jamie	G	6-1	278	6/14/64	3	Florida State	Orlando, Fla.	FA-'86	4/0
24	Emery, Larry	RB	5-9	195	7/13/64	2	Wisconsin	Macon, Ga.	D12-'87	5/0
39	Everett, Major	RB	5-10	218	1/4/60	5	Mississippi College	New Hebron, Miss.	FA-'87	10/3*
48	Flowers, Kenny	RB	6-0	210	3/14/64	2	Clemson	Daytona Beach, Fla.	D2-'87	8/1
79	Fralic, Bill	T-G	6-5	280	10/31/62	4	Pittsburgh	Penn Hills, Pa.	D1-'85	12/12
76	Gann, Mike	DE	6-5	275	10/19/63	4	Notre Dame	Lakewood, Colo.	D2-'85	12/12
41	Gordon, Tim	S	6-0	188	5/7/65	2	Tulsa	Ardmore, Okla.	FA-'87	11/8
99	Green, Tim	LB	6-2	245	12/16/63	3	Syracuse	Liverpool, N.Y.	D1b-'86	9/5
96	Hall, James	LB	6-1	252	1/27/63	2	Northwestern State, La.	Natchez, Miss.	FA-'88	3/0
21	Huff, Charles	CB	5-11	195	2/24/63	2	Presbyterian	Portal, Ga.	FA-'88	3/2
68	Jackson, Lawrence	G	6-1	275	8/10/64	2	Presbyterian	Atlanta, Ga.	FA-'88	3/3
84	†Jones, Joey	WR	5-8	165	10/29/62	2	Alabama	Mobile, Ala.	SD1-'84	0*
78	Kenn, Mike	T	6-7	277	2/9/56	11	Michigan	Evanston, Ill.	D1-'78	12/12
63	Kiewel, Jeff	G	6-3	277	9/27/60	3	Arizona	Tucson, Ariz.	FA-'85	12/0
14	Kramer, Erik	QB	6-0	192	11/6/64	2	North Carolina State	Encino, Calif.	FA-'87	3/2
52	†Kraynak, Rich	LB	6-1	230	1/20/61	6	Pittsburgh	Phoenixville, Pa.	FA-'87	9/8
20	Lavette, Robert	RB	5-11	190	9/8/63	3	Georgia Tech	Cartersville, Ga.	FA-'88	5/0*
83	†Matthews, Aubrey	WR	5-7	165	9/15/62	3	Delta State	Pascagoula, Miss.	FA-'86	12/6
87	†Middleton, Ron	TE	6-2	252	7/17/65	3	Auburn	Atmore, Ala.	FA-'86	12/4
62	Miller, Brett	T	6-7	300	10/2/58	6	Iowa	Glendale, Calif.	D5-'83	2/0
12	Miller, Chris	QB	6-2	195	8/9/65	2	Oregon	Eugene, Ore.	D1-'87	3/2
73	†Mitchell, Leonard	T	6-7	295	10/12/58	8	Houston	Houston, Tex.	T(Phil)-'87	12/12
34	†Moore, Robert	S	5-11	190	8/15/64	3	Northwestern State, La.	Shreveport, La.	FA-'86	12/12
67	Mraz, Mark	DE	6-4	255	2/9/65	2	Utah State	Glendora, Calif.	D5-'87	11/0
59	†Rade, John	LB	6-1	240	8/31/60	6	Boise State	Sierra Vista, Ariz.	D8-'83	11/11
55	†Radloff, Wayne	C	6-5	277	5/17/61	4	Georgia	Winter Park, Fla.	FA-'85	12/12
95	Reid, Michael	LB	6-2	226	6/25/64	2	Wisconsin	Albany, Ga.	D7-'87	11/1
42	Riggs, Gerald	RB	6-1	232	11/6/60	7	Arizona State	Las Vegas, Nev.	D1-'82	12/12
61	Scully, John	G	6-6	270	8/2/58	8	Notre Dame	Huntington, N.Y.	D4-'81	12/12
44	Settle, John	RB	5-9	207	6/2/65	2	Appalachian State	Ruffin, N.C.	FA-'87	9/1
37	Shelley, Elbert	S	5-11	180	12/24/64	2	Arkansas State	Trumann, Ark.	D11-'87	4/0
29	†Stamps, Sylvester	RB-KR	5-7	171	2/24/61	4	Jackson State	Vicksburg, Miss.	FA-'85	7/0
45	†Whisenhunt, Ken	TE	6-3	240	2/28/62	4	Georgia Tech	Augusta, Ga.	D12-'85	7/7
54	Williams, Joel	LB	6-1	227	12/13/56	10	Wisconsin-LaCrosse	Miami, Fla.	T(Phil)-'86	8/8

* Bohm played 3 games with St. Louis in '87; Everett played 3 games with Cleveland, 7 with Atlanta; Jones missed '87 season due to injury; Lavette played 4 games with Dallas, 1 with Philadelphia.

†Option playout; subject to developments.

Traded—Wide receiver Charlie Brown to Indianapolis; wide receiver-kick returner Billy Johnson to Indianapolis; defensive end Andrew Provence to Denver.

Retired—Buddy Curry, 8-year linebacker, 4 games in '87; Mick Luckhurst, 7-year kicker, 12 games in '87.

Also played with Falcons in '87—QB David Archer (9 games), C Doug Barnett (10), WR Milton Barney (3), P Louis Berry (2), DE Dwight Bingham (3), LB Ken Bowen (1), CB James Britt (12), LB Aaron Brown (6), WR Charlie Brown (6), RB Jerry Butler (1), S Wendell Cason (3), G Randy Clark (3), K Greg Davis (3), TE John Evans (1), WR Leon Gonzalez (2), RB Norm Granger (3), LB Paul Gray (2), WR Steve B. Griffin (3), WR Steve L. Griffin (2), WR Kwante Hampton (1), DE Dennis Harrison (11), C James Hendley (3), G Howard Hood (active for 1 game but did not play), DE Van Hughes (active for 1 game but did not play), WR Billy Johnson (12), CB Lyndell Jones (3), RB John Kamana (2), CB-S Leander Knight (1), LB Jim Laughlin (5), S Mike Lush (3), T Doug Mackie (3), RB Joe McIntosh (2), DE Buddy Moor (3), DE Dwaine Morris (3), S Gary Moss (3), S Jerome Norris (3), RB Darryl Oliver (2), TE Charles Phillips (active for 1 game but did not play), RB Shelley Poole (1), LB Art Price (3), G-T Greg Quick (1), T-G Don Robinson (2), G Pat Saindon (3), TE Dan Sharp (9), WR James Shibest (1), T Reggie Smith (2), LB Herb Spencer (3), P John Starnes (1), DE Mark Studaway (2), WR Lenny Taylor (3), CB Leon Thomasson (3), LB Jesse Tuggle (12), CB Jimmy Turner (2), QB Jeff Van Raaphorst (2), NT Emanuel Weaver (2), C Eric Wiegand (2), LB Reggie Wilkes (6), RB Mike Williams (3), S Brenard Wilson (8), DE Leonard Wingate (1), DT Mitchell Young (1), TE Geno Zimmerlink (3).

COACHING STAFF

Head Coach and Director of Football Operations, Marion Campbell

Pro Career: Enters his second season as Falcons head coach after rejoining and serving as defensive coordinator in 1986. Served as an assistant coach with the Boston Patriots 1962-63, Minnesota Vikings 1964-66, Los Angeles Rams 1967-68, Atlanta Falcons 1969-76 (head coach 1974-76), Philadelphia Eagles 1977-85 (head coach 1983-85). Campbell was a defensive tackle in the NFL with the San Francisco 49ers 1954-55 and Philadelphia Eagles 1956-61. Career record: 26-60-1.

Background: Campbell is serving as head coach with the Falcons for the second time. He's coached three teams with number-one ranked defenses in the NFL. He's been to an NFL championship as both a player and assistant coach. Campbell was an All-America defensive tackle at Georgia 1948-51.

Personal: Born May 25, 1929, Chester, S.C. Marion and his wife, June, have two children—Scott, 26, administrative assistant for the Falcons, and Alicia, 23.

Assistant Coaches

Tommy Brasher, defensive line; born December 30, 1940, El Dorado, Ark., lives in Dunwoody, Ga. Linebacker Arkansas 1961-63. No pro playing experience. College coach: Arkansas 1970, Virginia Tech 1971-73, Northeast Louisiana 1974, 1976, Southern Methodist 1977-81. Pro coach: Shreveport Steamer (WFL) 1975, New England Patriots 1982-84, Philadelphia Eagles 1985, joined Falcons in 1986.

Fred Bruney, assistant head coach/defense; born December 30, 1931, Martins Ferry, Ohio, lives in Atlanta. Back Ohio State 1949-52. Pro defensive back San Francisco 49ers 1953-56, Pittsburgh Steelers 1957, Washington Redskins 1958, Boston Patriots 1960-62. College coach: Ohio State 1959. Pro coach: Boston Patriots 1963, Philadelphia Eagles 1964-68, 1977-85, Atlanta Falcons 1969-76, rejoined Falcons in 1986.

Scott Campbell, administrative assistant, born August 16, 1961, Philadelphia, Pa., lives in Duluth, Ga. Tackle Georgia 1982-84. No pro playing experience. College coach: Auburn 1985-86. Pro coach: Joined Falcons in 1987.

Chuck Clausen, linebackers; born June 23, 1940, Anamosa, Iowa, lives in Roswell, Ga. Defensive lineman New Mexico 1961-63. No pro playing experience. College coach: William & Mary 1969-70, Ohio State 1971-75. Pro coach: Philadelphia Eagles 1976-85, joined Falcons in 1986.

Steve Crosby, running backs; born July 3, 1950, Great Bend, Kan., lives in Norcross, Ga. Running back Fort Hays (Kan.) State 1969-72. Pro running back New York Giants 1974-76. Pro coach: Miami Dolphins 1977-82, Atlanta Falcons 1983-84, Cleveland Browns 1985, rejoined Falcons in 1986.

Rod Dowhower, offensive coordinator; born April 15, 1943, Ord, Neb., lives in Atlanta. Quarterback San Diego State 1963-64. No pro playing experience. College coach: San Diego State 1966-72, UCLA 1974-75, Boise State 1976, Stanford 1977-79 (head coach 1979). Pro coach: St. Louis Cardinals 1973, 1982-84, Denver Broncos 1980-81, Indianapolis Colts 1985-86 (head coach), joined Falcons in 1987.

Foge Fazio, special teams/tight ends; born February 22, 1939, Dawmont, W. Va., lives in Atlanta. Linebacker-center Pittsburgh 1957-60. Pro linebacker Boston Patriots 1961. College coach: Boston University 1967, Harvard 1968, Pittsburgh 1969-72, 1977-81 (head coach), Cincinnati 1973-76, Notre Dame 1986-87. Pro coach: Joined Falcons in 1988.

Atlanta Falcons 1988 First-Year Roster

Name	Pos.	Ht.	Wt.	Birth-date	College	Hometown	How Acq.
Anderson, Anthony (1)	S	6-2	208	10/24/64	Grambling	Jonesboro, La.	FA
Armstrong, John (1)	CB-S	5-10	195	7/7/63	Richmond	Bruce, Miss.	FA
Bartley, Tony	T-G-C	6-6	275	2/17/65	Texas A&M	Atlanta, Ga.	FA
Brown, Ken (1)	WR	5-8	175	3/10/65	Southern Arkansas	Pine Bluff, Ark.	FA
Brown, Phillip	LB	6-2	230	5/30/64	Alabama	Birmingham, Ala.	D8
Bruce, Aundray	LB	6-5	245	4/30/66	Auburn	Montgomery, Ala.	D1
Byrd, Sylvester (1)	TE	6-2	225	5/1/63	Kansas	Kansas City, Kan.	FA
Carter, James (1)	G	6-3	260	10/21/63	Georgia Southern	Thomaston, Ga.	FA
Clayton, Stan	T	6-3	265	1/31/65	Penn State	Cherry Hill, N.J.	D10
Cotton, Marcus	LB	6-3	214	8/11/66	Southern California	Oakland, Calif.	D2
Davis, Greg (1)	K	5-11	197	11/29/65	Citadel	Rome, Ga.	FA
Dimry, Charles	CB	6-0	175	1/31/66	Nevada-Las Vegas	Oceanside, Calif.	D5
Dixon, Joe (1)	NT	6-3	275	1/8/64	Tulsa	Pocola, Okla.	FA
Griffin, Steve (1)	RB	5-10	185	12/24/64	Clemson	Miami, Fla.	FA
Hairston, Russell (1)	WR	6-4	193	2/10/64	Kentucky	Greenbelt, Md.	FA
Haynes, Michael	WR	6-0	180	12/24/65	Northern Arizona	New Orleans, La.	D7
Higdon, Alex	TE	6-5	247	9/9/66	Ohio State	Cincinnati, Ohio	D3
Hinson, Billy (1)	G	6-1	278	1/8/63	Florida	Folkston, Ga.	FA-'86
Hoover, Houston	G	6-2	262	6/2/65	Jackson State	Yazoo City, Miss.	D6b
Houghtlin, Robert	K	5-11	170	1/4/65	Iowa	Winnetka, Ill.	FA
Johnson, Walter (1)	NT	6-2	263	9/13/65	Pittsburgh	Pahokee, Fla.	FA
Knight, Leander (1)	CB-S	6-1	193	2/16/63	Montclair State	Newark, N.J.	FA
Land, Dan (1)	RB	6-0	195	7/3/65	Albany State	Donalsonville, Ga.	FA
Little, Steve (1)	DE	6-2	266	10/27/61	Iowa State	Peoria, Ill.	FA
McCluskey, David (1)	RB	6-0	220	10/5/63	Georgia	Rome, Ga.	FA
Meyers, Eddie (1)	RB	5-9	210	1/7/59	Navy	Pemberton, N.J.	FA-'87
Miller, Anthony	WR	6-2	210	5/27/66	James Madison	Petersburg, Va.	FA
Milling, James	WR	5-9	156	2/14/65	Maryland	Temple Hills, Md.	D11
Pettyjohn, Barry	G	6-5	270	3/29/64	Pittsburgh	Cincinnati, Ohio	FA
Primus, James	RB	5-11	196	5/18/64	UCLA	National City, Calif.	D9
Reese, Jerry (1)	TE	6-2	230	8/17/63	Illinois	Citrus Heights, Calif.	FA
Schamel, Duke (1)	NT	6-2	220	11/3/63	South Dakota	Glendale, Calif.	FA
Small, Fred (1)	LB	6-0	231	7/15/63	Washington	Los Angeles, Calif.	FA
Smith, Matt (1)	LB	6-2	233	9/1/65	West Virginia	Gahanna, Ohio	FA
Thomas, George	WR	5-9	169	6/11/64	Nevada-Las Vegas	Indio, Calif.	D6a
Ward, Jeffrey (1)	P	5-10	171	12/4/64	Texas	Austin, Tex.	FA
Wilkins, Gary (1)	TE	6-0	235	11/23/63	Georgia Tech	West Palm Beach, Fla.	FA
Wiley, Carter	S	6-2	213	4/26/64	Virginia Tech	Roanoke, Va.	D12
Witt, Billy (1)	DE	6-5	260	4/15/64	North Alabama	Russellville, Ala.	FA
Young, Mitchell (1)	DE	6-4	260	7/18/62	Arkansas State	Sardis, Miss.	FA

The term NFL Rookie is defined as a player who is in his first season of professional football and has not been on the roster of another professional football team for any regular-season or postseason games. A Rookie is designated by an "R" on NFL rosters. Players who have been active in another professional football league or players who have NFL experience, including either preseason training camp or being on an active roster for fewer than three regular-season or postseason games, are termed NFL First-Year Players. An NFL First-Year Player is designated by a "1" on NFL rosters. Thereafter, a player on an NFL active roster for at least three regular-season or postseason games is credited with an additional year of NFL playing experience.

NOTES

Jim Hanifan, assistant head coach-offense; born September 21, 1933, Compton, Calif., lives in Atlanta. Tight end California 1952-54. Pro tight end Toronto Argonauts (CFL) 1955. College coach: Glendale, Calif., J.C. 1964-66, Utah 1967-70, California 1971-72, San Diego State 1972-73. Pro coach: St. Louis Cardinals 1974-85 (head coach 1980-85), joined Falcons in 1987.

Claude Humphrey, defensive assistant; born November 19, 1947, Memphis, Tenn., lives in Atlanta. Defensive end Tennessee State 1965-67. Pro defensive end Atlanta Falcons 1968-77, Philadelphia Eagles 1977-81. Pro coach: Philadelphia 1982, joined Falcons in 1987.

Tim Jorgensen, strength and conditioning; born April 21, 1955, St. Louis, Mo., lives in Atlanta. Guard Southwest Missouri State 1974-76. No pro playing experience. College coach: Southwest Missouri State 1977-79, Alabama 1979-80, Louisiana State 1980-83. Pro coach: Philadelphia Eagles 1984-86, joined Falcons in 1987.

Jimmy Raye, receivers, born March 26, 1946, Fayetteville, N.C., lives in Atlanta. Quarterback Michigan State 1965-67. Pro defensive back Philadelphia Eagles 1969. College coach: Michigan State 1971-75, Wyoming 1976. Pro coach: San Francisco 49ers 1977, Detroit Lions 1978-79, Atlanta Falcons 1980-82, Los Angeles Rams 1983-84, Tampa Bay Buccaneers 1985-86, rejoined Falcons in 1987.

CHICAGO BEARS

National Football Conference
Central Division

Team Colors: Navy Blue, Orange, and White

Corporate Headquarters:
Halas Hall
250 North Washington
Lake Forest, Illinois 60045
Telephone: (312) 295-6600

Club Officials

Chairman of the Board: Edward W. McCaskey
President and Chief Executive Officer: Michael B. McCaskey
Vice President: Charles A. Brizzolara
Secretary: Virginia H. McCaskey
Vice President-Player Personnel: Bill Tobin
Director of Administration: Bill McGrane
Director of Community Involvement: Pat McCaskey
Director of Finance: Ted Phillips
Director of Public Relations: Ken Valdiserri
Assistant, Public Relations: Bryan Harlan
Assistant, Public Relations: John Bostrom
Ticket Manager: Gary Christenson
Video Director: Mitch Friedman
Trainer: Fred Caito
Assistant Trainer: Brian McCaskey
Strength Coordinator: Clyde Emrich
Equipment Manager: Gary Haeger
Assistant Equipment Manager: Tony Medlin
Scouts: Jim Parmer, Rod Graves, Don King, Ken Geiger

Stadium: Soldier Field • **Capacity:** 66,030
425 McFetridge Place
Chicago, Illinois 60605

Playing Surface: Grass

Training Camp: Wisconsin-Platteville
Platteville, Wisconsin 53818

1988 Schedule

Preseason

Aug. 6	**Miami**	6:00
Aug. 14	vs. Minnesota at Gothenburg, Sweden	7:00
Aug. 22	at Dallas	7:00
Aug. 26	**Los Angeles Raiders**	8:00

Regular Season

Sept. 4	**Miami**	12:00
Sept. 11	at Indianapolis	12:00
Sept. 18	**Minnesota**	12:00
Sept. 25	at Green Bay	12:00
Oct. 2	**Buffalo**	12:00
Oct. 9	at Detroit	1:00
Oct. 16	**Dallas**	12:00
Oct. 24	**San Francisco** (Monday)	8:00
Oct. 30	at New England	1:00
Nov. 6	**Tampa Bay**	12:00
Nov. 13	at Washington	1:00
Nov. 20	at Tampa Bay	1:00
Nov. 27	**Green Bay**	12:00
Dec. 5	at L.A. Rams (Monday)	6:00
Dec. 11	**Detroit**	12:00
Dec. 19	at Minnesota (Monday)	8:00

Bears Coaching History

Decatur Staleys 1920
Chicago Staleys 1921
(532-337-42)

1920-29	George Halas	84-31-19
1930-32	Ralph Jones	24-10-7
1933-42	George Halas*	89-24-4
1942-45	Hunk Anderson-Luke Johnsos**	23-12-2
1946-55	George Halas	76-43-2
1956-57	John (Paddy) Driscoll	14-10-1
1958-67	George Halas	76-53-6
1968-71	Jim Dooley	20-36-0
1972-74	Abe Gibron	11-30-1
1975-77	Jack Pardee	20-23-0
1978-81	Neill Armstrong	30-35-0
1982-87	Mike Ditka	65-30-0

*Retired after six games to enter U.S. Navy
**Co-coaches

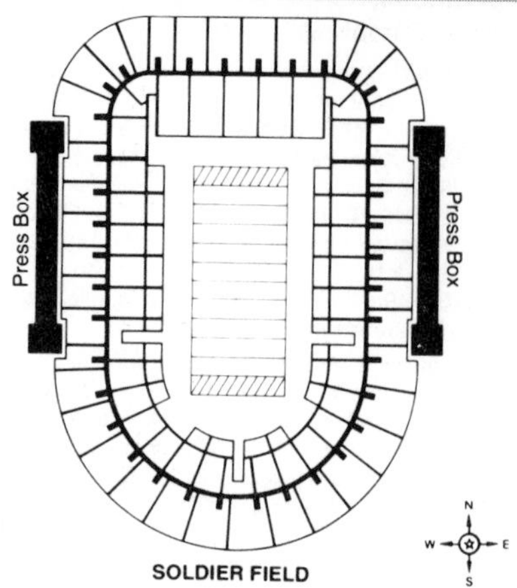

Record Holders

Individual Records—Career

Category	Name	Performance
Rushing (Yds.)	Walter Payton, 1975-1987	*16,726
Passing (Yds.)	Sid Luckman, 1939-1950	14,686
Passing (TDs)	Sid Luckman, 1939-1950	137
Receiving (No.)	Walter Payton, 1975-1987	492
Receiving (Yds.)	Johnny Morris, 1958-1967	5,059
Interceptions	Gary Fencik, 1976-1987	38
Punting (Avg.)	George Gulyanics, 1947-1952	44.5
Punt Return (Avg.)	Ray (Scooter) McLean, 1940-47	14.8
Kickoff Return (Avg.)	Gale Sayers, 1965-1971	30.6
Field Goals	Bob Thomas, 1975-1984	128
Touchdowns (Tot.)	Walter Payton, 1975-1987	125
Points	Walter Payton, 1975-1987	750

Individual Records—Single Season

Category	Name	Performance
Rushing (Yds.)	Walter Payton, 1977	1,852
Passing (Yds.)	Bill Wade, 1962	3,172
Passing (TDs)	Sid Luckman, 1943	28
Receiving (No.)	Johnny Morris, 1964	93
Receiving (Yds.)	Johnny Morris, 1964	1,200
Interceptions	Roosevelt Taylor, 1963	9
Punting (Avg.)	Bobby Joe Green, 1963	46.5
Punt Return (Avg.)	Harry Clark, 1943	15.8
Kickoff Return (Avg.)	Gale Sayers, 1967	37.7
Field Goals	Kevin Butler, 1985	31
Touchdowns (Tot.)	Gale Sayers, 1965	**22
Points	Kevin Butler, 1985	**144

Individual Records—Single Game

Category	Name	Performance
Rushing (Yds.)	Walter Payton, 11-20-77	*275
Passing (Yds.)	Johnny Lujack, 12-11-49	468
Passing (TDs)	Sid Luckman, 11-14-43	*7
Receiving (No.)	Jim Keane, 10-23-49	14
Receiving (Yds.)	Harlon Hill, 10-31-54	214
Interceptions	Many times	3
	Last time by Ross Brupbacher, 12-12-76	
Field Goals	Roger LeClerc, 12-3-61	5
	Mac Percival, 10-20-68	5
Touchdowns (Tot.)	Gale Sayers, 12-12-65	*6
Points	Gale Sayers, 12-12-65	36

*NFL Record
**NFL Rookie Record

1987 Team Record

Preseason (3-1)

Date	Result		Opponents
8/16	W	10- 3	at Miami
8/22	W	50-14	Pittsburgh
8/31	L	16-20	St. Louis
9/5	W	20-17	at L.A. Raiders
		96-54	

Regular Season (11-4)

Date	Result		Opponents	Att.
9/14	W	34-19	N.Y. Giants	65,704
9/20	W	20- 3	Tampa Bay	63,551
9/27	C		at Detroit	
10/4	W	35- 3	at Philadelphia	4,074
10/11	W	27- 7	Minnesota	32,113
10/18	L	17-19	New Orleans	46,813
10/25	W	27-26	at Tampa Bay	70,747
11/1	W	31-28	Kansas City	63,498
11/8	W	26-24	at Green Bay	53,320
11/16	L	29-31	at Denver	75,783
11/22	W	30-10	Detroit	63,357
11/29	W	23-10	Green Bay	61,638
12/6	W	30-24	at Minnesota	62,331
12/14	L	0-41	at San Francisco	63,509
12/20	L	21-34	Seattle	62,518
12/27	W	6- 3	at L.A. Raiders	78,019

C (Cancelled due to players' strike.)

Postseason (0-1)

Date	Result		Opponent	Att.
1/10	L	17-21	Washington	66,030

Score by Periods

Bears	72	126	59	99	0	—	356
Opponents	75	91	67	49	0	—	282

Attendance

Home 459,192 Away 407,783 Total 866,975
Single-game home record, 80,259 (11-24-66)
Single-season home record, 495,484 (1986)

1987 Team Statistics

	Bears	Opp.
Total First Downs	319	261
Rushing	121	77
Passing	156	158
Penalty	42	26
Third Down: Made/Att.	73/205	80/226
Fourth Down: Made/Att.	12/23	2/13
Total Net Yards	5044	4215
Avg. Per Game	336.3	281.0
Total Plays	1026	989
Avg. Per Play	4.9	4.3
Net Yards Rushing	1954	1413
Avg. Per Game	130.3	94.2
Total Rushes	485	412
Net Yards Passing	3090	2802
Avg. Per Game	206.0	186.8
Sacked/Yards Lost	48/330	70/484
Gross Yards	3420	3286
Att./Completions	493/272	507/255
Completion Pct.	55.2	50.3
Had Intercepted	24	13
Punts/Avg.	62/39.3	86/39.6
Net Punting Avg.	31.3	32.4
Penalties/Yards Lost	103/821	120/1108
Fumbles/Ball Lost	33/20	37/11
Touchdowns	42	33
Rushing	13	5
Passing	23	24
Returns	6	4
Avg. Time of Possession	31:58	28:02

1987 Individual Statistics

Scoring	TD R	TD P	TD Rt	PAT	FG	Saf	TP
Butler	0	0	0	28/30	19/28	0	85
Gault	0	7	0	0/0	0/0	0	42
Anderson	3	3	0	0/0	0/0	0	36
W. Payton	4	1	0	0/0	0/0	0	30
Lashar	0	0	0	10/10	3/4	0	19
Brewer	2	1	0	0/0	0/0	0	18
Kozlowski	0	3	0	0/0	0/0	0	18
McKinnon	0	1	2	0/0	0/0	0	18
Boso	0	2	0	0/0	0/0	0	12
Gentry	0	1	1	0/0	0/0	0	12
McMahon	2	0	0	0/0	0/0	0	12
Gayle	0	0	1	0/0	0/0	0	6
Heimuli	0	1	0	0/0	0/0	0	6
Kindt	0	1	0	0/0	0/0	0	6
McCray	0	0	1	0/0	0/0	0	6
Moorehead	0	1	0	0/0	0/0	0	6
Ro. Morris	0	1	0	0/0	0/0	0	6
Mosley	0	0	1	0/0	0/0	0	6
Sanders	1	0	0	0/0	0/0	0	6
Tomczak	1	0	0	0/0	0/0	0	6
Bears	13	23	6	38/42	22/32	0	356
Opponents	5	24	4	30/33	18/31	0	282

Passing	Att.	Comp.	Yds.	Pct.	TD	Int.	Tkld.	Rate
McMahon	210	125	1639	59.5	12	8	22/136	87.4
Tomczak	178	97	1220	54.5	5	10	9/59	62.0
Hohensee	52	28	343	53.8	4	1	3/19	92.1
S. Payton	23	8	79	34.8	0	1	7/47	27.3
Bradley	18	6	77	33.3	2	3	3/24	45.1
Harbaugh	11	8	62	72.7	0	0	4/45	86.2
W. Payton	1	0	0	0.0	0	1	0/0	0.0
Bears	493	272	3420	55.2	23	24	48/330	72.2
Opponents	507	255	3286	50.3	24	13	70/484	76.1

Rushing	Att.	Yds.	Avg.	LG	TD
Anderson	129	586	4.5	38t	3
W. Payton	146	533	3.7	17	4
Heimuli	34	128	3.8	12	0
Sanders	23	122	5.3	17	1
McMahon	22	88	4.0	13	2
Thomas	25	88	3.5	18	0
Mosley	18	80	4.4	16	0
Hohensee	9	56	6.2	26	0
Brewer	24	55	2.3	16	2
Tomczak	18	54	3.0	10	1
Gentry	6	41	6.8	12	0
S. Payton	1	28	28.0	28	0
Suhey	7	24	3.4	6	0
F. Harris	6	23	3.8	18	0
Gault	2	16	8.0	9	0
Harbaugh	4	15	3.8	9	0
Clark	5	11	2.2	5	0
Wolden	2	8	4.0	7	0
Marshall	1	1	1.0	1	0
Brown	1	0	0.0	0	0
Perry	1	0	0.0	0	0
Bradley	1	−3	−3.0	−3	0
Barnhardt, N.O.-Chi.	1	−13	−13.0	−13	0
Bears	485	1954	4.0	38t	13
Opponents	412	1413	3.4	25	5

Receiving	No.	Yds.	Avg.	LG	TD
Anderson	47	467	9.9	59t	3
Gault	35	705	20.1	56t	7
W. Payton	33	217	6.6	16	1
McKinnon	27	406	15.0	33	1
Moorehead	24	269	11.2	27	1
Ro. Morris	20	379	19.0	42t	1
Boso	17	188	11.1	31	2
Gentry	17	183	10.8	38t	1
Kozlowski	15	199	13.3	28	3
Suhey	7	54	7.7	12	0
Brewer	5	56	11.2	19	1
Heimuli	5	51	10.2	17	1
Kindt	5	34	6.8	11	1
Knapczyk	4	62	15.5	22	0
Sanders	3	53	17.7	25	0
Mullen	2	33	16.5	20	0
Glasgow	2	16	8.0	11	0
Mosley	2	16	8.0	16	0
Wolden	1	26	26.0	26	0
Bowers	1	6	6.0	6	0
Bears	272	3420	12.6	59t	23
Opponents	255	3286	12.9	75t	24

Interceptions	No.	Yds.	Avg.	LG	TD
Duerson	3	0	0.0	0	0
Rivera	2	19	9.5	15	0
Phillips	2	1	0.5	1	0
Douglass	2	0	0.0	0	0
McCray	1	23	23.0	23t	1
Gayle	1	20	20.0	20t	1
Norris	1	6	6.0	6	0
V. Jackson	1	0	0.0	0	0
Bears	13	69	5.3	23t	2
Opponents	24	334	13.9	70t	1

Punting	No.	Yds.	Avg.	In 20	LG
Barnhardt, N.O.-Chi.	17	719	42.3	6	52
Barnhardt, Chi.	6	236	39.3	2	50
Brown	18	742	41.2	4	58
Wagner	36	1461	40.6	9	71
Bears	62	2439	39.3	15	71
Opponents	86	3408	39.6	16	60

Punt Returns	No.	FC	Yds.	Avg.	LG	TD
McKinnon	40	4	405	10.1	94t	2
Duarte	8	1	64	8.0	16	0
Duerson	1	1	10	10.0	10	0
Jeffries	1	0	5	5.0	5	0
Bears	50	6	484	9.7	94t	2
Opponents	26	7	339	13.0	83t	1

Kickoff Returns	No.	Yds.	Avg.	LG	TD
Gentry	25	621	24.8	88t	1
Sanders	20	349	17.5	42	0
Kozlowski	3	72	24.0	31	0
Lynch	3	66	22.0	37	0
T. Bell	1	18	18.0	18	0
Knapczyk	1	14	14.0	14	0
Milton	1	10	10.0	10	0
Mosley	1	17	17.0	17	0
Suhey	1	9	9.0	9	0
White	1	17	17.0	17	0
Bears	57	1193	20.9	88t	1
Opponents	58	1054	18.2	42	0

Sacks	No.
Dent	12.5
McMichael	7.0
McInerney	6.5
Wilson	6.5
Marshall	5.0
Norvell	4.0
Althoff	3.5
B. Bell	3.5
Hampton	3.5
Duerson	3.0
Perry	3.0
Norris	2.0
Singletary	2.0
A. Harris	1.5
Teafatiller	1.5
T. Bell	1.0
January	1.0
Ra. Morris	1.0
Rivera	1.0
Bears	70.0
Opponents	48.0

Chicago Bears 1988 Veteran Roster

No.	Name	Pos.	Ht.	Wt.	Birth-date	NFL Exp.	College	Hometown	How Acq.	'87 Games/ Starts
54	Adickes, John	C	6-3	264	6/29/64	2	Baylor	Killeen, Tex.	D6-'87	6/0
47	Allen, Egypt	CB-S	6-0	203	7/28/64	2	Texas Christian	Dallas, Tex.	FA-'87	6/3
70	Althoff, Jim	DT	6-3	278	9/27/61	2	Winona State	McHenry, Ill.	FA-'87	4/3
35	Anderson, Neal	RB	5-11	210	8/14/64	3	Florida	Graceville, Fla.	D1-'86	11/10
81	†Barnes, Lew	WR	5-8	163	12/27/62	2	Oregon	Long Beach, Calif.	D5-'86	0*
17	Barnhardt, Tommy	P	6-3	205	6/11/63	2	North Carolina	Salisbury, N.C.	FA-'87	5/0*
79	Becker, Kurt	G	6-5	270	12/22/58	7	Michigan	Aurora, Ill.	D6-'82	12/1
68	Blair, Paul	T	6-4	295	3/8/63	3	Oklahoma State	Edmund, Okla.	D4-'86	10/2
62	Bortz, Mark	G	6-6	269	2/12/61	6	Iowa	Pardeeville, Wis.	D8-'83	12/12
86	Boso, Cap	TE	6-3	224	9/10/62	2	Illinois	Kansas City, Mo.	FA-'87	12/0
6	†Butler, Kevin	K	6-1	204	7/24/62	4	Georgia	Atlanta, Ga.	D4-'85	12/0
74	Covert, Jim	T	6-4	271	3/22/60	6	Pittsburgh	Conway, Pa.	D1-'83	9/9
95	Dent, Richard	DE	6-5	263	12/13/60	6	Tennessee State	Atlanta, Ga.	D8-'83	12/12
36	†Douglass, Maurice	CB-S	5-11	200	2/12/64	3	Kentucky	Trotwood, Ohio	FA-'86	12/1
22	Duerson, Dave	S	6-1	203	11/28/60	6	Notre Dame	Muncie, Ind.	D3-'83	12/12
83	†Gault, Willie	WR	6-1	183	9/5/60	6	Tennessee	Griffin, Ga.	D1-'83	12/12
23	Gayle, Shaun	CB	5-11	193	3/8/62	5	Ohio State	Hampton, Va.	D10-'84	8/0
29	†Gentry, Dennis	WR	5-8	181	2/10/59	7	Baylor	Lubbock, Tex.	D4-'82	12/0
99	Hampton, Dan	DE	6-5	267	9/19/57	10	Arkansas	Oklahoma City, Okla.	D1-'79	8/8
4	Harbaugh, Jim	QB	6-3	202	12/23/63	2	Michigan	Kalamazoo, Mich.	D1-'87	6/0
90	Harris, Al	LB	6-5	253	12/31/56	9	Arizona State	Bangor, Maine	D1-'79	12/5
63	†Hilgenberg, Jay	C	6-2	260	3/21/60	8	Iowa	Iowa City, Iowa	FA-'81	12/12
24	Jackson, Vestee	CB	6-0	186	8/14/63	3	Washington	Fresno, Calif.	D2-'86	12/12
31	†Jeffries, Eric	CB-S	5-10	161	7/25/64	2	Texas	Springfield, Mo.	D12-'87	3/0
93	Johnson, Will	LB	6-4	245	12/4/64	2	Northeast Louisiana	Monroe, La.	D5-'87	11/0
88	Kozlowski, Glen	WR	6-1	193	12/31/62	2	Brigham Young	Honolulu, Hawaii	D11-'86	3/3
43	Lynch, Lorenzo	CB-S	5-9	197	4/6/63	2	Cal State-Sacramento	Oakland, Calif.	FA-'87	3/3
85	†McKinnon, Dennis	WR	6-1	185	8/22/61	5	Florida State	Quitman, Ga.	FA-'83	12/0
9	McMahon, Jim	QB	6-1	190	8/21/59	7	Brigham Young	Jersey City, N.J.	FA-'82	7/6
76	†McMichael, Steve	DT	6-2	260	10/17/57	9	Texas	Houston, Tex.	FA-'81	12/12
87	†Moorehead, Emery	TE	6-2	220	3/22/54	12	Colorado	Evanston, Ill.	FA-'81	12/12
84	Morris, Ron	WR	6-1	187	11/14/64	2	Southern Methodist	Cooper, Tex.	D2-'87	12/12
51	†Morrissey, Jim	LB	6-3	215	12/24/62	4	Michigan State	Flint, Mich.	D11-'85	10/0
91	Norvell, Jay	LB	6-2	232	3/28/63	2	Iowa	Madison, Wis.	FA-'87	6/3
89	Ortego, Keith	WR	6-0	180	8/30/63	4	McNeese State	Eunice, Tex.	FA-'85	8/0
72	Perry, William	DT	6-2	325	12/16/62	4	Clemson	Aiken, S.C.	D1-'85	12/11
48	Phillips, Reggie	CB	5-10	170	12/12/60	4	Southern Methodist	Houston, Tex.	D2-'85	12/5
27	†Richardson, Mike	CB	6-0	188	5/23/61	6	Arizona State	Compton, Calif.	D2-'83	11/6
59	†Rivera, Ron	LB	6-3	239	1/7/62	5	California	Monterey, Calif.	D2-'84	12/5
53	†Rodenhauser, Mark	C	6-5	260	6/1/61	2	Illinois State	Elmhurst, Ill.	FA-'87	9/3
52	†Rubens, Larry	C	6-2	262	1/25/59	4	Montana State	Spokane, Wash.	FA-'86	0*
20	†Sanders, Thomas	RB	5-11	203	1/4/62	4	Texas A&M	Giddings, Tex.	D9-'85	12/0
50	Singletary, Mike	LB	6-0	228	10/9/58	8	Baylor	Houston, Tex.	D2-'81	12/12
97	Smith, Sean	DE	6-4	275	3/27/65	2	Grambling	Bogalusa, La.	D4-'87	10/0
26	Suhey, Matt	RB	5-11	216	7/7/58	9	Penn State	State College, Pa.	D2-'80	12/2
57	Thayer, Tom	G	6-4	261	8/16/61	4	Notre Dame	Joliet, Ill.	FA-'85	11/11
33	†Thomas, Calvin	RB	5-11	245	1/7/60	7	Illinois	St. Louis, Mo.	FA-'80	12/0
18	†Tomczak, Mike	QB	6-1	195	10/23/62	4	Ohio State	Calumet City, Ill.	FA-'85	12/6
78	†Van Horne, Keith	T	6-6	280	11/6/57	8	Southern California	Mt. Lebanon, Pa.	D1-'81	12/12
15	Wagner, Bryan	P	6-2	195	3/28/62	2	Cal State-Northridge	Chula Vista, Calif.	T(Den)-'87	10/0
55	†Wilson, Otis	LB	6-2	232	9/15/57	9	Louisville	New York, N.Y.	D1-'80	7/7
73	Wojciechowski, John	G	6-4	262	7/30/63	2	Michigan State	Detroit, Mich.	FA-'87	4/4

* Barnes and Rubens missed '87 season due to injury; Barnhardt played 3 games with New Orleans, 2 with Chicago in '87.

†Option playout; subject to developments.

Retired—Gary Fencik, 12-year safety, 12 games in '87; Walter Payton, 13-year running back, 12 games in '87.

Also played with Bears in '87—T John Arp (3 games), LB Bobby Bell (3), S Todd Bell (12), WR Todd Black (1), QB Steve Bradley (1), TE Sam Bowers (3), RB Chris Brewer (3), P Kevin Brown (3), RB Darryl Clark (3), CB-S George Duarte (3), DT Greg Fitzgerald (3), TE Brian Glasgow (3), T-G Charles Harris (3), RB Frank Harris (3), RB Lakei Heimuli (3), CB-S Mike Hintz (3), QB Mike Hohensee (3), DE Leonard Jackson (1), LB Mike January (3), C-G Brent Johnson (3), WR Herbert Johnson (3), TE Don Kindt (3), WR Ken Knapczyk (3), K Tim Lashar (3), LB Wilbur Marshall (12), CB-S Bruce McCray (3), DT Sean McInerney (3), LB Paul Migliazzo (3), LB Eldridge Milton (3), LB Raymond Morris (3), WR Gary Mullen (3), DE Jon Norris (3), T Jack Oliver (3), QB Sean Payton (3), G-T Stuart Rindy (2), CB-S Garland Rivers (2), G Jon Roehlk (3), LB Doug Rothschild (3), DT Gene Rowell (1), S Mike Stoops (3), DT Guy Teafatiller (3), S-CB Steve Trimble (3), WR Lawrence White (2), RB Alan Wolden (3).

COACHING STAFF

Head Coach, Mike Ditka

Pro Career: Became tenth head coach of Bears on January 20, 1982, after serving nine years as an offensive assistant with Dallas. Led Bears to first Super Bowl title following 15-1 1985 season. Bears shut out New York Giants and Los Angeles Rams in playoffs before routing New England 46-10 in Super Bowl XX. Under Ditka, Chicago has won four straight NFC Central titles and has posted 11-4 and 14-2 records the past two seasons. His 11-7 1984 record included a trip to NFC Championship Game at San Francisco (23-0 loss). The 48-year-old Ditka has won at least 10 games a season since 1984. Ditka is a 26-year veteran of the NFL as both a player and a coach. Had 12-year playing career as a tight end with Chicago (1961-66), Philadelphia (1967-68), and Dallas (1969-72). A first-round draft choice by Chicago in 1961, Ditka was NFL rookie of the year, all-NFL (1961-64), and played in five Pro Bowls (1962-66). He joined Cowboys coaching staff in 1973. In addition to working with Dallas special teams, Ditka coached Cowboys' receivers. During his NFL career, he has been in the playoffs 14 seasons and been a member of five NFC champions and three NFL champions. He became the first tight end to be inducted into the Pro Football Hall of Fame in July, 1988. Career record: 65-30.

Background: Played at Pittsburgh from 1958-60 and was a unanimous All-America his senior year. A two-way performer, he played both tight end and linebacker. He also was one of the nation's leading punters with a 40-plus-yard average over three years.

Personal: Born October 18, 1939, Carnegie, Pa. Mike and his wife, Diana, live in Grayslake, Ill., and have four children—Michael, Mark, Megan, and Matt.

Assistant Coaches

Jim Dooley, research and quality control; born February 8, 1930, Stoutsville, Mo., lives in Chicago. End Miami 1949-51. Pro receiver Chicago Bears 1952-61. Pro coach: Chicago Bears 1962-71 (head coach 1968-71), Buffalo Bills 1972, rejoined Bears in 1981.

Ed Hughes, offensive coordinator; born October 23, 1927, Buffalo, N.Y., lives in Libertyville, Ill. Halfback Tulsa 1952-53. Pro defensive back Los Angeles Rams 1954-55, New York Giants 1956-58. Pro coach: Dallas Texans 1960-62, Denver Broncos 1963, Washington Redskins 1964-67, San Francisco 49ers 1968-70, Houston Oilers 1971 (head coach), St. Louis Cardinals 1972, Dallas Cowboys 1973-76, Detroit Lions 1977, New Orleans Saints 1978-80, Philadelphia Eagles 1981, joined Bears in 1982.

Steve Kazor, special teams/tight ends; born February 24, 1948, New Kensington, Pa., lives in Vernon Hills, Ill. Nose tackle Westminister College 1967-70. No pro playing experience. College coach: Emporia State 1973 (head coach), Texas-Arlington 1974, Colorado State 1975, Wyoming 1976, Texas 1976-78, Texas-El Paso 1979-80. Pro coach: Joined Bears in 1982.

Greg Landry, quarterbacks-receivers; born December 18, 1946, Nashua, N.H., lives in Libertyville, Ill. Quarterback Massachusetts 1965-67. Pro quarterback Detroit Lions 1968-78, Baltimore Colts 1979-81, Chicago Blitz/Arizona Wranglers (USFL) 1983-84, Chicago Bears 1984. Pro coach: Cleveland Browns 1985, joined Bears in 1986.

Jim LaRue, defensive backfield; born August 11, 1925, Clinton, Okla., lives in Libertyville, Ill. Halfback Carson-Newman 1943, Duke 1944-45, Maryland 1947-49. No pro playing experience. College coach: Maryland 1950, Kansas State 1951-54, Houston 1955-56, Southern Methodist 1957-58, Arizona 1959-66 (head coach), Utah 1967-73, Wake Forest 1974-75. Pro coach: Buffalo Bills 1976-77, joined Bears in 1978.

Chicago Bears 1988 First-Year Roster

Name	Pos.	Ht.	Wt.	Birth-date	College	Hometown	How Acq.
Chapura, Dick (1)	DT	6-3	280	6/15/64	Missouri	Sarasota, Fla.	D10-'87
Clark, Greg	LB	6-0	221	3/5/65	Arizona State	Torrance, Calif.	D12
Davis, Wendell	WR	5-11	188	1/3/66	Louisiana State	Shreveport, La.	D1b
Forch, Steve	LB	6-1	238	12/29/64	Nebraska	McCook, Neb.	D11
Jarvis, Ralph	DE	6-3	240	6/1/65	Temple	Philadelphia, Pa.	D3
Johnson, Troy	LB	6-0	228	11/10/64	Oklahoma	Houston, Tex.	D5
Jones, Dante	LB	6-1	228	3/23/65	Oklahoma	Dallas, Tex.	D2
Lilja, David (1)	TE	6-4	240	8/14/64	Indiana	Palos Park, Ill.	FA
Magee, Rogie	WR	6-2	203	8/28/64	Louisiana State	Bogalusa, La.	D9
Mosley, Anthony (1)	RB	5-9	204	12/25/65	Fresno State	Selma, Calif.	FA-'87
Muster, Brad	RB	6-3	231	4/11/65	Stanford	San Martin, Calif.	D1a
Patterson, Votie	WR	5-11	185	3/11/64	West Texas State	Fresno, Calif.	FA
Porter, Joel	T	6-3	268	9/11/65	Baylor	Arkadelphia, Ark.	D10
Reed, Harvey	RB	5-11	181	9/2/65	Howard	Miami, Fla.	D8b
Rentie, Ceasar	T	6-3	293	11/10/64	Oklahoma	Hartshorne, Okla.	D7
Smith, Keith (1)	DE-TE	6-5	240	2/18/58	Texas-El Paso	New York, N.Y.	FA
Stinson, Lemuel	CB-S	5-9	165	5/10/66	Texas Tech	Houston, Tex.	D6
Tate, David	CB-S	6-0	178	11/22/64	Colorado	Cooper, Tex.	D8a
Thornton, James	TE	6-2	245	2/8/65	Cal State-Fullerton	Santa Rosa, Calif.	D4

The term NFL Rookie is defined as a player who is in his first season of professional football and has not been on the roster of another professional football team for any regular-season or postseason games. A Rookie is designated by an "R" on NFL rosters. Players who have been active in another professional football league or players who have NFL experience, including either preseason training camp or being on an active roster for fewer than three regular-season or postseason games, are termed NFL First-Year Players. An NFL First-Year Player is designated by a "1" on NFL rosters. Thereafter, a player on an NFL active roster for at least three regular-season or postseason games is credited with an additional year of NFL playing experience.

NOTES

John Levra, defensive line; born October 2, 1937, Arma, Kan., lives in Libertyville, Ill. Guard-linebacker Pittsburg (Kan.) State 1963-65. No pro playing experience. College coach: Stephen F. Austin 1971-74, Kansas 1975-78, North Texas State 1979. Pro coach: British Columbia Lions (CFL) 1980, New Orleans Saints 1981-85, joined Bears in 1986.

David McGinnis, linebackers; born August 7, 1951, Independence, Kan., lives in Lake Forest, Ill. Defensive back Texas Christian 1970-72. No pro playing experience. College coach: Texas Christian 1973-74, 1982, Missouri 1975-77, Indiana State 1978-81, Kansas State 1983-85. Pro coach: Joined Bears in 1986.

Johnny Roland, offensive backs; born May 21, 1943, Corpus Christi, Tex., lives in Vernon Hills, Ill. Running back Missouri 1963-65. Pro running back St. Louis Cardinals 1966-72, New York Giants 1973. College coach: Notre Dame 1975. Pro coach: Green Bay Packers 1974, Philadelphia Eagles 1976-78, joined Bears in 1983.

Dick Stanfel, offensive line; born July 20, 1927, San Francisco, Calif., lives in Libertyville, Ill. Guard San Francisco 1948-51. Pro guard Detroit Lions 1952-55, Washington Redskins 1956-58. College coach: Notre Dame 1959-62, California 1963. Pro coach: Philadelphia Eagles 1964-70, San Francisco 49ers 1971-75, New Orleans Saints 1976-80 (head coach, 4 games in 1980), joined Bears in 1981.

Vince Tobin, defensive coordinator; born September 29, 1943, in Burlington Junction, Mo., lives in Libertyville, Ill. Defensive back-running back Missouri 1961-64. No pro playing experience. College coach: Missouri 1967-76. Pro coach: British Columbia Lions (CFL) 1977-82, Philadelphia/Baltimore Stars (USFL) 1983-85, joined Bears in 1986.

National Football Conference Eastern Division

Team Colors: Royal Blue, Metallic Silver Blue, and White

Cowboys Center
One Cowboys Parkway
Irving, Texas 75063
Telephone: (214) 556-9900

Club Officials

General Partner: H.R. Bright
President-General Manager: Texas E. Schramm
Vice President-Personnel Development: Gil Brandt
Vice President-Treasurer: Don Wilson
Vice President-Administration: Joe Bailey
Vice President-Pro Personnel: Bob Ackles
Public Relations Director: Doug Todd
Marketing Director: Greg Aiello
Business Services: Billy Hicks
Director of Counseling Services: Larry Wansley
Ticket Manager: Steve Orsini
Trainers: Don Cochren, Ken Locker
Equipment Manager: William T. (Buck) Buchanan
Cheerleaders Director: Suzanne Mitchell

Stadium: Texas Stadium • **Capacity:** 63,855
Irving, Texas 75062

Playing Surface: Texas Turf

Training Camp: California Lutheran University
Thousand Oaks, California 91360

1988 Schedule

Preseason

Aug. 6	at San Diego	6:00
Aug. 13	at Los Angeles Raiders	1:00
Aug. 22	**Chicago**	7:00
Aug. 27	**Houston**	8:00

Regular Season

Sept. 4	at Pittsburgh	1:00
Sept. 12	at Phoenix (Monday)	6:00
Sept. 18	**New York Giants**	3:00
Sept. 25	**Atlanta**	12:00
Oct. 3	at New Orleans (Monday)	8:00
Oct. 9	**Washington**	12:00
Oct. 16	at Chicago	12:00
Oct. 23	at Philadelphia	1:00
Oct. 30	**Phoenix**	12:00
Nov. 6	at New York Giants	1:00
Nov. 13	**Minnesota**	7:00
Nov. 20	**Cincinnati**	12:00
Nov. 24	**Houston** (Thanksgiving)	3:00
Dec. 4	at Cleveland	1:00
Dec. 11	at Washington	1:00
Dec. 18	**Philadelphia**	12:00

Cowboys Coaching History

(267-165-6)

1960-87 Tom Landry 267-165-6

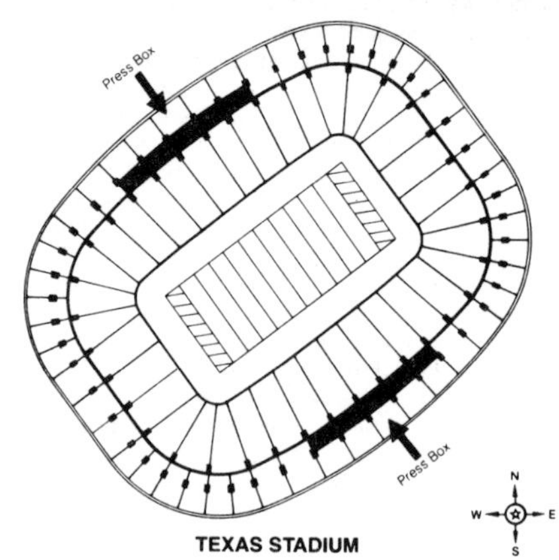

TEXAS STADIUM

Record Holders

Individual Records—Career

Category	Name	Performance
Rushing (Yds.)	Tony Dorsett, 1977-1987	12,036
Passing (Yds.)	Roger Staubach, 1969-1979	22,700
Passing (TDs)	Danny White, 1976-1987	154
Receiving (No.)	Drew Pearson, 1973-1983	489
Receiving (Yds.)	Tony Hill, 1977-1986	7,988
Interceptions	Mel Renfro, 1964-1977	52
Punting (Avg.)	Sam Baker, 1962-63	45.1
Punt Return (Avg.)	Bob Hayes, 1965-1974	11.1
Kickoff Return (Avg.)	Mel Renfro, 1964-1977	26.4
Field Goals	Rafael Septien, 1978-1986	162
Touchdowns (Tot.)	Tony Dorsett, 1977-1987	86
Points	Rafael Septien, 1978-1986	874

Individual Records—Single Season

Category	Name	Performance
Rushing (Yds.)	Tony Dorsett, 1981	1,646
Passing (Yds.)	Danny White, 1983	3,980
Passing (TDs)	Danny White, 1983	29
Receiving (No.)	Herschel Walker, 1985	76
Receiving (Yds.)	Bob Hayes, 1966	1,232
Interceptions	Everson Walls, 1981	11
Punting (Avg.)	Sam Baker, 1962	45.4
Punt Return (Avg.)	Bob Hayes, 1968	20.8
Kickoff Return (Avg.)	Mel Renfro, 1965	30.0
Field Goals	Rafael Septien, 1981	27
Touchdowns (Tot.)	Dan Reeves, 1966	16
Points	Rafael Septien, 1983	123

Individual Records—Single Game

Category	Name	Performance
Rushing (Yds.)	Tony Dorsett, 12-4-77	206
Passing (Yds.)	Don Meredith, 11-10-63	460
Passing (TDs)	Many times	5
	Last time by Danny White, 10-30-83	
Receiving (No.)	Lance Rentzel, 11-19-67	13
Receiving (Yds.)	Bob Hayes, 11-13-66	246
Interceptions	Herb Adderley, 9-26-71	3
	Lee Roy Jordan, 11-4-73	3
	Dennis Thurman, 12-13-81	3
Field Goals	Roger Ruzek, 12-21-87	5
Touchdowns (Tot.)	Many times	4
	Last time by Duane Thomas, 12-18-71	
Points	Many times	24
	Last time by Duane Thomas, 12-18-71	

1987 Team Record

Preseason (1-3)

Date	Result		Opponents
8/15	L	0-29	at San Diego
8/22	W	13- 3	at San Francisco
8/30	L	10-34	L.A. Raiders
9/5	L	13-18	Houston
		36-84	

Regular Season (7-8)

Date	Result		Opponents	Att.
9/13	L	13-24	at St. Louis	47,241
9/20	W	16-14	at N.Y. Giants	73,426
9/27	C		Buffalo	
10/4	W	38-24	at N.Y. Jets	12,370
10/11	W	41-22	Philadelphia	40,622
10/19	L	7-13	Washington	60,415
10/25	L	20-37	at Philadelphia	61,630
11/2	W	33-24	N.Y. Giants	55,730
11/8	L	17-27	at Detroit	45,325
11/15	W	23-17	at New Eng. (OT)	60,567
11/22	L	14-20	Miami	56,519
11/26	L	38-44	Minnesota (OT)	54,229
12/6	L	10-21	Atlanta	40,103
12/13	L	20-24	at Washington	54,882
12/21	W	29-21	at L.A. Rams	60,700
12/27	W	21-16	St. Louis	36,788

(OT) Overtime
C (Cancelled due to players' strike.)

Score by Periods

Cowboys	71	108	78	77	6	—	340
Opponents	84	68	79	111	6	—	348

Attendance

Home 344,406 Away 416,141 Total 760,547
Single-game home record, 80,259 (11-24-66)
Single-season home record, 511,541 (1981)

1987 Team Statistics

	Cowboys	Opp.
Total First Downs	293	294
Rushing	93	85
Passing	176	175
Penalty	24	34
Third Down: Made/Att.	86/222	96/223
Fourth Down: Made/Att.	3/9	6/14
Total Net Yards	5056	5061
Avg. Per Game	337.1	337.4
Total Plays	1017	1012
Avg. Per Play	5.0	5.0
Net Yards Rushing	1865	1617
Avg. Per Game	124.3	107.8
Total Rushes	465	459
Net Yards Passing	3191	3444
Avg. Per Game	212.7	229.6
Sacked/Yards Lost	52/403	51/337
Gross Yards	3594	3781
Att./Completions	500/288	502/269
Completion Pct.	57.6	53.6
Had Intercepted	20	23
Punts/Avg.	84/39.6	75/40.6
Net Punting Avg.	33.7	34.0
Penalties/Yards Lost	131/1091	100/851
Fumbles/Ball Lost	30/20	29/20
Touchdowns	38	42
Rushing	17	19
Passing	19	21
Returns	2	2
Avg. Time of Possession	30:41	29:19

1987 Individual Statistics

Scoring

Scoring	TD R	TD P	TD Rt	PAT	FG	Saf	TP
Ruzek	0	0	0	26/26	22/25	0	92
H. Walker	7	1	0	0/0	0/0	0	48
Edwards	1	3	0	0/0	0/0	0	24
Newsome	2	2	0	0/0	0/0	0	24
Renfro	0	4	0	0/0	0/0	0	24
Zendejas	0	0	0	10/10	3/4	0	19
Blount	3	0	0	0/0	0/0	0	18
Cosbie	0	3	0	0/0	0/0	0	18
Burbage	0	2	0	0/0	0/0	0	12
Dorsett	1	1	0	0/0	0/0	0	12
Adams	1	0	0	0/0	0/0	0	6
Banks	0	1	0	0/0	0/0	0	6
Barksdale	0	1	0	0/0	0/0	0	6
Chandler	0	1	0	0/0	0/0	0	6
Francis	0	0	1	0/0	0/0	0	6
Jeffcoat	0	0	1	0/0	0/0	0	6
Pelluer	1	0	0	0/0	0/0	0	6
D. White	1	0	0	0/0	0/0	0	6
Brady	0	0	0	1/1	0/0	0	1
Cowboys	17	19	2	37/37	25/29	0	340
Opponents	19	21	2	39/41	19/29	0	348

Passing

Passing	Att.	Comp.	Yds.	Pct.	TD	Int.	Tkld.	Rate
D. White	362	215	2617	59.4	12	17	44/353	73.2
Pelluer	101	55	642	54.5	3	2	5/35	75.6
Sweeney	28	14	291	50.0	4	1	3/15	111.8
Snyder	9	4	44	44.4	0	0	0/0	59.5
Cowboys	500	288	3594	57.6	19	20	52/403	76.0
Opponents	502	269	3781	53.6	21	23	51/337	73.0

Rushing

Rushing	Att.	Yds.	Avg.	LG	TD
H. Walker	209	891	4.3	60t	7
Dorsett	130	456	3.5	24	1
Pelluer	25	142	5.7	21	1
Blount	46	125	2.7	15	3
Newsome	25	121	4.8	24t	2
Edwards	2	61	30.5	62t	1
Adams	7	49	7.0	27t	1
D. White	10	14	1.4	8	1
Sweeney	5	8	1.6	5	0
E.J. Jones	2	7	3.5	5	0
Snyder	2	0	0.0	0	0
G. White	1	−4	−4.0	−4	0
Cosbie	1	−5	−5.0	−5	0
Cowboys	465	1865	4.0	62t	17
Opponents	459	1617	3.5	52t	19

Receiving

Receiving	No.	Yds.	Avg.	LG	TD
H. Walker	60	715	11.9	44	1
Renfro	46	662	14.4	43	4
Cosbie	36	421	11.7	30	3
Edwards	34	521	15.3	38t	3
Newsome	34	274	8.1	30	2
Dorsett	19	177	9.3	33	1
Banks	15	231	15.4	34	1
Barksdale	12	165	13.8	22	1
Burbage	7	168	24.0	77t	2
K. Martin	5	103	20.6	33	0
G. White	5	46	9.2	14	0
Chandler	5	25	5.0	9	1
E.J. Jones	3	16	5.3	10	0
Spivey	2	34	17.0	25	0
C. Scott	1	11	11.0	11	0
Adams	1	8	8.0	8	0
Fowler	1	6	6.0	6	0
Lavette	1	6	6.0	6	0
Blount	1	5	5.0	5	0
Cowboys	288	3594	12.5	77t	19
Opponents	269	3781	14.1	62t	21

Interceptions

Interceptions	No.	Yds.	Avg.	LG	TD
Walls	5	38	7.6	30	0
Downs	4	56	14.0	27	0
Bates	3	28	9.3	28	0
Haynes	3	7	2.3	7	0
Francis	2	18	9.0	18t	1
Jeffcoat	1	26	26.0	26t	1
Penn	1	21	21.0	21	0
Lockhart	1	13	13.0	13	0
V. Scott	1	1	1.0	1	0
Green	1	0	0.0	0	0
R. White	1	0	0.0	0	0
Cowboys	23	208	9.0	30	2
Opponents	20	279	14.0	69	0

Punting

Punting	No.	Yds.	Avg.	In 20	LG
Sawyer	16	639	39.9	1	54
Saxon	68	2685	39.5	20	63
Cowboys	84	3324	39.6	21	63
Opponents	75	3042	40.6	13	64

Punt Returns

Punt Returns	No.	FC	Yds.	Avg.	LG	TD
K. Martin	22	2	216	9.8	38	0
Edwards	8	1	75	9.4	13	0
Banks	5	1	33	6.6	12	0
Burbage	5	1	29	5.8	13	0
Livingston	1	0	0	0.0	0	0
Lavette	0	1	0	—	0	0
Cowboys	41	6	353	8.6	38	0
Opponents	45	17	376	8.4	78t	1

Kickoff Returns

Kickoff Returns	No.	Yds.	Avg.	LG	TD
Clack	29	635	21.9	48	0
K. Martin	12	237	19.8	38	0
Edwards	7	155	22.1	32	0
Adams	6	113	18.8	27	0
Lavette	4	72	18.0	22	0
Newsome	2	22	11.0	12	0
Spivey	2	49	24.5	29	0
Borresen	1	5	5.0	5	0
Chandler	1	7	7.0	7	0
Cowboys	64	1295	20.2	48	0
Opponents	65	1281	19.7	45	0

Sacks

Sacks	No.
"Too Tall" Jones	10.0
R. White	6.0
Jeffcoat	5.0
Rohrer	4.0
Bates	3.0
Brooks	3.0
Haynes	3.0
Hegman	3.0
Watts	3.0
Duliban	2.0
Lockhart	2.0
Perkins	2.0
Dwyer	1.0
Johnson	1.0
Noonan	1.0
Walen	1.0
Cowboys	51.0
Opponents	52.0

Dallas Cowboys 1988 Veteran Roster

No.	Name	Pos.	Ht.	Wt.	Birth-date	NFL Exp.	College	Hometown	How Acq.	'87 Games/ Starts
36	Albritton, Vince	S	6-2	217	7/23/62	5	Washington	Oakland, Calif.	FA-'84	11/1
2	Alexander, Ray	WR	6-4	196	1/8/62	2	Florida A&M	Mobile, Ala.	FA-'87	0*
87	Banks, Gordon	WR	5-10	170	3/12/58	6	Stanford	Los Angeles, Calif.	FA-'85	5/4
80	Barksdale, Rod	WR	6-1	193	9/8/62	3	Arizona	Los Angeles, Calif.	T(Raid)-'87	12/1
40	Bates, Bill	S	6-1	199	6/6/61	6	Tennessee	Knoxville, Tenn.	FA-'83	12/11
99	Brooks, Kevin	DE	6-6	278	2/9/63	4	Michigan	Detroit, Mich.	D1-'85	13/12
15	Burbage, Cornell	WR	5-10	181	2/22/65	2	Kentucky	Lexington, Ky.	FA-'88	3/2
57	Burton, Ron	LB	6-1	245	5/2/64	2	North Carolina	Highland Springs, Va.	FA-'87	12/2
85	Chandler, Thornton	TE	6-5	242	11/27/63	3	Alabama	Jacksonville, Fla.	D6a-'86	12/1
70	Cisowski, Steve	T	6-5	275	1/23/63	2	Santa Clara	Campbell, Calif.	FA-'87	3/3
42	Clack, Darryl	RB	5-10	220	10/29/63	3	Arizona State	Security, Colo.	D2-'86	12/0
84	Cosbie, Doug	TE	6-6	241	3/27/56	10	Santa Clara	Mountain View, Calif.	D3-'79	12/12
55	†DeOssie, Steve	LB	6-2	249	11/22/62	5	Boston College	Roslindale, Mass.	D4-'84	11/2
26	†Downs, Michael	S	6-3	212	6/9/59	8	Rice	Dallas, Tex.	FA-'81	12/12
81	Edwards, Kelvin	WR	6-2	205	7/19/64	3	Liberty	Eastpoint, Ga.	FA-'87	13/9
85	Folsom, Steve	TE	6-5	236	3/21/58	3	Utah	Santa Fe, Calif.	FA-'87	9/0
46	Fowler, Todd	RB	6-3	222	6/9/62	4	Stephen F. Austin	Van, Tex.	SD1-'84	12/1
38	Francis, Ron	CB	5-9	199	4/7/64	2	Baylor	LaMarque, Tex.	D2-'87	11/11
66	Gogan, Kevin	T	6-7	310	11/2/64	2	Washington	Pacifica, Calif.	D8-'87	11/10
27	Haynes, Tommy	S	6-0	190	2/6/63	2	Southern California	Covina, Calif.	FA-'88	3/3
58	Hegman, Mike	LB	6-1	226	1/17/53	13	Tennessee State	Memphis, Tenn.	D7-'75	10/10
45	Hendrix, Manny	CB-S	5-10	181	10/20/64	3	Utah	Phoenix, Ariz.	FA-'86	12/1
52	Hurd, Jeff	LB	6-2	245	5/25/64	2	Kansas State	Kansas City, Mo.	FA-'87	5/0
53	Jax, Garth	LB	6-2	222	9/16/63	3	Florida State	Houston, Tex.	D11-'86	3/0
77	Jeffcoat, Jim	DE	6-5	263	4/1/61	6	Arizona State	Cliffwood, N.J.	D1-'83	12/12
72	Jones, Ed	DE	6-9	275	2/23/51	14	Tennessee State	Jackson, Tenn.	D1a-'74	15/14
68	Ker, Crawford	G	6-3	283	5/5/62	4	Florida	Dunedin, Fla.	D3-'85	12/12
67	Lilja, George	C	6-4	282	3/3/58	7	Michigan	Orland Park, Ill.	FA-'87	5/0
56	Lockhart, Eugene	LB	6-2	230	3/8/61	5	Houston	Crockett, Tex.	D6a-'84	9/9
14	†McDonald, Paul	QB	6-2	182	2/23/58	9	Southern California	Montebello, Calif.	FA-'86	0*
83	Martin, Kelvin	WR	5-9	163	5/14/65	2	Boston College	Jacksonville, Fla.	D4-'87	7/0
30	Newsome, Timmy	RB	6-1	235	5/17/58	9	Winston-Salem State	Ahoskie, N.C.	D6-'80	11/8
67	Newton, Nate	G	6-3	315	12/20/61	3	Florida A&M	Orlando, Fla.	FA-'86	11/11
73	Noonan, Danny	DT	6-4	270	7/14/65	2	Nebraska	Lincoln, Neb.	D1-'87	11/0
16	Pelluer, Steve	QB	6-4	208	7/29/62	5	Washington	Bellevue, Wash.	D5a-'84	12/4
59	Penn, Jesse	LB	6-3	224	9/6/62	4	Virginia Tech	Martinsville, Va.	D2-'85	11/1
64	Rafferty, Tom	C	6-3	263	8/2/54	13	Penn State	Fayetteville, N.Y.	D4-'76	12/12
82	Renfro, Mike	WR	6-0	184	6/19/55	11	Texas Christian	Fort Worth, Tex.	T(Hou)-'84	14/11
50	Rohrer, Jeff	LB	6-2	222	12/25/58	7	Yale	Manhattan Beach, Calif.	D2-'82	12/12
9	Ruzek, Roger	K	6-1	190	12/17/60	2	Weber State	San Francisco, Calif.	FA-'87	12/0
4	Saxon, Mike	P	6-3	193	7/10/62	4	San Diego State	Arcadia, Calif.	FA-'85	12/0
22	Scott, Victor	CB-S	6-0	203	6/1/62	5	Colorado	East St. Louis, Ill.	D2-'84	6/0
86	Sherrard, Mike	WR	6-2	187	6/21/63	2	UCLA	Chico, Calif.	D1-'86	0*
60	Smerek, Don	DT	6-7	266	12/10/57	7	Nevada-Reno	Henderson, Nev.	FA-'80	8/3
79	Smith, Daryle	T	6-5	278	1/18/64	2	Tennessee	Knoxville, Tenn.	FA-'87	9/7
19	Sweeney, Kevin	QB	6-0	193	11/16/63	2	Fresno State	Fresno, Calif.	D7-'87	3/2
63	Titensor, Glen	G	6-4	275	2/21/58	7	Brigham Young	Garden Grove, Calif.	D3-'81	0*
71	Tuinei, Mark	C	6-5	282	3/31/60	6	Hawaii	Honolulu, Hawaii	FA-'83	8/8
95	Walen, Mark	DT	6-5	262	3/10/63	2	UCLA	Burlingame, Calif.	D3-'86	9/0
34	Walker, Herschel	RB	6-1	225	3/3/62	3	Georgia	Wrightsville, Ga.	D5a-'85	12/11
24	Walls, Everson	CB	6-1	192	12/28/59	8	Grambling	Dallas, Tex.	FA-'81	12/12
94	Watts, Randy	DE	6-6	305	6/22/63	2	Catawba	Sandersville, Ga.	FA-'88	5/0
65	White, Bob	T	6-5	267	4/9/63	2	Rhode Island	Lunenburg, Mass.	FA-'87	4/3
11	White, Danny	QB	6-3	198	2/9/52	13	Arizona State	Mesa, Ariz.	D3a-'74	11/9
37	White, Gerald	RB	5-11	223	12/9/64	2	Michigan	Titusville, Fla.	FA-'88	3/3
54	White, Randy	DT	6-4	263	1/15/53	14	Maryland	Wilmington, Del.	D1a-'75	15/14
23	Williams, Robert	CB-S	5-10	195	10/2/62	2	Baylor	Galveston, Tex.	FA-'87	11/3
76	Zimmerman, Jeff	T	6-3	316	1/10/65	2	Florida	Orlando, Fla.	D3-'87	11/1

* Alexander, Sherrard, and Titensor missed entire '87 season due to injury; McDonald was active for 12 games in '87 but did not play.

†Option playout; subject to developments.

Traded—Running back Tony Dorsett to Denver.

Retired—Kurt Petersen, 7-year guard, missed '87 season due to injury; Phil Pozderac, 6-year tackle, 2 games in '87.

Also played with Cowboys in '87—RB David Adams (3 games), CB Jimmy Armstrong (2), T-G Brian Baldinger (3), RB Alvin Blount (2), TE Rich Borresen (3), K Kerry Brady (1), T Dave Burnette (1), G Sal Cesario (3), CB-S Anthony Coleman (3), WR Vince Courville (2), LB Chris Duliban (3), DT John Dutton (4), DT Mike Dwyer (3), LB Harry Flaherty (2), S Alex Green (3), TE Tim Hendrix (3), CB Bill Hill (3), T Glen Howe (active for 1 game but did not play), DT-DE Walter Johnson (1), LB Dale Jones (3), RB E.J. Jones (3), RB Robert Lavette (4), CB-S Bruce Livingston (3), DE Ray Perkins (2), P Buzz Sawyer (3), WR Chuck Scott (2), C Joe Shearin (1), T-G Jon Shields (1), LB Victor Simmons (3), QB Loren Snyder (2), WR Sebron Spivey (2), LB Russ Swan (5), LB Kirk Timmer (1), T-G Gary Walker (1), K Luis Zendejas (2), C Joe Zentic (3).

COACHING STAFF

Head Coach, Tom Landry

Pro Career: Landry, the Cowboys' only head coach in their 28-year history, compiled 20 consecutive winning seasons from 1966 through 1985, and his overall record of 267-165-6 is second only to Don Shula among active coaches. Cowboys became the fourth team in NFL to win a second Super Bowl. They defeated Denver 27-10 in Super Bowl XII on January 15, 1978, at Louisiana Superdome. Dallas has played in four other Super Bowls (V, VI, X, and XIII), winning Game VI 24-3 over Miami. Pro defensive back with New York Yanks (AAFC) 1949, New York Giants 1950-55. Player-coach with Giants 1954-55, named all-pro in 1954. Defensive assistant coach with Giants 1956-59 before moving to Dallas as head coach in 1960. Career record: 267-165-6.

Background: Fullback and defensive back at University of Texas 1947-48. He played in Longhorns' victories over Alabama in 1948 Sugar Bowl and Georgia in 1949 Orange Bowl.

Personal: Born September 11, 1924, Mission, Tex. A World War II bomber pilot. Tom and his wife, Alicia, live in Dallas and have three children—Tom, Jr., Kitty, and Lisa.

Assistant Coaches

Neill Armstrong, research and development; born March 9, 1926, Tishomingo, Okla., lives in Roanoke, Tex. End Oklahoma State 1943-46. Pro end-defensive back Philadelphia Eagles 1947-51, Winnipeg Blue Bombers (CFL) 1951, 1953-54. College coach: Oklahoma State 1955-61. Pro coach: Houston Oilers 1962-63, Edmonton Eskimos (CFL) 1964-69 (head coach), Minnesota Vikings 1970-77, Chicago Bears 1978-81 (head coach), joined Cowboys in 1982.

Jim Erkenbeck, offensive line; born September 10, 1931, Los Angeles, Calif., lives in Roanoke, Tex. Fullback San Diego State 1949-52. No pro playing experience. College coach: San Diego State 1960-63, Grossmont, Calif., J.C. 1964-67, Utah State 1968, Washington State 1969-71, California 1972-76. Pro coach: Winnipeg Blue Bombers (CFL) 1977, Montreal Alouettes (CFL) 1978-81, Calgary Stampeders (CFL) 1982, Philadelphia/Baltimore Stars (USFL) 1983-85, New Orleans Saints 1986, joined Cowboys in 1987.

Paul Hackett, pass offense coordinator; born July 5, 1947, Burlington, Vt., lives in Southlake, Tex. Quarterback Cal-Davis 1965-68. No pro playing experience. College coach: Cal-Davis 1970-71, California 1972-75, Southern California 1976-80. Pro coach: Cleveland Browns 1981-82, San Francisco 49ers 1983-85, joined Cowboys in 1986.

Al Lavan, running backs; born September 13, 1946, Pierce, Fla., lives in Plano, Tex. Defensive back Colorado State 1965-67. Pro defensive back Philadelphia Eagles 1968, Atlanta Falcons 1969-70. College coach: Colorado State 1972, Louisville 1973, Iowa State 1974, Georgia Tech 1977-78, Stanford 1979. Pro coach: Atlanta Falcons 1975-76, joined Cowboys in 1980.

Alan Lowry, receivers; born November 21, 1950, Irving, Tex., lives in Roanoke, Tex. Defensive back-quarterback Texas 1970-72. No pro playing experience. College coach: Virginia Tech 1974, Wyoming 1975, Texas 1976-81. Pro coach: Joined Cowboys in 1982.

Dick Nolan, defensive backs; born March 26, 1932, Pittsburgh, Pa., lives in Roanoke, Tex. Offensive-defensive back Maryland 1951-53. Pro defensive back New York Giants 1954-57, 1959-61, St. Louis Cardinals 1958, Dallas 1962 (player-coach). Pro coach: Dallas Cowboys 1963-67, San Francisco 49ers 1968-75 (head coach), New Orleans Saints 1977-80 (head coach), Houston Oilers 1981, rejoined Cowboys in 1982.

Mike Solari, special teams; born January 16, 1955, Daly City, Calif., lives in Grapevine, Tex. Offensive lineman San Diego State 1975-76. No pro playing experience. College coach: Mira Vista, Calif., J.C. 1977-78, U.S. International 1979, Boise State 1980, Cincinnati 1981-82, Kansas 1983-85, Pittsburgh 1986. Pro coach: Joined Cowboys in 1987.

Dallas Cowboys 1988 First-Year Roster

Name	Pos.	Ht.	Wt.	Birth-date	College	Hometown	How Acq.
Bedford, Brian	WR	6-3	209	6/29/65	California	Sacramento, Calif.	D9
Gay, Everett (1)	WR	6-2	204	10/23/64	Texas	Houston, Tex.	D5-'87
Hennings, Chad	DE-DT	6-5	251	10/20/65	Air Force	Elberon, Iowa	D11
Higgs, Mark	RB	5-7	188	4/11/66	Kentucky	Owensboro, Ky.	D8
Hooven, Owen	T	6-8	302	8/11/66	Oregon State	Arcata, Calif.	D7
Hummel, Ben	LB	6-4	234	8/22/66	UCLA	Rockwall, Tex.	D12
Hutson, Mark	G	6-3	292	8/29/66	Oklahoma	Fort Smith, Ark.	D3
Irvin, Michael	WR	6-2	198	3/5/66	Miami	Fort Lauderdale, Fla.	D1
Norton, Ken	LB	6-2	224	9/29/66	UCLA	Los Angeles, Calif.	D2
Owens, Billy	CB-S	6-1	198	12/2/65	Pittsburgh	Syracuse, N.Y.	D10
Secules, Scott	QB	6-3	220	11/8/64	Virginia	Centreville, Va.	D6
Smith, Vernice (1)	G	6-2	275	10/24/65	Florida A&M	Orlando, Fla.	FA
Widell, Dave	T	6-6	297	5/14/65	Boston College	Hartford, Conn.	D4

The term NFL Rookie is defined as a player who is in his first season of professional football and has not been on the roster of another professional football team for any regular-season or postseason games. A Rookie is designated by an "R" on NFL rosters. Players who have been active in another professional football league or players who have NFL experience, including either preseason training camp or being on an active roster for fewer than three regular-season or postseason games, are termed NFL First-Year Players. An NFL First-Year Player is designated by a "1" on NFL rosters. Thereafter, a player on an NFL active roster for at least three regular-season or postseason games is credited with an additional year of NFL playing experience.

NOTES

Ernie Stautner, defensive coordinator-defensive line; born April 2, 1927, Cham, Bavaria, lives in Dallas. Tackle Boston College 1946-49. Pro defensive tackle Pittsburgh Steelers 1950-63 (player-coach 1963). Pro coach: Pittsburgh Steelers 1964, Washington Redskins 1965, joined Cowboys in 1966.

Jerry Tubbs, linebackers; born January 23, 1935, Breckenridge, Tex., lives in Dallas. Center-linebacker Oklahoma 1954-56. Pro linebacker Chicago Cardinals 1957, San Francisco 49ers 1958-59, Dallas Cowboys 1960-67. Pro coach: Joined Cowboys in 1966 (player-coach 1966-67).

Bob Ward, conditioning; born July 4, 1933, Huntington Park, Calif., lives in Dallas. Fullback-quarterback Whitworth College 1952-54. Doctorate in physical education, Indiana University. No pro playing experience. College coach: Fullerton, Calif., J.C. (track) 1965-75. Pro coach: Joined Cowboys in 1975.

National Football Conference Central Division

Team Colors: Honolulu Blue and Silver

Pontiac Silverdome
1200 Featherstone Road — Box 4200
Pontiac, Michigan 48057
Telephone: (313) 335-4131

Club Officials

President-Owner: William Clay Ford
Executive Vice President-General Manager: Russell Thomas
Director of Football Operations-Head Coach: Darryl Rogers
Vice President/Finance: Charles Schmidt
Vice President/Player Personnel: Jerome R. Vainisi
Director of Player Personnel: Joe Bushofsky
Scouts: Dirk Dierking, Allen Hughes, Ron Hughes, Scott McEwen, Jim Owens, Jerry Neri, John Trump
Director of Public Relations: Bill Keenist
Director of Communications: Tim Pendell
Assistant Director of Public Relations: Arthur Triche
Ticket Manager: Fred Otto
Trainer: Kent Falb
Strength and Conditioning: Don Clemons
Equipment Manager: Dan Jaroshewich

Stadium: Pontiac Silverdome • **Capacity:** 80,638
1200 Featherstone Road
Pontiac, Michigan 48057

Playing Surface: AstroTurf

Training Camp: Oakland University
Rochester, Michigan 48063

1988 Schedule

Preseason

Aug. 6	at Cleveland	7:00
Aug. 11	**Seattle**	7:30
Aug. 20	at Cincinnati	7:30
Aug. 25	**Philadelphia**	7:30

Regular Season

Sept. 4	**Atlanta**	1:00
Sept. 11	at Los Angeles Rams	1:00
Sept. 18	**New Orleans**	1:00
Sept. 25	**New York Jets**	1:00
Oct. 2	at San Francisco	1:00
Oct. 9	**Chicago**	1:00
Oct. 16	at New York Giants	1:00
Oct. 23	at Kansas City	12:00
Oct. 30	**New York Giants**	4:00
Nov. 6	at Minnesota	12:00
Nov. 13	**Tampa Bay**	1:00
Nov. 20	vs. Green Bay at Milwaukee	12:00
Nov. 24	**Minnesota** (Thanksgiving)	12:30
Dec. 4	**Green Bay**	1:00
Dec. 11	at Chicago	12:00
Dec. 18	at Tampa Bay	1:00

Lions Coaching History

Portsmouth Spartans 1930-33 (364-367-32)

1930	Hal (Tubby) Griffen	5- 6-3
1931-36	George (Potsy) Clark	49-20-6
1937-38	Earl (Dutch) Clark	14-8-0
1939	Elmer (Gus) Henderson	6-5-0
1940	George (Potsy) Clark	5-5-1
1941-42	Bill Edwards*	4-9-1
1942	John Karcis	0-8-0
1943-47	Charles (Gus) Dorais	20-31-2
1948-50	Alvin (Bo) McMillin	12-24-0
1951-56	Raymond (Buddy) Parker	50-24-2
1957-64	George Wilson	55-45-6
1965-66	Harry Gilmer	10-16-2
1967-72	Joe Schmidt	43-35-7
1973	Don McCafferty	6-7-1
1974-76	Rick Forzano**	15-17-0
1976-77	Tommy Hudspeth	11-13-0
1978-84	Monte Clark	43-63-1
1985-87	Darryl Rogers	16-31-0

*Released after three games in 1942
**Resigned after four games in 1976

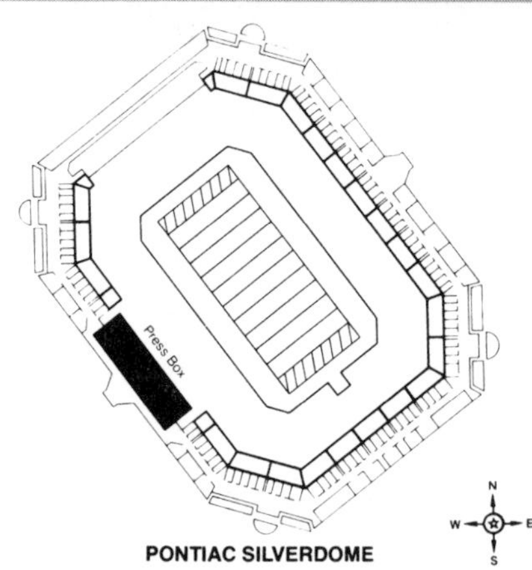

PONTIAC SILVERDOME

Record Holders

Individual Records—Career

Category	Name	Performance
Rushing (Yds.)	Billy Sims, 1980-84	5,106
Passing (Yds.)	Bobby Layne, 1950-58	15,710
Passing (TDs)	Bobby Layne, 1950-58	118
Receiving (No.)	Charlie Sanders, 1968-1977	336
Receiving (Yds.)	Gail Cogdill, 1960-68	5,220
Interceptions	Dick LeBeau, 1959-1972	62
Punting (Avg.)	Yale Lary, 1952-53, 1956-1964	44.3
Punt Return (Avg.)	Jack Christiansen, 1951-58	12.8
Kickoff Return (Avg.)	Pat Studstill, 1961-67	25.7
Field Goals	Eddie Murray, 1980-87	172
Touchdowns (Tot.)	Billy Sims, 1980-84	47
Points	Eddie Murray, 1980-87	765

Individual Records—Single Season

Category	Name	Performance
Rushing (Yds.)	Billy Sims, 1981	1,437
Passing (Yds.)	Gary Danielson, 1980	3,223
Passing (TDs)	Bobby Layne, 1951	26
Receiving (No.)	James Jones, 1984	77
Receiving (Yds.)	Pat Studstill, 1966	1,266
Interceptions	Don Doll, 1950	12
	Jack Christiansen, 1953	12
Punting (Avg.)	Yale Lary, 1963	48.9
Punt Return (Avg.)	Jack Christiansen, 1952	21.5
Kickoff Return (Avg.)	Tom Watkins, 1965	34.4
Field Goals	Eddie Murray, 1980	27
Touchdowns (Tot.)	Billy Sims, 1980	16
Points	Doak Walker, 1950	128

Individual Records—Single Game

Category	Name	Performance
Rushing (Yds.)	Bob Hoernschemeyer, 11-23-50	198
Passing (Yds.)	Bobby Layne, 11-5-50	374
Passing (TDs)	Gary Danielson, 12-9-78	5
Receiving (No.)	Cloyce Box, 12-3-50	12
	James Jones, 9-28-86	12
Receiving (Yds.)	Cloyce Box, 12-3-50	302
Interceptions	Don Doll, 10-23-49	*4
Field Goals	Garo Yepremian, 11-13-66	6
Touchdowns (Tot.)	Cloyce Box, 12-3-50	4
Points	Cloyce Box, 12-3-50	24

*NFL Record

1987 Team Record

Preseason (2-2)

Date	Result		Opponents
8/15	L	19-22	Indianapolis
8/22	W	23- 9	Cincinnati
8/28	L	10-38	at Seattle
9/3	W	36- 3	at Philadelphia
		88-72	

Regular Season (4-11)

Date	Result		Opponents	Att.
9/13	L	19-34	at Minnesota	57,061
9/20	L	7-27	at L.A. Raiders	50,300
9/27	C		Chicago	
10/4	L	27-31	Tampa Bay	4,919
10/11	W	19-16	at Green Bay (OT)	35,779
10/18	L	14-37	Seattle	8,310
10/25	L	33-34	Green Bay	27,278
11/1	L	0-34	at Denver	75,172
11/8	W	27-17	Dallas	45,325
11/15	L	13-20	at Washington	53,593
11/22	L	10-30	at Chicago	63,357
11/26	L	20-27	Kansas City	43,820
12/6	L	16-37	L.A. Rams	33,413
12/13	W	20-10	at Tampa Bay	41,699
12/20	L	14-17	Minnesota	27,693
12/27	W	30-13	at Atlanta	13,906

(OT) Overtime
C (Cancelled due to players' strike.)

Score by Periods

Lions	56	90	45	75	3	—	269
Opponents	89	153	68	74	0	—	384

Attendance

Home 190,758 Away 390,867 Total 581,625
Single-game home record, 80,444 (12-20-81)
Single-season home record, 622,593 (1980)

1987 Team Statistics

	Lions	Opp.
Total First Downs	270	314
Rushing	81	122
Passing	156	162
Penalty	33	30
Third Down: Made/Att.	59/191	81/201
Fourth Down: Made/Att.	5/15	2/5
Total Net Yards	4391	5273
Avg. Per Game	292.7	351.5
Total Plays	933	1005
Avg. Per Play	4.7	5.2
Net Yards Rushing	1435	2070
Avg. Per Game	95.7	138.0
Total Rushes	398	504
Net Yards Passing	2956	3203
Avg. Per Game	197.1	213.5
Sacked/Yards Lost	26/194	42/355
Gross Yards	3150	3558
Att./Completions	509/275	459/259
Completion Pct.	54.0	56.4
Had Intercepted	26	19
Punts/Avg.	70/41.8	65/37.9
Net Punting Avg.	37.6	31.4
Penalties/Yards Lost	86/737	115/907
Fumbles/Ball Lost	29/11	36/13
Touchdowns	27	43
Rushing	9	18
Passing	16	23
Returns	2	2
Avg. Time of Possession	28:19	31:41

1987 Individual Statistics

Scoring	TD R	TD P	TD Rt	PAT	FG	Saf	TP
Murray	0	0	0	21/21	20/32	0	81
Mandley	0	7	0	0/0	0/0	0	42
Ellerson	3	1	0	0/0	0/0	0	24
James	4	0	0	0/0	0/0	0	24
Prindle	0	0	0	6/6	6/7	0	24
Bernard	2	0	0	0/0	0/0	0	12
Bradley	0	2	0	0/0	0/0	0	12
Grymes	0	2	0	0/0	0/0	0	12
Bland	0	1	0	0/0	0/0	0	6
King	0	0	1	0/0	0/0	0	6
Rubick	0	1	0	0/0	0/0	0	6
Smith	0	0	1	0/0	0/0	0	6
Truvillion	0	1	0	0/0	0/0	0	6
S. Williams	0	1	0	0/0	0/0	0	6
Jamison	0	0	0	0/0	0/0	1	2
Lions	9	16	2	27/27	26/39	1	269
Opponents	18	23	2	42/43	28/34	0	384

Passing	Att.	Comp.	Yds.	Pct.	TD	Int.	Tkld.	Rate
Long	416	232	2598	55.8	11	20	17/127	63.4
Hons	92	43	552	46.7	5	5	9/67	61.5
Jones	1	0	0	0.0	0	1	0/0	0.0
Lions	509	275	3150	54.0	16	26	26/194	62.1
Opponents	459	259	3558	56.4	23	19	42/355	80.9

Rushing	Att.	Yds.	Avg.	LG	TD
Jones	96	342	3.6	19	0
James	82	270	3.3	17	4
Ellerson	47	196	4.2	33	3
Bernard	45	187	4.2	14	2
Wester	33	113	3.4	14	0
Woolfolk	12	82	6.8	31	0
Edwards	32	69	2.2	13	0
Long	22	64	2.9	15	0
Hons	5	49	9.8	23	0
S. Williams	8	29	3.6	8	0
Dollinger	8	22	2.8	8	0
Paige	4	13	3.3	6	0
Mandley	1	3	3.0	3	0
Kowgios	1	2	2.0	2	0
Black	1	0	0.0	0	0
Chadwick	1	−6	−6.0	−6	0
Lions	398	1435	3.6	33	9
Opponents	504	2070	4.1	39t	18

Receiving	No.	Yds.	Avg.	LG	TD
Mandley	58	720	12.4	41	7
Jones	34	262	7.7	35	0
Chadwick	30	416	13.9	36	0
Lee	19	308	16.2	53	0
Woolfolk	19	166	8.7	13	0
James	16	215	13.4	46	0
Rubick	13	147	11.3	22	1
Bernard	13	91	7.0	12	0
Truvillion	12	207	17.3	53t	1
Grymes	9	140	15.6	36t	2
Nichols	7	87	12.4	23	0
Edwards	7	82	11.7	21	0
Bradley	7	50	7.1	14	2
Giles	6	62	10.3	25	0
Kab	5	54	10.8	28	0
Ellerson	5	48	9.6	23	1
S. Williams	4	16	4.0	7	1
Dollinger	3	25	8.3	15	0
Wheeler	2	17	8.5	9	0
Bland	2	14	7.0	11t	1
Paige	2	1	0.5	3	0
Witte	1	19	19.0	19	0
Kowgios	1	3	3.0	3	0
Lions	275	3150	11.5	53t	16
Opponents	259	3558	13.7	81t	23

Interceptions	No.	Yds.	Avg.	LG	TD
Griffin	6	130	21.7	29	0
Galloway	3	46	15.3	30	0
McNorton	3	20	6.7	20	0
J. Williams	2	51	25.5	48	0
Smith	1	34	34.0	34t	1
Gibson	1	5	5.0	5	0
Benson	1	2	2.0	2	0
Cherry	1	2	2.0	2	0
Sheffield, Pitt.-Det.	1	2	2.0	2	0
Hall	1	0	0.0	0	0
Lions	19	290	15.3	48	1
Opponents	26	335	12.9	56	2

Punting	No.	Yds.	Avg.	In 20	LG
Erxleben	1	52	52.0	0	52
Arnold	46	2007	43.6	17	60
Misko	6	242	40.3	1	51
Black	6	233	38.8	1	47
Murray	4	155	38.8	1	46
Kinzer	7	238	34.0	2	42
Lions	70	2927	41.8	22	60
Opponents	65	2461	37.9	10	60

Punt Returns	No.	FC	Yds.	Avg.	LG	TD
Mandley	23	6	250	10.9	54	0
Bradley	12	5	53	4.4	13	0
Bland	0	1	0	—	0	0
Lions	35	12	303	8.7	54	0
Opponents	34	9	177	5.2	23	0

Kickoff Returns	No.	Yds.	Avg.	LG	TD
Lee	32	719	22.5	50	0
Woolfolk	11	219	19.9	44	0
Bradley	9	188	20.9	27	0
Hall	6	105	17.5	25	0
Bernard	4	54	13.5	32	0
Saleaumua	3	57	19.0	21	0
Ball	2	23	11.5	20	0
Bland	2	44	22.0	22	0
Glover	1	19	19.0	19	0
Green	1	0	0.0	0	0
Lions	71	1428	20.1	50	0
Opponents	56	1089	19.4	53	0

Sacks	No.
Cofer	8.5
K. Ferguson	6.0
J. Williams	4.0
Green	2.5
Carr	2.0
Gay	2.0
McDuffie	2.0
Saleaumua	2.0
Thompson	2.0
Eric M. Williams	2.0
Ball	1.0
Benson	1.0
Boyd	1.0
Federico	1.0
Gibson	1.0
Griffin	1.0
Jamison	1.0
Lockett	1.0
Ross	1.0
Lions	42.0
Opponents	26.0

Detroit Lions 1988 Veteran Roster

No.	Name	Pos.	Ht.	Wt.	Birth-date	NFL Exp.	College	Hometown	How Acq.	'87 Games/ Starts
6	†Arnold, Jim	P	6-3	211	1/31/61	6	Vanderbilt	Dalton, Ga.	FA-'86	11/0
68	†Baack, Steve	G	6-4	265	11/16/60	5	Oregon	John Day, Ore.	D3c-'84	7/0
93	Ball, Jerry	NT	6-1	283	12/15/64	2	Southern Methodist	Beaumont, Tex.	D3-'87	12/12
61	Barrows, Scott	G-C	6-2	278	3/31/63	3	West Virginia	Marietta, Ohio	FA-'86	12/10
69	Benson, Charles	DE	6-1	267	11/21/60	4	Baylor	Houston, Tex.	FA-'88	3/3
25	Bernard, Karl	RB	5-11	205	10/12/64	2	Southwest Louisiana	Baton Rouge, La.	FA-'87	8/3
80	Bland, Carl	WR	5-11	182	8/17/61	5	Virginia Union	Richmond, Va.	FA-'84	10/0
75	Brown, Lomas	T	6-4	282	3/30/63	4	Florida	Miami, Fla.	D1-'85	11/11
96	Butcher, Paul	LB	6-0	219	11/8/63	3	Wayne State	Dearborn, Mich.	FA-'86	12/0
95	Carr, Carl	LB	6-3	230	3/26/64	2	North Carolina	Alexandria, Va.	FA-'88	3/3
89	Chadwick, Jeff	WR	6-3	190	12/16/60	6	Grand Valley State	Dearborn Heights, Mich.	FA-'83	8/8
45	Cherry, Raphel	S	6-0	194	12/19/61	3	Hawaii	Little Rock, Ark.	FA-'87	10/10
55	Cofer, Michael	LB	6-5	245	4/7/60	6	Tennessee	Knoxville, Tenn.	D3-'83	11/11
92	Davis, Jerome	NT	6-1	260	2/27/62	2	Ball State	Cincinnati, Ohio	FA-'88	3/3
70	Dorney, Keith	G-T	6-5	285	12/3/57	10	Penn State	Macungie, Pa.	D1-'79	5/5
42	†Ellerson, Gary	RB-KR	5-11	220	7/17/63	4	Wisconsin	Albany, Ga.	FA-'87	8/2
77	†Ferguson, Keith	DE	6-5	260	4/3/59	8	Ohio State	Miami, Fla.	W(SD)-'85	12/9
40	†Galloway, Duane	CB-S	5-8	181	11/7/61	3	Arizona State	Los Angeles, Calif.	FA-'85	10/7
98	Gibson, Dennis	LB	6-2	240	2/8/64	2	Iowa State	Ankeny, Iowa	D8-'87	12/12
53	†Glover, Kevin	C-G	6-2	267	6/17/63	4	Maryland	Upper Marlboro, Md.	D2-'85	12/9
62	†Green, Curtis	DE-NT	6-3	265	6/3/57	8	Alabama State	Quincy, Fla.	D2-'81	12/0
34	Griffin, James	S	6-2	197	9/7/61	6	Middle Tennessee State	Camilla, Ga.	FA-'86	12/12
17	Hipple, Eric	QB	6-2	198	9/16/57	8	Utah State	Downey, Calif.	D4-'80	0*
32	James, Garry	RB	5-10	214	9/4/63	3	Louisiana State	Gretna, La.	D2-'86	8/7
95	Jamison, George	LB	6-1	226	9/30/62	2	Cincinnati	Bridgeton, N.J.	SD3-'86	12/0
23	Johnson, Earl	CB	6-0	190	10/20/63	2	South Carolina	Daytona Beach, Fla.	FA-'88	0*
30	Jones, James	RB	6-2	229	3/21/61	6	Florida	Pompano Beach, Fla.	D1-'83	11/11
87	†Kab, Vyto	TE	6-5	240	12/23/59	6	Penn State	Wayne, N.J.	FA-'87	7/2
83	Lee, Gary	WR-KR	6-1	202	2/12/65	2	Georgia Tech	Albany, Ga.	D12-'87	12/3
81	Lewis, Mark	TE	6-2	250	5/5/61	3	Texas A&M	Houston, Tex.	FA-'87	10/2*
50	Lockett, Danny	LB	6-2	228	7/11/64	2	Arizona	Ft. Valley, Ga.	D6-'87	13/1
16	Long, Chuck	QB	6-4	211	2/18/63	3	Iowa	Wheaton, Ill.	D1-'86	12/12
82	Mandley, Pete	WR-KR	5-10	191	7/29/61	5	Northern Arizona	Mesa, Ariz.	D2-'84	12/12
57	Maxwell, Vernon	LB	6-2	235	10/25/61	6	Arizona State	Los Angeles, Calif.	FA-'85	12/1
72	McDuffie, George	DE	6-6	270	1/20/63	2	Findlay	Lima, Ohio	FA-'88	3/2
29	McNorton, Bruce	CB	5-11	175	2/28/59	7	Georgetown, Ky.	Daytona Beach, Fla.	D4-'82	12/12
74	Milinichik, Joe	G-T	6-5	275	3/30/63	2	North Carolina State	Macungie, Pa.	D3-'86	11/0
31	Mitchell, Devon	S	6-1	194	12/30/62	2	Iowa	Brooklyn, N.Y.	D4-'86	0*
52	Mott, Steve	C	6-3	270	3/24/61	6	Alabama	New Orleans, La.	D5-'83	11/11
3	Murray, Ed	K	5-10	175	8/29/56	9	Tulane	Victoria, British Columbia	D7-'80	12/0
86	Nichols, Mark	WR	6-2	208	10/29/59	7	San Jose State	Bakersfield, Calif.	D1-'81	12/1
49	†Paige, Tony	RB	5-10	230	10/14/62	5	Virginia Tech	Washington, D.C.	FA-'87	5/0
51	†Robinson, Shelton	LB	6-2	236	9/14/60	7	North Carolina	Pikeville, N.C.	T(Sea)-'86	12/12
60	Rogers, Reggie	DE	6-6	272	1/21/64	2	Washington	Sacramento, Calif.	D1-'87	6/0
84	†Rubick, Rob	TE	6-3	234	9/27/60	7	Grand Valley State	Newberry, Mich.	D12-'82	9/8
97	Saleaumua, Dan	NT	6-0	285	11/11/65	2	Arizona State	San Diego, Calif.	D7-'87	9/0
73	Salem, Harvey	G	6-6	285	1/15/61	6	California	El Cerrito, Calif.	T(Hou)-'86	11/11
64	Sanders, Eric	T-G	6-7	280	10/22/58	8	Nevada-Reno	Reno, Nev.	W(Atl)-'86	12/0
28	Sheffield, Chris	CB	6-1	200	1/9/63	3	Albany State	Cairo, Ga.	FA-'87	11/0*
41	Smith, Ricky	WR-CB	6-0	188	7/20/60	5	Alabama State	Quincy, Fla.	FA-'87	12/0
27	Watkins, Bobby	CB	5-10	184	5/31/60	7	Southwest Texas State	Dallas, Tex.	D2-'82	5/5
32	Wester, Cleve	RB	5-8	188	6/14/64	2	Concordia, Neb.	Lake Worth, Fla.	FA-'88	3/1
48	Wheeler, Mark	TE	6-2	232	6/15/64	2	Kentucky	Arlington, Va.	FA-'88	3/0
76	Williams, Eric	NT	6-4	280	2/24/62	5	Washington State	Stockton, Calif.	D3a-'84	11/11
59	Williams, Jimmy	LB	6-3	230	11/15/60	7	Nebraska	Washington, D.C.	D1-'82	12/12
38	†Williams, Scott	RB	6-2	234	7/21/62	3	Georgia	Charlotte, N.C.	FA-'86	5/2
21	†Woolfolk, Butch	RB	6-1	212	3/1/60	7	Michigan	Westfield, N.J.	FA-'87	12/0

* Hipple and Mitchell missed '87 season due to injury; Johnson last played with Denver in '86; Lewis played 1 game with Green Bay, 9 with Detroit in '87; Sheffield played 5 games with Pittsburgh, 6 with Detroit.

†Option playout; subject to developments.

Also played with Lions in '87—LB Ernest Adams (3 games), WR Stan Baker (active for 1 game but did not play), P Mike Black (1), LB Steve Boadway (2), CB Jon Bostic (3), LB Thomas Boyd (4), WR Danny Bradley (3), C Pat Cain (3), CB-S Dexter Clark (2), TE Jerry Diorio (2), RB Tony Dollinger (2), RB Stan Edwards (3), P Russell Erxleben (1), RB Kelvin Farmer (active for 1 game but did not play), S Creig Federico (3), G Joe Felton (2), QB Joe Ferguson (active for 12 games but did not play), CB Anthony Fields (3), QB Brendon Folmar (1), DE William Gay (11), G Chris Geile (3), TE Jimmie Giles (4), S William Graham (2), WR Darrell Grymes (2), S Alvin Hall (3), CB Maurice Harvey (2), CB-S Ivan Hicks (1), LB Mark Hicks (1), CB Steve Hirsch (3), QB Todd Hons (3), WR Mel Hoover (2), T Mark Jenkins (active for 1 game but did not play), WR Gilvanni Johnson (3), T Rick Johnson (1), NT Jeff Kacmarek (3), LB Angelo King (1), P Matt Kinzer (1), G Paul Kiser (1), RB Nick Kowgios (3), CB-S Bob McDonough (3), P John Misko (1), LB Anthony Office (3), G Greg Orton (3), K Mike Prindle (3), T Jerry Quaerna (3), TE Derrick Ramsey (1), LB Tom Ross (3), C Chuck Steele (3), T Rich Strenger (3), S Ivory Sully (11), NT Stuart Tolle (1), WR Eric Truvillion (3), T Jim Warne (3), CB Eric T. Williams (1), TE Mark Witte (3).

COACHING STAFF

Head Coach, Darryl Rogers

Pro Career: Became Lions' sixteenth head coach and director of football operations on February 6, 1985. No pro playing experience. Career record: 16-31-0.

Background: Wide receiver who gained all-West Coast honors while playing at Fresno State. Served in U.S. Marine Corps and later earned his master's degree in physical education from Fresno State. Spent twenty years coaching in the collegiate ranks at Hayward State 1965, Fresno State 1966-72, San Jose State 1973-75 (head coach), Michigan State 1976-79 (head coach), Arizona State 1980-84 (head coach). Named national college coach of the year in 1978 while at Michigan State. Ranked as one of the winningest coaches in the college ranks with a 129-84-7 mark.

Personal: Born May 28, 1935, Los Angeles, Calif. Darryl and his wife, Marsha, live in Bloomfield Hills, Mich., and have three daughters—Jamie, Keely, and Stacy.

Assistant Coaches

Bob Baker, offensive coordinator; born November 28, 1927, Lima, Ohio, lives in Rochester Hills, Mich. Quarterback Ball State 1947-51. No pro playing experience. College coach: Indiana 1966-73, Michigan State 1977-79, Arizona State 1980-82. Pro coach: Calgary Stampeders (CFL) 1974-76 (head coach 1976), Los Angeles Rams 1983-84, joined Lions in 1985.

Carl Battershell, special teams-secondary; born November 5, 1948, Alliance, Ohio, lives in Rochester, Mich. Offensive tackle Bowling Green 1966-69. No pro playing experience. College coach: Bowling Green 1973-76, Syracuse 1977-79, West Virginia 1980-82, Arizona State 1983-84. Pro coach: Joined Lions in 1985.

Lew Carpenter, receivers; born January 12, 1932, Hayti, Mo., lives in Rochester, Mich. Running back-end Arkansas 1950-52. Pro running back-defensive back-end Detroit Lions 1953-55, Cleveland Browns 1957-58, Green Bay Packers 1959-63. Pro coach: Minnesota Vikings 1964-66, Atlanta Falcons 1967-68, Washington Redskins 1969-70, St. Louis Cardinals 1971-72, Houston Oilers 1973-74, Green Bay Packers 1975-85, joined Lions in 1987.

Don Doll, administrative assistant to coaching staff-tight ends; born August 29, 1926, Los Angeles, Calif., lives in Birmingham, Mich. Defensive back Southern California 1944, 1946-48. Pro defensive back Detroit Lions 1949-52, Washington Redskins 1953, Los Angeles Rams 1954. College coach: Washington 1955, Contra Costa, Calif., J.C. 1956, Southern California 1957-58, Notre Dame 1959-62. Pro coach: Detroit Lions 1963-64, Los Angeles Rams 1965, Washington Redskins 1966-70, Green Bay Packers 1971-73, Baltimore Colts 1974, Miami Dolphins 1975-76, rejoined Lions in 1978.

Wayne Fontes, defensive coordinator; born February 17, 1940, New Bedford, Mass., lives in Rochester, Mich. Defensive back Michigan State 1959-61. Pro defensive back New York Titans (AFL) 1962. College coach: Dayton 1967-68, Iowa 1969-70, Southern California 1971-75. Pro coach: Tampa Bay Buccaneers 1976-84, joined Lions in 1985.

Dick Modzelewski, defensive line; born January 16, 1931, West Natrona, Pa., lives in Rochester Hills, Mich. Tackle Maryland 1950-52. Pro defensive tackle Washington Redskins 1953-54, Pittsburgh Steelers 1955, New York Giants 1956-63, Cleveland Browns 1964-66. Pro coach: Cleveland Browns 1968-77, New York Giants 1978, Cincinnati Bengals 1979-83, Green Bay Packers 1984-87, joined Lions in 1988.

Bill Muir, offensive line; born October 26, 1942, Pittsburgh, Pa., lives in Rochester Hills, Mich. Tackle Susquehanna 1962-64. No pro playing experience. College coach: Susquehanna 1965, Delaware Valley 1966-67, Rhode Island 1970-71, Idaho State 1972-73, Southern Methodist 1976-77. Pro coach: Orlando (Continental Football League) 1968-69, Houston-Shreveport Steamer (WFL) 1975, New England Patriots 1982-84, joined Lions in 1985.

Detroit Lions 1988 First-Year Roster

Name	Pos.	Ht.	Wt.	Birth-date	College	Hometown	How Acq.
Andolsek, Eric	G	6-2	281	8/22/66	Louisiana State	Thibodaux, La.	D5
Beaty, Douglas	RB	6-1	221	9/17/65	Appalachian State	Anderson, S.C.	FA
Beemer, Bob (1)	DE	6-5	231	5/14/63	Toledo	Jackson, Mich.	FA-'87
Blades, Bennie	CB-S	6-1	216	9/3/66	Miami	Ft. Lauderdale, Fla.	D1
Brown, Ray (1)	WR	5-9	185	7/25/65	South Carolina	Greensboro, S.C.	FA-'87
Bryant, Willie	CB-S	6-0	195	3/10/66	Louisiana State	Ft. Walton Beach, Fla.	FA
Carter, Pat	TE	6-4	263	8/1/66	Florida State	Sarasota, Fla.	D2b
Corrington, Kip	S	6-0	175	4/12/65	Texas A&M	College Station, Tex.	D9a
Craig, Paco	WR	5-10	170	2/2/65	UCLA	Santa Maria, Calif.	D10
Garner, Dene	K	5-9	165	9/21/64	Utah State	Sandy, Utah	FA
Hadd, Gary	NT	6-4	270	10/19/65	Minnesota	Burnsville, Minn.	D8
Henry, Ken	WR	6-2	197	11/7/65	Southern California	Fresno, Calif.	FA
Irvin, Todd	T	6-5	288	2/1/65	Mississippi	Aberdeen, Miss.	D9b
James, Jeff	WR	5-11	179	3/25/65	Stanford	Beverly Hills, Calif.	D7
Johnson, Michael	LB	6-2	222	3/2/66	Texas Tech	Lubbock, Tex.	FA
Johnson, Rick (1)	T	6-6	255	12/12/63	Grand Valley State	Ionia, Mich.	FA-'87
Kosor, Ron (1)	C	6-2	270	12/2/62	North Carolina State	Greensburg, Pa.	FA-'87
McCoin, Danny	QB	6-3	206	8/31/64	Cincinnati	Livingston, Tenn.	D11
Painter, Carl	RB	5-9	184	5/10/64	Hampton Institute	Norfolk, Va.	D6
Reveiz, Louis	K	5-10	175	11/14/65	Carson-Newman	Miami, Fla.	FA
Roundtree, Ray	WR	6-0	180	4/19/66	Penn State	Aiken, S.C.	D3
Saltz, Lee	QB	6-1	195	9/25/63	Temple	Randolph, N.J.	FA-'87
Shafer, Donald	K	5-10	175	6/15/64	Southern California	Logan, Utah	FA
Snyder, Don (1)	T	6-5	290	5/24/63	Tennessee Tech	Scott, Kan.	FA-'87
Spielman, Chris	LB	6-0	234	10/11/65	Ohio State	Massillon, Ohio	D2a
Spielman, Rick (1)	LB	6-0	230	12/2/62	Southern Illinois	Massillon, Ohio	FA
Walker, Kevin	CB-S	5-10	185	10/20/63	East Carolina	Greensboro, N.C.	FA
Warren, John	CB-S	5-9	174	4/25/63	Virginia Union	Washington, D.C.	FA
White, William	CB	5-10	189	2/19/66	Ohio State	Lima, Ohio	D4

The term NFL Rookie is defined as a player who is in his first season of professional football and has not been on the roster of another professional football team for any regular-season or postseason games. A Rookie is designated by an "R" on NFL rosters. Players who have been active in another professional football league or players who have NFL experience, including either preseason training camp or being on an active roster for fewer than three regular-season or postseason games, are termed NFL First-Year Players. An NFL First-Year Player is designated by a "1" on NFL rosters. Thereafter, a player on an NFL active roster for at least three regular-season or postseason games is credited with an additional year of NFL playing experience.

NOTES

Mike Murphy, linebackers; born September 25, 1944, New York, N.Y., lives in Rochester, Mich. Guard-linebacker Huron, S.D., College 1962-65. No pro playing experience. College coach: Vermont 1970-73, Idaho State 1974-76, Western Illinois 1977-78. Pro coach: Saskatchewan Roughriders (CFL) 1979-83, Chicago Blitz (USFL) 1984, joined Lions in 1985.

Vic Rapp, running backs; born December 23, 1935, Marionville, Mo., lives in Rochester, Mich. Running back Southwest Missouri State 1954-57. No pro playing experience. College coach: Arizona 1965-66, Missouri 1967-71. Pro coach: Edmonton Eskimos (CFL) 1972-76, British Columbia Lions (CFL) 1977-82 (head coach), Houston Oilers 1983, Los Angeles Rams 1984, Tampa Bay Buccaneers 1985-86, joined Lions in 1987.

Willie Shaw, defensive backs; born January 11, 1944, Glenmora, La., lives in Rochester, Mich. Defensive back New Mexico 1966-68. No pro playing experience. College coach: San Diego City College 1970-72, Stanford 1973-76, Long Beach State 1977-78, Oregon 1979, Arizona State 1980-84. Pro coach: Joined Lions in 1985.

GREEN BAY PACKERS

National Football Conference Central Division

Team Colors: Dark Green, Gold, and White

1265 Lombardi Avenue
P.O. Box 10628
Green Bay, Wisconsin 54307-0628
Telephone: (414) 494-2351

Club Officials

Chairman of the Board: Dominic Olejniczak
President, CEO: Robert J. Parins
Vice President: Tony Canadeo
Secretary: Peter M. Platten III
Treasurer: Phil Hendrickson
Executive Vice President, Administration: Bob Harlan
Executive Vice President, Football Operations: Tom Braatz
Director of Public Relations: Lee Remmel
Assistant Director of Public Relations: Scott Berchtold
Green Bay Ticket Director: Mark Wagner
Accountant: Dick Blasczyk
Director of College Scouting: Dick Corrick
Video Director: Al Treml
Trainer: Domenic Gentile
Equipment Manager: Bob Noel

Stadium: Lambeau Field • **Capacity:** 57,093
P.O. Box 10628
1265 Lombardi Avenue
Green Bay, Wisconsin 54307-0628
Milwaukee County Stadium • **Capacity:** 56,051
Highway I-94
Milwaukee, Wisconsin 53214

Playing Surfaces: Grass

Training Camp: St. Norbert College
DePere, Wisconsin 54115

1988 Schedule

Preseason

Aug. 6	**New York Giants**	7:00
Aug. 13	at Indianapolis	7:30
Aug. 19	vs. Kansas City at Milw.	7:00
Aug. 27	vs. N.Y. Jets at Madison, Wis.	1:00

Regular Season

Sept. 4	**Los Angeles Rams**	12:00
Sept. 11	**Tampa Bay**	12:00
Sept. 18	at Miami	1:00
Sept. 25	**Chicago**	12:00
Oct. 2	at Tampa Bay	1:00
Oct. 9	**New England** at Milw.	12:00
Oct. 16	at Minnesota	12:00
Oct. 23	**Washington** at Milwaukee	12:00
Oct. 30	at Buffalo	1:00
Nov. 6	at Atlanta	1:00
Nov. 13	**Indianapolis**	12:00
Nov. 20	**Detroit** at Milwaukee	12:00
Nov. 27	at Chicago	12:00
Dec. 4	at Detroit	1:00
Dec. 11	**Minnesota**	12:00
Dec. 18	at Phoenix	2:00

Packers Coaching History

(465-373-36)

1921-49	Earl (Curly) Lambeau	212-106-21
1950-53	Gene Ronzani*	14-31-1
1953	Hugh Devore- Ray (Scooter) McLean**	0-2-0
1954-57	Lisle Blackbourn	17-31-0
1958	Ray (Scooter) McLean	1-10-1
1959-67	Vince Lombardi	98-30-4
1968-70	Phil Bengtson	20-21-1
1971-74	Dan Devine	25-28-4
1975-83	Bart Starr	53-77-3
1984-87	Forrest Gregg	25-37-1

*Released after 10 games in 1953
**Co-coaches

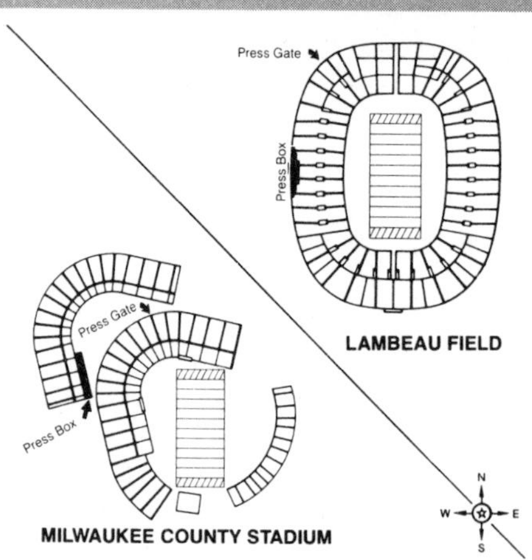

Record Holders

Individual Records—Career

Category	Name	Performance
Rushing (Yds.)	Jim Taylor, 1958-1966	8,207
Passing (Yds.)	Bart Starr, 1956-1971	23,718
Passing (TDs)	Bart Starr, 1956-1971	152
Receiving (No.)	James Lofton, 1978-1986	530
Receiving (Yds.)	James Lofton, 1978-1986	9,656
Interceptions	Bobby Dillon, 1952-59	52
Punting (Avg.)	Dick Deschaine, 1955-57	42.6
Punt Return (Avg.)	Billy Grimes, 1950-52	13.2
Kickoff Return (Avg.)	Travis Williams, 1967-1970	26.7
Field Goals	Chester Marcol, 1972-1980	120
Touchdowns (Tot.)	Don Hutson, 1935-1945	105
Points	Don Hutson, 1935-1945	823

Individual Records—Single Season

Category	Name	Performance
Rushing (Yds.)	Jim Taylor, 1962	1,407
Passing (Yds.)	Lynn Dickey, 1983	4,458
Passing (TDs)	Lynn Dickey, 1983	32
Receiving (No.)	Don Hutson, 1942	74
Receiving (Yds.)	James Lofton, 1984	1,361
Interceptions	Irv Comp, 1943	10
Punting (Avg.)	Jerry Norton, 1963	44.7
Punt Return (Avg.)	Billy Grimes, 1950	19.1
Kickoff Return (Avg.)	Travis Williams, 1967	41.1
Field Goals	Chester Marcol, 1972	33
Touchdowns (Tot.)	Jim Taylor, 1962	19
Points	Paul Hornung, 1960	*176

Individual Records—Single Game

Category	Name	Performance
Rushing (Yds.)	Jim Taylor, 12-3-61	186
Passing (Yds.)	Lynn Dickey, 10-12-80	418
Passing (TDs)	Many times Last time by Lynn Dickey, 9-4-83	5
Receiving (No.)	Don Hutson, 11-22-42	14
Receiving (Yds.)	Bill Howton, 10-21-56	257
Interceptions	Bobby Dillon, 11-26-53	*4
	Willie Buchanon, 9-24-78	*4
Field Goals	Many times Last time by Al Del Greco, 9-22-86	4
Touchdowns (Tot.)	Paul Hornung, 12-12-65	5
Points	Paul Hornung, 10-8-61	33

*NFL Record

1987 Team Record

Preseason (0-4)

Date	Result		Opponents
8/15	L	14-20	vs. Denver at Tempe, Ariz.
8/22	L	0-33	vs. Washington at Madison, Wis.
8/29	L	20-28	Cincinnati
9/5	L	24-30	vs. Clev. at Milw. (OT)
		58-111	

Regular Season (5-9-1)

Date	Result		Opponents	Att.
9/13	L	0-20	L.A. Raiders	54,983
9/20	T	17-17	Denver (OT)	50,624
9/27	C		at Tampa Bay	
10/4	W	23-16	at Minnesota	13,911
10/11	L	16-19	Detroit (OT)	35,779
10/18	W	16-10	Philadelphia (OT)	35,842
10/25	W	34-33	at Detroit	27,278
11/1	L	17-23	Tampa Bay	50,308
11/8	L	24-26	Chicago	53,320
11/15	L	13-24	at Seattle	60,963
11/22	W	23- 3	at Kansas City	34,611
11/29	L	10-23	at Chicago	61,638
12/6	L	12-23	San Francisco	51,118
12/13	W	16-10	Minnesota	47,059
12/19	L	10-20	at N.Y. Giants	51,013
12/27	L	24-33	at New Orleans	68,364

(OT) Overtime
C (Cancelled due to players' strike.)

Score by Periods

Packers	80	75	42	52	6	—	255
Opponents	40	98	71	88	3	—	300

Attendance

Home 379,033 Away 317,778 Total 696,811
Single-game home record, 56,895 (11-3-85; Lambeau Field), 56,258 (9-28-80, Milwaukee County Stadium)
Single-season home record, 435,521 (1980)

1987 Team Statistics

	Packers	Opp.
Total First Downs	248	296
Rushing	97	118
Passing	133	152
Penalty	18	26
Third Down: Made/Att.	68/217	86/220
Fourth Down: Made/Att.	2/8	10/14
Total Net Yards	4482	4923
Avg. Per Game	298.8	328.2
Total Plays	964	1024
Avg. Per Play	4.6	4.8
Net Yards Rushing	1801	1920
Avg. Per Game	120.1	128.0
Total Rushes	464	521
Net Yards Passing	2681	3003
Avg. Per Game	178.7	200.2
Sacked/Yards Lost	45/296	34/197
Gross Yards	2977	3200
Att./Completions	455/234	469/279
Completion Pct.	51.4	59.5
Had Intercepted	17	18
Punts/Avg.	93/39.3	77/40.1
Net Punting Avg.	33.5	34.0
Penalties/Yards Lost	135/1103	104/852
Fumbles/Ball Lost	35/18	42/24
Touchdowns	28	31
Rushing	13	15
Passing	15	14
Returns	0	2
Avg. Time of Possession	29:02	30:58

1987 Individual Statistics

Scoring	TD R	TD P	TD Rt	PAT	FG	Saf	TP
Zendejas	0	0	0	13/15	16/19	0	61
Fullwood	5	0	0	0/0	0/0	0	30
Del Greco	0	0	0	11/11	5/10	0	26
Carruth	3	1	0	0/0	0/0	0	24
Davis	3	0	0	0/0	0/0	0	18
Neal	0	3	0	0/0	0/0	0	18
Stanley	0	3	0	0/0	0/0	0	18
Epps	0	2	0	0/0	0/0	0	12
Clark	0	1	0	0/0	0/0	0	6
Hargrove	1	0	0	0/0	0/0	0	6
Le. Morris	0	1	0	0/0	0/0	0	6
Paskett	0	1	0	0/0	0/0	0	6
Risher	1	0	0	0/0	0/0	0	6
Summers	0	1	0	0/0	0/0	0	6
Thomas	0	1	0	0/0	0/0	0	6
West	0	1	0	0/0	0/0	0	6
Packers	13	15	0	24/27	21/29	0	255
Opponents	15	14	2	29/31	27/36	2	300

Passing	Att.	Comp.	Yds.	Pct.	TD	Int.	Tkld.	Rate
Wright	247	132	1507	53.4	6	11	20/128	61.6
Majkowski	127	55	875	43.3	5	3	10/77	70.2
Risher	74	44	564	59.5	3	3	12/77	80.0
Gillus	5	2	28	40.0	0	0	3/14	58.8
Carruth	1	1	3	100.0	1	0	0/0	118.8
Neal	1	0	0	0.0	0	0	0/0	39.6
Packers	455	234	2977	51.4	15	17	45/296	67.6
Opponents	469	279	3200	59.5	14	18	34/197	74.0

Rushing	Att.	Yds.	Avg.	LG	TD
Davis	109	413	3.8	39t	3
Fullwood	84	274	3.3	18	5
Willhite	53	251	4.7	61	0
Clark	56	211	3.8	57	0
Carruth	64	192	3.0	23	3
Majkowski	15	127	8.5	33	0
Wright	13	70	5.4	27	0
Risher	11	64	5.8	15	1
Hargrove	11	38	3.5	7	1
Stanley	4	38	9.5	24	0
Parker	8	33	4.1	17	0
Weigel	10	26	2.6	7	0
Sterling	5	20	4.0	9	0
Thomas	5	19	3.8	5	0
La. Morris	8	18	2.3	10	0
Cook	2	3	1.5	2	0
Le. Morris	2	2	1.0	4	0
Scott	1	2	2.0	2	0
Epps	1	0	0.0	0	0
Hunter	1	0	0.0	0	0
Neal	1	0	0.0	0	0
Packers	464	1801	3.9	61	13
Opponents	521	1920	3.7	57t	15

Receiving	No.	Yds.	Avg.	LG	TD
Stanley	38	672	17.7	70t	3
Neal	36	420	11.7	38	3
Epps	34	516	15.2	40	2
Clark	22	119	5.4	19	1
West	19	261	13.7	40	1
Le. Morris	16	259	16.2	46t	1
Davis	14	110	7.9	35	0
Paskett	12	188	15.7	47t	1
Carruth	10	78	7.8	19	1
Scott	8	79	9.9	16	0
Summers	7	83	11.9	17	1
Willhite	6	37	6.2	12	0
Parker	3	22	7.3	13	0
Thomas	2	52	26.0	30t	1
Harden	2	29	14.5	15	0
Fullwood	2	11	5.5	12	0
Redick	1	18	18.0	18	0
Weigel	1	17	17.0	17	0
Hargrove	1	6	6.0	6	0
Packers	234	2977	12.7	70t	15
Opponents	279	3200	11.5	63t	14

Interceptions	No.	Yds.	Avg.	LG	TD
J. Morris	3	135	45.0	73	0
D. Brown	3	16	5.3	11	0
J. Anderson	2	22	11.0	13	0
Holland	2	4	2.0	4	0
Mansfield	1	14	14.0	14	0
Greene	1	11	11.0	11	0
Noble	1	10	10.0	10	0
Carreker	1	6	6.0	6	0
K. Johnson	1	2	2.0	2	0
Harrison	1	0	0.0	0	0
Lee	1	0	0.0	0	0
Melka	1	0	0.0	0	0
Packers	18	220	12.2	73	0
Opponents	17	115	6.8	35t	1

Punting	No.	Yds.	Avg.	In 20	LG
Bracken	72	2947	40.9	13	65
Renner	20	712	35.6	4	49
Packers	93	3659	39.3	17	65
Opponents	77	3084	40.1	22	71

Punt Returns	No.	FC	Yds.	Avg.	LG	TD
Stanley	28	4	173	6.2	48	0
Scott	6	2	71	11.8	36	0
Le. Morris	1	0	1	1.0	1	0
Packers	35	6	245	7.0	48	0
Opponents	54	8	422	7.8	37	0

Kickoff Returns	No.	Yds.	Avg.	LG	TD
Fullwood	24	510	21.3	46	0
Cook	10	147	14.7	38	0
Le. Morris	6	104	17.3	28	0
Harden	4	72	18.0	20	0
Neal	4	44	11.0	18	0
Stanley	3	47	15.7	29	0
Jefferson	2	30	15.0	18	0
Scott	2	32	16.0	23	0
Carruth	1	8	8.0	8	0
Cherry	1	0	0.0	0	0
Sterling	1	0	0.0	0	0
Weishuhn	1	1	1.0	1	0
Willhite	0	37	—	37	0
Packers	59	1032	17.5	46	0
Opponents	61	1140	18.7	74	0

Sacks	No.
Harris	7.0
J. Anderson	4.0
Carreker	4.0
R. Brown	3.0
Boyarsky	2.0
Drost	2.0
E. Johnson	2.0
Murphy	2.0
Browner	1.0
Holland	1.0
K. Johnson	1.0
Jordan	1.0
Martin	1.0
J. Morris	1.0
Noble	1.0
Caldwell	0.5
Sullivan	0.5
Packers	34.0
Opponents	45.0

Green Bay Packers 1988 Veteran Roster

No.	Name	Pos.	Ht.	Wt.	Birth-date	NFL Exp.	College	Hometown	How Acq.	'87 Games/ Starts
59	Anderson, John	LB	6-3	228	2/14/56	11	Michigan	Waukesham, Wis.	D1b-'78	12/12
61	†Boyarsky, Jerry	NT	6-3	290	5/15/59	8	Pittsburgh	Scranton, Pa.	FA-'87	12/8
17	Bracken, Don	P	6-0	211	2/16/62	4	Michigan	Thermopolis, Wyo.	FA-'85	12/0
32	Brown, David	CB	6-1	197	1/16/53	14	Michigan	Akron, Ohio	T(Sea)-'87	12/12
93	†Brown, Robert	DE	6-2	267	5/21/60	7	Virginia Tech	Edenton, N.C.	D4-'82	12/12
79	†Browner, Ross	DE	6-3	265	3/22/54	11	Notre Dame	Warren, Ohio	FA-'87	11/2
58	†Cannon, Mark	C	6-3	258	6/14/62	5	Texas-Arlington	Austin, Tex.	D11-'84	12/12
76	†Carreker, Alphonso	DE	6-6	271	5/25/62	5	Florida State	Columbus, Ohio	D1-'84	12/12
30	Carruth, Paul Ott	RB	6-1	220	7/22/61	3	Alabama	McComb, Miss.	FA-'86	12/5
69	†Cherry, Bill	C-G	6-4	277	1/5/61	3	Middle Tennessee State	Dover, Tenn.	FA-'86	12/0
33	†Clark, Jessie	RB	6-0	228	1/3/60	6	Arkansas	Crossett, Ark.	D7-'83	12/10
64	Collier, Steve	T	6-7	342	4/19/63	2	Bethune-Cookman	Chicago, Ill.	FA-'87	10/6
20	Cook, Kelly	RB	5-10	225	8/20/62	2	Oklahoma State	Cushing, Okla.	FA-'87	11/0
36	Davis, Kenneth	RB	5-10	209	4/16/62	3	Texas Christian	Temple, Tex.	D2-'86	10/8
56	Dent, Burnell	LB	6-1	236	3/16/63	3	Tulane	St. Rose, La.	D6-'86	9/0
99	Dorsey, John	LB	6-2	243	8/31/60	5	Connecticut	Leonardtown, Md.	D4-'84	12/0
85	†Epps, Phillip	WR	5-10	165	11/11/59	7	Texas Christian	Atlanta, Tex.	D12-'82	10/9
21	Fullwood, Brent	RB	5-11	209	10/10/63	2	Auburn	St. Cloud, Fla.	D1-'87	11/1
23	†Greene, Tiger	CB-S	6-0	194	2/15/62	4	Western Carolina	Hendersonville, N.C.	FA-'86	11/1
89	Hackett, Joey	TE	6-5	267	9/29/58	3	Elon College	Greensboro, N.C.	FA-'87	11/0
65	†Hallstrom, Ron	G	6-6	290	6/11/59	7	Iowa	Moline, Ill.	D1-'82	12/12
97	Harris, Tim	LB	6-5	235	9/10/64	3	Memphis State	Birmingham, Ala.	D4a-'86	12/12
50	Holland, Johnny	LB	6-2	221	3/11/65	2	Texas A&M	Hempstead, Tex.	D2-'87	12/12
38	Jefferson, Norman	CB-S	5-10	183	8/7/64	2	Louisiana State	Marrero, La.	D12-'87	12/0
39	Johnson, Kenneth	CB	6-0	185	12/28/63	2	Mississippi State	Weir, Miss.	FA-'87	12/0
22	†Lee, Mark	CB-S	5-11	189	3/20/58	9	Washington	Hanford, Calif.	D2-'80	12/12
7	Majkowski, Don	QB	6-2	197	2/25/64	2	Virginia	Depew, N.Y.	D10-'87	7/5
44	Mandeville, Chris	S	6-1	213	2/1/65	2	California-Davis	Irvine, Calif.	FA-'87	4/0
98	†Moore, Brent	LB	6-5	242	1/9/63	2	Southern California	Novato, Calif.	D9-'86	4/0
57	†Moran, Rich	C-G	6-2	275	3/19/62	4	San Diego State	Pleasanton, Calif.	D3-'85	12/12
47	Morris, Jim Bob	CB-S	6-3	211	5/17/61	2	Kansas State	Hamilton, Kan.	FA-'87	11/2
81	Morris, Lee	WR	5-10	180	7/14/64	2	Oklahoma	Oklahoma City, Okla.	FA-'87	5/3
37	Murphy, Mark	S	6-2	201	4/22/58	7	West Liberty	Canton, Ohio	FA-'84	12/12
80	Neal, Frankie	WR	6-1	202	10/1/65	2	Fort Hays State	Okeechobee, Fla.	FA-'87	12/3
72	†Neville, Tom	T-G	6-5	306	9/4/61	3	Fresno State	Salcha, Alaska	FA-'86	12/0
91	†Noble, Brian	LB	6-3	252	9/6/62	4	Arizona State	Anaheim, Calif.	D5-'85	12/12
82	Paskett, Keith	WR	5-11	180	12/7/64	2	Western Kentucky	Nashville, Tenn.	FA-'87	12/0
77	Robison, Tommy	G	6-4	290	11/17/61	2	Texas A&M	Gregory, Tex.	T(Clev)-'85	3/0
75	Ruettgers, Ken	T	6-5	280	8/20/62	4	Southern California	Bakersfield, Calif.	D1-'85	12/12
83	Scott, Patrick	WR	5-10	170	9/13/64	2	Grambling	Ringgold, La.	FA-'87	8/3
87	†Stanley, Walter	WR-KR	5-9	179	11/5/62	4	Mesa College, Colo.	Chicago, Ill.	D4-'85	12/12
54	Stephen, Scott	LB	6-2	232	6/18/64	2	Arizona State	Los Angeles, Calif.	D3b-'87	8/0
29	Stills, Ken	CB-S	5-10	186	9/6/63	4	Wisconsin	Oceanside, Calif.	D8-'85	11/11
48	Summers, Don	TE	6-4	235	2/22/61	3	Boise State	Medford, Ore.	FA-'87	3/1
92	Thomas, Ben	DE-NT	6-4	275	7/2/61	3	Auburn	Ashburn, Ga.	W(NE)-'86	0*
70	Uecker, Keith	G-T	6-5	284	6/29/60	6	Auburn	Hollywood, Fla.	W(Den)-'84	8/8
73	†Veingrad, Alan	T-G	6-5	277	7/24/63	3	East Texas State	Miami, Fla.	FA-'86	11/2
28	Watts, Elbert	CB	6-1	205	3/20/63	2	Southern California	Carson, Calif.	W(Rams)-'86	0*
52	†Weddington, Mike	LB	6-4	245	10/9/60	3	Oklahoma	Temple, Tex.	FA-'86	12/0
51	Weishuhn, Clayton	LB	6-1	218	10/7/59	5	Angelo State	San Angelo, Tex.	FA-'87	9/0
86	West, Ed	TE	6-1	243	8/2/61	5	Auburn	Leighton, Ala.	FA-'84	12/11
35	Willhite, Kevin	RB	5-11	208	5/4/63	2	Oregon	Rancho Cordova, Calif.	FA-'87	3/3
68	t-Winter, Blaise	DE	6-3	274	1/31/62	4	Syracuse	Blauvelt, N.Y.	T(SD)-'88	3/3
16	†Wright, Randy	QB	6-2	203	1/12/61	5	Wisconsin	St. Charles, Ill.	D6-'84	9/7
8	Zendejas, Max	K	5-11	184	9/2/63	3	Arizona	Chino, Calif.	FA-'87	10/0

* Thomas and Watts missed '87 season due to injury.

†Option playout; subject to developments.

t-Packers traded for Winter (San Diego).

Also played with Packers in '87—LB Eric Anderson (3 games), LB Todd Auer (3), LB Warren Bone (1), NT David Caldwell (3), LB Putt Choate (2), CB-S Chuck Compton (2), K Al Del Greco (5), NT Jeff Drost (2), S Tony Elliott (1), G Mike Estep (1), TE Kevin Fitzgerald (1), QB Willie Gillus (1), T Bob Gruber (1), WR Derrick Harden (3), RB Jimmy Hargrove (2), S Anthony Harrison (3), G Perry Hartnett (1), CB-S Carlos Henderson (active for 1 game but did not play), G Jim Hobbins (3), RB Tony Hunter (1), TE Craig Jay (3), G Greg Jensen (1), DE Ezra Johnson (6), LB Kenneth Jordan (3), CB-S David King (3), T Ed Konopasek (3), DE Tony Leiker (1), TE Mark Lewis (1), NT Dave Logan (2), LB Rydell Malancon (3), CB-S Von Mansfield (3), DE Charles Martin (2), LB Stan Mataele (2), QB John McCarthy (active for 1 game but did not play), G John McGary (2), DE Sylvester McGrew (3), LB James Melka (1), T Jim Meyer (2), LB John Miller (1), LB Ron Monaco (2), RB Larry Morris (2), RB Freddie Parker (1), LB John Pointer (3), C Vince Rafferty (3), CB-S Louis Rash (3), WR Cornelius Redick (1), P Bill Renner (3), QB Alan Risher (3), C Travis Simpson (3), WR Wes Smith (1), RB John Sterling (2), DE Carl Sullivan (3), NT Vince Villanucci (2), DE Calvin Wallace (1), CB-S Charles Washington (3), RB Lee Weigel (2).

COACHING STAFF

Head Coach, Lindy Infante

Pro Career: Named Packers' head coach on February 3, 1988, after serving as offensive coordinator of Cleveland Browns in 1986-87. In that two-year span the Browns won more games (22) than any other team in the AFC. Was previously head coach of the Jacksonville Bulls (USFL) in 1984-85, compiling a 15-21 record. Earlier had been quarterback/receivers coach of the Cincinnati Bengals in 1980-81 and offensive coordinator in 1982, helping Bengals gain Super Bowl XVI in 1981 and compile the best record in the NFL over the 1981-82 seasons (19-6). Began pro coaching career with Charlotte Hornets (WFL) in 1975, later moving into the NFL with the New York Giants in 1978.

Background: Running back and defensive back at University of Florida (1960-62), winning second-team All-Southeastern Conference honors as senior, when he also was a team captain. Entered coaching at Miami High School (1965). College assistant at Florida 1966-71, Memphis State 1972-74, Tulane 1976, 1979.

Personal: Born May 27, 1940, in Miami, Fla. Attended Miami High School. He and his wife, Stephanie, live in Green Bay and have two sons, Brett, 16, and Brad, 15.

Assistant Coaches

Greg Blache, defensive line; born March 9, 1949, New Orleans, La., lives in Green Bay. No college or pro playing experience. College coach: Notre Dame 1973-75, 1981-83, Tulane 1976-80, Southern University 1986, Kansas 1987. Pro coach: Jacksonville (USFL) 1984-85, joined Packers in 1988.

Hank Bullough, defensive coordinator; born January 24, 1934, Scranton, Pa., lives in Green Bay. Offensive guard Michigan State 1952-54. Pro offensive guard Green Bay Packers 1955, 1958. College coach: Michigan State 1959-69. Pro coach: Baltimore Colts 1970-72, New England Patriots 1973-79, Cincinnati Bengals 1980-83, Pittsburgh Maulers (USFL) 1984-85, Buffalo Bills 1985-86 (compiled 4-17 record as head coach from October 1, 1985, through November 3, 1986), joined Packers in 1988.

Charlie Davis, offensive line; born August 7, 1944, San Diego, lives in Green Bay. Linebacker San Diego City College 1961, UCLA 1962-64. No pro playing experience. College coach: San Francisco State 1967-70, Xavier 1971-73, Ball State 1974-75, Tulane 1976-80. Pro coach: Jacksonville Bulls (USFL) 1984-85, Cleveland Browns 1986-87, joined Packers in 1988.

Buddy Geis, receivers; born September 16, 1946, Altoona, Pa., lives in Green Bay. Running back Lock Haven State 1967-69. No pro playing experience. College coach: Arizona 1973-76, Tulane 1977-82, Memphis State 1986-87. Pro coach: Jacksonville Bulls (USFL) 1984-85, joined Packers in 1988.

Dick Jauron, defensive backfield; born October 7, 1950, Swampscott, Mass., lives in Green Bay. Defensive back Yale 1970-72. Pro defensive back Detroit Lions 1973-77, Cincinnati Bengals 1978-80. Pro coach: Buffalo Bills 1985, joined Packers in 1986.

Virgil Knight, strength-conditioning; born January 30, 1948, Clarksville, Ark., lives in Green Bay. Tight end Northeastern Oklahoma 1968-70. No pro playing experience. College coach: Arkansas Tech 1975-78, Florida 1979-80, Auburn 1981-83. Pro coach: Joined Packers in 1984.

Dick Moseley, outside linebackers; born August 1, 1933, Detroit, Mich., lives in Green Bay. Running back-defensive back Eastern Michigan 1953-55. No pro playing experience. College coach: Eastern Michigan 1968-70, Wichita State 1971, Minnesota 1972-78, Colorado 1979-81. Pro coach: New Jersey Generals (USFL) 1982, Pittsburgh Maulers (USFL) 1983, Buffalo Bills 1984-85, Chicago Bruisers (Arena Football) 1987, joined Packers in 1988.

Green Bay Packers 1988 First-Year Roster

Name	Pos.	Ht.	Wt.	Birth-date	College	Hometown	How Acq.
Armentrout, Joe (1)	RB	6-0	225	11/4/64	Wisconsin	Elgin, Ill.	FA
Bolton, Scott	WR	6-0	188	1/4/65	Auburn	Theodore, Ala.	D12
Bosco, Robbie (1)	QB	6-2	198	1/11/63	Brigham Young	Roseville, Calif.	D3-'86
Cecil, Chuck	S	6-0	184	11/8/64	Arizona	San Diego, Calif.	D4b
Collins, Patrick	RB	5-10	185	8/4/66	Oklahoma	Tulsa, Okla.	D8
Croston, Dave (1)	T	6-5	280	11/10/63	Iowa	Sioux City, Iowa	D3a-'87
Drost, Jeff (1)	NT	6-5	286	1/27/64	Iowa	Indianola, Iowa	D8-'87
Elliott, Tony (1)	CB-S	5-10	195	1/10/64	Central Michigan	Detroit, Mich.	FA-'87
Fitzgerald, Pat (1)	WR	6-3	197	10/13/63	Boise State	Bellevue, Wash.	FA-'87
Harris, Gregg (1)	G	6-4	279	4/8/66	Wake Forest	Norfolk, Va.	D9-'87
Hill, Nate	DE	6-4	273	2/22/66	Auburn	LaGrange, Ga.	D6
Hopkins, Leonard	WR	6-1	190	9/8/64	Norfolk State	Richmond, Va.	FA
Kemp, C. Perry	WR	5-11	170	12/31/61	California State, Pa.	Canonsburg, Pa.	FA
Keyes, Bud	QB	6-2	211	3/3/66	Wisconsin	Green Bay, Wis.	D10
King, Don (1)	CB-S	5-11	200	2/10/64	Southern Methodist	Dallas, Tex.	FA-'87
Marshall, Willie (1)	WR	6-1	190	5/23/64	Temple	Browns Mill, N.J.	D6-'87
Mataele, Stan (1)	NT	6-2	290	6/24/63	Arizona	Laie, Hawaii	FA
Mayes, Tony	CB-S	6-0	195	5/19/64	Kentucky	Paintsville, Ky.	FA
Nelson, Bob	NT	6-4	275	3/3/59	Miami	Baltimore, Md.	FA
Patterson, Shawn	NT-DE	6-5	261	4/6/65	Arizona State	Tempe, Ariz.	D2
Porell, Thomas	NT-DE	6-3	275	9/23/64	Boston College	Winchester, Mass.	FA
Putzier, Rollin	NT	6-4	279	12/10/65	Oregon	Post Falls, Idaho	D4a
Reed, Darrell	LB	6-1	225	7/28/65	Oklahoma	Cypress, Tex.	D5
Richard, Gary	CB	5-9	171	10/9/65	Pittsburgh	Denver, Colo.	D7
Sharpe, Sterling	WR-KR	5-11	202	4/6/65	South Carolina	Glennville, Ga.	D1
Thomas, Lavale (1)	RB	6-0	205	12/12/63	Fresno State	Tulare, Calif.	FA-'87
Twombly, Darren	C-G	6-4	270	5/14/65	Boston College	Manchester, Mass.	FA
Walter, David	QB	6-3	220	12/9/64	Michigan Tech	Sanford, Mich.	FA
Wilkinson, Neal	TE	6-5	226	10/2/64	James Madison	Annandale, Va.	D9
Woodside, Keith	RB	5-11	203	7/29/64	Texas A&M	Vidalia, La.	D3

The term NFL Rookie is defined as a player who is in his first season of professional football and has not been on the roster of another professional football team for any regular-season or postseason games. A Rookie is designated by an "R" on NFL rosters. Players who have been active in another professional football league or players who have NFL experience, including either preseason training camp or being on an active roster for fewer than three regular-season or postseason games, are termed NFL First-Year Players. An NFL First-Year Player is designated by a "1" on NFL rosters. Thereafter, a player on an NFL active roster for at least three regular-season or postseason games is credited with an additional year of NFL playing experience.

NOTES

Willie Peete, offensive backfield; born July 14, 1937, Mesa, Ariz., lives in Green Bay. Tight end-defensive end Arizona 1956-59. No pro playing experience. College coach: Arizona 1960-62, 1971-82. Pro coach: Kansas City Chiefs 1983-86, joined Packers in 1987.

Howard Tippett, special teams; born September 23, 1938, Tallassee, Ala., lives in Green Bay. Quarterback/safety East Tennessee State 1956-58. No pro playing experience. College coach: Tulane 1963-65, West Virginia 1966, 1970-71, Houston 1967-69, Washington State 1976, UCLA 1980, Illinois 1987. Pro coach: Jacksonville Express (WFL) 1974-75, Tampa Bay Buccaneers 1981-86, joined Packers in 1988.

National Football Conference Western Division

Team Colors: Royal Blue, Gold, and White

Business Address:
2327 West Lincoln Avenue
Anaheim, California 92801

Ticket Office:
Anaheim Stadium
1900 State College Boulevard
Anaheim, California 92806
Telephone: (714) 535-7267
or (213) 585-5400

Club Officials

President: Georgia Frontiere
Vice President, Finance: John Shaw
General Counsel: Jay Zygmunt
Administrator, Football Operations: Jack Faulkner
Director of Operations: Dick Beam
Director of Player Personnel: John Math
Administrative Assistant/Consultant: Paul (Tank) Younger
Administration: Jack Youngblood
Director of Community Relations: Marshall Klein
Director of Administration: Barbara Robinson
Director of Promotions/Sales: Pete Donovan
Director of Public Relations: John Oswald
Public Relations Assistant: Doug Ward
Trainers: George Menefee, Jim Anderson, Garrett Giemont
Equipment Managers: Don Hewitt, Todd Hewitt

Stadium: Anaheim Stadium • **Capacity:** 69,007
Anaheim, California 92806

Playing Surface: Grass

Training Camp: Cal State-Fullerton
Fullerton, California 92634

1988 Schedule

Preseason

July 30	vs. Cincinnati at Canton, Ohio	2:30
Aug. 3	**Denver**	7:00
Aug. 13	**San Diego**	8:00
Aug. 20	**Houston**	7:00
Aug. 26	at San Diego	8:00

Regular Season

Sept. 4	at Green Bay	12:00
Sept. 11	**Detroit**	1:00
Sept. 18	at Los Angeles Raiders	1:00
Sept. 25	at New York Giants	4:00
Oct. 2	**Phoenix**	1:00
Oct. 9	at Atlanta	1:00
Oct. 16	**San Francisco**	1:00
Oct. 23	**Seattle**	1:00
Oct. 30	at New Orleans	12:00
Nov. 6	at Philadelphia	1:00
Nov. 13	**New Orleans**	1:00
Nov. 20	**San Diego**	1:00
Nov. 27	at Denver	2:00
Dec. 5	**Chicago** (Monday)	6:00
Dec. 11	**Atlanta**	1:00
Dec. 18	at San Francisco	5:00

Rams Coaching History

Cleveland 1937-45
(365-299-20)

1937-38	Hugo Bezdek*	1-13-0
1938	Art Lewis	4-4-0
1939-42	Earl (Dutch) Clark	16-26-2
1944	Aldo (Buff) Donelli	4-6-0
1945-46	Adam Walsh	16-5-1
1947	Bob Snyder	6-6-0
1948-49	Clark Shaughnessy	14-8-3
1950-52	Joe Stydahar**	19-9-0
1952-54	Hamp Pool	23-11-2
1955-59	Sid Gillman	28-32-1
1960-62	Bob Waterfield***	9-24-1
1962-65	Harland Svare	14-31-3
1966-70	George Allen	49-19-4
1971-72	Tommy Prothro	14-12-2
1973-77	Chuck Knox	57-20-1
1978-82	Ray Malavasi	43-36-0
1983-87	John Robinson	48-37-0

*Released after three games in 1938
**Resigned after one game in 1952
***Resigned after eight games in 1962

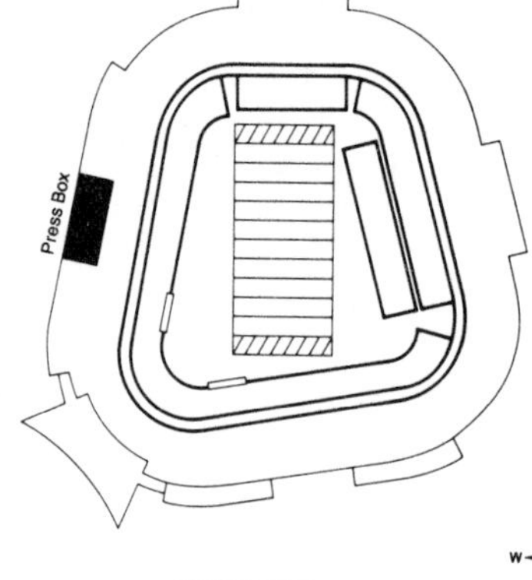

ANAHEIM STADIUM

Record Holders

Individual Records—Career

Category	Name	Performance
Rushing (Yds.)	Eric Dickerson, 1983-87	7,245
Passing (Yds.)	Roman Gabriel, 1962-1972	22,223
Passing (TDs)	Roman Gabriel, 1962-1972	154
Receiving (No.)	Tom Fears, 1948-1956	400
Receiving (Yds.)	Elroy (Crazylegs) Hirsch, 1949-1957	6,289
Interceptions	Ed Meador, 1959-1970	46
Punting (Avg.)	Danny Villanueva, 1960-64	44.2
Punt Return (Avg.)	Henry Ellard, 1983-87	12.1
Kickoff Return (Avg.)	Tom Wilson, 1956-1961	27.1
Field Goals	Bruce Gossett, 1964-69	120
Touchdowns (Tot.)	Eric Dickerson, 1983-87	58
Points	Bob Waterfield, 1946-1952	573

Individual Records—Single Season

Category	Name	Performance
Rushing (Yds.)	Eric Dickerson, 1984	*2,105
Passing (Yds.)	Vince Ferragamo, 1983	3,276
Passing (TDs)	Vince Ferragamo, 1980	30
Receiving (No.)	Tom Fears, 1950	84
Receiving (Yds.)	Elroy (Crazylegs) Hirsch, 1951	1,425
Interceptions	Dick (Night Train) Lane, 1952	*14
Punting (Avg.)	Danny Villanueva, 1962	45.5
Punt Return (Avg.)	Woodley Lewis, 1952	18.5
Kickoff Return (Avg.)	Verda (Vitamin T) Smith, 1950	33.7
Field Goals	David Ray, 1973	30
Touchdowns (Tot.)	Eric Dickerson, 1983	20
Points	David Ray, 1973	130

Individual Records—Single Game

Category	Name	Performance
Rushing (Yds.)	Eric Dickerson, 1-4-86	248
Passing (Yds.)	Norm Van Brocklin, 9-28-51	*554
Passing (TDs)	Many times	5
	Last time by Vince Ferragamo, 10-23-83	
Receiving (No.)	Tom Fears, 12-3-50	*18
Receiving (Yds.)	Jim Benton, 11-22-45	303
Interceptions	Many times	3
	Last time by Pat Thomas, 10-7-79	
Field Goals	Bob Waterfield, 12-9-51	5
Touchdowns (Tot.)	Bob Shaw, 12-11-49	4
	Elroy (Crazylegs) Hirsch, 9-28-51	4
	Harold Jackson, 10-14-73	4
Points	Bob Shaw, 12-11-49	24
	Elroy (Crazylegs) Hirsch, 9-28-51	24
	Harold Jackson, 10-14-73	24

*NFL Record

1987 Team Record

Preseason (3-2)

Date	Result		Opponents
8/9	W	28-27	vs. Denver at London, England
8/13	W	23-14	Seattle
8/23	W	23-21	at San Diego
8/29	L	20-24	Denver
9/3	L	14-26	Washington
		108-112	

Regular Season (6-9)

Date	Result		Opponents	Att.
9/13	L	16-20	at Houston	33,186
9/20	L	16-21	Minnesota	63,367
9/27	C		Cincinnati	
10/4	L	10-37	at New Orleans	29,745
10/11	W	31-21	Pittsburgh	20,219
10/18	L	20-24	at Atlanta	15,813
10/26	L	17-30	at Cleveland	76,933
11/1	L	10-31	San Francisco	55,328
11/8	L	14-31	New Orleans	43,379
11/15	W	27-24	at St. Louis	27,730
11/23	W	30-26	at Washington	53,614
11/29	W	35- 3	Tampa Bay	45,188
12/6	W	37-16	at Detroit	33,413
12/13	W	33- 0	Atlanta	43,310
12/21	L	21-29	Dallas	60,700
12/27	L	0-48	at San Francisco	57,950

C (Cancelled due to players' strike.)

Score by Periods

Rams	77	92	88	60	0	—	317
Opponents	79	132	57	93	0	—	361

Attendance

Home 331,491 Away 328,384 Total 659,875
Single-game home record, 102,368 (11-10-57; L.A. Coliseum), 67,037 (12-23-84; Anaheim Stadium)
Single-season home record, 519,175 (1973; L.A. Coliseum), 500,403 (1980; Anaheim Stadium)

1987 Team Statistics

	Rams	Opp.
Total First Downs	276	279
Rushing	118	95
Passing	136	162
Penalty	22	22
Third Down: Made/Att.	75/204	77/203
Fourth Down: Made/Att.	4/17	3/8
Total Net Yards	4651	5121
Avg. Per Game	310.1	341.4
Total Plays	957	961
Avg. Per Play	4.9	5.3
Net Yards Rushing	2097	1732
Avg. Per Game	139.8	115.5
Total Rushes	512	419
Net Yards Passing	2554	3389
Avg. Per Game	170.3	225.9
Sacked/Yards Lost	25/196	38/304
Gross Yards	2750	3693
Att./Completions	420/220	504/281
Completion Pct.	52.4	55.8
Had Intercepted	18	16
Punts/Avg.	77/40.8	83/37.3
Net Punting Avg.	35.6	33.2
Penalties/Yards Lost	91/677	100/888
Fumbles/Ball Lost	26/15	28/11
Touchdowns	38	43
Rushing	15	8
Passing	16	31
Returns	7	4
Avg. Time of Possession	29:59	30:01

1987 Individual Statistics

Scoring

Scoring	TD R	TD P	TD Rt	PAT	FG	Saf	TP
Lansford	0	0	0	36/38	17/21	0	87
White	11	0	0	0/0	0/0	0	66
Ro. Brown	0	2	1	0/0	0/0	0	18
Ellard	0	3	0	0/0	0/0	0	18
Baty, N.E.-Rams	0	2	0	0/0	0/0	0	12
Francis	0	2	0	0/0	0/0	0	12
D. Johnson	0	2	0	0/0	0/0	0	12
J. McDonald	0	2	0	0/0	0/0	0	12
Bell	0	1	0	0/0	0/0	0	6
Dickerson	1	0	0	0/0	0/0	0	6
Everett	1	0	0	0/0	0/0	0	6
Gray	0	0	1	0/0	0/0	0	6
Greene	0	0	1	0/0	0/0	0	6
Guman	1	0	0	0/0	0/0	0	6
House	0	1	0	0/0	0/0	0	6
Irvin	0	0	1	0/0	0/0	0	6
Jackson	0	0	1	0/0	0/0	0	6
J. Johnson	0	0	1	0/0	0/0	0	6
McGee	1	0	0	0/0	0/0	0	6
Mobley	0	1	0	0/0	0/0	0	6
Moore	0	1	0	0/0	0/0	0	6
Wilcher	0	0	1	0/0	0/0	0	6
Young	0	1	0	0/0	0/0	0	6
Stewart	0	0	0	0/0	0/0	1	2
Rams	15	16	7	36/38	17/21	1	317
Opponents	8	31	4	40/43	21/24	0	361

Passing

Passing	Att.	Comp.	Yds.	Pct.	TD	Int.	Tkld.	Rate
Everett	302	162	2064	53.6	10	13	17/139	68.4
Dils	114	56	646	49.1	5	4	7/51	66.6
Quarles	3	1	40	33.3	1	1	0/0	81.9
Millen	1	1	0	100.0	0	0	1/6	79.2
Rams	420	220	2750	52.4	16	18	25/196	67.9
Opponents	504	281	3693	55.8	31	16	38/304	86.4

Rushing

Rushing	Att.	Yds.	Avg.	LG	TD
White	324	1374	4.2	58	11
Dickerson	60	277	4.6	57	1
Francis	35	138	3.9	23	0
Guman	36	98	2.7	7	1
Bell, Buff.-Rams	22	86	3.9	13	0
Bell, Rams	8	26	3.3	13	0
Everett	18	83	4.6	16	1
Tyrrell	11	44	4.0	13	0
Ro. Brown	2	22	11.0	11	0
Evans	3	10	3.3	5	0
Williams	2	9	4.5	7	0
Quarles	1	8	8.0	8	0
McGee	3	6	2.0	2t	1
Ellard	1	4	4.0	4	0
Bryant	1	2	2.0	2	0
Dils	7	−4	−0.6	5	0
Rams	512	2097	4.1	58	15
Opponents	419	1732	4.1	46	8

Receiving

Receiving	No.	Yds.	Avg.	LG	TD
Ellard	51	799	15.7	81t	3
Ro. Brown	26	521	20.0	52	2
White	23	121	5.3	20	0
Guman	22	263	12.0	33	0
D. Johnson	21	198	9.4	20	2
Baty, N.E.-Rams	18	175	9.7	22	2
Baty, Rams	3	37	12.3	20	0
Hill	11	105	9.5	24	0
Bell, Buff.-Rams	9	96	10.7	32t	1
Bell, Rams	5	59	11.8	32t	1
Mobley	8	107	13.4	40t	1
Francis	8	38	4.8	7	2
McGee	7	40	5.7	12	0
Moore	6	107	17.8	26	1
House	6	63	10.5	15t	1
Tyrrell	6	59	9.8	16	0
Dickerson	5	38	7.6	13	0
Young	4	56	14.0	26	1
J. McDonald	4	31	7.8	13	2
P. Smith	3	95	31.7	51	0
Henry	1	13	13.0	13	0
Rams	220	2750	12.5	81t	16
Opponents	281	3693	13.1	82t	31

Interceptions

Interceptions	No.	Yds.	Avg.	LG	TD
Irvin	2	47	23.5	47t	1
Gray	2	35	17.5	35	0
Cromwell	2	28	14.0	28	0
H. Johnson	1	49	49.0	49	0
Jackson	1	36	36.0	36	0
Williamson	1	28	28.0	28	0
Owens	1	26	26.0	26	0
Greene	1	25	25.0	25t	1
Wilcher	1	11	11.0	11	0
Hicks	1	9	9.0	9	0
Ekern	1	7	7.0	7	0
Sutton	1	4	4.0	4	0
J. Johnson	1	0	0.0	0	0
Rams	16	305	19.1	49	2
Opponents	18	226	12.6	68	1

Punting

Punting	No.	Yds.	Avg.	In 20	LG
Hatcher	76	3140	41.3	19	62
Rams	77	3140	40.8	19	62
Opponents	83	3097	37.3	21	56

Punt Returns

Punt Returns	No.	FC	Yds.	Avg.	LG	TD
Ellard	15	6	107	7.1	29	0
Hicks	13	1	110	8.5	26	0
S. Johnson	4	1	−4	−1.0	5	0
Rutledge	3	0	10	3.3	7	0
P. Smith	2	0	5	2.5	5	0
Irvin	1	0	0	0.0	0	0
J. Johnson	1	0	5	5.0	5	0
Mobley	1	0	12	12.0	12	0
Sutton	0	2	0	—	0	0
Rams	40	10	245	6.1	29	0
Opponents	43	10	317	7.4	48	0

Kickoff Returns

Kickoff Returns	No.	Yds.	Avg.	LG	TD
Ro. Brown	27	581	21.5	95t	1
Tiumalu	8	158	19.8	25	0
Adams, Dall.-Rams	6	113	18.8	27	0
Tyrrell	6	116	19.3	30	0
Williams	5	114	22.8	47	0
Hicks	4	119	29.8	53	0
M. McDonald	3	31	10.3	15	0
White	3	73	24.3	26	0
Guman	2	18	9.0	12	0
Sutton	2	37	18.5	19	0
Ri. Brown	1	15	15.0	15	0
Cox	1	12	12.0	12	0
Ellard	1	8	8.0	8	0
Rams	63	1282	20.3	95t	1
Opponents	57	1112	19.5	71	0

Sacks

Sacks	No.
Jeter	7.0
Greene	6.5
Miller	6.0
Wilcher	5.0
Meisner	3.0
Borland	2.0
Reed	2.0
Wright	2.0
Collins	1.0
Cromwell	1.0
Edwards	1.0
Owens	1.0
Stokes	0.5
Rams	38.0
Opponents	25.0

Los Angeles Rams 1988 Veteran Roster

No.	Name	Pos.	Ht.	Wt.	Birth-date	NFL Exp.	College	Hometown	How Acq.	'87 Games/ Starts
31	Adams, David	RB	5-6	170	6/24/64	2	Arizona	Tucson, Ariz.	FA-'88	3/0*
84	†Baty, Greg	TE	6-5	241	8/28/64	3	Stanford	Sparta, N.J.	W(NE)-'87	9/0*
42	†Bell, Greg	RB	5-10	210	8/1/62	5	Notre Dame	Columbus, Ohio	T(Buff)-'87	4/3*
92	Brown, Richard	LB	6-3	240	9/21/65	2	San Diego State	Westminster, Calif.	FA-'87	8/0
50	Collins, Jim	LB	6-2	230	6/11/58	7	Syracuse	Mendham, N.J.	D2-'81	15/15
72	Cox, Robert	T	6-5	258	12/30/63	2	UCLA	Dublin, Calif.	D6a-'86	10/0
21	†Cromwell, Nolan	S	6-1	200	1/30/55	12	Kansas	Ransom, Kan.	D2-'77	15/8
8	Dils, Steve	QB	6-1	191	12/8/55	10	Stanford	Vancouver, Wash.	T(Minn)-'84	15/4
55	Ekern, Carl	LB	6-3	222	5/27/54	12	San Jose State	Sunnyvale, Calif.	D5-'76	11/11
80	Ellard, Henry	WR	5-11	175	7/21/61	6	Fresno State	Fresno, Calif.	D2-'83	12/12
11	Everett, Jim	QB	6-5	212	1/3/63	3	Purdue	Albuquerque, N.M.	T(Hou)-'86	11/11
35	Francis, Jon	RB	5-11	207	6/21/64	2	Boise State	Corvallis, Ore.	FA-'87	9/0
19	Gaynor, Doug	QB	6-2	205	7/5/63	2	Long Beach State	Fresno, Calif.	FA-'88	0*
25	Gray, Jerry	CB	6-0	185	12/2/62	4	Texas	Lubbock, Tex.	D1-'85	12/12
91	†Greene, Kevin	LB	6-3	238	7/31/62	4	Auburn	Granite City, Ill.	D5-'85	9/0
44	Guman, Mike	RB	6-2	218	4/21/58	9	Penn State	Bethlehem, Pa.	D6-'80	12/8
5	†Hatcher, Dale	P	6-2	200	4/5/63	4	Clemson	Cheraw, S.C.	D3-'85	15/0
38	Heimuli, Lakei	RB	5-11	219	6/24/65	2	Brigham Young	Laie, Hawaii	FA-'87	3/3*
28	Hicks, Cliff	CB	5-10	188	8/18/64	2	Oregon	San Diego, Calif.	D3-'87	11/0
81	t-Holohan, Pete	TE	6-4	232	7/25/59	8	Notre Dame	Liverpool, N.Y.	T(SD)-'88	12/4
83	†House, Kevin	WR	6-1	185	12/20/57	9	Southern Illinois	St. Louis, Mo.	W(TB)-'86	12/1
47	Irvin, LeRoy	CB	5-11	184	9/15/57	9	Kansas	Augusta, Ga.	D5-'80	10/9
59	†Jerue, Mark	LB	6-3	232	1/15/60	6	Washington	Seattle, Wash.	T(Ind)-'83	4/0
77	Jeter, Gary	DE	6-4	260	3/24/55	12	Southern California	Cleveland, Ohio	T(NYG)-'83	12/0
86	†Johnson, Damone	TE	6-4	230	3/2/62	3	Cal Poly-SLO	Santa Monica, Calif.	D6-'85	12/5
20	Johnson, Johnnie	S	6-1	183	10/8/56	9	Texas	LaGrange, Tex.	D1-'80	7/7
52	Kelm, Larry	LB	6-4	226	11/29/64	2	Texas A&M	Corpus Christi, Tex.	D4-'87	12/1
1	Lansford, Mike	K	6-0	183	7/20/58	7	Washington	Arcadia, Calif.	FA-'82	15/0
67	Love, Duval	G	6-3	263	6/24/63	4	UCLA	Fountain Valley, Calif.	D10-'85	10/4
90	McDonald, Mike	LB	6-1	235	6/22/58	4	Southern California	Burbank, Calif.	FA-'88	10/0
24	McGee, Buford	RB	6-0	206	8/16/60	5	Mississippi	Durant, Miss.	T(SD)-'87	3/1
69	†Meisner, Greg	NT	6-3	253	4/23/59	8	Pittsburgh	New Kensington, Pa.	D3-'81	15/15
98	†Miller, Shawn	NT	6-4	255	3/14/61	5	Utah State	Ogden, Utah	FA-'84	6/6
45	Moore, Malcolm	TE	6-3	236	6/24/61	2	Southern California	Los Angeles, Calif.	FA-'88	3/1
66	Newberry, Tom	G	6-2	279	12/20/62	3	Wisconsin-LaCrosse	Onalaska, Wis.	D2-'86	12/12
22	Newsome, Vince	S	6-1	179	1/22/61	6	Washington	Vacaville, Calif.	D4-'83	8/8
58	†Owens, Mel	LB	6-2	224	12/7/58	8	Michigan	Detroit, Mich.	D1-'81	12/12
75	Pankey, Irv	T	6-4	267	12/15/58	9	Penn State	Aberdeen, Pa.	D2-'80	12/12
93	†Reed, Doug	DE	6-3	262	7/16/60	5	San Diego State	San Diego, Calif.	D4-'83	12/12
78	Slater, Jackie	T	6-4	271	5/27/54	13	Jackson State	Meridian, Miss.	D3-'76	12/12
61	Slaton, Tony	C	6-3	265	4/12/61	4	Southern California	Merced, Calif.	FA-'84	11/0
56	Smith, Doug	C	6-3	260	11/25/56	11	Bowling Green	Columbus, Ohio	FA-'78	12/12
23	Stewart, Michael	S	5-11	195	7/21/65	2	Fresno State	Bakersfield, Calif.	D8-'87	12/4
65	Stokes, Fred	DE	6-3	262	3/14/64	2	Georgia Southern	Vidalia, Ga.	D12-'86	8/0
49	†Sutton, Mickey	CB	5-8	165	8/28/60	3	Montana	Union City, Calif.	FA-'86	12/3
70	Teafatiller, Guy	NT	6-2	285	5/10/64	2	Illinois	Downey, Calif.	FA-'88	3/2*
68	Tuiasosopo, Navy	C	6-2	285	5/24/64	2	Utah State	Carson, Calif.	FA-'88	3/3
32	†Tyrrell, Tim	RB	6-1	201	2/19/61	5	Northern Illinois	Hoffman Estates, Ill.	FA-'86	11/0
51	†Vann, Norwood	LB	6-1	237	2/18/62	5	East Carolina	Magnolia, S.C.	D10-'84	11/0
73	Walker, Jeff	T	6-4	295	1/22/63	2	Memphis State	Olive Branch, Miss.	T(SD)-'87	0*
41	Wattelet, Frank	S	6-0	190	10/25/58	8	Kansas	Abilene, Kan.	FA-'87	7/0*
33	White, Charles	RB	5-10	190	1/22/58	8	Southern California	Los Angeles, Calif.	FA-'85	15/12
54	†Wilcher, Mike	LB	6-3	235	3/20/60	6	North Carolina	Washington, D.C.	D2-'83	12/12
99	†Wright, Alvin	NT	6-2	265	2/5/61	3	Jacksonville State	Nedonee, Ala.	FA-'86	15/3
88	Young, Michael	WR	6-1	185	2/2/62	4	UCLA	Visalia, Calif.	D6-'85	12/0

* Adams played 3 games with Dallas in '87; Baty played 5 games with New England, 4 with L.A. Rams; Bell played 2 games with Buffalo, 2 with L.A. Rams; Gaynor last active with Cincinnati in '86; Heimuli played 3 games with Chicago; Teafatiller played 3 games with Chicago; Walker missed '87 season due to injury; Wattelet played 2 games with New Orleans, 5 with L.A. Rams.

†Option playout; subject to developments.

t-Rams traded for Holohan (San Diego).

Retired—Ron Brown, 4-year wide receiver, 12 games in '87; Dennis Harrah, 13-year guard, 8 games in '87.

Also played with Rams in '87—LB Sam Anno (3 games), LB David Aupiu (1), LB Kyle Borland (2), RB Cullen Bryant (3), LB Dan Clark (1), T Tom Cox (3), LB Rick DiBernardo (3), RB Eric Dickerson (3), DE Reggie Doss (12), NT Dennis Edwards (3), TE Jon Embree (1), DE Donald Evans (1), RB Owen Gill (1), T Hank Goebel (3), CB-S Darryl Hall (1), WR Bernard Henry (3), DE Tom Hensley (active for 1 game but did not play), TE David Hill (12), LB Neil Hope (3), CB Kirby Jackson (5), WR Samuel Johnson (3), LB Jim Kalafat (1), NT Marion Knight (2), WR Steve Marks (active for 1 game but did not play), G Chris Matau (3), TE James McDonald (5), WR Stacey Mobley (3), G-T Joe Murray (3), TE Don Noble (2), NT Christopher Pacheco (3), NT Dave Purling (1), S Reggie Richardson (3), TE Joe Rose (1), S Craig Rutledge (3), T Greg Sinnott (1), LB Tommy Taylor (3), T Kelly Thomas (3), RB Casey Tiumalu (3), LB Cary Whittingham (3), LB Kyle Whittingham (3), RB Alonzo Williams (3), CB Greg Williamson (3), CB-S Ed Zeman (3).

COACHING STAFF

Head Coach, John Robinson

Pro Career: Begins his sixth season as Rams head coach, most ever by any coach in team history. Has guided team to playoffs in four out of last five seasons. Became seventeenth head coach in club history on February 14, 1983. Arrived with 23 years of coaching experience, including one on professional level with the Raiders in 1975. No pro playing experience. Career record: 48-37.

Background: Played end at Oregon 1955-58. Began coaching career with his alma mater from 1960-71. Became an assistant at Southern California from 1972-74. Returned as head coach in 1976 before resigning after the 1982 season. Compiled seven-year .819 winning percentage at Southern California with 67 wins, 14 losses, and 2 ties.

Personal: Born July 25, 1935, in Chicago, Ill. John and his wife, Barbara, live in Fullerton, Calif., and have four children—Teresa, Lynn, David, and Christopher.

Assistant Coaches

Larry Brooks, assistant defensive line; born June 10, 1950, Prince George, Va., lives in Fountain Valley, Calif. Defensive tackle Virginia State 1968-71. Pro defensive tackle Los Angeles Rams 1972-82. Pro coach: Joined Rams in 1983.

Dick Coury, quarterbacks; born September 29, 1929, Athens, Ohio, lives in Anaheim, Calif. No college or pro playing experience. College coach: Southern California 1965-67, Cal State-Fullerton 1968-70 (head coach). Pro coach: Denver Broncos 1971-73, Portland Storm (WFL) 1974 (head coach), San Diego Chargers 1975, Philadelphia Eagles 1976-81, Boston/Portland Breakers (USFL) 1983-85 (head coach), joined Rams in 1986.

Artie Gigantino, special teams; born June 14, 1951, Edison, N.J., lives in Anaheim, Calif. Linebacker Bridgeport 1969-72. No pro playing experience. College coach: California 1973-78, Southern California 1979-86. Pro coach: Joined the Rams in 1987.

Marv Goux, defensive line; born September 8, 1932, Santa Barbara, Calif., lives in Long Beach, Calif. Linebacker Southern California 1952, 1954-55. No pro playing experience. College coach: Southern California 1957-82. Pro coach: Joined Rams in 1983.

Gil Haskell, running backs; born September 24, 1943, San Francisco, Calif., lives in Diamond Bar, Calif. Defensive back San Francisco State 1961, 1963-65. No pro playing experience. College coach: Southern California 1978-82. Pro coach: Joined Rams in 1983.

Hudson Houck, offensive line; born January 7, 1943, Los Angeles, Calif., lives in Long Beach, Calif. Center Southern California 1962-64. No pro playing experience. College coach: Southern California 1970-72, 1976-82, Stanford 1973-75. Pro coach: Joined Rams in 1983.

Steve Shafer, defensive backs; born December 8, 1940, Glendale, Calif., lives in Laguna Niguel, Calif. Quarterback-defensive back Utah State 1961-62. Pro defensive back British Columbia Lions (CFL) 1963-67. College coach: San Mateo, Calif., J.C. 1968-74 (head coach 1973-74), San Diego State 1975-82. Pro coach: Joined Rams in 1983.

Fritz Shurmur, defensive coordinator-inside linebackers; born July 15, 1932, Riverview, Mich., lives in Diamond Bar, Calif. Center Albion 1951-53. No pro playing experience. College coach: Albion 1956-61, Wyoming 1962-74 (head coach 1971-74). Pro coach: Detroit Lions 1975-77, New England Patriots 1978-81, joined Rams in 1982.

Norval Turner, tight ends-wide receivers; born May 17, 1952, Martinez, Calif., lives in Huntington Beach, Calif. Quarterback Oregon 1972-74. No pro playing experience. College coach: Oregon 1975, Southern California 1976-84. Pro coach: Joined Rams in 1985.

Fred Whittingham, outside linebackers; born February 4, 1942, Boston, Mass., lives in Anaheim, Calif. Linebacker Cal Poly-SLO 1960-62. Pro linebacker Los Angeles Rams 1964, Philadelphia Eagles 1965-66, 1971, New Orleans Saints 1967-68, Dallas Cowboys 1969-70. College coach: Brigham Young 1973-81. Pro coach: Joined Rams in 1982.

Ernie Zampese, offensive coordinator; born March 12, 1936, Santa Barbara, Calif., lives in Anaheim, Calif. Halfback Southern California 1956-58. No pro playing experience. College coach: Hancock, Calif., J.C. 1962-65, Cal Poly-SLO 1966, San Diego State 1967-75. Pro coach: San Diego Chargers 1976, 1979-86, New York Jets 1977-78 (scout), joined Rams in 1987.

Los Angeles Rams 1988 First-Year Roster

Name	Pos.	Ht.	Wt.	Birth-date	College	Hometown	How Acq.
Anderson, Gary	C-G	6-4	265	2/19/64	Utah	Salt Lake City, Utah	FA
Anderson, Willie	WR	6-0	169	3/7/65	UCLA	Paulsboro, N.J.	D2b
Beathard, Jeff	RB	5-9	190	6/9/64	Southern Oregon St.	Vienna, Va.	D12
Brookhart, Joe	WR	5-11	195	10/17/64	Colorado State	Englewood, Colo.	FA
Cox, Aaron	WR	5-9	174	3/13/65	Arizona State	Los Angeles, Calif.	D1b
Delpino, Robert	RB	6-0	198	11/2/65	Missouri	Dodge City, Kan.	D5a
Diaz-Infante, David (1)	C-G	6-2	280	3/31/64	San Jose State	San Jose, Calif.	FA
Esene, Levi (1)	NT	5-11	270	7/31/63	San Diego State	Nanakuli, Hawaii	FA
Foster, Pat	DE	6-5	255	12/2/64	Montana	Savage, Mont.	D9
Franklin, Darryl	WR	5-10	187	2/4/65	Washington	Tacoma, Wash.	D8
Frasch, Phillip	S-CB	6-3	200	7/19/66	Bakersfield J.C.	Bakersfield, Calif.	FA
Glenn, Ledell	CB	5-11	185	7/28/63	Oklahoma	Santa Ana, Calif.	FA
Green, Gaston	RB	5-10	189	8/1/66	UCLA	Gardena, Calif.	D1a
Henley, Thomas (1)	WR	5-10	180	7/28/65	Stanford	LaVerne, Calif.	FA
Jones, Keith	RB	5-9	179	2/5/66	Nebraska	Omaha, Neb.	D6a
Knapton, Jeff	NT	6-5	236	8/28/66	Wyoming	Yuma, Colo.	D6b
Lambert, Darren	LB	5-9	170	8/31/65	Brigham Young	Las Vegas, Nev.	FA
Millen, Hugh (1)	QB	6-5	216	11/22/63	Washington	Seattle, Wash.	D3-'86
Mullin, R.C.	T	6-6	316	6/28/65	S.W. Louisiana	Port Arthur, Tex.	D10
Myers, Bryan (1)	P	6-2	200	9/29/59	Ball State	Fort Wayne, Ind.	FA
Newman, Anthony	S-CB	6-0	199	11/21/65	Oregon	Beaverton, Ore.	D2a
Nicholas, Rey	WR	6-1	185	2/6/65	California	San Diego, Calif.	FA
Piel, Mike	NT	6-4	263	9/21/65	Illinois	El Toro, Calif.	D3
Quarles, Bernard (1)	QB	6-2	215	1/4/60	Hawaii	Los Angeles, Calif.	FA
Rill, David	LB	6-0	220	6/30/66	Washington	Port Orchard, Wash.	FA
Roskopf, Greg	NT	6-3	275	6/27/64	Northern Arizona	Prescott, Ariz.	FA
Seawright, James (1)	LB	6-3	236	3/30/62	South Carolina	Simpsonville, S.C.	FA
Shields, Jon (1)	G	6-5	285	4/30/64	Portland State	Vancouver, Wash.	FA
Strickland, Fred	LB	6-2	244	8/15/66	Purdue	Lakeland, N.J.	D2c
Terry, Joe	LB	6-2	229	11/10/65	Texas-El Paso	Odessa, Tex.	FA
Washington, James	S	6-1	191	1/10/65	UCLA	Los Angeles, Calif.	D5b

The term NFL Rookie is defined as a player who is in his first season of professional football and has not been on the roster of another professional football team for any regular-season or postseason games. A Rookie is designated by an "R" on NFL rosters. Players who have been active in another professional football league or players who have NFL experience, including either preseason training camp or being on an active roster for fewer than three regular-season or postseason games, are termed NFL First-Year Players. An NFL First-Year Player is designated by a "1" on NFL rosters. Thereafter, a player on an NFL active roster for at least three regular-season or postseason games is credited with an additional year of NFL playing experience.

NOTES

National Football Conference Central Division

Team Colors: Purple, Gold, and White

9520 Viking Drive
Eden Prairie, Minnesota 55344
Telephone: (612) 828-6500

Club Officers

Chairman of the Board: John Skoglund
President: Wheelock Whitney
Senior Vice President: Jack Steele
Senior Vice President and Treasurer: Jaye F. Dyer
Secretary: Sheldon Kaplan
Executive Vice President: Mike Lynn

Club Officials

General Manager: Mike Lynn
Assistant to the General Manager/Director of Operations: Jeff Diamond
Director of Administration: Harley Peterson
Ticket Manager: Harry Randolph
Director of Football Operations: Jerry Reichow
Director of Player Personnel: Frank Gilliam
Director of Pro Personnel: Bob Hollway
Head Scout: Ralph Kohl
Assistant Head Scout: Don Deisch
Regional Scout: John Carson
Regional Scout: Conrad Cardano
Director of Public Relations: Merrill Swanson
Director of Communications and Community Relations: Kernal Buhler
Public Relations Assistant: Katie Hogan
Public Relations Assistant: Daniel Endy
Trainer: Fred Zamberletti
Equipment Manager: Dennis Ryan

Stadium: Hubert H. Humphrey Metrodome • **Capacity:** 63,000
500 11th Avenue So.
Minneapolis, Minnesota 55415

Playing Surface: AstroTurf

Training Camp: Mankato State University
Mankato, Minnesota 56001

1988 Schedule

Preseason

Aug. 7	**New Orleans**	7:00
Aug. 14	vs. Chicago at Gothenburg, Sweden	7:00
Aug. 21	at Phoenix	5:00
Aug. 26	**Miami**	7:00

Regular Season

Sept. 4	at Buffalo	1:00
Sept. 11	**New England**	3:00
Sept. 18	at Chicago	12:00
Sept. 25	**Philadelphia**	12:00
Oct. 2	at Miami	4:00
Oct. 9	**Tampa Bay**	12:00
Oct. 16	**Green Bay**	12:00
Oct. 23	at Tampa Bay	1:00
Oct. 30	at San Francisco	1:00
Nov. 6	**Detroit**	12:00
Nov. 13	at Dallas	7:00
Nov. 20	**Indianapolis**	12:00
Nov. 24	at Detroit (Thanksgiving)	12:30
Dec. 4	**New Orleans**	12:00
Dec. 11	at Green Bay	12:00
Dec. 19	**Chicago** (Monday)	8:00

Vikings Coaching History

(219-187-9)

1961-66	Norm Van Brocklin	29-51-4
1967-83	Bud Grant	161-99-5
1984	Les Steckel	3-13-0
1985	Bud Grant	7-9-0
1986-87	Jerry Burns	19-15-0

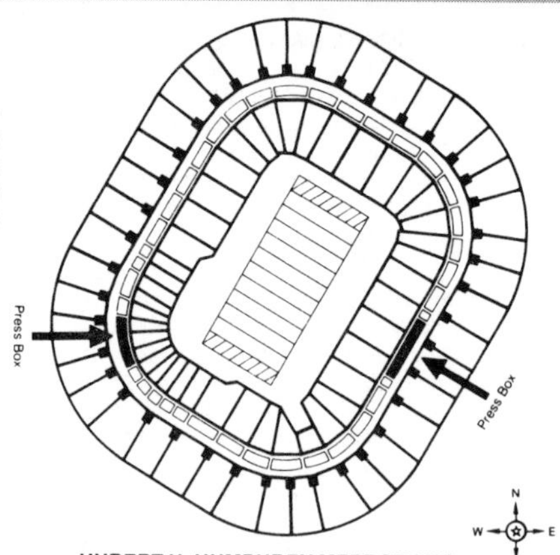

HUBERT H. HUMPHREY METRODOME

Record Holders

Individual Records—Career

Category	Name	Performance
Rushing (Yds.)	Chuck Foreman, 1973-79	5,879
Passing (Yds.)	Fran Tarkenton, 1961-66, 1972-78	33,098
Passing (TDs)	Fran Tarkenton, 1961-66, 1972-78	239
Receiving (No.)	Ahmad Rashad, 1976-1982	400
Receiving (Yds.)	Sammy White, 1976-1985	5,925
Interceptions	Paul Krause, 1968-1979	53
Punting (Avg.)	Bobby Walden, 1964-67	42.9
Punt Return (Avg.)	Leo Lewis, 1981-87	11.4
Kickoff Return (Avg.)	Bob Reed, 1962-63	27.1
Field Goals	Fred Cox, 1963-1977	282
Touchdowns (Tot.)	Bill Brown, 1962-1974	76
Points	Fred Cox, 1963-1977	1,365

Individual Records—Single Season

Category	Name	Performance
Rushing (Yds.)	Chuck Foreman, 1976	1,155
Passing (Yds.)	Tommy Kramer, 1981	3,912
Passing (TDs)	Tommy Kramer, 1981	26
Receiving (No.)	Rickey Young, 1978	88
Receiving (Yds.)	Ahmad Rashad, 1979	1,156
Interceptions	Paul Krause, 1975	10
Punting (Avg.)	Bobby Walden, 1964	46.4
Punt Return (Avg.)	Leo Lewis, 1987	12.5
Kickoff Return (Avg.)	John Gilliam, 1972	26.3
Field Goals	Fred Cox, 1970	30
Touchdowns (Tot.)	Chuck Foreman, 1975	22
Points	Chuck Foreman, 1975	132

Individual Records—Single Game

Category	Name	Performance
Rushing (Yds.)	Chuck Foreman, 10-24-76	200
Passing (Yds.)	Tommy Kramer, 11-2-86	490
Passing (TDs)	Joe Kapp, 9-28-69	*7
Receiving (No.)	Rickey Young, 12-16-79	15
Receiving (Yds.)	Sammy White, 11-7-76	210
Interceptions	Many times	3
	Last time by Willie Teal, 11-28-82	
Field Goals	Fred Cox, 9-23-73	5
	Jan Stenerud, 9-23-84	5
Touchdowns (Tot.)	Chuck Foreman, 12-20-75	4
	Ahmad Rashad, 9-2-79	4
Points	Chuck Foreman, 12-20-75	24
	Ahmad Rashad, 9-2-79	24

*NFL Record

1987 Team Record

Preseason (2-2)

Date	Result		Opponents
8/15	L	17-23	at New Orleans
8/22	W	37-19	Indianapolis
8/29	L	27-38	New England
9/3	W	27-17	at Denver
		108-97	

Regular Season (8-7)

Date	Result		Opponents	Att.
9/13	W	34-19	Detroit	57,061
9/20	W	21-16	at L.A. Rams	63,367
9/27	C		at Kansas City	
10/4	L	16-23	Green Bay	13,911
10/11	L	7-27	at Chicago	32,113
10/18	L	10-20	at Tampa Bay	20,850
10/26	W	34-27	Denver	51,011
11/1	L	17-28	at Seattle	61,134
11/8	W	31-20	L.A. Raiders	57,150
11/15	W	23-17	Tampa Bay	48,605
11/22	W	24-13	Atlanta	53,866
11/26	W	44-38	at Dallas (OT)	54,229
12/6	L	24-30	Chicago	62,331
12/13	L	10-16	at Green Bay	47,059
12/20	W	17-14	at Detroit	27,693
12/26	L	24-27	Washington (OT)	59,160

(OT) Overtime

C (Cancelled due to players' strike.)

Postseason (2-1)

Date	Result		Opponents	Att.
1/3	W	44-10	at New Orleans	68,127
1/9	W	36-24	at San Francisco	62,547
1/17	L	17-10	at Washington	55,212

Score by Periods

Vikings	52	81	100	97	6	—	336
Opponents	36	106	87	103	3	—	335

Attendance

Home 403,095 Away 306,445 Total 709,540

Single-game home record, 62,851 (10-19-86)

Single-season home record, 464,902 (1983)

1987 Team Statistics

	Vikings	Opp.
Total First Downs	293	281
Rushing	129	95
Passing	136	159
Penalty	28	27
Third Down: Made/Att.	76/205	76/206
Fourth Down: Made/Att.	6/12	2/10
Total Net Yards	4809	4824
Avg. Per Game	320.6	321.6
Total Plays	980	979
Avg. Per Play	4.9	4.9
Net Yards Rushing	1983	1724
Avg. Per Game	132.2	114.9
Total Rushes	482	440
Net Yards Passing	2826	3100
Avg. Per Game	188.4	206.7
Sacked/Yards Lost	52/359	41/307
Gross Yards	3185	3407
Att./Completions	446/232	498/278
Completion Pct.	52.0	55.8
Had Intercepted	23	26
Punts/Avg.	79/38.9	74/39.9
Net Punting Avg.	32.3	31.5
Penalties/Yards Lost	96/814	107/964
Fumbles/Ball Lost	28/10	30/11
Touchdowns	42	38
Rushing	20	9
Passing	21	24
Returns	1	5
Avg. Time of Possession	29:20	30:40

1987 Individual Statistics

Scoring	TD R	TD P	TD Rt	PAT	FG	Saf	TP
C. Nelson	0	0	0	36/37	13/24	0	75
Carter	0	7	0	0/0	0/0	0	42
Dozier	5	2	0	0/0	0/0	0	42
W. Wilson	5	0	0	0/0	0/0	0	30
Brim	1	2	0	0/0	0/0	0	18
Lewis	0	2	1	0/0	0/0	0	18
Anderson	2	0	0	0/0	0/0	0	12
Fenney	2	0	0	0/0	0/0	0	12
Hilton	0	2	0	0/0	0/0	0	12
H. Jones	0	2	0	0/0	0/0	0	12
Jordan	0	2	0	0/0	0/0	0	12
Kramer	2	0	0	0/0	0/0	0	12
D. Nelson	2	0	0	0/0	0/0	0	12
Rice	1	1	0	0/0	0/0	0	12
Dawson	0	0	0	4/4	1/5	0	7
Womack	0	1	0	0/0	0/0	0	6
Stepanek	0	0	0	0/0	0/0	1	2
Vikings	20	21	1	40/41	14/29	1	336
Opponents	9	24	5	35/38	24/31	0	335

Passing	Att.	Comp.	Yds.	Pct.	TD	Int.	Tkld.	Rate
W. Wilson	264	140	2106	53.0	14	13	26/194	76.7
Adams	89	49	607	55.1	3	5	18/120	64.2
Kramer	81	40	452	49.4	4	3	7/35	67.5
Gannon	6	2	18	33.3	0	1	0/0	2.8
Miller	6	1	2	16.7	0	1	1/10	0.0
Vikings	446	232	3185	52.0	21	23	52/359	69.4
Opponents	498	278	3407	55.8	24	26	41/307	71.4

Rushing	Att.	Yds.	Avg.	LG	TD
D. Nelson	131	642	4.9	72	2
Anderson	68	319	4.7	27	2
W. Wilson	41	263	6.4	38	5
Dozier	69	257	3.7	19	5
Fenney	42	174	4.1	12	2
Rice	51	131	2.6	13	1
Kramer	10	44	4.4	15	2
Brim	2	36	18.0	38t	1
Adams	11	31	2.8	12	0
A. Walker	5	24	4.8	11	0
Womack	9	20	2.2	13	0
B. Wilson	5	16	3.2	6	0
J. Smith	7	13	1.9	5	0
Moore	4	11	2.8	4	0
Harrell	5	8	1.6	4	0
Frye	4	4	1.0	2	0
A. Thomas	6	4	0.7	5	0
S. Harris	4	3	0.8	2	0
Miller	1	−1	−1.0	−1	0
Gustafson	1	−2	−2.0	−2	0
Lewis	5	−7	−1.4	4	0
Scribner	1	−7	−7.0	−7	0
Vikings	482	1983	4.1	72	20
Opponents	440	1724	3.9	29	9

Receiving	No.	Yds.	Avg.	LG	TD
Carter	38	922	24.3	73t	7
Jordan	35	490	14.0	38	2
D. Nelson	26	129	5.0	13	0
Lewis	24	383	16.0	36	2
Rice	19	201	10.6	24	1
Brim	18	282	15.7	63t	2
Dozier	12	89	7.4	20t	2
H. Jones	7	189	27.0	58t	2
Anderson	7	69	9.9	22	0
Fenney	7	27	3.9	18	0
Womack	5	46	9.2	23t	1
Gustafson	4	55	13.8	23	0
Finch	3	54	18.0	20	0
Parks	3	46	15.3	19	0
Frye	3	25	8.3	12	0
Harrell	3	20	6.7	8	0
Gillespie	2	28	14.0	14	0
Daugherty	2	21	10.5	13	0
S. Harris	2	17	8.5	16	0
Hilton	2	16	8.0	8t	2
B. Wilson	2	14	7.0	9	0
A. Thomas	2	13	6.5	10	0
A. Walker	2	3	1.5	2	0
May	1	22	22.0	22	0
Schenk	1	10	10.0	10	0
Moore	1	8	8.0	8	0
Mularkey	1	6	6.0	6	0
Vikings	232	3185	13.7	73t	21
Opponents	278	3407	12.3	64t	24

Interceptions	No.	Yds.	Avg.	LG	TD
Browner	6	67	11.2	23	0
Henderson	4	33	8.3	17	0
Lee	3	53	17.7	36	0
Harris	3	20	6.7	14	0
Studwell	2	26	13.0	14	0
Holt	2	7	3.5	7	0
Solomon	1	30	30.0	30	0
Guggemos	1	26	26.0	26	0
W. Smith	1	24	24.0	24	0
Louallen	1	16	16.0	16	0
Howard	1	1	1.0	1	0
H. Thomas	1	0	0.0	0	0
Vikings	26	303	11.7	36	0
Opponents	23	399	17.3	100t	3

Punting	No.	Yds.	Avg.	In 20	LG
Scribner	20	827	41.3	4	54
G. Coleman	45	1786	39.7	5	54
Bruno	13	464	35.7	2	53
Vikings	79	3077	38.9	11	54
Opponents	74	2954	39.9	13	58

Punt Returns	No.	FC	Yds.	Avg.	LG	TD
Lewis	22	7	275	12.5	78t	1
Bess	7	3	86	12.3	28	0
Richardson	4	2	19	4.8	7	0
Carter	3	0	40	13.3	22	0
Vikings	36	12	420	11.7	78t	1
Opponents	44	7	424	9.6	40	0

Kickoff Returns	No.	Yds.	Avg.	LG	TD
Guggemos	36	808	22.4	42	0
Bess	10	169	16.9	33	0
D. Nelson	7	164	23.4	42	0
Womack	5	77	15.4	20	0
Richardson	4	76	19.0	24	0
Dozier	2	23	11.5	13	0
Rice	2	29	14.5	18	0
J. Smith	2	42	21.0	22	0
Harrell	1	4	4.0	4	0
Hilton	1	13	13.0	13	0
Mularkey	1	16	16.0	16	0
Vikings	71	1421	20.0	42	0
Opponents	64	1173	18.3	40	0

Sacks	No.
Doleman	11.0
D. Martin	9.0
Mays	7.0
Millard	3.5
H. Thomas	2.5
D. Coleman	2.0
Solomon	2.0
Browner	1.0
Molden	1.0
Studwell	1.0
J. Walker	1.0
Vikings	41.0
Opponents	52.0

Minnesota Vikings 1988 Veteran Roster

No.	Name	Pos.	Ht.	Wt.	Birth-date	NFL Exp.	College	Hometown	How Acq.	'87 Games/ Starts
46	Anderson, Alfred	RB	6-1	219	8/4/61	5	Baylor	Waco, Tex.	D3-'84	10/10
53	Anno, Sam	LB	6-2	230	1/26/65	2	Southern California	Santa Monica, Calif.	FA-'87	9/0*
58	Ashley, Walker Lee	LB	6-0	240	7/28/60	5	Penn State	Jersey City, N.J.	D3-'83	12/0
50	Berry, Ray	LB	6-2	230	10/28/63	2	Baylor	Abilene, Tex.	D2-'87	11/0
19	Brim, James	WR	6-3	187	2/28/63	2	Wake Forest	Mt. Airy, N.C.	FA-'87	3/3
47	Browner, Joey	S	6-2	212	5/15/60	6	Southern California	Warren, Ohio	D1-'83	12/12
81	Carter, Anthony	WR	5-11	166	9/17/60	4	Michigan	Riviera Beach, Fla.	T(Mia)-'85	12/11
8	Coleman, Greg	P	6-0	181	9/9/54	12	Florida A&M	Jacksonville, Fla.	FA-'78	9/0
56	Doleman, Chris	DE	6-5	250	10/16/61	4	Pittsburgh	York, Pa.	D1-'85	12/12
42	Dozier, D.J.	RB	6-0	198	9/21/65	2	Penn State	Virginia Beach, Va.	D1-'87	9/3
31	Fenney, Rick	RB	6-1	240	12/7/64	2	Washington	Everett, Wash.	D8-'87	11/0
62	†Foote, Chris	C	6-4	265	12/2/56	6	Southern California	Boulder, Colo.	T(NYG)-'87	6/0
22	Freeman, Steve	S	5-11	185	5/8/53	14	Mississippi State	Memphis, Tenn.	T(Buff)-'87	12/0
16	†Gannon, Rich	QB	6-3	197	12/20/65	2	Delaware	Philadelphia, Pa.	T(NE)-'87	5/0
41	†Guggemos, Neal	S	6-0	187	6/14/64	3	St. Thomas	Winsted, Minn.	FA-'86	12/1
80	†Gustafson, Jim	WR	6-1	181	3/16/61	3	St. Thomas	Minneapolis, Minn.	FA-'85	12/0
44	Harris, John	S	6-2	198	6/13/56	11	Arizona State	Miami, Fla.	T(Sea)-'86	12/12
24	Henderson, Wymon	CB-S	5-10	186	12/15/61	2	Nevada-Las Vegas	North Miami Beach, Fla.	FA-'87	12/8
82	Hilton, Carl	TE	6-3	232	2/28/64	3	Houston	Galveston, Tex.	D7-'86	11/1
30	Holt, Issiac	CB	6-1	197	10/4/62	4	Alcorn State	Birmingham, Ala.	D2-'85	9/6
51	Howard, David	LB	6-2	228	12/8/61	4	Long Beach State	Long Beach, Calif.	SD3-'84	10/7
72	†Huffman, David	G	6-6	283	4/4/57	9	Notre Dame	Dallas, Tex.	FA-'85	12/12
76	Irwin, Tim	T	6-6	289	12/13/58	8	Tennessee	Knoxville, Tenn.	D3-'81	12/12
84	Jones, Hassan	WR	6-0	195	7/2/64	3	Florida State	Clearwater, Fla.	D5-'86	12/0
83	Jordan, Steve	TE	6-3	236	1/10/61	7	Brown	Phoenix, Ariz.	D7-'82	12/12
68	†Koch, Greg	T	6-4	276	6/14/55	12	Arkansas	Houston, Tex.	T(Mia)-'87	10/7*
9	Kramer, Tommy	QB	6-2	207	3/7/55	12	Rice	San Antonio, Tex.	D1-'77	6/5
39	Lee, Carl	CB	5-11	184	4/6/61	6	Marshall	South Charleston, W.Va.	D7-'83	12/12
87	Lewis, Leo	WR	5-8	171	9/17/56	8	Missouri	Columbia, Mo.	FA-'81	12/12
63	†Lowdermilk, Kirk	C	6-3	263	4/10/63	4	Ohio State	Salem, Ohio	D3a-'85	12/12
71	MacDonald, Mark	G	6-4	267	4/30/61	4	Boston College	West Roxbury, Mass.	D5-'85	12/1
56	†Martin, Chris	LB	6-2	233	12/19/60	6	Auburn	Huntsville, Ala.	W(NO)-'84	12/4
79	†Martin, Doug	DE	6-3	270	5/22/57	9	Washington	Fairfield, Calif.	D1-'80	12/12
73	Mays, Stafford	DE	6-2	264	3/13/58	9	Washington	Tacoma, Wash.	FA-'87	12/7
75	Millard, Keith	DT	6-6	260	3/18/62	4	Washington State	Pullman, Wash.	D1-'84	9/8
86	Mularkey, Mike	TE	6-4	238	11/19/61	6	Florida	Ft. Lauderdale, Fla.	W(SF)-'83	9/0
77	Mullaney, Mark	DE	6-6	246	4/30/53	13	Colorado State	Denver, Colo.	D1-'75	0*
1	Nelson, Chuck	K	5-11	172	2/23/60	5	Washington	Seattle, Wash.	FA-'86	12/0
20	Nelson, Darrin	RB	5-9	183	1/2/59	7	Stanford	Downey, Calif.	D1-'82	10/9
96	Newton, Tim	DT	6-0	283	3/23/63	4	Florida	Orlando, Fla.	D6b-'85	9/0
52	Rasmussen, Randy	C-G	6-1	254	9/27/60	5	Minnesota	Minneapolis, Minn.	FA-'87	5/0
36	Rice, Allen	RB	5-10	203	4/5/62	5	Baylor	Houston, Tex.	D5-'84	12/2
95	Robinson, Gerald	DE	6-3	256	5/4/63	3	Auburn	Notasulga, Ala.	D1-'86	4/0
48	Rutland, Reggie	S	6-1	195	6/20/64	2	Georgia Tech	East Point, Ga.	D4-'87	7/0
13	Scribner, Bucky	P	6-0	205	7/11/60	4	Kansas	Lawrence, Kan.	FA-'87	4/0
40	†Smith, Wayne	CB	6-0	170	5/9/57	9	Purdue	Chicago, Ill.	FA-'87	6/1
54	Solomon, Jesse	LB	6-0	235	11/4/63	3	Florida State	Madison, Fla.	D12-'86	12/12
55	Studwell, Scott	LB	6-2	228	8/27/54	12	Illinois	Evansville, Ind.	D9-'77	12/11
67	†Swilley, Dennis	C	6-3	257	6/28/55	11	Texas A&M	Pine Bluff, Ark.	D2-'77	6/0
66	Tausch, Terry	T	6-5	275	2/5/59	7	Texas	New Braunfels, Tex.	D2-'82	5/5
97	Thomas, Henry	NT	6-2	268	1/12/65	2	Louisiana State	Houston, Tex.	D3-'87	12/11
11	Wilson, Wade	QB	6-3	208	2/1/59	8	East Texas State	Commerce, Tex.	D8-'81	12/7
65	†Zimmerman, Gary	T	6-6	277	12/13/61	3	Oregon	Fullerton, Calif.	T(NYG)-'86	12/12

* Anno played 3 games with L.A. Rams, 6 with Minnesota in '87; Koch played 1 game with Miami, 9 with Minnesota; Mullaney missed '87 season due to injury.

†Option playout; subject to developments.

Also played with Vikings in '87—LB Steve Ache (3 games), QB Tony Adams (3), CB Rufus Bess (3), QB Keith Bishop (active for 3 games but did not play), DT Don Bramlett (3), WR Larry Brown (1), P Dave Bruno (2), LB Tim Bryant (1), T Derek Burton (3), S Chuck Clanton (active for 1 game but did not play), DE Daniel Coleman (3), LB Fabray Collins (3), WR Ron Daugherty (3), K Dale Dawson (3), LB Jim Dick (3), TE Clifton Eley (2), CB David Evans (3), WR Steve Finch (1), CB-S Jamie Fitzgerald (2), RB Phil Frye (1), WR Willie Gillespie (1), G Mark Hanson (1), RB Sam Harrell (1), RB Steve Harris (2), DE Mike Hartenstine (5), G Wayne Jones (6), WR Keith Kidd (1), WR Terry LeCount (1), S Fletcher Louallen (3), CB-S Terry Love (1), TE Marc May (3), G Mike McCurry (3) DE Phil Micech (3), LB Larry Miller (2), G Ted Million (1), DT Fred Molden (2), RB Leonard Moore (1), LB Pete Najarian (5), DE Tony Norman (2), G Frank Ori (3), WR Rickey Parks (2), DT Kurt Ploeger (1), LB Kelly Quinn (3), S Ted Rosnagle (3), T John Scardina (3), TE Ed Schenk (3), LB Randy Scott (2), G Ron Selesky (2), CB-S Mike Slaton (1), RB Jimmy Smith (1), CB-S Tim Starks (1), DT Joe Stepanek (1), RB Andre Thomas (1), CB-S John Turner (2), CB-S Mike Turner (2), RB Adam Walker (2), DT Jimmy Walker (2), C Kevin Webster (3), DT Brad White (1), RB Brett Wilson (3), RB Jeff Womack (2).

COACHING STAFF

Head Coach, Jerry Burns

Pro Career: Named fourth head coach in Vikings' history on January 6, 1986. Served as Vikings' assistant head coach and offensive coordinator under Bud Grant in 1985. Since his arrival in Minnesota as offensive coordinator in 1968, became known as an innovator and was credited with popularizing such changes as the one-back offense and short passing game. Has coached in six Super Bowls. Directed Vikings' offense in Super Bowls IV, VIII, IX, and XI, and coached defensive backs for Vince Lombardi on Green Bay's Super Bowl champions in Super Bowls I and II. No pro playing experience. Career record: 19-15-0.

Background: Quarterback at Michigan 1949-50. Began coaching career at Hawaii in 1951 as backfield coach for football team and head baseball coach. Moved to Whittier (Calif.) College in 1952 as backfield coach before returning to native Detroit in 1953 as head football coach at St. Mary's of Redford High School. Assistant coach at Iowa from 1954-60 before being named Hawkeyes head coach in 1961. Iowa was 16-27-2 in five seasons under Burns. He coached with the Packers in 1966-67 before joining the Vikings in 1968.

Personal: Born January 24, 1927, in Detroit, Mich. Graduated from Michigan with bachelor of science degree in physical education. Jerry and his wife, Marlyn, live in Eden Prairie, Minn., and have five children—Michael, Erin, Kelly, Kathy, and Kerry.

Assistant Coaches

Tom Batta, tight ends-special teams; born October 6, 1942, Youngstown, Ohio, lives in Bloomington, Minn. Offensive-defensive lineman Kent State 1961-63. No pro playing experience. College coach: Akron 1973, Colorado 1974-78, Kansas 1979-82, North Carolina State 1983. Pro coach: Joined Vikings in 1984.

Jerry Brown, offensive assistant; born September 28, 1949, Kent, Ohio, lives in Eden Prairie, Minn. Defensive back Northwestern 1969-72. No pro playing experience. College coach: Eastern Illinois 1977-79, Cal State-Fullerton 1980-87. Pro coach: Joined Vikings in 1988.

John Brunner, running backs; born September 6, 1937, Perkasie, Pa., lives in Eden Prairie, Minn. Running back Maryland 1955-56, East Stroudsburg State 1958-59. No pro playing experience. College coach: Villanova 1967-69, Temple 1970-73, 1976-79, Princeton 1974-75. Pro coach: Detroit Lions 1980-82, Green Bay Packers 1983, Tampa Bay Buccaneers 1984, New England 1985-86 (scout), joined Vikings in 1987.

Pete Carroll, secondary; born September 15, 1951, San Francisco, Calif., lives in Bloomington, Minn. Defensive back Pacific 1969-72. No pro playing experience. College coach: Arkansas 1977, Iowa State 1978, Ohio State 1979, North Carolina State 1980-82, Pacific 1983. Pro coach: Buffalo Bills 1984, joined Vikings in 1985.

Monte Kiffin, linebackers; born February 29, 1940, Lexington, Neb., lives in Bloomington, Minn. Defensive end Nebraska 1961-63. Pro defensive end Winnipeg Blue Bombers (CFL) 1965-66. College coach: Nebraska 1966-76, Arkansas 1977-79, North Carolina State 1980-82 (head coach). Pro coach: Green Bay Packers 1983, Buffalo Bills 1984-85, joined Vikings in 1986.

John Michels, offensive line; born February 15, 1931, Philadelphia, Pa., lives in Bloomington, Minn. Guard Tennessee 1949-52. Pro guard Philadelphia Eagles 1953, 1956, Winnipeg Blue Bombers (CFL) 1957. College coach: Texas A&M 1958. Pro coach: Winnipeg Blue Bombers (CFL) 1959-66, joined Vikings in 1967.

Minnesota Vikings 1988 First-Year Roster

Name	Pos.	Ht.	Wt.	Birth-date	College	Hometown	How Acq.
Beckman, Brad	TE	6-2	236	12/31/64	Nebraska-Omaha	Omaha, Neb.	D7
Cain, Joe	LB	6-1	228	6/11/65	Oregon Tech	Compton, Calif.	D8
Edwards, Brad	S	6-1	198	2/22/66	South Carolina	Fayetteville, N.C.	D2
Floyd, Norman	S	5-11	198	2/10/66	South Carolina	Greenville, S.C.	D11
Fullington, Darrell	S	6-1	183	4/17/64	Miami	New Smyrna Beach, Fla.	D5
Habib, Brian	NT	6-6	271	12/2/64	Washington	Ellensburg, Wash.	D10
Kalis, Todd	G	6-5	269	5/10/65	Arizona State	Phoenix, Ariz.	D4
McDaniel, Randall	G	6-3	268	12/19/64	Arizona State	Avondale, Ariz.	D1
McGowan, Paul	LB	5-11	221	1/13/66	Florida State	Orlando, Fla.	D9
Molden, Fred (1)	DE	6-2	272	8/12/63	Jackson State	Singing River, Miss.	FA
Noga, Al	NT	6-1	245	9/16/66	Hawaii	Honolulu, Hawaii	D3
Truelove, Tony (1)	RB	5-11	205	3/24/64	Livingston	Salligent, Ala.	FA-'87
White, Derrick	CB	5-8	185	11/11/65	Oklahoma	Lubbock, Tex.	D6
Yancey, Lloyd (1)	T	6-4	275	12/8/62	Temple	Philadelphia, Pa.	FA

The term NFL Rookie is defined as a player who is in his first season of professional football and has not been on the roster of another professional football team for any regular-season or postseason games. A Rookie is designated by an "R" on NFL rosters. Players who have been active in another professional football league or players who have NFL experience, including either preseason training camp or being on an active roster for fewer than three regular-season or postseason games, are termed NFL First-Year Players. An NFL First-Year Player is designated by a "1" on NFL rosters. Thereafter, a player on an NFL active roster for at least three regular-season or postseason games is credited with an additional year of NFL playing experience.

NOTES

Floyd Peters, defensive coordinator; born May 21, 1936, Council Bluffs, Iowa, lives in Bloomington, Minn. Defensive tackle-guard San Francisco State 1954-57. Pro defensive lineman Baltimore Colts 1958, Cleveland Browns 1959-62, Detroit Lions 1963, Philadelphia Eagles 1964-69, Washington Redskins 1970 (player/coach). Pro scout: Miami Dolphins 1971-73. Pro coach: New York Giants 1974-75, San Francisco 49ers 1976-77, Detroit Lions 1978-81, St. Louis Cardinals 1982-85, joined Vikings in 1986.

Dick Rehbein, receivers; born November 22, 1955, Green Bay, Wis., lives in Edina, Minn. Center Ripon 1973-77. No pro playing experience. Pro coach: Green Bay Packers 1979-83, Los Angeles Express (USFL) 1984, joined Vikings in 1984.

Bob Schnelker, offensive coordinator; born October 17, 1928, Galion, Ohio, lives in Eden Prairie, Minn. Tight end Bowling Green 1946-49. Pro tight end Cleveland Browns 1953, New York Giants 1954-59, Minnesota Vikings 1961, Pittsburgh Steelers 1961. Pro coach: Los Angeles Rams 1963-65, Green Bay Packers 1966-71, 1982-85, San Diego Chargers 1972-73, Miami Dolphins 1974, Kansas City Chiefs 1975-77, Detroit Lions 1978-81, joined Vikings in 1986.

Paul Wiggin, defensive line; born November 18, 1934, Modesto, Calif., lives in Eden Prairie, Minn. Offensive-defensive tackle Stanford 1953-56. Pro defensive end Cleveland Browns 1957-67. College coach: Stanford 1980-83 (head coach). Pro coach: San Francisco 49ers 1968-74, Kansas City Chiefs 1975-77 (head coach), New Orleans Saints 1978-79, joined Vikings in 1985.

NEW ORLEANS SAINTS

National Football Conference Western Division

Team Colors: Old Gold, Black, and White

1500 Poydras Street
New Orleans, Louisiana 70112
Telephone: (504) 733-0255

Club Officials

Owner/General Partner: Tom Benson
President/General Manager: Jim Finks
Vice President/Administration: Jim Miller
Business Manager/Controller: Bruce Broussard
Director of Player Personnel: Bill Kuharich
Director of Public Relations/Marketing: Greg Suit
Director of Media Services: Rusty Kasmiersky
Director of Travel/Entertainment: Barra Birrcher
Assistant Director of Marketing: Bill Ferrante
Public Relations/Marketing Assistant: Sylvia Alfortish
Player Personnel Scouts: Bill Baker, Hamp Cook, Hokie Gajan, Tom Marino, Carmen Piccone
Ticket Manager: Sandy King
Trainer: Dean Kleinschmidt
Equipment Manager: Dan Simmons
Video Director: Albert Aucoin

Stadium: Louisiana Superdome • **Capacity:** 69,548
1500 Poydras Street
New Orleans, Louisiana 70112

Playing Surface: AstroTurf

Training Camp: University of Wisconsin-LaCrosse
LaCrosse, Wisconsin 54601

1988 Schedule

Preseason

Aug. 7	at Minnesota	7:00
Aug. 12	at Phoenix	7:30
Aug. 20	at Indianapolis	7:30
Aug. 27	**Pittsburgh**	11:30 A.M.

Regular Season

Sept. 4	**San Francisco**	12:00
Sept. 11	at Atlanta	1:00
Sept. 18	at Detroit	1:00
Sept. 25	**Tampa Bay**	12:00
Oct. 3	**Dallas** (Monday)	8:00
Oct. 9	at San Diego	1:00
Oct. 16	at Seattle	1:00
Oct. 23	**Los Angeles Raiders**	12:00
Oct. 30	**Los Angeles Rams**	12:00
Nov. 6	at Washington	4:00
Nov. 13	at Los Angeles Rams	1:00
Nov. 20	**Denver**	12:00
Nov. 27	**New York Giants**	7:00
Dec. 4	at Minnesota	12:00
Dec. 11	at San Francisco	1:00
Dec. 18	**Atlanta**	12:00

Saints Coaching History

(102-200-5)

1967-70	Tom Fears*	13-34-2
1970-72	J.D. Roberts	7-25-3
1973-75	John North**	11-23-0
1975	Ernie Hefferle	1-7-0
1976-77	Hank Stram	7-21-0
1978-80	Dick Nolan***	15-29-0
1980	Dick Stanfel	1-3-0
1981-85	O.A. (Bum) Phillips****	27-42-0
1985	Wade Phillips	1-3-0
1986-87	Jim Mora	19-13-0

*Released after seven games in 1970
**Released after six games in 1975
***Released after 12 games in 1980
****Resigned after 12 games in 1985

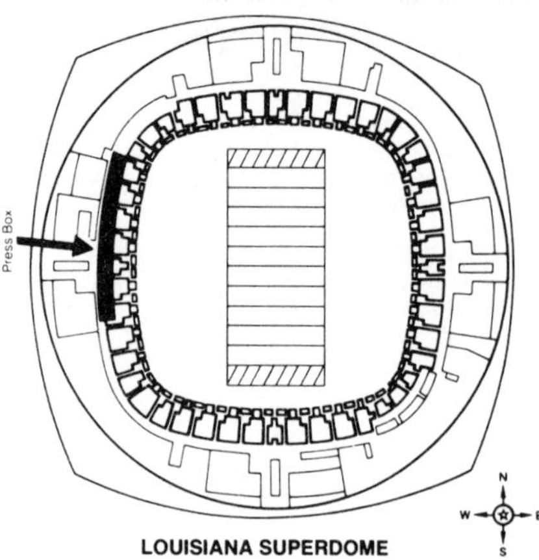

LOUISIANA SUPERDOME

Record Holders

Individual Records—Career

Category	Name	Performance
Rushing (Yds.)	George Rogers, 1981-84	4,267
Passing (Yds.)	Archie Manning, 1971-1982	21,734
Passing (TDs)	Archie Manning, 1971-1982	115
Receiving (No.)	Dan Abramowicz, 1967-1973	309
Receiving (Yds.)	Dan Abramowicz, 1967-1973	4,875
Interceptions	Tommy Myers, 1972-1982	36
Punting (Avg.)	Brian Hansen, 1984-87	42.4
Punt Return (Avg.)	Mel Gray, 1987	14.7
Kickoff Return (Avg.)	Walter Roberts, 1967	26.3
Field Goals	Morten Andersen, 1982-87	125
Touchdowns (Tot.)	Dan Abramowicz, 1967-1973	37
Points	Morten Andersen, 1982-87	546

Individual Records—Single Season

Category	Name	Performance
Rushing (Yds.)	George Rogers, 1981	1,674
Passing (Yds.)	Archie Manning, 1980	3,716
Passing (TDs)	Archie Manning, 1980	23
Receiving (No.)	Tony Galbreath, 1978	74
Receiving (Yds.)	Wes Chandler, 1979	1,069
Interceptions	Dave Whitsell, 1967	10
Punting (Avg.)	Brian Hansen, 1984	43.8
Punt Return (Avg.)	Mel Gray, 1987	14.7
Kickoff Return (Avg.)	Don Shy, 1969	27.9
Field Goals	Morten Andersen, 1985	31
Touchdowns (Tot.)	George Rogers, 1981	13
Points	Morten Andersen, 1987	121

Individual Records—Single Game

Category	Name	Performance
Rushing (Yds.)	George Rogers, 9-4-83	206
Passing (Yds.)	Archie Manning, 12-7-80	377
Passing (TDs)	Billy Kilmer, 11-2-69	6
Receiving (No.)	Tony Galbreath, 9-10-78	14
Receiving (Yds.)	Wes Chandler, 9-2-79	205
Interceptions	Tommy Myers, 9-3-78	3
	Dave Waymer, 10-6-85	3
	Reggie Sutton, 10-18-87	3
Field Goals	Morten Andersen, 12-1-85	5
	Morten Andersen, 11-15-87	5
Touchdowns (Tot.)	Many times	3
	Last time by Wayne Wilson, 1-2-83	
Points	Many times	18
	Last time by Wayne Wilson, 1-2-83	

1987 Team Record

Preseason (3-1)

Date	Result		Opponents
8/15	W	23-17	Minnesota
8/22	L	13-16	Houston
8/29	W	31-28	Pittsburgh
9/4	W	26-14	at Cincinnati
		93-75	

Regular Season (12-3)

Date	Result		Opponents	Att.
9/13	W	28-21	Cleveland	59,900
9/20	L	17-27	at Philadelphia	57,485
9/27	C		Atlanta	
10/4	W	37-10	L.A. Rams	29,745
10/11	L	19-24	at St. Louis	11,795
10/18	W	19-17	at Chicago	46,813
10/25	L	22-24	San Francisco	60,497
11/1	W	38- 0	at Atlanta	42,196
11/8	W	31-14	at L.A. Rams	43,379
11/15	W	26-24	at San Francisco	60,436
11/22	W	23-14	N.Y. Giants	67,639
11/29	W	20-16	at Pittsburgh	47,896
12/6	W	44-34	Tampa Bay	66,471
12/13	W	24-10	Houston	68,257
12/20	W	41-24	at Cincinnati	43,424
12/27	W	33-24	Green Bay	68,364

C (Cancelled due to players' strike.)

Postseason (0-1)

Date	Result		Opponent	Att.
1/3	L	10-44	Minnesota	68,127

Score by Periods

Saints	93	107	104	118	0	—	422
Opponents	69	95	58	61	0	—	283

Attendance

Home 420,873 Away 353,424 Total 774,297
Single-game home record, 70,940 (11-4-79)
Single-season home record, 529,878 (1979)

1987 Team Statistics

	Saints	Opp.
Total First Downs	304	270
Rushing	128	81
Passing	151	155
Penalty	25	34
Third Down: Made/Att.	99/221	57/182
Fourth Down: Made/Att.	1/6	6/15
Total Net Yards	4964	4350
Avg. Per Game	330.9	290.0
Total Plays	1009	924
Avg. Per Play	4.9	4.7
Net Yards Rushing	2190	1550
Avg. Per Game	146.0	103.3
Total Rushes	569	388
Net Yards Passing	2774	2800
Avg. Per Game	184.9	186.7
Sacked/Yards Lost	29/213	47/355
Gross Yards	2987	3155
Att./Completions	411/227	489/246
Completion Pct.	55.2	50.3
Had Intercepted	12	30
Punts/Avg.	63/41.1	73/37.5
Net Punting Avg.	35.7	30.0
Penalties/Yards Lost	107/994	84/685
Fumbles/Ball Lost	33/16	31/18
Touchdowns	46	35
Rushing	20	6
Passing	23	25
Returns	3	4
Avg. Time of Possession	34:01	25:59

1987 Individual Statistics

Scoring	TD R	TD P	TD Rt	PAT	FG	Saf	TP
Andersen	0	0	0	37/37	28/36	0	121
Hilliard	7	1	0	0/0	0/0	0	48
Martin	0	7	0	0/0	0/0	0	42
Tice	0	6	0	0/0	0/0	0	36
Mayes	5	0	0	0/0	0/0	0	30
M. Jones	0	3	0	0/0	0/0	0	18
Kempf	0	0	0	1/1	4/5	0	13
Beverly	2	0	0	0/0	0/0	0	12
Brenner	0	2	0	0/0	0/0	0	12
Hill	0	2	0	0/0	0/0	0	12
Jordan	2	0	0	0/0	0/0	0	12
Word	2	0	0	0/0	0/0	0	12
Cofer	0	0	0	5/7	1/1	0	8
Alexander	1	0	0	0/0	0/0	0	6
Gray	1	0	0	0/0	0/0	0	6
O'Neal	0	1	0	0/0	0/0	0	6
Poe	0	0	1	0/0	0/0	0	6
R. Sutton	0	0	1	0/0	0/0	0	6
Toles	0	0	1	0/0	0/0	0	6
Waters	0	1	0	0/0	0/0	0	6
B. Clark	0	0	0	0/0	0/0	1	2
Maxie	0	0	0	0/0	0/0	1	2
Saints	20	23	3	43/46	33/42	2	422
Opponents	6	25	4	35/35	12/18	1	283

Passing	Att.	Comp.	Yds.	Pct.	TD	Int.	Tkld.	Rate
Hebert	294	164	2119	55.8	15	9	20/119	82.9
J. Fourcade	89	48	597	53.9	4	3	6/67	75.9
Wilson	24	13	243	54.2	2	0	2/21	117.2
Ingram	2	1	5	50.0	1	0	1/6	95.8
Hilliard	1	1	23	100.0	1	0	0/0	158.3
Riordan	1	0	0	0.0	0	0	0/0	39.6
Saints	411	227	2987	55.2	23	12	29/213	84.9
Opponents	489	246	3155	50.3	25	30	47/355	62.4

Rushing	Att.	Yds.	Avg.	LG	TD
Mayes	243	917	3.8	38	5
Hilliard	123	508	4.1	30t	7
Beverly	62	217	3.5	25	2
J. Fourcade	19	134	7.1	18	0
Word	36	133	3.7	20	2
Hebert	13	95	7.3	19	0
Alexander	21	71	3.4	16	1
Gray	8	37	4.6	12	1
Jordan	12	36	3.0	8t	2
Rodenberger	17	35	2.1	5	0
Jean-Batiste	8	18	2.3	7	0
Ingram	2	14	7.0	9	0
Riordan	1	3	3.0	3	0
Hansen	2	−6	−3.0	−3	0
Hill	1	−9	−9.0	−9	0
Barnhardt	1	−13	−13.0	−13	0
Saints	569	2190	3.8	38	20
Opponents	388	1550	4.0	33	6

Receiving	No.	Yds.	Avg.	LG	TD
Martin	44	778	17.7	67	7
M. Jones	27	420	15.6	43t	3
Hilliard	23	264	11.5	38t	1
Brenner	20	280	14.0	29	2
Hill	19	322	16.9	36	2
Tice	16	181	11.3	27t	6
Mayes	15	68	4.5	16	0
Dawsey	13	142	10.9	29	0
Pattison	9	132	14.7	36	0
Word	6	54	9.0	17	0
Scott	6	35	5.8	11	0
Gray	6	30	5.0	12	0
Waters	5	140	28.0	82t	1
Clark	3	38	12.7	14	0
O'Neal	3	10	3.3	5	1
Rodenberger	2	17	8.5	11	0
Alexander	2	15	7.5	10	0
Walker	2	15	7.5	8	0
Jordan	2	13	6.5	11	0
Benson	2	11	5.5	6	0
C. Thomas	1	14	14.0	14	0
Beverly	1	8	8.0	8	0
Saints	227	2987	13.2	82t	23
Opponents	246	3155	12.8	50t	25

Interceptions	No.	Yds.	Avg.	LG	TD
Waymer	5	78	15.6	35	0
R. Sutton	5	68	13.6	26	0
Mack	4	32	8.0	26	0
Jakes	3	32	10.7	27	0
Maxie	3	17	5.7	10	0
Atkins	3	12	4.0	8	0
Jackson	2	4	2.0	4	0
Gibson	1	17	17.0	17	0
S. Leach	1	10	10.0	10	0
Swilling	1	10	10.0	10	0
Poe	1	0	0.0	0	0
V. Johnson	1	0	0.0	0	0
Saints	30	280	9.3	35	0
Opponents	12	173	14.4	35	1

Punting	No.	Yds.	Avg.	In 20	LG
Barnhardt	11	483	43.9	4	52
Hansen	52	2104	40.5	19	60
Saints	63	2587	41.1	23	60
Opponents	73	2740	37.5	10	57

Punt Returns	No.	FC	Yds.	Avg.	LG	TD
Gray	24	5	352	14.7	80	0
Martin	14	2	88	6.3	15	0
Cook	1	0	3	3.0	3	0
Jordan	1	0	13	13.0	13	0
Maxie	1	0	12	12.0	12	0
Saints	41	7	468	11.4	80	0
Opponents	29	8	199	6.9	29	0

Kickoff Returns	No.	Yds.	Avg.	LG	TD
Gray	30	636	21.2	43	0
Hilliard	10	248	24.8	74	0
Adams	4	52	13.0	20	0
Beverly	3	46	15.3	21	0
Word	3	100	33.3	64	0
Jordan	2	28	14.0	16	0
Brock	1	11	11.0	11	0
Martin	1	15	15.0	15	0
C. Thomas	1	11	11.0	11	0
Saints	55	1147	20.9	74	0
Opponents	55	1115	20.3	47	0

Sacks	No.
Swilling	10.5
Jackson	9.5
Warren	6.0
Wilks	5.5
B. Clark	4.5
To. Elliott	2.0
Maxie	2.0
McCoy	2.0
S. Leach	1.5
Deforest	1.0
V. Johnson	1.0
Swoopes	1.0
Taylor	0.5
Saints	47.0
Opponents	29.0

New Orleans Saints 1988 Veteran Roster

No.	Name	Pos.	Ht.	Wt.	Birth-date	NFL Exp.	College	Hometown	How Acq.	'87 Games/ Starts
40	Adams, Michael	CB	5-10	195	4/5/64	2	Arkansas State	Cleveland, Miss.	D3-'87	7/3
7	Andersen, Morten	K	6-2	221	8/19/60	7	Michigan State	Indianapolis, Ind.	D4-'82	12/0
28	Atkins, Gene	CB-S	6-1	200	8/31/64	2	Florida A&M	Tallahassee, Fla.	D7-'87	13/5
83	Benson, Cliff	TE	6-4	240	8/28/61	4	Purdue	Palos Heights, Ill.	W(Wash)-'87	10/3*
85	†Brenner, Hoby	TE	6-4	240	6/2/59	8	Southern California	Fullerton, Calif.	D3b-'81	12/10
67	Brock, Stan	T	6-6	292	6/8/58	9	Colorado	Beaverton, Ore.	D1-'80	12/12
59	Campen, James	C	6-3	260	6/11/64	2	Tulane	Sacramento, Calif.	FA-'87	3/3
75	Clark, Bruce	DE	6-3	275	3/31/58	7	Penn State	New Castle, Pa.	T(GB)-'82	15/15
66	Commiskey, Chuck	G	6-4	290	3/2/58	3	Mississippi	Pascagoula, Miss.	FA-'86	12/4
70	Contz, Bill	T	6-5	270	5/12/61	6	Penn State	Belle Vernon, Pa.	FA-'86	3/0
41	Cook, Toi	S	5-11	188	12/3/64	2	Stanford	Canoga Park, Calif.	D8-'87	7/0
26	Dawsey, Stacey	WR	5-9	154	10/24/65	2	Indiana	Bradenton, Fla.	FA-'87	3/3
72	Dombrowski, Jim	T	6-5	298	10/19/63	3	Virginia	Williamsville, N.Y.	D1-'86	10/10
63	†Edelman, Brad	G	6-6	270	9/3/60	7	Missouri	Creve Coeur, Mo.	D2-'82	11/9
99	Elliott, Tony	NT	6-2	295	4/28/59	7	North Texas State	Bridgeport, Conn.	D5-'82	14/14
11	Fourcade, John	QB	6-1	208	10/11/60	2	Mississippi	Marrero, La.	FA-'87	3/3
97	†Geathers, James	DE	6-7	290	4/26/60	4	Wichita State	Georgetown, S.C.	D2-'84	1/0
27	†Gibson, Antonio	S	6-3	204	7/5/62	3	Cincinnati	Jackson, Miss.	FA-'86	10/10
77	Gilbert, Daren	T	6-6	295	10/3/63	4	Cal State-Fullerton	Compton, Calif.	D2-'85	6/5
37	†Gray, Mel	RB	5-9	166	3/16/61	3	Purdue	Williamsburg, Va.	SD2-'84	12/1
10	Hansen, Brian	P	6-3	209	10/18/60	5	Sioux Falls	Hawarden, Iowa	D9-'84	12/0
80	Harris, Herbert	WR	6-1	206	5/4/61	2	Lamar	Houston, Tex.	FA-'88	2/0
92	Haynes, James	LB	6-2	233	8/9/60	5	Mississippi Valley State	Tallulah, La.	FA-'84	12/0
3	Hebert, Bobby	QB	6-4	215	8/19/60	4	Northwestern State, La.	Cut Off, La.	FA-'85	12/12
61	Hilgenberg, Joel	C-G	6-2	252	7/10/62	5	Iowa	Iowa City, Iowa	D4-'84	12/12
87	Hill, Lonzell	WR	5-11	189	9/25/65	2	Washington	Stockton, Calif.	D2-'87	10/1
21	Hilliard, Dalton	RB	5-8	204	1/21/64	3	Louisiana State	Patterson, La.	D2-'86	12/1
57	Jackson, Rickey	LB	6-2	243	3/20/58	8	Pittsburgh	Pahokee, Fla.	D2-'81	12/12
22	†Jakes, Van	CB	6-0	190	5/10/61	5	Kent State	Buffalo, N.Y.	FA-'86	12/10
53	†Johnson, Vaughan	LB	6-3	235	3/24/62	3	North Carolina State	Morehead City, N.C.	SD1-'84	12/12
86	Jones, Mike	WR	5-11	183	4/14/60	6	Tennessee State	Chattanooga, Tenn.	T(Minn)-'86	12/7
23	†Jordan, Buford	RB	6-0	223	6/26/62	3	McNeese State	Iota, La.	FA-'86	12/4
71	Kaplan, Ken	T	6-5	270	1/12/60	4	New Hampshire	Brockton, Mass.	FA-'88	3/3
78	Knight, Shawn	DE	6-6	288	6/4/64	2	Brigham Young	Sparks, Nev.	D1-'87	10/0
55	†Kohlbrand, Joe	LB	6-4	242	3/18/63	4	Miami	Merritt Island, Fla.	D8-'85	12/0
60	†Korte, Steve	C	6-2	260	1/15/60	6	Arkansas	Littleton, Colo.	D2-'83	3/0
24	Mack, Milton	CB	5-11	182	9/20/63	2	Alcorn State	Jackson, Miss.	D5-'87	13/0
84	Martin, Eric	WR	6-1	207	11/8/61	4	Louisiana State	Van Vleck, Tex.	D7-'85	15/11
39	†Maxie, Brett	S	6-2	194	1/13/62	4	Texas Southern	Dallas, Tex.	FA-'85	12/10
36	Mayes, Rueben	RB	5-11	200	6/16/63	3	Washington State	N. Battleford, Saskatchewan	D3a-'86	12/12
51	Mills, Sam	LB	5-9	225	6/3/59	3	Montclair State	Long Branch, N.J.	FA-'86	12/12
	Nelson, Edmund	NT-DE	6-3	266	4/30/60	7	Auburn	Tampa, Fla.	T(Pitt)-'88	10/8*
88	†Pattison, Mark	WR	6-2	190	12/13/61	3	Washington	Seattle, Wash.	W(Raid)-'87	9/4
29	†Sutton, Reggie	CB	5-10	180	2/15/65	2	Miami	Miami, Fla.	D5-'86	11/3
56	Swilling, Pat	LB	6-3	242	10/25/64	3	Georgia Tech	Toccoa, Ga.	D3b-'87	12/12
69	Swoopes, Patrick	NT	6-4	280	3/4/64	2	Mississippi State	Bradshaw, Miss.	FA-'87	9/3
82	Tice, John	TE	6-5	249	6/22/60	6	Maryland	Central Islip, N.Y.	D3a-'83	12/8
54	Toles, Alvin	LB	6-1	227	3/23/63	4	Tennessee	Forsythe, Ga.	D1-'85	12/0
65	Trapilo, Steve	G	6-5	281	9/20/64	2	Boston College	Milton, Mass.	D4-'87	11/11
73	†Warren, Frank	DE	6-4	290	9/14/59	8	Auburn	Birmingham, Ala.	D3a-'81	12/0
33	Waters, Mike	TE	6-2	230	3/15/62	3	San Diego State	Ridgecrest, Calif.	FA-'87	5/0
44	Waymer, Dave	CB	6-1	188	7/1/58	9	Notre Dame	Charlotte, N.C.	D2-'80	12/12
94	Wilks, Jim	DE	6-5	266	3/12/58	8	San Diego State	Pasadena, Calif.	D12-'81	12/12
18	Wilson, Dave	QB	6-3	206	4/27/59	7	Illinois	Anaheim, Calif.	SD1-'81	4/0
34	Word, Barry	RB	6-2	220	7/17/64	2	Virginia	Long Island, Va.	D3c-'86	12/1

* Benson played 2 games with Washington, 8 with New Orleans in '87; Nelson played 10 games with Pittsburgh.

†Option playout; subject to developments.

Also played with Saints in '87—RB Vincent Alexander (1 game), NT Sheldon Andrus (3), P Tommy Barnhardt (3), RB Dwight Beverly (3), DE Robert Brannon (1), K Mike Cofer (2), LB Joe DeForest (3), NT Ted Elliott (3), LB Keith Fourcade (2), TE Darren Gottschalk (1), WR Vic Harrison (3), T-G Walter Housman (3), QB Kevin Ingram (2), C Phillip James (3), RB Garland Jean-Batiste (3), RB Nate Johnson (1), K Florian Kempf (1), LB Scott Leach (3), G-T William Leach (1), G Greg Loberg (3), LB Ken Marchiol (3), LB Larry McCoy (3), TE Ken O'Neal (3), CB Johnnie Poe (12), QB Tim Riordan (1), RB Jeff Rodenberger (3), LB Bill Roe (3), TE Malcolm Scott (3), CB-S John Sutton (2), S Derrick Taylor (3), WR Curtland Thomas (2), G Henry Thomas (3), WR Joe Thomas (1), CB-S Junior Thurman (3), CB-S Darrell Toussaint (2), WR Dwight Walker (2), S Frank Wattelet (2), LB Ron Weissenhofer (1), S Scott Woerner (1), DE Kevin Young (1).

COACHING STAFF

Head Coach, Jim Mora

Pro Career: Begins third year as NFL coach, after leading Saints to 12-4 record in 1987 and earning NFL coach of the year honors. Came to New Orleans following a three-year career as the winningest coach in USFL history as head coach of the Philadelphia/Baltimore Stars. Directed Stars to championship game in each of his three seasons and won league championship in 1984 and 1985. He won coach of the year honors following the 1984 season. Mora began his pro coaching career in 1978 as defensive line coach of the Seattle Seahawks. In 1982, he became defensive coordinator of the New England Patriots and played a vital role in the Patriots' march to the playoffs that year. No pro playing experience. Career record: 19-13.

Background: Played tight end and defensive end at Occidental College. Assistant coach at Occidental 1960-63 and head coach 1964-67. Linebacker coach at Stanford on a staff that included former Eagles head coach Dick Vermeil. Defensive assistant at Colorado 1968-73. Linebacker coach under Vermeil at UCLA 1974. Defensive coordinator at Washington 1975-77. Received bachelor's degree in physical education from Occidental in 1957. Also holds master's degree in education from Southern California.

Personal: Born May 24, 1935, in Glendale, Calif. Jim and his wife, Connie, live in Metairie, La., and have three sons—Michael, Stephen, and Jim, a defensive assistant for the San Diego Chargers.

Assistant Coaches

Paul Boudreau, offensive line; born December 30, 1949, Somerville, Mass., lives in Metairie, La. Guard Boston College 1971-73. No pro playing experience. College coach: Boston College 1974-76, Maine 1977-78, Dartmouth 1979-81, Navy 1983. Pro coach: Edmonton Eskimos (CFL) 1983-86, joined Saints in 1987.

Dom Capers, defensive backs; born August 7, 1950, Cambridge, Ohio, lives in Metairie, La. Defensive back Mount Union College 1968-71. No pro playing experience. College coach: Hawaii 1975-76, San Jose State 1977, California 1978-79, Tennessee 1980-81, Ohio State 1982-83. Pro coach: Philadelphia/Baltimore Stars (USFL) 1984-85, joined Saints in 1986.

Vic Fangio, outside linebackers; born August 22, 1958, Dunmore, Pa., lives in Destrehan, La. Defensive back East Stroudsburg 1976-78. No pro playing experience. College coach: North Carolina 1983. Pro coach: Philadelphia/Baltimore Stars (USFL) 1983-85, joined Saints in 1986.

Joe Marciano, tight ends-special teams; born February 10, 1954, Scranton, Pa., lives in Metairie, La. Quarterback Temple 1972-75. No pro playing experience. College coach: East Stroudsburg 1977, Rhode Island 1978-79, Villanova 1980, Penn State 1981, Temple 1982. Pro coach: Philadelphia/Baltimore Stars (USFL) 1983-85, joined Saints in 1986.

Russell Paternostro, strength and conditioning; born July 21, 1940, New Orleans, La., lives in Jefferson, La. San Diego State. No college or pro playing experience. Pro coach: Joined Saints in 1981.

John Pease, defensive line; born October 14, 1943, Pittsburgh, Pa., lives in Kenner, La. Wingback Utah 1963-64. No pro playing experience. College coach: Fullerton, Calif., J.C. 1970-73, Long Beach State 1974-76, Utah 1977, Washington 1978-83. Pro coach: Philadelphia/Baltimore Stars (USFL) 1983-85, joined Saints in 1986.

Steve Sidwell, defensive coordinator-inside linebackers; born August 30, 1944, Winfield, Kan., lives in Destrehan, La. Linebacker Colorado 1962-65. No pro playing experience. College coach: Colorado 1966-73, Nevada-Las Vegas 1974-75, Southern Methodist 1976-81. Pro coach: New England Patriots 1982-84, Indianapolis Colts 1985, joined Saints in 1986.

New Orleans Saints 1988 First-Year Roster

Name	Pos.	Ht.	Wt.	Birth-date	College	Hometown	How Acq.
Booker, Darrell	LB	5-11	221	12/19/64	Delaware	Willingboro, N.J.	FA
Brannon, Robert	DE	6-7	245	3/26/61	Arkansas	Portland, Ore.	FA
Carr, Lydell	RB	6-0	226	5/27/65	Oklahoma	Enid, Okla.	D4
Clark, Robert (1)	WR	5-11	175	8/8/65	No. Carolina Central	Richmond, Va.	D10-'87
Couch, Gary	WR	5-11	171	1/2/66	Minnesota	Davenport, Iowa	D11
Craig, Chad	T	6-6	267	2/3/65	Tulsa	Guymon, Okla.	FA
Crow, Mike	P	6-2	200	6/16/64	Northwestern St., La.	Little Rock, Ark.	FA
DeForest, Joe	LB	6-1	240	4/17/65	Southwest Louisiana	Titusville, Fla.	FA
Derby, Glenn	T	6-6	290	6/7/64	Wisconsin	Oconomowoc, Wis.	D8
Evans, Vince	RB	5-10	216	9/8/63	North Carolina State	Fayetteville, N.C.	FA-'87
Fizer, Vincent	LB	6-4	250	10/10/65	Southern	Minden, La.	D10b
Forde, Brian	LB	6-2	225	11/1/63	Washington State	Montreal, Canada	D7
Fourcade, Keith	LB	5-11	225	10/20/61	Mississippi	Marrero, La.	FA
Genilla, Sal	QB	6-2	207	1/8/65	Pittsburgh	San Mateo, Calif.	FA
Hammond, Darryl	CB-S	6-1	207	9/24/66	Virginia	Center Cross, Va.	FA
Henderson, Keith	CB	5-9	183	9/11/65	Texas Tech	Terrell, Tex.	FA
Henderson, Rod	CB-S	5-9	175	8/31/66	Youngstown State	Miami, Fla.	FA
Heyward, Craig	RB	5-11	251	9/26/66	Pittsburgh	Passaic, N.J.	D1
Holloway, Derek	WR	5-6	165	1/17/61	Arkansas	Palmyra, N.J.	FA
Hopkins, Joe	WR	5-9	181	4/28/65	East Texas State	Monroe, La.	FA
Jones, Chris	WR	6-1	186	8/5/64	Northeast Louisiana	Lake Charles, La.	FA
Jones, Kirk	RB	5-9	204	1/5/65	Nevada-Las Vegas	Long Beach, Calif.	FA
Jurgensen, Paul	DE	6-5	243	11/16/65	Georgia Tech	Savannah, Ga.	D12
Keith, Jeff	G	6-2	274	10/26/65	Texas Tech	Arlington, Tex.	FA
Knutson, Mike	G	6-3	266	5/25/65	San Diego State	Anaheim, Calif.	FA
Mandarich, John	NT	6-4	281	8/1/61	Kent State	Oakville, Canada	FA
McCabe, Jim	LB	6-2	223	1/16/65	Morningside	Milford, Iowa	FA
Nunn, Clarence	CB	5-10	176	12/29/64	San Diego State	Gardena, Calif.	D9
Orndorff, Dave	C	6-0	285	4/4/64	Oregon State	Kent, Wash.	FA
Perriman, Brett	WR	5-9	175	10/10/65	Miami	Miami, Fla.	D2
Robinson, Anthony	WR	6-3	178	4/15/66	Elizabeth City State	Wheaton, Md.	FA
Santos, Todd	QB	6-2	207	2/12/64	San Diego State	Fresno, Calif.	D10a
Scales, Greg	TE	6-4	253	5/9/66	Wake Forest	Winston-Salem, N.C.	D5a
Schonyers, Toran	LB	6-1	228	1/2/65	Temple	Burlington, N.J.	FA
Sims, Bob	G	6-3	269	9/2/66	Florida	Fountain Valley, Calif.	D6
Solon, Dave	T	6-5	268	2/15/66	St. Cloud	Columbia Heights, Minn.	FA
Squires, Chris	LB	6-1	223	9/21/64	Tennessee Tech	Merritt, N.C.	FA
Steele, Todd (1)	RB	6-3	245	12/3/63	Southern California	Kingsburg, Calif.	FA-'87
Stephens, Tony	NT	6-3	306	12/13/64	Clemson	Walterboro, S.C.	D3
Taylor, Keith	CB-S	5-11	193	12/21/64	Illinois	Pennsauken, N.J.	D5b
Young, Nay	CB-S	5-9	187	2/10/65	Georgia Southern	Savannah, Ga.	FA

The term NFL Rookie is defined as a player who is in his first season of professional football and has not been on the roster of another professional football team for any regular-season or postseason games. A Rookie is designated by an "R" on NFL rosters. Players who have been active in another professional football league or players who have NFL experience, including either preseason training camp or being on an active roster for fewer than three regular-season or postseason games, are termed NFL First-Year Players. An NFL First-Year Player is designated by a "1" on NFL rosters. Thereafter, a player on an NFL active roster for at least three regular-season or postseason games is credited with an additional year of NFL playing experience.

NOTES

Jim Skipper, running backs; born January 23, 1949, Breaux Bridge, La., lives in Metairie, La. Defensive back Whittier College 1971-72. No pro playing experience. College coach: Cal Poly-Pomona 1974-76, San Jose State 1977-78, Pacific 1979, Oregon 1980-82. Pro coach: Philadelphia/Baltimore Stars (USFL) 1983-85, joined Saints in 1986.

Carl Smith, offensive coordinator-quarterbacks; born April 26, 1948, Wasco, Calif., lives in Metairie, La. Defensive back Cal Poly-SLO 1968-70. No pro playing experience. College coach: Cal Poly-SLO 1971, Colorado 1972-73, Southwestern Louisiana 1974-78, Lamar 1979-81, North Carolina State 1982. Pro coach: Philadelphia/Baltimore Stars (USFL) 1983-85, joined Saints in 1986.

Steve Walters, wide receivers; born June 16, 1948, Jonesboro, Ark., lives in Metairie, La. Quarterback-defensive back Arkansas 1967-70. No pro playing experience. College coach: Tampa 1973, Northeast Louisiana 1974-75, Morehead State 1976, Tulsa 1977-78, Memphis State 1979, Southern Methodist 1980-81, Alabama 1985. Pro coach: New England Patriots 1982-84, joined Saints in 1986.

NEW YORK GIANTS

National Football Conference Eastern Division

Team Colors: Blue, Red, and White

Giants Stadium
East Rutherford, New Jersey 07073
Telephone: (201) 935-8111

Club Officials

President: Wellington T. Mara
Vice President-Treasurer: Timothy J. Mara
Vice President-Secretary: Raymond J. Walsh
Vice President-General Manager: George Young
Assistant General Manager: Harry Hulmes
Controller: John Pasquali
Director of Player Personnel: Tom Boisture
Director of Pro Personnel: Tim Rooney
Director of Media Services: Ed Croke
Director of Promotions: Tom Power
Director of Special Projects: Victor Del Guercio
Box Office Treasurer: Jim Gleason
Trainer Emeritus: John Dziegiel
Head Trainer: Ronnie Barnes
Assistant Trainers: John Johnson, Jim Madaleno
Equipment Manager: Ed Wagner, Jr.

Stadium: Giants Stadium • **Capacity:** 76,891
East Rutherford, New Jersey 07073

Playing Surface: AstroTurf

Training Camp: Fairleigh Dickinson-Madison
Florham Park, N.J. 07932

1988 Schedule

Preseason

Aug. 6	at Green Bay	7:00
Aug. 13	**New York Jets**	8:00
Aug. 20	**Pittsburgh**	8:00
Aug. 26	at Cleveland	9:00

Regular Season

Sept. 5	**Washington** (Monday)	9:00
Sept. 11	**San Francisco**	1:00
Sept. 18	at Dallas	3:00
Sept. 25	**Los Angeles Rams**	4:00
Oct. 2	at Washington	1:00
Oct. 10	at Philadelphia (Monday)	9:00
Oct. 16	**Detroit**	1:00
Oct. 23	at Atlanta	1:00
Oct. 30	at Detroit	4:00
Nov. 6	**Dallas**	1:00
Nov. 13	at Phoenix	2:00
Nov. 20	**Philadelphia**	4:00
Nov. 27	at New Orleans	7:00
Dec. 4	**Phoenix**	1:00
Dec. 11	**Kansas City**	1:00
Dec. 18	at New York Jets	1:00

Giants Coaching History

(442-376-32)

1925	Bob Folwell	8-4-0
1926	Joe Alexander	8-4-1
1927-28	Earl Potteiger	15-8-3
1929-30	LeRoy Andrews	26-5-1
1931-53	Steve Owen	153-108-17
1954-60	Jim Lee Howell	54-29-4
1961-68	Allie Sherman	57-54-4
1969-73	Alex Webster	29-40-1
1974-76	Bill Arnsparger*	7-28-0
1976-78	John McVay	14-23-0
1979-82	Ray Perkins	24-35-0
1983-87	Bill Parcells	47-38-1

*Released after seven games in 1976

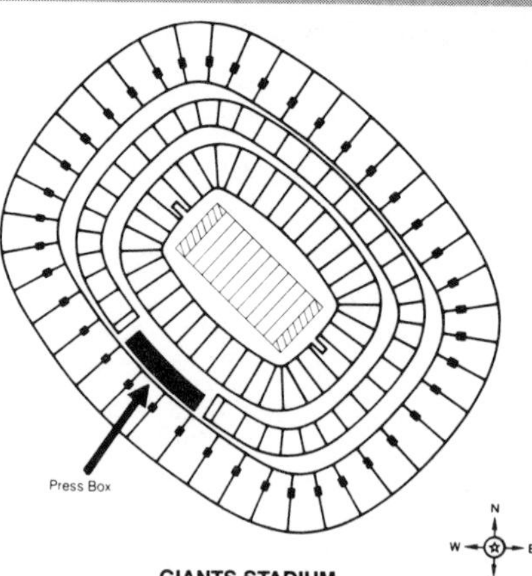

GIANTS STADIUM

Record Holders

Individual Records—Career

Category	Name	Performance
Rushing (Yds.)	Alex Webster, 1955-1964	4,638
Passing (Yds.)	Phil Simms, 1979-1987	19,815
Passing (TDs)	Charlie Conerly, 1948-1961	173
Receiving (No.)	Joe Morrison, 1959-1972	395
Receiving (Yds.)	Frank Gifford, 1952-1960, 1962-64	5,434
Interceptions	Emlen Tunnell, 1948-1958	74
Punting (Avg.)	Don Chandler, 1956-1964	43.8
Punt Return (Avg.)	Bob Hammond, 1976-78	9.1
Kickoff Return (Avg.)	Rocky Thompson, 1971-72	27.2
Field Goals	Pete Gogolak, 1966-1974	126
Touchdowns (Tot.)	Frank Gifford, 1952-1960, 1962-64	78
Points	Pete Gogolak, 1966-1974	646

Individual Records—Single Season

Category	Name	Performance
Rushing (Yds.)	Joe Morris, 1986	1,516
Passing (Yds.)	Phil Simms, 1984	4,044
Passing (TDs)	Y.A. Tittle, 1963	36
Receiving (No.)	Earnest Gray, 1983	78
Receiving (Yds.)	Homer Jones, 1967	1,209
Interceptions	Otto Schnellbacher, 1951	11
	Jim Patton, 1958	11
Punting (Avg.)	Don Chandler, 1959	46.6
Punt Return (Avg.)	Merle Hapes, 1942	15.5
Kickoff Return (Avg.)	John Salscheider, 1949	31.6
Field Goals	Ali Haji-Sheikh, 1983	*35
Touchdowns (Tot.)	Joe Morris, 1985	21
Points	Ali Haji-Sheikh, 1983	127

Individual Records—Single Game

Category	Name	Performance
Rushing (Yds.)	Gene Roberts, 11-12-50	218
Passing (Yds.)	Phil Simms, 10-13-85	513
Passing (TDs)	Y.A. Tittle, 10-28-62	*7
Receiving (No.)	Mark Bavaro, 10-13-85	12
Receiving (Yds.)	Del Shofner, 10-28-62	269
Interceptions	Many times	3
	Last time by Terry Kinard, 9-27-87	
Field Goals	Joe Danelo, 10-18-81	6
Touchdowns (Tot.)	Ron Johnson, 10-2-72	4
	Earnest Gray, 9-7-80	4
Points	Ron Johnson, 10-2-72	24
	Earnest Gray, 9-7-80	24

*NFL Record

1987 Team Record

Preseason (3-1)

Date	Result		Opponents
8/16	W	19-17	at New England
8/22	W	24-10	Cleveland
8/29	L	23-30	N.Y. Jets
9/4	W	26-20	at Cincinnati
		92-77	

Regular Season (6-9)

Date	Result		Opponents	Att.
9/14	L	19-34	at Chicago	65,704
9/20	L	14-16	Dallas	73,426
9/27	C		at Miami	
10/5	L	21-41	San Francisco	16,471
10/11	L	12-38	Washington	9,123
10/18	L	3- 6	at Buffalo (OT)	15,737
10/25	W	30- 7	St. Louis	74,391
11/2	L	24-33	at Dallas	55,730
11/8	W	17-10	New England	73,817
11/15	W	20-17	at Philadelphia	66,172
11/22	L	14-23	at New Orleans	67,639
11/29	L	19-23	at Washington	45,815
12/6	W	23-20	Philadelphia (OT)	65,874
12/13	L	24-27	at St. Louis	29,623
12/19	W	20-10	Green Bay	51,013
12/27	W	20- 7	N.Y. Jets	68,318

(OT) Overtime
C (Cancelled due to players' strike.)

Score by Periods

Giants	62	83	75	57	3	—	280
Opponents	53	85	60	111	3	—	312

Attendance

Home 432,433 Away 346,420 Total 778,853
Single-game home record, 76,633 (1-11-87)
Single-season home record, 594,433 (1986)

1987 Team Statistics

	Giants	Opp.
Total First Downs	266	275
Rushing	80	97
Passing	168	148
Penalty	18	30
Third Down: Made/Att.	76/217	77/237
Fourth Down: Made/Att.	9/14	6/15
Total Net Yards	4659	4658
Avg. Per Game	310.6	310.5
Total Plays	1000	1056
Avg. Per Play	4.7	4.4
Net Yards Rushing	1457	1768
Avg. Per Game	97.1	117.9
Total Rushes	440	493
Net Yards Passing	3202	2890
Avg. Per Game	213.5	192.7
Sacked/Yards Lost	61/443	55/382
Gross Yards	3645	3272
Att./Completions	499/265	508/292
Completion Pct.	53.1	57.5
Had Intercepted	22	20
Punts/Avg.	91/39.6	96/38.1
Net Punting Avg.	29.2	31.3
Penalties/Yards Lost	100/835	97/802
Fumbles/Ball Lost	38/20	31/14
Touchdowns	32	35
Rushing	4	14
Passing	26	17
Returns	2	4
Avg. Time of Possession	28:20	31:40

1987 Individual Statistics

Scoring

Scoring	TD R	TD P	TD Rt	PAT	FG	Saf	TP
Allegre	0	0	0	25/26	17/27	0	76
Bavaro	0	8	0	0/0	0/0	0	48
Manuel	0	6	0	0/0	0/0	0	36
Morris	3	0	0	0/0	0/0	0	18
Adams	1	1	0	0/0	0/0	0	12
Baker	0	2	0	0/0	0/0	0	12
Benyola	0	0	0	3/3	3/5	0	12
Lovelady	0	2	0	0/0	0/0	0	12
Robinson	0	2	0	0/0	0/0	0	12
Bennett	0	1	0	0/0	0/0	0	6
Flynn	0	0	1	0/0	0/0	0	6
Kinard	0	0	1	0/0	0/0	0	6
McGowan	0	1	0	0/0	0/0	0	6
Mowatt	0	1	0	0/0	0/0	0	6
Rouson	0	1	0	0/0	0/0	0	6
Turner	0	1	0	0/0	0/0	0	6
Giants	4	26	2	28/32	20/32	0	280
Opponents	14	17	4	33/35	23/34	0	312

Passing

Passing	Att.	Comp.	Yds.	Pct.	TD	Int.	Tkld.	Rate
Simms	282	163	2230	57.8	17	9	35/225	90.0
Rutledge	155	79	1048	51.0	5	11	17/129	53.9
Busch	47	17	278	36.2	3	2	7/72	60.4
Crocicchia	15	6	89	40.0	1	0	2/17	82.4
Giants	499	265	3645	53.1	26	22	61/443	75.8
Opponents	508	292	3272	57.5	17	20	55/382	71.6

Rushing

Rushing	Att.	Yds.	Avg.	LG	TD
Morris	193	658	3.4	34	3
Adams	61	169	2.8	14	1
Rouson	41	155	3.8	14	0
V. Williams	29	108	3.7	17	0
DiRico	25	90	3.6	14	0
Galbreath	10	74	7.4	17	0
Carthon	26	60	2.3	10	0
Simms	14	44	3.1	20	0
Rutledge	15	31	2.1	20	0
Beecham	5	22	4.4	10	0
Baker	1	18	18.0	18	0
Lovelady	2	11	5.5	8	0
Park	6	11	1.8	4	0
Anderson	2	6	3.0	4	0
Crocicchia	4	5	1.3	7	0
DiRenzo	1	5	5.0	5	0
Covington	4	0	0.0	2	0
Manuel	1	−10	−10.0	−10	0
Giants	440	1457	3.3	34	4
Opponents	493	1768	3.6	30	14

Receiving

Receiving	No.	Yds.	Avg.	LG	TD
Bavaro	55	867	15.8	38	8
Adams	35	298	8.5	25	1
Manuel	30	545	18.2	50t	6
Galbreath	26	248	9.5	21	0
Baker	15	277	18.5	50	2
McConkey	11	186	16.9	31	0
Rouson	11	129	11.7	26t	1
Morris	11	114	10.4	25	0
Turner	10	195	19.5	36	1
Bennett	10	184	18.4	46t	1
Lovelady	10	125	12.5	23t	2
Carthon	8	71	8.9	25	0
J. Smith	6	72	12.0	19	0
Robinson	6	58	9.7	14	2
V. Williams	5	36	7.2	12	0
McGowan	4	111	27.8	63t	1
Mowatt	3	39	13.0	29	1
Ingram	2	32	16.0	18	0
DiRico	2	22	11.0	15	0
Anderson	2	16	8.0	9	0
Covington	1	9	9.0	9	0
Park	1	6	6.0	6	0
Coleman	1	5	5.0	5	0
Giants	265	3645	13.8	63t	26
Opponents	292	3272	11.2	64t	17

Interceptions

Interceptions	No.	Yds.	Avg.	LG	TD
Kinard	5	163	32.6	70t	1
Taylor	3	16	5.3	15	0
Collins	2	28	14.0	28	0
Headen	2	25	12.5	20	0
Welch	2	7	3.5	7	0
Rehage	1	14	14.0	14	0
DeRose	1	10	10.0	10	0
Brown	1	4	4.0	4	0
Hill	1	1	1.0	1	0
Banks	1	0	0.0	0	0
P. Williams	1	−5	−5.0	−5	0
Giants	20	263	13.2	70t	1
Opponents	22	164	7.5	28	1

Punting

Punting	No.	Yds.	Avg.	In 20	LG
Landeta	65	2773	42.7	13	64
Moore	14	486	34.7	0	46
Miller	10	345	34.5	1	53
Giants	91	3604	39.6	14	64
Opponents	96	3653	38.1	14	56

Punt Returns

Punt Returns	No.	FC	Yds.	Avg.	LG	TD
McConkey	42	14	394	9.4	37	0
Lovelady	10	0	38	3.8	14	0
Baker	3	0	16	5.3	6	0
Giants	55	14	448	8.1	37	0
Opponents	51	11	811	15.9	94t	2

Kickoff Returns

Kickoff Returns	No.	Yds.	Avg.	LG	TD
Rouson	22	497	22.6	49	0
Adams	9	166	18.4	27	0
Ingram	6	114	19.0	25	0
Byrd	4	99	24.8	34	0
Norris	4	70	17.5	29	0
Beecham	3	70	23.3	30	0
DiRico	2	31	15.5	25	0
Bavaro	1	16	16.0	16	0
Coleman	1	20	20.0	20	0
Cummings	1	11	11.0	11	0
Dorsey	1	13	13.0	13	0
McConkey	1	8	8.0	8	0
Urch	1	13	13.0	13	0
Giants	56	1128	20.1	49	0
Opponents	68	1463	21.5	64	0

Sacks

Sacks	No.
Taylor	12.0
Banks	9.0
Marshall	8.0
E. Howard	5.5
Martin	5.0
Berthusen, Cin.-Giants	2.5
Headen	2.5
Burt	2.0
Thompson	2.0
Collins	1.5
Lasker	1.5
Carson	1.0
Dorsey	1.0
Hill	1.0
P. Johnson	1.0
Reasons	1.0
Washington	1.0
Giants	55.0
Opponents	61.0

New York Giants 1988 Veteran Roster

No.	Name	Pos.	Ht.	Wt.	Birth-date	NFL Exp.	College	Hometown	How Acq.	'87 Games/ Starts
59	Abraham, Robert	LB	6-1	236	7/13/60	6	North Carolina State	Myrtle Beach, S.C.	FA-'88	2/0*
33	Adams, George	RB	6-1	225	12/22/62	3	Kentucky	Lexington, Ky.	D1-'85	12/7
2	Allegre, Raul	K	5-10	167	6/15/59	6	Texas	Torreon, Mexico	FA-'86	12/0
24	Anderson, Ottis	RB	6-2	225	11/19/57	10	Miami	West Palm Beach, Fla.	T(StL)-'86	4/0
67	Ard, Bill	G	6-3	270	3/12/59	8	Wake Forest	Watchung, N.J.	D8c-'81	12/12
85	Baker, Stephen	WR	5-8	160	8/30/64	2	Fresno State	San Antonio, Tex.	D3-'87	12/5
58	†Banks, Carl	LB	6-4	235	8/29/62	5	Michigan State	Flint, Mich.	D1-'84	12/12
89	†Bavaro, Mark	TE	6-4	245	4/28/63	4	Notre Dame	Danvers, Mass.	D4-'85	12/12
79	Berthusen, Bill	NT	6-5	285	6/26/64	2	Iowa State	Grinnell, Iowa	D12-'87	4/3*
47	Brown, Don	CB	5-11	189	11/28/63	3	Maryland	Annapolis, Md.	FA-'87	3/3
64	Burt, Jim	NT	6-1	260	6/7/59	8	Miami	Orchard Park, N.Y.	FA-'81	8/8
35	Byrd, Boris	CB-S	6-0	210	4/15/62	2	Austin Peay	Bowling Green, Ky.	FA-'88	3/0
53	Carson, Harry	LB	6-2	240	11/26/53	13	South Carolina State	Florence, N.C.	D4-'76	12/12
44	†Carthon, Maurice	RB	6-1	225	4/24/61	4	Arkansas State	Osceola, Ark.	FA-'85	11/5
21	†Clayton, Harvey	CB	5-9	186	4/4/61	5	Florida State	Florida City, Fla.	FA-'87	2/0
25	Collins, Mark	CB	5-10	190	1/16/64	3	Cal State-Fullerton	San Bernardino, Calif.	D2-'86	11/11
77	Dorsey, Eric	DE	6-5	280	8/5/64	3	Notre Dame	McLean, Va.	D1-'86	12/3
28	Flynn, Tom	S	6-0	195	3/24/62	5	Pittsburgh	Verona, Pa.	FA-'87	12/0
30	Galbreath, Tony	RB	6-0	228	1/29/54	13	Missouri	Fulton, Mo.	T(Minn)-'84	12/0
61	†Godfrey, Chris	G	6-3	265	5/17/58	6	Michigan	Detroit, Mich.	FA-'84	8/5
37	Haddix, Wayne	CB	6-1	203	7/23/65	2	Liberty	Bolivar, Tenn.	FA-'87	5/0
54	†Headen, Andy	LB	6-5	242	7/8/60	6	Clemson	Asheboro, N.C.	D8-'83	12/2
48	Hill, Kenny	S	6-0	195	7/25/58	8	Yale	Oak Grove, La.	T(Raid)-'84	12/12
15	Hostetler, Jeff	QB	6-3	212	4/22/61	4	West Virginia	Johnston, Pa.	D3-'84	0*
74	Howard, Erik	NT	6-4	268	11/12/64	3	Washington State	San Jose, Calif.	D2a-'86	12/4
57	Hunt, Byron	LB	6-5	242	12/17/58	8	Southern Methodist	Longview, Tex.	D9-'81	12/0
82	Ingram, Mark	WR	5-10	188	8/23/65	2	Michigan State	Flint, Mich.	D1-'87	9/0
68	†Johnson, Damian	T	6-5	290	12/18/62	3	Kansas State	Great Bend, Kan.	FA-'86	12/7
52	Johnson, Thomas	LB	6-3	248	7/29/64	3	Ohio State	Detroit, Mich.	D2b-'86	12/12
59	Johnston, Brian	C	6-3	275	11/26/62	3	North Carolina	Highland, Md.	D3a-'85	5/0
51	Jones, Robbie	LB	6-2	230	12/25/59	5	Alabama	Demopolis, Ala.	D12-'84	12/0
43	Kinard, Terry	S	6-1	200	11/24/59	6	Clemson	Sumter, S.C.	D1-'83	12/12
5	†Landeta, Sean	P	6-0	200	1/6/62	4	Towson State	Baltimore, Md.	FA-'85	12/0
46	Lasker, Greg	S	6-0	200	9/28/64	3	Arkansas	Conway, Ark.	D2c-'86	11/0
86	Manuel, Lionel	WR	5-11	180	4/13/62	5	Pacific	La Puente, Calif.	D7-'84	12/12
70	Marshall, Leonard	DE	6-3	285	10/22/61	6	Louisiana State	Franklin, La.	D2-'83	10/10
75	Martin, George	DE	6-4	255	2/16/53	14	Oregon	Fairfield, Calif.	D11-'75	12/9
80	McConkey, Phil	WR	5-10	170	2/24/57	5	Navy	Buffalo, N.Y.	FA-'84	12/0
20	Morris, Joe	RB	5-7	195	9/15/60	7	Syracuse	Ayer, Mass.	D2-'82	11/10
84	Mowatt, Zeke	TE	6-3	240	3/5/61	5	Florida State	Wauchula, Fla.	FA-'83	12/1
63	†Nelson, Karl	T	6-6	285	6/14/60	4	Iowa State	De Kalb, Ill.	D2-'83	0*
65	Oates, Bart	C	6-3	265	12/16/58	4	Brigham Young	Albany, Ga.	FA-'85	12/12
55	Reasons, Gary	LB	6-4	234	2/18/62	5	Northwestern State, La.	Crowley, Tex.	D4a-'84	10/0
72	Riesenberg, Doug	T	6-5	275	7/22/65	2	California	Moscow, Idaho	D6a-'87	8/0
66	†Roberts, William	T	6-5	280	8/5/62	4	Ohio State	Miami, Fla.	D1a-'84	12/12
81	Robinson, Stacy	WR	5-11	186	2/19/62	4	North Dakota State	St. Paul, Minn.	D2-'85	5/4
22	Rouson, Lee	RB	6-1	222	10/18/62	4	Colorado	Greensboro, N.C.	D8-'85	12/2
17	Rutledge, Jeff	QB	6-1	195	1/22/57	10	Alabama	Birmingham, Ala.	T(Rams)-'82	13/4
31	Sanders, Charles	RB	6-1	230	4/24/64	3	Slippery Rock	Pittsburgh, Pa.	FA-'88	5/0*
11	Simms, Phil	QB	6-3	214	11/3/56	9	Morehead State	Louisville, Ky.	D1-'79	9/9
56	Taylor, Lawrence	LB	6-3	243	2/4/59	8	North Carolina	Williamsburg, Va.	D1-'81	12/11
83	Turner, Odessa	WR	6-3	205	10/12/64	2	Northwestern State, La.	Monroe, La.	D4-'87	7/2
34	Varajon, Michael	RB	6-1	232	7/12/64	2	Toledo	Detroit, Mich.	FA-'87	3/0*
73	Washington, John	DE	6-4	275	2/20/63	3	Oklahoma State	Houston, Tex.	D3-'86	12/2
27	Welch, Herb	CB-S	5-11	180	1/12/61	4	UCLA	Downey, Calif.	D12-'85	12/2
36	White, Adrian	S	6-0	200	4/6/64	2	Florida	Orange Park, Fla.	D2-'87	6/1
23	Williams, Perry	CB	6-2	203	5/12/61	5	North Carolina State	Hamlet, N.C.	D7-'83	10/10

* Abraham played 2 games with Houston in '87; Berthusen played 3 games with Cincinnati, 1 with N.Y. Giants; Hostetler active for 2 games but did not play; Nelson missed '87 season due to illness; Sanders played 5 games with Pittsburgh; Varajon played 3 games with San Francisco in '87.

†Option playout; subject to developments.

Retired—Tackle Brad Benson, 10-year veteran, 12 games in '87.

Also played with Giants in '87—WR Beau Almodobar (2), RB Earl Beecham (1), WR Lewis Bennett (3), K George Benyola (3), CB Don Brown (3), LB Charlie Burgess (2), QB Mike Busch (2), DE Reggie Carr (3), TE Charles Coleman (3), RB Jamie Covington (2), QB Jim Crocicchia (1), WR Mack Cummings (1), LB Chris Davis (3), G Kelvin Davis (1), LB Dan DeRose (3), RB Fred DiRenzo (1), RB Robert DiRico (3), G William Dugan (3), DE Curtis Garrett (3), G Anthony Howard (3), C Chris Jones (3), DE James Jones (active for 1 game but did not play), QB Paul Kelly (active for 2 games but did not play), LB Jerry Kimmel (2), WR Edwin Lovelady (3), WR Reggie McGowan (3), T Kevin Meuth (3), P Jim Miller (1), C Russell Mitchell (3), P Dana Moore (2), G Dan Morgan (2), S Pat Morrison (1), LB Frank Nicholson (3), CB Jimmy Norris (3), RB Kaulana Park (2), CB Elvis Patterson (1), T Marty Peterson (active for 1 game but did not play), S Robert Porter (3), S Steve Rehage (3), WR Warren Seitz (2), DE Brian Sisley (3), CB Doug Smith (3), TE Jeff Smith (3), DE Torin Smith (1), T Frank Sutton (2), T Gregg Swartwoudt (1), DE Joe Taibi (3), LB Warren Thompson (3), LB Jeff Tootle (3), G Scott Urch (3), RB Van Williams (3), S Jim Yarbrough (3).

COACHING STAFF

Head Coach, Bill Parcells

Pro Career: Became twelfth head coach in New York Giants history on December 15, 1982. Parcells begins sixth campaign as head coach after spending two seasons as the Giants' defensive coordinator and linebacker coach. Led Giants to Super Bowl XXI victory over Denver 39-20 after Wild Card playoff berths in both 1984 and 1985. Started pro coaching career in 1980 as linebacker coach with New England Patriots. Career record: 47-38-1.

Background: Linebacker at Wichita State 1961-63. College assistant Hastings (Neb.) 1964, Wichita State 1965, Army 1966-69, Florida State 1970-72, Vanderbilt 1973-74, Texas Tech 1975-77, Air Force 1978 (head coach).

Personal: Born August 22, 1941, Englewood, N.J. Bill and his wife, Judy, live in Upper Saddle River, N.J., and have three daughters—Suzy, Jill, and Dallas.

Assistant Coaches

Bill Belichick, defensive coordinator; born April 16, 1952, Nashville, Tenn., lives in Chatham, N.J. Center-tight end Wesleyan 1972-74. No pro playing experience. Pro coach: Baltimore Colts 1975, Detroit Lions 1976-77, Denver Broncos 1978, joined Giants in 1979.

Tom Coughlin, receivers; born August 31, 1946, Waterloo, N.Y., lives in East Rutherford, N.J. Halfback Syracuse 1965-67. No pro playing experience. College coach: Rochester Tech 1969-73 (head coach), Syracuse 1974-80, Boston College 1981-83. Pro coach: Philadelphia Eagles 1984-85, Green Bay Packers 1986-87, joined Giants in 1988.

Romeo Crennell, special teams; born June 18, 1947, Lynchburg, Va., lives in Montvale, N.J. Defensive lineman Western Kentucky 1966-69. No pro playing experience. College coach: Western Kentucky 1970-74, Texas Tech 1975-77, Mississippi 1978-79, Georgia Tech 1980. Pro coach: Joined Giants in 1981.

Ron Erhardt, offensive coordinator; born February 27, 1932, Mandan, N.D., lives in Wykoff, N.J. Quarterback Jamestown (N.D.) College 1951-54. No pro playing experience. College coach: North Dakota State 1963-72 (head coach 1966-72). Pro coach: New England Patriots 1973-81 (head coach 1979-81), joined Giants in 1982.

Len Fontes, defensive backfield; born March 8, 1938, New Bedford, Mass., lives in Dover, N.J. Defensive back Ohio State 1958-59. No pro playing experience. College coach: Eastern Michigan 1968, Dayton 1969-72, Navy 1973-76, Miami 1977-79. Pro coach: Cleveland Browns 1980-82, joined Giants in 1983.

Ray Handley, running backs; born October 8, 1944, Artesia, N.M., lives in West Orange, N.J. Running back Stanford 1963-65. No pro playing experience. College coach: Stanford 1967, 1971-74, 1979-83, Army 1968-69, Air Force 1975-78. Pro coach: Joined Giants in 1984.

Fred Hoaglin, offensive line; born January 28, 1944, Alliance, Ohio, lives in Sparta, N.J. Center Pittsburgh 1962-65. Pro center Cleveland Browns 1966-72, Baltimore Colts 1973, Houston Oilers 1974-75, Seattle Seahawks 1976. Pro coach: Detroit Lions 1978-84, joined Giants in 1985.

Lamar Leachman, defensive line; born August 7, 1934, Cartersville, Ga., lives in Ridgewood, N.J. Center-linebacker Tennessee 1952-55. No pro playing experience. College coach: Richmond 1966-67, Georgia Tech 1968-71, Memphis State 1972, South Carolina 1973. Pro coach: New York Stars (WFL) 1974, Toronto Argonauts (CFL) 1975-77, Montreal Alouettes (CFL) 1978-79, joined Giants in 1980.

Johnny Parker, strength and conditioning; born February 1, 1947, Greenville, S.C., lives in Montvale, N.J. No pro playing experience. Graduate of Mississippi, master's degree from Delta State University. College coach: South Carolina 1974-76, Indiana 1977-79, Louisiana State 1980, Mississippi 1981-83. Pro coach: Joined Giants in 1984.

Mike Pope, tight ends; born March 15, 1942, Monroe, N.C., lives in River Vale, N.J. Quarterback Lenoir Rhyne 1962-64. No pro playing experience. College coach: Florida State 1970-74, Texas Tech 1975-77, Mississippi 1978-82. Pro coach: Joined Giants in 1983.

Mike Sweatman, assistant special teams; born October 23, 1946, Kansas City, Mo., lives in Wayne, N.J. Linebacker Kansas 1964-67. No pro playing experience. College coach: Kansas 1973-74, 1979-82, Tulsa 1977-78, Tennessee 1983. Pro coach: Minnesota Vikings 1984, joined Giants in 1985.

New York Giants 1988 First-Year Roster

Name	Pos.	Ht.	Wt.	Birth-date	College	Hometown	How Acq.
Ariey, Mike	T	6-6	285	3/12/64	San Diego State	Bakersfield, Calif.	FA
Black, Mike (1)	T	6-4	280	8/24/64	Cal St.-Sacramento	Auburn, Calif.	FA-'87
Borcky, Dennis (1)	NT	6-3	284	9/14/64	Memphis State	Trainer, Pa.	FA-'87
Brown, Henry	NT	6-3	265	10/1/65	Florida	Fort Myers, Fla.	FA
Brownlee, Brandy	K	6-1	225	12/9/65	Washington	Dallas, Tex.	FA
Carter, Jon	DE	6-4	260	3/12/65	Pittsburgh	Angie, La.	D5
Compton, J.R.	RB	6-0	214	11/4/65	West Texas State	Hale Centre, Tex.	FA
Dominic, Steve	DE	6-5	262	6/10/66	Cal State-Northridge	San Diego, Calif.	FA
Donovan, Mark	QB	6-4	205	2/15/66	Brown	Pittsburgh, Pa.	FA
Elliott, John	T	6-7	305	4/1/65	Michigan	Lake Ronkonkoma, N.Y.	D2
Futrell, David	DE	6-1	265	3/20/66	Brigham Young	Baytown, Tex.	D12a
Harris, Greg	WR	5-9	160	12/30/65	Troy State	Okeechobee, Fla.	D11
Hickerson, Eric	CB-S	6-2	215	10/4/65	Indiana	New Albany, Ind.	D10a
Howard, Stanley	WR	5-10	171	5/22/65	Murray State	Jersey City, N.J.	FA
Houle, David	G	6-4	278	1/20/65	Michigan State	Detroit, Mich.	D6
Johnson, Thomas	TE	6-6	257	7/9/64	New Hampshire	Garden Grove, Calif.	FA
Lilly, Sammy	CB-S	5-9	172	2/12/65	Georgia Tech	Anchorage, Ala.	D8
Martin, Andrew	LB	6-3	245	6/24/66	Holy Cross	Detroit, Mich.	FA
McCormack, Brendan	DE	6-6	270	3/17/66	South Carolina	Chicago, Ill.	D12b
McLean, Ronald	DE	6-3	274	3/13/63	Cal State-Fullerton	Santa Maria, Calif.	FA
Medlock, James	RB	6-2	225	11/17/64	Purdue	Waycross, Ga.	FA
Morrow, Terry	RB	5-8	198	3/17/66	Central State, Mo.	St. Louis, Mo.	FA
Moore, Eric	T	6-5	290	1/21/65	Indiana	Berkeley, Mo.	D1
Nave, Stevan	G	6-2	265	8/29/63	Kansas	Nowata, Okla.	FA
Neal, Michael	DE	6-3	273	9/26/64	Weber State	Tallah, La.	FA
Oglesby, Eric	WR	5-9	168	7/30/65	Northern Colorado	Tallahassee, Fla.	FA
Oliver, Tommy	DE	6-4	257	8/4/64	Alabama State	Troy, Ala.	FA
Perez, Mike	QB	6-1	210	3/7/65	San Jose State	Denver, Colo.	D7a
Salonoa, Thor	LB	6-1	249	7/9/65	Brigham Young	Honolulu, Hawaii	FA
Shaw, Ricky	LB	6-4	240	7/28/65	Oklahoma State	Fayetteville, N.C.	D4
Stewart, Michael	WR	6-3	198	11/1/64	Pittsburgh	Cleveland, Ohio	FA
Thaxton, Galand	LB	6-1	240	10/23/64	Wyoming	London, England	FA
Williams, John	WR	6-0	180	4/5/64	Kansas State	Lakeland, Fla.	FA
Whitaker, Danta	TE	6-3	240	3/14/65	Mississippi Valley St.	Atlanta, Ga.	D7b
White, Sheldon	CB-S	5-11	188	3/1/65	Miami, Ohio	Dayton, Ohio	D3
Wilkes, Steve	TE	6-5	250	5/18/66	Appalachian State	Thomasville, N.C.	D10b
Wimbley, Keenan	LB	6-1	234	7/9/66	Central Florida	Miami, Fla.	FA

The term NFL Rookie is defined as a player who is in his first season of professional football and has not been on the roster of another professional football team for any regular-season or postseason games. A Rookie is designated by an "R" on NFL rosters. Players who have been active in another professional football league or players who have NFL experience, including either preseason training camp or being on an active roster for fewer than three regular-season or postseason games, are termed NFL First-Year Players. An NFL First-Year Player is designated by a "1" on NFL rosters. Thereafter, a player on an NFL active roster for at least three regular-season or postseason games is credited with an additional year of NFL playing experience.

NOTES

National Football Conference Eastern Division

Team Colors: Kelly Green, Silver, and White

Veterans Stadium
Broad Street and Pattison Avenue
Philadelphia, Pennsylvania 19148
Telephone: (215) 463-2500

Club Officials

Owner: Norman Braman
President-Chief Operating Officer: Harry Gamble
Vice President-Chief Financial Officer: Mimi Box
Vice President-Marketing and Development: Decker Uhlhorn
Vice President-Player Personnel: Bill Davis
Assistants to the President: George Azar, Patrick Forte
Director of Player Personnel: Joe Woolley
Talent Scouts: Bill Baker, Lou Blumling, King Hill
Director of Public Relations: Ron Howard
Associate Directors of Sales and Marketing: Jim Gallagher, Leslie Stephenson
Director of Administration: Vicki Chatley
Ticket Manager: Leo Carlin
Director of Penthouse Sales: Lou Scheinfeld
Assistant Director of Penthouse Sales: Ken Iman
Trainer: Otho Davis
Assistant Trainer: David Price
Player Relations Consultant: Lem Burnham, Ph.D.
Equipment Manager: Rusty Sweeney
Video Director: Mike Dougherty

Stadium: Veterans Stadium • **Capacity:** 65,356
Broad Street and Pattison Avenue
Philadelphia, Pennsylvania 19148

Playing Surface: AstroTurf-8

Training Camp: West Chester University
West Chester, Pennsylvania 19382

1988 Schedule

Preseason

Aug. 6	**New York Jets**	7:30
Aug. 14	at Pittsburgh	8:00
Aug. 20	**New England**	7:30
Aug. 25	at Detroit	7:30

Regular Season

Sept. 4	at Tampa Bay	1:00
Sept. 11	**Cincinnati**	4:00
Sept. 18	at Washington	1:00
Sept. 25	at Minnesota	12:00
Oct. 2	**Houston**	1:00
Oct. 10	**New York Giants** (Monday)	9:00
Oct. 16	at Cleveland	1:00
Oct. 23	**Dallas**	1:00
Oct. 30	**Atlanta**	1:00
Nov. 6	**Los Angeles Rams**	1:00
Nov. 13	at Pittsburgh	1:00
Nov. 20	at New York Giants	4:00
Nov. 27	**Phoenix**	1:00
Dec. 4	**Washington**	1:00
Dec. 10	at Phoenix (Saturday)	2:00
Dec. 18	at Dallas	12:00

Eagles Coaching History

(302-394-24)

1933-35	Lud Wray	9-21-1
1936-40	Bert Bell	10-44-2
1941-50	Earle (Greasy) Neale*	66-44-5
1951	Alvin (Bo) McMillin**	2-0-0
1951	Wayne Millner	2-8-0
1952-55	Jim Trimble	25-20-3
1956-57	Hugh Devore	7-16-1
1958-60	Lawrence (Buck) Shaw	20-16-1
1961-63	Nick Skorich	15-24-3
1964-68	Joe Kuharich	28-41-1
1969-71	Jerry Williams***	7-22-2
1971-72	Ed Khayat	8-15-2
1973-75	Mike McCormack	16-25-1
1976-82	Dick Vermeil	57-51-0
1983-85	Marion Campbell****	17-29-1
1985	Fred Bruney	1-0-0
1986-87	Buddy Ryan	12-18-1

*Co-coach with Walt Kiesling in Philadelphia-Pittsburgh merger in 1943
**Retired after two games in 1951
***Released after three games in 1971
****Released after 15 games in 1985

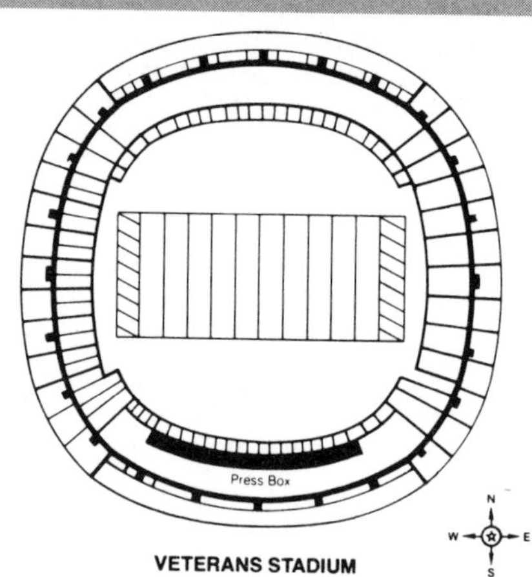

VETERANS STADIUM

Record Holders

Individual Records—Career

Category	Name	Performance
Rushing (Yds.)	Wilbert Montgomery, 1977-1984	6,538
Passing (Yds.)	Ron Jaworski, 1977-1986	26,963
Passing (TDs)	Ron Jaworski, 1977-1986	175
Receiving (No.)	Harold Carmichael, 1971-1983	589
Receiving (Yds.)	Harold Carmichael, 1971-1983	8,978
Interceptions	Bill Bradley, 1969-1976	34
Punting (Avg.)	Joe Muha, 1946-1950	42.9
Punt Return (Avg.)	Steve Van Buren, 1944-1951	13.9
Kickoff Return (Avg.)	Steve Van Buren, 1944-1951	26.7
Field Goals	Paul McFadden, 1984-87	91
Touchdowns (Tot.)	Harold Carmichael, 1971-1983	79
Points	Bobby Walston, 1951-1962	881

Individual Records—Single Season

Category	Name	Performance
Rushing (Yds.)	Wilbert Montgomery, 1979	1,512
Passing (Yds.)	Sonny Jurgensen, 1961	3,723
Passing (TDs)	Sonny Jurgensen, 1961	32
Receiving (No.)	Mike Quick, 1985	71
Receiving (Yds.)	Mike Quick, 1983	1,409
Interceptions	Bill Bradley, 1971	11
Punting (Avg.)	Joe Muha, 1948	47.2
Punt Return (Avg.)	Steve Van Buren, 1944	15.3
Kickoff Return (Avg.)	Al Nelson, 1972	29.1
Field Goals	Paul McFadden, 1984	30
Touchdowns (Tot.)	Steve Van Buren, 1945	18
Points	Paul McFadden, 1984	116

Individual Records—Single Game

Category	Name	Performance
Rushing (Yds.)	Steve Van Buren, 11-27-49	205
Passing (Yds.)	Bobby Thomason, 11-18-53	437
Passing (TDs)	Adrian Burk, 10-17-54	*7
Receiving (No.)	Don Looney, 12-1-40	14
Receiving (Yds.)	Tommy McDonald, 12-10-60	237
Interceptions	Russ Craft, 9-24-50	*4
Field Goals	Tom Dempsey, 11-12-72	6
Touchdowns (Tot.)	Many times Last time by Wilbert Montgomery, 10-7-79	4
Points	Bobby Walston, 10-17-54	25

*NFL Record

1987 Team Record

Preseason (1-3)

Date	Result		Opponents
8/15	L	10-13	at N.Y. Jets
8/23	W	19-13	at New England (OT)
8/29	L	3-35	Miami
9/3	L	3-36	Detroit
		35-97	

Regular Season (7-8)

Date	Result		Opponents	Att.
9/13	L	24-34	at Washington	52,188
9/20	W	27-17	New Orleans	57,485
9/27	C		at San Francisco	
10/4	L	3-35	Chicago	4,074
10/11	L	22-41	at Dallas	40,622
10/18	L	10-16	at Green Bay (OT)	35,842
10/25	W	37-20	Dallas	61,630
11/1	W	28-23	at St. Louis	24,586
11/8	W	31-27	Washington	63,609
11/15	L	17-20	N.Y. Giants	66,172
11/22	L	19-31	St. Louis	55,592
11/29	W	34-31	at New Eng. (OT)	54,198
12/6	L	20-23	at N.Y. Giants (OT)	65,874
12/13	L	10-28	Miami	63,841
12/20	W	38-27	at N.Y. Jets	30,572
12/27	W	17- 7	Buffalo	57,547

(OT) Overtime
C (Cancelled due to players' strike.)

Score by Periods

Eagles	46	118	86	84	3	—	337
Opponents	88	133	65	85	9	—	380

Attendance

Home 429,950 Away 303,882 Total 733,832
Single-game home record, 72,111 (11-1-81)
Single-season home record, 557,325 (1980)

1987 Team Statistics

	Eagles	Opp.
Total First Downs	289	301
Rushing	112	85
Passing	154	186
Penalty	23	30
Third Down: Made/Att.	75/241	69/216
Fourth Down: Made/Att.	8/19	7/17
Total Net Yards	5077	5249
Avg. Per Game	338.5	349.9
Total Plays	1101	1046
Avg. Per Play	4.6	5.0
Net Yards Rushing	2027	1643
Avg. Per Game	135.1	109.5
Total Rushes	509	428
Net Yards Passing	3050	3606
Avg. Per Game	203.3	240.4
Sacked/Yards Lost	72/511	57/452
Gross Yards	3561	4058
Att./Completions	520/283	561/305
Completion Pct.	54.4	54.4
Had Intercepted	16	21
Punts/Avg.	102/37.0	88/37.1
Net Punting Avg.	31.4	33.4
Penalties/Yards Lost	116/919	105/830
Fumbles/Ball Lost	44/19	41/27
Touchdowns	40	47
Rushing	12	16
Passing	26	29
Returns	2	2
Avg. Time of Possession	31:41	28:19

1987 Individual Statistics

Scoring	TD R	TD P	TD Rt	PAT	FG	Saf	TP
McFadden	0	0	0	36/36	16/26	0	84
Quick	0	11	0	0/0	0/0	0	66
Toney	5	1	0	0/0	0/0	o	36
Byars	3	1	0	0/0	0/0	0	24
Cunningham	3	0	0	0/0	0/0	0	18
Jackson	0	3	0	0/0	0/0	0	18
Carter	0	2	0	0/0	0/0	0	12
Garrity	0	2	0	0/0	0/0	0	12
Spagnola	0	2	0	0/0	0/0	0	12
Jacobs	0	0	0	2/4	3/5	0	11
Bowman	0	1	0	0/0	0/0	0	6
Clemons	0	1	0	0/0	0/0	0	6
Giles	0	1	0	0/0	0/0	0	6
Joyner	0	0	1	0/0	0/0	0	6
Ross	1	0	0	0/0	0/0	0	6
Siano	0	1	0	0/0	0/0	0	6
White	0	0	1	0/0	0/0	0	6
Eagles	12	26	2	38/40	19/31	1	337
Opponents	16	29	2	44/46	18/29	0	380

Passing	Att.	Comp.	Yds.	Pct.	TD	Int.	Tkld.	Rate
Cunningham	406	223	2786	54.9	23	12	54/380	83.0
Tinsley	86	48	637	55.8	3	4	6/55	71.7
Merkens	14	7	70	50.0	0	0	10/62	64.6
Horn	11	5	68	45.5	0	0	1/7	65.7
Carter	1	0	0	0.0	0	0	0/0	39.6
Grant	1	0	0	0.0	0	0	0/0	39.6
Toney	1	0	0	0.0	0	0	0/0	39.6
Teltschik	0	0	0	—	0	0	1/7	0.0
Eagles	520	283	3561	54.4	26	16	72/511	79.8
Opponents	561	305	4058	54.4	29	21	57/452	79.2

Rushing	Att.	Yds.	Avg.	LG	TD
Cunningham	76	505	6.6	45	3
Toney	127	473	3.7	36	5
Byars	116	426	3.7	30	3
Haddix	59	165	2.8	11	0
R. Brown	39	136	3.5	23	0
Robinson	24	114	4.8	18	0
Tautalatasi	26	69	2.7	17	0
Ross	14	54	3.9	12	1
Teltschik	3	32	10.7	23	0
Jackson	6	27	4.5	10	0
Grant	1	20	20.0	20	0
Morse	6	14	2.3	7	0
Tinsley	4	2	0.5	2	0
Clemons	3	0	0.0	3	0
Horn	1	0	0.0	0	0
Cavanaugh	1	−2	−2.0	−2	0
Merkens	3	−8	−2.7	1	0
Eagles	509	2027	4.0	45	12
Opponents	428	1643	3.8	62t	16

Receiving	No.	Yds.	Avg.	LG	TD
Quick	46	790	17.2	61t	11
Toney	39	341	8.7	33	1
Spagnola	36	350	9.7	22	2
Tautalatasi	25	176	7.0	22	0
Jackson	21	471	22.4	70t	3
Byars	21	177	8.4	30	1
Grant	16	280	17.5	41	0
Giles, Det.-Phil.	13	157	12.1	40t	1
Giles, Phil.	7	95	13.6	40t	1
Garrity	12	242	20.2	41	2
Siano	9	137	15.2	34	1
Bailey	8	69	8.6	19	0
R. Brown	8	53	6.6	14	0
Haddix	7	58	8.3	23	0
Bowman	6	127	21.2	62t	1
Carter	5	84	16.8	25	2
Repko	5	46	9.2	12	0
Ross	5	41	8.2	17	0
Robinson	2	9	4.5	5	0
Clemons	1	13	13.0	13t	1
Little	1	8	8.0	8	0
Morse	1	8	8.0	8	0
Lavette, Dall.-Phil.	1	6	6.0	6	0
Cunningham	1	−3	−3.0	−3	0
Singletary	1	−11	−11.0	−11	0
Eagles	283	3561	12.6	70t	26
Opponents	305	4058	13.3	77t	29

Interceptions	No.	Yds.	Avg.	LG	TD
Foules	4	6	1.5	6	0
Waters	3	63	21.0	63	0
Joyner	2	42	21.0	29	0
Kullman	2	25	12.5	13	0
Brown	2	7	3.5	6	0
Hoage	2	3	1.5	3	0
Cooper	2	0	0.0	0	0
Young	1	30	30.0	30	0
Evans	1	12	12.0	12	0
C. Brown	1	9	9.0	7	0
West	1	0	0.0	0	0
Eagles	21	197	9.4	63	0
Opponents	16	68	4.3	25	0

Punting	No.	Yds.	Avg.	In 20	LG
Royals, St.L.-Phil.	11	431	39.2	3	48
Royals, Phil.	5	209	41.8	1	48
Teltschik	82	3131	38.2	13	60
Jacobs	10	369	36.9	4	44
Merkens	2	61	30.5	0	38
Eagles	102	3770	37.0	18	60
Opponents	88	3262	37.1	20	65

Punt Returns	No.	FC	Yds.	Avg.	LG	TD
Morse	20	13	121	6.1	23	0
Bowman	4	1	43	10.8	37	0
Garrity	4	10	16	4.0	10	0
Caterbone	2	0	13	6.5	13	0
Ulmer	2	0	10	5.0	5	0
C. Brown	1	0	−1	−1.0	−1	0
A. Johnson	1	0	0	0.0	0	0
Lavette, Dall.-Phil.	0	1	0	—	0	0
Eagles	34	24	202	5.9	37	0
Opponents	54	17	469	8.7	45	0

Kickoff Returns	No.	Yds.	Avg.	LG	TD
Morse	24	386	16.1	28	0
Carter	12	241	20.1	33	0
Bowman	7	153	21.9	32	0
Lavette, Dall.-Phil.	6	109	18.2	22	0
Lavette, Phil.	2	37	18.5	19	0
Cooper	5	86	17.2	24	0
Reid	4	58	14.5	19	0
Tautalatasi	3	53	17.7	32	0
Haddix	2	16	8.0	9	0
Alexander	1	6	6.0	6	0
C. Brown	1	13	13.0	13	0
R. Brown	1	20	20.0	20	0
Clemons	1	0	0.0	0	0
Siano	1	13	13.0	13	0
Turrall	1	21	21.0	21	0
Ulmer	1	8	8.0	8	0
Reeves	0	1	—	1	0
Eagles	66	1112	16.8	33	0
Opponents	59	1276	21.6	54	0

Sacks	No.
White	21.0
Simmons	6.0
Brown	4.0
Joyner	4.0
Smalls	2.5
Grooms	2.0
Phillips	2.0
Pitts	2.0
Clarke	1.5
Jiles	1.5
Battaglia	1.0
C. Brown	1.0
Cobb	1.0
Frizzell	1.0
Griffin	1.0
Hoage	1.0
Lee	1.0
McMillen, Raiders-Phil.	1.0
R. Mitchell	1.0
Reichenbach	1.0
West	1.0
Auer	0.5
Eagles	57.0
Opponents	72.0

Philadelphia Eagles 1988 Veteran Roster

No.	Name	Pos.	Ht.	Wt.	Birth-date	NFL Exp.	College	Hometown	How Acq.	'87 Games/ Starts
72	Alexander, David	T	6-3	275	7/28/64	2	Tulsa	Broken Arrow, Okla.	D5-'87	12/0
58	Allert, Ty	LB	6-2	233	7/23/63	3	Texas	Rosenberg, Tex.	W(SD)-'87	10/0*
87	Bailey, Eric	TE	6-5	240	5/12/63	2	Kansas State	Fort Worth, Tex.	FA-'87	3/3
63	†Baker, Ron	G	6-4	274	11/19/54	11	Oklahoma State	Emerson, Ind.	T(Balt)-'80	10/10
23	†Brown, Cedrick	CB	5-10	182	9/6/64	2	Washington State	Compton, Calif.	FA-'86	12/0
99	Brown, Jerome	DT	6-2	288	2/4/65	2	Miami	Brooksville, Fla.	D1-'87	12/8
41	Byars, Keith	RB	6-1	238	10/14/63	3	Ohio State	Dayton, Ohio	D1-'86	10/8
80	Carter, Cris	WR	6-3	194	11/25/65	2	Ohio State	Middletown, Ohio	SD4-'87	9/0
6	Cavanaugh, Matt	QB	6-2	210	10/27/56	11	Pittsburgh	Youngstown, Ohio	T(SF)-'86	3/0
71	Clarke, Ken	DT	6-2	296	8/28/56	11	Syracuse	Boston, Mass.	FA-'78	11/10
27	Clemmons, Topper	RB	5-11	205	9/16/63	2	Wake Forest	Palmyra, N.J.	FA-'87	3/0
50	†Cobb, Garry	LB	6-2	230	3/16/57	10	Southern California	Stamford, Conn.	T(Det)-'85	12/7
79	†Conwell, Joe	T	6-5	286	2/24/61	3	North Carolina	Ardmore, Pa.	T(SF)-'86	12/12
21	Cooper, Evan	S	5-11	194	6/28/62	5	Michigan	Miami, Fla.	D4-'84	12/1
45	Crawford, Charles	RB	6-2	243	3/8/64	2	Oklahoma State	Bristow, Okla.	SD7-'86	2/0
12	†Cunningham, Randall	QB	6-4	201	3/27/63	4	Nevada-Las Vegas	Santa Barbara, Calif.	D2-'85	12/12
78	Darwin, Matt	T	6-4	275	3/11/63	3	Texas A&M	Spring, Tex.	D4-'86	12/12
93	†Dumbauld, Jonathan	DE	6-4	259	2/14/63	3	Kentucky	Troy, Ohio	W(NO)-'87	6/0
56	Evans, Byron	LB	6-2	225	2/23/64	2	Arizona	Phoenix, Ariz.	D4-'87	12/3
67	Feehery, Gerry	C	6-2	270	3/9/60	6	Syracuse	Springfield, Pa.	FA-'83	12/12
29	Foules, Elbert	CB	5-11	193	7/4/61	6	Alcorn State	Greenville, Miss.	FA-'83	9/8
33	Frizzell, William	S	6-3	205	9/8/62	5	North Carolina Central	Greenville, N.C.	FA-'86	12/5
86	Garrity, Gregg	WR	5-10	169	11/24/61	6	Penn State	Bradford Woods, Pa.	FA-'84	12/0
38	Gary, Russell	S	5-11	200	7/31/59	8	Nebraska	Minneapolis, Minn.	FA-'87	12/0
83	†Giles, Jimmie	TE	6-3	240	11/8/54	12	Alcorn State	Greenville, Miss.	T(Det)-'87	12/1*
90	†Golic, Mike	DE-DT	6-5	275	12/12/62	3	Notre Dame	Cleveland, Ohio	W(Hou)-'87	8/0*
26	Haddix, Michael	RB	6-2	227	12/27/61	6	Mississippi State	Walnut, Miss.	D1-'83	12/4
62	Haden, Nick	G	6-2	270	11/7/62	2	Penn State	McKees Rocks, Pa.	W(Raid)-'86	0*
34	†Hoage, Terry	S	6-3	201	4/11/62	5	Georgia	Huntsville, Tex.	FA-'86	11/11
48	Hopkins, Wes	S	6-1	212	9/26/61	5	Southern Methodist	Birmingham, Ala.	D2a-'83	0*
81	†Jackson, Kenny	WR	6-0	180	2/15/62	5	Penn State	South River, N.J.	D1-'84	12/12
53	†Jiles, Dwayne	LB	6-4	250	11/23/61	4	Texas Tech	Linden, Tex.	D5-'85	9/5
54	Johnson, Alonzo	LB	6-3	222	4/4/63	3	Florida	Panama City, Fla.	D2b-'86	3/0
85	Johnson, Ron	WR	6-3	186	9/21/58	4	Long Beach State	Monterey, Calif.	FA-'85	3/0
59	†Joyner, Seth	LB	6-2	248	11/18/64	3	Texas-El Paso	Spring Valley, N.Y.	D8-'86	12/12
64	Kelley, Mike	G-C	6-5	280	2/27/62	3	Notre Dame	Westfield, Mass.	FA-'87	1/0*
97	Klingel, John	DE	6-3	267	12/21/63	2	Kentucky	Cardington, Ohio	FA-'87	5/0
65	†Landsee, Bob	G-C	6-4	273	3/21/64	2	Wisconsin	Iron Mountain, Mich.	D6-'86	3/1
89	†Little, Dave	TE	6-2	226	4/18/61	5	Middle Tennessee State	Fresno, Calif.	FA-'85	12/0
8	†McFadden, Paul	K	5-11	166	9/24/61	5	Youngstown State	Euclid, Ohio	D12-'84	12/0
36	Morse, Bobby	RB-KR	5-10	213	10/3/65	2	Michigan State	Muskegon, Mich.	D12-'87	11/0
74	Pitts, Mike	DT	6-5	277	9/25/60	6	Alabama	Baltimore, Md.	T(Atl)-'87	12/6
82	Quick, Mike	WR	6-2	190	5/14/59	7	North Carolina State	Richmond, N.C.	D1-'82	12/12
66	†Reeves, Ken	T-G	6-5	270	10/4/61	4	Texas A&M	Pittsburg, Tex.	D6b-'85	10/0
55	Reichenbach, Mike	LB	6-2	230	9/14/61	5	East Stroudsburg	Bethlehem, Pa.	FA-'84	11/9
76	Schreiber, Adam	G	6-4	277	2/20/62	5	Texas	Huntsville, Ala.	FA-'86	12/12
95	†Schulz, Jody	LB	6-3	235	8/17/60	5	East Carolina	Centreville, Md.	D2b-'83	7/0
96	Simmons, Clyde	DE	6-6	276	8/4/64	3	Western Carolina	Wilmington, N.C.	D9-'86	12/12
68	Singletary, Reggie	G	6-3	280	1/17/64	3	North Carolina State	Whiteville, N.C.	D12a-'86	12/0
88	Spagnola, John	TE	6-4	242	8/1/57	9	Yale	Bethlehem, Pa.	FA-'79	12/12
37	Tautalatasi, Junior	RB	5-10	210	3/24/62	3	Washington State	Alameda, Calif.	D10-'86	12/1
10	Teltschik, John	P	6-2	209	3/8/64	3	Texas	Floresville, Tex.	W(Chi)-'86	12/0
25	Toney, Anthony	RB	6-0	227	9/23/62	3	Texas A&M	Salinas, Calif.	D2a-'86	11/11
20	Waters, Andre	S	5-11	199	3/10/62	5	Cheyney State	Pahokee, Fla.	FA-'84	12/12
92	White, Reggie	DE	6-5	285	12/19/61	4	Tennessee	Chattanooga, Tenn.	SD1-'84	12/12
43	Young, Roynell	CB	6-1	185	12/1/57	9	Alcorn State	New Orleans, La.	D1-'80	11/11

* Allert played 3 games with San Diego, 7 with Philadelphia in '87; Giles played 4 games with Detroit, 8 with Philadelphia; Golic played 2 games with Houston, 6 with Philadelphia; Haden and Hopkins missed '87 season due to injury; Kelley played 1 game with Houston in '87.

†Option playout; subject to developments.

Also played with Eagles in '87—G Jim Angelo (1 game), DE Jim Auer (1), DE Marvin Ayers (2), LB Matt Battaglia (3), CB Vic Bellamy (3), WR Jesse Bendross (3), DT Gary Bolden (2), WR Kevin Bowman (3), LB Carlos Bradley (3), LB Dave Brown (1), RB Reggie Brown (3), CB Thomas Caterbone (2), DT Ray Conlin (1), LB George Cumby (1), TE Ron Fazio (1), S Chris Gerhard (3), LB Chuck Gorecki (3), WR Otis Grant (3), S Jeff Griffin (2), DE-DT Elois Grooms (3), DT Skip Hamilton (1), CB-S Greg Harding (1), QB Marty Horn (1), K Dave Jacobs (3), CB Angelo James (3), CB-S Christopher Johnson (2), LB Kelly Kirchbaum (3), S Mike Kullman (3), RB Robert Lavette (1), LB Byron Lee (3), G Scott Leggett (2), DE Greg Liter (1), C Matt Long (3), TE Mike McCloskey (1), DE Dan McMillen (1), QB Guido Merkens (3), NT Mike Mitchell (active for 1 game but did not play), NT Randall Mitchell (3), DE Tim Mooney (2), G Mike Nease (2), T Mike Perrino (3), DE-LB Ray Phillips (3), RB Alan Reid (1), TE Jay Repko (3), RB Jacque Robinson (3), RB Alvin Ross (2), P Mark Royals (1), C Paul Ryczek (3), WR Mike Siano (3), LB Fred Smalls (3), C-G Ben Tamburello (2), QB Scott Tinsley (3), RB Willie Turrall (1), CB-S Mike Ulmer (1), G Pete Walters (3), T Jeff Wenzel (3), S Troy West (3), CB Brenard Wilson (1).

COACHING STAFF

Head Coach, Buddy Ryan

Pro Career: Ryan was named head coach of the Eagles on January 29, 1986, after eight seasons as the defensive coordinator of the Chicago Bears. An NFL assistant coach for 18 years, Ryan has been on the staffs of three Super Bowl teams: Jets, 1968; Vikings, 1976; and Bears, 1985. He served as defensive line coach under Bud Grant with the Minnesota Vikings in 1976-77 before joining Chicago. From 1968-75, he was on the defensive staff of the New York Jets under coach Weeb Ewbank. In Ryan's eight seasons as defensive coordinator with Chicago, his defenses ranked among the NFL's top 10 six times. He devised the "46 defense" with its multiple variations of alignments and coverages. Career record: 12-18-1.

Background: Ryan was a four-year letterman at Oklahoma State from 1952-55 as an offensive guard. While serving in the U.S. Army in Korea, Ryan played on the Fourth Army championship team in Japan. He served as an assistant at the University of Buffalo from 1961-65, Vanderbilt 1966, and the University of the Pacific 1967. Ryan has a master's degree in education from Middle Tennessee State.

Personal: Born James Ryan on February 17, 1934, in Frederick, Okla. Buddy and his wife, Joan, live in Cherry Hill, N.J., and have three sons: Jimmy, Jr., Rex, and Robert.

Assistant Coaches

Dave Atkins, offensive backfield; born May 18, 1949, Victoria, Tex., lives in Marlton, N.J. Running back Texas-El Paso 1970-72. Pro running back San Francisco 49ers 1973, Honolulu Hawaiians (WFL) 1974, San Diego Chargers 1975. College coach: Texas-El Paso 1979-80, San Diego State 1981-85. Pro coach: Joined Eagles in 1986.

Jeff Fisher, defensive backs; born February 25, 1958, Culver City, Calif., lives in Voorhees, N.J. Defensive back Southern California 1978-80. Pro defensive back-punt returner Chicago Bears 1981-85. Pro coach: Joined Eagles in 1986.

Dale Haupt, defensive line; born April 12, 1929, Manitowoc, Wis., lives in Cherry Hill, N.J. Defensive lineman-linebacker Wyoming 1950-53. No pro playing experience. College coach: Tennessee 1960-63, Iowa State 1964-65, Richmond 1966-71, North Carolina State 1972-76, Duke 1977. Pro coach: Chicago Bears 1978-85, joined Eagles in 1986.

Ronnie Jones, strength and conditioning; born October 17, 1955, Dumas, Tex., lives in Cherry Hill, N.J. Running back Northwestern State (Okla.) 1974-77. College coach: Northeastern State (Okla.) 1979-83, Tulsa 1984, Arizona State 1985-86. Pro coach: Joined Eagles in 1987.

Dan Neal, assistant offensive line; born August 30, 1949, Corbin, Ky., lives in Cherry Hill, N.J. Center Kentucky 1970-72. Pro center Baltimore Colts 1973-74, Chicago Bears 1975-83. Pro coach: Joined Eagles in 1986.

Wade Phillips, defensive coordinator-linebackers; born June 21, 1947, Orange, Tex., lives in Mt. Laurel, N.J. Linebacker Houston 1966-68. No pro playing experience. College coach: Houston 1969, Oklahoma State 1973-74, Kansas 1975. Pro coach: Houston Oilers 1976-80, New Orleans Saints 1981-85 (head coach last four games of 1985), joined Eagles in 1986.

Ted Plumb, assistant head coach-offense; born August 20, 1939, Reno, Nev., lives in Cherry Hill, N.J. Wide receiver Baylor 1960-61. Pro wide receiver Buffalo Bills 1962. College coach: Cerritos, Calif., J.C. 1966-67, Texas Christian 1968-70, Tulsa 1971, Kansas 1972-73. Pro coach: New York Giants 1974-76, Atlanta Falcons 1977-79, Chicago Bears 1980-85, joined Eagles in 1986.

Al Roberts, special teams; born January 6, 1944, Fresno, Calif., lives in Marlton, N.J. Running back Washington 1964-65, Puget Sound 1967-68. No pro playing experience. College coach: Washington 1977-82, Purdue 1986, Wyoming 1987. Pro coach: Los Angeles Express (USFL) 1983-84, Houston Oilers 1984-85, joined Eagles in 1988.

Doug Scovil, quarterbacks; born July 1, 1927, Anacortes, Wash., lives in Voorhees, N.J. Quarterback Stockton, Calif., J.C. and Pacific 1948-51. No pro playing experience. College coach: San Mateo, Calif., J.C. 1958-62 (head coach), Navy 1963-65, Pacific 1966-69 (head coach), Brigham Young 1976-77, 1979-80, San Diego State 1981-85 (head coach). Pro coach: San Francisco 49ers 1970-75, Chicago Bears 1978, joined Eagles in 1986.

Bill Walsh, offensive line; born September 8, 1927, Phillipsburg, N.J., lives in Marlton, N.J. Center Notre Dame 1945-48. Pro center Pittsburgh Steelers 1949-54. College coach: Notre Dame 1955-58, Kansas State 1959. Pro coach: Dallas Texans-Kansas City Chiefs 1960-74, Atlanta Falcons 1975-82, Houston Oilers 1983-86, joined Eagles in 1987.

Philadelphia Eagles 1988 First-Year Roster

Name	Pos.	Ht.	Wt.	Birth-date	College	Hometown	How Acq.
Allen, Eric	CB	5-10	181	11/11/65	Arizona State	San Diego, Calif.	D2
Anglim, Patrick	G	6-4	255	4/6/65	Connecticut	Fairfield, Conn.	FA
Antoine, Tamlin	WR	5-11	185	9/25/64	Morehouse	Hyattsvile, Md.	FA
Booker, Martin (1)	WR	6-1	191	3/8/63	Villanova	Camden, N.J.	FA-'86
Curtis, Scott	LB	6-1	230	12/26/64	New Hampshire	Lynnfield, Mass.	FA
Dorsey, Dean (1)	K	5-11	195	3/13/57	Toronto	Toronto, Canada	FA
Downey, Charles	KR	5-8	175	12/4/65	Stonybrook	Deer Park, N.Y.	FA
Everett, Eric	CB	5-10	161	7/13/66	Texas Tech	Dangerfield, Tex.	D5
Gilmore, Corey (1)	RB	6-1	220	12/9/64	San Diego State	Pasadena, Calif.	FA-'87
Giongo, Michael	LB	6-2	245	12/27/64	Syracuse	Philadelphia, Pa.	FA
Jackson, Keith	TE	6-2	250	4/19/65	Oklahoma	Little Rock, Ark.	D1
Jackson, Troy	LB	6-2	225	4/12/64	Indiana, Pa.	Pittsburgh, Pa.	FA
Jenkins, Izel	CB	5-10	191	5/27/64	North Carolina State	Wilson, N.C.	D11
Kaufusi, Steve	DE	6-4	260	10/17/63	Brigham Young	Salt Lake City, Utah	D12
Lambiotte, Ken (1)	QB	6-3	191	10/17/63	William & Mary	Woodstock, Va.	D9-'87
McPherson, Don	QB	6-1	183	4/2/65	Syracuse	Hempstead, N.Y.	D6a
Moten, Ron (1)	LB	6-1	230	9/15/64	Florida	Clearwater, Fla.	D6a-'87
Patchan, Matt	T	6-4	275	8/11/65	Miami	Penn Hills, Pa.	D3
Reid, Alan (1)	RB	5-8	197	9/6/60	Minnesota	El Paso, Tex.	FA-'87
Schuster, Joe	DT	6-4	260	12/30/64	Iowa	Faribault, Minn.	D10
Smith, David	RB	6-1	225	11/3/65	Western Kentucky	Dallas, Tex.	D8
Sterling, Rob	CB-S	5-11	195	2/11/66	Maine	Silver Spring, Md.	D6b
Tamburello, Ben (1)	G-C	6-3	278	9/9/64	Auburn	Birmingham, Ala.	D3-'87
Walsh, Steven	T-G-C	6-4	315	3/22/65	Western Kentucky	Voluntown, Conn.	FA
White, Todd	WR-KR	6-0	196	9/15/65	Cal State-Fullerton	Santa Fe Springs, Calif.	D7
Widmeyer, Kelly	T	6-7	315	7/3/60	Weber State	Ogden, Utah	FA
Yates, Bo	LB	6-1	222	1/2/65	Washington	Lebanon, Ore.	FA

The term NFL Rookie is defined as a player who is in his first season of professional football and has not been on the roster of another professional football team for any regular-season or postseason games. A Rookie is designated by an "R" on NFL rosters. Players who have been active in another professional football league or players who have NFL experience, including either preseason training camp or being on an active roster for fewer than three regular-season or postseason games, are termed NFL First-Year Players. An NFL First-Year Player is designated by a "1" on NFL rosters. Thereafter, a player on an NFL active roster for at least three regular-season or postseason games is credited with an additional year of NFL playing experience.

NOTES

PHOENIX CARDINALS

National Football Conference
Eastern Division

Team Colors: Cardinal Red, Black, and White

P.O. Box 888
Phoenix, Arizona 85001-0888
Telephone: (602) 967-1010

Club Officials

Chairman/President: William V. Bidwill
Vice President/Administration: Curt Mosher
Secretary and General Counsel: Thomas J. Guilfoil
Treasurer: Charley Schlegel
Director of Pro Personnel: Larry Wilson
Director of Player Personnel: George Boone
Public Relations Director: Bob Rose
Media Coordinator: Greg Gladysiewski
Director of Community Relations: Adele Harris
Ticket Manager: Steve Walsh
Trainer: John Omohundro
Assistant Trainers: Jim Shearer, Jeff Herndon
Equipment Manager: Mark Ahlemeier

Stadium: Sun Devil Stadium • **Capacity:** 74,000
Fifth Street
Tempe, Arizona 85287

Playing Surface: Grass

Training Camp: Northern Arizona University
Flagstaff, Arizona 86011

1988 Schedule

Preseason

Aug. 4	at Seattle	7:30
Aug. 12	**New Orleans**	7:30
Aug. 21	**Minnesota**	5:00
Aug. 25	at Kansas City	7:30

Regular Season

Sept. 4	at Cincinnati	1:00
Sept. 12	**Dallas** (Monday)	6:00
Sept. 18	at Tampa Bay	1:00
Sept. 25	**Washington**	1:00
Oct. 2	at Los Angeles Rams	1:00
Oct. 9	**Pittsburgh**	1:00
Oct. 16	at Washington	1:00
Oct. 23	**Cleveland**	1:00
Oct. 30	at Dallas	12:00
Nov. 6	**San Francisco**	2:00
Nov. 13	**New York Giants**	2:00
Nov. 20	at Houston	12:00
Nov. 27	at Philadelphia	1:00
Dec. 4	at New York Giants	1:00
Dec. 10	**Philadelphia** (Saturday)	2:00
Dec. 18	**Green Bay**	2:00

Cardinals Coaching History

Chicago 1920-59
St. Louis 1960-87
(354-462-39)

1920-22	John (Paddy) Driscoll	17-8-4
1923-24	Arnold Horween	13-8-1
1925-26	Norman Barry	16-8-2
1927	Guy Chamberlin	3-7-1
1928	Fred Gillies	1-5-0
1929	Dewey Scanlon	6-6-1
1930	Ernie Nevers	5-6-2
1931	LeRoy Andrews*	0-2-0
1931	Ernie Nevers	5-2-0
1932	Jack Chevigny	2-6-2
1933-34	Paul Schissler	6-15-1
1935-38	Milan Creighton	16-26-4
1939	Ernie Nevers	1-10-0
1940-42	Jimmy Conzelman	8-22-3
1943-45	Phil Handler**	1-29-0
1946-48	Jimmy Conzelman	27-10-0
1949	Phil Handler-Buddy Parker***	2-4-0
1949	Raymond (Buddy) Parker	4-1-1
1950-51	Earl (Curly) Lambeau****	7-15-0
1951	Phil Handler-Cecil Isbell#	1-1-0
1952	Joe Kuharich	4-8-0
1953-54	Joe Stydahar	3-20-1
1955-57	Ray Richards	14-21-1
1958-61	Frank (Pop) Ivy##	17-29-2
1961	Chuck Drulis-Ray Prochaska-Ray Willsey###	2-0-0
1962-65	Wally Lemm	27-26-3
1966-70	Charley Winner	35-30-5
1971-72	Bob Hollway	8-18-2
1973-77	Don Coryell	42-29-1
1978-79	Bud Wilkinson####	9-20-0
1979	Larry Wilson	2-1-0
1980-85	Jim Hanifan	39-50-1
1986-87	Gene Stallings	11-19-1

*Resigned after two games in 1931
**Co-coach with Walt Kiesling in Chicago Cardinals-Pittsburgh merger in 1944
***Co-coaches for first six games in 1949
****Resigned after 10 games in 1951
#Co-coaches
##Resigned after 12 games in 1961
###Co-coaches
####Released after 13 games in 1979

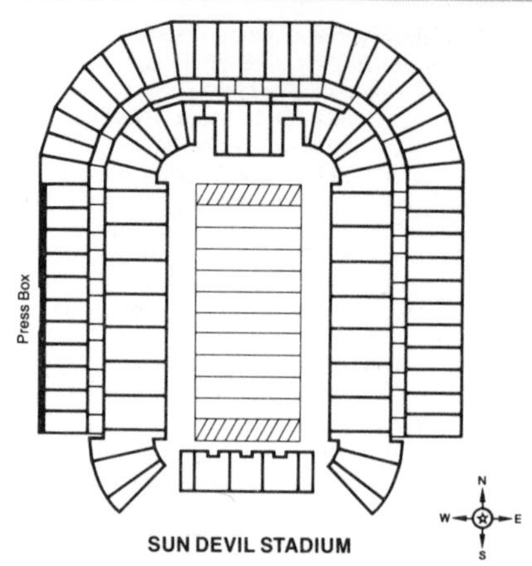

SUN DEVIL STADIUM

Record Holders

Individual Records—Career

Category	Name	Performance
Rushing (Yds.)	Ottis Anderson, 1979-1986	7,999
Passing (Yds.)	Jim Hart, 1966-1983	34,639
Passing (TDs)	Jim Hart, 1966-1983	209
Receiving (No.)	Jackie Smith, 1963-1977	480
Receiving (Yds.)	Jackie Smith, 1963-1977	7,918
Interceptions	Larry Wilson, 1960-1972	52
Punting (Avg.)	Jerry Norton, 1959-1961	44.9
Punt Return (Avg.)	Charley Trippi, 1947-1955	13.7
Kickoff Return (Avg.)	Ollie Matson, 1952, 1954-58	28.5
Field Goals	Jim Bakken, 1962-1978	282
Touchdowns (Tot.)	Sonny Randle, 1959-1966	60
Points	Jim Bakken, 1962-1978	1,380

Individual Records—Single Season

Category	Name	Performance
Rushing (Yds.)	Ottis Anderson, 1979	1,605
Passing (Yds.)	Neil Lomax, 1984	4,614
Passing (TDs)	Charley Johnson, 1963	28
	Neil Lomax, 1984	28
Receiving (No.)	J.T. Smith, 1987	91
Receiving (Yds.)	Roy Green, 1984	1,555
Interceptions	Bob Nussbaumer, 1949	12
Punting (Avg.)	Jerry Norton, 1960	45.6
Punt Return (Avg.)	John (Red) Cochran, 1949	20.9
Kickoff Return (Avg.)	Ollie Matson, 1958	35.5
Field Goals	Jim Bakken, 1967	27
Touchdowns (Tot.)	John David Crow, 1962	17
Points	Jim Bakken, 1967	117
	Neil O'Donoghue, 1984	117

Individual Records—Single Game

Category	Name	Performance
Rushing (Yds.)	John David Crow, 12-18-60	203
Passing (Yds.)	Neil Lomax, 12-16-84	468
Passing (TDs)	Jim Hardy, 10-2-50	6
	Charley Johnson, 9-26-65	6
	Charley Johnson, 11-2-69	6
Receiving (No.)	Sonny Randle, 11-4-62	16
Receiving (Yds.)	Sonny Randle, 11-4-62	256
Interceptions	Bob Nussbaumer, 11-13-49	*4
	Jerry Norton, 11-20-60	*4
Field Goals	Jim Bakken, 9-24-67	*7
Touchdowns (Tot.)	Ernie Nevers, 11-28-29	*6
Points	Ernie Nevers, 11-28-29	*40

*NFL Record

1987 Team Record

Preseason (2-2)

Date	Result		Opponents
8/15	L	16-31	at Cleveland
8/22	W	28-21	Seattle
8/31	W	20-16	at Chicago
9/6	L	10-13	vs. Kansas City at Memphis, Tenn. (OT)
		74-81	

Regular Season (7-8)

Date	Result		Opponents	Att.
9/13	W	24-13	Dallas	47,241
9/20	L	24-28	at San Diego	47,988
9/27	C		Indianapolis	
10/4	L	21-28	at Washington	27,728
10/11	W	24-19	New Orleans	11,795
10/18	L	28-34	at San Francisco	38,094
10/25	L	7-30	at N.Y. Giants	74,391
11/1	L	23-28	Philadelphia	24,586
11/8	W	31-28	Tampa Bay	22,449
11/15	L	24-27	L.A. Rams	27,730
11/22	W	31-19	at Philadelphia	55,592
11/29	W	34-21	at Atlanta	15,909
12/6	L	17-34	Washington	31,324
12/13	W	27-24	N.Y. Giants	29,623
12/20	W	31-14	at Tampa Bay	32,046
12/27	L	16-21	at Dallas	36,788

(OT) Overtime
C (Cancelled due to players' strike.)

Score by Periods

Cardinals	67	127	61	107	0	—	362
Opponents	90	88	103	87	0	—	368

Attendance

Home 194,748 Away 328,536 Total 523,284
Single-game home record, 51,010 (11-4-84)
Single-season home record, 384,375 (1981)

1987 Team Statistics

	Cardinals	Opp.
Total First Downs	325	306
Rushing	115	116
Passing	189	168
Penalty	21	22
Third Down: Made/Att.	79/211	100/217
Fourth Down: Made/Att.	11/18	8/17
Total Net Yards	5326	5384
Avg. Per Game	355.1	358.9
Total Plays	1045	1023
Avg. Per Play	5.1	5.3
Net Yards Rushing	1873	2001
Avg. Per Game	124.9	133.4
Total Rushes	462	492
Net Yards Passing	3453	3383
Avg. Per Game	230.2	225.5
Sacked/Yards Lost	54/397	41/285
Gross Yards	3850	3668
Att./Completions	529/305	490/276
Completion Pct.	57.7	56.3
Had Intercepted	15	14
Punts/Avg.	70/38.0	74/41.2
Net Punting Avg.	29.6	32.1
Penalties/Yards Lost	101/797	88/718
Fumbles/Ball Lost	23/12	34/19
Touchdowns	46	48
Rushing	15	16
Passing	25	30
Returns	6	2
Avg. Time of Possession	30:33	29:27

1987 Individual Statistics

Scoring	TD R	TD P	TD Rt	PAT	FG	Saf	TP
Gallery	0	0	0	30/31	9/19	0	57
J. Smith	0	8	0	0/0	0/0	0	48
Del Greco, G.B.-St.L.	0	0	0	19/20	9/15	0	46
Del Greco, St.L.	0	0	0	8/9	4/5	0	20
Ferrell	7	0	0	0/0	0/0	0	42
Awalt	0	6	0	0/0	0/0	0	36
Mitchell	3	2	0	0/0	0/0	0	30
Green	0	4	0	0/0	0/0	0	24
McAdoo	3	0	1	0/0	0/0	0	24
Novacek	0	3	0	0/0	0/0	0	18
T. Johnson	0	2	0	0/0	0/0	0	12
Staurovsky	0	0	0	6/6	1/3	0	9
Garza	1	0	0	0/0	0/0	0	6
Jackson	0	0	1	0/0	0/0	0	6
N. Noga	0	0	1	0/0	0/0	0	6
P. Noga	0	0	1	0/0	0/0	0	6
Sikahema	0	0	1	0/0	0/0	0	6
Le. Smith	0	0	1	0/0	0/0	0	6
Wolfley	1	0	0	0/0	0/0	0	6
Cardinals	15	25	6	44/46	14/27	0	362
Opponents	16	30	2	45/48	11/18	1	368

Passing	Att.	Comp.	Yds.	Pct.	TD	Int.	Tkld.	Rate
Lomax	463	275	3387	59.4	24	12	48/350	88.5
Halloran	42	18	263	42.9	0	1	5/34	54.0
Garza	20	11	183	55.0	1	2	1/13	63.1
Mitchell	3	1	17	33.3	0	0	0/0	53.5
Stoudt	1	0	0	0.0	0	0	0/0	39.6
Cardinals	529	305	3850	57.7	25	15	54/397	84.4
Opponents	490	276	3668	56.3	30	14	41/285	88.7

Rushing	Att.	Yds.	Avg.	LG	TD
Mitchell	203	781	3.8	42	3
Ferrell	113	512	4.5	35t	7
McAdoo	53	230	4.3	17	3
Lomax	29	107	3.7	19	0
Sargent	18	90	5.0	16	0
Wolfley	26	87	3.3	8	1
Green	2	34	17.0	26	0
Garza	8	31	3.9	10	1
Ro. Brown	1	9	9.0	9	0
T. Johnson	1	9	9.0	9	0
Cater	2	3	1.5	11	0
Stoudt	1	−2	−2.0	−2	0
Awalt	2	−9	−4.5	−1	0
Halloran	3	−9	−3.0	2	0
Cardinals	462	1873	4.1	42	15
Opponents	492	2001	4.1	47t	16

Receiving	No.	Yds.	Avg.	LG	TD
J. Smith	91	1117	12.3	38	8
Mitchell	45	397	8.8	39	2
Green	43	731	17.0	57	4
Awalt	42	526	12.5	35	6
Ferrell	23	262	11.4	36	0
Novacek	20	254	12.7	25	3
T. Johnson	15	308	20.5	49t	2
Holmes	11	132	12.0	23	0
Wolfley	8	68	8.5	16	0
Sargent	2	19	9.5	10	0
Ro. Brown	2	16	8.0	9	0
McAdoo	2	12	6.0	6	0
Harris	1	8	8.0	8	0
Cardinals	305	3850	12.6	57	25
Opponents	276	3668	13.3	88t	30

Interceptions	No.	Yds.	Avg.	LG	TD
Curtis	5	65	13.0	31	0
Mack	2	0	0.0	0	0
P. Noga	1	60	60.0	60t	1
Junior	1	25	25.0	25	0
Bell	1	13	13.0	13	0
Mathis	1	4	4.0	4	0
Carter	1	0	0.0	0	0
Saddler	1	0	0.0	0	0
Young	1	0	0.0	0	0
Cardinals	14	167	11.9	60t	1
Opponents	15	227	15.1	63	0

Punting	No.	Yds.	Avg.	In 20	LG
Horne, Cin.-St.L.	43	1730	40.2	6	57
Horne, St.L.	24	971	40.5	4	51
Cater	39	1470	37.7	10	68
Royals	6	222	37.0	2	46
Cardinals	70	2663	38.0	16	68
Opponents	74	3049	41.2	18	63

Punt Returns	No.	FC	Yds.	Avg.	LG	TD
Sikahema	44	7	550	12.5	76t	1
Cardinals	44	7	550	12.5	76t	1
Opponents	36	8	489	13.6	81t	1

Kickoff Returns	No.	Yds.	Avg.	LG	TD
Sikahema	34	761	22.4	50	0
McAdoo	23	444	19.3	30	0
Sargent	3	37	12.3	27	0
Ro. Brown	1	40	40.0	40	0
Ferrell	1	10	10.0	10	0
Holmes	1	25	25.0	25	0
Cardinals	63	1317	20.9	50	0
Opponents	59	1063	18.0	66	0

Sacks	No.
Nunn	11.0
Greer	6.0
Clasby	4.5
N. Noga	3.0
Saddler	3.0
Garalczyk	2.5
Junior	2.0
Scotts	2.0
Le. Smith	2.0
Alvord	1.5
Bell	1.0
Galloway	1.0
Mack	1.0
Dulin	0.5
Cardinals	41.0
Opponents	54.0

Phoenix Cardinals 1988 Veteran Roster

No.	Name	Pos.	Ht.	Wt.	Birth-date	NFL Exp.	College	Hometown	How Acq.	'87 Games/ Starts
60	Alvord, Steve	DT	6-4	272	10/2/64	2	Washington	Bellingham, Wash.	D8-'87	12/6
80	Awalt, Robert	TE	6-5	248	4/9/64	2	San Diego State	Sacramento, Calif.	D3-'87	12/9
52	†Baker, Charlie	LB	6-2	234	9/26/57	9	New Mexico	Odessa, Tex.	D3-'80	14/3
55	Bell, Anthony	LB	6-3	231	7/2/64	3	Michigan State	Miami, Fla.	D1-'86	12/12
71	Bostic, Joe	G	6-3	268	4/20/57	10	Clemson	Greensboro, N.C.	D3-'79	9/4
62	Brown, Ray	G-T	6-5	280	12/12/62	3	Arkansas State	Marion, Ark.	D8-'86	7/3
82	Brown, Ron	WR	5-10	186	1/11/63	2	Colorado	Pasadena, Calif.	FA-'87	3/0
41	Carter, Carl	CB	5-11	180	3/7/64	3	Texas Tech	Fort Worth, Tex.	D4-'86	12/12
74	Chilton, Gene	T	6-3	271	3/27/64	3	Texas	Houston, Tex.	D3-'86	11/0
79	†Clasby, Bob	DT	6-5	260	9/28/60	3	Notre Dame	Milton, Mass.	FA-'86	12/12
20	Curtis, Travis	S	5-10	180	9/27/65	2	West Virginia	Potomac, Md.	FA-'87	13/1
53	Davis, Wayne	LB	6-1	213	3/10/64	2	Alabama	Gordo, Ala.	D9-'87	12/1
17	Del Greco, Al	K	5-10	191	3/2/62	5	Auburn	Coral Gables, Fla.	FA-'87	8/0*
73	Duda, Mark	DT	6-3	279	2/4/61	6	Maryland	Plymouth, Pa.	D4-'83	3/3
31	†Ferrell, Earl	RB	6-0	240	3/27/58	7	East Tennessee State	Halifax, Va.	D5-'82	11/11
13	Gallery, Jim	K	6-1	190	9/15/61	2	Minnesota	Redwood Falls, Minn.	W(NE)-'87	13/0
65	Galloway, David	DE	6-3	279	2/16/59	7	Florida	Brandon, Fla.	D2-'82	4/3
76	Garalczyk, Mark	DT	6-5	272	8/12/65	2	Western Michigan	Roseville, Mich.	D6-'87	11/3
81	Green, Roy	WR	6-0	195	6/30/57	10	Henderson State	Magnolia, Ark.	D4-'79	12/12
75	†Greer, Curtis	DE	6-4	258	11/10/57	8	Michigan	Detroit, Mich.	D1-'80	10/9
89	Harris, William	TE	6-4	243	2/10/65	2	Texas	Houston, Tex.	FA-'87	10/3
82	†Holmes, Don	WR	5-10	180	4/1/61	3	Mesa College, Colo.	Grand Junction, Colo.	W(Ind)-'86	11/1
11	Horne, Greg	P	6-0	188	11/22/64	2	Arkansas	Russellville, Ark.	FA-'87	9/0*
21	Jackson, Mark	CB	5-9	180	3/16/62	2	Abilene Christian	Amarillo, Tex.	FA-'87	11/4
50	Jarostchuk, Ilia	LB	6-3	231	8/1/64	2	New Hampshire	Utica, N.Y.	D5-'87	12/0
27	†Johnson, Greggory	CB-S	6-1	195	10/20/58	6	Oklahoma State	Houston, Tex.	FA-'87	8/0
87	†Johnson, Troy	WR	6-1	175	10/20/62	3	Southern	Houma, La.	FA-'86	14/2
54	Junior, E.J.	LB	6-3	235	12/8/59	8	Alabama	Nashville, Tenn.	D1-'81	13/13
70	†Kennard, Derek	C	6-3	285	9/9/62	3	Nevada-Reno	Stockton, Calif.	SD2-'84	12/11
15	Lomax, Neil	QB	6-3	215	2/17/59	8	Portland State	Portland, Ore.	D2-'81	12/12
47	†Mack, Cedric	CB	6-0	194	9/14/60	6	Baylor	Freeport, Tex.	D2-'83	10/10
33	McAdoo, Derrick	RB	5-10	198	4/2/65	2	Baylor	Tallahassee, Fla.	FA-'87	15/2
46	McDonald, Tim	S	6-2	207	1/6/65	2	Southern California	Fresno, Calif.	D2-'87	3/0
30	Mitchell, Stump	RB	5-9	188	3/15/59	8	Citadel	St. Mary's, Ga.	D9-'81	12/12
68	Morris, Michael	G	6-5	275	2/22/61	2	Northeast Missouri State	Centerville, Iowa	FA-'87	14/0
57	Noga, Niko	LB	6-1	235	3/2/62	5	Hawaii	Honolulu, Hawaii	D8-'84	12/12
85	†Novacek, Jay	TE	6-4	235	10/24/62	4	Wyoming	Gothenburg, Neb.	D6-'85	7/4
78	Nunn, Freddie Joe	DE	6-4	255	4/9/62	4	Mississippi	Louisville, Miss.	D1-'85	12/12
64	Peat, Todd	G	6-2	294	5/20/64	2	Northern Illinois	Champaign, Ill.	D11-'87	12/8
63	Robbins, Tootie	T	6-5	302	6/2/58	7	East Carolina	Windsor, N.C.	D4-'82	14/14
51	†Ruether, Mike	C	6-4	275	9/20/62	3	Texas	Inglewood, Calif.	SD1-'84	12/1
72	Saddler, Rod	DE	6-5	276	9/26/65	2	Texas A&M	Atlanta, Ga.	D4-'87	12/3
39	†Sargent, Broderick	RB	5-10	215	9/16/62	3	Baylor	Waxahachie, Tex.	FA-'86	15/1
69	Scotts, Colin	DT	6-5	263	4/26/63	2	Hawaii	Sydney, Australia	D3-'87	7/3
67	Sharpe, Luis	T	6-4	260	6/16/60	7	UCLA	Detroit, Mich.	D1-'82	12/12
36	Sikahema, Vai	RB-KR	5-9	191	8/29/62	3	Brigham Young	American Samoa	D10-'86	15/0
84	Smith, J.T.	WR	6-2	185	10/29/55	11	North Texas State	Leonard, Tex.	FA-'85	15/14
61	Smith, Lance	G	6-2	262	11/1/63	4	Louisiana State	Kannapolis, N.C.	D3-'85	15/15
45	Smith, Leonard	S	5-11	202	9/2/60	6	McNeese State	Baton Rouge, La.	D1-'83	15/15
18	†Stoudt, Cliff	QB	6-4	215	3/27/55	10	Youngstown State	Oberlin, Ohio	T(Pitt)-'86	12/0
66	Welter, Tom	T	6-5	280	2/24/64	2	Nebraska	Yankton, S.D.	FA-'87	3/3
24	†Wolfley, Ron	RB	6-0	222	10/14/62	4	West Virginia	Orchard Park, N.Y.	D4-'85	12/4
43	Young, Lonnie	S	6-1	182	7/18/63	4	Michigan State	Flint, Mich.	D12-'85	12/12

* Del Greco played 5 games with Green Bay, 3 with St. Louis in '87; Horne played 4 games with Cincinnati, 5 with St. Louis.

†Option playout; subject to developments.

Also played with Cardinals in '87—S Dwayne Anderson (1 game), LB Terrence Anthony (1), LB Joe Bock (1), DE Ron Bohm (3), LB Tony Buford (2), DT Anthony Burke (1), DT Victor Burnett (3), LB Jimmie Carter (1), P Greg Cater (9), WR Clarence Collins (1), RB Larry Cowan (active for 3 games but did not play), DE Gary Dulin (3), LB Phil Forney (3), RB Don Goodman (3), QB Shawn Halloran (3), CB Johnny Holloway (3), TE Bob Keseday (3), LB Terrence Mack (5), CB Mark Mathis (2), S Tony Mayes (3), WR Adrian McBride (3), LB Peter Noga (3), LB Jeff Paine (1), G Ron Pasquale (1), DT Victor Perry (1), S John Preston (5), C Keith Radecic (3), P Mark Royals (1), S Ed Scott (3), CB Ken Sims (3), K Jason Staurovsky (2), QB Gregg Tipton (active for 3 games but did not play), CB Charles Wright (3).

Coaching Staff

Head Coach, Gene Stallings

Pro Career: Named head coach on February 10, 1986. Became thirtieth head coach in the history of the franchise dating back to 1920. Defensive backfield coach with Dallas from 1972-85. No pro playing experience. Career record: 11-19-1.

Background: Played end at Texas A&M from 1954-57 and was All-Southwest Conference receiver at Texas A&M under Paul "Bear" Bryant and tri-captain on undefeated 1956 team. College coach: Texas A&M 1957, 1965-71 (head coach), Alabama 1958-64. Assistant under just two coaches in career: Bryant at Alabama, and Tom Landry at Dallas.

Personal: Born March 2, 1935, in Paris, Tex. Gene and his wife, Ruth Ann, live in Phoenix and have five children: Anna Lee, Laurie, John Mark, Jacklyn, and Martha Kate.

Assistant Coaches

Marv Braden, special teams; born January 25, 1938, Kansas City, Mo., lives in Phoenix. Linebacker Southwest Missouri State 1956-59. No pro playing experience. College coach: Parsons 1963-66, Northeast Missouri State 1967-68 (head coach), U.S. International 1969-72, Iowa State 1973, Southern Methodist 1974-75, Michigan State 1976. Pro coach: Denver Broncos 1977-80, San Diego Chargers 1981-85, joined Cardinals in 1986.

Tom Bresnahan, offensive line; born January 21, 1935, Springfield, Mass., lives in Phoenix. Tackle Holy Cross 1953-55. No pro playing experience. College coach: Williams 1963-67, Columbia 1968-72, Navy 1973-80. Pro coach: Kansas City Chiefs 1981-82, New York Giants 1983-84, joined Cardinals in 1986.

LeBaron Caruthers, strength and conditioning; born April 20, 1954, Nashville, Tenn., lives in Phoenix. Tackle East Carolina 1972-73. No pro playing experience. College coach: Auburn 1978-79, Southern Methodist 1980-81. Pro coach: New England Patriots 1982-84, joined Cardinals in 1986.

Jim Johnson, defensive line; born May 26, 1941, Maywood, Ill., lives in Phoenix. Quarterback Missouri 1959-62. Pro tight end Buffalo Bills 1963-64. College coach: Missouri Southern 1967-68 (head coach), Drake 1969-72, Indiana 1973-76, Notre Dame 1977-80. Pro coach: Oklahoma Outlaws (USFL) 1984, Jacksonville Bulls (USFL) 1985, joined Cardinals in 1986.

Hank Kuhlmann, running backs; born October 6, 1937, St. Louis, Mo., lives in Phoenix. Running back Missouri 1956-59. No pro playing experience. College coach: Missouri 1963-71, Notre Dame 1975-77. Pro coach: Green Bay Packers 1972-74, Chicago Bears 1978-82, Birmingham Stallions (USFL) 1983-85, joined Cardinals in 1986.

Leon McLaughlin, special assistant-quality control; born May 30, 1925, San Diego, Calif., lives in Phoenix. Center-linebacker UCLA 1946-49. Pro center Los Angeles Rams 1951-55. College coach: Washington State 1956, Stanford 1959-65, San Fernando Valley State 1969-70 (head coach). Pro coach: Pittsburgh Steelers 1966-68, Los Angeles Rams 1971-72, Detroit Lions 1973-74, Green Bay Packers 1975-76, New England Patriots 1977, joined Cardinals in 1978.

Mal Moore, receivers; born December 19, 1939, Dozier, Ala., lives in Phoenix. Quarterback-defensive back Alabama 1958-62. No pro playing experience. College coach: Montana State 1963, Alabama 1964-82, Notre Dame 1983-85. Pro coach: Joined Cardinals in 1986.

Joe Pascale, linebackers; born April 4, 1946, New York, N.Y., lives in Phoenix. Linebacker Connecticut 1963-66. No pro playing experience. College coach: Connecticut 1967-68, Rhode Island 1969-73, Idaho State 1974-76 (head coach 1976), Princeton 1977-79. Pro coach: Montreal Alouettes (CFL) 1980-81, Ottawa Rough Riders (CFL) 1982-83, New Jersey Generals (USFL) 1984-85, joined Cardinals in 1986.

Jim Shofner, offensive coordinator; born December 18, 1935, Grapevine, Tex., lives in Phoenix. Running back Texas Christian 1955-57. Pro defensive back Cleveland Browns 1958-63. College coach: Texas Christian 1964-66, 1974-76 (head coach). Pro coach: San Francisco 49ers 1967-73, 1977, Cleveland Browns 1978-80, Houston Oilers 1981-82, Dallas Cowboys 1983-85, joined Cardinals in 1986.

Dennis Thurman, defensive backs; born April 14, 1956, Los Angeles, Calif., lives in Phoenix. Safety Southern California 1974-77. Pro defensive back Dallas Cowboys 1978-85, St. Louis Cardinals 1986. Pro coach: Joined Cardinals in 1988.

Phoenix Cardinals 1988 First-Year Roster

Name	Pos.	Ht.	Wt.	Birth-date	College	Hometown	How Acq.
Brim, Michael	CB	6-0	186	1/23/66	Virginia Union	Danville, Va.	D4
Carrier, Chris	S	6-5	215	4/4/64	Louisiana State	Eunice, La.	D12
Dill, Scott	G	6-5	272	4/5/66	Memphis State	Birmingham, Ala.	D9
Garza, Sammy (1)	QB	6-1	184	9/30/65	Texas-El Paso	Harlingen, Tex.	FA-'87
Gaines, Chris	LB	6-0	238	2/3/65	Vanderbilt	Nashville, Tenn.	D5a
Jordan, Tony	RB	6-2	220	5/5/65	Kansas State	Rochester, N.Y.	D5b
Jones, Ernie	WR	5-11	186	12/15/64	Indiana	Elkhart, Ind.	D7
Harvey, Ken	LB	6-2	225	5/6/65	California	Austin, Tex.	D1
Jeffrey, Tony	RB	5-11	208	7/8/64	Texas Christian	Gladewater, Tex.	D2
McCoy, Keith	CB	5-11	172	11/27/64	Fresno State	Compton, Calif.	D11
Mimbs, Robert	RB	5-10	197	8/6/64	Kansas	Kansas City, Mo.	FA
Moore, Tim	LB	6-2	218	1/1/65	Michigan State	Detroit, Mich.	D8
Neighbors, Wes	C	6-1	255	2/28/64	Alabama	Huntsville, Ala.	FA
Phillips, Jon	G	6-3	280	12/30/64	Oklahoma	Tulsa, Okla.	D6
Royals, Mark	P	6-5	216	6/22/63	Appalachian State	Mathews, Va.	FA
Schillinger, Andy	WR	5-11	179	11/22/64	Miami, Ohio	Avon Lake, Ohio	D10
Tupa, Tom	QB-P	6-4	220	9/6/66	Ohio State	Brecksville, Ohio	D3
Van Dyke, Ralph	T	6-6	270	1/19/64	Nebraska	Chicago Heights, Ill.	FA
Webster, Kennedy	CB-S	6-1	200	11/28/63	Texas-El Paso	Helena, Ark.	FA

The term NFL Rookie is defined as a player who is in his first season of professional football and has not been on the roster of another professional football team for any regular-season or postseason games. A Rookie is designated by an "R" on NFL rosters. Players who have been active in another professional football league or players who have NFL experience, including either preseason training camp or being on an active roster for fewer than three regular-season or postseason games, are termed NFL First-Year Players. An NFL First-Year Player is designated by a "1" on NFL rosters. Thereafter, a player on an NFL active roster for at least three regular-season or postseason games is credited with an additional year of NFL playing experience.

NOTES

SAN FRANCISCO 49ERS

National Football Conference Western Division

Team Colors: Forty Niners Gold and Scarlet

4949 Centennial Boulevard
Santa Clara, California 95054
Telephone: (408) 562-4949

Club Officials

Owner/President: Edward J. DeBartolo, Jr.
Head Coach: Bill Walsh
Vice President-General Manager: John McVay
Vice President-General Counsel: Carmen Policy
Business Manager: Keith Simon
Executive Administrative Assistant: Norb Hecker
Director of Pro Scouting: Alan Webb
Director of College Scouting: Tony Razzano
Director of Public Relations: Jerry Walker
Publications Coordinator: Rodney Knox
Coordinator of Football Operations: Neal Dahlen
Ticket Manager: Ken Dargel
Marketing/Promotions Coordinator: Laurie Welling
Trainer: Lindsy McLean
Equipment Manager: Bronco Hinek

Stadium: Candlestick Park • **Capacity:** 64,252
San Francisco, California 94124

Playing Surface: Grass

Training Camp: Sierra Community College
Rocklin, California 95677

1988 Schedule

Preseason

July 31	vs. Miami at London, Eng.	6:00
Aug. 6	**Los Angeles Raiders**	6:00
Aug. 13	at Denver	7:00
Aug. 20	at San Diego	6:00
Aug. 26	**Seattle**	6:00

Regular Season

Sept. 4	at New Orleans	12:00
Sept. 11	at New York Giants	1:00
Sept. 18	**Atlanta**	1:00
Sept. 25	at Seattle	1:00
Oct. 2	**Detroit**	1:00
Oct. 9	**Denver**	1:00
Oct. 16	at Los Angeles Rams	1:00
Oct. 24	at Chicago (Monday)	8:00
Oct. 30	**Minnesota**	1:00
Nov. 6	at Phoenix	2:00
Nov. 13	**Los Angeles Raiders**	1:00
Nov. 21	**Washington** (Monday)	6:00
Nov. 27	at San Diego	1:00
Dec. 4	at Atlanta	1:00
Dec. 11	**New Orleans**	1:00
Dec. 18	**Los Angeles Rams**	5:00

49ers Coaching History

(269-257-13)

1950-54	Lawrence (Buck) Shaw	33-25-2
1955	Norman (Red) Strader	4-8-0
1956-58	Frankie Albert	19-17-1
1959-63	Howard (Red) Hickey*	27-27-1
1963-67	Jack Christiansen	26-38-3
1968-75	Dick Nolan	56-56-5
1976	Monte Clark	8-6-0
1977	Ken Meyer	5-9-0
1978	Pete McCulley**	1-8-0
1978	Fred O'Connor	1-6-0
1979-87	Bill Walsh	89-57-1

*Resigned after three games in 1963
**Released after nine games in 1978

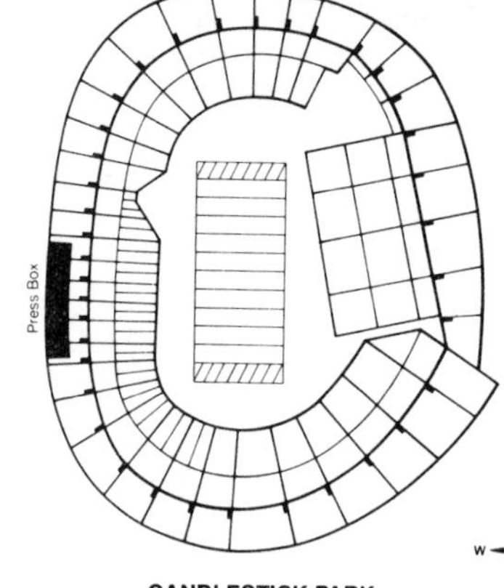

CANDLESTICK PARK

Record Holders

Individual Records—Career

Category	Name	Performance
Rushing (Yds.)	Joe Perry, 1950-1960, 1963	7,344
Passing (Yds.)	John Brodie, 1957-1973	31,548
Passing (TDs)	John Brodie, 1957-1973	214
Receiving (No.)	Dwight Clark, 1979-1987	506
Receiving (Yds.)	Dwight Clark, 1979-1987	6,750
Interceptions	Jimmy Johnson, 1961-1976	47
Punting (Avg.)	Tommy Davis, 1959-1969	44.7
Punt Return (Avg.)	Manfred Moore, 1974-75	14.7
Kickoff Return (Avg.)	Abe Woodson, 1958-1964	29.4
Field Goals	Ray Wersching, 1977-1987	190
Touchdowns (Tot.)	Ken Willard, 1965-1973	61
Points	Ray Wersching, 1977-1987	979

Individual Records—Single Season

Category	Name	Performance
Rushing (Yds.)	Wendell Tyler, 1984	1,262
Passing (Yds.)	Joe Montana, 1983	3,910
Passing (TDs)	Joe Montana, 1987	31
Receiving (No.)	Roger Craig, 1985	92
Receiving (Yds.)	Jerry Rice, 1986	1,570
Interceptions	Dave Baker, 1960	10
	Ronnie Lott, 1986	10
Punting (Avg.)	Tommy Davis, 1965	45.8
Punt Return (Avg.)	Dana McLemore, 1982	22.3
Kickoff Return (Avg.)	Joe Arenas, 1953	34.4
Field Goals	Bruce Gossett, 1973	26
Touchdowns (Tot.)	Jerry Rice, 1987	23
Points	Jerry Rice, 1987	138

Individual Records—Single Game

Category	Name	Performance
Rushing (Yds.)	Delvin Williams, 10-31-76	194
Passing (Yds.)	Joe Montana, 11-17-86	441
Passing (TDs)	John Brodie, 11-23-65	5
	Steve Spurrier, 11-19-72	5
	Joe Montana, 10-6-85	5
Receiving (No.)	Many times	12
	Last time by Roger Craig, 12-1-86	
Receiving (Yds.)	Jerry Rice, 12-9-85	241
Interceptions	Dave Baker, 12-4-60	*4
Field Goals	Ray Wersching, 10-16-83	6
Touchdowns (Tot.)	Billy Kilmer, 10-15-61	4
Points	Gordy Soltau, 10-27-51	26

*NFL Record

1987 Team Record

Preseason (3-2)

Date	Result		Opponents
8/8	W	20- 7	vs. Kansas City at Canton, Ohio
8/15	W	42-16	at L.A. Raiders
8/22	W	3-13	Dallas
8/27	W	17- 3	San Diego
9/4	L	10-34	at Seattle
		92-73	

Regular Season (13-2)

Date	Result		Opponents	Att.
9/13	L	17-30	at Pittsburgh	55,735
9/20	W	27-26	at Cincinnati	53,498
9/27	C		Philadelphia	
10/5	W	41-21	at N.Y. Giants	16,471
10/11	W	25-17	at Atlanta	8,684
10/18	W	34-28	St. Louis	38,094
10/25	W	24-22	at New Orleans	60,497
11/1	W	31-10	at L.A. Rams	55,328
11/8	W	27-20	Houston	59,740
11/15	L	24-26	New Orleans	60,436
11/22	W	24-10	at Tampa Bay	63,211
11/29	W	38-24	Cleveland	60,248
12/6	W	23-12	at Green Bay	51,118
12/14	W	41- 0	Chicago	63,509
12/20	W	35- 7	Atlanta	54,698
12/27	W	48- 0	L.A. Rams	57,950

C (Cancelled due to players' strike.)

Postseason (0-1)

Date	Result		Opponent	Att.
1/9	L	24-36	Minnesota	62,547

Score by Periods

49ers	81	150	89	139	0	— 459
Opponents	53	69	60	71	0	— 253

Attendance

Home 394,675 Away 364,542 Total 759,217
Single-game home record, 63,509 (12-14-87)
Single-season home record, 470,506 (1985)

1987 Team Statistics

	49ers	Opp.
Total First Downs	357	250
Rushing	134	95
Passing	202	132
Penalty	21	23
Third Down: Made/Att.	97/203	58/201
Fourth Down: Made/Att.	7/9	14/24
Total Net Yards	5987	4095
Avg. Per Game	399.1	273.0
Total Plays	1054	933
Avg. Per Play	5.7	4.4
Net Yards Rushing	2237	1611
Avg. Per Game	149.1	107.4
Total Rushes	524	429
Net Yards Passing	3750	2484
Avg. Per Game	250.0	165.6
Sacked/Yards Lost	29/205	37/287
Gross Yards	3955	2771
Att./Completions	501/322	467/224
Completion Pct.	64.3	48.0
Had Intercepted	14	25
Punts/Avg.	68/37.4	72/39.6
Net Punting Avg.	32.1	32.8
Penalties/Yards Lost	88/792	80/660
Fumbles/Ball Lost	25/12	30/13
Touchdowns	59	26
Rushing	11	8
Passing	44	13
Returns	4	5
Avg. Time of Possession	31:43	28:17

1987 Individual Statistics

Scoring	TD R	TD P	TD Rt	PAT	FG	Saf	TP
Rice	1	22	0	0/0	0/0	0	138
Wersching	0	0	0	44/46	13/17	0	83
Clark	0	5	0	0/0	0/0	0	30
Wilson	0	5	0	0/0	0/0	0	30
Craig	3	1	0	0/0	0/0	0	24
Rathman	1	3	0	0/0	0/0	0	24
Brockhaus	0	0	0	11/13	3/6	0	20
Frank	0	3	0	0/0	0/0	0	18
Heller	0	3	0	0/0	0/0	0	18
Cribbs	1	0	1	0/0	0/0	0	12
Cherry	1	0	0	0/0	0/0	0	6
Greer	0	1	0	0/0	0/0	0	6
McLemore	0	0	1	0/0	0/0	0	6
Monroe	0	1	0	0/0	0/0	0	6
Montana	1	0	0	0/0	0/0	0	6
Rodgers	1	0	0	0/0	0/0	0	6
Stevens	1	0	0	0/0	0/0	0	6
Taylor	0	0	1	0/0	0/0	0	6
Wells	0	0	1	0/0	0/0	0	6
Young	1	0	0	0/0	0/0	0	6
Fuller	0	0	0	0/0	0/0	1	2
49ers	11	44	4	55/59	16/23	1	459
Opponents	8	13	5	25/26	24/35	0	253

Passing	Att.	Comp.	Yds.	Pct.	TD	Int.	Tkld.	Rate
Montana	398	266	3054	66.8	31	13	22/158	102.1
Young	69	37	570	53.6	10	0	3/25	120.8
Gagliano	29	16	229	55.2	1	1	4/22	78.1
Stevens	4	2	52	50.0	1	0	0/0	135.4
Sydney	1	1	50	100.0	1	0	0/0	158.3
49ers	501	322	3955	64.3	44	14	29/205	106.2
Opponents	467	224	2771	48.0	13	25	37/287	53.8

Rushing	Att.	Yds.	Avg.	LG	TD
Craig	215	815	3.8	25	3
Cribbs	70	300	4.3	20	1
Rathman	62	257	4.1	35	1
Young	26	190	7.3	29t	1
Montana	35	141	4.0	20	1
Sydney	29	125	4.3	15	0
Varajon	18	82	4.6	11	0
Cherry	13	65	5.0	16	1
Rice	8	51	6.4	17	1
Hardy	7	48	6.9	14	0
Rodgers	11	46	4.2	15	1
Stevens	10	45	4.5	16	1
DuBose	10	33	3.3	11	0
Monroe	2	26	13.0	17	0
Flagler	6	11	1.8	5	0
Frank	1	2	2.0	2	0
Blount	1	0	0.0	0	0
49ers	524	2237	4.3	35	11
Opponents	429	1611	3.8	57	8

Receiving	No.	Yds.	Avg.	LG	TD
Craig	66	492	7.5	35t	1
Rice	65	1078	16.6	57t	22
Rathman	30	329	11.0	29	3
Wilson	29	450	15.5	46t	5
Frank	26	296	11.4	27	3
Clark	24	290	12.1	40t	5
Francis	22	202	9.2	19	0
Heller	12	165	13.8	39t	3
Taylor	9	151	16.8	34	0
Cribbs	9	70	7.8	16	0
Greer	6	111	18.5	50	1
Gladney	4	60	15.0	19	0
DuBose	4	37	9.3	14	0
Monroe	3	66	22.0	39t	1
Varajon	3	25	8.3	12	0
Rodgers	2	45	22.5	24	0
Jones	2	35	17.5	22	0
Flagler	2	28	14.0	24	0
Dressel	1	8	8.0	8	0
Hardy	1	7	7.0	7	0
Margerum	1	7	7.0	7	0
Sydney	1	3	3.0	3	0
49ers	322	3955	12.3	57t	44
Opponents	224	2771	12.4	63t	13

Interceptions	No.	Yds.	Avg.	LG	TD
Lott	5	62	12.4	34	0
Griffin	5	1	0.2	1	0
McLemore	2	35	17.5	25	0
McKyer	2	0	0.0	0	0
Courtney	1	30	30.0	30	0
Williamson	1	17	17.0	17	0
Walter	1	16	16.0	16	0
Turner	1	15	15.0	15	0
Martin	1	12	12.0	12	0
Cousineau	1	11	11.0	11	0
Nixon	1	5	5.0	5	0
Shell	1	1	1.0	1	0
J. Fahnhorst	1	0	0.0	0	0
Holmoe	1	0	0.0	0	0
McColl	1	0	0.0	0	0
49ers	25	205	8.2	34	0
Opponents	14	258	18.4	38	0

Punting	No.	Yds.	Avg.	In 20	LG
Runager	55	2157	39.2	13	56
Asmus	12	384	32.0	3	51
49ers	68	2541	37.4	16	56
Opponents	72	2850	39.6	13	68

Punt Returns	No.	FC	Yds.	Avg.	LG	TD
McLemore	21	7	265	12.6	83t	1
Griffin	9	2	79	8.8	29	0
Martin	2	0	12	6.0	9	0
Pollard	1	0	0	0.0	0	0
Taylor	1	0	9	9.0	9	0
49ers	34	9	365	10.7	83t	1
Opponents	29	10	195	6.7	26	0

Kickoff Returns	No.	Yds.	Avg.	LG	TD
Rodgers	17	358	21.1	50	0
Cribbs	13	327	25.2	92t	1
Sydney	12	243	20.3	30	0
Monroe	5	91	18.2	24	0
Flagler	3	31	10.3	16	0
Rathman	2	37	18.5	21	0
Henley	1	21	21.0	21	0
McLemore	1	23	23.0	23	0
Varajon	1	13	13.0	13	0
49ers	55	1144	20.8	92t	1
Opponents	76	1598	21.0	97t	1

Sacks	No.
Haley	6.5
Kugler	4.5
Stover	3.5
Turner	3.0
Roberts	2.5
Board	2.0
Collins	2.0
Fagan	2.0
Fuller	2.0
Glover	2.0
Korff	1.5
Carter	1.0
Courtney	1.0
McColl	1.0
Shell	1.0
Browner	0.5
49ers	37.0
Opponents	29.0

San Francisco 49ers 1988 Veteran Roster

No.	Name	Pos.	Ht.	Wt.	Birth-date	NFL Exp.	College	Hometown	How Acq.	'87 Games/ Starts
79	Barton, Harris	T	6-4	280	4/19/64	2	North Carolina	Atlanta, Ga.	D1a-'87	12/9
76	Board, Dwaine	DE	6-5	248	11/29/56	9	North Carolina A&T	Rocky Mount, Va.	FA-'79	14/12
65	Bregel, Jeff	G	6-4	280	5/1/64	2	Southern California	Granada Hills, Calif.	D2a-'87	5/0
95	Carter, Michael	NT	6-2	285	10/29/60	5	Southern Methodist	Dallas, Tex.	D5a-'84	12/12
	t-Chandler, Wes	WR	6-0	188	8/22/56	11	Florida	New Smyrna Beach, Fla.	T(SD)-'88	12/11
69	†Collie, Bruce	T-G	6-6	275	6/27/62	4	Texas-Arlington	San Antonio, Tex.	D5-'85	11/8
59	Comeaux, Darren	LB	6-1	227	4/15/60	7	Arizona State	San Diego, Calif.	FA-'87	8/0
52	Cooper, George	LB	6-2	225	12/24/58	2	Michigan State	Detroit, Mich.	FA-'87	10/2
57	Cousineau, Tom	LB	6-3	225	5/6/57	7	Ohio State	Lakewood, Ohio	FA-'86	4/3
33	Craig, Roger	RB	6-0	224	7/10/60	6	Nebraska	Davenport, Iowa	D2-'83	14/14
83	†Crawford, Derrick	WR-KR	5-10	185	9/3/60	2	Memphis State	Memphis, Tenn.	FA-'86	0*
28	Cribbs, Joe	RB	5-11	193	1/5/58	8	Auburn	Sulligent, Ala.	T(Buff)-'86	11/2
51	Cross, Randy	G	6-3	265	4/25/54	13	UCLA	Encino, Calif.	D2-'76	12/12
57	Dean, Kevin	LB	6-1	235	2/5/65	2	Texas Christian	Newton, Tex.	FA-'87	4/1
	t-Eason, Bo	S	6-2	205	3/10/61	5	California-Davis	Clarksburg, Calif.	T(Hou)-'88	3/0
50	Ellison, Riki	LB	6-2	225	8/15/60	6	Southern California	Tucson, Ariz.	D5-'83	3/1
75	Fagan, Kevin	DE	6-3	260	4/25/63	2	Miami	Lake Worth, Fla.	D4c-'87	7/2
55	†Fahnhorst, Jim	LB	6-4	230	11/8/58	5	Minnesota	St. Cloud, Minn.	FA-'87	11/10
32	Flagler, Terrence	RB	6-0	200	9/24/64	2	Clemson	Fernandia Beach, Fla.	D1b-'87	3/1
86	Frank, John	TE	6-3	225	4/17/62	5	Ohio State	Mt. Lebanon, Pa.	D2-'84	12/6
49	Fuller, Jeff	S	6-2	216	8/8/62	5	Texas A&M	Dallas, Tex.	D5b-'84	14/13
11	Gagliano, Bob	QB	6-3	205	9/5/58	5	Utah State	Glendale, Calif.	FA-'87	3/1
93	Glover, Clyde	DE	6-6	280	7/16/60	2	Fresno State	Las Vegas, Nev.	FA-'87	13/1
29	Griffin, Don	CB	6-0	176	3/17/64	3	Middle Tennessee State	Pelham, Ga.	D6-'86	12/10
54	Hadley, Ron	LB	6-2	240	11/9/63	2	Washington	Boise, Idaho	FA-'87	3/2
94	Haley, Charles	DE-LB	6-5	230	1/6/64	3	James Madison	Campbell County, Va.	D4a-'86	12/2
89	Heller, Ron	TE	6-3	235	9/18/63	2	Oregon State	Clarkfork, Idaho	FA-'87	13/6
46	Holmoe, Tom	S	6-2	195	3/7/60	5	Brigham Young	La Crescenta, Calif.	D4-'83	11/0
88	Jones, Brent	TE	6-4	230	2/12/63	2	Santa Clara	San Jose, Calif.	FA-'87	4/0
67	Kugler, Pete	NT-DE	6-4	255	8/9/59	6	Penn State	Cherry Hill, N.J.	FA-'86	11/8
42	†Lott, Ronnie	S	6-0	200	5/8/59	8	Southern California	Rialto, Calif.	D1-'81	12/12
84	Margerum, Ken	WR	6-0	180	10/5/58	6	Stanford	Fountain Valley, Calif.	FA-'86	2/0
53	†McColl, Milt	LB	6-6	230	8/28/59	8	Stanford	Covina, Calif.	FA-'81	12/10
62	McIntyre, Guy	G	6-3	264	2/17/61	5	Georgia	Thomasville, Ga.	D3-'84	3/3
22	McKyer, Tim	CB	6-0	174	9/5/63	3	Texas-Arlington	Port Arthur, Tex.	D3b-'86	12/12
43	McLemore, Dana	CB-KR	5-10	183	7/1/60	7	Hawaii	Venice, Calif.	FA-'87	12/2
97	Mikolas, Doug	NT	6-1	270	6/7/62	2	Portland State	Scio, Ore.	FA-'87	8/2
16	Montana, Joe	QB	6-2	195	6/11/56	10	Notre Dame	Monongahela, Pa.	D3-'79	13/11
20	Nixon, Tory	CB	5-11	186	2/24/62	4	San Diego State	Phoenix, Ariz.	T(Wash)-'85	12/0
77	Paris, Bubba	T	6-6	299	10/6/60	6	Michigan	Louisville, Ky.	D2-'82	11/8
44	Rathman, Tom	RB	6-1	232	10/7/62	3	Nebraska	Grand Island, Neb.	D3a-'86	12/7
80	Rice, Jerry	WR	6-2	200	10/13/62	4	Mississippi Valley State	Crawford, Miss.	D1-'85	12/12
91	Roberts, Larry	DE	6-3	264	6/2/63	3	Alabama	Dothan, Ala.	D2-'86	11/2
4	†Runager, Max	P	6-1	189	3/24/56	10	South Carolina	Orangeburg, S.C.	FA-'84	12/0
61	†Sapolu, Jesse	G-C	6-4	260	3/10/61	3	Hawaii	Honolulu, Hawaii	D11-'83	12/9
90	†Shell, Todd	LB	6-4	225	6/24/62	4	Brigham Young	Mesa, Ariz.	D1-'84	6/2
72	Stover, Jeff	DE	6-5	275	5/22/58	7	Oregon	Corning, Calif.	FA-'82	12/5
24	Sydney, Harry	RB	6-0	217	6/26/59	2	Kansas	Faye, N.C.	FA-'87	14/0
82	Taylor, John	WR	6-1	185	3/31/62	2	Delaware State	Pensauken, N.J.	D3c-'87	12/2
60	Thomas, Chuck	C	6-3	280	12/24/60	3	Oklahoma	Houston, Tex.	FA-'87	7/3
58	†Turner, Keena	LB	6-2	222	10/22/58	9	Purdue	Chicago, Ill.	D2-'80	10/10
74	Wallace, Steve	T	6-5	276	12/27/64	3	Auburn	Atlanta, Ga.	D4b-'86	11/4
99	Walter, Michael	LB	6-3	238	11/30/60	6	Oregon	Eugene, Ore.	FA-'84	12/12
14	Wersching, Ray	K	5-11	215	8/21/50	16	California	Downey, Calif.	FA-'77	12/0
81	t-Williams, Dokie	WR	5-11	180	8/25/60	6	UCLA	Oceanside, Calif.	T(Raid)-'88	11/5
27	†Williamson, Carlton	S	6-0	204	6/12/58	8	Pittsburgh	Atlanta, Ga.	D3-'81	8/1
85	Wilson, Mike	WR	6-3	215	12/19/58	8	Washington State	Carson, Calif.	FA-'81	11/8
21	Wright, Eric	CB	6-1	185	4/18/59	7	Missouri	East St. Louis, Ill.	D2b-'81	2/2
8	Young, Steve	QB	6-2	200	10/11/61	4	Brigham Young	Greenwich, Conn.	T(TB)-'87	8/3

* Crawford missed '87 season due to injury.

†Option playout; subject to developments.

Retired—Dwight Clark, 9-year wide receiver, 13 games in '87; Keith Fahnhorst, 14-year tackle, 3 games in '87.

t-49ers traded for Chandler (San Diego), Eason (Houston), Williams (L.A. Raiders).

Traded—Center Fred Quillan to San Diego.

Also played with 49ers in '87—K Jim Asmus (3 games), QB Ed Blount (1), K Jeff Brockhaus (3), RB Raynard Brown (1), LB Keith Browner (1), S John Butler (3), RB Tony Cherry (1), T Mark Cochran (3), DE Glen Collins (3), CB Matt Courtney (3), NT Joe Drake (3), TE Chris Dressel (1), G Michael Durrette (3), S John Faylor (3), TE Russ Francis (8), T Tracy Franz (3), WR Tony Gladney (2), WR Terry Greer (3), RB Andre Hardy (1), WR Thomas Henley (1), T Gary Hoffman (3), LB James Johnson (1), LB Jerry Keeble (3), LB Carl Keever (3), LB Mark Korff (2), DE Greg Liter (1), C Tim Long (2), CB Derrick Martin (3), WR Carl Monroe (3), T Limbo Parks (3), NT Reno Patterson (1), CB Darryl Pollard (3), G Kevin Reach (3), DE Elston Ridgle (3), RB Del Rodgers (7), CB Jonathan Shelley (1), QB Mark Stevens (2), S John Sullivan (1), RB Mike Varajon (3), TE Mike Wells (1).

COACHING STAFF

Head Coach, Bill Walsh

Pro Career: Begins tenth season as an NFL head coach. Directed 49ers to NFC championship in 1981 and 1984 and to victories in Super Bowl XVI (26-21 over Cincinnati) and Super Bowl XIX (38-16 over Miami). Started pro coaching career in 1966 as offensive backfield coach for the Oakland Raiders. He then spent eight seasons (1968-75) in Cincinnati, where he was responsible for coaching the Bengals' quarterbacks and receivers. His tenure in Cincinnati was followed by a season with the San Diego Chargers as offensive coordinator. While at Cincinnati he tutored Ken Anderson, who became the first NFL quarterback to lead the league in passing two straight years. At San Diego, he helped develop the talents of quarterback Dan Fouts. No pro playing experience. Career record: 89-57-1.

Background: End at San Jose State in 1953-54. Started college coaching career at California, where he served under Marv Levy from 1960-62. In 1963, he joined John Ralston's Stanford staff and worked with the defensive backfield for three seasons. Returned to Stanford as head coach in 1977 and directed the Cardinal to a two-year record of 17-7, including wins in the Sun and Bluebonnet Bowls. Received his master's degree in history from San Jose State in 1959.

Personal: Born November 30, 1931, in Los Angeles, Calif. He and his wife, Geri, live in Menlo Park, Calif., and have three children—Steve, Craig, and Elizabeth.

Assistant Coaches

Jerry Attaway, conditioning; born January 3, 1946, Susanville, Calif., lives in San Carlos, Calif. Defensive back Yuba, Calif., J.C. 1964-65, Cal-Davis 1967. No pro playing experience. College coach: Cal-Davis 1970-71, Idaho 1972-74, Utah State 1975-77, Southern California 1978-82. Pro coach: Joined 49ers in 1983.

Dennis Green, receivers; born February 17, 1949, Harrisburg, Pa., lives in Santa Cruz, Calif. Running back Iowa 1968-70. Pro running back British Columbia Lions (CFL) 1971. College coach: Iowa 1972, 1974-76, Dayton 1973, Stanford 1977-78, 1980, Northwestern 1981-85 (head coach). Pro coach: San Francisco 49ers 1979, rejoined 49ers in 1986.

Mike Holmgren, quarterbacks; born June 15, 1948, San Francisco, Calif., lives in San Jose, Calif. Quarterback Southern California 1966-69. No pro playing experience. College coach: San Francisco State 1981, Brigham Young 1982-85. Pro coach: Joined 49ers in 1986.

Sherman Lewis, running backs, born June 29, 1942, Louisville, Ky., lives in Sunnyvale, Calif. Running back Michigan State 1961-63. Pro running back Toronto Argonauts (CFL) 1964-65, New York Jets 1966. College coach: Michigan State 1969-82. Pro coach: Joined 49ers in 1983.

Bobb McKittrick, offensive line; born December 29, 1935, Baker, Ore., lives in San Mateo, Calif. Guard Oregon State 1955-57. No pro playing experience. College coach: Oregon State 1961-64, UCLA 1965-70. Pro coach: Los Angeles Rams 1971-72, San Diego Chargers 1974-78, joined 49ers in 1979.

Bill McPherson, linebackers; born October 24, 1931, Santa Clara, Calif., lives in San Jose, Calif. Tackle Santa Clara 1950-52. No pro playing experience. College coach: Santa Clara 1963-74, UCLA 1975-77. Pro coach: Philadelphia Eagles 1978, joined 49ers in 1979.

Ray Rhodes, defensive backfield; born October 20, 1950, Mexia, Tex., lives in Fremont, Calif. Running back-wide receiver Texas Christian 1969-70, Tulsa 1972-73. Pro defensive back New York Giants 1974-79, San Francisco 49ers 1980. Pro coach: Joined 49ers in 1981.

George Seifert, defensive coordinator; born January 22, 1940, San Francisco, Calif., lives in Sunnyvale, Calif. Linebacker Utah 1960-62. No pro playing experience. College coach: Westminster 1965 (head coach), Iowa 1966, Oregon 1967-71, Stanford 1972-74, 1977-79, Cornell 1975-76 (head coach). Pro coach: Joined 49ers in 1980.

Lynn Stiles, special teams; born April 12, 1941, Kermit, Tex., lives in Sunnyvale, Calif. Guard Utah 1961-62. No pro playing experience. College coach: Utah 1963-65, Iowa 1966-70, UCLA 1971-75, San Jose State 1976-78 (head coach). Pro coach: Philadelphia Eagles 1979-85, joined 49ers in 1987.

Fred vonAppen, defensive line; born March 22, 1942, Eugene, Ore., lives in Cupertino, Calif. Lineman Linfield College 1960-63. No pro playing experience. College coach: Linfield 1967-68, Arkansas 1969, 1981, UCLA 1970, Virginia Tech 1971, Oregon 1972-76, Stanford 1977-78, 1982. Pro coach: Green Bay Packers 1979-80, joined 49ers in 1983.

San Francisco 49ers 1988 First-Year Roster

Name	Pos.	Ht.	Wt.	Birth-date	College	Hometown	How Acq.
Allen, Dennis	WR	6-1	182	7/7/63	Kansas State	Dallas, Tex.	FA
Bankston, Bobby	WR	5-7	170	1/20/63	East Texas State	El Campo, Tex.	FA
Belluomini, Paul	C	6-0	210	3/31/57	California-Davis	Concord, Calif.	FA
Biggers, Kevin	CB	5-11	185	5/6/62	Nebraska	Gardena, Calif.	FA
Bonner, Brian	LB	6-1	220	10/9/65	Minnesota	Minneapolis, Minn.	D9
Brooks, Chet	CB	5-11	191	1/1/66	Texas A&M	Midland, Tex.	D11
Bryant, Kevin	LB	6-2	223	4/19/65	Delaware State	Passaic, N.J.	D7
Clarkson, Larry	T	6-7	303	3/11/65	Montana	Abbotsford, Canada	D8
Cofer, Mike	K	6-1	190	2/19/64	North Carolina State	Charlotte, N.C.	FA
DuBose, Doug (1)	RB	5-11	190	3/14/64	Nebraska	New London, Conn.	FA
Eccles, Scott	TE	6-4	240	6/28/63	Eastern New Mexico	San Jose, Calif.	FA
Foley, Tim	K	5-10	210	2/22/65	Georgia Southern	Miami, Fla.	D10
Gilcrest, Stacey	CB-S	5-10	185	9/5/63	San Jose State	Torrance, Calif.	FA
Hammond, Curtis	CB	6-1	195	8/31/66	Southeast Missouri	St. Petersburg, Fla.	FA
Helton, Barry	P	6-3	205	1/2/65	Colorado	Simla, Colo.	D4a
Holt, Pierce	DE-NT	6-4	280	1/1/62	Angelo State	Rosenberg, Tex.	D2b
Kennedy, Sam	LB	6-3	235	7/10/64	San Jose State	Aptos, Calif.	FA
Lilly, Kevin (1)	DE	6-4	265	5/14/63	Tulsa	Tulsa, Okla.	FA-'87
Miller, Mike	DE	6-4	275	9/8/64	California Lutheran	La Canada, Calif.	FA
Mira, George, Jr.	LB	6-0	230	6/13/65	Miami	Key West, Fla.	D12
Nicholas, Calvin (1)	WR	6-4	208	6/11/64	Grambling	Baton Rouge, La.	D11b-'87
Paye, John (1)	QB	6-3	205	3/30/65	Stanford	Atherton, Calif.	D10-'87
Rivers, Garland	S	6-1	181	11/3/64	Michigan	Canton, Ohio	FA
Romanowski, Bill	LB	6-4	231	4/2/66	Boston College	Vernon, Conn.	D3
Spangler, Rich	K	6-1	195	10/29/63	Ohio State	Geneva, Ohio	FA
Stubbs, Danny	DE	6-4	260	1/3/65	Miami	Red Bank, N.J.	D2a
Thomas, Sean (1)	S-CB	5-11	192	4/12/62	Texas Christian	Sacramento, Calif.	FA-'87

The term NFL Rookie is defined as a player who is in his first season of professional football and has not been on the roster of another professional football team for any regular-season or postseason games. A Rookie is designated by an "R" on NFL rosters. Players who have been active in another professional football league or players who have NFL experience, including either preseason training camp or being on an active roster for fewer than three regular-season or postseason games, are termed NFL First-Year Players. An NFL First-Year Player is designated by a "1" on NFL rosters. Thereafter, a player on an NFL active roster for at least three regular-season or postseason games is credited with an additional year of NFL playing experience.

NOTES

TAMPA BAY BUCCANEERS

National Football Conference Central Division

Team Colors: Florida Orange, White, and Red

One Buccaneer Place
Tampa, Florida 33607
Telephone: (813) 870-2700

Club Officials

Owner-President: Hugh F. Culverhouse
Vice President: Joy Culverhouse
Vice President-Head Coach: Ray Perkins
Vice President-Community Relations: Gay Culverhouse
Secretary-Treasurer: Ward Holland
Vice-President-Administration: Gen. William E. Klein
Assistant to the President: Phil Krueger
Assistant to the Head Coach-Director of Pro Personnel: Erik Widmark
Director of Player Personnel: Jerry Angelo
Director of Ticket Operations: Terry Wooten
Director of Public Relations: Rick Odioso
Director of Marketing & Advertising: Fred Doremus
Assistant Director-Media Relations: Mike McCall
College Personnel: James Harris, Tom Heckert, Dean Rossi, Tim Ruskell, Steve Verderosa
Comptroller: Ed Easom
Trainer: Chris Smith
Assistant Trainer: Joe Joe Petrone
Equipment Manager: Frank Pupello
Assistant Equipment Manager: Carl Melchior
Video Director: Dave Levy
Assistant Video Director: Mike Perkins

Stadium: Tampa Stadium • **Capacity:** 74,315
North Dale Mabry
Tampa, Florida 33607

Playing Surface: Grass

Training Camp: University of Tampa
401 W. Kennedy Boulevard
Tampa, Florida 33606

1988 Schedule

Preseason

Aug. 6	**Indianapolis**	7:00
Aug. 13	**Cleveland**	7:00
Aug. 20	at Atlanta	7:30
Aug. 25	vs. Buffalo at Nashville, Tenn.	7:00

Regular Season

Sept. 4	**Philadelphia**	1:00
Sept. 11	at Green Bay	12:00
Sept. 18	**Phoenix**	1:00
Sept. 25	at New Orleans	12:00
Oct. 2	**Green Bay**	1:00
Oct. 9	at Minnesota	12:00
Oct. 16	at Indianapolis	12:00
Oct. 23	**Minnesota**	1:00
Oct. 30	**Miami**	1:00
Nov. 6	at Chicago	12:00
Nov. 13	at Detroit	1:00
Nov. 20	**Chicago**	1:00
Nov. 27	at Atlanta	1:00
Dec. 4	**Buffalo**	1:00
Dec. 11	at New England	1:00
Dec. 18	**Detroit**	1:00

Buccaneers Coaching History

(53-130-1)

1976-84	John McKay	45-91-1
1985-86	Leeman Bennett	4-28-0
1987	Ray Perkins	4-11-0

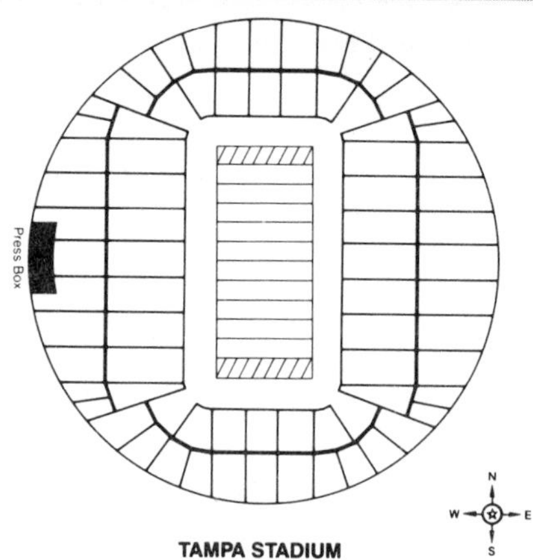

TAMPA STADIUM

Record Holders

Individual Records—Career

Category	Name	Performance
Rushing (Yds.)	James Wilder, 1981-87	5,370
Passing (Yds.)	Doug Williams, 1978-1982	12,648
Passing (TDs)	Doug Williams, 1978-1982	73
Receiving (No.)	James Wilder, 1981-87	379
Receiving (Yds.)	Kevin House, 1980-86	4,928
Interceptions	Cedric Brown, 1977-1984	29
Punting (Avg.)	Frank Garcia, 1983-87	41.1
Punt Return (Avg.)	John Holt, 1981-83	7.5
Kickoff Ret. (Avg.)	Isaac Hagins, 1976-1980	21.9
Field Goals	Donald Igwebuike, 1985-87	53
Touchdowns (Tot.)	James Wilder, 1981-87	42
Points	James Wilder, 1981-87	252

Individual Records—Single Season

Category	Name	Performance
Rushing (Yds.)	James Wilder, 1984	1,544
Passing (Yds.)	Doug Williams, 1981	3,563
Passing (TDs)	Doug Williams, 1980	20
Receiving (No.)	James Wilder, 1984	85
Receiving (Yds.)	Kevin House, 1981	1,176
Interceptions	Cedric Brown, 1981	9
Punting (Avg.)	Larry Swider, 1981	42.7
Punt Return (Avg.)	Leon Bright, 1985	10.3
Kickoff Return (Avg.)	Isaac Hagins, 1977	23.5
Field Goals	Donald Igwebuike, 1985	22
Touchdowns (Tot.)	James Wilder, 1984	13
Points	Donald Igwebuike, 1985	96

Individual Records—Single Game

Category	Name	Performance
Rushing (Yds.)	James Wilder, 11-6-83	219
Passing (Yds.)	Doug Williams, 11-16-80	486
Passing (TDs)	Steve DeBerg, 9-13-87	5
Receiving (No.)	James Wilder, 9-15-85	13
Receiving (Yds.)	Mark Carrier, 12-6-87	212
Interceptions	Many times	2
	Last time by Paul Tripoli, 10-4-87	
Field Goals	Bill Capece, 1-2-83	4
	Bill Capece, 10-30-83	4
	Donald Igwebuike, 11-24-85	4
Touchdowns	Jimmie Giles, 10-20-85	4
Points	Jimmie Giles, 10-20-85	24

1987 Team Record

Preseason (2-2)

Date	Result		Opponents
8/15	L	30-31	Cincinnati
8/22	W	29-27	N.Y. Jets
8/29	W	17-10	Washington
9/5	L	6-23	at Indianapolis
		82-91	

Regular Season (4-11)

Date	Result		Opponents	Att.
9/13	W	48-10	Atlanta	51,250
9/20	L	3-20	at Chicago	63,551
9/27	C		Green Bay	
10/4	W	31-27	at Detroit	4,919
10/11	L	13-17	San Diego	23,873
10/18	W	20-10	Minnesota	20,850
10/25	L	26-27	Chicago	70,747
11/1	W	23-17	at Green Bay	50,308
11/8	L	28-31	at St. Louis	22,449
11/15	L	17-23	at Minnesota	48,605
11/22	L	10-24	San Francisco	63,211
11/29	L	3-35	at L.A. Rams	45,188
12/6	L	34-44	at New Orleans	66,471
12/13	L	10-20	Detroit	41,699
12/20	L	14-31	St. Louis	32,046
12/27	L	6-24	at Indianapolis	60,468

C (Cancelled due to players' strike.)

Score by Periods

Buccaneers	78	66	81	61	0	—	286
Opponents	69	98	67	126	0	—	360

Attendance

Home 303,676 Away 361,959 Total 665,635
Single-game home record, 72,033 (1-6-80)
Single-season home record, 545,980 (1979)

1987 Team Statistics

	Buccaneers	Opp.
Total First Downs	263	314
Rushing	62	124
Passing	168	163
Penalty	33	27
Third Down: Made/Att.	85/215	90/200
Fourth Down: Made/Att.	3/6	6/9
Total Net Yards	4381	4987
Avg. Per Game	292.1	332.5
Total Plays	954	996
Avg. Per Play	4.6	5.0
Net Yards Rushing	1365	2038
Avg. Per Game	91.0	135.9
Total Rushes	394	500
Net Yards Passing	3016	2949
Avg. Per Game	201.1	196.6
Sacked/Yards Lost	43/361	39/306
Gross Yards	3377	3255
Att./Completions	517/264	457/271
Completion Pct.	51.1	59.3
Had Intercepted	17	16
Punts/Avg.	88/39.3	64/41.2
Net Punting Avg.	29.9	35.0
Penalties/Yards Lost	115/894	125/926
Fumbles/Ball Lost	35/14	42/20
Touchdowns	33	44
Rushing	7	18
Passing	22	23
Returns	4	3
Avg. Time of Possession	28:37	31:23

1987 Individual Statistics

Scoring

Scoring	TD R	TD P	TD Rt	PAT	FG	Saf	TP
Igwebuike	0	0	0	24/26	14/18	0	66
G. Carter	0	5	0	0/0	0/0	0	30
J. Smith	2	2	0	0/0	0/0	0	24
Tiffin	0	0	0	7/7	5/6	0	22
Carrier	0	3	0	0/0	0/0	0	18
Magee	0	3	0	0/0	0/0	0	18
Freeman	0	2	0	0/0	0/0	0	12
Hill	0	2	0	0/0	0/0	0	12
E. Hunter, Jets-T.B.	0	2	0	0/0	0/0	0	12
Streater	0	2	0	0/0	0/0	0	12
Austin	1	0	0	0/0	0/0	0	6
Bartalo	1	0	0	0/0	0/0	0	6
Hall	0	1	0	0/0	0/0	0	6
Howard	1	0	0	0/0	0/0	0	6
Moss	0	0	1	0/0	0/0	0	6
Ricks	1	0	0	0/0	0/0	0	6
Testaverde	1	0	0	0/0	0/0	0	6
Tripoli	0	0	1	0/0	0/0	0	6
K. Walker	0	0	1	0/0	0/0	0	6
Wells	0	0	1	0/0	0/0	0	6
Wilder	0	1	0	0/0	0/0	0	6
Wright	0	1	0	0/0	0/0	0	6
Buccaneers	7	22	4	31/33	19/24	0	286
Opponents	18	23	3	42/44	18/30	0	360

Passing

Passing	Att.	Comp.	Yds.	Pct.	TD	Int.	Tkld.	Rate
DeBerg	275	159	1891	57.8	14	7	20/185	85.3
Testaverde	165	71	1081	43.0	5	6	18/140	60.2
Zorn	36	20	199	55.6	0	2	1/6	48.3
Hold	24	8	123	33.3	2	1	3/18	61.6
Reaves	16	6	83	37.5	1	0	1/12	75.8
Bartalo	1	0	0	0.0	0	1	0/0	0.0
Buccaneers	517	264	3377	51.1	22	17	43/361	72.3
Opponents	457	271	3255	59.3	23	16	39/306	83.4

Rushing

Rushing	Att.	Yds.	Avg.	LG	TD
Wilder	106	488	4.6	21	0
J. Smith	100	309	3.1	46	2
E. Hunter, Jets-T.B.	56	210	3.8	23	0
E. Hunter, T.B.	8	41	5.1	11	0
Wright	37	112	3.0	11	0
Howard	30	100	3.3	31	1
Ricks	24	76	3.2	14	1
Hold	7	69	9.9	35	0
Testaverde	13	50	3.8	17	1
Austin	19	32	1.7	8	1
Bartalo	9	30	3.3	6	1
Gladman	12	29	2.4	6	0
Land	9	20	2.2	6	0
Streater	1	5	5.0	5	0
Zorn	4	4	1.0	5	0
Hill	3	3	1.0	9	0
Boone	1	2	2.0	2	0
Thomas	1	2	2.0	2	0
Freeman	1	1	1.0	1	0
Criswell	1	0	0.0	0	0
DeBerg	8	−8	−1.0	0	0
Buccaneers	394	1365	3.5	46	7
Opponents	500	2038	4.1	38t	18

Receiving

Receiving	No.	Yds.	Avg.	LG	TD
Wilder	40	328	8.2	32	1
G. Carter	38	586	15.4	57	5
Magee	34	424	12.5	37	3
Carrier	26	423	16.3	38	3
Hill	23	403	17.5	40	2
J. Smith	20	197	9.9	34t	2
Hall	16	169	10.6	29	1
Wright	13	98	7.5	15t	1
S. Holloway	10	127	12.7	26	0
Howard	10	123	12.3	45	0
Freeman	8	141	17.6	64t	2
E. Hunter, Jets-T.B.	7	28	4.0	8t	2
E. Hunter, T.B.	2	4	2.0	4	0
Streater	5	117	23.4	61t	2
Miller	5	97	19.4	33	0
Austin	5	51	10.2	20	0
G. Taylor	2	21	10.5	11	0
Gladman	2	8	4.0	5	0
Dixon	1	18	18.0	18	0
Walls	1	13	13.0	13	0
S. Carter	1	12	12.0	12	0
Ricks	1	12	12.0	12	0
Bartalo	1	5	5.0	5	0
Buccaneers	264	3377	12.8	64t	22
Opponents	271	3255	12.0	67	23

Interceptions

Interceptions	No.	Yds.	Avg.	LG	TD
Tripoli	3	17	5.7	15t	1
Isom	2	67	33.5	38	0
Woods	2	63	31.5	42	0
Futrell	2	46	23.0	23	0
K. Walker	2	30	15.0	30t	1
Jones	2	9	4.5	9	0
Kemp	1	11	11.0	11	0
Gant	1	5	5.0	5	0
Montoute	1	0	0.0	0	0
Buccaneers	16	248	15.5	42	2
Opponents	17	227	13.4	50	0

Punting

Punting	No.	Yds.	Avg.	In 20	LG
Criswell	26	1046	40.2	3	61
Garcia	62	2409	38.9	12	58
Buccaneers	88	3455	39.3	15	61
Opponents	64	2634	41.2	15	60

Punt Returns

Punt Returns	No.	FC	Yds.	Avg.	LG	TD
Futrell	24	6	213	8.9	22	0
Walls	4	2	12	3.0	11	0
Curry	3	0	32	10.7	14	0
Buccaneers	31	8	257	8.3	22	0
Opponents	50	10	621	12.4	80	1

Kickoff Returns

Kickoff Returns	No.	Yds.	Avg.	LG	TD
Futrell	31	609	19.6	40	0
E. Hunter, Jets-T.B.	8	123	15.4	27	0
Walls	6	136	22.7	39	0
J. Smith	5	84	16.8	21	0
Curry	3	53	17.7	20	0
Miller	3	68	22.7	25	0
Bartalo	1	15	15.0	15	0
Carrier	1	0	0.0	0	0
Gladman	1	16	16.0	16	0
Hill	1	8	8.0	8	0
Howard	1	5	5.0	5	0
Ricks	1	26	26.0	26	0
K. Walker	1	0	0.0	0	0
Wright	1	17	17.0	17	0
Buccaneers	56	1037	18.5	40	0
Opponents	61	1242	20.4	45	0

Sacks

Sacks	No.
Holmes	8.0
Washington	6.5
Kellin	3.5
Turner	3.5
Jarvis	3.0
Cannon	2.0
Riggins	2.0
Turpin	2.0
Montoute	1.5
Moss	1.5
M. Clark	1.0
Harris	1.0
McCallister	1.0
Nordgren	1.0
Keys	0.5
Buccaneers	39.0
Opponents	43.0

Tampa Bay Buccaneers 1988 Veteran Roster

No.	Name	Pos.	Ht.	Wt.	Birth-date	NFL Exp.	College	Hometown	How Acq.	'87 Games/ Starts
20	Austin, Cliff	RB	6-0	190	3/2/60	6	Clemson	Avondale, Ga.	T(Atl)-'87	3/2
42	Bartalo, Steve	RB	5-9	200	7/15/64	2	Colorado State	Colorado Springs, Colo.	D6-'87	9/0
52	†Brantley, Scot	LB	6-1	230	2/24/58	9	Florida	Ocala, Fla.	D3-'80	12/2
78	†Cannon, John	DE	6-5	260	7/30/60	7	William & Mary	Long Branch, N.J.	D3-'82	11/11
89	Carrier, Mark	WR	6-0	182	10/28/65	2	Nicholls State	Church Point, La.	D3-'87	10/6
87	Carter, Gerald	WR	6-1	190	6/19/57	9	Texas A&M	Bryan, Tex.	D9-'80	12/12
71	†Cooper, Mark	T	6-5	270	2/14/60	6	Miami	Miami, Fla.	FA-'87	9/2*
58	†Davis, Jeff	LB	6-0	230	1/26/60	7	Clemson	Greensboro, N.C.	D5-'82	11/10
96	t-Edwards, Randy	DE	6-4	266	3/9/61	5	Alabama	Atlanta, Ga.	T(Sea)-'88	7/0
12	t-Ferguson, Joe	QB	6-1	195	4/23/50	16	Arkansas	Shreveport, La.	T(Ind)-'88	0*
81	†Freeman, Phil	WR	5-11	185	12/9/62	4	Arizona	Los Angeles, Calif.	D8-'85	8/4
36	†Futrell, Bobby	CB-S	5-11	190	8/4/62	3	Elizabeth City State	Ahoskie, N.C.	FA-'86	12/1
91	Gant, Brian	LB	6-0	235	9/6/65	2	Illinois State	Gary, Ind.	FA-'87	11/3
79	†Goode, Conrad	T-G-C	6-6	285	1/9/62	4	Missouri	Creve Coeur, Mo.	FA-'87	11/2
31	Gordon, Sonny	S	5-11	192	7/30/65	2	Ohio State	Middletown, Ohio	FA-'87	7/0
60	†Grimes, Randy	C	6-4	270	7/20/60	6	Baylor	Tyler, Tex.	D2-'83	12/12
82	Hall, Ron	TE	6-4	238	3/15/64	2	Hawaii	Escondido, Calif.	D4b-'87	10/3
84	Hill, Bruce	WR	6-0	175	2/29/64	2	Arizona State	Lancaster, Calif.	D4c-'87	8/1
90	Holmes, Ron	DE	6-4	255	8/26/63	4	Washington	Lacey, Wash.	D1-'85	10/8
25	Howard, Bobby	RB	6-0	210	6/1/64	3	Indiana	Pittsburgh, Pa.	FA-'86	12/0
37	Hunter, Eddie	RB	5-10	195	1/20/65	2	Virginia Tech	Oxen Hill, Md.	FA-'87	6/3*
1	Igwebuike, Donald	K	5-9	185	12/27/60	4	Clemson	Anambra, Nigeria	D10-'85	12/0
28	Isom, Ray	S	5-9	190	12/27/65	2	Penn State	Harrisburg, Pa.	FA-'87	6/6
22	Jones, Rod	CB	6-0	175	3/31/64	3	Southern Methodist	Dallas, Tex.	D1b-'86	11/11
75	Kellin, Kevin	DE	6-5	250	11/16/59	3	Minnesota	Grand Rapids, Minn.	FA-'86	7/1
33	†Kemp, Bobby	S	6-0	190	5/29/59	8	Cal State-Fullerton	Pomona, Calif.	W(Cin)-'87	12/12
77	†Maarleveld, J.D.	T	6-6	300	10/24/61	3	Maryland	Rutherford, N.J.	D5-'86	11/3
86	Magee, Calvin	TE	6-3	240	4/23/63	4	Southern	New Orleans, La.	FA-'85	11/11
68	†Mallory, Rick	G	6-2	265	10/21/60	4	Washington	Renton, Wash.	D9-'84	12/12
99	McHale, Tom	DE	6-4	275	2/25/63	2	Cornell	Gaithersburg, Md.	FA-'87	3/1
83	Miller, Solomon	WR	6-1	185	12/6/64	3	Utah State	Los Angeles, Calif.	FA-'87	8/0
57	Moss, Winston	LB	6-3	235	12/24/65	2	Miami	Miami, Fla.	D2b-'87	12/6
59	Murphy, Kevin	LB	6-2	230	9/8/63	3	Oklahoma	Plano, Tex.	D2-'86	9/0
54	Randle, Ervin	LB	6-1	250	10/12/62	4	Baylor	Hearne, Tex.	D3-'85	12/12
29	Reynolds, Ricky	CB	5-11	182	1/19/65	2	Washington State	Sacramento, Calif.	D2a-'87	12/12
93	Sileo, Dan	NT	6-2	282	1/3/64	2	Miami	Stamford, Conn.	SD3-'87	10/10
35	Smith, Jeff	RB	5-9	204	3/22/62	4	Nebraska	Wichita, Kan.	T(KC)-'87	12/8
94	†Stensrud, Mike	NT	6-5	280	2/19/56	10	Iowa State	Lake Mills, Iowa	W(Minn)-'87	12/12
70	Swayne, Harry	DE	6-5	268	2/2/65	2	Rutgers	Philadelphia, Pa.	D7b-'87	8/2
85	Taylor, Gene	WR	6-2	189	11/12/62	2	Fresno State	Oakland, Calif.	W(NE)-'87	8/0
72	Taylor, Rob	T	6-6	285	11/14/60	3	Northwestern	St. Charles, Ill.	FA-'86	5/5
14	Testaverde, Vinny	QB	6-5	220	11/13/63	2	Miami	Elmont, N.Y.	D1-'87	6/4
24	†Tripoli, Paul	S	6-0	197	12/14/61	2	Alabama	Syracuse, N.Y.	FA-'88	13/4
50	Turk, Dan	C	6-4	260	6/25/62	3	Wisconsin	Milwaukee, Wis.	T(Pitt)-'87	13/3
56	Walker, Jackie	LB	6-5	245	11/3/62	3	Jackson State	Monroe, La.	D2-'86	12/6
51	Washington, Chris	LB	6-4	230	3/6/62	5	Iowa State	Chicago, Ill.	D6-'84	12/12
32	†Wilder, James	RB	6-3	225	5/12/58	8	Missouri	Sikeston, Mo.	D2-'82	12/12
3	Williams, Keith	RB	5-10	173	9/8/63	2	Southwest Missouri	Springfield, Mo.	FA-'87	0*
66	†Yarno, George	G	6-2	265	8/12/57	9	Washington State	Spokane, Wash.	FA-'85	11/8

* Cooper played 5 games with Denver, 4 with Tampa Bay in '87; Ferguson active for 12 games with Detroit but did not play; Hunter played 3 games with N.Y. Jets, 3 games with Tampa Bay; Williams missed '87 season due to injury.

†Option playout; subject to developments.

t-Buccaneers traded for Edwards (Seattle), Ferguson (Indianapolis).

Traded—Quarterback Steve DeBerg to Kansas City, tackle Ron Heller to Seattle.

Also played with Buccaneers in '87—CB Don Anderson (11 games), RB Greg Boone (2), G Rufus Brown (2), WR Steve Carter (3), DE Walter Carter (2), DE Mike Clark (3), CB-S Torin Clark (2), CB Ivory Curry (3), WR Dwayne Dixon (2), CB-S David Evans (active for 1 game but did not play), P Frank Garcia (12), CB Jeff George (2), RB Charles Gladman (2), DE Roy Harris (3), T Dave Heffernan (2), WR Derek Holloway (1), TE Steve Holloway (6), G Jim Huddleston (1), G John Hunt (1), WR David Jackson (1), LB Cam Jacobs (3), T David Johnson (1), G David Jordan (3), DE Tyrone Keys (3), CB Tim King (3), RB Dan Land (3), LB Fred McCallister (3), CB Vito McKeever (1), TE Jeff Modesitt (1), LB Sankar Montoute (3), NT Fred Nordgren (3), G Paul O'Connor (2), CB Lee Paige (3), LB Leon Pennington (3), C Chuck Pitcock (2), T Marvin Powell (6), T Don Pumphrey (3), DE James Ramey (3), QB John Reaves (2), DE Charles Riggins (3), WR Stanley Shakespeare (1), T Reggie Smith (3), WR Eric Streater (3), S Craig Swoope (1), LB Pat Teague (1), RB Derrick Thomas (1), K Van Tiffin (3), LB Miles Turner (3), CB Kevin Walker (3), WR Herkie Walls (2), TE Arthur Wells (2), S Rick Woods (5), QB Jim Zorn (1).

COACHING STAFF

Head Coach, Ray Perkins

Pro Career: Named third head coach in Tampa Bay Buccaneers history on December 31, 1986. Previous head coaching experience in the NFL came with New York Giants where he compiled a 24-35 record between 1979 and 1982. Perkins built the Giants into a playoff team by 1981, his third season. It marked the Giants' first playoff appearance in 18 years. Worked five years as an assistant in the NFL, spending 1974-77 as receivers coach with New England Patriots and 1978 as offensive coordinator with San Diego Chargers. Drafted by Baltimore Colts in seventh round of 1967, and played five seasons there. Career record: 28-46.

Background: Bear Bryant's hand-picked successor at University of Alabama, where he compiled a 32-15-1 record between 1983-86, including three bowl game victories. College receiver at Alabama 1964-66 and All-America as a senior. College assistant at Mississippi State (1973).

Personal: Born November 6, 1941, in Mt. Olive, Mississippi. Ray and his wife, Carolyn, live in Tampa and have two sons—Tony and Mike.

Assistant Coaches

Larry Beightol, offensive line; born November 21, 1942, Morrisdale, Pa., lives in Tampa. Guard-linebacker Catawba College 1961-63. No pro playing experience. College coach: William & Mary 1968-71, North Carolina State 1972-75, Auburn 1976, Arkansas 1977-78, 1980-82, Louisiana Tech 1979 (head coach), Missouri 1983-84. Pro coach: Atlanta Falcons 1985-86, joined Buccaneers in 1987.

John Bobo, offensive assistant; born February 18, 1958, Alapaha, Ga., lives in Tampa. Tight end-defensive end Maryville 1976-79. No pro playing experience. College coach: Alabama 1985-86. Pro coach: Joined Buccaneers in 1987.

Sylvester Croom, running backs; born September 25, 1954, Tuscaloosa, Ala., lives in Tampa. Center Alabama 1971-74. Pro center New Orleans Saints 1975. College coach: Alabama 1976-86. Pro coach: Joined Buccaneers in 1987.

Mike DuBose, defensive line; born January 5, 1953, Opp, Ala., lives in Tampa. Defensive lineman Alabama 1971-73. No pro playing experience. College coach: Alabama 1974-75, 1983-86, Tennessee-Chattanooga 1980-81, Southern Mississippi 1982. Pro coach: Joined Buccaneers in 1987.

Doug Graber, defensive coordinator-secondary; born September 26, 1944, Detroit, Mich., lives in Clearwater, Fla. Defensive back Wayne State 1963-66. No pro playing experience. College coach: Michigan Tech 1969-71, Eastern Michigan 1972-75, Ball State 1976-77, Wisconsin 1978-81, Montana State 1982 (head coach). Pro coach: Kansas City Chiefs 1983-86, joined Buccaneers in 1987.

Kent Johnson, strength and conditioning; born February 21, 1956, Mexia, Tex., lives in Tampa. Defensive back Stephen F. Austin 1974-77. No pro playing experience. College coach: Northeast Louisiana 1979, Northwestern State (La.) 1980-81, Alabama 1983-86. Pro coach: Joined Buccaneers in 1987.

Joe Kines, outside linebackers; born July 13, 1944, Piedmont, Ala., lives in Tampa. Linebacker Jacksonville (Ala.) State 1963-65. No pro playing experience. College coach: Jacksonville State 1966, 1972-76, Clemson 1977-78, Florida 1979-84, Alabama 1985-86. Pro coach: Joined Buccaneers in 1987.

Herb Paterra, inside linebackers; born November 8, 1940, Glassport, Pa., lives in Tampa. Offensive guard-linebacker Michigan State 1960-62. Pro linebacker Buffalo Bills 1963-64, Hamilton Tiger-Cats (CFL) 1965-68. College coach: Michigan State 1969-71, Wyoming 1972-74. Pro coach: Charlotte Hornets (WFL) 1975, Hamilton Tiger-Cats (CFL) 1978-79, Los Angeles Rams 1980-82, Edmonton Eskimos (CFL) 1983, Green Bay Packers 1984-85, Buffalo Bills 1986, joined Buccaneers in 1987.

Tampa Bay Buccaneers 1988 First-Year Roster

Name	Pos.	Ht.	Wt.	Birth-date	College	Hometown	How Acq.
Bruhin, John	G	6-4	285	12/9/64	Tennessee	Nashville, Tenn.	D4b
Carney, John (1)	K	5-11	170	4/20/64	Notre Dame	Jupiter, Fla.	FA
Davis, Reuben	DE	6-3	295	5/7/65	North Carolina	Greensboro, N.C.	D9
Evans, James (1)	RB	6-0	220	8/14/63	Southern	Mobile, Ala.	W(KC)-'87
Francis, Cazzy (1)	WR	5-10	175	12/17/63	Arkansas State	Orange, Tex.	FA
Goff, Robert	DE	6-3	265	10/2/65	Auburn	Bradenton, Fla.	D4a
Goode, Kerry	RB	6-1	200	7/28/65	Alabama	Town Creek, Ala.	D7
Graham, Don (1)	LB	6-2	244	1/31/64	Penn State	Pittsburgh, Pa.	D4a-'87
Gruber, Paul	T	6-5	290	2/24/65	Wisconsin	Prairie du Sac, Wis.	D1
Hold, Mike (1)	QB	5-11	190	3/16/63	South Carolina	Tempe, Ariz.	FA
Howard, William	RB	6-0	245	6/2/64	Tennessee	Lima, Ohio	D5
Jarvis, Curt (1)	NT-DE	6-2	266	1/28/65	Alabama	Gardendale, Ala.	D7a-'87
Jones, Bruce (1)	CB-S	5-11	195	12/26/62	North Alabama	Courtland, Ala.	FA
Jones, Victor	LB	6-2	245	10/19/66	Virginia Tech	Rockville, Md.	D12
Lee, Shawn	NT	6-3	265	10/24/66	North Alabama	Brooklyn, N.Y.	D6
Pidgeon, Tim (1)	LB	6-0	235	9/20/65	Syracuse	Oneonta, N.Y.	FA
Pillow, Frank	WR	5-10	170	4/11/65	Tennessee State	Nashville, Tenn.	D11
Ransdell, Bill (1)	QB	6-2	210	4/15/63	Kentucky	Elizabethtown, Ky.	FA
Robbins, Monte	P	6-4	200	9/19/64	Michigan	Great Bend, Kan.	D4c
Rolling, Henry (1)	LB	6-2	210	9/8/65	Nevada-Reno	Henderson, Nev.	D5-'87
Seals, Ray	TE	6-3	245	6/17/65	None	Syracuse, N.Y.	FA
Simmonds, Mike (1)	G	6-4	281	8/12/64	Indiana State	Belleville, Ill.	D10-'87
Simpson, Anthony	RB	5-10	245	12/21/64	East Carolina	Brooklyn, N.Y.	D8
Smith, Bill (1)	P	6-3	225	6/9/65	Mississippi	Little Rock, Ark.	FA
Smith, Don (1)	RB	5-11	200	10/30/63	Mississippi State	Hamilton, Miss.	D2-'87
Sowell, Brent (1)	T-G	6-5	285	3/27/63	Alabama	Clearwater, Fla.	FA
Tate, Lars	RB	6-2	215	2/2/66	Georgia	Indianapolis, Ind.	D2
Teague, Pat (1)	LB	6-1	230	10/22/63	North Carolina State	Raleigh, N.C.	FA
Thomas, Kevin (1)	C	6-2	268	7/27/64	Arizona State	Tucson, Ariz.	FA-'87

The term NFL Rookie is defined as a player who is in his first season of professional football and has not been on the roster of another professional football team for any regular-season or postseason games. A Rookie is designated by an "R" on NFL rosters. Players who have been active in another professional football league or players who have NFL experience, including either preseason training camp or being on an active roster for fewer than three regular-season or postseason games, are termed NFL First-Year Players. An NFL First-Year Player is designated by a "1" on NFL rosters. Thereafter, a player on an NFL active roster for at least three regular-season or postseason games is credited with an additional year of NFL playing experience.

NOTES

Mike Shula, offensive assistant; born June 3, 1965, Baltimore, Md. Lives in Tampa. Quarterback Alabama 1984-86. Pro quarterback Tampa Bay 1987. Pro coach: Joined Buccaneers in 1988.

Rodney Stokes, special teams; born February 3, 1953, Brookhaven, Miss., lives in Tampa. Linebacker Delta State 1976-77. No pro playing experience. College coach: Alabama 1983-86. Pro coach: Joined Buccaneers in 1987.

Richard Williamson, receivers; born April 13, 1941, Fort Deposit, Ala., lives in Tampa. Receiver Alabama 1959-62. No pro playing experience. College coach: Alabama 1963-67, 1970-71, Arkansas 1968-69, 1972-74, Memphis State 1975-80 (head coach). Pro coach: Kansas City Chiefs 1983-86, joined Buccaneers in 1987.

WASHINGTON REDSKINS

National Football Conference Eastern Division

Team Colors: Burgundy and Gold

Redskin Park
P.O. Box 17247
Dulles International Airport
Washington, D.C. 20041
Telephone: (703) 471-9100

Club Officials

Chairman of the Board-Chief Operating Executive: Jack Kent Cooke
Executive Vice President: John Kent Cooke
Secretary: Robert N. Eisman
Controller: Doug Porter
Board of Directors: Jack Kent Cooke, John Kent Cooke, James Lacher, William A. Shea, Esq., The Honorable John W. Warner
General Manager: Bobby Beathard
Asst. General Managers: Bobby Mitchell, Charles Casserly
Director of Player Personnel: Dick Daniels
Director of Pro Scouting: Kirk Mee
Scouts: Billy Devaney, George Saimes, Jerry Fauls
V.P.-Communications: Charlie Dayton
Director of Information: John C. Konoza
Director of Public Relations: Marty Hurney
Director of Marketing and Stadium Operations: Paul Denfeld
Director of Video: Donnie Schoenmann
Ticket Manager: Sue Barton
Head Trainer: Lamar (Bubba) Tyer
Asst. Trainers: Joe Kuczo, Keoki Kamau, Al Bellamy
Equipment Manager: Jay Brunetti

Stadium: Robert F. Kennedy Stadium • **Capacity:** 55,670
East Capitol Street
Washington, D.C. 20003

Playing Surface: Grass (PAT)

Training Camp: Dickinson College
Carlisle, Pennsylvania 17013

1988 Schedule

Preseason

Aug. 5	**Pittsburgh**	8:00
Aug. 13	at Miami	8:00
Aug. 20	at Los Angeles Raiders	7:00
Aug. 27	vs. Atl. at Birmingham, Ala.	7:00

Regular Season

Sept. 5	at N.Y. Giants (Monday)	9:00
Sept. 11	**Pittsburgh**	1:00
Sept. 18	**Philadelphia**	1:00
Sept. 25	at Phoenix	1:00
Oct. 2	**New York Giants**	1:00
Oct. 9	at Dallas	12:00
Oct. 16	**Phoenix**	1:00
Oct. 23	vs. Green Bay at Milw.	12:00
Oct. 30	at Houston	7:00
Nov. 6	**New Orleans**	4:00
Nov. 13	**Chicago**	1:00
Nov. 21	at San Francisco (Monday)	6:00
Nov. 27	**Cleveland**	1:00
Dec. 4	at Philadelphia	1:00
Dec. 11	**Dallas**	1:00
Dec. 17	at Cincinnati (Saturday)	12:30

Redskins Coaching History

Boston 1932-36
(391-333-26)

1932	Lud Wray	4-4-2
1933-34	William (Lone Star) Dietz	11-11-2
1935	Eddie Casey	2-8-1
1936-42	Ray Flaherty	56-23-3
1943	Arthur (Dutch) Bergman	7-4-1
1944-45	Dudley DeGroot	14-6-1
1946-48	Glen (Turk) Edwards	16-18-1
1949	John Whelchel*	3-3-1
1949-51	Herman Ball**	4-16-0
1951	Dick Todd	5-4-0
1952-53	Earl (Curly) Lambeau	10-13-1
1954-58	Joe Kuharich	26-32-2
1959-60	Mike Nixon	4-18-2
1961-65	Bill McPeak	21-46-3
1966-68	Otto Graham	17-22-3
1969	Vince Lombardi	7-5-2
1970	Bill Austin	6-8-0
1971-77	George Allen	69-35-1
1978-80	Jack Pardee	24-24-0
1981-87	Joe Gibbs	85-33-0

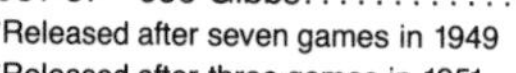

*Released after seven games in 1949
**Released after three games in 1951

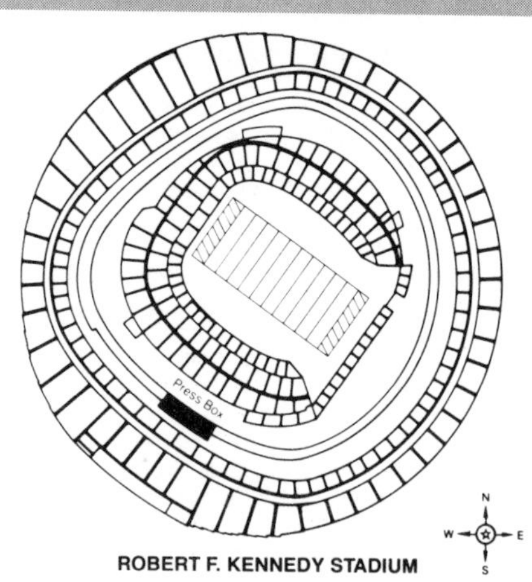

ROBERT F. KENNEDY STADIUM

Record Holders

Individual Records—Career

Category	Name	Performance
Rushing (Yds.)	John Riggins, 1976-79, 1981-85	7,472
Passing (Yds.)	Joe Theismann, 1974-1985	25,206
Passing (TDs)	Sonny Jurgensen, 1964-1974	209
Receiving (No.)	Charley Taylor, 1964-1977	649
Receiving (Yds.)	Charley Taylor, 1964-1977	9,140
Interceptions	Brig Owens, 1966-1977	36
Punting (Avg.)	Sammy Baugh, 1937-1952	45.1
Punt Return (Avg.)	Johnny Williams, 1952-53	12.8
Kickoff Return (Avg.)	Bobby Mitchell, 1962-68	28.5
Field Goals	Mark Moseley, 1974-1986	263
Touchdowns (Tot.)	Charley Taylor, 1964-1977	90
Points	Mark Moseley, 1974-1986	1,206

Individual Records—Single Season

Category	Name	Performance
Rushing (Yds.)	John Riggins, 1983	1,347
Passing (Yds.)	Jay Schroeder, 1986	4,109
Passing (TDs)	Sonny Jurgensen, 1967	31
Receiving (No.)	Art Monk, 1984	*106
Receiving (Yds.)	Bobby Mitchell, 1963	1,436
Interceptions	Dan Sandifer, 1948	13
Punting (Avg.)	Sammy Baugh, 1940	*51.4
Punt Return (Avg.)	Johnny Williams, 1952	15.3
Kickoff Return (Avg.)	Mike Nelms, 1981	29.7
Field Goals	Mark Moseley, 1983	33
Touchdowns (Tot.)	John Riggins, 1983	*24
Points	Mark Moseley, 1983	161

Individual Records—Single Game

Category	Name	Performance
Rushing (Yds.)	George Rogers, 12-21-85	206
Passing (Yds.)	Sammy Baugh, 10-31-43	446
Passing (TDs)	Sammy Baugh, 10-31-43	6
	Sammy Baugh, 11-23-47	6
Receiving (No.)	Art Monk, 12-15-85	13
	Kelvin Bryant, 12-7-86	13
Receiving (Yds.)	Anthony Allen, 10-4-87	255
Interceptions	Sammy Baugh, 11-14-43	*4
	Dan Sandifer, 10-31-48	*4
Field Goals	Many times	5
	Last time by Mark Moseley, 10-26-80	
Touchdowns (Tot.)	Dick James, 12-17-61	4
	Larry Brown, 12-4-73	4
Points	Dick James, 12-17-61	24
	Larry Brown, 12-4-73	24

*NFL Record

WASHINGTON REDSKINS

1987 Team Record

Preseason (3-1)

Date	Result		Opponents
8/14	W	23-17	Pittsburgh
8/22	W	33- 0	vs. Green Bay at Madison, Wis.
8/29	L	10-17	at Tampa Bay
9/5	W	26-14	at L.A. Rams
		92-48	

Regular Season (11-4)

Date	Result		Opponents	Att.
9/13	W	34-24	Philadelphia	52,188
9/20	L	20-21	at Atlanta	50,882
9/27	C		New England	
10/4	W	28-21	St. Louis	27,728
10/11	W	38-12	at N.Y. Giants	9,123
10/19	W	13- 7	at Dallas	60,415
10/25	W	17-16	N.Y. Jets	53,497
11/1	W	27- 7	at Buffalo	71,640
11/8	L	27-31	at Philadelphia	63,609
11/15	W	20-13	Detroit	53,593
11/23	L	26-30	L.A. Rams	53,614
11/29	W	23-19	N.Y. Giants	45,815
12/6	W	34-17	at St. Louis	31,324
12/13	W	24-20	Dallas	54,882
12/20	L	21-23	at Miami	65,715
12/26	W	27-24	at Minnesota (OT)	59,160

(OT) Overtime
C (Cancelled due to players' strike.)

Postseason (3-0)

Date	Result		Opponents	Att.
1/10	W	21-17	at Chicago	66,030
1/17	W	17-10	Minnesota	55,212
1/31	W	42-10	Denver	73,302

Score by Periods

Redskins	66	118	108	84	3	—	379
Opponents	54	68	94	69	0	—	285

Attendance

Home 341,317 Away 411,868 Total 753,185
Single-game home record, 55,750 (11-10-85)
Single-season home record, 434,854 (1986)

1987 Team Statistics

	Redskins	Opp.
Total First Downs	301	296
Rushing	119	104
Passing	153	177
Penalty	29	15
Third Down: Made/Att.	84/210	72/214
Fourth Down: Made/Att.	3/4	5/11
Total Net Yards	5597	5022
Avg. Per Game	373.1	334.8
Total Plays	1005	1021
Avg. Per Play	5.6	4.9
Net Yards Rushing	2102	1679
Avg. Per Game	140.1	111.9
Total Rushes	500	441
Net Yards Passing	3495	3343
Avg. Per Game	233.0	222.9
Sacked/Yards Lost	27/223	53/424
Gross Yards	3718	3767
Att./Completions	478/247	527/276
Completion Pct.	51.7	52.4
Had Intercepted	18	23
Punts/Avg.	78/39.1	91/39.2
Net Punting Avg.	34.1	31.4
Penalties/Yards Lost	82/691	97/801
Fumbles/Ball Lost	26/19	22/11
Touchdowns	47	33
Rushing	18	10
Passing	27	19
Returns	2	4
Avg. Time of Possession	30:30	29:30

1987 Individual Statistics

Scoring	TD R	TD P	TD Rt	PAT	FG	Saf	TP
Haji-Sheikh	0	0	0	29/32	13/19	0	68
Clark	0	7	0	0/0	0/0	0	42
Bryant	1	5	0	0/0	0/0	0	36
Monk	0	6	0	0/0	0/0	0	36
Rogers	6	0	0	0/0	0/0	0	36
Allen	0	3	0	0/0	0/0	0	18
Sanders	0	3	0	0/0	0/0	0	18
Schroeder	3	0	0	0/0	0/0	0	18
Ariri	0	0	0	6/6	3/5	0	15
Vital	2	0	0	0/0	0/0	0	12
T. Wilson	1	1	0	0/0	0/0	0	12
W. Wilson	2	0	0	0/0	0/0	0	12
Branch	1	0	0	0/0	0/0	0	6
Cox	0	0	0	3/3	1/2	0	6
Didier	0	1	0	0/0	0/0	0	6
Green	0	0	1	0/0	0/0	0	6
Griffin	0	1	0	0/0	0/0	0	6
Jessie	1	0	0	0/0	0/0	0	6
Wilburn	0	0	1	0/0	0/0	0	6
D. Williams	1	0	0	0/0	0/0	0	6
Atkinson	0	0	0	1/1	1/1	0	4
Toibin	0	0	0	4/4	0/2	0	4
Redskins	18	27	2	43/47	18/29	0	379
Opponents	10	19	4	30/33	19/28	0	285

Passing	Att.	Comp.	Yds.	Pct.	TD	Int.	Tkld.	Rate
Schroeder	267	129	1878	48.3	12	10	17/149	71.0
D. Williams	143	81	1156	56.6	11	5	7/53	94.0
Rubbert	49	26	532	53.1	4	1	1/9	110.2
Robinson	18	11	152	61.1	0	2	2/12	48.6
Bryant	1	0	0	0.0	0	0	0/0	39.6
Redskins	478	247	3718	51.7	27	18	27/223	80.7
Opponents	527	276	3767	52.4	19	23	53/424	69.3

Rushing	Att.	Yds.	Avg.	LG	TD
Rogers	163	613	3.8	29	6
Bryant	77	406	5.3	28	1
Vital	80	346	4.3	22t	2
Griffin	62	242	3.9	13	0
Smith	29	126	4.3	15	0
Schroeder	26	120	4.6	31	3
Monk	6	63	10.5	26	0
W. Wilson	18	55	3.1	11	2
Jessie	10	37	3.7	14t	1
Rubbert	9	31	3.4	14	0
T. Wilson	2	28	14.0	16t	1
Verdin	1	14	14.0	14	0
Branch	4	9	2.3	3	1
D. Williams	7	9	1.3	7	1
Holman	2	7	3.5	5	0
Clark	1	0	0.0	0	0
Robinson	2	0	0.0	2	0
Sanders	1	−4	−4.0	−4	0
Redskins	500	2102	4.2	31	18
Opponents	441	1679	3.8	45	10

Receiving	No.	Yds.	Avg.	LG	TD
Clark	56	1066	19.0	84t	7
Bryant	43	490	11.4	39	5
Monk	38	483	12.7	62	6
Sanders	37	630	17.0	57	3
Allen	13	337	25.9	88t	3
Didier	13	178	13.7	25	1
McEwen	12	164	13.7	42	0
Warren	7	43	6.1	9	0
T. Wilson	5	112	22.4	64t	1
Rogers	4	23	5.8	8	0
Orr	3	35	11.7	23	0
Griffin	3	13	4.3	6t	1
Verdin	2	62	31.0	55	0
Caravello	2	29	14.5	22	0
W. Wilson	2	16	8.0	9	0
Dennison	2	8	4.0	5	0
Vital	1	13	13.0	13	0
Jessie	1	8	8.0	8	0
Johnson	1	5	5.0	5	0
Yarber	1	5	5.0	5	0
Smith	1	−2	−2.0	−2	0
Redskins	247	3718	15.1	88t	27
Opponents	276	3767	13.6	59t	19

Interceptions	No.	Yds.	Avg.	LG	TD
Wilburn	9	135	15.0	100t	1
Bowles	4	24	6.0	24	0
Green	3	65	21.7	56	0
Walton	3	28	9.3	24	0
Coleman	2	53	26.5	28	0
Mitchell	1	17	17.0	17	0
Gage	1	7	7.0	7	0
Redskins	23	329	14.3	100t	1
Opponents	18	193	10.7	60t	1

Punting	No.	Yds.	Avg.	In 20	LG
Cox	63	2571	40.8	14	77
Weil	14	482	34.4	5	51
Redskins	78	3053	39.1	19	77
Opponents	91	3569	39.2	11	62

Punt Returns	No.	FC	Yds.	Avg.	LG	TD
Yarber	37	9	273	7.4	33	0
T. Wilson	8	0	143	17.9	40	0
Shepard	6	0	146	24.3	73	0
Green	5	1	53	10.6	15	0
Redskins	56	10	615	11.0	73	0
Opponents	37	11	231	6.2	45	0

Kickoff Returns	No.	Yds.	Avg.	LG	TD
Griffin	25	478	19.1	54	0
Verdin	12	244	20.3	38	0
Branch	4	61	15.3	19	0
Jessie	4	73	18.3	24	0
Orr	4	62	15.5	19	0
Sanders	4	118	29.5	39	0
Vital	2	31	15.5	18	0
W. Wilson	2	32	16.0	18	0
Shepard	1	20	20.0	20	0
T. Wilson	1	20	20.0	20	0
Redskins	59	1139	19.3	54	0
Opponents	63	1352	21.5	95t	1

Sacks	No.
Mann	9.5
Manley	8.5
Martin	5.0
Coleman	4.0
Butz	3.0
Walton	3.0
Benish	2.0
Cofer	2.0
Grant	2.0
Kaufman	2.0
Koch	2.0
Olkewicz	2.0
Curtis	1.0
Hamilton	1.0
Karras	1.0
Milot	1.0
Rose	1.0
Sagnella	1.0
Thompson	1.0
Waechter	1.0
Redskins	53.0
Opponents	27.0

Washington Redskins 1988 Veteran Roster

No.	Name	Pos.	Ht.	Wt.	Birth-date	NFL Exp.	College	Hometown	How Acq.	'87 Games/ Starts
89	Allen, Anthony	WR-RB	5-11	182	6/29/59	4	Washington	Seattle, Wash.	FA-'87	3/3
4	Atkinson, Jess	K	5-9	168	12/11/61	3	Maryland	Temple Hills, Md.	FA-'86	1/0
95	†Benish, Dan	DT	6-5	275	11/21/60	6	Clemson	Youngstown, Ohio	FA-'87	3/3
53	Bostic, Jeff	C	6-2	260	9/18/58	9	Clemson	Greensboro, N.C.	FA-'80	12/5
23	Bowles, Todd	S	6-2	203	11/18/63	3	Temple	Elizabeth, N.J.	FA-'86	12/12
29	†Branch, Reggie	RB	5-11	235	10/22/62	3	East Carolina	Sanford, Fla.	FA-'86	12/0
75	Brilz, Darrick	G	6-3	264	2/14/64	2	Oregon State	Richmond, Calif.	FA-'87	7/4
24	Bryant, Kelvin	RB	6-2	195	9/26/60	3	North Carolina	Tarboro, N.C.	FA-'86	11/1
65	Butz, Dave	DT	6-7	295	6/23/50	15	Purdue	Park Ridge, Ill.	FA-'75	12/12
50	Caldwell, Ravin	LB	6-3	229	8/4/63	2	Arkansas	Ft. Smith, Ark.	D5-'86	12/0
88	Caravello, Joe	TE	6-3	270	6/6/63	2	Tulane	El Segundo, Calif.	FA-'87	11/5
79	Carlson, Mark	T	6-6	284	6/6/63	2	So. Connecticut State	Milford, Conn.	FA-'87	3/3
84	Clark, Gary	WR	5-9	173	5/1/62	4	James Madison	Dublin, Va.	FA-'85	12/11
51	†Coleman, Monte	LB	6-2	230	11/4/57	10	Central Arkansas	Pine Bluff, Ark.	D11-'79	12/12
56	†Copeland, Anthony	LB	6-2	250	4/14/63	2	Louisville	East Point, Ga.	FA-'86	3/0
12	Cox, Steve	P-K	6-4	195	5/11/58	8	Arkansas	Charleston, Ark.	FA-'85	12/0
56	Coyle, Eric	C	6-3	260	10/26/63	2	Colorado	Longmont, Colo.	FA-'87	3/3
34	Davis, Brian	CB	6-2	190	8/31/63	2	Nebraska	Phoenix, Ariz.	D2a-'87	7/0
86	†Didier, Clint	TE	6-5	240	4/4/59	7	Portland State	Pasco, Wash.	D12-'81	9/6
48	Gage, Steve	S	6-3	210	5/10/64	2	Tulsa	Tulsa, Okla.	D6-'87	4/1
54	Gouveia, Kurt	LB	6-1	227	9/14/64	2	Brigham Young	Waianae, Hawaii	D8-'86	11/1
77	†Grant, Darryl	DT	6-1	275	11/22/59	8	Rice	San Antonio, Tex.	D9-'81	12/11
28	Green, Darrell	CB	5-8	170	2/15/60	6	Texas A&I	Houston, Tex.	D1-'83	12/12
35	†Griffin, Keith	RB	5-8	185	10/26/61	5	Miami	Eastmoor, Ohio	D10-'84	9/2
68	†Grimm, Russ	C-G	6-3	275	5/2/59	8	Pittsburgh	Southmoreland, Pa.	D3-'81	6/5
6	†Haji-Sheikh, Ali	K	6-0	172	1/11/61	5	Michigan	Ann Arbor, Mich.	FA-'87	11/0
78	Hamel, Dean	DT	6-3	290	7/7/61	4	Tulsa	Warren, Mich.	D12-'85	12/1
64	†Hamilton, Steve	DE-DT	6-4	270	9/28/61	4	East Carolina	Williamsville, N.Y.	D2-'84	12/0
	Hitchcock, Ray	C-G	6-2	289	6/20/65	2	Minnesota	Pine Bluff, Ark.	D12-'87	5/0
66	Jacoby, Joe	T	6-7	305	7/6/59	8	Louisville	Louisville, Ky.	FA-'81	12/12
21	Jessie, Tim	RB	5-11	190	3/1/63	2	Auburn	Opp, Ala.	FA-'87	3/0
82	Jones, Anthony	TE	6-3	248	5/16/60	4	Wichita State	Baltimore, Md.	D11-'84	2/0
55	Kaufman, Mel	LB	6-2	230	2/24/58	7	Cal Poly-SLO	Santa Monica, Calif.	FA-'81	12/12
61	Kehr, Rick	G	6-3	285	6/18/59	2	Carthage	Phoenixville, Pa.	FA-'87	5/0
74	Koch, Markus	DE	6-5	275	2/13/63	3	Boise State	Ontario, Canada	D2a-'86	12/2
72	Manley, Dexter	DE	6-3	257	2/2/59	8	Oklahoma State	Houston, Tex.	D5-'81	11/10
71	Mann, Charles	DE	6-6	270	4/12/61	6	Nevada-Reno	Sacramento, Calif.	D3-'83	12/12
58	#Marshall, Wilber	LB	6-1	225	4/18/62	5	Florida	Titusville, Fla.	FA-'88	12/12*
73	May, Mark	T	6-6	295	11/2/59	8	Pittsburgh	Oneonta, N.Y.	D1-'81	10/10
98	McEwen, Craig	TE	6-1	220	12/16/65	2	Utah	Queens, N.Y.	FA-'87	4/3
63	McKenzie, Raleigh	G	6-2	275	2/8/63	4	Tennessee	Knoxville, Tenn.	D11-'85	12/12
60	McQuaid, Dan	T	6-7	278	10/4/60	3	Nevada-Las Vegas	Clarksburg, Calif.	T(Rams)-'85	1/0
81	Monk, Art	WR	6-3	209	12/5/57	9	Syracuse	White Plains, N.Y.	D1-'80	9/9
52	†Olkewicz, Neal	LB	6-0	233	1/30/57	10	Maryland	Phoenixville, Pa.	FA-'79	10/6
87	†Orr, Terry	TE	6-3	227	9/27/61	3	Texas	Abilene, Tex.	D10-'85	10/1
11	†Rypien, Mark	QB	6-4	234	10/2/62	2	Washington State	Spokane, Wash.	D6-'86	0*
83	Sanders, Ricky	WR	5-11	180	8/30/62	3	Southwest Texas State	Temple, Tex.	T(NE)-'86	12/5
10	Schroeder, Jay	QB	6-4	215	6/28/61	5	UCLA	Pacific Palisades, Calif.	D3-'84	11/10
76	Simmons, Ed	T	6-5	280	12/31/63	2	Eastern Washington	Stockton, Calif.	D6b-'87	5/3
36	Smith, Timmy	RB	5-11	216	1/21/64	2	Texas Tech	Hobbs, N.M.	D5-'87	7/0
69	†Thielemann, R.C.	G	6-4	272	8/12/55	12	Arkansas	Houston, Tex.	T(Atl)-'85	12/12
31	Vaughn, Clarence	S	6-0	202	7/17/64	2	Northern Illinois	Chicago, Ill.	D8-'87	5/0
40	Walton, Alvin	S	6-0	180	3/14/64	3	Kansas	Banning, Calif.	D3-'86	12/12
85	Warren, Don	TE	6-4	242	5/5/56	10	San Diego State	Covina, Calif.	D4-'79	12/12
45	†Wilburn, Barry	CB	6-3	186	12/9/63	4	Mississippi	Memphis, Tenn.	D8-'85	12/12
17	Williams, Doug	QB	6-4	220	8/9/55	8	Grambling	Zachary, La.	T(TB)-'86	5/2
46	Woodberry, Dennis	CB	5-10	183	4/22/61	3	Southern Arkansas	Texarkana, Ark.	FA-'87	12/3
80	Yarber, Eric	WR-KR	5-8	156	9/22/63	2	Idaho	Los Angeles, Calif.	D12-'86	12/0

* Marshall played 12 games with Chicago in '87; Rypien active for 5 games but did not play.

†Option playout; subject to developments.

#Marshall signed as free agent; Chicago waived right of first refusal.

Traded—Wide receiver Clarence Verdin to Indianapolis.

Retired—David Jones, 3-year center, 5 games in '87.

Also played with Redskins in '87—K Obed Ariri (2 games), TE Cliff Benson (2), WR Keiron Bigby (1), LB Derek Bunch (3), S Danny Burmeister (3), S Joe Cofer (3), C John Cowne (3), LB Bobby Curtis (3), CB Vernon Dean (12), TE Glenn Dennison (2), TE K.D. Dunn (3), CB David Etherly (3), G Frank Frazier (3), DT Alec Gibson (3), RB Allen Harvin (1), RB Walter Holman (3), S Charles Jackson (1), WR Richard Johnson (1), DT Ted Karras (1), CB Garry Kimble (3), LB Jcn Kimmel (1), S Skip Lane (3), DT Kit Lathrop (1), QB Babe Laufenberg (active for 1 game but did not play), DE Steve Martin (3), DT Curtis McGriff (1), LB Rich Milot (9), CB Michael Mitchell (3), CB Tim Morrison (7), G Phil Pettey (3), WR Joe Phillips (2), QB Tony Robinson (1), RB George Rogers (11), LB Carlton Rose (2), QB Ed Rubbert (3), DT Anthony Sagnella (3), G Willard Scissum (3), LB Tony Settles (3), WR Derrick Shepard (3), QB Jack Stanley (active for 3 games but did not play), DT Steve Thompson (1), K Brendan Toibin (1), TE Dave Truitt (1), RB Lionel Vital (3), DT Henry Waechter (1), P Jack Weil (3), TE Marvin Williams (2), LB Eric Wilson (3), WR Ted Wilson (3), RB Wayne Wilson (2), LB David Windham (3), C Mike Wooten (3).

COACHING STAFF

Head Coach, Joe Gibbs

Pro Career: Enters eighth year as Redskins coach. Led Washington to 14-4 record and Super Bowl XXII victory. Team set 19 Super Bowl records in 42-10 win over Denver, and has now appeared in postseason play in five of last six seasons. The Redskins are the only NFL club to appear in three Super Bowls in the 1980's. Named head coach on January 13, 1981, after spending eight years as an NFL assistant coach and nine seasons on the college level. Came to Redskins from the San Diego Chargers where he was offensive coordinator in 1979 and 1980. Prior to that, he was offensive coordinator for the Tampa Bay Buccaneers in 1978 and offensive backfield coach for the St. Louis Cardinals from 1973-77. While he was with San Diego, the Chargers won the AFC West title and led the NFL in passing two straight years. No pro playing experience. Career record: 85-33.

Background: Played tight end, linebacker, and guard under Don Coryell at San Diego State in 1961 and 1962 after spending two years at Cerritos, Calif., J.C. 1959-60. Started his college coaching career at San Diego State 1964-66, followed by stints at Florida State 1967-68, Southern California 1969-70, and Arkansas 1971-72.

Personal: Born November 25, 1940, in Mocksville, N.C. Graduated from Santa Fe Springs, Calif., High School. Two-time national racquetball champion and ranked second in the over-35 category in 1978. He and his wife, Pat, live in Vienna, Va., and have two sons—J.D. and Coy.

Assistant Coaches

Chuck Banker, special teams; born March 12, 1941, Prescott, Ariz. Linebacker-tight end Pasadena C.C. 1959-60. No pro playing experience. College coach: Glendale, Calif., J.C. 1962-65, Utah 1966-67, 1974-75, Westminster 1968-70, Boise State 1976-79, Iowa State 1986. Pro coach: St. Louis Cardinals 1980-85, joined Redskins in 1987.

Don Breaux, offensive backs; born August 3, 1940, Jennings, La., lives in Centerville, Va. Quarterback McNeese State 1959-61. Pro quarterback Denver Broncos 1963, San Diego Chargers 1964-65. College coach: Florida State 1966-67, Arkansas 1968-71, 1977-80, Florida 1973-74, Texas 1975-76. Pro coach: Joined Redskins in 1981.

Joe Bugel, assistant head coach-offense; born March 10, 1940, Pittsburgh, Pa., lives in Oakton, Va. Guard Western Kentucky 1960-62. No pro playing experience. College coach: Western Kentucky 1964-68, Navy 1969-72, Iowa State 1973, Ohio State 1974. Pro coach: Detroit Lions 1975-76, Houston Oilers 1977-80, joined Redskins in 1981.

Dan Henning, offensive assistant-receivers, born June 21, 1942, Bronx, N.Y., lives in Reston, Va. Quarterback William & Mary 1960-63. Pro quarterback San Diego Chargers 1964-67. College coach: Florida State 1968-70, 1974, Virginia Tech 1971, 1973. Pro coach: Houston Oilers 1972, New York Jets 1976-78, Miami Dolphins 1979-80, Washington Redskins 1981-82, Atlanta Falcons 1983-86 (head coach), rejoined Redskins in 1987.

Bill Hickman, administrative assistant; born June 21, 1923, Baltimore, Md., lives in Leesburg, Va. Halfback Virginia 1946-48. No pro playing experience. College coach: Virginia 1949, Duke 1950, North Carolina State 1951, Vanderbilt 1953, North Carolina 1966-72. Pro coach: Washington Redskins 1973-77, Los Angeles Rams 1978-80, rejoined Redskins in 1981.

Larry Peccatiello, defensive coordinator; born December 21, 1935, Newark, N.J., lives in Warrenton, Va. Receiver William & Mary 1955-58. No pro playing experience. College coach: William & Mary 1961-68, Navy 1969-70, Rice 1971. Pro coach: Houston Oilers 1972-75, Seattle Seahawks 1976-80, joined Redskins in 1981.

Washington Redskins 1988 First-Year Roster

Name	Pos.	Ht.	Wt.	Birth-date	College	Hometown	How Acq.
Adams, Marvin	DE	6-5	270	12/30/64	Washington State	Modesto, Calif.	FA
Alexander, Dave	G	6-2	264	7/19/64	Iowa	Sterling, Ill.	FA
Annexstad, Scott	G	6-4	272	7/8/64	Mankato State	St. Peter, Minn.	FA
Austin, Teryl	S	6-0	195	3/3/65	Pittsburgh	Sharon, Pa.	FA
Banderas, Tom	TE	6-2	247	6/6/65	Nebraska	Oak Grove, Mo.	FA
Berkemeier, Roy	T	6-3	285	3/21/65	Austin Peay	Pisgah, Ala.	FA
Blondell, Jim	DT	6-2	270	2/17/65	Illinois	Glenview, Ill.	FA
Brown, Henry	T	6-4	262	1/27/65	Ohio State	Queens, N.Y.	D10
Corse, Cedric	LB	6-2	227	12/24/64	Mississippi State	Atlanta, Ga.	FA
Davis, Donald	CB	5-9	177	1/23/65	Idaho State	Duarte, Calif.	FA
Demerest, Chris	S	6-2	200	2/9/65	Northeastern	Keyport, N.J.	FA
Donaldson, Duke	WR	5-10	170	5/16/66	Auburn	Cairo, Ga.	FA
Duckens, Mark	DT	6-4	260	3/4/65	Arizona State	Wichita, Kan.	FA
Grant, African	CB	6-0	198	8/2/65	Illinois	Englewood, N.J.	FA
Green, Rod	WR	5-8	168	3/23/65	Oregon	Palo Alto, Calif.	FA
Harbour, Dave	G-C	6-4	265	10/23/65	Illinois	Naperville, Ill.	FA
Hawkins, Gilbert	WR	5-10	180	10/24/64	Oregon State	San Diego, Calif.	FA
Hicks, Harold	CB-S	6-0	200	12/7/65	San Diego State	Hollywood, Calif.	D7
Holmes, Carl	T	6-6	280	5/29/65	Temple	Philadelphia, Pa.	FA
Humphries, Stan	QB	6-2	223	4/14/65	N.E. Louisiana	Shreveport, La.	D6
Jackson, Cecil	LB	6-3	212	11/13/63	Eastern New Mexico	Lynchburg, Va.	FA
Karamanos, Ted	G	6-2	282	6/12/65	Northern Illinois	Oaklawn, Ill.	FA
Kleine, Wally (1)	DT	6-9	320	10/22/64	Notre Dame	Midland, Tex.	D2b-'87
Knighton, Rodney	RB	5-11	205	5/17/65	Louisville	Miami, Fla.	FA
Koch, Curt	DE	6-8	270	8/3/65	Colorado	Littleton, Colo.	D11
Krumm, Todd	S	6-0	189	12/18/65	Michigan State	West Bloomfield, Mich.	FA
Lohmiller, Chip	K	6-3	213	7/16/66	Minnesota	Springfield, Mo.	D2
Maiden, Petey	TE	6-2	220	9/7/65	Utah State	Seaside, Calif.	FA
Manusky, Greg	LB	6-1	242	8/12/66	Colgate	Wyoming, Pa.	FA
McDonald, Tim	DE	6-3	260	2/16/65	Kansas State	Leawood, Kan.	FA
McGill, Darryl	RB	5-10	210	3/28/66	Wake Forest	Durham, N.C.	D8
Mims, Carl	CB	5-10	180	10/28/65	Sam Houston State	Gainesville, Tex.	D5
Morris, Jamie	RB	5-7	188	6/6/65	Michigan	Ayer, Mass.	D4
Newton, Grady	LB	6-1	225	12/20/64	Kansas State	Edwardsville, Kan.	FA
Oliphant, Mike	RB-KR	5-10	183	5/19/63	Puget Sound	Auburn, Wash.	D3
Peterson, Blake	LB	6-4	245	5/14/66	Mesa College, Colo.	Broomfield, Colo.	D9
Reese, Albert (1)	TE	6-4	245	2/15/65	Southern Methodist	Temple, Tex.	FA-'87
Robinson, Kenneth (1)	LB	6-1	234	12/4/63	South Carolina	Charleston, S.C.	FA-'87
Robison, Doug	P	6-4	217	5/29/66	Stanford	Oklahoma City, Okla.	FA
Rose, Carlton (1)	LB	6-2	220	2/8/62	Michigan	Ft. Lauderdale, Fla.	FA
Ross, Wayne	P	6-3	210	2/8/65	San Diego State	San Diego, Calif.	D12
Scully, Mike	C	6-5	280	11/1/65	Illinois	Mt. Prospect, Ill.	FA
Smith, Warren	CB	5-11	175	6/12/65	Wake Forest	Sevren, Md.	FA
Stewart, Chris	CB-S	5-10	183	2/20/66	Bethune-Cookman	Cumberland, Md.	FA
Thompson, Steve (1)	DT	6-2	285	6/24/65	Minnesota	Aurora, Ill.	FA
White, Robb	DE	6-4	270	5/26/65	South Dakota	Aberdeen, S.D.	FA

The term NFL Rookie is defined as a player who is in his first season of professional football and has not been on the roster of another professional football team for any regular-season or postseason games. A Rookie is designated by an "R" on NFL rosters. Players who have been active in another professional football league or players who have NFL experience, including either preseason training camp or being on an active roster for fewer than three regular-season or postseason games, are termed NFL First-Year Players. An NFL First-Year Player is designated by a "1" on NFL rosters. Thereafter, a player on an NFL active roster for at least three regular-season or postseason games is credited with an additional year of NFL playing experience.

NOTES

Richie Petitbon, assistant head coach-defense; born April 18, 1938, New Orleans, La., lives in Vienna, Va. Back Tulane 1955-58. Pro defensive back Chicago Bears 1959-67, Los Angeles Rams 1969-70, Washington Redskins 1971-73. Pro coach: Houston Oilers 1974-77, joined Redskins in 1978.

Dan Riley, conditioning; born October 19, 1949, Syracuse, N.Y., lives in Herndon, Va. No college or pro playing experience. College coach: Army 1973-76, Penn State 1977-81. Pro coach: Joined Redskins in 1982.

Warren Simmons, tight ends; born February 25, 1942, Poughkeepsie, N.Y., lives in Centerville, Va. Center San Diego State 1963-65. No pro playing experience. College coach: Cal State-Fullerton 1972-75, Cerritos, Calif., J.C. 1976-80. Pro coach: Joined Redskins in 1981.

Charley Taylor, wide receivers; born September 28, 1942, Grand Prairie, Tex., lives in Sterling, Va. Running back Arizona State 1961-63. Pro running back-wide receiver Washington Redskins 1964-76. Pro coach: Joined Redskins in 1982.

Emmitt Thomas, defensive assistant; born June 4, 1943, Angleton, Tex., lives in Reston, Va. Quarterback-wide receiver Bishop (Tex.) College 1963-65. Pro defensive back Kansas City Chiefs 1966-78. College coach: Central Missouri State 1979-80. Pro coach: St. Louis Cardinals 1981-85, joined Redskins in 1986.

LaVern Torgeson, defensive line; born February 28, 1929, LaCrosse, Wash., lives in Fairfax, Va. Center-linebacker Washington State 1948-50. Pro linebacker Detroit Lions 1951-54, Washington Redskins 1955-58. Pro coach: Washington Redskins 1959-61, 1971-77, Pittsburgh Steelers 1962-68, Los Angeles Rams 1969-70, 1978-80, rejoined Redskins in 1981.

1987 SEASON IN REVIEW

Trades 142
Preseason Standings and Results 143
Regular Season Standings and Results 144
Week by Week Game Summaries 146
Pro Football Awards 165
All-Pro Teams 166
Rushing, Passing, and Receiving Leaders 168
Team and Individual Statistics 172
Paid Attendance Breakdown 209

Trades

1987 Interconference Trades

Defensive back **Ron Fellows** from Dallas to the Los Angeles Raiders for wide receiver **Rod Barksdale** (8/5).

Linebacker **Jack Del Rio** from New Orleans to Kansas City for a draft choice (8/18).

Tight end **Glenn Dennison** from New England to Washington for a draft choice (8/20).

Wide receiver **Bobby Johnson** from the New York Giants to San Diego for a draft choice (8/21).

Defensive back **Demetrious Johnson** from Detroit to Indianapolis for a draft choice (8/25).

Tackle **Ron Essink** from Seattle to Dallas for a draft choice (8/26).

Guard **Stephan Humphries** from Chicago to Denver for punter **Bryan Wagner** (8/26).

Punter **Barry Bowman** from the Los Angeles Rams to Seattle for cash (8/26).

Defensive back **Dave Brown** from Seattle to Green Bay for a draft choice (8/26).

Tackle **Greg Feasel** from Green Bay to Houston for a draft choice (9/1).

Defensive end **Willard Goff** from the Los Angeles Raiders to San Francisco for a draft choice (9/1).

Linebacker **David Brandon** and a draft choice from Buffalo to San Diego for wide receiver **Trumaine Johnson** and a draft choice (9/1).

Tight end **Derrick Ramsey** from Indianapolis to Detroit for a draft choice (9/1).

Defensive back **Rick Woods** from Pittsburgh to Tampa Bay for a draft choice (9/1).

Kicker **Rolf Benirschke** from San Diego to Dallas for a draft choice (9/2).

Defensive tackle **Jerome Sally** from the New York Giants to Indianapolis for a draft choice (9/3).

Running back **Jeff Smith** from Kansas City to Tampa Bay for a draft choice (9/3).

Defensive end **Al Baker** from St. Louis to Cleveland for a draft choice (9/4).

Defensive back **Harvey Clayton** from Pittsburgh to Detroit for a draft choice (9/7).

Guard-tackle **Jeff Walker** from San Diego to the Los Angeles Rams for a draft choice (9/9).

Kicker **John Diettrich** from Green Bay to Houston for cash (10/2).

Guard **Mitch Geier** from Tampa Bay to the New York Jets for cash (10/6).

Linebacker **Keith Browner** from San Francisco to the Los Angeles Raiders for cash (10/7).

Running back **Andre Hardy** from San Francisco to Seattle for a draft choice (10/7).

Quarterback **Doug Flutie** from Chicago to New England for a draft choice (10/13).

Linebacker **James Johnson** from San Francisco to San Diego for a past consideration (10/13).

Defensive tackle **Van Hughes** from Seattle to Atlanta for cash (10/14).

Running back **Kirk Jones** and defensive end **Robert Brannon** from Cleveland to New Orleans for two draft choices (10/15).

Center **Joe Bock** from St. Louis to Buffalo for cash (10/16).

Tackle **Greg Koch** from Miami to Minnesota for two draft choices (10/20).

Quarterback **John Witkowski** from Houston to Green Bay for a past consideration (10/20).

Running back **Eric Dickerson** from the Los Angeles Rams to the Indianapolis Colts. The rights to linebacker **Cornelius Bennett** (Alabama) from Indianapolis to Buffalo. Colts running back **Owen Gill** and Indianapolis's first- and second-round choices in 1988 and first-round choice in 1989, plus Bills running back **Greg Bell** and Buffalo's first-round choice in 1988 and first- and second-round choices in 1989 to the Rams (10/31).

1988 Interconference Trades

Philadelphia traded the rights to defensive end **Chris Pike** (Tulsa) to Cleveland for defensive back **D.D. Hoggard** and the Browns' sixth-round choice in 1988. Philadelphia selected defensive back **Rob Sterling** (Maine) (3/24).

Wide receiver **Clarence Verdin** from Washington to Indianapolis for the Colts' sixth-round choice in 1988.Washington selected quarterback **Stan Humphries** (Northeast Louisiana) (3/29).

Quarterback **Steve DeBerg** from Tampa Bay to Kansas City for defensive back **Mark Robinson,** the Chiefs' fourth-round choice in 1988, and Tampa Bay's eighth-round choice in 1988. Tampa Bay selected guard **John Bruhin** (Tennessee) and running back **Anthony Simpson** (East Carolina) (4/7).

Detroit's first-round choice in 1988 to Kansas City for the Chiefs' first- and second-round choices in 1988. Kansas City selected defensive end **Neil Smith** (Nebraska). Detroit selected defensive back **Bennie Blades** (Miami) and linebacker **Chris Spielman** (Ohio State) (4/22).

Phoenix traded the rights to quarterback **Kelly Stouffer** (Colorado State) to Seattle for Dallas's fifth-round choice in 1988 and Seattle's first- and fifth-round choices in 1989. Phoenix selected linebacker **Chris Gaines** (Vanderbilt) (4/23).

San Francisco traded its first-round choice in 1988 to the Los Angeles Raiders for wide receiver **Dokie Williams,** the Raiders' second-round choice in 1988, and Houston's fourth-round choice in 1988. The Raiders selected defensive end **Scott Davis** (Illinois). San Francisco selected defensive end **Dan Stubbs** (Miami) and punter **Barry Helton** (Colorado) (4/24).

Minnesota traded its second-round choice in 1988 to Denver for the Broncos' second-, fourth-, and sixth-round choices in 1988. Denver selected tackle **Gerald Perry** (Southern). Minnesota selected defensive back **Brad Edwards** (South Carolina), guard **Todd Kalis** (Arizona State), and defensive back **Derrick White** (Oklahoma) (4/24).

New Orleans traded its third-round choice in 1988 to Denver for the Broncos' third- and tenth-round choices in 1988. Denver selected defensive back **Kevin Guidry** (Louisiana State). New Orleans selected nose tackle **Tony Stephens** (Clemson) and linebacker **Vincent Fizer** (Southern) (4/24).

San Diego traded tight end **Pete Holohan** to the Los Angeles Rams for the Rams' fourth-round choice in 1988. San Diego selected defensive end **Joe Campbell** (New Mexico State) (4/24).

New England traded its fifth-round choice in 1988 to Washington for the Redskins' fourth-round choice in 1989. Washington selected defensive back **Carl Mims** (Sam Houston State) (4/24).

New England traded Minnesota's eleventh-round choice in 1988, which it previously obtained, to Minnesota for Minnesota's ninth-round choice in 1989. Minnesota selected defensive back **Norman Floyd** (South Carolina) (4/25).

1987 AFC Trades

Center **Jim Romano** from Houston to New England for a draft choice (8/13).

Guard **Larry Lee** from Miami to Denver for a draft choice (8/20).

Defensive back **Martin Bayless** from Buffalo to San Diego for defensive back **Wayne Davis** (8/26).

Linebacker **Ken Woodard** from Denver to Pittsburgh for a draft choice (8/28).

Tackle **Brian Holloway** from New England to the Los Angeles Raiders for a draft choice (9/2).

Defensive tackle **Don Smith** from Buffalo to the New York Jets for a draft choice (9/7).

Defensive end **Mark Smythe** from Indianapolis to Pittsburgh for cash (10/1).

1988 AFC Trades

Defensive end **Barry Bennett** from the New York Jets to the Los Angeles Raiders for a 1989 draft choice (3/9).

Tackle **Emil Slovacek** from San Diego to Denver for a past consideration (3/25).

Quarterback **Todd Blackledge** from Kansas City to Pittsburgh for Steelers' fourth-round choice in 1988. Kansas City selected wide receiver **J.R. Ambrose** (Mississippi) (3/30).

Defensive end **Sean Jones,** Houston's second-round choice in 1988, and the Raiders' third-round choice in 1988 from the Los Angeles Raiders to Houston for the Los Angeles Rams' first-round choice in 1988 and the Oilers' third- and fourth-round choices in 1988. The Raiders selected defensive back **Terry McDaniel** (Tennessee) and traded Houston's third-round choice to the New York Jets and Houston's fourth-round choice to San Francisco (4/22).

Houston traded the Los Angeles Raiders' third-round choice in 1988 to San Diego for the Chargers' third- and fifth-round choices in 1988. San Diego selected wide receiver **Quinn Early** (Iowa). Houston selected punter Greg Montgomery (Michigan State) and defensive back **Cris Dishman** (Purdue) (4/24).

The Los Angeles Raiders traded Houston's third-round choice in 1988 to the New York Jets for the Jets' fourth-round choice in 1988 and Seattle's fifth-round choice in 1988. The Jets selected defensive back **James Hasty** (Washington State). The Raiders selected defensive tackle **Tim Rother** (Nebraska) and defensive back **Dennis Price** (UCLA) (4/24).

San Diego traded quarterback **Mark Herrmann** to Indianapolis for a 1989 draft choice (4/27).

1987 NFC Trades

Tackle **Leonard Mitchell** from Philadelphia to Atlanta for a draft choice (8/10).

Running back **Keith Williams** from Atlanta to Tampa Bay for a draft choice (8/13).

Defensive back **Dennis Woodberry** from Atlanta to Green Bay for cash (8/25).

Running back **Cliff Austin** from Atlanta to Tampa Bay for a draft choice (9/7).

Defensive end **Greg Brown** from Philadelphia to Atlanta for defensive end **Mike Pitts** (9/8).

Defensive back **Eric Jeffries** from Washington to Chicago for cash (10/6).

Defensive back **Jonathan Sutton** from New Orleans to Tampa Bay for a past consideration (10/15).

1988 NFC Trades

Washington's first-round choices in 1988 and 1989 to Chicago as compensation for linebacker **Wilber Marshall.** Chicago selected wide receiver **Wendell Davis** (Louisiana State) (3/21).

Tampa Bay traded its second-round choice in 1988 to Philadelphia for the Eagles' second-round choice in 1988 and Atlanta's fourth-round choice in 1988. Philadelphia selected defensive back **Eric Allen** (Arizona State). Tampa Bay traded Philadelphia's second-round choice to San Francisco and also selected defensive end **Robert Goff** (Auburn) (4/24).

The Los Angeles Rams traded their third-round choice in 1988 to Washington for the Redskins' third-, fifth-, and sixth-round choices in 1988. Washington selected kick returner **Mike Oliphant** (Puget Sound). The Rams selected defensive tackle **Mike Piel** (Illinois), defensive back **James Washington** (UCLA), and defensive tackle **Jeff Knapton** (Wyoming) (4/24).

Tampa Bay traded Philadelphia's second-round choice in 1988 to San Francisco for the 49ers' second- and fourth-round choices in 1988. San Francisco selected defensive tackle **Pierce Holt** (Angelo State). Tampa Bay selected running back **Lars Tate** (Georgia) and punter **Monte Robbins** (Michigan) (4/24).

The Los Angeles Rams traded their twelfth-round choice in 1988 to Washington for the Redskins' twelfth-round choice in 1988 and eleventh-round choice in 1989. Washington selected punter **Wayne Ross** (San Diego State). The Rams selected wide receiver **Jeff Beathard** (Southern Oregon) (4/25).

1987 PRESEASON STANDINGS

American Football Conference

Eastern Division

	W	L	T	Pct.	Pts.	OP
Indianapolis	3	1	0	.750	81	68
Miami	2	2	0	.500	100	64
New England	2	2	0	.500	82	78
N.Y. Jets	2	2	0	.500	76	92
Buffalo	1	3	0	.250	55	90

Central Division

	W	L	T	Pct.	Pts.	OP
Cleveland	3	1	0	.750	94	67
Cincinnati	2	2	0	.500	82	99
Houston	2	2	0	.500	60	75
Pittsburgh	0	4	0	.000	79	130

Western Division

	W	L	T	Pct.	Pts.	OP
Kansas City*	4	1	0	.800	99	74
Denver**	3	2	0	.600	119	117
San Diego	2	2	0	.500	83	46
Seattle	2	2	0	.500	107	71
L.A. Raiders	1	3	0	.250	70	79

National Football Conference

Eastern Division

	W	L	T	Pct.	Pts.	OP
N.Y. Giants	3	1	0	.750	92	77
Washington	3	1	0	.750	92	48
St. Louis	2	2	0	.500	74	81
Dallas	1	3	0	.250	36	84
Philadelphia	1	3	0	.250	35	97

Central Division

	W	L	T	Pct.	Pts.	OP
Chicago	3	1	0	.750	96	54
Detroit	2	2	0	.500	88	72
Minnesota	2	2	0	.500	108	97
Tampa Bay	2	2	0	.500	82	91
Green Bay	0	4	0	.000	58	111

Western Division

	W	L	T	Pct.	Pts.	OP
New Orleans	3	1	0	.750	93	75
L.A. Rams**	3	2	0	.600	108	112
San Fran.*	3	2	0	.600	92	73
Atlanta	1	3	0	.250	45	64

**Includes Hall of Fame Game*
***Includes American Bowl '87 in London, England*

AFC Preseason Results—Team By Team

Eastern Division

BUFFALO (1-3)		
14	Atlanta	19
7	L.A. Raiders	3
14	Kansas City	34
20	Miami	34
55		90

INDIANAPOLIS (3-1)		
22	Detroit	19
19	Minnesota	37
17	*Houston	6
23	*Tampa Bay	6
81		68

MIAMI (2-2)		
3	*Chicago	10
28	Denver	31
35	Philadelphia	3
34	*Buffalo	20
100		64

NEW ENGLAND (2-2)		
17	*N.Y. Giants	19
13	*Philadelphia (OT)	19
38	Minnesota	27
14	Atlanta	13
82		78

N.Y. JETS (2-2)		
13	*Philadelphia	10
27	Tampa Bay	29
30	N.Y. Giants	23
6	San Diego	30
76		92

Central Division

CINCINNATI (2-2)		
31	Tampa Bay	30
9	Detroit	23
28	Green Bay	20
14	*New Orleans	26
82		99

CLEVELAND (3-1)		
31	*St. Louis	16
10	N.Y. Giants	24
23	Atlanta	3
30	Green Bay (OT)	24
94		67

HOUSTON (2-2)		
20	*Kansas City	32
16	New Orleans	13
6	Indianapolis	17
18	Dallas	13
60		75

PITTSBURGH (0-4)		
17	Washington	23
14	Chicago	50
28	New Orleans	31
20	*N.Y. Giants	26
79		130

Western Division

DENVER (3-2)		
27	L.A. Rams (AB)	28
20	Green Bay	14
31	*Miami	28
24	L.A. Rams	20
17	*Minnesota	27
119		117

KANSAS CITY (4-1)		
7	San Fran. (HOF)	20
32	Houston	20
13	*Atlanta	10
34	*Buffalo	14
13	St. Louis (OT)	10
99		74

L.A. RAIDERS (1-3)		
16	*San Francisco	42
3	*Buffalo	7
34	Dallas	10
17	*Chicago	20
70		79

SAN DIEGO (2-2)		
29	*Dallas	0
21	*L.A. Rams	23
3	San Francisco	17
30	*N.Y. Jets	6
83		46

SEATTLE (2-2)		
14	L.A. Rams	23
21	St. Louis	28
38	*Detroit	10
34	*San Francisco	10
107		71

NFC Preseason Results —Team By Team

Eastern Division

DALLAS (1-3)		
0	San Diego	29
13	San Francisco	3
10	*L.A. Raiders	34
13	*Houston	18
36		84

N.Y. GIANTS (3-1)		
19	New England	17
24	*Cleveland	10
23	*N.Y. Jets	30
26	Pittsburgh	20
92		77

PHILADELPHIA (1-3)		
10	N.Y. Jets	13
19	New Eng. (OT)	13
3	*Miami	35
3	*Detroit	36
35		97

ST. LOUIS (2-2)		
16	Cleveland	31
28	*Seattle	21
20	Chicago	16
10	Kansas City (OT)	13
74		81

WASHINGTON (3-1)		
23	*Pittsburgh	17
33	Green Bay	0
10	Tampa Bay	17
26	L.A. Rams	14
92		48

Central Division

CHICAGO (3-1)		
10	Miami	3
50	*Pittsburgh	14
16	*St. Louis	20
20	L.A. Raiders	17
96		54

DETROIT (2-2)		
19	*Indianapolis	22
23	*Cincinnati	9
10	Seattle	38
36	Philadelphia	3
88		72

GREEN BAY (0-4)		
14	Denver	20
0	*Washington	33
20	*Cincinnati	28
24	*Cleveland (OT)	30
58		111

MINNESOTA (2-2)		
17	New Orleans	23
37	*Indianapolis	19
27	*New England	38
27	Denver	17
108		97

TAMPA BAY (2-2)		
30	*Cincinnati	31
29	*N.Y. Jets	27
17	*Washington	10
6	Indianapolis	23
82		91

Western Division

ATLANTA (1-3)		
19	*Buffalo	14
10	Kansas City	13
3	*Cleveland	23
13	New England	14
45		64

L.A. RAMS (3-2)		
28	Denver (AB)	27
23	*Seattle	14
23	San Diego	21
20	*Denver	24
14	*Washington	26
108		112

NEW ORLEANS (3-1)		
23	*Minnesota	17
13	*Houston	16
31	*Pittsburgh	28
26	Cincinnati	14
93		75

SAN FRANCISCO (3-2)		
20	Kansas City (HOF)	7
42	L.A. Raiders	16
3	*Dallas	13
17	*San Diego	3
10	Seattle	34
92		73

**denotes home game*
(OT) denotes overtime
(HOF) denotes Hall of Fame Game
(AB) denotes American Bowl '87 Game

1987 NFL STANDINGS

American Football Conference

Eastern Division

	W	L	T	Pct.	Pts.	OP
Indianapolis	9	6	0	.600	300	238
New England	8	7	0	.533	320	293
Miami	8	7	0	.533	362	335
Buffalo	7	8	0	.467	270	305
N.Y. Jets	6	9	0	.400	334	360

Central Division

	W	L	T	Pct.	Pts.	OP
Cleveland	10	5	0	.667	390	239
Houston*	9	6	0	.600	345	349
Pittsburgh	8	7	0	.533	285	299
Cincinnati	4	11	0	.267	285	370

Western Division

	W	L	T	Pct.	Pts.	OP
Denver	10	4	1	.700	379	288
Seattle*	9	6	0	.600	371	314
San Diego	8	7	0	.533	253	317
L.A. Raiders	5	10	0	.333	301	289
Kansas City	4	11	0	.267	273	388

National Football Conference

Eastern Division

	W	L	T	Pct.	Pts.	OP
Washington	11	4	0	.733	379	285
Dallas	7	8	0	.467	340	348
St. Louis	7	8	0	.467	362	368
Philadelphia	7	8	0	.467	337	380
N.Y. Giants	6	9	0	.400	280	312

Central Division

	W	L	T	Pct.	Pts.	OP
Chicago	11	4	0	.733	356	282
Minnesota*	8	7	0	.533	336	335
Green Bay	5	9	1	.367	255	300
Tampa Bay	4	11	0	.267	286	360
Detroit	4	11	0	.267	269	384

Western Division

	W	L	T	Pct.	Pts.	OP
San Francisco	13	2	0	.867	459	253
New Orleans*	12	3	0	.800	422	283
L.A. Rams	6	9	0	.400	317	361
Atlanta	3	12	0	.200	205	436

**Wild Card qualifier for playoffs*

Houston gained first AFC Wild Card position on better conference record (7-4) over Seattle (5-6).

First-Round Playoffs

AFC .... Houston 23, Seattle 20 (OT), January 3, at Houston

NFC .... Minnesota 44, New Orleans 10, January 3, at New Orleans

Divisional Playoffs

AFC .... Cleveland 38, Indianapolis 21, January 9, at Cleveland
Denver 34, Houston 10, January 10, at Denver

NFC .... Minnesota 36, San Francisco 24, January 9, at San Francisco
Washington 21, Chicago 17, January 10, at Chicago

Championship Games

AFC .... Denver 38, Cleveland 33, January 17, at Denver

NFC .... Washington 17, Minnesota 10, January 17, at Washington

SUPER BOWL XXII .... Washington 42, Denver 10, January 31, at San Diego Jack Murphy Stadium, San Diego, California

AFC-NFC PRO BOWL .. AFC 15, NFC 6, February 7, at Aloha Stadium, Honolulu, Hawaii

AFC Season Records—Team by Team

BUFFALO (7-8)

28	*New York Jets	31
34	*Houston	30
	at Dallas	C
6	*Indianapolis	47
7	at New England	14
6	*N.Y. Giants (OT)	3
34	at Miami (OT)	31
7	*Washington	27
21	*Denver	14
21	at Cleveland	27
17	at N.Y. Jets	14
27	*Miami	0
21	at L.A. Raiders	34
27	at Indianapolis	3
7	*New England	13
7	at Philadelphia	17
270		305

CINCINNATI (4-11)

23	at Indianapolis	21
26	*San Francisco	27
	at L.A. Rams	C
9	*San Diego	10
17	at Seattle	10
0	*Cleveland	34
20	at Pittsburgh	23
29	*Houston	31
14	*Miami	20
16	at Atlanta	10
16	*Pittsburgh	30
20	at N.Y. Jets	27
30	*Kansas City (OT)	27
24	at Cleveland	38
24	*New Orleans	41
17	at Houston	21
285		370

CLEVELAND (10-5)

21	at New Orleans	28
34	*Pittsburgh	10
	*Denver	C
20	at New England	10
10	*Houston	15
34	at Cincinnati	0
30	*L.A. Rams	17
24	at San Diego (OT)	27
38	*Atlanta	3
27	*Buffalo	21
40	at Houston	7
24	at San Francisco	38
7	*Indianapolis	9
38	*Cincinnati	24
24	at L.A. Raiders	17
19	at Pittsburgh	13
390		239

DENVER (10-4-1)

40	*Seattle	17
17	at Green Bay (OT)	17
	at Cleveland	C
10	*Houston	40
30	*L.A. Raiders	14
26	at Kansas City	17
27	at Minnesota	34
34	*Detroit	0
14	at Buffalo	21
31	*Chicago	29
23	at L.A. Raiders	17
31	at San Diego	17
31	*New England	20
21	at Seattle	28
20	*Kansas City	17
24	*San Diego	0
379		288

HOUSTON (9-6)

20	*L.A. Rams	16
30	at Buffalo	34
	*L.A. Raiders	C
40	at Denver	10
15	at Cleveland	10
7	*New England	21
37	*Atlanta	33
31	at Cincinnati	29
20	at San Francisco	27
23	at Pittsburgh	3
7	*Cleveland	40
27	at Indianapolis	51
33	*San Diego	18
10	at New Orleans	24
24	*Pittsburgh	16
21	*Cincinnati	17
345		349

INDIANAPOLIS (9-6)

21	*Cincinnati	23
10	*Miami	23
	at St. Louis	C
47	at Buffalo	6
6	*N.Y. Jets	0
7	at Pittsburgh	21
30	*New England	16
19	at N.Y. Jets	14
13	*San Diego	16
40	at Miami	21
0	at New England	24
51	*Houston	27
9	at Cleveland	7
3	*Buffalo	27
20	at San Diego	7
24	*Tampa Bay	6
300		238

KANSAS CITY (4-11)

20	*San Diego	13
14	at Seattle	43
	*Minnesota	C
17	at L.A. Raiders	35
0	at Miami	42
17	*Denver	26
21	at San Diego	42
28	at Chicago	31
16	*Pittsburgh	17
9	*N.Y. Jets	16
3	*Green Bay	23
27	at Detroit	20
27	at Cincinnati (OT)	30
16	*L.A. Raiders	10
17	at Denver	20
41	*Seattle	20
273		388

L.A. RAIDERS (5-10)

20	at Green Bay	0
27	*Detroit	7
	at Houston	C
35	*Kansas City	17
14	at Denver	30
17	*San Diego	23
13	*Seattle	35
23	at New England	26
20	at Minnesota	31
14	at San Diego	16
17	*Denver	23
37	at Seattle	14
34	*Buffalo	21
10	at Kansas City	16
17	*Cleveland	24
3	*Chicago	6
301		289

MIAMI (8-7)

21	at New England	28
23	at Indianapolis	10
	*N.Y. Giants	C
20	at Seattle	24
42	*Kansas City	0
31	at N.Y. Jets (OT)	37
31	*Buffalo (OT)	34
35	*Pittsburgh	24
20	at Cincinnati	14
21	*Indianapolis	40
20	at Dallas	14
0	at Buffalo	27
37	*N.Y. Jets	28
28	at Philadelphia	10
23	*Washington	21
10	*New England	24
362		335

NEW ENGLAND (8-7)

28	*Miami	21
24	at N.Y. Jets	43
	at Washington	C
10	*Cleveland	20
14	*Buffalo	7
21	at Houston	7
16	at Indianapolis	30
26	*L.A. Raiders	23
10	at N.Y. Giants	17
17	*Dallas (OT)	23
24	*Indianapolis	0
31	*Philadelphia (OT)	34
20	at Denver	31
42	*N.Y. Jets	20
13	at Buffalo	7
24	at Miami	10
320		293

N.Y. JETS (6-9)

31	at Buffalo	28
43	*New England	24
	at Pittsburgh	C
24	*Dallas	38
0	at Indianapolis	6
37	*Miami (OT)	31
16	at Washington	17
14	*Indianapolis	19
30	*Seattle	14
16	at Kansas City	9
14	*Buffalo	17
27	*Cincinnati	20
28	at Miami	37
20	at New England	42
27	*Philadelphia	38
7	at N.Y. Giants	20
334		360

PITTSBURGH (8-7)

30	*San Francisco	17
10	at Cleveland	34
	*N.Y. Jets	C
28	at Atlanta	12
21	at L.A. Rams	31
21	*Indianapolis	7
23	*Cincinnati	20
24	at Miami	35
17	at Kansas City	16
3	*Houston	23
30	at Cincinnati	16
16	*New Orleans	20
13	*Seattle	9
20	at San Diego	16
16	at Houston	24
13	*Cleveland	19
285		299

SAN DIEGO (8-7)

13	at Kansas City	20
28	*St. Louis	24
	*Seattle	C
10	at Cincinnati	9
17	at Tampa Bay	13
23	at L.A. Raiders	17
42	*Kansas City	21
27	*Cleveland (OT)	24
16	at Indianapolis	13
16	*L.A. Raiders	14
3	at Seattle	34
17	*Denver	31
18	at Houston	33
16	*Pittsburgh	20
7	*Indianapolis	20
0	at Denver	24
253		317

SEATTLE (9-6)

17	at Denver	40
43	*Kansas City	14
	at San Diego	C
24	*Miami	20
10	*Cincinnati	17
37	at Detroit	14
35	at L.A. Raiders	13
28	*Minnesota	17
14	at N.Y. Jets	30
24	*Green Bay	13
34	*San Diego	3
14	*L.A. Raiders	37
9	at Pittsburgh	13
28	*Denver	21
34	at Chicago	21
20	at Kansas City	41
371		314

**denotes home game*
(OT) denotes overtime
C denotes game cancelled due to players' strike

NFC Season Records—Team by Team

ATLANTA (3-12)

10	at Tampa Bay	48
21	*Washington	20
	at New Orleans	C
12	*Pittsburgh	28
17	*San Francisco	25
24	*L.A. Rams	20
33	at Houston	37
0	*New Orleans	38
3	at Cleveland	38
10	*Cincinnati	16
13	at Minnesota	24
21	*St. Louis	34
21	at Dallas	10
0	at L.A. Rams	33
7	at San Francisco	35
13	*Detroit	30
205		436

CHICAGO (11-4)

34	*N.Y. Giants	19
20	*Tampa Bay	3
	at Detroit	C
35	at Philadelphia	3
27	*Minnesota	7
17	*New Orleans	19
27	at Tampa Bay	26
31	*Kansas City	28
26	at Green Bay	24
29	at Denver	31
30	*Detroit	10
23	*Green Bay	10
30	at Minnesota	24
0	at San Francisco	41
21	*Seattle	34
6	at L.A. Raiders	3
356		282

DALLAS (7-8)

13	at St. Louis	24
16	at N.Y. Giants	14
	*Buffalo	C
38	at N.Y. Jets	24
41	*Philadelphia	22
7	*Washington	13
20	at Philadelphia	37
33	*N.Y. Giants	24
17	at Detroit	27
23	at New Eng. (OT)	17
14	*Miami	20
38	*Minnesota (OT)	44
10	*Atlanta	21
20	at Washington	24
29	at L.A. Rams	21
21	*St. Louis	16
340		348

DETROIT (4-11)

19	at Minnesota	34
7	at L.A. Raiders	27
	*Chicago	C
27	*Tampa Bay	31
19	at Green Bay (OT)	16
14	*Seattle	37
33	*Green Bay	34
0	at Denver	34
27	*Dallas	17
13	at Washington	20
10	at Chicago	30
20	*Kansas City	27
16	*L.A. Rams	37
20	at Tampa Bay	10
14	*Minnesota	17
30	at Atlanta	13
269		384

GREEN BAY (5-9-1)

0	*L.A. Raiders	20
17	*Denver (OT)	17
	at Tampa Bay	C
23	at Minnesota	16
16	*Detroit (OT)	19
16	*Philadelphia (OT)	10
34	at Detroit	33
17	*Tampa Bay	23
24	*Chicago	26
13	at Seattle	24
23	at Kansas City	3
10	at Chicago	23
12	*San Francisco	23
16	*Minnesota	10
10	at N.Y. Giants	20
24	at New Orleans	33
255		300

L.A. RAMS (6-9)

16	at Houston	20
16	*Minnesota	21
	*Cincinnati	C
10	at New Orleans	37
31	*Pittsburgh	21
20	at Atlanta	24
17	at Cleveland	30
10	*San Francisco	31
14	*New Orleans	31
27	at St. Louis	24
30	at Washington	26
35	*Tampa Bay	3
37	at Detroit	16
33	*Atlanta	0
21	*Dallas	29
0	at San Francisco	48
317		361

MINNESOTA (8-7)

34	*Detroit	19
21	at L.A. Rams	16
	at Kansas City	C
16	*Green Bay	23
7	at Chicago	27
10	at Tampa Bay	20
34	*Denver	27
17	at Seattle	28
31	*L.A. Raiders	20
23	*Tampa Bay	17
24	*Atlanta	13
44	at Dallas (OT)	38
24	*Chicago	30
10	at Green Bay	16
17	at Detroit	14
24	*Washington (OT)	27
336		335

NEW ORLEANS (12-3)

28	*Cleveland	21
17	at Philadelphia	27
	*Atlanta	C
37	*L.A. Rams	10
19	at St. Louis	24
19	at Chicago	17
22	*San Francisco	24
38	at Atlanta	0
31	at L.A. Rams	14
26	at San Francisco	24
23	*N.Y. Giants	14
20	at Pittsburgh	16
44	*Tampa Bay	34
24	*Houston	10
41	at Cincinnati	24
33	*Green Bay	24
422		283

N.Y. GIANTS (6-9)

19	at Chicago	34
14	*Dallas	16
	at Miami	C
21	*San Francisco	41
12	*Washington	38
3	at Buffalo (OT)	6
30	*St. Louis	7
24	at Dallas	33
17	*New England	10
20	at Philadelphia	17
14	at New Orleans	23
19	at Washington	23
23	*Philadelphia (OT)	20
24	at St. Louis	27
20	*Green Bay	10
20	*N.Y. Jets	7
280		312

PHILADELPHIA (7-8)

24	at Washington	34
27	*New Orleans	17
	at San Francisco	C
3	*Chicago	35
22	at Dallas	41
10	at Green Bay (OT)	16
37	*Dallas	20
28	at St. Louis	23
31	*Washington	27
17	*N.Y. Giants	20
19	*St. Louis	31
34	at New Eng. (OT)	31
20	at N.Y. Giants (OT)	23
10	*Miami	28
38	at N.Y. Jets	27
17	*Buffalo	7
337		380

ST. LOUIS (7-8)

24	*Dallas	13
24	at San Diego	28
	*Indianapolis	C
21	at Washington	28
24	*New Orleans	19
28	at San Francisco	34
7	at N.Y. Giants	30
23	*Philadelphia	28
31	*Tampa Bay	28
24	*L.A. Rams	27
31	at Philadelphia	19
34	at Atlanta	21
17	*Washington	34
27	*N.Y. Giants	24
31	at Tampa Bay	14
16	at Dallas	21
362		368

SAN FRANCISCO (13-2)

17	at Pittsburgh	30
27	at Cincinnati	26
	*Philadelphia	C
41	at N.Y. Giants	21
25	at Atlanta	17
34	*St. Louis	28
24	at New Orleans	22
31	at L.A. Rams	10
27	*Houston	20
24	*New Orleans	26
24	at Tampa Bay	10
38	*Cleveland	24
23	at Green Bay	12
41	*Chicago	0
35	*Atlanta	7
48	*L.A. Rams	0
459		253

TAMPA BAY (4-11)

48	*Atlanta	10
3	at Chicago	20
	*Green Bay	C
31	at Detroit	27
13	*San Diego	17
20	*Minnesota	10
26	*Chicago	27
23	at Green Bay	17
28	at St. Louis	31
17	at Minnesota	23
10	*San Francisco	24
3	at L.A. Rams	35
34	at New Orleans	44
10	*Detroit	20
14	*St. Louis	31
6	at Indianapolis	24
286		360

WASHINGTON (11-4)

34	*Philadelphia	24
20	at Atlanta	21
	*New England	C
28	*St. Louis	21
38	at N.Y. Giants	12
13	at Dallas	7
17	*N.Y. Jets	16
27	at Buffalo	7
27	at Philadelphia	31
20	*Detroit	13
26	*L.A. Rams	30
23	*N.Y. Giants	19
34	at St. Louis	17
24	*Dallas	20
21	at Miami	23
27	at Minnesota (OT)	24
379		285

** denotes home game*
(OT) denotes overtime
C denotes game cancelled due to players' strike

Attendances as they appear in the following, and in the club-by-club sections starting on page 26, are turnstile counts and not paid attendance. Paid attendance totals are on page 209.

First Week Summaries

Standings

American Football Conference

Eastern Division

	W	L	T	Pct.	Pts.	OP
New England	1	0	0	1.000	28	21
N.Y. Jets	1	0	0	1.000	31	28
Buffalo	0	1	0	.000	28	31
Indianapolis	0	1	0	.000	21	23
Miami	0	1	0	.000	21	28
Central Division						
Cincinnati	1	0	0	1.000	23	21
Houston	1	0	0	1.000	20	16
Pittsburgh	1	0	0	1.000	30	17
Cleveland	0	1	0	.000	21	28
Western Division						
Denver	1	0	0	1.000	40	17
Kansas City	1	0	0	1.000	20	13
L.A. Raiders	1	0	0	1.000	20	0
San Diego	0	1	0	.000	13	20
Seattle	0	1	0	.000	17	40

National Football Conference

Eastern Division

	W	L	T	Pct.	Pts.	OP
St. Louis	1	0	0	1.000	24	13
Washington	1	0	0	1.000	34	24
Dallas	0	1	0	.000	13	24
N.Y. Giants	0	1	0	.000	19	34
Philadelphia	0	1	0	.000	24	34
Central Division						
Chicago	1	0	0	1.000	34	19
Minnesota	1	0	0	1.000	34	19
Tampa Bay	1	0	0	1.000	48	10
Detroit	0	1	0	.000	19	34
Green Bay	0	1	0	.000	0	20
Western Division						
New Orleans	1	0	0	1.000	28	21
Atlanta	0	1	0	.000	10	48
L.A. Rams	0	1	0	.000	16	20
San Francisco	0	1	0	.000	17	30

Sunday, September 13

Tampa Bay 48, Atlanta 10—At Tampa Stadium, attendance 51,250. Steve DeBerg completed 24 of 34 passes for 333 yards and a team-record five touchdowns as the Buccaneers rolled over the Falcons in Ray Perkins's debut as Tampa Bay head coach. Four of DeBerg's scoring passes came in the first half to spark a 27-3 Tampa Bay lead. Phil Freeman and Calvin Magee each caught 11-yard touchdowns, while Gerald Carter added six- and three-yard scores. The Buccaneers increased their lead to 41-3 on a one-yard scoring run by Cliff Austin and a two-yard reception by Mark Carrier. Tampa Bay's defense held Atlanta to 197 total yards. DeBerg earned NFC offensive player of the week honors.

Atlanta	0	3	0	7	— 10
Tampa Bay	14	13	7	14	— 48

TB —Freeman 11 pass from DeBerg (Igwebuike kick)
TB —Carter 6 pass from DeBerg (Igwebuike kick)
Atl —FG Luckhurst 50
TB —Magee 11 pass from DeBerg (Igwebuike kick)
TB —Carter 3 pass from DeBerg (kick failed)
TB —Austin 1 run (Igwebuike kick)
TB —Carrier 2 pass from DeBerg (Igwebuike kick)
Atl —Bailey 34 pass from Campbell (Luckhurst kick)
TB —Bartalo 3 run (Igwebuike kick)

Cincinnati 23, Indianapolis 21—At Hoosier Dome, attendance 59,387. Boomer Esiason completed 17 of 26 passes for 236 yards and two touchdowns to help Cincinnati edge Indianapolis. Esiason threw first-quarter touchdown passes of 61 yards to Rodney Holman and 18 yards to James Brooks. Indianapolis answered with Jack Trudeau's 52-yard scoring pass to Bill Brooks and a two-yard touchdown run by Albert Bentley. Jim Breech's 20-yard field goal and James Brooks's second touchdown, a one-yard run in the fourth quarter, capped the Cincinnati victory.

Cincinnati	13	0	0	10	— 23
Indianapolis	7	0	7	7	— 21

Cin —J. Brooks 18 pass from Esiason (Breech kick)
Cin —Holman 61 pass from Esiason (kick failed)
Ind —B. Brooks 52 pass from Trudeau (Biasucci kick)
Ind —Bentley 2 run (Biasucci kick)
Cin —FG Breech 20
Cin —J. Brooks 1 run (Breech kick)
Ind —Sherwin 1 pass from Trudeau (Biasucci kick)

New Orleans 28, Cleveland 21—At Louisiana Superdome, attendance 62,339. Bobby Hebert completed two touchdown passes and the Saints' defense produced two fourth-quarter safeties to lead New Orleans over Cleveland. Hebert broke a 7-7 halftime tie with a seven-yard scoring pass to tight end Hoby Brenner. Dalton Hilliard's five-yard scoring run increased New Orleans's lead to 21-14 in the third quarter. Bernie Kosar completed 28 of 44 passes for 314 yards and two touchdowns for the Browns and also scored on a three-yard run in the fourth quarter. Bruce Clark and Brett Maxie each sacked Kosar in the end zone for safeties. It marked the first time New Orleans registered two safeties in one game in its 21-year history.

Cleveland	0	7	7	7	— 21
New Orleans	7	0	14	7	— 28

NO —Brenner 5 pass from Hebert (Andersen kick)
Clev —Weathers 7 pass from Kosar (Jaeger kick)
NO —Brenner 7 pass from Hebert (Andersen kick)
Clev —Brennan 30 pass from Kosar (Jaeger kick)
NO —Hilliard 5 run (Andersen kick)
Clev —Kosar 3 run (Jaeger kick)
NO —Safety, Clark tackled Kosar in end zone
NO —Safety, Maxie tackled Kosar in end zone
NO —FG Andersen 39

St. Louis 24, Dallas 13—At Busch Stadium, attendance 42,241. Neil Lomax and Roy Green combined for two touchdowns within 65 seconds to help St. Louis record its first home-opener victory since 1975. Trailing 13-3 late in the fourth quarter, Lomax, who completed 17 of 33 passes for 270 yards, hit Green on a 16-yard scoring play. He then connected on a 25-yard pass to Stump Mitchell on the Cardinals' next series to set up Green's second touchdown reception from 22 yards. St. Louis recorded eight sacks, including three by Curtis Greer, who was named NFC defensive player of the week.

Dallas	0	6	0	7	— 13
St. Louis	3	0	0	21	— 24

StL —FG Gallery 23
Dall —FG Ruzek 22
Dall —FG Ruzek 29
Dall —Banks 20 pass from D. White (Ruzek kick)
StL —Green 16 pass from Lomax (Gallery kick)
StL —Green 22 pass from Lomax (Gallery kick)
StL —Ferrell 15 run (Gallery kick)

Minnesota 34, Detroit 19—At Metrodome, attendance 57,061. Rookie running back D.J. Dozier scored a pair of touchdowns in his first NFL game to help the Vikings notch their 200th regular-season victory. Trailing 19-10 in the third quarter, Minnesota quarterback Wade Wilson fired touchdown passes to Anthony Carter (73 yards) and Leo Lewis (24), and Dozier's one-yard run helped Minnesota take a 31-19 third-quarter lead. Chuck Nelson's 22-yard field goal in the fourth quarter finished the Vikings' scoring. Dozier also scored on a two-yard reception in the second quarter. Detroit's Eddie Murray kicked field goals of 26, 27, 24, and 34 yards for the Lions.

Detroit	6	10	3	0	— 19
Minnesota	0	10	21	3	— 34

Det —FG Murray 26
Det —FG Murray 27
Minn —FG C. Nelson 27
Det —FG Murray 24
Det —Mandley 5 pass from Long (Murray kick)
Minn —Dozier 2 pass from Wilson (C. Nelson kick)
Det —FG Murray 34
Minn —Carter 73 pass from Wilson (C. Nelson kick)
Minn —Dozier 1 run (C. Nelson kick)
Minn —Lewis 24 pass from Wilson (C. Nelson kick)
Minn —FG C. Nelson 22

Los Angeles Raiders 20, Green Bay 0—At Lambeau Field, attendance 54,983. Marcus Allen carried a career-high 33 times for 136 yards and one touchdown as the Raiders handed the Packers their first shutout in 122 games. Allen opened the scoring with a one-yard run with 2:52 remaining in the first half. Vann McElroy returned an interception 35 yards and Chris Bahr kicked field goals of 40 and 27 yards to finish the Raiders' scoring. Los Angeles's defense held the Packers to 147 total yards. Green Bay was last shut out by Chicago on December 10, 1978.

L.A. Raiders	0	7	7	6	— 20
Green Bay	0	0	0	0	— 0

Raiders —Allen 1 run (Bahr kick)
Raiders —McElroy 35 interception return (Bahr kick)
Raiders —FG Bahr 40
Raiders —FG Bahr 27

Houston 20, Los Angeles Rams 16—At Astrodome, attendance 33,186. Warren Moon threw for 310 yards and two touchdowns to lead the Oilers over the Rams. Los Angeles jumped out to a 13-0 second-quarter lead on two Mike Lansford field goals from 28 and 44 yards, and a 25-yard interception return for a touchdown by Kevin Greene. Moon countered with touchdown passes of 3 yards to Jamie Williams and 54 yards to Ernest Givins in the fourth quarter. Tony Zendejas kicked field goals of 44 and 19 yards. Keith Bostic's interception with 38 seconds remaining sealed the Oilers' victory.

L.A. Rams	6	7	3	0	— 16
Houston	0	3	0	17	— 20

Rams —FG Lansford 28
Rams —FG Lansford 44
Rams —Greene 25 interception return (Lansford kick)
Hou —FG Zendejas 44
Rams —FG Lansford 47
Hou —Williams 3 pass from Moon (Zendejas kick)
Hou —Givins 54 pass from Moon (Zendejas kick)
Hou —FG Zendejas 19

New England 28, Miami 21—At Sullivan Stadium, attendance 54,642. The Patriots scored two third-quarter touchdowns within a 50-second span to post a 28-21 comeback win over the Dolphins. Miami led 21-7 in the second quarter when New England quarterback Steve Grogan connected on a 17-yard touchdown pass to Irving Fryar to cut the Dolphins' margin to 21-14. The Patriots' third-quarter scoring came on a seven-yard run by Tony Collins and a 20-yard interception return by Ronnie Lippett.

Miami	7	14	0	0	— 21
New England	7	7	14	0	— 28

Mia —Duper 9 pass from Marino (Reveiz kick)
NE —Collins 4 run (Franklin kick)
Mia —Duper 25 pass from Marino (Reveiz kick)
Mia —Davenport 1 pass from Marino (Reveiz kick)
NE —Fryar 17 pass from Grogan (Franklin kick)
NE —Collins 7 run (Franklin kick)
NE —Lippett 20 interception return (Franklin kick)

New York Jets 31, Buffalo 28—At Rich Stadium, attendance 75,718. Ken O'Brien passed for two touchdowns and Johnny Hector ran for two more as the Jets edged the Bills. After a scoreless first quarter, Buffalo opened the scoring with a 26-yard touchdown pass from Jim Kelly to Trumaine Johnson. O'Brien then connected with Wesley Walker (55 yards) and Mickey Shuler (4) to give New York a 14-7 halftime lead. Hector opened the fourth quarter with a two-yard scoring run. Bob Crable's interception then set up Hector's one-yard touchdown run with less than three minutes remaining in the game. Buffalo's Jim Kelly completed 25 of 42 passes for 305 yards and three touchdowns.

N.Y. Jets	0	14	10	7	— 31
Buffalo	0	7	7	14	— 28

Buff —T. Johnson 26 pass from Kelly (Norwood kick)
NYJ —Walker 55 pass from O'Brien (Leahy kick)
NYJ —Shuler 4 pass from O'Brien (Leahy kick)
NYJ —FG Leahy 29
Buff —Burkett 6 pass from Kelly (Norwood kick)
NYJ —Hector 2 run (Leahy kick)
Buff —Riddick 2 run (Norwood kick)
NYJ —Hector 1 run (Leahy kick)
Buff —Riddick 1 pass from Kelly (Norwood kick)

Washington 34, Philadelphia 24—At Robert F. Kennedy Stadium, attendance 52,188. Reserve quarterback Doug Williams came off the bench to relieve injured Jay Schroeder in the first quarter and completed 17 of 27 passes for 272 yards and two touchdowns as the Redskins defeated the Eagles. Williams's scoring pass of six yards to Art Monk, and Jess Atkinson's 27-yard field goal, gave Washington a 10-0 first-quarter lead. Reggie Branch scored on a one-yard run and Monk added a 39-yard touchdown pass from Williams in the second half. Punter Steve Cox replaced Atkinson and kicked a 40-yard field goal midway through the fourth quarter to seal the victory. It was the 158th straight sellout crowd at Washington's Robert F. Kennedy Stadium.

Philadelphia	0	10	14	0	— 24
Washington	10	7	7	10	— 34

Wash —FG Atkinson 27
Wash —Monk 6 pass from Williams (Atkinson kick)
Phil —Quick 30 pass from Cunningham (McFadden kick)
Phil —FG McFadden 33
Wash —Rogers 1 run (Cox kick)
Wash —Branch 1 run (Cox kick)
Phil —Cunningham 2 run (McFadden kick)
Phil —White 70 fumble recovery return (McFadden kick)
Wash —Monk 39 pass from Williams (Cox kick)
Wash —FG Cox 40

Kansas City 20, San Diego 16—At Arrowhead Stadium, attendance 56,940. Rookie Paul Palmer returned a kickoff 95 yards for a touchdown late in the fourth quarter as the Chiefs defeated the Chargers to post their fifth straight opening-day win. Kansas City took a 10-0 halftime lead on Nick Lowery's 25-yard field goal and rookie Christian Okoye's 43-yard run. After trading field goals, Dan Fouts's 34-yard touchdown pass to Gary Anderson brought the Chargers to within 13-10. Vince Abbott's 33-yard field goal tied the game, but Palmer then returned the ensuing kickoff for the winning score. Okoye became the first Kansas City player to rush for over 100 yards (105) in his first NFL game.

San Diego	0	0	3	10	— 13
Kansas City	3	7	0	10	— 20

KC — FG Lowery 25
KC — Okoye 43 run (Lowery kick)
SD — FG Abbott 32
KC — FG Lowery 29
SD — Anderson 34 pass from Fouts (Abbott kick)
SD — FG Abbott 33
KC — Palmer 95 kickoff return (Lowery kick)

Pittsburgh 30, San Francisco 17—At Three Rivers Stadium, attendance 55,735. The Steelers converted three of four takeaways into 13 points to defeat San Francisco. Rookie Delton Hall returned a fumble 50 yards midway through the first quarter to open the scoring. Mark Malone's two-yard touchdown pass to Preston Gothard and two Gary Anderson field goals from 50 and 41 yards put the Steelers ahead 20-3 at halftime. Anderson's third field goal (44 yards) and Walter Abercrombie's 28-yard touchdown run put the game away. Pittsburgh held San Francisco to 47 net rushing yards. Steelers linebacker Mike Merriweather, who had nine solo tackles, one interception, and one forced fumble, was named AFC defensive player of the week. Joe Montana completed 24 of 49 passes for 316 yards and two touchdowns for San Francisco.

San Francisco	0	3	7	7	—	17
Pittsburgh	7	10	3	10	—	30

Pitt — Hall 50 fumble recovery return (Anderson kick)
SF — FG Wersching 43
Pitt — Gothard 2 pass from Malone (Anderson kick)
Pitt — FG Anderson 50
Pitt — FG Anderson 41
SF — Frank 1 pass from Montana (Wersching kick)
Pitt — FG Anderson 44
Pitt — Abercrombie 28 run (Anderson kick)
SF — Rice 3 pass from Montana (Wersching kick)

Denver 40, Seattle 17—At Mile High Stadium, attendance 75,999. John Elway threw for 338 yards and four touchdowns as the Broncos defeated the Seahawks. Denver trailed 17-7 in the second quarter before Rich Karlis kicked field goals of 37 and 42 yards. Elway then connected with Steve Watson on a four-yard scoring play to give Denver a 20-17 edge at the half. Dennis Smith's fourth-quarter interception set up Elway's five-yard touchdown pass to Orson Mobley. Elway, who completed 22 of 33 passes, also had a 72-yard bomb to Steve Sewell and a 59-yarder to Vance Johnson. Karlis's fourth-quarter field goals of 25 and 29 yards completed the scoring.

Seattle	14	3	0	0	—	17
Denver	7	13	14	6	—	40

Sea — Turner 20 pass from Krieg (Johnson kick)
Den — Sewell 72 pass from Elway (Karlis kick)
Sea — Warner 10 pass from Krieg (Johnson kick)
Sea — FG Johnson 25
Den — FG Karlis 37
Den — FG Karlis 42
Den — Watson 4 pass from Elway (Karlis kick)
Den — Mobley 5 pass from Elway (Karlis kick)
Den — Johnson 59 pass from Elway (Karlis kick)
Den — FG Karlis 25
Den — FG Karlis 29

Monday, September 14

Chicago 34, New York Giants 19—At Soldier Field, attendance 65,704. Mike Tomczak completed 20 of 34 passes for 292 yards and two touchdowns to propel the Bears past the Giants. Tomczak scored on a one-yard run in the final seconds of the first half that put Chicago ahead 10-7. The Bears broke the game wide open in the second half when Tomczak connected on touchdown passes to Ron Morris (42 yards) and Willie Gault (56) to give Chicago a 24-7 lead. Dennis McKinnon added a club-record 94-yard punt return for a touchdown in the fourth quarter. Chicago's defense held New York to 203 yards total offense and registered eight sacks, including two each by linebackers Mike Singletary and Wilber Marshall.

N.Y. Giants	7	0	6	6	—	19
Chicago	3	7	14	10	—	34

NYG — Flynn recovered blocked punt in end zone (Allegre kick)
Chi — FG Butler 24
Chi — Tomczak 1 run (Butler kick)
Chi — Morris 42 pass from Tomczak (Butler kick)
Chi — Gault 56 pass from Tomczak (Butler kick)
NYG — Kinard 70 interception return (kick blocked)
Chi — McKinnon 94 punt return (Butler kick)
NYG — Robinson 5 pass from Simms (pass failed)
Chi — FG Butler 25

Second Week Summaries

Standings

American Football Conference

Eastern Division	W	L	T	Pct.	Pts.	OP
N.Y. Jets	2	0	0	1.000	74	52
Buffalo	1	1	0	.500	62	61
Miami	1	1	0	.500	44	38
New England	1	1	0	.500	52	64
Indianapolis	0	2	0	.000	31	46
Central Division						
Cincinnati	1	1	0	.500	49	48
Cleveland	1	1	0	.500	55	38
Houston	1	1	0	.500	50	50
Pittsburgh	1	1	0	.500	40	51
Western Division						
L.A. Raiders	2	0	0	1.000	47	7
Denver	1	0	1	.750	57	34
Kansas City	1	1	0	.500	34	56
San Diego	1	1	0	.500	41	44
Seattle	1	1	0	.500	60	54

National Football Conference

Eastern Division	W	L	T	Pct.	Pts.	OP
Dallas	1	1	0	.500	29	38
Philadelphia	1	1	0	.500	51	51
St. Louis	1	1	0	.500	48	41
Washington	1	1	0	.500	54	45
N.Y. Giants	0	2	0	.000	33	50
Central Division						
Chicago	2	0	0	1.000	54	22
Minnesota	2	0	0	1.000	55	35
Tampa Bay	1	1	0	.500	51	30
Green Bay	0	1	1	.250	17	37
Detroit	0	2	0	.000	26	61
Western Division						
Atlanta	1	1	0	.500	31	68
New Orleans	1	1	0	.500	45	48
San Francisco	1	1	0	.500	44	56
L.A. Rams	0	2	0	.000	32	41

Sunday, September 20

Dallas 16, New York Giants 14—At Giants Stadium, attendance 73,426. Roger Ruzek kicked a pair of second-half field goals to help the Cowboys end their longest regular-season losing streak since 1963. Trailing 14-10 midway through the third period, Ruzek connected on a 43-yard field goal and added a game-clinching 28-yarder with 5:12 remaining. He also had a 46-yarder in the first quarter. The Giants almost pulled the game out but Raul Allegre's 46-yard field-goal attempt sailed wide left with six seconds to play.

Dallas	3	7	3	3	—	16
N.Y. Giants	7	0	7	0	—	14

NYG — Robinson 5 pass from Simms (Allegre kick)
Dall — FG Ruzek 46
Dall — Chandler 1 pass from D. White (Ruzek kick)
NYG — Bavaro 1 pass from Simms (Allegre kick)
Dall — FG Ruzek 43
Dall — FG Ruzek 28

Denver 17, Green Bay 17—At Milwaukee County Stadium, attendance 50,624. The Broncos and Packers played to only the eleventh tie game since overtime play began in 1974. Green Bay led 14-3 at halftime before Denver cut the deficit to 14-10 in the third quarter on Gene Lang's three-yard touchdown run. After the Packers extended their lead to 17-10 on a 32-yard field goal by Al Del Greco, John Elway led the Broncos on an 18-play, 80-yard drive that concluded with Steve Sewell's two-yard touchdown run to send the game into overtime. Don Majkowski, making his first NFL start for Green Bay, completed 10 of 20 passes for 121 yards and one touchdown. Elway hit on 30 of 48 passes for 285 yards, but suffered three interceptions.

Denver	0	3	7	7	0	—	17
Green Bay	7	7	0	3	0	—	17

GB — Fullwood 2 run (Del Greco kick)
GB — Carruth 7 pass from Majkowski (Del Greco kick)
Den — FG Karlis 38
Den — Lang 3 run (Karlis kick)
GB — FG Del Greco 32
Den — Sewell 2 run (Karlis kick)

Los Angeles Raiders 27, Detroit 7—At Memorial Coliseum, attendance 50,300. Rusty Hilger completed 20 of 39 passes for 234 yards and one touchdown as the Raiders beat the Lions. The Raiders, who trailed 7-6 at halftime, broke the game open by scoring 21 unanswered points in the second half. Hilger hit Dokie Williams on a 14-yard scoring pass, and Marcus Allen and Vance Mueller added a pair of one-yard touchdown runs to account for the 21 points. The Raiders outrushed the Lions 171 to 47, and had a time-of-possession advantage of 37:04 to 22:56.

Detroit	0	7	0	0	—	7
L.A. Raiders	6	0	7	14	—	27

Raiders — FG Bahr 38
Raiders — FG Bahr 34
Det — S. Williams 2 pass from Long (Murray kick)
Raiders — D. Williams 14 pass from Hilger (Bahr kick)
Raiders — Allen 1 run (Bahr kick)
Raiders — Mueller 1 run (Bahr kick)

Buffalo 34, Houston 30—At Rich Stadium, attendance 56,534. Jim Kelly passed for 293 yards and three touchdowns to lift the Bills over the Oilers. Buffalo scored 21 points in the fourth quarter to overcome a 20-13 deficit. Kelly completed an eight-yard touchdown pass to Andre Reed, and Robb Riddick's two-yard scoring run brought the Bills to within three, 30-27. Kelly threw his third touchdown pass, a two-yarder to Ronnie Harmon with 57 seconds remaining, for the win. Mike Rozier had 150 yards rushing for the Oilers.

Houston	3	14	3	10	—	30
Buffalo	3	10	0	21	—	34

Buff — FG Norwood 45
Hou — FG Zendejas 52
Hou — Hill 2 pass from Moon (Zendejas kick)
Buff — FG Norwood 38
Hou — Rozier 8 run (Zendejas kick)
Buff — Riddick 11 pass from Kelly (Norwood kick)
Hou — FG Zendejas 27
Buff — Reed 8 pass from Kelly (Norwood kick)
Hou — Givins 12 pass from Moon (Zendejas kick)
Hou — FG Zendejas 30
Buff — Riddick 2 run (Norwood kick)
Buff — Harmon 2 pass from Kelly (Norwood kick)

Seattle 43, Kansas City 14—At Kingdome, attendance 61,667. Dave Krieg threw three touchdown passes and Norm Johnson kicked a team-record five field goals as the Seahawks rolled over the Chiefs. Krieg completed second-quarter touchdown passes of 9 and 17 yards to Daryl Turner, and added a two-yarder to Mike Tice in the third quarter. Johnson's field goals came from 34, 25, 46, 27, and 49 yards. Seattle's John L. Williams rushed 15 times for 112 yards and one touchdown for his first NFL 100-yard rushing game.

Kansas City	0	7	0	7	—	14
Seattle	3	14	20	6	—	43

Sea — FG Johnson 34
Sea — Turner 9 pass from Krieg (Johnson kick)
KC — Carson 10 pass from Blackledge (Lowery kick)
Sea — Turner 17 pass from Krieg (Johnson kick)
Sea — Tice 2 pass from Krieg (Johnson kick)
Sea — FG Johnson 25
Sea — Williams 1 run (Johnson kick)
Sea — FG Johnson 46
Sea — FG Johnson 27
Sea — FG Johnson 49
KC — Carson 10 pass from Kenney (Lowery kick)

Miami 23, Indianapolis 10—At Hoosier Dome, attendance 57,524. Dan Marino threw for 254 yards and three touchdowns to lead the Dolphins over the Colts. Marino completed scoring passes to Troy Stradford (18 yards), Jim Jenson (6), and Mark Clayton (10), and Fuad Reveiz kicked a 27-yard field goal, to give Miami a commanding 23-7 lead. Marino tied Daryle Lamonica by throwing a touchdown pass in his twenty-fifth consecutive game, the third-longest streak in NFL history. The win gave the Dolphins 14 straight victories over the Colts, the longest current win streak by one team in the NFL.

Miami	7	9	7	0	—	23
Indianapolis	0	7	3	0	—	10

Mia — Stradford 18 pass from Marino (Reveiz kick)
Mia — FG Reveiz 27
Ind — Bouza 17 pass from Hogeboom (Biasucci kick)
Mia — Jensen 6 pass from Marino (kick failed)
Mia — Clayton 10 pass from Marino (Reveiz kick)
Ind — FG Biasucci 50

Minnesota 21, Los Angeles Rams 16—At Anaheim Stadium, attendance 63,567. Wade Wilson, who came off the bench to relieve an injured Tommy Kramer, threw for 285 yards and three touchdowns to lift the Vikings over the Rams. Wilson completed a 41-yard scoring pass to Hassan Jones with only 30 seconds left to win the game. Minnesota opened a 14-0 lead in the first half on Wilson touchdown passes to Carl Hilton (8 yards) and Anthony Carter (46). The Rams closed the gap on Buford McGee's two-yard touchdown run and Johnnie Johnson's blocked punt, which he returned 20 yards for a touchdown. Los Angeles took the lead when Mike Lansford kicked a 27-yard field goal 5:05 into the fourth quarter. Wilson then engineered the Vikings' winning 80-yard drive.

Minnesota	7	7	0	7	—	21
L.A. Rams	0	0	7	9	—	16

Minn — Hilton 8 pass from Wilson (C. Nelson kick)
Minn — Carter 46 pass from Wilson (C. Nelson kick)
Rams — McGee 2 run (Lansford kick)
Rams — Johnson 20 blocked punt return (kick failed)
Rams — FG Lansford 27
Minn — Jones 41 pass from Wilson (C. Nelson kick)

Philadelphia 27, New Orleans 17—At Veterans Stadium, attendance 57,485. Randall Cunningham threw for two touchdowns and the Eagles' defense forced five turnovers to highlight Philadelphia's comeback victory over New Orleans. Trailing 10-0 in the first quarter, the Eagles took a 17-10 halftime lead on Paul McFadden's 30-yard field goal and Cunningham's touchdown passes to Mike Quick (19 yards) and Kenny Jackson (25). Philadelphia's five takeaways included Seth Joyner's fumble recovery return for a touchdown in the fourth quarter.

New Orleans	10	0	0	7	—	17
Philadelphia	0	17	3	7	—	27

NO — FG Andersen 45
NO — Tice 6 pass from Hebert (Andersen kick)
Phil — FG McFadden 30
Phil — Quick 19 pass from Cunningham (McFadden kick)
Phil — Jackson 25 pass from Cunningham (McFadden kick)
Phil — FG McFadden 30

Phil — Joyner 18 fumble recovery return (McFadden kick)
NO — Tice 27 pass from Wilson (Andersen kick)

Cleveland 34, Pittsburgh 10—At Cleveland Stadium, attendance 79,543. The Browns' defense had three sacks and five interceptions to lead Cleveland past the Steelers. With the score tied 10-10 in the third quarter, the Browns took the lead for good 17-10, when Mike Johnson intercepted Mark Malone to set up Bernie Kosar's 11-yard touchdown pass to Gerald McNeil. Clay Matthews then returned an interception 26 yards for a score in the fourth quarter for his first NFL touchdown. Kosar's 37-yard touchdown pass to Clarence Weathers completed the scoring. Pittsburgh's only touchdown came when Donnie Shell recovered a fumble and ran 19 yards for a score early in the third quarter.

Pittsburgh	0	3	7	0	— 10
Cleveland	0	10	7	17	— 34

Clev — FG Jaeger 29
Clev — Mack 1 run (Jaeger kick)
Pitt — FG Anderson 27
Pitt — Shell 19 fumble recovery return (Anderson kick)
Clev — McNeil 11 pass from Kosar (Jaeger kick)
Clev — FG Jaeger 23
Clev — Matthews 26 interception return (Jaeger kick)
Clev — Weathers 37 pass from Kosar (Jaeger kick)

San Diego 28, St. Louis 24—At San Diego Jack Murphy Stadium, attendance 47,988. The Chargers scored 28 points in the first half and held on to edge the Cardinals. Lionel James scored on an 81-yard punt return the first time San Diego touched the ball. Gary Anderson added a five-yard touchdown run and Dan Fouts connected with Wes Chandler (26 yards) to give the Chargers a 21-0 second-quarter lead. Following an interception by Billy Ray Smith, James scored his second touchdown on a seven-yard run for a 28-0 halftime lead. St. Louis scored on four straight drives in the second half. Cardinals quarterback Neil Lomax completed 32 of 61 passes for 457 yards and three touchdowns to bring St. Louis back.

St. Louis	0	0	10	14	— 24
San Diego	14	14	0	0	— 28

SD — James 81 punt return (Abbott kick)
SD — Anderson 5 run (Abbott kick)
SD — Chandler 26 pass from Fouts (Abbott kick)
SD — James 7 run (Abbott kick)
StL — Green 8 pass from Lomax (Gallery kick)
StL — FG Gallery 38
StL — Novacek 21 pass from Lomax (Gallery kick)
StL — Mitchell 17 pass from Lomax (Gallery kick)

San Francisco 27, Cincinnati 26—At Riverfront Stadium, attendance 53,498. Joe Montana completed a 25-yard touchdown pass to Jerry Rice with no time left on the clock, and Ray Wersching kicked the extra point, to give the 49ers a 27-26 win. The Bengals, who failed to get a first down on their own 25-yard line with two seconds left in the game, gave the 49ers one last try for the victory. Trailing 20-7 in the third quarter, Montana threw a 34-yard touchdown pass to Rice, and Wersching added two field goals from 24 and 31 yards, to deadlock the score, 20-20. Cincinnati's Jim Breech kicked a pair of field goals to give the Bengals a six-point advantage late in the fourth quarter.

San Francisco	0	7	13	7	— 27
Cincinnati	10	10	0	6	— 26

Cin — Kinnebrew 2 run (Breech kick)
Cin — FG Breech 23
SF — Wilson 38 pass from Montana (Wersching kick)
Cin — Holman 46 pass from Esiason (Breech kick)
Cin — FG Breech 42
SF — Rice 34 pass from Montana (Wersching kick)
SF — FG Wersching 24
SF — FG Wersching 31
Cin — FG Breech 41
Cin — FG Breech 46
SF — Rice 25 pass from Montana (Wersching kick)

Chicago 20, Tampa Bay 3—At Soldier Field, attendance 63,551. Walter Payton set an NFL record by rushing for his 107th career touchdown to help Chicago defeat Tampa Bay. The Bears marched 78 yards in the first quarter to set up Payton's one-yard scoring run. After the Buccaneers scored on a 43-yard field goal by Donald Igwebuike, Chicago's Neal Anderson ran 27 yards for the Bears' second touchdown to give Chicago a 14-3 lead at the half. Payton finished the scoring in the fourth quarter on a nine-yard pass from Mike Tomczak.

Tampa Bay	0	0	0	3	— 3
Chicago	7	7	0	6	— 20

Chi — Payton 1 run (Butler kick)
TB — FG Igwebuike 43
Chi — Anderson 27 run (Butler kick)
Chi — Payton 9 pass from Tomczak (run failed)

Atlanta 21, Washington 20—At Atlanta-Fulton County Stadium, attendance 63,567. Quarterback Scott Campbell made his first start for the Falcons and threw for 271 yards and two touchdowns as Atlanta edged Washington. Campbell completed scoring passes of 22 yards to Floyd Dixon and 23 yards to Stacey Bailey. With the Redskins trailing by one point in the fourth quarter, Doug Williams hit Art Monk on a six-yard touchdown pass to take a 20-14 lead. Gerald Riggs's four-yard run 5:01 later proved to be the game-winning score.

Washington	7	0	6	7	— 20
Atlanta	7	0	7	7	— 21

Wash — Bryant 17 pass from Williams (Haji-Sheikh kick)
Atl — Dixon 22 pass from Campbell (Luckhurst kick)
Wash — Clark 18 pass from Williams (kick failed)
Atl — Bailey 23 pass from Campbell (Luckhurst kick)
Wash — Monk 6 pass from Williams (Haji-Sheikh kick)
Atl — Riggs 4 run (Luckhurst kick)

Monday, September 21

New York Jets 43, New England 24—At Giants Stadium, attendance 70,847. Ken O'Brien completed 19 of 26 passes for 313 yards and one touchdown as the Jets overpowered the Patriots. After only three first-half field goals, the two teams combined for 58 points in the second half. With New York leading 6-3 in the third quarter, O'Brien connected on a 58-yard touchdown pass to Al Toon. Johnny Hector then ran for two scores from five and nine yards to give the Jets a commanding 27-3 lead. Nuu Faaola added two one-yard touchdown blasts in the final quarter to finish New York's scoring. The Jets' defense had five sacks, including two each by Bob Crable and Alex Gordon, and held the Patriots to only 48 yards rushing.

New England	0	3	7	14	— 24
N.Y. Jets	6	0	21	16	— 43

NYJ — FG Leahy 37
NYJ — FG Leahy 34
NE — FG Franklin 32
NYJ — Toon 58 pass from O'Brien (Leahy kick)
NYJ — Hector 5 run (Leahy kick)
NE — Tippett 29 fumble recovery return (Franklin kick)
NYJ — Hector 9 run (Leahy kick)
NYJ — Safety, Lyons tackled Tatupu in end zone
NE — Baty 1 pass from Eason (Franklin kick)
NYJ — Faaola 1 run (Leahy kick)
NE — Starring 12 pass from Eason (Franklin kick)
NYJ — Faaola 1 run (Leahy kick)

Third Week Summaries

The 14 games of the third week of the season were cancelled due to a players' strike. The players union initiated a strike action on Tuesday, September 22, following the New England-New York Jets game, and called off the work stoppage on Thursday, October 15. NFL games on the fourth, fifth, and sixth weeks were played with replacement teams that included some regulars.

Fourth Week Summaries

Standings

American Football Conference

Eastern Division

	W	L	T	Pct.	Pts.	OP
N.Y. Jets	2	1	0	.667	98	90
Buffalo	1	2	0	.333	68	108
Indianapolis	1	2	0	.333	78	52
Miami	1	2	0	.333	64	62
New England	1	2	0	.333	62	84

Central Division

	W	L	T	Pct.	Pts.	OP
Cleveland	2	1	0	.667	75	48
Houston	2	1	0	.667	90	60
Pittsburgh	2	1	0	.667	68	63
Cincinnati	1	2	0	.333	58	58

Western Division

	W	L	T	Pct.	Pts.	OP
L.A. Raiders	3	0	0	1.000	82	24
San Diego	2	1	0	.667	51	53
Seattle	2	1	0	.667	84	74
Denver	1	1	1	.500	67	74
Kansas City	1	2	0	.333	51	91

National Football Conference

Eastern Division

	W	L	T	Pct.	Pts.	OP
Dallas	2	1	0	.667	67	62
Washington	2	1	0	.667	82	66
Philadelphia	1	2	0	.333	54	86
St. Louis	1	2	0	.333	69	69
N.Y. Giants	0	3	0	.000	54	91

Central Division

	W	L	T	Pct.	Pts.	OP
Chicago	3	0	0	1.000	89	25
Minnesota	2	1	0	.667	71	58
Tampa Bay	2	1	0	.667	82	57
Green Bay	1	1	1	.500	40	53
Detroit	0	3	0	.000	53	92

Western Division

	W	L	T	Pct.	Pts.	OP
New Orleans	2	1	0	.667	82	58
San Francisco	2	1	0	.667	85	77
Atlanta	1	2	0	.333	43	96
L.A. Rams	0	3	0	.000	42	78

Sunday, October 4

Chicago 35, Philadelphia 3—At Veterans Stadium, attendance 4,074. The Bears exploded for 28 second-quarter points to highlight their victory over the Eagles. Leading 7-3, Chicago's Mike Hohensee completed a 20-yard touchdown pass to Glen Kozlowski, and Chris Brewer added a one-yard run to increase their lead to 21-3. Anthony Mosley blocked a punt and returned it nine yards for another Bears touchdown one minute later. Hohensee's three-yard touchdown pass to Don Kindt capped the scoring.

Chicago	7	28	0	0	— 35
Philadelphia	0	3	0	0	— 3

Chi — Heimuli 9 pass from Hohensee (Lashar kick)
Phil — FG Jacobs 27
Chi — Kozlowski 20 pass from Hohensee (Lashar kick)
Chi — Brewer 1 run (Lashar kick)
Chi — Mosley 9 blocked punt return (Lashar kick)
Chi — Kindt 3 pass from Hohensee (Lashar kick)

Cleveland 20, New England 10—At Sullivan Stadium, attendance 14,830. Larry Mason carried 32 times for 133 yards and had two one-yard touchdown runs to lead the Browns over the Patriots. After a scoreless first quarter, Eric Schubert's 23-yard field goal and Bob Bleier's six-yard pass to Larry Linne gave New England a 10-0 lead. Cleveland narrowed the 10-point halftime deficit in the third quarter to 10-6 on Brian Franco's 28- and 21-yard field goals. Mason's two scoring runs in the fourth quarter sealed the Browns' win. Cleveland outrushed New England 217 yards to 31 and maintained a 37:01 to 22:59 time-of-possession advantage.

Cleveland	0	0	6	14	— 20
New England	0	10	0	0	— 10

NE — FG Schubert 23
NE — Linne 6 pass from Bleier (Schubert kick)
Clev — FG Franco 28
Clev — FG Franco 21
Clev — Mason 1 run (Kelley pass from Walters)
Clev — Mason 1 run (Franco kick)

Dallas 38, New York Jets 24—At Giants Stadium, attendance 12,370. Dallas quarterback Kevin Sweeney threw for three touchdowns, including a pair to wide receiver Kelvin Edwards, as the Cowboys defeated the Jets. Dallas's two touchdowns in the third quarter, Alvin Blount's one-yard run and Sweeney's 35-yard pass to Edwards, put the game away. The Jets' Michael Harper returned a punt 78 yards for a touchdown late in the fourth quarter to finish the scoring. The Cowboys' defense recorded 11 sacks.

Dallas	7	17	14	0	— 38
N.Y. Jets	3	7	7	7	— 24

NYJ — FG Ragusa 20
Dall — Burbage 13 pass from Sweeney (Zendejas kick)
Dall — FG Zendejas 33
Dall — Adams 27 run (Zendejas kick)
Dall — Edwards 33 pass from Sweeney (Zendejas kick)
NYJ — Kurisko 41 pass from Norrie (Ragusa kick)
NYJ — Chirico 3 run (Ragusa kick)
Dall — Blount 1 run (Zendejas kick)
Dall — Edwards 35 pass from Sweeney (Zendejas kick)
NYJ — Harper 78 punt return (Ragusa kick)

Green Bay 23, Minnesota 16—At Metrodome, attendance 13,911. Quarterback Alan Risher threw for one touchdown and ran for another to lead the Packers over the Vikings. Risher opened the scoring with a 30-yard pass to Lavelle Thomas. Max Zendejas then kicked field goals of 35 and 43 yards, and Risher ran 13 yards for a touchdown, to give the Packers a 20-7 halftime lead. Minnesota cut the deficit to 20-16 when James Brim ran 38 yards for a score and Joe Stepanek tackled Risher in the end zone for a safety. Zendejas kicked his third field goal of the game from 34 yards midway through the fourth quarter, to cap the scoring.

Green Bay	7	13	0	3	— 23
Minnesota	0	7	7	2	— 16

GB — Thomas 30 pass from Risher (Zendejas kick)
GB — FG Zendejas 35
GB — FG Zendejas 43
Minn — Brim 63 pass from Adams (Dawson kick)
GB — Risher 13 run (Zendejas kick)
Minn — Brim 38 run (Dawson kick)
Minn — Safety, Stepanek tackled Risher in end zone
GB — FG Zendejas 34

Houston 40, Denver 10—At Mile High Stadium, attendance 38,494. John Diettrich kicked four field goals, and Eugene Seale returned an interception 73 yards for a touchdown, as the Oilers crushed the Broncos. Houston opened a 17-10 halftime lead on quarterback Brent Pease's one-yard keeper, Diettrich's 43-yard field goal, and Andrew Jackson's 16-yard run. Ken Karcher's 21-yard pass to Rick Massie, and Mike Clendenen's 28-yard field goal, gave Denver its only points. Pease completed 15 of 25 passes for 260 yards and one touchdown, a 31-yarder to Mark Gehring in the fourth quarter for the Oilers. Houston's defense held Denver to 38 rushing yards and recorded five sacks.

Houston	7	10	10	13	— 40
Denver	0	10	0	0	— 10

Hou — Pease 1 run (Diettrich kick)
Den — FG Clendenen 28
Hou — FG Diettrich 43
Hou — Jackson 16 run (Diettrich kick)
Den — Massie 21 pass from Karcher (Clendenen kick)
Hou — FG Diettrich 39
Hou — Seale 73 interception return (Diettrich kick)
Hou — Gehring 31 pass from Pease (Diettrich kick)
Hou — FG Diettrich 44
Hou — FG Diettrich 27

Indianapolis 47, Buffalo 6—At Rich Stadium, attendance 9,860. Gary Hogeboom tied a team record with five touchdown passes, including two each to Walter Murray and James Noble, to help Indianapolis defeat Buffalo. Hogeboom connected on touchdown passes to Murray (37 and 11 yards), Joe Jones (4), and Noble (18) to give the Colts a 28-0 halftime advantage. Indianapolis added 19 points in the third quarter. Jim Perryman intercepted a pass to set up the Colts' first score and blocked a punt to set up a safety in the third quarter. The Colts' defense recovered four fumbles and had three interceptions. Hogeboom was named AFC offensive player of the week.

Indianapolis	7	21	19	0	— 47
Buffalo	0	0	0	6	— 6

Ind — Murray 37 pass from Hogeboom (Jordan kick)
Ind — Murray 11 pass from Hogeboom (Jordan kick)
Ind — Jones 4 pass from Hogeboom (Jordan kick)
Ind — Noble 18 pass from Hogeboom (Jordan kick)
Ind — Noble 18 pass from Hogeboom (Jordan kick)
Ind — Safety, Leiding tackled Clark in end zone
Ind — FG Jordan 36
Ind — G. Brown 18 run (Jordan kick)
Buff — M. Brown 8 pass from Totten (kick failed)

Los Angeles Raiders 35, Kansas City 17—At Memorial Coliseum, attendance 10,708. Vince Evans completed 10 of 18 attempts for 248 yards and two touchdowns as the Raiders rolled over the Chiefs. Los Angeles opened a 14-0 lead on Evans's 27-yard touchdown pass to Carl Aikens and Craig Ellis's two-yard scoring run. Evans also gained 63 yards on four carries, including a four-yard touchdown run in the second quarter. The Chiefs scored 14 points in the third quarter on Bob Harris's blocked punt return for a touchdown and Matt Stevens's four-yard pass to Rod Jones. Los Angeles outgained Kansas City 500 total yards to 268.

Kansas City	0	0	14	3	— 17
L.A. Raiders	14	7	7	7	— 35

Raiders — Aikens 27 pass from Evans (Hardy kick)
Raiders — C. Ellis 2 run (Hardy kick)
Raiders — Evans 4 run (Hardy kick)
KC — B. Harris 23 blocked punt return (Hamrick kick)
Raiders — Horton 32 pass from Evans (Hardy kick)
KC — R. Jones 4 pass from Stevens (Hamrick kick)
Raiders — C. Ellis 8 run (Hardy kick)
KC — FG Hamrick 40

New Orleans 37, Los Angeles Rams 10—At Louisiana Superdome, attendance 29,745. John Fourcade fired three touchdown passes and Vincent Alexander ran for another to power New Orleans past Los Angeles. The Saints took command of the game by scoring 20 points in the second quarter. Reggie Sutton returned a blocked punt 13 yards for a score, Fourcade connected on an 11-yard pass to Eric Martin, and Alexander ran one yard for a score for a 27-0 lead at the half. Fourcade's third scoring pass was a club-record 82-yarder to Mike Waters early in the fourth quarter.

L.A. Rams	0	0	3	7	— 10
New Orleans	7	20	3	7	— 37

NO — O'Neal 1 pass from Fourcade (Cofer kick)
NO — R. Sutton 13 blocked punt return (kick failed)
NO — Martin 11 pass from Fourcade (Cofer kick)
NO — Alexander 1 run (Cofer kick)
Rams — FG Lansford 37
NO — FG Cofer 27
NO — Waters 82 pass from Fourcade (Cofer kick)
Rams — Mobley 40 pass from Quarles (Lansford kick)

Seattle 24, Miami 20—At Kingdome, attendance 19,448. Running back Rick Parros scored on a one-yard run with 1:30 remaining in the game to lift the Seahawks over the Dolphins. Trailing 20-17, Seahawks quarterback Bruce Mathison threw a 47-yard pass to Jimmy Teal to set up the winning score. Mathison, who completed 20 of 42 passes for 326 yards and two touchdowns, had a 25-yard touchdown pass to Curtis Pardridge in the first quarter. Charles Glaze had two sacks, one interception, five tackles, and defensed one pass for the Seahawks.

Miami	7	0	6	7	— 20
Seattle	7	3	0	14	— 24

Mia — Douglas 14 pass from Mackey (Beecher kick)
Sea — Pardridge 25 pass from Mathison (Hagler kick)
Sea — FG Hagler 20
Mia — FG Beecher 34
Mia — FG Beecher 40
Sea — Keel 24 pass from Mathison (Hagler kick)
Mia — Tagliaferri 2 run (Beecher kick)
Sea — Parros 1 run (Hagler kick)

Pittsburgh 28, Atlanta 12—At Atlanta-Fulton County Stadium, attendance 16,667. Earnest Jackson rushed 29 times for 104 yards and one touchdown as the Steelers downed the Falcons. Pittsburgh took a 14-3 halftime lead on Jackson's one-yard run and Steve Bono's five-yard pass to Russell Hairston. After Atlanta scored a safety, Bono scored on a one-yard run to put the Steelers ahead 21-5 in the fourth quarter. Pittsburgh's Joey Clinkscales, who had six receptions for 150 yards, scored on an 11-yard pass from backup quarterback Reggie Collier. Ray Williams had one interception and seven tackles for the Steelers.

Pittsburgh	0	14	0	14	— 28
Atlanta	3	0	2	7	— 12

Atl — FG Davis 27
Pitt — Jackson 1 run (Trout kick)
Pitt — Hairston 5 pass from Bono (Trout kick)
Atl — Safety, Bono intentionally grounded ball in end zone
Pitt — Bono 1 run (Trout kick)
Pitt — Clinkscales 11 pass from Collier (Trout kick)
Atl — Barney 19 pass from Van Raaphorst (Davis kick)

Washington 28, St. Louis 21—At Robert F. Kennedy Stadium, attendance 27,728. Anthony Allen caught seven passes for a club-record 255 yards and three touchdowns to lead the Redskins past the Cardinals. Ed Rubbert and Allen connected on scoring passes of 34 and 88 yards to give Washington a 14-7 halftime lead. Lionel Vital rushed 27 times for 82 yards for the Redskins, including an eight-yard scoring run in the third quarter. Rubbert was 14 of 24 for 334 yards and three touchdowns. Allen was named NFC offensive player of the week for his performance.

St. Louis	0	7	7	7	— 21
Washington	7	7	14	0	— 28

Wash — Allen 34 pass from Rubbert (Toibin kick)
StL — Ferrell 1 run (Staurovsky kick)
Wash — Allen 88 pass from Rubbert (Toibin kick)
StL — Ferrell 1 run (Staurovsky kick)
Wash — Vital 8 run (Toibin kick)
Wash — Allen 48 pass from Rubbert (Toibin kick)
StL — P. Noga 60 interception return (Staurovsky kick)

San Diego 10, Cincinnati 9—At Riverfront Stadium, attendance 18,074. Jeff Gaffney kicked a 24-yard field goal with 2:44 remaining to help the Chargers edge the Bengals. Cincinnati quarterback Adrian Breen connected on a four-yard touchdown pass to Wade Russell, and Scott Schutt tackled San Diego quarterback Rick Neuheisel in the end zone for a safety, to give Cincinnati a 9-0 halftime lead. Chargers quarterback Mike Kelley then directed an eight-play, 86-yard drive capped by Frank Middleton's one-yard scoring run to cut the Bengals' lead to 9-7 early in the fourth quarter.

San Diego	0	0	0	10	— 10
Cincinnati	7	2	0	0	— 9

Cin — Russell 4 pass from Breen (Manca kick)
Cin — Safety, Schutt tackled Neuheisel in end zone
SD — Middleton 1 run (Neuheisel run)
SD — FG Gaffney 24

Tampa Bay 31, Detroit 27—At Pontiac Silverdome, attendance 4,919. The Buccaneers overcame a 17-point first-quarter deficit to post a come-from-behind victory over the Lions. Mike Hold's 15-yard touchdown pass to Adrian Wright, and Paul Tripoli's 15-yard interception return for a score, cut the Lions' lead to 17-14 early in the second quarter. Hold then fired a 61-yard scoring bomb to Eric Streater with two minutes left in the half to cut the Buccaneers' deficit to 24-21. Tampa Bay recovered a fumbled punt on Detroit's 3-yard line late in the third period to set up Harold Ricks's decisive one-yard touchdown run.

Tampa Bay	0	21	10	0	— 31
Detroit	17	7	0	3	— 27

Det — Grymes 36 pass from Hons (Prindle kick)
Det — FG Prindle 23
Det — King 9 fumble recovery return (Prindle kick)
TB — Wright 15 pass from Hold (Tiffin kick)
TB — Tripoli 15 interception return (Tiffin kick)
Det — Truvillion 53 pass from Hons (Prindle kick)
TB — Streater 61 pass from Hold (Tiffin kick)
TB — FG Tiffin 21
TB — Ricks 1 run (Tiffin kick)
Det — FG Prindle 35

Monday, October 5

San Francisco 41, New York Giants 21—At Giants Stadium, attendance 16,471. The 49ers scored 14 points within a 30-second span late in the first half and went on to defeat the Giants. Trailing 7-3 in the second quarter, Del Rodgers ran two yards for a touchdown, and Mike Wells returned a blocked punt for another score, to give the 49ers a 17-7 lead they never relinquished. San Francisco quarterback Mark Stevens connected on a 39-yard touchdown pass to Carl Monroe and also scored on a nine-yard run early in the fourth quarter. The 49ers held a 40:17 to 19:43 time-of-possession advantage over New York.

San Francisco	3	14	10	14	— 41
N.Y. Giants	0	7	0	14	— 21

SF — FG Brockhaus 39
NYG — Bennett 46 pass from Crocicchia (Benyola kick)
SF — Rodgers 2 run (Brockhaus kick)
SF — Wells 1 blocked punt return (Brockhaus kick)
SF — Monroe 39 pass from Stevens (Brockhaus kick)
SF — FG Brockhaus 22
SF — Stevens 9 run (Brockhaus kick)
NYG — McGowan 63 pass from Busch (Benyola kick)
SF — Cherry 13 run (Brockhaus kick)
NYG — Lovelady 7 pass from Busch (Benyola kick)

Fifth Week Summaries

Standings

American Football Conference

Eastern Division

	W	L	T	Pct.	Pts.	OP
Indianapolis	2	2	0	.500	84	52
Miami	2	2	0	.500	106	62
New England	2	2	0	.500	76	91
N.Y. Jets	2	2	0	.500	98	96
Buffalo	1	3	0	.250	75	122

Central Division

	W	L	T	Pct.	Pts.	OP
Houston	3	1	0	.750	105	70
Cincinnati	2	2	0	.500	75	68
Cleveland	2	2	0	.500	85	63
Pittsburgh	2	2	0	.500	89	94

Western Division

	W	L	T	Pct.	Pts.	OP
L.A. Raiders	3	1	0	.750	96	54
San Diego	3	1	0	.750	68	66
Denver	2	1	1	.625	97	88
Seattle	2	2	0	.500	94	91
Kansas City	1	3	0	.250	51	133

National Football Conference

Eastern Division

	W	L	T	Pct.	Pts.	OP
Dallas	3	1	0	.750	108	84
Washington	3	1	0	.750	120	78
St. Louis	2	2	0	.500	93	88
Philadelphia	1	3	0	.250	76	127
N.Y. Giants	0	4	0	.000	66	129

Central Division

	W	L	T	Pct.	Pts.	OP
Chicago	4	0	0	1.000	116	32
Minnesota	2	2	0	.500	78	85
Tampa Bay	2	2	0	.500	95	74
Green Bay	1	2	1	.375	56	72
Detroit	1	3	0	.250	72	108

Western Division

	W	L	T	Pct.	Pts.	OP
San Francisco	3	1	0	.750	110	94
New Orleans	2	2	0	.500	101	82
Atlanta	1	3	0	.250	60	121
L.A. Rams	1	3	0	.250	73	99

Sunday, October 11

San Francisco 25, Atlanta 17—At Atlanta-Fulton County Stadium, attendance 8,684. Joe Montana threw for one touchdown and Roger Craig ran for another to lead the 49ers over the Falcons. Craig carried 17 times for 91 yards and scored on a one-yard run in the first quarter. Montana's six-yard pass to Dwight Clark, and Bob Gagliano's five-yard completion to Terry Greer, helped San Francisco build a 20-0 halftime lead. Jeff Fuller tackled Erik Kramer in the end zone for a safety to finish San Francisco's scoring. The 49ers' defense held the Falcons to 50 yards rushing.

San Francisco	6	14	0	5	— 25
Atlanta	0	0	10	7	— 17

SF — Craig 1 run (kick failed)
SF — Clark 6 pass from Montana (Brockhaus kick)
SF — Greer 5 pass from Gagliano (Brockhaus kick)
Atl — Badanjek 3 run (Davis kick)
Atl — FG Davis 42
SF — FG Brockhaus 20
SF — Safety, Fuller tackled Kramer in end zone
Atl — Kamana 4 pass from Kramer (Davis kick)

New England 14, Buffalo 7—At Sullivan Stadium, attendance 11,878. Mike LeBlanc ran for 146 yards on 35 carries to help the Patriots defeat the Bills. New England opened the scoring on Carl Woods's four-yard scoring run and added another touchdown in the third quarter on Bob Bleier's one-yard run. The Bills' Willie Totten completed a 13-yard touchdown pass to Thad McFadden early in the fourth quarter to prevent the shutout.

Buffalo	0	0	0	7	— 7
New England	7	0	7	0	— 14

NE — Woods 4 run (Franklin kick)
NE — Bleier 1 run (Franklin kick)
Buff — McFadden 13 pass from Totten (Schlopy kick)

Cincinnati 17, Seattle 10—At Kingdome, attendance 31,739. Cincinnati running backs Marc Logan and David McCluskey combined for 173 yards rushing and two touchdowns to power the Bengals over the Seahawks. Logan, who gained 103 yards on 16 carries, opened the scoring with a five-yard touchdown run in the second quarter. McCluskey added a one-yard scoring run, and Massimo Manca kicked a 28-yard field goal, for a 17-0 halftime lead. Seattle narrowed the margin to 17-10 on Scott Hagler's 24-yard field goal and Bruce Mathison's eight-yard touchdown pass to Jimmy Teal. Rob Niehoff intercepted Mathison with

28 seconds remaining to halt Seattle's final drive. Reggie Williams recorded two of Cincinnati's five sacks.

Cincinnati	0	17	0	0 —	17
Seattle	0	0	3	7 —	10

Cin —Logan 5 run (Manca kick)
Cin —McCluskey 1 run (Manca kick)
Cin —FG Manca 28
Sea —FG Hagler 24
Sea —Teal 8 pass from Mathison (Hagler kick)

Detroit 19, Green Bay 16—At Lambeau Field, attendance 35,779. Mike Prindle kicked a 31-yard field goal 2:34 into overtime to lift the Lions over the Packers. Green Bay quarterback Alan Risher connected with Don Summers on a 10-yard scoring pass to give the Packers a 13-6 lead early in the fourth quarter. Detroit tied the game when Todd Hons threw a seven-yard scoring pass to Darrell Grymes. Prindle put Detroit ahead 16-13 with a 27-yard field goal with 1:20 to play, but Max Zendejas's 45-yard field goal with four seconds left in regulation sent the game into overtime.

Detroit	3	0	3	10	3 —	19
Green Bay	0	6	0	10	0 —	16

Det —FG Prindle 23
GB —FG Zendejas 39
GB —FG Zendejas 28
Det —FG Prindle 32
GB —Summers 10 pass from Risher (Zendejas kick)
Det —Grymes 7 pass from Hons (Prindle kick)
Det —FG Prindle 27
GB —FG Zendejas 45
Det —FG Prindle 31

Houston 15, Cleveland 10—At Cleveland Stadium, attendance 38,927. Herman Hunter carried 28 times for 121 yards to help the Oilers snap a six-game losing streak to the Browns. Leading 7-3 on Brent Pease's 15-yard touchdown pass to Keith McDonald, John Diettrich kicked field goals from 45 and 23 yards to give Houston a 13-3 lead. Jesse Baker tackled Jeff Christensen in the end zone for a safety early in the fourth quarter to complete the Oilers' scoring. Houston maintained a 40:36 to 19:24 time-of-possession advantage and limited the Browns to 50 yards rushing.

Houston	0	7	6	2 —	15
Cleveland	3	0	0	7 —	10

Clev —FG Franco 26
Hou —McDonald 15 pass from Pease (Diettrich kick)
Hou —FG Diettrich 45
Hou —FG Diettrich 23
Clev —Mason 5 pass from Christensen (Franco kick)
Hou —Safety, Baker tackled Christensen in end zone

Miami 42, Kansas City 0—At Joe Robbie Stadium, attendance 25,867. Ron Scott ran for three touchdowns, and the Dolphins' defense added two more scores, to highlight their 42-0 victory over the Chiefs. Scott gained 99 yards rushing and had touchdown runs of two, four, and three yards. Miami's Liffort Hobley returned a fumble 55 yards for a score in the third quarter, and on Kansas City's next possession, Trell Hooper returned a fumble 59 yards for another touchdown. The Dolphins outgained the Chiefs 344 total yards to 132. Hobley, who also had two interceptions, was named AFC defensive player of the week.

Kansas City	0	0	0	0 —	0
Miami	7	7	21	7 —	42

Mia —Isom 6 run (Beecher kick)
Mia —R. Scott 2 run (Beecher kick)
Mia —R. Scott 4 run (Beecher kick)
Mia —Hobley 55 fumble recovery return (Beecher kick)
Mia —Hooper 59 fumble recovery return (Beecher kick)
Mia —R. Scott 3 run (Beecher kick)

Chicago 27, Minnesota 7—At Soldier Field, attendance 32,113. Mike Hohensee threw for a touchdown, and Tim Lashar kicked two field goals, as the Bears downed the Vikings to remain the NFL's only undefeated team. Hohensee opened the scoring with a nine-yard pass to Glen Kozlowski in the second quarter. Chris Brenner's one-yard run and Lashar's 26-yard field goal gave Chicago a 17-0 third-quarter lead. Bruce McCray returned an interception 23 yards for a touchdown to cap the Bears' scoring. Sean McInerney had three-and-a-half of the Bears' nine sacks and was named NFC defensive player of the week. Chicago outgained Minnesota 344 total yards to 151.

Minnesota	0	0	0	7 —	7
Chicago	0	7	10	10 —	27

Chi —Kozlowski 9 pass from Hohensee (Lashar kick)
Chi —Brewer 1 run (Lashar kick)
Chi —FG Lashar 26
Minn —Brim 11 pass from Adams (Dawson kick)
Chi —FG Lashar 27
Chi —McCray 23 interception return (Lashar kick)

St. Louis 24, New Orleans 19—At Busch Stadium, attendance 11,795. Mark Jackson and Leonard Smith each returned fumbles for touchdowns to propel the Cardinals over the Saints. Jackson's fumble return covered 77 yards, while Smith sped 29 yards for his score to give St. Louis a 17-6 halftime lead. The Cardinals tackled punter Tommy Barnhart on the Saints' 26-yard line to set up Sammy Garza's two-yard scoring run in the fourth quarter. New Orleans's Dwight Beverly rushed for 139 yards on 35 carries and two touchdowns.

New Orleans	0	6	6	7 —	19
St. Louis	10	7	0	7 —	24

StL —Jackson 77 fumble recovery return (Staurovsky kick)
StL —FG Staurovsky 24
StL —L. Smith 29 fumble recovery return (Staurovsky kick)
NO —Martin 5 pass from Ingram (kick blocked)
NO —Beverly 3 run (kick failed)
StL —Garza 2 run (Staurovsky kick)
NO —Beverly 5 run (Cofer kick)

Indianapolis 6, New York Jets 0—At Hoosier Dome, attendance 34,927. Steve Jordan kicked field goals from 35 and 25 yards to help the Colts record their first shutout victory in 11 years. Mike Prior intercepted Jets quarterback David Norrie's pass with 17 seconds remaining to preserve the win. Chuck Banks carried 25 times for 159 yards to lead Indianapolis's offense. Bryant Jones had two interceptions and nine tackles to pace the Colts' defense. Indianapolis's last shutout was a 20-0 blanking of the Jets on October 24, 1976.

N.Y. Jets	0	0	0	0 —	0
Indianapolis	0	3	3	0 —	6

Ind —FG Jordan 35
Ind —FG Jordan 25

Dallas 41, Philadelphia 22—At Texas Stadium, attendance 40,622. The Cowboys scored three touchdowns in their first five offensive plays to defeat the Eagles. Kelvin Edwards scampered 62 yards for a score on Dallas's first possession of the game. Alvin Blount added an eight-yard scoring run, and Cornell Burbage's 77-yard touchdown catch gave the Cowboys a 21-0 advantage. Luis Zendejas added field goals of 44 and 50 yards. Tony Dorsett rushed for 162 yards on 40 carries to move into fourth place on the NFL's all-time list with 11,742 career yards.

Philadelphia	3	7	6	6 —	22
Dallas	21	6	14	0 —	41

Dall —Edwards 62 run (Zendejas kick)
Dall —Blount 8 run (Zendejas kick)
Dall —Burbage 77 pass from Sweeney (Zendejas kick)
Phil —FG Jacobs 40
Phil —Bowman 62 pass from Tinsley (Jacobs kick)
Dall —FG Zendejas 44
Dall —FG Zendejas 50
Dall —Dorsett 10 run (Zendejas kick)
Dall —Blount 1 run (Zendejas kick)
Phil —Siano 13 pass from Tinsley (kick failed)
Phil —Clemons 13 pass from Tinsley (kick blocked)

Los Angeles Rams 31, Pittsburgh 21—At Anaheim Stadium, attendance 20,218. Charles White ran for a career-high 166 yards and one touchdown to power the Rams past the Steelers. Los Angeles took a 7-0 lead in the opening two minutes of the game when Nolan Cromwell blocked a Steelers punt and Kirby Jackson recovered it in the end zone for a touchdown. Steve Dils completed 13 of 19 passes for 148 yards and two touchdowns for the Rams. Mike Lansford's 39-yard field goal in the fourth quarter finished Los Angeles's scoring.

Pittsburgh	7	7	0	7 —	21
L.A. Rams	7	14	7	3 —	31

Rams —Jackson recovered blocked punt in end zone (Lansford kick)
Pitt —Alston 22 pass from Bono (Trout kick)
Pitt —Carter 10 pass from Bono (Trout kick)
Rams —White 2 run (Lansford kick)
Rams —McDonald 1 pass from Dils (Lansford kick)
Rams —Moore 11 pass from Dils (Lansford kick)
Rams —FG Lansford 39
Pitt —Alston 42 pass from Collier (Trout kick)

San Diego 17, Tampa Bay 13—At Tampa Stadium, attendance 23,878. Quarterback Rick Neuheisel led three second-half scoring drives to give the Chargers a come-from-behind victory over the Buccaneers. Trailing 10-0 at halftime, San Diego scored on its first possession of the second half on Jeff Gaffney's 27-yard field goal. Martin Sartin ran two yards for a score late in the third quarter to tie the game 10-10. Neuheisel then completed a 19-yard touchdown pass to Tim Moffett two minutes into the final period for the winning score. San Diego held Tampa Bay to 72 passing yards and seven first downs.

San Diego	0	0	10	7 —	17
Tampa Bay	7	3	0	3 —	13

TB —Streater 26 pass from Reaves (Tiffin kick)
TB —FG Tiffin 41
SD —FG Gaffney 27
SD —Sartin 2 run (Gaffney kick)
SD —Moffett 19 pass from Neuheisel (Gaffney kick)
TB —FG Tiffin 45

Washington 38, New York Giants 12—At Giants Stadium, attendance 9,123. Lionel Vital rushed for 128 yards on 27 carries and scored on a 22-yard touchdown run as the Redskins beat the Giants. Wayne Wilson added a pair of scoring runs (one and three yards) to give Washington a 24-3 first-half lead. Washington's Ted Wilson gained 142 yards on seven punt returns and caught a 64-yard pass from Ed Rubbert for a score in the fourth quarter. The Redskins' defense held the Giants to 47 yards rushing.

Washington	3	21	7	7 —	38
N.Y. Giants	3	0	9	0 —	12

NYG —FG Benyola 45
Wash —FG Ariri 22
Wash —W. Wilson 1 run (Ariri kick)
Wash —Vital 22 run (Ariri kick)
Wash —W. Wilson 3 run (Ariri kick)
NYG —Lovelady 23 pass from Busch (kick failed)
Wash —T. Wilson 64 pass from Rubbert (Ariri kick)
NYG —FG Benyola 20
Wash —Jessie 14 run (Ariri kick)

Monday, October 12

Denver 30, Los Angeles Raiders 14—At Mile High Stadium, attendance 61,230. Joe Dudek ran for two first-quarter touchdowns to highlight the Broncos' victory over the Raiders. Dudek, who carried 23 times for 128 yards, opened Denver's scoring with touchdown runs of seven and three yards in the first quarter. Ken Karcher threw a 10-yard touchdown pass to Rick Massie and Nathan Poole ran one yard for a score in the second half to complete the Broncos' scoring. The Raiders' only scoring came in the second quarter when Vince Evans threw a three-yard touchdown pass to Mario Perry and Rick Calhoun returned a punt 55 yards for a score. The Broncos' defense had three interceptions and two fumble recoveries.

L.A. Raiders	0	14	0	0 —	14
Denver	14	3	6	7 —	30

Den —Dudek 7 run (Clendenen kick)
Den —Dudek 3 run (Clendenen kick)
Raiders —Perry 3 pass from Evans (Hardy kick)
Raiders —Calhoun 55 punt return (Hardy kick)
Den —FG Clendenen 31
Den —Massie 10 pass from Karcher (kick failed)
Den —Poole 1 run (Clendenen kick)

Sixth Week Summaries

Standings

American Football Conference

Eastern Division

	W	L	T	Pct.	Pts.	OP
New England	3	2	0	.600	97	98
N.Y. Jets	3	2	0	.600	135	127
Buffalo	2	3	0	.400	81	125
Indianapolis	2	3	0	.400	91	73
Miami	2	3	0	.400	137	99

Central Division

	W	L	T	Pct.	Pts.	OP
Cleveland	3	2	0	.600	119	63
Houston	3	2	0	.600	112	91
Pittsburgh	3	2	0	.600	110	101
Cincinnati	2	3	0	.400	75	102

Western Division

	W	L	T	Pct.	Pts.	OP
San Diego	4	1	0	.800	91	83
Denver	3	1	1	.700	123	105
L.A. Raiders	3	2	0	.600	113	77
Seattle	3	2	0	.600	131	105
Kansas City	1	4	0	.200	68	159

National Football Conference

Eastern Division

	W	L	T	Pct.	Pts.	OP
Washington	4	1	0	.800	133	85
Dallas	3	2	0	.600	115	97
St. Louis	2	3	0	.400	121	122
Philadelphia	1	4	0	.200	86	143
N.Y. Giants	0	5	0	.000	69	135

Central Division

	W	L	T	Pct.	Pts.	OP
Chicago	4	1	0	.800	133	51
Tampa Bay	3	2	0	.600	115	84
Green Bay	2	2	1	.500	72	82
Minnesota	2	3	0	.400	88	105
Detroit	1	4	0	.200	86	145

Western Division

	W	L	T	Pct.	Pts.	OP
San Francisco	4	1	0	.800	144	122
New Orleans	3	2	0	.600	120	99
Atlanta	2	3	0	.400	84	141
L.A. Rams	1	4	0	.200	93	123

Sunday, October 18

Cleveland 34, Cincinnati 0—At Riverfront Stadium, attendance 40,179. Gary Danielson completed 25 of 31 passes for 281 yards and four touchdowns as Cleveland blanked Cincinnati. Danielson's scoring passes to Brian Brennan (6 yards), Derek Tennell (3), and Perry Kemp (22), along with Jeff Jaeger's 45-yard field goal, gave the Browns a commanding 24-0 first-half lead. Jaeger added a 33-yard field goal and Kemp caught his second touchdown, a 19-yarder from Danielson, to cap the scoring. Brennan had a career-high 10 receptions for 139 yards. The Browns held the Bengals to six first downs and 95 yards total offense.

Cleveland	7	17	3	7 —	34
Cincinnati	0	0	0	0 —	0

Clev —Brennan 6 pass from Danielson (Jaeger kick)
Clev —Tennell 3 pass from Danielson (Jaeger kick)
Clev —FG Jaeger 45
Clev —Kemp 22 pass from Danielson (Jaeger kick)
Clev —FG Jaeger 33
Clev —Kemp 19 pass from Danielson (Jaeger kick)

Denver 26, Kansas City 17—At Arrowhead Stadium, attendance 20,296. Denver's Bobby Micho caught nine passes for 105 yards and two touchdowns to help the Broncos defeat the Chiefs. Ken Karcher completed 25 of 39 attempts for 275 yards for Denver, including scoring passes to Micho of 26 and 5 yards. Jim Ryan sacked Doug Hudson in the end zone for a safety in the first quarter to open Denver's scoring. Shane Swanson, who caught a 35-yard touchdown pass from Karcher in the second quarter, set a team record with 290 all-purpose yards. Kansas City linebacker Bob Harris made 23 tackles, including 16 solo stops.

Denver	9	10	0	7	— 26
Kansas City	7	7	3	0	— 17

Den —Safety, Ryan tackled Hudson in end zone
Den —Micho 26 pass from Karcher (Clendenen kick)
KC —Fields 85 punt return (Hamrick kick)
Den —FG Clendenen 35
KC —Parker 4 run (Hamrick kick)
Den —Swanson 35 pass from Karcher (Clendenen kick)
KC —FG Hamrick 25
Den —Micho 5 pass from Karcher (Clendenen kick)

Pittsburgh 21, Indianapolis 7—At Three Rivers Stadium, attendance 34,627. Steve Bono threw for two touchdowns, and the Steelers' defense had five takeaways, to lead Pittsburgh past Indianapolis. Gerald Williams's fumble recovery in the first quarter set up Bono's three-yard scoring pass to John Stallworth for a 7-0 lead. Bono's 20-yard scoring pass to Merril Hoge broke a 7-7 tie in the fourth quarter. Chuck Sanders ran 10 yards for a score with three minutes to play to seal the win. Stallworth caught five passes for 54 yards to become the eighteenth NFL player to catch over 500 passes in a career (504). Earnest Jackson carried 24 times for 134 yards in his third 100-yard game of the season.

Indianapolis	0	7	0	0	— 7
Pittsburgh	7	0	0	14	— 21

Pitt —Stallworth 3 pass from Bono (Trout kick)
Ind —Murray 20 pass from Kiel (Jordan kick)
Pitt —Hoge 20 pass from Bono (Trout kick)
Pitt —Sanders 10 run (Trout kick)

Atlanta 24, Los Angeles Rams 20—At Atlanta-Fulton County Stadium, attendance 15,813. Erik Kramer threw for 338 yards and three second-half touchdowns to rally the Falcons to a 24-20 come-from-behind victory. Trailing 17-0 in the third quarter, Kramer connected on scoring passes to Milton Barney (five yards) and Joe McIntosh (one). Greg Davis added a 35-yard field goal to narrow the deficit to 20-17. Lenny Taylor then scored on a 19-yard pass from Kramer for the go-ahead score. Lyndell Jones's interception on the final play of the game preserved the win.

L.A. Rams	7	10	3	0	— 20
Atlanta	0	0	7	17	— 24

Rams —Francis 2 pass from Dils (Lansford kick)
Rams —McDonald 13 pass from Dils (Lansford kick)
Rams —FG Lansford 40
Atl —Barney 5 pass from Kramer (Davis kick)
Rams —FG Lansford 40
Atl —McIntosh 1 pass from Kramer (Davis kick)
Atl —FG Davis 35
Atl —Taylor 19 pass from Kramer (Davis kick)

New York Jets 37, Miami 31—At Giants Stadium, attendance 18,249. Pat Ryan's eight-yard touchdown pass to Eddie Hunter with 34 seconds remaining in overtime lifted the Jets to a 37-31 victory over the Dolphins. With Miami leading 10-0 in the second quarter, Ryan threw scoring passes of 35 yards to Michael Harper and 7 yards to Hunter. Pat Ragusa added a 34-yard field goal to give New York a 17-10 lead at halftime. Dennis Bligen ran seven yards for a score and Ryan connected with Stan Hunter on a five-yard touchdown pass to give the Jets a 31-17 lead. But the Dolphins scored two touchdowns in the final four minutes of regulation play to force overtime. George Radachowsky's interception return to Miami's 31-yard line set up the Jets' winning score.

Miami	10	0	7	14	0	— 31
N.Y. Jets	0	17	0	14	6	— 37

Mia —FG Beecher 19
Mia —Smith 5 pass from Mackey (Beecher kick)
NYJ —Harper 35 pass from Ryan (Ragusa kick)
NYJ —E. Hunter 7 pass from Ryan (Ragusa kick)
NYJ —FG Ragusa 34
Mia —Mackey 1 run (Beecher kick)
NYJ —Bligen 7 run (Ragusa kick)
NYJ —S. Hunter 5 pass from Ryan (Ragusa kick)
Mia —Mackey 5 run (Beecher kick)
Mia —Lewis 1 pass from Mackey (Beecher kick)
NYJ —E. Hunter 8 pass from Ryan (no kick)

New England 21, Houston 7—At Astrodome, attendance 26,294. Doug Flutie, who threw for 199 yards and rushed for 43 more in his first game with the Patriots, led New England to the win. Flutie fired a 27-yard scoring pass to Larry Linne to give the Patriots an early first-quarter lead, but Houston tied the score on Brent Pease's 36-yard touchdown pass to Oliver Williams. The Patriots regained the lead when Michael LeBlanc ran for a three-yard score. Andre Tippett blocked Tony Zendejas's field-goal attempt in the last two minutes of the first half, and Raymond Clayborn returned it 71 yards for the final score of the game.

New England	14	7	0	0	— 21
Houston	7	0	0	0	— 7

NE —Linne 27 pass from Flutie (Franklin kick)
Hou —Williams 36 pass from Pease (Zendejas kick)
NE —LeBlanc 3 run (Franklin kick)
NE —Clayborn 71 blocked field goal return (Franklin kick)

New Orleans 19, Chicago 17—At Soldier Field, attendance 46,813. Florian Kempf kicked four field goals, including a 21-yarder with 4:30 to play, to help the Saints knock the Bears from the unbeaten ranks. Chicago jumped to a 10-point lead on Tim Lashar's 22-yard field goal and Chris Brewer's eight-yard scoring catch. New Orleans cut the Bears' lead to 17-10 when Kempf kicked a 48-yard field goal and John Fourcade completed a 14-yard touchdown pass to Eric Martin. Kempf also kicked field goals of 31 and 42 yards in the second half.

New Orleans	0	10	3	6	— 19
Chicago	10	7	0	0	— 17

Chi —FG Lashar 22
Chi —Brewer 8 pass from Bradley (Lashar kick)
NO —FG Kempf 48
Chi —Kozlowski 18 pass from Bradley (Lashar kick)
NO —Martin 14 pass from Fourcade (Kempf kick)
NO —FG Kempf 31
NO —FG Kempf 42
NO —FG Kempf 21

Buffalo 6, New York Giants 3—At Rich Stadium, attendance 15,737. Todd Schlopy's 27-yard field goal with 19 seconds remaining in overtime lifted the Bills over the Giants. After three plays from the one-yard line in the fourth quarter, the Giants settled on George Benyola's 22-yard field goal to give New York a 3-0 edge. Buffalo drove 56 yards to tie the score on Schlopy's 31-yard field goal. The Giants had a chance to win the game in regulation time, but Benyola's 40-yard field-goal attempt was wide left. Buffalo running back Carl Byrum had 139 yards on 25 carries, including a 30-yard run to set up Schlopy's winning kick.

N.Y. Giants	0	0	0	3	0	— 3
Buffalo	0	0	0	3	3	— 6

NYG —FG Benyola 22
Buff —FG Schlopy 31
Buff —FG Schlopy 27

Green Bay 16, Philadelphia 10—At Lambeau Field, attendance 35,842. James Hargrove ran five yards for a touchdown 5:04 into overtime as the Packers defeated the Eagles. Kevin Willhite rushed for 100 yards on 16 carries and Lee Morris caught six passes for 132 yards, including a 46-yard touchdown catch from Alan Risher in the third quarter, to spark the Packers' victory. Philadelphia sent the game into overtime on Dave Jacobs's 44-yard field goal with 3:58 to play. Hargrove's winning score capped a 10-play, 76-yard drive on the Packers' first possession of overtime.

Philadelphia	7	0	0	3	0	— 10
Green Bay	0	3	7	0	6	— 16

Phil —Ross 5 pass from Tinsley (Jacobs kick)
GB —FG Zendejas 42
GB —Lee Morris 46 pass from Risher (Zendejas kick)
Phil —FG Jacobs 44
GB —Hargrove 5 run (no kick)

San Francisco 34, St. Louis 28—At Candlestick Park, attendance 38,094. Joe Montana threw for four touchdowns as the 49ers rallied to defeat the Cardinals and take sole possession of first place in the NFC West. Trailing 14-0 in the second quarter, Montana, who completed 31 of 39 passes for 334 yards, connected on scoring passes of 22 and 8 yards to Dwight Clark. Roger Craig then added two touchdowns on a one-yard run and a 36-yard reception from Montana to tie the game in the fourth quarter. Ron Heller caught a three-yard pass from Montana with 9:39 to play for the winning score.

St. Louis	7	14	7	0	— 28
San Francisco	0	14	7	13	— 34

StL —McAdoo 1 run (Gallery kick)
StL —Johnson 38 pass from Garza (Gallery kick)
SF —Clark 22 pass from Montana (Brockhaus kick)
StL —McAdoo 6 run (Gallery kick)
SF —Clark 8 pass from Montana (Brockhaus kick)
SF —Craig 1 run (Brockhaus kick)
StL —McAdoo 1 run (Gallery kick)
SF —Craig 36 pass from Montana (Brockhaus kick)
SF —Heller 3 pass from Montana (kick failed)

San Diego 23, Los Angeles Raiders 17—At Memorial Coliseum, attendance 23,541. Elvis Patterson returned an interception 75 yards for a touchdown with 18 seconds remaining to give the Chargers a 23-17 win over the Raiders. San Diego took a 7-0 lead on quarterback Rick Neuheisel's eight-yard touchdown run. The Raiders then rallied to take a 14-7 halftime advantage on quarterback Vince Evans's scoring passes of 7 and 32 yards to Carl Aikens. Al Williams's seven-yard scoring reception tied the game 17-17. The Chargers' victory marked their first win ever over the Raiders in Los Angeles.

San Diego	7	0	0	16	— 23
L.A. Raiders	0	14	0	3	— 17

SD —Neuheisel 8 run (Gaffney kick)
Raiders —Aikens 7 pass from Evans (Bahr kick)
Raiders —Aikens 32 pass from Evans (Bahr kick)
SD —FG Gaffney 21
Raiders —FG Bahr 33
SD —A. Williams 7 pass from Kelley (Gaffney kick)
SD —Patterson 75 interception return (kick failed)

Seattle 37, Detroit 14—At Pontiac Silverdome, attendance 8,310. Jeff Kemp completed 20 of 27 passes for 344 yards and a career-high four touchdowns to lead the Seahawks to victory. Seattle opened a 21-0 lead in the first quarter on Kemp's scoring passes of 19, 21, and 2 yards to Steve Largent. Jimmy Teal caught a 12-yard touchdown pass, and Norm Johnson kicked a 43-yard field goal, as the Seahawks built a 30-7 halftime lead. Michael Morton ran one yard for a touchdown to cap Seattle's scoring. Largent broke his own club records with 15 receptions for 261 yards, and notched his fortieth career 100-yard game.

Seattle	21	9	7	0	— 37
Detroit	0	7	0	7	— 14

Sea —Largent 19 pass from Kemp (Johnson kick)
Sea —Largent 21 pass from Kemp (Johnson kick)
Sea —Largent 2 pass from Kemp (Johnson kick)
Det —Bradley 5 pass from Hons (Prindle kick)
Sea —Teal 12 pass from Kemp (pass failed)
Sea —FG Johnson 43
Sea —Morton 1 run (Johnson kick)
Det —Bradley 3 pass from Hons (Prindle kick)

Tampa Bay 20, Minnesota 10—At Tampa Stadium, attendance 20,850. The Buccaneers' defense turned a fumble recovery and an interception into 14 points to highlight Tampa Bay's win over the Vikings. With the score tied 3-3 in the third quarter, Arthur Wells recovered a Minnesota fumble in the end zone for a score. The Vikings answered with a touchdown on Tony Adams's 23-yard pass to Jeff Womack, but Kevin Walker's 30-yard interception return for a touchdown late in the third quarter put the Buccaneers ahead for good.

Minnesota	3	0	7	0	— 10
Tampa Bay	3	0	14	3	— 20

Minn —FG Dawson 34
TB —FG Tiffin 50
TB —Wells recovered fumble in end zone (Tiffin kick)
Minn —Womack 23 pass from Adams (Dawson kick)
TB —Walker 30 interception return (Tiffin kick)
TB —FG Tiffin 37

Monday, October 19

Washington 13, Dallas 7—At Texas Stadium, attendance 60,415. Obed Ariri kicked two field goals and Ted Wilson ran for a touchdown as the Redskins defeated the Cowboys. Ariri's first field goal, a 19-yarder, was set up by Bobby Curtis's fumble recovery. Wilson's 16-yard scoring run on the Redskins' opening drive of the second half gave Washington a 10-0 lead. Ariri's 39-yard field goal in the fourth quarter completed the scoring. Lionel Vital's 136 yards rushing helped Washington maintain a 36:05 to 23:55 time-of-possession advantage.

Washington	3	0	7	3	— 13
Dallas	0	0	7	0	— 7

Wash —FG Ariri 19
Wash —Wilson 16 run (Ariri kick)
Dall —Edwards 38 pass from D. White (Brady kick)
Wash —FG Ariri 39

Seventh Week Summaries

Standings

American Football Conference

Eastern Division

	W	L	T	Pct.	Pts.	OP
Buffalo	3	3	0	.500	115	156
Indianapolis	3	3	0	.500	121	89
New England	3	3	0	.500	113	128
N.Y. Jets	3	3	0	.500	151	144
Miami	2	4	0	.333	168	133

Central Division

	W	L	T	Pct.	Pts.	OP
Cleveland	4	2	0	.667	149	80
Houston	4	2	0	.667	149	124
Pittsburgh	4	2	0	.667	133	121
Cincinnati	2	4	0	.333	95	125

Western Division

	W	L	T	Pct.	Pts.	OP
San Diego	5	1	0	.833	133	104
Seattle	4	2	0	.667	166	118
Denver	3	2	1	.583	150	139
L.A. Raiders	3	3	0	.500	126	112
Kansas City	1	5	0	.200	89	201

National Football Conference

Eastern Division

	W	L	T	Pct.	Pts.	OP
Washington	5	1	0	.833	150	101
Dallas	3	3	0	.500	135	134
Philadelphia	2	4	0	.333	123	163
St. Louis	2	4	0	.333	128	152
N.Y. Giants	1	5	0	.167	99	142

Central Division

Chicago	5	1	0	.833	160	77
Green Bay	3	2	1	.583	106	115
Minnesota	3	3	0	.500	122	132
Tampa Bay	3	3	0	.500	141	111
Detroit	1	5	0	.167	119	179

Western Division

San Francisco	5	1	0	.833	168	144
New Orleans	3	3	0	.500	142	123
Atlanta	2	4	0	.333	117	178
L.A. Rams	1	5	0	.167	110	153

Sunday, October 25

Houston 37, Atlanta 33—At Astrodome, attendance 29,062. Warren Moon threw three touchdown passes, including a 14-yarder to Clyde Duncan with 27 seconds remaining, to rally the Oilers past the Falcons. Moon, who completed 15 of 34 passes for 242 yards, also fired a 41-yard scoring pass to Duncan late in the second quarter to tie the game 13-13. Mike Rozier ran for 144 yards and tied the score 27-27 on a 14-yard touchdown run early in the fourth quarter. Mick Luckhurst kicked four field goals for the Falcons, including an 18-yarder late in the fourth quarter to give the Falcons a 33-30 lead, before Moon drove the Oilers 80 yards for the decisive score.

Atlanta	3	10	14	6	— 33
Houston	3	10	7	17	— 37

Atl —FG Luckhurst 39
Hou —FG Zendejas 31
Atl —FG Luckhurst 37
Hou —FG Zendejas 43
Atl —Dixon 10 pass from Campbell (Luckhurst kick)
Hou —Duncan 41 pass from Moon (Zendejas kick)
Hou —Givins 8 pass from Moon (Zendejas kick)
Atl —Bailey 29 pass from Campbell (Luckhurst kick)
Atl —Whisenhunt 3 pass from Campbell (Luckhurst kick)
Hou —Rozier 14 run (Zendejas kick)
Hou —FG Zendejas 24
Atl —FG Luckhurst 45
Atl —FG Luckhurst 18
Hou —Duncan 14 pass from Moon (Zendejas kick)

Buffalo 34, Miami 31—At Joe Robbie Stadium, attendance 61,295. Scott Norwood's 27-yard field goal 4:12 into overtime gave the Bills a dramatic come-from-behind win over the Dolphins. Dan Marino completed 24 of 46 passes for 303 yards and had three scoring passes to give Miami a 21-3 lead at halftime. Robb Riddick led Buffalo's comeback by running for two scores, and added another on a 17-yard pass from Jim Kelly, to give the Bills a 31-24 fourth-quarter lead. Kelly, who completed 29 of 39 for 359 yards, also threw a 14-yard touchdown pass to Chris Burkett. Marino's 12-yard touchdown pass to Mark Clayton, which sent the game into overtime, capped an 11-play, 80-yard drive in the final 63 seconds.

Buffalo	0	3	14	14	3	— 34
Miami	14	7	0	10	0	— 31

Mia —Duper 5 pass from Marino (Reveiz kick)
Mia —Pruitt 25 pass from Marino (Reveiz kick)
Mia —Hardy 2 pass from Marino (Reveiz kick)
Buff —FG Norwood 41
Buff —Riddick 1 run (Norwood kick)
Buff —Burkett 14 pass from Kelly (Norwood kick)
Mia —FG Reveiz 46
Buff —Riddick 1 run (Norwood kick)
Buff —Riddick 17 pass from Kelly (Norwood kick)
Mia —Clayton 12 pass from Marino (Reveiz kick)
Buff —FG Norwood 27

Chicago 27, Tampa Bay 26—At Tampa Stadium, attendance 70,747. Jim McMahon, who relieved an injured Mike Tomczak in the second half, threw for one touchdown and ran for another to help the Bears edge the Buccaneers. Tampa Bay jumped to a 20-0 lead in the first quarter on Steve DeBerg touchdown passes of seven yards to Calvin Magee and 28 yards to Jeff Smith, and Winston Moss recovered a Tomczak fumble in the end zone. Neal Anderson scored on a 38-yard run, and Dennis McKinnon returned a punt 65 yards for a score, to narrow Chicago's deficit to 20-14. Tampa Bay took a 26-14 lead midway through the third quarter on Donald Igwebuike's field goals of 46 and 37 yards. McMahon scored on a one-yard keeper, and then drove the Bears 72 yards to set up a six-yard pass to Anderson for the winning score.

Chicago	0	14	0	13	— 27
Tampa Bay	20	3	3	0	— 26

TB —Magee 7 pass from DeBerg (Igwebuike kick)
TB —Smith 28 pass from DeBerg (Igwebuike kick)
TB —Moss recovered fumble in end zone (kick blocked)
Chi —Anderson 38 run (Butler kick)
Chi —McKinnon 65 punt return (Butler kick)
TB —FG Igwebuike 46
TB —FG Igwebuike 37
Chi —McMahon 1 run (kick failed)
Chi —Anderson 6 pass from McMahon (Butler kick)

Pittsburgh 23, Cincinnati 20—At Three Rivers Stadium, attendance 53,692. Gary Anderson's third field goal of the day, a 20-yarder with 1:47 remaining, lifted the Steelers over the Bengals. Trailing 20-10, Pittsburgh scored 13 unanswered points in the fourth quarter for the win. Anderson kicked a 21-yard field goal and John Stallworth caught a 12-yard pass from Mark Malone to tie the game 20-20. After Bryan Hinkle intercepted a Boomer Esiason pass, Malone hit Stallworth on a 45-yard bomb to set up Anderson's winning kick. Stallworth's seven catches for 100 yards marked his twenty-fifth 100-yard game. Esiason completed 20 of 32 passes for 303 yards and two touchdowns.

Cincinnati	7	7	6	0	— 20
Pittsburgh	3	0	7	13	— 23

Cin —Kinnebrew 2 run (Breech kick)
Pitt —FG Anderson 45
Cin —Martin 41 pass from Esiason (Breech kick)
Pitt —Hall 25 run with lateral after Hinkle intercepted pass (Anderson kick)
Cin —Jennings 9 pass from Esiason (kick failed)
Pitt —FG Anderson 21
Pitt —Stallworth 12 pass from Malone (Anderson kick)
Pitt —FG Anderson 20

Philadelphia 37, Dallas 20—At Veterans Stadium, attendance 60,497. Randall Cunningham and John Spagnola connected on a pair of touchdown passes, and Paul McFadden kicked three field goals, to power the Eagles over the Cowboys. McFadden kicked field goals from 46 and 45 yards, and Cunningham hit Spagnola for a 10-yard pass to give Philadelphia a 13-10 halftime edge. Anthony Toney ran one yard for a score to cap a nine-play, 75-yard drive in the third quarter. McFadden's 21-yard field goal, and Spagnola's five-yard pass from Cunningham, extended the Eagles' lead to 30-13. Philadelphia's Clyde Simmons had two sacks, one fumble recovery, and blocked a field goal to earn NFC defensive player of the week honors.

Dallas	3	7	3	7	— 20
Philadelphia	3	10	7	17	— 37

Dall —FG Ruzek 23
Phil —FG McFadden 46
Phil —FG McFadden 45
Phil —Spagnola 10 pass from Cunningham (McFadden kick)
Dall —Walker 1 run (Ruzek kick)
Dall —FG Ruzek 25
Phil —Toney 1 run (McFadden kick)
Phil —FG McFadden 21
Phil —Spagnola 5 pass from Cunningham (McFadden kick)
Dall —Dorsett 19 pass from D. White (Ruzek kick)
Phil —Byars 1 run (McFadden kick)

Green Bay 34, Detroit 33—At Pontiac Silverdome, attendance 27,278. Al Del Greco's 45-yard field goal with one minute remaining lifted the Packers over the Lions. Green Bay took a 21-point lead in the first quarter on scoring runs by Brent Fullwood (1 yard) and Kenneth Davis (39), and Don Majkowski's 70-yard pass to Walter Stanley. Del Greco's 22-yard field goal and Davis's 28-yard touchdown run put the Packers ahead 31-7 in the second quarter. But Chuck Long completed touchdown passes of 12 and 22 yards to Pete Mandley to narrow the Lions' deficit to 31-26. The Lions pulled ahead 33-31 on Garry James's two-yard touchdown run. Green Bay's defense held Detroit to 17 yards rushing.

Green Bay	21	10	0	3	— 34
Detroit	0	16	3	14	— 33

GB —Fullwood 1 run (Del Greco kick)
GB —Stanley 70 pass from Majkowski (Del Greco kick)
GB —Davis 39 run (Del Greco kick)
GB —FG Del Greco 22
Det —Bland 11 pass from Long (Murray kick)
GB —Davis 28 run (Del Greco kick)
Det —Mandley 12 pass from Long (Murray kick)
Det —Safety, Jamison tackled Stanley in end zone
Det —FG Murray 23
Det —Mandley 22 pass from Long (Murray kick)
Det —James 2 run (Murray kick)
GB —FG Del Greco 45

San Diego 42, Kansas City 21—At San Diego Jack Murphy Stadium, attendance 47,972. Dan Fouts threw two touchdown passes and ran for another as the Chargers defeated the Chiefs to remain in first place in the AFC West. Fouts, who completed 24 of 34 passes for 293 yards, threw scoring passes to Wes Chandler (10 yards) and Kellen Winslow (19). Les Miller recovered a fumble in the end zone, and Gary Anderson and Fouts each ran one yard for a score to give San Diego a commanding 35-14 halftime lead. Anderson added a one-yard run in the fourth quarter to cap the scoring. Kansas City quarterback Bill Kenney completed 22 of 38 for 328 yards and threw touchdown passes of 14 and 63 yards to Carlos Carson.

Kansas City	0	14	7	0	— 21
San Diego	14	21	0	7	— 42

SD —Chandler 10 pass from Fouts (Abbott kick)
SD —Anderson 1 run (Abbott kick)
SD —Miller fumble recovery in end zone (Abbott kick)
SD —Fouts 1 run (Abbott kick)
KC —Carson 14 pass from Kenney (Lowery kick)
SD —Winslow 19 pass from Fouts (Abbott kick)
KC —Carson 63 pass from Kenney (Lowery kick)
KC —Okoye 1 run (Lowery kick)
SD —Anderson 1 run (Abbott kick)

Indianapolis 30, New England 16—At Hoosier Dome, attendance 48,850. Jack Trudeau completed 17 of 28 passes for 239 yards and one touchdown, and Dean Biasucci kicked three field goals, to help the Colts defeat the Patriots. Trudeau hit Matt Bouza with a 25-yard scoring pass and Biasucci kicked a 48-yard field goal to give Indianapolis a 10-6 halftime edge, which they never relinquished. Biasucci added field goals of 48 and 24 yards in the third quarter, and Donnell Thompson returned a fumble 28 yards for another score to give the Colts a 23-6 lead. Terry Wright blocked a punt in the fourth quarter to set up the Colts' final score, a 12-yard touchdown run by Albert Bentley. Patriots wide receiver Stanley Morgan caught seven passes for 102 yards.

New England	3	3	7	3	— 16
Indianapolis	0	10	13	7	— 30

NE —FG Franklin 38
NE —FG Franklin 31
Ind —Bouza 25 pass from Trudeau (Biasucci kick)
Ind —FG Biasucci 48
Ind —FG Biasucci 48
Ind —FG Biasucci 24
Ind —Thompson 28 fumble recovery return (Biasucci kick)
NE —Morgan 27 pass from Eason (Franklin kick)
NE —FG Franklin 49
Ind —Bentley 12 run (Biasucci kick)

Washington 17, New York Jets 16—At Robert F. Kennedy Stadium, attendance 53,497. Ali Haji-Sheikh's 28-yard field goal with 54 seconds remaining lifted the Redskins to a 17-16 victory over the Jets and into sole possession of first place in the NFC East. Washington opened the scoring on Jay Schroeder's 20-yard pass to Gary Clark. The Jets answered with a pair of Pat Leahy field goals from 33 and 23 yards, and Mickey Shuler's 15-yard touchdown catch from Ken O'Brien. Leahy's 21-yard field goal in the fourth quarter put the Jets ahead 16-7. But Schroeder hit Kelvin Bryant with a two-yard scoring pass with less than six minutes remaining, and then drove Washington 68 yards in nine plays to set up Haji-Sheikh's winning kick. Charles Mann registered three of the Redskins' six sacks.

N.Y. Jets	0	3	10	3	— 16
Washington	0	7	0	10	— 17

Wash —Clark 20 pass from Schroeder (Haji-Sheikh kick)
NYJ —FG Leahy 33
NYJ —FG Leahy 23
NYJ —Shuler 15 pass from O'Brien (Leahy kick)
NYJ —FG Leahy 21
Wash —Bryant 2 pass from Schroeder (Haji-Sheikh kick)
Wash —FG Haji-Sheikh 28

New York Giants 30, St. Louis 7—At Giants Stadium, attendance 74,391. Phil Simms completed 17 of 21 passes for 253 yards and three touchdowns as the defending Super Bowl champions registered their first win of the season. Simms hit Mark Bavaro with a three-yard scoring pass early in the first quarter. He also completed touchdown passes of 16 and 28 yards to Lionel Manuel that put the Giants ahead 27-0 in the fourth quarter. Raul Allegre kicked field goals of 28, 35, and 32 yards for the Giants. Neil Lomax hit Jay Novacek with an 18-yard pass late in the game to prevent the shutout. The Giants' defense held the Cardinals to 51 yards rushing. Phil Simms was named NFC offensive player of the week.

St. Louis	0	0	0	7	— 7
N.Y. Giants	14	3	3	10	— 30

NYG —Bavaro 3 pass from Simms (Allegre kick)
NYG —Manuel 16 pass from Simms (Allegre kick)
NYG —FG Allegre 28
NYG —FG Allegre 35
NYG —Manuel 28 pass from Simms (Allegre kick)
NYG —FG Allegre 32
StL —Novacek 18 pass from Lomax (Gallery kick)

San Francisco 24, New Orleans 22—At Louisiana Superdome, attendance 60,497. Joe Montana threw for 256 yards and three touchdowns as the 49ers edged the Saints. San Francisco took a 17-6 halftime lead on Montana's scoring passes of eight yards to Jerry Rice and 39 yards to Ron Heller. Saints kicker Morten Andersen, who tied his club record by kicking five field goals, connected on a pair of 19-yarders, and Alvin Toles returned a blocked punt 11 yards for a score to give the Saints a 19-17 edge. Montana's 14-yard touchdown pass to Mike Wilson early in the fourth quarter proved to be decisive.

San Francisco	7	10	0	7	— 24
New Orleans	3	3	6	10	— 22

NO —FG Andersen 39
SF —Rice 8 pass from Montana (Wersching kick)
SF —Heller 39 pass from Montana (Wersching kick)
SF —FG Wersching 31
NO —FG Andersen 49
NO —FG Andersen 19
NO —FG Andersen 19
NO —Toles 11 blocked punt return (Andersen kick)
SF —Wilson 14 pass from Montana (Wersching kick)
NO —FG Andersen 37

Seattle 35, Los Angeles Raiders 13—At Memorial Coliseum, attendance 52,735. Curt Warner and Ray Butler each scored a pair of touchdowns to power the Seahawks past the Raiders. Warner, who rushed for 112 yards on 29 carries, ran for touchdowns of one and six yards in the first half. Butler had scoring catches of 15 and 31 yards on passes from Dave Krieg. Fredd Young's 50-yard interception return for a score gave Seattle a commanding 28-0 halftime lead. Seattle's defense held the Raiders to 44 yards rushing, while the Seahawks maintained a 37:47 to 22:13 time-of-possession advantage.

Seattle	7	21	0	7	— 35
L.A. Raiders	0	0	7	6	— 13

Sea —Warner 1 run (Johnson kick)
Sea —R. Butler 15 pass from Krieg (Johnson kick)
Sea —Warner 6 run (Johnson kick)
Sea —Young 50 interception return (Johnson kick)
Raiders —Christensen 7 pass from Wilson (Bahr kick)
Raiders —D. Williams 14 pass from Wilson (kick blocked)
Sea —R. Butler 31 pass from Krieg (Johnson kick)

Monday, October 26

Cleveland 30, Los Angeles Rams 17—At Cleveland Stadium, attendance 76,933. Felix Wright returned one of his two interceptions for a touchdown to highlight the Browns' victory over the Rams. Wright's 68-yard interception set up the only score of the first quarter, a 23-yard field goal by Jeff Jaeger. Wright's second interception, which he returned 40 yards for a score, helped Cleveland to a 23-7 halftime lead. Bernie Kosar's 53-yard scoring pass to Brian Brennan two plays into the second half capped the Browns' scoring.

L.A. Rams	0	7	10	0	— 17
Cleveland	3	20	7	0	— 30

Clev —FG Jaeger 23
Clev —Mack 16 run (Jaeger kick)
Clev —Wright 40 interception return (Jaeger kick)
Clev —FG Jaeger 48
Rams —Dickerson 27 run (Lansford kick)
Clev —FG Jaeger 41
Clev —Brennan 53 pass from Kosar (Jaeger kick)
Rams —White 1 run (Lansford kick)
Rams —FG Lansford 27

Minnesota 34, Denver 27—At Metrodome, attendance 51,011. D.J. Dozier tied a club record by rushing for three touchdowns (from one, three, and five yards) to help the Vikings defeat the Broncos. Wade Wilson added a one-yard run and also hit Leo Lewis with a five-yard scoring pass in the fourth quarter to give Minnesota a 34-17 lead. Darrin Nelson gained 98 yards on 11 carries, including a 72-yard run to set up Dozier's three-yard touchdown run. Nelson's 72-yard run from scrimmage without a touchdown set a club record. The Vikings-Broncos game was played on Monday due to a conflict with the Twins-Cardinals World Series game on Sunday.

Denver	7	10	0	10	— 27
Minnesota	7	7	13	7	— 34

Den —Johnson 25 pass from Elway (Karlis kick)
Minn —W. Wilson 1 run (C. Nelson kick)
Den —Elway 1 run (Karlis kick)
Minn —Dozier 1 run (C. Nelson kick)
Den —FG Karlis 43
Minn —Dozier 3 run (kick failed)
Minn —Dozier 5 run (C. Nelson kick)
Minn —Lewis 5 pass from W. Wilson (C. Nelson kick)
Den —Lang 4 pass from Elway (Karlis kick)
Den —FG Karlis 51

Eighth Week Summaries

Standings

American Football Conference

Eastern Division	W	L	T	Pct.	Pts.	OP
Indianapolis	4	3	0	.571	140	103
New England	4	3	0	.571	139	151
Buffalo	3	4	0	.429	122	183
Miami	3	4	0	.429	203	157
N.Y. Jets	3	4	0	.429	165	163
Central Division						
Houston	5	2	0	.714	180	153
Cleveland	4	3	0	.571	173	107
Pittsburgh	4	3	0	.571	157	156
Cincinnati	2	5	0	.286	124	156
Western Division						
San Diego	6	1	0	.857	160	128
Seattle	5	2	0	.714	194	135
Denver	4	2	1	.643	184	139
L.A. Raiders	3	4	0	.429	149	138
Kansas City	1	6	0	.143	117	232

National Football Conference

Eastern Division	W	L	T	Pct.	Pts.	OP
Washington	6	1	0	.857	177	108
Dallas	4	3	0	.571	168	158
Philadelphia	3	4	0	.429	151	186
St. Louis	2	5	0	.286	151	180
N.Y. Giants	1	6	0	.143	123	175
Central Division						
Chicago	6	1	0	.857	191	105
Tampa Bay	4	3	0	.571	164	128
Green Bay	3	3	1	.500	123	138
Minnesota	3	4	0	.429	139	160
Detroit	1	6	0	.143	119	213
Western Division						
San Francisco	6	1	0	.857	199	154
New Orleans	4	3	0	.571	180	123
Atlanta	2	5	0	.286	117	216
L.A. Rams	1	6	0	.143	120	184

Sunday, November 1

San Diego 27, Cleveland 24—At San Diego Jack Murphy Stadium, attendance 55,381. Vince Abbott kicked a 33-yard field goal 2:16 into overtime to lift the Chargers over the Browns. San Diego rallied from a 24-14 third-quarter deficit to force the extra period on Dan Fouts's 22-yard touchdown pass to Lionel James and Abbott's 20-yard field goal. Fouts, who completed 25 of 42 passes for 315 yards, also had a 10-yard touchdown pass to Rod Bernstine in the first quarter. Vencie Glenn returned an interception 30 yards to Cleveland's 20-yard line to set up Abbott's winning kick.

Cleveland	7	7	10	0	0	— 24
San Diego	14	0	0	10	3	— 27

SD —James 15 run (Abbott kick)
Clev —Slaughter 20 pass from Kosar (Jaeger kick)
SD —Bernstine 10 pass from Fouts (Abbott kick)
Clev —Brennan 41 pass from Kosar (Jaeger kick)
Clev —FG Jaeger 41
Clev —Byner 1 run (Jaeger kick)
SD —James 22 pass from Fouts (Abbott kick)
SD —FG Abbott 20
SD —FG Abbott 33

Denver 34, Detroit 0—At Mile High Stadium, attendance 75,172. John Elway ran for two touchdowns and threw for another as the Broncos shut out the Lions. Elway, who scored on runs of three and seven yards, also completed a 35-yard scoring pass to Vance Johnson. Sammy Winder had 94 yards rushing, including a two-yard touchdown run, as Denver outgained Detroit 212 rushing yards to 63. Rich Karlis added field goals of 28 and 29 yards for the Broncos. The game marked Denver's first shutout since a 21-0 victory over Kansas City on September 23, 1984.

Detroit	0	0	0	0	— 0
Denver	17	7	0	10	— 34

Den —Elway 3 run (Karlis kick)
Den —FG Karlis 28
Den —Winder 2 run (Karlis kick)
Den —Johnson 35 pass from Elway (Karlis kick)
Den —Elway 7 run (Karlis kick)
Den —FG Karlis 29

Houston 31, Cincinnati 29—At Riverfront Stadium, attendance 52,700. Warren Moon's one-yard touchdown run with 55 seconds remaining helped the Oilers defeat the Bengals and move into first place in the AFC Central. Trailing 29-14 with less than seven minutes to play, Tony Zendejas kicked a 47-yard field goal and Spencer Tillman added a one-yard touchdown run to narrow the Bengals' lead to five points. Moon, who threw for 191 yards, also completed touchdown passes of seven yards to Jamie Williams and 16 yards to Curtis Duncan. Cincinnati's Boomer Esiason threw for a career-high 387 yards, and kicker Jim Breech kicked five field goals to tie Horst Muhlmann's club record.

Houston	7	0	7	17	— 31
Cincinnati	3	6	7	13	— 29

Cin —FG Breech 32
Hou —J. Williams 7 pass from Moon (Zendejas kick)
Cin —FG Breech 33
Cin —FG Breech 26
Cin —Brown 47 pass from Esiason (Breech kick)
Hou —Duncan 16 pass from Moon (Zendejas kick)
Cin —FG Breech 39
Cin —FG Breech 32
Cin —Muñoz 3 pass from Esiason (Breech kick)
Hou —FG Zendejas 47
Hou —Tillman 1 run (Zendejas kick)
Hou —Moon 1 run (Zendejas kick)

Indianapolis 19, New York Jets 14—At Giants Stadium, attendance 60,863. Albert Bentley rushed for 145 yards on 29 carries, and Dean Biasucci kicked a career-high four field goals, to lead the Colts over the Jets. Indianapolis took a 10-7 lead at the half on Biasucci's 36-yard field goal and Jack Trudeau's 44-yard flea-flicker touchdown pass to Matt Bouza. Biasucci added field goals of 44, 38, and 33 yards in the second half. Johnny Hector scored on runs of 12 and 20 yards for the Jets. Duane Bickett registered four of the Colts' seven sacks and was named AFC defensive player of the week.

Indianapolis	3	7	3	6	— 19
N.Y. Jets	0	7	0	7	— 14

Ind —FG Biasucci 36
Ind —Bouza 44 pass from Trudeau (Biasucci kick)
NYJ —Hector 12 run (Leahy kick)
Ind —FG Biasucci 44
Ind —FG Biasucci 38
Ind —FG Biasucci 33
NYJ —Hector 20 run (Leahy kick)

Chicago 31, Kansas City 28—At Soldier Field, attendance 63,498. Jim McMahon threw for three touchdowns, including two in the fourth quarter, as the Bears defeated the Chiefs. Bill Kenney got Kansas City off to a quick start by throwing scoring passes to Carlos Carson (29 yards) and Jonathan Hayes (15) to give the Chiefs a 14-0 lead. Chicago tied the game in the second quarter on Dennis Gentry's 88-yard kickoff return for a touchdown and McMahon's 28-yard scoring pass to Cap Boso. The Chiefs went ahead by 14 points again, but Kevin Butler kicked a 27-yard field goal and McMahon fired two fourth-quarter touchdowns to Willie Gault (25 and 38 yards) for the win. The game marked McMahon's first start of the 1987 season.

Kansas City	14	7	7	0	— 28
Chicago	7	7	3	14	— 31

KC —Carson 29 pass from Kenney (Lowery kick)
KC —Hayes 15 pass from Kenney (Lowery kick)
Chi —Gentry 88 kickoff return (Butler kick)
Chi —Boso 28 pass from McMahon (Butler kick)
KC —Moriarty 4 pass from Kenney (Lowery kick)
KC —Paige 43 pass from Kenney (Lowery kick)
Chi —FG Butler 27
Chi —Gault 25 pass from McMahon (Butler kick)
Chi —Gault 38 pass from McMahon (Butler kick)

New England 26, Los Angeles Raiders 23—At Sullivan Stadium, attendance 60,664. Tony Franklin kicked four field goals, including a 29-yarder with one second remaining, to lift the Patriots over the Raiders. New England went ahead 10-6 at the half on Franklin's 50-yard field goal and Tony Collins's 15-yard reception from running back Mosi Tatupu. Franklin added a pair of field goals from 25 and 27 yards in the third quarter, and Steve Grogan hit Irving Fryar on a 25-yard scoring pass to increase the Patriots' lead to 23-6. But Los Angeles scored 17 points in the final 12 minutes to tie the game, before Grogan marched New England to the Raiders' 24-yard line to set up Franklin's winning kick.

L.A. Raiders	3	3	0	17	— 23
New England	3	7	6	10	— 26

Raiders —FG Bahr 31
NE —FG Franklin 50
NE —Collins 15 pass from Tatupu (Franklin kick)
Raiders —FG Bahr 31
NE —FG Franklin 27
NE —FG Franklin 25
NE —Fryar 25 pass from Grogan (Franklin kick)
Raiders —Christensen 8 pass from Hilger (Bahr kick)
Raiders —Allen 2 run (Bahr kick)
Raiders —FG Bahr 39
NE —FG Franklin 29

Seattle 28, Minnesota 17—at Kingdome, attendance 61,134. Dave Krieg threw for three touchdowns, and Jeff Kemp added a fourth, to lead the Seahawks past the Vikings. Krieg opened the scoring with a four-yard pass to Daryl Turner. Curt Warner, who gained 94 yards on 23 carries, caught a 30-yard touchdown pass from Krieg in the second quarter to give Seattle a 14-10 halftime edge. Steve Largent's 27-yard scoring catch in the third quarter extended his NFL record for consecutive games with a reception to 144. Kemp, relieving Krieg in the fourth quarter, hit Ray Butler with a 28-yard touchdown pass to finish the Seahawks' scoring.

Minnesota	7	3	0	7	— 17
Seattle	7	7	7	7	— 28

Sea —Turner 4 pass from Krieg (Johnson kick)
Minn —Wilson 1 run (C. Nelson kick)
Sea —Warner 30 pass from Krieg (Johnson kick)
Minn —FG C. Nelson 29
Sea —Largent 27 pass from Krieg (Johnson kick)
Minn —Dozier 5 run (C. Nelson kick)
Sea —Butler 28 pass from Kemp (Johnson kick)

New Orleans 38, Atlanta 0—At Atlanta-Fulton County Stadium, attendance 42,196. Dalton Hilliard ran for two touchdowns, and Bobby Hebert passed for another as the Saints shut out the Falcons. New Orleans took a 21-0 halftime lead on Hebert's seven-yard pass to Mike Jones, Barry Word's one-yard scoring run, and Hilliard's five-yard touchdown jaunt. Hilliard (30-yard run), Morten Andersen (49-yard field goal), and Mel Gray (three-yard run) added second-half scores to complete the onslaught. Rueben Mayes ran for 119 yards on 19 carries for the Saints.

New Orleans	14	7	3	14	— 38
Atlanta	0	0	0	0	— 0

NO —Jones 7 pass from Hebert (Andersen kick)
NO —Word 1 run (Andersen kick)
NO —Hilliard 5 run (Andersen kick)
NO —FG Andersen 49
NO —Hilliard 30 run (Andersen kick)
NO —Gray 3 run (Andersen kick)

Philadelphia 28, St. Louis 23—At Busch Stadium, attendance 24,586. Randall Cunningham threw for three touchdowns, including a nine-yarder with 40 seconds remaining to Gregg Garrity, to lead the Eagles over the Cardinals. Cunningham, who completed 17 of 32 passes for 291 yards, completed a 70-yard scoring pass to Kenny Jackson to give Philadelphia a 21-6 lead in the third quarter. Jim Gallery's 43-yard field goal, and Neil Lomax's touchdown passes to J.T. Smith (14 yards) and Robert Awalt (eight), gave St. Louis a 23-21 edge. One minute and ten seconds later, Cunningham capped a 70-yard drive with the game-winning touchdown pass.

Philadelphia	0	7	14	7	— 28
St. Louis	6	0	7	10	— 23

StL — Ferrell 8 run (kick failed)
Phil — Carter 22 pass from Cunningham (McFadden kick)
Phil — Byars 2 run (McFadden kick)
Phil — Jackson 70 pass from Cunningham (McFadden kick)
StL — J.T. Smith 14 pass from Lomax (Gallery kick)
StL — FG Gallery 43
StL — Awalt 8 pass from Lomax (Gallery kick)
Phil — Garrity 9 pass from Cunningham (McFadden kick)

Miami 35, Pittsburgh 24—At Joe Robbie Stadium, attendance 52,578. Dan Marino completed 25 of 31 passes for 332 yards and four touchdowns to rally the Dolphins past the Steelers. With Miami trailing 21-7 in the third quarter, Marino connected with Mark Clayton on touchdown passes of 41 and 33 yards, and completed a 50-yard bomb to Mark Duper to give the Dolphins a 28-24 lead. Troy Stradford carried 19 times for 110 yards, including a five-yard touchdown run in the fourth quarter to finish the scoring.

Pittsburgh	14	7	3	0	— 24
Miami	0	7	14	14	— 35

Pitt — Lockett 10 pass from Malone (Anderson kick)
Pitt — Shell 50 interception return (Anderson kick)
Mia — Hardy 2 pass from Marino (Reveiz kick)
Pitt — Pollard 1 run (Anderson kick)
Mia — Clayton 41 pass from Marino (Reveiz kick)
Pitt — FG Anderson 43
Mia — Duper 50 pass from Marino (Reveiz kick)
Mia — Clayton 33 pass from Marino (Reveiz kick)
Mia — Stradford 5 run (Reveiz kick)

San Francisco 31, Los Angeles Rams 10—At Anaheim Stadium, attendance 55,328. Joe Montana threw three touchdown passes to help the 49ers notch their sixth straight victory. Tom Rathman opened the scoring with a nine-yard run in the first quarter to cap an 80-yard drive. San Francisco took a commanding 24-3 lead in the second quarter on Ray Wersching's 22-yard field goal and Montana's scoring passes to Mike Wilson (17 yards) and John Frank (two). Montana hit Jerry Rice with a 51-yard touchdown pass in the fourth quarter. The 49ers' defense held the Rams to 62 yards rushing.

San Francisco	7	17	0	7	— 31
L.A. Rams	3	0	0	7	— 10

SF — Rathman 9 run (Wersching kick)
Rams — FG Lansford 22
SF — FG Wersching 22
SF — Wilson 17 pass from Montana (Wersching kick)
SF — Frank 2 pass from Montana (Wersching kick)
SF — Rice 51 pass from Montana (Wersching kick)
Rams — Young 7 pass from Everett (Lansford kick)

Tampa Bay 23, Green Bay 17—At Milwaukee County Stadium, attendance 50,308. Donald Igwebuike kicked three field goals (from 48, 36, and 46 yards) to lead the Buccaneers past the Packers. Jeff Smith ran one yard for a score, Steve DeBerg connected on a five-yard scoring pass to Gerald Carter, and Igwebuike's field goals gave Tampa Bay a commanding 23-3 lead with 10 minutes to play.

Tampa Bay	0	3	17	3	— 23
Green Bay	0	0	3	14	— 17

TB — FG Igwebuike 48
TB — Smith 1 run (Igwebuike kick)
TB — Carter 5 pass from DeBerg (Igwebuike kick)
TB — FG Igwebuike 36
GB — FG Del Greco 36
TB — FG Igwebuike 46
GB — Neal 4 pass from Wright (Del Greco kick)
GB — Fullwood 1 run (Del Greco kick)

Washington 27, Buffalo 7—At Rich Stadium, attendance 71,640. Jay Schroeder threw for a pair of touchdowns and ran for another to power the Redskins over the Bills. Washington took a 17-0 halftime lead on Ali Haji-Sheikh's 30-yard field goal, Kelvin Bryant's 12-yard touchdown catch, and Schroeder's 13-yard run for a score. Schroeder also connected with Bryant on a seven-yard touchdown pass, and Haji-Sheikh kicked a 33-yard field goal to put the game away. Buffalo quarterback Jim Kelly's 17-yard scoring pass to Andre Reed in the fourth quarter prevented the shutout. George Rogers rushed 30 times for 125 yards for his twenty-seventh career 100-yard game.

Washington	3	14	10	0	— 27
Buffalo	0	0	0	7	— 7

Wash — FG Haji-Sheikh 30
Wash — Bryant 12 pass from Schroeder (Haji-Sheikh kick)
Wash — Schroeder 13 run (Haji-Sheikh kick)
Wash — Bryant 7 pass from Schroeder (Haji-Sheikh kick)
Wash — FG Haji-Sheikh 33
Buff — Reed 17 pass from Kelly (Norwood kick)

Monday, November 2

Dallas 33, New York Giants 24—At Texas Stadium, attendance 55,730. Roger Ruzek tied an NFL record by kicking four field goals in one quarter, and defensive end Jim Jeffcoat returned an interception for a touchdown, as the Cowboys downed the Giants. Herschel Walker's one-yard run, and Danny White's two-yard scoring pass to Doug Cosbie, gave Dallas a 14-10 halftime edge. Phil Simms then hit Lionel Manuel on a pair of scoring passes covering 50 and 33 yards to give New York a 24-14 lead, but a pair of Ruzek field goals from 34 and 49 yards, and Jeffcoat's 26-yard interception return for a score, put the Cowboys back in front 27-24. Dallas then took advantage of three New York fumbles to set up Ruzek field goals of 40 and 35 yards.

N.Y. Giants	0	10	7	7	— 24
Dallas	7	7	0	19	— 33

Dall — Walker 1 run (Ruzek kick)
NYG — Morris 5 run (Allegre kick)
NYG — FG Allegre 35
Dall — Cosbie 2 pass from D. White (Ruzek kick)
NYG — Manuel 50 pass from Simms (Allegre kick)
NYG — Manuel 33 pass from Simms (Allegre kick)
Dall — FG Ruzek 34
Dall — Jeffcoat 26 interception return (Ruzek kick)
Dall — FG Ruzek 49
Dall — FG Ruzek 40
Dall — FG Ruzek 35

Ninth Week Summaries

Standings

American Football Conference

Eastern Division	W	L	T	Pct.	Pts.	OP
Buffalo	4	4	0	.500	143	197
Indianapolis	4	4	0	.500	153	119
Miami	4	4	0	.500	223	171
New England	4	4	0	.500	149	168
N.Y. Jets	4	4	0	.500	195	177
Central Division						
Cleveland	5	3	0	.625	211	110
Houston	5	3	0	.625	200	180
Pittsburgh	5	3	0	.625	174	172
Cincinnati	2	6	0	.250	138	176
Western Division						
San Diego	7	1	0	.875	176	141
Seattle	5	3	0	.625	208	165
Denver	4	3	1	.563	198	160
L.A. Raiders	3	5	0	.375	169	169
Kansas City	1	7	0	.125	133	249

National Football Conference

Eastern Division	W	L	T	Pct.	Pts.	OP
Washington	6	2	0	.750	204	139
Dallas	4	4	0	.500	185	185
Philadelphia	4	4	0	.500	182	213
St. Louis	3	5	0	.375	182	208
N.Y. Giants	2	6	0	.250	140	185
Central Division						
Chicago	7	1	0	.875	217	129
Minnesota	4	4	0	.500	170	180
Tampa Bay	4	4	0	.500	192	159
Green Bay	3	4	1	.438	147	164
Detroit	2	6	0	.250	146	230
Western Division						
San Francisco	7	1	0	.875	226	174
New Orleans	5	3	0	.625	211	137
Atlanta	2	6	0	.250	120	254
L.A. Rams	1	7	0	.125	134	215

Sunday, November 8

Cleveland 38, Atlanta 3—At Cleveland Stadium, attendance 71,135. Earnest Byner scored three touchdowns to lead the Browns past the Falcons. Cleveland led 14-3 at halftime on Bernie Kosar's 54-yard bomb to Webster Slaughter and Kevin Mack's one-yard run. The Browns took a commanding 35-3 third-quarter lead on Byner's scoring runs of three and five yards, and his four-yard touchdown reception from Kosar. Jeff Jaeger added a 38-yard field goal in the fourth quarter to complete Cleveland's scoring. The Browns' defense recorded seven sacks. Byner was named AFC offensive player of the week for his performance.

Atlanta	0	3	0	0	— 3
Cleveland	0	14	21	3	— 38

Clev — Slaughter 54 pass from Kosar (Jaeger kick)
Clev — Mack 1 run (Jaeger kick)
Atl — FG Luckhurst 42
Clev — Byner 3 run (Jaeger kick)
Clev — Byner 5 run (Jaeger kick)
Clev — Byner 4 pass from Kosar (Jaeger kick)
Clev — FG Jaeger 38

Chicago 26, Green Bay 24—At Lambeau Field, attendance 53,320. Kevin Butler kicked four field goals, including a 52-yarder with four seconds remaining, as the Bears rallied to beat the Packers 26-24. Trailing 21-13 in the fourth quarter, Walter Payton scored on a one-yard run, and Butler kicked a 24-yard field goal to put Chicago ahead 23-21. Al Del Greco's 47-yard field goal with one minute to play gave Green Bay a 24-23 edge. But Jim McMahon drove the Bears to the Packers' 35-yard line to set up Butler's winning kick. Neal Anderson caught five passes for 102 yards for Chicago, including a 59-yard scoring pass from McMahon in the first quarter.

Chicago	7	6	0	13	— 26
Green Bay	14	7	0	3	— 24

Chi — Anderson 59 pass from McMahon (Butler kick)
GB — West 27 pass from Wright (Del Greco kick)
GB — Fullwood 2 run (Del Greco kick)
Chi — FG Butler 27
Chi — FG Butler 29
GB — Epps 26 pass from Wright (Del Greco kick)
Chi — Payton 1 run (Butler kick)
Chi — FG Butler 24
GB — FG Del Greco 47
Chi — FG Butler 52

Detroit 27, Dallas 17—At Pontiac Silverdome, attendance 45,325. Garry James rushed for two touchdowns and Eddie Murray kicked two field goals to lead the Lions over the Cowboys. Detroit jumped to a 10-0 lead on Murray's 30-yard field goal and Rob Rubick's 20-yard scoring pass from Chuck Long. Dallas answered with Timmy Newsome's one-yard touchdown run and Roger Ruzek's 38-yard field goal to tie the game at halftime, 10-10. James opened the second half with a two-yard scoring run, and James Griffins's 29-yard interception return set up James's four-yard touchdown run for the go-ahead score. Murray's 19-yard field goal finished the Lions' scoring.

Dallas	0	10	0	7	— 17
Detroit	10	0	7	10	— 27

Det — FG Murray 30
Det — Rubick 20 pass from Long (Murray kick)
Dall — Newsome 1 run (Ruzek kick)
Dall — FG Ruzek 38
Det — James 2 run (Murray kick)
Dall — Newsome 24 run (Ruzek kick)
Det — James 4 run (Murray kick)
Det — FG Murray 19

Buffalo 21, Denver 14—At Rich Stadium, attendance 63,698. Robb Riddick ran for a touchdown and blocked a punt for a safety as the Bills downed the Broncos. Buffalo opened an 18-0 second-quarter lead on touchdowns by Andre Reed (nine-yard reception) and Riddick (one-yard run), plus safeties by Riddick and Steve Tasker after each blocked punts through the end zone. Scott Norwood kicked a 30-yard field goal in the fourth quarter to complete the Bills' scoring. Buffalo held Denver to 76 yards rushing, and maintained a 37:37 to 22:23 time-of-possession advantage. Rookie Cornelius Bennett had one of the Bills' three sacks in his NFL debut.

Denver	0	0	7	7	— 14
Buffalo	0	18	3	0	— 21

Buff — Reed 9 pass from Kelly (Norwood kick)
Buff — Safety, Riddick blocked punt through end zone
Buff — Riddick 1 run (Norwood kick)
Buff — Safety, Tasker blocked punt through end zone
Buff — FG Norwood 30
Den — Winder 6 run (Karlis kick)
Den — Johnson 15 pass from Elway (Karlis kick)

San Francisco 27, Houston 20—At Candlestick Park, attendance 59,740. Joe Montana completed 32 of 46 passes for 289 yards and three touchdowns to pace the 49ers over the Oilers. Montana completed an eight-yard scoring pass to Tom Rathman to cap a 90-yard drive in the first quarter and threw a one-yard touchdown pass to Jerry Rice to give San Francisco a 14-6 halftime lead. Montana connected with Rathman again for a three-yard scoring play, and Ray Wersching kicked field goals of 28 and 38 yards in the fourth quarter to complete the scoring.

Houston	3	3	7	7	— 20
San Francisco	7	7	7	6	— 27

Hou — FG Zendejas 20
SF — Rathman 8 pass from Montana (Wersching kick)
Hou — FG Zendejas 48
SF — Rice 1 pass from Montana (Wersching kick)
SF — Rathman 3 pass from Montana (Wersching kick)
Hou — Duncan 5 pass from Moon (Zendejas kick)
SF — FG Wersching 28
SF — FG Wersching 38
Hou — Givins 8 pass from Moon (Zendejas kick)

Minnesota 31, Los Angeles Raiders 20—At Metrodome, attendance 57,150. Wade Wilson threw two touchdown passes and ran for another to lift the Vikings over the Raiders. Wilson, who came off the bench in the second half to replace starter Tommy Kramer, scored on a one-yard run that was set up by Carl Lee's interception. Wilson added a 58-yard scoring pass to Hassan Jones, but Marc Wilson's nine-yard pass to James Lofton, and Chris Bahr's 35-yard field goal, narrowed Minnesota's lead to 21-13. Chuck Nelson's 27-yard field goal and Wilson's scoring pass to Steve Jordan completed the Vikings' scoring.

L.A. Raiders	3	0	10	7	— 20
Minnesota	0	7	14	10	— 31

Raiders — FG Bahr 21
Minn — Kramer 1 run (C. Nelson kick)
Minn — W. Wilson 1 run (C. Nelson kick)
Minn — H. Jones 58 pass from W. Wilson (C. Nelson kick)

Raiders — Lofton 9 pass from M. Wilson (Bahr kick)
Raiders — FG Bahr 35
Minn — FG C. Nelson 27
Minn — Jordan 11 pass from W. Wilson (C. Nelson kick)
Raiders — D. Williams 27 pass from M. Wilson (Bahr kick)

Miami 20, Cincinnati 14—At Riverfront Stadium, attendance 53,848. Dan Marino and rookie Troy Stradford each accounted for touchdowns to help the Dolphins defeat the Bengals. Miami took a 10-7 first-half lead on Stradford's one-yard run and Fuad Reveiz's 47-yard field goal. Marino, who completed 26 of 41 passes for 262 yards, threw a 30-yard scoring pass to Mark Clayton to put the Dolphins ahead 17-7 in the third quarter. Reveiz's second field goal, a 34-yarder, finished the scoring.

Miami	0	10	7	3	— 20
Cincinnati	7	0	0	7	— 14

Cin — Kattus 17 pass from Esiason (Breech kick)
Mia — Stradford 1 run (Reveiz kick)
Mia — FG Reveiz 47
Mia — Clayton 30 pass from Marino (Reveiz kick)
Cin — Johnson 6 run (Breech kick)
Mia — FG Reveiz 34

New Orleans 31, Los Angeles Rams 14—At Anaheim Stadium, attendance 43,379. Running back Dalton Hilliard ran for one touchdown and threw another as the Saints downed the Rams. Hilliard, who scored on a 38-yard pass from Bobby Hebert, also completed a 23-yard scoring strike to Mike Tice to give New Orleans a 17-0 lead. Los Angeles cut the deficit to 17-14 in the third quarter on Jim Everett's touchdown passes to Damone Johnson (eight yards) and Greg Bell (32). New Orleans rebounded on Rueben Mayes's two-yard scoring run and Hebert's three-yard touchdown pass to Lonzell Hill. Hilliard also rushed for 92 yards on 14 carries and had four receptions for 84 yards to earn NFC offensive player of the week honors.

New Orleans	10	7	7	7	— 31
L.A. Rams	0	7	7	0	— 14

NO — FG Andersen 32
NO — Hilliard 38 pass from Hebert (Andersen kick)
NO — Tice 23 pass from Hilliard (Andersen kick)
Rams — Johnson 8 pass from Everett (Lansford kick)
Rams — Bell 32 pass from Everett (Lansford kick)
NO — Mayes 2 run (Andersen kick)
NO — L. Hill 3 pass from Hebert (Andersen kick)

Pittsburgh 17, Kansas City 16—At Arrowhead Stadium, attendance 45,249. Rodney Carter caught a pair of touchdown passes, and Gary Anderson kicked a 44-yard field goal late in the fourth quarter, to give the Steelers a 17-16 comeback win. Mark Malone's scoring passes of 4 and 26 yards to Carter gave Pittsburgh a 14-10 lead in the third quarter. But Nick Lowery's field goals from 27 and 38 yards put Kansas City ahead 16-14. Pittsburgh's Gerald Williams recovered a fumble on the Kansas City 27-yard line to set up Anderson's winning kick.

Pittsburgh	0	7	7	3	— 17
Kansas City	7	3	0	6	— 16

KC — Maas 6 fumble recovery return (Lowery kick)
Pitt — Carter 4 pass from Malone (Anderson kick)
KC — FG Lowery 41
Pitt — Carter 26 pass from Malone (Anderson kick)
KC — FG Lowery 27
KC — FG Lowery 38
Pitt — FG Anderson 44

San Diego 16, Indianapolis 13—At Hoosier Dome, attendance 60,459. Vince Abbott kicked a 39-yard field goal with 12 seconds remaining to rally the Chargers to a 16-13 come-from-behind win over the Colts. Indianapolis opened a 13-0 halftime lead on Dean Biasucci field goals of 37 and 27 yards and Albert Bentley's eight-yard run. Abbott connected on field goals of 42 and 37 yards, and Dan Fouts threw a five-yard scoring pass to Lionel James, to deadlock the game 13-13 early in the fourth quarter. Eric Dickerson rushed for 138 yards on 35 carries in his first game for the Colts.

San Diego	0	0	6	10	— 16
Indianapolis	3	10	0	0	— 13

Ind — FG Biasucci 37
Ind — FG Biasucci 27
Ind — Bentley 8 run (Biasucci kick)
SD — FG Abbott 42
SD — FG Abbott 37
SD — L. James 5 pass from Fouts (Abbott kick)
SD — FG Abbott 39

St. Louis 31, Tampa Bay 28—At Busch Stadium, attendance 22,449. Neil Lomax's 17-yard touchdown pass to J.T. Smith with 2:01 remaining rallied the Cardinals over the Buccaneers. Trailing 28-3 in the fourth quarter, Lomax threw a four-yard scoring pass to Robert Awalt, and Niko Noga returned a fumble 24 yards for a touchdown to cut the deficit to 28-17. Lomax, who completed 25 of 36 passes for 314 yards, also hit Smith on an 11-yard touchdown pass with 8:18 remaining.

Tampa Bay	7	7	14	0	— 28
St. Louis	0	3	0	28	— 31

TB — Carrier 5 pass from DeBerg (Igwebuike kick)
TB — Carter 3 pass from DeBerg (Igwebuike kick)
StL — FG Gallery 31
TB — Je. Smith 34 pass from DeBerg (Igwebuike kick)
TB — Je. Smith 3 run (Igwebuike kick)
StL — Awalt 4 pass from Lomax (Gallery kick)
StL — Noga 24 fumble recovery return (Gallery kick)
StL — J.T. Smith 11 pass from Lomax (Gallery kick)
StL — J.T. Smith 17 pass from Lomax (Gallery kick)

Philadelphia 31, Washington 27—At Veterans Stadium, attendance 66,398. Randall Cunningham's third touchdown pass of the day, a 40-yarder to Gregg Garrity with 1:06 left, lifted the Eagles past the Redskins. Cunningham's 32-yard scoring pass to Mike Quick gave Philadelphia a 24-21 edge early in the fourth quarter. Jay Schroeder connected with Gary Clark on a 47-yard scoring pass to put the Redskins ahead 27-24 with 2:29 remaining, but Cunningham drove the Eagles 77 yards on six plays to set up Garrity's decisive reception.

Washington	7	14	0	6	— 27
Philadelphia	7	10	0	14	— 31

Phil — Toney 5 run (McFadden kick)
Wash — Rogers 3 run (Haji-Sheikh kick)
Wash — Monk 19 pass from Schroeder (Haji-Sheikh kick)
Wash — Green 26 fumble recovery return (Haji-Sheikh kick)
Phil — FG McFadden 37
Phil — Quick 6 pass from Cunningham (McFadden kick)
Phil — Quick 32 pass from Cunningham (McFadden kick)
Wash — Clark 47 pass from Schroeder (kick failed)
Phil — Garrity 40 pass from Cunningham (McFadden kick)

New York Giants 17, New England 10—At Giants Stadium, attendance 73,817. Jeff Rutledge passed for two touchdowns and Raul Allegre kicked a field goal to lead the Giants over the Patriots. After a scoreless first quarter, New York took a 14-0 halftime lead when Rutledge threw scoring passes of 16 yards to Mark Bavaro and nine yards to George Adams. Allegre's 19-yard field goal completed the Giants' scoring. Lawrence Taylor, who recorded two sacks, intercepted a pass with 1:09 remaining to secure the victory.

New England	0	0	7	3	— 10
N.Y. Giants	0	14	3	0	— 17

NYG — Bavaro 16 pass from Rutledge (Allegre kick)
NYG — Adams 9 pass from Rutledge (Allegre kick)
NE — Baty 15 pass from Grogan (Franklin kick)
NYG — FG Allegre 19
NE — FG Franklin 46

Monday, November 9

New York Jets 30, Seattle 14—At Giants Stadium, attendance 60,452. Pat Leahy kicked three field goals and JoJo Townsell returned a punt for a touchdown to highlight the Jets' win over the Seahawks. Townsell's 91-yard punt return and Leahy's 35-yard field goal gave New York a 10-0 halftime advantage. Seattle took a 14-13 third-quarter lead on Curt Warner's three-yard scoring run and Dave Krieg's 29-yard scoring pass to Steve Largent. The Jets regained the lead when Ken O'Brien hit Billy Griggs with a four-yard scoring pass and Johnny Hector ran one yard for a touchdown. Leahy's 26-yard field goal completed the Jets' scoring.

Seattle	0	0	14	0	— 14
N.Y. Jets	0	10	10	10	— 30

NYJ — Townsell 91 punt return (Leahy kick)
NYJ — FG Leahy 35
NYJ — FG Leahy 36
Sea — Warner 3 run (Johnson kick)
Sea — Largent 29 pass from Krieg (Johnson kick)
NYJ — Griggs 4 pass from O'Brien (Leahy kick)
NYJ — Hector 1 run (Leahy kick)
NYJ — FG Leahy 26

Tenth Week Summaries

Standings

American Football Conference

Eastern Division

	W	L	T	Pct.	Pts.	OP
Indianapolis	5	4	0	.556	193	140
N.Y. Jets	5	4	0	.556	211	186
Buffalo	4	5	0	.444	164	224
Miami	4	5	0	.444	244	211
New England	4	5	0	.444	166	191

Central Division

	W	L	T	Pct.	Pts.	OP
Cleveland	6	3	0	.667	238	131
Houston	6	3	0	.667	223	183
Pittsburgh	5	4	0	.556	177	195
Cincinnati	3	6	0	.333	154	186

Western Division

	W	L	T	Pct.	Pts.	OP
San Diego	8	1	0	.889	192	155
Seattle	6	3	0	.667	232	178
Denver	5	3	1	.611	229	189
L.A. Raiders	3	6	0	.333	183	185
Kansas City	1	8	0	.111	142	265

National Football Conference

Eastern Division

	W	L	T	Pct.	Pts.	OP
Washington	7	2	0	.778	224	152
Dallas	5	4	0	.556	208	202
Philadelphia	4	5	0	.444	199	233
N.Y. Giants	3	6	0	.333	160	202
St. Louis	3	6	0	.333	206	235

Central Division

	W	L	T	Pct.	Pts.	OP
Chicago	7	2	0	.778	246	160
Minnesota	5	4	0	.556	193	197
Tampa Bay	4	5	0	.444	209	182
Green Bay	3	5	1	.389	160	188
Detroit	2	7	0	.222	159	250

Western Division

	W	L	T	Pct.	Pts.	OP
San Francisco	7	2	0	.778	250	200
New Orleans	6	3	0	.667	237	161
Atlanta	2	7	0	.222	130	270
L.A. Rams	2	7	0	.222	161	239

Sunday, November 15

Cleveland 27, Buffalo 21—At Cleveland Stadium, attendance 78,409. Bernie Kosar threw for 346 yards and two touchdowns to lead the Browns over the Bills. Cleveland took a 17-7 halftime lead on Jeff Jaeger's 22-yard field goal, Ray Ellis's 27-yard fumble recovery for a score, and Kosar's 15-yard touchdown pass to Reggie Langhorne. Kosar also fired a 52-yard scoring pass to Webster Slaughter to open the second half. Jaeger kicked a 40-yard field goal to complete the Browns' scoring.

Buffalo	7	0	0	14	— 21
Cleveland	3	14	7	3	— 27

Clev — FG Jaeger 22
Buff — Kelso 56 fumble recovery return (Norwood kick)
Clev — Ellis 27 fumble recovery return (Jaeger kick)
Clev — Langhorne 15 pass from Kosar (Jaeger kick)
Clev — Slaughter 52 pass from Kosar (Jaeger kick)
Clev — FG Jaeger 40
Buff — Burkett 13 pass from Kelly (Norwood kick)
Buff — Reed 10 pass from Kelly (Norwood kick)

Cincinnati 16, Atlanta 10—At Atlanta-Fulton County Stadium, attendance 25,758. Larry Kinnebrew's two-yard touchdown run with 23 seconds remaining lifted the Bengals over the Falcons. With Cincinnati trailing 10-6 in the fourth quarter, Jim Breech kicked his third field goal of the game, a 30-yarder, to cut Atlanta's lead to 10-9 with 3:42 remaining. Kinnebrew gained 100 yards on 27 carries. Atlanta's Gerald Riggs rushed for 112 yards on 23 carries for his twenty-third 100-yard game in the NFL.

Cincinnati	3	0	0	13	— 16
Atlanta	0	0	7	3	— 10

Cin — FG Breech 31
Atl — Dixon 44 pass from Campbell (Luckhurst kick)
Cin — FG Breech 22
Atl — FG Luckhurst 44
Cin — FG Breech 30
Cin — Kinnebrew 2 run (Breech kick)

Dallas 23, New England 17—At Sullivan Stadium, attendance 60,567. Herschel Walker ran for 173 yards on 28 carries, including a 60-yard touchdown run 1:50 into overtime, to power the Cowboys past the Patriots. Dallas took a 14-7 halftime lead on Ron Francis's 18-yard interception return for a touchdown and Danny White's three-yard scoring pass to Doug Cosbie. New England went ahead 17-14 in the third quarter on Tony Franklin's 41-yard field goal and Tom Ramsey's five-yard scoring pass to Stanley Morgan. White rallied the Cowboys and mounted a 78-yard, 11-play drive to set up Roger Ruzek's 20-yard field goal with 28 seconds remaining, to send the game into overtime.

Dallas	7	7	0	3	6	— 23
New England	0	7	0	10	0	— 17

Dall — Francis 18 interception return (Ruzek kick)
NE — Grogan 2 run (Franklin kick)
Dall — Cosbie 3 pass from D. White (Ruzek kick)
NE — FG Franklin 41
NE — Morgan 5 pass from Ramsey (Franklin kick)
Dall — FG Ruzek 20
Dall — Walker 60 run (no kick)

Washington 20, Detroit 13—At Robert F. Kennedy Stadium, attendance 53,593. Doug Williams came off the bench midway through the second quarter and threw two touchdown passes to help the Redskins defeat the Lions. Washington took a 17-3 halftime lead on Ali Haji-Sheikh's 33-yard field goal and Williams's two scoring passes to Kelvin Bryant (16 yards) and Gary Clark (47). Detroit closed the gap to seven points in the fourth quarter, but Darrell Green's interception sealed the Redskins' win.

Detroit	3	0	10	0	— 13
Washington	0	17	3	0	— 20

Det — FG Murray 40
Wash — FG Haji-Sheikh 33
Wash — Bryant 16 pass from Williams (Haji-Sheikh kick)
Wash — Clark 42 pass from Williams (Haji-Sheikh kick)

Det — FG Murray 41
Wash — FG Haji-Sheikh 41
Det — Bernard 2 run (Murray kick)

Seattle 24, Green Bay 13—At Kingdome, attendance 60,963. Curt Warner rushed for 123 yards on 25 carries to lead Seattle over Green Bay. Warner's 57-yard touchdown run, along with Eugene Robinson's eight-yard blocked punt return, and Dave Krieg's eight-yard scoring run, staked Seattle to a 21-13 lead at the half. Norm Johnson kicked a 24-yard field goal in the fourth quarter for the only points in the second half.

Green Bay	3	10	0	0	— 13
Seattle	0	21	0	3	— 24

GB — FG Zendejas 31
Sea — Warner 57 run (Johnson kick)
GB — Paskett 47 pass from Wright (Zendejas kick)
GB — FG Zendejas 48
Sea — Robinson 8 blocked punt return (Johnson kick)
Sea — Krieg 8 run (Johnson kick)
Sea — FG Johnson 24

Houston 23, Pittsburgh 3—At Three Rivers Stadium, attendance 56,177. Warren Moon threw two touchdown passes as the Oilers rolled over the Steelers. With the score tied 3-3 midway through the third quarter, Moon, who completed 18 of 24 passes for 252 yards, blew the game open by throwing scoring passes to Curtis Duncan (14 yards) and Drew Hill (42) to give Houston a 17-3 lead. Tony Zendejas added field goals of 20 and 40 yards to finish the scoring. The Oilers' defense held the Steelers to 170 total yards. The win was Houston's first at Three Rivers Stadium since 1978.

Houston	0	3	14	6	— 23
Pittsburgh	3	0	0	0	— 3

Pitt — FG Anderson 22
Hou — FG Zendejas 34
Hou — Duncan 14 pass from Moon (Zendejas kick)
Hou — D. Hill 42 pass from Moon (Zendejas kick)
Hou — FG Zendejas 20
Hou — FG Zendejas 40

Indianapolis 40, Miami 21—At Joe Robbie Stadium, attendance 65,433. Albert Bentley ran for a pair of touchdowns and Dean Biasucci kicked four field goals in the second half as the Colts snapped a 14-game losing streak to the Dolphins. Miami got out to a 14-0 first-quarter lead, but Eric Dickerson's four-yard scoring run and Gary Hogeboom's seven-yard touchdown pass to Bill Brooks tied the score, 14-14. Biasucci kicked two field goals from 22 and 32 yards, but Dan Marino's 10-yard scoring pass to Fred Banks gave Miami a 21-20 edge at halftime. Biasucci added field goals of 25 and 23 yards, and Bentley had touchdown runs of 17 and 2 yards in the second half, to help Indianapolis put the game away.

Indianapolis	7	13	3	17	— 40
Miami	14	7	0	0	— 21

Mia — Hampton 6 run (Reveiz kick)
Mia — D. Johnson 4 pass from Marino (Reveiz kick)
Ind — Dickerson 4 run (Biasucci kick)
Ind — Brooks 7 pass from Hogeboom (Biasucci kick)
Ind — FG Biasucci 22
Mia — Banks 10 pass from Marino (Reveiz kick)
Ind — FG Biasucci 32
Ind — FG Biasucci 25
Ind — FG Biasucci 23
Ind — Bentley 17 run (Biasucci kick)
Ind — Bentley 2 run (Biasucci kick)

Los Angeles Rams 27, St. Louis 24—At Busch Stadium, attendance 27,730. Mike Lansford's 20-yard field goal with no time remaining lifted the Rams over the Cardinals. Los Angeles tied the game 24-24 in the third quarter when Jerry Gray recovered a blocked punt in the end zone and Lansford kicked a 28-yard field goal. Charles White, who had 34 carries for 213 yards, ran 47 yards for a touchdown in the first quarter. White gained 62 yards on the Rams' final drive to set up the winning kick.

L.A. Rams	14	0	10	3	— 27
St. Louis	3	14	7	0	— 24

Rams — White 47 run (Lansford kick)
StL — FG Gallery 44
Rams — Johnson 10 pass from Everett (Lansford kick)
StL — Mitchell 5 run (Gallery kick)
StL — Awalt 19 pass from Lomax (Gallery kick)
StL — McAdoo fumble recovery in end zone (Gallery kick)
Rams — Gray recovered blocked punt in end zone (Lansford kick)
Rams — FG Lansford 28
Rams — FG Lansford 20

Minnesota 23, Tampa Bay 17—At Tampa Stadium, attendance 48,605. Tommy Kramer came off the bench in the second half to rally the Vikings over the Buccaneers. The Vikings overcame a 7-6 halftime deficit on Rick Fenney's one-yard scoring run and Chuck Nelson's 26-yard field goal. Kramer's two-yard scoring pass to Steve Jordan gave the Vikings a commanding 23-10 fourth-quarter lead. Nelson also had field goals from 29 and 27 yards. Minnesota held Tampa Bay to 15 yards rushing, and maintained a 37:59 to 22:01 time-of-possession advantage.

Tampa Bay	0	7	3	7	— 17
Minnesota	0	6	10	7	— 23

TB — Magee 20 pass from DeBerg (Igwebuike kick)
Minn — FG C. Nelson 29
Minn — FG C. Nelson 27
Minn — Fenney 1 run (C. Nelson kick)
TB — FG Igwebuike 26
Minn — FG C. Nelson 26
Minn — Jordan 2 pass from Kramer (C. Nelson kick)
TB — Freeman 64 pass from DeBerg (Igwebuike kick)

New Orleans 26, San Francisco 24—At Candlestick Park, attendance 68,436. Morten Andersen's fourth field goal of the day, a 40-yarder with 1:06 remaining in the game, helped the Saints edge the 49ers. Leading 9-7 in the third quarter, Saints quarterback Bobby Hebert threw a 43-yard scoring pass to Mike Jones and Johnnie Poe returned a blocked field goal 61 yards for a touchdown to give New Orleans a 23-14 lead. San Francisco pulled ahead 24-23 on Ray Wersching's 35-yard field goal and Joe Montana's 29-yard touchdown pass to Ron Heller. Andersen also kicked field goals from 40, 27, and 51 yards in the first half.

New Orleans	3	6	14	3	— 26
San Francisco	7	0	7	10	— 24

NO — FG Andersen 40
SF — Rice 46 pass from Young (Wersching kick)
NO — FG Andersen 27
NO — FG Andersen 51
NO — Jones 43 pass from Hebert (Andersen kick)
SF — Rice 50 pass from Sydney (Wersching kick)
NO — Poe 61 blocked field goal return (Andersen kick)
SF — FG Wersching 35
SF — Heller 29 pass from Montana (Wersching kick)
NO — FG Andersen 40

New York Giants 20, Philadelphia 17—At Veterans Stadium, attendance 66,172. Mark Bavaro and Lionel Manuel combined for 207 yards receiving, and Raul Allegre kicked two field goals, as the Giants downed the Eagles. Philadelphia took a 10-0 lead on Randall Cunningham's four-yard run and Paul McFadden's 25-yard field goal. Jeff Rutledge brought the Giants back with a 36-yard scoring pass to Manuel, and Allegre kicked a 53-yard field goal to tie the game 10-10 at halftime. After the Eagles regained the lead 17-10 in the third quarter, George Adams ran one yard for a touchdown to tie the score 17-17. Allegre added a decisive 52-yard field goal early in the fourth quarter. The Giants' defense registered six sacks, including two by Lawrence Taylor.

N.Y. Giants	7	3	7	3	— 20
Philadelphia	10	0	7	0	— 17

Phil — Cunningham 4 run (McFadden kick)
Phil — FG McFadden 25
NYG — Manuel 36 pass from Rutledge (Allegre kick)
NYG — FG Allegre 53
Phil — Byars 8 pass from Cunningham (McFadden kick)
NYG — Adams 1 run (Allegre kick)
NYG — FG Allegre 52

New York Jets 16, Kansas City 9—At Arrowhead Stadium, attendance 40,718. Freeman McNeil rushed 26 times for 184 yards and Pat Leahy kicked three field goals as the Jets downed the Chiefs. It was a battle of kickers for three quarters, as Nick Lowery's three field goals staked Kansas City to a 9-6 lead. But the Jets scored 10 unanswered points in the fourth quarter on Ken O'Brien's 18-yard touchdown pass to Al Toon and Leahy's third field goal, a 21-yarder. New York's defense recorded five sacks. Cornerback Carl Howard had two interceptions.

N.Y. Jets	3	0	3	10	— 16
Kansas City	0	3	6	0	— 9

NYJ — FG Leahy 39
KC — FG Lowery 42
KC — FG Lowery 43
NYJ — FG Leahy 24
KC — FG Lowery 18
NYJ — Toon 18 pass from O'Brien (Leahy kick)
NYJ — FG Leahy 21

San Diego 16, Los Angeles Raiders 14—At San Diego Jack Murphy Stadium, attendance 60,639. Vince Abbott kicked three field goals, and Dan Fouts threw one touchdown pass, to give the Chargers their eighth straight victory. An interception by Billy Ray Smith set up Fouts's nine-yard scoring pass to Kellen Winslow. Abbott added second-quarter field goals of 38, 47, and 39 yards to give San Diego a 16-0 halftime lead. The Raiders rebounded with two fourth-quarter touchdowns, but could get no closer. James Lofton caught three passes for 84 yards to become the sixth NFL player to surpass 10,000 career receiving yards (10,054).

L.A. Raiders	0	0	0	14	— 14
San Diego	7	9	0	0	— 16

SD — Winslow 9 pass from Fouts (Abbott kick)
SD — FG Abbott 38
SD — FG Abbott 47
SD — FG Abbott 39
Raiders — Williams 5 pass from Wilson (Bahr kick)
Raiders — Lofton 47 pass from Wilson (Bahr kick)

Monday, November 16

Denver 31, Chicago 29—At Mile High Stadium, attendance 75,783. John Elway completed 21 of 40 passes for 341 yards and three touchdowns to help the Broncos past the Bears. Trailing 14-0 in the second quarter, Elway threw scoring passes of 22 yards each to Vance Johnson and Mark Jackson, and completed a 35-yarder to Ricky Nattiel to give Denver a 21-14 halftime lead. Chicago went ahead 29-21 in the third quarter on Willie Gault's 26-yard scoring pass from Jim McMahon, McMahon's one-yard run for a score, and Kevin Butler's 42-yard field goal. Rich Karlis's 27-yard field goal cut Denver's deficit to 29-24. Rookie K.C. Clark's interception set up Steve Sewell's game-winning four-yard run with 4:58 remaining.

Chicago	14	0	15	0	— 29
Denver	0	21	0	10	— 31

Chi — Gault 51 pass from McMahon (Butler kick)
Chi — Boso 6 pass from McMahon (Butler kick)
Den — Johnson 22 pass from Elway (Karlis kick)
Den — Jackson 22 pass from Elway (Karlis kick)
Den — Nattiel 35 pass from Elway (Karlis kick)
Chi — Gault 26 pass from McMahon (run failed)
Chi — McMahon 1 run (kick failed)
Chi — FG Butler 42
Den — FG Karlis 27
Den — Sewell 4 run (Karlis kick)

Eleventh Week Summaries

Standings

American Football Conference

Eastern Division	W	L	T	Pct.	Pts.	OP
Buffalo	5	5	0	.500	181	238
Indianapolis	5	5	0	.500	193	164
Miami	5	5	0	.500	264	225
New England	5	5	0	.500	190	191
N.Y. Jets	5	5	0	.500	225	203
Central Division						
Cleveland	7	3	0	.700	278	138
Houston	6	4	0	.600	230	223
Pittsburgh	6	4	0	.600	207	211
Cincinnati	3	7	0	.300	170	216
Western Division						
San Diego	8	2	0	.800	195	189
Seattle	7	3	0	.700	266	181
Denver	6	3	1	.650	252	206
L.A. Raiders	3	7	0	.300	200	208
Kansas City	1	9	0	.100	145	288

National Football Conference

Eastern Division	W	L	T	Pct.	Pts.	OP
Washington	7	3	0	.700	250	182
Dallas	5	5	0	.500	222	222
Philadelphia	4	6	0	.400	218	264
St. Louis	4	6	0	.400	237	254
N.Y. Giants	3	7	0	.300	174	225
Central Division						
Chicago	8	2	0	.800	276	170
Minnesota	6	4	0	.600	217	210
Green Bay	4	5	1	.450	183	191
Tampa Bay	4	6	0	.400	219	206
Detroit	2	8	0	.200	169	280
Western Division						
San Francisco	8	2	0	.800	274	210
New Orleans	7	3	0	.700	260	175
L.A. Rams	3	7	0	.300	191	265
Atlanta	2	8	0	.200	143	294

Sunday, November 22

Minnesota 24, Atlanta 13—At Metrodome, attendance 53,866. Leo Lewis returned a punt 78 yards for a touchdown to highlight the Vikings' victory over the Falcons. Minnesota held a 10-7 halftime edge on Wade Wilson's eight-yard touchdown pass to Carl Hilton and Chuck Nelson's 51-yard field goal. Minnesota increased its lead in the third quarter to 17-7 on Lewis's punt return. Hilton also blocked a punt to set up Allen Rice's two-yard scoring run late in the fourth quarter to secure the win. Lewis's scoring return was Minnesota's first since November 3, 1968, when Charlie West returned a punt 98 yards for a touchdown.

Atlanta	0	7	6	0	— 13
Minnesota	0	10	7	7	— 24

Minn — Hilton 8 pass from Wilson (C. Nelson kick)
Atl — Campbell 7 run (Luckhurst kick)
Minn — FG C. Nelson 51
Minn — Lewis 78 punt return (C. Nelson kick)
Atl — Matthews 23 pass from Campbell (run failed)
Minn — Rice 2 run (C. Nelson kick)

Buffalo 17, New York Jets 14—At Giants Stadium, attendance 58,407. The Bills snapped a seven-game losing streak to the Jets by defeating New York 17-14. New York opened the scoring on Ken O'Brien's 32-yard scoring pass to Mickey Shuler. But Buffalo tied the game 7-7 on Walter Broughton's 25-yard touchdown catch. Rookie Jamie Mueller's first NFL score on a two-yard run, and Scott Norwood's 42-yard field goal, put the Bills ahead 17-7. Fred

Raiders —FG Bahr 23
Raiders —Allen 3 run (Bahr kick)
KC —FG Lowery 39
KC —FG Lowery 22
KC —FG Lowery 35

Miami 28, Philadelphia 10—At Veterans Stadium, attendance 63,841. Dan Marino completed 25 of 39 passes for 376 yards and three touchdowns as the Dolphins overpowered the Eagles. Miami took a 14-10 halftime lead on Marino's 20-yard scoring pass to Mark Duper and Ron Davenport's one-yard touchdown run. Marino also completed touchdown passes of 11 and 20 yards to Mark Clayton within a five-minute span in the third quarter to secure the win. Clayton finished with seven receptions for 104 yards.

Miami	0	14	14	0	— 28
Philadelphia	0	10	0	0	— 10

Phil —Quick 44 pass from Cunningham (McFadden kick)
Mia —Duper 20 pass from Marino (Tiffin kick)
Phil —FG McFadden 27
Mia —Davenport 1 run (Tiffin kick)
Mia —Clayton 11 pass from Marino (Tiffin kick)
Mia —Clayton 20 pass from Marino (Tiffin kick)

Green Bay 16, Minnesota 10—At Milwaukee County Stadium, attendance 47,059. Kenneth Davis's seven-yard touchdown run with 1:09 remaining in the game lifted the Packers over the Vikings. Trailing 7-0 in the second quarter, Paul Ott Carruth ran one yard for a score to tie the game at halftime. John Anderson's fumble recovery set up Max Zendejas's 47-yard field goal in the third quarter to give Green Bay a 10-7 edge. Minnesota tied the game on Chuck Nelson's 34-yard field goal in the fourth quarter.

Minnesota	7	0	0	3	— 10
Green Bay	0	7	3	6	— 16

Minn —Carter 40 pass from Kramer (C. Nelson kick)
GB —Carruth 1 run (Zendejas kick)
GB —FG Zendejas 47
Minn —FG C. Nelson 34
GB —Davis 7 run (kick failed)

St. Louis 27, New York Giants 24—At Busch Stadium, attendance 29,623. Vai Sikahema returned a punt 76 yards for a touchdown and had a 48-yard kickoff return to set up another score as the Cardinals downed the Giants for the first time since 1984. Sikahema's kickoff return set up Ron Wolfley's six-yard scoring run to give St. Louis a 14-7 lead in the first quarter. After New York closed the gap to 14-10, Neil Lomax threw a 20-yard scoring pass to Robert Awalt, and Stump Mitchell ran six yards for a touchdown, to give St. Louis a 27-10 halftime lead. New York's Phil Simms threw for 359 yards, including touchdown passes of 11 yards to Mark Bavaro and 14 yards to Lionel Manuel. Bavaro caught a team season-high 11 passes for 137 yards.

N.Y. Giants	7	3	7	7	— 24
St. Louis	14	13	0	0	— 27

StL —Sikahema 76 punt return (Del Greco kick)
NYG —Bavaro 11 pass from Simms (Allegre kick)
StL —Wolfley 6 run (Del Greco kick)
NYG —FG Allegre 29
StL —Awalt 20 pass from Lomax (Del Greco kick)
StL —Mitchell 6 run (kick failed)
NYG —Manuel 14 pass from Simms (Allegre kick)
NYG —Morris 1 run (Allegre kick)

New England 42, New York Jets 20—At Sullivan Stadium, attendance 60,617. Steve Grogan threw four touchdown passes and ran for another as the Patriots beat the Jets. Grogan, who completed 11 of 18 passes for 180 yards, connected with Cedric Jones on touchdowns of 16 and 17 yards, and added scoring passes to Irving Fryar (26 yards) and Stephen Starring (28). He also scored on a two-yard touchdown run, the thirty-fourth rushing touchdown of his career, to give New England a commanding 35-6 lead at the half. Reggie Dupard ran seven yards for a score in the third quarter for the Patriots' final touchdown. The Jets' Al Toon led all receivers with 110 yards on eight catches, including a 28-yard touchdown from Ken O'Brien.

N.Y. Jets	3	3	0	14	— 20
New England	14	21	7	0	— 42

NE —Jones 16 pass from Grogan (Franklin kick)
NYJ —FG Leahy 42
NE —Grogan 2 run (Franklin kick)
NE —Fryar 26 pass from Grogan (Franklin kick)
NYJ —FG Leahy 24
NE —Starring 28 pass from Grogan (Franklin kick)
NE —Jones 17 pass from Grogan (Franklin kick)
NE —Dupard 7 run (Franklin kick)
NYJ —Hector 6 run (Leahy kick)
NYJ —Toon 28 pass from O'Brien (Leahy kick)

Pittsburgh 20, San Diego 16—At San Diego Jack Murphy Stadium, attendance 51,605. Mark Malone and Frank Pollard each rushed for touchdowns, and Gary Anderson kicked two field goals, as the Steelers downed the Chargers. Trailing 9-0 in the second quarter, Pollard ran eight yards for a score to cut the deficit to 9-7. Malone then hit Weegie Thompson with a 47-yard pass to set up his own seven-yard scoring run. Gary Anderson kicked field goals of 43 and 33 yards to complete Pittsburgh's scoring. San Diego's Dan Fouts threw for 334 yards, his fifty-first 300-yard game.

Pittsburgh	0	7	10	3	— 20
San Diego	9	0	0	7	— 16

SD —Brandon recovered blocked punt in end zone (Abbott kick)
SD —Safety, Ehin tackled Malone in end zone
Pitt —Pollard 8 run (Anderson kick)
Pitt —Malone 7 run (Anderson kick)
Pitt —FG Anderson 43
Pitt —FG Anderson 33
SD —James 15 pass from Fouts (Abbott kick)

Seattle 28, Denver 21—At Kingdome, attendance 61,759. Dave Krieg completed three touchdown passes, including two to Ray Butler, as the Seahawks outlasted the Broncos. After a scoreless first quarter, Seattle took a 14-0 halftime lead on Curt Warner's three-yard run and Krieg's three-yard pass to Butler. Denver answered with 14 points in the third quarter on Sammy Winder's 11-yard run and John Elway's 39-yard touchdown pass to Rick Massie. Butler's second scoring reception, a 40-yarder, put Seattle back in front 21-14. Krieg's seven-yard touchdown pass to John L. Williams sealed the win for the Seahawks.

Denver	0	0	14	7	— 21
Seattle	0	14	7	7	— 28

Sea —Warner 3 run (Johnson kick)
Sea —Butler 3 pass from Krieg (Johnson kick)
Den —Winder 11 run (Karlis kick)
Den —Massie 39 pass from Elway (Karlis kick)
Sea —Butler 40 pass from Krieg (Johnson kick)
Sea —Williams 7 pass from Krieg (Johnson kick)
Den —Winder 1 run (Karlis kick)

Monday, December 14

San Francisco 41, Chicago 0—At Candlestick Park, attendance 63,509. Steve Young came off the bench to replace an injured Joe Montana and threw four touchdown passes as the 49ers handed the Bears their first regular-season shutout since 1982. Young entered the game seven minutes into the first quarter after Montana injured a leg. San Francisco took a 20-0 halftime lead on Young's one-yard scoring pass to Jerry Rice, his 13-yarder to Dwight Clark, and Ray Wersching's field goals of 20 and 45 yards. Dana McLemore returned a punt 83 yards for a touchdown, and Young hit Rice on touchdown passes of 16 and 2 yards in the second half, to complete the scoring. Rice tied NFL records for most touchdown catches in a season (18) and most consecutive games with a touchdown reception (11).

Chicago	0	0	0	0	— 0
San Francisco	10	10	14	7	— 41

SF —Rice 1 pass from Young (Wersching kick)
SF —FG Wersching 20
SF —FG Wersching 45
SF —Clark 13 pass from Young (Wersching kick)
SF —McLemore 83 punt return (Wersching kick)
SF —Rice 16 pass from Young (Wersching kick)
SF —Rice 2 pass from Young (Wersching kick)

Fifteenth Week Summaries

Standings

American Football Conference

Eastern Division

	W	L	T	Pct.	Pts.	OP
Indianapolis	8	6	0	.571	276	232
Miami	8	6	0	.571	352	311
Buffalo	7	7	0	.500	263	288
New England	7	7	0	.500	296	283
N.Y. Jets	6	8	0	.429	327	340

Central Division

	W	L	T	Pct.	Pts.	OP
Cleveland	9	5	0	.643	371	226
Houston	8	6	0	.571	324	332
Pittsburgh	8	6	0	.571	272	280
Cincinnati	4	10	0	.286	268	349

Western Division

	W	L	T	Pct.	Pts.	OP
Denver	9	4	1	.679	355	288
Seattle	9	5	0	.643	351	273
San Diego	8	6	0	.571	253	293
L.A. Raiders	5	9	0	.357	298	283
Kansas City	3	11	0	.214	232	368

National Football Conference

Eastern Division

	W	L	T	Pct.	Pts.	OP
Washington	10	4	0	.714	352	261
St. Louis	7	7	0	.500	346	347
Dallas	6	8	0	.429	319	332
Philadelphia	6	8	0	.429	320	373
N.Y. Giants	5	9	0	.357	260	305

Central Division

	W	L	T	Pct.	Pts.	OP
Chicago	10	4	0	.714	350	279
Minnesota	8	6	0	.571	312	308
Green Bay	5	8	1	.393	231	267
Tampa Bay	4	10	0	.286	280	336
Detroit	3	11	0	.214	239	371

Western Division

	W	L	T	Pct.	Pts.	OP
San Francisco	12	2	0	.857	411	253
New Orleans	11	3	0	.786	389	259
L.A. Rams	6	8	0	.429	317	313
Atlanta	3	11	0	.214	192	406

Saturday, December 19

New York Giants 20, Green Bay 10—At Giants Stadium, attendance 51,013. Phil Simms completed two touchdown passes and became the Giants' all-time passing yardage leader. Joe Morris ran three yards for a score and Lee Rouson caught a 26-yard touchdown pass from Simms to give New York a 13-0 lead at halftime. Zeke Mowatt's one-yard touchdown catch extended the Giants' lead to 20-0 in the third quarter. Morris, who gained 37 yards rushing to total 4,081 in his career, joined Alex Webster (4,638) as the only Giants players to gain over 4,000 yards. Simms's 19,551 career passing yards surpassed Charlie Conerly's club-record 19,488. Simms completed 21 of 26 passes for 233 yards in the game.

Green Bay	0	0	3	7	— 10
N.Y. Giants	0	13	7	0	— 20

NYG —Morris 3 run (run failed)
NYG —Rouson 26 pass from Simms (Allegre kick)
NYG —Mowatt 1 pass from Simms (Allegre kick)
GB —FG Zendejas 26
GB —Clark 3 pass from Carruth (Zendejas kick)

Denver 20, Kansas City 17—At Mile High Stadium, attendance 75,053. The Broncos opened a 17-3 halftime lead and held on to defeat the Chiefs and clinch at least a Wild Card playoff berth. Denver took its lead on a three-yard touchdown run by Gene Lang, a 20-yard field goal by Rich Karlis, and John Elway's eight-yard scoring pass to Sammy Winder. Kansas City cut the lead to 20-17 in the second half on Herman Heard's 64-yard run and Bill Kenney's eight-yard touchdown pass to Stephone Paige. The Chiefs had a chance to tie the game, but Nick Lowery's 37-yard field-goal attempt with 34 seconds remaining sailed wide right.

Kansas City	0	3	7	7	— 17
Denver	7	10	3	0	— 20

Den —Lang 3 run (Karlis kick)
Den —FG Karlis 20
KC —FG Lowery 33
Den —Winder 8 pass from Elway (Karlis kick)
KC —Heard 64 run (Lowery kick)
Den —FG Karlis 43
KC —Paige 8 pass from Kenney (Lowery kick)

Sunday, December 20

Cleveland 24, Los Angeles Raiders 17—At Memorial Coliseum, attendance 40,275. Bernie Kosar threw for 294 yards and two touchdowns to help the Browns defeat the Raiders and clinch a playoff berth. Cleveland took a 17-3 halftime lead on Kosar's two-yard touchdown pass to Earnest Byner, Byner's 15-yard touchdown run, and Matt Bahr's 20-yard field goal. Webster Slaughter, who caught seven passes for 115 yards, scored on an 18-yard pass from Kosar in the third quarter to complete the Browns' scoring.

Cleveland	7	10	7	0	— 24
L.A. Raiders	3	0	0	14	— 17

Raiders —FG C. Bahr 39
Clev —Byner 2 pass from Kosar (M. Bahr kick)
Clev —FG M. Bahr 20
Clev —Byner 15 run (M. Bahr kick)
Clev —Slaughter 18 pass from Kosar (M. Bahr kick)
Raiders —Toran 48 interception return (C. Bahr kick)
Raiders —Lofton 28 pass from Wilson (C. Bahr kick)

Indianapolis 20, San Diego 7—At San Diego Jack Murphy Stadium, attendance 46,211. The Colts' defense registered five sacks and had three interceptions to upend the Chargers. Jack Trudeau and Bill Brooks teamed up on a 42-yard scoring pass to tie the game 7-7 in the first quarter. Indianapolis went ahead 20-7 on Dean Biasucci's field goals from 36 and 41 yards and Albert Bentley's three-yard run. The Colts' defense held the Chargers to 59 yards rushing. Eric Dickerson (1,092) topped the 1,000-yard mark for the fifth straight season by gaining 115 yards on 23 carries.

Indianapolis	7	6	0	7	— 20
San Diego	7	0	0	0	— 7

SD —Fouts 1 run (Abbott kick)
Ind —Brooks 42 pass from Trudeau (Biasucci kick)
Ind —FG Biasucci 36
Ind —FG Biasucci 41
Ind —Bentley 3 run (Biasucci kick)

Minnesota 17, Detroit 14—At Pontiac Silverdome, attendance 27,693. Wade Wilson threw for one touchdown and ran for another as the Vikings snapped a two-game losing streak. Wilson opened the scoring with a 20-yard touchdown pass to D. J. Dozier. Chuck Nelson then kicked a 22-yard field goal to give Minnesota a 10-7 halftime edge. Wilson, who also led the Vikings in rushing with 55 yards, ran two yards for a score in the fourth quarter to give Minnesota a 17-7 lead. Safety Joey Browner had two of the Vikings' three interceptions.

Minnesota	0	10	0	7	— 17
Detroit	0	7	0	7	— 14

Minn —Dozier 20 pass from Wilson (C. Nelson kick)
Det —Mandley 4 pass from Long (Murray kick)
Minn —FG C. Nelson 22
Minn —Wilson 2 run (C. Nelson kick)
Det —James 16 run (Murray kick)

New England 13, Buffalo 7—At Rich Stadium, attendance 74,945. Reggie Dupard and Cedric Jones each scored touchdowns as the Patriots overcame a steady rain and a 25-mile-an-hour wind to defeat the Bills. New England opened the scoring on Jones's seven-yard touchdown pass from Steve Grogan. Dupard's 36-yard scoring run gave the Patriots a 13-0 halftime lead. Buffalo defensive end Sean McNanie's 14-yard fumble return for a touchdown prevented the shutout. The Patriots' defense held the Bills to just 148 yards total offense and ended Jim Kelly's streak of 19 straight games with a touchdown pass.

New England	7	6	0	0 —	13
Buffalo	0	0	7	0 —	7

NE —Jones 7 pass from Grogan (Franklin kick)
NE —Dupard 36 run (kick failed)
Buff —McNanie 14 fumble recovery return (Norwood kick)

New Orleans 41, Cincinnati 24—At Riverfront Stadium, attendance 43,424. Buford Jordan ran for two touchdowns as the Saints rallied for 38 unanswered points to defeat the Bengals. Dave Wilson, replacing an injured Bobby Hebert, completed a 29-yard touchdown pass to Mike Jones, and Dalton Hilliard ran two yards for a score, as New Orleans tied the game in the third quarter 24-24. The Saints then exploded for 17 points in the fourth quarter to put the game away on Morten Andersen's 30-yard field goal and Jordan's scoring runs of one and eight yards.

New Orleans	3	7	14	17 —	41
Cincinnati	14	10	0	0 —	24

Cin —Brown 10 pass from Esiason (Breech kick)
NO —FG Andersen 21
Cin —Jennings 1 pass from Esiason (Breech kick)
Cin —FG Breech 43
Cin —Kinnebrew 1 run (Breech kick)
NO —Hilliard 2 run (Andersen kick)
NO —Jones 29 pass from Wilson (Andersen kick)
NO —Hilliard 3 run (Andersen kick)
NO —FG Andersen 30
NO —Jordan 1 run (Andersen kick)
NO —Jordan 8 run (Andersen kick)

Philadelphia 38, New York Jets 27—At Giants Stadium, attendance 30,572. Randall Cunningham threw three touchdown passes, including two to Mike Quick, as the Eagles downed the Jets. With Philadelphia trailing 17-10 in the second quarter, the Eagles came back to take a 24-17 lead on scoring passes from Cunningham to Quick (45 and 13 yards). Keith Byars's two-yard run and Cris Carter's 14-yard touchdown reception extended Philadelphia's lead to 38-20. The Eagles' defense held the Jets to 78 yards rushing. New York's Al Toon had 10 catches for 168 yards in his third straight 100-yard game.

Philadelphia	10	14	14	0 —	38
N.Y. Jets	3	17	0	7 —	27

Phil —Toney 3 run (McFadden kick)
Phil —FG McFadden 38
NYJ —FG Leahy 42
NYJ —Sohn 9 pass from O'Brien (Leahy kick)
NYJ —Vick 5 run (Leahy kick)
Phil —Quick 45 pass from Cunningham (McFadden kick)
Phil —Quick 13 pass from Cunningham (McFadden kick)
NYJ —FG Leahy 29
Phil —Byars 2 run (McFadden kick)
Phil —Carter 14 pass from Cunningham (McFadden kick)
NYJ —Toon 51 pass from O'Brien (Leahy kick)

Houston 24, Pittsburgh 16—At Astrodome, attendance 38,683. Warren Moon threw for 240 yards and two touchdowns as the Oilers completed their first-ever season-sweep of the Steelers. Moon hit Drew Hill with a 52-yard scoring pass in the second quarter and Tony Zendejas kicked a 34-yard field goal to give Houston a 10-6 halftime edge. Allen Pinkett ran five yards for a touchdown and Hill, who had four receptions for 109 yards, caught a 30-yard touchdown pass to complete the scoring.

Pittsburgh	3	3	7	3 —	16
Houston	0	10	7	7 —	24

Pitt —FG Anderson 25
Pitt —FG Anderson 35
Hou —Hill 52 pass from Moon (Zendejas kick)
Hou —FG Zendejas 34
Pitt —Malone 1 run (Anderson kick)
Hou —Pinkett 5 run (Zendejas kick)
Pitt —FG Anderson 20
Hou —Hill 30 pass from Moon (Zendejas kick)

St. Louis 31, Tampa Bay 14—At Tampa Stadium, attendance 32,046. Neil Lomax completed three touchdown passes, and Stump Mitchell ran for another, to power the Cardinals over the Buccaneers. Cedric Mack's two fumble recoveries set up Lomax's 15-yard scoring pass to Jay Novacek and Al Del Greco's 28-yard field goal. Lomax, who hit on 22 of 29 passes for 233 yards, also completed scoring passes to J.T. Smith (eight yards) and Robert Awalt (five). Mitchell rushed for 101 yards on 23 carries, including a three-yard touchdown run in the fourth quarter. St. Louis's defense recorded six sacks and had two interceptions.

St. Louis	0	14	10	7 —	31
Tampa Bay	7	0	0	7 —	14

TB —Hall 1 pass from Testaverde (Igwebuike kick)
StL —Novacek 15 pass from Lomax (Del Greco kick)
StL —J.T. Smith 8 pass from Lomax (Del Greco kick)
StL —FG Del Greco 28
StL —Awalt 5 pass from Lomax (Del Greco kick)
StL —Mitchell 3 run (Del Greco kick)
TB —Carter 26 pass from Testaverde (Igwebuike kick)

San Francisco 35, Atlanta 7—At Candlestick Park, attendance 54,275. Jerry Rice set two NFL records and caught three touchdown passes as the 49ers beat the Falcons. Rice's scoring catches of 5, 20, and 1 yards gave him 21 for the season, breaking Mark Clayton's previous NFL record of 18 set in 1984. It was also Rice's twelfth straight game with a touchdown catch, bettering the previous record of 11 held by Elroy (Crazylegs) Hirsch and Buddy Dial. Atlanta's Sylvester Stamps (97 yards) and San Francisco's Joe Cribbs (92) had back-to-back kickoff returns for touchdowns in the third quarter to tie an NFL mark. Steve Young, who started at quarterback for the 49ers, passed for 216 yards and rushed for 83 more.

Atlanta	0	0	7	0 —	7
San Francisco	0	7	14	14 —	35

SF —Rice 5 pass from Young (Wersching kick)
SF —Rice 20 pass from Young (Wersching kick)
Atl —Stamps 97 kickoff return (Luckhurst kick)
SF —Cribbs 92 kickoff return (Wersching kick)
SF —Young 29 run (Wersching kick)
SF —Rice 1 pass from Young (Wersching kick)

Seattle 34, Chicago 21—At Soldier Field, attendance 62,518. Dave Krieg threw two touchdown passes, and Norm Johnson kicked two field goals, to lead the Seahawks. With the score tied 7-7 at halftime, Brian Bosworth recovered a fumble to set up Curt Warner's one-yard touchdown run. John L. Williams caught a 75-yard touchdown pass from Krieg, and Johnson added field goals of 45 and 29 yards to give Seattle a 27-14 third-quarter lead. Warner rushed four yards for a touchdown to finish the Seahawks' scoring. Chicago's Walter Payton, playing in his last regular-season game at Soldier Field, had touchdown runs of three and five yards and led all rushers with 79 yards.

Seattle	0	7	20	7 —	34
Chicago	0	7	7	7 —	21

Sea —Turner 12 pass from Krieg (Johnson kick)
Chi —Moorehead 3 pass from Tomczak (Butler kick)
Sea —Warner 1 run (Johnson kick)
Chi —Payton 3 run (Butler kick)
Sea —Williams 75 pass from Krieg (Johnson kick)
Sea —FG Johnson 45
Sea —FG Johnson 29
Chi —Payton 5 run (Butler kick)
Sea —Warner 4 run (Johnson kick)

Miami 23, Washington 21—At Joe Robbie Stadium, attendance 65,715. Dan Marino threw for 393 yards and completed three scoring passes to Mark Duper to highlight the Dolphins' victory over the Redskins. After a scoreless first quarter, Fuad Reveiz kicked a 48-yard field goal and Marino fired a 26-yard scoring pass to Duper to give Miami a 9-7 halftime lead. Washington rebounded to a 14-9 edge on Jay Schroeder's six-yard run, but Miami regained the lead 16-14 as Marino found Duper on a 59-yard scoring bomb. Duper's six-yard reception with 1:07 to play proved to be the game-winner. The Redskins' defense was held without a sack for the first time in 68 games.

Washington	0	7	7	7 —	21
Miami	0	9	0	14 —	23

Mia —FG Reveiz 48
Wash —Bryant 6 run (Haji-Sheikh kick)
Mia —Duper 26 pass from Marino (kick failed)
Wash —Schroeder 6 run (Haji-Sheikh kick)
Mia —Duper 59 pass from Marino (Reveiz kick)
Wash —Rogers 2 run (Haji-Sheikh kick)
Mia —Duper 6 pass from Marino (Reveiz kick)

Monday, December 22

Dallas 29, Los Angeles Rams 21—At Anaheim Stadium, attendance 60,700. Roger Ruzek kicked a club-record five field goals, and Herschel Walker ran for 108 yards and a touchdown, to lead the Cowboys over the Rams. Walker's one-yard run and Ruzek's field goals from 24, 42, and 44 yards gave Dallas a 16-7 halftime lead. The Cowboys increased their advantage to 26-7 in the third quarter on Ruzek's 47-yard field goal and Doug Cosbie's 27-yard touchdown catch. Ruzek added his club-record fifth field goal, a 37-yarder, in the fourth quarter. Dallas's defense held the Rams to just 74 yards rushing.

Dallas	10	6	10	3 —	29
L.A. Rams	7	0	7	7 —	21

Dall —Walker 1 run (Ruzek kick)
Rams —White 8 run (Lansford kick)
Dall —FG Ruzek 24
Dall —FG Ruzek 42
Dall —FG Ruzek 44
Dall —FG Ruzek 47
Dall —Cosbie 27 pass from Pelluer (Ruzek kick)
Rams —Everett 1 run (Lansford kick)
Dall —FG Ruzek 37
Rams —House 15 pass from Dils (Lansford kick)

Sixteenth Week Summaries

Standings

American Football Conference

Eastern Division	W	L	T	Pct.	Pts.	OP
Indianapolis*	9	6	0	.600	300	238
New England	8	7	0	.533	320	293
Miami	8	7	0	.533	362	335
Buffalo	7	8	0	.467	270	305
N.Y. Jets	6	9	0	.400	334	360
Central Division						
Cleveland*	10	5	0	.667	390	239
Houston*	9	6	0	.600	345	349
Pittsburgh	8	7	0	.533	285	299
Cincinnati	4	11	0	.267	285	370
Western Division						
Denver*	10	4	1	.700	379	288
Seattle*	9	6	0	.600	371	314
San Diego	8	7	0	.533	253	317
L.A. Raiders	5	10	0	.333	301	289
Kansas City	4	11	0	.267	273	388

National Football Conference

Eastern Division	W	L	T	Pct.	Pts.	OP
Washington*	11	4	0	.733	379	285
Dallas	7	8	0	.467	340	348
St. Louis	7	8	0	.467	362	368
Philadelphia	7	8	0	.467	337	380
N.Y. Giants	6	9	0	.400	280	312
Central Division						
Chicago*	11	4	0	.733	356	282
Minnesota*	8	7	0	.533	336	335
Green Bay	5	9	1	.367	255	300
Tampa Bay	4	11	0	.267	286	360
Detroit	4	11	0	.267	269	384
Western Division						
San Francisco*	13	2	0	.867	459	253
New Orleans*	12	3	0	.800	422	283
L.A. Rams	6	9	0	.400	317	361
Atlanta	3	12	0	.200	205	436

**Denotes Playoff Team*

New England finished second in the AFC East because of better division record (6-2 vs. 2-6 by Miami). Dallas finished second in NFC East because of better division record (4-4 vs. 3-5 by St. Louis and Philadelphia). St. Louis finished third in NFC East because of better conference record (7-7 vs. 4-7 by Philadelphia). Tampa Bay finished fourth in NFC Central because of better division record (3-4 vs. 2-5 by Detroit).

Saturday, December 26

Cleveland 19, Pittsburgh 13—At Three Rivers Stadium, attendance 56,394. Bernie Kosar threw for 241 yards and one touchdown and the Browns' defense held the Steelers to 221 total yards as Cleveland notched its third straight AFC Central title. Matt Bahr's 31-yard field goal and Kosar's two-yard touchdown pass to Derek Tennell gave the Browns a 9-3 first-half lead. Bahr kicked a 30-yard field goal and Earnest Byner ran two yards for a touchdown to complete Cleveland's scoring. Pittsburgh's only touchdown came on a 45-yard interception return by Cornell Gowdy with 7:33 remaining in the game.

Cleveland	3	6	3	7 —	19
Pittsburgh	0	3	0	10 —	13

Clev —FG Bahr 31
Clev —Tennell 2 pass from Kosar (kick failed)
Pitt —FG Anderson 39
Clev —FG Bahr 30
Pitt —FG Anderson 27
Clev —Byner 2 run (Bahr kick)
Pitt —Gowdy 45 interception return (Anderson kick)

Washington 27, Minnesota 24—At Metrodome, attendance 59,160. Ali Haji-Sheikh's 26-yard field goal with 12:51 remaining in overtime lifted the Redskins to a 27-24 win over the Vikings. Washington gained a 14-7 advantage in the third quarter on Barry Wilburn's club-record 100-yard interception return and Ricky Sanders's 46-yard scoring pass from Doug Williams. Minnesota rallied for 17 points in the fourth quarter to overtake the Redskins 24-14. But Washington tied the score 24-24 on Haji-Sheikh's 37-yard field goal and Williams's 51-yard pass to Sanders. Sanders led all receivers with eight catches for 164 yards.

Washington	0	7	7	10	3 —	27
Minnesota	7	0	0	17	0 —	24

Minn —Anderson 9 run (C. Nelson kick)
Wash —Wilburn 100 interception return (Haji-Sheikh kick)
Wash —Sanders 46 pass from Williams (Haji-Sheikh kick)
Minn —Anderson 1 run (C. Nelson kick)
Minn —Wilson 1 run (C. Nelson kick)
Minn —FG C. Nelson 20
Wash —FG Haji-Sheikh 37
Wash —Sanders 51 pass from Williams (Haji-Sheikh kick)
Wash —FG Haji-Sheikh 26

Sunday, December 27

Philadelphia 17, Buffalo 7—At Veterans Stadium, attendance 57,547. Anthony Toney caught one touchdown pass and ran for another as the Eagles downed the Bills. After a scoreless first quarter, Philadelphia took a 10-0 halftime lead on Byron Evans's interception that set up Paul McFadden's 39-yard field goal, and Randall Cunningham's 18-yard scoring pass to Toney. Toney ran two yards for a touchdown in the third quarter to extend Philadelphia's lead to 17-0. Reggie White had two sacks, and the Eagles' defense held the Bills to 57 yards rushing.

Buffalo 0 0 0 7 — 7
Philadelphia 0 10 7 0 — 17

Phil —FG McFadden 39
Phil —Toney 18 pass from Cunningham (McFadden kick)
Phil —Toney 2 run (McFadden kick)
Buff —Reed 4 pass from Kelly (Norwood kick)

Chicago 6, Los Angeles Raiders 3—At Memorial Coliseum, attendance 78,019. Kevin Butler kicked two field goals as the NFC Central champion Bears edged the Raiders. Chris Bahr's 48-yard field goal opened the scoring in the first quarter. Butler's first field goal, a 38-yarder in the second quarter, tied the game 3-3 at halftime. Chicago drove 60 yards in 13 plays to set up Butler's 30-yard field goal with less than five minutes left to play. Richard Dent had a career-high four-and-a-half sacks and was named NFC defensive player of the week. Walter Payton, playing in his final regular-season game, led all rushers with 82 yards.

Chicago 0 3 0 3 — 6
L.A. Raiders 3 0 0 0 — 3

Raiders —FG Bahr 48
Chi —FG Butler 38
Chi —FG Butler 30

Houston 21, Cincinnati 17—At Astrodome, attendance 49,275. Alonzo Highsmith scored the first two touchdowns of his NFL career and Warren Moon ran for another as the Oilers defeated the Bengals to clinch their first playoff berth since 1980. Highsmith caught a 33-yard touchdown pass and scored on a one-yard run, and Moon added a one-yard touchdown run to give Houston a 21-7 halftime advantage. Cincinnati scored 10 points in the second half to narrow Houston's lead to 21-17, but Oilers defensive end Ray Childress sacked Bengals quarterback Boomer Esiason with 5:19 left to play, forcing Cincinnati to surrender the ball. Mike Rozier gained 103 yards on 20 carries, and Drew Hill caught six passes for 109 yards for the Oilers.

Cincinnati 7 0 7 3 — 17
Houston 7 14 0 0 — 21

Cin —Jennings 1 run (Breech kick)
Hou —Highsmith 33 pass from Moon (Zendejas kick)
Hou —Moon 1 run (Zendejas kick)
Hou —Highsmith 1 run (Zendejas kick)
Cin —Martin 25 pass from Esiason (Breech kick)
Cin —FG Breech 43

Detroit 30, Atlanta 13—At Atlanta-Fulton County Stadium, attendance 13,906. Gary Ellerson ran for two touchdowns and Eddie Murray kicked three field goals as the Lions beat the Falcons. Ellerson's eight-yard touchdown run gave Detroit an early 7-0 edge. Detroit came back from a 13-10 halftime deficit to take a 23-13 lead on Ellerson's two-yard scoring run and Murray field goals of 23 and 46 yards. The Lions' defense recorded two sacks and had four interceptions, including Ricky Smith's 34-yard touchdown return midway through the fourth quarter.

Detroit 7 3 10 10 — 30
Atlanta 0 13 0 0 — 13

Det —Ellerson 8 run (Murray kick)
Atl —FG Luckhurst 50
Det —FG Murray 45
Atl —Dixon 51 pass from Miller (Luckhurst kick)
Atl —FG Luckhurst 28
Det —Ellerson 2 run (Murray kick)
Det —FG Murray 23
Det —FG Murray 46
Det —Smith 34 interception return (Murray kick)

New Orleans 33, Green Bay 24—At Louisiana Superdome, attendance 68,364. Morten Andersen kicked four first-half field goals, and the Saints exploded for three touchdowns in the second half, as New Orleans won its ninth straight. With the Packers holding a 17-12 lead in the third quarter, Dalton Hilliard ran 23 yards to set up Rueben Mayes's three-yard touchdown run, giving New Orleans a 19-17 edge. The Packers regained the lead 24-19, but Hilliard returned the ensuing kickoff 74 yards to set up Bobby Hebert's five-yard scoring pass to John Tice. Hilliard's one-yard touchdown run midway through the fourth quarter clinched the victory.

Green Bay 14 3 7 0 — 24
New Orleans 9 3 14 7 — 33

NO —FG Andersen 31
GB —Stanley 29 pass from Majkowski (Zendejas kick)
GB —Stanley 39 pass from Majkowski (Zendejas kick)
NO —FG Andersen 52
NO —FG Andersen 48
GB —FG Zendejas 24
NO —FG Andersen 32
NO —Mayes 3 run (Andersen kick)
GB —Epps 20 pass from Majkowski (Zendejas kick)
NO —Tice 5 pass from Hebert (Andersen kick)
NO —Hilliard 1 run (Andersen kick)

New York Giants 20, New York Jets 7—At Giants Stadium, attendance 68,318. Joe Morris rushed for over 100 yards for the first time in 1987 as the Giants downed the Jets. Trailing 7-3 in the second quarter, Phil Simms completed scoring passes of 12 yards to Mark Bavaro and 16 yards to Odessa Turner to give the Giants a 17-7 lead. Raul Allegre added a 23-yard field goal in the fourth quarter to finish the Giants' scoring. Morris gained 132 yards on 26 carries, while Bavaro had six receptions for 109 yards. The Giants' defense held the Jets to 68 yards rushing, while maintaining a 34:54 to 25:06 time-of-possession advantage.

N.Y. Jets 7 0 0 0 — 7
N.Y. Giants 0 17 3 0 — 20

NYJ —Hector 14 run (Leahy kick)
NYG —FG Allegre 29
NYG —Bavaro 12 pass from Simms (Allegre kick)
NYG —Turner 16 pass from Simms (Allegre kick)
NYG —FG Allegre 23

Dallas 21, St. Louis 16—At Texas Stadium, attendance 36,788. Herschel Walker rushed for 137 yards and scored two second-quarter touchdowns as the Cowboys eliminated the Cardinals from the playoffs. Walker's pair of 11-yard scoring runs gave Dallas a 14-10 halftime advantage. Steve Pelluer scored on a five-yard run in the fourth quarter for Dallas's decisive points. St. Louis got as close as the Cowboys' 22-yard line with less than two minutes remaining, but Manny Hendrix knocked down Neil Lomax's fourth-down pass attempt to preserve the win. Walker was named NFC offensive player of the week for his performance.

St. Louis 3 7 0 6 — 16
Dallas 0 14 0 7 — 21

StL —FG Del Greco 32
Dall —Walker 11 run (Ruzek kick)
Dall —Walker 11 run (Ruzek kick)
StL —Smith 2 pass from Lomax (Del Greco kick)
StL —FG Del Greco 28
Dall —Pelluer 5 run (Ruzek kick)
StL —FG Del Greco 37

Denver 24, San Diego 0—At Mile High Stadium, attendance 37,500. K.C. Clark returned a punt for a touchdown, and Ricky Hunley returned an interception for a score, as the AFC West champion Broncos blanked the Chargers to earn the home-field advantage throughout the playoffs. On Denver's first possession of the game, Clark scored on a 71-yard punt return. Sammy Winder added a one-yard scoring run in the first quarter to put Denver up 14-0. The Broncos added 10 points in the fourth quarter on Rich Karlis's 26-yard field goal and Hunley's 52-yard interception return for a score.

San Diego 0 0 0 0 — 0
Denver 14 0 0 10 — 24

Den —Clark 71 punt return (Karlis kick)
Den —Winder 1 run (Karlis kick)
Den —FG Karlis 26
Den —Hunley 52 interception return (Karlis kick)

Kansas City 41, Seattle 20—At Arrowhead Stadium, attendance 20,370. Bill Kenney threw for 320 yards and three touchdowns as the Chiefs overpowered the Seahawks. Kansas City jumped to a 17-7 first-quarter lead on Herman Heard's (12 carries for 107 yards) 37-yard run, Carlos Carson's (four receptions for 120 yards) 81-yard touchdown catch, and Nick Lowery's 35-yard field goal. The Chiefs increased their lead to 27-20 at the half on Paul Palmer's 92-yard kickoff return for a touchdown and Lowery's 44-yard field goal. Kenney fired touchdowns to tackle-eligible Mark Adickes (three yards) and Stephone Paige (46) for the only scoring in the second half. Paige finished with seven catches for 100 yards.

Seattle 7 13 0 0 — 20
Kansas City 17 10 7 7 — 41

KC —Heard 37 run (Lowery kick)
Sea —Largent 15 pass from Krieg (Johnson kick)
KC —FG Lowery 35
KC —Carson 81 pass from Kenney (Lowery kick)
Sea —Skansi 8 pass from Krieg (Johnson kick)
KC —Palmer 92 kickoff return (Lowery kick)
Sea —FG Johnson 39
Sea —FG Johnson 24
KC —FG Lowery 44
KC —Adickes 3 pass from Kenney (Lowery kick)
KC —Paige 46 pass from Kenney (Lowery kick)

Indianapolis 24, Tampa Bay 6—At Hoosier Dome, attendance 60,468. Eric Dickerson carried 33 times for 196 yards and two touchdowns as the Colts defeated the Buccaneers to capture their first AFC East title since 1977. Dickerson scored on runs of 6 and 34 yards, and Dean Biasucci kicked a 30-yard field goal for a 17-3 lead after three quarters. Albert Bentley added a two-yard touchdown run in the fourth quarter to put the game away. Dickerson rushed for a club-record six 100-yard games, in 1987, surpassing Lydell Mitchell's five in 1975.

Tampa Bay 3 0 0 3 — 6
Indianapolis 7 3 7 7 — 24

Ind —Dickerson 6 run (Biasucci kick)
TB —FG Igwebuike 38
Ind —FG Biasucci 30
Ind —Dickerson 34 run (Biasucci kick)
TB —FG Igwebuike 39
Ind —Bentley 2 run (Biasucci kick)

San Francisco 48, Los Angeles Rams 0—At Candlestick Park, attendance 57,950. Jerry Rice caught two touchdown passes as the 49ers defeated the Rams to claim their fifth NFC West title in seven years. San Francisco took a commanding 27-0 halftime lead on Steve Young's touchdown passes of 22 and 50 yards to Rice and 7 yards to Mike Wilson, and Roger Craig's one-yard run for a score. Joe Montana came off the bench in the second half and added two more scoring passes. Rice increased his two NFL records to 22 touchdown catches and at least one touchdown catch in 13 straight games.

L.A. Rams 0 0 0 0 — 0
San Francisco 13 14 7 14 — 48

SF —Craig 1 run (kick failed)
SF —Rice 22 pass from Young (Wersching kick)
SF —Rice 50 pass from Young (Wersching kick)
SF —Wilson 7 pass from Young (Wersching kick)
SF —Frank 11 pass from Montana (Wersching kick)
SF —Wilson 46 pass from Montana (Wersching kick)
SF —Taylor 26 fumble recovery return (Wersching kick)

Monday, December 28

New England 24, Miami 10—At Joe Robbie Stadium, attendance 61,192. Steve Grogan, playing with a broken bone in his left hand, threw for 238 yards and two touchdowns to lead the Patriots over the Dolphins. New England took a 24-3 lead at halftime on Grogan's scoring passes of three yards to Irving Fryar and 34 yards to Stephen Starring, Tony Collins's five-yard touchdown run, and Tony Franklin's 31-yard field goal. The Patriots held a 37:48 to 22:12 time-of-possession advantage over Miami.

New England 14 10 0 0 — 24
Miami 3 0 0 7 — 10

NE —Fryar 3 pass from Grogan (Franklin kick)
Mia —FG Reveiz 47
NE —Starring 34 pass from Grogan (Franklin kick)
NE —Collins 5 run (Franklin kick)
NE —FG Franklin 31
Mia —Pruitt 9 pass from Marino (Reveiz kick)

Seventeenth Week Summaries

Sunday, January 3, 1988
AFC First-Round Playoff Game

Houston 23, Seattle 20—At Astrodome, attendance 50,519. Oilers kicker Tony Zendejas atoned for a fourth-quarter 29-yard field-goal miss by converting a 42-yarder 8:05 into overtime to help Houston advance to the divisional playoffs for the first time since 1980. Quarterback Warren Moon completed 21 of 32 passes for 273 yards and one touchdown in his initial NFL playoff game. Drew Hill and Ernest Givins combined for 13 catches for 173 yards, including six for 71 on third downs. Wide receiver Willie Drewrey's first NFL touchdown catch, a 29-yarder, gave the Oilers a 20-13 lead in the third quarter. However, Seattle quarterback Dave Krieg hit wide receiver Steve Largent on a 12-yard scoring pass in the final 1:47 to tie the score and send the game into overtime. Houston held a 47:44 to 20:21 time-of-possession advantage over Seattle and outgained the Seahawks 437 yards to 250.

Seattle 7 3 3 7 0 — 20
Houston 3 10 7 0 3 — 23

Sea —Largent 20 pass from Krieg (Johnson kick)
Hou —FG Zendejas 47
Hou —Rozier 1 run (Zendejas kick)
Hou —FG Zendejas 49
Sea —FG Johnson 33
Sea —FG Johnson 41
Hou —Drewrey 29 pass from Moon (Zendejas kick)
Sea —Largent 12 pass from Krieg (Johnson kick)
Hou —FG Zendejas 42

Sunday, January 3, 1988
NFC First-Round Playoff Game

Minnesota 44, New Orleans 10—At Louisiana Superdome, attendance 68,546. Minnesota scored the most points ever in a Wild Card game in downing host New Orleans. The Vikings compiled 417 yards, and yielded only 149 in advancing to the divisional playoffs. Minnesota held a time-of-possession advantage of 41:18 to 18:42. In addition, the defense had four interceptions, two fumble recoveries, and two sacks. Vikings wide receiver Anthony Carter caught six passes for 79 yards, including a 10-yard touchdown. His 84-yard punt return for a touchdown broke the previous NFL playoff record of 81 yards by the Bears' Hugh Gallarneau in 1941. Darrin Nelson carried 17 times for 73 yards for Minnesota.

Minnesota 10 21 3 10 — 44
New Orleans 7 3 0 0 — 10

NO —Martin 10 pass from Hebert (Andersen kick)
Minn —FG C. Nelson 42
Minn —Carter 84 punt return (C. Nelson kick)

Minn —Jordan 5 pass from Wilson (C. Nelson kick)
Minn —Carter 10 pass from Rice (C. Nelson kick)
NO —FG Andersen 40
Minn —Jones 44 pass from Wilson (C. Nelson kick)
Minn —FG C. Nelson 32
Minn —FG C. Nelson 19
Minn —Dozier 8 run (C. Nelson kick)

Eighteenth Week Summaries

Saturday, January 9, 1988
AFC Divisional Playoff Game

Cleveland 38, Indianapolis 21—At Cleveland Stadium, attendance 79,372. Quarterback Bernie Kosar threw for three touchdowns, and running back Earnest Byner rushed for 122 yards and scored two touchdowns, as the Browns advanced to their second straight AFC Championship Game with a 38-21 triumph over the Colts. Cleveland took the opening kickoff and drove 86 yards for a touchdown. Kosar capped the 15-play drive with a 10-yard scoring pass to Byner. After Indianapolis tied the score 7-7, Kosar hit wide receiver Reggie Langhorne on a 39-yard scoring pass with 1:51 to go in the first half. But Jack Trudeau's 19-yard touchdown pass to Eric Dickerson, 42 seconds before halftime, tied the score 14-14. The turning point in the game came midway through the third quarter when safety Felix Wright intercepted a Trudeau pass at the Cleveland 14-yard line. The Browns then concluded another 86-yard drive on Byner's two-yard run. Kosar (20 of 31 passes for 229 yards) threw three touchdown passes for the first time in his four postseason games. Cornerback Frank Minnifield returned an interception 48 yards for the game's final touchdown with 39 seconds left. The Browns averaged 6.2 yards per play in gaining 404 yards. Cleveland converted 11 of 14 third-down plays.

Indianapolis	7	7	0	7	— 21
Cleveland	7	7	7	17	— 38

Clev —Byner 10 pass from Kosar (Bahr kick)
Ind —Beach 2 pass from Trudeau (Biasucci kick)
Clev —Langhorne 39 pass from Kosar (Bahr kick)
Ind —Dickerson 19 pass from Trudeau (Biasucci kick)
Clev —Byner 2 run (Bahr kick)
Clev —FG Bahr 22
Clev —Brennan 2 pass from Kosar (Bahr kick)
Ind —Bentley 1 run (Biasucci kick)
Clev —Minnifield 48 interception return (Bahr kick)

Saturday, January 9, 1988
NFC Divisional Playoff

Minnesota 36, San Francisco 24—At Candlestick Park, attendance 63,008. Minnesota advanced to its first NFC Championship Game since 1977 by defeating San Francisco 36-24. Wide receiver Anthony Carter established an NFL playoff record with 227 receiving yards on 10 receptions. The old record of 198 yards was set by Tom Fears of the Los Angeles Rams in 1950. Quarterback Wade Wilson played the entire game, completing 20 of 34 passes for 298 yards. Kicker Chuck Nelson made all five of his field goals from 21, 23, 40, 46, and 23 yards. Rookie cornerback Reggie Rutland added a 45-yard interception return for a touchdown. The Vikings' defense had four sacks and two interceptions.

Minnesota	3	17	10	6	— 36
San Francisco	3	0	14	7	— 24

Minn —FG C. Nelson 21
SF —FG Wersching 43
Minn —Hilton 7 pass from Wilson (C. Nelson kick)
Minn —FG C. Nelson 23
Minn —Rutland 45 interception return (C. Nelson kick)
SF —Fuller 48 interception return (Wersching kick)
Minn —Jones 5 pass from Wilson (C. Nelson kick)
SF —Young 5 run (Wersching kick)
Minn —FG C. Nelson 40
Minn —FG C. Nelson 46
SF —Frank 16 pass from Young (Wersching kick)
Minn —FG C. Nelson 23

Sunday, January 10, 1988
AFC Divisional Playoff

Denver 34, Houston 10—At Mile High Stadium, attendance 75,440. Denver quarterback John Elway passed for two touchdowns and ran for a third as the Broncos defeated the Oilers 34-10 to become the first AFC West team since the San Diego Chargers of 1980 and 1981 to play in consecutive AFC Championship Games. Denver capitalized on two Houston turnovers to take a 14-0 first-quarter lead. Safety Steve Wilson recovered Warren Moon's lateral to Mike Rozier at the Oilers' 1-yard line to set up Gene Lang's one-yard touchdown run. Karl Mecklenburg's interception on Houston's next possession led to Elway's first touchdown pass, a 27-yarder to Clarence Kay. Kay also caught a one-yarder in the second quarter for the first two-touchdown game of his four-year career. Elway, who completed 14 of 25 passes for 259 yards, scored on a three-yard run with 4:23 remaining to seal the win. Wide receiver Vance Johnson caught four passes for 105 yards, including a 55-yarder to set up Kay's second score. The Broncos held the Oilers to 73 rushing yards.

Houston	0	3	0	7	— 10
Denver	14	10	3	7	— 34

Den —Lang 1 run (Karlis kick)
Den —Kay 27 pass from Elway (Karlis kick)
Den —FG Karlis 43
Hou —FG Zendejas 46
Den —Kay 1 pass from Elway (Karlis kick)
Den —FG Karlis 23
Hou —Givins 19 pass from Moon (Zendejas kick)
Den —Elway 3 run (Karlis kick)

Sunday, January 10, 1988
NFC Divisional Playoff

Washington 21, Chicago 17—At Soldier Field, attendance 65,268. NFC East champion Washington qualified for its fourth NFC Championship Game in the past six seasons by coming from behind to edge NFC Central titlist Chicago 21-17. The Bears jumped to a 14-0 lead midway through the second quarter. However, the Redskins rallied to tie the game by halftime on running back George Rogers's three-yard touchdown run and tight end Clint Didier's 18-yard touchdown reception from quarterback Doug Williams. The deciding score came with 3:20 elapsed in the third quarter when cornerback Darrell Green returned a Bears punt 52 yards for a touchdown. Williams completed 14 of 29 passes for 207 yards and one touchdown. Wide receiver Ricky Sanders, starting for the injured Art Monk, caught six passes for 92 yards.

Washington	0	14	7	0	— 21
Chicago	7	7	3	0	— 17

Chi —Thomas 2 run (Butler kick)
Chi —Morris 14 pass from McMahon (Butler kick)
Wash —Rogers 3 run (Haji-Sheikh kick)
Wash —Didier 18 pass from Williams (Haji-Sheikh kick)
Wash —Green 52 punt return (Haji-Sheikh kick)
Chi —FG Butler 25

Nineteenth Week Summaries

Sunday, January 17, 1988
AFC Championship Game

Denver 38, Cleveland 33—At Mile High Stadium, attendance 76,197. AFC West champion Denver became the first team to win back-to-back AFC titles since Pittsburgh in 1978-79 by defeating Cleveland for the second straight year, 38-33. Reserve cornerback Jeremiah Castille forced and then recovered a fumble by Cleveland running back Earnest Byner at the Broncos' 3-yard line with 65 seconds to play to insure Denver's third Super Bowl appearance. The Broncos jumped to a 21-3 halftime lead. Defensive end Freddie Gilbert halted Cleveland's first drive of the game by intercepting a Bernie Kosar pass. That set up John Elway's eight-yard touchdown pass to wide receiver Ricky Nattiel. Running backs Steve Sewell and Gene Lang each scored on one-yard runs to give Denver its lead. The Browns roared back in the second half by scoring 28 points in the first 19:22. Kosar fired scoring passes to wide receiver Reggie Langhorne (18 yards) and Byner (32), who also scored on a four-yard run. Kosar's four-yard strike to wide receiver Webster Slaughter on the Browns' opening drive of the fourth quarter tied the score 31-31 with 10:38 to play. But Elway, who completed 14 of 26 passes for 281 yards and three touchdowns, finished off a 75-yard drive with a 20-yard touchdown pass to running back Sammy Winder with 4:01 remaining for the decisive score. Kosar completed an AFC Championship Game record 26 of 41 passes for 356 yards and three touchdowns. Byner caught seven passes for 120 yards and a touchdown. Denver wide receiver Mark Jackson had four receptions for 134 yards, including a club postseason-record 80-yard scoring catch.

Cleveland	0	3	21	9	— 33
Denver	14	7	10	7	— 38

Den —Nattiel 8 pass from Elway (Karlis kick)
Den —Sewell 1 run (Karlis kick)
Clev —FG Bahr 24
Den —Lang 1 run (Karlis kick)
Clev —Langhorne 18 pass from Kosar (Bahr kick)
Den —Jackson 80 pass from Elway (Karlis kick)
Clev —Byner 32 pass from Kosar (Bahr kick)
Clev —Byner 4 run (Bahr kick)
Den —FG Karlis 38
Clev —Slaughter 4 pass from Kosar (Bahr kick)
Den —Winder 20 pass from Elway (Karlis kick)
Clev —Safety, Denver punter Horan ran out of end zone

Sunday, January 17, 1988
NFC Championship Game

Washington 17, Minnesota 10—At Robert F. Kennedy Stadium, attendance 55,212. NFC East champion Washington advanced to its third Super Bowl in the past six seasons by downing Minnesota 17-10. The Redskins consistently applied pressure to Vikings quarterback Wade Wilson and accumulated eight sacks, one off the NFL playoff record of nine. Defensive tackle Dave Butz, with two sacks, and defensive end Dexter Manley, with one-and-a-half sacks, led the defense. Washington also limited Minnesota to 259 total yards. The Redskins scored first when quarterback Doug Williams threw a 42-yard touchdown pass to Kelvin Bryant to complete an eight-play, 98-yard drive. Redskins linebacker Mel Kaufman had an interception in the third quarter and returned it to the Vikings' 17-yard line to set up a 28-yard field goal by Ali Haji-Sheikh that gave Washington a 10-7 lead. Early in the final period, the Vikings' Anthony Carter had a 26-yard punt return to midfield which preceded Chuck Nelson's 18-yard field goal. The Redskins responded with an 18-play, 70-yard drive that concluded with wide receiver Gary Clark's seven-yard touchdown catch with 5:06 remaining. Minnesota drove to the Washington 6-yard line, but couldn't score, throwing an incomplete pass on fourth down with 52 seconds left.

Minnesota	0	7	0	3	— 10
Washington	7	0	3	7	— 17

Wash —Bryant 42 pass from Williams (Haji-Sheikh kick)
Minn —Lewis 23 pass from W. Wilson (C. Nelson kick)
Wash —FG Haji-Sheikh 28
Minn —FG C. Nelson 18
Wash —Clark 7 pass from Williams (Haji-Sheikh kick)

Twentieth Week Summary

Sunday, January 31, 1988
Super Bowl XXII
San Diego, California

Washington 42, Denver 10—At San Diego Jack Murphy Stadium, attendance 73,302. NFC champion Washington won Super Bowl XXII and its second NFL championship of the 1980's with a 42-10 decision over AFC champion Denver. The Redskins, who also won Super Bowl XVII, enjoyed a record-setting second quarter en route to the victory. The Broncos broke in front 10-0 when quarterback John Elway threw a 56-yard touchdown pass to wide receiver Ricky Nattiel on the Broncos' first pay from scrimmage. Following a Washington punt, Denver's Rich Karlis kicked a 24-yard field goal to cap a seven-play, 61-yard scoring drive. The Redskins then erupted for 35 points on five straight possessions in the second period and coasted thereafter. Redskins quarterback Doug Williams led the second-period explosion by throwing a Super Bowl record-tying four touchdown passes, including 80- and 50-yarders to wide receiver Ricky Sanders, a 27-yarder to wide receiver Gary Clark, and an 8-yarder to tight end Clint Didier. Also in the second period, Washington scored five touchdowns in 18 plays with total time of possession of 5:47. Overall, Williams completed 18 of 29 passes for 340 yards and was named the game's most valuable player. His passing-yardage total eclipsed the previous Super Bowl record of 331 yards by Joe Montana of San Francisco in Super Bowl XIX. Sanders ended with 193 yards on eight catches, breaking the previous Super Bowl yardage record of 161 yards by Lynn Swann of Pittsburgh in Game X. Rookie running back Timmy Smith of Washington was the game's leading rusher with 22 carries for a Super Bowl record 204 yards, breaking the previous mark of 191 yards by Marcus Allen of the Raiders in Game XVIII. Smith also scored twice on runs of 58 (in the second quarter) and 4 yards. Washington's six touchdowns and 602 total yards gained also set Super Bowl records.

Washington	0	35	0	7	— 42
Denver	10	0	0	0	— 10

Den —Nattiel 56 pass from Elway (Karlis kick)
Den —FG Karlis 24
Wash —Sanders 80 pass from Williams (Haji-Sheikh kick)
Wash —Clark 27 pass from Williams (Haji-Sheikh kick)
Wash —Smith 58 run (Haji-Sheikh kick)
Wash —Sanders 50 pass from Williams (Haji-Sheikh kick)
Wash —Didier 8 pass from Williams (Haji-Sheikh kick)
Wash —Smith 4 run (Haji-Sheikh kick)

Twenty-First Week Summary

Sunday, February 7, 1988
AFC-NFC Pro Bowl
Honolulu, Hawaii

AFC 15, NFC 6—At Aloha Stadium, attendance 50,113. Led by a tenacious pass rush, the AFC defeated the NFC for the second consecutive year, 15-6, before the ninth straight sellout crowd in Honolulu's Aloha Stadium. Buffalo quarterback Jim Kelly scored the game's lone touchdown, capping an 89-yard drive with a one-yard run for a 7-6 half-time lead. Colts kicker Dean Biasucci added field goals from 37 and 30 yards. Saints kicker Morten Andersen had 25- and 36-yard field goals to account for the NFC's points. AFC defenders held the NFC to 213 yards and recorded eight sacks. Bills defensive end Bruce Smith, who had five tackles and two sacks, was voted the game's outstanding player. Oilers running back Mike Rozier led all rushers with 49 yards on nine carries. Jets wide receiver Al Toon had five receptions for 75 yards. The AFC generated 341 yards total offense and held a time-of-possession advantage of 34:14 to 25:46. By winning, the AFC cut the NFC's lead in the Pro Bowl series to 10-8.

NFC	0	6	0	0	— 6
AFC	0	7	6	2	— 15

NFC —FG Andersen 25
AFC —Kelly 1 run (Biasucci kick)
NFC —FG Andersen 36
AFC —FG Biasucci 37
AFC —FG Biasucci 30
AFC —Safety, Montana forced out of end zone

1987 Professional Football Awards

	NFL	AFC	NFC
Professional Football Writers of America			
Most Valuable Player	Jerry Rice		
Rookie of the Year	Shane Conlan		
Coach of the Year		Ron Meyer	Jim Mora
Associated Press			
Most Valuable Player	John Elway		
Offensive Player of the Year	Jerry Rice		
Defensive Player of the Year	Reggie White		
Rookie of the Year—Offensive	Troy Stradford		
Rookie of the Year—Defensive	Shane Conlan		
Coach of the Year	Jim Mora		
United Press International			
Offensive Player of the Year		John Elway	Jerry Rice
Defensive Player of the Year		Bruce Smith	Reggie White
Coach of the Year		Ron Meyer	Jim Mora
The Sporting News			
Player of the Year	Jerry Rice		
Rookie of the Year	Robert Awalt		
Coach of the Year	Jim Mora		
Football News			
Player of the Year		John Elway	Jerry Rice
Coach of the Year		Ron Meyer	Jim Mora
Pro Football Weekly			
Offensive Player of the Year	Jerry Rice		
Defensive Player of the Year	Reggie White		
Offensive Rookie of the Year	Troy Stradford		
Defensive Rookie of the Year	Shane Conlan		
Comeback Player of the Year	Charles White		
Coach of the Year	Jim Mora		
Football Digest			
Player of the Year	Jerry Rice		
Offensive Rookie of the Year	Bo Jackson		
Defensive Rookie of the Year	Shane Conlan		
Coach of the Year	Jim Mora		
Maxwell Club			
Player of the Year (Bert Bell Trophy)	Jerry Rice		
Super Bowl XXII Most Valuable Player			
(Selected by Sport Magazine)	Doug Williams		
AFC-NFC Pro Bowl			
Player of the Game (Dan McGuire Award)	Bruce Smith		

AFC-NFC Players of the Week:

	AFC Offense	AFC Defense	NFC Offense	NFC Defense
Week 1	QB John Elway, Den.	LB Mike Merriweather, Pitt.	QB Steve DeBerg, TB	DE Curtis Greer, StL
Week 2	QB Jim Kelly, Buff.	LB Fredd Young, Sea.	QB Wade Wilson, Minn.	S Bill Bates, Dall.
Week 3	Games Cancelled Due to Players' Strike			
Week 4	QB Gary Hogeboom, Ind.	LB Eugene Seale, Hou.	WR Anthony Allen, Wash.	S Paul Tripoli, TB
Week 5	RB Joe Dudek, Den.	CB Liffort Hobley, Mia.	WR Kelvin Edwards, Dall.	DE Sean McInerney, Chi.
Week 6	WR Steve Largent, Sea.	LB Andre Tippett, NE	WR Lee Morris, GB	CB Kevin Walker, TB
Week 7	QB Jim Kelly, Buff.	CB-S Felix Wright, Clev.	QB Phil Simms, NYG	DE Clyde Simmons, Phil.
Week 8	QB Dan Fouts, SD	LB Duane Bickett, Ind.	QB Randall Cunningham, Phil.	DE Ed Jones, Dall.
Week 9	RB Earnest Byner, Clev.	LB Mike Merriweather, Pitt.	RB Dalton Hilliard, NO	DE Chris Doleman, Minn.
Week 10	RB Freeman McNeil, NYJ	LB Cliff Odom, Ind.	RB Charles White, Rams	CB Darrell Green, Wash.
Week 11	RB Troy Stradford, Mia.	CB Frank Minnifield, Clev.	WR Jerry Rice, SF	DE Jim Wilks, NO
Week 12	RB Bo Jackson, Raiders	Bills Defense	QB Joe Montana, SF	DE Al Harris, Chi.
Week 13	QB Boomer Esiason, Cin.	LB Karl Mecklenburg, Den.	QB Jim Everett, Rams	LB Carl Banks, NYG
Week 14	QB Bernie Kosar, Clev.	DE Bruce Smith, Buff.	QB Bobby Hebert, NO	DE Charles Mann, Wash.
Week 15	WR Mark Duper, Mia.	LB Brian Bosworth, Sea.	QB Neil Lomax, StL	LB Rickey Jackson, NO
Week 16	RB Eric Dickerson, Ind.	LB Cornelius Bennett, Buff.	RB Herschel Walker, Dall.	DE Richard Dent, Chi.

1987 ALL-PRO TEAMS

1987 PFWA All-Pro Team

Selected by the Professional Football Writers of America

Offense

Jerry Rice, San Francisco .... Wide Receiver
Steve Largent, Seattle .... Wide Receiver
Mark Bavaro, New York Giants .... Tight End
Anthony Muñoz, Cincinnati .... Tackle
Gary Zimmerman, Minnesota .... Tackle
Bill Fralic, Atlanta .... Guard
Mike Munchak, Houston .... Guard
Dwight Stephenson, Miami .... Center
Joe Montana, San Francisco .... Quarterback
Eric Dickerson, Indianapolis .... Running Back
Charles White, Los Angeles Rams .... Running Back
Morten Andersen, New Orleans .... Kicker
Dennis Gentry, Chicago .... Kick Returner
Mel Gray, New Orleans .... Punt Returner

Defense

Reggie White, Philadelphia .... Defensive End
Bruce Smith, Buffalo .... Defensive End
Steve McMichael, Chicago .... Defensive Tackle
Michael Carter, San Francisco .... Nose Tackle
Carl Banks, New York Giants .... Outside Linebacker
Andre Tippett, New England .... Outside Linebacker
Mike Singletary, Chicago .... Inside Linebacker
Fredd Young, Seattle .... Inside Linebacker
Hanford Dixon, Cleveland .... Cornerback
Frank Minnifield, Cleveland .... Cornerback
Joey Browner, Minnesota .... Safety
Ronnie Lott, San Francisco .... Safety
Jim Arnold, Detroit .... Punter

1987 Associated Press All-Pro Team

Offense

Jerry Rice, San Francisco .... Wide Receiver
Gary Clark, Washington .... Wide Receiver
Mark Bavaro, New York Giants .... Tight End
Anthony Muñoz, Cincinnati .... Tackle
Gary Zimmerman, Minnesota .... Tackle
Bill Fralic, Atlanta .... Guard
Mike Munchak, Houston .... Guard
Dwight Stephenson, Miami .... Center
Joe Montana, San Francisco .... Quarterback
Eric Dickerson, Indianapolis .... Running Back
Charles White, Los Angeles Rams .... Running Back
Morten Andersen, New Orleans .... Kicker
Vai Sikahema, St. Louis .... Kick Returner

Defense

Reggie White, Philadelphia .... Defensive End
Bruce Smith, Buffalo .... Defensive End
Steve McMichael, Chicago .... Defensive Tackle
Michael Carter, San Francisco .... Nose Tackle
Carl Banks, New York Giants .... Outside Linebacker
Andre Tippett, New England .... Outside Linebacker
Mike Singletary, Chicago .... Inside Linebacker
Fredd Young, Seattle .... Inside Linebacker
Hanford Dixon, Cleveland .... Cornerback
Barry Wilburn, Washington .... Cornerback
Joey Browner, Minnesota .... Safety
Ronnie Lott, San Francisco .... Safety
Jim Arnold, Detroit .... Punter

1987 All-NFL Team

Selected by the Associated Press and Professional Football Writers of America

Offense

Jerry Rice, San Francisco (AP, PFWA) .... Wide Receiver
Gary Clark, Washington (AP) .... Wide Receiver
Steve Largent, Seattle (PFWA) .... Wide Receiver
Mark Bavaro, New York Giants (AP, PFWA) .... Tight End
Anthony Muñoz, Cincinnati (AP, PFWA) .... Tackle
Gary Zimmerman, Minnesota (AP, PFWA) .... Tackle
Mike Munchak, Houston (AP, PFWA) .... Guard
Bill Fralic, Atlanta (AP, PFWA) .... Guard
Dwight Stephenson, Miami (AP, PFWA) .... Center
Joe Montana, San Francisco (AP, PFWA) .... Quarterback
Eric Dickerson, Indianapolis (AP, PFWA) .... Running Back
Charles White, Los Angeles Rams (AP, PFWA) .... Running Back

Defense

Reggie White, Philadelphia (AP, PFWA) .... Defensive End
Bruce Smith, Buffalo (AP, PFWA) .... Defensive End
Steve McMichael, Chicago (AP, PFWA) .... Defensive Tackle
Michael Carter, San Francisco (AP, PFWA) .... Nose Tackle
Carl Banks, New York Giants (AP, PFWA) .... Outside Linebacker
Andre Tippett, New England (AP, PFWA) .... Outside Linebacker
Fredd Young, Seattle (AP, PFWA) .... Inside Linebacker
Mike Singletary, Chicago (AP, PFWA) .... Inside Linebacker
Hanford Dixon, Cleveland (AP, PFWA) .... Cornerback
Barry Wilburn, Washington (AP) .... Cornerback
Frank Minnifield, Cleveland (PFWA) .... Cornerback
Joey Browner, Minnesota (AP, PFWA) .... Safety
Ronnie Lott, San Francisco (AP, PFWA) .... Safety

Specialists

Morten Andersen, New Orleans (AP, PFWA) .... Kicker
Jim Arnold, Detroit (AP, PFWA) .... Punter
Vai Sikahema, St. Louis (AP) .... Kick Returner
Dennis Gentry, Chicago (PFWA) .... Kick Returner
Mel Gray, New Orleans (PFWA) .... Punt Returner

1987 UPI All-AFC Team

Selected by United Press International

Offense

Steve Largent, Seattle .... Wide Receiver
Al Toon, New York Jets .... Wide Receiver
Kellen Winslow, San Diego .... Tight End
Anthony Muñoz, Cincinnati .... Tackle
Jim Lachey, San Diego .... Tackle
Mike Munchak, Houston .... Guard
Ron Solt, Indianapolis .... Guard
Dwight Stephenson, Miami .... Center
John Elway, Denver .... Quarterback
Eric Dickerson, Indianapolis .... Running Back
Curt Warner, Seattle .... Running Back
Dean Biasucci, Indianapolis .... Kicker

Defense

Bruce Smith, Buffalo .... Defensive End
Jacob Green, Seattle .... Defensive End
Bill Maas, Kansas City .... Defensive Tackle
Andre Tippett, New England .... Outside Linebacker
Duane Bickett, Indianapolis .... Outside Linebacker
Fredd Young, Seattle .... Inside Linebacker
Karl Mecklenburg, Denver .... Inside Linebacker
Frank Minnifield, Cleveland .... Cornerback
Hanford Dixon, Cleveland .... Cornerback
Vann McElroy, Los Angeles Raiders .... Safety
Keith Bostic, Houston .... Safety
Ralf Mojsiejenko, San Diego .... Punter

1987 UPI All-NFC Team

Selected by United Press International

Offense

Jerry Rice, San Francisco .... Wide Receiver
J.T. Smith, St. Louis .... Wide Receiver
Mark Bavaro, New York Giants .... Tight End
Jackie Slater, Los Angeles Rams .... Tackle
Jim Covert, Chicago .... Tackle
Bill Fralic, Atlanta .... Guard
Tom Newberry, Los Angeles Rams .... Guard
Jay Hilgenberg, Chicago .... Center
Joe Montana, San Francisco .... Quarterback
Charles White, Los Angeles Rams .... Running Back
Rueben Mayes, New Orleans .... Running Back
Morten Andersen, New Orleans .... Kicker

Defense

Reggie White, Philadelphia .... Defensive End
Chris Doleman, Minnesota .... Defensive End
Michael Carter, San Francisco .... Defensive Tackle
Carl Banks, New York Giants .... Outside Linebacker
Pat Swilling, New Orleans .... Outside Linebacker
Mike Singletary, Chicago .... Inside Linebacker
Vaughan Johnson, New Orleans .... Inside Linebacker
Barry Wilburn, Washington .... Cornerback
Dave Waymer, New Orleans .... Cornerback
Ronnie Lott, San Francisco .... Safety
Joey Browner, Minnesota .... Safety
Jim Arnold, Detroit .... Punter

1987 PFWA All-Rookie Team

Selected by Professional Football Writers of America

Offense

Ricky Nattiel, Denver .... Wide Receiver
Frankie Neal, Green Bay .... Wide Receiver
Robert Awalt, St. Louis .... Tight End
Harris Barton, San Francisco .... Tackle
Bruce Armstrong, New England .... Tackle
Steve Trapilo, New Orleans .... Guard
Todd Peat, St. Louis .... Guard
Frank Winters, Cleveland .... Center
Vinny Testaverde, Tampa Bay .... Quarterback
Troy Stradford, Miami .... Running Back
Christian Okoye, Kansas City .... Running Back
Jeff Jaeger, Cleveland .... Kicker

Defense

John Bosa, Miami .... Defensive End
Shawn Knight, New Orleans .... Defensive End
Jerome Brown, Philadelphia .... Defensive Tackle
Jerry Ball, Detroit .... Defensive Tackle
Cornelius Bennett, Buffalo .... Outside Linebacker
Alex Gordon, New York Jets .... Outside Linebacker
Shane Conlan, Buffalo .... Inside Linebacker
Brian Bosworth, Seattle .... Inside Linebacker
Delton Hall, Pittsburgh .... Cornerback
Nate Odomes, Buffalo .... Cornerback
Gene Atkins, New Orleans .... Safety
Thomas Everett, Pittsburgh .... Safety
Ruben Rodriguez, Seattle .... Punter

1987 UPI All-Rookie Team

Selected by United Press International

Offense

Ricky Nattiel, Denver .... Wide Receiver
Mark Carrier, Tampa Bay .... Wide Receiver
Robert Awalt, St. Louis .... Tight End
Bruce Armstrong, New England .... Tackle
Harris Barton, San Francisco .... Tackle
Todd Peat, St. Louis .... Guard
Steve Trapilo, New Orleans .... Guard
Gregg Rakoczy, Cleveland .... Center
Vinny Testaverde, Tampa Bay .... Quarterback
Troy Stradford, Miami .... Running Back
Bo Jackson, Los Angeles Raiders .... Running Back
Roger Ruzek, Dallas .... Kicker

Defense

John Bosa, Miami .... Defensive End
Jerome Brown, Philadelphia .... Defensive Tackle
Henry Thomas, Minnesota .... Defensive Tackle
Cornelius Bennett, Buffalo .... Outside Linebacker
Johnny Holland, Green Bay .... Outside Linebacker
Shane Conlan, Buffalo .... Inside Linebacker
Brian Bosworth, Seattle .... Inside Linebacker
Nate Odomes, Buffalo .... Cornerback
Delton Hall, Pittsburgh .... Cornerback
Fred Robinson, Indianapolis .... Safety
Thomas Everett, Pittsburgh .... Safety
Scott Fulhage, Cincinnati .... Punter

Ten Best Rushing Performances, 1987

	Attempts	Yards	TD
1. Bo Jackson L.A. Raiders vs. Seattle, November 30	18	221	2
2. Charles White L.A. Rams vs. St. Louis, November 15	34	213	1
3. Eric Dickerson Indianapolis vs. Tampa Bay, December 27	33	196	2
4. Freeman McNeil N.Y. Jets vs. Kansas City, November 15	26	184	0
5. Herschel Walker Dallas vs. New England, November 15	28	173	1
6. Troy Stradford Miami vs. Dallas, November 22	17	169	1
7. Charles White L.A. Rams vs. Pittsburgh, October 11	33	166	1
8. Chuck Banks Indianapolis vs. N.Y. Jets, October 11	25	159	0
Charles White L.A. Rams vs. Atlanta, December 13	29	159	2
10. Charles White L.A. Rams vs. Atlanta, October 18	31	155	0

100-Yard Rushing Performances, 1987

First Week	
Eric Dickerson, L.A. Rams	149 yards vs. Houston
Rueben Mayes, New Orleans	147 yards vs. Cleveland
Marcus Allen, L.A. Raiders	136 yards vs. Green Bay
Christian Okoye, Kansas City	105 yards vs. San Diego
Earnest Jackson, Pittsburgh	103 yards vs. San Francisco
Second Week	
Mike Rozier, Houston	150 yards vs. Buffalo
Gerald Riggs, Atlanta	120 yards vs. Washington
Neal Anderson, Chicago	117 yards vs. Tampa Bay
John L. Williams, Seattle	112 yards vs. Kansas City
Third Week	
Games cancelled due to players' strike.	
Fourth Week	
Larry Mason, Cleveland	133 yards vs. New England
Earnest Jackson, Pittsburgh	104 yards vs. Atlanta
Fifth Week	
Charles White, L.A. Rams	166 yards vs. Pittsburgh
Chuck Banks, Indianapolis	159 yards vs. N.Y. Jets
Mike LeBlanc, New England	146 yards vs. Buffalo
Dwight Beverly, New Orleans	139 yards vs. St. Louis
Joe Dudek, Denver	128 yards vs. L.A. Raiders
Lionel Vital, Washington	128 yards vs. N.Y. Giants
Herman Hunter, Houston	121 yards vs. Cleveland
Marc Logan, Cincinnati	103 yards vs. Seattle
Sixth Week	
Charles White, L.A. Rams	155 yards vs. Atlanta
Carl Byrum, Buffalo	139 yards vs. N.Y. Giants
Lionel Vital, Washington	136 yards vs. Dallas
Earnest Jackson, Pittsburgh	134 yards vs. Indianapolis
Derrick McAdoo, St. Louis	111 yards vs. San Francisco
Kevin Willhite, Green Bay	100 yards vs. Philadelphia
Seventh Week	
Rueben Mayes, New Orleans	144 yards vs. San Francisco
Mike Rozier, Houston	144 yards vs. Atlanta
Kenneth Davis, Green Bay	129 yards vs. Detroit
Gerald Riggs, Atlanta	113 yards vs. Houston
Curt Warner, Seattle	112 yards vs. L.A. Raiders
Eighth Week	
Albert Bentley, Indianapolis	145 yards vs. N.Y. Jets
George Rogers, Washington	125 yards vs. Buffalo
Rueben Mayes, New Orleans	112 yards vs. Atlanta
Troy Stradford, Miami	110 yards vs. Pittsburgh
Roger Craig, San Francisco	104 yards vs. L.A. Rams
Ninth Week	
Eric Dickerson, Indianapolis	138 yards vs. San Diego
Earnest Jackson, Pittsburgh	125 yards vs. Kansas City
Tenth Week	
Charles White, L.A. Rams	213 yards vs. St. Louis
Freeman McNeil, N.Y. Jets	184 yards vs. Kansas City
Herschel Walker, Dallas	173 yards vs. New England
Eric Dickerson, Indianapolis	154 yards vs. Miami
Curt Warner, Seattle	123 yards vs. Green Bay
Gerald Riggs, Atlanta	112 yards vs. Cincinnati
Mike Rozier, Houston	112 yards vs. Pittsburgh
Darrin Nelson, Minnesota	103 yards vs. Tampa Bay
Larry Kinnebrew, Cincinnati	100 yards vs. Atlanta
Eleventh Week	
Troy Stradford, Miami	169 yards vs. Dallas
Curt Warner, Seattle	119 yards vs. San Diego
Eric Dickerson, Indianapolis	117 yards vs. New England
Kevin Mack, Cleveland	114 yards vs. Houston
Charles White, L.A. Rams	112 yards vs. Washington
Freeman McNeil, N.Y. Jets	103 yards vs. Buffalo
Twelfth Week	
Bo Jackson, L.A. Raiders	221 yards vs. Seattle
Charles White, L.A. Rams	137 yards vs. Tampa Bay
Eric Dickerson, Indianapolis	136 yards vs. Houston
Anthony Toney, Philadelphia	123 yards vs. New England
Mike Rozier, Houston	122 yards vs. Indianapolis
Ronnie Harmon, Buffalo	119 yards vs. Miami
Darrin Nelson, Minnesota	118 yards vs. Dallas
Thirteenth Week	
George Rogers, Washington	133 yards vs. St. Louis
Troy Stradford, Miami	120 yards vs. N.Y. Jets
Gerald Riggs, Atlanta	119 yards vs. Dallas
Frank Pollard, Pittsburgh	106 yards vs. Seattle
Charles White, L.A. Rams	102 yards vs. Detroit
Stump Mitchell, St. Louis	101 yards vs. Washington
Fourteenth Week	
Charles White, L.A. Rams	159 yards vs. Atlanta
Kevin Mack, Cleveland	133 yards vs. Cincinnati
Stump Mitchell, St. Louis	111 yards vs. N.Y. Giants
Johnny Hector, N.Y. Jets	104 yards vs. New England
Fifteenth Week	
Eric Dickerson, Indianapolis	115 yards vs. San Diego
Herschel Walker, Dallas	108 yards vs. L.A. Rams
Stump Mitchell, St. Louis	101 yards vs. Tampa Bay
Sixteenth Week	
Eric Dickerson, Indianapolis	196 yards vs. Tampa Bay
Herschel Walker, Dallas	137 yards vs. St. Louis
Joe Morris, N.Y. Giants	132 yards vs. N.Y. Jets
Herman Heard, Kansas City	107 yards vs. Seattle
Mike Rozier, Houston	103 yards vs. Cincinnati
Keith Byars, Philadelphia	102 yards vs. Buffalo

Times 100 or More
Dickerson, White, 7; Jackson, Riggs, Rozier, 4; Mayes, Mitchell, Stradford, H. Walker, Warner, 3; Rogers, Mack, McNeil, D. Nelson, Vital, 2.

Ten Best Passing Yardage Performances, 1987

	Att.	Comp.	Yards	TD
1. Neil Lomax St. Louis vs. San Diego, September 20	61	32	457	3
2. Boomer Esiason Cincinnati vs. Pittsburgh, November 22	53	30	409	0
3. Tom Ramsey New England vs. Philadelphia, November 29	53	34	402	3
4. Dan Marino Miami vs. Washington, December 20	50	22	393	3
5. Boomer Esiason Cincinnati vs. Houston, November 1	41	26	387	2
6. Dan Marino Miami vs. Philadelphia, December 13	39	25	376	3
7. Neil Lomax St. Louis vs. Atlanta, November 29	42	25	369	2
Vinny Testaverde Tampa Bay vs. New Orleans, December 6	47	22	369	2
9. Boomer Esiason Cincinnati vs. Kansas City, December 6	44	28	368	2
10. Chuck Long Detroit vs. Green Bay, October 25	47	33	362	3

300-Yard Passing Performances, 1987

First Week

John Elway, Denver	338 yards vs. Seattle
Steve DeBerg, Tampa Bay	333 yards vs. Atlanta
Joe Montana, San Francisco	316 yards vs. Pittsburgh
Bernie Kosar, Cleveland	314 yards vs. New Orleans
Warren Moon, Houston	310 yards vs. L.A. Rams
Jim Kelly, Buffalo	305 yards vs. N.Y. Jets

Second Week

Neil Lomax, St. Louis	457 yards vs. San Diego
Ken O'Brien, N.Y. Jets	313 yards vs. New England

Third Week

Games cancelled due to players' strike.

Fourth Week

Ed Rubbert, Washington	334 yards vs. St. Louis
Bruce Mathison, Seattle	326 yards vs. Miami

Fifth Week

Scott Tinsley, Philadelphia	338 yards vs. Dallas

Sixth Week

Jeff Kemp, Seattle	344 yards vs. Detroit
Erik Kramer, Atlanta	335 yards vs. L.A. Rams
Joe Montana, San Francisco	334 yards vs. St. Louis
Pat Ryan, N.Y. Jets	301 yards vs. Miami

Seventh Week

Chuck Long, Detroit	362 yards vs. Green Bay
Jim Kelly, Buffalo	359 yards vs. Miami
Bill Kenney, Kansas City	328 yards vs. San Diego
Don Majkowski, Green Bay	323 yards vs. Detroit
Boomer Esiason, Cincinnati	303 yards vs. Pittsburgh
Dan Marino, Miami	303 yards vs. Buffalo

Eighth Week

Boomer Esiason, Cincinnati	387 yards vs. Houston
Dan Marino, Miami	332 yards vs. Pittsburgh
Dan Fouts, San Diego	315 yards vs. Cleveland

Ninth Week

Neil Lomax, St. Louis	314 yards vs. Tampa Bay
Steve DeBerg, Tampa Bay	303 yards vs. St. Louis

Tenth Week

Bernie Kosar, Cleveland	346 yards vs. Buffalo
John Elway, Denver	341 yards vs. Chicago
Jim McMahon, Chicago	311 yards vs. Denver

Eleventh Week

Boomer Esiason, Cincinnati	409 yards vs. Pittsburgh
Doug Williams, Washington	308 yards vs. L.A. Rams
Joe Montana, San Francisco	304 yards vs. Tampa Bay

Twelfth Week

Tom Ramsey, New England	402 yards vs. Philadelphia
Neil Lomax, St. Louis	369 yards vs. Atlanta
John Elway, Denver	347 yards vs. San Diego
Joe Montana, San Francisco	342 yards vs. Cleveland
Danny White, Dallas	341 yards vs. Minnesota
Jay Schroeder, Washington	331 yards vs. N.Y. Giants
Warren Moon, Houston	327 yards vs. Indianapolis
Dan Fouts, San Diego	322 yards vs. Denver
Randall Cunningham, Philadelphia	314 yards vs. New England

Thirteenth Week

Vinny Testaverde, Tampa Bay	369 yards vs. New Orleans
Boomer Esiason, Cincinnati	368 yards vs. Kansas City
Marc Wilson, L.A. Raiders	337 yards vs. Buffalo
Jim Everett, L.A. Rams	324 yards vs. Detroit
Jim Kelly, Buffalo	315 yards vs. L.A. Raiders
Joe Montana, San Francisco	308 yards vs. Green Bay

Fourteenth Week

Dan Marino, Miami	376 yards vs. Philadelphia
Boomer Esiason, Cincinnati	361 yards vs. Cleveland
Phil Simms, N.Y. Giants	359 yards vs. St. Louis
Danny White, Dallas	359 yards vs. Washington
Marc Wilson, L.A. Raiders	339 yards vs. Kansas City
John Elway, Denver	335 yards vs. Seattle
Dan Fouts, San Diego	334 yards vs. Pittsburgh

Fifteenth Week

Dan Marino, Miami	393 yards vs. Washington
Ken O'Brien, N.Y. Jets	301 yards vs. Philadelphia

Sixteenth Week

Bill Kenney, Kansas City	320 yards vs. Seattle
Neil Lomax, St. Louis	314 yards vs. Dallas

Times 300 or More

Esiason, Montana, 5; Elway, Lomax, Marino, 4; Fouts, Kelly, 3; DeBerg, Kenney, Moon, O'Brien, D. White, M. Wilson, 2.

Ten Best Receiving Yardage Performances, 1987

		Yards	No.	TD
1.	Steve Largent Seattle vs. Detroit, October 18	261	15	3
2.	Anthony Allen Washington vs. St. Louis, October 4	255	7	3
3.	Mark Carrier Tampa Bay vs. New Orleans, December 6	212	8	1
4.	Carlos Carson Kansas City vs. San Diego, October 25	197	9	2
5.	Gary Clark Washington vs. Dallas, December 13	187	9	1
6.	Anthony Carter Minnesota vs. Dallas, November 26	184	8	2
7.	Henry Ellard L.A. Rams vs. Detroit, December 6	171	7	1
8.	Mark Duper Miami vs. Washington, December 20	170	6	3
9.	Al Toon N.Y. Jets vs. Philadelphia, December 20	168	10	1
10.	Ricky Sanders Washington vs. Minnesota, December 26	164	8	2

100-Yard Receiving Performances, 1987

(Number in parentheses is receptions.)

First Week

Bill Brooks, Indianapolis — 146 yards (6) vs. Cincinnati
Mark Duper, Miami — 123 yards (9) vs. New England
Ernest Givins, Houston — 117 yards (6) vs. L.A. Rams
Jerry Rice, San Francisco — 106 yards (8) vs. Pittsburgh
Gary Clark, Washington — 102 yards (8) vs. Philadelphia
Lionel James, San Diego — 100 yards (6) vs. Kansas City

Second Week

Roy Green, St. Louis — 139 yards (7) vs. San Diego
Anthony Carter, Minnesota — 117 yards (4) vs. L.A. Rams
Chris Burkett, Buffalo — 115 yards (7) vs. Houston
Pete Mandley, Detroit — 110 yards (7) vs. L.A. Raiders
Floyd Dixon, Atlanta — 105 yards (5) vs. Washington
Mike Wilson, San Francisco — 104 yards (7) vs. Cincinnati
Jay Novacek, St. Louis — 101 yards (7) vs. San Diego

Third Week

Games cancelled due to players' strike.

Fourth Week

Anthony Allen, Washington — 255 yards (7) vs. St. Louis
Walter Murray, Indianapolis — 161 yards (7) vs. Buffalo
Joey Clinkscales, Pittsburgh — 150 yards (6) vs. Atlanta
James Brim, Minnesota — 144 yards (6) vs. Green Bay
Jimmy Teal, Seattle — 137 yards (9) vs. Miami
J.T. Smith, St. Louis — 116 yards (6) vs. Washington

Fifth Week

Kevin Bowman, Philadelphia — 123 yards (5) vs. Dallas
Cornell Burbage, Dallas — 110 yards (3) vs. Philadelphia
Al Williams, San Diego — 110 yards (5) vs. Tampa Bay
Leonard Harris, Houston — 104 yards (6) vs. Cleveland
Eric Martin, New Orleans — 101 yards (7) vs. St. Louis
Kelvin Edwards, Dallas — 100 yards (6) vs. Philadelphia

Sixth Week

Steve Largent, Seattle — 261 yards (15) vs. Detroit
Brian Brennan, Cleveland — 139 yards (10) vs. Cincinnati
Otis Grant, Philadelphia — 135 yards (7) vs. Green Bay
Lee Morris, Green Bay — 132 yards (6) vs. Philadelphia
Oliver Williams, Houston — 124 yards (9) vs. New England
Milton Barney, Atlanta — 109 yards (6) vs. L.A. Rams
Craig McEwen, Washington — 108 yards (7) vs. Dallas
Steve Holloway, Tampa Bay — 107 yards (8) vs. Minnesota
Bobby Micho, Denver — 105 yards (9) vs. Kansas City
Kelvin Edwards, Dallas — 104 yards (6) vs. Washington

Seventh Week

Carlos Carson, Kansas City — 197 yards (9) vs. San Diego
Walter Stanley, Green Bay — 150 yards (6) vs. Detroit
Chris Burkett, Buffalo — 130 yards (9) vs. Miami
Todd Christensen, L.A. Raiders — 124 yards (8) vs. Seattle
Stanley Morgan, New England — 102 yards (7) vs. Indianapolis
John Stallworth, Pittsburgh — 100 yards (7) vs. Cincinnati

Eighth Week

Lionel Manuel, N.Y. Giants — 151 yards (7) vs. Dallas
Stanley Morgan, New England — 146 yards (6) vs. L.A. Raiders
Cris Collinsworth, Cincinnati — 121 yards (8) vs. Houston
Stephone Paige, Kansas City — 121 yards (5) vs. Chicago
Carlos Carson, Kansas City — 117 yards (7) vs. Chicago
J.T. Smith, St. Louis — 112 yards (10) vs. Philadelphia
Andre Reed, Buffalo — 108 yards (8) vs. Washington
Irving Fryar, New England — 107 yards (6) vs. L.A. Raiders
James Brooks, Cincinnati — 103 yards (8) vs. Houston
Mark Duper, Miami — 100 yards (5) vs. Pittsburgh

Ninth Week

Phillip Epps, Green Bay — 139 yards (6) vs. Chicago
James Lofton, L.A. Raiders — 128 yards (4) vs. Minnesota
Robert Awalt, St. Louis — 124 yards (9) vs. Tampa Bay
Gary Clark, Washington — 119 yards (5) vs. Philadelphia
Eddie Brown, Cincinnati — 105 yards (8) vs. Miami
Neal Anderson, Chicago — 102 yards (5) vs. Green Bay
Drew Hill, Houston — 101 yards (4) vs. San Francisco

Tenth Week

Willie Gault, Chicago — 133 yards (5) vs. Denver
Jerry Rice, San Francisco — 108 yards (4) vs. New Orleans
Drew Hill, Houston — 107 yards (4) vs. Pittsburgh
Jonathan Hayes, Kansas City — 105 yards (5) vs. N.Y. Jets
Lionel Manuel, N.Y. Giants — 105 yards (4) vs. Philadelphia
Mark Bavaro, N.Y. Giants — 102 yards (7) vs. Philadelphia

Eleventh Week

Tim McGee, Cincinnati — 139 yards (8) vs. Pittsburgh
Ernest Givins, Houston — 126 yards (3) vs. Cleveland
Vance Johnson, Denver — 115 yards (5) vs. L.A. Raiders
Jerry Rice, San Francisco — 103 yards (7) vs. Tampa Bay
Stanley Morgan, New England — 102 yards (5) vs. Indianapolis
Stephen Baker, N.Y. Giants — 100 yards (4) vs. New Orleans

Twelfth Week

Anthony Carter, Minnesota — 184 yards (8) vs. Dallas
Drew Hill, Houston — 134 yards (7) vs. Indianapolis
Jerry Rice, San Francisco — 126 yards (7) vs. Cleveland
Mike Quick, Philadelphia — 121 yards (5) vs. New England
Ricky Nattiel, Denver — 118 yards (4) vs. San Diego
Aubrey Matthews, Atlanta — 115 yards (7) vs. St. Louis
Gary Clark, Washington — 112 yards (7) vs. N.Y. Giants
J.T. Smith, St. Louis — 109 yards (10) vs. Atlanta
Tony Collins, New England — 100 yards (11) vs. Philadelphia
Mike Renfro, Dallas — 100 yards (7) vs. Minnesota

Thirteenth Week

Mark Carrier, Tampa Bay — 212 yards (8) vs. New Orleans
Henry Ellard, L.A. Rams — 171 yards (7) vs. Detroit
Andre Reed, Buffalo — 153 yards (7) vs. L.A. Raiders
Wes Chandler, San Diego — 140 yards (10) vs. Houston
Mark Bavaro, N.Y. Giants — 133 yards (6) vs. Philadelphia
James Lofton, L.A. Raiders — 132 yards (6) vs. Buffalo
Gary Clark, Washington — 130 yards (5) vs. St. Louis
Anthony Carter, Minnesota — 106 yards (3) vs. Chicago
Eric Martin, New Orleans — 101 yards (2) vs. Tampa Bay
Al Toon, N.Y. Jets — 100 yards (5) vs. Miami

Fourteenth Week

Gary Clark, Washington — 187 yards (9) vs. Dallas
Carlos Carson, Kansas City — 142 yards (4) vs. L.A. Raiders
Mark Bavaro, N.Y. Giants — 137 yards (11) vs. St. Louis
Eric Martin, New Orleans — 130 yards (6) vs. Houston
Webster Slaughter, Cleveland — 119 yards (5) vs. Cincinnati
Tim McGee, Cincinnati — 117 yards (4) vs. Cleveland
Wes Chandler, San Diego — 116 yards (7) vs. Pittsburgh
James Lofton, L.A. Raiders — 112 yards (5) vs. Kansas City
Al Toon, N.Y. Jets — 110 yards (8) vs. New England
Ray Butler, Seattle — 107 yards (6) vs. Denver
Mark Clayton, Miami — 104 yards (7) vs. Philadelphia
Drew Hill, Houston — 102 yards (4) vs. New Orleans

Fifteenth Week

Mark Duper, Miami — 170 yards (6) vs. Washington
Al Toon, N.Y. Jets — 168 yards (10) vs. Philadelphia
Mike Quick, Philadelphia — 148 yards (6) vs. N.Y. Jets
John L. Williams, Seattle — 117 yards (8) vs. Chicago
Gerald Carter, Tampa Bay — 116 yards (5) vs. St. Louis
Webster Slaughter, Cleveland — 115 yards (7) vs. L.A. Raiders
Drew Hill, Houston — 109 yards (4) vs. Pittsburgh

Sixteenth Week

Ricky Sanders, Washington	164 yards (8) vs. Minnesota
Carlos Carson, Kansas City	120 yards (4) vs. Seattle
Cris Collinsworth, Cincinnati	119 yards (4) vs. Houston
Roy Green, St. Louis	112 yards (7) vs. Dallas
Stephone Paige, Kansas City	110 yards (7) vs. Seattle
Mark Bavaro, N.Y. Giants	109 yards (6) vs. N.Y. Jets
Drew Hill, Houston	109 yards (6) vs. Cincinnati
Walter Stanley, Green Bay	109 yards (4) vs. New Orleans
J.T. Smith, St. Louis	102 yards (11) vs. Dallas

Times 100 or More

D. Hill, 6; Bavaro, Carson, Clark, Rice, J.T. Smith, 4; Carter, Duper, Lofton, Martin, Morgan, Toon, 3; Burkett, Chandler, Collinsworth, Edwards, Givins, Green, Manuel, McGee, Paige, Quick, Reed, Slaughter, Stanley, 2.

American Football Conference Offense

	Buff.	Cin.	Clev.	Den.	Hou.	Ind.	K.C.	Raid.	Mia.	N.E.	N.Y.J.	Pitt.	S.D.	Sea.
First Downs	294	319	310	331	294	285	265	300	331	266	292	263	264	301
Rushing	111	130	110	132	118	122	97	107	109	84	97	114	68	120
Passing	151	159	171	173	150	138	141	158	197	158	169	126	175	154
Penalty	32	30	29	26	26	25	27	35	25	24	26	23	21	27
Rushes	465	538	474	510	486	497	419	475	408	513	458	517	396	496
Net Yds. Gained	1840	2164	1745	1970	1923	2143	1799	2197	1662	1771	1671	2144	1308	2023
Avg. Gain	4.0	4.0	3.7	3.9	4.0	4.3	4.3	4.6	4.1	3.5	3.6	4.1	3.3	4.1
Avg. Yds. per Game	122.7	144.3	116.3	131.3	128.2	142.9	119.9	146.5	110.8	118.1	111.4	142.9	87.2	134.9
Passes Attempted	516	475	482	530	482	447	432	457	584	440	517	429	516	405
Completed	292	255	291	285	240	255	236	247	338	236	302	198	303	237
% Completed	56.6	53.7	60.4	53.8	49.8	57.0	54.6	54.0	57.9	53.6	58.4	46.2	58.7	58.5
Total Yds. Gained	3246	3468	3625	3874	3534	3042	2985	3429	3977	2929	3402	2464	3602	3028
Times Sacked	37	32	29	30	30	24	48	53	13	33	66	27	39	36
Yds. Lost	345	255	170	220	234	190	366	359	101	246	443	198	322	316
Net Yds. Gained	2901	3213	3455	3654	3300	2852	2619	3070	3876	2683	2959	2266	3280	2712
Avg. Yds. per Game	193.4	214.2	230.3	243.6	220.0	190.1	174.6	204.7	258.4	178.9	197.3	151.1	218.7	180.8
Net Yds. per Pass Play	5.25	6.34	6.76	6.53	6.45	6.06	5.46	6.02	6.49	5.67	5.08	4.97	5.91	3.15
Yds. Gained per Comp.	11.12	13.60	12.46	13.59	14.73	11.93	12.65	13.88	11.77	12.41	11.26	12.44	11.89	12.78
Combined Net Yds. Gained	4741	5377	5200	5624	5223	4995	4418	5267	5538	4454	4630	4410	4588	4735
% Total Yds. Rushing	38.8	40.2	33.6	35.0	36.8	42.9	40.7	41.7	30.0	39.8	36.1	48.6	28.5	42.7
% Total Yds. Passing	61.2	59.8	66.4	65.0	63.2	57.1	59.3	58.3	70.0	60.2	63.9	51.4	71.5	57.3
Avg. Yds. per Game	316.1	358.5	346.7	374.9	348.2	333.0	294.5	351.1	369.2	296.9	308.7	294.0	305.9	315.7
Ball Control Plays	1018	1045	985	1070	998	968	899	985	1005	986	1041	973	951	937
Avg. Yds. per Play	4.7	5.1	5.3	5.3	5.2	5.2	4.9	5.3	5.5	4.5	4.4	4.5	4.8	5.1
Avg. Time of Poss.	28:41	30:24	31:44	31:52	30:17	30:10	27:11	30:45	29:43	29:37	30:28	29:45	28:08	30:35
Third Down Efficiency	37.0	37.5	41.6	47.1	35.1	34.8	40.1	37.5	47.5	37.3	40.6	39.7	30.1	48.7
Had Intercepted	19	20	12	19	23	16	17	18	20	18	15	25	23	21
Yds. Opp. Returned	177	336	173	362	225	181	141	371	298	160	210	330	266	146
Ret. by Opp. for TD	0	2	2	2	1	1	0	2	2	2	0	1	1	0
Punts	83	73	57	65	75	78	69	71	63	89	82	82	84	61
Yds. Punted	3173	2995	2102	2595	2929	2941	2789	2796	2424	3350	3046	3297	3529	2370
Avg. Yds. per Punt	38.2	41.0	36.9	39.9	39.1	37.7	40.4	39.4	38.5	37.6	37.1	40.2	42.0	38.9
Punt Returns	31	34	44	48	37	38	32	44	37	25	42	36	45	32
Yds. Returned	232	293	487	486	249	210	346	356	290	213	497	244	508	322
Avg. Yds. per Return	7.5	8.6	11.1	10.1	6.7	5.5	10.8	8.1	7.8	8.5	11.8	6.8	11.3	10.1
Returned for TD	0	0	0	1	0	0	1	1	0	0	2	0	1	0
Kickoff Returns	45	67	48	46	67	55	70	60	54	48	65	56	62	64
Yds. Returned	872	1161	846	952	1225	1115	1437	1174	952	901	1221	1060	1137	1236
Avg. Yds. per Return	19.4	17.3	17.6	20.7	18.3	20.3	20.5	19.6	17.6	18.8	18.8	18.9	18.3	19.3
Returned for TD	0	0	0	0	0	0	2	0	0	0	0	0	0	0
Fumbles	41	29	33	29	32	36	41	24	37	36	33	37	38	31
Lost	24	12	17	17	14	18	24	13	17	13	19	8	20	15
Out of Bounds	0	0	1	0	3	5	3	1	2	2	1	1	1	0
Own Rec. for TD	0	0	0	0	0	0	0	0	0	0	0	0	0	0
Opp. Rec. by	14	12	13	19	14	25	17	15	16	21	11	17	15	21
Opp. Rec. for TD	3	0	2	0	1	1	1	0	2	1	1	2	1	0
Penalties	94	99	100	95	114	90	108	114	76	64	135	105	98	79
Yds. Penalized	762	791	857	812	1029	742	861	1048	634	506	1055	801	743	668
Total Points Scored	270	285	390	379	345	300	273	301	362	320	334	285	253	371
Total TDs	33	30	47	45	38	31	30	35	47	39	39	31	29	46
TDs Rushing	9	13	16	18	12	14	7	13	16	12	17	11	11	13
TDs Passing	21	17	27	24	24	16	17	19	29	22	18	13	13	31
TDs on Ret. and Rec.	3	0	4	3	2	1	6	3	2	5	4	7	5	2
Extra Points	32	28	45	44	37	31	30	34	44	38	38	31	27	44
Safeties	2	1	0	1	1	1	0	0	0	0	1	1	2	0
Field Goals Made	12	25	21	21	26	27	21	19	12	16	20	22	16	17
Field Goals Attempted	20	32	31	29	32	32	25	30	16	28	26	29	28	22
% Successful	60.0	78.1	67.7	72.4	81.3	84.4	84.0	63.3	75.0	57.1	76.9	75.9	57.1	77.3

American Football Conference Defense

	Buff.	Cin.	Clev.	Den.	Hou.	Ind.	K.C.	Raid.	Mia.	N.E.	N.Y.J.	Pitt.	S.D.	Sea.
First Downs	297	286	251	277	287	276	344	267	314	293	300	289	280	297
Rushing	114	99	86	103	98	97	139	98	115	112	117	94	120	133
Passing	162	169	134	148	153	161	172	135	176	159	153	170	136	148
Penalty	21	18	31	26	36	18	33	34	23	22	30	25	24	16
Rushes	541	441	401	454	446	463	535	469	498	490	476	455	522	472
Net Yds. Gained	2052	1641	1433	2017	1848	1790	2333	1637	2198	1778	1835	1610	2171	2201
Avg. Gain	3.8	3.7	3.6	4.4	4.1	3.9	4.4	3.5	4.4	3.6	3.9	3.5	4.2	4.7
Avg. Yds. per Game	136.8	109.4	95.5	134.5	123.2	119.3	155.5	109.1	146.5	118.5	122.3	107.3	144.7	146.7
Passes Attempted	447	456	467	456	495	501	484	425	494	520	488	481	441	445
Completed	249	267	246	261	266	250	279	224	295	273	260	290	227	255
% Completed	55.7	58.6	52.7	57.2	53.7	49.9	57.6	52.7	59.7	52.5	53.3	60.3	51.5	57.3
Total Yds. Gained	3121	3359	3088	3040	3416	3073	3473	3088	3430	3438	3412	3506	3080	3196
Times Sacked	34	40	34	31	35	39	26	44	21	43	29	26	45	37
Yds. Lost	267	303	257	244	271	313	167	361	183	339	206	196	298	238
Net Yds. Gained	2854	3056	2831	2796	3145	2760	3306	2727	3247	3099	3206	3310	2782	2958
Avg. Yds. per Game	190.3	203.7	188.7	186.4	209.7	184.0	220.4	181.8	216.5	206.6	213.7	220.7	185.5	197.2
Net Yds. per Pass Play	5.93	6.16	5.65	5.74	5.93	5.11	6.48	5.81	6.30	5.50	6.20	6.53	5.72	6.14
Yds. Gained per Comp.	12.53	12.58	12.55	11.65	12.84	12.29	12.45	13.79	11.63	12.59	13.12	12.09	13.57	12.53
Combined Net Yds. Gained	4906	4697	4264	4813	4993	4550	5639	4364	5445	4877	5041	4920	4953	5159
% Total Yds. Rushing	41.8	34.9	33.6	41.9	37.0	39.3	41.4	37.5	40.4	36.5	36.4	32.7	43.8	42.7
% Total Yds. Passing	58.2	65.1	66.4	58.1	63.0	60.7	58.6	62.5	59.6	63.5	63.6	67.3	56.2	57.3
Avg. Yds. per Game	327.1	313.1	284.3	320.9	332.9	303.3	375.9	290.9	363.0	325.1	336.1	328.0	330.2	343.9
Ball Control Plays	1022	937	902	941	976	1003	1045	938	1013	1053	993	962	1008	954
Avg. Yds. per Play	4.8	5.0	4.7	5.1	5.1	4.5	5.4	4.7	5.4	4.6	5.1	5.1	4.9	5.4
Avg. Time of Poss.	31:19	29:36	28:16	28:09	29:43	29:50	32:49	29:15	30:17	30:23	29:32	30:15	31:52	29:25
Third Down Efficiency	37.3	40.7	35.5	35.0	32.3	39.0	44.7	39.1	45.5	36.8	38.6	34.4	34.9	43.4
Intercepted by	17	14	23	28	23	20	11	13	16	21	18	27	13	17
Yds. Returned by	93	187	366	403	274	212	140	178	135	307	239	336	291	289
Returned for TD	0	0	2	2	1	0	0	2	0	2	0	5	2	1
Punts	88	75	81	75	77	82	56	78	71	77	80	70	89	63
Yds. Punted	3229	3017	3035	3158	3033	3048	2260	3321	2753	2937	3073	2741	3694	2465
Avg. Yds. per Punt	36.7	40.2	37.5	42.1	39.4	37.2	40.4	42.6	38.8	38.1	38.4	39.2	41.5	39.1
Punt Returns	35	42	17	34	43	39	43	34	26	41	33	46	43	32
Yds. Returned	179	299	93	424	454	376	442	256	141	397	162	395	429	251
Avg. Yds. per Return	5.1	7.1	5.5	12.5	10.6	9.6	10.3	7.5	5.4	9.7	4.9	8.6	10.0	7.8
Returned for TD	0	0	0	2	0	0	0	0	0	0	0	0	1	1
Kickoff Returns	43	62	72	61	57	60	55	59	67	63	54	65	50	67
Yds. Returned	679	1145	1343	1168	1177	1068	1263	1136	1222	1130	1013	1083	985	1379
Avg. Yds. per Return	15.8	18.5	18.7	19.1	20.6	17.8	23.0	19.3	18.2	17.9	18.8	16.7	19.7	20.6
Returned for TD	0	0	0	0	0	0	1	0	0	0	0	0	1	1
Fumbles	37	26	26	35	37	43	24	28	32	42	23	41	26	38
Lost	14	12	13	19	14	25	17	15	16	21	11	17	15	21
Out of Bounds	3	1	1	1	2	0	2	3	2	2	0	4	1	0
Own Rec. for TD	0	0	0	0	0	0	0	0	0	0	0	0	0	0
Opp. Rec. by	24	12	17	17	14	18	24	13	17	13	19	8	20	15
Opp. Rec. for TD	1	0	2	0	0	1	3	0	1	2	1	1	1	0
Penalties	103	79	120	96	101	85	112	95	103	110	96	95	107	104
Yds. Penalized	840	669	1008	785	874	689	936	652	850	846	881	771	869	890
Total Points Scored	305	370	239	288	349	238	388	289	335	293	360	299	317	314
Total TDs	37	43	26	35	37	28	45	33	42	34	43	34	37	36
TDs Rushing	11	15	7	16	10	6	16	12	18	13	15	8	14	14
TDs Passing	25	24	15	15	25	19	25	18	21	17	27	22	19	20
TDs on Ret. and Rec.	1	4	4	4	2	3	4	3	3	4	1	4	4	2
Extra Points	36	43	26	32	35	25	44	31	41	33	42	31	36	35
Safeties	1	0	3	2	1	0	1	0	0	1	0	2	1	0
Field Goals Made	15	23	17	14	30	15	24	20	14	18	20	20	19	21
Field Goals Attempted	20	26	25	21	36	26	35	29	22	27	29	26	29	26
% Successful	75.0	88.5	68.0	66.7	83.3	57.7	68.6	69.0	63.6	66.7	69.0	76.9	65.5	80.8

National Football Conference Offense

	Atl.	Chi.	Dall.	Det.	G.B.	Rams	Minn.	N.O.	N.Y.G.	Phil.	St.L.	S.F.	T.B.	Wash.
First Downs	230	319	293	270	248	276	293	304	266	289	325	357	263	301
Rushing	73	121	93	81	97	118	129	128	80	112	115	134	62	119
Passing	139	156	176	156	133	136	136	151	168	154	189	202	168	153
Penalty	18	42	24	33	18	22	28	25	18	23	21	21	33	29
Rushes	333	485	465	398	464	512	482	569	440	509	462	524	394	500
Net Yds. Gained	1298	1954	1865	1435	1801	2097	1983	2190	1457	2027	1873	2237	1365	2102
Avg. Gain	3.9	4.0	4.0	3.6	3.9	4.1	4.1	3.8	3.3	4.0	4.1	4.3	3.5	4.2
Avg. Yds. per Game	86.5	130.3	124.3	95.7	120.1	139.8	132.2	146.0	97.1	135.1	124.9	149.1	91.0	140.1
Passes Attempted	501	493	500	509	455	420	446	411	499	520	529	501	517	478
Completed	247	272	288	275	234	220	232	227	265	283	305	322	264	247
% Completed	49.3	55.2	57.6	54.0	51.4	52.4	52.0	55.2	53.1	54.4	57.7	64.3	51.1	51.7
Total Yds. Gained	3108	3420	3594	3150	2977	2750	3185	2987	3645	3561	3850	3955	3377	3718
Times Sacked	46	48	52	26	45	25	52	29	61	72	54	29	43	27
Yds. Lost	340	330	403	194	296	196	359	213	443	511	397	205	361	223
Net Yds. Gained	2768	3090	3191	2956	2681	2554	2826	2774	3202	3050	3453	3750	3016	3495
Avg. Yds. per Game	184.5	206.0	212.7	197.1	178.7	170.3	188.4	184.9	213.5	203.3	230.2	250.0	201.1	233.0
Net Yds. per Pass Play	5.06	5.71	5.78	5.53	5.36	5.74	5.67	6.30	5.72	5.15	5.92	7.08	5.39	6.92
Yds. Gained per Comp.	12.58	12.57	12.48	11.45	12.72	12.50	13.73	13.16	13.75	12.58	12.62	12.28	12.79	15.05
Combined Net Yds. Gained	4066	5044	5056	4391	4482	4651	4809	4964	4659	5077	5326	5987	4381	5597
% Total Yds. Rushing	31.9	38.7	36.9	32.7	40.2	45.1	41.2	44.1	31.3	39.9	35.2	37.4	31.2	37.6
% Total Yds. Passing	68.1	61.3	63.1	67.3	59.8	54.9	58.8	55.9	68.7	60.1	64.8	62.6	68.8	62.4
Avg. Yds. per Game	271.1	336.3	337.1	292.7	298.8	310.1	320.6	330.9	310.6	338.5	355.1	399.1	292.1	373.1
Ball Control Plays	880	1026	1017	933	964	957	980	1009	1000	1101	1045	1054	954	1005
Avg. Yds. per Play	4.6	4.9	5.0	4.7	4.6	4.9	4.9	4.9	4.7	4.6	5.1	5.7	4.6	5.6
Avg. Time of Poss.	26:01	31:58	30:41	28:19	29:02	29:59	29:20	34:01	28:20	31:41	30:33	31:43	28:37	30:30
Third Down Efficiency	30.5	35.6	38.7	30.9	31.3	36.8	37.1	44.8	35.0	31.1	37.4	47.8	39.5	40.0
Had Intercepted	32	24	20	26	17	18	23	12	22	16	15	14	17	18
Yds. Opp. Returned	342	334	279	335	115	226	399	173	164	68	227	258	227	193
Ret. by Opp. for TD	2	1	0	2	1	1	3	1	1	0	0	0	0	1
Punts	83	62	84	70	93	77	79	63	91	102	70	68	88	78
Yds. Punted	3375	2439	3324	2927	3659	3140	3077	2587	3604	3770	2663	2541	3455	3053
Avg. Yds. per Punt	40.7	39.3	39.6	41.8	39.3	40.8	38.9	41.1	39.6	37.0	38.0	37.4	39.3	39.1
Punt Returns	31	50	41	35	35	40	36	41	55	34	44	34	31	56
Yds. Returned	221	484	353	303	245	245	420	468	448	202	550	365	257	615
Avg. Yds. per Return	7.1	9.7	8.6	8.7	7.0	6.1	11.7	11.4	8.1	5.9	12.5	10.7	8.3	11.0
Returned for TD	0	2	0	0	0	0	1	0	0	0	1	1	0	0
Kickoff Returns	79	57	64	71	59	63	71	55	56	66	63	55	56	59
Yds. Returned	1700	1193	1295	1428	1032	1282	1421	1147	1128	1112	1317	1144	1037	1139
Avg. Yds. per Return	21.5	20.9	20.2	20.1	17.5	20.3	20.0	20.9	20.1	16.8	20.9	20.8	18.5	19.3
Returned for TD	1	1	0	0	0	1	0	0	0	0	0	1	0	0
Fumbles	27	33	30	29	35	26	28	33	38	44	23	25	35	26
Lost	17	20	20	11	18	15	10	16	20	19	12	12	14	19
Out of Bounds	1	0	0	3	1	2	5	3	4	2	3	0	0	2
Own Rec. for TD	0	0	0	0	0	0	0	0	0	0	0	1	0	0
Opp. Rec. by	12	11	20	13	24	11	11	18	14	27	19	13	19	11
Opp. Rec. for TD	1	0	0	1	0	1	0	0	0	2	4	0	2	1
Penalties	98	103	131	86	135	91	96	107	100	116	101	88	115	82
Yds. Penalized	807	821	1091	737	1103	677	814	994	835	919	797	792	894	691
Total Points Scored	205	356	340	269	255	317	336	422	280	337	362	459	286	379
Total TDs	24	42	38	27	28	38	42	46	32	40	46	59	33	47
TDs Rushing	5	13	17	9	13	15	20	20	4	12	15	11	7	18
TDs Passing	17	23	19	16	15	16	21	23	26	26	25	44	22	27
TDs on Ret. and Rec.	2	6	2	2	0	7	1	3	2	2	6	4	4	2
Extra Points	23	38	37	27	24	36	40	43	28	38	44	55	31	43
Safeties	1	0	0	1	0	1	1	2	0	1	0	1	0	0
Field Goals Made	12	22	25	26	21	17	14	33	20	19	14	16	19	18
Field Goals Attempted	17	32	29	39	29	21	29	42	32	31	27	23	24	29
% Successful	70.6	68.8	86.2	66.7	72.4	81.0	48.3	78.6	62.5	61.3	51.9	69.6	79.2	62.1

National Football Conference Defense

	Atl.	Chi.	Dall.	Det.	G.B.	Rams	Minn.	N.O.	N.Y.G.	Phil.	St.L.	S.F.	T.B.	Wash.
First Downs	354	261	294	314	296	279	281	270	275	301	306	250	314	296
Rushing	162	77	85	122	118	95	95	81	97	85	116	95	124	104
Passing	164	158	175	162	152	162	159	155	148	186	168	132	163	177
Penalty	28	26	34	30	26	22	27	34	30	30	22	23	27	15
Rushes	600	412	459	504	521	419	440	388	493	428	492	429	500	441
Net Yds. Gained	2734	1413	1617	2070	1920	1732	1724	1550	1768	1643	2001	1611	2038	1679
Avg. Gain	4.6	3.4	3.5	4.1	3.7	4.1	3.9	4.0	3.6	3.8	4.1	3.8	4.1	3.8
Avg. Yds. per Game	182.3	94.2	107.8	138.0	128.0	115.5	114.9	103.3	117.9	109.5	133.4	107.4	135.9	111.9
Passes Attempted	453	507	502	459	469	504	498	489	508	561	490	467	457	527
Completed	243	255	269	259	279	281	278	246	292	305	276	224	271	276
% Completed	53.6	50.3	53.6	56.4	59.5	55.8	55.8	50.3	57.5	54.4	56.3	48.0	59.3	52.4
Total Yds. Gained	3291	3286	3781	3558	3200	3693	3407	3155	3272	4058	3668	2771	3255	3767
Times Sacked	17	70	51	42	34	38	41	47	55	57	41	37	39	53
Yds. Lost	118	484	337	355	197	304	307	355	382	452	285	287	306	424
Net Yds. Gained	3173	2802	3444	3203	3003	3389	3100	2800	2890	3606	3383	2484	2949	3343
Avg. Yds. per Game	211.5	186.8	229.6	213.5	200.2	225.9	206.7	186.7	192.7	240.4	225.5	165.6	196.6	222.9
Net Yds. per Pass Play	6.75	4.86	6.23	6.39	5.97	6.25	5.75	5.22	5.13	5.83	6.37	4.93	5.95	5.76
Yds. Gained per Comp.	13.54	12.89	14.06	13.74	11.47	13.14	12.26	12.83	11.21	13.30	13.29	12.37	12.01	13.65
Combined Net Yds. Gained	5907	4215	5061	5273	4923	5121	4824	4350	4658	5249	5384	4095	4987	5022
% Total Yds. Rushing	46.3	33.5	32.0	39.3	39.0	33.8	35.7	35.6	38.0	31.3	37.2	39.3	40.9	33.4
% Total Yds. Passing	53.7	66.5	68.0	60.7	61.0	66.2	64.3	64.4	62.0	68.7	62.8	60.7	59.1	66.6
Avg. Yds. per Game	393.8	281.0	337.4	351.5	328.2	341.4	321.6	290.0	310.5	349.9	358.9	273.0	332.5	334.8
Ball Control Plays	1070	989	1012	1005	1024	961	979	924	1056	1046	1023	933	996	1021
Avg. Yds. per Play	5.5	4.3	5.0	5.2	4.8	5.3	4.9	4.7	4.4	5.0	5.3	4.4	5.0	4.9
Avg. Time of Poss.	33:59	28:02	29:19	31:41	30:58	30:01	30:40	25:59	31:40	28:19	29:27	28:17	31:23	29:30
Third Down Efficiency	50.9	35.4	43.0	40.3	39.1	37.9	36.9	31.3	32.5	31.9	46.1	28.9	45.0	33.6
Intercepted by	15	13	23	19	18	16	26	30	20	21	14	25	16	23
Yds. Returned by	182	69	208	290	220	305	303	280	263	197	167	205	248	329
Returned for TD	0	2	2	1	0	2	0	0	1	0	1	0	2	1
Punts	60	86	75	65	77	83	74	73	96	88	74	72	64	91
Yds. Punted	2383	3408	3042	2461	3084	3097	2954	2740	3653	3262	3049	2850	2634	3569
Avg. Yds. per Punt	39.7	39.6	40.6	37.9	40.1	37.3	39.9	37.5	38.1	37.1	41.2	39.6	41.2	39.2
Punt Returns	48	26	45	34	54	43	44	29	51	54	36	29	50	37
Yds. Returned	541	339	376	177	422	317	424	199	811	469	489	195	621	231
Avg. Yds. per Return	11.3	13.0	8.4	5.2	7.8	7.4	9.6	6.9	15.9	8.7	13.6	6.7	12.4	6.2
Returned for TD	1	1	1	0	0	0	0	0	2	0	1	0	1	0
Kickoff Returns	44	58	65	56	61	57	64	55	68	59	59	76	61	63
Yds. Returned	915	1054	1281	1089	1140	1112	1173	1115	1463	1276	1063	1598	1242	1352
Avg. Yds. per Return	20.8	18.2	19.7	19.4	18.7	19.5	18.3	20.3	21.5	21.6	18.0	21.0	20.4	21.5
Returned for TD	1	0	0	0	0	0	0	0	0	0	0	1	0	1
Fumbles	18	37	29	36	42	28	30	31	31	41	34	30	42	22
Lost	12	11	20	13	24	11	11	18	14	27	19	13	20	11
Out of Bounds	2	2	1	1	2	4	0	2	3	0	2	1	2	2
Own Rec. for TD	0	0	0	0	0	1	0	0	0	0	0	0	0	0
Opp. Rec. by	17	20	20	11	18	15	10	16	20	19	11	12	14	19
Opp. Rec. for TD	0	1	1	0	0	1	1	3	0	1	0	2	2	2
Penalties	92	120	100	115	104	100	107	84	97	105	88	80	125	97
Yds. Penalized	729	1108	851	907	852	888	964	685	802	830	718	660	926	801
Total Points Scored	436	282	348	384	300	361	335	283	312	380	368	253	360	285
Total TDs	54	33	42	43	31	43	38	35	35	47	48	26	44	33
TDs Rushing	24	5	19	18	15	8	9	6	14	16	16	8	18	10
TDs Passing	26	24	21	23	14	31	24	25	17	29	30	13	23	19
TDs on Ret. and Rec.	4	4	2	2	2	4	5	4	4	2	2	5	3	4
Extra Points	51	30	39	42	29	40	35	35	33	44	45	25	42	30
Safeties	2	0	0	0	2	0	0	1	0	0	1	0	0	0
Field Goals Made	19	18	19	28	27	21	24	12	23	18	11	24	18	19
Field Goals Attempted	30	31	29	34	36	24	31	18	34	29	18	35	30	28
% Successful	63.3	58.1	65.5	82.4	75.0	87.5	77.4	66.7	67.6	62.1	61.1	68.6	60.0	67.9

AFC, NFC, and NFL Summary

	AFC Offense Total	AFC Offense Average	AFC Defense Total	AFC Defense Average	NFC Offense Total	NFC Offense Average	NFC Defense Total	NFC Defense Average	NFL Total	NFL Average
First Downs	4115	293.9	4058	289.9	4034	288.1	4091	292.2	8149	291.0
Rushing	1519	108.5	1525	108.9	1462	104.4	1456	104.0	2981	106.5
Passing	2220	158.6	2176	155.4	2217	158.4	2261	161.5	4437	158.5
Penalty	376	26.9	357	25.5	355	25.4	374	26.7	731	26.1
Rushes	6652	475.1	6663	475.9	6537	466.9	6526	466.1	13,189	471.0
Net Yds. Gained	26,360	1882.9	26,544	1896.0	25,684	1834.6	25,500	1821.4	52,044	1858.7
Avg. Gain	—	4.0	—	4.0	—	3.9	—	3.9	—	3.9
Avg. Yds. per Game	—	125.5	—	126.4	—	122.3	—	121.4	—	123.9
Passes Attempted	6712	479.4	6600	471.4	6779	484.2	6891	492.2	13,491	481.8
Completed	3715	265.4	3642	260.1	3681	262.9	3754	268.1	7396	264.1
% Completed	—	55.3	—	55.2	—	54.3	—	54.5	—	54.8
Total Yds. Gained	46,605	3328.9	45,720	3265.7	47,277	3376.9	48,162	3440.1	93,882	3352.9
Times Sacked	497	35.5	484	34.6	609	43.5	622	44.4	1106	39.5
Yds. Lost	3765	268.9	3643	260.2	4471	319.4	4593	328.1	8236	294.1
Net Yds. Gained	42,840	3060.0	42,077	3005.5	42,806	3057.6	43,569	3112.1	85,646	3058.8
Avg. Yds. per Game	—	204.0	—	200.4	—	203.8	—	207.5	—	203.9
Net Yds. per Pass Play	—	5.94	—	5.94	—	5.79	—	5.80	—	5.87
Yds. Gained per Comp.	—	12.55	—	12.55	—	12.84	—	12.83	—	12.69
Combined Net Yds.Gained	69,200	4942.9	68,621	4901.5	68,490	4892.1	69,069	4933.5	137,690	4917.5
% Total Yds. Rushing	—	38.1	—	38.7	—	37.5	—	36.9	—	37.8
% Total Yds. Passing	—	61.9	—	61.3	—	62.5	—	63.1	—	62.2
Avg. Yds. per Game	—	329.5	—	326.8	—	326.1	—	328.9	—	327.8
Ball Control Plays	13,861	990.1	13,747	981.9	13,925	994.6	14,039	1002.8	27,786	992.4
Avg. Yds. per Play	—	5.0	—	5.0	—	4.9	—	4.9	—	5.0
Third Down Efficiency	—	39.6	—	38.4	—	36.9	—	38.1	—	38.3
Interceptions	261	18.6	266	19.0	279	19.9	274	19.6	540	19.3
Yds. Returned	3450	246.4	3376	241.1	3266	233.3	3340	238.6	6716	239.9
Returned for TD	17	1.2	16	1.1	12	0.9	13	0.9	29	1.0
Punts	1032	73.7	1062	75.9	1108	79.1	1078	77.0	2140	76.4
Yds. Punted	40,336	2881.1	41,764	2983.1	43,614	3115.3	42,186	3013.3	83,950	2998.2
Avg. Yds. per Punt	—	39.1	—	39.3	—	39.4	—	39.1	—	39.2
Punt Returns	525	37.5	508	36.3	563	40.2	580	41.4	1088	38.9
Yds. Returned	4733	338.1	4298	307.0	5176	369.7	5611	400.8	9909	353.9
Avg. Yds. per Return	—	9.0	—	8.5	—	9.2	—	9.7	—	9.1
Returned for TD	6	0.4	4	0.3	5	0.4	7	0.5	11	0.4
Kickoff Returns	807	57.6	835	59.6	874	62.4	846	60.4	1681	60.0
Yds. Returned	15,289	1092.1	15,791	1127.9	17,375	1241.1	16,873	1205.2	32,664	1166.6
Avg. Yds. per Return	—	18.9	—	18.9	—	19.9	—	19.9	—	19.4
Returned for TD	2	0.1	3	0.2	4	0.3	3	0.2	6	0.2
Fumbles	477	34.1	458	32.7	432	30.9	451	32.2	909	32.5
Lost	231	16.5	230	16.4	223	15.9	224	16.0	454	16.2
Out of Bounds	20	1.4	22	1.6	26	1.9	24	1.7	46	1.6
Own Rec. for TD	0	0.0	0	0.0	1	0.1	1	0.1	1	0.0
Opp. Rec.	230	16.4	231	16.5	223	15.9	222	15.9	453	16.2
Opp. Rec. for TD	15	1.1	13	0.9	12	0.9	14	1.0	27	1.0
Penalties	1371	97.9	1406	100.4	1449	103.5	1414	101.0	2820	100.7
Yds. Penalized	11,309	807.8	11,560	825.7	11,972	855.1	11,721	837.2	23,281	831.5
Total Points Scored	4468	319.1	4384	313.1	4603	328.8	4687	334.8	9071	324.0
Total TDs	520	37.1	510	36.4	542	38.7	552	39.4	1062	37.9
TDs Rushing	182	13.0	175	12.5	179	12.8	186	13.3	361	12.9
TDs Passing	291	20.8	292	20.9	320	22.9	319	22.8	611	21.8
TDs on Ret. and Rec.	47	3.4	43	3.1	43	3.1	47	3.4	90	3.2
Extra Points	503	35.9	490	35.0	507	36.2	520	37.1	1010	36.1
Safeties	10	0.7	12	0.9	8	0.6	6	0.4	18	0.6
Field Goals Made	275	19.6	270	19.3	276	19.7	281	20.1	551	19.7
Field Goals Attempted	380	27.1	377	26.9	404	28.9	407	29.1	784	28.0
% Successful	—	72.4	—	71.6	—	68.3	—	69.0	—	70.3

Club Leaders

	Offense	Defense
First Downs	S.F. 357	S.F. 250
Rushing	S.F. 134	Chi. 77
Passing	S.F. 202	S.F. 132
Penalty	Chi. 42	Wash. 15
Rushes	N.O. 569	N.O. 388
Net Yds. Gained	S.F. 2297	Chi. 1413
Avg. Gain	Raiders 4.6	Chi. 3.4
Passes Attempted	Mia. 584	Raiders 425
Completed	Mia. 338	Raiders & S.F. 224
% Completed	S.F. 64.3	S.F. 48.0
Total Yds. Gained	Mia. 3977	S.F. 2771
Times Sacked	Mia. 13	Chi. 70
Yds. Lost	Mia. 101	Chi. 484
Net Yds. Gained	Mia. 3876	S.F. 2484
Net Yds. per Pass Play	S.F. 7.08	Chi. 4.86
Yds. Gained per Comp.	Wash. 15.05	N.Y.G. 11.21
Combined Net Yds. Gained	S.F. 5987	S.F. 4095
% Total Yds. Rushing	Pitt. 48.6	Phil. 31.3
% Total Yds. Passing	S.D. 71.5	Atl. 53.7
Ball Control Plays	Phil. 1101	Clev. 902
Avg. Yds. per Play	S.F. 5.7	Chi. 4.3
Avg. Time of Poss.	N.O. 34:01	—
Third Down Efficiency	Sea. 48.7	S.F. 28.9
Interceptions	—	N.O. 30
Yds. Returned	—	Den. 403
Returned for TD	—	Pitt. 5
Punts	Phil. 102	—
Yds. Punted	Phil. 3770	—
Avg. Yds. per Punt	S.D. 42.0	—
Punt Returns	Wash. 56	Clev. 17
Yds. Returned	Wash. 615	Clev. 93
Avg. Yds. per Return	St.L. 12.5	N.Y.J. 4.9
Returned for TD	Chi. & N.Y.J. 2	—
Kickoff Returns	Atl. 79	Buff. 43
Yds. Returned	Atl. 1700	Buff. 679
Avg. Yds. per Return	Atl. 21.5	Buff. 15.8
Returned for TD	K.C. 2	—
Total Points Scored	S.F. 459	Ind. 238
Total TDs	S.F. 59	Clev. & S.F. 26
TDs Rushing	Minn. & N.O. 20	Chi. 5
TDs Passing	S.F. 44	S.F. 13
TDs on Ret. and Rec.	Pitt. & Rams 7	Buff. & N.Y.J. 1
Extra Points	S.F. 55	Ind. & S.F. 25
Safeties	Three with 2	—
Field Goals Made	N.O. 33	St.L. 11
Field Goals Attempted	N.O. 42	N.O. & St.L. 18
% Successful	Dall. 86.2	Ind. 57.7

National Football League Club Rankings by Yards

	Offense			Defense		
Team	Total	Rush	Pass	Total	Rush	Pass
Atlanta	28	28	22	28	28	18
Buffalo	16	17	18	12	22	9
Chicago	12	13	12	2	*1	7
Cincinnati	5	4	9	8	8	14
Cleveland	9	21	5	3	2	8
Dallas	11	16	11	20	6	27
Denver	2	12	3	9	20	5
Detroit	26	25	17	24	23	19
Green Bay	22	18	25	14	18	13
Houston	8	14	7	17	17	17
Indianapolis	13	6	19	6	15	3
Kansas City	24	19	26	27	27	22
Los Angeles Raiders	7	2	13	5	7	2
Los Angeles Rams	19	8	27	21	12	26
Miami	4	23	*1	26	25	21
Minnesota	15	11	20	10	11	16
New England	23	20	24	11	14	15
New Orleans	14	3	21	4	3	6
New York Giants	18	24	10	7	13	10
New York Jets	20	22	16	19	16	20
Philadelphia	10	9	14	23	9	28
Pittsburgh	25	5	28	13	4	23
St. Louis	6	15	6	25	19	25
San Diego	21	27	8	15	24	4
San Francisco	*1	*1	2	*1	5	*1
Seattle	17	10	23	22	26	12
Tampa Bay	27	26	15	16	21	11
Washington	3	7	4	18	10	24

*—League leader

AFC Takeaways/Giveaways

	Takeaways			Giveaways			Net
	Int.	Fum.	Total	Int.	Fum.	Total	Diff.
Denver	28	19	47	19	17	36	11
Indianapolis	20	25	45	16	18	34	11
New England	21	21	42	18	13	31	11
Pittsburgh	27	17	44	25	8	33	11
Cleveland	23	13	36	12	17	29	7
Seattle	17	21	38	21	15	36	2
Houston	23	14	37	23	14	37	0
Los Angeles Raiders	13	15	28	18	13	31	– 3
New York Jets	18	11	29	15	19	34	– 5
Miami	16	16	32	20	17	37	– 5
Cincinnati	14	12	26	20	12	32	– 6
Buffalo	17	14	31	19	24	43	–12
Kansas City	11	17	28	17	24	41	–13
San Diego	13	15	28	23	20	43	–15

NFC Takeaways/Giveaways

	Takeaways			Giveaways			Net
	Int.	Fum.	Total	Int.	Fum.	Total	Diff.
New Orleans	30	18	48	12	16	28	20
Philadelphia	21	27	48	16	19	35	13
San Francisco	25	13	38	14	12	26	12
Green Bay	18	24	42	17	18	35	7
St. Louis	14	19	33	15	12	27	6
Tampa Bay	16	20	36	17	14	31	5
Minnesota	26	11	37	23	10	33	4
Dallas	23	20	43	20	20	40	3
Washington	23	11	34	18	19	37	– 3
Detroit	19	13	32	26	11	37	– 5
Los Angeles Rams	16	11	27	18	15	33	– 6
New York Giants	20	14	34	22	20	42	– 8
Chicago	13	11	24	24	20	44	–20
Atlanta	15	12	27	32	17	49	–22

Scoring

Points
NFC: 138—Jerry Rice, San Francisco
AFC: 97—Jim Breech, Cincinnati

Touchdowns
NFC: 23—Jerry Rice, San Francisco
AFC: 11—Johnny Hector, N.Y. Jets

Extra Points
NFC: 44—Ray Wersching, San Francisco
AFC: 40—Norm Johnson, Seattle

Field Goals
NFC: 28—Morten Andersen, New Orleans
AFC: 24—Dean Biasucci, Indianapolis
24—Jim Breech, Cincinnati

Field Goal Attempts
NFC: 36—Morten Andersen, New Orleans
AFC: 30—Jim Breech, Cincinnati

Longest Field Goal
AFC: 54—Nick Lowery, Kansas City at Detroit, November 26
NFC: 53—Raul Allegre, N.Y. Giants at Philadelphia, November 15
53—Ed Murray, Detroit vs. L.A. Rams, December 6

Most Points, Game
AFC: 19—Norm Johnson, Seattle vs. Kansas City, September 20 (4 PAT, 5 FG)
NFC: 18—Anthony Allen, Washington vs. St. Louis, October 4 (3 TD)
18—Derrick McAdoo, St. Louis at San Francisco, October 18 (3 TD)
18—D.J. Dozier, Minnesota vs. Denver, October 26 (3 TD)
18—Jerry Rice, San Francisco at Tampa Bay, November 22 (3 TD)
18—Mike Renfro, Dallas vs. Minnesota, November 26 [OT] (3 TD)
18—Jerry Rice, San Francisco vs. Cleveland, November 29 (3 TD)
18—Jerry Rice, San Francisco vs. Chicago, December 14 (3 TD)
18—Jerry Rice, San Francisco vs. Atlanta, December 20 (3 TD)

Team Leaders, Points
AFC: BUFFALO: 61, Scott Norwood; CINCINNATI: 97, Jim Breech; CLEVELAND: 75, Jeff Jaeger; DENVER: 91, Rich Karlis; HOUSTON: 92, Tony Zendejas; INDIANAPOLIS: 96, Dean Biasucci; KANSAS CITY: 83, Nick Lowery; L.A. RAIDERS: 84, Chris Bahr; MIAMI: 55, Fuad Reveiz; NEW ENGLAND: 82, Tony Franklin; N.Y. JETS: 85, Pat Leahy; PITTSBURGH: 87, Gary Anderson; SAN DIEGO: 61, Vince Abbott; SEATTLE: 85, Norm Johnson.
NFC: ATLANTA: 44, Mick Luckhurst; CHICAGO: 85, Kevin Butler; DALLAS: 92, Roger Ruzek; DETROIT: 81, Ed Murray; GREEN BAY: 61, Max Zendejas; L.A. RAMS: 87, Mike Lansford; MINNESOTA: 75, Chuck Nelson; NEW ORLEANS: 121, Morten Andersen; N.Y. GIANTS: 76, Raul Allegre; PHILADELPHIA: 84, Paul McFadden; ST. LOUIS: 57, Jim Gallery; SAN FRANCISCO: 138, Jerry Rice; TAMPA BAY: 66, Donald Igwebuike; WASHINGTON: 68, Ali Haji-Sheikh.

Team Champions
NFC: 459—San Francisco
AFC: 390—Cleveland

AFC Scoring—Team

	TD	TDR	TDP	TD Misc.	PAT	PAT Att.	FG	FG Att.	SAF	TP
Cleveland	47	16	27	4	45	47	21	31	0	390
Denver	45	18	24	3	44	45	21	29	1	379
Seattle	46	13	31	2	44	46	17	22	0	371
Miami	47	16	29	2	44	47	12	16	0	362
Houston	38	12	24	2	37	38	26	32	1	345
N.Y. Jets	39	17	18	4	38	38	20	26	1	334
New England	39	12	22	5	38	39	16	28	0	320
L.A. Raiders	35	13	19	3	34	35	19	30	0	301
Indianapolis	31	14	16	1	31	31	27	32	1	300
Cincinnati	30	13	17	0	28	30	25	32	1	285
Pittsburgh	31	11	13	7	31	31	22	29	1	285
Kansas City	30	7	17	6	30	30	21	25	0	273
Buffalo	33	9	21	3	32	33	12	20	2	270
San Diego	29	11	13	5	27	29	16	28	2	253
AFC Total	520	182	291	47	503	519	275	380	10	4468
AFC Average	37.1	13.0	20.8	3.4	35.9	37.1	19.6	27.1	0.7	319.1

NFC Scoring—Team

	TD	TDR	TDP	TD Misc.	PAT	PAT Att.	FG	FG Att.	SAF	TP
San Francisco	59	11	44	4	55	59	16	23	1	459
New Orleans	46	20	23	3	43	46	33	42	2	422
Washington	47	18	27	2	43	47	18	29	0	379
St. Louis	46	15	25	6	44	46	14	27	0	362
Chicago	42	13	23	6	38	42	22	32	0	356
Dallas	38	17	19	2	37	37	25	29	0	340
Philadelphia	40	12	26	2	38	40	19	31	1	337
Minnesota	42	20	21	1	40	41	14	29	1	336
L.A. Rams	38	15	16	7	36	38	17	21	1	317
Tampa Bay	33	7	22	4	31	33	19	24	0	286
N.Y. Giants	32	4	26	2	28	32	20	32	0	280
Detroit	27	9	16	2	27	27	26	39	1	269
Green Bay	28	13	15	0	24	27	21	29	0	255
Atlanta	24	5	17	2	23	24	12	17	1	205
NFC Total	542	179	320	43	507	539	276	404	8	4603
NFC Average	38.7	12.8	22.9	3.1	36.2	38.5	19.7	28.9	0.6	328.8
League Total	1062	361	611	90	1010	1058	551	784	18	9071
League Avg.	37.9	12.9	21.8	3.2	36.1	37.8	19.7	28.0	0.6	324.0

NFL Top 10 Scorers—Touchdowns

	TD	TDR	TDP	TD Misc.	TP
Rice, Jerry, San Francisco	23	1	22	0	138
Hector, Johnny, N.Y. Jets	11	11	0	0	66
Quick, Mike, Philadelphia	11	0	11	0	66
White, Charles, L.A. Rams	11	11	0	0	66
Byner, Earnest, Cleveland	10	8	2	0	60
Warner, Curt, Seattle	10	8	2	0	60
Bentley, Albert, Indianapolis	9	7	2	0	54
Riddick, Robb, Buffalo	8	5	3	0	50
Bavaro, Mark, N.Y. Giants	8	0	8	0	48
Duper, Mark, Miami	8	0	8	0	48
Hilliard, Dalton, New Orleans	8	7	1	0	48
Kinnebrew, Larry, Cincinnati	8	8	0	0	48
Largent, Steve, Seattle	8	0	8	0	48
Smith, J.T., St.Louis	8	0	8	0	48
Walker, Herschel, Dallas	8	7	1	0	48

NFL Top 10 Scorers—Kicking

	PAT	PAT Att.	FG	FG Att.	TP
Andersen, Morten, New Orleans	37	37	28	36	121
Breech, Jim, Cincinnati	25	27	24	30	97
Biasucci, Dean, Indianapolis	24	24	24	27	96
Ruzek, Roger, Dallas	26	26	22	25	92
Zendejas, Tony, Houston	32	33	20	26	92
Karlis, Rich, Denver	37	37	18	25	91
Anderson, Gary, Pittsburgh	21	21	22	27	87
Lansford, Mike, L.A. Rams	36	38	17	21	87
Butler, Kevin, Chicago	28	30	19	28	85
Johnson, Norm, Seattle	40	40	15	20	85
Leahy, Pat, N.Y. Jets	31	31	18	22	85

AFC Scoring—Individual

Kickers	PAT	PAT Att.	FG	FG Att.	TP
Breech, Jim, Cincinnati	25	27	24	30	97
Biasucci, Dean, Indianapolis	24	24	24	27	96
Zendejas, Tony, Houston	32	33	20	26	92
Karlis, Rich, Denver	37	37	18	25	91
Anderson, Gary, Pittsburgh	21	21	22	27	87
Johnson, Norm, Seattle	40	40	15	20	85
Leahy, Pat, N.Y. Jets	31	31	18	22	85
Bahr, Chris, L.A. Raiders	27	28	19	29	84
Lowery, Nick, Kansas City	26	26	19	23	83
Franklin, Tony, New England	37	38	15	26	82
Jaeger, Jeff, Cleveland	33	33	14	22	75
Abbott, Vince, San Diego	22	23	13	22	61
Norwood, Scott, Buffalo	31	31	10	15	61
Reveiz, Fuad, Miami	28	30	9	11	55
Tiffin, Van, Tampa Bay-Miami	11	11	5	7	26
Diettrich, John, Houston	5	5	6	6	23
Bahr, Matt, Cleveland	9	10	4	5	21
Beecher, Willie, Miami	12	12	3	4	21
Clendenen, Mike, Denver	7	7	3	4	16
Jordan, Steve, Indianapolis	7	7	3	5	16
Gaffney, Jeff, San Diego	4	5	3	6	13
Ragusa, Pat, N.Y. Jets	7	7	2	4	13
Franco, Brian, Cleveland	2	2	3	4	11
Hagler, Scott, Seattle	4	4	2	2	10
Hamrick, James, Kansas City	4	4	2	2	10
Trout, David, Pittsburgh	10	10	0	2	10
Hardy, David, L.A. Raiders	7	7	0	1	7
Schlopy, Todd, Buffalo	1	2	2	5	7
Manca, Massimo, Cincinnati	3	3	1	2	6
Schubert, Eric, New England	1	1	1	2	4
Kelley, Chris, Cleveland	1	1	0	0	1

Non-Kickers	TD	TDR	TDP	TD Misc.	TP
Hector, Johnny, N.Y. Jets	11	11	0	0	66
Byner, Earnest, Cleveland	10	8	2	0	60
Warner, Curt, Seattle	10	8	2	0	60
Bentley, Albert, Indianapolis	9	7	2	0	54

	TD	TDR	TDP	TD Misc.	TP
Riddick, Robb, Buffalo	8	5	3	0	*50
Duper, Mark, Miami	8	0	8	0	48
Kinnebrew, Larry, Cincinnati	8	8	0	0	48
Largent, Steve, Seattle	8	0	8	0	48
Carson, Carlos, Kansas City	7	0	7	0	42
Clayton, Mark, Miami	7	0	7	0	42
Johnson, Vance, Denver	7	0	7	0	42
Slaughter, Webster, Cleveland	7	0	7	0	42
Stradford, Troy, Miami	7	6	1	0	42
Winder, Sammy, Denver	7	6	1	0	42
Brennan, Brian, Cleveland	6	0	6	0	36
Collins, Tony, New England	6	3	3	0	36
Dickerson, Eric, L.A. Rams-Indianapolis	6	6	0	0	36
Givins, Ernest, Houston	6	0	6	0	36
Hill, Drew, Houston	6	0	6	0	36
Jackson, Bo, L.A. Raiders	6	4	2	0	36
James, Lionel, San Diego	6	2	3	1	36
Mack, Kevin, Cleveland	6	5	1	0	36
Turner, Daryl, Seattle	6	0	6	0	36
Allen, Marcus, L.A. Raiders	5	5	0	0	30
Anderson, Gary, San Diego	5	3	2	0	30
Butler, Raymond, Seattle	5	0	5	0	30
Duncan, Curtis, Houston	5	0	5	0	30
Fryar, Irving, New England	5	0	5	0	30
Lofton, James, L.A. Raiders	5	0	5	0	30
Reed, Andre, Buffalo	5	0	5	0	30
Toon, Al, N.Y. Jets	5	0	5	0	30
Williams, Dokie, L.A. Raiders	5	0	5	0	30
Bouza, Matt, Indianapolis	4	0	4	0	24
Burkett, Chris, Buffalo	4	0	4	0	24
Elway, John, Denver	4	4	0	0	24
Harmon, Ronnie, Buffalo	4	2	2	0	24
Lang, Gene, Denver	4	2	2	0	24
Massie, Rick, Denver	4	0	4	0	24
Paige, Stephone, Kansas City	4	0	4	0	24
Williams, John L., Seattle	4	1	3	0	24
Aikens, Carl, L.A. Raiders	3	0	3	0	18
Brooks, Bill, Indianapolis	3	0	3	0	18
Brooks, James, Cincinnati	3	1	2	0	18
Brown, Eddie, Cincinnati	3	0	3	0	18
Carter, Rodney, Pittsburgh	3	0	3	0	18
Dupard, Reggie, New England	3	3	0	0	18
Heard, Herman, Kansas City	3	3	0	0	18
Jennings, Stanford, Cincinnati	3	1	2	0	18
Jones, Cedric, New England	3	0	3	0	18
Malone, Mark, Pittsburgh	3	3	0	0	18
Martin, Mike, Cincinnati	3	0	3	0	18
Mason, Larry, Cleveland	3	2	1	0	18
Moon, Warren, Houston	3	3	0	0	18
Morgan, Stanley, New England	3	0	3	0	18
Murray, Walter, Indianapolis	3	0	3	0	18
Okoye, Christian, Kansas City	3	3	0	0	18
Pollard, Frank, Pittsburgh	3	3	0	0	18
Pruitt, James, Miami	3	0	3	0	18
Rozier, Mike, Houston	3	3	0	0	18
Scott, Ronald, Miami	3	3	0	0	18
Sewell, Steve, Denver	3	2	1	0	18
Shuler, Mickey, N.Y. Jets	3	0	3	0	18
Starring, Stephen, New England	3	0	3	0	18
Tennell, Derek, Cleveland	3	0	3	0	18
Williams, Jamie, Houston	3	0	3	0	18
Winslow, Kellen, San Diego	3	0	3	0	18
Abercrombie, Walter, Pittsburgh	2	2	0	0	12
Alston, Lyneal, Pittsburgh	2	0	2	0	12
Baty, Greg, New England	2	0	2	0	12
Chandler, Wes, San Diego	2	0	2	0	12
Christensen, Todd, L.A. Raiders	2	0	2	0	12
Davenport, Ron, Miami	2	1	1	0	12
Dudek, Joe, Denver	2	2	0	0	12
Ellis, Craig, L.A. Raiders	2	2	0	0	12
Faaola, Nuu, N.Y. Jets	2	2	0	0	12
Fouts, Dan, San Diego	2	2	0	0	12
Grogan, Steve, New England	2	2	0	0	12
Hall, Delton, Pittsburgh	2	0	0	2	12
Hardy, Bruce, Miami	2	0	2	0	12
Harper, Michael, N.Y. Jets	2	0	1	1	12
Hayes, Jonathan, Kansas City	2	0	2	0	12
Highsmith, Alonzo, Houston	2	1	1	0	12
Holman, Rodney, Cincinnati	2	0	2	0	12
Hunter, Eddie, N.Y. Jets	2	0	2	0	12
Jackson, Mark, Denver	2	0	2	0	12
Johnson, Dan, Miami	2	0	2	0	12
Johnson, Trumaine, Buffalo	2	0	2	0	12
Kattus, Eric, Cincinnati	2	0	2	0	12
Kemp, Perry, Cleveland	2	0	2	0	12
Krieg, Dave, Seattle	2	2	0	0	12
Linne, Larry, New England	2	0	2	0	12
Lippett, Ronnie, New England	2	0	0	2	12
Mackey, Kyle, Miami	2	2	0	0	12

	TD	TDR	TDP	TD Misc.	TP
McNeil, Gerald, Cleveland	2	0	2	0	12
Micho, Bobby, Denver	2	0	2	0	12
Mueller, Jamie, Buffalo	2	2	0	0	12
Nattiel, Ricky, Denver	2	0	2	0	12
Noble, James, Indianapolis	2	0	2	0	12
Palmer, Paul, Kansas City	2	0	0	2	12
Pinkett, Allen, Houston	2	2	0	0	12
Rolle, Butch, Buffalo	2	0	2	0	12
Scott, Willie, New England	2	0	1	1	12
Shell, Donnie, Pittsburgh	2	0	0	2	12
Sohn, Kurt, N.Y. Jets	2	0	2	0	12
Stallworth, John, Pittsburgh	2	0	2	0	12
Teal, Jimmy, Seattle	2	0	2	0	12
Tice, Mike, Seattle	2	0	2	0	12
Weathers, Clarence, Cleveland	2	0	2	0	12
Neuheisel, Rick, San Diego	1	1	0	0	#7
Adams, Curtis, San Diego	1	1	0	0	6
Adickes, Mark, Kansas City	1	0	1	0	6
Banks, Fred, Miami	1	0	1	0	6
Bernstine, Rod, San Diego	1	0	1	0	6
Bleier, Bob, New England	1	1	0	0	6
Bligen, Dennis, N.Y. Jets	1	1	0	0	6
Boddie, Tony, Denver	1	1	0	0	6
Bono, Steve, Pittsburgh	1	1	0	0	6
Brandon, David, San Diego	1	0	0	1	6
Broughton, Walter, Buffalo	1	0	1	0	6
Brown, Gordon, Indianapolis	1	1	0	0	6
Brown, Marc, Buffalo	1	0	1	0	6
Calhoun, Rick, L.A. Raiders	1	0	0	1	6
Chirico, John, N.Y. Jets	1	1	0	0	6
Clark, Kevin, Denver	1	0	0	1	6
Clayborn, Raymond, New England	1	0	0	1	6
Clinkscales, Joey, Pittsburgh	1	0	1	0	6
Coffman, Paul, Kansas City	1	0	1	0	6
Douglas, Leland, Miami	1	0	1	0	6
Ellis, Ray, Cleveland	1	0	0	1	6
Evans, Vince, L.A. Raiders	1	1	0	0	6
Fields, Jitter, Kansas City	1	0	0	1	6
Gehring, Mark, Houston	1	0	1	0	6
Glenn, Vencie, San Diego	1	0	0	1	6
Gothard, Preston, Pittsburgh	1	0	1	0	6
Gowdy, Cornell, Pittsburgh	1	0	0	1	6
Grayson, Dave, Cleveland	1	0	0	1	6
Griggs, Billy, N.Y. Jets	1	0	1	0	6
Hairston, Russell, Pittsburgh	1	0	1	0	6
Hampton, Lorenzo, Miami	1	1	0	0	6
Harris, Bob, Kansas City	1	0	0	1	6
Haynes, Mark, Denver	1	0	0	1	6
Hobley, Liffort, Miami	1	0	0	1	6
Hoge, Merril, Pittsburgh	1	0	1	0	6
Hooper, Trell, Miami	1	0	0	1	6
Horton, Ethan, L.A. Raiders	1	0	1	0	6
Humphery, Bobby, N.Y. Jets	1	0	0	1	6
Hunley, Ricky, Denver	1	0	0	1	6
Hunter, Stan, N.Y. Jets	1	0	1	0	6
Isom, Rickey, Miami	1	1	0	0	6
Jackson, Andrew, Houston	1	1	0	0	6
Jackson, Earnest, Pittsburgh	1	1	0	0	6
Jensen, Jim, Miami	1	0	1	0	6
Johnson, Bill, Cincinnati	1	1	0	0	6
Jones, Joe, Indianapolis	1	0	1	0	6
Jones, Rod, Kansas City	1	0	1	0	6
Keel, Mark, Seattle	1	0	1	0	6
Kelso, Mark, Buffalo	1	0	0	1	6
Kosar, Bernie, Cleveland	1	1	0	0	6
Kurisko, Jamie, N.Y. Jets	1	0	1	0	6
Langhorne, Reggie, Cleveland	1	0	1	0	6
LeBlanc, Michael, New England	1	1	0	0	6
Lewis, David, Miami	1	0	1	0	6
Lockett, Charles, Pittsburgh	1	0	1	0	6
Logan, Marc, Cincinnati	1	1	0	0	6
Lyles, Robert, Houston	1	0	0	1	6
Maas, Bill, Kansas City	1	0	0	1	6
Marino, Dan, Miami	1	1	0	0	6
Matthews, Clay, Cleveland	1	0	0	1	6
McCluskey, David, Cincinnati	1	1	0	0	6
McDonald, Keith, Houston	1	0	1	0	6
McElroy, Vann, L.A. Raiders	1	0	0	1	6
McFadden, Thad, Buffalo	1	0	1	0	6
McGee, Tim, Cincinnati	1	0	1	0	6
McNanie, Sean, Buffalo	1	0	0	1	6
McNeil, Freeman, N.Y. Jets	1	0	1	0	6
Miano, Rich, N.Y. Jets	1	0	0	1	6
Middleton, Frank, San Diego	1	1	0	0	6
Miller, Les, San Diego	1	0	0	1	6
Mobley, Orson, Denver	1	0	1	0	6
Moffett, Tim, San Diego	1	0	1	0	6
Moriarty, Larry, Kansas City	1	0	1	0	6
Morton, Michael, Seattle	1	1	0	0	6

	TD	TDR	TDP	TD Misc.	TP
Mueller, Vance, L.A. Raiders	1	1	0	0	6
Muñoz, Anthony, Cincinnati	1	0	1	0	6
Pardridge, Curt, Seattle	1	0	1	0	6
Parker, Robert, Kansas City	1	1	0	0	6
Parros, Rick, Seattle	1	1	0	0	6
Patterson, Elvis, San Diego	1	0	0	1	6
Pease, Brent, Houston	1	1	0	0	6
Perry, Mario, L.A. Raiders	1	0	1	0	6
Poole, Nathan, Denver	1	1	0	0	6
Ramsey, Tom, New England	1	1	0	0	6
Robinson, Eugene, Seattle	1	0	0	1	6
Ross, Kevin, Kansas City	1	0	0	1	6
Russell, Wade, Cincinnati	1	0	1	0	6
Ryan, Pat, N.Y. Jets	1	1	0	0	6
Sanders, Chuck, Pittsburgh	1	1	0	0	6
Sartin, Martin, San Diego	1	1	0	0	6
Seale, Eugene, Houston	1	0	0	1	6
Sherwin, Tim, Indianapolis	1	0	1	0	6
Skansi, Paul, Seattle	1	0	1	0	6
Smith, Bruce, Buffalo	1	0	0	1	6
Smith, Willie, Miami	1	0	1	0	6
Swanson, Shane, Denver	1	0	1	0	6
Tagliaferri, John, Miami	1	1	0	0	6
Thompson, Donnell, Indianapolis	1	0	0	1	6
Thompson, Weegie, Pittsburgh	1	0	1	0	6
Tillman, Spencer, Houston	1	1	0	0	6
Tippett, Andre, New England	1	0	0	1	6
Toran, Stacey, L.A. Raiders	1	0	0	1	6
Townsell, JoJo, N.Y. Jets	1	0	0	1	6
Vick, Roger, N.Y. Jets	1	1	0	0	6
Walker, Wesley, N.Y. Jets	1	0	1	0	6
Watson, Steve, Denver	1	0	1	0	6
Williams, Alphonso, San Diego	1	0	1	0	6
Williams, Oliver, Houston	1	0	1	0	6
Wonsley, George, Indianapolis	1	1	0	0	6
Woodruff, Dwayne, Pittsburgh	1	0	0	1	6
Woods, Carl, New England	1	1	0	0	6
Woodson, Rod, Pittsburgh	1	0	0	1	6
Wright, Felix, Cleveland	1	0	0	1	6
Young, Fredd, Seattle	1	0	0	1	6
Baker, Jesse, Houston	0	0	0	0	*2
Carr, Gregg, Pittsburgh	0	0	0	0	*2
Leiding, Jeff, Indianapolis	0	0	0	0	*2
Lyons, Marty, N.Y. Jets	0	0	0	0	*2
Ryan, Jim, Denver	0	0	0	0	*2
Schutt, Scott, Cincinnati	0	0	0	0	*2
Tasker, Steve, Buffalo	0	0	0	0	*2
Williams, Lee, San Diego	0	0	0	0	*2

**indicates safety scored.*
#indicates extra point scored.

NFC Scoring—Individual

Kickers	PAT	PAT Att.	FG	FG Att.	TP
Andersen, Morten, New Orleans	37	37	28	36	121
Ruzek, Roger, Dallas	26	26	22	25	92
Lansford, Mike, L.A. Rams	36	38	17	21	87
Butler, Kevin, Chicago	28	30	19	28	85
McFadden, Paul, Philadelphia	36	36	16	26	84
Wersching, Ray, San Francisco	44	46	13	17	83
Murray, Ed, Detroit	21	21	20	32	81
Allegre, Raul, N.Y. Giants	25	26	17	27	76
Nelson, Chuck, Minnesota	36	37	13	24	75
Haji-Sheikh, Ali, Washington	29	32	13	19	68
Igwebuike, Donald, Tampa Bay	24	26	14	18	66
Zendejas, Max, Green Bay	13	15	16	19	61
Gallery, Jim, St. Louis	30	31	9	19	57
Del Greco, Al, Green Bay-St. Louis	19	20	9	15	46
Luckhurst, Mick, Atlanta	17	17	9	13	44
Prindle, Mike, Detroit	6	6	6	7	24
Brockhaus, Jeff, San Francisco	11	13	3	6	20
Lashar, Tim, Chicago	10	10	3	4	19
Zendejas, Luis, Dallas	10	10	3	4	19
Ariri, Obed, Washington	6	6	3	5	15
Davis, Greg, Atlanta	6	6	3	4	15
Kempf, Florian, New Orleans	1	1	4	5	13
Benyola, George, N.Y. Giants	3	3	3	5	12
Jacobs, Dave, Philadelphia	2	4	3	5	11
Staurovsky, Jason, St. Louis	6	6	1	3	9
Cofer, Mike, New Orleans	5	7	1	1	8
Dawson, Dale, Minnesota	4	4	1	5	7
Cox, Steve, Washington	3	3	1	2	6
Atkinson, Jess, Washington	1	1	1	1	4
Toibin, Brendan, Washington	4	4	0	2	4
Brady, Kerry, Dallas	1	1	0	0	1

Non-Kickers	TD	TDR	TDP	TD Misc.	TP
Rice, Jerry, San Francisco	23	1	22	0	138
Quick, Mike, Philadelphia	11	0	11	0	66
White, Charles, L.A. Rams	11	11	0	0	66
Bavaro, Mark, N.Y. Giants	8	0	8	0	48
Hilliard, Dalton, New Orleans	8	7	1	0	48
Smith, J.T., St. Louis	8	0	8	0	48
Walker, Herschel, Dallas	8	7	1	0	48
Carter, Anthony, Minnesota	7	0	7	0	42
Clark, Gary, Washington	7	0	7	0	42
Dozier, D.J., Minnesota	7	5	2	0	42
Ferrell, Earl, St. Louis	7	7	0	0	42
Gault, Willie, Chicago	7	0	7	0	42
Mandley, Pete, Detroit	7	0	7	0	42
Martin, Eric, New Orleans	7	0	7	0	42
Anderson, Neal, Chicago	6	3	3	0	36
Awalt, Robert, St. Louis	6	0	6	0	36
Bryant, Kelvin, Washington	6	1	5	0	36
Manuel, Lionel, N.Y. Giants	6	0	6	0	36
Monk, Art, Washington	6	0	6	0	36
Rogers, George, Washington	6	6	0	0	36
Tice, John, New Orleans	6	0	6	0	36
Toney, Anthony, Philadelphia	6	5	1	0	36
Carter, Gerald, Tampa Bay	5	0	5	0	30
Clark, Dwight, San Francisco	5	0	5	0	30
Dixon, Floyd, Atlanta	5	0	5	0	30
Fullwood, Brent, Green Bay	5	5	0	0	30
Mayes, Rueben, New Orleans	5	5	0	0	30
Mitchell, Stump, St. Louis	5	3	2	0	30
Payton, Walter, Chicago	5	4	1	0	30
Wilson, Mike, San Francisco	5	0	5	0	30
Wilson, Wade, Minnesota	5	5	0	0	30
Byars, Keith, Philadelphia	4	3	1	0	24
Carruth, Paul Ott, Green Bay	4	3	1	0	24
Craig, Roger, San Francisco	4	3	1	0	24
Edwards, Kelvin, Dallas	4	1	3	0	24
Ellerson, Gary, Detroit	4	3	1	0	24
Green, Roy, St. Louis	4	0	4	0	24
James, Garry, Detroit	4	4	0	0	24
McAdoo, Derrick, St. Louis	4	3	0	1	24
Newsome, Tim, Dallas	4	2	2	0	24
Rathman, Tom, San Francisco	4	1	3	0	24
Renfro, Mike, Dallas	4	0	4	0	24
Smith, Jeff, Tampa Bay	4	2	2	0	24
Allen, Anthony, Washington	3	0	3	0	18
Bailey, Stacey, Atlanta	3	0	3	0	18
Blount, Alvin, Dallas	3	3	0	0	18
Brewer, Chris, Chicago	3	2	1	0	18
Brim, James, Minnesota	3	1	2	0	18
Brown, Ron, L.A. Rams	3	0	2	1	18
Carrier, Mark, Tampa Bay	3	0	3	0	18
Cosbie, Doug, Dallas	3	0	3	0	18
Cunningham, Randall, Philadelphia	3	3	0	0	18
Davis, Kenneth, Green Bay	3	3	0	0	18
Ellard, Henry, L.A. Rams	3	0	3	0	18
Frank, John, San Francisco	3	0	3	0	18
Heller, Ron, San Francisco	3	0	3	0	18
Jackson, Kenny, Philadelphia	3	0	3	0	18
Jones, Mike, New Orleans	3	0	3	0	18
Kozlowski, Glen, Chicago	3	0	3	0	18
Lewis, Leo, Minnesota	3	0	2	1	18
Magee, Calvin, Tampa Bay	3	0	3	0	18
Matthews, Aubrey, Altanta	3	0	3	0	18
McKinnon, Dennis, Chicago	3	0	1	2	18
Morris, Joe, N.Y. Giants	3	3	0	0	18
Neal, Frankie, Green Bay	3	0	3	0	18
Novacek, Jay, St. Louis	3	0	3	0	18
Sanders, Ricky, Washington	3	0	3	0	18
Schroeder, Jay, Washington	3	3	0	0	18
Stanley, Walter, Green Bay	3	0	3	0	18
Adams, George, N.Y. Giants	2	1	1	0	12
Anderson, Alfred, Minnesota	2	2	0	0	12
Baker, Stephen, N.Y. Giants	2	0	2	0	12
Barney, Milton, Atlanta	2	0	2	0	12
Bernard, Karl, Detroit	2	2	0	0	12
Beverly, Dwight, New Orleans	2	2	0	0	12
Boso, Cap, Chicago	2	0	2	0	12
Bradley, Danny, Detroit	2	0	2	0	12
Brenner, Hoby, New Orleans	2	0	2	0	12
Burbage, Cornell, Dallas	2	0	2	0	12
Campbell, Scott, Altanta	2	2	0	0	12
Carter, Cris, Philadelphia	2	0	2	0	12
Cribbs, Joe, San Francisco	2	1	0	1	12
Dorsett, Tony, Dallas	2	1	1	0	12
Epps, Phillip, Green Bay	2	0	2	0	12
Fenney, Rick, Minnesota	2	2	0	0	12
Francis, Jon, L.A. Rams	2	0	2	0	12
Freeman, Phil, Tampa Bay	2	0	2	0	12
Garrity, Gregg, Philadelphia	2	0	2	0	12
Gentry, Dennis, Chicago	2	0	1	1	12

	TD	TDR	TDP	TD Misc.	TP
Grymes, Darrell, Detroit	2	0	2	0	12
Hill, Bruce, Tampa Bay	2	0	2	0	12
Hill, Lonzell, New Orleans	2	0	2	0	12
Hilton, Carl, Minnesota	2	0	2	0	12
Johnson, Damone, L.A. Rams	2	0	2	0	12
Johnson, Troy, St. Louis	2	0	2	0	12
Jones, Hassan, Minnesota	2	0	2	0	12
Jordan, Buford, New Orleans	2	2	0	0	12
Jordan, Steve, Minnesota	2	0	2	0	12
Kramer, Tommy, Minnesota	2	2	0	0	12
Lovelady, Edwin, N.Y. Giants	2	0	2	0	12
McDonald, James, L.A. Rams	2	0	2	0	12
McMahon, Jim, Chicago	2	2	0	0	12
Nelson, Darrin, Minnesota	2	2	0	0	12
Rice, Allen, Minnesota	2	1	1	0	12
Riggs, Gerald, Atlanta	2	2	0	0	12
Robinson, Stacy, N.Y. Giants	2	0	2	0	12
Spagnola, John, Philadelphia	2	0	2	0	12
Streater, Eric, Tampa Bay	2	0	2	0	12
Vital, Lionel, Washington	2	2	0	0	12
Wilson, Ted, Washington	2	1	1	0	12
Wilson, Wayne, Washington	2	2	0	0	12
Word, Barry, New Orleans	2	2	0	0	12
Adams, David, Dallas	1	1	0	0	6
Alexander, Vincent, New Orleans	1	1	0	0	6
Austin, Cliff, Tampa Bay	1	1	0	0	6
Badanjek, Rick, Atlanta	1	1	0	0	6
Banks, Gordon, Dallas	1	0	1	0	6
Barksdale, Rod, Dallas	1	0	1	0	6
Bartalo, Steve, Tampa Bay	1	1	0	0	6
Bell, Greg, L.A. Rams	1	0	1	0	6
Bennett, Lewis, N.Y. Giants	1	0	1	0	6
Bland, Carl, Detroit	1	0	1	0	6
Bowman, Kevin, Philadelphia	1	0	1	0	6
Branch, Reggie, Washington	1	1	0	0	6
Chandler, Thornton, Dallas	1	0	1	0	6
Cherry, Tony, San Francisco	1	1	0	0	6
Clark, Jessie, Green Bay	1	0	1	0	6
Clemons, Topper, Philadelphia	1	0	1	0	6
Didier, Clint, Washington	1	0	1	0	6
Everett, Jim, L.A. Rams	1	1	0	0	6
Flynn, Tom, N.Y. Giants	1	0	0	1	6
Francis, Ron, Dallas	1	0	0	1	6
Garza, Sammy, St. Louis	1	1	0	0	6
Gayle, Shaun, Chicago	1	0	0	1	6
Giles, Jimmie, Philadelphia	1	0	1	0	6
Gray, Jerry, L.A. Rams	1	0	0	1	6
Gray, Mel, New Orleans	1	1	0	0	6
Green, Darrell, Washington	1	0	0	1	6
Greene, Kevin, L.A. Rams	1	0	0	1	6
Greer, Terry, San Francisco	1	0	1	0	6
Griffin, Keith, Washington	1	0	1	0	6
Guman, Mike, L.A. Rams	1	1	0	0	6
Hall, Ron, Tampa Bay	1	0	1	0	6
Hargrove, Jimmy, Green Bay	1	1	0	0	6
Heimuli, Lakei, Chicago	1	0	1	0	6
House, Kevin, L.A. Rams	1	0	1	0	6
Howard, Bobby, Tampa Bay	1	1	0	0	6
Irvin, LeRoy, L.A. Rams	1	0	0	1	6
Jackson, Kirby, L.A. Rams	1	0	0	1	6
Jackson, Mark, St. Louis	1	0	0	1	6
Jeffcoat, Jim, Dallas	1	0	0	1	6
Jessie, Tim, Washington	1	1	0	0	6
Johnson, Johnnie, L.A. Rams	1	0	0	1	6
Joyner, Seth, Philadelphia	1	0	0	1	6
Kamana, John, Atlanta	1	0	1	0	6
Kinard, Terry, N.Y. Giants	1	0	0	1	6
Kindt, Don, Chicago	1	0	1	0	6
King, Angelo, Detroit	1	0	0	1	6
McCray, Bruce, Chicago	1	0	0	1	6
McGee, Buford, L.A. Rams	1	1	0	0	6
McGowan, Reggie, N.Y. Giants	1	0	1	0	6
McIntosh, Joe, Atlanta	1	0	1	0	6
McLemore, Dana, San Francisco	1	0	0	1	6
Mobley, Stacey, L.A. Rams	1	0	1	0	6
Monroe, Carl, San Francisco	1	0	1	0	6
Montana, Joe, San Francisco	1	1	0	0	6
Moore, Malcolm, L.A. Rams	1	0	1	0	6
Moore, Robert, Atlanta	1	0	0	1	6
Moorehead, Emery, Chicago	1	0	1	0	6
Morris, Lee, Green Bay	1	0	1	0	6
Morris, Ron, Chicago	1	0	1	0	6
Mosley, Anthony, Chicago	1	0	0	1	6
Moss, Winston, Tampa Bay	1	0	0	1	6
Mowatt, Zeke, N.Y. Giants	1	0	1	0	6
Noga, Niko, St. Louis	1	0	0	1	6
Noga, Pete, St. Louis	1	0	0	1	6
O'Neal, Ken, New Orleans	1	0	1	0	6
Paskett, Keith, Green Bay	1	0	1	0	6
Pelluer, Steve, Dallas	1	1	0	0	6
Poe, Johnnie, New Orleans	1	0	0	1	6
Ricks, Harold, Tampa Bay	1	1	0	0	6
Risher, Alan, Green Bay	1	1	0	0	6
Rodgers, Del, San Francisco	1	1	0	0	6
Ross, Alvin, Philadelphia	1	1	0	0	6
Rouson, Lee, N.Y. Giants	1	0	1	0	6
Rubick, Rob, Detroit	1	0	1	0	6
Sanders, Thomas, Chicago	1	1	0	0	6
Siano, Mike, Philadelphia	1	0	1	0	6
Sikahema, Vai, St. Louis	1	0	0	1	6
Smith, Leonard, St. Louis	1	0	0	1	6
Smith, Ricky, Detroit	1	0	0	1	6
Stamps, Sylvester, Atlanta	1	0	0	1	6
Stevens, Mark, San Francisco	1	1	0	0	6
Summers, Don, Green Bay	1	0	1	0	6
Sutton, Reggie, New Orleans	1	0	0	1	6
Taylor, John, San Francisco	1	0	0	1	6
Taylor, Lenny, Atlanta	1	0	1	0	6
Testaverde, Vinny, Tampa Bay	1	1	0	0	6
Thomas, Lavale, Green Bay	1	0	1	0	6
Toles, Alvin, New Orleans	1	0	0	1	6
Tomczak, Mike, Chicago	1	1	0	0	6
Tripoli, Paul, Tampa Bay	1	0	0	1	6
Truvillion, Eric, Detroit	1	0	1	0	6
Turner, Odessa, N.Y. Giants	1	0	1	0	6
Walker, Kevin, Tampa Bay	1	0	0	1	6
Waters, Mike, New Orleans	1	0	1	0	6
Wells, Arthur, Tampa Bay	1	0	0	1	6
Wells, Mike, San Francisco	1	0	0	1	6
West, Ed, Green Bay	1	0	1	0	6
Whisenhunt, Ken, Atlanta	1	0	1	0	6
White, Danny, Dallas	1	1	0	0	6
White, Reggie, Philadelphia	1	0	0	1	6
Wilburn, Barry, Washington	1	0	0	1	6
Wilcher, Mike, L.A. Rams	1	0	0	1	6
Wilder, James, Tampa Bay	1	0	1	0	6
Williams, Doug, Washington	1	1	0	0	6
Williams, Scott, Detroit	1	0	1	0	6
Wolfley, Ron, St. Louis	1	1	0	0	6
Womack, Jeff, Minnesota	1	0	1	0	6
Wright, Adrian, Tampa Bay	1	0	1	0	6
Young, Mike, L.A. Rams	1	0	1	0	6
Young, Steve, San Francisco	1	1	0	0	6
Clark, Bruce, New Orleans	0	0	0	0	*2
Fuller, Jeff, San Francisco	0	0	0	0	*2
Maxie, Brett, New Orleans	0	0	0	0	*2
Stepanek, Joe, Minnesota	0	0	0	0	*2
Stewart, Michael, L.A. Rams	0	0	0	0	*2

**indicates safety scored.*
#indicates extra point scored.

Field Goals

Best Percentage
AFC: .889—Dean Biasucci, Indianapolis
NFC: .880—Roger Ruzek, Dallas

Made
NFC: 28—Morten Andersen, New Orleans
AFC: 24—Dean Biasucci, Indianapolis
24—Jim Breech, Cincinnati

Attempts
NFC: 36—Morten Andersen, New Orleans
AFC: 30—Jim Breech, Cincinnati

Longest
AFC: 54—Nick Lowery, Kansas City vs. Detroit, November 26
NFC: 53—Raul Allegre, N.Y. Giants vs. Philadelphia, November 15
53—Ed Murray, Detroit vs. L.A. Rams, December 6

Average Yards Made
NFC: 38.8—Donald Igwebuike, Tampa Bay
AFC: 35.9—Nick Lowery, Kansas City

AFC Field Goals—Team

	Made	Att.	Pct.	Long
Indianapolis	27	32	.844	50
Kansas City	21	25	.840	54
Houston	26	32	.813	52
Cincinnati	25	32	.781	46
Seattle	17	22	.773	49
N.Y. Jets	20	26	.769	42
Pittsburgh	22	29	.759	52
Miami	12	16	.750	48
Denver	21	29	.724	51
Cleveland	21	31	.677	48
L.A. Raiders	19	30	.633	48
Buffalo	12	20	.600	45
New England	16	28	.571	50
San Diego	16	28	.571	47
AFC Totals	275	380	—	54
AFC Average	19.6	27.1	.724	—

NFC Field Goals—Team

	Made	Att.	Pct.	Long
Dallas	25	29	.862	50
L.A. Rams	17	21	.810	48
Tampa Bay	19	24	.792	50
New Orleans	33	42	.786	52
Green Bay	21	29	.724	48
Atlanta	12	17	.706	50
San Francisco	16	23	.696	45
Chicago	22	32	.688	52
Detroit	26	39	.667	53
N.Y. Giants	20	32	.625	53
Washington	18	29	.621	41
Philadelphia	19	31	.613	49
St. Louis	14	27	.519	48
Minnesota	14	29	.483	51
NFC Totals	276	404	—	53
NFC Average	19.7	28.9	.683	—
League Totals	551	784	—	54
League Average	19.7	28.0	.703	—

AFC Field Goals—Individual

	1-19	20-29	30-39	40-49	50 & Over	Totals	Avg. Yds. Att.	Avg. Yds. Made	Avg. Yds. Miss	Long
Biasucci, Dean,	0-0	5-6	12-12	6-7	1-2	24-27	36.4	35.7	42.3	50
Indianapolis	—	.833	1.000	.857	.500	.889				
Lowery, Nick,	1-1	4-4	8-10	4-6	2-2	19-23	37.1	35.9	42.5	54
Kansas City	1.000	1.000	.800	.667	1.000	.826				
Leahy, Pat,	0-0	11-11	5-6	2-4	0-1	18-22	32.7	29.3	48.3	42
N.Y. Jets	—	1.000	.833	.500	.000	.818				
Anderson, Gary,	0-0	8-9	5-5	7-11	2-2	22-27	36.1	35.0	40.6	52
Pittsburgh	—	.889	1.000	.636	1.000	.815				
Breech, Jim,	0-0	6-7	12-12	6-11	0-0	24-30	34.9	33.3	41.5	46
Cincinnati	—	.857	1.000	.545	—	.800				
Zendejas, Tony,	2-2	5-5	4-6	8-12	1-1	20-26	36.5	34.6	42.8	52
Houston	1.000	1.000	.667	.667	1.000	.769				
Johnson, Norm,	0-0	7-7	4-7	4-5	0-1	15-20	35.6	33.3	42.4	49
Seattle	—	1.000	.571	.800	.000	.750				
Karlis, Rich,	0-0	9-9	4-6	4-7	1-3	18-25	36.4	33.3	44.4	51
Denver	—	1.000	.667	.571	.333	.720				
Norwood, Scott,	0-0	3-4	4-6	3-5	0-0	10-15	36.0	35.4	37.2	45
Buffalo	—	.750	.667	.600	—	.667				
Bahr, Chris,	0-0	6-6	10-13	3-10	0-0	19-29	35.7	32.7	41.3	48
L.A. Raiders	—	1.000	.769	.300	—	.655				
Jaeger, Jeff,	0-0	6-6	3-6	5-9	0-1	14-22	36.9	33.1	43.5	48
Cleveland	—	1.000	.500	.556	.000	.636				
Abbott, Vince,	0-0	2-3	9-10	2-6	0-3	13-22	38.5	34.8	43.9	47
San Diego	—	.667	.900	.333	.000	.591				
Franklin, Tony,	0-0	5-5	6-11	3-7	1-3	15-26	37.8	34.5	42.3	50
New England	—	1.000	.545	.429	.333	.577				
Non-Qualifiers (Less than 15 attempts)										
Diettrich, John,	0-0	2-2	1-1	3-3	0-0	6-6	36.8	36.8	0.0	45
Houston	—	1.000	1.000	1.000	—	1.000				
Hagler, Scott,	0-0	2-2	0-0	0-0	0-0	2-2	22.0	22.0	0.0	24
Seattle	—	1.000	—	—	—	1.000				
Hamrick, James,	0-0	1-1	0-0	1-1	0-0	2-2	32.5	32.5	0.0	40
Kansas City	—	1.000	—	1.000	—	1.000				
Reveiz, Fuad,	1-1	2-2	2-2	4-6	0-0	9-11	38.2	36.3	46.5	48
Miami	1.000	1.000	1.000	.667	—	.818				
Bahr, Matt,	0-0	2-2	2-3	0-0	0-0	4-5	29.0	27.0	37.0	31
Cleveland	—	1.000	.667	—	—	.800				
Beecher, Willie,	1-1	0-0	1-1	1-2	0-0	3-4	35.5	31.0	40.0	40
Miami	1.000	—	1.000	.500	—	.750				
Clendenen, Mike,	0-0	1-1	2-2	0-1	0-0	3-4	33.5	31.3	40.0	35
Denver	—	1.000	1.000	.000	—	.750				
Franco, Brian,	0-0	3-3	0-1	0-0	0-0	3-4	28.0	25.0	37.0	28
Cleveland	—	1.000	.000	—	—	.750				
Tiffin, Van,	0-0	1-1	1-2	2-3	1-1	5-7	38.7	38.8	38.5	50
Tampa Bay-Miami	—	1.000	.500	.667	1.000	.714				
Jordan, Steve,	0-0	1-1	2-2	0-2	0-0	3-5	36.0	32.0	42.0	36
Indianapolis	—	1.000	1.000	.000	—	.600				
Gaffney, Jeff,	0-0	3-3	0-3	0-0	0-0	3-6	29.3	24.0	34.7	27
San Diego	—	1.000	.000	—	—	.500				
Manca, Massimo,	0-0	1-1	0-0	0-1	0-0	1-2	36.5	28.0	45.0	28
Cincinnati	—	1.000	—	.000	—	.500				
Ragusa, Pat,	0-0	1-1	1-2	0-1	0-0	2-4	33.3	27.0	39.5	34
N.Y. Jets	—	1.000	.500	.000	—	.500				
Schubert, Eric,	0-0	1-1	0-0	0-1	0-0	1-2	31.5	23.0	40.0	23
New England	—	1.000	—	.000	—	.500				
Schlopy, Todd,	0-0	1-1	1-3	0-1	0-0	2-5	33.4	29.0	36.3	31
Buffalo	—	1.000	.333	.000	—	.400				
Hardy, David,	0-0	0-0	0-1	0-0	0-0	0-1	34.0	0.0	34.0	—
L.A. Raiders	—	—	.000	—	—	.000				
Trout, David,	0-0	0-1	0-1	0-0	0-0	0-2	30.5	0.0	30.5	—
Pittsburgh	—	.000	.000	—	—	.000				
AFC Totals	5-5	98-104	98-132	66-120	8-19	275-380	35.7	33.4	41.8	54
	1.000	.942	.742	.550	.421	.724				
League Totals	14-14	196-211	181-248	140-260	20-51	551-784	36.1	33.7	41.9	54
	1.000	.929	.730	.538	.392	.703				

NFC Field Goals — Individual

	1-19	20-29	30-39	40-49	50 & Over	Totals	Avg. Yds. Att.	Avg. Yds. Made	Avg. Yds. Miss	Long
Ruzek, Roger,	0-0	8-8	6-7	8-10	0-0	22-25	35.8	34.9	42.7	49
Dallas	—	1.000	.857	.800	—	.880				
Zendejas, Max,	0-0	3-3	6-7	7-8	0-1	16-19	37.8	36.8	43.0	48
Green Bay	—	1.000	.857	.875	.000	.842				
Lansford, Mike,	1-1	6-6	3-4	7-9	0-1	17-21	36.6	35.2	42.8	48
L.A. Rams	1.000	1.000	.750	.788	.000	.810				
Andersen, Morten,	3-3	6-6	9-9	8-12	2-6	28-36	37.6	34.7	48.0	52
New Orleans	1.000	1.000	1.000	.667	.333	.778				
Igwebuike, Donald,	0-0	2-2	6-6	6-9	0-1	14-18	41.0	38.8	48.8	48
Tampa Bay	—	1.000	1.000	.667	.000	.778				
Wersching, Ray,	0-0	5-5	5-5	3-7	0-0	13-17	35.3	32.5	44.3	45
San Francisco	—	1.000	1.000	.429	—	.765				
Haji-Sheikh, Ali,	0-0	5-5	6-10	2-4	0-0	13-19	33.5	31.6	37.5	41
Washington	—	1.000	.600	.500	—	.684				
Butler, Kevin,	0-0	11-11	5-5	1-6	2-6	19-28	36.9	31.3	48.8	52
Chicago	—	1.000	1.000	.167	.333	.679				
Allegre, Raul,	1-1	7-8	4-5	3-9	2-4	17-27	36.6	33.5	41.9	53
N.Y. Giants	1.000	.875	.800	.333	.500	.630				
Murray, Ed,	1-1	6-6	7-12	5-11	1-2	20-32	37.0	34.4	41.4	53
Detroit	1.000	1.000	.583	.455	.500	.625				
McFadden, Paul,	1-1	3-4	6-10	6-9	0-2	16-26	38.0	35.8	41.7	49
Philadelphia	1.000	.750	.600	.667	.000	.615				
Del Greco, Al,	0-0	3-5	4-6	2-4	0-0	9-15	35.3	34.1	37.2	47
Green Bay-St. Louis	—	.600	.667	.500	—	.600				
Nelson, Chuck,	0-0	10-12	2-4	0-6	1-2	13-24	33.7	28.8	39.5	51
Minnesota	—	.833	.500	.000	.500	.542				
Gallery, Jim,	0-0	4-5	2-7	3-7	0-0	9-19	36.1	33.9	38.1	48
St. Louis	—	.800	.286	.429	—	.474				
Non-Qualifiers (Less than 15 attempts)										
Atkinson, Jess,	0-0	1-1	0-0	0-0	0-0	1-1	27.0	27.0	0.0	27
Washington	—	1.000	—	—	—	1.000				
Cofer, Mike,	0-0	1-1	0-0	0-0	0-0	1-1	27.0	27.0	0.0	27
New Orleans	—	1.000	—	—	—	1.000				
Prindle, Mike,	0-0	3-3	3-3	0-1	0-0	6-7	30.4	28.5	42.0	35
Detroit	—	1.000	1.000	.000	—	.857				
Kempf, Florian,	0-0	1-1	1-2	2-2	0-0	4-5	35.0	35.5	33.0	48
New Orleans	—	1.000	.500	1.000	—	.800				
Davis, Greg,	0-0	1-1	1-1	1-2	0-0	3-4	37.3	34.7	45.0	42
Atlanta	—	1.000	1.000	.500	—	.750				
Lashar, Tim,	0-0	3-3	0-0	0-1	0-0	3-4	29.3	25.0	42.0	27
Chicago	—	1.000	—	.000	—	.750				
Zendejas, Luis,	0-0	0-0	1-1	1-2	1-1	3-4	44.0	42.3	49.0	50
Dallas	—	—	1.000	.500	1.000	.750				
Luckhurst, Mick,	1-1	1-1	2-2	3-5	2-4	9-13	41.4	39.2	46.3	50
Atlanta	1.000	1.000	1.000	.600	.500	.692				
Ariri, Obed,	1-1	1-1	1-1	0-2	0-0	3-5	33.0	26.7	42.5	39
Washington	1.000	1.000	1.000	.000	—	.600				
Benyola, George,	0-0	2-2	0-1	1-2	0-0	3-5	32.8	29.0	38.5	45
N.Y. Giants	—	1.000	.000	.500	—	.600				
Jacobs, Dave,	0-0	1-1	0-1	2-3	0-0	3-5	38.2	37.0	40.0	44
Philadelphia	—	1.000	.000	.667	—	.600				
Brockhaus, Jeff,	0-0	2-3	1-2	0-1	0-0	3-6	31.3	27.0	35.7	39
San Francisco	—	.667	.500	.000	—	.500				
Cox, Steve,	0-0	0-0	0-0	1-1	0-1	1-2	53.5	40.0	67.0	40
Washington	—	—	—	1.000	.000	.500				
Staurovsky, Jason,	0-0	1-2	0-0	0-1	0-0	1-3	30.0	24.0	33.0	24
St. Louis	—	.500	—	.000	—	.333				
Dawson, Dale,	0-0	0-0	1-2	0-3	0-0	1-5	39.4	34.0	40.8	34
Minnesota	—	—	.500	.000	—	.200				
Toibin, Brendan,	0-0	0-0	0-1	0-1	0-0	0-2	39.5	0.0	39.5	—
Washington	—	—	.000	.000	—	.000				
NFC Totals	9-9	98-107	83-116	74-140	12-32	276-404	36.5	34.0	42.0	53
	1.000	.916	.716	.529	.375	.683				
League Totals	14-14	196-211	181-248	140-260	20-51	551-784	36.1	33.7	41.9	54
	1.000	.929	.730	.538	.392	.703				

Rushing

Individual Champions

NFC: 1,374—Charles White, L.A. Rams
AFC: 1,011—Eric Dickerson, Indianapolis

Attempts

NFC: 324—Charles White, L.A. Rams
AFC: 234—Curt Warner, Seattle

Most Attempts, Game

AFC: 35—Mike LeBlanc, New England vs. Buffalo, October 11 (146 yards)
35—Eric Dickerson, Indianapolis vs. San Diego, November 8 (138 yards)
NFC: 35—Dwight Beverly, New Orleans at St. Louis, October 11 (139 yards)
35—Charles White, L.A. Rams at Washington, November 23 (112 yards)

Yards Per Attempt

NFC: 4.9—Darrin Nelson, Minnesota
AFC: 4.5—Eric Dickerson, Indianapolis

Most Yards, Game

AFC: 221—Bo Jackson, L.A. Raiders at Seattle, November 30 (18 attempts)
NFC: 213—Charles White, L.A. Rams at St. Louis, November 15 (34 attempts)

Longest

AFC: 91—Bo Jackson, L.A. Raiders at Seattle, November 30 (TD)
NFC: 72—Darrin Nelson, Minnesota vs. Denver, October 26

Touchdowns

AFC: 11—Johnny Hector, N.Y. Jets
NFC: 11—Charles White, L.A. Rams

Team Leaders, Yards

AFC: BUFFALO: 485, Ronnie Harmon; CINCINNATI: 570, Larry Kinnebrew; CLEVELAND: 735, Kevin Mack; DENVER: 741, Sammy Winder; HOUSTON: 957, Mike Rozier; INDIANAPOLIS: 1,011, Eric Dickerson; KANSAS CITY: 660, Christian Okoye; L.A. RAIDERS: 754, Marcus Allen; MIAMI: 619, Troy Stradford; NEW ENGLAND: 474, Tony Collins; N.Y. JETS: 530, Freeman McNeil; PITTSBURGH: 696, Earnest Jackson; SAN DIEGO: 343, Curtis Adams; SEATTLE: 985, Curt Warner.

NFC: ATLANTA: 875, Gerald Riggs; CHICAGO: 586, Neal Anderson; DALLAS: 891, Herschel Walker; DETROIT: 342, James Jones; GREEN BAY: 413, Kenneth Davis; L.A. RAMS: 1,374, Charles White; MINNESOTA: 642, Darrin Nelson; NEW ORLEANS: 917, Rueben Mayes; GIANTS: 658, Joe Morris; PHILADELPHIA: 505, Randall Cunningham; ST. LOUIS: 781, Stump Mitchell; SAN FRANCISCO: 815, Roger Craig; TAMPA BAY: 488, James Wilder; WASHINGTON: 613, George Rogers.

Team Champions

NFC: 2,237—San Francisco
AFC: 2,197—L.A. Raiders

AFC Rushing—Team

	Att.	Yards	Avg.	Long	TD
L.A. Raiders	475	2197	4.6	91t	13
Cincinnati	538	2164	4.0	52	13
Pittsburgh	517	2144	4.1	51	11
Indianapolis	497	2143	4.3	53	14
Seattle	496	2023	4.1	57t	13
Denver	510	1970	3.9	29	18
Houston	486	1923	4.0	41	12
Buffalo	465	1840	4.0	30	9
Kansas City	419	1799	4.3	64t	7
New England	513	1771	3.5	49	12
Cleveland	474	1745	3.7	35	16
N.Y. Jets	458	1671	3.6	32	17
Miami	408	1662	4.1	51	16
San Diego	396	1308	3.3	25	11
AFC Total	6,652	26,360	—	91t	182
AFC Average	475.1	1,882.9	4.0	—	13.0

NFC Rushing—Team

	Att.	Yards	Avg.	Long	TD
San Francisco	524	2237	4.3	35	11
New Orleans	569	2190	3.8	38	20
Washington	500	2102	4.2	31	18
L.A. Rams	512	2097	4.1	58	15
Philadelphia	509	2027	4.0	45	12
Minnesota	482	1983	4.1	72	20
Chicago	485	1954	4.0	38t	13
St. Louis	462	1873	4.1	42	15
Dallas	465	1865	4.0	62t	17
Green Bay	464	1801	3.9	61	13
N.Y. Giants	440	1457	3.3	34	4
Detroit	398	1435	3.6	33	9
Tampa Bay	394	1365	3.5	46	7
Atlanta	333	1298	3.9	44	5
NFC Total	6,537	25,684	—	72	179
NFC Average	466.9	1834.6	3.9	—	12.8
League Total	13,189	52,044	—	91t	361
League Average	471.0	1858.7	3.9	—	12.9

NFL Top 10 Rushers

	Att.	Yards	Avg.	Long	TD
White, Charles, L.A. Rams	324	1374	4.2	58	11
Dickerson, Eric, L.A. Rams-Ind.	283	1288	4.6	57	6
Warner, Curt, Seattle	234	985	4.2	57t	8
Rozier, Mike, Houston	229	957	4.2	41	3
Mayes, Rueben, New Orleans	243	917	3.8	38	5
Walker, Herschel, Dallas	209	891	4.3	60t	7
Riggs, Gerald, Atlanta	203	875	4.3	44	2
Craig, Roger, San Francisco	215	815	3.8	25	3
Mitchell, Stump, St. Louis	203	781	3.8	42	3
Allen, Marcus, L.A. Raiders	200	754	3.8	44	5

AFC Rushing—Individual

	Att.	Yards	Avg.	Long	TD
Dickerson, Eric, L.A. Rams-Ind.	283	1288	4.6	57	6
Warner, Curt, Seattle	234	985	4.2	57t	8
Rozier, Mike, Houston	229	957	4.2	41	3
Allen, Marcus, L.A. Raiders	200	754	3.8	44	5
Winder, Sammy, Denver	196	741	3.8	19	6
Mack, Kevin, Cleveland	201	735	3.7	22t	5
Jackson, Earnest, Pittsburgh	180	696	3.9	39	1
Okoye, Christian, Kansas City	157	660	4.2	43t	3
Bentley, Albert, Indianapolis	142	631	4.4	17t	7
Stradford, Troy, Miami	145	619	4.3	51	6
Kinnebrew, Larry, Cincinnati	145	570	3.9	52	8
Jackson, Bo, L.A. Raiders	81	554	6.8	91t	4
Pollard, Frank, Pittsburgh	128	536	4.2	33	3
McNeil, Freeman, N.Y. Jets	121	530	4.4	30	0
Williams, John L., Seattle	113	500	4.4	48	1
Harmon, Ronnie, Buffalo	116	485	4.2	21	2
Collins, Tony, New England	147	474	3.2	19	3
Heard, Herman, Kansas City	82	466	5.7	64t	3
Abercrombie, Walter, Pittsburgh	123	459	3.7	28t	2
Hector, Johnny, N.Y. Jets	111	435	3.9	20t	11
Byner, Earnest, Cleveland	105	432	4.1	21	8
Mueller, Jamie, Buffalo	82	354	4.3	20	2
Adams, Curtis, San Diego	90	343	3.8	24	1
Dupard, Reggie, New England	94	318	3.4	49	3
Jennings, Stanford, Cincinnati	70	314	4.5	18	1
Elway, John, Denver	66	304	4.6	29	4
Lang, Gene, Denver	89	303	3.4	28	2
Brooks, James, Cincinnati	94	290	3.1	18	1
Hampton, Lorenzo, Miami	75	289	3.9	34	1
Byrum, Carl, Buffalo	66	280	4.2	30	0
Anderson, Gary, San Diego	80	260	3.3	25	3
Vick, Roger, N.Y. Jets	77	257	3.3	14	1
Tatupu, Mosi, New England	79	248	3.1	19	0
Banks, Chuck, Indianapolis	50	245	4.9	35	0
Esiason, Boomer, Cincinnati	52	241	4.6	19	0
Jackson, Andrew, Houston	60	232	3.9	16t	1
Spencer, Tim, San Diego	73	228	3.1	16	0
Riddick, Robb, Buffalo	59	221	3.7	25	5
Mason, Larry, Cleveland	56	207	3.7	22	2
Johnson, Bill, Cincinnati	39	205	5.3	20	1
Logan, Marc, Cincinnati	37	203	5.5	51	1
Scott, Ronald, Miami	47	199	4.2	24	3
Perryman, Bob, New England	41	187	4.6	48	0
Porter, Ricky, Buffalo	47	177	3.8	13	0
Mueller, Vance, L.A. Raiders	37	175	4.7	35	1
LeBlanc, Michael, New England	49	170	3.5	42	1
Malone, Mark, Pittsburgh	34	162	4.8	42t	3
Krieg, Dave, Seattle	36	155	4.3	17	2
Palmer, Paul, Kansas City	24	155	6.5	35	0
Dudek, Joe, Denver	35	154	4.4	16	2
Parker, Robert, Kansas City	47	150	3.2	10	1
Pinkett, Allen, Houston	31	149	4.8	22	2
Evans, Vince, L.A. Raiders	11	144	13.1	24	1
Hunter, Herman, Houston	34	144	4.2	21	0
Willhite, Gerald, Denver	26	141	5.4	29	0
Ellis, Craig, L.A. Raiders	33	138	4.2	14	2
Stone, Dwight, Pittsburgh	17	135	7.9	51	0
Kelly, Jim, Buffalo	29	133	4.6	24	0
Bligen, Dennis, N.Y. Jets	31	128	4.1	15	1
Poole, Nathan, Denver	28	126	4.5	15	1
Manoa, Tim, Cleveland	23	116	5.0	35	0
Davenport, Ron, Miami	32	114	3.6	27	1
Smith, Chris, Kansas City	26	114	4.4	11	0
Moon, Warren, Houston	34	112	3.3	20	3
Strachan, Steve, L.A. Raiders	28	108	3.9	20	0
Moriarty, Larry, Kansas City	30	107	3.6	11	0
Highsmith, Alonzo, Houston	29	106	3.7	25	1
Bennett, Woody, Miami	25	102	4.1	18	0
James, Lionel, San Diego	27	102	3.8	15t	2
Wallace, Ray, Houston	19	102	5.4	19	0
Mackey, Kyle, Miami	17	98	5.8	17	2
Everett, Major, Cleveland	34	95	2.8	16	0
Horton, Ethan, L.A. Raiders	31	95	3.1	14	0
McCluskey, David, Cincinnati	29	94	3.2	12	1
Wilson, Marc, L.A. Raiders	17	91	5.4	16	0
Jenkins, Keyvan, San Diego	22	88	4.0	9	0
Brown, Gordon, Indianapolis	19	85	4.5	18t	1
Sewell, Steve, Denver	19	83	4.4	17	2
Green, Boyce, Seattle	21	77	3.7	17	0
Ramsey, Tom, New England	13	75	5.8	19	1
Middleton, Frank, San Diego	28	74	2.6	21	1
Wright, Dana, Cincinnati	24	74	3.1	10	0
Morris, Randall, Seattle	21	71	3.4	13	0
Wonsley, George, Indianapolis	18	71	3.9	12	1
Walter, Dave, Cincinnati	16	70	4.4	16	0
Sanders, Chuck, Pittsburgh	11	65	5.9	14	1
O'Brien, Ken, N.Y. Jets	30	61	2.0	11	0
Rice, Dan, Cincinnati	18	59	3.3	8	0
McLemore, Chris, Indianapolis	17	58	3.4	9	0
Bailey, Clarence, Miami	10	55	5.5	13	0
Caldwell, Scott, Denver	16	53	3.3	7	0
Fryar, Irving, New England	9	52	5.8	16	0
Morton, Michael, Seattle	19	52	2.7	10	1
Sartin, Martin, San Diego	19	52	2.7	10	1
Harrison, Rob, L.A. Raiders	9	49	5.4	13	0
Lacy, Kenneth, Kansas City	14	49	3.5	17	0
Konecny, Mark, Miami	6	46	7.7	19	0
Tagliaferri, John, Miami	13	45	3.5	7	1
Hansen, Bruce, New England	16	44	2.8	7	0
Bell, Ken, Denver	13	43	3.3	11	0
Davis, Elgin, New England	9	43	4.8	27	0
Faaola, Nuu, N.Y. Jets	14	43	3.1	18	2
Flutie, Doug, New England	6	43	7.2	13	0
Shepherd, Johnny, Buffalo	12	42	3.5	19	0
Christensen, Jeff, Cleveland	11	41	3.7	15	0
Isom, Rickey, Miami	9	41	4.6	8	1
Neuheisel, Rick, San Diego	6	41	6.8	18	1
Lane, Eric, Seattle	13	40	3.1	7	0
Grogan, Steve, New England	20	37	1.9	8	2
Burse, Tony, Seattle	7	36	5.1	16	0
Calhoun, Rick, L.A. Raiders	7	36	5.1	18	0
Redden, Barry, San Diego	11	36	3.3	7	0
Fontenot, Herman, Cleveland	15	33	2.2	14	0
Largent, Steve, Seattle	2	33	16.5	21	0
Pease, Brent, Houston	15	33	2.2	8	1
Seurer, Frank, Kansas City	9	33	3.7	11	0
Parros, Rick, Seattle	13	32	2.5	7	1
Driver, Stacey, Cleveland	9	31	3.4	16	0
Kiel, Blair, Indianapolis	4	30	7.5	16	0
Tillman, Spencer, Houston	12	29	2.4	13	1
King, Bruce, Buffalo	9	28	3.1	8	0

	Att.	Yards	Avg.	Long	TD
Bono, Steve, Pittsburgh	8	27	3.4	23	1
Eason, Tony, New England	3	25	8.3	13	0
Williams, Leonard, Buffalo	9	25	2.8	9	0
Hawkins, Frank, L.A. Raiders	4	24	6.0	7	0
Spencer, Todd, San Diego	14	24	1.7	5	0
Cobble, Eric, Houston	9	23	2.6	12	0
McSwain, Chuck, New England	9	23	2.6	9	0
Chirico, John, N.Y. Jets	12	22	1.8	4	1
Kosar, Bernie, Cleveland	15	22	1.5	7	1
Moore, Ricky, Houston	7	22	3.1	11	0
Blackledge, Todd, Kansas City	5	21	4.2	11	0
Collier, Reggie, Pittsburgh	4	20	5.0	12	0
Nathan, Tony, Miami	4	20	5.0	8	0
Woods, Carl, New England	4	20	5.0	13	1
Meehan, Greg, Cincinnati	4	19	4.8	17	0
Breen, Adrian, Cincinnati	6	18	3.0	9	0
Jensen, Jim, Miami	4	18	4.5	9	0
Smith, Steve, L.A. Raiders	5	18	3.6	15	0
Bennett, Ben, Cincinnati	2	17	8.5	9	0
Harris, Leonard, Houston	1	17	17.0	17	0
Holland, Jamie, San Diego	1	17	17.0	17	0
Kelley, Mike, San Diego	4	17	4.3	10	0
McNeil, Gerald, Cleveland	1	17	17.0	17	0
Goodburn, Kelly, Kansas City	1	16	16.0	16	0
Newsome, Harry, Pittsburgh	2	16	8.0	16	0
Pippens, Woodie, Kansas City	3	16	5.3	11	0
Mathison, Bruce, Seattle	5	15	3.0	10	0
Moore, Alvin, Detroit	3	15	5.0	13	0
Nattiel, Ricky, Denver	2	13	6.5	10	0
Partridge, Rick, Buffalo	1	13	13.0	13	0
Starring, Stephen, New England	2	13	6.5	10	0
Carter, Rodney, Pittsburgh	5	12	2.4	4	0
Totten, Willie, Buffalo	12	11	0.9	7	0
Williams, Alphonso, San Diego	1	11	11.0	11	0
James, Craig, New England	4	10	2.5	5	0
Roth, Pete, Miami	3	10	3.3	9	0
Valentine, Ira, Houston	5	10	2.0	4	0
Bernstine, Rod, San Diego	1	9	9.0	9	0
Foster, Derrick, N.Y. Jets	1	9	9.0	9	0
Kemp, Jeff, Seattle	5	9	1.8	12	0
Verser, David, Cleveland	1	9	9.0	9	0
Clayton, Mark, Miami	2	8	4.0	4	0
Hilger, Rusty, L.A. Raiders	8	8	1.0	6	0
Hoge, Merril, Pittsburgh	3	8	2.7	5	0
Micho, Bobby, Denver	4	8	2.0	5	0
Reeder, Dan, Pittsburgh	2	8	4.0	4	0
Boddie, Tony, Denver	3	7	2.3	4	1
Clemons, Michael, Kansas City	2	7	3.5	7	0
Davis, Johnny, Cleveland	1	7	7.0	7	0
Stevens, Matt, Kansas City	3	7	2.3	6	0
Trudeau, Jack, Indianapolis	15	7	0.5	9	0
Manucci, Dan, Buffalo	4	6	1.5	9	0
Espinoza, Alex, Kansas City	1	5	5.0	5	0
Jennings, Dave, N.Y. Jets	2	5	2.5	4	0
Norrie, David, N.Y. Jets	5	5	1.0	2	0
Ryan, Pat, N.Y. Jets	4	5	1.3	8t	1
Briggs, Walter, N.Y. Jets	1	4	4.0	4	0
McClure, Brian, Buffalo	2	4	2.0	3	0
Brown, Tom, Miami	3	3	1.0	3	0
Carver, Mel, Indianapolis	2	3	1.5	3	0
Hagen, Mike, Seattle	2	3	1.5	4	0
Hogeboom, Gary, Indianapolis	3	3	1.0	2	0
Karcher, Ken, Denver	9	3	0.3	8	0
Kubiak, Gary, Denver	1	3	3.0	3	0
Steels, Anthony, San Diego	1	3	3.0	3	0
Zachary, Ken, San Diego	1	3	3.0	3	0
Stockemer, Ralph, Kansas City	1	2	2.0	2	0
Aikens, Carl, L.A. Raiders	1	1	1.0	1	0
Browne, Jim, L.A. Raiders	2	1	0.5	2	0
Lofton, James, L.A. Raiders	1	1	1.0	1	0
Moffett, Tim, San Diego	1	1	1.0	1	0
Nugent, Terry, Indianapolis	2	1	0.5	3	0
Reed, Andre, Buffalo	1	1	1.0	1	0
Brown, Eddie, Cincinnati	1	0	0.0	0	0
Camarillo, Rich, New England	1	0	0.0	0	0
Danielson, Gary, Cleveland	1	0	0.0	0	0
Fouts, Dan, San Diego	12	0	0.0	2	2
Griffith, Russell, Seattle	1	0	0.0	0	0
Hudson, Doug, Kansas City	1	0	0.0	0	0
Katolin, Mike, Cleveland	1	0	0.0	0	0
Porter, Kerry, Buffalo	2	0	0.0	1	0
Roby, Reggie, Miami	1	0	0.0	0	0
Rodriguez, Ruben, Seattle	1	0	0.0	0	0
Herrmann, Mark, San Diego	4	−1	−0.3	0	0
Brooks, Bill, Indianapolis	2	−2	−1.0	1	0
Kenney, Bill, Kansas City	12	−2	−0.2	6	0
Townsell, JoJo, N.Y. Jets	1	−2	−2.0	−2	0
May, Dean, Denver	2	−4	−2.0	−2	0
Bleier, Bob, New England	5	−5	−1.0	1t	1
Marino, Dan, Miami	12	−5	−0.4	5t	1
Whitten, Todd, New England	2	−6	−3.0	−2	0
Carson, Carlos, Kansas City	1	−7	−7.0	−7	0
Johnson, Vance, Denver	1	−8	−8.0	−8	0
McGee, Tim, Cincinnati	1	−10	−10.0	−10	0
Givins, Ernest, Houston	1	−13	−13.0	−13	0

t indicates touchdown.
Leader based on most yards gained.

NFC Rushing—Individual

	Att.	Yards	Avg.	Long	TD
White, Charles, L.A. Rams	324	1374	4.2	58	11
Mayes, Rueben, New Orleans	243	917	3.8	38	5
Walker, Herschel, Dallas	209	891	4.3	60t	7
Riggs, Gerald, Atlanta	203	875	4.3	44	2
Craig, Roger, San Francisco	215	815	3.8	25	3
Mitchell, Stump, St. Louis	203	781	3.8	42	3
Morris, Joe, N.Y. Giants	193	658	3.4	34	3
Nelson, Darrin, Minnesota	131	642	4.9	72	2
Rogers, George, Washington	163	613	3.8	29	6
Anderson, Neal, Chicago	129	586	4.5	38t	3
Payton, Walter, Chicago	146	533	3.7	17	4
Ferrell, Earl, St. Louis	113	512	4.5	35t	7
Hilliard, Dalton, New Orleans	123	508	4.1	30t	7
Cunningham, Randall, Philadelphia	76	505	6.6	45	3
Wilder, James, Tampa Bay	106	488	4.6	21	0
Toney, Anthony, Philadelphia	127	473	3.7	36	5
Dorsett, Tony, Dallas	130	456	3.5	24	1
Byars, Keith, Philadelphia	116	426	3.7	30	3
Davis, Kenneth, Green Bay	109	413	3.8	39t	3
Bryant, Kelvin, Washington	77	406	5.3	28	1
Vital, Lionel, Washington	80	346	4.3	22t	2
Jones, James, Detroit	96	342	3.6	19	0
Anderson, Alfred, Minnesota	68	319	4.7	27	2
Smith, Jeff, Tampa Bay	100	309	3.1	46	2
Cribbs, Joe, San Francisco	70	300	4.3	20	1
Fullwood, Brent, Green Bay	84	274	3.3	18	5
James, Garry, Detroit	82	270	3.3	17	4
Wilson, Wade, Minnesota	41	263	6.4	38	5
Dozier, D.J., Minnesota	69	257	3.7	19	5
Rathman, Tom, San Francisco	62	257	4.1	35	1
Willhite, Kevin, Green Bay	53	251	4.7	61	0
Griffin, Keith, Washington	62	242	3.9	13	0
McAdoo, Derrick, St. Louis	53	230	4.3	17	3
Beverly, Dwight, New Orleans	62	217	3.5	25	2
Clark, Jessie, Green Bay	56	211	3.8	57	0
Hunter, Eddie, N.Y. Jets-Tampa Bay	56	210	3.8	23	0
Ellerson, Gary, Detroit	47	196	4.2	33	3
Carruth, Paul Ott, Green Bay	64	192	3.0	23	3
Young, Steve, San Francisco	26	190	7.3	29t	1
Bernard, Karl, Detroit	45	187	4.2	14	2
Fenney, Rick, Minnesota	42	174	4.1	12	2
Adams, George, N.Y. Giants	61	169	2.8	14	1
Haddix, Michael, Philadelphia	59	165	2.8	11	0
Rouson, Lee, N.Y. Giants	41	155	3.8	14	0
Pelluer, Steve, Dallas	25	142	5.7	21	1
Montana, Joe, San Francisco	35	141	4.0	20	1
Francis, Jon, L.A. Rams	35	138	3.9	23	0
Brown, Reggie, Philadelphia	39	136	3.5	23	0
Fourcade, John, New Orleans	19	134	7.1	18	0
Word, Barry, New Orleans	36	133	3.7	20	2
Rice, Allen, Minnesota	51	131	2.6	13	1
Heimuli, Lakei, Chicago	34	128	3.8	12	0
Majkowski, Don, Green Bay	15	127	8.5	33	0
Smith, Timmy, Washington	29	126	4.3	15	0
Blount, Alvin, Dallas	46	125	2.7	15	3
Sydney, Harry, San Francisco	29	125	4.3	15	0
Sanders, Thomas, Chicago	23	122	5.3	17	1
Newsome, Tim, Dallas	25	121	4.8	24t	2
Schroeder, Jay, Washington	26	120	4.6	31	3
Robinson, Jacque, Philadelphia	24	114	4.8	18	0
Wester, Cleve, Detroit	33	113	3.4	14	0
Wright, Adrian, Tampa Bay	37	112	3.0	11	0
Williams, Van, N.Y. Giants	29	108	3.7	17	0
Lomax, Neil, St. Louis	29	107	3.7	19	0
Campbell, Scott, Atlanta	21	102	4.9	24	2
Howard, Bobby, Tampa Bay	30	100	3.3	31	1
Guman, Mike, L.A. Rams	36	98	2.7	7	1
Hebert, Bobby, New Orleans	13	95	7.3	19	0
DiRico, Bob, N.Y. Giants	25	90	3.6	14	0
Sargent, Broderick, St. Louis	18	90	5.0	16	0
McMahon, Jim, Chicago	22	88	4.0	13	2
Thomas, Calvin, Chicago	25	88	3.5	18	0
Badanjek, Rick, Atlanta	29	87	3.0	31	1
Wolfley, Ron, St. Louis	26	87	3.3	8	1
Bell, Greg, Buffalo-L.A. Rams	22	86	3.9	13	0
Everett, Jim, L.A. Rams	18	83	4.6	16	1
Varajon, Mike, San Francisco	18	82	4.6	11	0
Woolfolk, Butch, Detroit	12	82	6.8	31	0

	Att.	Yards	Avg.	Long	TD
Mosley, Anthony, Chicago	18	80	4.4	16	0
Ricks, Harold, Tampa Bay	24	76	3.2	14	1
Galbreath, Tony, N.Y. Giants	10	74	7.4	17	0
Settle, John, Atlanta	19	72	3.8	12	0
Alexander, Vincent, New Orleans	21	71	3.4	16	1
Wright, Randy, Green Bay	13	70	5.4	27	0
Edwards, Stan, Detroit	32	69	2.2	13	0
Hold, Mike, Tampa Bay	7	69	9.9	35	0
Tautalatasi, Junior, Philadelphia	26	69	2.7	17	0
Cherry, Tony, San Francisco	13	65	5.0	16	1
Long, Chuck, Detroit	22	64	2.9	15	0
Risher, Alan, Green Bay	11	64	5.8	15	1
Monk, Art, Washington	6	63	10.5	26	0
Edwards, Kelvin, Dallas	2	61	30.5	62t	1
Flowers, Kenny, Atlanta	14	61	4.4	14	0
Carthon, Maurice, N.Y. Giants	26	60	2.3	10	0
Hohensee, Mike, Chicago	9	56	6.2	26	0
Brewer, Chris, Chicago	24	55	2.3	16	2
Wilson, Wayne, Washington	18	55	3.1	11	2
Ross, Alvin, Philadelphia	14	54	3.9	12	1
Tomczak, Mike, Chicago	18	54	3.0	10	1
Rice, Jerry, San Francisco	8	51	6.4	17	1
Testaverde, Vinny, Tampa Bay	13	50	3.8	17	1
Adams, David, Dallas	7	49	7.0	27t	1
Hons, Todd, Detroit	5	49	9.8	23	0
Williams, Michael, Atlanta	14	49	3.5	9	0
Hardy, Andre, San Francisco	7	48	6.9	14	0
Rodgers, Del, San Francisco	11	46	4.2	15	1
Stevens, Mark, San Francisco	10	45	4.5	16	1
Kramer, Tommy, Minnesota	10	44	4.4	15	2
Simms, Phil, N.Y. Giants	14	44	3.1	20	0
Tyrrell, Tim, L.A. Rams	11	44	4.0	13	0
Gentry, Dennis, Chicago	6	41	6.8	12	0
Hargrove, Jimmy, Green Bay	11	38	3.5	7	1
Stanley, Walter, Green Bay	4	38	9.5	24	0
Gray, Mel, New Orleans	8	37	4.6	12	1
Jessie, Tim, Washington	10	37	3.7	14t	1
Brim, James, Minnesota	2	36	18.0	38t	1
Jordan, Buford, New Orleans	12	36	3.0	8t	2
Rodenberger, Jeff, New Orleans	17	35	2.1	5	0
Green, Roy, St. Louis	2	34	17.0	26	0
DuBose, Doug, San Francisco	10	33	3.3	11	0
Parker, Freddie, Green Bay	8	33	4.1	17	0
Austin, Cliff, Tampa Bay	19	32	1.7	8	1
Teltschik, John, Philadelphia	3	32	10.7	23	0
Adams, Tony, Minnesota	11	31	2.8	12	0
Garza, Sammy, St. Louis	8	31	3.9	10	1
Rubbert, Ed, Washington	9	31	3.4	14	0
Rutledge, Jeff, N.Y. Giants	15	31	2.1	20	0
Bartalo, Steve, Tampa Bay	9	30	3.3	6	1
Gladman, Charles, Tampa Bay	12	29	2.4	6	0
Williams, Scott, Detroit	8	29	3.6	8	0
Payton, Sean, Chicago	1	28	28.0	28	0
Wilson, Ted, Washington	2	28	14.0	16t	1
Jackson, Kenny, Philadelphia	6	27	4.5	10	0
Monroe, Carl, San Francisco	2	26	13.0	17	0
Weigel, Lee, Green Bay	10	26	2.6	7	0
Suhey, Matt, Chicago	7	24	3.4	6	0
Walker, Adam, Minnesota	5	24	4.8	11	0
Harris, Frank, Chicago	6	23	3.8	18	0
Beecham, Earl, N.Y. Giants	5	22	4.4	10	0
Brown, Ron, L.A. Rams	2	22	11.0	11	0
Dollinger, Tony, Detroit	8	22	2.8	8	0
Miller, Chris, Atlanta	4	21	5.3	11	0
Grant, Otis, Philadelphia	1	20	20.0	20	0
Land, Dan, Tampa Bay	9	20	2.2	6	0
Sterling, John, Green Bay	5	20	4.0	9	0
Womack, Jeff, Minnesota	9	20	2.2	13	0
Thomas, Lavale, Green Bay	5	19	3.8	5	0
Baker, Stephen, N.Y. Giants	1	18	18.0	18	0
Jean-Batiste, Garland, New Orleans	8	18	2.3	7	0
Morris, Larry, Green Bay	8	18	2.3	10	0
Gault, Willie, Chicago	2	16	8.0	9	0
Wilson, Brett, Minnesota	5	16	3.2	6	0
Harbaugh, James, Chicago	4	15	3.8	9	0
Ingram, Kevin, New Orleans	2	14	7.0	9	0
Morse, Bobby, Philadelphia	6	14	2.3	7	0
Verdin, Clarence, Washington	1	14	14.0	14	0
White, Danny, Dallas	10	14	1.4	8	1
Paige, Tony, Detroit	4	13	3.3	6	0
Smith, Jimmy, Minnesota	7	13	1.9	5	0
Granger, Norm, Atlanta	6	12	2.0	6	0
Clark, Daryl, Chicago	5	11	2.2	5	0
Flagler, Terrence, San Francisco	6	11	1.8	5	0
Lovelady, Edwin, N.Y. Giants	2	11	5.5	8	0
McIntosh, Joe, Atlanta	5	11	2.2	5	0
Moore, Leonard, Minnesota	4	11	2.8	4	0
Park, Kaulana, N.Y. Giants	6	11	1.8	4	0

	Att.	Yards	Avg.	Long	TD
Evans, Donald, L.A. Rams	3	10	3.3	5	0
Kramer, Erik, Atlanta	2	10	5.0	11	0
Branch, Reggie, Washington	4	9	2.3	3	1
Brown, Ron, St. Louis	1	9	9.0	9	0
Johnson, Troy, St. Louis	1	9	9.0	9	0
Williams, Alonzo, L.A. Rams	2	9	4.5	7	0
Williams, Doug, Washington	7	9	1.3	7	1
Archer, David, Atlanta	2	8	4.0	7	0
Harrell, Samuel, Minnesota	5	8	1.6	4	0
Quarles, Bernard, L.A. Rams	1	8	8.0	8	0
Sweeney, Kevin, Dallas	5	8	1.6	5	0
Wolden, Al, Chicago	2	8	4.0	7	0
Holman, Walter, Washington	2	7	3.5	5	0
Jones, E.J., Dallas	2	7	3.5	5	0
Anderson, Ottis, N.Y. Giants	2	6	3.0	4	0
McGee, Buford, L.A. Rams	3	6	2.0	2t	1
Stamps, Sylvester, Altanta	1	6	6.0	6	0
Van Raaphorst, Jeff, Atlanta	1	6	6.0	6	0
Crocicchia, Jim, N.Y. Giants	4	5	1.3	7	0
DiRenzo, Fred, N.Y. Giants	1	5	5.0	5	0
Emery, Larry, Atlanta	1	5	5.0	5	0
Streater, Eric, Tampa Bay	1	5	5.0	5	0
Ellard, Henry, L.A. Rams	1	4	4.0	4	0
Frye, Phil, Minnesota	4	4	1.0	2	0
Thomas, Andre, Minnesota	6	4	0.7	5	0
Zorn, Jim, Tampa Bay	4	4	1.0	5	0
Cater, Greg, St. Louis	2	3	1.5	11	0
Cook, Kelly, Green Bay	2	3	1.5	2	0
Harris, Steve, Minnesota	4	3	0.8	2	0
Hill, Bruce, Tampa Bay	3	3	1.0	9	0
Mandley, Pete, Detroit	1	3	3.0	3	0
Riordan, Tim, New Orleans	1	3	3.0	3	0
Boone, Greg, Tampa Bay	1	2	2.0	2	0
Bryant, Cullen, L.A. Rams	1	2	2.0	2	0
Frank, John, San Francisco	1	2	2.0	2	0
Kowgios, Nick, Detroit	1	2	2.0	2	0
Morris, Lee, Green Bay	2	2	1.0	4	0
Scott, Patrick, Green Bay	1	2	2.0	2	0
Thomas, Derrick, Tampa Bay	1	2	2.0	2	0
Tinsley, Scott, Philadelphia	4	2	0.5	2	0
Butler, Jerry, Atlanta	1	1	1.0	1	0
Freeman, Phil, Tampa Bay	1	1	1.0	1	0
Marshall, Wilber, Chicago	1	1	1.0	1	0
Black, Mike, Detroit	1	0	0.0	0	0
Blount, Ed, San Francisco	1	0	0.0	0	0
Brown, Kevin, Chicago	1	0	0.0	0	0
Clark, Gary, Washington	1	0	0.0	0	0
Clemons, Topper, Philadelphia	3	0	0.0	3	0
Covington, Jamie, N.Y. Giants	4	0	0.0	2	0
Criswell, Ray, Tampa Bay	1	0	0.0	0	0
Epps, Phillip, Green Bay	1	0	0.0	0	0
Horn, Marty, Philadelphia	1	0	0.0	0	0
Hunter, Tony, Green Bay	1	0	0.0	0	0
Neal, Frankie, Green Bay	1	0	0.0	0	0
Oliver, Darryl, Atlanta	1	0	0.0	0	0
Perry, William, Chicago	1	0	0.0	0	0
Robinson, Tony, Washington	2	0	0.0	2	0
Snyder, Loren, Dallas	2	0	0.0	0	0
Miller, Larry, Minnesota	1	−1	−1.0	−1	0
Cavanaugh, Matt, Philadelphia	1	−2	−2.0	−2	0
Griffin, Steve B., Atlanta	1	−2	−2.0	−2	0
Gustafson, Jim, Minnesota	1	−2	−2.0	−2	0
Stoudt, Cliff, St. Louis	1	−2	−2.0	−2	0
Bradley, Steve, Chicago	1	−3	−3.0	−3	0
Dixon, Floyd, Atlanta	3	−3	−1.0	7	0
Dils, Steve, L.A. Rams	7	−4	−0.6	5	0
Matthews, Aubrey, Atlanta	1	−4	−4.0	−4	0
Sanders, Ricky, Washington	1	−4	−4.0	−4	0
White, Gerald, Dallas	1	−4	−4.0	−4	0
Cosbie, Doug, Dallas	1	−5	−5.0	−5	0
Chadwick, Jeff, Detroit	1	−6	−6.0	−6	0
Donnelly, Rick, Atlanta	3	−6	−2.0	0	0
Hansen, Brian, New Orleans	2	−6	−3.0	−3	0
Lewis, Leo, Minnesota	5	−7	−1.4	4	0
Scribner, Bucky, Minnesota	1	−7	−7.0	−7	0
DeBerg, Steve, Tampa Bay	8	−8	−1.0	0	0
Merkens, Guido, Philadelphia	3	−8	−2.7	1	0
Awalt, Robert, St. Louis	2	−9	−4.5	−1	0
Halloran, Shawn, St. Louis	3	−9	−3.0	2	0
Hill, Lonzell, New Orleans	1	−9	−9.0	−9	0
Manuel, Lionel, N.Y. Giants	1	−10	−10.0	−10	0
Barnhardt, Tommy, New Orleans	1	−13	−13.0	−13	0
Taylor, Lenny, Atlanta	1	−13	−13.0	−13	0

t indicates touchdown.
Leader based on most yards gained.

Passing

Individual Champions (Rating Points)
NFC: 102.1—Joe Montana, San Francisco
AFC: 95.4—Bernie Kosar, Cleveland

Attempts
NFC: 463—Neil Lomax, St. Louis
AFC: 444—Dan Marino, Miami

Completions
NFC: 275—Neil Lomax, St. Louis
AFC: 263—Dan Marino, Miami

Completion Percentage
NFC: 66.8—Joe Montana, San Francisco
AFC: 62.0—Bernie Kosar, Cleveland

Yards
NFC: 3,387—Neil Lomax, St. Louis
AFC: 3,321—Boomer Esiason, Cincinnati

Most Yards, Game
NFC: 457—Neil Lomax, St. Louis vs. San Diego, September 20 (61 attempts, 32 completions)
AFC: 409—Boomer Esiason, Cincinnati vs. Pittsburgh, November 22 (53 attempts, 30 completions)

Yards Per Attempt
NFC: 7.98—Wade Wilson, Minnesota
AFC: 7.80—John Elway, Denver

Touchdown Passes
NFC: 31—Joe Montana, San Francisco
AFC: 26—Dan Marino, Miami

Most Touchdown Passes, Game
AFC: 5—Gary Hogeboom, Indianapolis vs. Buffalo, October 4
NFC: 5—Steve DeBerg, Tampa Bay vs. Atlanta, September 13

Longest
NFC: 88—Ed Rubbert (to Anthony Allen), Washington vs. St. Louis, October 4 (TD)
AFC: 83—Warren Moon (to Ernest Givins), Houston vs. Cleveland, November 22 (TD)

Lowest Interception Percentage
AFC: 2.0—Ken O'Brien, N.Y. Jets
NFC: 2.5—Steve DeBerg, Tampa Bay

Team Champions
AFC: 3,876—Miami
NFC: 3,750—San Francisco

AFC Passing—Team

	Att.	Comp.	Pct. Comp.	Gross Yards	Tkd.	Yards Lost	Net Yards	TD	Pct. TD	Long	Int.	Pct. Int.	Avg. Yds. Att.	Avg. Yds. Comp.
Miami	584	338	57.9	3977	13	101	3876	29	5.0	59t	20	3.4	6.81	11.77
Denver	530	285	53.8	3874	30	220	3654	24	4.5	72t	19	3.6	7.31	13.59
Cleveland	482	291	60.4	3625	29	170	3455	27	5.6	54t	12	2.5	7.52	12.46
Houston	482	240	49.8	3534	30	234	3300	24	5.0	83t	23	4.8	7.33	14.73
San Diego	516	303	58.7	3602	39	322	3280	13	2.5	67	23	4.5	6.98	11.89
Cincinnati	475	255	53.7	3468	32	255	3213	17	3.6	61t	20	4.2	7.30	13.60
L.A. Raiders	457	247	54.0	3429	53	359	3070	19	4.2	49	18	3.9	7.50	13.88
N.Y. Jets	517	302	58.4	3402	66	443	2959	18	3.5	59	15	2.9	6.58	11.26
Buffalo	516	292	56.6	3246	37	345	2901	21	4.1	47	19	3.7	6.29	11.12
Indianapolis	447	255	57.0	3042	24	190	2852	16	3.6	72t	16	3.6	6.81	11.93
Seattle	405	237	58.5	3028	36	316	2712	31	7.7	75t	21	5.2	7.48	12.78
New England	440	236	53.6	2929	33	246	2683	22	5.0	45	18	4.1	6.66	12.41
Kansas City	432	236	54.6	2985	48	366	2619	17	3.9	81t	17	3.9	6.91	12.65
Pittsburgh	429	198	46.2	2464	27	198	2266	13	3.0	63	25	5.8	5.74	12.44
AFC Total	6,712	3,715	—	46,605	497	3,765	42,840	291	—	83t	266	—	—	—
AFC Average	479.4	265.4	55.3	3,328.9	35.5	268.9	3,060.0	20.8	4.3	—	19.0	4.0	6.94	12.55

NFC Passing—Team

	Att.	Comp.	Pct. Comp.	Gross Yards	Tkd.	Yards Lost	Net Yards	TD	Pct. TD	Long	Int.	Pct. Int.	Avg. Yds. Att.	Avg. Yds. Comp.
San Francisco	501	322	64.3	3955	29	205	3750	44	8.8	57t	14	2.8	7.89	12.28
Washington	478	247	51.7	3718	27	223	3495	27	5.6	88t	18	3.8	7.78	15.05
St. Louis	529	305	57.7	3850	54	397	3453	25	4.7	57	15	2.8	7.28	12.62
N.Y. Giants	499	265	53.1	3645	61	443	3202	26	5.2	63t	22	4.4	7.30	13.75
Dallas	500	288	57.6	3594	52	403	3191	19	3.8	77t	20	4.0	7.19	12.48
Chicago	493	272	55.2	3420	48	330	3090	23	4.7	59t	24	4.9	6.94	12.57
Philadelphia	520	283	54.4	3561	72	511	3050	26	5.0	70t	16	3.1	6.85	12.58
Tampa Bay	517	264	51.1	3377	43	361	3016	22	4.3	64t	17	3.3	6.53	12.79
Detroit	509	275	54.0	3150	26	194	2956	16	3.1	53t	26	5.1	6.19	11.45
Minnesota	446	232	52.0	3185	52	359	2826	21	4.7	73t	23	5.2	7.14	13.73
New Orleans	411	227	55.2	2987	29	213	2774	23	5.6	82t	12	2.9	7.27	13.16
Atlanta	501	247	49.3	3108	46	340	2768	17	3.4	57	32	6.4	6.20	12.58
Green Bay	455	234	51.4	2977	45	296	2681	15	3.3	70t	17	3.7	6.54	12.72
L.A. Rams	420	220	52.4	2750	25	196	2554	16	3.8	81t	18	4.3	6.55	12.50
NFC Total	6,779	3,681	—	47,277	609	4,471	42,806	320	—	88t	274	—	—	—
NFC Average	484.2	262.9	54.3	3,376.9	43.5	319.4	3,057.6	22.9	4.7	—	19.6	4.0	6.97	12.84
League Total	13,491	7,396	—	93,882	1,106	8,236	85,646	611	—	88t	540	—	—	—
League Average	481.8	264.1	54.8	3,352.9	39.5	294.1	3,058.8	21.8	4.5	—	19.3	4.0	6.96	12.69

Leader based on net yards.

NFL Top 10 Individual Qualifiers

	Att.	Comp.	Pct. Comp.	Yards	Avg. Gain	TD	Pct. TD	Long	Int.	Pct. Int.	Rating Points
Montana, Joe, San Francisco	398	266	66.8	3054	7.67	31	7.8	57t	13	3.3	102.1
Kosar, Bernie, Cleveland	389	241	62.0	3033	7.80	22	5.7	54t	9	2.3	95.4
Simms, Phil, N.Y. Giants	282	163	57.8	2230	7.91	17	6.0	50t	9	3.2	90.0
Marino, Dan, Miami	444	263	59.2	3245	7.31	26	5.9	59t	13	2.9	89.2
Lomax, Neil, St. Louis	463	275	59.4	3387	7.32	24	5.2	57	12	2.6	88.5
Krieg, Dave, Seattle	294	178	60.5	2131	7.25	23	7.8	75t	15	5.1	87.6
McMahon, Jim, Chicago	210	125	59.5	1639	7.80	12	5.7	59t	8	3.8	87.4
Kenney, Bill, Kansas City	273	154	56.4	2107	7.72	15	5.5	81t	9	3.3	85.8
DeBerg, Steve, Tampa Bay	275	159	57.8	1891	6.88	14	5.1	64t	7	2.5	85.3
Wilson, Marc, L.A. Raiders	266	152	57.1	2070	7.78	12	4.5	47t	8	3.0	84.6

AFC Passing — Individual Qualifiers

	Att.	Comp.	Pct. Comp.	Yards	Avg. Gain	TD	Pct. TD	Long	Int.	Pct. Int.	Rating Points
Kosar, Bernie, Cleveland	389	241	62.0	3033	7.80	22	5.7	54t	9	2.3	95.4
Marino, Dan, Miami	444	263	59.2	3245	7.31	26	5.9	59t	13	2.9	89.2
Krieg, Dave, Seattle	294	178	60.5	2131	7.25	23	7.8	75t	15	5.1	87.6
Kenney, Bill, Kansas City	273	154	56.4	2107	7.72	15	5.5	81t	9	3.3	85.8
Wilson, Marc, L.A. Raiders	266	152	57.1	2070	7.78	12	4.5	47t	8	3.0	84.6
Kelly, Jim, Buffalo	419	250	59.7	2798	6.68	19	4.5	47	11	2.6	83.8
Elway, John, Denver	410	224	54.6	3198	7.80	19	4.6	72t	12	2.9	83.4
O'Brien, Ken, N.Y. Jets	393	234	59.5	2696	6.86	13	3.3	59	8	2.0	82.8
Trudeau, Jack, Indianapolis	229	128	55.9	1587	6.93	6	2.6	55	6	2.6	75.4
Moon, Warren, Houston	368	184	50.0	2806	7.63	21	5.7	83t	18	4.9	74.2
Esiason, Boomer, Cincinnati	440	240	54.5	3321	7.55	16	3.6	61t	19	4.3	73.1
Fouts, Dan, San Diego	364	206	56.6	2517	6.91	10	2.7	46	15	4.1	70.0
Malone, Mark, Pittsburgh	336	156	46.4	1896	5.64	6	1.8	63	19	5.7	46.7

Non-qualifiers	Att.	Comp.	Pct. Comp.	Yards	Avg. Gain	TD	Pct. TD	Long	Int.	Pct. Int.	Rating Points
Danielson, Gary, Cleveland	33	25	75.8	281	8.52	4	12.1	23	0	0.0	140.3
Kemp, Jeff, Seattle	33	23	69.7	396	12.00	5	15.2	55	1	3.0	137.1
Kelley, Mike, San Diego	29	17	58.6	305	10.52	1	3.4	67	0	0.0	106.3
Flutie, Doug, New England	25	15	60.0	199	7.96	1	4.0	30	0	0.0	98.6
Ryan, Pat, N.Y. Jets	53	32	60.4	314	5.92	4	7.5	35t	2	3.8	86.5
Hogeboom, Gary, Indianapolis	168	99	58.9	1145	6.82	9	5.4	72t	5	3.0	85.0
Neuheisel, Rick, San Diego	59	40	67.8	367	6.22	1	1.7	32	1	1.7	83.1
Grogan, Steve, New England	161	93	57.8	1183	7.35	10	6.2	40	9	5.6	78.2
Bono, Steve, Pittsburgh	74	34	45.9	438	5.92	5	6.8	57	2	2.7	76.3
Karcher, Ken, Denver	102	56	54.9	628	6.16	5	4.9	49	4	3.9	73.5
Evans, Vince, L.A. Raiders	83	39	47.0	630	7.59	5	6.0	47	4	4.8	72.9
Eason, Tony, New England	79	42	53.2	453	5.73	3	3.8	45	2	2.5	72.4
Stevens, Matt, Kansas City	57	32	56.1	315	5.53	1	1.8	23	1	1.8	70.4
Ramsey, Tom, New England	134	71	53.0	898	6.70	6	4.5	40	6	4.5	70.4
Walter, Dave, Cincinnati	21	10	47.6	113	5.38	0	0.0	35	0	0.0	64.2
Pease, Brent, Houston	113	56	49.6	728	6.44	3	2.7	51	5	4.4	60.6
Blackledge, Todd, Kansas City	31	15	48.4	154	4.97	1	3.2	19	1	3.2	60.4
Mackey, Kyle, Miami	109	57	52.3	604	5.54	3	2.8	30	5	4.6	58.8
Hilger, Rusty, L.A. Raiders	106	55	51.9	706	6.66	2	1.9	49	6	5.7	55.8
Herrmann, Mark, San Diego	57	37	64.9	405	7.11	1	1.8	34	5	8.8	55.1
Mathison, Bruce, Seattle	76	36	47.4	501	6.59	3	3.9	47	5	6.6	54.8
Strock, Don, Miami	23	13	56.5	114	4.96	0	0.0	26	1	4.3	51.7
Totten, Willie, Buffalo	33	13	39.4	155	4.70	2	6.1	37	2	6.1	49.4
Bleier, Bob, New England	39	14	35.9	181	4.64	1	2.6	35	1	2.6	49.2
Norrie, David, N.Y. Jets	68	35	51.5	376	5.53	1	1.5	41t	4	5.9	48.4
Christensen, Jeff, Cleveland	58	24	41.4	297	5.12	1	1.7	34	3	5.2	42.1
Kiel, Blair, Indianapolis	33	17	51.5	195	5.91	1	3.0	21	3	9.1	41.9
Salisbury, Sean, Indianapolis	12	8	66.7	68	5.67	0	0.0	11	2	16.7	41.7
Seurer, Frank, Kansas City	55	26	47.3	340	6.18	0	0.0	33	4	7.3	36.9
Espinoza, Alex, Kansas City	14	9	64.3	69	4.93	0	0.0	16	2	14.3	36.6
McClure, Brian, Buffalo	38	20	52.6	181	4.76	0	0.0	30	3	7.9	32.9
Manucci, Dan, Buffalo	21	7	33.3	68	3.24	0	0.0	15	2	9.5	3.8
Brister, Bubby, Pittsburgh	12	4	33.3	20	1.67	0	0.0	10	3	25.0	2.8

Less than 10 attempts	Att.	Comp.	Pct. Comp.	Yards	Avg. Gain	TD	Pct. TD	Long	Int.	Pct. Int.	Rating Points
Allen, Marcus, L.A. Raiders	2	1	50.0	23	11.50	0	0.0	23	0	0.0	91.7
Bennett, Ben, Cincinnati	6	2	33.3	25	4.17	0	0.0	18	1	16.7	7.6
Breen, Adrian, Cincinnati	8	3	37.5	9	1.13	1	12.5	6	0	0.0	85.4
Briggs, Walter, N.Y. Jets	2	0	0.0	0	0.00	0	0.0	0	1	50.0	0.0
Collier, Reggie, Pittsburgh	7	4	57.1	110	15.71	2	28.6	49	1	14.3	101.8
Fontenot, Herman, Cleveland	1	1	100.0	14	14.00	0	0.0	14	0	0.0	118.8
Hill, Drew, Houston	1	0	0.0	0	0.00	0	0.0	0	0	0.0	39.6
Hillary, Ira, Cincinnati	0	0	—	0	—	0	—	0	0	—	0.0
Hudson, Doug, Kansas City	1	0	0.0	0	0.00	0	0.0	0	0	0.0	39.6
Jaeger, Jeff, Cleveland	1	0	0.0	0	0.00	0	0.0	0	0	0.0	39.6
Jennings, Dave, N.Y. Jets	1	1	100.0	16	16.00	0	0.0	16	0	0.0	118.8
Johnson, Vance, Denver	1	0	0.0	0	0.00	0	0.0	0	0	0.0	39.6
Jones, Cedric, New England	1	0	0.0	0	0.00	0	0.0	0	0	0.0	39.6
Kidd, John, Buffalo	1	0	0.0	0	0.00	0	0.0	0	0	0.0	39.6
Kubiak, Gary, Denver	7	3	42.9	25	3.57	0	0.0	17	2	28.6	13.1
Lang, Gene, Denver	1	0	0.0	0	0.00	0	0.0	0	0	0.0	39.6
Largent, Steve, Seattle	2	0	0.0	0	0.00	0	0.0	0	0	0.0	39.6
May, Dean, Denver	5	0	0.0	0	0.00	0	0.0	0	1	20.0	0.0
McGuire, Monte, Denver	3	2	66.7	23	7.67	0	0.0	13	0	0.0	89.6
Miller, Mark, Buffalo	3	1	33.3	9	3.00	0	0.0	9	1	33.3	2.8
Nugent, Terry, Indianapolis	5	3	60.0	47	9.40	0	0.0	21	0	0.0	91.3
Palmer, Paul, Kansas City	1	0	0.0	0	0.00	0	0.0	0	0	0.0	39.6
Riddick, Robb, Buffalo	1	1	100.0	35	35.00	0	0.0	35	0	0.0	118.8
Sewell, Steve, Denver	0	0	—	0	—	0	—	0	0	—	0.0
Smith, Billy Ray, San Diego	1	0	0.0	0	0.00	0	0.0	0	1	100.0	0.0
Stankavage, Scott, Miami	7	4	57.1	8	1.14	0	0.0	8	1	14.3	22.6
Stradford, Troy, Miami	1	1	100.0	6	6.00	0	0.0	6	0	0.0	91.7
Tatupu, Mosi, New England	1	1	100.0	15	15.00	1	100.0	15t	0	0.0	158.3
Vlasic, Mark, San Diego	6	3	50.0	8	1.33	0	0.0	7	1	16.7	16.7
Willhite, Gerald, Denver	1	0	0.0	0	0.00	0	0.0	0	0	0.0	39.6

t indicates touchdown.

Leader based on rating points, minimum 210 attempts.

NFC Passing — Individual Qualifiers

	Att.	Comp.	Pct. Comp.	Yards	Avg. Gain	TD	Pct. TD	Long	Int.	Pct. Int.	Rating Points
Montana, Joe, San Francisco	398	266	66.8	3054	7.67	31	7.8	57t	13	3.3	102.1
Simms, Phil, N.Y. Giants	282	163	57.8	2230	7.91	17	6.0	50t	9	3.2	90.0
Lomax, Neil, St. Louis	463	275	59.4	3387	7.32	24	5.2	57	12	2.6	88.5
McMahon, Jim, Chicago	210	125	59.5	1639	7.80	12	5.7	59t	8	3.8	87.4
DeBerg, Steve, Tampa Bay	275	159	57.8	1891	6.88	14	5.1	64t	7	2.5	85.3
Cunningham, Randall, Philadelphia	406	223	54.9	2786	6.86	23	5.7	70t	12	3.0	83.0
Hebert, Bobby, New Orleans	294	164	55.8	2119	7.21	15	5.1	67	9	3.1	82.9
Wilson, Wade, Minnesota	264	140	53.0	2106	7.98	14	5.3	73t	13	4.9	76.7
White, Danny, Dallas	362	215	59.4	2617	7.23	12	3.3	43	17	4.7	73.2
Schroeder, Jay, Washington	267	129	48.3	1878	7.03	12	4.5	84t	10	3.7	71.0
Everett, Jim, L.A. Rams	302	162	53.6	2064	6.83	10	3.3	81t	13	4.3	68.4
Campbell, Scott, Atlanta	260	136	52.3	1728	6.65	11	4.2	44t	14	5.4	65.0
Long, Chuck, Detroit	416	232	55.8	2598	6.25	11	2.6	53	20	4.8	63.4
Wright, Randy, Green Bay	247	132	53.4	1507	6.10	6	2.4	66	11	4.5	61.6

Non-qualifiers	Att.	Comp.	Pct. Comp.	Yards	Avg. Gain	TD	Pct. TD	Long	Int.	Pct. Int.	Rating Points
Young, Steve, San Francisco	69	37	53.6	570	8.26	10	14.5	50t	0	0.0	120.8
Wilson, Dave, New Orleans	24	13	54.2	243	10.13	2	8.3	38	0	0.0	117.2
Sweeney, Kevin, Dallas	28	14	50.0	291	10.39	4	14.3	77t	1	3.6	111.8
Rubbert, Ed, Washington	49	26	53.1	532	10.86	4	8.2	88t	1	2.0	110.2
Williams, Doug, Washington	143	81	56.6	1156	8.08	11	7.7	62	5	3.5	94.0
Hohensee, Mike, Chicago	52	28	53.8	343	6.60	4	7.7	28	1	1.9	92.1
Harbaugh, James, Chicago	11	8	72.7	62	5.64	0	0.0	21	0	0.0	86.2
Crocicchia, Jim, N.Y. Giants	15	6	40.0	89	5.93	1	6.7	46t	0	0.0	82.4
Risher, Alan, Green Bay	74	44	59.5	564	7.62	3	4.1	46t	3	4.1	80.0
Gagliano, Bob, San Francisco	29	16	55.2	229	7.90	1	3.4	50	1	3.4	78.1
Fourcade, John, New Orleans	89	48	53.9	597	6.71	4	4.5	82t	3	3.4	75.9
Reaves, John, Tampa Bay	16	6	37.5	83	5.19	1	6.3	26t	0	0.0	75.8
Pelluer, Steve, Dallas	101	55	54.5	642	6.36	3	3.0	44	2	2.0	75.6
Tinsley, Scott, Philadelphia	86	48	55.8	637	7.41	3	3.5	62t	4	4.7	71.7
Majkowski, Don, Green Bay	127	55	43.3	875	6.89	5	3.9	70t	3	2.4	70.2
Kramer, Tommy, Minnesota	81	40	49.4	452	5.58	4	4.9	40t	3	3.7	67.5
Dils, Steve, L.A. Rams	114	56	49.1	646	5.67	5	4.4	51	4	3.5	66.6
Horn, Marty, Philadelphia	11	5	45.5	68	6.18	0	0.0	23	0	0.0	65.7
Merkens, Guido, Philadelphia	14	7	50.0	70	5.00	0	0.0	17	0	0.0	64.6
Adams, Tony, Minnesota	89	49	55.1	607	6.82	3	3.4	63t	5	5.6	64.2
Garza, Sammy, St. Louis	20	11	55.0	183	9.15	1	5.0	38t	2	10.0	63.1
Tomczak, Mike, Chicago	178	97	54.5	1220	6.85	5	2.8	56t	10	5.6	62.0
Hold, Mike, Tampa Bay	24	8	33.3	123	5.13	2	8.3	61t	1	4.2	61.6
Hons, Todd, Detroit	92	43	46.7	552	6.00	5	5.4	53t	5	5.4	61.5
Busch, Mike, N.Y. Giants	47	17	36.2	278	5.91	3	6.4	63t	2	4.3	60.4
Testaverde, Vinny, Tampa Bay	165	71	43.0	1081	6.55	5	3.0	40	6	3.6	60.2
Kramer, Erik, Atlanta	92	45	48.9	559	6.08	4	4.3	33	5	5.4	60.0
Halloran, Shawn, St. Louis	42	18	42.9	263	6.26	0	0.0	49	1	2.4	54.0
Rutledge, Jeff, N.Y. Giants	155	79	51.0	1048	6.76	5	3.2	50	11	7.1	53.9
Van Raaphorst, Jeff, Atlanta	34	18	52.9	174	5.12	1	2.9	24	2	5.9	52.8
Robinson, Tony, Washington	18	11	61.1	152	8.44	0	0.0	42	2	11.1	48.6
Zorn, Jim, Tampa Bay	36	20	55.6	199	5.53	0	0.0	26	2	5.6	48.3
Bradley, Steve, Chicago	18	6	33.3	77	4.28	2	11.1	18t	3	16.7	45.1
Payton, Sean, Chicago	23	8	34.8	79	3.43	0	0.0	20	1	4.3	27.3
Miller, Chris, Atlanta	92	39	42.4	552	6.00	1	1.1	57	9	9.8	26.4
Archer, David, Atlanta	23	9	39.1	95	4.13	0	0.0	33	2	8.7	15.7

Less than 10 attempts	Att.	Comp.	Pct. Comp.	Yards	Avg. Gain	TD	Pct. TD	Long	Int.	Pct. Int.	Rating Points
Bartalo, Steve, Tampa Bay	1	0	0.0	0	0.00	0	0.0	0	1	100.0	0.0
Bryant, Kelvin, Washington	1	0	0.0	0	0.00	0	0.0	0	0	0.0	39.6
Carruth, Paul Ott, Green Bay	1	1	100.0	3	3.00	1	100.0	3t	0	0.0	118.8
Carter, Cris, Philadelphia	1	0	0.0	0	0.00	0	0.0	0	0	0.0	39.6
Gannon, Rich, Minnesota	6	2	33.3	18	3.00	0	0.0	12	1	16.7	2.8
Gillus, Willie, Green Bay	5	2	40.0	28	5.60	0	0.0	15	0	0.0	58.8
Grant, Otis, Philadelphia	1	0	0.0	0	0.00	0	0.0	0	0	0.0	39.6
Hilliard, Dalton, New Orleans	1	1	100.0	23	23.00	1	100.0	23t	0	0.0	158.3
Ingram, Kevin, New Orleans	2	1	50.0	5	2.50	1	50.0	5t	0	0.0	95.8
Jones, James, Detroit	1	0	0.0	0	0.00	0	0.0	0	1	100.0	0.0
Millen, Hugh, L.A. Rams	1	1	100.0	0	0.00	0	0.0	0	0	0.0	79.2
Miller, Larry, Minnesota	6	1	16.7	2	0.33	0	0.0	2	1	16.7	0.0
Mitchell, Stump, St. Louis	3	1	33.3	17	5.67	0	0.0	17	0	0.0	53.5
Neal, Frankie, Green Bay	1	0	0.0	0	0.00	0	0.0	0	0	0.0	39.6
Payton, Walter, Chicago	1	0	0.0	0	0.00	0	0.0	0	1	100.0	0.0
Quarles, Bernard, L.A. Rams	3	1	33.3	40	13.33	1	33.3	40t	1	33.3	81.9
Riordan, Tim, New Orleans	1	0	0.0	0	0.00	0	0.0	0	0	0.0	39.6
Snyder, Loren, Dallas	9	4	44.4	44	4.89	0	0.0	22	0	0.0	59.5
Stevens, Mark, San Francisco	4	2	50.0	52	13.00	1	25.0	39t	0	0.0	135.4
Stoudt, Cliff, St. Louis	1	0	0.0	0	0.00	0	0.0	0	0	0.0	39.6
Sydney, Harry, San Francisco	1	1	100.0	50	50.00	1	100.0	50t	0	0.0	158.3
Teltschik, John, Philadelphia	0	0	—	0	—	0	—	0	0	—	0.0
Toney, Anthony, Philadelphia	1	0	0.0	0	0.00	0	0.0	0	0	0.0	39.6

t indicates touchdown.

Leader based on rating points, minimum 210 attempts.

Pass Receiving

Individual Champions

NFC: 91—J.T. Smith, St. Louis
AFC: 68—Al Toon, N.Y. Jets

Most Receptions, Game

AFC: 15—Steve Largent, Seattle at Detroit, October 18 (261 yards)
NFC: 11—Mark Bavaro, N.Y. Giants at St. Louis, December 13 (137 yards)
11—J.T. Smith, St. Louis at Dallas, December 27 (102 yards)

Yards

NFC: 1,117—J.T. Smith, St. Louis
AFC: 1,044—Carlos Carson, Kansas City

Most Yards, Game

AFC: 261—Steve Largent, Seattle vs. Detroit, October 18 (15 receptions)
NFC: 255—Anthony Allen, Washington vs. St. Louis, October 4 (7 receptions)

Yards Per Reception

NFC: 24.3—Anthony Carter, Minnesota
AFC: 21.5—James Lofton, L.A. Raiders

Longest

NFC: 88—Anthony Allen (from Ed Rubbert), Washington vs. St. Louis, September 20 (TD)
AFC: 83—Ernest Givins (from Warren Moon), Houston vs. Cleveland, November 22 (TD)

Touchdowns

NFC: 22—Jerry Rice, San Francisco
AFC: 8—Mark Duper, Miami
8—Steve Largent, Seattle

Team Leaders, Receptions

AFC: BUFFALO: 57, Andre Reed; CINCINNATI: 44, Eddie Brown; CLEVELAND: 52, Earnest Byner; DENVER: 42, Vance Johnson; HOUSTON: 53, Ernest Givins; INDIANAPOLIS: 51, Bill Brooks; KANSAS CITY: 55, Carlos Carson; L.A. RAIDERS: 51, Marcus Allen; MIAMI: 48, Troy Stradford; NEW ENGLAND: 44, Tony Collins; N.Y. JETS: 68, Al Toon; PITTSBURGH: 41, John Stallworth; SAN DIEGO: 53, Kellen Winslow; SEATTLE: 58, Steve Largent.

NFC: ATLANTA: 36, Floyd Dixon; CHICAGO: 47, Neal Anderson; DALLAS: 60, Herschel Walker; DETROIT: 58, Pete Mandley; GREEN BAY: 38, Walter Stanley; L.A. RAMS: 51, Henry Ellard; MINNESOTA: 38, Anthony Carter; NEW ORLEANS: 44, Eric Martin; N.Y. GIANTS: 55, Mark Bavaro; PHILADELPHIA: 46, Mike Quick; ST. LOUIS: 91, J.T. Smith; SAN FRANCISCO: 66, Roger Craig; TAMPA BAY: 40, James Wilder; WASHINGTON: 56, Gary Clark.

NFL Top 10 Pass Receivers

	No.	Yards	Avg.	Long	TD
Smith, J. T., St. Louis	91	1117	12.3	38	8
Toon, Al, N.Y. Jets	68	976	14.4	58t	5
Craig, Roger, San Francisco	66	492	7.5	35t	1
Rice, Jerry, San Francisco	65	1078	16.6	57t	22
Walker, Herschel, Dallas	60	715	11.9	44	1
Largent, Steve, Seattle	58	912	15.7	55	8
Mandley, Pete, Detroit	58	720	12.4	41	7
Reed, Andre, Buffalo	57	752	13.2	40	5
Clark, Gary, Washington	56	1066	19.0	84t	7
Burkett, Chris, Buffalo	56	765	13.7	47	4
Harmon, Ronnie, Buffalo	56	477	8.5	42	2

NFL Top 10 Pass Receivers By Yards

	Yards	No.	Avg.	Long	TD
Smith, J. T., St. Louis	1117	91	12.3	38	8
Rice, Jerry, San Francisco	1078	65	16.6	57t	22
Clark, Gary, Washington	1066	56	19.0	84t	7
Carson, Carlos, Kansas City	1044	55	19.0	81t	7
Hill, Drew, Houston	989	49	20.2	52t	6
Toon, Al, N.Y. Jets	976	68	14.4	58t	5
Givins, Ernest, Houston	933	53	17.6	83t	6
Carter, Anthony, Minnesota	922	38	24.3	73t	7
Largent, Steve, Seattle	912	58	15.7	55	8
Lofton, James, L.A. Raiders	880	41	21.5	49	5

AFC Pass Receiving—Individual

	No.	Yards	Avg.	Long	TD
Toon, Al, N.Y. Jets	68	976	14.4	58t	5
Largent, Steve, Seattle	58	912	15.7	55	8
Reed, Andre, Buffalo	57	752	13.2	40	5
Burkett, Chris, Buffalo	56	765	13.7	47	4
Harmon, Ronnie, Buffalo	56	477	8.5	42	2
Carson, Carlos, Kansas City	55	1044	19.0	81t	7
Givins, Ernest, Houston	53	933	17.6	83t	6
Winslow, Kellen, San Diego	53	519	9.8	30	3
Byner, Earnest, Cleveland	52	552	10.6	37	2
Brooks, Bill, Indianapolis	51	722	14.2	52t	3
Allen, Marcus, L.A. Raiders	51	410	8.0	39	0
Hill, Drew, Houston	49	989	20.2	52t	6
Stradford, Troy, Miami	48	457	9.5	34	1
Slaughter, Webster, Cleveland	47	806	17.1	54t	7
Christensen, Todd, L.A. Raiders	47	663	14.1	33	2
Anderson, Gary, San Diego	47	503	10.7	38	2
Clayton, Mark, Miami	46	776	16.9	43	7
Brown, Eddie, Cincinnati	44	608	13.8	47t	3
Collins, Tony, New England	44	347	7.9	29	3
Paige, Stephone, Kansas City	43	707	16.4	51	4
Brennan, Brian, Cleveland	43	607	14.1	53t	6
Shuler, Mickey, N.Y. Jets	43	434	10.1	32t	3
Johnson, Vance, Denver	42	684	16.3	59t	7
Bouza, Matt, Indianapolis	42	569	13.5	44t	4
Lofton, James, L.A. Raiders	41	880	21.5	49	5
James, Lionel, San Diego	41	593	14.5	46	3
Stallworth, John, Pittsburgh	41	521	12.7	45	2
Morgan, Stanley, New England	40	672	16.8	45	3
Chandler, Wes, San Diego	39	617	15.8	27	2
Williams, John L., Seattle	38	420	11.1	75t	3
Jennings, Stanford, Cincinnati	35	277	7.9	24	2
Bentley, Albert, Indianapolis	34	447	13.1	72t	2
Newsome, Ozzie, Cleveland	34	375	11.0	25	0
Duper, Mark, Miami	33	597	18.1	59t	8
Butler, Raymond, Seattle	33	465	14.1	40t	5
Hector, Johnny, N.Y. Jets	32	249	7.8	27	0
Mack, Kevin, Cleveland	32	223	7.0	17	1
Nattiel, Ricky, Denver	31	630	20.3	54	2
Collinsworth, Cris, Cincinnati	31	494	15.9	53	0
Fryar, Irving, New England	31	467	15.1	40	5
Kay, Clarence, Denver	31	440	14.2	30	0
Holman, Rodney, Cincinnati	28	438	15.6	61t	2
Hardy, Bruce, Miami	28	292	10.4	31	2
Metzelaars, Pete, Buffalo	28	290	10.4	34	0
Beach, Pat, Indianapolis	28	239	8.5	16	0
Davenport, Ron, Miami	27	249	9.2	29	1
Rozier, Mike, Houston	27	192	7.1	27	0
Jackson, Mark, Denver	26	436	16.8	52	2
Pruitt, James, Miami	26	404	15.5	37	3
Jensen, Jim, Miami	26	221	8.5	20	1
Jones, Cedric, New England	25	388	15.5	29	3
Micho, Bobby, Denver	25	242	9.7	26t	2
McNeil, Freeman, N.Y. Jets	24	262	10.9	57	1
Abercrombie, Walter, Pittsburgh	24	209	8.7	24	0
Okoye, Christian, Kansas City	24	169	7.0	22	0
McGee, Tim, Cincinnati	23	408	17.7	49	1
Sohn, Kurt, N.Y. Jets	23	261	11.3	31	2
Hampton, Lorenzo, Miami	23	223	9.7	24	0
Brooks, James, Cincinnati	22	272	12.4	46	2
Williams, Dokie, L.A. Raiders	21	330	15.7	33	5
Hayes, Jonathan, Kansas City	21	272	13.0	33	2
Martin, Mike, Cincinnati	20	394	19.7	54t	3
Murray, Walter, Indianapolis	20	339	17.0	43	3
Langhorne, Reggie, Cleveland	20	288	14.4	25	1
Holohan, Pete, San Diego	20	239	12.0	18	0
Skansi, Paul, Seattle	19	207	10.9	25	1
Harper, Michael, N.Y. Jets	18	225	12.5	35t	1
Kattus, Eric, Cincinnati	18	217	12.1	57	2
Dickerson, Eric, L.A. Rams-Indianapolis	18	171	9.5	28	0
Thompson, Weegie, Pittsburgh	17	313	18.4	63	1
Starring, Stephen, New England	17	289	17.0	34t	3
Warner, Curt, Seattle	17	167	9.8	30t	2
Lang, Gene, Denver	17	130	7.6	29	2
Spencer, Tim, San Diego	17	123	7.2	18	0
Mobley, Orson, Denver	16	228	14.3	28	1
Sweeney, Calvin, Pittsburgh	16	217	13.6	34	0
Carter, Rodney, Pittsburgh	16	180	11.3	26t	3
Jackson, Bo, L.A. Raiders	16	136	8.5	23	2
Johnson, Trumaine, Buffalo	15	186	12.4	26t	2
Holman, Scott, N.Y. Jets	15	155	10.3	30	0
Tatupu, Mosi, New England	15	136	9.1	23	0
Riddick, Robb, Buffalo	15	96	6.4	17t	3
Fernandez, Mervyn, L.A. Raiders	14	236	16.9	47	0
Teal, Jimmy, Seattle	14	198	14.1	47	2
Turner, Daryl, Seattle	14	153	10.9	20t	6
Klever, Rocky, N.Y. Jets	14	152	10.9	30	0
Heard, Herman, Kansas City	14	118	8.4	15	0
Tice, Mike, Seattle	14	106	7.6	27	2
Pollard, Frank, Pittsburgh	14	77	5.5	17	0
Winder, Sammy, Denver	14	74	5.3	13	1
Massie, Rick, Denver	13	244	18.8	39t	4
Clinkscales, Joey, Pittsburgh	13	240	18.5	57	1
Duncan, Curtis, Houston	13	237	18.2	48	5
Sewell, Steve, Denver	13	209	16.1	72t	1
Williams, Jamie, Houston	13	158	12.2	25	3
Vick, Roger, N.Y. Jets	13	108	8.3	23	0
Williams, Alphonso, San Diego	12	247	20.6	57	1
Kemp, Perry, Cleveland	12	224	18.7	34	2
Lee, Danzell, Pittsburgh	12	124	10.3	24	0
Tagliaferri, John, Miami	12	117	9.8	27	0
Dawson, Lin, New England	12	81	6.8	14	0
Watson, Steve, Denver	11	167	15.2	49	1
Williams, Oliver, Houston	11	165	15.0	36t	1
Lipps, Louis, Pittsburgh	11	164	14.9	27	0
Linne, Larry, New England	11	158	14.4	30	2

	No.	Yards	Avg.	Long	TD
Weathers, Clarence, Cleveland	11	153	13.9	37t	2
Drewrey, Willie, Houston	11	148	13.5	35	0
Mueller, Vance, L.A. Raiders	11	95	8.6	14	0
Bligen, Dennis, N.Y. Jets	11	81	7.4	19	0
Harris, Leonard, Houston	10	164	16.4	39	0
Marshall, Henry, Kansas City	10	126	12.6	19	0
Noble, James, Indianapolis	10	78	7.8	18t	2
Nathan, Tony, Miami	10	77	7.7	14	0
Bernstine, Rod, San Diego	10	76	7.6	15	1
Boyer, Mark, Indianapolis	10	73	7.3	15	0
Jackson, Andrew, Houston	10	44	4.4	16	0
Moriarty, Larry, Kansas City	10	37	3.7	8	1
Walker, Wesley, N.Y. Jets	9	190	21.1	59	1
Brown, Marc, Buffalo	9	120	13.3	30	1
Gaines, Sheldon, Buffalo	9	115	12.8	37	0
Kinnebrew, Larry, Cincinnati	9	114	12.7	25	0
Tennell, Derek, Cleveland	9	102	11.3	24	3
Douglas, Leland, Miami	9	92	10.2	17	1
Sherwin, Tim, Indianapolis	9	86	9.6	32	1
Boddie, Tony, Denver	9	85	9.4	26	0
McKeller, Keith, Buffalo	9	80	8.9	22	0
Porter, Ricky, Buffalo	9	70	7.8	26	0
Banks, Chuck, Indianapolis	9	50	5.6	18	0
Willhite, Gerald, Denver	9	25	2.8	6	0
Pardridge, Curt, Seattle	8	145	18.1	47	1
Aikens, Carl, L.A. Raiders	8	134	16.8	32t	3
McNeil, Gerald, Cleveland	8	120	15.0	39t	2
Keel, Mark, Seattle-Kansas City	8	97	12.1	24t	1
Jones, Rod, Kansas City	8	76	9.5	16	1
Sampleton, Lawrence, Miami	8	64	8.0	19	0
Middleton, Frank, San Diego	8	43	5.4	17	0
Everett, Major, Cleveland	8	41	5.1	10	0
Jenkins, Keyvan, San Diego	8	40	5.0	7	0
Lockett, Charles, Pittsburgh	7	116	16.6	25	1
Chavis, Eddie, Miami	7	108	15.4	27	0
Hoge, Merril, Pittsburgh	7	97	13.9	27	1
Juma, Kevin, Seattle	7	95	13.6	26	0
Jeffires, Haywood, Houston	7	89	12.7	23	0
Holt, Harry, San Diego	7	56	8.0	17	0
Jackson, Earnest, Pittsburgh	7	52	7.4	23	0
Redden, Barry, San Diego	7	46	6.6	13	0
Parker, Robert, Kansas City	7	44	6.3	14	0
Dudek, Joe, Denver	7	41	5.9	19	0
Wallace, Ray, Houston	7	34	4.9	7	0
Holland, Jamie, San Diego	6	138	23.0	45	0
Swanson, Shane, Denver	6	87	14.5	35t	1
Lewis, David, Miami	6	53	8.8	22	1
Hunter, Stan, N.Y. Jets	6	50	8.3	12	1
Rome, Tag, San Diego	6	49	8.2	13	0
Konecny, Mark, Miami	6	26	4.3	10	0
Sartin, Martin, San Diego	6	19	3.2	8	0
Walters, Joey, Houston	5	99	19.8	51	0
Lathan, Greg, L.A. Raiders	5	98	19.6	33	0
Broughton, Walter, Buffalo	5	90	18.0	39	1
Moffett, Tim, San Diego	5	80	16.0	25	1
Reilly, Dameon, Miami	5	70	14.0	20	0
Bellini, Mark, Indianapolis	5	69	13.8	19	0
Brown, Eric, Kansas City	5	69	13.8	23	0
Hillary, Ira, Cincinnati	5	65	13.0	23	0
Gehring, Mark, Houston	5	64	12.8	31t	1
Wonsley, George, Indianapolis	5	48	9.6	16	0
Montagne, Dave, Kansas City	5	47	9.4	16	0
Coffman, Paul, Kansas City	5	42	8.4	13t	1
Ellis, Craig, L.A. Raiders	5	39	7.8	15	0
Brandes, John, Indianapolis	5	35	7.0	13	0
Scott, Willie, New England	5	35	7.0	15	1
Mason, Larry, Cleveland	5	26	5.2	15	1
Williams, David, L.A. Raiders	4	104	26.0	44	0
McDonald, Keith, Houston	4	56	14.0	24	1
Highsmith, Alonzo, Houston	4	55	13.8	33t	1
Andrews, Mitch, Denver	4	53	13.3	20	0
Riley, Eric, N.Y. Jets	4	42	10.5	16	0
Strachan, Steve, L.A. Raiders	4	42	10.5	14	0
McFadden, Thad, Buffalo	4	41	10.3	13t	1
Brown, Laron, Denver	4	40	10.0	18	0
Fontenot, Herman, Cleveland	4	40	10.0	25	0
Trahan, John, Kansas City	4	40	10.0	14	0
Adams, Curtis, San Diego	4	38	9.5	21	0
Townsell, JoJo, N.Y. Jets	4	37	9.3	11	0
Johnson, Dan, Miami	4	35	8.8	22	2
Caldwell, Scott, Denver	4	34	8.5	14	0
Lane, Eric, Seattle	4	30	7.5	12	0
Wright, Dana, Cincinnati	4	28	7.0	11	0
Palmer, Paul, Kansas City	4	27	6.8	10	0
Bennett, Woody, Miami	4	18	4.5	6	0
Chirico, John, N.Y. Jets	4	18	4.5	8	0
Alston, Lyneal, Pittsburgh	3	84	28.0	42t	2
Coffey, Wayne, New England	3	66	22.0	35	0
Wheeler, Ron, L.A. Raiders	3	61	20.3	29	0
Kearse, Tim, Indianapolis	3	56	18.7	21	0
Gadbois, Dennis, New England	3	51	17.0	20	0
Smith, Steve, L.A. Raiders	3	46	15.3	32	0
Sweet, Tony, N.Y. Jets	3	45	15.0	22	0
Horton, Ethan, L.A. Raiders	3	44	14.7	32t	1
Hawthorne, Greg, Indianapolis	3	41	13.7	21	0
Williams, Derwin, New England	3	30	10.0	12	0
Arnold, Walt, Kansas City	3	26	8.7	10	0
Jones, Joe, Indianapolis	3	25	8.3	13	1
Meehan, Greg, Cincinnati	3	25	8.3	12	0
Estell, Richard, Kansas City	3	24	8.0	11	0
Byrum, Carl, Buffalo	3	23	7.7	20	0
Colbert, Darrell, Kansas City	3	21	7.0	9	0
Moore, Ricky, Houston	3	21	7.0	10	0
Johnson, Bill, Cincinnati	3	19	6.3	9	0
Hunter, Herman, Houston	3	17	5.7	11	0
Logan, Marc, Cincinnati	3	14	4.7	18	0
Mueller, Jamie, Buffalo	3	13	4.3	11	0
Perryman, Bob, New England	3	13	4.3	7	0
Dupard, Reggie, New England	3	1	0.3	2	0
Muhammad, Calvin, San Diego	2	87	43.5	67	0
Spencer, Todd, San Diego	2	47	23.5	45	0
Caterbone, Michael, Miami	2	46	23.0	30	0
Pleasant, Marquis, Cincinnati	2	45	22.5	35	0
Ware, Timmie, San Diego	2	38	19.0	23	0
Bengen, Brant, Seattle	2	33	16.5	24	0
Russell, Wade, Cincinnati	2	27	13.5	23	1
Koss, Stein, Kansas City	2	25	12.5	14	0
Bynum, Reggie, Buffalo	2	24	12.0	17	0
Frain, Todd, New England	2	22	11.0	11	0
Nash, Kenny, Kansas City	2	22	11.0	14	0
Pierce, Steve, Cleveland	2	21	10.5	13	0
Smith, Chris, Kansas City	2	21	10.5	16	0
Harrison, Rob, L.A. Raiders	2	18	9.0	15	0
Griggs, Billy, N.Y. Jets	2	17	8.5	13	1
Hairston, Russell, Pittsburgh	2	16	8.0	11	1
Junkin, Trey, L.A. Raiders	2	15	7.5	8	0
Munoz, Anthony, Cincinnati	2	15	7.5	12	1
Smith, Willie, Miami	2	13	6.5	8	1
Pippens, Woodie, Kansas City	2	12	6.0	7	0
Valentine, Ira, Houston	2	10	5.0	7	0
Young, Theo, Pittsburgh	2	10	5.0	6	0
Gothard, Preston, Pittsburgh	2	9	4.5	7	1
McLemore, Chris, Indianapolis	2	9	4.5	5	0
Browne, Jim, L.A. Raiders	2	8	4.0	5	0
Scott, Ronald, Miami	2	7	3.5	5	0
Rolle, Butch, Buffalo	2	6	3.0	3t	2
LeBlanc, Michael, New England	2	3	1.5	3	0
Kurisko, Jamie, N.Y. Jets	1	41	41.0	41t	1
Darrington, Chris, Houston	1	38	38.0	38	0
Kelly, Jim, Buffalo	1	35	35.0	35	0
Hester, Jessie, L.A. Raiders	1	30	30.0	30	0
Hansen, Bruce, New England	1	22	22.0	22	0
Stone, Dwight, Pittsburgh	1	22	22.0	22	0
Calhoun, Rick, L.A. Raiders	1	17	17.0	17	0
Tinsley, Keith, Cleveland	1	17	17.0	17	0
Faaola, Nuu, N.Y. Jets	1	16	16.0	16	0
Johnson, Kelley, Indianapolis	1	15	15.0	15	0
James, Arrike, Houston	1	14	14.0	14	0
Woods, Chris, L.A. Raiders	1	14	14.0	14	0
Watson, Remi, Cleveland	1	13	13.0	13	0
Bryant, Steve, Indianapolis	1	12	12.0	12	0
Isom, Rickey, Miami	1	11	11.0	11	0
Sanders, Chuck, Pittsburgh	1	11	11.0	11	0
Banks, Fred, Miami	1	10	10.0	10t	1
Gaffney, Derrick, N.Y. Jets	1	10	10.0	10	0
Pickering, Clay, New England	1	10	10.0	10	0
Chetti, Joseph, Buffalo	1	9	9.0	9	0
Foster, Derrick, N.Y. Jets	1	9	9.0	9	0
Poole, Nathan, Denver	1	9	9.0	9	0
Watson, Louis, Cleveland	1	9	9.0	9	0
Bell, Ken, Denver	1	8	8.0	8	0
Manoa, Tim, Cleveland	1	8	8.0	8	0
McCluskey, David, Cincinnati	1	8	8.0	8	0
Payne, Russell, Denver	1	8	8.0	8	0
Belk, Veno, Buffalo	1	7	7.0	7	0
Franklin, Byron, Seattle	1	7	7.0	7	0
Parros, Rick, Seattle	1	7	7.0	7	0
Pinkett, Allen, Houston	1	7	7.0	7	0
Brown, Tom, Miami	1	6	6.0	6	0
Hawkins, Frank, L.A. Raiders	1	6	6.0	6	0
Farmer, George, Miami	1	5	5.0	5	0
Williams, Leonard, Buffalo	1	5	5.0	5	0
Steels, Anthony, San Diego	1	4	4.0	4	0
Stockemer, Ralph, Kansas City	1	4	4.0	4	0
Adickes, Mark, Kansas City	1	3	3.0	3t	1
King, Bruce, Buffalo	1	3	3.0	3	0
Perry, Mario, L.A. Raiders	1	3	3.0	3t	1
Bono, Steve, Pittsburgh	1	2	2.0	2	0

	No.	Yards	Avg.	Long	TD
Shepherd, Johnny, Buffalo	1	2	2.0	2	0
Boyle, Jim, Pittsburgh	1	0	0.0	0	0
Utt, Ben, Indianapolis	1	−4	−4.0	−4	0
Millard, Bryan, Seattle	1	−5	−5.0	−5	0

t indicates touchdown.
Leader based on most passes caught.

NFC Pass Receiving — Individual

	No.	Yards	Avg.	Long	TD
Smith, J.T., St. Louis	91	1117	12.3	38	8
Craig, Roger, San Francisco	66	492	7.5	35t	1
Rice, Jerry, San Francisco	65	1078	16.6	57t	22
Walker, Herschel, Dallas	60	715	11.9	44	1
Mandley, Pete, Detroit	58	720	12.4	41	7
Clark, Gary, Washington	56	1066	19.0	84t	7
Bavaro, Mark, N.Y. Giants	55	867	15.8	38	8
Ellard, Henry, L.A. Rams	51	799	15.7	81t	3
Anderson, Neal, Chicago	47	467	9.9	59t	3
Quick, Mike, Philadelphia	46	790	17.2	61t	11
Renfro, Mike, Dallas	46	662	14.4	43	4
Mitchell, Stump, St. Louis	45	397	8.8	39	2
Martin, Eric, New Orleans	44	778	17.7	67	7
Green, Roy, St. Louis	43	731	17.0	57	4
Bryant, Kelvin, Washington	43	490	11.4	39	5
Awalt, Robert, St. Louis	42	526	12.5	35	6
Wilder, James, Tampa Bay	40	328	8.2	32	1
Toney, Anthony, Philadelphia	39	341	8.7	33	1
Carter, Anthony, Minnesota	38	922	24.3	73t	7
Stanley, Walter, Green Bay	38	672	17.7	70t	3
Carter, Gerald, Tampa Bay	38	586	15.4	57	5
Monk, Art, Washington	38	483	12.7	62	6
Sanders, Ricky, Washington	37	630	17.0	57	3
Dixon, Floyd, Atlanta	36	600	16.7	51t	5
Cosbie, Doug, Dallas	36	421	11.7	30	3
Neal, Frankie, Green Bay	36	420	11.7	38	3
Spagnola, John, Philadelphia	36	350	9.7	22	2
Gault, Willie, Chicago	35	705	20.1	56t	7
Jordan, Steve, Minnesota	35	490	14.0	38	2
Adams, George, N.Y. Giants	35	298	8.5	25	1
Edwards, Kelvin, Dallas	34	521	15.3	38t	3
Epps, Phillip, Green Bay	34	516	15.2	40	2
Magee, Calvin, Tampa Bay	34	424	12.5	37	3
Newsome, Tim, Dallas	34	274	8.1	30	2
Jones, James, Detroit	34	262	7.7	35	0
Payton, Walter, Chicago	33	217	6.6	16	1
Matthews, Aubrey, Atlanta	32	537	16.8	57	3
Manuel, Lionel, N.Y. Giants	30	545	18.2	50t	6
Chadwick, Jeff, Detroit	30	416	13.9	36	0
Rathman, Tom, San Francisco	30	329	11.0	29	3
Wilson, Mike, San Francisco	29	450	15.5	46t	5
Jones, Mike, New Orleans	27	420	15.6	43t	3
McKinnon, Dennis, Chicago	27	406	15.0	33	1
Brown, Ron, L.A. Rams	26	521	20.0	52	2
Carrier, Mark, Tampa Bay	26	423	16.3	38	3
Frank, John, San Francisco	26	296	11.4	27	3
Galbreath, Tony, N.Y. Giants	26	248	9.5	21	0
Nelson, Darrin, Minnesota	26	129	5.0	13	0
Riggs, Gerald, Atlanta	25	199	8.0	48	0
Tautalatasi, Junior, Philadelphia	25	176	7.0	22	0
Lewis, Leo, Minnesota	24	383	16.0	36	2
Clark, Dwight, San Francisco	24	290	12.1	40t	5
Moorehead, Emery, Chicago	24	269	11.2	27	1
Hill, Bruce, Tampa Bay	23	403	17.5	40	2
Hilliard, Dalton, New Orleans	23	264	11.5	38t	1
Ferrell, Earl, St. Louis	23	262	11.4	36	0
White, Charles, L.A. Rams	23	121	5.3	20	0
Guman, Mike, L.A. Rams	22	263	12.0	33	0
Francis, Russ, San Francisco	22	202	9.2	19	0
Clark, Jessie, Green Bay	22	119	5.4	19	1
Jackson, Kenny, Philadelphia	21	471	22.4	70t	3
Johnson, Damone, L.A. Rams	21	198	9.4	20	2
Byars, Keith, Philadelphia	21	177	8.4	30	1
Morris, Ron, Chicago	20	379	19.0	42t	1
Bailey, Stacey, Atlanta	20	325	16.3	35	3
Brenner, Hoby, New Orleans	20	280	14.0	29	2
Novacek, Jay, St. Louis	20	254	12.7	25	3
Smith, Jeff, Tampa Bay	20	197	9.9	34t	2
Hill, Lonzell, New Orleans	19	322	16.9	36	2
Lee, Gary, Detroit	19	308	16.2	53	0
West, Ed, Green Bay	19	261	13.7	40	1
Rice, Allen, Minnesota	19	201	10.6	24	1
Dorsett, Tony, Dallas	19	177	9.3	33	1
Woolfolk, Butch, Detroit	19	166	8.7	13	0
Brim, James, Minnesota	18	282	15.7	63t	2
Baty, Greg, New England-L.A. Rams	18	175	9.7	22	2
Boso, Cap, Chicago	17	188	11.1	31	2
Gentry, Dennis, Chicago	17	183	10.8	38t	1
Whisenhunt, Ken, Atlanta	17	145	8.5	26	1
Grant, Otis, Philadelphia	16	280	17.5	41	0
Morris, Lee, Green Bay	16	259	16.2	46t	1
James, Garry, Detroit	16	215	13.4	46	0
Tice, John, New Orleans	16	181	11.3	27t	6
Hall, Ron, Tampa Bay	16	169	10.6	29	1
Johnson, Troy, St. Louis	15	308	20.5	49t	2
Baker, Stephen, N.Y. Giants	15	277	18.5	50	2
Banks, Gordon, Dallas	15	231	15.4	34	1
Kozlowski, Glen, Chicago	15	199	13.3	28	3
Mayes, Rueben, New Orleans	15	68	4.5	16	0
Davis, Kenneth, Green Bay	14	110	7.9	35	0
Allen, Anthony, Washington	13	337	25.9	88t	3
Didier, Clint, Washington	13	178	13.7	25	1
Giles, Jimmie, Detroit-Philadelphia	13	157	12.1	40t	1
Rubick, Rob, Detroit	13	147	11.3	22	1
Dawsey, Stacey, New Orleans	13	142	10.9	29	0
Wright, Adrian, Tampa Bay	13	98	7.5	15t	1
Bernard, Karl, Detroit	13	91	7.0	12	0
Garrity, Gregg, Philadelphia	12	242	20.2	41	2
Truvillion, Eric, Detroit	12	207	17.3	53t	1
Paskett, Keith, Green Bay	12	188	15.7	47t	1
Taylor, Lenny, Atlanta	12	171	14.3	28	1
Barksdale, Rod, Dallas	12	165	13.8	22	1
Heller, Ron, San Francisco	12	165	13.8	39t	3
McEwen, Craig, Washington	12	164	13.7	42	0
Dozier, D.J., Minnesota	12	89	7.4	20t	2
McConkey, Phil, N.Y. Giants	11	186	16.9	31	0
Settle, John, Atlanta	11	153	13.9	36	0
Holmes, Don, St. Louis	11	132	12.0	23	0
Rouson, Lee, N.Y. Giants	11	129	11.7	26t	1
Morris, Joe, N.Y. Giants	11	114	10.4	25	0
Hill, David, L.A. Rams	11	105	9.5	24	0
Cox, Arthur, Atlanta	11	101	9.2	19	0
Turner, Odessa, N.Y. Giants	10	195	19.5	36	1
Bennett, Lewis, N.Y. Giants	10	184	18.4	46t	1
Barney, Milton, Atlanta	10	175	17.5	32	2
Holloway, Steve, Tampa Bay	10	127	12.7	26	0
Lovelady, Edwin, N.Y. Giants	10	125	12.5	23t	2
Howard, Bobby, Tampa Bay	10	123	12.3	45	0
Carruth, Paul Ott, Green Bay	10	78	7.8	19	1
Taylor, John, San Francisco	9	151	16.8	34	0
Grymes, Darrell, Detroit	9	140	15.6	36t	2
Siano, Mike, Philadelphia	9	137	15.2	34	1
Pattison, Mark, New Orleans	9	132	14.7	36	0
Bell, Greg, Buffalo-L.A. Rams	9	96	10.7	32t	1
Cribbs, Joe, San Francisco	9	70	7.8	16	0
Williams, Michael, Atlanta	9	70	7.8	15	0
Freeman, Phil, Tampa Bay	8	141	17.6	64t	2
Mobley, Stacey, L.A. Rams	8	107	13.4	40t	1
Johnson, Billy, Atlanta	8	84	10.5	19	0
Scott, Patrick, Green Bay	8	79	9.9	16	0
Carthon, Maurice, N.Y. Giants	8	71	8.9	25	0
Bailey, Eric, Philadelphia	8	69	8.6	19	0
Wolfley, Ron, St. Louis	8	68	8.5	16	0
Brown, Reggie, Philadelphia	8	53	6.6	14	0
Francis, Jon, L.A. Rams	8	38	4.8	7	2
Jones, Hassan, Minnesota	7	189	27.0	58t	2
Burbage, Cornell, Dallas	7	168	24.0	77t	2
Byrd, Sylvester, Atlanta	7	125	17.9	33	0
Nichols, Mark, Detroit	7	87	12.4	23	0
Summers, Don, Green Bay	7	83	11.9	17	1
Edwards, Stan, Detroit	7	82	11.7	21	0
Anderson, Alfred, Minnesota	7	69	9.9	22	0
Haddix, Michael, Philadelphia	7	58	8.3	23	0
Suhey, Matt, Chicago	7	54	7.7	12	0
Kamana, John, Atlanta	7	51	7.3	15	1
Bradley, Danny, Detroit	7	50	7.1	14	2
Flowers, Kenny, Atlanta	7	50	7.1	24	0
Warren, Don, Washington	7	43	6.1	9	0
McGee, Buford, L.A. Rams	7	40	5.7	12	0
Hunter, Eddie, N.Y. Jets-Tampa Bay	7	28	4.0	8t	2
Fenney, Rick, Minnesota	7	27	3.9	18	0
Bowman, Kevin, Philadelphia	6	127	21.2	62t	1
Greer, Terry, San Francisco	6	111	18.5	50	1
Moore, Malcolm, L.A. Rams	6	107	17.8	26	1
Smith, Jeff, N.Y. Giants	6	72	12.0	19	0
House, Kevin, L.A. Rams	6	63	10.5	15t	1
Tyrrell, Tim, L.A. Rams	6	59	9.8	16	0
Robinson, Stacy, N.Y. Giants	6	58	9.7	14	2
Word, Barry, New Orleans	6	54	9.0	17	0
Willhite, Kevin, Green Bay	6	37	6.2	12	0
Badanjek, Rick, Atlanta	6	35	5.8	16	0
Scott, Malcolm, New Orleans	6	35	5.8	11	0
Gray, Mel, New Orleans	6	30	5.0	12	0
Waters, Mike, New Orleans	5	140	28.0	82t	1
Streater, Eric, Tampa Bay	5	117	23.4	61t	2
Wilson, Ted, Washington	5	112	22.4	64t	1
Brown, Charlie, Atlanta	5	103	20.6	23	0
Martin, Kelvin, Dallas	5	103	20.6	33	0

	No.	Yards	Avg.	Long	TD
Miller, Solomon, Tampa Bay	5	97	19.4	33	0
Carter, Cris, Philadelphia	5	84	16.8	25	2
Brewer, Chris, Chicago	5	56	11.2	19	1
Kab, Vyto, Detroit	5	54	10.8	28	0
Austin, Cliff, Tampa Bay	5	51	10.2	20	0
Heimuli, Lakei, Chicago	5	51	10.2	17	1
Ellerson, Gary, Detroit	5	48	9.6	23	1
Repko, Jay, Philadelphia	5	46	9.2	12	0
White, Gerald, Dallas	5	46	9.2	14	0
Womack, Jeff, Minnesota	5	46	9.2	23t	1
Ross, Alvin, Philadelphia	5	41	8.2	17	0
Williams, Van, N.Y. Giants	5	36	7.2	12	0
Kindt, Don, Chicago	5	34	6.8	11	1
Emery, Larry, Atlanta	5	31	6.2	13	0
Chandler, Thornton, Dallas	5	25	5.0	9	1
McGowan, Reggie, N.Y. Giants	4	111	27.8	63t	1
Knapczyk, Ken, Chicago	4	62	15.5	22	0
Gladney, Tony, San Francisco	4	60	15.0	19	0
Young, Mike, L.A. Rams	4	56	14.0	26	1
Gustafson, Jim, Minnesota	4	55	13.8	23	0
Stamps, Sylvester, Atlanta	4	40	10.0	19	0
DuBose, Doug, San Francisco	4	37	9.3	14	0
McDonald, James, L.A. Rams	4	31	7.8	13	2
Rogers, George, Washington	4	23	5.8	8	0
Williams, Scott, Detroit	4	16	4.0	7	1
Smith, Phil, L.A. Rams	3	95	31.7	51	0
Monroe, Carl, San Francisco	3	66	22.0	39t	1
Finch, Steve, Minnesota	3	54	18.0	20	0
Sanders, Thomas, Chicago	3	53	17.7	25	0
Parks, Rickey, Minnesota	3	46	15.3	19	0
Gonzalez, Leon, Atlanta	3	40	13.3	22	0
Mowatt, Zeke, N.Y. Giants	3	39	13.0	29	1
Clark, Robert, New Orleans	3	38	12.7	14	0
Orr, Terry, Washington	3	35	11.7	23	0
Dollinger, Tony, Detroit	3	25	8.3	15	0
Frye, Phil, Minnesota	3	25	8.3	12	0
Varajon, Mike, San Francisco	3	25	8.3	12	0
Parker, Freddie, Green Bay	3	22	7.3	13	0
Harrell, Samuel, Minnesota	3	20	6.7	8	0
Jones, E.J., Dallas	3	16	5.3	10	0
McIntosh, Joe, Atlanta	3	15	5.0	9	1
Griffin, Keith, Washington	3	13	4.3	6t	1
O'Neal, Ken, New Orleans	3	10	3.3	5	1
Verdin, Clarence, Washington	2	62	31.0	55	0
Thomas, Lavale, Green Bay	2	52	26.0	30t	1
Rodgers, Del, San Francisco	2	45	22.5	24	0
Jones, Brent, San Francisco	2	35	17.5	22	0
Granger, Norm, Atlanta	2	34	17.0	26	0
Spivey, Sebron, Dallas	2	34	17.0	25	0
Mullen, Gary, Chicago	2	33	16.5	20	0
Ingram, Mark, N.Y. Giants	2	32	16.0	18	0
Caravello, Joe, Washington	2	29	14.5	22	0
Harden, Derrick, Green Bay	2	29	14.5	15	0
Flagler, Terrence, San Francisco	2	28	14.0	24	0
Gillespie, Willie, Minnesota	2	28	14.0	14	0
DiRico, Bob, N.Y. Giants	2	22	11.0	15	0
Daugherty, Ron, Minnesota	2	21	10.5	13	0
Taylor, Gene, Tampa Bay	2	21	10.5	11	0
Sargent, Broderick, St. Louis	2	19	9.5	10	0
Harris, Steve, Minnesota	2	17	8.5	16	0
Rodenberger, Jeff, New Orleans	2	17	8.5	11	0
Wheeler, Mark, Detroit	2	17	8.5	9	0
Anderson, Ottis, N.Y. Giants	2	16	8.0	9	0
Brown, Ron, St. Louis	2	16	8.0	9	0
Glasgow, Brian, Chicago	2	16	8.0	11	0
Hilton, Carl, Minnesota	2	16	8.0	8t	2
Mosley, Anthony, Chicago	2	16	8.0	16	0
Wilson, Wayne, Washington	2	16	8.0	9	0
Alexander, Vincent, New Orleans	2	15	7.5	10	0
Walker, Dwight, New Orleans	2	15	7.5	8	0
Bland, Carl, Detroit	2	14	7.0	11t	1
Wilson, Brett, Minnesota	2	14	7.0	9	0
Jordan, Buford, New Orleans	2	13	6.5	11	0
Thomas, Andre, Minnesota	2	13	6.5	10	0
McAdoo, Derrick, St. Louis	2	12	6.0	6	0
Benson, Cliff, New Orleans	2	11	5.5	6	0
Fullwood, Brent, Green Bay	2	11	5.5	12	0
Robinson, Jacque, Philadelphia	2	9	4.5	5	0
Dennison, Glenn, Washington	2	8	4.0	5	0
Gladman, Charles, Tampa Bay	2	8	4.0	5	0
Butler, Jerry, Atlanta	2	7	3.5	4	0
Sharp, Dan, Atlanta	2	6	3.0	5	0
Walker, Adam, Minnesota	2	3	1.5	2	0
Paige, Tony, Detroit	2	1	0.5	3	0
Wolden, Al, Chicago	1	26	26.0	26	0
May, Marc, Minnesota	1	22	22.0	22	0
Witte, Mark, Detroit	1	19	19.0	19	0
Dixon, Dwayne, Tampa Bay	1	18	18.0	18	0
Redick, Corn, Green Bay	1	18	18.0	18	0
Weigel, Lee, Green Bay	1	17	17.0	17	0
Thomas, Curtland, New Orleans	1	14	14.0	14	0
Clemons, Topper, Philadelphia	1	13	13.0	13t	1
Henry, Bernard, L.A. Rams	1	13	13.0	13	0
Vital, Lionel, Washington	1	13	13.0	13	0
Walls, Herkie, Tampa Bay	1	13	13.0	13	0
Carter, Steve, Tampa Bay	1	12	12.0	12	0
Ricks, Harold, Tampa Bay	1	12	12.0	12	0
Scott, Chuck, Dallas	1	11	11.0	11	0
Schenk, Ed, Minnesota	1	10	10.0	10	0
Covington, Jamie, N.Y. Giants	1	9	9.0	9	0
Adams, David, Dallas	1	8	8.0	8	0
Bevelry, Dwight, New Orleans	1	8	8.0	8	0
Dressel, Chris, San Francisco	1	8	8.0	8	0
Evans, John, Atlanta	1	8	8.0	8	0
Harris, William, St. Louis	1	8	8.0	8	0
Jessie, Tim, Washington	1	8	8.0	8	0
Little, David, Philadelphia	1	8	8.0	8	0
Moore, Leonard, Minnesota	1	8	8.0	8	0
Morse, Bobby, Philadelphia	1	8	8.0	8	0
Hardy, Andre, San Francisco	1	7	7.0	7	0
Margerum, Ken, San Francisco	1	7	7.0	7	0
Bowers, Sam, Chicago	1	6	6.0	6	0
Fowler, Todd, Dallas	1	6	6.0	6	0
Hargrove, Jimmy, Green Bay	1	6	6.0	6	0
Lavette, Robert, Dallas	1	6	6.0	6	0
Mularkey, Mike, Minnesota	1	6	6.0	6	0
Park, Kaulana, N.Y. Giants	1	6	6.0	6	0
Bartalo, Steve, Tampa Bay	1	5	5.0	5	0
Blount, Alvin, Dallas	1	5	5.0	5	0
Coleman, Charles, N.Y. Giants	1	5	5.0	5	0
Johnson, Richard, Washington	1	5	5.0	5	0
Yarber, Eric, Washington	1	5	5.0	5	0
Kowgios, Nick, Detroit	1	3	3.0	3	0
Sydney, Harry, San Francisco	1	3	3.0	3	0
Oliver, Darryl, Atlanta	1	2	2.0	2	0
Middleton, Ron, Atlanta	1	1	1.0	1	0
Smith, Timmy, Washington	1	−2	−2.0	−2	0
Cunningham, Randall, Philadelphia	1	−3	−3.0	−3	0
Singletary, Reggie, Philadelphia	1	−11	−11.0	−11	0

t indicates touchdown.
Leader based on most passes caught.

Interceptions

Individual Champions
NFC: 9—Barry Wilburn, Washington
AFC: 6—Keith Bostic, Houston
6—Mark Kelso, Buffalo
6—Mike Prior, Indianapolis

Most Interceptions, Game
AFC: 3—Frank Minnifield, Cleveland vs. Houston, November 22
NFC: 3—Terry Kinard, N.Y. Giants vs. Dallas, September 20
3—Reggie Sutton, New Orleans vs. Chicago, October 18
3—Darrell Green, Washington vs. Detroit, November 15

Yards
AFC: 166—Vencie Glenn, San Diego
NFC: 163—Terry Kinard, N.Y. Giants

Longest
AFC: 103—Vencie Glenn, San Diego vs. Denver, November 29 (TD)
NFC: 100—Barry Wilburn, Washington at Minnesota, December 26 (TD)

Touchdowns
AFC: 2—Ronnie Lippett, New England
NFC: 1—By 12 players

Team Leaders, Interceptions
AFC: BUFFALO: 6, Mark Kelso; CINCINNATI: 3, Robert Jackson, David Fulcher; CLEVELAND: 4, Frank Minnifield, Felix Wright; DENVER: 4, Mike Harden; HOUSTON: 6, Keith Bostic; INDIANAPOLIS: 6, Mike Prior; KANSAS CITY: 3, Deron Cherry, Kevin Ross; L.A. RAIDERS: 4, Vann McElroy; MIAMI: 3, Glenn Blackwood, Paul Lankford; NEW ENGLAND: 4, Fred Marion; N.Y. JETS: 3, Harry Hamilton, Carl Howard, Rich Miano; PITTSBURGH: 5, Dwayne Woodruff; SAN DIEGO: 5, Billy Ray Smith; SEATTLE: 4, Ken Easley.
NFC: ATLANTA: 4, Bobby Butler; CHICAGO: 3, Dave Duerson; DALLAS: 5, Everson Walls; DETROIT: 6, James Griffin; GREEN BAY: 3, Dave Brown, Jim Bob Morris; L.A. RAMS: 2, Nolan Cromwell, Jerry Gray, LeRoy Irvin; MINNESOTA: 6, Joey Browner; NEW ORLEANS: 5, Reggie Sutton, Dave Waymer; N.Y. GIANTS: 5, Terry Kinard; PHILADELPHIA: 4, Elbert Foules; ST. LOUIS: 5, Travis Curtis; SAN FRANCISCO: 5, Don Griffin, Ronnie Lott; TAMPA BAY: 3, Paul Tripoli; WASHINGTON: 9, Barry Wilburn.

Team Champions
NFC: 30—New Orleans
AFC: 28—Denver

AFC Interceptions—Team

	No.	Yards	Avg.	Long	TD
Denver	28	403	14.4	52t	2
Pittsburgh	27	336	12.4	50t	5
Cleveland	23	366	15.9	76	2
Houston	23	274	11.9	73t	1
New England	21	307	14.6	51	2
Indianapolis	20	212	10.6	68	0
N.Y. Jets	18	239	13.3	45	0
Seattle	17	289	17.0	53	1
Buffalo	17	93	5.5	23	0
Miami	16	135	8.4	44	0
Cincinnati	14	187	13.4	44	0
San Diego	13	291	22.4	103t	2
L.A. Raiders	13	178	13.7	58	2
Kansas City	11	140	12.7	40	0
AFC Total	261	3450	—	103t	17
AFC Average	18.6	246.4	13.2	—	1.2

NFC Interceptions—Team

	No.	Yards	Avg.	Long	TD
New Orleans	30	280	9.3	35	0
Minnesota	26	303	11.7	36	0
San Francisco	25	205	8.2	34	0
Washington	23	329	14.3	100t	1
Dallas	23	208	9.0	30	2
Philadelphia	21	197	9.4	63	0
N.Y. Giants	20	263	13.2	70t	1
Detroit	19	290	15.3	48	1
Green Bay	18	220	12.2	73	0
L.A. Rams	16	305	19.1	49	2
Tampa Bay	16	248	15.5	42	2
Atlanta	15	182	12.1	40	0
St. Louis	14	167	11.9	60t	1
Chicago	13	69	5.3	23t	2
NFC Total	279	3266	—	100t	12
NFC Average	19.9	233.3	11.7	—	0.9
League Total	540	6716	—	103t	29
League Average	19.3	239.9	12.4	—	1.0

NFL Top 10 Interceptors

	No.	Yards	Avg.	Long	TD
Wilburn, Barry, Washington	9	135	15.0	100t	1
Griffin, James, Detroit	6	130	21.7	29	0
Browner, Joey, Minnesota	6	67	11.2	23	0
Prior, Mike, Indianapolis	6	57	9.5	38	0
Kelso, Mark, Buffalo	6	25	4.2	12	0
Bostic, Keith, Houston	6	−14	−2.3	7	0
Kinard, Terry, N.Y. Giants	5	163	32.6	70t	1
Woodruff, Dwayne, Pittsburgh	5	91	18.2	33t	1
Waymer, Dave, New Orleans	5	78	15.6	35	0
Sutton, Reggie, New Orleans	5	68	13.6	26	0
Curtis, Travis, St. Louis	5	65	13.0	31	0
Lott, Ronnie, San Francisco	5	62	12.4	34	0
Walls, Everson, Dallas	5	38	7.6	30	0
Smith, Billy Ray, San Diego	5	28	5.6	12	0
Griffin, Don, San Francisco	5	1	0.2	1	0

AFC Interceptions—Individual

	No.	Yards	Avg.	Long	TD
Prior, Mike, Indianapolis	6	57	9.5	38	0
Kelso, Mark, Buffalo	6	25	4.2	12	0
Bostic, Keith, Houston	6	−14	−2.3	7	0
Woodruff, Dwayne, Pittsburgh	5	91	18.2	33t	1
Smith, Billy Ray, San Diego	5	28	5.6	12	0
Glenn, Vencie, San Diego	4	166	41.5	103t	1
Wright, Felix, Cleveland	4	152	38.0	68	1
Harden, Mike, Denver	4	85	21.3	32	0
Bryant, Domingo, Houston	4	75	18.8	29	0
Marion, Fred, New England	4	53	13.3	25	0
Easley, Ken, Seattle	4	47	11.8	22	0
McElroy, Vann, L.A. Raiders	4	41	10.3	35t	1
Minnifield, Frank, Cleveland	4	24	6.0	27	0
Donaldson, Jeff, Houston	4	16	4.0	9	0
Clark, Kevin, Denver	3	105	35.0	50	0
Lippett, Ronnie, New England	3	103	34.3	45t	2
Robinson, Eugene, Seattle	3	75	25.0	44	0
Matthews, Clay, Cleveland	3	62	20.7	36	1
Cherry, Deron, Kansas City	3	58	19.3	30	0
Jackson, Robert, Cincinnati	3	49	16.3	29	0
Toran, Stacey, L.A. Raiders	3	48	16.0	48t	1
Jenkins, Mel, Seattle	3	46	15.3	34	0
Lankford, Paul, Miami	3	44	14.7	44	0
Ross, Kevin, Kansas City	3	40	13.3	40	0
Haynes, Mark, Denver	3	39	13.0	25	1
Fulcher, David, Cincinnati	3	30	10.0	28	0
Hall, Delton, Pittsburgh	3	29	9.7	25t	1
Howard, Carl, N.Y. Jets	3	29	9.7	29	0
Lilly, Tony, Denver	3	29	9.7	24	0
Hamilton, Harry, N.Y. Jets	3	25	8.3	25	0
Miano, Rich, N.Y. Jets	3	24	8.0	21	0
Mecklenburg, Karl, Denver	3	23	7.7	16	0
Everett, Thomas, Pittsburgh	3	22	7.3	21	0
Pitts, Ron, Buffalo	3	19	6.3	12	0
Blackwood, Glenn, Miami	3	17	5.7	17	0
Hinkle, Bryan, Pittsburgh	3	15	5.0	8	0
Robbins, Randy, Denver	3	9	3.0	9	0
Ryan, Jim, Denver	3	7	2.3	5	0
Dixon, Hanford, Cleveland	3	5	1.7	6	0
Tullis, Willie, Indianapolis	3	0	0.0	0	0
Robinson, Freddie, Indianapolis	2	86	43.0	68	0
Hunley, Ricky, Denver	2	64	32.0	52t	1
Glaze, Charles, Seattle	2	53	26.5	53	0
Gowdy, Cornell, Pittsburgh	2	50	25.0	45t	1
Breeden, Louis, Cincinnati	2	49	24.5	44	0
Brown, Steve, Houston	2	45	22.5	35	0
Radachowsky, George, N.Y. Jets	2	45	22.5	45	0
Lyles, Robert, Houston	2	42	21.0	27	0
Robinson, Mark, Kansas City	2	42	21.0	25	0
Daniel, Eugene, Indianapolis	2	34	17.0	34	0
Jones, Bryant, Indianapolis	2	26	13.0	23	0
Merriweather, Mike, Pittsburgh	2	26	13.0	15	0
Rockins, Chris, Cleveland	2	25	12.5	15	0
Clayborn, Raymond, New England	2	24	12.0	24	0
Smith, Dennis, Denver	2	21	10.5	15	0
Gibson, Ernest, New England	2	17	8.5	17	0
Harper, Mark, Cleveland	2	16	8.0	16	0
Randle, Tate, Miami	2	16	8.0	11	0
Burroughs, Derrick, Buffalo	2	11	5.5	14	0
Hooper, Trell, Miami	2	11	5.5	11	0
Judson, William, Miami	2	11	5.5	10	0
Haynes, Mike, L.A. Raiders	2	9	4.5	7	0
Hobley, Liffort, Miami	2	7	3.5	7	0
Radecic, Scott, Buffalo	2	4	2.0	4	0
Bowman, Jim, New England	2	3	1.5	3	0
Griffin, Larry, Pittsburgh	2	2	1.0	2	0
Smith, Daryl, Cincinnati	2	0	0.0	0	0
Patterson, Elvis, San Diego	1	75	75.0	75t	1
Seale, Eugene, Houston	1	73	73.0	73t	1
Anderson, Eddie, L.A. Raiders	1	58	58.0	58	0
Williams, Ed, New England	1	51	51.0	51	0
Shell, Donnie, Pittsburgh	1	50	50.0	50t	1
Young, Fredd, Seattle	1	50	50.0	50t	1
Woodson, Rod, Pittsburgh	1	45	45.0	45t	1
Robinson, Larry, N.Y. Jets	1	38	38.0	38	0
Allen, Patrick, Houston	1	37	37.0	24	0
Wilcots, Solomon, Cincinnati	1	37	37.0	37	0
Heath, Jo Jo, N.Y. Jets	1	35	35.0	35	0
Sowell, Robert, Miami	1	29	29.0	29	0
Horn, Alvin, Cleveland	1	28	28.0	28	0
James, Roland, New England	1	27	27.0	27	0
Clark, Steve, Buffalo	1	23	23.0	23	0
Banks, Chip, San Diego	1	20	20.0	20	0
Holmes, Jerry, N.Y. Jets	1	20	20.0	20	0
Niehoff, Robert, Cincinnati	1	19	19.0	19	0
McSwain, Rod, New England	1	17	17.0	17	0
Johnson, Eddie, Cleveland	1	11	11.0	11	0
Lucas, Tim, Denver	1	11	11.0	11	0
Taylor, Terry, Seattle	1	11	11.0	11	0
Dennison, Rick, Denver	1	10	10.0	10	0
Haslett, Jim, N.Y. Jets	1	9	9.0	9	0
Adams, Stefon, L.A. Raiders	1	8	8.0	8	0
Crable, Bob, N.Y. Jets	1	8	8.0	8	0
King, Linden, L.A. Raiders	1	8	8.0	8	0
Davis, Lee, Indianapolis	1	7	7.0	7	0
Schankweiler, Scott, Buffalo	1	7	7.0	7	0
Shegog, Ron, New England	1	7	7.0	7	0
Millen, Matt, L.A. Raiders	1	6	6.0	6	0
Hogan, Marc, N.Y. Jets	1	5	5.0	5	0
Caldwell, Tony, Seattle	1	4	4.0	4	0
Cokeley, Will, Buffalo	1	4	4.0	4	0
Holmes, Darryl, New England	1	4	4.0	4	0
Riley, Avon, Pittsburgh	1	4	4.0	4	0
Hunter, Patrick, Seattle	1	3	3.0	3	0
Johnson, Mike, Cleveland	1	3	3.0	3	0
Small, Donovan, Houston	1	3	3.0	3	0
Thomas, Eric, Cincinnati	1	3	3.0	3	0
Cooks, Johnie, Indianapolis	1	2	2.0	2	0
Plummer, Gary, San Diego	1	2	2.0	2	0
Sheffield, Chris, Pittsburgh	1	2	2.0	2	0
Rembert, Johnny, New England	1	1	1.0	1	0
Rose, Ken, N.Y. Jets	1	1	1.0	1	0
Brazley, Carl, San Diego	1	0	0.0	0	0
Brown, Bud, Miami	1	0	0.0	0	0

	No.	Yards	Avg.	Long	TD
Bryant, Trent, Kansas City	1	0	0.0	0	0
Bussey, Barney, Cincinnati	1	0	0.0	0	0
Cole, Robin, Pittsburgh	1	0	0.0	0	0
Cooper, Louis, Kansas City	1	0	0.0	0	0
Curry, Craig, Indianapolis	1	0	0.0	0	0
Davis, Wayne, Buffalo	1	0	0.0	0	0
Edwards, David, Pittsburgh	1	0	0.0	0	0
Glasgow, Nesby, Indianapolis	1	0	0.0	0	0
Johnson, Richard, Houston	1	0	0.0	0	0
Lewis, Albert, Kansas City	1	0	0.0	0	0
Moyer, Paul, Seattle	1	0	0.0	0	0
Perryman, Jim, Indianapolis	1	0	0.0	0	0
Peterson, Joe, New England	1	0	0.0	0	0
Robinson, DeJuan, Cleveland	1	0	0.0	0	0
Williams, Perry, New England	1	0	0.0	0	0
Williams, Ray, Pittsburgh	1	0	0.0	0	0
Wilson, Troy, Cleveland	1	0	0.0	0	0
Newsom, Tony, Houston	1	−3	−3.0	−3	0
Hairston, Carl, Cleveland	0	40	—	40	0

t indicates touchdown.
Leader based on most interceptions.

NFC Interceptions—Individual

	No.	Yards	Avg.	Long	TD
Wilburn, Barry, Washington	9	135	15.0	100t	1
Griffin, James, Detroit	6	130	21.7	29	0
Browner, Joey, Minnesota	6	67	11.2	23	0
Kinard, Terry, N.Y. Giants	5	163	32.6	70t	1
Waymer, Dave, New Orleans	5	78	15.6	35	0
Sutton, Reggie, New Orleans	5	68	13.6	26	0
Curtis, Travis, St. Louis	5	65	13.0	31	0
Lott, Ronnie, San Francisco	5	62	12.4	34	0
Walls, Everson, Dallas	5	38	7.6	30	0
Griffin, Don, San Francisco	5	1	0.2	1	0
Downs, Michael, Dallas	4	56	14.0	27	0
Butler, Bobby, Atlanta	4	48	12.0	31	0
Henderson, Wymon, Minnesota	4	33	8.3	17	0
Mack, Milton, New Orleans	4	32	8.0	26	0
Bowles, Todd, Washington	4	24	6.0	24	0
Foules, Elbert, Philadelphia	4	6	1.5	6	0
Morris, Jim Bob, Green Bay	3	135	45.0	73	0
Green, Darrell, Washington	3	65	21.7	56	0
Waters, Andre, Philadelphia	3	63	21.0	63	0
Lee, Carl, Minnesota	3	53	17.7	36	0
Galloway, Duane, Detroit	3	46	15.3	30	0
Jakes, Van, New Orleans	3	32	10.7	27	0
Bates, Bill, Dallas	3	28	9.3	28	0
Walton, Alvin, Washington	3	28	9.3	24	0
Harris, John, Minnesota	3	20	6.7	14	0
McNorton, Bruce, Detroit	3	20	6.7	20	0
Maxie, Brett, New Orleans	3	17	5.7	10	0
Tripoli, Paul, Tampa Bay	3	17	5.7	15t	1
Brown, Dave, Green Bay	3	16	5.3	11	0
Taylor, Lawrence, N.Y. Giants	3	16	5.3	15	0
Atkins, Gene, New Orleans	3	12	4.0	8	0
Haynes, Tommy, Dallas	3	7	2.3	7	0
Duerson, Dave, Chicago	3	0	0.0	0	0
Isom, Ray, Tampa Bay	2	67	33.5	38	0
Woods, Rick, Tampa Bay	2	63	31.5	42	0
Coleman, Monte, Washington	2	53	26.5	28	0
Williams, Jimmy, Detroit	2	51	25.5	48	0
Irvin, LeRoy, L.A. Rams	2	47	23.5	47t	1
Futrell, Bobby, Tampa Bay	2	46	23.0	23	0
Joyner, Seth, Philadelphia	2	42	21.0	29	0
Croudip, David, Atlanta	2	40	20.0	40	0
Gray, Jerry, L.A. Rams	2	35	17.5	35	0
McLemore, Dana, San Francisco	2	35	17.5	25	0
Walker, Kevin, Tampa Bay	2	30	15.0	30t	1
Collins, Mark, N.Y. Giants	2	28	14.0	28	0
Cromwell, Nolan, L.A. Rams	2	28	14.0	28	0
Gordon, Tim, Atlanta	2	28	14.0	27	0
Studwell, Scott, Minnesota	2	26	13.0	14	0
Headen, Andy, N.Y. Giants	2	25	12.5	20	0
Kullman, Mike, Philadelphia	2	25	12.5	13	0
Moore, Robert, Atlanta	2	23	11.5	18	0
Anderson, John, Green Bay	2	22	11.0	13	0
Rivera, Ron, Chicago	2	19	9.5	15	0
Francis, Ron, Dallas	2	18	9.0	18t	1
Huff, Charles, Atlanta	2	14	7.0	14	0
Jones, Rod, Tampa Bay	2	9	4.5	9	0
Brown, Jerome, Philadelphia	2	7	3.5	6	0
Holt, Issiac, Minnesota	2	7	3.5	7	0
Welch, Herb, N.Y. Giants	2	7	3.5	7	0
Holland, Johnny, Green Bay	2	4	2.0	4	0
Jackson, Rickey, New Orleans	2	4	2.0	4	0
Hoage, Terry, Philadelphia	2	3	1.5	3	0
Phillips, Reggie, Chicago	2	1	0.5	1	0
Cooper, Evan, Philadelphia	2	0	0.0	0	0
Douglass, Maurice, Chicago	2	0	0.0	0	0
Mack, Cedric, St. Louis	2	0	0.0	0	0
McKyer, Tim, San Francisco	2	0	0.0	0	0
Noga, Pete, St. Louis	1	60	60.0	60t	1
Johnson, Holbert, L.A. Rams	1	49	49.0	49	0
Jackson, Kirby, L.A. Rams	1	36	36.0	36	0
Smith, Ricky, Detroit	1	34	34.0	34t	1
Courtney, Matt, San Francisco	1	30	30.0	30	0
Solomon, Jesse, Minnesota	1	30	30.0	30	0
Young, Roynell, Philadelphia	1	30	30.0	30	0
Williamson, Greg, L.A. Rams	1	28	28.0	28	0
Guggemos, Neal, Minnesota	1	26	26.0	26	0
Jeffcoat, Jim, Dallas	1	26	26.0	26t	1
Owens, Mel, L.A. Rams	1	26	26.0	26	0
Greene, Kevin, L.A. Rams	1	25	25.0	25t	1
Junior, E.J., St. Louis	1	25	25.0	25	0
Smith, Wayne, Minnesota	1	24	24.0	24	0
McCray, Bruce, Chicago	1	23	23.0	23t	1
Penn, Jesse, Dallas	1	21	21.0	21	0
Gayle, Shaun, Chicago	1	20	20.0	20t	1
Moss, Gary, Atlanta	1	18	18.0	18	0
Gibson, Antonio, New Orleans	1	17	17.0	17	0
Mitchell, Michael, Washington	1	17	17.0	17	0
Williamson, Carlton, San Francisco	1	17	17.0	17	0
Louallen, Fletcher, Minnesota	1	16	16.0	16	0
Walter, Mike, San Francisco	1	16	16.0	16	0
Turner, Keena, San Francisco	1	15	15.0	15	0
Mansfield, Von, Green Bay	1	14	14.0	14	0
Rehage, Steve, N.Y. Giants	1	14	14.0	14	0
Bell, Anthony, St. Louis	1	13	13.0	13	0
Lockhart, Eugene, Dallas	1	13	13.0	13	0
Case, Scott, Atlanta	1	12	12.0	12	0
Evans, Byron, Philadelphia	1	12	12.0	12	0
Martin, Derrick, San Francisco	1	12	12.0	12	0
Cousineau, Tom, San Francisco	1	11	11.0	11	0
Greene, Tiger, Green Bay	1	11	11.0	11	0
Kemp, Bobby, Tampa Bay	1	11	11.0	11	0
Wilcher, Mike, L.A. Rams	1	11	11.0	11	0
DeRose, Dan, N.Y. Giants	1	10	10.0	10	0
Leach, Scott, New Orleans	1	10	10.0	10	0
Noble, Brian, Green Bay	1	10	10.0	10	0
Swilling, Pat, New Orleans	1	10	10.0	10	0
Brown, Cedrick, Philadelphia	1	9	9.0	9	0
Hicks, Cliff, L.A. Rams	1	9	9.0	9	0
Ekern, Carl, L.A. Rams	1	7	7.0	7	0
Gage, Steve, Washington	1	7	7.0	7	0
Carreker, Alphonso, Green Bay	1	6	6.0	6	0
Norris, Jon, Chicago	1	6	6.0	6	0
Gant, Brian, Tampa Bay	1	5	5.0	5	0
Gibson, Dennis, Detroit	1	5	5.0	5	0
Nixon, Tory, San Francisco	1	5	5.0	5	0
Brown, Donald, N.Y. Giants	1	4	4.0	4	0
Mathis, Mark, St. Louis	1	4	4.0	4	0
Sutton, Mickey, L.A. Rams	1	4	4.0	4	0
Benson, Charles, Detroit	1	2	2.0	2	0
Cherry, Raphel, Detroit	1	2	2.0	2	0
Johnson, Kenneth, Green Bay	1	2	2.0	2	0
Hill, Kenny, N.Y. Giants	1	1	1.0	1	0
Howard, David, Minnesota	1	1	1.0	1	0
Scott, Victor, Dallas	1	1	1.0	1	0
Shell, Todd, San Francisco	1	1	1.0	1	0
Banks, Carl, N.Y. Giants	1	0	0.0	0	0
Carter, Carl, St. Louis	1	0	0.0	0	0
Fahnhorst, Jim, San Francisco	1	0	0.0	0	0
Green, Alex, Dallas	1	0	0.0	0	0
Hall, Alvin, Detroit	1	0	0.0	0	0
Harrison, Anthony, Green Bay	1	0	0.0	0	0
Holmoe, Tom, San Francisco	1	0	0.0	0	0
Jackson, Vestee, Chicago	1	0	0.0	0	0
Johnson, Johnnie, L.A. Rams	1	0	0.0	0	0
Johnson, Vaughan, New Orleans	1	0	0.0	0	0
Lee, Mark, Green Bay	1	0	0.0	0	0
McColl, Milt, San Francisco	1	0	0.0	0	0
Melka, Jim, Green Bay	1	0	0.0	0	0
Montoute, Sankar, Tampa Bay	1	0	0.0	0	0
Poe, Johnnie, New Orleans	1	0	0.0	0	0
Saddler, Rod, St. Louis	1	0	0.0	0	0
Thomas, Henry, Minnesota	1	0	0.0	0	0
West, Troy, Philadelphia	1	0	0.0	0	0
White, Randy, Dallas	1	0	0.0	0	0
Young, Lonnie, St. Louis	1	0	0.0	0	0
Britt, James, Atlanta	1	−1	−1.0	4	0
Williams, Perry, N.Y. Giants	1	−5	−5.0	−5	0

t indicates touchdown.
Leader based on most interceptions.

Punting

Individual Champions
NFC: 44.0—Rick Donnelly, Atlanta
AFC: 42.9—Ralf Mojsiejenko, San Diego
Net Average
NFC: 39.6—Jim Arnold, Detroit
AFC: 35.6—Scott Fulhage, Cincinnati
Longest
AFC: 77—Reggie Roby, Miami at Buffalo, November 29
NFC: 77—Steve Cox, Washington at Buffalo, November 1
Most Punts
NFC: 82—John Teltschik, Philadelphia
AFC: 67—Ralf Mojsiejenko, San Diego
Most Punts, Game
NFC: 15—John Teltschik, Philadelphia vs. N.Y. Giants, December 6 (OT)
AFC: 10—Scott Fulhage, Cincinnati vs. San Diego, October 4
Team Champions
AFC: 42.0—San Diego
NFC: 41.8—Detroit

AFC Punting—Team

	Net Punts	Gross Yards	Long	Gross Avg.	TB	Blk.	Opp. Ret.	Ret. Yards	In 20	Net Avg.
San Diego	84	3529	57	42.0	13	0	43	429	16	33.8
Cincinnati	73	2995	58	41.0	9	0	42	299	13	34.5
Kansas City	69	2789	55	40.4	6	0	43	442	13	32.3
Pittsburgh	82	3297	57	40.2	17	2	46	395	13	31.2
Denver	65	2595	61	39.9	6	2	34	424	16	31.6
L.A. Raiders	71	2796	63	39.4	5	2	34	256	15	34.4
Houston	75	2929	59	39.1	6	1	43	454	7	31.4
Seattle	61	2370	63	38.9	5	0	32	251	18	33.1
Miami	63	2424	77	38.5	3	1	26	141	20	35.3
Buffalo	83	3173	67	38.2	9	1	35	179	23	33.9
Indianapolis	78	2941	63	37.7	8	3	39	376	15	30.8
New England	89	3350	73	37.6	12	2	41	397	15	30.5
N.Y. Jets	82	3046	58	37.1	7	0	33	162	14	33.5
Cleveland	57	2102	66	36.9	8	0	17	93	14	32.4
AFC Total	1,032	40,336	77	—	114	14	508	4,298	212	—
AFC Average	73.7	2,881.1	—	39.1	8.1	1.0	36.3	307.0	15.1	32.7

NFC Punting—Team

	Net Punts	Gross Yards	Long	Gross Avg.	TB	Blk.	Opp. Ret.	Ret. Yards	In 20	Net Avg.
Detroit	70	2927	60	41.8	6	0	34	177	22	37.6
New Orleans	63	2587	60	41.1	7	0	29	199	23	35.7
L.A. Rams	77	3140	62	40.8	4	1	43	317	19	35.6
Atlanta	83	3375	62	40.7	11	2	48	541	11	31.5
N.Y. Giants	91	3604	64	39.6	7	2	51	811	14	29.2
Dallas	84	3324	63	39.6	6	0	45	376	21	33.7
Green Bay	93	3659	65	39.3	6	1	54	422	17	33.5
Chicago	62	2439	71	39.3	8	2	26	339	15	31.3
Tampa Bay	88	3455	61	39.3	10	0	50	621	15	29.9
Washington	78	3053	77	39.1	8	1	37	231	19	34.1
Minnesota	79	3077	54	38.9	5	1	44	424	11	32.3
St. Louis	70	2663	68	38.0	5	1	36	489	16	29.6
San Francisco	68	2541	56	37.4	8	1	29	195	16	32.1
Philadelphia	102	3770	60	37.0	5	3	54	469	18	31.4
NFC Total	1,108	43,614	77	—	96	15	580	5,611	237	—
NFC Average	79.1	3,115.3	—	39.4	6.9	1.1	41.4	400.8	16.9	32.6
League Total	2,140	83,950	77	—	210	29	1,088	9,909	449	—
League Average	76.4	2,998.2	—	39.2	7.5	1.0	38.9	353.9	16.0	32.6

NFL Top 10 Punters

	Net Punts	Gross Yards	Long	Gross Avg.	Total Punts	TB	Blk.	Opp. Ret.	Ret. Yards	In 20	Net Avg.
Donnelly, Rick, Atlanta	61	2686	62	44.0	63	8	2	38	501	9	32.1
Arnold, Jim, Detroit	46	2007	60	43.6	46	4	0	22	104	17	39.6
Mojsiejenko, Ralf, San Diego	67	2875	57	42.9	67	12	0	37	392	15	33.5
Landeta, Sean, N.Y. Giants	65	2773	64	42.7	66	6	1	38	606	13	31.0
Newsome, Harry, Pittsburgh	64	2678	57	41.8	65	13	1	36	373	8	31.5
Fulhage, Scott, Cincinnati	52	2168	58	41.7	52	5	0	31	216	10	35.6
Hatcher, Dale, L.A. Rams	76	3140	62	41.3	77	4	1	43	317	19	35.6
Horan, Mike, Denver	44	1807	61	41.1	46	5	2	22	186	11	33.1
Bracken, Don, Green Bay	72	2947	65	40.9	73	5	1	45	354	13	34.2
Goodburn, Kelly, Kansas City	59	2412	55	40.9	59	5	0	39	403	13	32.4

AFC Punting—Individual

	Net Punts	Gross Yards	Long	Gross Avg.	Total Punts	TB	Blk.	Opp. Ret.	Ret. Yards	In 20	Net Avg.
Mojsiejenko, Ralf, San Diego	67	2875	57	42.9	67	12	0	37	392	15	33.5
Newsome, Harry, Pittsburgh	64	2678	57	41.8	65	13	1	36	373	8	31.5
Fulhage, Scott, Cincinnati	52	2168	58	41.7	52	5	0	31	216	10	35.6
Horan, Mike, Denver	44	1807	61	41.1	46	5	2	22	186	11	33.1
Goodburn, Kelly, Kansas City	59	2412	55	40.9	59	5	0	39	403	13	32.4
Talley, Stan, L.A. Raiders	56	2277	63	40.7	57	5	1	28	207	13	34.6
Gossett, Jeff, Cleveland-Houston	44	1777	55	40.4	45	6	1	23	234	4	31.6
Camarillo, Rich, New England	62	2489	73	40.1	63	8	1	34	333	14	31.7
Rodriguez, Ruben, Seattle	47	1880	63	40.0	47	5	0	22	182	17	34.0
Stark, Rohn, Indianapolis	61	2440	63	40.0	63	7	2	33	353	12	30.9
Johnson, Lee, Houston-Cleveland	50	1969	66	39.4	50	4	0	25	249	8	32.8
Kidd, John, Buffalo	64	2495	67	39.0	64	7	0	26	148	20	34.5
Jennings, Dave, N.Y. Jets	64	2444	58	38.2	64	6	0	24	100	12	34.8
Non-Qualifiers											
Roby, Reggie, Miami	32	1371	77	42.8	32	3	0	16	87	8	38.3
Herline, Alan, New England	25	861	50	34.4	26	4	1	7	64	1	27.6
Giacomarro, Ralph, Denver	18	757	50	42.1	18	1	0	12	238	4	27.7
O'Connor, Tom, N.Y. Jets	18	602	47	33.4	18	1	0	9	62	2	28.9
Winslow, George, Cleveland	18	616	45	34.2	18	2	0	6	11	5	31.4
Partridge, Rick, Buffalo	18	678	52	37.7	19	2	1	9	31	3	31.9
Prokop, Joe, San Diego	17	654	50	38.5	17	1	0	6	37	1	35.1
Bruno, John, Pittsburgh	16	619	56	38.7	17	4	1	10	22	5	30.4
Gore, Stacy, Miami	14	502	60	35.9	14	0	0	4	21	6	34.4
Gamache, Vince, L.A. Raiders	13	519	53	39.9	14	0	1	6	49	2	33.6
Kiel, Blair, Indianapolis	12	440	50	36.7	12	1	0	5	16	3	33.7
Griffith, Russell, Seattle	11	386	51	35.1	11	0	0	7	57	1	29.9
Walters, Dale, Cleveland	11	400	56	36.4	11	1	0	2	28	2	32.0
Colbert, Lewis, Kansas City	10	377	47	37.7	10	1	0	4	39	0	31.8
Strock, Don, Miami	9	277	44	30.8	9	0	0	1	0	5	30.8
Superick, Steve, Houston	8	269	45	33.6	8	1	0	4	25	2	28.0
Hayes, Jeff, Miami	7	274	51	39.1	8	0	1	5	33	1	30.1
Bowman, Barry, Seattle	3	104	36	34.7	3	0	0	3	12	0	30.7
Esiason, Boomer, Cincinnati	2	68	41	34.0	2	0	0	1	12	1	28.0
Colquitt, Craig, Indianapolis	2	61	33	30.5	3	0	1	1	7	0	18.0
Elway, John, Denver	1	31	31	31.0	1	0	0	0	0	1	31.0

Leader based on gross average, minimum 38 punts.

NFC Punting—Individual

	Net Punts	Gross Yards	Long	Gross Avg.	Total Punts	TB	Blk.	Opp. Ret.	Ret. Yards	In 20	Net Avg.
Donnelly, Rick, Atlanta	61	2686	62	44.0	63	8	2	38	501	9	32.1
Arnold, Jim, Detroit	46	2007	60	43.6	46	4	0	22	104	17	39.6
Landeta, Sean, N.Y. Giants	65	2773	64	42.7	66	6	1	38	606	13	31.0
Hatcher, Dale, L.A. Rams	76	3140	62	41.3	77	4	1	43	317	19	35.6
Bracken, Don, Green Bay	72	2947	65	40.9	73	5	1	45	354	13	34.2
Cox, Steve, Washington	63	2571	77	40.8	64	7	1	29	193	14	35.0
Hansen, Brian, New Orleans	52	2104	60	40.5	52	6	0	23	135	19	35.6
Horne, Greg, Cincinnati-St. Louis	43	1730	57	40.2	43	7	0	25	237	6	31.5
Coleman, Greg, Minnesota	45	1786	54	39.7	46	3	1	30	323	5	30.5
Saxon, Mike, Dallas	68	2685	63	39.5	68	5	0	36	260	20	34.2
Runager, Max, San Francisco	55	2157	56	39.2	56	7	1	23	167	13	33.0
Garcia, Frank, Tampa Bay	62	2409	58	38.9	62	5	0	38	553	12	28.3
Teltschik, John, Philadelphia	82	3131	60	38.2	83	4	1	47	399	13	32.0
Cater, Greg, St. Louis	39	1470	68	37.7	40	2	1	17	204	10	30.7
Non-Qualifiers											
Wagner, Bryan, Chicago	36	1461	71	40.6	37	4	1	12	195	9	32.1
Criswell, Ray, Tampa Bay	26	1046	61	40.2	26	5	0	12	68	3	33.8
Renner, Bill, Green Bay	20	712	49	35.6	20	1	0	9	68	4	31.2
Scribner, Bucky, Minnesota	20	827	54	41.3	20	1	0	10	79	4	36.4
Brown, Kevin, Chicago	18	742	58	41.2	19	4	1	11	108	4	29.2
Barnhardt, Tommy, New Orleans-Chicago	17	719	52	42.3	17	1	0	9	100	6	35.2
Sawyer, Buzz, Dallas	16	639	54	39.9	16	1	0	9	116	1	31.4
Weil, Jack, Washington	14	482	51	34.4	14	1	0	8	38	5	30.3
Moore, Dana, N.Y. Giants	14	486	46	34.7	15	0	1	9	154	0	22.1
Bruno, Dave, Minnesota	13	464	53	35.7	13	1	0	4	22	2	32.5
Asmus, Jim, San Francisco	12	384	51	32.0	12	1	0	6	28	3	28.0
Royals, Mark, St. Louis-Philadelphia	11	431	48	39.2	11	1	0	6	155	3	23.3
Miller, Jim, N.Y. Giants	10	345	53	34.5	10	1	0	4	51	1	27.4
Jacobs, Dave, Philadelphia	10	369	44	36.9	11	0	1	5	34	4	30.5
Berry, Louis, Atlanta	7	258	51	36.9	7	1	0	5	15	0	31.9
Kinzer, Matt, Detroit	7	238	42	34.0	7	0	0	3	35	2	29.0
Black, Mike, Detroit	6	233	47	38.8	6	0	0	4	12	1	36.8
Davis, Greg, Atlanta	6	191	55	31.8	6	1	0	2	6	0	27.5
Misko, John, Detroit	6	242	51	40.3	6	0	0	4	23	1	36.5
Starnes, John, Atlanta	6	203	49	33.8	6	0	0	3	19	2	30.7
Murray, Ed, Detroit	4	155	46	38.8	4	2	0	1	3	1	28.0
Merkens, Guido, Philadelphia	2	61	38	30.5	3	0	1	0	0	0	20.3
Erxleben, Russell, Detroit	1	52	52	52.0	1	0	0	0	0	0	52.0
Luckhurst, Mick, Atlanta	1	37	37	37.0	1	1	0	0	0	0	17.0

Leader based on gross average, minimum 38 punts.

Punt Returns

Individual Champions (Average)
NFC: 14.7—Mel Gray, New Orleans
AFC: 12.6—Bobby Joe Edmonds, Seattle

Yards
NFC: 550—Vai Sikahema, St. Louis
AFC: 400—Lionel James, San Diego

Most Yards, Game
AFC: 144—Kevin Clark, Denver vs. San Diego, December 27 (6 returns)
NFC: 142—Ted Wilson, Washington vs. N.Y. Giants, October 11 (7 returns)

Longest
NFC: 94—Dennis McKinnon, Chicago vs. N.Y. Giants, September 14 (TD)
AFC: 91—JoJo Townsell, N.Y. Jets vs. Seattle, November 9 (TD)

Most Returns
NFC: 44—Vai Sikahema, St. Louis
AFC: 34—Gerald McNeil, Cleveland

Most Returns, Game
NFC: 9—Phil McConkey, N.Y. Giants vs. Philadelphia, December 6 (OT) (112 yards)
AFC: 6—Louis Lipps, Pittsburgh vs. San Francisco, September 13 (42 yards)
6—Kenny Johnson, Houston vs. Denver, October 4 (56 yards)
6—Shane Swanson, Denver vs. Kansas City, October 18 (112 yards)
6—Chris Woods, L.A. Raiders vs. Minnesota, November 8 (29 yards)
6—Michael Clemons, Kansas City vs. Green Bay, November 22 (79 yards)
6—Lionel James, San Diego vs. Houston, December 6 (74 yards)
6—Kevin Clark, Denver vs. San Diego, December 27 (144 yards)

Fair Catches
NFC: 14—Phil McConkey, N.Y. Giants
AFC: 12—Ron Pitts, Buffalo

Touchdowns
NFC: 2—Dennis McKinnon, Chicago
AFC: 1—Rick Calhoun, L.A. Raiders
1—Kevin Clark, Denver
1—Jitter Fields, Kansas City
1—Michael Harper, N.Y. Jets
1—Lionel James, San Diego
1—JoJo Townsell, N.Y. Jets

Team Champions
NFC: 12.5—St. Louis
AFC: 11.8—N.Y. Jets

AFC Punt Returns—Team

	No.	FC	Yards	Avg.	Long	TD
N.Y. Jets	42	12	497	11.8	91t	2
San Diego	45	9	508	11.3	81t	1
Cleveland	44	12	487	11.1	40	0
Kansas City	32	8	346	10.8	85t	1
Denver	48	4	486	10.1	71t	1
Seattle	32	8	322	10.1	40	0
Cincinnati	34	9	293	8.6	21	0
New England	25	17	213	8.5	36	0
L.A. Raiders	44	7	356	8.1	55t	1
Miami	37	13	290	7.8	31	0
Buffalo	31	15	232	7.5	23	0
Pittsburgh	36	5	244	6.8	20	0
Houston	37	14	249	6.7	26	0
Indianapolis	38	12	210	5.5	17	0
AFC Total	525	145	4,733	—	91t	6
AFC Average	37.5	10.4	338.1	9.0	—	0.4

NFC Punt Returns—Team

	No.	FC	Yards	Avg.	Long	TD
St. Louis	44	7	550	12.5	76t	1
Minnesota	36	12	420	11.7	78t	1
New Orleans	41	7	468	11.4	80	0
Washington	56	10	615	11.0	73	0
San Francisco	34	9	365	10.7	83t	1
Chicago	50	6	484	9.7	94t	2
Detroit	35	12	303	8.7	54	0
Dallas	41	6	353	8.6	38	0
Tampa Bay	31	8	257	8.3	22	0
N.Y. Giants	55	14	448	8.1	37	0
Atlanta	31	7	221	7.1	45	0
Green Bay	35	6	245	7.0	48	0
L.A. Rams	40	10	245	6.1	29	0
Philadelphia	34	24	202	5.9	37	0
NFC Total	563	138	5,176	—	94t	5
NFC Average	40.2	9.9	369.7	9.2	—	0.4
League Total	1,088	283	9,909	—	94t	11
League Average	38.9	10.1	353.9	9.1	—	0.4

NFL Top 10 Punt Returners

	No.	FC	Yards	Avg.	Long	TD
Gray, Mel, New Orleans	24	5	352	14.7	80	0
McLemore, Dana, San Francisco	21	7	265	12.6	83t	1
Edmonds, Bobby Joe, Seattle	20	4	251	12.6	40	0
James, Lionel, San Diego	32	7	400	12.5	81t	1
Lewis, Leo, Minnesota	22	7	275	12.5	78t	1
Sikahema, Vai, St. Louis	44	7	550	12.5	76t	1
Townsell, JoJo, N.Y. Jets	32	11	381	11.9	91t	1
McNeil, Gerald, Cleveland	34	9	386	11.4	40	0
Mandley, Pete, Detroit	23	6	250	10.9	54	0
McKinnon, Dennis, Chicago	40	4	405	10.1	94t	2

AFC Punt Returns—Individual

	No.	FC	Yards	Avg.	Long	TD
Edmonds, Bobby Joe, Seattle	20	4	251	12.6	40	0
James, Lionel, San Diego	32	7	400	12.5	81t	1
Townsell, JoJo, N.Y. Jets	32	11	381	11.9	91t	1
McNeil, Gerald, Cleveland	34	9	386	11.4	40	0
Martin, Mike, Cincinnati	28	5	277	9.9	21	0
Clemons, Michael, Kansas City	19	4	162	8.5	44	0
Schwedes, Scott, Miami	24	6	203	8.5	31	0
Johnson, Kenny, Houston	24	5	196	8.2	26	0
Woods, Chris, L.A. Raiders	26	4	189	7.3	34	0
Pitts, Ron, Buffalo	23	12	149	6.5	19	0
Brooks, Bill, Indianapolis	22	9	136	6.2	17	0
Non-Qualifiers						
Clark, Kevin, Denver	18	1	233	12.9	71t	1
Fryar, Irving, New England	18	12	174	9.7	36	0
Woodson, Rod, Pittsburgh	16	1	135	8.4	20	0
Nattiel, Ricky, Denver	12	1	73	6.1	14	0
Wilson, Troy, Cleveland	10	3	101	10.1	17	0
Williams, Alphonso, San Diego	10	1	96	9.6	25	0
Swanson, Shane, Denver	9	1	132	14.7	33	0
Caterbone, Michael, Miami	9	4	78	8.7	21	0
Johnson, Kelley, Indianapolis	9	2	42	4.7	12	0
Fields, Jitter, Kansas City	8	3	161	20.1	85t	1
Calhoun, Rick, L.A. Raiders	8	1	92	11.5	55t	1
McFadden, Thad, Buffalo	8	3	83	10.4	23	0
Duncan, Curtis, Houston	8	2	23	2.9	9	0
Lipps, Louis, Pittsburgh	7	1	46	6.6	12	0
Anderson, Mel, Pittsburgh	7	1	38	5.4	10	0
Teal, Jimmy, Seattle	6	4	38	6.3	13	0
Hollis, David, Seattle	6	0	33	5.5	15	0
Adams, Stefon, L.A. Raiders	5	2	39	7.8	12	0
Linne, Larry, New England	5	2	22	4.4	16	0
Brown, Kenneth, Cincinnati	5	3	16	3.2	10	0
Harper, Michael, N.Y. Jets	4	1	93	23.3	78t	1
Tullis, Willie, Indianapolis	4	1	27	6.8	10	0
Everett, Thomas, Pittsburgh	4	2	22	5.5	11	0
Willhite, Gerald, Denver	4	1	22	5.5	9	0
Rome, Tag, San Diego	3	1	12	4.0	6	0
Drewrey, Willie, Houston	3	1	11	3.7	5	0
Fellows, Ron, L.A. Raiders	2	0	19	9.5	18	0
Walters, Joey, Houston	2	6	19	9.5	12	0
Harkey, Lance, L.A. Raiders	2	0	17	8.5	9	0
Harden, Mike, Denver	2	0	11	5.5	7	0
Smith, Reggie, N.Y. Jets	2	0	9	4.5	7	0
Brown, Bud, Miami	2	1	8	4.0	8	0
Foster, Derrick, N.Y. Jets	2	0	8	4.0	4	0
Lilly, Tony, Denver	2	0	6	3.0	4	0
Simmons, John, Indianapolis	2	0	5	2.5	5	0
Wyatt, Kevin, Kansas City	2	0	4	2.0	4	0
Lockett, Charles, Pittsburgh	2	0	3	1.5	5	0
Starring, Stephen, New England	1	1	17	17.0	17	0
Colbert, Darrell, Kansas City	1	0	11	11.0	11	0
Johnson, Vance, Denver	1	0	9	9.0	9	0
Montagne, Dave, Kansas City	1	1	8	8.0	8	0
Sohn, Kurt, N.Y. Jets	1	0	6	6.0	6	0
Blackwood, Glenn, Miami	1	1	1	1.0	1	0
Ahrens, Dave, Indianapolis	1	0	0	0.0	0	0
Cocroft, Sherman, Kansas City	1	0	0	0.0	0	0
Collins, Trent, N.Y. Jets	1	0	0	0.0	0	0
Davis, James, L.A. Raiders	1	0	0	0.0	0	0
Hooper, Trell, Miami	1	0	0	0.0	0	0
Horton, Ray, Cincinnati	1	0	0	0.0	0	0
Marion, Fred, New England	1	2	0	0.0	0	0
Jackson, Robert, Cincinnati	0	1	0	—	—	0
Stradford, Troy, Miami	0	1	0	—	—	0

t indicates touchdown.
Leader based on average return, minimum 19 returns.

NFC Punt Returns—Individual

	No.	FC	Yards	Avg.	Long	TD
Gray, Mel, New Orleans	24	5	352	14.7	80	0
McLemore, Dana, San Francisco	21	7	265	12.6	83t	1
Lewis, Leo, Minnesota	22	7	275	12.5	78t	1
Sikahema, Vai, St. Louis	44	7	550	12.5	76t	1
Mandley, Pete, Detroit	23	6	250	10.9	54	0
McKinnon, Dennis, Chicago	40	4	405	10.1	94t	2
Martin, Kelvin, Dallas	22	2	216	9.8	38	0
McConkey, Phil, N.Y. Giants	42	14	394	9.4	37	0
Futrell, Bobby, Tampa Bay	24	6	213	8.9	22	0
Johnson, Billy, Atlanta	21	6	168	8.0	45	0
Yarber, Eric, Washington	37	9	273	7.4	33	0
Stanley, Walter, Green Bay	28	4	173	6.2	48	0
Morse, Bobby, Philadelphia	20	13	121	6.1	23	0
Non-Qualifiers						
Ellard, Henry, L.A. Rams	15	6	107	7.1	29	0
Martin, Eric, New Orleans	14	2	88	6.3	15	0
Hicks, Cliff, L.A. Rams	13	1	110	8.5	26	0
Bradley, Danny, Detroit	12	5	53	4.4	13	0
Lovelady, Edwin, N.Y. Giants	10	0	38	3.8	14	0
Griffin, Don, San Francisco	9	2	79	8.8	29	0
Wilson, Ted, Washington	8	0	143	17.9	40	0
Edwards, Kelvin, Dallas	8	1	75	9.4	13	0
Duarte, George, Chicago	8	1	64	8.0	16	0
Bess, Rufus, Minnesota	7	3	86	12.3	28	0
Shepard, Derrick, Washington	6	0	146	24.3	73	0
Scott, Patrick, Green Bay	6	2	71	11.8	36	0
Green, Darrell, Washington	5	1	53	10.6	15	0
Banks, Gordon, Dallas	5	1	33	6.6	12	0
Burbage, Cornell, Dallas	5	1	29	5.8	13	0
Barney, Milton, Atlanta	5	0	28	5.6	11	0
Bowman, Kevin, Philadelphia	4	1	43	10.8	37	0
Richardson, Greg, Minnesota	4	2	19	4.8	7	0
Garrity, Gregg, Philadelphia	4	10	16	4.0	10	0
Walls, Herkie, Tampa Bay	4	2	12	3.0	11	0
Johnson, Sam, L.A. Rams	4	1	−4	−1.0	5	0
Carter, Anthony, Minnesota	3	0	40	13.3	22	0
Curry, Ivory, Tampa Bay	3	0	32	10.7	14	0
Baker, Stephen, N.Y. Giants	3	0	16	5.3	6	0
Moss, Gary, Atlanta	3	1	15	5.0	11	0
Rutledge, Craig, L.A. Rams	3	0	10	3.3	7	0
Caterbone, Thomas, Philadelphia	2	0	13	6.5	13	0
Martin, Derrick, San Francisco	2	0	12	6.0	9	0
Butler, Jerry, Atlanta	2	0	10	5.0	9	0
Ulmer, Mike, Philadelphia	2	0	10	5.0	5	0
Smith, Phil, L.A. Rams	2	0	5	2.5	5	0
Jordan, Buford, New Orleans	1	0	13	13.0	13	0
Maxie, Brett, New Orleans	1	0	12	12.0	12	0
Mobley, Stacey, L.A. Rams	1	0	12	12.0	12	0
Duerson, Dave, Chicago	1	1	10	10.0	10	0
Taylor, John, San Francisco	1	0	9	9.0	9	0
Jeffries, Eric, Chicago	1	0	5	5.0	5	0
Johnson, Johnnie, L.A. Rams	1	0	5	5.0	5	0
Cook, Toi, New Orleans	1	0	3	3.0	3	0
Morris, Lee, Green Bay	1	0	1	1.0	1	0
Irvin, LeRoy, L.A. Rams	1	0	0	0.0	0	0
Johnson, Alonzo, Philadelphia	1	0	0	0.0	0	0
Livingston, Bruce, Dallas	1	0	0	0.0	0	0
Pollard, Darryl, San Francisco	1	0	0	0.0	0	0
Brown, Cedrick, Philadelphia	1	0	−1	−1.0	−1	0
Bland, Carl, Detroit	0	1	0	—	—	0
Lavette, Robert, Dallas	0	1	0	—	—	0
Sutton, Mickey, L.A. Rams	0	2	0	—	—	0

t indicates touchdown.
Leader based on average return, minimum 19 returns.

Kickoff Returns

Individual Champions (Average)
NFC: 27.5—Sylvester Stamps, Atlanta
AFC: 24.3—Paul Palmer, Kansas City

Yards
AFC: 923—Paul Palmer, Kansas City
NFC: 808—Neal Guggemos, Minnesota

Most Yards, Game
AFC: 221—Paul Palmer, Kansas City at Seattle, September 20 (9 returns)
NFC: 193—Sylvester Stamps, Atlanta at Houston, October 25 (5 returns)

Longest
NFC: 97—Sylvester Stamps, Atlanta at San Francisco, December 20 (TD)
AFC: 95—Paul Palmer, Kansas City vs. San Diego, September 13 (TD)

Most Returns
AFC: 38—Paul Palmer, Kansas City
NFC: 36—Neal Guggemos, Minnesota

Most Returns, Game
AFC: 9—Paul Palmer, Kansas City at Seattle, September 20 (221 yards)
NFC: 7—Gary Lee, Detroit vs. Green Bay, October 25 (141 yards)

Touchdowns

AFC: 2—Paul Palmer, Kansas City
NFC: 1—Ron Brown, L.A. Rams
1—Joe Cribbs, San Francisco
1—Dennis Gentry, Chicago
1—Sylvester Stamps, Atlanta

Team Champions

NFC: 21.5—Atlanta
AFC: 20.7—Denver

AFC Kickoff Returns—Team

	No.	Yards	Avg.	Long	TD
Denver	46	952	20.7	50	0
Kansas City	70	1437	20.5	95t	2
Indianapolis	55	1115	20.3	45	0
L.A. Raiders	60	1174	19.6	50	0
Buffalo	45	872	19.4	40	0
Seattle	64	1236	19.3	43	0
Pittsburgh	56	1060	18.9	36	0
N.Y. Jets	65	1221	18.8	60	0
New England	48	901	18.8	43	0
San Diego	62	1137	18.3	46	0
Houston	67	1225	18.3	62	0
Miami	54	952	17.6	34	0
Cleveland	48	846	17.6	44	0
Cincinnati	67	1161	17.3	34	0
AFC Total	807	15,289	—	95t	2
AFC Average	57.6	1,092.1	18.9	—	0.1

NFC Kickoff Returns—Team

	No.	Yards	Avg.	Long	TD
Atlanta	79	1700	21.5	97t	1
Chicago	57	1193	20.9	88t	1
St. Louis	63	1317	20.9	50	0
New Orleans	55	1147	20.9	74	0
San Francisco	55	1144	20.8	92t	1
L.A. Rams	63	1282	20.3	95t	1
Dallas	64	1295	20.2	48	0
N.Y. Giants	56	1128	20.1	49	0
Detroit	71	1428	20.1	50	0
Minnesota	71	1421	20.0	42	0
Washington	59	1139	19.3	54	0
Tampa Bay	56	1037	18.5	40	0
Green Bay	59	1032	17.5	46	0
Philadelphia	66	1112	16.8	33	0
NFC Total	874	17,375	—	97t	4
NFC Average	62.4	1,241.1	19.9	—	0.3
League Total	1,681	32,664	—	97t	6
League Average	60.0	1,166.6	19.4	—	0.2

NFL Top 10 Kickoff Returners

	No.	Yards	Avg.	Long	TD
Stamps, Sylvester, Atlanta	24	660	27.5	97t	1
Gentry, Dennis, Chicago	25	621	24.8	88t	1
Palmer, Paul, Kansas City	38	923	24.3	95t	2
Bentley, Albert, Indianapolis	22	500	22.7	45	0
Rouson, Lee, N.Y. Giants	22	497	22.6	49	0
Lee, Gary, Detroit	32	719	22.5	50	0
Guggemos, Neal, Minnesota	36	808	22.4	42	0
Sikahema, Vai, St. Louis	34	761	22.4	50	0
Clack, Darryl, Dallas	29	635	21.9	48	0
Mueller, Vance, L.A. Raiders	27	588	21.8	46	0

AFC Kickoff Returns—Individual

	No.	Yards	Avg.	Long	TD
Palmer, Paul, Kansas City	38	923	24.3	95t	2
Bentley, Albert, Indianapolis	22	500	22.7	45	0
Mueller, Vance, L.A. Raiders	27	588	21.8	46	0
Holland, Jamie, San Diego	19	410	21.6	46	0
Edmonds, Bobby Joe, Seattle	27	564	20.9	43	0
Stone, Dwight, Pittsburgh	28	568	20.3	34	0
Anderson, Gary, San Diego	22	433	19.7	31	0
Duncan, Curtis, Houston	28	546	19.5	62	0
Starring, Stephen, New England	23	445	19.3	43	0
Bussey, Barney, Cincinnati	21	406	19.3	34	0
Non-Qualifiers					
Young, Glen, Cleveland	18	412	22.9	44	0
Humphery, Bobby, N.Y. Jets	18	357	19.8	47	0
Pinkett, Allen, Houston	17	322	18.9	30	0
Hampton, Lorenzo, Miami	16	304	19.0	32	0
Bell, Ken, Denver	15	323	21.5	42	0
McGee, Tim, Cincincati	15	242	16.1	24	0
Stradford, Troy, Miami	14	258	18.4	32	0
Williams, Dokie, L.A. Raiders	14	221	15.8	27	0
Woodson, Rod, Pittsburgh	13	290	22.3	36	0
Wright, Dana, Cincinnati	13	266	20.5	30	0
Townsell, JoJo, N.Y. Jets	11	272	24.7	60	0
McNeil, Gerald, Cleveland	11	205	18.6	33	0
Tasker, Steve, Buffalo	11	197	17.9	39	0
Hollis, David, Seattle	10	263	26.3	41	0
Daniel, Kenny, Indianapolis	10	225	22.5	29	0
Wright, Terry, Indianapolis	10	187	18.7	27	0
Swanson, Shane, Denver	9	234	26.0	50	0
Calhoun, Rick, L.A. Raiders	9	217	24.1	50	0
Schwedes, Scott, Miami	9	177	19.7	34	0
Morris, Randall, Seattle	9	149	16.6	20	0
Fontenot, Herman, Cleveland	9	130	14.4	24	0
Porter, Ricky, Buffalo	8	219	27.4	40	0
Martin, Tracy, N.Y. Jets	8	180	22.5	47	0
Drewrey, Willie, Houston	8	136	17.0	27	0
Hunter, Eddie, N.Y. Jets	8	123	15.4	27	0
Riddick, Robb, Buffalo	7	151	21.6	31	0
Johnson, Vance, Denver	7	140	20.0	34	0
McFadden, Thad, Buffalo	7	121	17.3	26	0
Fryar, Irving, New England	6	119	19.8	31	0
Sanchez, Lupe, Pittsburgh	6	116	19.3	27	0
Moriarty, Larry, Kansas City	6	102	17.0	24	0
Johnson, Kelley, Indianapolis	6	98	16.3	28	0
Teal, Jimmy, Seattle	6	95	15.8	23	0
Davis, Elgin, New England	5	134	26.8	43	0
Wyatt, Kevin, Kansas City	5	121	24.2	29	0
Sartin, Martin, San Diego	5	117	23.4	28	0
Robinson, Mark, Kansas City	5	97	19.4	25	0
Klever, Rocky, N.Y. Jets	5	85	17.0	29	0
Mueller, Jamie, Buffalo	5	74	14.8	20	0
Hardy, Bruce, Miami	5	62	12.4	18	0
Hunter, Herman, Houston	4	79	19.8	28	0
Lang, Gene, Denver	4	78	19.5	25	0
Nattiel, Ricky, Denver	4	78	19.5	25	0
Harper, Michael, N.Y. Jets	4	75	18.8	22	0
Dupard, Reggie, New England	4	61	15.3	21	0
Smith, Reggie, New York Jets	4	60	15.0	20	0
Lacy, Kenneth, Kansas City	4	44	11.0	20	0
Adams, Curtis, San Diego	4	32	8.0	11	0
Harris, Leonard, Houston	3	87	29.0	43	0
Adams, Stefon, L.A. Raiders	3	61	20.3	25	0
Brown, Laron, Denver	3	57	19.0	28	0
Farmer, George, Miami	3	56	18.7	23	0
Woods, Chris, L.A. Raiders	3	55	18.3	22	0
Martin, Mike, Cincinnati	3	51	17.0	20	0
Parker, Robert, Kansas City	3	49	16.3	25	0
Prior, Mike, Indianapolis	3	47	15.7	22	0
Sohn, Kurt, N.Y. Jets	3	47	15.7	18	0
Brown, Kenneth, Cincinnati	3	45	15.0	20	0
Perryman, Bob, New England	3	43	14.3	16	0
Logan, Marc, Cincinnati	3	31	10.3	16	0
Powell, Alvin, Seattle	3	23	7.7	14	0
Kirk, Randy, San Diego	3	15	5.0	10	0
Roth, Pete, Miami	2	49	24.5	26	0
Bengen, Brant, Seattle	2	47	23.5	36	0
Jenkins, Keyvan, San Diego	2	46	23.0	25	0
Brooks, James, Cincinnati	2	42	21.0	23	0
James, Lionel, San Diego	2	41	20.5	21	0
Jones, Bruce, Pittsburgh	2	38	19.0	22	0
Lane, Garcia, Kansas City	2	37	18.5	21	0
Brown, Marc, Buffalo	2	35	17.5	18	0
Noble, James, Indianapolis	2	35	17.5	18	0
Lane, Eric, Seattle	2	34	17.0	22	0
Clark, Kevin, Denver	2	33	16.5	25	0
Jennings, Stanford, Cincinnati	2	32	16.0	18	0
McSwain, Chuck, New England	2	32	16.0	24	0
LeBlanc, Michael, New England	2	31	15.5	24	0
Tinsley, Keith, Cleveland	2	31	15.5	18	0
Pardridge, Curt, Seattle	2	29	14.5	16	0
Rome, Tag, San Diego	2	28	14.0	17	0
Armstrong, John, Buffalo	2	25	12.5	18	0
Johnson, Kenny, Houston	2	24	12.0	18	0
Kattus, Eric, Cincinnati	2	22	11.0	13	0
Manoa, Tim, Cleveland	2	14	7.0	13	0
Johnson, Dan, Miami	2	13	6.5	10	0
Britt, Ralph, Pittsburgh	2	9	4.5	5	0
Ryan, Jim, Denver	2	9	4.5	9	0
Barber, Marion, N.Y. Jets	2	5	2.5	5	0
Pearson, Aaron, Kansas City	2	4	2.0	4	0
Harmon, Ronnie, Buffalo	1	30	30.0	30	0
Beauford, Clayton, Cleveland	1	22	22.0	22	0
Scott, Ronald, Miami	1	22	22.0	22	0
Green, Boyce, Seattle	1	20	20.0	20	0
Harkey, Lance, L.A. Raiders	1	20	20.0	20	0
Wonsley, George, Indianapolis	1	19	19.0	19	0
Clark, Mike, Pittsburgh	1	18	18.0	18	0
Colbert, Darrell, Kansas City	1	18	18.0	18	0
Collins, Tony, New England	1	18	18.0	18	0
Walters, Joey, Houston	1	18	18.0	18	0

	No.	Yards	Avg.	Long	TD
Driver, Stacey, Cleveland	1	16	16.0	16	0
Griffin, Stephen, Kansas City	1	16	16.0	16	0
Hillary, Ira, Cincinnati	1	15	15.0	15	0
Hansen, Bruce, New England	1	14	14.0	14	0
Radecic, Scott, Buffalo	1	14	14.0	14	0
Bernstine, Rod, San Diego	1	13	13.0	13	0
Fields, Jitter, Kansas City	1	13	13.0	13	0
Griggs, Billy, N.Y. Jets	1	13	13.0	13	0
Hoge, Merril, Pittsburgh	1	13	13.0	13	0
Valentine, Ira, Houston	1	13	13.0	13	0
Foster, Ron, L.A. Raiders	1	12	12.0	12	0
Isom, Rickey, Miami	1	11	11.0	11	0
Scholtz, Bruce, Seattle	1	11	11.0	11	0
Smith, Blane, Kansas City	1	10	10.0	10	0
Meehan, Greg, Cincinnati	1	9	9.0	9	0
Anderson, Mel, Pittsburgh	1	8	8.0	8	0
Langhorne, Reggie, Cleveland	1	8	8.0	8	0
Grayson, Dave, Cleveland	1	6	6.0	6	0
Rolle, Butch, Buffalo	1	6	6.0	6	0
Alexander, Rogers, New England	1	4	4.0	4	0
Faaola, Nuu, N.Y. Jets	1	4	4.0	4	0
Perryman, Jim, Indianapolis	1	4	4.0	4	0
Clemons, Michael, Kansas City	1	3	3.0	3	0
Byner, Earnest, Cleveland	1	2	2.0	2	0
Zachary, Ken, San Diego	1	2	2.0	2	0
Burse, Tony, Seattle	1	1	1.0	1	0
Davis, John, Houston	1	0	0.0	0	0
Fulcher, David, Cincinnati	1	0	0.0	0	0
Fuller, William, Houston	1	0	0.0	0	0
Gowdy, Cornell, Pittsburgh	1	0	0.0	0	0
Hunter, Daniel, San Diego	1	0	0.0	0	0
Lewis, David, Miami	1	0	0.0	0	0
Mason, Larry, Cleveland	1	0	0.0	0	0
Millen, Matt, L.A. Raiders	1	0	0.0	0	0
Riley, Avon, Pittsburgh	1	0	0.0	0	0
Tillman, Spencer, Houston	1	0	0.0	0	0
Washington, Ronnie, L.A. Raiders	1	0	0.0	0	0
Wallace, Ray, Houston	0(f)	0	—	—	0

t indicates touchdown.
(f) indicates fair catch.
Leader based on average return, minimum 19 returns.

NFC Kickoff Returns—Individual

	No.	Yards	Avg.	Long	TD
Stamps, Sylvester, Atlanta	24	660	27.5	97t	1
Gentry, Dennis, Chicago	25	621	24.8	88t	1
Rouson, Lee, N.Y. Giants	22	497	22.6	49	0
Lee, Gary, Detroit	32	719	22.5	50	0
Guggemos, Neal, Minnesota	36	808	22.4	42	0
Sikahema, Vai, St. Louis	34	761	22.4	50	0
Clack, Darryl, Dallas	29	635	21.9	48	0
Brown, Ron, L.A. Rams	27	581	21.5	95t	1
Fullwood, Brent, Green Bay	24	510	21.3	46	0
Gray, Mel, New Orleans	30	636	21.2	43	0
Emery, Larry, Atlanta	21	440	21.0	66	0
Futrell, Bobby, Tampa Bay	31	609	19.6	40	0
McAdoo, Derrick, St. Louis	23	444	19.3	30	0
Griffin, Keith, Washington	25	478	19.1	54	0
Sanders, Thomas, Chicago	20	349	17.5	42	0
Morse, Bobby, Philadelphia	24	386	16.1	28	0
Non-Qualifiers					
Rodgers, Del, San Francisco	17	358	21.1	50	0
Cribbs, Joe, San Francisco	13	327	25.2	92t	1
Verdin, Clarence, Washington	12	244	20.3	38	0
Sydney, Harry, San Francisco	12	243	20.3	30	0
Carter, Cris, Philadelphia	12	241	20.1	33	0
Martin, Kelvin, Dallas	12	237	19.8	38	0
Woolfolk, Butch, Detroit	11	219	19.9	44	0
Hilliard, Dalton, New Orleans	10	248	24.8	74	0
Bess, Rufus, Minnesota	10	169	16.9	33	0
Settle, John, Atlanta	10	158	15.8	22	0
Cook, Kelly, Green Bay	10	147	14.7	38	0
Bradley, Danny, Detroit	9	188	20.9	27	0
Adams, George, N.Y. Giants	9	166	18.4	27	0
Tiumalu, Casey, L.A. Rams	8	158	19.8	25	0
Nelson, Darrin, Minnesota	7	164	23.4	42	0
Edwards, Kelvin, Dallas	7	155	22.1	32	0
Bowman, Kevin, Philadelphia	7	153	21.9	32	0
Walls, Herkie, Tampa Bay	6	136	22.7	39	0
Tyrrell, Tim, L.A. Rams	6	116	19.3	30	0
Ingram, Mark, N.Y. Giants	6	114	19.0	25	0
Adams, David, Dallas	6	113	18.8	27	0
Lavette, Robert, Dallas-Philadelphia	6	109	18.2	22	0
Hall, Alvin, Detroit	6	105	17.5	25	0
Morris, Lee, Green Bay	6	104	17.3	28	0
Williams, Alonzo, L.A. Rams	5	114	22.8	47	0
Monroe, Carl, San Francisco	5	91	18.2	24	0
Oliver, Darryl, Atlanta	5	90	18.0	28	0

	No.	Yards	Avg.	Long	TD
Cooper, Evan, Philadelphia	5	86	17.2	24	0
Smith, Jeff, Tampa Bay	5	84	16.8	21	0
Womack, Jeff, Minnesota	5	77	15.4	20	0
Hicks, Cliff, L.A. Rams	4	119	29.8	53	0
Sanders, Ricky, Washington	4	118	29.5	39	0
Byrd, Boris, N.Y. Giants	4	99	24.8	34	0
Richardson, Greg, Minnesota	4	76	19.0	24	0
Jessie, Tim, Washington	4	73	18.3	24	0
Flowers, Kenny, Atlanta	4	72	18.0	20	0
Harden, Derrick, Green Bay	4	72	18.0	20	0
Norris, Jimmy, N.Y. Giants	4	70	17.5	29	0
Orr, Terry, Washington	4	62	15.5	19	0
Branch, Reggie, Washington	4	61	15.3	19	0
Reid, Alan, Philadelphia	4	58	14.5	19	0
Bernard, Karl, Detroit	4	54	13.5	32	0
Adams, Michael, New Orleans	4	52	13.0	20	0
Neal, Frankie, Green Bay	4	44	11.0	18	0
McIntosh, Joe, Atlanta	3	108	36.0	71	0
Word, Barry, New Orleans	3	100	33.3	64	0
White, Charles, L.A. Rams	3	73	24.3	26	0
Kozlowski, Glen, Chicago	3	72	24.0	31	0
Beecham, Earl, N.Y. Giants	3	70	23.3	30	0
Miller, Solomon, Tampa Bay	3	68	22.7	25	0
Lynch, Lorenzo, Chicago	3	66	22.0	37	0
Saleaumua, Dan, Detroit	3	57	19.0	21	0
Curry, Ivory, Tampa Bay	3	53	17.7	20	0
Tautalatasi, Junior, Philadelphia	3	53	17.7	32	0
Stanley, Walter, Green Bay	3	47	15.7	29	0
Beverly, Dwight, New Orleans	3	46	15.3	21	0
Sargent, Broderick, St. Louis	3	37	12.3	27	0
Flagler, Terrence, San Francisco	3	31	10.3	16	0
McDonald, Mike, L.A. Rams	3	31	10.3	15	0
Spivey, Sebron, Dallas	2	49	24.5	29	0
Bland, Carl, Detroit	2	44	22.0	22	0
Smith, Jimmy, Minnesota	2	42	21.0	22	0
Rathman, Tom, San Francisco	2	37	18.5	21	0
Sutton, Mickey, L.A. Rams	2	37	18.5	19	0
Everett, Major, Atlanta	2	33	16.5	18	0
Scott, Patrick, Green Bay	2	32	16.0	23	0
Wilson, Wayne, Washington	2	32	16.0	18	0
DiRico, Bob, N.Y. Giants	2	31	15.5	25	0
Vital, Lionel, Washington	2	31	15.5	18	0
Jefferson, Norman, Green Bay	2	30	15.0	18	0
Rice, Allen, Minnesota	2	29	14.5	18	0
Jordan, Buford, New Orleans	2	28	14.0	16	0
Badanjek, Rick, Atlanta	2	27	13.5	16	0
Ball, Jerry, Detroit	2	23	11.5	20	0
Dozier, D.J., Minnesota	2	23	11.5	13	0
Newsome, Tim, Dallas	2	22	11.0	12	0
Guman, Mike, L.A. Rams	2	18	9.0	12	0
Haddix, Michael, Philadelphia	2	16	8.0	9	0
Williams, Michael, Atlanta	2	15	7.5	15	0
Brown, Ron, St. Louis	1	40	40.0	40	0
Ricks, Harold, Tampa Bay	1	26	26.0	26	0
Holmes, Don, St. Louis	1	25	25.0	25	0
McLemore, Dana, San Francisco	1	23	23.0	23	0
Moss, Gary, Atlanta	1	23	23.0	23	0
Griffin, Steve B., Atlanta	1	21	21.0	21	0
Henley, Thomas, San Francisco	1	21	21.0	21	0
Turrall, Willie, Philadelphia	1	21	21.0	21	0
Brown, Reggie, Philadelphia	1	20	20.0	20	0
Coleman, Charles, N.Y. Giants	1	20	20.0	20	0
Shepard, Derrick, Washington	1	20	20.0	20	0
Wilson, Ted, Washington	1	20	20.0	20	0
Glover, Kevin, Detroit	1	19	19.0	19	0
Bell, Todd, Chicago	1	18	18.0	18	0
Croudip, David, Atlanta	1	18	18.0	18	0
Mosley, Anthony, Chicago	1	17	17.0	17	0
White, Lawrence, Chicago	1	17	17.0	17	0
Wright, Adrian, Tampa Bay	1	17	17.0	17	0
Bavaro, Mark, N.Y. Giants	1	16	16.0	16	0
Gladman, Charles, Tampa Bay	1	16	16.0	16	0
Mularkey, Mike, Minnesota	1	16	16.0	16	0
Bartalo, Steve, Tampa Bay	1	15	15.0	15	0
Brown, Richard, L.A. Rams	1	15	15.0	15	0
Martin, Eric, New Orleans	1	15	15.0	15	0
Knapczyk, Ken, Chicago	1	14	14.0	14	0
Brown, Cedrick, Philadelphia	1	13	13.0	13	0
Butler, Jerry, Atlanta	1	13	13.0	13	0
Dorsey, Eric, N.Y. Giants	1	13	13.0	13	0
Hilton, Carl, Minnesota	1	13	13.0	13	0
Siano, Mike, Philadelphia	1	13	13.0	13	0
Urch, Scott, N.Y. Giants	1	13	13.0	13	0
Varajon, Mike, San Francisco	1	13	13.0	13	0
Cox, Robert, L.A. Rams	1	12	12.0	12	0
Brock, Stan, New Orleans	1	11	11.0	11	0
Cox, Arthur, Atlanta	1	11	11.0	11	0
Cummings, Mack, N.Y. Giants	1	11	11.0	11	0

	No.	Yards	Avg.	Long	TD
Sharp, Dan, Atlanta	1	11	11.0	11	0
Thomas, Curtland, New Orleans	1	11	11.0	11	0
Ferrell, Earl, St. Louis	1	10	10.0	10	0
Milton, Eldridge, Chicago	1	10	10.0	10	0
Suhey, Matt, Chicago	1	9	9.0	9	0
Carruth, Paul Ott, Green Bay	1	8	8.0	8	0
Ellard, Henry, L.A. Rams	1	8	8.0	8	0
Hill, Bruce, Tampa Bay	1	8	8.0	8	0
McConkey, Phil, N.Y. Giants	1	8	8.0	8	0
Ulmer, Mike, Philadelphia	1	8	8.0	8	0
Chandler, Thornton, Dallas	1	7	7.0	7	0
Alexander, David, Philadelphia	1	6	6.0	6	0
Borresen, Rich, Dallas	1	5	5.0	5	0
Howard, Bobby, Tampa Bay	1	5	5.0	5	0
Harrell, Samuel, Minnesota	1	4	4.0	4	0
Weishuhn, Clayton, Green Bay	1	1	1.0	1	0
Carrier, Mark, Tampa Bay	1	0	0.0	0	0
Cherry, Bill, Green Bay	1	0	0.0	0	0
Clemons, Topper, Philadelphia	1	0	0.0	0	0
Green, Curtis, Detroit	1	0	0.0	0	0
Sterling, John, Green Bay	1	0	0.0	0	0
Walker, Kevin, Tampa Bay	1	0	0.0	0	0
Willhite, Kevin, Green Bay	0	37	—	37	0
Reeves, Ken, Philadelphia	0	1	—	1	0

t indicates touchdown.
Leader based on average return, minimum 19 returns.

Fumbles

Most Fumbles
NFC: 12—Randall Cunningham, Philadelphia
AFC: 11—Dave Krieg, Seattle
Most Fumbles, Game
AFC: 5—Willie Totten, Buffalo vs. Indianapolis, October 4
5—Dave Walter, Cincinnati vs. Seattle, October 11
NFC: 3—By 9 players
Own Fumbles Recovered
AFC: 6—Steve Grogan, New England
6—Warren Moon, Houston
NFC: 6—Randall Cunningham, Philadelphia
Most Own Fumbles Recovered, Game
AFC: 3—Dave Krieg, Seattle vs. Chicago, December 20
NFC: 2—By 10 players
Opponents' Fumbles Recovered
NFC: 5—Brian Noble, Green Bay
AFC: 4—Fredd Young, Seattle
Most Opponents' Fumbles Recovered, Game
AFC: 2—By 9 players
NFC: 2—By 9 players
Yards
NFC: 77—Mark Jackson, St. Louis
AFC: 59—Trell Hooper, Miami
Longest
NFC: 77—Mark Jackson, St. Louis vs. New Orleans, October 11 (TD)
AFC: 59—Trell Hooper, Miami vs. Kansas City, October 11 (TD)

AFC Fumbles—Team

	Fum.	Own Rec.	Fum. *O.B.	TD	Opp. Rec.	TD	Yds.	Tot. Rec.
L.A. Raiders	24	10	1	0	15	0	−7	25
Cincinnati	29	17	0	0	12	0	−34	29
Denver	29	12	0	0	19	0	34	31
Seattle	31	16	0	0	21	0	19	37
Houston	32	15	3	0	14	1	39	29
Cleveland	33	15	1	0	13	2	46	28
N.Y. Jets	33	13	1	0	11	1	25	24
Indianapolis	36	13	5	0	25	1	44	38
New England	36	21	2	0	21	1	35	42
Miami	37	18	2	0	16	2	87	34
Pittsburgh	37	28	1	0	17	2	80	45
San Diego	38	17	1	0	15	1	4	32
Buffalo	41	17	0	0	14	3	57	31
Kansas City	41	14	3	0	17	1	−20	31
AFC Total	477	226	20	0	230	15	409	456
AFC Average	34.1	16.1	1.4	0.0	16.4	1.1	29.2	32.6

NFC Fumbles—Team

	Fum.	Own Rec.	Fum. *O.B.	TD	Opp. Rec.	TD	Yds.	Tot. Rec.
St. Louis	23	8	3	0	19	4	127	27
San Francisco	25	13	0	1	13	0	63	26
L.A. Rams	26	9	2	0	11	1	47	20
Washington	26	5	2	0	11	1	35	16
Atlanta	27	9	1	0	12	1	57	21
Minnesota	28	13	5	0	11	0	42	24
Detroit	29	15	3	0	13	1	−30	28
Dallas	30	10	0	0	20	0	32	30
Chicago	33	13	0	0	11	0	22	24
New Orleans	33	14	3	0	18	0	52	32
Green Bay	35	16	1	0	24	0	−2	40
Tampa Bay	35	21	0	0	19	2	61	40
N.Y. Giants	38	14	4	0	14	0	−14	28
Philadelphia	44	23	2	0	27	2	189	50
NFC Total	432	183	26	1	223	12	681	406
NFC Average	30.9	13.1	1.9	0.7	15.9	0.9	48.6	29.0
League Total	909	409	46	1	453	27	1090	862
League Average	32.5	14.6	1.6	0.4	16.2	1.0	38.9	30.8

indicates fumbles out of bounds.

AFC Fumbles—Individual

	Fum.	Own Rec.	Opp. Rec.	Yds.	Tot. Rec.
Abercrombie, Walter, Pittsburgh	4	3	0	2	3
Ackerman, Rick, L.A. Raiders	0	0	1	0	1
Adams, Curtis, San Diego	1	0	0	0	0
Adickes, Mark, Kansas City	0	1	0	0	1
Ahrens, Dave, Indianapolis	0	0	2	0	2
Alexander, Dan, N.Y. Jets	0	2	0	0	2
Allen, Marcus, L.A. Raiders	3	0	0	0	0
Allen, Patrick, Houston	0	1	0	0	1
Anderson, Eddie, L.A. Raiders	0	1	0	0	1
Anderson, Gary, San Diego	4	1	0	0	1
Armstrong, Harvey, Indianapolis	0	1	1	0	2
Armstrong, John, Buffalo	1	0	0	0	0
Aydelette, Buddy, Pittsburgh	0	1	0	5	1
Ayers, John, Denver	0	1	0	0	1
Baker, Al, Cleveland	0	0	1	0	1
Baldinger, Rich, Kansas City	0	1	0	0	1
Banker, Ted, N.Y. Jets	0	1	0	0	1
Banks, Chip, San Diego	0	0	2	0	2
Banks, Chuck, Indianapolis	1	0	0	0	0
Baugh, Tom, Kansas City	1	2	0	0	2
Bell, Ken, Denver	2	1	0	0	1
Bell, Mike, Kansas City	0	0	2	0	2
Benjamin, Bill, Indianapolis	0	0	1	0	1
Benson, Thomas, San Diego	0	0	1	0	1
Bentley, Albert, Indianapolis	3	3	0	0	3
Bernstine, Rod, San Diego	0	1	0	0	1
Berthusen, Bill, Cincinnati	0	0	1	1	1
Bickett, Duane, Indianapolis	1	0	2	32	2
Billups, Lewis, Cincinnati	0	0	1	0	1
Blackledge, Todd, Kansas City	2	0	0	−6	0
Bleier, Bob, New England	2	2	0	0	2
Bligen, Dennis, N.Y. Jets	1	1	0	0	1
Boddie, Tony, Denver	0	0	1	0	1
Bono, Steve, Pittsburgh	5	3	0	0	3
Bosa, John, Miami	0	0	2	0	2
Bostic, Keith, Houston	1	0	1	2	1
Bosworth, Brian, Seattle	0	0	2	38	2
Bouza, Matt, Indianapolis	2	0	0	0	0
Bowman, Jim, New England	0	0	1	6	1
Brady, Ed, Cincinnati	0	0	1	0	1
Breen, Adrian, Cincinnati	1	1	0	0	1
Brennan, Brian, Cleveland	1	1	0	0	1
Britt, Ralph, Pittsburgh	1	1	0	0	1
Brooks, Bill, Indianapolis	3	0	0	0	0
Brooks, Michael, Denver	0	0	1	0	1
Brown, Arnold, Seattle	0	1	0	0	1
Brown, Bud, Miami	1	1	0	0	1
Brown, Eddie, Cincinnati	3	1	0	0	1
Brown, Gordon, Indianapolis	1	0	0	0	0
Brown, Mark, Miami	0	0	1	1	1
Brown, Ron, L.A. Raiders	0	0	1	0	1
Brown, Steve, Houston	1	0	1	0	1
Bryan, Bill, Denver	0	0	1	0	1
Bryant, Domingo, Houston	0	0	1	0	1
Bryant, Jeff, Seattle	0	0	1	0	1
Burkett, Chris, Buffalo	1	0	0	0	0
Burnham, Tim, Seattle	1	0	0	0	0
Burroughs, Derrick, Buffalo	0	1	0	0	1
Burse, Tony, Seattle	1	0	0	0	0
Bussey, Barney, Cincinnati	1	0	0	0	0
Butler, Keith, Seattle	0	0	1	0	1
Butler, Raymond, Seattle	1	0	0	0	0
Byner, Earnest, Cleveland	5	1	0	0	1
Byrd, Gill, San Diego	0	0	1	0	1
Byrum, Carl, Buffalo	4	1	0	0	1
Carson, Carlos, Kansas City	1	0	0	0	0
Carter, Russell, N.Y. Jets	0	0	1	0	1
Catchings, Toney, Cincinnati	0	0	1	0	1
Caterbone, Michael, Miami	1	1	0	0	1
Chandler, Wes, San Diego	1	1	0	0	1
Chapman, Ted, L.A. Raiders	0	0	1	0	1
Cherry, Deron, Kansas City	0	0	1	0	1
Childress, Ray, Houston	0	0	1	1	1
Chirico, John, N.Y. Jets	1	0	2	0	2
Christensen, Jeff, Cleveland	3	0	0	−3	0

	Fum.	Own Rec.	Opp. Rec.	Yds.	Tot. Rec.
Clancy, Sam, Cleveland	0	0	2	0	2
Clark, Kevin, Denver	1	1	0	0	1
Clay, John, L.A. Raiders	0	1	0	0	1
Clayborn, Raymond, New England	0	0	1	0	1
Clemons, Michael, Kansas City	3	1	0	0	1
Coffman, Paul, Kansas City	0	0	2	0	2
Cofield, Tim, Kansas City	0	0	1	0	1
Cole, Robin, Pittsburgh	0	0	1	0	1
Collins, Tony, New England	6	2	0	0	2
Collins, Trent, N.Y. Jets	1	0	1	0	1
Colton, George, New England	0	1	0	0	1
Cooks, Johnie, Indianapolis	1	0	1	0	1
Daniel, Kenny, Indianapolis	2	0	0	0	0
Danielson, Gary, Cleveland	2	2	0	−2	2
Davis, James, L.A. Raiders	1	0	1	0	1
Davis, John, Houston	1	0	0	0	0
Davis, Johnny, Cleveland	1	1	0	0	1
Davis, Lee, Indianapolis	0	1	0	0	1
DeAyala, Kiki, Cincinnati	0	1	1	0	2
Dellenbach, Jeff, Miami	1	0	0	−13	0
Dickerson, Eric, L.A. Rams-Indianapolis	7	3	0	0	3
Donaldson, Jeff, Houston	0	0	2	0	2
Drane, Dwight, Buffalo	0	0	1	0	1
Driver, Stacey, Cleveland	1	0	0	0	0
Dudek, Joe, Denver	4	1	0	0	1
Dunn, Gary, Pittsburgh	0	0	1	0	1
Dupard, Reggie, New England	2	1	0	0	1
Easley, Ken, Seattle	0	0	1	0	1
Eason, Tony, New England	1	0	0	0	0
Echols, Don, Cleveland	0	1	0	0	1
Edmonds, Bobby Joe, Seattle	1	1	0	0	1
Edwards, Eddie, Cincinnati	0	0	1	0	1
Ehin, Chuck, San Diego	1	0	1	27	1
Elko, Bill, Indianapolis	0	0	1	0	1
Ellis, Craig, L.A. Raiders	1	0	0	0	0
Ellis, Ray, Cleveland	0	1	1	27	2
Elway, John, Denver	2	0	0	−1	0
Esiason, Boomer, Cincinnati	10	4	0	−8	4
Everett, Thomas, Pittsburgh	1	2	0	7	2
Faaola, Nuu, N.Y. Jets	0	0	1	3	1
Farren, Paul, Cleveland	0	1	0	0	1
Feasel, Grant, Seattle	1	1	0	−19	1
Fernandez, Mervyn, L.A. Raiders	1	0	0	0	0
Fields, Joe, N.Y. Jets	0	1	0	0	1
Flaherty, Tom, Cincinnati	0	0	1	0	1
Fletcher, Simon, Denver	0	0	1	0	1
Flutie, Doug, New England	1	1	0	0	1
Foster, Roy, Miami	0	1	0	0	1
Fouts, Dan, San Diego	10	4	0	−10	4
Fryar, Irving, New England	2	0	0	0	0
Fulcher, David, Cincinnati	0	0	1	0	1
Fuller, William, Houston	0	0	1	0	1
Gaines, Greg, Seattle	0	0	1	0	1
Gaines, Sheldon, Buffalo	1	0	0	0	0
Gilbert, Freddie, Denver	0	0	1	0	1
Givins, Ernest, Houston	2	0	0	0	0
Glasgow, Nesby, Indianapolis	0	0	1	0	1
Glenn, Vencie, San Diego	0	0	1	0	1
Gowdy, Cornell, Pittsburgh	0	0	2	1	2
Graf, Rick, Miami	0	0	1	0	1
Graham, David, Seattle	0	0	2	0	2
Grayson, Dave, Cleveland	0	0	1	17	1
Green, Jacob, Seattle	0	0	1	0	1
Griffith, Russell, Seattle	0	1	0	0	1
Grimsley, Ed, Indianapolis	0	0	1	0	1
Grimsley, John, Houston	0	0	1	0	1
Grogan, Steve, New England	8	6	0	−6	6
Hairston, Carl, Cleveland	0	0	1	0	1
Hairston, Russell, Pittsburgh	1	0	0	0	0
Hall, Delton, Pittsburgh	1	0	2	50	2
Hamilton, Harry, N.Y. Jets	0	0	1	0	1
Hampton, Lorenzo, Miami	4	1	0	0	1
Hannah, Charley, L.A. Raiders	0	1	0	2	1
Hansen, Bruce, New England	0	1	0	0	1
Harden, Mike, Denver	0	0	1	14	1
Hardy, Bruce, Miami	1	0	0	−7	0
Harmon, Ronnie, Buffalo	2	0	0	0	0
Harrell, James, Kansas City	0	0	2	0	2
Harris, Bob, Kansas City	0	0	1	0	1
Harris, Walt, San Diego	0	0	1	0	1
Harrison, Rob, L.A. Raiders	2	0	0	0	0
Haslett, Jim, N.Y. Jets	0	0	1	0	1
Hayes, Jonathan, Kansas City	0	1	0	0	1
Haynes, Mark, Denver	0	0	1	24	1
Heard, Herman, Kansas City	5	2	0	0	2
Hector, Johnny, N.Y. Jets	2	1	0	0	1
Herrmann, Mark, San Diego	1	1	0	−5	1
Highsmith, Alonzo, Houston	2	0	0	0	0

	Fum.	Own Rec.	Opp. Rec.	Yds.	Tot. Rec.
Hilger, Rusty, L.A. Raiders	3	1	0	0	1
Hill, Drew, Houston	1	0	0	0	0
Hinkle, Bryan, Pittsburgh	1	0	1	0	1
Hinton, Chris, Indianapolis	0	0	1	0	1
Hobley, Liffort, Miami	0	1	3	55	4
Hogeboom, Gary, Indianapolis	1	1	0	−1	1
Holman, Rodney, Cincinnati	0	1	0	0	1
Holman, Scott, N.Y. Jets	1	0	0	0	0
Holmes, Darryl, New England	0	0	1	0	1
Holohan, Pete, San Diego	0	1	0	0	1
Holt, Harry, San Diego	1	0	0	0	0
Hooper, Trell, Miami	1	0	1	59	1
Horton, Ethan, L.A. Raiders	2	0	0	0	0
Howard, Todd, Kansas City	0	0	1	0	1
Hudson, Doug, Kansas City	1	1	0	−3	1
Humiston, Mike, San Diego	0	0	1	0	1
Humphery, Bobby, N.Y. Jets	1	1	1	46	2
Hunter, Daniel, San Diego	1	0	0	0	0
Hunter, Eddie, N.Y. Jets	3	0	0	−12	0
Hunter, Herman, Houston	1	0	0	0	0
Hyde, Glenn, Kansas City	1	0	1	0	1
Jackson, Bo, L.A. Raiders	2	1	0	0	1
Jackson, Earnest, Pittsburgh	2	3	0	0	3
Jackson, Jeff, San Diego	0	0	1	0	1
Jackson, Robert, Cincinnati	0	0	1	0	1
Jaeger, Jeff, Cleveland	0	1	0	0	1
James, Lionel, San Diego	6	0	0	−8	0
Jenkins, Mel, Seattle	1	0	0	0	0
Jennings, Stanford, Cincinnati	0	0	1	0	1
Jensen, Jim, Miami	1	0	3	2	3
Johnson, Dan, Miami	1	0	0	0	0
Johnson, Eddie, Cleveland	0	0	1	0	1
Johnson, Kelley, Indianapolis	1	0	0	0	0
Johnson, Kenny, Houston	3	0	1	0	1
Johnson, Mike, Cleveland	0	0	1	0	1
Johnson, Vance, Denver	1	0	0	0	0
Jones, Leonard, Denver	0	0	2	24	2
Jones, Rod, Kansas City	1	0	0	0	0
Jones, Sean, L.A. Raiders	0	0	2	0	2
Jordan, Tim, New England	0	1	0	0	1
Justin, Kerry, Seattle	0	0	1	0	1
Kaiser, John, Buffalo	0	0	1	0	1
Karcher, Ken, Denver	2	3	0	−11	3
Katolin, Mike, Cleveland	1	0	0	0	0
Kay, Clarence, Denver	3	0	0	0	0
Keel, Mark, Seattle	0	2	0	0	2
Kelly, Jim, Buffalo	6	2	0	0	2
Kelso, Mark, Buffalo	0	0	2	56	2
Kemp, Jeff, Seattle	2	1	0	−8	1
Kenney, Bill, Kansas City	8	2	0	−8	2
Kidd, Billy, Houston	0	1	0	0	1
Kimmel, Jamie, L.A. Raiders	0	1	0	0	1
King, Linden, L.A. Raiders	0	0	1	0	1
Kinnebrew, Larry, Cincinnati	1	0	0	0	0
Kirk, Randy, San Diego	1	1	0	0	1
Klecko, Joe, N.Y. Jets	0	0	1	0	1
Konecny, Mark, Miami	0	1	0	0	1
Kosar, Bernie, Cleveland	2	1	0	−3	1
Kowalski, Gary, San Diego	0	1	0	0	1
Kozerski, Bruce, Cincinnati	0	1	0	0	1
Kragen, Greg, Denver	0	0	1	0	1
Krauss, Barry, Indianapolis	0	0	2	0	2
Krieg, Dave, Seattle	11	5	0	−2	5
Lacy, Kenneth, Kansas City	2	0	0	0	0
Lankford, Paul, Miami	0	0	1	4	1
Largent, Steve, Seattle	2	0	0	0	0
LeBlanc, Michael, New England	2	0	0	0	0
Lee, Danzell, Pittsburgh	0	0	1	0	1
Lee, Larry, Denver	0	1	0	0	1
Lewis, Albert, Kansas City	0	0	1	0	1
Lilly, Tony, Denver	0	0	1	0	1
Lingner, Adam, Buffalo	0	0	1	0	1
Linne, Larry, New England	1	1	0	0	1
Little, David, Pittsburgh	0	0	1	0	1
Lockett, Charles, Pittsburgh	1	1	0	0	1
Long, Howie, L.A. Raiders	0	0	2	0	2
Lowry, Orlando, Indianapolis	0	0	1	0	1
Lucas, Tim, Denver	0	0	1	0	1
Lyles, Robert, Houston	0	0	3	55	3
Maas, Bill, Kansas City	0	0	1	6	1
Macek, Don, San Diego	1	1	0	0	1
Mack, Kevin, Cleveland	6	1	0	0	1
Mackey, Kyle, Miami	3	0	0	−6	0
Malone, Mark, Pittsburgh	10	5	0	−3	5
Manoa, Tim, Cleveland	1	1	0	0	1
Manos, Sam, Cincinnati	0	1	0	0	1
Manucci, Dan, Buffalo	1	0	0	−7	0
Marino, Dan, Miami	5	4	0	−25	4

	Fum.	Own Rec.	Opp. Rec.	Yds.	Tot. Rec.
Marion, Fred, New England	0	0	1	0	1
Martin, Charles, Houston	0	0	1	0	1
Martin, Mike, Cincinnati	1	0	0	0	0
Mason, Larry, Cleveland	4	1	0	0	1
Matthews, Clay, Cleveland	0	0	2	0	2
McCluskey, David, Cincinnati	2	0	0	0	0
McGrew, Larry, New England	0	0	1	0	1
McLemore, Chris, Indianapolis	1	0	0	0	0
McNanie, Sean, Buffalo	0	0	1	14	1
McNeil, Freeman, N.Y. Jets	1	0	0	0	0
McNeil, Gerald, Cleveland	2	0	0	0	0
McSwain, Chuck, New England	1	0	1	11	1
Mecklenburg, Karl, Denver	0	0	1	0	1
Meehan, Greg, Cincinnati	1	0	0	0	0
Merritts, Jim, Indianapolis	0	0	1	0	1
Merriweather, Mike, Pittsburgh	0	1	3	4	4
Mersereau, Scott, N.Y. Jets	0	0	1	0	1
Metzelaars, Pete, Buffalo	3	1	0	0	1
Micho, Bobby, Denver	1	0	0	0	0
Millard, Bryan, Seattle	0	2	0	0	2
Millen, Matt, L.A. Raiders	1	0	0	0	0
Miller, Les, San Diego	0	0	2	0	2
Mobley, Orson, Denver	1	0	0	0	0
Moon, Warren, Houston	8	6	0	−7	6
Moore, Greg, New England	0	0	1	0	1
Morriss, Guy, New England	1	0	0	0	0
Morton, Michael, Seattle	1	0	0	0	0
Moyer, Paul, Seattle	0	0	3	10	3
Mueller, Jamie, Buffalo	5	1	0	−22	1
Mueller, Vance, L.A. Raiders	3	1	0	0	1
Munchak, Mike, Houston	0	0	1	0	1
Munford, Marc, Denver	0	0	2	0	2
Nathan, Tony, Miami	1	0	0	0	0
Nattiel, Ricky, Denver	2	1	0	0	1
Nelson, Edmund, Pittsburgh	0	0	1	0	1
Nelson, Steve, New England	0	0	1	0	1
Nelson, Teddy, Kansas City	0	0	1	0	1
Neuheisel, Rick, San Diego	1	1	0	0	1
Newsome, Harry, Pittsburgh	1	1	0	−17	1
Nickerson, Hardy, Pittsburgh	0	1	0	0	1
Noble, James, Indianapolis	2	0	0	0	0
Noble, Mike, L.A. Raiders	0	0	1	0	1
Norrie, David, N.Y. Jets	4	2	0	−2	2
O'Brien, Ken, N.Y. Jets	8	1	0	−10	1
O'Connor, Tom, N.Y. Jets	1	1	0	0	1
Odom, Clifton, Indianapolis	0	0	3	8	3
Odomes, Nate, Buffalo	0	1	1	0	2
Okoye, Christian, Kansas City	5	0	0	0	0
Oubre, Louis, Miami	0	1	0	0	1
Palmer, Paul, Kansas City	2	0	0	0	0
Parker, Andy, L.A. Raiders	0	1	0	0	1
Parker, Robert, Kansas City	1	0	0	0	0
Partridge, Rick, Buffalo	0	1	0	0	1
Patterson, Elvis, San Diego	0	0	1	0	1
Pearson, Aaron, Kansas City	2	0	0	0	0
Pease, Brent, Houston	2	2	0	0	2
Peavey, Jack, Denver	1	0	0	−16	0
Pennison, Jay, Houston	1	1	0	−12	1
Perryman, Bob, New England	1	2	0	0	2
Perryman, Jim, Indianapolis	0	0	1	5	1
Peterson, Joe, New England	0	0	1	0	1
Pickel, Bill, L.A. Raiders	0	0	2	0	2
Pidgeon, Tim, Miami	0	0	1	17	1
Pinkett, Allen, Houston	1	0	0	0	0
Pitts, Ron, Buffalo	3	1	0	0	1
Pollard, Frank, Pittsburgh	3	1	0	1	1
Polley, Tom, Cleveland	0	0	1	0	1
Powell, Alvin, Seattle	1	0	0	0	0
Prior, Mike, Indianapolis	0	0	3	0	3
Pruitt, James, Miami	1	0	0	0	0
Radecic, Scott, Buffalo	0	0	2	0	2
Ramsey, Tom, New England	4	1	0	0	1
Reimers, Bruce, Cincinnati	0	1	0	0	1
Riddick, Robb, Buffalo	2	1	0	0	1
Riley, Avon, Pittsburgh	1	0	0	0	0
Riley, Eric, N.Y. Jets	0	0	1	0	1
Rimington, Dave, Cincinnati	2	0	0	−18	0
Robinson, DeJuan, Cleveland	0	1	0	10	1
Robinson, Eugene, Seattle	0	0	1	0	1
Robinson, Freddie, Indianapolis	0	0	1	0	1
Robinson, Greg, New England	0	1	0	0	1
Robinson, Mark, Kansas City	0	0	2	0	2
Roby, Reggie, Miami	0	1	0	0	1
Rockins, Chris, Cleveland	0	0	1	0	1
Romasko, Dave, Cincinnati	0	1	0	0	1
Rose, Don, Miami	0	0	1	0	1
Roth, Pete, Miami	0	0	1	0	1
Rozier, Mike, Houston	5	2	0	0	2

	Fum.	Own Rec.	Opp. Rec.	Yds.	Tot. Rec.
Rusinek, Mike, Cleveland	0	0	1	0	1
Ryan, Jim, Denver	1	1	1	0	2
Salisbury, Sean, Indianapolis	1	0	0	0	0
Sampleton, Lawrence, Miami	1	0	0	0	0
Sanchez, Lupe, Pittsburgh	1	0	0	0	0
Sartin, Martin, San Diego	2	1	0	0	1
Schulte, Rick, Buffalo	0	1	0	0	1
Schwedes, Scott, Miami	7	3	0	0	3
Scott, Ronald, Miami	1	1	0	0	1
Sealby, Randy, New England	0	0	1	0	1
Seale, Sam, L.A. Raiders	0	0	1	−9	1
Seurer, Frank, Kansas City	2	1	0	0	1
Sewell, Steve, Denver	1	0	0	0	0
Shell, Donnie, Pittsburgh	0	0	1	19	1
Shuler, Mickey, N.Y. Jets	2	0	0	0	0
Sims, Kenneth, New England	0	0	1	0	1
Skansi, Paul, Seattle	1	0	0	0	0
Slaughter, Webster, Cleveland	1	0	0	0	0
Smith, Billy Ray, San Diego	0	0	3	0	3
Smith, Blane, Kansas City	1	1	0	0	1
Smith, Bruce, Buffalo	0	0	2	15	2
Smith, Chris, Kansas City	2	0	0	0	0
Smith, Dallis, Seattle	0	0	2	0	2
Smith, Dennis, Denver	0	0	2	0	2
Smith, Reggie, N.Y. Jets	1	0	0	0	0
Smith, Steve, L.A. Raiders	0	1	0	0	1
Spencer, Tim, San Diego	1	0	0	0	0
Spencer, Todd, San Diego	2	2	0	0	2
Stallworth, John, Pittsburgh	1	0	0	0	0
Starring, Stephen, New England	2	1	0	0	1
Stephenson, Dwight, Miami	1	0	0	0	0
Stevens, Matt, Kansas City	0	1	0	−9	1
Stone, Dwight, Pittsburgh	0	0	1	0	1
Strachan, Steve, L.A. Raiders	1	0	0	0	0
Stradford, Troy, Miami	6	2	0	0	2
Swanson, Shane, Denver	1	0	0	0	0
Talley, Darryl, Buffalo	0	0	1	1	1
Tasker, Steve, Buffalo	2	0	0	0	0
Tatupu, Mosi, New England	1	0	0	0	0
Teal, Jimmy, Seattle	1	0	0	0	0
Thomas, Carlton, Kansas City	0	0	1	0	1
Thompson, Donnell, Indianapolis	0	0	1	28	1
Thompson, Weegie, Pittsburgh	0	1	0	0	1
Tillman, Spencer, Houston	1	0	0	0	0
Tippett, Andre, New England	0	0	3	29	3
Toran, Stacey, L.A. Raiders	0	0	1	0	1
Totten, Willie, Buffalo	9	3	0	0	3
Townsell, JoJo, N.Y. Jets	3	2	0	0	2
Trudeau, Jack, Indianapolis	10	2	0	−28	2
Turner, T.J., Miami	0	0	1	0	1
Utt, Ben, Indianapolis	0	2	0	0	2
Veris, Garin, New England	0	0	2	0	2
Vick, Roger, N.Y. Jets	3	0	0	0	0
Villa, Danny, New England	1	0	0	−13	0
Vlasic, Mark, San Diego	1	1	0	0	1
Vogler, Tim, Buffalo	0	2	0	0	2
Walczak, Mark, Buffalo	1	0	0	0	0
Wallace, Ray, Houston	1	1	0	0	1
Walter, Dave, Cincinnati	6	3	0	−9	3
Walter, Joe, Cincinnati	0	2	0	0	2
Warner, Curt, Seattle	4	1	0	0	1
Warren, Xavier, Pittsburgh	0	1	0	11	1
Watters, Scott, Buffalo	0	0	2	0	2
Wheeler, Ron, L.A. Raiders	1	0	0	0	0
Wichard, Murray, New England	0	0	2	0	2
Willhite, Gerald, Denver	1	0	0	0	0
Williams, Alphonso, San Diego	1	0	0	0	0
Williams, Bert, Pittsburgh	0	0	1	0	1
Williams, Derwin, New England	0	0	1	0	1
Williams, Dokie, L.A. Raiders	0	0	1	0	1
Williams, Ed, New England	0	0	2	8	2
Williams, Gerald, Pittsburgh	0	0	1	0	1
Williams, Jamie, Houston	0	1	0	0	1
Williams, John L., Seattle	2	1	0	0	1
Williams, Leonard, Buffalo	0	1	0	0	1
Williams, Oliver, Houston	1	0	0	0	0
Williams, Reggie, Cincinnati	0	0	2	0	2
Wilson, Marc, L.A. Raiders	1	0	0	0	0
Wilson, Troy, Cleveland	2	0	0	0	0
Winder, Sammy, Denver	5	2	0	0	2
Winn, Bryant, Denver	0	0	1	0	1
Winslow, Kellen, San Diego	1	0	0	0	0
Winters, Frank, Cleveland	1	0	0	0	0
Wolfley, Craig, Pittsburgh	0	1	0	0	1
Wonsley, George, Indianapolis	1	0	0	0	0
Woods, Chris, L.A. Raiders	2	1	0	0	1
Woods, Tony, Seattle	0	0	1	0	1
Woodson, Rod, Pittsburgh	3	2	0	0	2

	Fum.	Own Rec.	Opp. Rec.	Yds.	Tot. Rec.
Wright, Dana, Cincinnati	1	0	0	0	0
Wright, Felix, Cleveland	0	1	0	0	1
Wright, Terry, Indianapolis	0	0	1	0	1
Wyatt, Kevin, Kansas City	1	0	0	0	0
Young, Fredd, Seattle	0	0	4	0	4
Zachary, Ken, San Diego	1	0	0	0	0

Yards include aborted plays, own recoveries, and opponents' recoveries.
Touchdowns: Ray Ellis, Cleveland; Dave Grayson, Cleveland; Delton Hall, Pittsburgh; Liffort Hobley, Miami; Trell Hooper, Miami; Bobby Humphery, N.Y. Jets; Mark Kelso, Buffalo; Robert Lyles, Houston; Bill Maas, Kansas City; Sean McNanie, Buffalo; Les Miller, San Diego; Donnie Shell, Pittsburgh; Bruce Smith, Buffalo; Donnell Thompson, Indianapolis; Andre Tippett, New England.
Includes both offensive and defensive recoveries for touchdowns.

NFC Fumbles—Individual

	Fum.	Own Rec.	Opp. Rec.	Yds.	Tot. Rec.
Adams, David, Dallas	2	1	0	0	1
Adams, George, N.Y. Giants	3	1	0	0	1
Adams, Michael, New Orleans	1	1	1	0	2
Adams, Tony, Minnesota	3	0	0	0	0
Alexander, Vincent, New Orleans	2	0	0	0	0
Allen, Egypt, Chicago	0	0	2	0	2
Althoff, Jim, Chicago	0	0	1	0	1
Anderson, Alfred, Minnesota	1	0	0	0	0
Anderson, Don, Tampa Bay	0	0	1	38	1
Anderson, John, Green Bay	0	0	3	0	3
Anderson, Neal, Chicago	2	0	0	0	0
Atkins, Gene, New Orleans	0	0	1	0	1
Awalt, Robert, St. Louis	0	1	0	0	1
Badanjek, Rick, Atlanta	1	0	0	0	0
Bailey, Stacey, Atlanta	1	0	0	0	0
Baker, Ron, Philadelphia	0	1	0	0	1
Baker, Stephen, N.Y. Giants	1	0	0	0	0
Banks, Gordon, Dallas	1	1	0	0	1
Barney, Milton, Atlanta	1	0	0	0	0
Barrows, Scott, Detroit	0	1	0	0	1
Barton, Harris, San Francisco	0	1	0	0	1
Bavaro, Mark, N.Y. Giants	2	0	0	0	0
Bell, Anthony, St. Louis	1	0	0	0	0
Bell, Bobby, Chicago	0	0	1	0	1
Bell, Greg, L.A. Rams	1	0	0	0	0
Bell, Todd, Chicago	1	0	1	0	1
Benish, Dan, Washington	0	0	1	0	1
Bennett, Lewis, N.Y. Giants	0	0	1	0	1
Benson, Charles, Detroit	0	0	1	0	1
Bernard, Karl, Detroit	3	1	0	0	1
Berry, Ray, Minnesota	0	1	0	0	1
Bess, Rufus, Minnesota	4	0	0	0	0
Beverly, Dwight, New Orleans	1	0	0	0	0
Black, Mike, Detroit	1	1	0	0	1
Blount, Alvin, Dallas	1	0	0	0	0
Blount, Ed, San Francisco	1	1	0	−4	1
Board, Dwaine, San Francisco	0	0	1	0	1
Borcky, Dennis, N.Y. Giants	0	0	1	0	1
Bowles, Todd, Washington	0	0	1	0	1
Bowman, Kevin, Philadelphia	1	1	0	0	1
Bradley, Carlos, Philadelphia	0	0	2	0	2
Bradley, Danny, Detroit	2	2	0	0	2
Bramlett, Don, Minnesota	0	1	0	0	1
Brantley, Scot, Tampa Bay	0	0	1	0	1
Brooks, Kevin, Dallas	0	0	1	0	1
Brown, Aaron, Atlanta	0	0	1	0	1
Brown, Donald, N.Y. Giants	0	0	1	0	1
Brown, Jerome, Philadelphia	0	0	1	37	1
Brown, Kevin, Chicago	1	0	0	−6	0
Brown, Reggie, Philadelphia	2	1	1	0	2
Brown, Robert, Green Bay	0	0	4	0	4
Brown, Ron, L.A. Rams	2	1	0	0	1
Browner, Joey, Minnesota	0	0	1	0	1
Bryan, Rick, Atlanta	0	0	1	0	1
Bryant, Kelvin, Washington	4	1	0	0	1
Burton, Ron, Dallas	0	0	1	0	1
Butcher, Paul, Detroit	0	1	0	0	1
Byars, Keith, Philadelphia	3	2	0	0	2
Campbell, Scott, Atlanta	4	2	0	0	2
Campen, James, New Orleans	0	1	0	0	1
Cannon, John, Tampa Bay	0	0	1	0	1
Cannon, Mark, Green Bay	1	0	0	−8	0
Caravello, Joe, Washington	0	0	1	0	1
Carr, Carl, Detroit	0	0	1	0	1
Carson, Harry, N.Y. Giants	0	0	1	0	1
Carter, Carl, St. Louis	0	0	1	0	1
Carter, Steve, Tampa Bay	0	1	0	0	1
Casillas, Tony, Atlanta	0	0	1	0	1
Choate, Putt, Green Bay	0	0	1	4	1

	Fum.	Own Rec.	Opp. Rec.	Yds.	Tot. Rec.
Clack, Darryl, Dallas	1	0	0	0	0
Clark, Bruce, New Orleans	0	0	2	0	2
Clark, Dwight, San Francisco	1	0	0	0	0
Clark, Gary, Washington	3	0	0	0	0
Clasby, Bob, St. Louis	0	0	1	0	1
Cobb, Garry, Philadelphia	0	0	3	0	3
Cofer, Mike, Detroit	0	0	1	0	1
Collins, Jim, L.A. Rams	0	0	2	0	2
Cooper, Evan, Philadelphia	1	0	0	0	0
Courtney, Matt, San Francisco	0	0	2	0	2
Covert, Jimbo, Chicago	0	1	0	0	1
Cox, Arthur, Atlanta	2	0	0	0	0
Craig, Roger, San Francisco	5	2	0	0	2
Crawford, Charles, Philadelphia	0	0	1	0	1
Cribbs, Joe, San Francisco	1	0	0	0	0
Criswell, Ray, Tampa Bay	1	0	0	0	0
Crocicchia, Jim, N.Y. Giants	2	1	0	0	1
Cunningham, Randall, Philadelphia	12	6	0	−7	6
Curtis, Bobby, Washington	0	0	2	0	2
Darwin, Matt, Philadelphia	0	1	0	0	1
Davis, Brian, Washington	0	0	1	11	1
Davis, Chris, N.Y. Giants	0	0	2	0	2
Davis, Jeff, Tampa Bay	0	0	2	3	2
Davis, Kenneth, Green Bay	2	0	0	0	0
Dawsey, Stacey, New Orleans	2	1	0	9	1
Dean, Vernon, Washington	0	1	0	0	1
DeBerg, Steve, Tampa Bay	7	2	0	−2	2
Dent, Richard, Chicago	0	0	2	11	2
DiBernardo, Rick, L.A. Rams	0	0	2	5	2
Dils, Steve, L.A. Rams	2	1	0	−1	1
DiRico, Bob, N.Y. Giants	2	1	0	0	1
Donnelly, Rick, Atlanta	2	1	0	−4	1
Dorsett, Tony, Dallas	3	0	0	0	0
Douglass, Maurice, Chicago	0	1	0	0	1
Downs, Michael, Dallas	0	0	1	0	1
Dozier, D.J., Minnesota	2	0	0	0	0
Duarte, George, Chicago	1	1	0	0	1
Duerson, Dave, Chicago	0	0	1	10	1
Dwyer, Mike, Dallas	0	0	2	0	2
Edwards, Kelvin, Dallas	1	0	0	0	0
Edwards, Stan, Detroit	3	0	0	−23	0
Ellard, Henry, L.A. Rams	3	1	0	0	1
Epps, Phillip, Green Bay	1	0	0	0	0
Evans, Byron, Philadelphia	0	0	1	0	1
Evans, David, Minnesota	0	0	1	0	1
Everett, Jim, L.A. Rams	2	1	0	0	1
Fagan, Kevin, San Francisco	0	0	1	6	1
Ferguson, Keith, Detroit	0	0	1	0	1
Ferrell, Earl, St. Louis	0	1	0	0	1
Flagler, Terrence, San Francisco	2	1	0	0	1
Flowers, Kenny, Atlanta	1	1	0	0	1
Fourcade, John, New Orleans	1	0	0	0	0
Francis, Ron, Dallas	0	0	1	2	1
Frank, John, San Francisco	2	0	0	0	0
Freeman, Phil, Tampa Bay	1	0	0	0	0
Frizzell, William, Philadelphia	0	1	0	0	1
Fuller, Jeff, San Francisco	0	0	3	0	3
Fullwood, Brent, Green Bay	2	1	0	0	1
Futrell, Bobby, Tampa Bay	2	2	0	0	2
Galbreath, Tony, N.Y. Giants	1	0	0	0	0
Garalczyk, Mark, St. Louis	0	0	1	0	1
Garrity, Gregg, Philadelphia	2	0	0	0	0
Gary, Russell, Philadelphia	0	0	1	19	1
Garza, Sammy, St. Louis	1	0	0	0	0
Gault, Willie, Chicago	0	1	0	0	1
Gentry, Dennis, Chicago	2	0	0	0	0
Gogan, Kevin, Dallas	0	1	0	0	1
Goode, Conrad, Tampa Bay	0	1	0	0	1
Gordon, Tim, Atlanta	0	0	1	0	1
Granger, Norm, Atlanta	1	0	0	0	0
Grant, Darryl, Washington	0	0	1	0	1
Gray, Jerry, L.A. Rams	0	0	1	0	1
Gray, Mel, New Orleans	3	1	0	0	1
Green, Curtis, Detroit	1	0	0	0	0
Green, Darrell, Washington	0	0	1	26	1
Green, Roy, St. Louis	1	0	0	0	0
Green, Tim, Atlanta	0	0	2	35	2
Greene, Tiger, Green Bay	0	0	2	0	2
Griffin, Don, San Francisco	0	0	1	7	1
Griffin, Jeff, Philadelphia	0	0	1	0	1
Griffin, Keith, Washington	3	0	0	0	0
Guggemos, Neal, Minnesota	4	3	0	0	3
Haddix, Michael, Philadelphia	1	0	0	0	0
Hadley, Ron, San Francisco	0	0	1	0	1
Hall, Alvin, Detroit	1	1	0	0	1
Halloran, Shawn, St. Louis	1	0	0	0	0
Hallstrom, Ron, Green Bay	0	0	1	0	1
Hamilton, Steve, Washington	0	1	0	0	1

	Fum.	Own Rec.	Opp. Rec.	Yds.	Tot. Rec.
Harden, Derrick, Green Bay	1	0	0	0	0
Harrell, Samuel, Minnesota	1	0	0	0	0
Harris, John, Minnesota	0	0	1	0	1
Harris, Steve, Minnesota	0	1	0	0	1
Harrison, Anthony, Green Bay	0	0	1	0	1
Headen, Andy, N.Y. Giants	0	0	1	0	1
Hebert, Bobby, New Orleans	4	2	0	0	2
Hegman, Mike, Dallas	0	0	1	0	1
Heimuli, Lakei, Chicago	1	0	0	0	0
Heller, Ron, San Francisco	1	0	0	0	0
Hendrix, Manuel, Dallas	0	0	1	0	1
Hicks, Cliff, L.A. Rams	1	0	0	0	0
Hilgenberg, Joel, New Orleans	0	1	0	0	1
Hill, Bruce, Tampa Bay	1	1	0	0	1
Hill, David, L.A. Rams	0	1	0	0	1
Hill, Kenny, N.Y. Giants	0	0	1	6	1
Hill, Lonzell, New Orleans	0	1	0	0	1
Hilliard, Dalton, New Orleans	4	0	0	0	0
Hoage, Terry, Philadelphia	0	0	2	0	2
Hobbins, Jim, Green Bay	0	1	0	0	1
Hohensee, Mike, Chicago	2	2	0	0	2
Holland, Johnny, Green Bay	0	0	1	0	1
Holloway, Johnny, St. Louis	0	0	1	0	1
Holloway, Steve, Tampa Bay	0	1	0	0	1
Holmes, Ron, Tampa Bay	0	0	1	0	1
Hons, Todd, Detroit	2	2	0	−8	2
Horn, Marty, Philadelphia	1	0	0	0	0
Howard, Anthony, N.Y. Giants	0	0	2	0	2
Howard, Bobby, Tampa Bay	1	0	0	0	0
Howard, Erik, N.Y. Giants	0	0	1	0	1
Ingram, Kevin, New Orleans	2	0	0	0	0
Jackson, Kenny, Philadelphia	1	1	0	0	1
Jackson, Mark, St. Louis	0	0	1	77	1
Jakes, Van, New Orleans	0	0	1	30	1
James, Garry, Detroit	3	1	0	0	1
James, Phillip, New Orleans	0	1	0	0	1
January, Mike, Chicago	0	0	1	7	1
Jeffcoat, Jim, Dallas	0	0	2	8	2
Jefferson, Norman, Green Bay	2	0	1	0	1
Johnson, Alonzo, Philadelphia	1	0	0	0	0
Johnson, Billy, Atlanta	2	0	0	0	0
Johnson, Gregg, St. Louis	0	0	2	0	2
Johnson, Holbert, L.A. Rams	0	1	0	0	1
Johnson, Pepper, N.Y. Giants	0	0	1	0	1
Johnson, Sam, L.A. Rams	2	0	0	0	0
Johnson, Vaughan, New Orleans	0	0	1	0	1
Jones, Chris, N.Y. Giants	1	0	0	−18	0
Jones, Dale, Dallas	0	0	2	26	2
Jones, Ed (Too Tall), Dallas	0	0	1	0	1
Jones, James, Detroit	2	0	0	0	0
Jones, Mike, New Orleans	1	0	0	0	0
Jones, Rod, Tampa Bay	0	0	1	8	1
Jordan, David, Tampa Bay	0	1	0	0	1
Jordan, Steve, Minnesota	1	0	0	0	0
Joyner, Seth, Philadelphia	0	0	2	18	2
Junior, E.J., St. Louis	1	0	2	5	2
Kab, Vyto, Detroit	0	1	0	0	1
Kamana, John, Atlanta	1	0	0	0	0
Keever, Carl, San Francisco	0	0	1	0	1
Kennard, Derek, St. Louis	2	0	0	−4	0
King, Angelo, Detroit	0	0	1	9	1
Kirchbaum, Kelly, Philadelphia	0	0	1	0	1
Klingel, John, Philadelphia	0	0	1	0	1
Kramer, Tommy, Minnesota	2	0	0	0	0
Lee, Gary, Detroit	1	0	0	0	0
Lewis, Leo, Minnesota	1	2	0	0	2
Lilja, George, Dallas	1	0	0	0	0
Livingston, Bruce, Dallas	1	0	0	0	0
Lockett, Danny, Detroit	0	0	1	0	1
Lockhart, Eugene, Dallas	0	0	1	0	1
Lomax, Neil, St. Louis	7	3	0	−3	3
Long, Chuck, Detroit	8	3	0	−8	3
Lott, Ronnie, San Francisco	0	1	1	33	2
Lovelady, Edwin, N.Y. Giants	5	2	0	0	2
Mack, Cedric, St. Louis	0	0	2	0	2
Majkowski, Don, Green Bay	5	0	0	0	0
Mandley, Pete, Detroit	0	1	0	0	1
Mann, Charles, Washington	0	0	1	0	1
Mansfield, Von, Green Bay	1	0	0	0	0
Manuel, Lionel, N.Y. Giants	1	0	0	0	0
Marshall, Wilber, Chicago	0	0	1	0	1
Martin, Chris, Minnesota	0	0	1	0	1
Martin, Derrick, San Francisco	1	0	0	0	0
Martin, Eric, New Orleans	3	1	0	0	1
Martin, Kelvin, Dallas	1	0	0	0	0
Matthews, Aubrey, Atlanta	2	0	1	0	1
May, Marc, Minnesota	1	0	0	0	0
May, Mark, Washington	0	1	0	0	1

	Fum.	Own Rec.	Opp. Rec.	Yds.	Tot. Rec.
Mayes, Rueben, New Orleans	8	1	0	0	1
Mayes, Tony, St. Louis	0	0	1	0	1
Mays, Stafford, Minnesota	0	0	2	0	2
McAdoo, Derrick, St. Louis	2	1	2	0	3
McCallister, Fred, Tampa Bay	0	0	1	0	1
McConkey, Phil, N.Y. Giants	2	1	0	0	1
McHale, Tom, Tampa Bay	0	0	1	0	1
McKinnon, Dennis, Chicago	6	3	0	0	3
McLemore, Dana, San Francisco	1	1	0	0	1
McMahon, Jim, Chicago	2	0	0	0	0
Merkens, Guido, Philadelphia	3	1	0	0	1
Mikolas, Doug, San Francisco	0	0	1	0	1
Millard, Keith, Minnesota	0	0	2	8	2
Millen, Hugh, L.A. Rams	1	0	0	0	0
Mills, Sam, New Orleans	0	0	3	0	3
Milot, Rich, Washington	0	0	1	0	1
Mitchell, Stump, St. Louis	3	1	0	0	1
Monroe, Carl, San Francisco	1	1	0	0	1
Montana, Joe, San Francisco	3	2	0	−5	2
Moore, Robert, Atlanta	0	0	2	20	2
Moorehead, Emery, Chicago	1	0	0	0	0
Moran, Rich, Green Bay	1	1	0	3	1
Morris, Joe, N.Y. Giants	2	0	0	0	0
Morris, Lee, Green Bay	1	2	0	0	2
Morse, Bobby, Philadelphia	1	0	1	0	1
Moss, Winston, Tampa Bay	0	0	1	0	1
Murphy, Mark, Green Bay	0	0	2	0	2
Neal, Frankie, Green Bay	1	0	0	0	0
Nelson, Darrin, Minnesota	2	0	0	0	0
Neville, Tom, Green Bay	0	1	0	0	1
Newsome, Tim, Dallas	1	0	0	0	0
Newsome, Vince, L.A. Rams	0	0	1	7	1
Noble, Brian, Green Bay	0	0	5	0	5
Noga, Niko, St. Louis	0	0	1	23	1
Novacek, Jay, St. Louis	1	0	0	0	0
Oates, Bart, N.Y. Giants	0	1	0	0	1
Ori, Frank, Minnesota	0	2	0	0	2
Owens, Mel, L.A. Rams	0	0	1	0	1
Paige, Tony, Detroit	0	0	1	0	1
Payton, Sean, Chicago	1	0	0	0	0
Payton, Walter, Chicago	5	0	0	0	0
Penn, Jesse, Dallas	0	0	1	0	1
Perry, William, Chicago	1	0	0	0	0
Pitts, Mike, Philadelphia	0	0	4	21	4
Pointer, John, Green Bay	0	0	1	0	1
Quick, Mike, Philadelphia	3	1	0	0	1
Quinn, Marcus, Tampa Bay	0	0	1	0	1
Rafferty, Tom, Dallas	0	1	0	0	1
Randle, Ervin, Tampa Bay	0	0	1	0	1
Rathman, Tom, San Francisco	1	0	0	0	0
Reaves, John, Tampa Bay	1	0	0	0	0
Renfro, Mike, Dallas	1	0	0	0	0
Rice, Allen, Minnesota	1	1	0	0	1
Rice, Jerry, San Francisco	2	1	0	0	1
Richardson, Greg, Minnesota	1	0	0	0	0
Richardson, Reggie, L.A. Rams	0	0	1	0	1
Ricks, Harold, Tampa Bay	3	2	0	0	2
Riggs, Gerald, Atlanta	4	1	0	0	1
Risher, Alan, Green Bay	4	1	0	0	1
Robinson, Jacque, Philadelphia	1	1	0	0	1
Robinson, Shelton, Detroit	0	0	2	0	2
Rodenberger, Jeff, New Orleans	0	1	0	0	1
Rodgers, Del, San Francisco	1	0	0	0	0
Rogers, George, Washington	2	0	0	0	0
Rohrer, Jeff, Dallas	0	0	2	0	2
Rouson, Lee, N.Y. Giants	3	1	0	0	1
Rubbert, Ed, Washington	1	0	0	−2	0
Rutledge, Craig, L.A. Rams	1	0	0	0	0
Rutledge, Jeff, N.Y. Giants	7	3	0	−3	3
Saindon, Pat, Atlanta	0	1	0	6	1
Sanders, Thomas, Chicago	1	0	0	0	0
Sargent, Broderick, St. Louis	1	0	0	0	0
Schroeder, Jay, Washington	5	0	0	0	0
Scott, Patrick, Green Bay	2	2	0	0	2
Scott, Victor, Dallas	0	0	1	3	1
Scribner, Bucky, Minnesota	1	0	0	0	0
Settle, John, Atlanta	2	1	0	0	1
Sharpe, Luis, St. Louis	0	1	0	0	1
Simmons, Clyde, Philadelphia	0	0	1	0	1
Simms, Phil, N.Y. Giants	4	1	0	0	1
Singletary, Mike, Chicago	0	0	1	0	1
Smith, J.T., St. Louis	2	0	0	0	0
Smith, Jeff, Tampa Bay	2	0	0	0	0
Smith, Leonard, St. Louis	0	0	1	29	1
Smith, Phil, L.A. Rams	1	0	0	0	0
Smith, Sean, Chicago	0	1	0	0	1
Snyder, Loren, Dallas	1	0	0	0	0
Solomon, Jesse, Minnesota	0	0	1	33	1

	Fum.	Own Rec.	Opp. Rec.	Yds.	Tot. Rec.
Spagnola, John, Philadelphia	2	0	0	0	0
Stamps, Sylvester, Atlanta	1	1	0	0	1
Stanley, Walter, Green Bay	5	3	0	0	3
Stensrud, Mike, Tampa Bay	0	0	1	3	1
Sterling, John, Green Bay	1	0	0	0	0
Stills, Ken, Green Bay	0	1	0	0	1
Studwell, Scott, Minnesota	0	0	1	0	1
Sully, Ivory, Detroit	0	0	1	0	1
Sutton, Mickey, L.A. Rams	0	0	2	0	2
Sutton, Reggie, New Orleans	0	0	1	0	1
Sweeney, Kevin, Dallas	0	1	0	0	1
Swilling, Pat, New Orleans	0	0	3	1	3
Sydney, Harry, San Francisco	2	0	0	0	0
Tamburello, Ben, Philadelphia	0	1	0	0	1
Tautalatasi, Junior, Philadelphia	1	0	0	0	0
Taylor, John, San Francisco	0	1	0	26	1
Testaverde, Vinny, Tampa Bay	7	4	0	−3	4
Thomas, Calvin, Chicago	0	1	0	0	1
Thomas, Henry, Minnesota	0	0	1	0	1
Thomas, Kelly, L.A. Rams	0	1	0	1	1
Thomas, Lavale, Green Bay	0	1	1	3	2
Thomasson, Leon, Atlanta	0	0	1	0	1
Thompson, Robert, Detroit	0	0	1	0	1
Tinsley, Scott, Philadelphia	3	0	0	0	0
Tomczak, Mike, Chicago	6	1	0	0	1
Toney, Anthony, Philadelphia	5	3	0	0	3
Tripoli, Paul, Tampa Bay	0	0	3	0	3
Truvillion, Eric, Detroit	1	0	0	0	0
Tuinei, Mark, Dallas	0	1	0	0	1
Vann, Norwood, L.A. Rams	0	1	0	0	1
Van Raaphorst, Jeff, Atlanta	1	0	0	0	0
Vital, Lionel, Washington	3	0	0	0	0
Walker, Dwight, New Orleans	0	1	0	0	1
Walker, Herschel, Dallas	4	1	0	0	1
Wallace, Steve, San Francisco	0	1	0	0	1
Walls, Herkie, Tampa Bay	1	1	0	0	1
Walter, Mike, San Francisco	0	0	1	0	1
Washington, Charles, Green Bay	0	1	0	0	1
Waters, Andre, Philadelphia	0	0	2	11	2
Wattelet, Frank, New Orleans	0	0	1	0	1
Watts, Randy, Dallas	0	0	1	0	1
Waymer, Dave, New Orleans	0	0	3	2	3
Weaver, Emanuel, Atlanta	0	0	1	0	1
Weddington, Mike, Green Bay	0	0	1	0	1
Wells, Arthur, Tampa Bay	0	0	1	0	1
Wenzel, Jeff, Philadelphia	0	1	0	0	1
Whisenhunt, Ken, Atlanta	1	1	0	0	1
White, Bob, Dallas	2	0	0	0	0
White, Charles, L.A. Rams	8	1	0	0	1
White, Danny, Dallas	9	3	0	−7	3
White, Reggie, Philadelphia	0	0	1	70	1
Wilcher, Mike, L.A. Rams	0	0	1	35	1
Wilder, James, Tampa Bay	3	2	0	0	2
Wilks, Jim, New Orleans	0	0	1	10	1
Willhite, Kevin, Green Bay	2	0	0	0	0
Williams, Doug, Washington	3	0	0	0	0
Williams, Jimmy, Detroit	0	0	2	0	2
Williams, Perry, N.Y. Giants	0	0	2	1	2
Williams, Robert, Dallas	0	0	1	0	1
Williams, Van, N.Y. Giants	2	2	0	0	2
Wilson, Brenard, Atlanta	0	0	1	0	1
Wilson, Wade, Minnesota	3	0	0	−3	0
Wilson, Wayne, Washington	1	1	0	0	1
Wojciechowski, John, Chicago	0	1	0	0	1
Womack, Jeff, Minnesota	0	1	0	0	1
Woodberry, Dennis, Washington	0	0	1	0	1
Woods, Rick, Tampa Bay	1	0	2	14	2
Woolfolk, Butch, Detroit	1	0	0	0	0
Word, Barry, New Orleans	1	1	0	0	1
Wright, Adrian, Tampa Bay	1	1	0	0	1
Wright, Randy, Green Bay	3	1	0	−4	1
Yarber, Eric, Washington	1	0	0	0	0
Young, Lonnie, St. Louis	0	0	3	0	3
Young, Roynell, Philadelphia	0	1	1	20	2
Zimmerman, Gary, Minnesota	0	1	0	4	1
Zorn, Jim, Tampa Bay	3	2	0	0	2

Yards include aborted plays, own recoveries, and opponents' recoveries.
St. Louis fumbled ball through end zone; it was awarded to Tampa Bay.
Touchdowns: Darrell Green, Washington; Mark Jackson, St. Louis; Seth Joyner, Philadelphia; Angelo King, Detroit; Derrick McAdoo, St. Louis; Robert Moore, Atlanta; Winston Moss, Tampa Bay; Niko Noga, St. Louis; Leonard Smith, St. Louis; John Taylor, San Francisco; Arthur Wells, Tampa Bay; Reggie White, Philadelphia; Mike Wilcher, L.A. Rams.
Includes both offensive and defensive recoveries for touchdowns.

Sacks

Individual Champions
NFC: 21.0—Reggie White, Philadelphia
AFC: 12.5—Andre Tippett, New England

Most Sacks, Game
NFC: 4.5—Richard Dent, Chicago vs. L.A. Raiders, December 27
AFC: 4.0—Duane Bickett, Indianapolis vs. N.Y. Jets, November 1
4.0—Cornelius Bennett, Buffalo vs. Philadelphia, December 27

Team Champions
NFC: 70—Chicago
AFC: 45—San Diego

AFC Sacks—Team

	Sacks	Yards
San Diego	45	298
L.A. Raiders	44	361
New England	43	339
Cincinnati	40	303
Indianapolis	39	313
Seattle	37	238
Houston	35	271
Buffalo	34	267
Cleveland	34	257
Denver	31	244
N.Y. Jets	29	206
Kansas City	26	167
Pittsburgh	26	196
Miami	21	183
AFC Total	484	3,643
AFC Average	34.6	260.2

NFC Sacks—Team

	Sacks	Yards
Chicago	70	484
Philadelphia	57	452
N.Y. Giants	55	382
Washington	53	424
Dallas	51	337
New Orleans	47	355
Detroit	42	355
Minnesota	41	307
St. Louis	41	285
Tampa Bay	39	306
L.A. Rams	38	304
San Francisco	37	287
Green Bay	34	197
Atlanta	17	118
NFC Total	622	4,593
NFC Average	44.4	328.1
League Total	1,106	8,236
League Average	39.5	294.1

NFL Top 10 Individual Leaders in Sacks

	Total
White, Reggie, Philadelphia	21.0
Dent, Richard, Chicago	12.5
Tippett, Andre, New England	12.5
Smith, Bruce, Buffalo	12.0
Taylor, Lawrence, N.Y. Giants	12.0
Doleman, Chris, Minnesota	11.0
Nunn, Freddie Joe, St. Louis	11.0
Swilling, Pat, New Orleans	10.5
Jones, Ed (Too Tall), Dallas	10.0
Green, Jacob, Seattle	9.5
Jackson, Rickey, New Orleans	9.5
Mann, Charles, Washington	9.5

AFC Sacks—Individual

Tippett, Andre, New England 12.5
Smith, Bruce, Buffalo 12.0
Green, Jacob, Seattle 9.5
Young, Fredd, Seattle 9.0
Bennett, Cornelius, Buffalo 8.5
Townsend, Greg, L.A. Raiders 8.5
Bickett, Duane, Indianapolis 8.0
Hairston, Carl, Cleveland 8.0
Williams, Lee, San Diego 8.0
Jones, Rulon, Denver 7.0
Mecklenburg, Karl, Denver 7.0
Veris, Garin, New England 7.0
Bell, Mike, Kansas City 6.5
Childress, Ray, Houston 6.0
Jones, Sean, L.A. Raiders 6.0
Maas, Bill, Kansas City 6.0
Williams, Reggie, Cincinnati 6.0
Merriweather, Mike, Pittsburgh 5.5
Puzzuoli, Dave, Cleveland 5.5
Still, Art, Kansas City 5.5
Thompson, Donnell, Indianapolis 5.5
Cooks, Johnie, Indianapolis 5.0
Gordon, Alex, N.Y. Jets 5.0
Phillips, Joe, San Diego 5.0
Williams, Brent, New England 5.0
Gastineau, Mark, N.Y. Jets 4.5
King, Linden, L.A. Raiders 4.5
Robinson, Jerry, L.A. Raiders 4.5
Skow, Jim, Cincinnati 4.5
Williams, Toby, New England 4.5
Bosworth, Brian, Seattle 4.0
Bryant, Jeff, Seattle 4.0
Edwards, Eddie, Cincinnati 4.0
Fletcher, Simon, Denver 4.0
Gary, Keith, Pittsburgh 4.0
King, Emanuel, Cincinnati 4.0
Long, Howie, L.A. Raiders 4.0
Martin, Charles, Green Bay-Houston 4.0
Meads, Johnny, Houston 4.0
Turner, T.J., Miami 4.0
Winter, Blaise, San Diego 4.0
Baker, Al, Cleveland 3.5
Ehin, Chuck, San Diego 3.5
Krumrie, Tim, Cincinnati 3.5
Lyons, Marty, N.Y. Jets 3.5
Martin, Rod, L.A. Raiders 3.5
Nash, Joe, Seattle 3.5
Seals, Leon, Buffalo 3.5
Smith, Doug, Houston 3.5
Sochia, Brian, Miami 3.5
Banks, Chip, San Diego 3.0
Bosa, John, Miami 3.0
Bostic, Keith, Houston 3.0
Carr, Gregg, Pittsburgh 3.0
Crawford, Tim, Cleveland 3.0
Darby, Byron, Indianapolis 3.0
Del Rio, Jack, Kansas City 3.0
Fulcher, David, Cincinnati 3.0
Miller, Les, San Diego 3.0
Smith, Billy Ray, San Diego 3.0
Taylor, Malcolm, L.A. Raiders 3.0
Thorp, Don, Indianapolis 3.0
Willis, Keith, Pittsburgh 3.0
Baker, Jesse, Houston 2.5
Bayless, Martin, San Diego 2.5
Berthusen, Bill, Cincinnati 2.5
Catchings, Toney, Cincinnati 2.5
Crable, Bob, N.Y. Jets 2.5
Matthews, Clay, Cleveland 2.5
McNanie, Sean, Buffalo 2.5
Nichols, Gerald, N.Y. Jets 2.5
Unrein, Terry, San Diego 2.5
Armstrong, John, Buffalo 2.0
Brown, Ron, L.A. Raiders 2.0
Buck, Jason, Cincinnati 2.0
Bussey, Barney, Cincinnati 2.0
Clancy, Sam, Cleveland 2.0
Cooks, Rayford, Houston 2.0
Fuller, William, Houston 2.0
Glaze, Charles, Seattle 2.0
Hackett, Dino, Kansas City 2.0
Hinkle, Bryan, Pittsburgh 2.0
Howard, Carl, N.Y. Jets 2.0
Johnson, Byron, Houston 2.0
Johnson, Mike, Cleveland 2.0
Kragen, Greg, Denver 2.0
Krauss, Barry, Indianapolis 2.0
Lucas, Tim, Denver 2.0
Lyles, Robert, Houston 2.0
Readon, Ike, Miami 2.0
Rembert, Johnny, New England 2.0
Reynolds, Ed, New England 2.0
Snipes, Angelo, San Diego-Kansas City 2.0
Bennett, Barry, N.Y. Jets 1.5
Dorning, Dale, Seattle 1.5
Golic, Bob, Cleveland 1.5
Lambrecht, Mike, Miami 1.5
Little, David, Pittsburgh 1.5
Mersereau, Scott, N.Y. Jets 1.5
Offerdahl, John, Miami 1.5
Rose, Ken, N.Y. Jets 1.5
Ryan, Jim, Denver 1.5
Simmons, King, San Diego 1.5
Sims, Kenneth, New England 1.5
Tupper, Jeff, Denver 1.5
Ackerman, Rick, L.A. Raiders 1.0
Benjamin, Bill, Indianapolis 1.0
Benson, Thomas, San Diego 1.0
Bentley, Ray, Buffalo 1.0
Blackmon, Don, New England 1.0
Brooks, Michael, Denver 1.0
Brophy, Jay, N.Y. Jets 1.0
Brown, Mark, Miami 1.0
Brudzinski, Bob, Miami 1.0
Buczkowski, Bob, L.A. Raiders 1.0
Bulluck, Brian, Indianapolis 1.0
Byrd, Richard, Houston 1.0
Camp, Reggie, Cleveland 1.0
Carter, Alex, Cleveland 1.0
Charles, Mike, San Diego 1.0
Chatman, Ricky, Indianapolis 1.0
Cole, Robin, Pittsburgh 1.0
Cormier, Joe, L.A. Raiders 1.0
Dawkins, Tommy, Pittsburgh 1.0
Donaldson, Jeff, Houston 1.0
Drane, Dwight, Buffalo 1.0
Elko, Bill, Indianapolis 1.0
Fox, Scott, Houston 1.0
Frye, David, Miami 1.0
Graf, Rick, Miami 1.0
Grayson, Dave, Cleveland 1.0
Grimsley, Ed, Indianapolis 1.0
Hammerstein, Mike, Cincinnati 1.0
Hand, Jon, Indianapolis 1.0
Harper, Mark, Cleveland 1.0
Hodge, Milford, New England 1.0
Holmes, Jerry, N.Y. Jets 1.0
Hunley, Ricky, Denver 1.0
Hunter, Daniel, San Diego 1.0
Jackson, Jeff, San Diego 1.0
Johnson, Eddie, Cleveland 1.0
Kelly, Joe, Cincinnati 1.0
Kirk, Randy, San Diego 1.0
Klecko, Joe, N.Y. Jets 1.0
Leiding, Jeff, Indianapolis 1.0
Lippett, Ronnie, New England 1.0
Mangiero, Dino, New England 1.0
Martin, Dave, Buffalo 1.0
Mattiace, Frank, Indianapolis 1.0
McCabe, Jerry, New England 1.0
McGrew, Larry, New England 1.0
McMillen, Dan, L.A. Raiders 1.0
Millen, Matt, L.A. Raiders 1.0
Moyer, Paul, Seattle 1.0
Newsom, Tony, Houston 1.0
Perryman, Jim, Indianapolis 1.0
Pickel, Bill, L.A. Raiders 1.0
Prior, Mike, Indianapolis 1.0
Robbins, Randy, Denver 1.0
Ross, Kevin, Kansas City 1.0
Rusinek, Mike, Cleveland 1.0
Sally, Jerome, Indianapolis 1.0
Schutt, Scott, Cincinnati 1.0
Scott, Stanley, Miami 1.0
Seale, Eugene, Houston 1.0
Simmons, Tony, San Diego 1.0
Smerlas, Fred, Buffalo 1.0
Talley, Darryl, Buffalo 1.0
Thomas, Eric, Cincinnati 1.0
Townsend, Andre, Denver 1.0
Ward, David, Cincinnati 1.0
Warren, Xavier, Pittsburgh 1.0
Washington, Ronnie, L.A. Raiders 1.0
Wichard, Murray, New England 1.0
Wilburn, Steve, New England 1.0
Wiley, Charles, Seattle 1.0
Williams, Gerald, Pittsburgh 1.0
Williams, Joseph, Pittsburgh 1.0
Williams, Lester, Seattle 1.0
Wilson, Karl, San Diego 1.0
Wilson, Steve, Denver 1.0
Wright, Terry, Indianapolis 1.0
Zander, Carl, Cincinnati 1.0
Zordich, Mike, N.Y. Jets 1.0
Anderson, Anthony, San Diego 0.5
Bowman, Jim, New England 0.5
Bowyer, Walt, Denver 0.5
Conlan, Shane, Buffalo 0.5
Glasgow, Nesby, Indianapolis 0.5
Glenn, Kerry, N.Y. Jets 0.5
Glenn, Vencie, San Diego 0.5
Holle, Eric, Kansas City 0.5
Koch, Pete, Kansas City 0.5
Scholtz, Bruce, Seattle 0.5
Wimberly, Derek, Miami 0.5
Woodard, Ray, Denver 0.5

NFC Sacks—Individual

White, Reggie, Philadelphia 21.0
Dent, Richard, Chicago 12.5
Taylor, Lawrence, N.Y. Giants 12.0
Doleman, Chris, Minnesota 11.0
Nunn, Freddie Joe, St. Louis 11.0
Swilling, Pat, New Orleans 10.5
Jones, Ed (Too Tall), Dallas 10.0
Jackson, Rickey, New Orleans 9.5
Mann, Charles, Washington 9.5
Banks, Carl, N.Y. Giants 9.0
Martin, Doug, Minnesota 9.0
Cofer, Mike, Detroit 8.5
Manley, Dexter, Washington 8.5
Holmes, Ron, Tampa Bay 8.0
Marshall, Leonard, N.Y. Giants 8.0
Harris, Timothy, Green Bay 7.0
Jeter, Gary, L.A. Rams 7.0
Mays, Stafford, Minnesota 7.0
McMichael, Steve, Chicago 7.0
Greene, Kevin, L.A. Rams 6.5
Haley, Charles, San Francisco 6.5
McInerney, Sean, Chicago 6.5
Washington, Chris, Tampa Bay 6.5
Wilson, Otis, Chicago 6.5
Ferguson, Keith, Detroit 6.0
Greer, Curtis, St. Louis 6.0
Miller, Shawn, L.A. Rams 6.0
Simmons, Clyde, Philadelphia 6.0
Warren, Frank, New Orleans 6.0
White, Randy, Dallas 6.0
Howard, Erik, N.Y. Giants 5.5
Wilks, Jim, New Orleans 5.5
Jeffcoat, Jim, Dallas 5.0
Marshall, Wilber, Chicago 5.0
Martin, George, N.Y. Giants 5.0
Martin, Steve, Washington 5.0
Wilcher, Mike, L.A. Rams 5.0
Clark, Bruce, New Orleans 4.5
Clasby, Bob, St. Louis 4.5
Kugler, Pete, San Francisco 4.5
Anderson, John, Green Bay 4.0
Brown, Jerome, Philadelphia 4.0
Carreker, Alphonso, Green Bay 4.0
Coleman, Monte, Washington 4.0
Joyner, Seth, Philadelphia 4.0
Moor, Buddy, Atlanta 4.0
Norvell, Jay, Chicago 4.0
Rohrer, Jeff, Dallas 4.0
Williams, Jimmy, Detroit 4.0
Althoff, Jim, Chicago 3.5
Bell, Bobby, Chicago 3.5
Hampton, Dan, Chicago 3.5
Kellin, Kevin, Tampa Bay 3.5
Millard, Keith, Minnesota 3.5
Stover, Jeff, San Francisco 3.5
Turner, Calvin, Tampa Bay 3.5
Bates, Bill, Dallas 3.0
Brooks, Kevin, Dallas 3.0
Brown, Robert, Green Bay 3.0
Butz, Dave, Washington 3.0
Duerson, Dave, Chicago 3.0
Haynes, Tommy, Dallas 3.0
Hegman, Mike, Dallas 3.0
Jarvis, Curt, Tampa Bay 3.0
Meisner, Greg, L.A. Rams 3.0
Noga, Niko, St. Louis 3.0
Perry, William, Chicago 3.0
Saddler, Rod, St. Louis 3.0
Turner, Keena, San Francisco 3.0
Walton, Alvin, Washington 3.0
Watts, Randy, Dallas 3.0
Bryan, Rick, Atlanta 2.5
Garalczyk, Mark, St. Louis 2.5
Green, Curtis, Detroit 2.5
Headen, Andy, N.Y. Giants 2.5
Roberts, Larry, San Francisco 2.5
Smalls, Fred, Philadelphia 2.5
Thomas, Henry, Minnesota 2.5
Benish, Dan, Washington 2.0
Board, Dwaine, San Francisco 2.0
Borland, Kyle, L.A. Rams 2.0
Boyarsky, Jerry, Green Bay 2.0
Brown, Greg, Atlanta 2.0
Burt, Jim, N.Y. Giants 2.0
Cannon, John, Tampa Bay 2.0
Carr, Carl, Detroit 2.0
Casillas, Tony, Atlanta 2.0
Cofer, Joe, Washington 2.0
Coleman, Dan, Minnesota 2.0
Collins, Glen, San Francisco 2.0
Drost, Jeff, Green Bay 2.0
Duliban, Chris, Dallas 2.0
Elliott, Tony, New Orleans 2.0
Fagan, Kevin, San Francisco 2.0
Fuller, Jeff, San Francisco 2.0
Gay, William, Detroit 2.0
Glover, Clyde, San Francisco 2.0
Grant, Darryl, Washington 2.0
Grooms, Elois, Philadelphia 2.0
Johnson, Ezra, Green Bay 2.0
Junior, E.J., St. Louis 2.0
Kaufman, Mel, Washington 2.0
Koch, Markus, Washington 2.0
Lockhart, Eugene, Dallas 2.0
Maxie, Brett, New Orleans 2.0
McCoy, Larry, New Orleans 2.0
McDuffie, George, Detroit 2.0
Murphy, Mark, Green Bay 2.0
Norris, Jon, Chicago 2.0
Olkewicz, Neal, Washington 2.0
Perkins, Ray, Dallas 2.0
Phillips, Ray, Philadelphia 2.0
Pitts, Mike, Philadelphia 2.0
Reed, Doug, L.A. Rams 2.0
Riggins, Charles, Tampa Bay 2.0
Saleaumua, Dan, Detroit 2.0
Scotts, Colin, St. Louis 2.0
Singletary, Mike, Chicago 2.0
Smith, Leonard, St. Louis 2.0
Solomon, Jesse, Minnesota 2.0
Thompson, Robert, Detroit 2.0
Thompson, Warren, N.Y. Giants 2.0
Turpin, Miles, Tampa Bay 2.0
Williams, Eric M., Detroit 2.0
Wright, Alvin, L.A. Rams 2.0
Alvord, Steve, St. Louis 1.5
Clarke, Ken, Philadelphia 1.5
Collins, Mark, N.Y. Giants 1.5
Harris, Al, Chicago 1.5
Harrison, Dennis, Atlanta 1.5
Jiles, Dwayne, Philadelphia 1.5
Korff, Mark, San Francisco 1.5
Lasker, Greg, N.Y. Giants 1.5
Leach, Scott, New Orleans 1.5
Montoute, Sankar, Tampa Bay 1.5
Moss, Winston, Tampa Bay 1.5
Teafatiller, Guy, Chicago 1.5
Ball, Jerry, Detroit 1.0
Battaglia, Matt, Philadelphia 1.0
Bell, Anthony, St. Louis 1.0
Bell, Todd, Chicago 1.0
Benson, Charles, Detroit 1.0
Boyd, Thomas, Detroit 1.0
Brown, Cedrick, Philadelphia 1.0
Browner, Joey, Minnesota 1.0
Browner, Ross, Green Bay 1.0
Carson, Harry, N.Y. Giants 1.0
Carter, Michael, San Francisco 1.0
Clark, Mike, Tampa Bay 1.0
Cobb, Garry, Philadelphia 1.0
Collins, Jim, L.A. Rams 1.0
Courtney, Matt, San Francisco 1.0
Cromwell, Nolan, L.A. Rams 1.0
Curtis, Bobby, Washington 1.0
Deforest, Joe, New Orleans 1.0
Dorsey, Eric, N.Y. Giants 1.0

Dwyer, Mike, Dallas	1.0
Edwards, Dennis, L.A. Rams	1.0
Federico, Creig, Detroit	1.0
Frizzell, William, Philadelphia	1.0
Galloway, David, St. Louis	1.0
Gann, Mike, Atlanta	1.0
Gibson, Dennis, Detroit	1.0
Green, Tim, Atlanta	1.0
Griffin, James, Detroit	1.0
Griffin, Jeff, Philadelphia	1.0
Hamilton, Steve, Washington	1.0
Harris, Roy, Tampa Bay	1.0
Hill, Kenny, N.Y. Giants	1.0
Hoage, Terry, Philadelphia	1.0
Holland, Johnny, Green Bay	1.0
Jamison, George, Detroit	1.0
January, Mike, Chicago	1.0
Johnson, Kenneth, Green Bay	1.0
Johnson, Pepper, N.Y. Giants	1.0
Johnson, Vaughan, New Orleans	1.0
Johnson, Walter, Dallas	1.0
Jordan, Kenneth, Green Bay	1.0
Karras, Ted, Washington	1.0
Lee, Byron, Philadelphia	1.0
Lockett, Danny, Detroit	1.0
Mack, Cedric, St. Louis	1.0
McCallister, Fred, Tampa Bay	1.0
McColl, Milt, San Francisco	1.0
Milot, Rich, Washington	1.0
Mitchell, Randall, Philadelphia	1.0
Molden, Fred, Minnesota	1.0
Morris, Jim Bob, Green Bay	1.0
Morris, Raymond, Chicago	1.0
Noble, Brian, Green Bay	1.0
Noonan, Danny, Dallas	1.0
Nordgren, Fred, Tampa Bay	1.0
Owens, Mel, L.A. Rams	1.0
Rade, John, Atlanta	1.0
Reasons, Gary, N.Y. Giants	1.0
Reichenbach, Mike, Philadelphia	1.0
Rivera, Ron, Chicago	1.0
Rose, Carlton, Washington	1.0
Ross, Tim, Detroit	1.0
Sagnella, Tony, Washington	1.0
Shell, Todd, San Francisco	1.0
Studwell, Scott, Minnesota	1.0
Swoopes, Pat, New Orleans	1.0
Thompson, Steve, Washington	1.0
Tuggle, Jessie, Atlanta	1.0
Waechter, Henry, Washington	1.0
Walen, Mark, Dallas	1.0
Walker, Jimmy, Minnesota	1.0
Washington, John, N.Y. Giants	1.0
West, Troy, Philadelphia	1.0
Auer, Jim, Philadelphia	0.5
Browner, Keith, San Francisco	0.5
Caldwell, David, Green Bay	0.5
Dulin, Gary, St. Louis	0.5
Keys, Tyrone, Tampa Bay	0.5
Morris, Dwaine, Atlanta	0.5
Stokes, Fred, L.A. Rams	0.5
Studaway, Mark, Atlanta	0.5
Sullivan, Carl, Green Bay	0.5
Taylor, Derrick, New Orleans	0.5

1987 Paid Attendance Breakdown

	Games	Attendance	Average
AFC Preseason	7	360,906	51,558
NFC Preseason	7	427,072	61,010
AFC-NFC Preseason, Interconference	44	2,328,892	52,929
NFL Preseason Total	**58**	**3,116,870**	**53,739**
AFC Regular Season	82	4,575,262	55,796
NFC Regular Season	82	4,231,079	51,599
AFC-NFC Regular Season, Interconference	46	2,599,825	56,518
NFL Regular Season Total	***210**	**11,406,166**	**54,315**
AFC First-Round Playoff	1		
(Seattle-Houston)		50,519	
AFC Divisional Playoffs	2		
(Indianapolis-Cleveland)		79,372	
(Houston-Denver)		75,440	
AFC Championship Game	1		
(Cleveland-Denver)		76,197	
NFC First-Round Playoff	1		
(Minnesota-New Orleans)		68,546	
NFC Divisional Playoffs	2		
(Minnesota-San Francisco)		63,008	
(Washington-Chicago)		65,268	
NFC Championship Game	1		
(Minnesota-Washington)		55,212	
Super Bowl XXII at San Diego, California	1		
(Washington-Denver)		73,302	
AFC-NFC Pro Bowl at Honolulu, Hawaii	1	50,113	
NFL Postseason Total	**10**	**656,977**	**65,698**
NFL All Games	**278**	**15,180,013**	**54,604**

*1987 NFL regular season reduced from 224 games to 210 by players' strike.

INSIDE THE NUMBERS

NFL Home/Road Records, Past Five Seasons 212
Most Points in a Game by Each NFL Team 213
Teams That Have Scored Sixty Points in a Game 214
Youngest/Oldest Starters in NFL in 1987 214
NFL's Sixty-Ninth Season by the Numbers 214
Tony Dorsett's Rushing vs. Each Opponent 215
Eric Dickerson's Rushing vs. Each Opponent 215
Marcus Allen's Rushing vs. Each Opponent 215
Curt Warner's Rushing vs. Each Opponent 215
Joe Montana's Career Passing vs. Each Opponent 216
Phil Simms's Career Passing vs. Each Opponent 216
Dan Marino's Career Passing vs. Each Opponent 216
John Elway's Career Passing vs. Each Opponent 216
Steve Largent's Career Receiving Statistics 217
Starting Records of Active NFL Quarterbacks 217
Individual Leaders Over Last Two, Three, and Four Seasons 218
Longest Streaks in NFL History 218
Opening Day Records, 1933-1987 219
Teams' Records Trailing at Halftime/After Three Quarters 219
Oldest NFL Records 219
Largest Trades in NFL History 219
December Records Over Last 10 Years 220
Retired Uniform Numbers 220
1987 Score by Quarters 221
Active Players, Not Drafted, Eight Years Experience 221
Active Players, Not Drafted, Who Played in One Pro Bowl 221
Rushing in the 1980's 221
Greatest Comebacks in NFL History 222
Teams' Records in Out-of-Division Games, 1978-1987 224
Teams' Records Since AFL-NFL Merger 224
Longest Winning Streaks Since 1970 224

NFL Home/Road Records, Past 5 Seasons

AFC

BUFFALO

	Total	Home	Road	Playoffs
1983	8-8	3-5	5-3	None
1984	2-14	2-6	0-8	None
1985	2-14	2-6	0-8	None
1986	4-12	3-5	1-7	None
1987	7-8	4-4	3-4	None

CINCINNATI

	Total	Home	Road	Playoffs
1983	7-9	4-4	3-5	None
1984	8-8	5-3	3-5	None
1985	7-9	5-3	2-6	None
1986	10-6	6-2	4-4	None
1987	4-11	1-7	3-4	None

*Lost first-round game

CLEVELAND

	Total	Home	Road	Playoffs
1983	9-7	6-2	3-5	None
1984	5-11	2-6	3-5	None
1985	8-8	5-3	3-5	0-1*
1986	12-4	6-2	6-2	1-1**
1987	10-5	5-2	5-3	1-1**

*Lost divisional playoff game
**Lost AFC Championship Game

DENVER

	Total	Home	Road	Playoffs
1983	9-7	6-2	3-5	0-1*
1984	13-3	7-1	6-2	0-1**
1985	11-5	6-2	5-3	None
1986	11-5	7-1	4-4	2-1***
1987	10-4-1	7-1	3-3-1	2-1#

*Lost first-round game
**Lost divisional playoff game
***Lost Super Bowl XXI
#Lost Super Bowl XXII

HOUSTON

	Total	Home	Road	Playoffs
1983	2-14	2-6	0-8	None
1984	3-13	2-6	1-7	None
1985	5-11	4-4	1-7	None
1986	5-11	4-4	1-7	None
1987	9-6	5-2	4-4	1-1*

*Lost divisional playoff game

INDIANAPOLIS/BALTIMORE (1983)

	Total	Home	Road	Playoffs
1983	7-9	3-5	4-4	None
1984	4-12	2-6	2-6	None
1985	5-11	4-4	1-7	None
1986	3-13	1-7	2-6	None
1987	9-6	4-4	5-2	0-1*

*Lost divisional playoff game

KANSAS CITY

	Total	Home	Road	Playoffs
1983	6-10	5-3	1-7	None
1984	8-8	5-3	3-5	None
1985	6-10	5-3	1-7	None
1986	10-6	6-2	4-4	0-1*
1987	4-11	3-4	1-7	None

*Lost first-round game

LOS ANGELES RAIDERS

	Total	Home	Road	Playoffs
1983	12-4	6-2	6-2	3-0*
1984	11-5	6-2	5-3	0-1**
1985	12-4	7-1	5-3	0-1***
1986	8-8	3-5	5-3	None
1987	5-10	3-5	2-5	None

*Won Super Bowl XVIII
**Lost first-round game
***Lost divisional playoff game

MIAMI

	Total	Home	Road	Playoffs
1983	12-4	7-1	5-3	0-1*
1984	14-2	7-1	7-1	2-1**
1985	12-4	8-0	4-4	1-1***
1986	8-8	4-4	4-4	None
1987	8-7	4-3	4-4	None

*Lost divisional playoff game
**Lost Super Bowl XIX
***Lost AFC Championship Game

NEW ENGLAND

	Total	Home	Road	Playoffs
1983	8-8	5-3	3-5	None
1984	9-7	5-3	4-4	None
1985	11-5	7-1	4-4	3-1*
1986	11-5	4-4	7-1	0-1**
1987	8-7	5-3	3-4	None

*Lost Super Bowl XX
**Lost divisional playoff game

NEW YORK JETS

	Total	Home	Road	Playoffs
1983	7-9	2-6	5-3	None
1984	7-9	3-5	4-4	None
1985	11-5	7-1	4-4	0-1*
1986	10-6	5-3	5-3	1-1**
1987	6-9	4-4	2-5	None

*Lost first-round game
**Lost divisional playoff game

PITTSBURGH

	Total	Home	Road	Playoffs
1983	10-6	4-4	6-2	0-1*
1984	9-7	6-2	3-5	1-1**
1985	7-9	5-3	2-6	None
1986	6-10	4-4	2-6	None
1987	8-7	4-3	4-4	None

*Lost first-round game
**Lost AFC Championship Game

SAN DIEGO

	Total	Home	Road	Playoffs
1983	6-10	4-4	2-6	None
1984	7-9	4-4	3-5	None
1985	8-8	6-2	2-6	None
1986	4-12	2-6	2-6	None
1987	8-7	4-3	4-4	None

SEATTLE

	Total	Home	Road	Playoffs
1983	9-7	5-3	4-4	2-1*
1984	12-4	7-1	5-3	1-1**
1985	8-8	5-3	3-5	None
1986	10-6	7-1	3-5	None
1987	9-6	6-2	3-4	0-1***

*Lost AFC Championship Game
**Lost divisional playoff game
***Lost first-round game

NFC

ATLANTA

	Total	Home	Road	Playoffs
1983	7-9	4-4	3-5	None
1984	4-12	2-6	2-6	None
1985	4-12	3-5	1-7	None
1986	7-8-1	2-5-1	5-3	None
1987	3-12	2-6	1-6	None

CHICAGO

	Total	Home	Road	Playoffs
1983	8-8	5-3	3-5	None
1984	10-6	6-2	4-4	1-1*
1985	15-1	8-0	7-1	3-0**
1986	14-2	7-1	7-1	0-1***
1987	11-4	6-2	5-2	0-1***

*Lost NFC Championship Game
**Won Super Bowl XX
***Lost divisional playoff game

DALLAS

	Total	Home	Road	Playoffs
1983	12-4	6-2	6-2	0-1*
1984	9-7	5-3	4-4	None
1985	10-6	7-1	3-5	0-1**
1986	7-9	3-5	4-4	None
1987	7-8	3-4	4-4	None

*Lost first-round game
**Lost divisional playoff game

DETROIT

	Total	Home	Road	Playoffs
1983	9-7	6-2	3-5	0-1*
1984	4-11-1	2-5-1	2-6	None
1985	7-9	6-2	1-7	None
1986	5-11	1-7	4-4	None
1987	4-11	1-6	3-5	None

*Lost divisional playoff game

GREEN BAY

	Total	Home	Road	Playoffs
1983	8-8	5-3	3-5	None
1984	8-8	5-3	3-5	None
1985	8-8	5-3	3-5	None
1986	4-12	1-7	3-5	None
1987	5-9-1	2-5-1	3-4	None

LOS ANGELES RAMS

	Total	Home	Road	Playoffs
1983	9-7	5-3	4-4	1-1*
1984	10-6	5-3	5-3	0-1**
1985	11-5	6-2	5-3	1-1***
1986	10-6	6-2	4-4	0-1#
1987	6-9	3-4	3-5	None

*Lost divisional playoff game
**Lost first-round game
***Lost NFC Championship Game
#Lost first-round game

MINNESOTA

	Total	Home	Road	Playoffs
1983	8-8	3-5	5-3	None
1984	3-13	2-6	1-7	None
1985	7-9	4-4	3-5	None
1986	9-7	5-3	4-4	None
1987	8-7	5-3	3-4	2-1*

*Lost NFC Championship Game

NEW ORLEANS

	Total	Home	Road	Playoffs
1983	8-8	5-3	3-5	None
1984	7-9	3-5	4-4	None
1985	5-11	3-5	2-6	None
1986	7-9	4-4	3-5	None
1987	12-3	6-1	6-2	0-1*

*Lost first-round game

NEW YORK GIANTS

	Total	Home	Road	Playoffs
1983	3-12-1	1-7	2-5-1	None
1984	9-7	6-2	3-5	1-1*
1985	10-6	6-2	4-4	1-1**
1986	14-2	8-0	6-2	3-0***
1987	6-9	5-3	1-6	None

*Lost divisional playoff game
**Lost divisional playoff game
***Won Super Bowl XXI

PHILADELPHIA

	Total	Home	Road	Playoffs
1983	5-11	1-7	4-4	None
1984	6-9-1	5-3	1-6-1	None
1985	7-9	4-4	3-5	None
1986	5-10-1	2-5-1	3-5	None
1987	7-8	4-4	3-4	None

ST. LOUIS

	Total	Home	Road	Playoffs
1983	8-7-1	4-3-1	4-4	None
1984	9-7	5-3	4-4	None
1985	5-11	4-4	1-7	None
1986	4-11-1	3-5	1-6-1	None
1987	7-8	4-3	3-5	None

SAN FRANCISCO

	Total	Home	Road	Playoffs
1983	10-6	4-4	6-2	1-1*
1984	15-1	7-1	8-0	3-0**
1985	10-6	5-3	5-3	0-1***
1986	10-5-1	6-2	4-3-1	0-1#
1987	13-2	6-1	7-1	0-1#

*Lost NFC Championship Game
**Won Super Bowl XIX
***Lost first-round game
#Lost divisional playoff game

TAMPA BAY

	Total	Home	Road	Playoffs
1983	2-14	1-7	1-7	None
1984	6-10	6-2	0-8	None
1985	2-14	2-6	0-8	None
1986	2-14	1-7	1-7	None
1987	4-11	2-5	2-6	None

WASHINGTON

	Total	Home	Road	Playoffs
1983	14-2	7-1	7-1	2-1*
1984	11-5	7-1	4-4	0-1**
1985	10-6	5-3	5-3	None
1986	12-4	7-1	5-3	2-1***
1987	11-4	6-1	5-3	3-0#

*Lost Super Bowl XVIII
**Lost divisional playoff game
***Lost NFC Championship Game
#Won Super Bowl XXII

Records for Each Current NFL Team for Most Points in a Game (Regular Season Only)

Note: When the record has been achieved more than once, only the most recent game is shown; summaries are listed in alphabetical order by conference. Bold face indicates team holding record.

BUFFALO BILLS
September 18, 1966, at Buffalo

Miami.................. 3 7 0 14 — 24
Buffalo................ 21 27 3 7 — 58

TDs: Buff—Bobby Burnett 2, Butch Byrd 2, Jack Spikes 2, Bobby Crockett, Jack Kemp; Mia—Dave Kocourek, Bo Roberson, John Roderick. TD Passes: Buff—Jack Kemp, Daryle Lamonica; Mia—George Wilson 3. FGs: Buff—Booth Lusteg; Mia—Gene Mingo.

CINCINNATI BENGALS
December 17, 1972, at Houston

Cincinnati.............. 3 13 17 28 — 61
Houston................ 3 7 0 7 — 17

TDs: Cin—Doug Dressler 3, Lemar Parrish 2, Ken Anderson, Neal Craig; Hou—Ken Burrough, Fred Willis. TD Passes: Cin—Ken Anderson; Hou—Kent Nix 2. FGs: Cin—Horst Muhlmann 4; Hou—Skip Butler.

CLEVELAND BROWNS
November 7, 1954, at Cleveland

Washington............. 0 3 0 0 — 3
Cleveland............... 13 14 21 14 — 62

TDs: Clev—Darrell Brewster 2, Mo Bassett, Ken Gorgal, Otto Graham, Dub Jones, Dante Lavelli, Curley Morrison. TD Passes: Clev—George Ratterman 3, Otto Graham. FGs: Clev—Lou Groza 2; Wash—Vic Janowicz.

DENVER BRONCOS
October 6, 1963, at Denver

San Diego.............. 13 7 0 14 — 34
Denver................. 3 14 9 24 — 50

TDs: Den—Lionel Taylor 2, Goose Gonsoulin, Gene Prebola, Donnie Stone; SD—Keith Lincoln 2, Lance Alworth, Paul Lowe, Jacque MacKinnon. TD Passes: Den—John McCormick 3; SD—Tobin Rote 3, John Hadl 2. FGs: Den—Gene Mingo 5.

HOUSTON OILERS
October 14, 1962, at Houston

New York Titans......... 3 7 7 0 — 17
Houston................ 14 21 14 7 — 56

TDs: Hou—Bill Groman, 2, Bob McLeod 2, Dave Smith 2, Willard Dewveall, Charley Hennigan; NY—Dick Christy, Ed Cooke. TD Passes: Hou—George Blanda 6, Jacky Lee. FGs: NY—Bill Shockley.

INDIANAPOLIS COLTS
December 12, 1976, at Baltimore

Buffalo.................. 3 3 7 7 — 20
Baltimore Colts......... 7 13 28 10 — 58

TDs: Balt—Roger Carr, Raymond Chester, Glenn Doughty, Roosevelt Leaks, Derrel Luce, Lydell Mitchell, Howard Stevens; Buff—Bob Chandler, O.J. Simpson. TD Passes: Balt—Bert Jones 3; Buff—Gary Marangi. FGs: Balt—Toni Linhart 3; Buff—George Jakowenko 2.

KANSAS CITY CHIEFS
September 7, 1963, at Denver

Kansas City............ 14 14 21 10 — 59
Denver................. 0 7 0 0 — 7

TDs: KC—Chris Burford 2, Frank Jackson 2, Dave Grayson, Abner Haynes, Sherrill Headrick, Curtis McClinton; Den—Lionel Taylor. TD Passes: KC—Len Dawson 4, Curtis McClinton; Den—Mickey Slaughter. FG: KC—Tommy Brooker.

LOS ANGELES RAIDERS
December 22, 1963, at Oakland

Houston................ 14 21 14 0 — 49
Oakland Raiders........ 7 28 7 10 — 52

TDs: Oak—Art Powell 4, Clem Daniels, Claude Gibson, Ken Herock; Hou—Willard Dewveall 2, Dave Smith 2, Charley Hennigan, Bob McLeod, Charley Tolar. TD Passes: Oak—Tom Flores 6; Hou—George Blanda 5. FG: Oak—Mike Mercer.

MIAMI DOLPHINS
November 24, 1977, at St. Louis

Miami.................. 14 14 20 7 — 55
St. Louis............... 7 0 0 7 — 14

TDs: Mia—Nat Moore 3, Gary Davis, Duriel Harris, Leroy Harris, Benny Malone, Andre Tillman; StL—Ike Harris, Terry Metcalf. TD Passes: Mia—Bob Griese 6; StL—Jim Hart.

NEW ENGLAND PATRIOTS
September 9, 1979, at New England

New York Jets........... 3 0 0 0 — 3
New England........... 14 21 7 14 — 56

TDs: NE—Harold Jackson 3, Stanley Morgan 2, Allan Clark, Andy Johnson, Don Westbrook. TD Passes: NE—Steve Grogan 5, Tom Owen. FG: NYJ—Pat Leahy.

NEW YORK JETS
November 17, 1985, at New York

Tampa Bay.............. 14 7 7 0 — 28
New York Jets.......... 17 24 14 7 — 62

TDs: NYJ—Mickey Shuler 3, Johnny Hector 2, Tony Paige, Al Toon, Wesley Walker; TB—James Wilder 2, Kevin House, Calvin Magee. TD Passes: NYJ—Ken O'Brien 5; TB—Steve DeBerg 2. FGs: NYJ—Pat Leahy 2.

PITTSBURGH STEELERS
November 30, 1952, at Pittsburgh

New York Giants......... 0 0 7 0 — 7
Pittsburgh............. 14 14 7 28 — 63

TDs: Pitt—Lynn Chandnois 2, Dick Hensley 2, Jack Butler, George Hays, Ray Mathews, Ed Modzelewski, Elbie Nickel; NYG—Bill Stribling. TD Passes: Pitt—Jim Finks 4, Gary Kerkorian; NYG—Tom Landry.

SAN DIEGO CHARGERS
December 22, 1963, at San Diego

Denver................. 7 10 3 0 — 20
San Diego.............. 10 16 10 22 — 58

TDs: SD—Paul Lowe 2, Chuck Allen, Bobby Jackson, Dave Kocourek, Keith Lincoln, Jacque MacKinnon; Den—Billy Joe, Donnie Stone. TD Passes: SD—John Hadl, Tobin Rote; Den—Don Breaux. FGs: SD—George Blair 3; Den—Gene Mingo 2.

SEATTLE SEAHAWKS
October 30, 1977, at Seattle

Buffalo.................. 3 0 7 7 — 17
Seattle................. 14 28 7 7 — 56

TDs: Sea—Steve Largent 2, Duke Fergerson, Al Hunter, David Sims, Sherman Smith, Don Testerman, Jim Zorn; Buff—Joe Ferguson, John Kimbrough. TD Passes: Sea—Jim Zorn 4; Buff—Joe Ferguson. FG: Buff—Carson Long.

ATLANTA FALCONS
September 16, 1973, at New Orleans

Atlanta................. 0 24 21 17 — 62
New Orleans............. 0 0 7 0 — 7

TDs: Atl—Ken Burrow 2, Eddie Ray 2, Wes Chesson, Tom Hayes, Art Malone, Joe Profit; NO—Bill Butler. TD Passes: Atl—Dick Shiner 3, Bob Lee; NO—Archie Manning. FGs: Atl—Nick Mike-Mayer.

CHICAGO BEARS
December 7, 1980, at Chicago

Green Bay............... 0 7 0 0 — 7
Chicago................ 0 28 13 20 — 61

TDs: Chi—Walter Payton 3, Brian Baschnagel, Robin Earl, Roland Harper, Willie McClendon, Len Walterscheid, Rickey Watts; GB—James Lofton. TD Passes: Chi—Vince Evans 3; GB—Lynn Dickey.

DALLAS COWBOYS
October 12, 1980, at Dallas

San Francisco........... 0 7 0 7 — 14
Dallas.................. 14 24 14 7 — 59

TDs: Dall—Drew Pearson 3, Ron Springs 2, Tony Dorsett, Billy Joe DuPree, Robert Newhouse; SF—Dwight Clark 2. TD Passes: Dall—Danny White 4; SF—Steve DeBerg 2. FG: Dall—Rafael Septien.

DETROIT LIONS
October 26, 1952, at Green Bay

Detroit................. 14 14 14 10 — 52
Green Bay............... 7 3 7 0 — 17

TDs: Det—Jug Girard 2, Bob Hoernschemeyer 2, Jack Christiansen, Jim Smith, Bill Swiacki; GB—Billy Howton, Jim Keane. TD Passes: Det—Bobby Layne 3; GB—Babe Parilli, Tobin Rote. FGs: Det—Pat Harder; GB—Bill Reichardt.

GREEN BAY PACKERS
October 7, 1945, at Milwaukee

Detroit.................. 0 7 7 7 — 21
Green Bay............... 0 41 9 7 — 57

TDs: GB—Don Hutson 4, Charley Brock, Irv Comp, Ted Fritsch, Clyde Goodnight; Det—Chuck Fenenbock, John Greene, Bob Westfall. TD Passes: GB—Tex McKay 4, Lou Brock, Irv Comp; Det—Dave Ryan.

LOS ANGELES RAMS
October 22, 1950, at Los Angeles

Baltimore............... 13 0 7 7 — 27
Los Angeles............ 21 14 14 21 — 70

TDs: LA—Bob Boyd 2, Vitamin T. Smith 2, Tom Fears, Elroy (Crazylegs) Hirsch, Dick Hoerner, Ralph Pasquariello, Dan Towler, Bob Waterfield; Balt—Chet Mutryn 2, Adrian Burk, Billy Stone. TD Passes: LA—Norm Van Brocklin 2, Bob Waterfield 2, Glenn Davis; Balt—Adrian Burk 3.

MINNESOTA VIKINGS
October 18, 1970, at Minnesota

Dallas.................. 3 3 0 7 — 13
Minnesota.............. 14 20 17 3 — 54

TDs: Minn—Clint Jones 2, Ed Sharockman 2, John Beasley, Dave Osborn; Dall—Calvin Hill. TD Pass: Minn—Gary Cuozzo. FGs: Minn—Fred Cox 4; Dall—Mike Clark 2.

NEW ORLEANS SAINTS
November 21, 1976, at Seattle

New Orleans............ 3 17 28 3 — 51
Seattle.................. 6 0 7 14 — 27

TDs: NO—Bobby Douglass 2, Tony Galbreath, Chuck Muncie, Tom Myers, Elex Price; Sea—Sherman Smith 2, Steve Largent, Jim Zorn. TD Pass: Sea—Bill Munson. FGs: NO—Rich Szaro 3.

NEW YORK GIANTS
November 26, 1972, at New York

Philadelphia............ 3 7 0 0 — 10
New York Giants........ 14 24 10 14 — 62

TDs: NYG—Don Herrmann 2, Ron Johnson 2, Bob Tucker 2, Randy Johnson; Phil—Harold Jackson. TD Passes: NYG—Norm Snead 3, Randy Johnson 2; Phil—John Reaves. FGs: NYG—Pete Gogolak 2; Phil—Tom Dempsey.

PHILADELPHIA EAGLES
November 6, 1934, at Philadelphia

Cincinnati Reds.......... 0 0 0 0 — 0
Philadelphia............ 26 6 12 20 — 64

TDs: Phil—Joe Carter 3, Swede Hanson 3, Marvin Ellstrom, Roger Kirkman, Ed Matesic, Ed Storm. TD Passes: Phil—Ed Matesic 2, Albert Weiner 2, Marvin Elstrom.

ST. LOUIS CARDINALS
November 13, 1949, at New York

Chicago Cardinals...... 7 31 14 13 — 65
New York Bulldogs....... 7 0 6 7 — 20

TDs: Chi—Red Cochran 2, Pat Harder 2, Bill Dewell, Mel Kutner, Bob Ravensburg, Vic Schwall, Charlie Trippi; NY—Joe Golding, Frank Muehlheuser, Johnny Rauch. TD Passes: Chi—Paul Christman 3, Jim Hardy 3; NY—Bobby Layne. FG: Chi—Pat Harder.

SAN FRANCISCO 49ERS
September 19, 1965, at San Francisco

Chicago................. 3 0 0 21 — 24
San Francisco.......... 0 24 21 7 — 52

TDs: SF—Bernie Casey 2, John David Crow, Charlie Krueger, Gary Lewis, Dave Parks, Ken Willard; Chi—Charlie Bivins 2, Andy Livingston. TD Passes: SF—John Brodie 4; Chi—Rudy Bukich 2. FGs: SF—Tommy Davis; Chi—Roger LeClerc.

TAMPA BAY BUCCANEERS
September 13, 1987, at Tampa Bay

Atlanta.................. 0 3 0 7 — 10
Tampa Bay............. 14 13 7 14 — 48

TDs: TB—Gerald Carter 2, Cliff Austin, Steve Bartalo, Mark Carrier, Phil Freeman, Calvin Magee; Atl—Stacey Bailey. TD Passes: TB—Steve DeBerg 5; Atl—Scott Campbell. FG: Atl—Mick Luckhurst.

WASHINGTON REDSKINS
November 27, 1966, at Washington

New York Giants......... 0 14 14 13 — 41
Washington............ 13 21 14 24 — 72

TDs: Wash—A. D. Whitfield 3, Brig Owens 2, Charley Taylor 2, Rickie Harris, Joe Don Looney, Bobby Mitchell; NYG—Allen Jacobs, Homer Jones, Dan Lewis, Joe Morrison, Aaron Thomas, Gary Wood. TD Passes: Wash—Sonny Jurgensen 3; NYG—Gary Wood 2, Tom Kennedy. FG: Wash—Charlie Gogolak.

NFL Games In Which a Team Has Scored 60 or More Points

(Home team in capitals)

Regular Season

WASHINGTON 72, New York Giants 41	November 27, 1966
LOS ANGELES RAMS 70, Baltimore 27	October 22, 1950
Chicago Cardinals 65, NEW YORK BULLDOGS 20	November 13, 1949
LOS ANGELES RAMS 65, Detroit 24	October 29, 1950
PHILADELPHIA 64, Cincinnati 0	November 6, 1934
CHICAGO CARDINALS 63, New York Giants 35	October 17, 1948
AKRON 62, Oorang 0	October 29,1922
PITTSBURGH 62, New York Giants 7	November 30, 1952
CLEVELAND 62, New York Giants 14	December 6, 1953
CLEVELAND 62, Washington 3	November 7, 1954
NEW YORK GIANTS 62, Philadelphia 10	November 26, 1972
Atlanta 62, NEW ORLEANS 7	September 16, 1973
NEW YORK JETS 62, Tampa Bay 28	November 17, 1985
CHICAGO 61, San Francisco 20	December 12, 1965
Cincinnati 61, HOUSTON 17	December 17, 1972
CHICAGO 61, Green Bay 7	December 7, 1980
ROCK ISLAND 60, Evansville 0	October 15, 1922
CHICAGO CARDINALS 60, Rochester 0	October 7, 1923
Postseason	
Chicago Bears 73, WASHINGTON 0	December 8, 1940

Youngest and Oldest Regular Starters in NFL in 1987

Minimum: 8 Games Started

Five Youngest Regular Starters

	Birthdate	Games Started	Position
Bruce Armstrong, New England	9/7/65	12	T
Nate Odomes, Buffalo	8/25/65	12	CB
Tim Gordon, Atlanta	5/7/65	8	FS
Johnny Holland, Green Bay	3/11/65	12	LB
Brian Bosworth, Seattle	3/9/65	12	LB

Five Oldest Regular Starters

	Birthdate	Games Started	Position
Dave Butz, Washington	6/23/50	12	DT
Ed Jones, Dallas	2/23/51	14	DE
Steve Nelson, New England	4/26/51	11	LB
Dan Fouts, San Diego	6/10/51	10	QB
Danny White, Dallas	2/9/52	9	QB

Youngest and Oldest Regular Starters By Position

Minimum: 8 Games Started

	Youngest	Oldest
QB	11/25/63 Bernie Kosar, Clev.	6/10/51 Dan Fouts, S.D.
RB	11/23/64 John L. Williams, Sea.	7/25/54 Walter Payton, Chi.
WR	11/14/64 Ron Morris, Chi.	7/15/52 John Stallworth, Pitt.
TE	4/28/63 Mark Bavaro, Giants	3/22/54 Emery Moorehead, Chi.
C	4/10/63 Kirk Lowdermilk, Minn.	3/18/52 Mike Webster, Pitt.
G	9/20/64 Steve Trapilo, N.O.	3/9/53 Dennis Harrah, Rams
T	9/7/65 Bruce Armstrong, N.E.	2/23/54 Joe Devlin, Buff.
DE	8/4/64 Clyde Simmons, Phil.	2/23/51 Ed Jones, Dall.
DT	2/4/65 Jerome Brown, Phil.	6/23/50 Dave Butz, Wash.
LB	3/11/65 Johnny Holland, G.B.	4/26/51 Steve Nelson, N.E.
CB	8/25/65 Nate Odomes, Buff.	1/16/53 Dave Brown, G.B.
S	5/7/65 Tim Gordon, Atl.	8/26/52 Donnie Shell, Pitt.

NFL's 69th Season by the Numbers

0 Overtime games won by the Patriots (the only current NFL team never to have won one).

2.7 Number of interceptions for every 100 passes thrown by Joe Montana, the lowest rate by anyone in NFL history with at least 1,500 passes.

3 Number of players within 50 receptions of 600 for career: Ozzie Newsome (575), James Lofton (571), Wes Chandler (555).

4 Great players of the past to be inducted into the Pro Football Hall of Fame on July 30: Fred Biletnikoff, Mike Ditka, Jack Ham, and Alan Page.

5 Number of seasons in which Joe Montana has passed for 3,000+ yards, one season shy of Dan Fouts's NFL record.

6 Consecutive seasons that the Dolphins have allowed the fewest sacks in the NFL. No other team ever led for more than three years in succession.

6.7 Postseason rushing average for Timmy Smith, the top mark by anyone in NFL history (minimum: 50 postseason rushes).

7 Consecutive postseason games in which John Elway has thrown at least one touchdown pass, a streak three games short of Ken Stabler's record.

9 Consecutive postseason field goals made by Chuck Nelson last season; he is six short of Rafael Septien's record.

11 Total of tie games played in NFL in 14 seasons since sudden-death overtime was enacted for regular-season games.

13 Jerry Rice's streak of games scoring a touchdown, five shy of Lenny Moore's NFL record.

18.4 Anthony Carter's punt return average in postseason play, an NFL record.

20 Postseason games won by Dallas Cowboys, most by any team in NFL history.

23 Opponents' fumbles recovered by Reggie Williams, the most by any active player.

44 Touchdowns by Marcus Allen over last four seasons, most by any NFL player in that span.

44.5 The average yardage of Rohn Stark's 450 NFL punts, the top average by any active punter.

53 Interceptions by Dave Brown in his NFL career, the most by any active player.

73.5 Lawrence Taylor's sack total over the past six seasons, the highest among NFL players over that span.

79.6 Career field-goal percentage of Morten Andersen, the best by any kicker (with 100 field goals) in NFL history.

88 Dan Marino's thrown 88 more touchdowns than interceptions (168-80) in his first five NFL seasons, a total which exceeds every quarterback in the Hall of Fame.

95 Steve Largent's career total of touchdown catches, four short of Don Hutson's NFL record.

152 Consecutive games with a reception by Steve Largent, an NFL record.

174 Consecutive extra points by Gary Anderson, the longest current streak in the NFL.

216 Regular-season games played by Guy Morriss, the most among active NFL players.

255 Games won by Don Shula in regular-season play, just 64 short of George Halas's NFL record.

279 Career punt returns by Billy Johnson, the most by any punt returner in NFL history.

1,122 Points scored by Ray Wersching, the NFL's leading scorer among active players.

1950 Year of birth for Dave Butz, the oldest regular starter in the NFL last season.

8,256 Eric Dickerson's career rushing yardage, the highest five-year total in NFL history.

12,041 Steve Largent's career total of yards on receptions, 105 short of Charlie Joiner's NFL record.

Tony Dorsett's Career Rushing vs. Each Opponent

Opponent	Games	Rushes	Yards	Yards Per Rush	Yards Per Game	TD
Atlanta	3	40	209	5.2	69.7	1
Buffalo	2	45	187	4.2	93.5	0
Chicago	5	80	340	4.3	68.0	0
Cincinnati	2	37	183	4.9	91.5	0
Cleveland	3	49	247	5.0	82.3	2
Denver	2	34	112	3.3	56.0	0
Detroit	5	74	311	4.2	62.2	1
Green Bay	3	65	270	4.2	90.0	4
Houston	3	53	278	5.2	92.7	1
Indianapolis	3	69	426	6.2	142.0	0
Kansas City	1	18	108	6.0	108.0	2
L.A. Raiders	3	67	263	3.9	87.7	2
L.A. Rams	7	132	546	4.1	78.0	3
Miami	3	53	229	4.3	76.3	0
Minnesota	6	85	507	6.0	84.5	4
New England	4	54	265	4.9	66.3	1
New Orleans	4	88	461	5.2	115.3	4
N.Y. Giants	20	347	1389	4.0	69.5	8
N.Y. Jets	1	29	121	4.2	121.0	1
Philadelphia	21	348	1436	4.1	68.4	12
Pittsburgh	4	68	289	4.3	72.3	2
St. Louis	17	299	1487	5.0	87.5	11
San Diego	2	31	134	4.3	67.0	0
San Francisco	6	101	323	3.2	53.8	2
Seattle	3	64	283	4.4	94.3	5
Tampa Bay	4	69	292	4.2	73.0	0
Washington	20	356	1340	3.8	67.0	6
Totals	157	2755	12,036	4.4	76.7	72

Indianapolis totals include two games vs. Baltimore
L.A. Raiders totals include one game vs. Oakland

Eric Dickerson's Career Rushing vs. Each Opponent

Opponent	Games	Rushes	Yards	Yards Per Rush	Yards Per Game	TD
Atlanta	8	157	772	4.9	96.5	9
Buffalo	2	43	144	3.3	72.0	1
Chicago	3	91	387	4.3	129.0	4
Cincinnati	1	22	89	4.0	89.0	1
Cleveland	3	61	238	3.9	79.3	1
Dallas	2	49	244	5.0	122.0	1
Detroit	2	54	329	6.1	164.5	4
Green Bay	3	76	357	4.7	119.0	2
Houston	3	81	500	6.2	166.7	4
Indianapolis	1	25	121	4.8	121.0	1
Kansas City	1	26	68	2.6	68.0	1
L.A. Raiders	1	25	98	3.9	98.0	0
Miami	3	72	379	5.3	126.3	3
Minnesota	2	51	145	2.8	72.5	1
New England	3	78	313	4.0	104.3	0
New Orleans	8	176	853	4.8	106.6	6
N.Y. Giants	3	77	312	4.1	104.0	1
N.Y. Jets	3	69	337	4.9	112.3	3
Philadelphia	2	45	161	3.6	80.5	0
Pittsburgh	1	23	49	2.1	49.0	0
St. Louis	3	79	525	6.6	175.0	4
San Diego	2	58	253	4.4	126.5	0
San Francisco	8	151	726	4.8	90.8	3
Seattle	1	31	150	4.8	150.0	3
Tampa Bay	4	116	669	5.8	167.3	8
Washington	1	12	37	3.1	37.0	0
Totals	74	1748	8256	4.7	111.6	61

Marcus Allen's Career Rushing vs. Each Opponent

Opponent	Games	Rushes	Yards	Yards Per Rush	Yards Per Game	TD
Atlanta	2	40	212	5.3	106.0	1
Buffalo	2	41	136	3.3	68.0	2
Chicago	2	33	117	3.5	58.5	0
Cincinnati	3	56	182	3.3	60.7	2
Cleveland	3	47	172	3.7	57.3	0
Dallas	2	22	84	3.8	42.0	0
Denver	10	180	806	4.5	80.6	5
Detroit	2	39	135	3.5	67.5	1
Green Bay	2	53	217	4.1	108.5	2
Houston	2	38	177	4.7	88.5	1
Indianapolis	2	28	141	5.0	70.5	0
Kansas City	9	172	624	3.6	69.3	3
L.A. Rams	2	49	216	4.4	108.0	3
Miami	3	63	356	5.7	118.7	5
Minnesota	2	28	104	3.7	52.0	1
New England	2	37	139	3.8	69.5	1
New Orleans	1	28	107	3.8	107.0	2
N.Y. Giants	2	28	104	3.7	52.0	1
N.Y. Jets	1	20	76	3.8	76.0	2
Philadelphia	1	24	59	2.5	59.0	0
Pittsburgh	1	13	38	2.9	38.0	0
St. Louis	1	18	86	4.8	86.0	0
San Diego	10	199	877	4.4	87.7	14
San Francisco	2	35	175	5.0	87.5	1
Seattle	11	175	707	4.0	64.3	7
Washington	2	23	104	4.5	52.0	0
Totals	82	1489	6151	4.1	75.0	54

Curt Warner's Career Rushing vs. Each Opponent

Opponent	Games	Rushes	Yards	Yards Per Rush	Yards Per Game	TD
Atlanta	1	12	66	5.5	66.0	0
Chicago	1	17	75	4.4	75.0	2
Cincinnati	2	39	160	4.1	80.0	2
Cleveland	3	46	158	3.4	52.7	2
Dallas	2	34	144	4.2	72.0	2
Denver	8	168	922	5.5	115.3	5
Green Bay	1	25	123	4.9	123.0	1
Kansas City	8	147	656	4.5	82.0	5
L.A. Raiders	8	160	584	3.7	73.0	7
L.A. Rams	1	13	32	2.5	32.0	0
Minnesota	1	23	94	4.1	94.0	0
New England	3	68	294	4.3	98.0	2
New Orleans	1	23	47	2.0	47.0	1
N.Y. Giants	2	45	118	2.6	59.0	1
N.Y. Jets	4	54	242	4.5	60.5	3
Philadelphia	1	13	33	2.5	33.0	0
Pittsburgh	3	55	231	4.2	77.0	1
St. Louis	1	21	83	4.0	83.0	0
San Diego	7	176	799	4.5	114.1	7
San Francisco	1	19	48	2.5	48.0	0
Washington	2	31	140	4.5	70.0	1
Totals	61	1189	5049	4.2	82.8	42

Joe Montana's Career Passing vs. Each Opponent

Opponent	Games	Att.	Cmp.	Pct.	Yards	Avg. Gain	TD	Int.	Sacked
Atlanta	15	369	237	64.2	2574	6.98	22	11	19/142
Buffalo	2	64	43	67.2	381	5.95	2	0	6/46
Chicago	5	112	67	59.8	749	6.69	3	2	14/95
Cincinnati	3	115	71	61.7	738	6.42	7	5	7/60
Cleveland	3	103	71	68.9	818	7.94	6	4	5/40
Dallas	4	89	57	64.0	824	9.26	8	2	5/39
Denver	3	82	46	56.1	588	7.17	4	2	3/30
Detroit	4	90	55	61.1	531	5.90	2	2	7/36
Green Bay	3	67	49	73.1	528	7.88	2	1	3/21
Houston	3	107	75	70.1	846	7.91	7	3	3/13
Kansas City	2	69	43	62.3	488	7.07	2	2	3/16
L.A. Raiders	3	65	35	53.8	499	7.68	4	1	7/68
L.A Rams	17	492	318	64.6	4119	8.37	31	9	28/193
Miami	2	30	19	63.3	267	8.90	1	0	3/22
Minnesota	4	84	56	66.7	741	8.82	9	2	5/24
New England	3	86	53	61.6	613	7.13	5	2	6/39
New Orleans	15	353	214	60.6	2507	7.10	20	11	28/178
N.Y. Giants	5	130	83	63.8	843	6.48	5	3	5/31
N.Y. Jets	3	79	48	60.8	538	6.81	3	3	3/17
Philadelphia	2	20	10	50.0	118	5.90	0	1	1/9
Pittsburgh	3	120	80	66.7	762	6.35	3	6	2/17
St. Louis	6	141	95	67.4	1389	9.85	13	5	7/53
San Diego	2	46	31	67.4	356	7.74	3	2	0/0
Seattle	2	33	17	51.5	237	7.18	2	3	1/7
Tampa Bay	6	180	128	71.1	1364	7.58	5	3	6/45
Washington	4	150	83	55.3	1134	7.56	3	4	8/79
Totals	124	3276	2084	63.6	24,552	7.49	172	89	185/1320

L.A. Raiders totals include one game vs. Oakland.

Phil Simms's Career Passing vs. Each Opponent

Opponent	Games	Att.	Cmp.	Pct.	Yards	Avg. Gain	TD	Int.	Sacked
Atlanta	3	89	49	55.1	658	7.39	4	0	8/54
Chicago	1	28	15	53.6	181	6.46	1	0	8/53
Cincinnati	1	62	40	64.5	513	8.27	1	2	7/70
Cleveland	1	37	23	62.2	289	7.81	1	2	4/22
Dallas	14	385	190	49.4	3071	7.98	22	22	39/299
Denver	2	56	30	53.6	348	6.21	0	1	5/41
Green Bay	5	156	97	62.2	1302	8.35	11	4	16/111
Houston	1	24	13	54.2	234	9.75	2	1	0/0
Indianapolis	1	14	7	50.0	67	4.79	1	4	3/19
Kansas City	2	67	36	53.7	494	7.37	3	4	6/44
L.A. Raiders	1	30	18	60.0	239	7.97	2	2	4/34
L.A. Rams	4	122	58	47.5	806	6.61	4	4	16/135
Minnesota	1	38	25	65.8	310	8.16	1	2	2/17
New Orleans	5	155	90	58.1	1011	6.52	5	7	13/88
N.Y. Jets	3	102	60	58.8	698	6.84	2	2	13/107
Philadelphia	11	316	164	51.9	2201	6.97	12	10	34/264
Pittsburgh	1	16	10	62.5	106	6.63	1	1	3/24
St. Louis	12	348	176	50.6	2297	6.60	24	10	38/239
San Diego	2	66	32	48.5	435	6.59	1	3	6/58
San Francisco	4	141	83	58.9	1096	7.77	4	5	18/119
Seattle	2	52	26	50.0	293	5.63	2	5	8/52
Tampa Bay	6	177	101	57.1	960	5.42	5	5	17/189
Washington	11	293	146	49.8	2206	7.53	12	16	35/263
Totals	94	2774	1489	53.7	19,815	7.14	121	112	303/2302

Indianapolis totals include one game vs. Baltimore.

Dan Marino's Career Passing vs. Each Opponent

Opponent	Games	Att.	Cmp.	Pct.	Yards	Avg. Gain	TD	Int.	Sacked
Atlanta	1	40	20	50.0	303	7.58	2	4	0/0
Buffalo	9	306	201	65.7	2478	8.10	22	13	11/111
Chicago	1	27	14	51.9	270	10.00	3	1	3/25
Cincinnati	2	70	44	62.9	479	6.84	4	0	4/30
Cleveland	1	39	22	56.4	295	7.56	2	1	0/0
Dallas	2	79	45	57.0	605	7.66	5	3	2/19
Denver	1	43	25	58.1	390	9.07	3	0	3/25
Detroit	1	44	23	52.3	247	5.61	2	2	1/8
Green Bay	1	44	30	68.2	345	7.84	5	1	0/0
Houston	4	111	67	60.4	895	8.06	8	5	2/9
Indianapolis	10	331	196	59.2	2662	8.04	19	3	4/33
Kansas City	1	35	23	65.7	258	7.37	2	1	0/0
L.A. Raiders	3	106	66	62.3	846	7.98	9	4	5/49
L.A. Rams	2	84	54	64.3	682	8.12	7	2	1/4
New England	9	305	162	53.1	1895	6.21	15	16	7/64
New Orleans	2	63	39	61.9	391	6.21	4	1	1/6
N.Y. Jets	8	289	181	62.6	2366	8.19	23	8	12/72
Philadelphia	2	73	45	61.6	622	8.52	4	2	3/31
Pittsburgh	3	100	68	68.0	835	8.35	7	6	0/0
St. Louis	1	36	24	66.7	429	11.92	3	0	1/9
San Diego	2	77	51	66.2	628	8.16	5	1	4/29
San Francisco	2	75	42	56.0	495	6.60	3	4	3/29
Tampa Bay	1	39	27	69.2	302	7.74	3	1	0/0
Washington	2	78	43	55.1	704	9.03	8	1	0/0
Totals	71	2494	1512	60.6	19,422	7.79	168	80	67/553

Indianapolis totals include two games vs. Baltimore.

John Elway's Career Passing vs. Each Opponent

Opponent	Games	Att.	Cmp.	Pct.	Yards	Avg. Gain	TD	Int.	Sacked
Atlanta	1	38	19	50.0	291	7.66	3	2	2/11
Buffalo	2	53	25	47.2	311	5.87	3	0	4/25
Chicago	3	53	27	50.9	388	7.32	3	3	3/25
Cincinnati	2	47	30	63.8	355	7.55	4	1	2/13
Cleveland	2	59	31	52.5	454	7.69	4	2	1/6
Dallas	1	24	12	50.0	200	8.33	3	0	1/2
Detroit	2	52	32	61.5	456	8.77	2	1	4/40
Green Bay	2	68	41	60.3	386	5.68	0	4	1/4
Houston	1	35	17	48.6	256	7.31	3	3	2/15
Indianapolis	3	101	49	48.5	690	6.83	3	1	10/73
Kansas City	8	258	137	53.1	1594	6.18	4	16	18/127
L.A. Raiders	8	212	116	54.7	1400	6.60	8	6	19/172
L.A Rams	1	38	18	47.4	229	6.03	2	1	2/15
Miami	1	37	18	48.6	250	6.76	0	1	3/24
Minnesota	2	58	38	65.5	463	7.98	7	1	4/30
New England	3	111	61	55.0	768	6.92	6	3	6/35
New Orleans	1	43	28	65.1	353	8.21	4	1	3/26
N.Y. Giants	1	47	29	61.7	336	7.15	0	2	2/11
N.Y. Jets	1	28	13	46.4	145	5.18	0	1	5/27
Philadelphia	2	45	25	55.6	289	6.42	2	2	6/42
Pittsburgh	3	87	46	52.9	495	5.69	4	2	5/34
San Diego	9	296	160	54.1	1894	6.40	5	14	19/148
San Francisco	1	42	20	47.6	215	5.12	2	1	0/0
Seattle	9	291	156	53.6	2335	8.02	12	9	17/126
Washington	1	35	20	57.1	282	8.06	1	0	3/23
Totals	70	2158	1168	54.1	14,835	6.87	85	77	142/1054

Indianapolis totals include two games vs. Baltimore.

Steve Largent's Career Receiving vs. Each Opponent

Opponent	Games	Rec.	Yards	Yards Per Rec.	Yards Per Game	TD
Atlanta	3	17	252	14.8	84.0	1
Buffalo	2	9	240	26.7	120.0	4
Chicago	5	22	349	15.9	69.8	2
Cincinnati	6	32	454	14.2	75.7	3
Cleveland	9	35	512	14.6	56.9	5
Dallas	4	14	180	12.9	45.0	2
Denver	21	90	1421	15.8	67.7	8
Detroit	4	29	502	17.3	125.5	6
Green Bay	5	26	419	16.1	83.8	2
Houston	4	13	254	19.5	63.5	3
Indianapolis	2	8	130	16.3	65.0	0
Kansas City	19	79	1210	15.3	63.7	5
L.A. Raiders	18	67	1090	16.3	60.6	8
L.A. Rams	3	10	127	12.7	42.3	0
Miami	2	3	41	13.7	20.5	1
Minnesota	4	13	172	13.2	43.0	2
New England	7	28	490	17.5	70.0	3
New Orleans	3	20	357	17.9	119.0	3
N.Y. Giants	5	19	237	12.5	47.4	2
N.Y. Jets	10	48	698	14.5	69.8	4
Philadelphia	3	16	264	16.5	88.0	2
Pittsburgh	7	28	508	18.1	72.6	4
St. Louis	2	13	241	18.5	120.5	3
San Diego	18	77	1266	16.4	70.3	16
San Francisco	3	15	302	20.1	100.7	1
Tampa Bay	2	7	93	13.3	46.5	2
Washington	4	14	232	16.6	58.0	3
Totals	175	752	12,041	16.0	69.6	95

Indianapolis totals include two games vs. Baltimore
L.A. Raiders totals include eight games vs. Oakland

Steve Largent's Career Receiving By Passer

Passer	Rec.	Yards	Avg.	TD
Jim Zorn	455	7346	16.1	49
Dave Krieg	246	3862	15.7	35
Jeff Kemp	15	261	17.4	3
Gale Gilbert	14	234	16.7	2
Steve Myer	10	109	10.9	3
Bill Munson	6	84	14.0	1
Sam Adkins	5	102	20.4	1
David Sims	1	43	43.0	1
Totals	752	12,041	16.0	95

Steve Largent Milestones

Receptions

1st:	Sept. 12, 1976 vs. St. Louis	(1st game)
100th:	Sept. 17, 1978 vs. N.Y. Jets	(31st game)
200th:	Nov. 18, 1979 vs. New Orleans	(56th game)
300th:	Sept. 13, 1981 vs. Denver	(77th game)
400th:	Sept. 4, 1983 vs. Kansas City	(100th game)
500th:	Oct. 21, 1984 vs. Green Bay	(122nd game)
600th:	Nov. 17, 1985 vs. New England	(141st game)
700th:	Sept. 20, 1987 vs. Kansas City	(164th game)
751st:	Dec. 27, 1987 vs. Kansas City	(175th game)

Yards

1000th:	Oct. 30, 1977 vs. Buffalo	(20th game)
2000th:	Nov. 15, 1978 vs. Chicago	(38th game)
3000th:	Oct. 21, 1979 vs. Houston	(52nd game)
4000th:	Oct. 5, 1980 vs. Houston	(64th game)
5000th:	Sept. 20, 1981 vs. Oakland	(78th game)
6000th:	Dec. 20, 1981 vs. Cleveland	(91st game)
7000th:	Oct. 30, 1983 vs. L.A. Raiders	(107th game)
8000th:	Oct. 14, 1984 vs. Buffalo	(121st game)
9000th:	Sept. 23, 1985 vs. L.A. Rams	(133rd game)
10,000th:	Dec. 20, 1985 vs. Denver	(146th game)
11,000th:	Dec. 14, 1986 vs. San Diego	(161st game)
12,000th:	Dec. 27, 1987 vs. Kansas City	(175th game)

Touchdowns

1st:	Sept. 26, 1976 vs. San Francisco	(3rd game)
25th:	Oct. 21, 1979 vs. Houston	(52nd game)
50th:	Sept. 18, 1983 vs. San Diego	(102nd game)
75th:	Oct. 13, 1985 vs. Atlanta	(136th game)
95th:	Dec. 27, 1987 vs. Kansas City	(175th game)

Steve Largent's Number of Games by Reception Total

15 receptions:	1 game	5 receptions:	24 games
12 receptions:	1 game	4 receptions:	35 games
9 receptions:	2 games	3 receptions:	29 games
8 receptions:	11 games	2 receptions:	24 games
7 receptions:	13 games	1 reception:	13 games
6 receptions:	20 games	0 receptions:	2 games*

*Oct. 9, 1977 vs. New England
Nov. 13, 1977 vs. N.Y. Jets

Starting Records of Active NFL Quarterbacks

	W-L-T	Pct.
Mike Tomczak	11-2	.846
Jay Schroeder	24-7	.774
Jim McMahon	39-13	.750
Don Strock	14-6	.700
Dan Marino	48-21	.696
John Elway	46-21-1	.684
Joe Montana	67-31	.684
Danny White	62-30	.674
Pat Ryan	9-5	.643
Bernie Kosar	24-14	.632
Marc Wilson	31-19	.620
Dave Krieg	44-27	.620
Bobby Hebert	13-8	.619
Tony Eason	26-18	.591
Wade Wilson	10-7	.588
Steve Grogan	71-50	.587
Gary Hogeboom	13-10	.565
Phil Simms	51-40	.560
Turk Schonert	6-5	.545
Todd Blackledge	13-11	.542
Ken O'Brien	25-22	.532
Ron Jaworski	72-67-1	.518
Boomer Esiason	23-23	.500
Jim Everett	8-8	.500
Cliff Stoudt	9-9	.500
Doug Williams	33-35-1	.486
Bill Kenney	34-38	.472
Neil Lomax	40-45-2	.471
Tommy Kramer	47-53	.470
Mark Malone	21-24	.467
Randall Cunningham	9-11-1	.452
Steve Dils	10-14	.417
David Archer	9-13-1	.413
Dave Wilson	12-19	.387
Steve Pelluer	5-8	.385
Paul McDonald	8-13	.381
Jim Kelly	10-18	.357
Warren Moon	19-38	.333
Mike Pagel	15-31-1	.330
Jack Trudeau	5-14	.263
Steve DeBerg	20-60	.250
Randy Wright	6-19	.240
Steve Young	5-17	.227
Chuck Long	3-11	.214
Mark Herrmann	2-9	.182

Individual NFL Leaders During Last 2 Seasons, Last 3 Seasons, Last 4 Seasons

Last 2 Seasons	Last 3 Seasons	Last 4 Seasons
Points		
234, Jerry Rice	349, Morten Andersen	443, Morten Andersen
229, Morten Andersen	349, Kevin Butler	442, Tony Franklin
222, Tony Franklin	334, Tony Franklin	438, Gary Anderson
205, Kevin Butler	321, Gary Anderson	421, Jim Breech
199, Ray Wersching	318, Jim Breech	421, Ray Wersching
Touchdowns		
39, Jerry Rice	43, Jerry Rice	44, Marcus Allen
24, George Rogers	39, Joe Morris	43, Eric Dickerson
23, Curt Warner	32, Curt Warner	43, Joe Morris
22, Herschel Walker	31, Mike Quick	43, Jerry Rice*
21, Sammy Winder	31, George Rogers	40, Mike Quick
Field Goals		
54, Morten Andersen	85, Morten Andersen	105, Morten Andersen
47, Kevin Butler	78, Kevin Butler	100, Gary Anderson
47, Tony Franklin	76, Gary Anderson	93, Tony Franklin
43, Gary Anderson	71, Tony Franklin	91, Paul McFadden
42, Tony Zendejas	65, Jim Breech	87, Jim Breech
Rushes		
687, Eric Dickerson	979, Eric Dickerson	1358, Eric Dickerson
553, Curt Warner	943, Gerald Riggs	1296, Gerald Riggs
546, Gerald Riggs	844, Curt Warner	1172, Walter Payton
534, Joe Morris	828, Joe Morris	1068, James Wilder
529, Rueben Mayes	791, Walter Payton	1063, Marcus Allen
Rushing Yards		
3109, Eric Dickerson	4343, Eric Dickerson	6448, Eric Dickerson
2466, Curt Warner	3921, Gerald Riggs	5407, Gerald Riggs
2270, Rueben Mayes	3560, Curt Warner	5101, Walter Payton
2202, Gerald Riggs	3510, Joe Morris	4440, Marcus Allen
2174, Joe Morris	3417, Walter Payton	4036, James Wilder
Rushing TDs		
24, George Rogers	38, Joe Morris	43, Eric Dickerson
21, Curt Warner	31, George Rogers	42, Joe Morris
19, Johnny Hector	29, Eric Dickerson	34, Marcus Allen
19, Herschel Walker	29, Curt Warner	34, Larry Kinnebrew
17, Dickerson & Morris	25, Hector & Kinnebrew	34, Gerald Riggs
Passes		
1067, Dan Marino	1634, Dan Marino	2198, Dan Marino
920, Bernie Kosar	1519, John Elway	1915, Neil Lomax
914, John Elway	1363, Ken O'Brien	1899, John Elway
909, Boomer Esiason	1355, Neil Lomax	1778, Phil Simms
899, Jim Kelly	1340, Boomer Esiason	1731, Dan Fouts
Completions		
641, Dan Marino	977, Dan Marino	1339, Dan Marino
551, Bernie Kosar	831, John Elway	1125, Neil Lomax
535, Jim Kelly	831, Ken O'Brien	1045, John Elway
534, Ken O'Brien	780, Neil Lomax	1039, Joe Montana
515, Neil Lomax	764, Boomer Esiason	1029, Dan Fouts
Passing Yards		
7991, Dan Marino	12,128, Dan Marino	17,212, Dan Marino
7280, Boomer Esiason	10,723, Boomer Esiason	13,590, Phil Simms
6887, Bernie Kosar	10,574, John Elway	13,172, John Elway
6683, John Elway	10,274, Ken O'Brien	12,926, Dan Fouts
6391, Jim Kelly	9,546, Phil Simms	12,573, Joe Montana
TD Passes		
70, Dan Marino	100, Dan Marino	148, Dan Marino
44, Dave Krieg	71, Dave Krieg	103, Dave Krieg
41, Jim Kelly	67, Boomer Esiason	94, Joe Montana
40, Boomer Esiason	66, Joe Montana	83, Neil Lomax
39, Kosar & Montana	63, Ken O'Brien	82, Phil Simms
Receptions		
171, J.T. Smith	239, Roger Craig	310, Roger Craig
153, Al Toon	224, Todd Christensen	308, Art Monk
151, Jerry Rice	214, J.T. Smith	304, Todd Christensen
147, Roger Craig	207, Steve Largent	281, Steve Largent
142, Todd Christensen	202, G. Clark & Monk	256, Mickey Shuler
Reception Yards		
2648, Jerry Rice	3575, Jerry Rice	4433, Steve Largent
2331, Gary Clark	3270, Drew Hill	4311, Mark Clayton
2163, Stanley Morgan	3269, Steve Largent	4234, James Lofton
2152, Al Toon	3257, Gary Clark	4149, Art Monk
2131, J.T. Smith	2976, Mike Quick	4028, Mike Quick
Receiving TDs		
37, Jerry Rice	40, Jerry Rice	40, Mike Quick
20, Mike Quick	31, Mike Quick	40, Jerry Rice*
19, Mark Duper	26, Daryl Turner	39, Mark Clayton
17, Mark Clayton	25, Stephone Paige	36, Daryl Turner
17, Steve Largent	23, Steve Largent	35, Steve Largent
Interceptions		
15, Ronnie Lott	21, Ronnie Lott	26, Deron Cherry
14, Dave Waymer	20, Dave Waymer	25, Ronnie Lott
12, Deron Cherry	19, Deron Cherry	24, Dave Waymer
11, Lippett, McElroy, & Wilburn	17, Everson Walls	22, Dave Brown
	15, J. Griffin & Harden	21, Mike Harden

*Played only three of last four seasons.

Longest Streaks in NFL History

Games Played		
282	Jim Marshall	1960-79
240	Mick Tingelhoff	1962-78
234	Jim Bakken	1962-78
Games Scoring		
151	Fred Cox	1963-73
133	Garo Yepremian	1970-79
128	Rafael Septien	1977-85
Games Scoring Touchdowns		
18	Lenny Moore	1963-65
14	O.J. Simpson	1975
13	John Riggins	1982-83
	Jerry Rice	1986-87 (current)
Extra Points		
234	Tommy Davis	1959-65
221	Jim Turner	1967-74
201	George Blanda	1967-71
Games Scoring Field Goals		
31	Fred Cox	1968-70
28	Jim Turner	1970-72
21	Bruce Gossett	1970-72
	Ray Wersching	1986-87
Field Goals		
23	Mark Moseley	1981-82
22	Pat Leahy	1985-86
20	Garo Yepremian	1978-79
	Morten Andersen	1985-86
100-Yard Rushing Games		
11	Marcus Allen	1985-86
9	Walter Payton	1985
7	O.J. Simpson	1972-73
	Earl Campbell	1979
Games Rushing For Touchdowns		
13	John Riggins	1982-83
	George Rogers	1985-86
11	Lenny Moore	1963-64
9	Leroy Kelly	1968
Passes Completed		
22	Joe Montana	1987
20	Ken Anderson	1983
18	Steve DeBerg	1982
	Lynn Dickey	1983
	Joe Montana	1984
300-Yard Passing Games		
5	Joe Montana	1982
4	Dan Fouts	1979
	Bill Kenney	1983
Games Passing For Touchdowns		
47	Johnny Unitas	1956-60
30	Dan Marino	1985-87
28	Dave Krieg	1983-85
Passes Without Interception		
294	Bart Starr	1964-65
208	Milt Plum	1959-60
206	Roman Gabriel	1968-69
Games With Receptions		
152	Steve Largent	1977-87 (current)
127	Harold Carmichael	1972-80
	Ozzie Newsome	1979-87 (current)
121	Mel Gray	1973-82
100-Yard Receiving Games		
7	Charley Hennigan	1961
	Bill Groman	1961
6	Raymond Berry	1960
	Pat Studstill	1966
5	Elroy (Crazylegs) Hirsch	1951
	Bob Boyd	1954
	Terry Barr	1963
	Lance Alworth	1966
Games With Touchdown Receptions		
13	Jerry Rice	1986-87 (current)
11	Elroy (Crazylegs) Hirsch	1950-51
	Buddy Dial	1959-60
9	Lance Alworth	1963
Games With Interceptions		
8	Tom Morrow	1962-63
7	Paul Krause	1964
	Larry Wilson	1966
	Ben Davis	1968
Punts Without A Block		
623	Dave Jennings	1976-83
619	Ray Guy	1979-86
578	Bobby Walden	1964-72

Records of Teams on Opening Day, 1933-87

AFC	W	L	T	Pct.	Longest W Strk.	Longest L Strk.	Current Streak
Chargers	18	10	0	.643	6	4	L-1
Broncos	17	10	1	.630	3	4	W-2
Colts	20	15	0	.571	8	4	L-4
Raiders	16	12	0	.571	5	5	W-1
Browns	21	17	0	.553	5	5	L-5
Oilers	15	13	0	.536	4	3	W-3
Chiefs	15	13	0	.536	5	4	W-5
Steelers	26	23	4	.531	4	3	W-1
Bengals	10	10	0	.500	4	4	W-1
Dolphins	10	11	1	.476	4	3	L-3
Jets	13	15	0	.464	3	5	W-2
Patriots	13	15	0	.464	4	3	W-4
Bills	9	19	0	.321	3	5	L-5
Seahawks	3	9	0	.250	3	8	L-1

NFC	W	L	T	Pct.	Longest W Strk.	Longest L Strk.	Current Streak
Cowboys	22	5	1	.815	17	2	L-1
Vikings	16	10	1	.615	4	2	W-1
Falcons	13	9	0	.591	5	3	L-1
Giants	29	22	4	.569	3	3	L-2
Bears	30	24	1	.556	7	6	W-4
Lions	29	24	2	.547	7	4	L-1
Rams	27	23	0	.540	5	6	L-1
Packers	28	24	3	.538	5	6	L-3
Redskins	26	25	4	.510	6	5	W-2
Cardinals	24	29	1	.453	6	6	W-1
49ers	16	21	1	.432	4	3	L-1
Eagles	20	33	1	.377	5	9	L-4
Buccaneers	4	8	0	.333	3	5	W-1
Saints	4	17	0	.190	1	6	W-1

Note: All tied games occurred prior to 1972, when calculation of ties as half-win, half-loss was begun.

Records of all NFL teams for 1987 in each category of games:

	Status at Halftime			Status After 3 Quarters		
AFC	Leading	Tied	Trailing	Leading	Tied	Trailing
Buffalo	3-1	2-0	2-7	4-0	1-0	2-8
Cincinnati	4-5	0-0	0-6	2-3	0-3	2-5
Cleveland	9-0	0-2	1-3	9-1	0-0	1-4
Denver	9-1	0-0	1-3-1	8-0	0-0	2-4-1
Houston	5-1	2-0	2-5	6-1	0-0	3-5
Indianapolis	8-1	0-1	1-4	9-2	0-1	0-3
Kansas City	4-2	0-1	0-8	3-2	1-0	0-9
L.A. Raiders	3-1	0-1	2-8	5-1	0-2	0-7
Miami	7-3	0-0	1-4	7-2	0-1	1-4
New England	7-2	0-0	1-5	8-2	0-0	0-5
N.Y. Jets	5-0	1-1	0-8	3-1	2-0	1-8
Pittsburgh	3-2	1-1	4-4	5-2	1-0	2-5
San Diego	3-1	1-0	4-6	3-0	1-0	4-7
Seattle	8-1	1-0	0-5	8-1	0-0	1-5
NFC	Leading	Tied	Trailing	Leading	Tied	Trailing
Atlanta	1-1	1-1	1-10	2-2	0-0	1-10
Chicago	6-1	2-1	3-2	6-2	1-0	4-2
Dallas	7-1	0-1	0-6	5-1	0-1	2-6
Detroit	1-4	1-0	2-7	2-0	2-0	0-11
Green Bay	3-3-1	1-1	1-5	5-1-1	0-1	0-7
L.A. Rams	4-2	0-0	2-7	5-2	1-0	0-7
Minnesota	5-0	0-3	3-4	8-1	0-0	0-6
New Orleans	7-0	1-0	4-3	8-0	1-0	3-3
N.Y. Giants	5-1	1-1	0-7	5-4	1-1	0-4
Philadelphia	6-1	0-1	1-6	6-0	0-2	1-6
St. Louis	5-3	0-0	2-5	5-1	0-1	2-6
San Francisco	11-0	0-0	2-2	11-0	1-0	1-2
Tampa Bay	2-4	1-0	1-7	4-2	0-1	0-8
Washington	8-1	1-1	2-2	8-1	1-0	2-3

Trailing at Halftime

	1981–86	1987 ONLY
Home Teams	147-428-3 (.257)	21-65-0 (.244)
Road Teams	139-616-2 (.185)	22-84-1 (.210)
All Teams	286-1044-5 (.216)	43-149-1 (.225)

Trailing After 3 Quarters

	1981–86	1987 ONLY
Home Teams	121-474-2 (.204)	20-72-0 (.217)
Road Teams	111-664-3 (.145)	15-88-1 (.149)
All Teams	232-1138-5 (.171)	35-160-1 (.181)

Oldest Individual Single-Season or Single-Game Records in NFL Record & Fact Book

Regular-Season Records That Have Not Been Surpassed or Tied

Most Points, Game—40, Ernie Nevers, Chi. Cardinals vs. Chi. Bears, Nov. 28, 1929 (6-td, 4-pat)

Most Touchdowns Rushing, Game—6, Ernie Nevers, Chi. Cardinals vs. Chi. Bears, Nov. 28, 1929

Highest Average Gain, Rushing, Season (Qualifiers)—9.94, Beattie Feathers, Chi. Bears, 1934 (101-1,004)

Highest Punting Average, Season (Qualifiers)—51.40, Sammy Baugh, Washington, 1940 (35-1,799)

Highest Punting Average, Game (minimum: 4 punts)—61.75, Bob Cifers, Detroit vs. Chi. Bears, Nov. 24, 1946 (4-247)

Highest Average Gain, Pass Receptions, Season (minimum: 24 receptions)—32.58, Don Currivan, Boston, 1947 (24-782)

Highest Average Gain, Passing, Game (minimum: 20 passes)—18.58, Sammy Baugh, Washington vs. Boston, Oct. 31, 1948 (24-446)

Most Touchdowns, Fumble Recoveries, Game—2, Fred (Dippy) Evans, Chi. Bears vs. Washington, Nov. 28, 1948

Most Yards Gained, Intercepted Passes, Rookie, Season—301, Don Doll, Detroit, 1949

Most Passes Had Intercepted, Game—8, Jim Hardy, Chi. Cardinals vs. Philadelphia, Sept. 24, 1950

Highest Average Gain, Rushing, Game (minimum: 10 attempts)—17.09, Marion Motley, Cleveland vs. Pittsburgh, Oct. 29, 1950 (11-188)

Most Yards Gained, Kickoff Returns, Game—294, Wally Triplett, Detroit vs. Los Angeles, Oct. 29, 1950

Highest Kickoff Return Average, Game (minimum: 3 returns)—73.50, Wally Triplett, Detroit vs. Los Angeles, Oct. 29, 1950 (4-294)

Most Pass Receptions, Game—18, Tom Fears, Los Angeles vs. Green Bay, Dec. 3, 1950

Highest Punt Return Average, Season (Qualifiers)—23.00, Herb Rich, Baltimore, 1950 (12-276)

Highest Punt Return Average, Rookie, Season (Qualifiers)—23.00, Herb Rich, Baltimore, 1950 (12-276)

Most Yards Passing, Game—554, Norm Van Brocklin, Los Angeles vs. N.Y. Yanks, Sept. 28, 1951

Most Touchdowns, Punt Returns, Rookie, Season—4, Jack Christiansen, Detroit, 1951

Most Interceptions By, Season—14, Dick (Night Train) Lane, Los Angeles, 1952

Most Interceptions By, Rookie, Season—14, Dick (Night Train) Lane, Los Angeles, 1952

Highest Average Gain, Passing, Season (Qualifiers)—11.17, Tommy O'Connell, Cleveland, 1957 (110-1,229)

Most Points, Season—176, Paul Hornung, Green Bay, 1960 (15-td, 41-pat, 15-fg)

Highest Pass Rating, Season—110.4, Milt Plum, Cleveland, 1960

Most Yards Gained, Pass Receptions, Rookie, Season—1,473, Bill Groman, Houston, 1960

Largest Trades in NFL History

(Based on number of players or draft choices involved)

15—March 26, 1953—T Mike McCormack, DT Don Colo, LB Tom Catlin, DB John Petitbon, and G Herschell Forester from Baltimore to Cleveland for DB Don Shula, DB Bert Rechichar, DB Carl Taseff, LB Ed Sharkey, E Gern Nagler, QB Harry Agganis, T Dick Batten, T Stu Sheets, G Art Spinney, and G Elmer Willhoite.

15—January 28, 1971—LB Marlin McKeever, first- and third-round choices in 1971, and third-, fourth-, fifth-, sixth-, and seventh-round choices in 1972 from Washington to the Los Angeles Rams for LB Maxie Baughan, LB Jack Pardee, LB Myron Pottios, RB Jeff Jordan, G John Wilbur, DT Diron Talbert, and a fifth-round choice in 1971.

12—June 13, 1952—Selection rights to Les Richter from the Dallas Texans to the Los Angeles Rams for RB Dick Hoerner, DB Tom Keane, DB George Sims, C Joe Reid, HB Billy Baggett, T Jack Halliday, FB Dick McKissack, LB Vic Vasicek, E Richard Wilkins, C Aubrey Phillips, and RB Dave Anderson.

10—March 23, 1959—Ollie Matson from the Chicago Cardinals to the Los Angeles Rams for T Frank Fuller, DE Glenn Holtzman, T Ken Panfil, DT Art Hauser, E John Tracey, FB Larry Hickman, HB Don Brown, the Rams second-round choice in 1960, and a player to be delivered during the 1959 training camp.

10—October 31, 1987—RB Eric Dickerson from the Los Angeles Rams to Indianapolis. The rights to LB Cornelius Bennett from Indianapolis to Buffalo. Indianapolis running back Owen Gill and the Colts' first- and second-round choices in 1988 and first-round choice in 1989, plus Bills running back Greg Bell and Buffalo's first-round choice in 1988 and first- and second-round choices in 1989 to the Rams.

December Records Over Last 10 Years

AFC	1978	1979	1980	1981	1982	1983	1984	1985	1986	1987	Total	Pct.
Miami	3-0	1-1	2-1	3-0	3-1	3-0	2-1	4-0	2-1	3-1	26- 6	.813
Cincinnati	3-0	1-2	2-1	2-1	3-1	2-1	3-0	2-2	2-1	1-3	21-12	.636
L.A. Raiders	1-2	2-1	3-1	1-2	4-0	2-1	2-1	4-0	0-3	1-3	20-14	.588
San Diego	3-0	2-1	2-1	2-1	4-0	1-2	1-2	3-1	1-2	0-4	19-14	.576
Kansas City	1-2	2-1	2-1	1-2	1-3	1-2	3-0	2-2	3-0	2-2	18-15	.545
Denver	2-1	1-2	1-3	2-1	1-3	2-1	2-1	3-1	1-2	3-1	18-16	.529
Seattle	2-1	2-1	0-3	2-1	1-3	2-1	1-2	2-2	3-0	2-2	17-16	.515
New England	1-2	1-1	2-1	0-3	2-2	2-1	1-2	3-1	1-2	3-1	16-16	.500
Cleveland	1-2	1-2	2-1	0-3	2-2	1-2	1-2	2-2	3-0	3-1	16-17	.485
Pittsburgh	3-0	2-1	1-2	0-3	2-2	1-2	2-1	1-3	2-1	2-2	16-17	.485
N.Y. Jets	1-2	3-0	1-2	2-1	3-1	1-2	1-2	2-1	0-3	0-4	14-18	.438
Houston	1-2	1-2	3-0	2-1	0-4	1-2	1-2	0-4	2-1	3-1	14-19	.424
Indianapolis	0-3	1-2	0-3	1-2	0-3-1	1-2	0-3	2-2	3-0	3-1	11-21-1	.348
Buffalo	1-2	0-3	2-1	2-1	1-3	1-2	1-2	0-4	0-3	1-3	9-24	.273

NFC	1978	1979	1980	1981	1982	1983	1984	1985	1986	1987	Total	Pct.
Washington	0-3	2-1	3-0	3-0	3-1	3-0	2-0	3-1	1-2	3-1	23-9	.719
San Francisco	1-2	1-2	1-2	3-0	2-2	3-0	3-0	3-1	3-1	4-0	24-10	.706
Chicago	2-1	3-0	2-1	3-0	2-2	2-1	1-2	3-1	3-0	2-2	23-10	.697
St. Louis	2-1	2-1	1-2	1-2	3-1	3-0	2-1	1-2	1-1-1	2-2	18-13-1	.578
Dallas	3-0	3-0	2-1	2-1	3-1	1-2	1-2	1-2	0-3	2-2	18-14	.563
Green Bay	1-2	1-2	0-3	2-1	2-1-1	2-1	3-0	3-1	1-2	1-3	16-16-1	.500
N.Y. Giants	1-2	0-3	1-2	3-0	2-2	0-3	1-2	2-2	4-0	3-1	17-17	.500
L.A. Rams	2-1	2-1	2-1	1-2	0-4	1-2	2-1	2-2	1-2	2-2	15-18	.455
Atlanta	1-2	2-1	2-1	0-3	3-1	1-2	1-2	2-2	1-2	1-3	14-19	.424
Philadelphia	1-2	2-1	1-2	1-2	2-2	1-2	1-2	1-3	1-1-1	2-2	13-19-1	.409
Minnesota	1-2	1-2	2-1	0-3	2-2	1-2	0-2	2-2	2-1	1-3	12-20	.375
New Orleans	2-1	1-2	1-2	0-3	0-4	1-2	1-2	1-3	1-2	4-0	12-21	.364
Detroit	2-1	0-3	2-1	1-2	1-3	2-1	0-3	0-3	0-3	2-2	10-22	.313
Tampa Bay	0-3	1-2	0-3	2-1	3-1	0-3	2-1	0-4	0-3	0-4	8-25	.242

L.A. Raiders totals include Oakland, 1978-81
Indianapolis totals include Baltimore, 1978-83

Retired Uniform Numbers in NFL

AFC

Buffalo:	None	
Cincinnati:	Bob Johnson	54
Cleveland:	Otto Graham	14
	Jim Brown	32
	Ernie Davis	45
	Don Fleming	46
	Lou Groza	76
Denver:	Frank Tripucka	18
	Floyd Little	44
Houston:	Earl Campbell	34
	Jim Norton	43
	Elvin Bethea	65
Indianapolis:	Johnny Unitas	19
	Buddy Young	22
	Lenny Moore	24
	Art Donovan	70
	Jim Parker	77
	Raymond Berry	82
	Gino Marchetti	89
Kansas City:	Len Dawson	16
	Abner Haynes	28
	Stone Johnson	33
	Mack Lee Hill	36
	Bobby Bell	78
Los Angeles Raiders:	None	
Miami:	Bob Griese	12
New England:	Gino Cappelletti	20
	Jim Hunt	79
	Bob Dee	89
New York Jets:	Joe Namath	12
	Don Maynard	13
Pittsburgh:	None	
San Diego:	None	
Seattle:	"Fans/the twelfth man"	12

NFC

Atlanta:	Tommy Nobis	60
Chicago:	Bronko Nagurski	3
	George McAfee	5
	Willie Galimore	28
	Walter Payton	34
	Brian Piccolo	41
	Sid Luckman	42
	Bill Hewitt	56
	Bill George	61
	Bulldog Turner	66
	Red Grange	77
Dallas:	None	
Detroit:	Dutch Clark	7
	Bobby Layne	22
	Doak Walker	37
	Joe Schmidt	56
	Chuck Hughes	85
	Charlie Sanders	88
Green Bay:	Tony Canadeo	3
	Don Hutson	14
	Bart Starr	15
	Ray Nitschke	66
Los Angeles Rams:	Bob Waterfield	7
	Merlin Olsen	74
Minnesota:	Fran Tarkenton	10
New Orleans:	Jim Taylor	31
	Doug Atkins	81
New York Giants:	Ray Flaherty	1
	Mel Hein	7
	Y.A. Tittle	14
	Al Blozis	32
	Joe Morrison	40
	Charlie Conerly	42
	Ken Strong	50
Philadelphia:	Steve Van Buren	15
	Tom Brookshier	40
	Pete Retzlaff	44
	Chuck Bednarik	60
	Al Wistert	70
St. Louis:	Larry Wilson	8
	Stan Mauldin	77
	J.V. Cain	88
	Marshall Goldberg	99
San Francisco:	John Brodie	12
	Joe Perry	34
	Jimmy Johnson	37
	Hugh McElhenny	39
	Charlie Krueger	70
	Leo Nomellini	73
Tampa Bay:	Lee Roy Selmon	63
Washington:	Sammy Baugh	33

1987 NFL Score by Quarters

AFC Offense	1	2	3	4	OT	PTS
Cleveland	49	160	106	75	0	390
Denver	92	110	79	98	0	379
Seattle	79	132	95	65	0	371
Miami	90	100	89	83	0	362
Houston	47	97	89	112	0	345
N.Y. Jets	32	95	68	133	6	334
New England	76	111	72	61	0	320
L.A. Raiders	49	85	72	95	0	301
Indianapolis	48	120	61	71	0	300
Cincinnati	87	72	40	83	3	285
Pittsburgh	50	88	51	96	0	285
Kansas City	55	88	74	56	0	273
Buffalo	17	86	51	110	6	270
San Diego	79	55	25	91	3	253

NFC Offense	1	2	3	4	OT	PTS
San Francisco	81	150	89	139	0	459
New Orleans	93	107	104	118	0	422
Washington	66	118	108	84	3	379
St. Louis	67	127	61	107	0	362
Chicago	72	126	59	99	0	356
Dallas	71	108	78	77	6	340
Philadelphia	46	118	86	84	3	337
Minnesota	52	81	100	97	6	336
L.A. Rams	77	92	88	60	0	317
Tampa Bay	78	66	81	61	0	286
N.Y. Giants	62	83	75	57	3	280
Detroit	56	90	45	75	3	269
Green Bay	80	75	42	52	6	255
Atlanta	34	43	67	61	0	205

AFC Defense	1	2	3	4	OT	PTS
Indianapolis	61	52	48	77	0	238
Cleveland	41	56	54	85	3	239
Denver	70	110	64	44	0	288
L.A. Raiders	62	98	64	65	0	289
New England	39	68	71	106	9	293
Pittsburgh	45	79	77	98	0	299
Buffalo	54	113	77	61	0	305
Seattle	51	110	75	78	0	314
San Diego	68	104	68	77	0	317
Miami	63	105	61	97	9	335
Houston	75	117	71	86	0	349
N.Y. Jets	58	129	105	68	0	360
Cincinnati	44	106	96	124	0	370
Kansas City	88	116	93	88	3	388

NFC Defense	1	2	3	4	OT	PTS
San Francisco	53	69	60	71	0	253
Chicago	75	91	67	49	0	282
New Orleans	69	95	58	61	0	283
Washington	54	68	94	69	0	285
Green Bay	40	98	71	88	3	300
N.Y. Giants	53	85	60	111	3	312
Minnesota	36	106	87	103	3	335
Dallas	84	68	79	111	6	348
Tampa Bay	69	98	67	126	0	360
L.A. Rams	79	132	57	93	0	361
St. Louis	90	88	103	87	0	368
Philadelphia	88	133	65	85	9	380
Detroit	89	153	68	74	0	384
Atlanta	87	136	95	118	0	436

NFL TOTALS	1	2	3	4	OT	PTS
	1785	2783	2055	2400	48	9071

Team Leaders

Offense	Most Scored	Fewest Scored
1st Quarter	93, New Orleans	17, Buffalo
2nd Quarter	160, Cleveland	43, Atlanta
3rd Quarter	108, Washington	25, San Diego
4th Quarter	139, San Francisco	52, Green Bay

Defense	Most Allowed	Fewest Allowed
1st Quarter	90, St. Louis	36, Minnesota
2nd Quarter	153, Detroit	52, Indianapolis
3rd Quarter	105, N.Y. Jets	48, Indianapolis
4th Quarter	126, Tampa Bay	44, Denver

NFL Players Active in 1987 Who Were Not Drafted by an NFL Team But Have Played at Least 8 Years in NFL

	Yrs.	Pos.	Games	Starts
Walt Arnold, Kansas City	8	TE	5	4
Woody Bennett, Miami	9	RB	12	11
Rufus Bess, Minnesota	9	DB	3	2
Jeff Bostic, Washington	8	C	12	5
Ken Clarke, Philadelphia	10	NT	11	10
Paul Coffman, Kansas City	10	TE	12	1
Gary Danielson, Cleveland	10	QB	6	1
James Harrell, Kansas City	8	LB	11	4
Glenn Hyde, Kansas City	10	G	8	1
David Jennings, N.Y. Jets	14	P	12	0
Kerry Justin, Seattle	8	DB	7	0
Dave Krieg, Seattle	8	QB	12	12
Pat Leahy, N.Y. Jets	14	K	12	0
Nick Lowery, Kansas City	8	K	12	0
Guido Merkens, Philadelphia	9	QB	3	0
Neal Olkewicz, Washington	9	LB	10	6
Jim Ryan, Denver	9	LB	14	14
Donnie Shell, Pittsburgh	14	DB	13	13
Doug Smith, L.A. Rams	10	C	12	12
J.T. Smith, St. Louis	10	WR	15	14
Ivory Sully, Detroit	9	DB	11	1
Tim Vogler, Buffalo	9	G	12	12
Steve Watson, Denver	9	WR	5	1
Ray Wersching, San Francisco	15	K	12	0
Joel Williams, Atlanta	9	LB	8	8
Brenard Wilson, Atl.-Phil.	9	DB	9	1
Steve Wilson, Denver	9	DB	11	5
George Yarno, Tampa Bay	8	G	11	8

NFL Players Active in 1987 Who Were Not Drafted by an NFL Team But Have Played in at Least 1 AFC-NFC Pro Bowl

	Yrs.	Pos.	Pro Bowls
Bill Bates, Dallas	5	DB	1
Dean Biasucci, Indianapolis	3	K	1
Jeff Bostic, Washington	8	C	1
Jim Burt, N.Y. Giants	7	NT	1
Rich Camarillo, New England	7	P	1
Deron Cherry, Kansas City	7	DB	4
Paul Coffman, Kansas City	10	TE	3
Jay Hilgenberg, Chicago	7	C	3
Joe Jacoby, Washington	7	T	4
Dave Jennings, N.Y. Jets	14	P	4
Norm Johnson, Seattle	6	K	1
Dave Krieg, Seattle	8	QB	1
Sean Landeta, N.Y. Giants	3	P	1
Nick Lowery, Kansas City	8	K	1
Frank Minnifield, Cleveland	4	DB	2
Joe Nash, Seattle	6	NT	1
Donnie Shell, Pittsburgh	14	DB	5
Doug Smith, L.A. Rams	10	C	4
J.T. Smith, St. Louis	10	WR	1
Everson Walls, Dallas	7	DB	4
Steve Watson, Denver	9	WR	1

Rushing in the Eighties

100+ Yards Rushing By Two Teammates, Game

Sept. 7, 1980	Detroit (Billy Sims 153, Dexter Bussey 111)
Oct. 5, 1980	St. Louis (Ottis Anderson 126, Wayne Morris 102)
Nov. 23, 1980	New England (Don Calhoun 106, Vagas Ferguson 100)
Nov. 23, 1980	Green Bay (Eddie Lee Ivery 145, Gerry Ellis 101)
Nov. 14, 1983	L.A. Rams (Eric Dickerson 147, Barry Redden 110)
Nov. 20, 1983	Chicago (Matt Suhey 112, Walter Payton 106)
Oct. 7, 1985	Washington (George Rogers 104, John Riggins 103)
Nov. 3, 1985	Washington (Keith Griffin 164, George Rogers 124)
Nov. 10, 1985	Chicago (Walter Payton 107, Matt Suhey 102)
Nov. 17, 1985	Pittsburgh (Frank Pollard 123, Walter Abercrombie 107)
Oct. 26, 1986	Pittsburgh (Earnest Jackson 132, Walter Abercrombie 109)
Dec. 7, 1986	Cincinnati (James Brooks 163, Stanley Wilson 120)

300+ Yards Rushing, Team, Game

Sept. 7, 1980	Detroit vs. L.A. Rams	330
Oct. 5, 1980	St. Louis vs. New Orleans	330
Sept. 20, 1981	Pittsburgh vs. N.Y. Jets	343
Nov. 8, 1981	New Orleans vs. L.A. Rams	307
Dec. 6, 1981	Dallas vs. Baltimore	354
Sept. 18, 1983	New England vs. N.Y. Jets	328
Sept. 9, 1984	Chicago vs. Denver	302
Nov. 3, 1985	Washington vs. Atlanta	307
Dec. 7, 1986	Cincinnati vs. New England	300
Nov. 30, 1987	L.A. Raiders vs. Seattle	356

Greatest Comebacks in NFL History (Most Points Overcome To Win Game)

Regular-Season Games

From 28 points behind to win:
December 7, 1980, at San Francisco

New Orleans	14	21	0	0	0 — 35
San Francisco	0	7	14	14	3 — 38

NO —Harris 33 pass from Manning (Ricardo kick)
NO —Childs 21 pass from Manning (Ricardo kick)
NO —Holmes 1 run (Ricardo kick)
SF —Solomon 57 punt return (Wersching kick)
NO —Holmes 1 run (Ricardo kick)
NO —Harris 41 pass from Manning (Ricardo kick)
SF —Montana 1 run (Wersching kick)
SF —Clark 71 pass from Montana (Wersching kick)
SF —Solomon 14 pass from Montana (Wersching kick)
SF —Elliott 7 run (Wersching kick)
SF —FG Wersching 36

	N.O.	S.F.
First Downs	27	24
Total Yards	519	430
Yards Rushing	143	176
Yards Passing	376	254
Turnovers	3	0

From 25 points behind to win:
November 8, 1987, at St. Louis

Tampa Bay	7	7	14	0 — 28
St. Louis	0	3	0	28 — 31

TB —Carrier 5 pass from DeBerg (Igwebuike kick)
TB —Carter 3 pass from DeBerg (Igwebuike kick)
StL —FG Gallery 31
TB —Smith 34 pass from DeBerg (Igwebuike kick)
TB —Smith 3 run (Igwebuike kick)
StL —Awalt 4 pass from Lomax (Gallery kick)
StL —Noga 23 fumble recovery (Gallery kick)
StL —J. Smith 11 pass from Lomax (Gallery kick)
StL —J. Smith 17 pass from Lomax (Gallery kick)

	T.B.	St.L.
First Downs	26	26
Total Yards	377	415
Yards Rushing	83	137
Yards Passing	294	278
Turnovers	1	2

From 24 points behind to win:
October 27, 1946, at Washington

Philadelphia	0	0	14	14 — 28
Washington	10	14	0	0 — 24

Wash—Rosato 2 run (Poillon kick)
Wash—FG Poillon 28
Wash—Rosato 4 run (Poillon kick)
Wash—Lapka recovered fumble in end zone (Poillon kick)
Phil —Steele 1 run (Lio kick)
Phil —Pritchard 45 pass from Thompson (Lio kick)
Phil —Steinke 7 pass from Thompson (Lio kick)
Phil —Ferrante 30 pass from Thompson (Lio kick)

	Phil.	Wash.
First Downs	14	8
Total Yards	262	127
Yards Rushing	34	66
Yards Passing	228	61
Turnovers	6	3

From 24 points behind to win:
October 20, 1957, at Detroit

Baltimore	7	14	6	0 — 27
Detroit	0	3	7	21 — 31

Balt —Mutscheller 15 pass from Unitas (Rechichar kick)
Det —FG Martin 47
Balt —Moore 72 pass from Unitas (Rechichar kick)
Balt —Mutscheller 52 pass from Unitas (Rechichar kick)
Balt —Moore 4 pass from Unitas (kick failed)
Det —Junker 14 pass from Rote (Layne kick)
Det —Cassady 26 pass from Layne (Layne kick)
Det —Johnson 1 run (Layne kick)
Det —Cassady 29 pass from Layne (Layne kick)

	Balt.	Det.
First Downs	15	20
Total Yards	322	369
Yards Rushing	117	178
Yards Passing	205	191
Turnovers	6	4

From 24 points behind to win:
October 25, 1959, at Chicago

Philadelphia	0	0	21	7 — 28
Chi. Cardinals	7	10	7	0 — 24

Chi —Crow 10 pass from Roach (Conrad kick)
Chi —J. Hill 77 blocked field goal return (Conrad kick)
Chi —FG Conrad 15
Chi —Lane 37 interception return (Conrad kick)
Phil —Barnes 1 run (Walston kick)
Phil —McDonald 29 pass from Van Brocklin (Walston kick)
Phil —Barnes 2 run (Walston kick)
Phil —McDonald 22 pass from Van Brocklin (Walston kick)

	Phil.	Chi.
First Downs	22	14
Total Yards	399	313
Yards Rushing	168	163
Yards Passing	231	150
Turnovers	2	6

From 24 points behind to win:
October 23, 1960, at Denver

Boston	10	7	7	0 — 24
Denver	0	0	14	17 — 31

Bos —FG Cappelletti 12
Bos —Colclough 10 pass from Songin (Cappelletti kick)
Bos —Wells 6 pass from Songin (Cappelletti kick)
Bos —Miller 47 pass from Songin (Cappelletti kick)
Den—Carmichael 21 pass from Tripucka (Mingo kick)
Den—Jessup 19 pass from Tripucka (Mingo kick)
Den—Carmichael 35 lateral from Taylor, pass from Tripucka (Mingo kick)
Den—Taylor 8 pass from Tripucka (Mingo kick)
Den—FG Mingo 9

	Bos.	Den.
First Downs	19	16
Total Yards	434	326
Yards Rushing	211	65
Yards Passing	223	261
Turnovers	7	4

From 24 points behind to win:
December 15, 1974, at Miami

New England	21	3	0	3 — 27
Miami	0	17	7	10 — 34

NE —Hannah recovered fumble in end zone (J. Smith kick)
NE —Sanders 23 interception return (J. Smith kick)
NE —Herron 4 pass from Plunkett (J. Smith kick)
NE —FG J. Smith 46
Mia —Nottingham 1 run (Yepremian kick)
Mia —Baker 37 pass from Morrall (Yepremian kick)
Mia —FG Yepremian 28
Mia —Baker 46 pass from Morrall (Yepremian kick)
NE —FG J. Smith 34
Mia —Nottingham 2 run (Yepremian kick)
Mia —FG Yepremian 40

	N.E.	Mia.
First Downs	18	18
Total Yards	333	333
Yards Rushing	114	61
Yards Passing	219	272
Turnovers	3	4

From 24 points behind to win:
December 4, 1977, at Minnesota

San Francisco	0	10	14	3 — 27
Minnesota	0	0	7	21 — 28

SF —Delvin Williams 2 run (Wersching kick)
SF —FG Wersching 31
SF —Dave Williams 80 kickoff return (Wersching kick)
SF —Delvin Williams 5 run (Wersching kick)
Minn —McClanahan 15 pass from Lee (Cox kick)
Minn —Rashad 8 pass from Kramer (Cox kick)
Minn —Tucker 9 pass from Kramer (Cox kick)
SF —FG Wersching 31
Minn —S. White 69 pass from Kramer (Cox kick)

	S.F.	Minn.
First Downs	19	18
Total Yards	243	309
Yards Rushing	196	52
Yards Passing	47	257
Turnovers	2	5

From 24 points behind to win:
September 23, 1979, at Denver

Seattle	10	10	14	0 — 34
Denver	0	10	21	6 — 37

Sea — FG Herrera 28
Sea — Doornink 5 run (Herrera kick)
Den — FG Turner 27
Sea — Doornink 5 run (Herrera kick)
Den — Armstrong 2 run (Turner kick)
Sea — FG Herrera 22
Sea — McCullum 13 pass from Zorn (Herrera kick)
Sea — Smith 1 run (Herrera kick)
Den — Studdard 2 pass from Morton (Turner kick)
Den — Moses 11 pass from Morton (Turner kick)
Den — Upchurch 35 pass from Morton (Turner kick)
Den — Lytle 1 run (kick failed)

	Sea.	Den.
First Downs	22	23
Total Yards	350	344
Yards Rushing	153	90
Yards Passing	197	254
Turnovers	4	3

From 24 points behind to win:
September 23, 1979, at Cincinnati

Houston	0	10	17	0	3 — 30
Cincinnati	14	10	0	3	0 — 27

Cin — Johnson 1 run (Bahr kick)
Cin — Alexander 2 run (Bahr kick)
Cin — Johnson 1 run (Bahr kick)
Cin — FG Bahr 52
Hou — Burrough 35 pass from Pastorini (Fritsch kick)
Hou — FG Fritsch 33
Hou — Campbell 8 run (Fritsch kick)
Hou — Caster 22 pass from Pastorini (Fritsch kick)
Hou — FG Fritsch 47
Cin — FG Bahr 55
Hou — FG Fritsch 29

	Hou.	Cin.
First Downs	19	21
Total Yards	361	265
Yards Rushing	177	165
Yards Passing	184	100
Turnovers	3	2

From 24 points behind to win:
November 22, 1982, at Los Angeles

San Diego	10	14	0	0 — 24
L.A. Raiders	0	7	14	7 — 28

SD — FG Benirschke 19
SD — Scales 29 pass from Fouts (Benirschke kick)
SD — Muncie 2 run (Benirschke kick)
SD — Muncie 1 run (Benirschke kick)
Raiders — Christensen 1 pass from Plunkett (Bahr kick)
Raiders — Allen 3 run (Bahr kick)
Raiders — Allen 6 run (Bahr kick)
Raiders — Hawkins 1 run (Bahr kick)

	S.D.	Raiders
First Downs	26	23
Total Yards	411	326
Yards Rushing	72	181
Yards Passing	339	145
Turnovers	4	2

Postseason Games

From 20 points behind to win:
Western Conference Playoff Game
December 22, 1957, at San Francisco

Detroit	0	7	14	10 — 31
San Francisco	14	10	3	0 — 27

SF — Owens 34 pass from Tittle (Soltau kick)
SF — McElhenny 47 pass from Tittle (Soltau kick)
Det — Junker 4 pass from Rote (Martin kick)
SF — Wilson 12 pass from Tittle (Soltau kick)
SF — FG Soltau 25
SF — FG Soltau 10
Det — Tracy 2 run (Martin kick)
Det — Tracy 58 run (Martin kick)
Det — Gedman 3 run (Martin kick)
Det — FG Martin 14

	Det.	S.F.
First Downs	22	20
Total Yards	324	351
Yards Rushing	129	127
Yards Passing	195	224
Turnovers	5	4

From 18 points behind to win:
NFC Divisional Playoff Game
December 23, 1972, at San Francisco

Dallas	3	10	0	17 — 30
San Francisco	7	14	7	0 — 28

SF — Washington 97 kickoff return (Gossett kick)
Dall — FG Fritsch 37
SF — Schreiber 1 run (Gossett kick)
SF — Schreiber 1 run (Gossett kick)
Dall — FG Fritsch 45
Dall — Alworth 28 pass from Morton (Fritsch kick)
SF — Schreiber 1 run (Gossett kick)
Dall — FG Fritsch 27
Dall — Parks 20 pass from Staubach (Fritsch kick)
Dall — Sellers 10 pass from Staubach (Fritsch kick)

	Dall.	S.F.
First Downs	22	13
Total Yards	402	255
Yards Rushing	165	105
Yards Passing	237	150
Turnovers	5	3

From 18 points behind to win:
AFC Divisional Playoff Game
January 4, 1986, at Miami

Cleveland	7	7	7	0 — 21
Miami	3	0	14	7 — 24

Mia — FG Reveiz 51
Clev — Newsome 16 pass from Kosar (Bahr kick)
Clev — Byner 21 run (Bahr kick)
Clev — Byner 66 run (Bahr kick)
Mia — Moore 6 pass from Marino (Reveiz kick)
Mia — Davenport 31 run (Reveiz kick)
Mia — Davenport 1 run (Reveiz kick)

	Clev.	Mia.
First Downs	17	20
Total Yards	313	330
Yards Rushing	251	92
Yards Passing	62	238
Turnovers	1	1

From 14 points behind to win:
NFC Divisional Playoff Game
January 3, 1981, at Philadelphia

Minnesota	7	7	2	0 — 16
Philadelphia	0	7	14	10 — 31

Minn — S. White 30 pass from Kramer (Danmeier kick)
Minn — Brown 1 run (Danmeier kick)
Phil — Carmichael 9 pass from Jaworski (Franklin kick)
Phil — Montgomery 8 run (Franklin kick)
Minn — Safety, Jaworski tackled in end zone by Martin and Blair
Phil — Montgomery 5 run (Franklin kick)
Phil — FG Franklin 33
Phil — Harrington 2 run (Franklin kick)

	Minn.	Phil.
First Downs	14	24
Total Yards	215	305
Yards Rushing	36	126
Yards Passing	179	179
Turnovers	8	3

From 14 points behind to win:
NFC Divisional Playoff Game
January 4, 1981, at Atlanta

Dallas	3	7	0	20 — 30
Atlanta	10	7	7	3 — 27

Atl — FG Mazzetti 38
Atl — Jenkins 60 pass from Bartkowski (Mazzetti kick)
Dall — FG Septien 38
Dall — DuPree 5 pass from D. White (Mazzetti kick)
Atl — Cain 1 run (Mazzetti kick)
Atl — Andrews 5 pass from Bartkowski (Mazzetti kick)
Dall — Newhouse 1 run (Septien kick)
Atl — FG Mazzetti 34
Dall — D. Pearson 14 pass from D. White (Septien kick)
Dall — D. Pearson 23 pass from D. White (pass failed)

	Dall.	Atl.
First Downs	22	18
Total Yards	422	371
Yards Rushing	112	86
Yards Passing	310	283
Turnovers	2	2

From 14 points behind to win:
NFC Divisional Playoff Game
January 10, 1988, at Chicago

Washington	0	14	7	0 — 21
Chicago	7	7	3	0 — 17

Chi —Thomas 2 run (Butler kick)
Chi —Morris 14 pass from McMahon (Butler kick)
Wash —Rogers 3 run (Haji-Sheikh kick)
Wash —Didier 18 pass from Williams (Haji-Sheikh kick)
Wash —Green 52 punt return (Haji-Sheikh kick)
Chi —FG Butler 25

	Wash.	Chi.
First Downs	17	15
Total Yards	272	280
Yards Rushing	72	110
Yards Passing	200	170
Turnovers	2	3

Records of NFL Divisions in Out-of-Division Games 1978–87

Since 1978, teams in a five-team division have been scheduled for eight games against out-of-division opponents; teams in a four-team division have been scheduled for 10 such games. These charts indicate the annual records for each division's teams in games against teams from other divisions:

NFC East

	W	L	T	Pct.	Pos.
1978	21	19	0	.525	2T
1979	23	17	0	.575	3
1980	19	21	0	.475	4
1981	26	14	0	.650	1
1982	13	6	0	.684	1
1983	23	17	0	.575	1
1984	24	15	1	.613	2
1985	22	18	0	.550	2
1986	23	17	0	.575	1T
1987	18	17	0	.514	3T
Totals	212	161	1	.568	2

NFC Central

	W	L	T	Pct.	Pos.
1978	16	24	0	.400	6
1979	14	26	0	.350	5
1980	16	24	0	.400	6
1981	18	22	0	.450	4T
1982	12	12	1	.500	3T
1983	15	25	0	.375	6
1984	11	28	1	.288	6
1985	19	21	0	.475	4
1986	14	26	0	.350	6
1987	14	24	1	.372	6
Totals	149	232	3	.392	6

NFC West

	W	L	T	Pct.	Pos.
1978	18	22	0	.450	5
1979	13	27	0	.325	6
1980	18	22	0	.450	5
1981	18	22	0	.450	4T
1982	7	15	0	.318	6
1983	22	18	0	.550	2T
1984	24	16	0	.600	3
1985	18	22	0	.450	5
1986	23	17	0	.575	1T
1987	23	15	0	.605	1
Totals	184	196	0	.484	4

AFC East

	W	L	T	Pct.	Pos.
1978	20	20	0	.500	4
1979	19	21	0	.475	4
1980	20	20	0	.500	3
1981	16	24	0	.400	6
1982	10	10	1	.500	3T
1983	22	18	0	.550	2T
1984	16	24	0	.400	4
1985	21	19	0	.475	3
1986	16	24	0	.400	5
1987	18	17	0	.514	3T
Totals	178	197	1	.475	5

AFC Central

	W	L	T	Pct.	Pos.
1978	24	16	0	.600	1
1979	24	16	0	.600	2
1980	25	15	0	.625	1
1981	20	20	0	.500	3
1982	10	10	0	.500	3T
1983	16	24	0	.400	5
1984	13	27	0	.325	5
1985	15	25	0	.375	6
1986	21	19	0	.525	4
1987	19	17	0	.528	2
Totals	187	189	0	.497	3

AFC West

	W	L	T	Pct.	Pos.
1978	21	19	0	.525	2T
1979	27	13	0	.675	1
1980	22	18	0	.550	2
1981	22	18	0	.550	2
1982	12	11	0	.522	2
1983	22	18	0	.550	2T
1984	31	9	0	.775	1
1985	25	15	0	.625	1
1986	23	17	0	.575	1T
1987	17	19	1	.473	5
Totals	222	157	1	.586	1

Composite Standings for 10 Seasons

	W	L	T	Pct.
AFC West	222	157	1	.586
NFC East	212	161	1	.568
AFC Central	187	189	0	.497
NFC West	184	196	0	.484
AFC East	178	197	1	.475
NFC Central	149	232	3	.392

Records of NFL Teams Since 1970 AFL-NFL Merger

AFC	W-L-T	Pct.	Division Titles	Playoff Berths	Post-season Record	Super Bowl Record
Miami	184- 78-2	.702	9	12	14-10	2-3
L.A. Raiders	174- 84-6	.673	8	12	16-9	3-0
Pittsburgh	162-101-1	.616	9	11	15-7	4-0
Denver	149-109-6	.576	5	7	6-7	0-3
Cleveland	136-126-2	.519	5	7	2-7	0-0
Cincinnati	135-129-0	.511	3	5	2-5	0-1
New England	130-134-0	.492	2	5	3-5	0-1
Seattle*	87- 93-0	.483	0	3	3-3	0-0
San Diego	118-141-5	.456	3	4	3-4	0-0
Kansas City	114-145-5	.441	1	2	0-2	0-0
N.Y. Jets	114-149-1	.434	0	4	3-4	0-0
Indianapolis	110-152-2	.420	5	6	4-5	1-0
Houston	103-159-2	.393	0	4	5-4	0-0
Buffalo	99-163-2	.378	1	3	1-3	0-0

NFC	W-L-T	Pct.	Division Titles	Playoff Berths	Post-season Record	Super Bowl Record
Dallas	180- 84-0	.682	9	14	19-12	2-3
Washington	171- 92-1	.650	4	10	13-8	2-2
L.A. Rams	163- 97-4	.626	8	12	8-12	0-1
Minnesota	155-107-2	.591	9	11	10-11	0-3
San Francisco	140-121-3	.536	8	9	9-7	2-0
Chicago	134-129-1	.509	4	6	4-5	1-0
St. Louis	119-139-6	.462	2	3	0-3	0-0
Detroit	116-144-4	.447	1	3	0-3	0-0
Philadelphia	111-147-6	.431	1	4	3-4	0-1
Green Bay	108-148-8	.424	1	2	1-2	0-0
Atlanta	109-151-4	.420	1	3	1-3	0-0
N.Y. Giants	109-153-2	.417	1	4	6-3	1-0
New Orleans	90-170-4	.347	0	1	0-1	0-0
Tampa Bay*	52-127-1	.292	2	3	1-3	0-0

*entered NFL in 1976.

Indianapolis totals include Baltimore, 1970-83
L.A. Raiders totals include Oakland, 1970-81

Tie games before 1972 are not calculated in won-lost percentage.

In 1982, due to players' strike, the divisional format was abandoned. (L.A. Raiders and Washington won regular-season conference titles, not included in "Division Titles" totals listed above. Sixteen teams were awarded playoff berths, included in totals listed above.)

Longest Winning Streaks Since 1970

Regular-season games

16	Miami, 1971-73	(1 in 1971, 14 in 1972, 1 in 1973)
16	Miami, 1983-84	(5 in 1983, 11 in 1984)
14	Oakland, 1976-77	(10 in 1976, 4 in 1977)
13	Chicago, 1984-85	(1 in 1984, 12 in 1985)
13	Minnesota, 1974-75	(3 in 1974, 10 in 1975)
11	Pittsburgh, 1975	
11	Baltimore, 1975-76	(9 in 1975, 2 in 1976)
10	Miami, 1973	
10	Pittsburgh, 1976-77	(9 in 1976, 1 in 1977)
10	Denver, 1984	

HISTORY

Pro Football Hall of Fame 226
Chronology 230
Past NFL Standings 238
All-Time Team vs. Team Results 245
Super Bowl Game Summaries 269
Playoff Game Summaries 275
AFC-NFC Pro Bowl Game Summaries 282
All-Time Pro Bowl Results 286
AFC-NFC Interconference Games 287
Monday Night Results 288
Thursday-Sunday Night Results 290
History of Overtime Games 291
Chicago All-Star Games 295
NFL Playoff Bowls 295
Pro Football Hall of Fame Games 295
NFL International Games 295
NFL Paid Attendance 296
NFL's 10 Biggest Attendance Weekends 296
NFL's 10 Highest Scoring Weekends 296
Top 10 Televised Sports Events of All Time... 296
Ten Most Watched Programs in TV History.. 296
Number-One Draft Choices 297
First-Round Selections 298

PRO FOOTBALL HALL OF FAME

The Professional Football Hall of Fame is located in Canton, Ohio, site of the organizational meeting on September 17, 1920, from which the National Football League evolved. The NFL recognized Canton as the Hall of Fame site on April 27, 1961. Canton area individuals, foundations, and companies donated almost $400,000 in cash and services to provide funds for the construction of the original two-building complex, which was dedicated on September 7, 1963. The original Hall of Fame complex was almost doubled in size with the completion of a $620,000 expansion project that was dedicated on May 10, 1971. A second expansion project was completed on November 20, 1978. It now features four exhibition areas and a theater twice the size of the original one.

The Hall represents the sport of pro football in many ways—through four large and colorful exhibition galleries, in the twin enshrinement halls, with numerous fan-participation electronic devices, a research library, and an NFL gift shop.

In recent years, the Pro Football Hall of Fame has become an extremely popular tourist attraction. At the end of 1987, a total of 4,237,497 fans had visited the Pro Football Hall of Fame.

New members of the Pro Football Hall of Fame are elected annually by a 30-member National Board of Selectors, made up of media representatives from every league city, one at-large representative and the president of the Pro Football Writers of America. Between four and seven new members are elected each year. An affirmative vote of approximately 80 percent is needed for election.

Any fan may nominate any eligible player or contributor simply by writing to the Pro Football Hall of Fame. Players must be retired five years to be eligible, while a coach need only to be retired with no time limit specified. Contributors (administrators, owners, *et al.*) may be elected while they are still active.

The charter class of 17 enshrinees was elected in 1963 and the honor roll now stands at 144 with the election of a four-man class in 1988. That class consists of Fred Biletnikoff, Mike Ditka, Jack Ham, and Alan Page.

Roster of Members

HERB ADDERLEY
Defensive back. 6-1, 200. Born in Philadelphia, Pennsylvania, June 8, 1939. Michigan State. Inducted in 1980. 1961-69 Green Bay Packers, 1970-72 Dallas Cowboys.

LANCE ALWORTH
Wide receiver. 6-0, 184. Born in Houston, Texas, August 3, 1940. Arkansas. Inducted in 1978. 1962-70 San Diego Chargers, 1971-72 Dallas Cowboys.

DOUG ATKINS
Defensive end. 6-8, 275. Born in Humboldt, Tennessee, May 8, 1930. Tennessee. Inducted in 1982. 1953-54 Cleveland Browns, 1955-66 Chicago Bears, 1967-69 New Orleans Saints.

MORRIS (RED) BADGRO
End. 6-0, 190. Born in Orilla, Washington, December 1, 1902. Southern California. Inducted in 1981. 1927 New York Yankees, 1930-35 New York Giants, 1936 Brooklyn Dodgers.

CLIFF BATTLES
Halfback. 6-1, 201. Born in Akron, Ohio, May 1, 1910. Died April 28, 1981. West Virginia Wesleyan. Inducted in 1968. 1932 Boston Braves, 1933-36 Boston Redskins, 1937 Washington Redskins.

SAMMY BAUGH
Quarterback. 6-2, 180. Born in Temple, Texas, March 17, 1914. Texas Christian. Inducted in 1963. 1937-52 Washington Redskins.

CHUCK BEDNARIK
Center-linebacker. 6-3, 230. Born in Bethlehem, Pennsylvania, May 1, 1925. Pennsylvania. Inducted in 1967. 1949-62 Philadelphia Eagles.

BERT BELL
Team owner. Commissioner. Born in Philadelphia, Pennsylvania, February 25, 1895. Died October 11, 1959. Pennsylvania. Inducted in 1963. 1933-40 Philadelphia Eagles, 1941-42 Pittsburgh Steelers, 1943 Phil-Pitt, 1944-46 Pittsburgh Steelers. Commissioner, 1946-59.

BOBBY BELL
Linebacker. 6-4, 225. Born in Shelby, North Carolina, June 17, 1940. Minnesota. Inducted in 1983. 1963-74 Kansas City Chiefs.

RAYMOND BERRY
End. 6-2, 187. Born in Corpus Christi, Texas, February 27, 1933. Southern Methodist. Inducted in 1973. 1955-67 Baltimore Colts.

CHARLES W. BIDWILL, SR.
Team owner. Born in Chicago, Illinois, September 16, 1895. Died April 19, 1947. Loyola of Chicago. Inducted in 1967. 1933-43 Chicago Cardinals, 1944 Card-Pitt, 1945-47 Chicago Cardinals.

FRED BILETNIKOFF
Wide receiver. 6-1, 190. Born in Erie, Pennsylvania, February 23, 1943. Florida State. Inducted in 1988. 1965-78 Oakland Raiders.

GEORGE BLANDA
Quarterback-kicker. 6-2, 215. Born in Youngwood, Pennsylvania, September 17, 1927. Kentucky. Inducted in 1981. 1949-58 Chicago Bears, 1950 Baltimore Colts, 1960-66 Houston Oilers, 1967-75 Oakland Raiders.

JIM BROWN
Fullback. 6-2, 232. Born in St. Simons, Georgia, February 17, 1936. Syracuse. Inducted in 1971. 1957-65 Cleveland Browns.

PAUL BROWN
Coach. Born in Norwalk, Ohio, September 7, 1908. Miami, Ohio. Inducted in 1967. 1946-49 Cleveland Browns (AAFC), 1950-62 Cleveland Browns, 1968-75 Cincinnati Bengals.

ROOSEVELT BROWN
Tackle. 6-3, 255. Born in Charlottesville, Virginia, October 20, 1932. Morgan State. Inducted in 1975. 1953-65 New York Giants.

WILLIE BROWN
Defensive back. 6-1, 210. Born in Yazoo City, Mississippi, December 2, 1940. Grambling. Inducted in 1984. 1963-66 Denver Broncos, 1967-78 Oakland Raiders.

DICK BUTKUS
Linebacker. 6-3, 245. Born in Chicago, Illinois, December 9, 1942. Illinois. Inducted in 1979. 1965-73 Chicago Bears.

TONY CANADEO
Halfback. 5-11, 195. Born in Chicago, Illinois, May 5, 1919. Gonzaga. Inducted in 1974. 1941-44, 1946-52 Green Bay Packers.

JOE CARR
NFL president. Born in Columbus, Ohio, October 22, 1880. Died May 20, 1939. Did not attend college. Inducted in 1963. President, 1921-39 National Football League.

GUY CHAMBERLIN
End. Coach. 6-2, 210. Born in Blue Springs, Nebraska, January 16, 1894. Died April 4, 1967. Nebraska. Inducted in 1965. 1920 Decatur Staleys, 1921 Chicago Staleys, player-coach 1922-23 Canton Bulldogs, 1924 Cleveland Bulldogs, 1925-26 Frankford Yellow Jackets, 1927 Chicago Cardinals.

JACK CHRISTIANSEN
Defensive back. 6-1, 185. Born in Sublette, Kansas, December 20, 1928. Died June 29, 1986. Colorado State. Inducted in 1970. 1951-58 Detroit Lions.

EARL (DUTCH) CLARK
Quarterback. 6-0, 185. Born in Fowler, Colorado, October 11, 1906. Died August 5, 1978. Colorado College. Inducted in 1963. 1931-32 Portsmouth Spartans, 1934-38 Detroit Lions.

GEORGE CONNOR
Tackle-linebacker. 6-3, 240. Born in Chicago, Illinois, January 21, 1925. Holy Cross, Notre Dame. Inducted in 1975. 1948-55 Chicago Bears.

JIMMY CONZELMAN
Quarterback. Coach. Team owner. 6-0, 180. Born in St. Louis, Missouri, March 6, 1898. Died July 31, 1970. Washington, Missouri. Inducted in 1964. 1920 Decatur Staleys, 1921-22 Rock Island, Ill., Independents, 1923-24 Milwaukee Badgers; owner-coach, 1925-26 Detroit Panthers; player-coach 1927-29, coach 1930 Providence Steam Roller; coach, 1940-42 Chicago Cardinals, 1946-48 Chicago Cardinals.

LARRY CSONKA
Running back. 6-3, 235. Born in Stow, Ohio, December 25, 1946. Syracuse. Inducted in 1987. Miami Dolphins 1968-74, 1979, New York Giants 1976-78.

WILLIE DAVIS
Defensive end. 6-3, 245. Born in Lisbon, Louisiana, July 24, 1934. Grambling. Inducted in 1981. 1958-59 Cleveland Browns, 1960-69 Green Bay Packers.

LEN DAWSON
Quarterback. 6-0, 190. Born in Alliance, Ohio, June 20, 1935. Purdue. Inducted in 1987. Pittsburgh Steelers 1957-59, Cleveland Browns 1960-61, Dallas Texans 1962, Kansas City Chiefs 1963-75.

MIKE DITKA
Tight end. 6-3, 225. Born in Carnegie, Pennsylvania, October 18, 1939. Pittsburgh. Inducted in 1988. 1961-66 Chicago Bears, 1967-68 Philadelphia Eagles, 1969-72 Dallas Cowboys.

ART DONOVAN
Defensive tackle. 6-3, 265. Born in Bronx, New York, June 5, 1925. Boston College. Inducted in 1968. 1950 Baltimore Colts, 1951 New York Yanks, 1952 Dallas Texans, 1953-61 Baltimore Colts.

JOHN (PADDY) DRISCOLL
Quarterback. 5-11, 160. Born in Evanston, Illinois, January 11, 1896. Died June 29, 1968. Northwestern. Inducted in 1965. 1920 Decatur Staleys, 1920-25 Chicago Cardinals, 1926-29 Chicago Bears. Coach, 1956-57 Chicago Bears.

BILL DUDLEY
Halfback. 5-10, 176. Born in Bluefield, Virginia, December 24, 1921. Virginia. Inducted in 1966. 1942, 1945-46 Pittsburgh Steelers, 1947-49 Detroit Lions, 1950-51, 1953 Washington Redskins.

GLEN (TURK) EDWARDS
Tackle. 6-2, 260. Born in Mold, Washington, September 28, 1907. Died January 12, 1973. Washington State. Inducted in 1969. 1932 Boston Braves, 1933-36 Boston Redskins, 1937-40 Washington Redskins.

WEEB EWBANK
Coach. Born in Richmond, Indiana, May 6, 1907. Miami, Ohio. Inducted in 1978. 1954-62 Baltimore Colts, 1963-73 New York Jets.

TOM FEARS
End. 6-2, 215. Born in Los Angeles, California, December 3, 1923. Santa Clara, UCLA. Inducted in 1970. 1948-56 Los Angeles Rams.

RAY FLAHERTY
End. Coach. Born in Spokane, Washington, September 1, 1904. Gonzaga. Inducted in 1976. 1926 Los Angeles Wildcats (AFL), 1927-28 New York Yankees, 1928-29, 1931-35 New York Giants. Coach, 1936 Boston Redskins, 1937-42 Washington Redskins, 1946-48 New York Yankees (AAFC), 1949 Chicago Hornets (AAFC).

LEN FORD
End. 6-5, 260. Born in Washington, D.C., February 18, 1926. Died March 14, 1972. Michigan. Inducted in 1976. 1948-49 Los Angeles Dons (AAFC), 1950-57 Cleveland Browns, 1958 Green Bay Packers.

DAN FORTMANN
Guard. 6-0, 207. Born in Pearl River, New York, April 11, 1916. Colgate. In-

ducted in 1965. 1936-43 Chicago Bears.

FRANK GATSKI
Center. 6-3, 240. Born in Farmington, West Virginia, March 13, 1922. Marshall, Auburn. Inducted in 1985. 1946-49 Cleveland Browns (AAFC), 1950-56 Cleveland Browns, 1957 Detroit Lions.

BILL GEORGE
Linebacker. 6-2, 230. Born in Waynesburg, Pennsylvania, October 27, 1930. Died September 30, 1982. Wake Forest. Inducted in 1974. 1952-65 Chicago Bears, 1966 Los Angeles Rams.

FRANK GIFFORD
Halfback. 6-1, 195. Born in Santa Monica, California, August 16, 1930. Southern California. Inducted in 1977. 1952-60, 1962-64 New York Giants.

SID GILLMAN
Coach. Born in Minneapolis, Minnesota, October 26, 1911. Ohio State. Inducted in 1983. 1955-59 Los Angeles Rams, 1960 Los Angeles Chargers, 1961-69 San Diego Chargers, 1973-74 Houston Oilers.

OTTO GRAHAM
Quarterback. 6-1, 195. Born in Waukegan, Illinois, December 6, 1921. Northwestern. Inducted in 1965. 1946-49 Cleveland Browns (AAFC), 1950-55 Cleveland Browns.

HAROLD (RED) GRANGE
Halfback. 6-0, 185. Born in Forksville, Pennsylvania, June 13, 1903. Illinois. Inducted in 1963. 1925 Chicago Bears, 1926 New York Yankees (AFL), 1927 New York Yankees, 1929-34 Chicago Bears.

JOE GREENE
Defensive tackle. 6-4, 260. Born in Temple, Texas, September 24, 1946. North Texas State. Inducted in 1987. 1969-81 Pittsburgh Steelers.

FORREST GREGG
Tackle. 6-4, 250. Born in Birthright, Texas, October 18, 1933. Southern Methodist. Inducted in 1977. 1956, 1958-70 Green Bay Packers, 1971 Dallas Cowboys.

LOU GROZA
Tackle-kicker. 6-3, 250. Born in Martin's Ferry, Ohio, January 25, 1924. Ohio State. Inducted in 1974. 1946-49 Cleveland Browns (AAFC), 1950-59, 1961-67 Cleveland Browns.

JOE GUYON
Halfback. 6-1, 180. Born in Mahnomen, Minnesota, November 26, 1892. Died November 27, 1971. Carlisle, Georgia Tech. Inducted in 1966. 1920 Canton Bulldogs, 1921 Cleveland Indians, 1922-23 Oorang Indians, 1924 Rock Island, Ill., Independents, 1924-25 Kansas City Cowboys, 1927 New York Giants.

GEORGE HALAS
End. Coach. Team owner. Born in Chicago, Illinois, February 2, 1895. Died October 31, 1983. Illinois. Inducted in 1963. 1920 Decatur Staleys, 1921 Chicago Staleys, 1922-29 Chicago Bears; coach, 1933-42, 1946-55, 1958-67 Chicago Bears.

JACK HAM
Linebacker. 6-1, 225. Born in Johnstown, Pennsylvania, December 23, 1948. Penn State. Inducted in 1988. 1971-82 Pittsburgh Steelers.

ED HEALEY
Tackle. 6-3, 220. Born in Indian Orchard, Massachusetts, December 28, 1894. Died December 9, 1978. Dartmouth. Inducted in 1964. 1920-22 Rock Island, Ill., Independents, 1922-27 Chicago Bears.

MEL HEIN
Center. 6-2, 225. Born in Redding, California, August 22, 1909. Washington State. Inducted in 1963. 1931-45 New York Giants.

WILBUR (PETE) HENRY
Tackle. 6-0, 250. Born in Mansfield, Ohio, October 31, 1897. Died February 7, 1952. Washington & Jefferson. Inducted in 1963. 1920-23, 1925-26 Canton Bulldogs, 1927 New York Giants, 1927-28 Pottsville Maroons.

ARNIE HERBER
Quarterback. 6-1, 200. Born in Green Bay, Wisconsin, April 2, 1910. Died October 14, 1969. Wisconsin, Regis College. Inducted in 1966. 1930-40 Green Bay Packers, 1944-45 New York Giants.

BILL HEWITT
End. 5-11, 191. Born in Bay City, Michigan, October 8, 1909. Died January 14, 1947. Michigan. Inducted in 1971. 1932-36 Chicago Bears, 1937-39 Philadelphia Eagles, 1943 Phil-Pitt.

CLARKE HINKLE
Fullback. 5-11, 201. Born in Toronto, Ohio, April 10, 1910. Bucknell. Inducted in 1964. 1932-41 Green Bay Packers.

ELROY (CRAZYLEGS) HIRSCH
Halfback-end. 6-2, 190. Born in Wausau, Wisconsin, June 17, 1923. Wisconsin, Michigan. Inducted in 1968. 1946-48 Chicago Rockets (AAFC), 1949-57 Los Angeles Rams.

PAUL HORNUNG
Halfback. 6-2, 220. Born in Louisville, Kentucky, December 23, 1935. Notre Dame. Inducted in 1986. 1957-62, 1964-66 Green Bay Packers.

KEN HOUSTON
Safety. 6-3, 198. Born in Lufkin, Texas, November 12, 1944. Prairie View A&M. Inducted in 1986. 1967-72 Houston Oilers, 1973-80 Washington Redskins.

CAL HUBBARD
Tackle. 6-5, 250. Born in Keytesville, Missouri, October 31, 1900. Died October 17, 1977. Centenary, Geneva. Inducted in 1963. 1927-28 New York Giants, 1929-33, 1935 Green Bay Packers, 1936 New York Giants, 1936 Pittsburgh Pirates.

SAM HUFF
Linebacker. 6-1, 230. Born in Morgantown, West Virginia, October 4, 1934. West Virginia. Inducted in 1982. 1956-63 New York Giants, 1964-67, 1969 Washington Redskins.

LAMAR HUNT
Team owner. Born in El Dorado, Arkansas, August 2, 1932. Southern Methodist. Inducted in 1972. 1960-62 Dallas Texans, 1963-87 Kansas City Chiefs.

DON HUTSON
End. 6-1, 180. Born in Pine Bluff, Arkansas, January 31, 1913. Alabama. Inducted in 1963. 1935-45 Green Bay Packers.

JOHN HENRY JOHNSON
Fullback. 6-2, 225. Born in Waterproof, Louisiana, November 24, 1929. St. Mary's, Arizona State. Inducted in 1987. San Francisco 49ers 1954-56, Detroit Lions 1957-59, Pittsburgh Steelers 1960-65, Houston Oilers 1966.

DAVID (DEACON) JONES
Defensive end. 6-5, 250. Born in Eatonville, Florida, December 9, 1938. Mississippi Vocational. Inducted in 1980. 1961-71 Los Angeles Rams, 1972-73 San Diego Chargers, 1974 Washington Redskins.

SONNY JURGENSEN
Quarterback. 6-0, 203. Born in Wilmington, North Carolina, August 23, 1934. Duke. Inducted in 1983. 1957-63 Philadelphia Eagles, 1964-74 Washington Redskins.

WALT KIESLING
Guard. Coach. 6-2, 245. Born in St. Paul, Minnesota, March 27, 1903. Died March 2, 1962. St. Thomas (Minnesota). Inducted in 1966. 1926-27 Duluth Eskimos, 1928 Pottsville Maroons, 1929-33 Chicago Cardinals, 1934 Chicago Bears, 1935-36 Green Bay Packers, 1937-38 Pittsburgh Pirates; coach, 1939-42 Pittsburgh Steelers; co-coach, 1943 Phil-Pitt, 1944 Card-Pitt; coach, 1954-56 Pittsburgh Steelers.

FRANK (BRUISER) KINARD
Tackle. 6-1, 210. Born in Pelahatchie, Mississippi, October 23, 1914. Died September 7, 1985. Mississippi. Inducted in 1971. 1938-44 Brooklyn Dodgers-Tigers, 1946-47 New York Yankees (AAFC).

EARL (CURLY) LAMBEAU
Coach. Born in Green Bay, Wisconsin, April 9, 1898. Died June 1, 1965. Notre Dame. Inducted in 1963. 1919-49 Green Bay Packers, 1950-51 Chicago Cardinals, 1952-53 Washington Redskins.

DICK (NIGHT TRAIN) LANE
Defensive back. 6-2, 210. Born in Austin, Texas, April 16, 1928. Scottsbluff Junior College. Inducted in 1974. 1952-53 Los Angeles Rams, 1954-59 Chicago Cardinals, 1960-65 Detroit Lions.

JIM LANGER
Center. 6-2, 255. Born in Little Falls, Minnesota, May 16, 1948. South Dakota State. Inducted in 1987. Miami Dolphins 1970-79, Minnesota Vikings 1980-81.

WILLIE LANIER
Linebacker. 6-1, 245. Born in Clover, Virginia, August 21, 1945. Morgan State. Inducted in 1986. 1967-77 Kansas City Chiefs.

YALE LARY
Defensive back-punter. 5-11, 189. Born in Fort Worth, Texas, November 24, 1930. Texas A&M. Inducted in 1979. 1952-53, 1956-64 Detroit Lions.

DANTE LAVELLI
End. 6-0, 199. Born in Hudson, Ohio, February 23, 1923. Ohio State. Inducted in 1975. 1946-49 Cleveland Browns (AAFC), 1950-56 Cleveland Browns.

BOBBY LAYNE
Quarterback. 6-2, 190. Born in Santa Anna, Texas, December 19, 1926. Died December 1, 1986. Texas. Inducted in 1967. 1948 Chicago Bears, 1949 New York Bulldogs, 1950-58 Detroit Lions, 1958-62 Pittsburgh Steelers.

ALPHONSE (TUFFY) LEEMANS
Fullback. 6-0, 200. Born in Superior, Wisconsin, November 12, 1912. Died January 19, 1979. George Washington. Inducted in 1978. 1936-43 New York Giants.

BOB LILLY
Defensive tackle. 6-5, 260. Born in Olney, Texas, July 26, 1939. Texas Christian. Inducted in 1980. 1961-74 Dallas Cowboys.

VINCE LOMBARDI
Coach. Born in Brooklyn, New York, June 11, 1913. Died September 3, 1970. Fordham. Inducted in 1971. 1959-67 Green Bay Packers, 1969 Washington Redskins.

SID LUCKMAN
Quarterback. 6-0, 195. Born in Brooklyn, New York, November 21, 1916. Columbia. Inducted in 1965. 1939-50 Chicago Bears.

ROY (LINK) LYMAN
Tackle. 6-2, 252. Born in Table Rock, Nebraska, November 30, 1898. Died December 16, 1972. Nebraska. Inducted in 1964. 1922-23, 1925 Canton Bulldogs, 1924 Cleveland Bulldogs, 1925 Frankford Yellow Jackets, 1926-28, 1930-31, 1933-34 Chicago Bears.

TIM MARA
Team owner. Born in New York, New York, July 29, 1887. Died February 17, 1959. Did not attend college. Inducted in 1963. 1925-59 New York Giants.

GINO MARCHETTI
Defensive end. 6-4, 245. Born in Antioch, California, January 2, 1927. San Francisco. Inducted in 1972. 1952 Dallas Texans, 1953-64, 1966 Baltimore Colts.

GEORGE PRESTON MARSHALL
Team owner. Born in Grafton, West Virginia, October 11, 1897. Died August 9, 1969. Randolph-Macon. Inducted in 1963. 1932 Boston Braves, 1933-36 Boston Redskins, 1937-69 Washington Redskins.

OLLIE MATSON
Halfback. 6-2, 220. Born in Trinity, Texas, May 1, 1930. San Francisco. Inducted in 1972. 1952, 1954-58 Chicago Cardinals, 1959-62 Los Angeles Rams, 1963 Detroit Lions, 1964-66 Philadelphia Eagles.

DON MAYNARD
Wide receiver. 6-1, 180. Born in Crosbyton, Texas, January 25, 1937. Texas Western. Inducted in 1987. New York Giants 1958, New York Titans 1960-62, New York Jets 1963-72, St. Louis Cardinals 1973.

GEORGE McAFEE
Halfback. 6-0, 177. Born in Ironton, Ohio, March 13, 1918. Duke. Inducted in 1966. 1940-41, 1945-50 Chicago Bears.

MIKE McCORMACK
Tackle. 6-4, 248. Born in Chicago, Illinois, June 21, 1930. Kansas. Inducted in 1984. 1951 New York Yanks, 1954-62 Cleveland Browns.

HUGH McELHENNY
Halfback. 6-1, 198. Born in Los Angeles, California, December 31, 1928. Washington. Inducted in 1970. 1952-60 San Francisco 49ers, 1961-62 Minnesota Vikings, 1963 New York Giants, 1964 Detroit Lions.

JOHNNY BLOOD (McNALLY)
Halfback. 6-0, 185. Born in New Richmond, Wisconsin, November 27, 1903. Died November 28, 1985. St. John's (Minnesota). Inducted in 1963. 1925-26 Milwaukee Badgers, 1926-27 Duluth Eskimos, 1928 Pottsville Maroons, 1929-33 Green Bay Packers, 1934 Pittsburgh Pirates, 1935-36 Green Bay Packers; player-coach, 1937-39 Pittsburgh Pirates.

MIKE MICHALSKE
Guard. 6-0, 209. Born in Cleveland, Ohio, April 24, 1903. Died October 26, 1983. Penn State. Inducted in 1964. 1926 New York Yankees (AFL), 1927-28 New York Yankees, 1929-35, 1937 Green Bay Packers.

WAYNE MILLNER
End. 6-0, 191. Born in Roxbury, Massachusetts, January 31, 1913. Died November 19, 1976. Notre Dame. Inducted in 1968. 1936 Boston Redskins, 1937-41, 1945 Washington Redskins.

BOBBY MITCHELL
Running back-wide receiver. 6-0, 195. Born in Hot Springs, Arkansas, June 6, 1935. Illinois. Inducted in 1983. 1958-61 Cleveland Browns, 1962-68 Washington Redskins.

RON MIX
Tackle. 6-4, 250. Born in Los Angeles, California, March 10, 1938. Southern California. Inducted in 1979. 1960 Los Angeles Chargers, 1961-69 San Diego Chargers, 1971 Oakland Raiders.

LENNY MOORE
Back. 6-1, 198. Born in Reading, Pennsylvania, November 25, 1933. Penn State. Inducted in 1975. 1956-67 Baltimore Colts.

MARION MOTLEY
Fullback. 6-1, 238. Born in Leesburg, Georgia, June 5, 1920. South Carolina State, Nevada. Inducted in 1968. 1946-49 Cleveland Browns (AAFC), 1950-53 Cleveland Browns, 1955 Pittsburgh Steelers.

GEORGE MUSSO
Guard-tackle. 6-2, 270. Born in Collinsville, Illinois. April 8, 1910. Millikin. Inducted in 1982. 1933-44 Chicago Bears.

BRONKO NAGURSKI
Fullback. 6-2, 225. Born in Rainy River, Ontario, Canada, November 3, 1908. Minnesota. Inducted in 1963. 1930-37, 1943 Chicago Bears.

JOE NAMATH
Quarterback. 6-2, 200. Born in Beaver Falls, Pennsylvania, May 31, 1943. Alabama. Inducted in 1985. 1965-76 New York Jets, 1977 Los Angeles Rams.

EARLE (GREASY) NEALE
Coach. Born in Parkersburg, West Virginia, November 5, 1891. Died November 2, 1973. West Virginia Wesleyan. Inducted in 1969. 1941-42, 1944-50 Philadelphia Eagles; co-coach, Phil-Pitt 1943.

ERNIE NEVERS
Fullback. 6-1, 205. Born in Willow River, Minnesota, June 11, 1903. Died May 3, 1976. Stanford. Inducted in 1963. 1926-27 Duluth Eskimos, 1929-31 Chicago Cardinals.

RAY NITSCHKE
Linebacker. 6-3, 235. Born in Elmwood Park, Illinois, December 29, 1936. Illinois. Inducted in 1978. 1958-72 Green Bay Packers.

LEO NOMELLINI
Defensive tackle. 6-3, 264. Born in Lucca, Italy, June 19, 1924. Minnesota. Inducted in 1969. 1950-63 San Francisco 49ers.

MERLIN OLSEN
Defensive tackle. 6-5, 270. Born in Logan, Utah, September 15, 1940. Utah State. Inducted in 1982. 1962-76 Los Angeles Rams.

JIM OTTO
Center. 6-2, 255. Born in Wausau, Wisconsin, January 5, 1938. Miami. Inducted in 1980. 1960-74 Oakland Raiders.

STEVE OWEN
Tackle. Coach. 6-0, 235. Born in Cleo Springs, Oklahoma, April 21, 1898. Died May 17, 1964. Phillips. Inducted in 1966. 1924-25 Kansas City Cowboys, 1926-30 New York Giants; coach, 1931-53 New York Giants.

ALAN PAGE
Defensive tackle. 6-4, 225. Born in Canton, Ohio, August 7, 1945. Inducted in 1988. 1967-78 Minnesota Vikings, 1978-81 Chicago Bears.

CLARENCE (ACE) PARKER
Quarterback. 5-11, 168. Born in Portsmouth, Virginia, May 17, 1912. Duke. Inducted in 1972. 1937-41 Brooklyn Dodgers, 1945 Boston Yanks, 1946 New York Yankees (AAFC).

JIM PARKER
Guard-tackle. 6-3, 273. Born in Macon, Georgia, April 3, 1934. Ohio State. Inducted in 1973. 1957-67 Baltimore Colts.

JOE PERRY
Fullback. 6-0, 200. Born in Stevens, Arkansas, January 27, 1927. Compton Junior College. Inducted in 1969. 1948-49 San Francisco 49ers (AAFC), 1950-60, 1963 San Francisco 49ers, 1961-62 Baltimore Colts.

PETE PIHOS
End. 6-1, 210. Born in Orlando, Florida, October 22, 1923. Indiana. Inducted in 1970. 1947-55 Philadelphia Eagles.

HUGH (SHORTY) RAY
Supervisor of officials 1938-56. Born in Highland Park, Illinois, September 21, 1884. Died September 16, 1956. Illinois. Inducted in 1966.

DAN REEVES
Team owner. Born in New York, New York, June 30, 1912. Died April 15, 1971. Georgetown. Inducted in 1967. 1941-45 Cleveland Rams, 1946-71 Los Angeles Rams.

JIM RINGO
Center. 6-1, 235. Born in Orange, New Jersey, November 21, 1931. Syracuse. Inducted in 1981. 1953-63 Green Bay Packers, 1964-67 Philadelphia Eagles.

ANDY ROBUSTELLI
Defensive end. 6-0, 230. Born in Stamford, Connecticut, December 6, 1925. Arnold College. Inducted in 1971. 1951-55 Los Angeles Rams, 1956-64 New York Giants.

ART ROONEY
Team owner. Born in Coulterville, Pennsylvania, January 27, 1901. Georgetown, Duquesne. Inducted in 1964. 1933-40 Pittsburgh Pirates, 1941-42, 1949-88 Pittsburgh Steelers, 1943 Phil-Pitt, 1944 Card-Pitt.

PETE ROZELLE
Commissioner. Born in South Gate, California, March 1, 1926. San Francisco. Inducted in 1985. Commissioner 1960-88.

GALE SAYERS
Running back. 6-0, 200. Born in Wichita, Kansas, May 30, 1943. Kansas. Inducted in 1977. 1965-71 Chicago Bears.

JOE SCHMIDT
Linebacker. 6-0, 222. Born in Pittsburgh, Pennsylvania, January 19, 1932. Pittsburgh. Inducted in 1973. 1953-65 Detroit Lions.

O.J. SIMPSON
Running back. 6-1, 212. Born in San Francisco, California, July 9, 1947. Southern California. Inducted in 1985. 1969-77 Buffalo Bills, 1978-79 San Francisco 49ers.

BART STARR
Quarterback. 6-1, 200. Born in Montgomery, Alabama, January 9, 1934. Alabama. Inducted in 1977. 1956-71 Green Bay Packers; coach, 1975-83 Green Bay Packers.

ROGER STAUBACH
Quarterback. 6-3, 202. Born in Cincinnati, Ohio, February 5, 1942. Navy. Inducted in 1985. 1969-79 Dallas Cowboys.

ERNIE STAUTNER
Defensive tackle. 6-2, 235. Born in Prinzing-by-Cham, Bavaria, Germany, April 20, 1925. Boston College. Inducted in 1969. 1950-63 Pittsburgh Steelers.

KEN STRONG
Halfback. 5-11, 210. Born in New Haven, Connecticut, August 6, 1906. Died October 5, 1979. New York University. Inducted in 1967. 1929-32 Staten Island Stapletons, 1933-35, 1939, 1944-47 New York Giants, 1936-37 New York Yanks (AFL).

JOE STYDAHAR
Tackle. 6-4, 230. Born in Kaylor, Pennsylvania, March 3, 1912. Died March 23, 1977. West Virginia. Inducted in 1967. 1936-42, 1945-46 Chicago Bears.

FRAN TARKENTON
Quarterback. 6-0, 185. Born in Richmond, Virginia, February 3, 1940. Georgia. Inducted in 1986. 1961-66, 1972-78 Minnesota Vikings, 1967-71 New York Giants.

CHARLEY TAYLOR
Running back-wide receiver. 6-3, 210. Born in Grand Prairie, Texas, September 28, 1941. Arizona State. Inducted in 1984. 1964-75, 1977 Washington Redskins.

JIM TAYLOR
Fullback. 6-0, 216. Born in Baton Rouge, Louisiana, September 20, 1935. Louisiana State. Inducted in 1976. 1958-66 Green Bay Packers, 1967 New Orleans Saints.

JIM THORPE
Halfback. 6-1, 190. Born in Prague, Oklahoma, May 28, 1888. Died March 28, 1953. Carlisle. Inducted in 1963. 1920 Canton Bulldogs, 1921 Cleveland Indians, 1922-23 Oorang Indians, 1923 Toledo Maroons, 1924 Rock Island, Ill., Independents, 1925 New York Giants, 1926 Canton Bulldogs, 1928 Chicago Cardinals.

Y.A. TITTLE
Quarterback. 6-0, 200. Born in Marshall, Texas, October 24, 1926. Louisiana State. Inducted in 1971. 1948-49 Baltimore Colts (AAFC), 1950 Baltimore Colts, 1951-60 San Francisco 49ers, 1961-64 New York Giants.

GEORGE TRAFTON
Center. 6-2, 235. Born in Chicago, Illinois, December 6, 1896. Died September 5, 1971. Notre Dame. Inducted in 1964. 1920 Decatur Staleys, 1921 Chicago Staleys, 1922-32 Chicago Bears.

CHARLEY TRIPPI
Halfback. 6-0, 185. Born in Pittston, Pennsylvania, December 14, 1922. Georgia. Inducted in 1968. 1947-55 Chicago Cardinals.

EMLEN TUNNELL
Safety. 6-1, 200. Born in Bryn Mawr, Pennsylvania, March 29, 1925. Died July 23, 1975. Toledo, Iowa. Inducted in 1967. 1948-58 New York Giants, 1959-61 Green Bay Packers.

CLYDE (BULLDOG) TURNER
Center. 6-2, 235. Born in Sweetwater, Texas, November 10, 1919. Hardin-Simmons. Inducted in 1966. 1940-52 Chicago Bears.

JOHNNY UNITAS
Quarterback. 6-1, 195. Born in Pittsburgh, Pennsylvania, May 7, 1933. Louisville. Inducted in 1979. 1956-72 Baltimore Colts, 1973 San Diego Chargers.

GENE UPSHAW
Guard. 6-5, 255. Born in Robstown, Texas, August 15, 1945. Texas A & I. Inducted in 1987. Oakland Raiders 1967-81.

NORM VAN BROCKLIN
Quarterback. 6-1, 190. Born in Eagle Butte, South Dakota, March 15, 1926. Died May 2, 1983. Oregon. Inducted in 1971. 1949-57 Los Angeles Rams, 1958-60 Philadelphia Eagles.

STEVE VAN BUREN
Halfback. 6-1, 200. Born in La Ceiba, Honduras, December 28, 1920. Louisiana State. Inducted in 1965. 1944-51 Philadelphia Eagles.

DOAK WALKER
Halfback. 5-10, 172. Born in Dallas, Texas, January 1, 1927. Southern Methodist. Inducted in 1986. 1950-55 Detroit Lions.

PAUL WARFIELD
Wide receiver. 6-0, 188. Born in Warren, Ohio, November 28, 1942. Ohio State. Inducted in 1983. 1964-69, 1976-77 Cleveland Browns, 1970-74 Miami Dolphins.

BOB WATERFIELD
Quarterback. 6-2, 200. Born in Elmira, New York, July 26, 1920. Died March 25, 1983. UCLA. Inducted in 1965. 1945 Cleveland Rams, 1946-52 Los Angeles Rams.

ARNIE WEINMEISTER
Defensive tackle. 6-4, 235. Born in Rhein, Saskatchewan, Canada, March 23, 1923. Washington. Inducted in 1984. 1948-49 New York Yankees (AAFC), 1950-53 New York Giants.

BILL WILLIS
Guard. 6-2, 215. Born in Columbus, Ohio, October 5, 1921. Ohio State. Inducted in 1977. 1946-49 Cleveland Browns (AAFC), 1950-53 Cleveland Browns.

LARRY WILSON
Safety. 6-0, 190. Born in Rigby, Idaho, March 24, 1938. Utah. Inducted in 1978. 1960-72 St. Louis Cardinals.

ALEX WOJCIECHOWICZ
Center. 6-0, 235. Born in South River, New Jersey, August 12, 1915. Fordham. Inducted in 1968. 1938-46 Detroit Lions, 1946-50 Philadelphia Eagles.

A CHRONOLOGY OF PROFESSIONAL FOOTBALL

1869 Rutgers and Princeton played a college soccer football game, the first ever, November 6. The game used modified London Football Association rules. During the next seven years, rugby gained favor with the major eastern schools over soccer, and modern football began to develop from rugby.

1876 At the Massasoit convention, the first rules for American football were written. Walter Camp, who would become known as "the father of American football," first became involved with the game.

1892 In an era in which football was a major attraction of local athletic clubs, an intense competition between two Pittsburgh-area clubs, the Allegheny Athletic Association (AAA) and the Pittsburgh Athletic Club (PAC), led to the making of the first professional football player. Former Yale All-America guard William (Pudge) Heffelfinger was paid $500 by the AAA to play in a game against the PAC, becoming the first person to be paid to play football, November 12. The AAA won the game 4-0 when Heffelfinger picked up a PAC fumble and ran 35 yards for a touchdown.

1893 The Pittsburgh Athletic Club signed one of its players, probably halfback Grant Dibert, to the first known pro football contract, which covered all of the PAC's games for the year.

1895 John Brallier became the first football player to openly turn pro, accepting $10 and expenses to play for the Latrobe YMCA against the Jeannette Athletic Club.

1896 The Allegheny Athletic Association team fielded the first completely professional team for its abbreviated two-game season.

1897 The Latrobe Athletic Association football team went entirely professional, becoming the first team to play a full season with only professionals.

1898 A touchdown was changed from four points to five.

1899 Chris O'Brien formed a neighborhood team, which played under the name the Morgan Athletic Club, on the south side of Chicago. The team later became known as the Normals, then the Racine (for a street in Chicago) Cardinals, the Chicago Cardinals, the St. Louis Cardinals, and, in 1988, the Phoenix Cardinals. The team remains the oldest continuing operation in pro football.

1900 William C. Temple took over the team payments for the Duquesne Country and Athletic Club, becoming the first known individual club owner.

1902 Baseball's Philadelphia Athletics, managed by Connie Mack, and the Philadelphia Phillies formed professional football teams, joining the Pittsburgh Stars in the first attempt at a pro football league, named the National Football League. The Athletics won the first night football game ever played, 39-0 over Kanaweola AC at Elmira, New York, November 21.

All three teams claimed the pro championship for the year, but the league president, Dave Berry, named the Stars the champions. Pitcher Rube Waddell was with the Athletics, and pitcher Christy Mathewson a fullback for Pittsburgh.

The first World Series of pro football, actually a five-team tournament, was played among a team made up of players from both the Athletics and the Phillies, but simply named "New York;" the New York Knickerbockers; the Syracuse AC; the Warlow AC; and the Orange (New Jersey) AC at New York's original Madison Square Garden. New York and Syracuse played the first indoor football game before 3,000, December 28. Syracuse, with Glen (Pop) Warner at guard, won 6-0 and went on to win the tournament.

1903 The Franklin (Pa.) Athletic Club won the second and last World Series of pro football over the Oreos AC of Asbury Park, New Jersey; the Watertown Red and Blacks; and the Orange AC.

Pro football was popularized in Ohio when the Massillon Tigers, a strong amateur team, hired four Pittsburgh pros to play in the season-ending game against Akron. At the same time, pro football declined in the Pittsburgh area, and the emphasis on the pro game moved west from Pennsylvania to Ohio.

1904 A field goal was changed from five points to four.

Ohio had at least seven pro teams, with Massillon winning the Ohio Independent Championship, that is, the pro title. Talk surfaced about forming a state-wide league to end spiraling salaries brought about by constant bidding for players and to write universal rules for the game. The feeble attempt to start the league failed.

Halfback Charles Follis signed a contract with the Shelby AC, making him the first-known black pro football player.

1905 The Canton AC, later to become known as the Bulldogs, became a professional team. Massillon again won the Ohio League championship.

1906 The forward pass was legalized. The first authenticated pass completion in a pro game came on October 27, when George (Peggy) Parratt of Massillon threw a completion to Dan (Bullet) Riley in a victory over a combined Benwood-Moundsville team.

Archrivals Canton and Massillon, the two best pro teams in America, played twice, with Canton winning the first game but Massillon winning the second and the Ohio League championship. A betting scandal and the financial disaster wrought upon the two clubs by paying huge salaries caused a temporary decline in interest in pro football in the two cities and, somewhat, through Ohio.

1909 A field goal dropped from four points to three.

1912 A touchdown was increased from five points to six.

Jack Cusack revived a strong pro team in Canton.

1913 Jim Thorpe, a former football and track star at the Carlisle Indian School (Pa.) and a double gold medal winner at the 1912 Olympics in Stockholm, played for the Pine Village Pros in Indiana.

1915 Massillon again fielded a major team, reviving the old rivalry with Canton. Cusack signed Thorpe to play for Canton for $250 a game.

1916 With Thorpe and former Carlisle teammate Pete Calac starring, Canton went 9-0-1, won the Ohio League championship, and was acclaimed the pro football champion.

1917 Despite an upset by Massillon, Canton again won the Ohio League championship.

1919 Canton again won the Ohio League championship, despite the team having been turned over from Cusack to Ralph Hay. Thorpe and Calac were joined in the backfield by Joe Guyon.

Earl (Curly) Lambeau and George Calhoun organized the Green Bay Packers. Lambeau's employer at the Indian Packing Company provided $500 for equipment and allowed the team to use the company field for practices. The Packers went 10-1.

1920 Pro football was in a state of confusion due to three major problems: dramatically rising salaries; players continually jumping from one team to another following the highest offer; and the use of college players still enrolled in school. A league in which all the members would follow the same rules seemed the answer. An organizational meeting, at which the Akron Pros, Canton Bulldogs, Cleveland Indians, and Dayton Triangles were represented, was held in Canton, Ohio, August 20. This meeting resulted in the formation of the American Professional Football Conference.

A second organizational meeting was held in Canton, September 17. The teams were from four states—Akron, Canton, Cleveland, and Dayton from Ohio; the Hammond Pros and Muncie Flyers from Indiana; the Rochester Jeffersons from New York; and the Rock Island Independents, Decatur Staleys, and Racine Cardinals from Illinois. The name of the league was changed to the American Professional Football Association. Hoping to capitalize on his fame, the members elected Thorpe president; Stanley Cofall of Cleveland was elected vice president. A membership fee of $100 per team was charged to give an appearance of respectability, but no team ever paid it. Scheduling was left up to the teams, and there was a wide variation both in the overall number of games played and in the number played against APFA member teams.

Four other teams—the Buffalo All-Americans, Chicago Tigers, Columbus Panhandles, and Detroit Heralds—joined the league sometime during the year. On September 26, the first game featuring an APFA team was played at Rock Island's Douglas Park. A crowd of 800 watched the Independents defeat the St. Paul Ideals 48-0. A week later, October 3, the first game matching two APFA teams was held. At Triangle Park, Dayton defeated Columbus 14-0, with Lou Partlow of Dayton scoring the first touchdown in a game between Association teams. The same day, Rock Island defeated Muncie 45-0.

By the beginning of December, most of the teams in the APFA had abandoned their hopes for a championship, and some of them, including the Chicago Tigers and the Detroit Heralds, had finished their seasons, disbanded, and had their franchises canceled by the Association. Four teams—Akron, Buffalo, Canton, and Decatur—still had championship aspirations, but a series of late-season games among them left Akron as the only undefeated team in the Association. At one of these games, Akron sold tackle Bob Nash to Buffalo for $300 and five percent of the gate receipts—the first APFA player deal.

1921 At the league meeting in Akron, April 30, the championship of the 1920 season was awarded to the Akron Pros. The APFA was reorganized, with Joe Carr of the Columbus Panhandles named president and Carl Storck of Dayton secretary-treasurer. Carr moved the Association's headquarters to Columbus, drafted a league constitution and by-laws, gave teams territorial rights, restricted player movements, developed membership criteria for the franchises, and issued standings for the first time, so that the APFA would have a clear champion.

The Association's membership increased to 22 teams, including the Green Bay Packers, who were awarded to John Clair of the Acme Packing Company.

Thorpe moved from Canton to the Cleveland Indians, but he was hurt early in the season and played very little.

A.E. Staley turned the Decatur Staleys over to player-coach George Halas, who moved the team to Cubs Park in Chicago. Staley paid Halas $5,000 to keep the name "Staleys" for one more year. Halas made halfback Ed (Dutch) Sternaman his partner.

The Staleys claimed the APFA championship with a 9-1-1 record, as did Buffalo at 9-1-2. Carr ruled in favor of the Staleys, giving Halas his first championship.

1922 After admitting the use of players who had college eligibility remaining during the 1921 season, Clair and the Green Bay management withdrew from the APFA, January 28. Curly Lambeau promised to obey league rules and then used $50 of his own money to buy back the franchise. Bad weather and low attendance plagued the Packers, and Lambeau went broke, but local merchants arranged a $2,500 loan for the club. A public non-profit corporation was set up to operate the team, with Lambeau as head coach and manager.

The American Professional Football Association changed its name to the National Football League, June 24. The Chicago Staleys became the Chicago Bears.

The NFL fielded 18 teams, including the new Oorang Indians of Marion, Ohio, an all-Indian team featuring Thorpe, Joe Guyon, and Pete Calac, and sponsored by the Oorang dog kennels.

Canton, led by player-coach Guy Chamberlin and tackles Link Lyman and Wilbur (Pete) Henry, emerged as the league's first true powerhouse, going 10-0-2.

1923 For the first time, all of the franchises considered to be part of the NFL fielded teams. Thorpe played first for Oorang, then for the Toledo Maroons. Against the Bears, Thorpe fumbled, and Halas picked up the ball and returned it 98 yards for a touchdown, a record that would last until 1972.

Canton had its second consecutive undefeated season, going 11-0-1 for the NFL title.

1924 The league had 18 franchises, including new ones in Kansas City, Kenosha, and Frankford, a section of Philadelphia. League champion Canton, successful on the field but not at the box office, was purchased by the owner of the Cleveland franchise, who kept the Canton franchise inactive, while using the best players for his Cleveland team, which he renamed the Bulldogs. Cleveland won the title with a 7-1-1 record.

1925 Five new franchises were admitted to the NFL—the New York Giants, who were awarded to Tim Mara and Billy Gibson for $500; the Detroit Panthers, featuring Jimmy Conzelman as owner, coach, and tailback; the Providence Steam Roller; a new Canton Bulldogs team; and the Pottsville Maroons, who had been perhaps the most successful independent pro team. The NFL established its first player limit, at 16 players.

Late in the season, the NFL made its greatest coup in gaining national recognition. Shortly after the University of Illinois season ended in November, All-America halfback Harold (Red) Grange signed a contract to play with the Chicago Bears. On Thanksgiving Day, a crowd of 36,000—the largest in pro football history—watched Grange and the Bears play the Chicago Cardinals to a scoreless tie at Wrigley Field. At the beginning of December, the Bears left on a barnstorming tour that saw them play eight games in 12 days, in St. Louis, Philadelphia, New York City, Washington, Boston, Pittsburgh, Detroit, and Chicago. A crowd of 73,000 watched the game against the Giants at the Polo Grounds, helping assure the future of the troubled NFL franchise in New York. The Bears then played nine more games in the South and West, including a game in Los Angeles, in which 75,000 fans watched them defeat the Los Angeles Tigers in the Los Angeles Memorial Coliseum.

Pottsville and the Chicago Cardinals were the top contenders for the league title, with Pottsville winning a late-season meeting 21-7. Pottsville scheduled a game against a team of former Notre Dame players for Shibe Park in Philadelphia. Frankford lodged a protest not only because the game was in Frankford's "protected territory," but because it was being played the same day as a Yellow Jackets home game. Carr gave three different notices forbidding Pottsville to play the game, but Pottsville played anyway, December 12. That day, Carr fined the club, suspended it from all rights and privileges (including the right to play for the NFL championship), and returned its franchise to the league. The Cardinals, who ended the season with the best record in the league, were named the 1925 champions.

1926 Grange's manager, C.C. Pyle, told the Bears that Grange wouldn't play for them unless he was paid a five-figure salary and given one-third ownership of the team. The Bears refused. Pyle leased Yankee Stadium in New York City, then petitioned for an NFL franchise. After he was refused, he started the first American Football League. It lasted one season and included Grange's New York Yankees and eight other teams. The AFL champion Philadelphia Quakers played a December game against the New York Giants, seventh in the NFL, and the Giants won 31-0. At the end of the season, the AFL folded.

Halas pushed through a rule that prohibited any team from signing a player whose college class had not graduated.

The NFL grew to 22 teams, including the Duluth Eskimos, who signed All-America fullback Ernie Nevers of Stanford, giving the league a gate attraction to rival Grange. The 15-member Eskimos, dubbed the "Iron Men of the North," played 29 exhibition and league games, 28 on the road, and Nevers played in all but 29 minutes of them.

Frankford edged the Bears for the championship, despite Halas having obtained John (Paddy) Driscoll from the Cardinals. On December 4, the Yellow Jackets scored in the final two minutes to defeat the Bears 7-6 and move ahead of them in the standings.

1927 At a special meeting in Cleveland, April 23, Carr decided to secure the NFL's future by eliminating the financially weaker teams and consolidating the quality players onto a limited number of more successful teams. The new-look NFL dropped to 12 teams, and the center of gravity of the league left the Midwest, where the NFL had started, and began to emerge in the large cities of the East. One of the new teams was Grange's New York Yankees, but Grange suffered a knee injury and the Yankees finished in the middle of the pack. The NFL championship was won by the cross-town rival New York Giants, who posted 10 shutouts in 13 games.

1928 Grange and Nevers both retired from pro football, and Duluth disbanded, as the NFL was reduced to only 10 teams. The Providence Steam Roller of Jimmy Conzelman and Pearce Johnson won the championship, playing in the Cycledrome, a 10,000-seat oval that had been built for bicycle races.

1929 Chris O'Brien sold the Chicago Cardinals to David Jones, July 27.

The NFL added a fourth official, the field judge, July 28.

Grange and Nevers returned to the NFL. Nevers scored six rushing touchdowns and four extra points as the Cardinals beat Grange's Bears 40-6, November 28. The 40 points set a record that remains the NFL's oldest.

Providence became the first NFL team to host a game at night under floodlights, against the Cardinals, November 3.

The Packers added back Johnny Blood (McNally), tackle Cal Hubbard, and guard Mike Michalske, and won their first NFL championship, edging the Giants, who featured quarterback Benny Friedman.

1930 Dayton, the last of the NFL's original franchises, was purchased by John Dwyer, moved to Brooklyn, and renamed the Dodgers. The Portsmouth, Ohio, Spartans entered the league.

The Packers edged the Giants for the title, but the most improved team was the Bears. Halas retired as a player and replaced himself as coach of the Bears with Ralph Jones, who refined the T-formation by introducing wide ends and a halfback in motion. Jones also introduced rookie All-America fullback-tackle Bronko Nagurski.

The Giants defeated a team of former Notre Dame players coached by Knute Rockne 22-0 before 55,000 at the Polo Grounds, December 14. The proceeds went to the New York Unemployment Fund to help those suffering because of the Great Depression, and the easy victory helped give the NFL credibility with the press and the public.

1931 The NFL decreased to 10 teams, and halfway through the season the Frankford franchise folded. Carr fined the Bears, Packers, and Portsmouth $1,000 each for using players whose college classes had not graduated.

The Packers won an unprecedented third consecutive title, beating out the Spartans, who were led by rookie backs Earl (Dutch) Clark and Glenn Presnell.

1932 George Preston Marshall, Vincent Bendix, Jay O'Brien, and M. Dorland Doyle were awarded a franchise for Boston, July 9. Despite the presence of two rookies—halfback Cliff Battles and tackle Glen (Turk) Edwards—the new team, named the Braves, lost money and Marshall was left as the sole owner at the end of the year.

NFL membership dropped to eight teams, the lowest in history. Official statistics were kept for the first time. The Bears and the Spartans finished the season in the first-ever tie for first place. After the season finale, the league office arranged for the first playoff game in NFL history. The game was moved indoors to Chicago Stadium because of bitter cold and heavy snow. The arena allowed only an 80-yard field that came right to the walls. The goal posts were moved from the end lines to the goal lines and, for safety, inbounds lines or hashmarks where the ball would be put in play were drawn 10 yards from the walls that butted against the sidelines. The Bears won 9-0, December 18, scoring the winning touchdown on a two-yard pass from Nagurski to Grange. The Spartans claimed Nagurski's pass was thrown from less than five yards behind the line of scrimmage, violating the existing passing rule, but the play stood.

1933 The NFL, which long had followed the rules of college football, made a number of significant changes from the college game for the first time and began to independently develop rules serving its needs and the style of play it preferred. The innovations from the 1932 championship game—inbounds line or hashmarks and goal posts on the goal lines—were adopted. Also the forward pass was legalized from anywhere behind the line of scrimmage, February 25.

Marshall and Halas pushed through a proposal that divided the NFL into two divisions, with the winners to meet in an annual championship game, July 8.

Three new franchises joined the league—the Pittsburgh Pirates of Art Rooney, the Philadelphia Eagles of Bert Bell and Lud Wray, and the Cincinnati Reds. The Staten Island Stapletons suspended operations for a year, but never returned to the league.

Halas bought out Sternaman, became sole owner of the Bears, and reinstated himself as head coach. Marshall changed the name of the Boston Braves to the Redskins. David Jones sold the Chicago Cardinals to Charles W. Bidwill.

In the first NFL Championship Game scheduled before the season, the Western Division champion Bears defeated the Eastern Division champion Giants 23-21 at Wrigley Field, December 17.

1934 G.A. (Dick) Richards purchased the Portsmouth Spartans, moved them to Detroit, and renamed them the Lions.

Professional football gained new prestige when the Bears were matched against the best college football players in the first Chicago College All-Star Game, August 31. The game ended in a scoreless tie before 79,432 at Soldier Field.

The Cincinnati Reds lost their first eight games, then were suspended from the league for defaulting on payments. The St. Louis Gunners, an independent team, joined the NFL by buying the Cincinnati franchise and went 1-2 the last three weeks.

Rookie Beattie Feathers of the Bears became the NFL's first 1,000-yard rusher, gaining 1,004 on 101 carries. The Thanksgiving Day game between the Bears and the Lions became the first NFL game broadcast nationally, with Graham McNamee the announcer for CBS radio.

In the championship game, on an extremely cold and icy day at the Polo Grounds, the Giants trailed the Bears 13-3 in the third quarter before changing to basketball shoes for better footing. The Giants won 30-13 in what has come to be known as the "Sneakers Game," December 9.

The player waiver rule was adopted, December 10.

1935 The NFL adopted Bert Bell's proposal to hold an annual draft of college players, to begin in 1936, with teams selecting in an inverse order of finish, May 19. The inbounds line or hashmarks were moved nearer the center of the field, 15 yards from the sidelines.

All-America end Don Hutson of Alabama joined Green Bay. The Lions defeated the Giants 26-7 in the NFL Championship Game, December 15.

1936 There were no franchise transactions for the first year since the formation of the NFL. It also was the first year in which all member teams played the same number of games.

The Eagles made University of Chicago halfback and Heisman Trophy winner Jay Berwanger the first player ever selected in the NFL draft, February 8. The Eagles traded his rights to the Bears, but Berwanger never played pro football. The first player selected to actually sign was the number-two pick, Riley Smith of Alabama, who was selected by Boston.

A rival league was formed, and it became the second to call itself the American Football League. The Boston Shamrocks were its champions.

Due to poor attendance, Marshall, the owner of the host team, moved the Championship Game from Boston to the Polo Grounds in New York. Green Bay defeated the Redskins 21-6, December 13.

1937 Homer Marshman was granted a Cleveland franchise, named the Rams, February 12. Marshall moved the Redskins to Washington, D.C., February 13. The Redskins signed TCU All-America tailback Sammy Baugh, who led them to a 28-21 victory over the Bears in the NFL Championship Game, December 12.

The Los Angeles Bulldogs had an 8-0 record to win the AFL title, but then the two-year-old league folded.

1938 At the suggestion of Halas, Hugh (Shorty) Ray became a technical advisor on rules and officiating to the NFL. A new rule called for a 15-yard penalty for roughing the passer.

Rookie Byron (Whizzer) White of the Pittsburgh Pirates led the NFL in rushing. The Giants defeated the Packers 23-17 for the NFL title, December 11.

Marshall, *Los Angeles Times* sports editor Bill Henry, and promoter Tom Gallery established the Pro Bowl game between the NFL champion and a team of pro all-stars.

1939 The New York Giants defeated the Pro All-Stars 13-10 in the first Pro Bowl, at Wrigley Field, Los Angeles, January 15.

Carr, NFL president since 1921, died in Columbus, May 20. Carl Storck was named acting president, May 25.

An NFL game was televised for the first time when NBC broadcast the Brooklyn Dodgers-Philadelphia Eagles game from Ebbets Field to the approximately 1,000 sets then in New York.

Green Bay defeated New York 27-0 in the NFL Championship Game, December 10 at Milwaukee. NFL attendance exceeded one million in a season for the first time, reaching 1,071,200.

1940 A six-team rival league, the third to call itself the American Football League, was formed, and the Columbus Bullies won its championship.

Halas's Bears, with additional coaching by Clark Shaughnessy of Stanford, defeated the Redskins 73-0 in the NFL Championship Game, December 8. The game, which was the most decisive victory in NFL history, popularized the Bears' T-formation with a man-in-motion. It was the first championship carried on network radio, broadcast by Red Barber to 120 stations of the Mutual Broadcasting System, which paid $2,500 for the rights.

Art Rooney sold the Pittsburgh franchise to Alexis Thompson, December 9, then bought part interest in the Philadelphia Eagles.

1941 Elmer Layden was named the first Commissioner of the NFL, March 1; Storck, the acting president, resigned, April 5. NFL headquarters were moved to Chicago.

Bell and Rooney traded the Eagles to Thompson for the Pirates, then renamed their new team the Steelers. Homer Marshman sold the Rams to Daniel F. Reeves and Fred Levy, Jr.

The league by-laws were revised to provide for playoffs in case there were ties in division races, and sudden-death overtimes in case a playoff game was tied after four quarters. An official *NFL Record Manual* was published for the first time.

Columbus again won the championship of the AFL, but the two-year-old league then folded.

The Bears and the Packers finished in a tie for the Western Division championship, setting up the first divisional playoff game in league history. The Bears won 33-14, then defeated the Giants 37-9 for the NFL championship, December 21.

1942 Players departing for service in World War II depleted the rosters of NFL teams. Halas left the Bears in midseason to join the Navy, and Luke Johnsos and Heartley (Hunk) Anderson served as co-coaches as the Bears went 11-0 in the regular season. The Redskins defeated the Bears 14-6 in the NFL Championship Game, December 13.

1943 The Cleveland Rams, with co-owners Reeves and Levy in the service, were granted permission to suspend operations for one season, April 6. Levy transferred his stock in the team to Reeves, April 16.

The NFL adopted free substitution, April 7. The league also made the wearing of helmets mandatory and approved a 10-game schedule for all teams.

Philadelphia and Pittsburgh were granted permission to merge for one season, June 19. The team, known as Phil-Pitt (and called the Steagles by fans), divided home games between the two cities, and Earle (Greasy) Neale of Philadelphia and Walt Kiesling of Pittsburgh served as co-coaches. The merger automatically dissolved the last day of the season, December 5.

Ted Collins was granted a franchise for Boston, to become active in 1944.

Sammy Baugh led the league in passing, punting, and interceptions. He led the Redskins to a tie with the Giants for the Eastern Division title, and then to a 28-0 victory in a divisional playoff game. The Bears beat the Redskins 41-21 in the NFL Championship Game, December 26.

1944 Collins, who had wanted a franchise in Yankee Stadium in New York, named his new team in Boston the Yanks. Cleveland resumed operations. The Brooklyn Dodgers changed their name to the Tigers.

Coaching from the bench was legalized, April 20.

The Cardinals and the Steelers were granted permission to merge for one year under the name Card-Pitt, April 21. Phil Handler of the Cardinals and Walt Kiesling of the Steelers served as co-coaches. The merger automatically dissolved the last day of the season, December 3.

In the NFL Championship Game, Green Bay defeated the New York Giants 14-7, December 17.

1945 The inbounds lines or hashmarks were moved from 15 yards away from the sidelines to nearer the center of the field—20 yards from the sidelines.

Brooklyn and Boston merged into a team that played home games in both cities and was known simply as "The Yanks." The team was coached by former Boston head coach Herb Kopf. In December, the Brooklyn franchise withdrew from the NFL to join the new All-America Football Conference; all the players on its active and reserve lists were assigned to The Yanks, who once again became the Boston Yanks.

Halas rejoined the Bears late in the season after service with the U.S. Navy. Although Halas took over much of the coaching duties, Anderson and Johnsos remained the coaches of record throughout the season.

Steve Van Buren of Philadelphia led the NFL in rushing, kickoff returns, and scoring.

After the Japanese surrendered ending World War II, a count showed that the NFL service roster, limited to men who had played in league games, totaled 638, 21 of whom had died in action.

Rookie quarterback Bob Waterfield led Cleveland to a 15-14 victory over Washington in the NFL Championship Game, December 16.

1946 The contract of Commissioner Layden was not renewed, and Bert Bell, the co-owner of the Steelers, replaced him, January 11. Bell moved the league headquarters from Chicago to the Philadelphia suburb of Bala Cynwyd.

Free substitution was withdrawn and substitutions were limited to no more than three men at a time. Forward passes were made automatically incomplete upon striking the goal posts, January 11.

The NFL took on a truly national appearance for the first time when Reeves was granted permission by the league to move his NFL champion Rams to Los Angeles.

The rival All-America Football Conference began play with eight teams. The Cleveland Browns, coached by Paul Brown, won the AAFC's first championship, defeating the New York Yankees 14-9.

Bill Dudley of the Steelers led the NFL in rushing, interceptions, and punt returns, and won the league's most valuable player award.

Backs Frank Filchock and Merle Hapes of the Giants were questioned about an attempt by a New York man to fix the championship game with the Bears. Bell suspended Hapes but allowed Filchock to play; he played well, but Chicago won 24-14, December 15.

1947 The NFL added a fifth official, the back judge.

A bonus choice was made for the first time in the NFL draft. One team each year would select the special choice before the first round began. The Chicago Bears won a lottery and the rights to the first choice and drafted back Bob Fenimore of Oklahoma A&M.

The Cleveland Browns again won the AAFC title, defeating the New York Yankees 14-3.

Charles Bidwill, Sr., owner of the Cardinals, died April 19, but his wife and sons retained ownership of the team. On December 28, the Cardinals won the NFL Championship Game 28-21 over the Philadelphia Eagles, who had beaten Pittsburgh 21-0 in a playoff.

1948 Plastic helmets were prohibited. A flexible artificial tee was permitted at the kickoff. Officials other than the referee were equipped with whistles, not horns, January 14.

Fred Mandel sold the Detroit Lions to a syndicate headed by D. Lyle Fife, January 15.

Halfback Fred Gehrke of the Los Angeles Rams painted horns on the Rams' helmets, the first modern helmet emblems in pro football.

The Cleveland Browns won their third straight championship in the AAFC, going 14-0 and then defeating the Buffalo Bills 49-7.

In a blizzard, the Eagles defeated the Cardinals 7-0 in the NFL Championship Game, December 19.

1949 Alexis Thompson sold the champion Eagles to a syndicate headed by James P. Clark, January 15. The Boston Yanks became the New York Bulldogs, sharing the Polo Grounds with the Giants.

Free substitution was adopted for one year, January 20.

The NFL had two 1,000-yard rushers in the same season for the first time—Steve Van Buren of Philadelphia and Tony Canadeo of Green Bay.

The AAFC played its season with a one-division, seven-team format. On December 9, Bell announced a merger agreement in which three AAFC franchises—Cleveland, San Francisco, and Baltimore—would join the NFL in 1950. The Browns won their fourth consecutive AAFC title, defeating the 49ers 21-7, December 11.

In a heavy rain, the Eagles defeated the Rams 14-0 in the NFL Championship Game, December 18.

1950 Unlimited free substitution was restored, opening the way for the era of two platoons and specialization in pro football, January 20.

Curly Lambeau, founder of the franchise and Green Bay's head coach since 1921, resigned under fire, February 1.

The name National Football League was restored after about three months as the National-American Football League. The American and National conferences were created to replace the Eastern and Western divisions, March 3.

The New York Bulldogs became the Yanks and divided the players of the former AAFC Yankees with the Giants. A special allocation draft was held in which the 13 teams drafted the remaining AAFC players, with special consideration for Baltimore, which received 15 choices compared to 10 for other teams.

The Los Angeles Rams became the first NFL team to have all of its games—both home and away—televised. The Washington Redskins followed the Rams in arranging to televise their games; other teams made deals to put selected games on television.

In the first game of the season, former AAFC champion Cleveland defeated NFL champion Philadelphia 35-10. For the first time, deadlocks occurred in both conferences and playoffs were necessary. The Browns defeated the Giants in the American and the Rams defeated the Bears in the National. Cleveland defeated Los Angeles 30-28 in the NFL Championship Game, December 24.

1951 The Pro Bowl game, dormant since 1942, was revived under a new format matching the all-stars of each conference at the Los Angeles Memorial Coliseum. The American Conference defeated the National Conference 28-27, January 14.

Abraham Watner returned the Baltimore franchise and its player contracts back to the NFL for $50,000. Baltimore's former players were made available for drafting at the same time as college players, January 18.

A rule was passed that no tackle, guard, or center would be eligible to catch a forward pass, January 18.

The Rams reversed their television policy and televised only road games.

The NFL Championship Game was televised coast-to-coast for the first time, December 23. The DuMont Network paid $75,000 for the rights to the game, in which the Rams defeated the Browns 24-17.

1952 Ted Collins sold the New York Yanks' franchise back to the NFL, January 19. A new franchise was awarded to a group in Dallas after it purchased the assets of the Yanks, January 24. The new Texans went 1-11, with the owners turning the franchise back to the league in midseason. For the last five games of the season, the commissioner's office operated the Texans as a road team, using Hershey, Pennsylvania, as a home base. At the end of the season the franchise was cancelled, the last time an NFL team failed.

The Pittsburgh Steelers abandoned the Single-Wing for the T-formation, the last pro team to do so.

The Detroit Lions won their first NFL championship in 17 years, defeating the Browns 17-7 in the title game, December 28.

1953 A Baltimore group headed by Carroll Rosenbloom was granted a franchise and was awarded the holdings of the defunct Dallas organization, January 23. The team, named the Colts, put together the largest trade in league history, acquiring 10 players from Cleveland in exchange for five.

The names of the American and National conferences were changed to the Eastern and Western conferences, January 24.

Jim Thorpe died, March 28.

Mickey McBride, founder of the Cleveland Browns, sold the franchise to a syndicate headed by Dave R. Jones, June 10.

The NFL policy of blacking out home games was upheld by Judge Allan K. Grim of the U.S. District Court in Philadelphia, November 12.

The Lions again defeated the Browns in the NFL Championship Game, winning 17-16, December 27.

1954 The Canadian Football League began a series of raids on NFL teams, signing quarterback Eddie LeBaron and defensive end Gene Brito of Washington and defensive tackle Arnie Weinmeister of the Giants, among others.

Fullback Joe Perry of the 49ers became the first player in league history to gain 1,000 yards rushing in consecutive seasons.

Cleveland defeated Detroit 56-10 in the NFL Championship Game, December 26.

1955 The sudden-death overtime rule was used for the first time in a preseason game between the Rams and Giants at Portland, Oregon, August 28. The Rams won 23-17 three minutes into overtime.

A rule change declared the ball dead immediately if the ball carrier touched the ground with any part of his body except his hands or feet while in the grasp of an opponent.

The NFL Players Association was founded.

The Baltimore Colts made an 80-cent phone call to Johnny Unitas and signed him as a free agent. Another quarterback, Otto Graham, played his last game as the Browns defeated the Rams 38-14 in the NFL Championship Game, December 26. Graham had quarterbacked the Browns to 10 championship-game appearances in 10 years.

NBC replaced DuMont as the network for the title game, paying a rights fee of $100,000.

1956 Grabbing an opponent's facemask (other than the ball carrier) was made illegal. Using radio receivers to communicate with players on the field was prohibited. A natural leather ball with white end stripes replaced the white ball with black stripes for night games.

The Giants moved from the Polo Grounds to Yankee Stadium.

Halas retired as coach of the Bears, and was replaced by Paddy Driscoll.

CBS became the first network to broadcast some NFL regular-season games to selected television markets across the nation.

The Giants routed the Bears 47-7 in the NFL Championship Game, December 30.

1957 Pete Rozelle was named general manager of the Rams. Anthony J. Morabito, founder and co-owner of the 49ers, died of a heart attack during a game against the Bears at Kezar Stadium, October 28. An NFL-record crowd of 102,368 saw the 49ers-Rams game at the Los Angeles Memorial Coliseum, November 10.

The Lions came from 20 points down to post a 31-27 playoff victory over the 49ers, December 22. Detroit defeated Cleveland 59-14 in the NFL Championship Game, December 29.

1958 The bonus selection in the draft was eliminated, January 29. The last selection was quarterback King Hill of Rice by the Chicago Cardinals.

Halas reinstated himself as coach of the Bears.

Jim Brown of Cleveland gained an NFL record 1,527 yards rushing. In a divisional playoff game, the Giants held Brown to eight yards and defeated Cleveland 10-0.

Baltimore, coached by Weeb Ewbank, defeated the Giants 23-17 in the first sudden-death overtime in an NFL Championship Game, December 28. The game ended when Colts fullback Alan Ameche scored on a one-yard touchdown run after 8:15 of overtime.

1959 Vince Lombardi was named head coach of the Green Bay Packers, January 28. Tim Mara, the cofounder of the Giants, died, February 17.

Lamar Hunt of Dallas announced his intentions to form a second pro football league. The first meeting was held in Chicago, August 14, and consisted of Hunt representing Dallas; Bob Howsam, Denver; K.S. (Bud) Adams, Houston; Barron Hilton, Los Angeles; Max Winter and Bill Boyer, Minneapolis; and Harry Wismer, New York City. They made plans to begin play in 1960.

The new league was named the American Football League, August 22. Buffalo, owned by Ralph Wilson, became the seventh franchise, October 28. Boston, owned by William H. Sullivan, became the eighth team, November 22. The first AFL draft, lasting 33 rounds, was held, November 22. Joe Foss was named AFL Commissioner, November 30. An additional draft of 20 rounds was held by the AFL, December 2.

NFL Commissioner Bert Bell died of a heart attack suffered at Franklin Field, Philadelphia, during the last two minutes of a game between the Eagles and the Steelers, October 11. Treasurer Austin Gunsel was named president in the office of the commissioner, October 14.

The Colts again defeated the Giants in the NFL Championship Game, 31-16, December 27.

1960 Pete Rozelle was elected NFL Commissioner as a compromise choice on the twenty-third ballot, January 26. Rozelle moved the league offices to New York City.

Hunt was elected AFL president for 1960, January 26. Minneapolis withdrew from the AFL, January 27, and the same ownership was given an NFL franchise for Minnesota (to start in 1961), January 28. Dallas received an NFL franchise for 1960, January 28. Oakland received an AFL franchise, January 30.

The AFL adopted the two-point option on points after touchdown, January 28. A "no-tampering" verbal pact, relative to players' contracts, was agreed to between the NFL and AFL, February 9.

The NFL owners voted to allow the transfer of the Chicago Cardinals to St. Louis, March 13.

The AFL signed a five-year television contract with ABC, June 9.

The Boston Patriots defeated the Buffalo Bills 28-7 before 16,000 at Buffalo in the first AFL preseason game, July 30. The Denver Broncos defeated the Patriots 13-10 before 21,597 at Boston in the first AFL regular-season game, September 9.

Philadelphia defeated Green Bay 17-13 in the NFL Championship Game, December 26.

1961 The Houston Oilers defeated the Los Angeles Chargers 24-16 before 32,183 in the first AFL Championship Game, January 1.

Detroit defeated Cleveland 17-16 in the first Playoff Bowl, or Bert Bell Benefit Bowl, between second-place teams in each conference in Miami, January 7.

End Willard Dewveall of the Bears played out his option and joined the Oilers, becoming the first player to deliberately move from one league to the other, January 14.

Ed McGah, Wayne Valley, and Robert Osborne bought out their partners in the ownership of the Raiders, January 17. The Chargers were transferred to San Diego, February 10. Dave R. Jones sold the Browns to a group headed by Arthur B. Modell, March 22. The Howsam brothers sold the Broncos to a group headed by Calvin Kunz and Gerry Phipps, May 26.

NBC was awarded a two-year contract for radio and television rights to the NFL Championship Game for $615,000 annually, $300,000 of which was to go directly into the NFL Player Benefit Plan, April 5.

Canton, Ohio, where the league that became the NFL was formed in 1920, was chosen as the site of the Pro Football Hall of Fame, April 27. Dick McCann, a former Redskins executive, was named executive director.

A bill legalizing single-network television contracts by professional sports leagues was introduced in Congress by Representative Emanuel Celler. It passed the House and Senate and was signed into law by President John F. Kennedy, September 30.

Houston defeated San Diego 10-3 for the AFL championship, December 24. Green Bay won its first NFL championship since 1944, defeating the New York Giants 37-0, December 31.

1962 The Western Division defeated the Eastern Division 47-27 in the first AFL All-Star Game, played before 20,973 in San Diego, January 7.

Both leagues prohibited grabbing any player's facemask. The AFL voted to make the scoreboard clock the official timer of the game.

The NFL entered into a single-network agreement with CBS for telecasting all regular-season games for $4,650,000 annually, January 10.

Judge Roszel Thompson of the U.S. District Court in Baltimore ruled against the AFL in its antitrust suit against the NFL, May 21. The AFL had charged the NFL with monopoly and conspiracy in areas of expansion, television, and player signings. The case lasted two and a half years, the trial two months.

McGah and Valley acquired controlling interest in the Raiders, May 24. The AFL assumed financial responsibility for the New York Titans, November 8. With Commissioner Rozelle as referee, Daniel F. Reeves regained the ownership of the Rams, outbidding his partners in sealed-envelope bidding for the team, November 27.

The Dallas Texans defeated the Oilers 20-17 for the AFL championship at Houston after 17 minutes, 54 seconds of overtime on a 25-yard field goal by Tommy Brooker, December 23. The game lasted a record 77 minutes, 54 seconds.

Judge Edward Weinfeld of the U.S. District Court in New York City upheld the legality of the NFL's television blackout within a 75-mile radius of home games and denied an injunction that would have forced the championship game between the Giants and the Packers to be televised in the New York City area, December 28. The Packers beat the Giants 16-7 for the NFL title, December 30.

1963 The Dallas Texans transferred to Kansas City, becoming the Chiefs, February 8. The New York Titans were sold to a five-man syndicate headed by David (Sonny) Werblin, March 28. Weeb Ewbank became the Titans' new head coach and the team's name was changed to the Jets, April 15. They began play in Shea Stadium.

NFL Properties, Inc., was founded to serve as the licensing arm of the NFL.

Rozelle indefinitely suspended Green Bay halfback Paul Hornung and Detroit defensive tackle Alex Karras for placing bets on their own teams and on other NFL games; he also fined five other Detroit players $2,000 each for betting on one game in which they did not participate, and the Detroit Lions Football Company $2,000 on each of two counts for failure to report information promptly and for lack of sideline supervision.

Paul Brown, head coach of the Browns since their inception, was fired and replaced by Blanton Collier. Don Shula replaced Weeb Ewbank as head coach of the Colts.

The AFL allowed the Jets and Raiders to select players from other franchises in hopes of giving the league more competitive balance, May 11.

NBC was awarded exclusive network broadcasting rights for the 1963 AFL Championship Game for $926,000, May 23.

The Pro Football Hall of Fame was dedicated at Canton, Ohio, September 7.

The U.S. Fourth Circuit Court of Appeals reaffirmed the lower court's finding for the NFL in the $10-million suit brought by the AFL, ending three and a half years of litigation, November 21.

Jim Brown of Cleveland rushed for an NFL single-season record 1,863 yards.

Boston defeated Buffalo 26-8 in the first divisional playoff game in AFL history, December 28. The Chargers defeated the Patriots in the AFL Championship Game, January 5.

The Bears defeated the Giants 14-10 in the NFL Championship Game, a record sixth and last title for Halas in his thirty-sixth season as the Bears' coach, December 29.

1964 The Chargers defeated the Patriots in the AFL Championship Game, January 5.

William Clay Ford, the Lions' president since 1961, purchased the team, January 10. A group representing the late James P. Clark sold the Eagles to a group headed by Jerry Wolman, January 21. Carroll Rosenbloom, the majority owner of the Colts since 1953, acquired complete ownership of the team, January 23.

CBS submitted the winning bid of $14.1 million per year for the NFL regular-season television rights for 1964 and 1965, January 24. CBS acquired the rights to the championship games for 1964 and 1965 for $1.8 million per game, April 17.

The AFL signed a five-year, $36-million television contract with NBC to begin with the 1965 season, assuring each team approximately $900,000 a year from television rights, January 29.

Hornung and Karras were reinstated by Rozelle, March 16.

Pete Gogolak of Cornell signed a contract with Buffalo, becoming the first soccer-style kicker in pro football.

Buffalo defeated San Diego 20-7 in the AFL Championship Game, December 26. Cleveland defeated Baltimore 27-0 in the NFL Championship Game, December 27.

1965 The NFL teams pledged not to sign college seniors until completion of all their games, including bowl games, and empowered the Commissioner to discipline the clubs up to as much as the loss of an entire draft list for a violation of the pledge, February 15.

The NFL added a sixth official, the line judge, February 19. The color of the officials' penalty flags was changed from white to bright gold, April 5.

Atlanta was awarded an NFL franchise for 1966, with Rankin Smith, Sr., as owner, June 30. Miami was awarded an AFL franchise for 1966, with Joe Robbie and Danny Thomas as owners, August 16.

Green Bay defeated Baltimore 13-10 in sudden-death overtime in a Western Conference playoff game. Don Chandler kicked a 25-yard field goal for the Packers after 13 minutes, 39 seconds of overtime, December 26. The Packers then defeated the Browns 23-12 in the NFL Championship Game, January 2.

In the AFL Championship Game, the Bills again defeated the Chargers, 23-0, December 26.

CBS acquired the rights to the NFL regular-season games in 1966 and 1967, with an option for 1968, for $18.8 million per year, December 29.

1966 The AFL-NFL war reached its peak, as the leagues spent a combined $7 million to sign their 1966 draft choices. The NFL signed 75 percent of its 232 draftees, the AFL 46 percent of its 181. Of the 111 common draft choices, 79 signed with the NFL, 28 with the AFL, and 4 went unsigned.

The rights to the 1966 and 1967 NFL Championship Games were sold to CBS for $2 million per game, February 14.

Foss resigned as AFL Commissioner, April 7. Al Davis, the head coach and general manager of the Raiders, was named to replace him, April 8.

Goal posts offset from the goal line, painted bright yellow, and with uprights 20 feet above the crossbar were made standard in the NFL, May 16.

A series of secret meetings regarding a possible AFL-NFL merger were held in the spring between Hunt of Kansas City and Tex Schramm of Dallas. Rozelle announced the merger, June 8. Under the agreement, the two leagues would combine to form an expanded league with 24 teams, to be increased to 26 to 1968 and to 28 by 1970 or soon thereafter. All existing franchises would be retained, and no franchises would be transferred outside their metropolitan areas. While maintaining separate schedules through 1969, the leagues agreed to play an annual AFL-NFL World Championship Game beginning in January, 1967, and to hold a combined draft, also beginning in 1967. Preseason games would be held between teams of each league starting in 1967. Official regular-season play would start in 1970 when the two leagues would officially merge to form one league with two conferences. Rozelle was named Commissioner of the expanded league setup.

Davis rejoined the Raiders, and Milt Woodard was named president of the AFL, July 25.

The St. Louis Cardinals moved into newly constructed Busch Memorial Stadium.

Barron Hilton sold the Chargers to a group headed by Eugene Klein and Sam Schulman, August 25.

Congress approved the AFL-NFL merger, passing legislation exempting the agreement itself from antitrust action, October 21.

New Orleans was awarded an NFL franchise to begin play in 1967, November 1. John Mecom, Jr., of Houston was designated majority stockholder and president of the franchise, December 15.

The NFL was realigned for the 1967-69 seasons into the Capitol and Century Divisions in the Eastern Conference and the Central and Coastal Divisions in the Western Conference, December 2. New Orleans and the New York Giants agreed to switch divisions in 1968 and return to the 1967 alignment in 1969.

The rights to the Super Bowl for four years were sold to CBS and NBC for $9.5 million, December 13.

1967 Green Bay earned the right to represent the NFL in the first AFL-NFL World Championship Game by defeating Dallas 34-27, January 1. The same day, Kansas City defeated Buffalo 31-7 to represent the AFL. The Packers defeated the Chiefs 35-10 before 61,946 fans at the Los Angeles Memorial Coliseum in the first game between AFL and NFL teams, January 15. The winning players' share for the Packers was $15,000 each, and the losing players' share for the Chiefs was $7,500 each. The game was televised by both CBS and NBC.

The "sling-shot" goal post and a six-foot-wide border around the field were made standard in the NFL, February 22.

Baltimore made Bubba Smith, a Michigan State defensive lineman, the first choice in the first combined AFL-NFL draft, March 14.

The AFL awarded a franchise to begin play in 1968 to Cincinnati, May 24. A group with Paul Brown as part owner, general manager, and head coach, was awarded the Cincinnati franchise, September 27.

Arthur B. Modell, the president of the Cleveland Browns, was elected president of the NFL, May 28.

An AFL team defeated an NFL team for the first time, when Denver beat Detroit 13-7 in a preseason game, August 5.

Green Bay defeated Dallas 21-17 for the NFL championship on a last-minute one-yard quarterback sneak by Bart Starr in 13-below-zero temperature at Green Bay, December 31. The same day, Oakland defeated Houston 40-7 for the AFL championship.

1968 Green Bay defeated Oakland 33-14 in Super Bowl II at Miami, January 14. The game had the first $3-million gate in pro football history.

Vince Lombardi resigned as head coach of the Packers, but remained as general manager, January 28.

Werblin sold his shares in the Jets to his partners Don Lillis, Leon Hess, Townsend Martin, and Phil Iselin, May 21. Lillis assumed the presidency of the club, but then died July 23. Iselin was appointed president, August 6.

Halas retired for the fourth and last time as head coach of the Bears, May 27.

The Oilers left Rice Stadium for the Astrodome and became the first NFL team to play its home games in a domed stadium.

The movie "Heidi" became a footnote in sports history when NBC didn't show the last 1:05 of the Jets-Raiders game in order to permit the children's special to begin on time. The Raiders scored two touchdowns in the last 42 seconds to win 43-32, November 17.

Ewbank became the first coach to win titles in both the NFL and AFL when his Jets defeated the Raiders 27-23 for the AFL championship, December 29. The same day, Baltimore defeated Cleveland 34-0.

1969 The AFL established a playoff format for the 1969 season, with the winner in one division playing the runner-up in the other, January 11.

An AFL team won the Super Bowl for the first time, as the Jets defeated the Colts 16-7 at Miami, January 12 in Super Bowl III. The title "Super Bowl" was recognized by the NFL for the first time.

Vince Lombardi became part owner, executive vice-president, and head coach of the Washington Redskins, Feb. 7.

Wolman sold the Eagles to Leonard Tose, May 1.

Baltimore, Cleveland, and Pittsburgh agreed to join the AFL teams to form the 13-team American Football Conference of the NFL in 1970, May 17. The NFL also agreed on a playoff format that would include one "wild-card" team per conference—the second-place team with the best record.

Monday Night Football was signed for 1970. ABC acquired the rights to televise 13 NFL regular-season Monday night games in 1970, 1971, and 1972.

George Preston Marshall, president emeritus of the Redskins, died at 72, August 9.

The NFL marked its fiftieth year by the wearing of a special patch by each of the 16 teams.

1970 Kansas City defeated Minnesota 23-7 in Super Bowl IV at New Orleans, January 11. The gross receipts of approximately $3.8 million were the largest ever for a one-day sports event.

Four-year television contracts, under which CBS would televise all NFC games and NBC all AFC games (except Monday night games) and the two would divide televising the Super Bowl and AFC-NFC Pro Bowl games, were announced, January 26.

Art Modell resigned as president of the NFL, March 12. Milt Woodard resigned as president of the AFL, March 13. Lamar Hunt was elected president of the AFC and George Halas was elected president of the NFC, March 19.

The merged 26-team league adopted rules changes putting names on the backs of players' jerseys, making a point after touchdown worth only one point, and making the scoreboard clock the official timing device of the game, March 18.

The Players Negotiating Committee and the NFL Players Association announced a four-year agreement guaranteeing approximately $4,535,000 annually to player pension and insurance benefits, August 3. The owners also agreed to contribute $250,000 annually to improve or implement items such as disability payments, widows' benefits, maternity benefits, and dental benefits. The agreement also provided for increased preseason game and per diem payments, averaging approximately $2.6 million annually.

The Pittsburgh Steelers moved into Three Rivers Stadium. The Cincinnati Bengals moved to Riverfront Stadium.

Lombardi died of cancer at 57, September 3.

Tom Dempsey of New Orleans kicked a game-winning NFL-record 63-yard field goal against Detroit, November 8.

1971 Baltimore defeated Dallas 16-13 on Jim O'Brien's 32-yard field goal with five seconds to go in Super Bowl V at Miami, January 17. The NBC telecast was viewed in an estimated 23,980,000 homes, the largest audience ever for a one-day sports event.

The NFC defeated the AFC 27-6 in the first AFC-NFC Pro Bowl at Los Angeles, January 24.

The Boston Patriots changed their name to the New England Patriots, March 25. Their new stadium, Schaefer Stadium, was dedicated in a 20-14 preseason victory over the Giants.

The Philadelphia Eagles left Franklin Field and played their games at the new Veterans Stadium.

The San Francisco 49ers left Kezar Stadium and moved their games to Candlestick Park.

Daniel F. Reeves, the president and general manager of the Rams, died at 58, April 15.

The Dallas Cowboys moved from

the Cotton Bowl into their new home, Texas Stadium, October 24.

Miami defeated Kansas City 27-24 in sudden-death overtime in an AFC Divisional Playoff Game, December 25. Garo Yepremian kicked a 37-yard field goal for the Dolphins after 22 minutes, 40 seconds of overtime, as the game lasted 82 minutes, 40 seconds overall, making it the longest game in history.

1972 Dallas defeated Miami 24-3 in Super Bowl VI at New Orleans, January 16. The CBS telecast was viewed in an estimated 27,450,000 homes, the top-rated one-day telecast ever.

The inbounds lines or hashmarks were moved nearer the center of the field, 23 yards, 1 foot, 9 inches from the sidelines, March 23. The method of determining won-lost percentage in standings changed. Tie games, previously not counted in the standings, were made equal to a half-game won and a half-game lost, May 24.

Robert Irsay purchased the Los Angeles Rams and transferred ownership of the club to Carroll Rosenbloom in exchange for the Baltimore Colts, July 13.

William V. Bidwill purchased the stock of his brother Charles (Stormy) Bidwill to become the sole owner of the St. Louis Cardinals, September 2.

The National District Attorneys Association endorsed the position of professional leagues in opposing proposed legalization of gambling in professional team sports, September 28.

Franco Harris's "Immaculate Reception" gave the Steelers their first postseason win ever, 13-7 over the Raiders, December 23.

1973 Rozelle announced that all Super Bowl VII tickets were sold and that the game would be telecast in Los Angeles, the site of the game, on an experimental basis, January 3.

Miami defeated Washington 14-7 in Super Bowl VII at Los Angeles, completing a 17-0 season, the first perfect-record regular-season and postseason mark in NFL history, January 14. The NBC telecast was viewed by approximately 75 million people.

The AFC defeated the NFC 33-28 in the Pro Bowl in Dallas, the first time since 1942 that the game was played outside Los Angeles, January 21.

A jersey numbering system was adopted, April 5: 1-19 for quarterbacks and specialists, 20-49 for running backs and defensive backs, 50-59 for centers and linebackers, 60-79 for defensive linemen and interior offensive linemen other than centers, and 80-89 for wide receivers and tight ends. Players who had been in the NFL in 1972 could continue to use old numbers.

NFL Charities, a non-profit organization, was created to derive an income from monies generated from NFL Properties' licensing of NFL trademarks and team names, June 26. NFL Charities was set up to support education and charitable activities and to supply economic support to persons formerly associated with professional football who were no longer able to support themselves.

Congress adopted experimental legislation (for three years) requiring any NFL game that had been declared a sellout 72 hours prior to kick-off to be made available for local televising, September 14. The legislation provided for an annual review to be made by the Federal Communications Commission.

The Buffalo Bills moved their home games from War Memorial Stadium to Rich Stadium in nearby Orchard Park. The Giants tied the Eagles 23-23 in the final game in Yankee Stadium, September 23. The Giants played the rest of their home games at the Yale Bowl in New Haven, Connecticut.

A rival league, the World Football League, was formed and was reported in operation, October 2. It had plans to start play in 1974.

O.J. Simpson of Buffalo became the first player to rush for more than 2,000 yards in a season, gaining 2,003.

1974 Miami defeated Minnesota 24-7 in Super Bowl VIII at Houston, the second consecutive Super Bowl championship for the Dolphins, January 13. The CBS telecast was viewed by approximately 75 million people.

Rozelle was given a 10-year contract effective January 1, 1973, February 27.

Tampa Bay was awarded a franchise to begin operation in 1976, April 24.

Sweeping rules changes were adopted to add action and tempo to games: one sudden-death overtime period was added for preseason and regular-season games; the goal posts were moved from the goal line to the end lines; kickoffs were moved from the 40- to the 35-yard line; after missed field goals from beyond the 20, the ball was to be returned to the line of scrimmage; restrictions were placed on members of the punting team to open up return possibilities; roll-blocking and cutting of wide receivers was eliminated; the extent of downfield contact a defender could have with an eligible receiver was restricted; the penalties for offensive holding, illegal use of the hands, and tripping were reduced from 15 to 10 yards; wide receivers blocking back toward the ball within three yards of the line of scrimmage were prevented from blocking below the waist, April 25.

The Toronto Northmen of the WFL signed Larry Csonka, Jim Kiick, and Paul Warfield of Miami, March 31.

Seattle was awarded an NFL franchise to begin play in 1976, June 4. Lloyd W. Nordstrom, president of the Seattle Seahawks, and Hugh Culverhouse, president of the Tampa Bay Buccaneers, signed franchise agreements, December 5.

The Birmingham Americans defeated the Florida Blazers 22-21 in the WFL World Bowl, winning the league championship, December 5.

1975 Pittsburgh defeated Minnesota 16-6 in Super Bowl IX at New Orleans, the Steelers' first championship since entering the NFL in 1933. The NBC telecast was viewed by approximately 78 million people.

The divisional winners with the highest won-loss percentage were made the home team for the divisional playoffs, and the surviving winners with the highest percentage made home teams for the championship games, June 26.

Referees were equipped with wireless microphones for all preseason, regular-season, and playoff games.

The Lions moved to the new Pontiac Silverdome. The Giants played their home games in Shea Stadium. The Saints moved into the Louisiana Superdome.

The World Football League folded, October 22.

1976 Pittsburgh defeated Dallas 21-17 in Super Bowl X in Miami. The Steelers joined Green Bay and Miami as the only teams to win two Super Bowls; the Cowboys became the first wild-card team to play in the Super Bowl. The CBS telecast was viewed by an estimated 80 million people, the largest television audience in history.

Lloyd Nordstrom, the president of the Seahawks, died at 66, January 20. His brother Elmer succeeded him as majority representative of the team.

The owners awarded Super Bowl XII, to be played on January 15, 1978, to New Orleans. They also adopted the use of two 30-second clocks for all games, visible to both players and fans to note the official time between the ready-for-play signal and snap of the ball, March 16.

A veteran player allocation was held to stock the Seattle and Tampa Bay franchises with 39 players each, March 30-31. In the college draft, Seattle and Tampa Bay each received eight extra choices, April 8-9.

The Giants moved into new Giants Stadium in East Rutherford, New Jersey.

The Steelers defeated the College All-Stars in a storm-shortened Chicago College All-Star Game, the last of the series, July 23. St. Louis defeated San Diego 20-10 in a preseason game before 38,000 in Korakuen Stadium, Tokyo, in the first NFL game outside of North America, August 16.

1977 Oakland defeated Minnesota 32-14 before a record crowd of 100,421 in Super Bowl XI at Pasadena, January 9. The paid attendance was a pro record 103,438. The NBC telecast was viewed by 81.9 million people, the largest ever to view a sports event. The victory was the fifth consecutive for the AFC in the Super Bowl.

The NFL Players Association and the NFL Management Council ratified a collective bargaining agreement extending until 1982, covering five football seasons while continuing the pension plan—including years 1974, 1975, and 1976—with contributions totaling more than $55 million. The total cost of the agreement was estimated at $107 million. The agreement called for a college draft at least through 1986; contained a no-strike, no-suit clause; established a 43-man active player limit; reduced pension vesting to four years; provided for increases in minimum salaries and preseason and postseason pay; improved insurance, medical, and dental benefits; modified previous practices in player movement and control; and reaffirmed the NFL Commissioner's disciplinary authority. Additionally, the agreement called for the NFL member clubs to make payments totaling $16 million the next 10 years to settle various legal disputes, February 25.

The San Francisco 49ers were sold to Edward J. DeBartolo, Jr., March 28.

A 16-game regular season, 4-game preseason was adopted to begin in 1978, March 29. A second wild card team was adopted for the playoffs beginning in 1978, with the wild card teams to play each other and the winners advancing to a round of eight postseason series.

The Seahawks were permanently aligned in the AFC Western Division and the Buccaneers in the NFC Central Division, March 31.

The owners awarded Super Bowl XIII, to be played on January 21, 1979, to Miami to be played in the Orange Bowl; Super Bowl XIV, to be played January 20, 1980, was awarded to Pasadena, to be played in the Rose Bowl, June 14.

Rules changes were adopted to open up the passing game and to cut down on injuries. Defenders were permitted to make contact with eligible receivers only once; the head slap was outlawed; offensive linemen were prohibited from thrusting their hands to an opponent's neck, face, or head; and wide receivers were prohibited from clipping, even in the legal clipping zone.

Rozelle negotiated contracts with the three television networks to televise all NFL regular-season and postseason games, plus selected preseason games, for four years beginning with the 1978 season. ABC was awarded yearly rights to 16 Monday night games, four prime-time games, the AFC-NFC Pro Bowl, and the Hall of Fame games. CBS received the rights to all NFC regular-season and postseason games (except those in the ABC package) and to Super Bowls XIV and XVI. NBC received the rights to all AFC regular-season and postseason games (except those in the ABC package) and to Super Bowls XIII and XV. Industry sources considered it the largest single television package ever negotiated, October.

Chicago's Walter Payton set a single-game rushing record with 275 yards (40 carries) against Minnesota, November 20.

1978 Dallas defeated Denver 27-10 in Super Bowl XII, held indoors for the first time, at the Louisiana Superdome in New Orleans, January 15. The CBS telecast was viewed by more than 102 million people, meaning the game was watched by more viewers than any other show of any kind in the history of television. Dallas's victory was the first for the NFC in six years.

According to a Louis Harris Sports Survey, 70 percent of the nation's sports fans said they followed football, compared to 54 percent who followed baseball. Football increased its lead as the country's favorite, 26 percent to 16 percent for baseball, January 19.

A seventh official, the side judge, was added to the officiating crew, March 14.

The NFL continued a trend toward opening up the game. Rules changes permitted a defender to maintain contact with a receiver within five yards of the line of scrimmage, but restricted contact beyond that point. The pass-blocking rule was interpreted to permit the extending of arms and open hands, March 17.

A study on the use of instant replay as an officiating aid was made during seven nationally televised preseason games.

The NFL played for the first time in Mexico City, with the Saints defeating the Eagles 14-7 in a preseason game, August 5.

Bolstered by the expansion of the

regular-season schedule from 14 to 16 weeks, NFL paid attendance exceeded 12 million (12,771,800) for the first time. The per-game average of 57,017 was the third-highest in league history and the most since 1973.

1979 Pittsburgh defeated Dallas 35-31 in Super Bowl XIII at Miami to become the first team ever to win three Super Bowls, January 21. The NBC telecast was viewed in 35,090,000 homes, by an estimated 96.6 million fans.

The owners awarded three future Super Bowl sites: Super Bowl XV to the Louisiana Superdome in New Orleans, to be played on January 25, 1981; Super Bowl XVI to the Pontiac Silverdome in Pontiac, Michigan, to be played on January 24, 1982; and Super Bowl XVII to Pasadena's Rose Bowl, to be played on January 30, 1983, March 13.

NFL rules changes emphasized additional player safety. The changes prohibited players on the receiving team from blocking below the waist during kickoffs, punts, and field-goal attempts; prohibited the wearing of torn or altered equipment and exposed pads that could be hazardous; extended the zone in which there could be no crackback blocks; and instructed officials to quickly whistle a play dead when a quarterback was clearly in the grasp of a tackler, March 16.

Rosenbloom, the president of the Rams, drowned at 72, April 2. His widow, Georgia, assumed control of the club.

1980 Pittsburgh defeated the Los Angeles Rams 31-19 in Super Bowl XIV at Pasadena to become the first team to win four Super Bowls, January 20. The game was viewed in a record 35,330,000 homes.

The AFC-NFC Pro Bowl, won 37-27 by the NFC, was played before 48,060 fans at Aloha Stadium in Honolulu, Hawaii. It was the first time in the 30-year history of the Pro Bowl that the game was played in a non-NFL city.

Rules changes placed greater restrictions on contact in the area of the head, neck, and face. Under the heading of "personal foul," players were prohibited from directly striking, swinging, or clubbing on the head, neck, or face. Starting in 1980, a penalty could be called for such contact whether or not the initial contact was made below the neck area.

CBS, with a record bid of $12 million, won the national radio rights to 26 NFL regular-season games and all 10 postseason games for the 1980-83 seasons.

The Los Angeles Rams moved their home games to Anaheim Stadium in nearby Orange County, California.

The Oakland Raiders joined the Los Angeles Coliseum Commission's antitrust suit against the NFL. The suit contended the league violated antitrust laws in declining to approve a proposed move by the Raiders from Oakland to Los Angeles.

NFL regular-season attendance of nearly 13.4 million set a record for the third year in a row. The average paid attendance for the 224-game 1980 regular season was 59,787, the highest in the league's 61-year history. NFL games in 1980 were played before 92.4 percent of total stadium capacity.

Television ratings in 1980 were the second-best in NFL history, trailing only the combined ratings of the 1976 season. All three networks posted gains, and NBC's 15.0 rating was its best ever. CBS and ABC had their best ratings since 1977, with 15.3 and 20.8 ratings, respectively. CBS Radio reported a record audience of 7 million for Monday night and special games.

1981 Oakland defeated Philadelphia 27-10 in Super Bowl XV at the Louisiana Superdome in New Orleans, to become the first wild card team to win a Super Bowl, January 25.

Edgar F. Kaiser, Jr., purchased the Denver Broncos from Gerald and Allan Phipps, February 26.

The owners adopted a disaster plan for re-stocking a team should the club be involved in a fatal accident, March 20.

The owners awarded Super Bowl XVIII to Tampa to be played in Tampa Stadium on January 22, 1984, June 3.

A CBS-New York Times poll showed that 48 percent of sports fans preferred football to 31 percent for baseball.

The NFL teams hosted 167 representatives from 44 predominantly black colleges during training camps for a total of 289 days. The program was adopted for renewal during each training camp period.

NFL regular-season attendance—13.6 million for an average of 60,745—set a record for the fourth year in a row. It also was the first time the per-game average exceeded 60,000. NFL games in 1981 were played before 93.8 percent of total stadium capacity.

ABC and CBS set all-time rating highs. ABC finished with a 21.7 rating and CBS with a 17.5 rating. NBC was down slightly to 13.9.

1982 San Francisco defeated Cincinnati 26-21 in Super Bowl XVI at the Pontiac Silverdome, in the first Super Bowl held in the North, January 24. The CBS telecast achieved the highest rating of any televised sports event ever, 49.1 with a 73.0 share. The game was viewed by a record 110.2 million fans. CBS Radio reported a record 14 million listeners for the game.

The NFL signed a five-year contract with the three television networks (ABC, CBS, and NBC) to televise all NFL regular-season and postseason games starting with the 1982 season.

The owners awarded the 1983, 1984, and 1985 AFC-NFC Pro Bowls to Honolulu's Aloha Stadium.

A jury ruled against the NFL in the antitrust trial brought by the Los Angeles Coliseum Commission and the Oakland Raiders, May 7. The verdict cleared the way for the Raiders to move to Los Angeles, where they defeated Green Bay 24-3 in their first preseason game, August 29.

The 1982 season was reduced from a 16-game schedule to 9 as the result of a 57-day players' strike. The strike was called by the NFLPA at 12:00 midnight on Monday, September 20, following the Green Bay at New York Giants game. Play resumed November 21-22 following ratification of the Collective Bargaining Agreement by NFL owners, November 17 in New York.

Under the Collective Bargaining Agreement, which was to run through the 1986 season, the NFL draft was extended through 1992 and the veteran free-agent system was left basically unchanged. A minimum salary schedule for years of experience was established; training camp and postseason pay were increased; players' medical, insurance, and retirement benefits were increased; and a severance-pay system was introduced to aid in career transition, a first in professional sports.

Despite the players' strike, the average paid attendance in 1982 was 58,472, the fifth-highest in league history.

The owners awarded the sites of two Super Bowls, December 14: Super Bowl XIX, to be played on January 25, 1985, to Stanford University Stadium in Palo Alto, California, with San Francisco as host team; and Super Bowl XX, to be played on January 26, 1986, to the Louisiana Superdome in New Orleans.

1983 Because of the shortened season, the NFL adopted a format of 16 teams competing in a Super Bowl Tournament for the 1982 playoffs. The NFC's number-one seed, Washington, defeated the AFC's number-two seed, Miami, 27-17 in Super Bowl XVII at the Rose Bowl in Pasadena, January 30. The Redskins' victory marked only the second time the NFC had won consecutive Super Bowls.

Super Bowl XVII was the second-highest rated live television program of all time, giving the NFL a sweep of the top 10 live programs in television history. The game was viewed in more than 40 million homes, the largest ever for a live telecast.

Halas, the owner of the Bears and the last surviving member of the NFL's second organizational meeting, died at 88, October 31.

1984 The Los Angeles Raiders defeated Washington 38-9 in Super Bowl XVIII at Tampa Stadium, January 22. The game achieved a 46.4 rating and 71.0 share.

An 11-man group headed by H.R. (Bum) Bright purchased the Dallas Cowboys from Clint Murchison, Jr., March 20. Club president Tex Schramm was designated as managing general partner.

Patrick Bowlen purchased a majority interest in the Denver Broncos from Edgar Kaiser, Jr., March 21.

The Colts relocated to Indianapolis, March 28. Their new home became the Hoosier Dome.

The owners awarded two Super Bowl sites at their May 23-25 meetings: Super Bowl XXI, to be played on January 25, 1987, to the Rose Bowl in Pasadena; and Super Bowl XXII, to be played on January 31, 1988, to San Diego Jack Murphy Stadium.

The New York Jets moved their home games to Giants Stadium in East Rutherford, New Jersey.

Alex G. Spanos purchased a majority interest in the San Diego Chargers from Eugene V. Klein, August 28.

Houston defeated Pittsburgh 23-20 to mark the one-hundredth overtime game in regular-season play since overtime was adopted in 1974, December 2.

On the field, many all-time records were set: Dan Marino of Miami passed for 5,084 yards and 48 touchdowns; Eric Dickerson of the Los Angeles Rams rushed for 2,105 yards; Art Monk of Washington caught 106 passes; and Walter Payton of Chicago broke Jim Brown's career rushing mark, finishing the season with 13,309 yards.

According to a CBS Sports/New York Times survey, 53 percent of the nation's sports fans said they most enjoyed watching football, compared to 18 percent for baseball, December 2-4.

NFL paid attendance exceeded 13 million for the fifth consecutive complete regular season when 13,398,112, an average of 59,813, attended games. The figure was the second-highest in league history. Teams averaged 42.4 points per game, the second-highest total since the 1970 merger.

1985 San Francisco defeated Miami 38-16 in Super Bowl XIX at Stanford Stadium in Palo Alto, California, January 20. The game was viewed on television by more people than any other live event in history. President Ronald Reagan, who took his second oath of office before tossing the coin for the game, was one of 115,936,000 viewers. The game drew a 46.4 rating and a 63.0 share. In addition, 6 million people watched the Super Bowl in the United Kingdom and a similar number in Italy. Super Bowl XIX had a direct economic impact of $113.5 million on the San Francisco Bay area.

NBC Radio and the NFL entered into a two-year agreement granting NBC the radio rights to a 37-game package in each of the 1985-86 seasons, March 6. The package included 27 regular-season games and 10 postseason games.

The owners awarded two Super Bowl sites at their annual meeting, March 10-15: Super Bowl XXIII, to be played on January 22, 1989, to the proposed Dolphins Stadium in Miami; and Super Bowl XXIV, to be played on January 28, 1990, to the Louisiana Superdome in New Orleans.

Norman Braman, in partnership with Edward Leibowitz, bought the Philadelphia Eagles from Leonard Tose, April 29.

Bruce Smith, a Virginia Tech defensive lineman selected by Buffalo, was the first player chosen in the fiftieth NFL draft, April 30.

A group headed by Tom Benson, Jr., was approved to purchase the New Orleans Saints from John W. Mecom, Jr., June 3.

The NFL owners adopted a resolution calling for a series of overseas preseason games, beginning in 1986, with one game to be played in England/Europe and/or one game in Japan each year. The game would be a fifth preseason game for the clubs involved and all arrangements and selection of the clubs would be under the control of the Commissioner, May 23.

The league-wide conversion to videotape from movie film for coaching study was approved.

Commissioner Rozelle was authorized to extend the commitment to Honolulu's Aloha Stadium for the AFC-NFC Pro Bowl for 1988, 1989, and 1990, October 15.

The NFL set a single-weekend paid attendance record when 902,657 tickets were sold for the weekend of October 27-28.

A Louis Harris poll in December revealed that pro football remained the sport most followed by Americans. Fifty-nine percent of those surveyed followed pro football, compared with 54 percent who followed baseball.

The Chicago-Miami Monday game had the highest rating, 29.6, and share, 46.0, of any prime-time game in NFL history, December 2. The game was viewed in more than 25 million homes.

The NFL showed a ratings increase on all three networks for the season, gaining 4 percent on NBC, 10 on CBS, and 16 on ABC.

1986 Chicago defeated New England 46-10 in Super Bowl XX at the Louisiana Superdome, January 26. The Patriots had earned the right to play the Bears by becoming the first wild card team to win three consecutive games on the road. The NBC telecast replaced the final episode of M*A*S*H as the most-viewed television program in history, with an audience of 127 million viewers, according to A.C. Nielsen figures. In addition to drawing a 48.3 rating and a 70 percent share in the United States, Super Bowl XX was televised to 59 foreign countries and beamed via satellite to the QE II. An estimated 300 million Chinese viewed a tape delay of the game in March. NBC Radio figures indicated an audience of 10 million for the game.

Super Bowl XX injected more than $100 million into the New Orleans-area economy, and fans spent $250 per day and a record $17.69 per person on game day.

The owners adopted limited use of instant replay as an officiating aid, prohibited players from wearing or otherwise displaying equipment, apparel, or other items that carry commercial names, names of organizations, or personal messages of any type, March 11.

After an 11-week trial, a jury in U.S. District Court in New York awarded the United States Football League one dollar in its $1.7 billion antitrust suit against the NFL. The jury rejected all of the USFL's television-related claims, which were the self-proclaimed "heart" of the USFL's case, July 29.

Chicago defeated Dallas 17-6 at Wembley Stadium in London in the first American Bowl. The game drew a sellout crowd of 82,699 and the NBC national telecast in this country produced a 12.4 rating and 36 percent share, making it the second-highest-rated daytime preseason game and highest daytime preseason television audience ever with 10,650,000 viewers, August 3.

Monday Night Football became the longest-running prime-time series in the history of the ABC network.

Instant replay was used to reverse two plays in 31 preseason games. During the regular season, 374 plays were closely reviewed by replay officials, leading to 38 reversals in 224 games. Eighteen plays were closely reviewed by instant replay in 10 postseason games with three reversals.

1987 The New York Giants defeated Denver 39-20 in Super Bowl XXI and captured their first NFL title since 1956. The game, played in Pasadena's Rose Bowl, drew a sellout crowd of 101,063. According to A.C. Nielsen figures, the CBS broadcast of the game was viewed in the U.S. on television by 122,640,000 people, making the telecast the second most-watched television show of all-time behind Super Bowl XX. The game was watched live or on tape in 55 foreign countries and NBC Radio's broadcast of the game was heard by a record 10.1 million people.

The NFL set an all-time paid attendance mark of 17,304,463 for all games, including preseason, regular-season, and postseason. Average regular-season game attendance (60,663) exceeded the 60,000 figure for only the second time in league history.

New three-year TV contracts with ABC, CBS, and NBC were announced for 1987-89 at the NFL annual meeting in Maui, Hawaii, March 15. Commissioner Rozelle and Broadcast Committee Chairman Art Modell also announced a three-year contract with ESPN to televise a mini-series of 13 prime-time games each season. The ESPN contract was the first with a cable network. However, NFL games on ESPN also were scheduled for regular television in the city of the visiting team and in the home city if the game was sold out 72 hours in advance.

Owners also voted to continue in effect for one year the instant replay system used during the 1986 season.

A special payment program was adopted to benefit nearly 1,000 former NFL players who participated in the League before the current Bert Bell NFL Pension Plan was created and made retroactive to the 1959 season. Players covered by the new program spent at least five years in the League and played all or part of their career prior to 1959. Each vested player would receive $60 per month for each year of service in the League for life.

Possible sites for Super Bowl XXV were reduced to five locations by the NFL Super Bowl XXV Site Selection Committee: Anaheim Stadium, Los Angeles Memorial Coliseum, Joe Robbie Stadium, San Diego Jack Murphy Stadium, and Tampa Stadium.

NFL and CBS Radio jointly announced agreement granting CBS the radio rights to a 40-game package in each of the next three NFL seasons, 1987-89, April 7.

NFL owners awarded Super Bowl XXV, to be played on January 27, 1991, to Tampa Stadium, May 20.

Over 400 former NFL players from the pre-1959 era received first payments from NFL owners, July 1.

The NFL's debut on ESPN produced the two highest-rated and most-watched sports programs in basic cable history. The Chicago at Miami game on August 16 drew an 8.9 rating in 3.81 million homes. Those records fell two weeks later when the Los Angeles Raiders at Dallas game achieved a 10.2 cable rating in 4.36 million homes.

Fifty-eight preseason games drew a record paid attendance of 3,116,870.

The 1987 season was reduced from a 16-game season to 15 as the result of a 24-day players' strike. The strike was called by the NFLPA on Tuesday, September 22, following the New England at New York Jets game. Games scheduled for the third weekend were cancelled but the games of weeks four, five, and six were played with replacement teams. Striking players returned for the seventh week of the season, October 25.

In a three-team deal involving 10 players and/or draft choices, the Los Angeles Rams traded running back Eric Dickerson to the Indianapolis Colts for six draft choices and two players. Buffalo obtained the rights to linebacker Cornelius Bennett from Indianapolis, sending Greg Bell and three draft choices to the Rams. The Colts added Owen Gill and three draft choices of their own to complete the deal with the Rams, October 31.

The Chicago at Minnesota game became the highest rated and most-watched sports program in basic cable history when it drew a 14.4 cable rating in 6.5 million homes, December 6.

Instant replay was used to reverse eight plays in 52 preseason games. During the strike-shortened 210-game regular season, 490 plays were closely reviewed by replay officials, leading to 57 reversals. Eighteen plays were closely reviewed by instant replay in 10 postseason games, with three reversals.

1988 Washington defeated Denver 42-10 in Super Bowl XXII to earn a second victory this decade in the NFL Championship Game. The game, played for the first time in San Diego Jack Murphy Stadium, drew a sellout crowd of 73,302. According to A.C. Nielsen figures, the ABC broadcast of the game was viewed in the U.S. on television by 115,000,000 people. The game was seen live or on tape in 60 foreign countries, including the People's Republic of China, and NBC's radio broadcast of the game was heard by 13.7 million people.

A total of 811 players shared in the postseason pool of $16.9 million, the most ever distributed in a single season.

In a unanimous 3-0 decision, the 2nd Circuit Court of Appeals in New York upheld the verdict of the jury that in July, 1986, had awarded the United States Football League one dollar in its $1.7 billion antitrust suit against the NFL. In a 91-page opinion, Judge Ralph K. Winter said the USFL sought "through court decree the success it failed to gain among football fans," March 10.

By a 23-5 margin, owners voted to continue the instant replay system for the third consecutive season with the Instant Replay Official to be assigned to a regular seven-man, on-the-field crew. At the NFL annual meeting in Phoenix, Arizona, a 45-second clock was also approved to replace the 30-second clock. For a normal sequence of plays, the interval between plays was changed to 45 seconds from the time the ball is signaled dead until it is snapped on the succeeding play.

NFL owners approved the transfer of the Cardinals' franchise from St. Louis to Phoenix; approved two Supplemental Drafts each year—one prior to training camp and one prior to the regular season; and voted to initiate an annual series of games in Japan/Asia as early as the 1989 preseason, March 14-18.

The NFL Annual Selection Meeting returned to a separate two-day format and for the first time originated on a Sunday. ESPN drew a 3.6 rating during their seven-hour coverage of the draft, which was viewed in 1.6 million homes, April 24-25.

NFL COMMISSIONERS AND PRESIDENTS

1920 . . . . Jim Thorpe, President
1921-39 . . . . Joe Carr, President
1939-41 . . . . . Carl Storck, President
1941-46 . . . . Elmer Layden, Commissioner
1946-59 . . . Bert Bell, Commissioner
1959-60 . . . Austin Gunsel, President in the office of the Commissioner
1960-present . . . . Pete Rozelle, Commissioner

PAST STANDINGS

1987

American Conference

Eastern Division

	W	L	T	Pct.	Pts.	OP
Indianapolis	9	6	0	.600	300	238
New England	8	7	0	.533	320	293
Miami	8	7	0	.533	362	335
Buffalo	7	8	0	.467	270	305
N.Y. Jets	6	9	0	.400	334	360

Central Division

	W	L	T	Pct.	Pts.	OP
Cleveland	10	5	0	.667	390	239
Houston*	9	6	0	.600	345	349
Pittsburgh	8	7	0	.533	285	299
Cincinnati	4	11	0	.267	285	370

Western Division

	W	L	T	Pct.	Pts.	OP
Denver	10	4	1	.700	379	288
Seattle*	9	6	0	.600	371	314
San Diego	8	7	0	.533	253	317
L.A. Raiders	5	10	0	.333	301	289
Kansas City	4	11	0	.267	273	388

National Conference

Eastern Division

	W	L	T	Pct.	Pts.	OP
Washington	11	4	0	.733	379	285
Dallas	7	8	0	.467	340	348
St. Louis	7	8	0	.467	362	368
Philadelphia	7	8	0	.467	337	380
N.Y. Giants	6	9	0	.400	280	312

Central Division

	W	L	T	Pct.	Pts.	OP
Chicago	11	4	0	.733	356	282
Minnesota*	8	7	0	.533	336	335
Green Bay	5	9	1	.367	255	300
Tampa Bay	4	11	0	.267	286	360
Detroit	4	11	0	.267	269	384

Western Division

	W	L	T	Pct.	Pts.	OP
San Francisco	13	2	0	.867	459	253
New Orleans*	12	3	0	.800	422	283
L.A. Rams	6	9	0	.400	317	361
Atlanta	3	12	0	.200	205	436

**Wild Card qualifiers for playoffs*

Houston gained first AFC Wild Card position on better conference record (7-4) over Seattle (5-6).

First round playoff: HOUSTON 23, Seattle 20 (OT)
Divisional playoffs: CLEVELAND 38, Indianapolis 21
DENVER 34, Houston 10
AFC championship: DENVER 38, Cleveland 33
First round playoff: Minnesota 44, NEW ORLEANS 10
Divisional playoffs: Minnesota 36, SAN FRANCISCO 24
Washington 21, CHICAGO 17
NFC championship: WASHINGTON 17, Minnesota 10
Super Bowl XXII: Washington (NFC) 42, Denver (AFC) 10, at San Diego Jack Murphy Stadium, San Diego, Calif.

Note: 1987 regular season was reduced from 16 to 15 games for each team due to players' strike.

1986

American Conference

Eastern Division

	W	L	T	Pct.	Pts.	OP
New England	11	5	0	.688	412	307
N.Y. Jets*	10	6	0	.625	364	386
Miami	8	8	0	.500	430	405
Buffalo	4	12	0	.250	287	348
Indianapolis	3	13	0	.188	229	400

Central Division

	W	L	T	Pct.	Pts.	OP
Cleveland	12	4	0	.750	391	310
Cincinnati	10	6	0	.625	409	394
Pittsburgh	6	10	0	.375	307	336
Houston	5	11	0	.313	274	329

Western Division

	W	L	T	Pct.	Pts.	OP
Denver	11	5	0	.688	378	327
Kansas City*	10	6	0	.625	358	326
Seattle	10	6	0	.625	366	293
L.A. Raiders	8	8	0	.500	323	346
San Diego	4	12	0	.250	335	396

National Conference

Eastern Division

	W	L	T	Pct.	Pts.	OP
N.Y. Giants	14	2	0	.875	371	236
Washington*	12	4	0	.750	368	296
Dallas	7	9	0	.438	346	337
Philadelphia	5	10	1	.344	256	312
St. Louis	4	11	1	.281	218	351

Central Division

	W	L	T	Pct.	Pts.	OP
Chicago	14	2	0	.875	352	187
Minnesota	9	7	0	.563	398	273
Detroit	5	11	0	.313	277	326
Green Bay	4	12	0	.250	254	418
Tampa Bay	2	14	0	.125	239	473

Western Division

	W	L	T	Pct.	Pts.	OP
San Francisco	10	5	1	.656	374	247
L.A. Rams*	10	6	0	.625	309	267
Atlanta	7	8	1	.469	280	280
New Orleans	7	9	0	.438	288	287

**Wild Card qualifiers for playoffs*

New York Jets gained first AFC Wild Card position on better conference record (8-4) over Kansas City (9-5), Seattle (7-5), and Cincinnati (7-5). Kansas City gained second Wild Card based on better conference record (9-5) over Seattle (7-5) and Cincinnati (7-5).

First round playoff: NEW YORK JETS 35, Kansas City 15
Divisional playoffs: CLEVELAND 23, New York Jets 20 (OT)
DENVER 22, New England 17
AFC championship: Denver 23, CLEVELAND 20 (OT)
First round playoff: WASHINGTON 19, Los Angeles Rams 7
Divisional playoffs: Washington 27, CHICAGO 13
NEW YORK GIANTS 49, San Francisco 3
NFC championship: NEW YORK GIANTS 17, Washington 0
Super Bowl XXI: New York Giants (NFC) 39, Denver (AFC) 20, at Rose Bowl, Pasadena, Calif.

In the Past Standings section, home teams in playoff games are indicated by capital letters.

1985

American Conference

Eastern Division

	W	L	T	Pct.	Pts.	OP
Miami	12	4	0	.750	428	320
N.Y. Jets*	11	5	0	.688	393	264
New England*	11	5	0	.688	362	290
Indianapolis	5	11	0	.313	320	386
Buffalo	2	14	0	.125	200	381

Central Division

	W	L	T	Pct.	Pts.	OP
Cleveland	8	8	0	.500	287	294
Cincinnati	7	9	0	.438	441	437
Pittsburgh	7	9	0	.438	379	355
Houston	5	11	0	.313	284	412

Western Division

	W	L	T	Pct.	Pts.	OP
L.A. Raiders	12	4	0	.750	354	308
Denver	11	5	0	.688	380	329
Seattle	8	8	0	.500	349	303
San Diego	8	8	0	.500	467	435
Kansas City	6	10	0	.375	317	360

National Conference

Eastern Division

	W	L	T	Pct.	Pts.	OP
Dallas	10	6	0	.625	357	333
N.Y. Giants*	10	6	0	.625	399	283
Washington	10	6	0	.625	297	312
Philadelphia	7	9	0	.438	286	310
St. Louis	5	11	0	.313	278	414

Central Division

	W	L	T	Pct.	Pts.	OP
Chicago	15	1	0	.938	456	198
Green Bay	8	8	0	.500	337	355
Minnesota	7	9	0	.438	346	359
Detroit	7	9	0	.438	307	366
Tampa Bay	2	14	0	.125	294	448

Western Division

	W	L	T	Pct.	Pts.	OP
L.A. Rams	11	5	0	.688	340	277
San Francisco*	10	6	0	.625	411	263
New Orleans	5	11	0	.313	294	401
Atlanta	4	12	0	.250	282	452

**Wild Card qualifiers for playoffs*

New York Jets gained first AFC Wild Card position on better conference record (9-3) over New England (8-4) and Denver (8-4). New England gained second AFC Wild Card position based on better record vs. common opponents (4-2) than Denver (3-3). Dallas won NFC Eastern Division title based on better record (4-0) vs. New York Giants (1-3) and Washington (1-3). New York Giants gained first NFC Wild Card position based on better conference record (8-4) over San Francisco (7-5) and Washington (6-6). San Francisco gained second NFC Wild Card position based on head-to-head victory over Washington.

First round playoff: New England 26, NEW YORK JETS 14
Divisional playoffs: MIAMI 24, Cleveland 21;
New England 27, LOS ANGELES RAIDERS 20
AFC championship: New England 31, MIAMI 14
First round playoff: NEW YORK GIANTS 17, San Francisco 3
Divisional playoffs: LOS ANGELES RAMS 20, Dallas 0;
CHICAGO 21, New York Giants 0
NFC championship: CHICAGO 24, Los Angeles Rams 0
Super Bowl XX: Chicago (NFC) 46, New England (AFC) 10, at Louisiana Superdome, New Orleans, La.

1984

American Conference

Eastern Division

	W	L	T	Pct.	Pts.	OP
Miami	14	2	0	.875	513	298
New England	9	7	0	.563	362	352
N.Y. Jets	7	9	0	.438	332	364
Indianapolis	4	12	0	.250	239	414
Buffalo	2	14	0	.125	250	454

Central Division

	W	L	T	Pct.	Pts.	OP
Pittsburgh	9	7	0	.563	387	310
Cincinnati	8	8	0	.500	339	339
Cleveland	5	11	0	.313	250	297
Houston	3	13	0	.188	240	437

Western Division

	W	L	T	Pct.	Pts.	OP
Denver	13	3	0	.813	353	241
Seattle*	12	4	0	.750	418	282
L.A. Raiders*	11	5	0	.688	368	278
Kansas City	8	8	0	.500	314	324
San Diego	7	9	0	.438	394	413

National Conference

Eastern Division

	W	L	T	Pct.	Pts.	OP
Washington	11	5	0	.688	426	310
N.Y. Giants*	9	7	0	.563	299	301
St. Louis	9	7	0	.563	423	345
Dallas	9	7	0	.563	308	308
Philadelphia	6	9	1	.406	278	320

Central Division

	W	L	T	Pct.	Pts.	OP
Chicago	10	6	0	.625	325	248
Green Bay	8	8	0	.500	390	309
Tampa Bay	6	10	0	.375	335	380
Detroit	4	11	1	.281	283	408
Minnesota	3	13	0	.188	276	484

Western Division

	W	L	T	Pct.	Pts.	OP
San Francisco	15	1	0	.938	475	227
L.A. Rams*	10	6	0	.625	346	316
New Orleans	7	9	0	.438	298	361
Atlanta	4	12	0	.250	281	382

**Wild Card qualifiers for playoffs*

New York Giants clinched Wild Card berth based on 3-1 record vs. St. Louis's 2-2 and Dallas's 1-3. St. Louis finished ahead of Dallas based on better division record (5-3 to 3-5).

First round playoff: SEATTLE 13, Los Angeles Raiders 7
Divisional playoffs: MIAMI 31, Seattle 10; Pittsburgh 24, DENVER 17
AFC championship: MIAMI 45, Pittsburgh 28
First round playoff: New York Giants 16, LOS ANGELES RAMS 13
Divisional playoffs: SAN FRANCISCO 21, New York Giants 10;
Chicago 23, WASHINGTON 19
NFC championship: SAN FRANCISCO 23, Chicago 0
Super Bowl XIX: San Francisco (NFC) 38, Miami (AFC) 16, at Stanford Stadium, Stanford, Calif.

1983

American Conference

Eastern Division

	W	L	T	Pct.	Pts.	OP
Miami	12	4	0	.750	389	250
New England	8	8	0	.500	274	289
Buffalo	8	8	0	.500	283	351
Baltimore	7	9	0	.438	264	354
N.Y. Jets	7	9	0	.438	313	331

Central Division

	W	L	T	Pct.	Pts.	OP
Pittsburgh	10	6	0	.625	355	303
Cleveland	9	7	0	.563	356	342
Cincinnati	7	9	0	.438	346	302
Houston	2	14	0	.125	288	460

Western Division

	W	L	T	Pct.	Pts.	OP
L.A. Raiders	12	4	0	.750	442	338
Seattle*	9	7	0	.563	403	397
Denver*	9	7	0	.563	302	327
San Diego	6	10	0	.375	358	462
Kansas City	6	10	0	.375	386	367

National Conference

Eastern Division

	W	L	T	Pct.	Pts.	OP
Washington	14	2	0	.875	541	332
Dallas*	12	4	0	.750	479	360
St. Louis	8	7	1	.531	374	428
Philadelphia	5	11	0	.313	233	322
N.Y. Giants	3	12	1	.219	267	347

Central Division

	W	L	T	Pct.	Pts.	OP
Detroit	9	7	0	.563	347	286
Green Bay	8	8	0	.500	429	439
Chicago	8	8	0	.500	311	301
Minnesota	8	8	0	.500	316	348
Tampa Bay	2	14	0	.125	241	380

Western Division

	W	L	T	Pct.	Pts.	OP
San Francisco	10	6	0	.625	432	293
L.A. Rams*	9	7	0	.563	361	344
New Orleans	8	8	0	.500	319	337
Atlanta	7	9	0	.438	370	389

**Wild Card qualifiers for playoffs*

Seattle and Denver gained Wild Card berths over Cleveland because of their victories over the Browns.

First round playoff: SEATTLE 31, Denver 7
Divisional playoffs: Seattle 27, MIAMI 20; LOS ANGELES RAIDERS 38, Pittsburgh 10
AFC championship: LOS ANGELES RAIDERS 30, Seattle 14
First round playoff: Los Angeles Rams 24, DALLAS 17
Divisional playoffs: SAN FRANCISCO 24, Detroit 23; WASHINGTON 51, L.A. Rams 7
NFC championship: WASHINGTON 24, San Francisco 21
Super Bowl XVIII: Los Angeles Raiders (AFC) 38, Washington (NFC) 9, at Tampa Stadium, Tampa, Fla.

1982

American Conference

	W	L	T	Pct.	Pts.	OP
L.A. Raiders	8	1	0	.889	260	200
Miami	7	2	0	.778	198	131
Cincinnati	7	2	0	.778	232	177
Pittsburgh	6	3	0	.667	204	146
San Diego	6	3	0	.667	288	221
N.Y. Jets	6	3	0	.667	245	166
New England	5	4	0	.556	143	157
Cleveland	4	5	0	.444	140	182
Buffalo	4	5	0	.444	150	154
Seattle	4	5	0	.444	127	147
Kansas City	3	6	0	.333	176	184
Denver	2	7	0	.222	148	226
Houston	1	8	0	.111	136	245
Baltimore	0	8	1	.056	113	236

National Conference

	W	L	T	Pct.	Pts.	OP
Washington	8	1	0	.889	190	128
Dallas	6	3	0	.667	226	145
Green Bay	5	3	1	.611	226	169
Minnesota	5	4	0	.556	187	198
Atlanta	5	4	0	.556	183	199
St. Louis	5	4	0	.556	135	170
Tampa Bay	5	4	0	.556	158	178
Detroit	4	5	0	.444	181	176
New Orleans	4	5	0	.444	129	160
N.Y. Giants	4	5	0	.444	164	160
San Francisco	3	6	0	.333	209	206
Chicago	3	6	0	.333	141	174
Philadelphia	3	6	0	.333	191	195
L.A. Rams	2	7	0	.222	200	250

As the result of a 57-day players' strike, the 1982 NFL regular season schedule was reduced from 16 weeks to 9. At the conclusion of the regular season, the NFL conducted a 16-team postseason Super Bowl Tournament. Eight teams from each conference were seeded 1-8 based on their records during the season.

Miami finished ahead of Cincinnati based on better conference record (6-1 to 6-2). Pittsburgh won common games tie-breaker with San Diego (3-1 to 2-1) after New York Jets were eliminated from three-way tie based on conference record (Pittsburgh and San Diego 5-3 vs. Jets 2-3). Cleveland finished ahead of Buffalo and Seattle based on better conference record (4-3 to 3-3 to 3-5). Minnesota (4-1), Atlanta (4-3), St. Louis (5-4), Tampa Bay (3-3) seeds were determined by best won-lost record in conference games. Detroit finished ahead of New Orleans and the New York Giants based on better conference record (4-4 to 3-5 to 3-5).

First round playoff: MIAMI 28, New England 13
LOS ANGELES RAIDERS 27, Cleveland 10
New York Jets 44, CINCINNATI 17
San Diego 31, PITTSBURGH 28
Second round playoff: New York Jets 17, LOS ANGELES RAIDERS 14
MIAMI 34, San Diego 13
AFC championship: MIAMI 14, New York Jets 0
First round playoff: WASHINGTON 31, Detroit 7
GREEN BAY 41, St. Louis 16
MINNESOTA 30, Atlanta 24
DALLAS 30, Tampa Bay 17
Second round playoff: WASHINGTON 21, Minnesota 7
DALLAS 37, Green Bay 26
NFC championship: WASHINGTON 31, Dallas 17
Super Bowl XVII: Washington (NFC) 27, Miami (AFC) 17, at Rose Bowl, Pasadena, Calif.

1981

American Conference

Eastern Division

	W	L	T	Pct.	Pts.	OP
Miami	11	4	1	.719	345	275
N.Y. Jets*	10	5	1	.656	355	287
Buffalo*	10	6	0	.625	311	276
Baltimore	2	14	0	.125	259	533
New England	2	14	0	.125	322	370

Central Division

	W	L	T	Pct.	Pts.	OP
Cincinnati	12	4	0	.750	421	304
Pittsburgh	8	8	0	.500	356	297
Houston	7	9	0	.438	281	355
Cleveland	5	11	0	.313	276	375

Western Division

	W	L	T	Pct.	Pts.	OP
San Diego	10	6	0	.625	478	390
Denver	10	6	0	.625	321	289
Kansas City	9	7	0	.563	343	290
Oakland	7	9	0	.438	273	343
Seattle	6	10	0	.375	322	388

National Conference

Eastern Division

	W	L	T	Pct.	Pts.	OP
Dallas	12	4	0	.750	367	277
Philadelphia*	10	6	0	.625	368	221
N.Y. Giants*	9	7	0	.563	295	257
Washington	8	8	0	.500	347	349
St. Louis	7	9	0	.438	315	408

Central Division

	W	L	T	Pct.	Pts.	OP
Tampa Bay	9	7	0	.563	315	268
Detroit	8	8	0	.500	397	322
Green Bay	8	8	0	.500	324	361
Minnesota	7	9	0	.438	325	369
Chicago	6	10	0	.375	253	324

Western Division

	W	L	T	Pct.	Pts.	OP
San Francisco	13	3	0	.813	357	250
Atlanta	7	9	0	.438	426	355
Los Angeles	6	10	0	.375	303	351
New Orleans	4	12	0	.250	207	378

**Wild Card qualifiers for playoffs*

San Diego won AFC Western title over Denver on the basis of a better division record (6-2 to 5-3). Buffalo won a Wild Card playoff berth over Denver as the result of a 9-7 victory in head-to-head competition.

First round playoff: Buffalo 31, NEW YORK JETS 27
Divisional playoffs: San Diego 41, MIAMI 38 (OT); CINCINNATI 28, Buffalo 21
AFC championship: CINCINNATI 27, San Diego 7
First round playoff: New York Giants 27, PHILADELPHIA 21
Divisional playoffs: DALLAS 38, Tampa Bay 0; SAN FRANCISCO 38, New York Giants 24
NFC championship: SAN FRANCISCO 28, Dallas 27
Super Bowl XVI: San Francisco (NFC) 26, Cincinnati (AFC) 21, at Silverdome, Pontiac, Mich.

1980

American Conference

Eastern Division

	W	L	T	Pct.	Pts.	OP
Buffalo	11	5	0	.688	320	260
New England	10	6	0	.625	441	325
Miami	8	8	0	.500	266	305
Baltimore	7	9	0	.438	355	387
N.Y. Jets	4	12	0	.250	302	395

Central Division

	W	L	T	Pct.	Pts.	OP
Cleveland	11	5	0	.688	357	310
Houston*	11	5	0	.688	295	251
Pittsburgh	9	7	0	.563	352	313
Cincinnati	6	10	0	.375	244	312

Western Division

	W	L	T	Pct.	Pts.	OP
San Diego	11	5	0	.688	418	327
Oakland*	11	5	0	.688	364	306
Kansas City	8	8	0	.500	319	336
Denver	8	8	0	.500	310	323
Seattle	4	12	0	.250	291	408

National Conference

Eastern Division

	W	L	T	Pct.	Pts.	OP
Philadelphia	12	4	0	.750	384	222
Dallas*	12	4	0	.750	454	311
Washington	6	10	0	.375	261	293
St. Louis	5	11	0	.313	299	350
N.Y. Giants	4	12	0	.250	249	425

Central Division

	W	L	T	Pct.	Pts.	OP
Minnesota	9	7	0	.563	317	308
Detroit	9	7	0	.563	334	272
Chicago	7	9	0	.438	304	264
Tampa Bay	5	10	1	.344	271	341
Green Bay	5	10	1	.344	231	371

Western Division

	W	L	T	Pct.	Pts.	OP
Atlanta	12	4	0	.750	405	272
Los Angeles*	11	5	0	.688	424	289
San Francisco	6	10	0	.375	320	415
New Orleans	1	15	0	.063	291	487

**Wild Card qualifiers for playoffs*

Philadelphia won division title over Dallas on the basis of best net points in division games (plus 84 net points to plus 50). Minnesota won division title because of a better conference record than Detroit (8-4 to 9-5). Cleveland won division title because of a better conference record than Houston (8-4 to 7-5). San Diego won division title over Oakland on the basis of best net points in division games (plus 60 net points to plus 37).

First round playoff: OAKLAND 27, Houston 7
Divisional playoffs: SAN DIEGO 20, Buffalo 14; Oakland 14, CLEVELAND 12
AFC championship: Oakland 34, SAN DIEGO 27
First round playoff: DALLAS 34, Los Angeles 13
Divisional playoffs: PHILADELPHIA 31, Minnesota 16; Dallas 30, ATLANTA 27
NFC championship: PHILADELPHIA 20, Dallas 7
Super Bowl XV: Oakland (AFC) 27, Philadelphia (NFC) 10, at Louisiana Superdome, New Orleans, La.

1979

American Conference

Eastern Division

	W	L	T	Pct.	Pts.	OP
Miami	10	6	0	.625	341	257
New England	9	7	0	.563	411	326
N.Y. Jets	8	8	0	.500	337	383
Buffalo	7	9	0	.438	268	279
Baltimore	5	11	0	.313	271	351

Central Division

	W	L	T	Pct.	Pts.	OP
Pittsburgh	12	4	0	.750	416	262
Houston*	11	5	0	.688	362	331
Cleveland	9	7	0	.563	359	352
Cincinnati	4	12	0	.250	337	421

Western Division

	W	L	T	Pct.	Pts.	OP
San Diego	12	4	0	.750	411	246
Denver*	10	6	0	.625	289	262
Seattle	9	7	0	.563	378	372
Oakland	9	7	0	.563	365	337
Kansas City	7	9	0	.438	238	262

National Conference

Eastern Division

	W	L	T	Pct.	Pts.	OP
Dallas	11	5	0	.688	371	313
Philadelphia*	11	5	0	.688	339	282
Washington	10	6	0	.625	348	295
N.Y. Giants	6	10	0	.375	237	323
St. Louis	5	11	0	.313	307	358

Central Division

	W	L	T	Pct.	Pts.	OP
Tampa Bay	10	6	0	.625	273	237
Chicago*	10	6	0	.625	306	249
Minnesota	7	9	0	.438	259	337
Green Bay	5	11	0	.313	246	316
Detroit	2	14	0	.125	219	365

Western Division

	W	L	T	Pct.	Pts.	OP
Los Angeles	9	7	0	.563	323	309
New Orleans	8	8	0	.500	370	360
Atlanta	6	10	0	.375	300	388
San Francisco	2	14	0	.125	308	416

**Wild Card qualifiers for playoffs*

Dallas won division title because of a better conference record than Philadelphia (10-2 to 9-3). Tampa Bay won division title because of a better division record than Chicago (6-2 to 5-3). Chicago won a Wild Card berth over Washington on the basis of best net points in all games (plus 57 net points to plus 53).

First round playoff: HOUSTON 13, Denver 7

Divisional playoffs: Houston 17, SAN DIEGO 14; PITTSBURGH 34, Miami 14

AFC championship: PITTSBURGH 27, Houston 13

First round playoff: PHILADELPHIA 27, Chicago 17

Divisional playoffs: TAMPA BAY 24, Philadelphia 17; Los Angeles 21, DALLAS 19

NFC championship: Los Angeles 9, TAMPA BAY 0

Super Bowl XIV: Pittsburgh (AFC) 31, Los Angeles (NFC) 19, at Rose Bowl, Pasadena, Calif.

1978

American Conference

Eastern Division

	W	L	T	Pct.	Pts.	OP
New England	11	5	0	.688	358	286
Miami*	11	5	0	.688	372	254
N.Y. Jets	8	8	0	.500	359	364
Buffalo	5	11	0	.313	302	354
Baltimore	5	11	0	.313	239	421

Central Division

	W	L	T	Pct.	Pts.	OP
Pittsburgh	14	2	0	.875	356	195
Houston*	10	6	0	.625	283	298
Cleveland	8	8	0	.500	334	356
Cincinnati	4	12	0	.250	252	284

Western Division

	W	L	T	Pct.	Pts.	OP
Denver	10	6	0	.625	282	198
Oakland	9	7	0	.563	311	283
Seattle	9	7	0	.563	345	358
San Diego	9	7	0	.563	355	309
Kansas City	4	12	0	.250	243	327

National Conference

Eastern Division

	W	L	T	Pct.	Pts.	OP
Dallas	12	4	0	.750	384	208
Philadelphia*	9	7	0	.563	270	250
Washington	8	8	0	.500	273	283
St. Louis	6	10	0	.375	248	296
N.Y. Giants	6	10	0	.375	264	298

Central Division

	W	L	T	Pct.	Pts.	OP
Minnesota	8	7	1	.531	294	306
Green Bay	8	7	1	.531	249	269
Detroit	7	9	0	.438	290	300
Chicago	7	9	0	.438	253	274
Tampa Bay	5	11	0	.313	241	259

Western Division

	W	L	T	Pct.	Pts.	OP
Los Angeles	12	4	0	.750	316	245
Atlanta*	9	7	0	.563	240	290
New Orleans	7	9	0	.438	281	298
San Francisco	2	14	0	.125	219	350

**Wild Card qualifiers for playoffs*

New England won division title on the basis of a better division record than Miami (6-2 to 5-3). Minnesota won division title because of a better head-to-head record against Green Bay (1-0-1).

First round playoff: Houston 17, MIAMI 9

Divisional playoffs: Houston 31, NEW ENGLAND 14; PITTSBURGH 33, Denver 10

AFC championship: PITTSBURGH 34, Houston 5

First round playoff: ATLANTA 14, Philadelphia 13

Divisional playoffs: DALLAS 27, Atlanta 20; LOS ANGELES 34, Minnesota 10

NFC championship: Dallas 28, LOS ANGELES 0

Super Bowl XIII: Pittsburgh (AFC) 35, Dallas (NFC) 31, at Orange Bowl, Miami, Fla.

1977

American Conference

Eastern Division

	W	L	T	Pct.	Pts.	OP
Baltimore	10	4	0	.714	295	221
Miami	10	4	0	.714	313	197
New England	9	5	0	.643	278	217
N.Y. Jets	3	11	0	.214	191	300
Buffalo	3	11	0	.214	160	313

Central Division

	W	L	T	Pct.	Pts.	OP
Pittsburgh	9	5	0	.643	283	243
Houston	8	6	0	.571	299	230
Cincinnati	8	6	0	.571	238	235
Cleveland	6	8	0	.429	269	267

Western Division

	W	L	T	Pct.	Pts.	OP
Denver	12	2	0	.857	274	148
Oakland*	11	3	0	.786	351	230
San Diego	7	7	0	.500	222	205
Seattle	5	9	0	.357	282	373
Kansas City	2	12	0	.143	225	349

National Conference

Eastern Division

	W	L	T	Pct.	Pts.	OP
Dallas	12	2	0	.857	345	212
Washington	9	5	0	.643	196	189
St. Louis	7	7	0	.500	272	287
Philadelphia	5	9	0	.357	220	207
N.Y. Giants	5	9	0	.357	181	265

Central Division

	W	L	T	Pct.	Pts.	OP
Minnesota	9	5	0	.643	231	227
Chicago*	9	5	0	.643	255	253
Detroit	6	8	0	.429	183	252
Green Bay	4	10	0	.286	134	219
Tampa Bay	2	12	0	.143	103	223

Western Division

	W	L	T	Pct.	Pts.	OP
Los Angeles	10	4	0	.714	302	146
Atlanta	7	7	0	.500	179	129
San Francisco	5	9	0	.357	220	260
New Orleans	3	11	0	.214	232	336

**Wild Card qualifier for playoffs*

Baltimore won division title on the basis of a better conference record than Miami (9-3 to 8-4). Chicago won a Wild Card berth over Washington on the basis of best net points in conference games (plus 48 net points to plus 4).

Divisional playoffs: DENVER 34, Pittsburgh 21; Oakland 37, BALTIMORE 31 (OT)

AFC championship: DENVER 20, Oakland 17

Divisional playoffs: DALLAS 37, Chicago 7; Minnesota 14, LOS ANGELES 7

NFC championship: DALLAS 23, Minnesota 6

Super Bowl XII: Dallas (NFC) 27, Denver (AFC) 10, at Louisiana Superdome, New Orleans, La.

1976

American Conference

Eastern Division

	W	L	T	Pct.	Pts.	OP
Baltimore	11	3	0	.786	417	246
New England*	11	3	0	.786	376	236
Miami	6	8	0	.429	263	264
N.Y. Jets	3	11	0	.214	169	383
Buffalo	2	12	0	.143	245	363

Central Division

	W	L	T	Pct.	Pts.	OP
Pittsburgh	10	4	0	.714	342	138
Cincinnati	10	4	0	.714	335	210
Cleveland	9	5	0	.643	267	287
Houston	5	9	0	.357	222	273

Western Division

	W	L	T	Pct.	Pts.	OP
Oakland	13	1	0	.929	350	237
Denver	9	5	0	.643	315	206
San Diego	6	8	0	.429	248	285
Kansas City	5	9	0	.357	290	376
Tampa Bay	0	14	0	.000	125	412

National Conference

Eastern Division

	W	L	T	Pct.	Pts.	OP
Dallas	11	3	0	.786	296	194
Washington*	10	4	0	.714	291	217
St. Louis	10	4	0	.714	309	267
Philadelphia	4	10	0	.286	165	286
N.Y. Giants	3	11	0	.214	170	250

Central Division

	W	L	T	Pct.	Pts.	OP
Minnesota	11	2	1	.821	305	176
Chicago	7	7	0	.500	253	216
Detroit	6	8	0	.429	262	220
Green Bay	5	9	0	.357	218	299

Western Division

	W	L	T	Pct.	Pts.	OP
Los Angeles	10	3	1	.750	351	190
San Francisco	8	6	0	.571	270	190
Atlanta	4	10	0	.286	172	312
New Orleans	4	10	0	.286	253	346
Seattle	2	12	0	.143	229	429

**Wild Card qualifier for playoffs*

Baltimore won division title on the basis of a better division record than New England (7-1 to 6-2). Pittsburgh won division title because of a two-game sweep over Cincinnati. Washington won Wild Card berth over St. Louis because of a two-game sweep over Cardinals.

Divisional playoffs: OAKLAND 24, New England 21; Pittsburgh 40, BALTIMORE 14

AFC championship: OAKLAND 24, Pittsburgh 7

Divisional playoffs: MINNESOTA 35, Washington 20; Los Angeles 14, DALLAS 12

NFC championship: MINNESOTA 24, Los Angeles 13

Super Bowl XI: Oakland (AFC) 32, Minnesota (NFC) 14, at Rose Bowl, Pasadena, Calif.

1975

American Conference

Eastern Division

	W	L	T	Pct.	Pts.	OP
Baltimore	10	4	0	.714	395	269
Miami	10	4	0	.714	357	222
Buffalo	8	6	0	.571	420	355
New England	3	11	0	.214	258	358
N.Y. Jets	3	11	0	.214	258	433

Central Division

	W	L	T	Pct.	Pts.	OP
Pittsburgh	12	2	0	.857	373	162
Cincinnati*	11	3	0	.786	340	246
Houston	10	4	0	.714	293	226
Cleveland	3	11	0	.214	218	372

Western Division

	W	L	T	Pct.	Pts.	OP
Oakland	11	3	0	.786	375	255
Denver	6	8	0	.429	254	307
Kansas City	5	9	0	.357	282	341
San Diego	2	12	0	.143	189	345

National Conference

Eastern Division

	W	L	T	Pct.	Pts.	OP
St. Louis	11	3	0	.786	356	276
Dallas*	10	4	0	.714	350	268
Washington	8	6	0	.571	325	276
N.Y. Giants	5	9	0	.357	216	306
Philadelphia	4	10	0	.286	225	302

Central Division

	W	L	T	Pct.	Pts.	OP
Minnesota	12	2	0	.857	377	180
Detroit	7	7	0	.500	245	262
Chicago	4	10	0	.286	191	379
Green Bay	4	10	0	.286	226	285

Western Division

	W	L	T	Pct.	Pts.	OP
Los Angeles	12	2	0	.857	312	135
San Francisco	5	9	0	.357	255	286
Atlanta	4	10	0	.286	240	289
New Orleans	2	12	0	.143	165	360

**Wild Card qualifier for playoffs*

Baltimore won division title on the basis of a two-game sweep over Miami.

Divisional playoffs: PITTSBURGH 28, Baltimore 10; OAKLAND 31, Cincinnati 28

AFC championship: PITTSBURGH 16, Oakland 10

Divisional playoffs: LOS ANGELES 35, St. Louis 23; Dallas 17, MINNESOTA 14

NFC championship: Dallas 37, LOS ANGELES 7

Super Bowl X: Pittsburgh (AFC) 21, Dallas (NFC) 17, at Orange Bowl, Miami, Fla.

1974

American Conference

Eastern Division

	W	L	T	Pct.	Pts.	OP
Miami	11	3	0	.786	327	216
Buffalo*	9	5	0	.643	264	244
New England	7	7	0	.500	348	289
N.Y. Jets	7	7	0	.500	279	300
Baltimore	2	12	0	.143	190	329

Central Division

	W	L	T	Pct.	Pts.	OP
Pittsburgh	10	3	1	.750	305	189
Cincinnati	7	7	0	.500	283	259
Houston	7	7	0	.500	236	282
Cleveland	4	10	0	.286	251	344

Western Division

	W	L	T	Pct.	Pts.	OP
Oakland	12	2	0	.857	355	228
Denver	7	6	1	.536	302	294
Kansas City	5	9	0	.357	233	293
San Diego	5	9	0	.357	212	285

National Conference

Eastern Division

	W	L	T	Pct.	Pts.	OP
St. Louis	10	4	0	.714	285	218
Washington*	10	4	0	.714	320	196
Dallas	8	6	0	.571	297	235
Philadelphia	7	7	0	.500	242	217
N.Y. Giants	2	12	0	.143	195	299

Central Division

	W	L	T	Pct.	Pts.	OP
Minnesota	10	4	0	.714	310	195
Detroit	7	7	0	.500	256	270
Green Bay	6	8	0	.429	210	206
Chicago	4	10	0	.286	152	279

Western Division

	W	L	T	Pct.	Pts.	OP
Los Angeles	10	4	0	.714	263	181
San Francisco	6	8	0	.429	226	236
New Orleans	5	9	0	.357	166	263
Atlanta	3	11	0	.214	111	271

**Wild Card qualifier for playoffs*

St. Louis won division title because of a two-game sweep over Washington.

Divisional playoffs: OAKLAND 28, Miami 26; PITTSBURGH 32, Buffalo 14

AFC championship: Pittsburgh 24, OAKLAND 13

Divisional playoffs: MINNESOTA 30, St. Louis 14; LOS ANGELES 19, Washington 10

NFC championship: MINNESOTA 14, Los Angeles 10

Super Bowl IX: Pittsburgh (AFC) 16, Minnesota (NFC) 6, at Tulane Stadium, New Orleans, La.

1973

American Conference

Eastern Division

	W	L	T	Pct.	Pts.	OP
Miami	12	2	0	.857	343	150
Buffalo	9	5	0	.643	259	230
New England	5	9	0	.357	258	300
Baltimore	4	10	0	.286	226	341
N.Y. Jets	4	10	0	.286	240	306

Central Division

	W	L	T	Pct.	Pts.	OP
Cincinnati	10	4	0	.714	286	231
Pittsburgh*	10	4	0	.714	347	210
Cleveland	7	5	2	.571	234	255
Houston	1	13	0	.071	199	447

Western Division

	W	L	T	Pct.	Pts.	OP
Oakland	9	4	1	.679	292	175
Denver	7	5	2	.571	354	296
Kansas City	7	5	2	.571	231	192
San Diego	2	11	1	.179	188	386

National Conference

Eastern Division

	W	L	T	Pct.	Pts.	OP
Dallas	10	4	0	.714	382	203
Washington*	10	4	0	.714	325	198
Philadelphia	5	8	1	.393	310	393
St. Louis	4	9	1	.321	286	365
N.Y. Giants	2	11	1	.179	226	362

Central Division

	W	L	T	Pct.	Pts.	OP
Minnesota	12	2	0	.857	296	168
Detroit	6	7	1	.464	271	247
Green Bay	5	7	2	.429	202	259
Chicago	3	11	0	.214	195	334

Western Division

	W	L	T	Pct.	Pts.	OP
Los Angeles	12	2	0	.857	388	178
Atlanta	9	5	0	.643	318	224
New Orleans	5	9	0	.357	163	312
San Francisco	5	9	0	.357	262	319

**Wild Card qualifier for playoffs*

Cincinnati won division title on the basis of a better conference record than Pittsburgh (8-3 to 7-4). Dallas won division title on the basis of a better point differential vs. Washington (net 13 points).

Divisional playoffs: OAKLAND 33, Pittsburgh 14; MIAMI 34, Cincinnati 16
AFC championship: MIAMI 27, Oakland 10
Divisional playoffs: MINNESOTA 27, Washington 20; DALLAS 27, Los Angeles 16
NFC championship: Minnesota 27, DALLAS 10
Super Bowl VIII: Miami (AFC) 24, Minnesota (NFC) 7, at Rice Stadium, Houston, Tex.

1972

American Conference

Eastern Division

	W	L	T	Pct.	Pts.	OP
Miami	14	0	0	1.000	385	171
N.Y. Jets	7	7	0	.500	367	324
Baltimore	5	9	0	.357	235	252
Buffalo	4	9	1	.321	257	377
New England	3	11	0	.214	192	446

Central Division

	W	L	T	Pct.	Pts.	OP
Pittsburgh	11	3	0	.786	343	175
Cleveland*	10	4	0	.714	268	249
Cincinnati	8	6	0	.571	299	229
Houston	1	13	0	.071	164	380

Western Division

	W	L	T	Pct.	Pts.	OP
Oakland	10	3	1	.750	365	248
Kansas City	8	6	0	.571	287	254
Denver	5	9	0	.357	325	350
San Diego	4	9	1	.321	264	344

National Conference

Eastern Division

	W	L	T	Pct.	Pts.	OP
Washington	11	3	0	.786	336	218
Dallas*	10	4	0	.714	319	240
N.Y. Giants	8	6	0	.571	331	247
St. Louis	4	9	1	.321	193	303
Philadelphia	2	11	1	.179	145	352

Central Division

	W	L	T	Pct.	Pts.	OP
Green Bay	10	4	0	.714	304	226
Detroit	8	5	1	.607	339	290
Minnesota	7	7	0	.500	301	252
Chicago	4	9	1	.321	225	275

Western Division

	W	L	T	Pct.	Pts.	OP
San Francisco	8	5	1	.607	353	249
Atlanta	7	7	0	.500	269	274
Los Angeles	6	7	1	.464	291	286
New Orleans	2	11	1	.179	215	361

**Wild Card qualifier for playoffs*

Divisional playoffs: PITTSBURGH 13, Oakland 7; MIAMI 20, Cleveland 14
AFC championship: Miami 21, PITTSBURGH 17
Divisional playoffs: Dallas 30, SAN FRANCISCO 28; WASHINGTON 16, Green Bay 3
NFC championship: WASHINGTON 26, Dallas 3
Super Bowl VII: Miami (AFC) 14, Washington (NFC) 7, at Memorial Coliseum, Los Angeles, Calif.

1971

American Conference

Eastern Division

	W	L	T	Pct.	Pts.	OP
Miami	10	3	1	.769	315	174
Baltimore*	10	4	0	.714	313	140
New England	6	8	0	.429	238	325
N.Y. Jets	6	8	0	.429	212	299
Buffalo	1	13	0	.071	184	394

Central Division

	W	L	T	Pct.	Pts.	OP
Cleveland	9	5	0	.643	285	273
Pittsburgh	6	8	0	.429	246	292
Houston	4	9	1	.308	251	330
Cincinnati	4	10	0	.286	284	265

Western Division

	W	L	T	Pct.	Pts.	OP
Kansas City	10	3	1	.769	302	208
Oakland	8	4	2	.667	344	278
San Diego	6	8	0	.429	311	341
Denver	4	9	1	.308	203	275

National Conference

Eastern Division

	W	L	T	Pct.	Pts.	OP
Dallas	11	3	0	.786	406	222
Washington*	9	4	1	.692	276	190
Philadelphia	6	7	1	.462	221	302
St. Louis	4	9	1	.308	231	279
N.Y. Giants	4	10	0	.286	228	362

Central Division

	W	L	T	Pct.	Pts.	OP
Minnesota	11	3	0	.786	245	139
Detroit	7	6	1	.538	341	286
Chicago	6	8	0	.429	185	276
Green Bay	4	8	2	.333	274	298

Western Division

	W	L	T	Pct.	Pts.	OP
San Francisco	9	5	0	.643	300	216
Los Angeles	8	5	1	.615	313	260
Atlanta	7	6	1	.538	274	277
New Orleans	4	8	2	.333	266	347

**Wild Card qualifier for playoffs*

Divisional playoffs: Miami 27, KANSAS CITY 24 (OT); Baltimore 20, CLEVELAND 3
AFC championship: MIAMI 21, Baltimore 0
Divisional playoffs: Dallas 20, MINNESOTA 12; SAN FRANCISCO 24, Washington 20
NFC championship: DALLAS 14, San Francisco 3
Super Bowl VI: Dallas (NFC) 24, Miami (AFC) 3, at Tulane Stadium, New Orleans, La.

1970

American Conference

Eastern Division

	W	L	T	Pct.	Pts.	OP
Baltimore	11	2	1	.846	321	234
Miami*	10	4	0	.714	297	228
N.Y. Jets	4	10	0	.286	255	286
Buffalo	3	10	1	.231	204	337
Boston Patriots	2	12	0	.143	149	361

Central Division

	W	L	T	Pct.	Pts.	OP
Cincinnati	8	6	0	.571	312	255
Cleveland	7	7	0	.500	286	265
Pittsburgh	5	9	0	.357	210	272
Houston	3	10	1	.231	217	352

Western Division

	W	L	T	Pct.	Pts.	OP
Oakland	8	4	2	.667	300	293
Kansas City	7	5	2	.583	272	244
San Diego	5	6	3	.455	282	278
Denver	5	8	1	.385	253	264

National Conference

Eastern Division

	W	L	T	Pct.	Pts.	OP
Dallas	10	4	0	.714	299	221
N.Y. Giants	9	5	0	.643	301	270
St. Louis	8	5	1	.615	325	228
Washington	6	8	0	.429	297	314
Philadelphia	3	10	1	.231	241	332

Central Division

	W	L	T	Pct.	Pts.	OP
Minnesota	12	2	0	.857	335	143
Detroit*	10	4	0	.714	347	202
Chicago	6	8	0	.429	256	261
Green Bay	6	8	0	.429	196	293

Western Division

	W	L	T	Pct.	Pts.	OP
San Francisco	10	3	1	.769	352	267
Los Angeles	9	4	1	.692	325	202
Atlanta	4	8	2	.333	206	261
New Orleans	2	11	1	.154	172	347

**Wild Card qualifier for playoffs*

Divisional playoffs: BALTIMORE 17, Cincinnati 0; OAKLAND 21, Miami 14
AFC championship: BALTIMORE 27, Oakland 17
Divisional playoffs: DALLAS 5, Detroit 0; San Francisco 17, MINNESOTA 14
NFC championship: Dallas 17, SAN FRANCISCO 10
Super Bowl V: Baltimore (AFC) 16, Dallas (NFC) 13, at Orange Bowl, Miami, Fla.

1969 NFL

Eastern Conference

Capitol Division

	W	L	T	Pct.	Pts.	OP
Dallas	11	2	1	.846	369	223
Washington	7	5	2	.583	307	319
New Orleans	5	9	0	.357	311	393
Philadelphia	4	9	1	.308	279	377

Century Division

	W	L	T	Pct.	Pts.	OP
Cleveland	10	3	1	.769	351	300
N.Y. Giants	6	8	0	.429	264	298
St. Louis	4	9	1	.308	314	389
Pittsburgh	1	13	0	.071	218	404

Western Conference

Coastal Division

	W	L	T	Pct.	Pts.	OP
Los Angeles	11	3	0	.786	320	243
Baltimore	8	5	1	.615	279	268
Atlanta	6	8	0	.429	276	268
San Francisco	4	8	2	.333	277	319

Central Division

	W	L	T	Pct.	Pts.	OP
Minnesota	12	2	0	.857	379	133
Detroit	9	4	1	.692	259	188
Green Bay	8	6	0	.571	269	221
Chicago	1	13	0	.071	210	339

Conference championships: Cleveland 38, DALLAS 14; MINNESOTA 23, Los Angeles 20
NFL championship: MINNESOTA 27, Cleveland 7
Super Bowl IV: Kansas City (AFL) 23, Minnesota (NFL) 7, at Tulane Stadium, New Orleans, La.

1969 AFL

Eastern Division

	W	L	T	Pct.	Pts.	OP
N.Y. Jets	10	4	0	.714	353	269
Houston	6	6	2	.500	278	279
Boston Patriots	4	10	0	.286	266	316
Buffalo	4	10	0	.286	230	359
Miami	3	10	1	.231	233	332

Western Division

	W	L	T	Pct.	Pts.	OP
Oakland	12	1	1	.923	377	242
Kansas City	11	3	0	.786	359	177
San Diego	8	6	0	.571	288	276
Denver	5	8	1	.385	297	344
Cincinnati	4	9	1	.308	280	367

Divisional Playoffs: Kansas City 13, N.Y. JETS 6; OAKLAND 56, Houston 7
AFL championship: Kansas City 17, OAKLAND 7

1968 NFL

Eastern Conference

Capitol Division

	W	L	T	Pct.	Pts.	OP
Dallas	12	2	0	.857	431	186
N.Y. Giants	7	7	0	.500	294	325
Washington	5	9	0	.357	249	358
Philadelphia	2	12	0	.143	202	351

Century Division

	W	L	T	Pct.	Pts.	OP
Cleveland	10	4	0	.714	394	273
St. Louis	9	4	1	.692	325	289
New Orleans	4	9	1	.308	246	327
Pittsburgh	2	11	1	.154	244	397

Western Conference

Coastal Division

	W	L	T	Pct.	Pts.	OP
Baltimore	13	1	0	.929	402	144
Los Angeles	10	3	1	.769	312	200
San Francisco	7	6	1	.538	303	310
Atlanta	2	12	0	.143	170	389

Central Division

	W	L	T	Pct.	Pts.	OP
Minnesota	8	6	0	.571	282	242
Chicago	7	7	0	.500	250	333
Green Bay	6	7	1	.462	281	227
Detroit	4	8	2	.333	207	241

Conference championships: CLEVELAND 31, Dallas 20; BALTIMORE 24, Minnesota 14
NFL championship: Baltimore 34, CLEVELAND 0
Super Bowl III: N.Y. Jets (AFL) 16, Baltimore (NFL) 7, at Orange Bowl, Miami, Fla.

1968 AFL

Eastern Division

	W	L	T	Pct.	Pts.	OP
N.Y. Jets	11	3	0	.786	419	280
Houston	7	7	0	.500	303	248
Miami	5	8	1	.385	276	355
Boston Patriots	4	10	0	.286	229	406
Buffalo	1	12	1	.077	199	367

Western Division

	W	L	T	Pct.	Pts.	OP
Oakland	12	2	0	.857	453	233
Kansas City	12	2	0	.857	371	170
San Diego	9	5	0	.643	382	310
Denver	5	9	0	.357	255	404
Cincinnati	3	11	0	.214	215	329

Western Division playoff: OAKLAND 41, Kansas City 6
AFL championship: N.Y. JETS 27, Oakland 23

1967 NFL

Eastern Conference

Capitol Division

	W	L	T	Pct.	Pts.	OP
Dallas	9	5	0	.643	342	268
Philadelphia	6	7	1	.462	351	409
Washington	5	6	3	.455	347	353
New Orleans	3	11	0	.214	233	379

Century Division

	W	L	T	Pct.	Pts.	OP
Cleveland	9	5	0	.643	334	297
N.Y. Giants	7	7	0	.500	369	379
St. Louis	6	7	1	.462	333	356
Pittsburgh	4	9	1	.308	281	320

Western Conference

Coastal Division

	W	L	T	Pct.	Pts.	OP
Los Angeles	11	1	2	.917	398	196
Baltimore	11	1	2	.917	394	198
San Francisco	7	7	0	.500	273	337
Atlanta	1	12	1	.077	175	422

Central Division

	W	L	T	Pct.	Pts.	OP
Green Bay	9	4	1	.692	332	209
Chicago	7	6	1	.538	239	218
Detroit	5	7	2	.417	260	259
Minnesota	3	8	3	.273	233	294

Los Angeles won division title on the basis of advantage in points (58-34) in two games vs. Baltimore.

Conference championships: DALLAS 52, Cleveland 14; GREEN BAY 28, Los Angeles 7

NFL championship: GREEN BAY 21, Dallas 17

Super Bowl II: Green Bay (NFL) 33, Oakland (AFL) 14, at Orange Bowl, Miami, Fla.

1967 AFL

Eastern Division

	W	L	T	Pct.	Pts.	OP
Houston	9	4	1	.692	258	199
N.Y. Jets	8	5	1	.615	371	329
Buffalo	4	10	0	.286	237	285
Miami	4	10	0	.286	219	407
Boston Patriots	3	10	1	.231	280	389

Western Division

	W	L	T	Pct.	Pts.	OP
Oakland	13	1	0	.929	468	233
Kansas City	9	5	0	.643	408	254
San Diego	8	5	1	.615	360	352
Denver	3	11	0	.214	256	409

AFL championship: OAKLAND 40, Houston 7

1966 NFL

Eastern Conference

	W	L	T	Pct.	Pts.	OP
Dallas	10	3	1	.769	445	239
Cleveland	9	5	0	.643	403	259
Philadelphia	9	5	0	.643	326	340
St. Louis	8	5	1	.615	264	265
Washington	7	7	0	.500	351	355
Pittsburgh	5	8	1	.385	316	347
Atlanta	3	11	0	.214	204	437
N.Y. Giants	1	12	1	.077	263	501

Western Conference

	W	L	T	Pct.	Pts.	OP
Green Bay	12	2	0	.857	335	163
Baltimore	9	5	0	.643	314	226
Los Angeles	8	6	0	.571	289	212
San Francisco	6	6	2	.500	320	325
Chicago	5	7	2	.417	234	272
Detroit	4	9	1	.308	206	317
Minnesota	4	9	1	.308	292	304

NFL championship: Green Bay 34, DALLAS 27

Super Bowl I: Green Bay (NFL) 35, Kansas City (AFL) 10, at Memorial Coliseum, Los Angeles, Calif.

1966 AFL

Eastern Division

	W	L	T	Pct.	Pts.	OP
Buffalo	9	4	1	.692	358	255
Boston Patriots	8	4	2	.677	315	283
N.Y. Jets	6	6	2	.500	322	312
Houston	3	11	0	.214	335	396
Miami	3	11	0	.214	213	362

Western Division

	W	L	T	Pct.	Pts.	OP
Kansas City	11	2	1	.846	448	276
Oakland	8	5	1	.615	315	288
San Diego	7	6	1	.538	335	284
Denver	4	10	0	.286	196	381

AFL championship: Kansas City 31, BUFFALO 7

1965 NFL

Eastern Conference

	W	L	T	Pct.	Pts.	OP
Cleveland	11	3	0	.786	363	325
Dallas	7	7	0	.500	325	280
N.Y. Giants	7	7	0	.500	270	338
Washington	6	8	0	.429	257	301
Philadelphia	5	9	0	.357	363	359
St. Louis	5	9	0	.357	296	309
Pittsburgh	2	12	0	.143	202	397

Western Conference

	W	L	T	Pct.	Pts.	OP
Green Bay	10	3	1	.769	316	224
Baltimore	10	3	1	.769	389	284
Chicago	9	5	0	.643	409	275
San Francisco	7	6	1	.538	421	402
Minnesota	7	7	0	.500	383	403
Detroit	6	7	1	.462	257	295
Los Angeles	4	10	0	.286	269	328

Western Conference playoff: GREEN BAY 13, Baltimore 10 (OT)

NFL championship: GREEN BAY 23, Cleveland 12

1965 AFL

Eastern Division

	W	L	T	Pct.	Pts.	OP
Buffalo	10	3	1	.769	313	226
N.Y. Jets	5	8	1	.385	285	303
Boston Patriots	4	8	2	.333	244	302
Houston	4	10	0	.286	298	429

Western Division

	W	L	T	Pct.	Pts.	OP
San Diego	9	2	3	.818	340	227
Oakland	8	5	1	.615	298	239
Kansas City	7	5	2	.583	322	285
Denver	4	10	0	.286	303	392

AFL championship: Buffalo 23, SAN DIEGO 0

1964 NFL

Eastern Conference

	W	L	T	Pct.	Pts.	OP
Cleveland	10	3	1	.769	415	293
St. Louis	9	3	2	.750	357	331
Philadelphia	6	8	0	.429	312	313
Washington	6	8	0	.429	307	305
Dallas	5	8	1	.385	250	289
Pittsburgh	5	9	0	.357	253	315
N.Y. Giants	2	10	2	.167	241	399

Western Conference

	W	L	T	Pct.	Pts.	OP
Baltimore	12	2	0	.857	428	225
Green Bay	8	5	1	.615	342	245
Minnesota	8	5	1	.615	355	296
Detroit	7	5	2	.583	280	260
Los Angeles	5	7	2	.417	283	339
Chicago	5	9	0	.357	260	379
San Francisco	4	10	0	.286	236	330

NFL championship: CLEVELAND 27, Baltimore 0

1964 AFL

Eastern Division

	W	L	T	Pct.	Pts.	OP
Buffalo	12	2	0	.857	400	242
Boston Patriots	10	3	1	.769	365	297
N.Y. Jets	5	8	1	.385	278	315
Houston	4	10	0	.286	310	355

Western Division

	W	L	T	Pct.	Pts.	OP
San Diego	8	5	1	.615	341	300
Kansas City	7	7	0	.500	366	306
Oakland	5	7	2	.417	303	350
Denver	2	11	1	.154	240	438

AFL championship: BUFFALO 20, San Diego 7

1963 NFL

Eastern Conference

	W	L	T	Pct.	Pts.	OP
N.Y. Giants	11	3	0	.786	448	280
Cleveland	10	4	0	.714	343	262
St. Louis	9	5	0	.643	341	283
Pittsburgh	7	4	3	.636	321	295
Dallas	4	10	0	.286	305	378
Washington	3	11	0	.214	279	398
Philadelphia	2	10	2	.167	242	381

Western Conference

	W	L	T	Pct.	Pts.	OP
Chicago	11	1	2	.917	301	144
Green Bay	11	2	1	.846	369	206
Baltimore	8	6	0	.571	316	285
Detroit	5	8	1	.385	326	265
Minnesota	5	8	1	.385	309	390
Los Angeles	5	9	0	.357	210	350
San Francisco	2	12	0	.143	198	391

NFL championship: CHICAGO 14, N.Y. Giants 10

1963 AFL

Eastern Division

	W	L	T	Pct.	Pts.	OP
Boston Patriots	7	6	1	.538	317	257
Buffalo	7	6	1	.538	304	291
Houston	6	8	0	.429	302	372
N.Y. Jets	5	8	1	.385	249	399

Western Division

	W	L	T	Pct.	Pts.	OP
San Diego	11	3	0	.786	399	256
Oakland	10	4	0	.714	363	288
Kansas City	5	7	2	.417	347	263
Denver	2	11	1	.154	301	473

Eastern Division playoff: Boston 26, BUFFALO 8

AFL championship: SAN DIEGO 51, Boston 10

1962 NFL

Eastern Conference

	W	L	T	Pct.	Pts.	OP
N.Y. Giants	12	2	0	.857	398	283
Pittsburgh	9	5	0	.643	312	363
Cleveland	7	6	1	.538	291	257
Washington	5	7	2	.417	305	376
Dallas Cowboys	5	8	1	.385	398	402
St. Louis	4	9	1	.308	287	361
Philadelphia	3	10	1	.231	282	356

Western Conference

	W	L	T	Pct.	Pts.	OP
Green Bay	13	1	0	.929	415	148
Detroit	11	3	0	.786	315	177
Chicago	9	5	0	.643	321	287
Baltimore	7	7	0	.500	293	288
San Francisco	6	8	0	.429	282	331
Minnesota	2	11	1	.154	254	410
Los Angeles	1	12	1	.077	220	334

NFL championship: Green Bay 16, N.Y. GIANTS 7

1962 AFL

Eastern Division

	W	L	T	Pct.	Pts.	OP
Houston	11	3	0	.786	387	270
Boston Patriots	9	4	1	.692	346	295
Buffalo	7	6	1	.538	309	272
N.Y. Titans	5	9	0	.357	278	423

Western Division

	W	L	T	Pct.	Pts.	OP
Dallas Texans	11	3	0	.786	389	233
Denver	7	7	0	.500	353	334
San Diego	4	10	0	.286	314	392
Oakland	1	13	0	.071	213	370

AFL championship: Dallas Texans 20, HOUSTON 17 (OT)

1961 NFL

Eastern Conference

	W	L	T	Pct.	Pts.	OP
N.Y. Giants	10	3	1	.769	368	220
Philadelphia	10	4	0	.714	361	297
Cleveland	8	5	1	.615	319	270
St. Louis	7	7	0	.500	279	267
Pittsburgh	6	8	0	.429	295	287
Dallas Cowboys	4	9	1	.308	236	380
Washington	1	12	1	.077	174	392

Western Conference

	W	L	T	Pct.	Pts.	OP
Green Bay	11	3	0	.786	391	223
Detroit	8	5	1	.615	270	258
Baltimore	8	6	0	.571	302	307
Chicago	8	6	0	.571	326	302
San Francisco	7	6	1	.538	346	272
Los Angeles	4	10	0	.286	263	333
Minnesota	3	11	0	.214	285	407

NFL championship: GREEN BAY 37, N.Y. Giants 0

1961 AFL

Eastern Division

	W	L	T	Pct.	Pts.	OP
Houston	10	3	1	.769	513	242
Boston Patriots	9	4	1	.692	413	313
N.Y. Titans	7	7	0	.500	301	390
Buffalo	6	8	0	.429	294	342

Western Division

	W	L	T	Pct.	Pts.	OP
San Diego	12	2	0	.857	396	219
Dallas Texans	6	8	0	.429	334	343
Denver	3	11	0	.214	251	432
Oakland	2	12	0	.143	237	458

AFL championship: Houston 10, SAN DIEGO 3

1960 NFL

Eastern Conference

	W	L	T	Pct.	Pts.	OP
Philadelphia	10	2	0	.833	321	246
Cleveland	8	3	1	.727	362	217
N.Y. Giants	6	4	2	.600	271	261
St. Louis	6	5	1	.545	288	230
Pittsburgh	5	6	1	.455	240	275
Washington	1	9	2	.100	178	309

Western Conference

	W	L	T	Pct.	Pts.	OP
Green Bay	8	4	0	.667	332	209
Detroit	7	5	0	.583	239	212
San Francisco	7	5	0	.583	208	205
Baltimore	6	6	0	.500	288	234
Chicago	5	6	1	.455	194	299
L.A. Rams	4	7	1	.364	265	297
Dallas Cowboys	0	11	1	.000	177	369

NFL championship: PHILADELPHIA 17, Green Bay 13

1960 AFL

Eastern Conference

	W	L	T	Pct.	Pts.	OP
Houston	10	4	0	.714	379	285
N.Y. Titans	7	7	0	.500	382	399
Buffalo	5	8	1	.385	296	303
Boston	5	9	0	.357	286	349

Western Conference

	W	L	T	Pct.	Pts.	OP
L.A. Chargers	10	4	0	.714	373	336
Dallas Texans	8	6	0	.571	362	253
Oakland	6	8	0	.429	319	388
Denver	4	9	1	.308	309	393

AFL championship: HOUSTON 24, L.A. Chargers 16

1959

Eastern Conference

	W	L	T	Pct.	Pts.	OP
N.Y. Giants	10	2	0	.833	284	170
Cleveland	7	5	0	.583	270	214
Philadelphia	7	5	0	.583	268	278
Pittsburgh	6	5	1	.545	257	216
Washington	3	9	0	.250	185	350
Chi. Cardinals	2	10	0	.167	234	324

Western Conference

	W	L	T	Pct.	Pts.	OP
Baltimore	9	3	0	.750	374	251
Chi. Bears	8	4	0	.667	252	196
Green Bay	7	5	0	.583	248	246
San Francisco	7	5	0	.583	255	237
Detroit	3	8	1	.273	203	275
Los Angeles	2	10	0	.167	242	315

NFL championship: BALTIMORE 31, N.Y. Giants 16

1958

Eastern Conference

	W	L	T	Pct.	Pts.	OP
N.Y. Giants	9	3	0	.750	246	183
Cleveland	9	3	0	.750	302	217
Pittsburgh	7	4	1	.636	261	230
Washington	4	7	1	.364	214	268
Chi. Cardinals	2	9	1	.182	261	356
Philadelphia	2	9	1	.182	235	306

Western Conference

	W	L	T	Pct.	Pts.	OP
Baltimore	9	3	0	.750	381	203
Chi. Bears	8	4	0	.667	298	230
Los Angeles	8	4	0	.667	344	278
San Francisco	6	6	0	.500	257	324
Detroit	4	7	1	.364	261	276
Green Bay	1	10	1	.091	193	382

Eastern Conference playoff: N.Y. GIANTS 10, Cleveland 0
NFL championship: Baltimore 23, N.Y. GIANTS 17 (OT)

1957

Eastern Conference

	W	L	T	Pct.	Pts.	OP
Cleveland	9	2	1	.818	269	172
N.Y. Giants	7	5	0	.583	254	211
Pittsburgh	6	6	0	.500	161	178
Washington	5	6	1	.455	251	230
Philadelphia	4	8	0	.333	173	230
Chi. Cardinals	3	9	0	.250	200	299

Western Conference

	W	L	T	Pct.	Pts.	OP
Detroit	8	4	0	.667	251	231
San Francisco	8	4	0	.667	260	264
Baltimore	7	5	0	.583	303	235
Los Angeles	6	6	0	.500	307	278
Chi. Bears	5	7	0	.417	203	211
Green Bay	3	9	0	.250	218	311

Western Conference playoff: Detroit 31, SAN FRANCISCO 27
NFL championship: DETROIT 59, Cleveland 14

1956

Eastern Conference

	W	L	T	Pct.	Pts.	OP
N.Y. Giants	8	3	1	.727	264	197
Chi. Cardinals	7	5	0	.583	240	182
Washington	6	6	0	.500	183	225
Cleveland	5	7	0	.417	167	177
Pittsburgh	5	7	0	.417	217	250
Philadelphia	3	8	1	.273	143	215

Western Conference

	W	L	T	Pct.	Pts.	OP
Chi. Bears	9	2	1	.818	363	246
Detroit	9	3	0	.750	300	188
San Francisco	5	6	1	.455	233	284
Baltimore	5	7	0	.417	270	322
Green Bay	4	8	0	.333	264	342
Los Angeles	4	8	0	.333	291	307

NFL championship: N.Y. GIANTS 47, Chi. Bears 7

1955

Eastern Conference

	W	L	T	Pct.	Pts.	OP
Cleveland	9	2	1	.818	349	218
Washington	8	4	0	.667	246	222
N.Y. Giants	6	5	1	.545	267	223
Chi. Cardinals	4	7	1	.364	224	252
Philadelphia	4	7	1	.364	248	231
Pittsburgh	4	8	0	.333	195	285

Western Conference

	W	L	T	Pct.	Pts.	OP
Los Angeles	8	3	1	.727	260	231
Chi. Bears	8	4	0	.667	294	251
Green Bay	6	6	0	.500	258	276
Baltimore	5	6	1	.455	214	239
San Francisco	4	8	0	.333	216	298
Detroit	3	9	0	.250	230	275

NFL championship: Cleveland 38, LOS ANGELES 14

1954

Eastern Conference

	W	L	T	Pct.	Pts.	OP
Cleveland	9	3	0	.750	336	162
Philadelphia	7	4	1	.636	284	230
N.Y. Giants	7	5	0	.583	293	184
Pittsburgh	5	7	0	.417	219	263
Washington	3	9	0	.250	207	432
Chi. Cardinals	2	10	0	.167	183	347

Western Conference

	W	L	T	Pct.	Pts.	OP
Detroit	9	2	1	.818	337	189
Chi. Bears	8	4	0	.667	301	279
San Francisco	7	4	1	.636	313	251
Los Angeles	6	5	1	.545	314	285
Green Bay	4	8	0	.333	234	251
Baltimore	3	9	0	.250	131	279

NFL championship: CLEVELAND 56, Detroit 10

1953

Eastern Conference

	W	L	T	Pct.	Pts.	OP
Cleveland	11	1	0	.917	348	162
Philadelphia	7	4	1	.636	352	215
Washington	6	5	1	.545	208	215
Pittsburgh	6	6	0	.500	211	263
N.Y. Giants	3	9	0	.250	179	277
Chi. Cardinals	1	10	1	.091	190	337

Western Conference

	W	L	T	Pct.	Pts.	OP
Detroit	10	2	0	.833	271	205
San Francisco	9	3	0	.750	372	237
Los Angeles	8	3	1	.727	366	236
Chi. Bears	3	8	1	.273	218	262
Baltimore	3	9	0	.250	182	350
Green Bay	2	9	1	.182	200	338

NFL championship: DETROIT 17, Cleveland 16

1952

American Conference

	W	L	T	Pct.	Pts.	OP
Cleveland	8	4	0	.667	310	213
N.Y. Giants	7	5	0	.583	234	231
Philadelphia	7	5	0	.583	252	271
Pittsburgh	5	7	0	.417	300	273
Chi. Cardinals	4	8	0	.333	172	221
Washington	4	8	0	.333	240	287

National Conference

	W	L	T	Pct.	Pts.	OP
Detroit	9	3	0	.750	344	192
Los Angeles	9	3	0	.750	349	234
San Francisco	7	5	0	.583	285	221
Green Bay	6	6	0	.500	295	312
Chi. Bears	5	7	0	.417	245	326
Dallas Texans	1	11	0	.083	182	427

National Conference playoff: DETROIT 31, Los Angeles 21
NFL championship: Detroit 17, CLEVELAND 7

1951

American Conference

	W	L	T	Pct.	Pts.	OP
Cleveland	11	1	0	.917	331	152
N.Y. Giants	9	2	1	.818	254	161
Washington	5	7	0	.417	183	296
Pittsburgh	4	7	1	.364	183	235
Philadelphia	4	8	0	.333	234	264
Chi. Cardinals	3	9	0	.250	210	287

National Conference

	W	L	T	Pct.	Pts.	OP
Los Angeles	8	4	0	.667	392	261
Detroit	7	4	1	.636	336	259
San Francisco	7	4	1	.636	255	205
Chi. Bears	7	5	0	.583	286	282
Green Bay	3	9	0	.250	254	375
N.Y. Yanks	1	9	2	.100	241	382

NFL championship: LOS ANGELES 24, Cleveland 17

1950

American Conference

	W	L	T	Pct.	Pts.	OP
Cleveland	10	2	0	.833	310	144
N.Y. Giants	10	2	0	.833	268	150
Philadelphia	6	6	0	.500	254	141
Pittsburgh	6	6	0	.500	180	195
Chi. Cardinals	5	7	0	.417	233	287
Washington	3	9	0	.250	232	326

National Conference

	W	L	T	Pct.	Pts.	OP
Los Angeles	9	3	0	.750	466	309
Chi. Bears	9	3	0	.750	279	207
N.Y. Yanks	7	5	0	.583	366	367
Detroit	6	6	0	.500	321	285
Green Bay	3	9	0	.250	244	406
San Francisco	3	9	0	.250	213	300
Baltimore	1	11	0	.083	213	462

American Conference playoff: CLEVELAND 8, N.Y. Giants 3
National Conference playoff: LOS ANGELES 24, Chi. Bears 14
NFL championship: CLEVELAND 30, Los Angeles 28

1949

Eastern Division

	W	L	T	Pct.	Pts.	OP
Philadelphia	11	1	0	.917	364	134
Pittsburgh	6	5	1	.545	224	214
N.Y. Giants	6	6	0	.500	287	298
Washington	4	7	1	.364	268	339
N.Y. Bulldogs	1	10	1	.091	153	365

Western Division

	W	L	T	Pct.	Pts.	OP
Los Angeles	8	2	2	.800	360	239
Chi. Bears	9	3	0	.750	332	218
Chi. Cardinals	6	5	1	.545	360	301
Detroit	4	8	0	.333	237	259
Green Bay	2	10	0	.167	114	329

NFL championship: Philadelphia 14, LOS ANGELES 0

1948

Eastern Division

	W	L	T	Pct.	Pts.	OP
Philadelphia	9	2	1	.818	376	156
Washington	7	5	0	.583	291	287
N.Y. Giants	4	8	0	.333	297	388
Pittsburgh	4	8	0	.333	200	243
Boston	3	9	0	.250	174	372

Western Division

	W	L	T	Pct.	Pts.	OP
Chi. Cardinals	11	1	0	.917	395	226
Chi. Bears	10	2	0	.833	375	151
Los Angeles	6	5	1	.545	327	269
Green Bay	3	9	0	.250	154	290
Detroit	2	10	0	.167	200	407

NFL championship: PHILADELPHIA 7, Chi. Cardinals 0

1947

Eastern Division

	W	L	T	Pct.	Pts.	OP
Philadelphia	8	4	0	.667	308	242
Pittsburgh	8	4	0	.667	240	259
Boston	4	7	1	.364	168	256
Washington	4	8	0	.333	295	367
N.Y. Giants	2	8	2	.200	190	309

Western Division

	W	L	T	Pct.	Pts.	OP
Chi. Cardinals	9	3	0	.750	306	231
Chi. Bears	8	4	0	.667	363	241
Green Bay	6	5	1	.545	274	210
Los Angeles	6	6	0	.500	259	214
Detroit	3	9	0	.250	231	305

Eastern Division playoff: Philadelphia 21, PITTSBURGH 0
NFL championship: CHI. CARDINALS 28, Philadelphia 21

1946

Eastern Division

	W	L	T	Pct.	Pts.	OP
N.Y. Giants	7	3	1	.700	236	162
Philadelphia	6	5	0	.545	231	220
Washington	5	5	1	.500	171	191
Pittsburgh	5	5	1	.500	136	117
Boston	2	8	1	.200	189	273

Western Division

	W	L	T	Pct.	Pts.	OP
Chi. Bears	8	2	1	.800	289	193
Los Angeles	6	4	1	.600	277	257
Green Bay	6	5	0	.545	148	158
Chi. Cardinals	6	5	0	.545	260	198
Detroit	1	10	0	.091	142	310

NFL championship: Chi. Bears 24, N.Y. GIANTS 14

1945

Eastern Division

	W	L	T	Pct.	Pts.	OP
Washington	8	2	0	.800	209	121
Philadelphia	7	3	0	.700	272	133
N.Y. Giants	3	6	1	.333	179	198
Boston	3	6	1	.333	123	211
Pittsburgh	2	8	0	.200	79	220

Western Division

	W	L	T	Pct.	Pts.	OP
Cleveland	9	1	0	.900	244	136
Detroit	7	3	0	.700	195	194
Green Bay	6	4	0	.600	258	173
Chi. Bears	3	7	0	.300	192	235
Chi. Cardinals	1	9	0	.100	98	228

NFL championship: CLEVELAND 15, Washington 14

1944

Eastern Division

	W	L	T	Pct.	Pts.	OP
N.Y. Giants	8	1	1	.889	206	75
Philadelphia	7	1	2	.875	267	131
Washington	6	3	1	.667	169	180
Boston	2	8	0	.200	82	233
Brooklyn	0	10	0	.000	69	166

Western Division

	W	L	T	Pct.	Pts.	OP
Green Bay	8	2	0	.800	238	141
Chi. Bears	6	3	1	.667	258	172
Detroit	6	3	1	.667	216	151
Cleveland	4	6	0	.400	188	224
Card-Pitt	0	10	0	.000	108	328

NFL championship: Green Bay 14, N.Y. GIANTS 7

1943

Eastern Division

	W	L	T	Pct.	Pts.	OP
Washington	6	3	1	.667	229	137
N.Y. Giants	6	3	1	.667	197	170
Phil-Pitt	5	4	1	.556	225	230
Brooklyn	2	8	0	.200	65	234

Western Division

	W	L	T	Pct.	Pts.	OP
Chi. Bears	8	1	1	.889	303	157
Green Bay	7	2	1	.778	264	172
Detroit	3	6	1	.333	178	218
Chi. Cardinals	0	10	0	.000	95	238

Eastern Division playoff: Washington 28, N.Y. GIANTS 0
NFL championship: CHI. BEARS 41, Washington 21

1942

Eastern Division

	W	L	T	Pct.	Pts.	OP
Washington	10	1	0	.909	227	102
Pittsburgh	7	4	0	.636	167	119
N.Y. Giants	5	5	1	.500	155	139
Brooklyn	3	8	0	.273	100	168
Philadelphia	2	9	0	.182	134	239

Western Division

	W	L	T	Pct.	Pts.	OP
Chi. Bears	11	0	0	1.000	376	84
Green Bay	8	2	1	.800	300	215
Cleveland	5	6	0	.455	150	207
Chi. Cardinals	3	8	0	.273	98	209
Detroit	0	11	0	.000	38	263

NFL championship: WASHINGTON 14, Chi. Bears 6

1941

Eastern Division

	W	L	T	Pct.	Pts.	OP
N.Y. Giants	8	3	0	.727	238	114
Brooklyn	7	4	0	.636	158	127
Washington	6	5	0	.545	176	174
Philadelphia	2	8	1	.200	119	218
Pittsburgh	1	9	1	.100	103	276

Western Division

	W	L	T	Pct.	Pts.	OP
Chi. Bears	10	1	0	.909	396	147
Green Bay	10	1	0	.909	258	120
Detroit	4	6	1	.400	121	195
Chi. Cardinals	3	7	1	.300	127	197
Cleveland	2	9	0	.182	116	244

Western Division playoff: CHI. BEARS 33, Green Bay 14
NFL championship: CHI. BEARS 37, N.Y. Giants 9

1940

Eastern Division

	W	L	T	Pct.	Pts.	OP
Washington	9	2	0	.818	245	142
Brooklyn	8	3	0	.727	186	120
N.Y. Giants	6	4	1	.600	131	133
Pittsburgh	2	7	2	.222	60	178
Philadelphia	1	10	0	.091	111	211

Western Division

	W	L	T	Pct.	Pts.	OP
Chi. Bears	8	3	0	.727	238	152
Green Bay	6	4	1	.600	238	155
Detroit	5	5	1	.500	138	153
Cleveland	4	6	1	.400	171	191
Chi. Cardinals	2	7	2	.222	139	222

NFL championship: Chi. Bears 73, WASHINGTON 0

1939

Eastern Division

	W	L	T	Pct.	Pts.	OP
N.Y. Giants	9	1	1	.900	168	85
Washington	8	2	1	.800	242	94
Brooklyn	4	6	1	.400	108	219
Philadelphia	1	9	1	.100	105	200
Pittsburgh	1	9	1	.100	114	216

Western Division

	W	L	T	Pct.	Pts.	OP
Green Bay	9	2	0	.818	233	153
Chi. Bears	8	3	0	.727	298	157
Detroit	6	5	0	.545	145	150
Cleveland	5	5	1	.500	195	164
Chi. Cardinals	1	10	0	.091	84	254

NFL championship: GREEN BAY 27, N.Y. Giants 0

1938

Eastern Division

	W	L	T	Pct.	Pts.	OP
N.Y. Giants	8	2	1	.800	194	79
Washington	6	3	2	.667	148	154
Brooklyn	4	4	3	.500	131	161
Philadelphia	5	6	0	.455	154	164
Pittsburgh	2	9	0	.182	79	169

Western Division

	W	L	T	Pct.	Pts.	OP
Green Bay	8	3	0	.727	223	118
Detroit	7	4	0	.636	119	108
Chi. Bears	6	5	0	.545	194	148
Cleveland	4	7	0	.364	131	215
Chi. Cardinals	2	9	0	.182	111	168

NFL championship: N.Y. GIANTS 23, Green Bay 17

1937

Eastern Division

	W	L	T	Pct.	Pts.	OP
Washington	8	3	0	.727	195	120
N.Y. Giants	6	3	2	.667	128	109
Pittsburgh	4	7	0	.364	122	145
Brooklyn	3	7	1	.300	82	174
Philadelphia	2	8	1	.200	86	177

Western Division

	W	L	T	Pct.	Pts.	OP
Chi. Bears	9	1	1	.900	201	100
Green Bay	7	4	0	.636	220	122
Detroit	7	4	0	.636	180	105
Chi. Cardinals	5	5	1	.500	135	165
Cleveland	1	10	0	.091	75	207

NFL championship: Washington 28, CHI. BEARS 21

1936

Eastern Division

	W	L	T	Pct.	Pts.	OP
Boston	7	5	0	.583	149	110
Pittsburgh	6	6	0	.500	98	187
N.Y. Giants	5	6	1	.455	115	163
Brooklyn	3	8	1	.273	92	161
Philadelphia	1	11	0	.083	51	206

Western Division

	W	L	T	Pct.	Pts.	OP
Green Bay	10	1	1	.909	248	118
Chi. Bears	9	3	0	.750	222	94
Detroit	8	4	0	.667	235	102
Chi. Cardinals	3	8	1	.273	74	143

NFL championship: Green Bay 21, Boston 6, at Polo Grounds, N.Y.

1935

Eastern Division

	W	L	T	Pct.	Pts.	OP
N. Y. Giants	9	3	0	.750	180	96
Brooklyn	5	6	1	.455	90	141
Pittsburgh	4	8	0	.333	100	209
Boston	2	8	1	.200	65	123
Philadelphia	2	9	0	.182	60	179

Western Division

	W	L	T	Pct.	Pts.	OP
Detroit	7	3	2	.700	191	111
Green Bay	8	4	0	.667	181	96
Chi. Bears	6	4	2	.600	192	106
Chi. Cardinals	6	4	2	.600	99	97

NFL championship: DETROIT 26, N.Y. Giants 7
One game between Boston and Philadelphia was canceled.

1934

Eastern Division

	W	L	T	Pct.	Pts.	OP
N.Y. Giants	8	5	0	.615	147	107
Boston	6	6	0	.500	107	94
Brooklyn	4	7	0	.364	61	153
Philadelphia	4	7	0	.364	127	85
Pittsburgh	2	10	0	.167	51	206

Western Division

	W	L	T	Pct.	Pts.	OP
Chi. Bears	13	0	0	1.000	286	86
Detroit	10	3	0	.769	238	59
Green Bay	7	6	0	.538	156	112
Chi. Cardinals	5	6	0	.455	80	84
St. Louis	1	2	0	.333	27	61
Cincinnati	0	8	0	.000	10	243

NFL championship: N.Y. GIANTS 30, Chi. Bears 13

1933

Eastern Division

	W	L	T	Pct.	Pts.	OP
N.Y. Giants	11	3	0	.786	244	101
Brooklyn	5	4	1	.556	93	54
Boston	5	5	2	.500	103	97
Philadelphia	3	5	1	.375	77	158
Pittsburgh	3	6	2	.333	67	208

Western Division

	W	L	T	Pct.	Pts.	OP
Chi. Bears	10	2	1	.833	133	82
Portsmouth	6	5	0	.545	128	87
Green Bay	5	7	1	.417	170	107
Cincinnati	3	6	1	.333	38	110
Chi. Cardinals	1	9	1	.100	52	101

NFL championship: CHI. BEARS 23, N.Y. Giants 21

1932

	W	L	T	Pct.
Chicago Bears	7	1	6	.875
Green Bay Packers	10	3	1	.769
Portsmouth Spartans	6	2	4	.750
Boston Braves	4	4	2	.500
New York Giants	4	6	2	.400
Brooklyn Dodgers	3	9	0	.250
Chicago Cardinals	2	6	2	.250
Staten Island Stapletons	2	7	3	.222

NFL championship:
CHI. BEARS 9, Portsmouth 0

1931

	W	L	T	Pct.
Green Bay Packers	12	2	0	.857
Portsmouth Spartans	11	3	0	.786
Chicago Bears	8	5	0	.615
Chicago Cardinals	5	4	0	.556
New York Giants	7	6	1	.538
Providence Steam Roller	4	4	3	.500
Staten Island Stapletons	4	6	1	.400
Cleveland Indians	2	8	0	.200
Brooklyn Dodgers	2	12	0	.143
Frankford Yellow Jackets	1	6	1	.143

1930

	W	L	T	Pct.
Green Bay Packers	10	3	1	.769
New York Giants	13	4	0	.765
Chicago Bears	9	4	1	.692
Brooklyn Dodgers	7	4	1	.636
Providence Steam Roller	6	4	1	.600
Staten Island Stapletons	5	5	2	.500
Chicago Cardinals	5	6	2	.455
Portsmouth Spartans	5	6	3	.455
Frankford Yellow Jackets	4	13	1	.222
Minneapolis Red Jackets	1	7	1	.125
Newark Tornadoes	1	10	1	.091

1929

	W	L	T	Pct.
Green Bay Packers	12	0	1	1.000
New York Giants	13	1	1	.929
Frankford Yellow Jackets	9	4	5	.692
Chicago Cardinals	6	6	1	.500
Boston Bulldogs	4	4	0	.500
Orange Tornadoes	3	4	4	.429
Staten Island Stapletons	3	4	3	.429
Providence Steam Roller	4	6	2	.400
Chicago Bears	4	9	2	.308
Buffalo Bisons	1	7	1	.125
Minneapolis Red Jackets	1	9	0	.100
Dayton Triangles	0	6	0	.000

1928

	W	L	T	Pct.
Providence Steam Roller	8	1	2	.889
Frankford Yellow Jackets	11	3	2	.786
Detroit Wolverines	7	2	1	.778
Green Bay Packers	6	4	3	.600
Chicago Bears	7	5	1	.583
New York Giants	4	7	2	.364
New York Yankees	4	8	1	.333
Pottsville Maroons	2	8	0	.200
Chicago Cardinals	1	5	0	.167
Dayton Triangles	0	7	0	.000

1927

	W	L	T	Pct.
New York Giants	11	1	1	.917
Green Bay Packers	7	2	1	.778
Chicago Bears	9	3	2	.750
Cleveland Bulldogs	8	4	1	.667
Providence Steam Roller	8	5	1	.615
New York Yankees	7	8	1	.467
Frankford Yellow Jackets	6	9	3	.400
Pottsville Maroons	5	8	0	.385
Chicago Cardinals	3	7	1	.300
Dayton Triangles	1	6	1	.143
Duluth Eskimos	1	8	0	.111
Buffalo Bisons	0	5	0	.000

1926

	W	L	T	Pct.
Frankford Yellow Jackets	14	1	1	.933
Chicago Bears	12	1	3	.923
Pottsville Maroons	10	2	1	.833
Kansas City Cowboys	8	3	0	.727
Green Bay Packers	7	3	3	.700
Los Angeles Buccaneers	6	3	1	.667
New York Giants	8	4	1	.667
Duluth Eskimos	6	5	3	.545
Buffalo Rangers	4	4	2	.500
Chicago Cardinals	5	6	1	.455
Providence Steam Roller	5	7	1	.417
Detroit Panthers	4	6	2	.400
Hartford Blues	3	7	0	.300
Brooklyn Lions	3	8	0	.273
Milwaukee Badgers	2	7	0	.222
Akron Pros	1	4	3	.200
Dayton Triangles	1	4	1	.200
Racine Tornadoes	1	4	0	.200
Columbus Tigers	1	6	0	.143
Canton Bulldogs	1	9	3	.100
Hammond Pros	0	4	0	.000
Louisville Colonels	0	4	0	.000

1925

	W	L	T	Pct.
Chicago Cardinals	11	2	1	.846
Pottsville Maroons	10	2	0	.833
Detroit Panthers	8	2	2	.800
New York Giants	8	4	0	.667
Akron Indians	4	2	2	.667
Frankford Yellow Jackets	13	7	0	.650
Chicago Bears	9	5	3	.643
Rock Island Independents	5	3	3	.625
Green Bay Packers	8	5	0	.615
Providence Steam Roller	6	5	1	.545
Canton Bulldogs	4	4	0	.500
Cleveland Bulldogs	5	8	1	.385
Kansas City Cowboys	2	5	1	.286
Hammond Pros	1	4	0	.250
Buffalo Bisons	1	6	2	.143
Duluth Kelleys	0	3	0	.000
Rochester Jeffersons	0	6	1	.000
Milwaukee Badgers	0	6	0	.000
Dayton Triangles	0	7	1	.000
Columbus Tigers	0	9	0	.000

1924

	W	L	T	Pct.
Cleveland Bulldogs	7	1	1	.875
Chicago Bears	6	1	4	.857
Frankford Yellow Jackets	11	2	1	.846
Duluth Kelleys	5	1	0	.833
Rock Island Independents	6	2	2	.750
Green Bay Packers	7	4	0	.636
Racine Legion	4	3	3	.571
Chicago Cardinals	5	4	1	.556
Buffalo Bisons	6	5	0	.545
Columbus Tigers	4	4	0	.500
Hammond Pros	2	2	1	.500
Milwaukee Badgers	5	8	0	.385
Akron Indians	2	6	0	.333
Dayton Triangles	2	6	0	.333
Kansas City Blues	2	7	0	.222
Kenosha Maroons	0	5	1	.000
Minneapolis Marines	0	6	0	.000
Rochester Jeffersons	0	7	0	.000

1923

	W	L	T	Pct.
Canton Bulldogs	11	0	1	1.000
Chicago Bears	9	2	1	.818
Green Bay Packers	7	2	1	.778
Milwaukee Badgers	7	2	3	.778
Cleveland Indians	3	1	3	.750
Chicago Cardinals	8	4	0	.667
Duluth Kelleys	4	3	0	.571
Columbus Tigers	5	4	1	.556
Buffalo All-Americans	4	4	3	.500
Racine Legion	4	4	2	.500
Toledo Maroons	2	3	2	.400
Rock Island Independents	2	3	3	.400
Minneapolis Marines	2	5	2	.286
St. Louis All-Stars	1	4	2	.200
Hammond Pros	1	5	1	.167
Dayton Triangles	1	6	1	.143
Akron Indians	1	6	0	.143
Oorang Indians	1	10	0	.091
Rochester Jeffersons	0	2	0	.000
Louisville Brecks	0	3	0	.000

1922

	W	L	T	Pct.
Canton Bulldogs	10	0	2	1.000
Chicago Bears	9	3	0	.750
Chicago Cardinals	8	3	0	.727
Toledo Maroons	5	2	2	.714
Rock Island Independents	4	2	1	.667
Racine Legion	6	4	1	.600
Dayton Triangles	4	3	1	.571
Green Bay Packers	4	3	3	.571
Buffalo All-Americans	5	4	1	.556
Akron Pros	3	5	2	.375
Milwaukee Badgers	2	4	3	.333
Oorang Indians	2	6	0	.250
Minneapolis Marines	1	3	0	.250
Louisville Brecks	1	3	0	.250
Evansville Crimson Giants	0	3	0	.000
Rochester Jeffersons	0	4	1	.000
Hammond Pros	0	5	1	.000
Columbus Panhandles	0	7	0	.000

1921

	W	L	T	Pct.
Chicago Staleys	9	1	1	.900
Buffalo All-Americans	9	1	2	.900
Akron Pros	8	3	1	.727
Canton Bulldogs	5	2	3	.714
Rock Island Independents	4	2	1	.667
Evansville Crimson Giants	3	2	0	.600
Green Bay Packers	3	2	1	.600
Dayton Triangles	4	4	1	.500
Chicago Cardinals	3	3	2	.500
Rochester Jeffersons	2	3	0	.400
Cleveland Indians	3	5	0	.375
Washington Senators	1	2	0	.333
Cincinnati Celts	1	3	0	.250
Hammond Pros	1	3	1	.250
Minneapolis Marines	1	3	1	.250
Detroit Heralds	1	5	1	.167
Columbus Panhandles	1	8	0	.111
Tonawanda Kardex	0	1	0	.000
Muncie Flyers	0	2	0	.000
Louisville Brecks	0	2	0	.000
New York Giants	0	2	0	.000

1920

	W	L	T	Pct.
Akron Pros	8	0	3	1.000
Decatur Staleys	10	1	2	.909
Buffalo All-Americans	9	1	1	.900
Chicago Cardinals	6	2	2	.750
Rock Island Independents	6	2	2	.750
Dayton Triangles	5	2	2	.714
Rochester Jeffersons	6	3	2	.667
Canton Bulldogs	7	4	2	.636
Detroit Heralds	2	3	3	.400
Cleveland Tigers	2	4	2	.333
Chicago Tigers	2	5	1	.286
Hammond Pros	2	5	0	.286
Columbus Panhandles	2	6	2	.250
Muncie Flyers	0	1	0	.000

ALL-TIME TEAM VS. TEAM RESULTS

ATLANTA vs. BUFFALO
Series tied, 2-2
1973—Bills, 17-6 (A)
1977—Bills, 3-0 (B)
1980—Falcons, 30-14 (B)
1983—Falcons, 31-14 (A)
(Points—Falcons 67, Bills 48)
ATLANTA vs. CHICAGO
Falcons lead series, 9-6
1966—Bears, 23-6 (C)
1967—Bears, 23-14 (A)
1968—Falcons, 16-13 (C)
1969—Falcons, 48-31 (A)
1970—Bears, 23-14 (A)
1972—Falcons, 37-21 (C)
1973—Falcons, 46-6 (A)
1974—Falcons, 13-10 (A)
1976—Falcons, 10-0 (C)
1977—Falcons, 16-10 (C)
1978—Bears, 13-7 (C)
1980—Falcons, 28-17 (A)
1983—Falcons, 20-17 (C)
1985—Bears, 36-0 (C)
1986—Bears, 13-10 (A)
(Points—Falcons 285, Bears 256)
ATLANTA vs. CINCINNATI
Bengals lead series, 5-1
1971—Falcons, 9-6 (C)
1975—Bengals, 21-14 (A)
1978—Bengals, 37-7 (C)
1981—Bengals, 30-28 (A)
1984—Bengals, 35-14 (C)
1987—Bengals, 16-10 (A)
(Points—Bengals 145, Falcons 82)
ATLANTA vs. CLEVELAND
Browns lead series, 7-1
1966—Browns, 49-17 (A)
1968—Browns, 30-7 (C)
1971—Falcons, 31-14 (C)
1976—Browns, 20-17 (A)
1978—Browns, 24-16 (A)
1981—Browns, 28-17 (C)
1984—Browns, 23-7 (A)
1987—Browns, 38-3 (C)
(Points—Browns 226, Falcons 115)
ATLANTA vs. DALLAS
Cowboys lead series, 8-3
1966—Cowboys, 47-14 (A)
1967—Cowboys, 37-7 (D)
1969—Cowboys, 24-17 (A)
1970—Cowboys, 13-0 (D)
1974—Cowboys, 24-0 (A)
1976—Falcons, 17-10 (A)
1978—*Cowboys, 27-20 (D)
1980—*Cowboys, 30-27 (A)
1985—Cowboys, 24-10 (D)
1986—Falcons, 37-35 (D)
1987—Falcons, 21-10 (D)
(Points—Cowboys 281, Falcons 170)
**NFC Divisional Playoff*
ATLANTA vs. DENVER
Series tied, 3-3
1970—Broncos, 24-10 (D)
1972—Falcons, 23-20 (A)
1975—Falcons, 35-21 (A)
1979—Broncos, 20-17 (A) OT
1982—Falcons, 34-27 (D)
1985—Broncos, 44-28 (A)
(Points—Broncos 156, Falcons 147)
ATLANTA vs. DETROIT
Lions lead series, 13-5
1966—Lions, 28-10 (D)
1967—Lions, 24-3 (D)
1968—Lions, 24-7 (A)
1969—Lions, 27-21 (D)
1971—Lions, 41-38 (D)
1972—Lions, 26-23 (A)
1973—Lions, 31-6 (D)
1975—Lions, 17-14 (A)
1976—Lions, 24-10 (D)
1977—Falcons, 17-6 (A)
1978—Falcons, 14-0 (A)
1979—Lions, 24-23 (D)
1980—Falcons, 43-28 (A)
1983—Falcons, 30-14 (D)
1984—Lions, 27-24 (A) OT
1985—Lions, 28-27 (A)
1986—Falcons, 20-6 (D)
1987—Lions, 30-13 (A)
(Points—Lions 405, Falcons 343)
ATLANTA vs. GREEN BAY
Packers lead series, 8-6
1966—Packers, 56-3 (Mil)
1967—Packers, 23-0 (Mil)
1968—Packers, 38-7 (A)
1969—Packers, 28-10 (GB)
1970—Packers, 27-24 (GB)
1971—Falcons, 28-21 (A)
1972—Falcons, 10-9 (Mil)
1974—Falcons, 10-3 (A)
1975—Packers, 22-13 (GB)
1976—Packers, 24-20 (A)
1979—Falcons, 25-7 (A)
1981—Falcons, 31-17 (GB)
1982—Packers, 38-7 (A)
1983—Falcons, 47-41 (A) OT
(Points—Packers 354, Falcons 235)
ATLANTA vs. HOUSTON
Falcons lead series, 4-2
1972—Falcons, 20-10 (A)
1976—Oilers, 20-14 (H)
1978—Falcons, 20-14 (A)
1981—Falcons, 31-27 (H)
1984—Falcons, 42-10 (A)
1987—Oilers, 37-33 (H)
(Points—Falcons 160, Oilers 118)
ATLANTA vs. *INDIANAPOLIS
Colts lead series, 9-0
1966—Colts, 19-7 (A)
1967—Colts, 38-31 (B)
Colts, 49-7 (A)
1968—Colts, 28-20 (A)
Colts, 44-0 (B)
1969—Colts, 21-14 (A)
Colts, 13-6 (B)
1974—Colts, 17-7 (A)
1986—Colts, 28-23 (A)
(Points—Colts 257, Falcons 115)
**Franchise in Baltimore prior to 1984*
ATLANTA vs. KANSAS CITY
Chiefs lead series, 2-0
1972—Chiefs, 17-14 (A)
1985—Chiefs, 38-10 (KC)
(Points—Chiefs 55, Falcons 24)
ATLANTA vs. *L.A. RAIDERS
Raiders lead series, 4-1
1971—Falcons, 24-13 (A)
1975—Raiders, 37-34 (O) OT
1979—Raiders, 50-19 (O)
1982—Raiders, 38-14 (A)
1985—Raiders, 34-24 (A)
(Points—Raiders 172, Falcons 115)
**Franchise in Oakland prior to 1982*
ATLANTA vs. L.A. RAMS
Rams lead series, 30-10-2
1966—Rams, 19-14 (A)
1967—Rams, 31-3 (A)
Rams, 20-3 (LA)
1968—Rams, 27-14 (LA)
Rams, 17-10 (A)
1969—Rams, 17-7 (LA)
Rams, 38-6 (A)
1970—Tie, 10-10 (LA)
Rams, 17-7 (A)
1971—Tie, 20-20 (LA)
Rams, 24-16 (A)
1972—Falcons, 31-3 (A)
Rams, 20-7 (LA)
1973—Rams, 31-0 (LA)
Falcons, 15-13 (A)
1974—Rams, 21-0 (LA)
Rams, 30-7 (A)
1975—Rams, 22-7 (LA)
Rams, 16-7 (A)
1976—Rams, 30-14 (A)
Rams, 59-0 (LA)
1977—Falcons, 17-6 (A)
Rams, 23-7 (LA)
1978—Rams, 10-0 (LA)
Falcons, 15-7 (A)
1979—Rams, 20-14 (LA)
Rams, 34-13 (A)
1980—Falcons, 13-10 (A)
Rams, 20-17 (LA) OT
1981—Rams, 37-35 (A)
Rams, 21-16 (LA)
1982—Falcons, 34-17 (A)
1983—Rams, 27-21 (LA)
Rams, 36-13 (A)
1984—Falcons, 30-28 (LA)
Rams, 24-10 (A)
1985—Rams, 17-6 (LA)
Falcons, 30-14 (A)
1986—Falcons, 26-14 (A)
Rams, 14-7 (LA)
1987—Falcons, 24-20 (A)
Rams, 33-0 (LA)
(Points—Rams 917, Falcons 546)
ATLANTA vs. MIAMI
Dolphins lead series, 4-1
1970—Dolphins, 20-7 (A)
1974—Dolphins, 42-7 (M)
1980—Dolphins, 20-17 (A)
1983—Dolphins, 31-24 (M)
1986—Falcons, 20-14 (M)
(Points—Dolphins 127, Falcons 75)
ATLANTA vs. MINNESOTA
Vikings lead series, 10-6
1966—Falcons, 20-13 (M)
1967—Falcons, 21-20 (A)
1968—Vikings, 47-7 (M)
1969—Falcons, 10-3 (A)
1970—Vikings, 37-7 (A)
1971—Vikings, 24-7 (M)
1973—Falcons, 20-14 (A)
1974—Vikings, 23-10 (M)
1975—Vikings, 38-0 (M)
1977—Vikings, 14-7 (A)
1980—Vikings, 24-23 (M)
1981—Falcons, 31-30 (A)
1982—*Vikings, 30-24 (M)
1984—Vikings, 27-20 (M)
1985—Falcons, 14-13 (A)
1987—Vikings, 24-13 (M)
(Points—Vikings 381, Falcons 234)
**NFC First Round Playoff*
ATLANTA vs. NEW ENGLAND
Patriots lead series, 3-2
1972—Patriots, 21-20 (NE)
1977—Patriots, 16-10 (A)
1980—Falcons, 37-21 (NE)
1983—Falcons, 24-13 (A)
1986—Patriots, 25-17 (NE)
(Points—Falcons 108, Patriots 96)
ATLANTA vs. NEW ORLEANS
Falcons lead series, 24-13
1967—Saints, 27-24 (NO)
1969—Falcons, 45-17 (A)
1970—Falcons, 14-3 (NO)
Falcons, 32-14 (A)
1971—Falcons, 28-6 (A)
Falcons, 24-20 (NO)
1972—Falcons, 21-14 (NO)
Falcons, 36-20 (A)
1973—Falcons, 62-7 (NO)
Falcons, 14-10 (A)
1974—Saints, 14-13 (NO)
Saints, 13-3 (A)
1975—Falcons, 14-7 (A)
Saints, 23-7 (NO)
1976—Saints, 30-0 (NO)
Falcons, 23-20 (A)
1977—Saints, 21-20 (NO)
Falcons, 35-7 (A)
1978—Falcons, 20-17 (NO)
Falcons, 20-17 (A)
1979—Falcons, 40-34 (NO) OT
Saints, 37-6 (A)
1980—Falcons, 41-14 (NO)
Falcons, 31-13 (A)
1981—Falcons, 27-0 (A)
Falcons, 41-10 (NO)
1982—Falcons, 35-0 (A)
Saints, 35-6 (NO)
1983—Saints, 19-17 (A)
Saints, 27-10 (NO)
1984—Falcons, 36-28 (NO)
Saints, 17-13 (A)
1985—Falcons, 31-24 (A)
Falcons, 16-10 (NO)
1986—Falcons, 31-10 (NO)
Saints, 14-9 (A)
1987—Saints, 38-0 (A)
(Points—Falcons 845, Saints 637)
ATLANTA vs. N.Y. GIANTS
Falcons lead series, 6-5
1966—Falcons, 27-16 (NY)
1968—Falcons, 24-21 (A)
1971—Giants, 21-17 (A)
1974—Falcons, 14-7 (New Haven)
1977—Falcons, 17-3 (A)
1978—Falcons, 23-20 (A)
1979—Giants, 24-3 (NY)
1981—Giants, 27-24 (A) OT
1982—Falcons, 16-14 (NY)
1983—Giants, 16-13 (A) OT
1984—Giants, 19-7 (A)
(Points—Giants 188, Falcons 185)
ATLANTA vs. N.Y. JETS
Series tied, 2-2
1973—Falcons, 28-20 (NY)
1980—Jets, 14-7 (A)
1983—Falcons, 27-21 (NY)
1986—Jets, 28-14 (A)
(Points—Jets 83, Falcons 76)
ATLANTA vs. PHILADELPHIA
Eagles lead series, 7-6-1
1966—Eagles, 23-10 (P)
1967—Eagles, 38-7 (A)
1969—Falcons, 27-3 (P)
1970—Tie, 13-13 (P)
1973—Falcons, 44-27 (P)
1976—Eagles, 14-13 (A)
1978—*Falcons, 14-13 (A)
1979—Falcons, 14-10 (P)
1980—Falcons, 20-17 (P)
1981—Eagles, 16-13 (P)
1983—Eagles, 28-24 (A)
1984—Falcons, 26-10 (A)
1985—Eagles, 23-17 (P) OT
1986—Eagles, 16-0 (A)
(Points—Eagles 251, Falcons 242)
**NFC First Round Playoff*
ATLANTA vs. PITTSBURGH
Steelers lead series, 7-1
1966—Steelers, 57-33 (A)
1968—Steelers, 41-21 (A)
1970—Falcons, 27-16 (A)
1974—Steelers, 24-17 (P)
1978—Steelers, 31-7 (P)
1981—Steelers, 34-20 (A)
1984—Steelers, 35-10 (P)
1987—Steelers, 28-12 (A)
(Points—Steelers 266, Falcons 147)
ATLANTA vs. ST. LOUIS
Cardinals lead series, 7-4
1966—Falcons, 16-10 (A)
1968—Cardinals, 17-12 (StL)
1971—Cardinals, 26-9 (A)
1973—Cardinals, 32-10 (A)
1975—Cardinals, 23-20 (StL)
1978—Cardinals, 42-21 (StL)
1980—Falcons, 33-27 (StL) OT
1981—Falcons, 41-20 (A)
1982—Cardinals, 23-20 (A)
1986—Falcons, 33-13 (A)
1987—Cardinals, 34-21 (A)
(Points—Cardinals 267, Falcons 236)
ATLANTA vs. SAN DIEGO
Falcons lead series, 2-0
1973—Falcons, 41-0 (SD)
1979—Falcons, 28-26 (SD)
(Points—Falcons 69, Chargers 26)
ATLANTA vs. SAN FRANCISCO
49ers lead series, 24-17-1
1966—49ers, 44-7 (A)
1967—49ers, 38-7 (SF)
49ers, 34-28 (A)
1968—49ers, 28-13 (SF)
49ers, 14-12 (A)
1969—Falcons, 24-12 (A)
Falcons, 21-7 (SF)
1970—Falcons, 21-20 (A)
49ers, 24-20 (SF)
1971—Falcons, 20-17 (A)
49ers, 24-3 (SF)
1972—49ers, 49-14 (A)
49ers, 20-0 (SF)
1973—49ers, 13-9 (A)
Falcons, 17-3 (SF)
1974—49ers, 16-10 (A)
49ers, 27-0 (SF)
1975—Falcons, 17-3 (SF)
Falcons, 31-9 (A)
1976—49ers, 15-0 (SF)
Falcons, 21-16 (A)
1977—Falcons, 7-0 (SF)
49ers, 10-3 (A)
1978—Falcons, 20-17 (SF)
Falcons, 21-10 (A)
1979—49ers, 20-15 (SF)
Falcons, 31-21 (A)
1980—Falcons, 20-17 (SF)
Falcons, 35-10 (A)
1981—Falcons, 34-17 (A)
49ers, 17-14 (SF)
1982—Falcons, 17-7 (SF)
1983—49ers, 24-20 (SF)
Falcons, 28-24 (A)
1984—49ers, 14-5 (SF)
49ers, 35-17 (A)
1985—49ers, 35-16 (SF)
49ers, 38-17 (A)
1986—Tie, 10-10 (A) OT
49ers, 20-0 (SF)
1987—49ers, 25-17 (A)
49ers, 35-7 (SF)
(Points—49ers 839, Falcons 649)
ATLANTA vs. SEATTLE
Seahawks lead series, 3-0
1976—Seahawks, 30-13 (S)
1979—Seahawks, 31-28 (A)
1985—Seahawks, 30-26 (S)
(Points—Seahawks 91, Falcons 67)
ATLANTA vs. TAMPA BAY
Buccaneers lead series, 4-3
1977—Falcons, 17-0 (TB)
1978—Buccaneers, 14-9 (TB)
1979—Falcons, 17-14 (A)
1981—Buccaneers, 24-23 (TB)
1984—Buccaneers, 23-6 (TB)
1986—Falcons, 23-20 (TB) OT
1987—Buccaneers, 48-10 (TB)
(Points—Buccaneers 143, Falcons 105)
ATLANTA vs. WASHINGTON
Redskins lead series, 9-3-1
1966—Redskins, 33-20 (W)
1967—Tie, 20-20 (A)
1969—Redskins, 27-20 (W)
1972—Redskins, 24-13 (W)

1975—Redskins, 30-27 (A)
1977—Redskins, 10-6 (W)
1978—Falcons, 20-17 (A)
1979—Redskins, 16-7 (A)
1980—Falcons, 10-6 (A)
1983—Redskins, 37-21 (W)
1984—Redskins, 27-14 (W)
1985—Redskins, 44-10 (A)
1987—Falcons, 21-20 (A)
(Points—Redskins 311, Falcons 209)

BUFFALO vs. ATLANTA
Series tied, 2-2;
See Atlanta vs. Buffalo

BUFFALO vs. CHICAGO
Bears lead series, 2-1
1970—Bears, 31-13 (C)
1974—Bills, 16-6 (B)
1979—Bears, 7-0 (B)
(Points—Bears 44, Bills 29)

BUFFALO vs. CINCINNATI
Bengals lead series, 9-5
1968—Bengals, 34-23 (C)
1969—Bills, 16-13 (B)
1970—Bengals, 43-14 (B)
1973—Bengals, 16-13 (B)
1975—Bengals, 33-24 (C)
1978—Bills, 5-0 (B)
1979—Bills, 51-24 (B)
1980—Bills, 14-0 (C)
1981—Bengals, 27-24 (C) OT
*Bengals, 28-21 (C)
1983—Bills, 10-6 (C)
1984—Bengals, 52-21 (C)
1985—Bengals, 23-17 (B)
1986—Bengals, 36-33 (C) OT
(Points—Bengals 335, Bills 286)
**AFC Divisional Playoff*

BUFFALO vs. CLEVELAND
Browns lead series, 7-2
1972—Browns, 27-10 (C)
1974—Bills, 15-10 (C)
1977—Browns, 27-16 (B)
1978—Browns, 41-20 (C)
1981—Bills, 22-13 (B)
1984—Browns, 13-10 (B)
1985—Browns, 17-7 (C)
1986—Browns, 21-17 (B)
1987—Browns, 27-21 (C)
(Points—Browns 196, Bills 138)

BUFFALO vs. DALLAS
Cowboys lead series, 3-1
1971—Cowboys, 49-37 (B)
1976—Cowboys, 17-10 (D)
1981—Cowboys, 27-14 (D)
1984—Bills, 14-3 (B)
(Points—Cowboys 96, Bills 75)

BUFFALO vs. DENVER
Bills lead series, 14-9-1
1960—Broncos, 27-21 (B)
Tie, 38-38 (D)
1961—Broncos, 22-10 (B)
Bills, 23-10 (D)
1962—Broncos, 23-20 (B)
Bills, 45-38 (D)
1963—Bills, 30-28 (D)
Bills, 27-17 (B)
1964—Bills, 30-13 (B)
Bills, 30-19 (D)
1965—Bills, 30-15 (D)
Bills, 31-13 (B)
1966—Bills, 38-21 (B)
1967—Bills, 17-16 (D)
Broncos, 21-20 (B)
1968—Broncos, 34-32 (D)
1969—Bills, 41-28 (B)
1970—Broncos, 25-10 (B)
1975—Bills, 38-14 (B)
1977—Broncos, 26-6 (D)
1979—Broncos, 19-16 (B)
1981—Bills, 9-7 (B)
1984—Broncos, 37-7 (B)
1987—Bills, 21-14 (B)
(Points—Bills 590, Broncos 525)

BUFFALO vs. DETROIT
Series tied, 1-1-1
1972—Tie, 21-21 (B)
1976—Lions, 27-14 (D)
1979—Bills, 20-17 (D)
(Points—Lions 65, Bills 55)

BUFFALO vs. GREEN BAY
Bills lead series, 2-1
1974—Bills, 27-7 (GB)
1979—Bills, 19-12 (B)
1982—Packers, 33-21 (Mil)
(Points—Bills 67, Packers 52)

BUFFALO vs. HOUSTON
Oilers lead series, 18-10
1960—Bills, 25-24 (B)
Oilers, 31-23 (H)
1961—Bills, 22-12 (H)
Oilers, 28-16 (B)
1962—Oilers, 28-23 (B)
Oilers, 17-14 (H)
1963—Oilers, 31-20 (B)
Oilers, 28-14 (H)
1964—Bills, 48-17 (H)
Bills, 24-10 (B)
1965—Oilers, 19-17 (B)
Bills, 29-18 (H)
1966—Bills, 27-20 (B)
Bills, 42-20 (H)
1967—Oilers, 20-3 (B)
Oilers, 10-3 (H)
1968—Oilers, 30-7 (B)
Oilers, 35-6 (H)
1969—Oilers, 17-3 (B)
Oilers, 28-14 (H)
1971—Oilers, 20-14 (B)
1974—Oilers, 21-9 (B)
1976—Oilers, 13-3 (B)
1978—Oilers, 17-10 (H)
1983—Bills, 30-13 (B)
1985—Bills, 20-0 (B)
1986—Oilers, 16-7 (H)
1987—Bills, 34-30 (B)
(Points—Oilers 573, Bills 507)

BUFFALO vs. *INDIANAPOLIS
Series tied, 17-17-1
1970—Tie, 17-17 (Balt)
Colts, 20-14 (Buff)
1971—Colts, 43-0 (Buff)
Colts, 24-0 (Balt)
1972—Colts, 17-0 (Buff)
Colts, 35-7 (Balt)
1973—Bills, 31-13 (Buff)
Bills, 24-17 (Balt)
1974—Bills, 27-14 (Balt)
Bills, 6-0 (Buff)
1975—Bills, 38-31 (Balt)
Colts, 42-35 (Buff)
1976—Colts, 31-13 (Buff)
Colts, 58-20 (Balt)
1977—Colts, 17-14 (Balt)
Colts, 31-13 (Buff)
1978—Bills, 24-17 (Buff)
Bills, 21-14 (Balt)
1979—Bills, 31-13 (Balt)
Colts, 14-13 (Buff)
1980—Colts, 17-12 (Buff)
Colts, 28-24 (Balt)
1981—Bills, 35-3 (Balt)
Bills, 23-17 (Buff)
1982—Bills, 20-0 (Buff)
1983—Bills, 28-23 (Buff)
Bills, 30-7 (Balt)
1984—Colts, 31-17 (I)
Bills, 21-15 (Buff)
1985—Colts, 49-17 (I)
Bills, 21-9 (Buff)
1986—Bills, 24-13 (Buff)
Colts, 24-14 (I)
1987—Colts, 47-6 (Buff)
Bills, 27-3 (I)
(Points—Colts 754, Bills 667)
**Franchise in Baltimore prior to 1984*

BUFFALO vs. *KANSAS CITY
Bills lead series, 15-12-1
1960—Texans, 45-28 (B)
Texans, 24-7 (D)
1961—Bills, 27-24 (B)
Bills, 30-20 (D)
1962—Texans, 41-21 (D)
Bills, 23-14 (B)
1963—Tie, 27-27 (B)
Bills, 35-26 (KC)
1964—Bills, 34-17 (B)
Bills, 35-22 (KC)
1965—Bills, 23-7 (KC)
Bills, 34-25 (B)
1966—Chiefs, 42-20 (B)
Bills, 29-14 (KC)
**Chiefs, 31-7 (B)
1967—Chiefs, 23-13 (KC)
1968—Chiefs, 18-7 (B)
1969—Chiefs, 29-7 (B)
Chiefs, 22-19 (KC)
1971—Chiefs, 22-9 (KC)
1973—Bills, 23-14 (B)
1976—Bills, 50-17 (B)
1978—Bills, 28-13 (B)
Chiefs, 14-10 (KC)
1982—Bills, 14-9 (B)
1983—Bills, 14-9 (KC)
1986—Chiefs, 20-17 (B)
Bills, 17-14 (KC)
(Points—Chiefs 608, Bills 603)
**Franchise in Dallas prior to 1963 and known as Texans*
***AFL Championship*

BUFFALO vs. *L.A. RAIDERS
Raiders lead series, 13-11
1960—Bills, 38-9 (B)
Raiders, 20-7 (O)
1961—Raiders, 31-22 (B)
Bills, 26-21 (O)
1962—Bills, 14-6 (B)
Bills, 10-6 (O)
1963—Raiders, 35-17 (O)
Bills, 12-0 (B)
1964—Bills, 23-20 (B)
Raiders, 16-13 (O)
1965—Bills, 17-12 (B)
Bills, 17-14 (O)
1966—Bills, 31-10 (O)
1967—Raiders, 24-20 (B)
Raiders, 28-21 (O)
1968—Raiders, 48-6 (B)
Raiders, 13-10 (O)
1969—Raiders, 50-21 (O)
1972—Raiders, 28-16 (O)
1974—Bills, 21-20 (B)
1977—Raiders, 34-13 (O)
1980—Bills, 24-7 (B)
1983—Raiders, 27-24 (B)
1987—Raiders, 34-21 (LA)
(Points—Raiders 513, Bills 444)
**Franchise in Oakland prior to 1982*

BUFFALO vs. L.A. RAMS
Rams lead series, 3-1
1970—Rams, 19-0 (B)
1974—Rams, 19-14 (LA)
1980—Bills, 10-7 (B) OT
1983—Rams, 41-17 (LA)
(Points—Rams 86, Bills 41)

BUFFALO vs. MIAMI
Dolphins lead series, 34-9-1
1966—Bills, 58-24 (B)
Bills, 29-0 (M)
1967—Bills, 35-13 (B)
Dolphins, 17-14 (M)
1968—Tie, 14-14 (M)
Dolphins, 21-17 (B)
1969—Dolphins, 24-6 (M)
Bills, 28-3 (B)
1970—Dolphins, 33-14 (B)
Dolphins, 45-7 (M)
1971—Dolphins, 29-14 (B)
Dolphins, 34-0 (M)
1972—Dolphins, 24-23 (M)
Dolphins, 30-16 (B)
1973—Dolphins, 27-6 (M)
Dolphins, 17-0 (B)
1974—Dolphins, 24-16 (B)
Dolphins, 35-28 (M)
1975—Dolphins, 35-30 (B)
Dolphins, 31-21 (M)
1976—Dolphins, 30-21 (B)
Dolphins, 45-27 (M)
1977—Dolphins, 13-0 (B)
Dolphins, 31-14 (M)
1978—Dolphins, 31-24 (M)
Dolphins, 25-24 (B)
1979—Dolphins, 9-7 (B)
Dolphins, 17-7 (M)
1980—Bills, 17-7 (B)
Dolphins, 17-14 (M)
1981—Bills, 31-21 (B)
Dolphins, 16-6 (M)
1982—Dolphins, 9-7 (B)
Dolphins, 27-10 (M)
1983—Dolphins, 12-0 (B)
Bills, 38-35 (M) OT
1984—Dolphins, 21-17 (B)
Dolphins, 38-7 (M)
1985—Dolphins, 23-14 (B)
Dolphins, 28-0 (M)
1986—Dolphins, 27-14 (M)
Dolphins, 34-24 (B)
1987—Bills, 34-31 (M) OT
Bills, 27-0 (B)
(Points—Dolphins 1,027, Bills 760)

BUFFALO vs. MINNESOTA
Vikings lead series, 4-1
1971—Vikings, 19-0 (M)
1975—Vikings, 35-13 (B)
1979—Vikings, 10-3 (M)
1982—Bills, 23-22 (B)
1985—Vikings, 27-20 (B)
(Points—Vikings 113, Bills 59)

BUFFALO vs. *NEW ENGLAND
Patriots lead series, 32-23-1
1960—Bills, 13-0 (Bos)
Bills, 38-14 (Buff)
1961—Patriots, 23-21 (Buff)
Patriots, 52-21 (Bos)
1962—Tie, 28-28 (Buff)
Patriots, 21-10 (Bos)
1963—Bills, 28-21 (Buff)
Patriots, 17-7 (Bos)
**Patriots, 26-8 (Buff)
1964—Patriots, 36-28 (Buff)
Bills, 24-14 (Bos)
1965—Bills, 24-7 (Buff)
Bills, 23-7 (Bos)
1966—Patriots, 20-10 (Buff)
Patriots, 14-3 (Bos)
1967—Patriots, 23-0 (Buff)
Bills, 44-16 (Bos)
1968—Patriots, 16-7 (Buff)
Patriots, 23-6 (Bos)
1969—Bills, 23-16 (Buff)
Patriots, 35-21 (Bos)
1970—Bills, 45-10 (Bos)
Patriots, 14-10 (Buff)
1971—Patriots, 38-33 (NE)
Bills, 27-20 (Buff)
1972—Bills, 38-14 (Buff)
Bills, 27-24 (NE)
1973—Bills, 31-13 (NE)
Bills, 37-13 (Buff)
1974—Bills, 30-28 (Buff)
Bills, 29-28 (NE)
1975—Bills, 45-31 (Buff)
Bills, 34-14 (NE)
1976—Patriots, 26-22 (Buff)
Patriots, 20-10 (NE)
1977—Bills, 24-14 (NE)
Patriots, 20-7 (Buff)
1978—Patriots, 14-10 (Buff)
Patriots, 26-24 (NE)
1979—Patriots, 26-6 (Buff)
Bills, 16-13 (NE) OT
1980—Bills, 31-13 (Buff)
Patriots, 24-2 (NE)
1981—Bills, 20-17 (Buff)
Bills, 19-10 (NE)
1982—Patriots, 30-19 (NE)
1983—Patriots, 31-0 (Buff)
Patriots, 21-7 (NE)
1984—Patriots, 21-17 (Buff)
Patriots, 38-10 (NE)
1985—Patriots, 17-14 (Buff)
Patriots, 14-3 (NE)
1986—Patriots, 23-3 (Buff)
Patriots, 22-19 (NE)
1987—Patriots, 14-7 (NE)
Patriots, 13-7 (Buff)
(Points—Patriots 1,143, Bills 1,070)
**Franchise in Boston prior to 1971*
***Division Playoff*

BUFFALO vs. NEW ORLEANS
Bills lead series, 2-1
1973—Saints, 13-0 (NO)
1980—Bills, 35-26 (NO)
1983—Bills, 27-21 (B)
(Points—Bills 62, Saints 60)

BUFFALO vs. N.Y. GIANTS
Series tied, 2-2
1970—Giants, 20-6 (NY)
1975—Giants, 17-14 (B)
1978—Bills, 41-17 (B)
1987—Bills, 6-3 (B) OT
(Points—Bills 67, Giants 57)

BUFFALO vs. *N.Y. JETS
Jets lead series, 28-27
1960—Titans, 27-3 (NY)
Titans, 17-13 (B)
1961—Bills, 41-31 (B)
Titans, 21-14 (NY)
1962—Titans, 17-6 (B)
Bills, 20-3 (NY)
1963—Bills, 45-14 (B)
Bills, 19-10 (NY)
1964—Bills, 34-24 (B)
Bills, 20-7 (NY)
1965—Bills, 33-21 (B)
Jets, 14-12 (NY)
1966—Bills, 33-23 (NY)
Bills, 14-3 (B)
1967—Bills, 20-17 (B)
Jets, 20-10 (NY)
1968—Bills, 37-35 (B)
Jets, 25-21 (NY)
1969—Jets, 33-19 (B)
Jets, 16-6 (NY)
1970—Bills, 34-31 (B)
Bills, 10-6 (NY)
1971—Jets, 28-17 (NY)
Jets, 20-7 (B)
1972—Jets, 41-24 (B)
Jets, 41-3 (NY)
1973—Bills, 9-7 (B)
Bills, 34-14 (NY)
1974—Bills, 16-12 (B)
Jets, 20-10 (NY)
1975—Bills, 42-14 (B)
Bills, 24-23 (NY)
1976—Jets, 17-14 (NY)
Jets, 19-14 (B)
1977—Jets, 24-19 (B)
Bills, 14-10 (NY)
1978—Jets, 21-20 (B)
Jets, 45-14 (NY)
1979—Bills, 46-31 (B)
Bills, 14-12 (NY)
1980—Bills, 20-10 (B)
Bills, 31-24 (NY)
1981—Bills, 31-0 (B)
Jets, 33-14 (NY)
**Bills, 31-27 (NY)

1983—Jets, 34-10 (B)
Bills, 24-17 (NY)
1984—Jets, 28-26 (B)
Jets, 21-17 (NY)
1985—Jets, 42-3 (NY)
Jets, 27-7 (B)
1986—Jets, 28-24 (B)
Jets, 14-13 (NY)
1987—Jets, 31-28 (B)
Bills, 17-14 (NY)
(Points—Jets 1,164, Bills 1,101)
Jets known as Titans prior to 1963
***AFC First Round Playoff*

BUFFALO vs. PHILADELPHIA
Eagles lead series, 4-1
1973—Bills, 27-26 (B)
1981—Eagles, 20-14 (B)
1984—Eagles, 27-17 (B)
1985—Eagles, 21-17 (P)
1987—Eagles, 17-7 (P)
(Points—Eagles 111, Bills 82)

BUFFALO vs. PITTSBURGH
Steelers lead series, 6-4
1970—Steelers, 23-10 (P)
1972—Steelers, 38-21 (B)
1974—*Steelers, 32-14 (P)
1975—Bills, 30-21 (P)
1978—Steelers, 28-17 (B)
1979—Steelers, 28-0 (P)
1980—Bills, 28-13 (B)
1982—Bills, 13-0 (B)
1985—Steelers, 30-24 (P)
1986—Bills, 16-12 (B)
(Points—Steelers 225, Bills 173)
*AFC Divisional Playoff

BUFFALO vs. ST. LOUIS
Cardinals lead series, 3-2
1971—Cardinals, 28-23 (B)
1975—Bills, 32-14 (StL)
1981—Cardinals, 24-0 (StL)
1984—Cardinals, 37-7 (StL)
1986—Bills, 17-10 (B)
(Points—Cardinals 113, Bills 79)

BUFFALO vs. *SAN DIEGO
Chargers lead series, 17-9-2
1960—Chargers, 24-10 (B)
Bills, 32-3 (LA)
1961—Chargers, 19-11 (B)
Chargers, 28-10 (SD)
1962—Bills, 35-10 (B)
Bills, 40-20 (SD)
1963—Chargers, 14-10 (SD)
Chargers, 23-13 (B)
1964—Bills, 30-3 (B)
Bills, 27-24 (SD)
**Bills, 20-7 (B)
1965—Chargers, 34-3 (B)
Tie, 20-20 (SD)
**Bills, 23-0 (SD)
1966—Chargers, 27-7 (SD)
Tie, 17-17 (B)
1967—Chargers, 37-17 (B)
1968—Chargers, 21-6 (B)
1969—Chargers, 45-6 (SD)
1971—Chargers, 20-3 (SD)
1973—Chargers, 34-7 (SD)
1976—Chargers, 34-13 (B)
1979—Chargers, 27-19 (SD)
1980—Bills, 26-24 (SD)
***Chargers, 20-14 (SD)
1981—Bills, 28-27 (SD)
1985—Chargers, 14-9 (B)
Chargers, 40-7 (SD)
(Points—Chargers 616, Bills 463)
*Franchise in Los Angeles prior to 1961
**AFL Championship
***AFC Divisional Playoff

BUFFALO vs. SAN FRANCISCO
Bills lead series, 2-1
1972—Bills, 27-20 (B)
1980—Bills, 18-13 (SF)
1983—49ers, 23-10 (B)
(Points—49ers 56, Bills 55)

BUFFALO vs. SEATTLE
Seahawks lead series, 2-0
1977—Seahawks, 56-17 (S)
1984—Seahawks, 31-28 (S)
(Points—Seahawks 87, Bills 45)

BUFFALO vs. TAMPA BAY
Buccaneers lead series, 3-1
1976—Bills, 14-9 (TB)
1978—Buccaneers, 31-10 (TB)
1982—Buccaneers, 24-23 (TB)
1986—Buccaneers, 34-28 (TB)
(Points—Buccaneers 98, Bills 75)

BUFFALO vs. WASHINGTON
Redskins lead series, 3-2
1972—Bills, 24-17 (W)
1977—Redskins, 10-0 (B)
1981—Bills, 21-14 (B)
1984—Redskins, 41-14 (W)
1987—Redskins, 27-7 (B)
(Points—Redskins 109, Bills 66)

CHICAGO vs. ATLANTA
Falcons lead series, 9-6;
See Atlanta vs. Chicago

CHICAGO vs. BUFFALO
Bears lead series, 2-1;
See Buffalo vs. Chicago

CHICAGO vs. CINCINNATI
Bengals lead series, 2-1
1972—Bengals, 13-3 (Chi)
1980—Bengals, 17-14 (Chi) OT
1986—Bears, 44-7 (Cin)
(Points—Bears 61, Bengals 37)

CHICAGO vs. CLEVELAND
Browns lead series, 6-3
1951—Browns, 42-21 (Cle)
1954—Browns, 39-10 (Chi)
1960—Browns, 42-0 (Cle)
1961—Bears, 17-14 (Chi)
1967—Browns, 24-0 (Cle)
1969—Browns, 28-24 (Chi)
1972—Bears, 17-0 (Cle)
1980—Browns, 27-21 (Cle)
1986—Bears, 41-31 (Chi)
(Points—Browns 247, Bears 151)

CHICAGO vs. DALLAS
Cowboys lead series, 8-5
1960—Bears, 17-7 (C)
1962—Bears, 34-33 (D)
1964—Cowboys, 24-10 (C)
1968—Cowboys, 34-3 (C)
1971—Bears, 23-19 (C)
1973—Cowboys, 20-17 (C)
1976—Cowboys, 31-21 (D)
1977—*Cowboys, 37-7 (D)
1979—Cowboys, 24-20 (D)
1981—Cowboys, 10-9 (D)
1984—Cowboys, 23-14 (C)
1985—Bears, 44-0 (D)
1986—Bears, 24-10 (D)
(Points—Cowboys 272, Bears 243)
*NFC Divisional Playoff

CHICAGO vs. DENVER
Series tied, 4-4
1971—Broncos, 6-3 (D)
1973—Bears, 33-14 (D)
1976—Broncos, 28-14 (C)
1978—Broncos, 16-7 (D)
1981—Bears, 35-24 (C)
1983—Bears, 31-14 (C)
1984—Bears, 27-0 (C)
1987—Broncos, 31-29 (D)
(Points—Bears 179, Broncos 133)

CHICAGO vs. *DETROIT
Bears lead series, 67-44-5
1930—Spartans, 7-6 (P)
Bears, 14-6 (C)
1931—Bears, 9-6 (C)
Spartans, 3-0 (P)
1932—Tie, 13-13 (C)
Tie, 7-7 (P)
**Bears, 9-0 (C)
1933—Bears, 17-14 (C)
Bears, 17-7 (P)
1934—Bears, 19-16 (D)
Bears, 10-7 (C)
1935—Tie, 20-20 (C)
Lions, 14-2 (D)
1936—Bears, 12-10 (C)
Lions, 13-7 (D)
1937—Bears, 28-20 (C)
Bears, 13-0 (D)
1938—Lions, 13-7 (C)
Lions, 14-7 (D)
1939—Lions, 10-0 (C)
Bears, 23-13 (D)
1940—Bears, 7-0 (C)
Lions, 17-14 (D)
1941—Bears, 49-0 (C)
Bears, 24-7 (D)
1942—Bears, 16-0 (C)
Bears, 42-0 (D)
1943—Bears, 27-21 (D)
Bears, 35-14 (C)
1944—Tie, 21-21 (C)
Lions, 41-21 (D)
1945—Lions, 16-10 (D)
Lions, 35-28 (C)
1946—Bears, 42-6 (C)
Bears, 45-24 (D)
1947—Bears, 33-24 (C)
Bears, 34-14 (D)
1948—Bears, 28-0 (C)
Bears, 42-14 (D)
1949—Bears, 27-24 (C)
Bears, 28-7 (D)
1950—Bears, 35-21 (D)
Bears, 6-3 (C)
1951—Bears, 28-23 (D)
Lions, 41-28 (C)
1952—Bears, 24-23 (C)
Lions, 45-21 (D)
1953—Lions, 20-16 (C)
Lions, 13-7 (D)
1954—Lions, 48-23 (D)
Bears, 28-24 (C)
1955—Bears, 24-14 (D)
Bears, 21-20 (C)
1956—Lions, 42-10 (D)
Bears, 38-21 (C)
1957—Bears, 27-7 (D)
Lions, 21-13 (C)
1958—Bears, 20-7 (D)
Bears, 21-16 (C)
1959—Bears, 24-14 (D)
Bears, 25-14 (C)
1960—Bears, 28-7 (C)
Lions, 36-0 (D)
1961—Bears, 31-17 (D)
Lions, 16-15 (C)
1962—Lions, 11-3 (D)
Bears, 3-0 (C)
1963—Bears, 37-21 (D)
Bears, 24-14 (C)
1964—Lions, 10-0 (C)
Bears, 27-24 (D)
1965—Bears, 38-10 (C)
Bears, 17-10 (D)
1966—Lions, 14-3 (D)
Tie, 10-10 (C)
1967—Bears, 14-3 (C)
Bears, 27-13 (D)
1968—Lions, 42-0 (D)
Lions, 28-10 (C)
1969—Lions, 13-7 (D)
Lions, 20-3 (C)
1970—Lions, 28-14 (D)
Lions, 16-10 (C)
1971—Bears, 28-23 (D)
Lions, 28-3 (C)
1972—Lions, 38-24 (C)
Lions, 14-0 (D)
1973—Lions, 30-7 (C)
Lions, 40-7 (D)
1974—Bears, 17-9 (C)
Lions, 34-17 (D)
1975—Lions, 27-7 (D)
Bears, 25-21 (C)
1976—Bears, 10-3 (C)
Lions, 14-10 (D)
1977—Bears, 30-20 (C)
Bears, 31-14 (D)
1978—Bears, 19-0 (D)
Lions, 21-17 (C)
1979—Bears, 35-7 (C)
Lions, 20-0 (D)
1980—Bears, 24-7 (C)
Bears, 23-17 (D) OT
1981—Lions, 48-17 (D)
Lions, 23-7 (C)
1982—Lions, 17-10 (D)
Bears, 20-17 (C)
1983—Lions, 31-17 (D)
Lions, 38-17 (C)
1984—Bears, 16-14 (C)
Bears, 30-13 (D)
1985—Bears, 24-3 (C)
Bears, 37-17 (D)
1986—Bears, 13-7 (C)
Bears, 16-13 (D)
1987—Bears, 30-10 (C)
(Points—Bears 2,161, Lions 1,936)
Franchise in Portsmouth prior to 1934 and known as the Spartans
***Championship*

***CHICAGO vs. GREEN BAY**
Bears lead series, 74-55-6
1921—Staleys, 20-0 (C)
1923—Bears, 3-0 (GB)
1924—Bears, 3-0 (C)
1925—Packers, 14-10 (GB)
Bears, 21-0 (C)
1926—Tie, 6-6 (GB)
Bears, 19-13 (C)
Tie, 3-3 (C)
1927—Bears, 7-6 (GB)
Bears, 14-6 (C)
1928—Tie, 12-12 (GB)
Packers, 16-6 (C)
Packers, 6-0 (C)
1929—Packers, 23-0 (GB)
Packers, 14-0 (C)
Packers, 25-0 (C)
1930—Packers, 7-0 (GB)
Packers, 13-12 (C)
Bears, 21-0 (C)
1931—Packers, 7-0 (GB)
Packers, 6-2 (C)
Bears, 7-6 (C)
1932—Tie, 0-0 (GB)
Packers, 2-0 (C)
Bears, 9-0 (C)
1933—Bears, 14-7 (GB)
Bears, 10-7 (C)
Bears, 7-6 (C)
1934—Bears, 24-10 (GB)
Bears, 27-14 (C)
1935—Packers, 7-0 (GB)
Packers, 17-14 (C)
1936—Bears, 30-3 (GB)
Packers, 21-10 (C)
1937—Bears, 14-2 (GB)
Packers, 24-14 (C)
1938—Bears, 2-0 (GB)
Packers, 24-17 (C)
1939—Packers, 21-16 (GB)
Bears, 30-27 (C)
1940—Bears, 41-10 (GB)
Bears, 14-7 (C)
1941—Bears, 25-17 (GB)
Packers, 16-14 (C)
**Bears, 33-14 (C)
1942—Bears, 44-28 (GB)
Bears, 38-7 (C)
1943—Tie, 21-21 (GB)
Bears, 21-7 (C)
1944—Packers, 42-28 (GB)
Bears, 21-0 (C)
1945—Packers, 31-21 (GB)
Bears, 28-24 (C)
1946—Bears, 30-7 (GB)
Bears, 10-7 (C)
1947—Packers, 29-20 (GB)
Bears, 20-17 (C)
1948—Bears, 45-7 (GB)
Bears, 7-6 (C)
1949—Bears, 17-0 (GB)
Bears, 24-3 (C)
1950—Packers, 31-21 (GB)
Bears, 28-14 (C)
1951—Bears, 31-20 (GB)
Bears, 24-13 (C)
1952—Bears, 24-14 (GB)
Packers, 41-28 (C)
1953—Bears, 17-13 (GB)
Tie, 21-21 (C)
1954—Bears, 10-3 (GB)
Bears, 28-23 (C)
1955—Packers, 24-3 (GB)
Bears, 52-31 (C)
1956—Bears, 37-21 (GB)
Bears, 38-14 (C)
1957—Packers, 21-17 (GB)
Bears, 21-14 (C)
1958—Bears, 34-20 (GB)
Bears, 24-10 (C)
1959—Packers, 9-6 (GB)
Bears, 28-17 (C)
1960—Bears, 17-14 (GB)
Packers, 41-13 (C)
1961—Packers, 24-0 (GB)
Packers, 31-28 (C)
1962—Packers, 49-0 (GB)
Packers, 38-7 (C)
1963—Bears, 10-3 (GB)
Bears, 26-7 (C)
1964—Packers, 23-12 (GB)
Packers, 17-3 (C)
1965—Packers, 23-14 (GB)
Bears, 31-10 (C)
1966—Packers, 17-0 (C)
Packers, 13-6 (GB)
1967—Packers, 13-10 (GB)
Packers, 17-13 (C)
1968—Bears, 13-10 (GB)
Packers, 28-27 (C)
1969—Packers, 17-0 (GB)
Packers, 21-3 (C)
1970—Packers, 20-19 (GB)
Bears, 35-17 (C)
1971—Packers, 17-14 (C)
Packers, 31-10 (GB)
1972—Packers, 20-17 (GB)
Packers, 23-17 (C)
1973—Bears, 31-17 (GB)
Packers, 21-0 (C)
1974—Bears, 10-9 (C)
Packers, 20-3 (Mil)
1975—Bears, 27-14 (C)
Packers, 28-7 (GB)
1976—Bears, 24-13 (C)
Bears, 16-10 (GB)
1977—Bears, 26-0 (GB)
Bears, 21-10 (C)
1978—Packers, 24-14 (GB)
Bears, 14-0 (C)
1979—Bears, 6-3 (C)
Bears, 15-14 (GB)
1980—Packers, 12-6 (GB) OT
Bears, 61-7 (C)
1981—Packers, 16-9 (C)
Packers, 21-17 (GB)
1983—Packers, 31-28 (GB)
Bears, 23-21 (C)
1984—Bears, 9-7 (GB)
Packers, 20-14 (C)
1985—Bears, 23-7 (C)
Bears, 16-10 (GB)
1986—Bears, 25-12 (GB)
Bears, 12-10 (C)

1987—Bears, 26-24 (GB)
Bears, 23-10 (C)
(Points—Bears 2,269, Packers 1,984)
*Bears known as Staleys prior to 1922
**Division Playoff

CHICAGO vs. HOUSTON
Series tied, 2-2
1973—Bears, 35-14 (C)
1977—Oilers, 47-0 (H)
1980—Oilers, 10-6 (C)
1986—Bears, 20-7 (H)
(Points—Oilers 78, Bears 61)

CHICAGO vs. *INDIANAPOLIS
Colts lead series, 21-14
1953—Colts, 13-9 (B)
Colts, 16-14 (C)
1954—Bears, 28-9 (C)
Bears, 28-13 (B)
1955—Colts, 23-17 (B)
Bears, 38-10 (C)
1956—Colts, 28-21 (B)
Bears, 58-27 (C)
1957—Colts, 21-10 (B)
Colts, 29-14 (C)
1958—Colts, 51-38 (B)
Colts, 17-0 (C)
1959—Bears, 26-21 (B)
Colts, 21-7 (C)
1960—Colts, 42-7 (B)
Colts, 24-20 (C)
1961—Bears, 24-10 (C)
Bears, 21-20 (B)
1962—Bears, 35-15 (C)
Bears, 57-0 (B)
1963—Bears, 10-3 (C)
Bears, 17-7 (B)
1964—Colts, 52-0 (B)
Colts, 40-24 (C)
1965—Colts, 26-21 (C)
Bears, 13-0 (B)
1966—Bears, 27-17 (C)
Colts, 21-16 (B)
1967—Colts, 24-3 (C)
1968—Colts, 28-7 (B)
1969—Colts, 24-21 (C)
1970—Colts, 21-20 (B)
1975—Colts, 35-7 (C)
1983—Colts, 22-19 (B) OT
1985—Bears, 17-10 (C)
(Points—Colts 740, Bears 694)
*Franchise in Baltimore prior to 1984

CHICAGO vs. KANSAS CITY
Bears lead series, 3-1
1973—Chiefs, 19-7 (KC)
1977—Bears, 28-27 (C)
1981—Bears, 16-13 (KC) OT
1987—Bears, 31-28 (C)
(Points—Chiefs 87, Bears 82)

CHICAGO vs. *L.A. RAIDERS
Series tied, 3-3
1972—Raiders, 28-21 (O)
1976—Raiders, 28-27 (C)
1978—Raiders, 25-19 (C) OT
1981—Bears, 23-6 (O)
1984—Bears, 17-6 (C)
1987—Bears, 6-3 (LA)
(Points—Bears 113, Raiders 96)
*Franchise in Oakland prior to 1982

CHICAGO vs. *L.A. RAMS
Bears lead series, 43-28-3
1937—Bears, 20-2 (Clev)
Bears, 15-7 (C)
1938—Rams, 14-7 (C)
Rams, 23-21 (Clev)
1939—Bears, 30-21 (Clev)
Bears, 35-21 (C)
1940—Bears, 21-14 (Clev)
Bears, 47-25 (C)
1941—Bears, 48-21 (Clev)
Bears, 31-13 (C)
1942—Bears, 21-7 (Clev)
Bears, 47-0 (C)
1944—Rams, 19-7 (Clev)
Bears, 28-21 (C)
1945—Rams, 17-0 (Clev)
Rams, 41-21 (C)
1946—Tie, 28-28 (C)
Bears, 27-21 (LA)
1947—Bears, 41-21 (LA)
Rams, 17-14 (C)
1948—Bears, 42-21 (C)
Bears, 21-6 (LA)
1949—Rams, 31-16 (C)
Rams, 27-24 (LA)
1950—Bears, 24-20 (LA)
Bears, 24-14 (C)
**Rams, 24-14 (LA)
1951—Rams, 42-17 (C)
1952—Rams, 31-7 (LA)
Rams, 40-24 (C)
1953—Rams, 38-24 (LA)
Bears, 24-21 (C)
1954—Rams, 42-38 (LA)
Bears, 24-13 (C)
1955—Bears, 31-20 (LA)
Bears, 24-3 (C)
1956—Bears, 35-24 (LA)
Bears, 30-21 (C)
1957—Bears, 34-26 (C)
Bears, 16-10 (LA)
1958—Bears, 31-10 (C)
Rams, 41-35 (LA)
1959—Rams, 28-21 (C)
Bears, 26-21 (LA)
1960—Bears, 34-27 (C)
Tie, 24-24 (LA)
1961—Bears, 21-17 (LA)
Bears, 28-24 (C)
1962—Bears, 27-23 (LA)
Bears, 30-14 (C)
1963—Bears, 52-14 (LA)
Bears, 6-0 (C)
1964—Bears, 38-17 (C)
Bears, 34-24 (LA)
1965—Rams, 30-28 (LA)
Bears, 31-6 (C)
1966—Rams, 31-17 (LA)
Bears, 17-10 (C)
1967—Rams, 28-17 (C)
1968—Bears, 17-16 (LA)
1969—Rams, 9-7 (C)
1971—Rams, 17-3 (LA)
1972—Tie, 13-13 (C)
1973—Rams, 26-0 (C)
1975—Rams, 38-10 (LA)
1976—Rams, 20-12 (LA)
1977—Bears, 24-23 (C)
1979—Bears, 27-23 (C)
1981—Rams, 24-7 (C)
1982—Bears, 34-26 (LA)
1983—Rams, 21-14 (LA)
1984—Rams, 29-13 (LA)
1985—***Bears, 24-0 (C)
1986—Rams, 20-17 (C)
(Points—Bears 1,741, Rams 1,521)
*Franchise in Cleveland prior to 1946
**Conference Playoff
***NFC Championship

CHICAGO vs. MIAMI
Dolphins lead series, 4-0
1971—Dolphins, 34-3 (M)
1975—Dolphins, 46-13 (C)
1979—Dolphins, 31-16 (M)
1985—Dolphins, 38-24 (M)
(Points—Dolphins 149, Bears 56)

CHICAGO vs. MINNESOTA
Vikings lead series, 26-25-2
1961—Vikings, 37-13 (M)
Bears, 52-35 (C)
1962—Bears, 13-0 (M)
Bears, 31-30 (C)
1963—Bears, 28-7 (M)
Tie, 17-17 (C)
1964—Bears, 34-28 (M)
Vikings, 41-14 (C)
1965—Bears, 45-37 (M)
Vikings, 24-17 (C)
1966—Bears, 13-10 (M)
Bears, 41-28 (C)
1967—Bears, 17-7 (M)
Tie, 10-10 (C)
1968—Bears, 27-17 (M)
Bears, 26-24 (C)
1969—Vikings, 31-0 (C)
Vikings, 31-14 (M)
1970—Vikings, 24-0 (C)
Vikings, 16-13 (M)
1971—Bears, 20-17 (M)
Vikings, 27-10 (C)
1972—Bears, 13-10 (C)
Vikings, 23-10 (M)
1973—Vikings, 22-13 (C)
Vikings, 31-13 (M)
1974—Vikings, 11-7 (M)
Vikings, 17-0 (C)
1975—Vikings, 28-3 (M)
Vikings, 13-9 (C)
1976—Vikings, 20-19 (M)
Bears, 14-13 (C)
1977—Vikings, 22-16 (M) OT
Bears, 10-7 (C)
1978—Vikings, 24-20 (C)
Vikings, 17-14 (M)
1979—Bears, 26-7 (C)
Vikings, 30-27 (M)
1980—Vikings, 34-14 (C)
Vikings, 13-7 (M)
1981—Vikings, 24-21 (M)
Bears, 10-9 (C)
1982—Vikings, 35-7 (M)
1983—Vikings, 23-14 (C)
Bears, 19-13 (M)
1984—Bears, 16-7 (C)
Bears, 34-3 (M)
1985—Bears, 33-24 (M)
Bears, 27-9 (C)
1986—Bears, 23-0 (C)
Vikings, 23-7 (M)
1987—Bears, 27-7 (C)
Bears, 30-24 (M)
(Points—Vikings 1,041, Bears 958)

CHICAGO vs. NEW ENGLAND
Bears lead series, 3-2
1973—Patriots, 13-10 (C)
1979—Patriots, 27-7 (C)
1982—Bears, 26-13 (C)
1985—Bears, 20-7 (C)
*Bears, 46-10 (New Orleans)
(Points—Bears 109, Patriots 70)
*Super Bowl XX

CHICAGO vs. NEW ORLEANS
Bears lead series, 7-5
1968—Bears, 23-17 (NO)
1970—Bears, 24-3 (NO)
1971—Bears, 35-14 (C)
1973—Saints, 21-16 (NO)
1974—Bears, 24-10 (C)
1975—Bears, 42-17 (NO)
1977—Saints, 42-24 (C)
1980—Bears, 22-3 (C)
1982—Saints, 10-0 (C)
1983—Saints, 34-31 (NO) OT
1984—Bears, 20-7 (C)
1987—Saints, 19-17 (C)
(Points—Bears 278, Saints 197)

CHICAGO vs. N.Y. GIANTS
Bears lead series, 28-16-2
1925—Bears, 19-7 (NY)
Giants, 9-0 (C)
1926—Bears, 7-0 (C)
1927—Giants, 13-7 (NY)
1928—Bears, 13-0 (C)
1929—Giants, 26-14 (C)
Giants, 34-0 (NY)
Giants, 14-9 (C)
1930—Giants, 12-0 (C)
Bears, 12-0 (NY)
1931—Bears, 6-0 (C)
Bears, 12-6 (NY)
Giants, 25-6 (C)
1932—Bears, 28-8 (NY)
Bears, 6-0 (C)
1933—Bears, 14-10 (C)
Giants, 3-0 (NY)
*Bears, 23-21 (C)
1934—Bears, 27-7 (C)
Bears, 10-9 (NY)
*Giants, 30-13 (NY)
1935—Bears, 20-3 (NY)
Giants, 3-0 (C)
1936—Bears, 25-7 (NY)
1937—Tie, 3-3 (NY)
1939—Giants, 16-13 (NY)
1940—Bears, 37-21 (NY)
1941—*Bears, 37-9 (C)
1942—Bears, 26-7 (NY)
1943—Bears, 56-7 (NY)
1946—Giants, 14-0 (NY)
*Bears, 24-14 (NY)
1948—Bears, 35-14 (C)
1949—Giants, 35-28 (NY)
1956—Tie, 17-17 (NY)
*Giants, 47-7 (NY)
1962—Giants, 26-24 (C)
1963—*Bears, 14-10 (C)
1965—Bears, 35-14 (NY)
1967—Bears, 34-7 (C)
1969—Giants, 28-24 (NY)
1970—Bears, 24-16 (NY)
1974—Bears, 16-13 (C)
1977—Bears, 12-9 (NY) OT
1985—**Bears, 21-0 (C)
1987—Bears, 34-19 (C)
(Points—Bears 792, Giants 593)
*NFL Championship
**NFC Divisional Playoff

CHICAGO vs. N.Y. JETS
Bears lead series, 2-1
1974—Jets, 23-21 (C)
1979—Bears, 23-13 (C)
1985—Bears, 19-6 (NY)
(Points—Bears 63, Jets 42)

CHICAGO vs. PHILADELPHIA
Bears lead series, 21-4-1
1933—Tie, 3-3 (P)
1935—Bears, 39-0 (P)
1936—Bears, 17-0 (P)
Bears, 28-7 (P)
1938—Bears, 28-6 (P)
1939—Bears, 27-14 (C)
1941—Bears, 49-14 (P)
1942—Bears, 45-14 (C)
1944—Bears, 28-7 (P)
1946—Bears, 21-14 (C)
1947—Bears, 40-7 (C)
1948—Eagles, 12-7 (P)
1949—Bears, 38-21 (C)
1955—Bears, 17-10 (C)
1961—Eagles, 16-14 (P)
1963—Bears, 16-7 (C)
1968—Bears, 29-16 (P)
1970—Bears, 20-16 (C)
1972—Bears, 21-12 (P)
1975—Bears, 15-13 (C)
1979—*Eagles, 27-17 (P)
1980—Eagles, 17-14 (P)
1983—Bears, 7-6 (P)
Bears, 17-14 (C)
1986—Bears, 13-10 (C) OT
1987—Bears, 35-3 (P)
(Points—Bears 605, Eagles 286)
*NFC First Round Playoff

CHICAGO vs. *PITTSBURGH
Bears lead series, 14-4-1
1934—Bears, 28-0 (P)
1935—Bears, 23-7 (P)
1936—Bears, 27-9 (P)
Bears, 26-6 (C)
1937—Bears, 7-0 (P)
1939—Bears, 32-0 (P)
1941—Bears, 34-7 (C)
1945—Bears, 28-7 (P)
1947—Bears, 49-7 (C)
1949—Bears, 30-21 (C)
1958—Steelers, 24-10 (P)
1959—Bears, 27-21 (C)
1963—Tie, 17-17 (P)
1967—Steelers, 41-13 (P)
1969—Bears, 38-7 (C)
1971—Bears, 17-15 (C)
1975—Steelers, 34-3 (P)
1980—Steelers, 38-3 (P)
1986—Bears, 13-10 (C) OT
(Points—Bears 425, Steelers 271)
*Steelers known as Pirates prior to 1941

***CHICAGO vs. **ST. LOUIS**
Bears lead series, 50-25-6
(NP denotes Normal Park;
Wr denotes Wrigley Field;
Co denotes Comiskey Park;
So denotes Soldier Field;
all Chicago)
1920—Cardinals, 7-6 (NP)
Staleys, 10-0 (Wr)
1921—Tie, 0-0 (Wr)
1922—Cardinals, 6-0 (Co)
Cardinals, 9-0 (Co)
1923—Bears, 3-0 (Wr)
1924—Bears, 6-0 (Wr)
Bears, 21-0 (Co)
1925—Cardinals, 9-0 (Co)
Tie, 0-0 (Wr)
1926—Bears, 16-0 (Wr)
Bears, 10-0 (So)
Tie, 0-0 (Wr)
1927—Bears, 9-0 (NP)
Cardinals, 3-0 (Wr)
1928—Bears, 15-0 (NP)
Bears, 34-0 (Wr)
1929—Tie, 0-0 (Wr)
Cardinals, 40-6 (Co)
1930—Bears, 32-6 (Co)
Bears, 6-0 (Wr)
1931—Bears, 26-13 (Wr)
Bears, 18-7 (Wr)
1932—Tie, 0-0 (Wr)
Bears, 34-0 (Wr)
1933—Bears, 12-9 (Wr)
Bears, 22-6 (Wr)
1934—Bears, 20-0 (Wr)
Bears, 17-6 (Wr)
1935—Tie, 7-7 (Wr)
Bears, 13-0 (Wr)
1936—Bears, 7-3 (Wr)
Cardinals, 14-7 (Wr)
1937—Bears, 16-7 (Wr)
Bears, 42-28 (Wr)
1938—Bears, 16-13 (So)
Bears, 34-28 (Wr)
1939—Bears, 44-7 (Wr)
Bears, 48-7 (Co)
1940—Cardinals, 21-7 (Co)
Bears, 31-23 (Wr)
1941—Bears, 53-7 (Wr)
Bears, 34-24 (Co)
1942—Bears, 41-14 (Wr)
Bears, 21-7 (Co)
1943—Bears, 20-0 (Wr)
Bears, 35-24 (Co)
1945—Cardinals, 16-7 (Wr)
Bears, 28-20 (Co)
1946—Bears, 34-17 (Co)
Cardinals, 35-28 (Wr)
1947—Cardinals, 31-7 (Co)
Cardinals, 30-21 (Wr)
1948—Bears, 28-17 (Co)
Cardinals, 24-21 (Wr)
1949—Bears, 17-7 (Co)
Bears, 52-21 (Wr)
1950—Bears, 27-6 (Wr)
Cardinals, 20-10 (Co)
1951—Cardinals, 28-14 (Co)

Cardinals, 24-14 (Wr)
1952—Cardinals, 21-10 (Co)
Bears, 10-7 (Wr)
1953—Cardinals, 24-17 (Wr)
1954—Bears, 29-7 (Co)
1955—Cardinals, 53-14 (Co)
1956—Bears, 10-3 (Wr)
1957—Bears, 14-6 (Co)
1958—Bears, 30-14 (Wr)
1959—Bears, 31-7 (So)
1965—Bears, 34-13 (Wr)
1966—Cardinals, 24-17 (StL)
1967—Bears, 30-3 (Wr)
1969—Cardinals, 20-17 (StL)
1972—Bears, 27-10 (StL)
1975—Cardinals, 34-20 (So)
1977—Cardinals, 16-13 (StL)
1978—Bears, 17-10 (So)
1979—Bears, 42-6 (So)
1982—Cardinals, 10-7 (So)
1984—Cardinals, 38-21 (StL)
(Points—Bears 1,517, Cardinals 977)
**Franchise in Decatur prior to 1921; Bears known as Staleys prior to 1922*
***Franchise in Chicago prior to 1960*

CHICAGO vs. SAN DIEGO
Chargers lead series, 4-1
1970—Chargers, 20-7 (C)
1974—Chargers, 28-21 (SD)
1978—Chargers, 40-7 (SD)
1981—Bears, 20-17 (C) OT
1984—Chargers, 20-7 (SD)
(Points—Chargers 125, Bears 62)

CHICAGO vs. SAN FRANCISCO
Series tied, 24-24-1
1950—Bears, 32-20 (SF)
Bears, 17-0 (C)
1951—Bears, 13-7 (C)
1952—49ers, 40-16 (C)
Bears, 20-17 (SF)
1953—49ers, 35-28 (C)
49ers, 24-14 (SF)
1954—49ers, 31-24 (C)
Bears, 31-27 (SF)
1955—49ers, 20-19 (C)
Bears, 34-23 (SF)
1956—Bears, 31-7 (C)
Bears, 38-21 (SF)
1957—49ers, 21-17 (C)
49ers, 21-17 (SF)
1958—Bears, 28-6 (C)
Bears, 27-14 (SF)
1959—49ers, 20-17 (SF)
Bears, 14-3 (C)
1960—Bears, 27-10 (C)
49ers, 25-7 (SF)
1961—Bears, 31-0 (C)
49ers, 41-31 (SF)
1962—Bears, 30-14 (SF)
49ers, 34-27 (C)
1963—49ers, 20-14 (SF)
Bears, 27-7 (C)
1964—49ers, 31-21 (SF)
Bears, 23-21 (C)
1965—49ers, 52-24 (SF)
Bears, 61-20 (C)
1966—Tie, 30-30 (C)
49ers, 41-14 (SF)
1967—Bears, 28-14 (SF)
1968—Bears, 27-19 (C)
1969—49ers, 42-21 (SF)
1970—49ers, 37-16 (C)
1971—49ers, 13-0 (SF)
1972—49ers, 34-21 (C)
1974—49ers, 34-0 (C)
1975—49ers, 31-3 (SF)
1976—Bears, 19-12 (SF)
1978—Bears, 16-13 (SF)
1979—Bears, 28-27 (SF)
1981—49ers, 28-17 (SF)
1983—Bears, 13-3 (C)
1984—*49ers, 23-0 (SF)
1985—Bears, 26-10 (SF)
1987—49ers, 41-0 (SF)
(Points—49ers 1,084, Bears 1,039)
**NFC Championship*

CHICAGO vs. SEATTLE
Seahawks lead series, 4-1
1976—Bears, 34-7 (S)
1978—Seahawks, 31-29 (C)
1982—Seahawks, 20-14 (S)
1984—Seahawks, 38-9 (S)
1987—Seahawks, 34-21 (C)
(Points—Seahawks 130, Bears 107)

CHICAGO vs. TAMPA BAY
Bears lead series, 16-4
1977—Bears, 10-0 (TB)
1978—Buccaneers, 33-19 (TB)
Bears, 14-3 (C)
1979—Buccaneers, 17-13 (C)
Bears, 14-0 (TB)
1980—Bears, 23-0 (C)
Bears, 14-13 (TB)
1981—Bears, 28-17 (C)
Buccaneers, 20-10 (TB)
1982—Buccaneers, 26-23 (TB) OT
1983—Bears, 17-10 (C)
Bears, 27-0 (TB)
1984—Bears, 34-14 (C)
Bears, 44-9 (TB)
1985—Bears, 38-28 (C)
Bears, 27-19 (TB)
1986—Bears, 23-3 (TB)
Bears, 48-14 (C)
1987—Bears, 20-3 (C)
Bears, 27-26 (TB)
(Points—Bears 473, Buccaneers 255)

CHICAGO vs. *WASHINGTON
Bears lead series, 20-13-1
1932—Tie, 7-7 (B)
1933—Bears, 7-0 (C)
Redskins, 10-0 (B)
1934—Bears, 21-0 (B)
1935—Bears, 30-14 (B)
1936—Bears, 26-0 (B)
1937—**Redskins, 28-21 (C)
1938—Bears, 31-7 (C)
1940—Redskins, 7-3 (W)
**Bears, 73-0 (W)
1941—Bears, 35-21 (C)
1942—**Redskins, 14-6 (W)
1943—Redskins, 21-7 (W)
**Bears, 41-21 (C)
1945—Redskins, 28-21 (W)
1946—Bears, 24-20 (C)
1947—Bears, 56-20 (W)
1948—Bears, 48-13 (C)
1949—Bears, 31-21 (W)
1951—Bears, 27-0 (W)
1953—Bears, 27-24 (W)
1957—Redskins, 14-3 (C)
1964—Redskins, 27-20 (W)
1968—Redskins, 38-28 (C)
1971—Bears, 16-15 (C)
1974—Redskins, 42-0 (W)
1976—Bears, 33-7 (C)
1978—Bears, 14-10 (W)
1980—Bears, 35-21 (C)
1981—Redskins, 24-7 (C)
1984—***Bears, 23-19 (W)
1985—Bears, 45-10 (C)
1986—***Redskins, 27-13 (C)
1987—***Redskins, 21-17 (C)
(Points—Bears 796, Redskins 551)
**Franchise in Boston prior to 1937 and known as Braves prior to 1933*
***NFL Championship*
****NFC Divisional Playoff*

CINCINNATI vs. ATLANTA
Bengals lead series, 5-1;
See Atlanta vs. Cincinnati

CINCINNATI vs. BUFFALO
Bengals lead series, 9-5;
See Buffalo vs. Cincinnati

CINCINNATI vs. CHICAGO
Bengals lead series, 2-1;
See Chicago vs. Cincinnati

CINCINNATI vs. CLEVELAND
Browns lead series, 18-17
1970—Browns, 30-27 (Cle)
Bengals, 14-10 (Cin)
1971—Browns, 27-24 (Cin)
Browns, 31-27 (Cle)
1972—Browns, 27-6 (Cle)
Browns, 27-24 (Cin)
1973—Browns, 17-10 (Cle)
Bengals, 34-17 (Cin)
1974—Bengals, 33-7 (Cin)
Bengals, 34-24 (Cle)
1975—Bengals, 24-17 (Cin)
Browns, 35-23 (Cle)
1976—Bengals, 45-24 (Cle)
Bengals, 21-6 (Cin)
1977—Browns, 13-3 (Cin)
Bengals, 10-7 (Cle)
1978—Browns, 13-10 (Cle) OT
Bengals, 48-16 (Cin)
1979—Browns, 28-27 (Cle)
Bengals, 16-12 (Cin)
1980—Browns, 31-7 (Cle)
Browns, 27-24 (Cin)
1981—Browns, 20-17 (Cin)
Bengals, 41-21 (Cle)
1982—Bengals, 23-10 (Cin)
1983—Browns, 17-7 (Cle)
Bengals, 28-21 (Cin)
1984—Bengals, 12-9 (Cin)
Bengals, 20-17 (Cle) OT
1985—Bengals, 27-10 (Cin)
Browns, 24-6 (Cle)
1986—Bengals, 30-13 (Cle)
Browns, 34-3 (Cin)
1987—Browns, 34-0 (Cin)
Browns, 38-24 (Cle)
(Points—Bengals 729, Browns 714)

CINCINNATI vs. DALLAS
Cowboys lead series, 2-1
1973—Cowboys, 38-10 (D)
1979—Cowboys, 38-13 (D)
1985—Bengals, 50-24 (C)
(Points—Cowboys 100, Bengals 73)

CINCINNATI vs. DENVER
Broncos lead series, 9-6
1968—Bengals, 24-10 (C)
Broncos, 10-7 (D)
1969—Broncos, 30-23 (C)
Broncos, 27-16 (D)
1971—Bengals, 24-10 (D)
1972—Bengals, 21-10 (C)
1973—Broncos, 28-10 (D)
1975—Bengals, 17-16 (D)
1976—Bengals, 17-7 (C)
1977—Broncos, 24-13 (C)
1979—Broncos, 10-0 (D)
1981—Bengals, 38-21 (C)
1983—Broncos, 24-17 (D)
1984—Broncos, 20-17 (D)
1986—Broncos, 34-28 (D)
(Points—Broncos 281, Bengals 272)

CINCINNATI vs. DETROIT
Series tied, 2-2
1970—Lions, 38-3 (D)
1974—Lions, 23-19 (C)
1983—Bengals, 17-9 (C)
1986—Bengals, 24-17 (D)
(Points—Lions 87, Bengals 63)

CINCINNATI vs. GREEN BAY
Bengals lead series, 4-2
1971—Packers, 20-17 (GB)
1976—Bengals, 28-7 (C)
1977—Bengals, 17-7 (Mil)
1980—Packers, 14-9 (GB)
1983—Bengals, 34-14 (C)
1986—Bengals, 34-28 (Mil)
(Points—Bengals 139, Packers 90)

CINCINNATI vs. HOUSTON
Bengals lead series, 21-16-1
1968—Oilers, 27-17 (C)
1969—Tie, 31-31 (H)
1970—Oilers, 20-13 (C)
Bengals, 30-20 (H)
1971—Oilers, 10-6 (H)
Bengals, 28-13 (C)
1972—Bengals, 30-7 (C)
Bengals, 61-17 (H)
1973—Bengals, 24-10 (C)
Bengals, 27-24 (H)
1974—Oilers, 34-21 (C)
Oilers, 20-3 (H)
1975—Bengals, 21-19 (H)
Bengals, 23-19 (C)
1976—Bengals, 27-7 (H)
Bengals, 31-27 (C)
1977—Bengals, 13-10 (C) OT
Oilers, 21-16 (H)
1978—Bengals, 28-13 (C)
Oilers, 17-10 (H)
1979—Oilers, 30-27 (C) OT
Oilers, 42-21 (H)
1980—Oilers, 13-10 (C)
Oilers, 23-3 (H)
1981—Oilers, 17-10 (H)
Bengals, 34-21 (C)
1982—Bengals, 27-6 (C)
Bengals, 35-27 (H)
1983—Bengals, 55-14 (H)
Bengals, 38-10 (C)
1984—Bengals, 13-3 (C)
Bengals, 31-13 (H)
1985—Oilers, 44-27 (H)
Bengals, 45-27 (C)
1986—Bengals, 31-28 (C)
Oilers, 32-28 (H)
1987—Oilers, 31-29 (C)
Oilers, 21-17 (H)
(Points—Bengals 941, Oilers 768)

CINCINNATI vs. *INDIANAPOLIS
Series tied, 5-5
1970—**Colts, 17-0 (B)
1972—Colts, 20-19 (C)
1974—Bengals, 24-14 (B)
1976—Colts, 28-27 (B)
1979—Colts, 38-28 (B)
1980—Bengals, 34-33 (C)
1981—Bengals, 41-19 (B)
1982—Bengals, 20-17 (B)
1983—Colts, 34-31 (C)
1987—Bengals, 23-21 (I)
(Points—Bengals 247, Colts 241)
**Franchise in Baltimore prior to 1984*
***AFC Divisional Playoff*

CINCINNATI vs. KANSAS CITY
Chiefs lead series, 9-8
1968—Chiefs, 13-3 (KC)
Chiefs, 16-9 (C)
1969—Bengals, 24-19 (C)
Chiefs, 42-22 (KC)
1970—Chiefs, 27-19 (C)
1972—Bengals, 23-16 (KC)
1973—Bengals, 14-6 (C)
1974—Bengals, 33-6 (C)
1976—Bengals, 27-24 (KC)
1977—Bengals, 27-7 (KC)
1978—Chiefs, 24-23 (C)
1979—Chiefs, 10-7 (C)
1980—Bengals, 20-6 (KC)
1983—Chiefs, 20-15 (KC)
1984—Chiefs, 27-22 (C)
1986—Chiefs, 24-14 (KC)
1987—Bengals, 30-27 (C) OT
(Points—Bengals 332, Chiefs 314)

CINCINNATI vs. *L.A. RAIDERS
Raiders lead series, 12-4
1968—Raiders, 31-10 (O)
Raiders, 34-0 (C)
1969—Bengals, 31-17 (C)
Raiders, 37-17 (O)
1970—Bengals, 31-21 (C)
1971—Raiders, 31-27 (O)
1972—Raiders, 20-14 (C)
1974—Raiders, 30-27 (O)
1975—Bengals, 14-10 (C)
**Raiders, 31-28 (O)
1976—Raiders, 35-20 (O)
1978—Raiders, 34-21 (C)
1980—Raiders, 28-17 (O)
1982—Bengals, 31-17 (C)
1983—Raiders, 20-10 (C)
1985—Raiders, 13-6 (LA)
(Points—Raiders 409, Bengals 304)
**Franchise in Oakland prior to 1982*
***AFC Divisional Playoff*

CINCINNATI vs. L.A. RAMS
Bengals lead series, 3-2
1972—Rams, 15-12 (LA)
1976—Bengals, 20-12 (C)
1978—Bengals, 20-19 (LA)
1981—Bengals, 24-10 (C)
1984—Rams, 24-14 (C)
(Points—Bengals 90, Rams 80)

CINCINNATI vs. MIAMI
Dolphins lead series, 8-3
1968—Dolphins, 24-22 (C)
Bengals, 38-21 (M)
1969—Bengals, 27-21 (C)
1971—Dolphins, 23-13 (C)
1973—*Dolphins, 34-16 (M)
1974—Dolphins, 24-3 (M)
1977—Bengals, 23-17 (C)
1978—Dolphins, 21-0 (M)
1980—Dolphins, 17-16 (M)
1983—Dolphins, 38-14 (M)
1987—Dolphins, 20-14 (C)
(Points—Dolphins 260, Bengals 186)
**AFC Divisional Playoff*

CINCINNATI vs. MINNESOTA
Bengals lead series, 3-2
1973—Bengals, 27-0 (C)
1977—Vikings, 42-10 (M)
1980—Bengals, 14-0 (C)
1983—Vikings, 20-14 (M)
1986—Bengals, 24-20 (C)
(Points—Bengals 89, Vikings 82)

CINCINNATI vs. *NEW ENGLAND
Patriots lead series, 6-4
1968—Patriots, 33-14 (B)
1969—Patriots, 25-14 (C)
1970—Bengals, 45-7 (C)
1972—Bengals, 31-7 (NE)
1975—Bengals, 27-10 (C)
1978—Patriots, 10-3 (C)
1979—Patriots, 20-14 (C)
1984—Patriots, 20-14 (NE)
1985—Patriots, 34-23 (NE)
1986—Bengals, 31-7 (NE)
(Points—Bengals 216, Patriots 173)
**Franchise in Boston prior to 1971*

CINCINNATI vs. NEW ORLEANS
Series tied, 3-3
1970—Bengals, 26-6 (C)
1975—Bengals, 21-0 (NO)
1978—Saints, 20-18 (C)
1981—Saints, 17-7 (NO)
1984—Bengals, 24-21 (NO)
1987—Saints, 41-24 (C)
(Points—Bengals 120, Saints 105)

CINCINNATI vs. N.Y. GIANTS
Bengals lead series, 3-0
1972—Bengals, 13-10 (C)
1977—Bengals, 30-13 (C)
1985—Bengals, 35-30 (C)
(Points—Bengals 78, Giants 53)

CINCINNATI vs. N.Y. JETS
Jets lead series, 8-4
1968—Jets, 27-14 (NY)
1969—Jets, 21-7 (C)
Jets, 40-7 (NY)
1971—Jets, 35-21 (NY)
1973—Bengals, 20-14 (C)
1976—Bengals, 42-3 (NY)
1981—Bengals, 31-30 (NY)

1982—*Jets, 44-17 (C)
1984—Jets, 43-23 (NY)
1985—Jets, 29-20 (C)
1986—Bengals, 52-21 (C)
1987—Jets, 27-20 (NY)
(Points—Jets 334, Bengals 274)
*AFC First Round Playoff

CINCINNATI vs. PHILADELPHIA
Bengals lead series, 4-0
1971—Bengals, 37-14 (C)
1975—Bengals, 31-0 (P)
1979—Bengals, 37-13 (C)
1982—Bengals, 18-14 (P)
(Points—Bengals 123, Eagles 41)

CINCINNATI vs. PITTSBURGH
Steelers lead series, 20-15
1970—Steelers, 21-10 (P)
Bengals, 34-7 (C)
1971—Steelers, 21-10 (P)
Steelers, 21-13 (C)
1972—Bengals, 15-10 (C)
Steelers, 40-17 (P)
1973—Bengals, 19-7 (C)
Steelers, 20-13 (P)
1974—Bengals, 17-10 (C)
Steelers, 27-3 (P)
1975—Steelers, 30-24 (C)
Steelers, 35-14 (P)
1976—Steelers, 23-6 (P)
Steelers, 7-3 (C)
1977—Steelers, 20-14 (P)
Bengals, 17-10 (C)
1978—Steelers, 28-3 (C)
Steelers, 7-6 (P)
1979—Bengals, 34-10 (C)
Steelers, 37-17 (P)
1980—Bengals, 30-28 (C)
Bengals, 17-16 (P)
1981—Bengals, 34-7 (C)
Bengals, 17-10 (P)
1982—Steelers, 26-20 (P) OT
1983—Steelers, 24-14 (C)
Bengals, 23-10 (P)
1984—Steelers, 38-17 (P)
Bengals, 22-20 (C)
1985—Bengals, 37-24 (P)
Bengals, 26-21 (C)
1986—Bengals, 24-22 (C)
Steelers, 30-9 (P)
1987—Steelers, 23-20 (P)
Steelers, 30-16 (C)
(Points—Steelers 720, Bengals 615)

CINCINNATI vs. ST. LOUIS
Bengals lead series, 2-1
1973—Bengals, 42-24 (C)
1979—Bengals, 34-28 (C)
1985—Cardinals, 41-27 (StL)
(Points—Bengals 103, Cardinals 93)

CINCINNATI vs. SAN DIEGO
Chargers lead series, 11-7
1968—Chargers, 29-13 (SD)
Chargers, 31-10 (C)
1969—Bengals, 34-20 (C)
Chargers, 21-14 (SD)
1970—Bengals, 17-14 (SD)
1971—Bengals, 31-0 (C)
1973—Bengals, 20-13 (SD)
1974—Chargers, 20-17 (C)
1975—Bengals, 47-17 (C)
1977—Chargers, 24-3 (SD)
1978—Chargers, 22-13 (SD)
1979—Chargers, 26-24 (C)
1980—Chargers, 31-14 (C)
1981—Bengals, 40-17 (SD)
*Bengals, 27-7 (C)
1982—Chargers, 50-34 (SD)
1985—Chargers, 44-41 (C)
1987—Chargers, 10-9 (C)
(Points—Bengals 408, Chargers 396)
*AFC Championship

CINCINNATI vs. SAN FRANCISCO
49ers lead series, 5-1
1974—Bengals, 21-3 (SF)
1978—49ers, 28-12 (SF)
1981—49ers, 21-3 (C)
*49ers, 26-21 (Detroit)
1984—49ers, 23-17 (SF)
1987—49ers, 27-26 (C)
(Points—49ers 128, Bengals 100)
*Super Bowl XVI

CINCINNATI vs. SEATTLE
Bengals lead series, 5-2
1977—Bengals, 42-20 (C)
1981—Bengals, 27-21 (C)
1982—Bengals, 24-10 (C)
1984—Seahawks, 26-6 (C)
1985—Seahawks, 28-24 (C)
1986—Bengals, 34-7 (C)
1987—Bengals, 17-10 (S)
(Points—Bengals 174, Seahawks 122)

CINCINNATI vs. TAMPA BAY
Bengals lead series, 2-1
1976—Bengals, 21-0 (C)
1980—Buccaneers, 17-12 (C)
1983—Bengals, 23-17 (TB)
(Points—Bengals 56, Buccaneers 34)

CINCINNATI vs. WASHINGTON
Redskins lead series, 3-1
1970—Redskins, 20-0 (W)
1974—Bengals, 28-17 (C)
1979—Redskins, 28-14 (W)
1985—Redskins, 27-24 (W)
(Points—Redskins 92, Bengals 66)

CLEVELAND vs. ATLANTA
Browns lead series, 7-1;
See Atlanta vs. Cleveland

CLEVELAND vs. BUFFALO
Browns lead series, 7-2;
See Buffalo vs. Cleveland

CLEVELAND vs. CHICAGO
Browns lead series, 6-3;
See Chicago vs. Cleveland

CLEVELAND vs. CINCINNATI
Browns lead series, 18-17;
See Cincinnati vs. Cleveland

CLEVELAND vs. DALLAS
Browns lead series, 15-9
1960—Browns, 48-7 (D)
1961—Browns, 25-7 (C)
Browns, 38-17 (D)
1962—Browns, 19-10 (C)
Cowboys, 45-21 (D)
1963—Browns, 41-24 (D)
Browns, 27-17 (C)
1964—Browns, 27-6 (C)
Browns, 20-16 (D)
1965—Browns, 23-17 (C)
Browns, 24-17 (D)
1966—Browns, 30-21 (C)
Cowboys, 26-14 (D)
1967—Cowboys, 21-14 (C)
*Cowboys, 52-14 (D)
1968—Cowboys, 28-7 (C)
*Browns, 31-20 (C)
1969—Browns, 42-10 (C)
*Browns, 38-14 (D)
1970—Cowboys, 6-2 (C)
1974—Cowboys, 41-17 (D)
1979—Browns, 26-7 (C)
1982—Cowboys, 31-14 (D)
1985—Cowboys, 20-7 (D)
(Points—Browns 569, Cowboys 480)
*Conference Championship

CLEVELAND vs. DENVER
Broncos lead series, 10-3
1970—Browns, 27-13 (D)
1971—Broncos, 27-0 (C)
1972—Browns, 27-20 (D)
1974—Browns, 23-21 (C)
1975—Broncos, 16-15 (D)
1976—Broncos, 44-13 (D)
1978—Broncos, 19-7 (C)
1980—Broncos, 19-16 (C)
1981—Broncos, 23-20 (D) OT
1983—Broncos, 27-6 (D)
1984—Broncos, 24-14 (C)
1986—*Broncos, 23-20 (C) OT
1987—*Broncos, 38-33 (D)
(Points—Broncos 314, Browns 221)
*AFC Championship

CLEVELAND vs. DETROIT
Lions lead series, 12-4
1952—Lions, 17-6 (D)
*Lions, 17-7 (C)
1953—*Lions, 17-16 (D)
1954—Lions, 14-10 (C)
*Browns, 56-10 (C)
1957—Lions, 20-7 (D)
*Lions, 59-14 (D)
1958—Lions, 30-10 (C)
1963—Lions, 38-10 (D)
1964—Browns, 37-21 (C)
1967—Lions, 31-14 (D)
1969—Lions, 28-21 (C)
1970—Lions, 41-24 (C)
1975—Lions, 21-10 (D)
1983—Browns, 31-26 (D)
1986—Browns, 24-21 (C)
(Points—Lions 411, Browns 297)
*NFL Championship

CLEVELAND vs. GREEN BAY
Packers lead series, 8-5
1953—Browns, 27-0 (Mil)
1955—Browns, 41-10 (C)
1956—Browns, 24-7 (Mil)
1961—Packers, 49-17 (C)
1964—Packers, 28-21 (Mil)
1965—*Packers, 23-12 (GB)
1966—Packers, 21-20 (C)
1967—Packers, 55-7 (Mil)
1969—Browns, 20-7 (C)
1972—Packers, 26-10 (C)
1980—Browns, 26-21 (C)
1983—Packers, 35-21 (Mil)
1986—Packers, 17-14 (C)
(Points—Packers 299, Browns 260)
*NFL Championship

CLEVELAND vs. HOUSTON
Browns lead series, 23-12
1970—Browns, 28-14 (C)
Browns, 21-10 (H)
1971—Browns, 31-0 (C)
Browns, 37-24 (H)
1972—Browns, 23-17 (H)
Browns, 20-0 (C)
1973—Browns, 42-13 (C)
Browns, 23-13 (H)
1974—Browns, 20-7 (C)
Oilers, 28-24 (H)
1975—Oilers, 40-10 (C)
Oilers, 21-10 (H)
1976—Browns, 21-7 (H)
Browns, 13-10 (C)
1977—Browns, 24-23 (H)
Oilers, 19-15 (C)
1978—Oilers, 16-13 (C)
Oilers, 14-10 (H)
1979—Oilers, 31-10 (H)
Browns, 14-7 (C)
1980—Oilers, 16-7 (C)
Browns, 17-14 (H)
1981—Oilers, 9-3 (C)
Oilers, 17-13 (H)
1982—Browns, 20-14 (H)
1983—Browns, 25-19 (C) OT
Oilers, 34-27 (H)
1984—Browns, 27-10 (C)
Browns, 27-20 (H)
1985—Browns, 21-6 (H)
Browns, 28-21 (C)
1986—Browns, 23-20 (H)
Browns, 13-10 (C) OT
1987—Oilers, 15-10 (C)
Browns, 40-7 (H)
(Points—Browns 710, Oilers 546)

CLEVELAND vs. *INDIANAPOLIS
Browns lead series, 12-6
1956—Colts, 21-7 (C)
1959—Browns, 38-31 (B)
1962—Colts, 36-14 (C)
1964—**Browns, 27-0 (C)
1968—Browns, 30-20 (B)
**Colts, 34-0 (C)
1971—Browns, 14-13 (B)
***Colts, 20-3 (C)
1973—Browns, 24-14 (C)
1975—Colts, 21-7 (B)
1978—Browns, 45-24 (B)
1979—Browns, 13-10 (C)
1980—Browns, 28-27 (B)
1981—Browns, 42-28 (C)
1983—Browns, 41-23 (C)
1986—Browns, 24-9 (I)
1987—Colts, 9-7 (C)
***Browns, 38-21 (C)
(Points—Browns 402, Colts 361)
*Franchise in Baltimore prior to 1984
**NFL Championship
***AFC Divisional Playoff

CLEVELAND vs. KANSAS CITY
Series tied, 5-5-1
1971—Chiefs, 13-7 (KC)
1972—Chiefs, 31-7 (C)
1973—Tie, 20-20 (KC)
1975—Browns, 40-14 (C)
1976—Chiefs, 39-14 (KC)
1977—Browns, 44-7 (C)
1978—Chiefs, 17-3 (KC)
1979—Browns, 27-24 (KC)
1980—Browns, 20-13 (C)
1984—Chiefs, 10-6 (KC)
1986—Browns, 20-7 (C)
(Points—Browns 208, Chiefs 195)

CLEVELAND vs. *L.A.RAIDERS
Raiders lead series, 10-2
1970—Raiders, 23-20 (O)
1971—Raiders, 34-20 (C)
1973—Browns, 7-3 (O)
1974—Raiders, 40-24 (C)
1975—Raiders, 38-17 (O)
1977—Raiders, 26-10 (C)
1979—Raiders, 19-14 (O)
1980—**Raiders, 14-12 (C)
1982—***Raiders, 27-10 (LA)
1985—Raiders, 21-20 (C)
1986—Raiders, 27-14 (LA)
1987—Browns, 24-17 (LA)
(Points—Raiders 289, Browns 192)
*Franchise in Oakland prior to 1982
**AFC Divisional Playoff
***AFC First Round Playoff

CLEVELAND vs. L.A. RAMS
Browns lead series, 9-7
1950—*Browns, 30-28 (C)
1951—Browns, 38-23 (LA)
*Rams, 24-17 (LA)
1952—Browns, 37-7 (C)
1955—*Browns, 38-14 (LA)
1957—Browns, 45-31 (C)
1958—Browns, 30-27 (LA)
1963—Browns, 20-6 (C)
1965—Rams, 42-7 (LA)
1968—Rams, 24-6 (C)
1973—Rams, 30-17 (LA)
1977—Rams, 9-0 (C)
1978—Browns, 30-19 (C)
1981—Rams, 27-16 (LA)
1984—Rams, 20-17 (LA)
1987—Browns, 30-17 (C)
(Points—Browns 378, Rams 348)
*NFL Championship

CLEVELAND vs. MIAMI
Browns lead series, 4-3
1970—Browns, 28-0 (M)
1972—*Dolphins, 20-14 (M)
1973—Dolphins, 17-9 (C)
1976—Browns, 17-13 (C)
1979—Browns, 30-24 (C) OT
1985—*Dolphins, 24-21 (M)
1986—Browns, 26-16 (C)
(Points—Browns 145, Dolphins 114)
*AFC Divisional Playoff

CLEVELAND vs. MINNESOTA
Vikings lead series, 7-2
1965—Vikings, 27-17 (C)
1967—Browns, 14-10 (C)
1969—Vikings, 51-3 (M)
*Vikings, 27-7 (M)
1973—Vikings, 26-3 (M)
1975—Vikings, 42-10 (C)
1980—Vikings, 28-23 (M)
1983—Vikings, 27-21 (C)
1986—Browns, 23-20 (M)
(Points—Vikings 258, Browns 121)
*NFL Championship

CLEVELAND vs. NEW ENGLAND
Browns lead series, 7-2
1971—Browns, 27-7 (C)
1974—Browns, 21-14 (NE)
1977—Browns, 30-27 (C) OT
1980—Patriots, 34-17 (NE)
1982—Browns, 10-7 (C)
1983—Browns, 30-0 (NE)
1984—Patriots, 17-16 (C)
1985—Browns, 24-20 (C)
1987—Browns, 20-10 (NE)
(Points—Browns 195, Patriots 136)

CLEVELAND vs. NEW ORLEANS
Browns lead series, 8-2
1967—Browns, 42-7 (NO)
1968—Browns, 24-10 (NO)
Browns, 35-17 (C)
1969—Browns, 27-17 (NO)
1971—Browns, 21-17 (NO)
1975—Browns, 17-16 (C)
1978—Browns, 24-16 (NO)
1981—Browns, 20-17 (C)
1984—Saints, 16-14 (C)
1987—Saints, 28-21 (NO)
(Points—Browns 245, Saints 161)

CLEVELAND vs. N.Y. GIANTS
Browns lead series, 26-16-2
1950—Giants, 6-0 (C)
Giants, 17-13 (NY)
*Browns, 8-3 (C)
1951—Browns, 14-13 (C)
Browns, 10-0 (NY)
1952—Giants, 17-9 (C)
Giants, 37-34 (NY)
1953—Browns, 7-0 (NY)
Browns, 62-14 (C)
1954—Browns, 24-14 (C)
Browns, 16-7 (NY)
1955—Browns, 24-14 (C)
Tie, 35-35 (NY)
1956—Giants, 21-9 (C)
Browns, 24-7 (NY)
1957—Browns, 6-3 (C)
Browns, 34-28 (NY)
1958—Giants, 21-17 (C)
Giants, 13-10 (NY)
*Giants, 10-0 (NY)
1959—Giants, 10-6 (C)
Giants, 48-7 (NY)
1960—Giants, 17-13 (C)
Browns, 48-34 (NY)
1961—Giants, 37-21 (C)
Tie, 7-7 (NY)
1962—Browns, 17-7 (C)
Giants, 17-13 (NY)
1963—Browns, 35-24 (NY)
Giants, 33-6 (C)
1964—Browns, 42-20 (C)
Browns, 52-20 (NY)
1965—Browns, 38-14 (NY)
Browns, 34-21 (C)
1966—Browns, 28-7 (NY)
Browns, 49-40 (C)
1967—Giants, 38-34 (NY)
Browns, 24-14 (C)
1968—Browns, 45-10 (C)

1969—Browns, 28-17 (C)
Giants, 27-14 (NY)
1973—Browns, 12-10 (C)
1977—Browns, 21-7 (NY)
1985—Browns, 35-33 (NY)
(Points—Browns 985, Giants 792)
Conference Playoff

CLEVELAND vs. N.Y. JETS
Browns lead series, 8-3
1970—Browns, 31-21 (C)
1972—Browns, 26-10 (NY)
1976—Browns, 38-17 (C)
1978—Browns, 37-34 (C) OT
1979—Browns, 25-22 (NY) OT
1980—Browns, 17-14 (C)
1981—Jets, 14-13 (C)
1983—Browns, 10-7 (C)
1984—Jets, 24-20 (C)
1985—Jets, 37-10 (NY)
1986—*Browns, 23-20 (C) OT
(Points—Browns 250, Jets 220)
AFC Divisional Playoff

CLEVELAND vs. PHILADELPHIA
Browns lead series, 29-11-1
1950—Browns, 35-10 (P)
Browns, 13-7 (C)
1951—Browns, 20-17 (C)
Browns, 24-9 (NY)
1952—Browns, 49-7 (P)
Eagles, 28-20 (C)
1953—Browns, 37-13 (C)
Eagles, 42-27 (P)
1954—Eagles, 28-10 (P)
Browns, 6-0 (C)
1955—Browns, 21-17 (C)
Eagles, 33-17 (P)
1956—Browns, 16-0 (P)
Browns, 17-14 (C)
1957—Browns, 24-7 (C)
Eagles, 17-7 (P)
1958—Browns, 28-14 (C)
Browns, 21-14 (P)
1959—Browns, 28-7 (C)
Browns, 28-21 (P)
1960—Browns, 41-24 (P)
Eagles, 31-29 (C)
1961—Eagles, 27-20 (P)
Browns, 45-24 (C)
1962—Eagles, 35-7 (P)
Tie, 14-14 (C)
1963—Browns, 37-7 (C)
Browns, 23-17 (P)
1964—Browns, 28-20 (P)
Browns, 38-24 (C)
1965—Browns, 35-17 (P)
Browns, 38-34 (C)
1966—Browns, 27-7 (C)
Eagles, 33-21 (P)
1967—Eagles, 28-24 (P)
1968—Browns, 47-13 (C)
1969—Browns, 27-20 (P)
1972—Browns, 27-17 (P)
1976—Browns, 24-3 (C)
1979—Browns, 24-19 (P)
1982—Eagles, 24-21 (C)
(Points—Browns 1,045, Eagles 743)

CLEVELAND vs. PITTSBURGH
Browns lead series, 45-31
1950—Browns, 30-17 (P)
Browns, 45-7 (C)
1951—Browns, 17-0 (C)
Browns, 28-0 (P)
1952—Browns, 21-20 (P)
Browns, 29-28 (C)
1953—Browns, 34-16 (C)
Browns, 20-16 (P)
1954—Steelers, 55-27 (P)
Browns, 42-7 (C)
1955—Browns, 41-14 (C)
Browns, 30-7 (P)
1956—Browns, 14-10 (P)
Steelers, 24-16 (C)
1957—Browns, 23-12 (P)
Browns, 24-0 (C)
1958—Browns, 45-12 (P)
Browns, 27-10 (C)
1959—Steelers, 17-7 (P)
Steelers, 21-20 (C)
1960—Browns, 28-20 (C)
Steelers, 14-10 (P)
1961—Browns, 30-28 (P)
Steelers, 17-13 (C)
1962—Browns, 41-14 (P)
Browns, 35-14 (C)
1963—Browns, 35-23 (C)
Steelers, 9-7 (P)
1964—Steelers, 23-7 (C)
Browns, 30-17 (P)
1965—Browns, 24-19 (C)
Browns, 42-21 (P)
1966—Browns, 41-10 (C)
Steelers, 16-6 (P)
1967—Browns, 21-10 (C)
Browns, 34-14 (P)
1968—Browns, 31-24 (C)
Browns, 45-24 (P)
1969—Browns, 42-31 (C)
Browns, 24-3 (P)
1970—Browns, 15-7 (C)
Steelers, 28-9 (P)
1971—Browns, 27-17 (C)
Steelers, 26-9 (P)
1972—Browns, 26-24 (C)
Steelers, 30-0 (P)
1973—Steelers, 33-6 (P)
Browns, 21-16 (C)
1974—Steelers, 20-16 (P)
Steelers, 26-16 (C)
1975—Steelers, 42-6 (C)
Steelers, 31-17 (P)
1976—Steelers, 31-14 (P)
Browns, 18-16 (C)
1977—Steelers, 28-14 (C)
Steelers, 35-31 (P)
1978—Steelers, 15-9 (P) OT
Steelers, 34-14 (C)
1979—Steelers, 51-35 (C)
Steelers, 33-30 (P) OT
1980—Browns, 27-26 (C)
Steelers, 16-13 (P)
1981—Steelers, 13-7 (P)
Steelers, 32-10 (C)
1982—Browns, 10-9 (C)
Steelers, 37-21 (P)
1983—Steelers, 44-17 (P)
Browns, 30-17 (C)
1984—Browns, 20-10 (C)
Steelers, 23-20 (P)
1985—Browns, 17-7 (C)
Steelers, 10-9 (P)
1986—Browns, 27-24 (P)
Browns, 37-31 (C) OT
1987—Browns, 34-10 (C)
Browns, 19-13 (P)
(Points—Browns 1,737, Steelers 1,509)

CLEVELAND vs. *ST. LOUIS
Browns lead series, 30-10-3
1950—Browns, 34-24 (Cle)
Browns, 10-7 (Chi)
1951—Browns, 34-17 (Chi)
Browns, 49-28 (Cle)
1952—Browns, 28-13 (Cle)
Browns, 10-0 (Chi)
1953—Browns, 27-7 (Chi)
Browns, 27-16 (Cle)
1954—Browns, 31-7 (Cle)
Browns, 35-3 (Chi)
1955—Browns, 26-20 (Chi)
Browns, 35-24 (Cle)
1956—Cardinals, 9-7 (Chi)
Cardinals, 24-7 (Cle)
1957—Browns, 17-7 (Chi)
Browns, 31-0 (Cle)
1958—Browns, 35-28 (Cle)
Browns, 38-24 (Chi)
1959—Browns, 34-7 (Chi)
Browns, 17-7 (Cle)
1960—Browns, 28-27 (Cle)
Tie, 17-17 (StL)
1961—Browns, 20-17 (Cle)
Browns, 21-10 (StL)
1962—Browns, 34-7 (StL)
Browns, 38-14 (Cle)
1963—Cardinals, 20-14 (Cle)
Browns, 24-10 (StL)
1964—Tie, 33-33 (Cle)
Cardinals, 28-19 (StL)
1965—Cardinals, 49-13 (Cle)
Browns, 27-24 (StL)
1966—Cardinals, 34-28 (Cle)
Browns, 38-10 (StL)
1967—Browns, 20-16 (Cle)
Browns, 20-16 (StL)
1968—Cardinals, 27-21 (Cle)
Cardinals, 27-16 (StL)
1969—Tie, 21-21 (Cle)
Browns, 27-21 (StL)
1974—Cardinals, 29-7 (StL)
1979—Browns, 38-20 (StL)
1985—Cardinals, 27-24 (Cle) OT
(Points—Browns 1,080, Cardinals 776)
Franchise in Chicago prior to 1960

CLEVELAND vs. SAN DIEGO
Chargers lead series, 6-5-1
1970—Chargers, 27-10 (C)
1972—Browns, 21-17 (SD)
1973—Tie, 16-16 (C)
1974—Chargers, 36-35 (SD)
1976—Browns, 21-17 (C)
1977—Chargers, 37-14 (SD)
1981—Chargers, 44-14 (C)
1982—Chargers, 30-13 (C)
1983—Browns, 30-24 (SD) OT
1985—Browns, 21-7 (SD)
1986—Browns, 47-17 (C)
1987—Chargers, 27-24 (SD) OT
(Points—Chargers 299, Browns 266)

CLEVELAND vs. SAN FRANCISCO
Browns lead series, 8-5
1950—Browns, 34-14 (C)
1951—49ers, 24-10 (SF)
1953—Browns, 23-21 (C)
1955—Browns, 38-3 (SF)
1959—49ers, 21-20 (C)
1962—Browns, 13-10 (SF)
1968—Browns, 33-21 (SF)
1970—49ers, 34-31 (SF)
1974—Browns, 7-0 (C)
1978—Browns, 24-7 (C)
1981—Browns, 15-12 (SF)
1984—49ers, 41-7 (C)
1987—49ers, 38-24 (SF)
(Points—Browns 279, 49ers 246)

CLEVELAND vs. SEATTLE
Seahawks lead series, 7-2
1977—Seahawks, 20-19 (S)
1978—Seahawks, 47-24 (S)
1979—Seahawks, 29-24 (C)
1980—Browns, 27-3 (S)
1981—Seahawks, 42-21 (S)
1982—Browns, 21-7 (S)
1983—Seahawks, 24-9 (C)
1984—Seahawks, 33-0 (S)
1985—Seahawks, 31-13 (S)
(Points—Seahawks 236, Browns 158)

CLEVELAND vs. TAMPA BAY
Browns lead series, 3-0
1976—Browns, 24-7 (TB)
1980—Browns, 34-27 (TB)
1983—Browns, 20-0 (C)
(Points—Browns 78, Buccaneers 34)

CLEVELAND vs. WASHINGTON
Browns lead series, 31-8-1
1950—Browns, 20-14 (C)
Browns, 45-21 (W)
1951—Browns, 45-0 (C)
1952—Browns, 19-15 (C)
Browns, 48-24 (W)
1953—Browns, 30-14 (W)
Browns, 27-3 (C)
1954—Browns, 62-3 (C)
Browns, 34-14 (W)
1955—Redskins, 27-17 (C)
Browns, 24-14 (W)
1956—Redskins, 20-9 (W)
Redskins, 20-17 (C)
1957—Browns, 21-17 (C)
Tie, 30-30 (W)
1958—Browns, 20-10 (W)
Browns, 21-14 (C)
1959—Browns, 34-7 (C)
Browns, 31-17 (W)
1960—Browns, 31-10 (W)
Browns, 27-16 (C)
1961—Browns, 31-7 (C)
Browns, 17-6 (W)
1962—Redskins, 17-16 (C)
Redskins, 17-9 (W)
1963—Browns, 37-14 (C)
Browns, 27-20 (W)
1964—Browns, 27-13 (W)
Browns, 34-24 (C)
1965—Browns, 17-7 (W)
Browns, 24-16 (C)
1966—Browns, 38-14 (W)
Browns, 14-3 (C)
1967—Browns, 42-37 (C)
1968—Browns, 24-21 (W)
1969—Browns, 27-23 (C)
1971—Browns, 20-13 (W)
1975—Redskins, 23-7 (C)
1979—Redskins, 13-9 (C)
1985—Redskins, 14-7 (C)
(Points—Browns 1,039, Redskins 612)

DALLAS vs. ATLANTA
Cowboys lead series, 8-3;
See Atlanta vs. Dallas

DALLAS vs. BUFFALO
Cowboys lead series, 3-1;
See Buffalo vs. Dallas

DALLAS vs. CHICAGO
Cowboys lead series, 8-5;
See Chicago vs. Dallas

DALLAS vs. CINCINNATI
Cowboys lead series, 2-1;
See Cincinnati vs. Dallas

DALLAS vs. CLEVELAND
Browns lead series, 15-9;
See Cleveland vs. Dallas

DALLAS vs. DENVER
Cowboys lead series, 3-2
1973—Cowboys, 22-10 (Den)
1977—Cowboys, 14-6 (Dal)
*Cowboys, 27-10 (New Orleans)
1980—Broncos, 41-20 (Den)
1986—Broncos, 29-14 (Den)
(Points—Cowboys 97, Broncos 96)
Super Bowl XII

DALLAS vs. DETROIT
Cowboys lead series, 7-4
1960—Lions, 23-14 (Det)
1963—Cowboys, 17-14 (Dal)
1968—Cowboys, 59-13 (Dal)
1970—*Cowboys, 5-0 (Dal)
1972—Cowboys, 28-24 (Dal)
1975—Cowboys, 36-10 (Det)
1977—Cowboys, 37-0 (Dal)
1981—Lions, 27-24 (Det)
1985—Lions, 26-21 (Det)
1986—Cowboys, 31-7 (Det)
1987—Lions, 27-17 (Det)
(Points—Cowboys 289, Lions 171)
NFC Divisional Playoff

DALLAS vs. GREEN BAY
Packers lead series, 8-5
1960—Packers, 41-7 (GB)
1964—Packers, 45-21 (D)
1965—Packers, 13-3 (Mil)
1966—*Packers, 34-27 (D)
1967—*Packers, 21-17 (GB)
1968—Packers, 28-17 (D)
1970—Cowboys, 16-3 (D)
1972—Packers, 16-13 (Mil)
1975—Packers, 19-17 (D)
1978—Cowboys, 42-14 (Mil)
1980—Cowboys, 28-7 (Mil)
1982—**Cowboys, 37-26 (D)
1984—Cowboys, 20-6 (D)
(Points—Packers 273, Cowboys 265)
NFL Championship
***NFC Second Round Playoff*

DALLAS vs. HOUSTON
Cowboys lead series, 4-1
1970—Cowboys, 52-10 (D)
1974—Cowboys, 10-0 (H)
1979—Oilers, 30-24 (D)
1982—Cowboys, 37-7 (H)
1985—Cowboys, 17-10 (H)
(Points—Cowboys 140, Oilers 57)

DALLAS vs. *INDIANAPOLIS
Cowboys lead series, 6-3
1960—Colts, 45-7 (D)
1967—Colts, 23-17 (B)
1969—Cowboys, 27-10 (D)
1970—**Colts, 16-13 (Miami)
1972—Cowboys, 21-0 (B)
1976—Cowboys, 30-27 (D)
1978—Cowboys, 38-0 (D)
1981—Cowboys, 37-13 (B)
1984—Cowboys, 22-3 (D)
(Points—Cowboys 212, Colts 137)
Franchise in Baltimore prior to 1984
***Super Bowl V*

DALLAS vs. KANSAS CITY
Cowboys lead series, 2-1
1970—Cowboys, 27-16 (KC)
1975—Chiefs, 34-31 (D)
1983—Cowboys, 41-21 (D)
(Points—Cowboys 99, Chiefs 71)

DALLAS vs. *L.A. RAIDERS
Raiders lead series, 3-1
1974—Raiders, 27-23 (O)
1980—Cowboys, 19-13 (O)
1983—Raiders, 40-38 (D)
1986—Raiders, 17-13 (D)
(Points—Raiders 97, Cowboys 93)
Franchise in Oakland prior to 1982

DALLAS vs. L.A. RAMS
Series tied, 11-11
1960—Rams, 38-13 (D)
1962—Cowboys, 27-17 (LA)
1967—Rams, 35-13 (D)
1969—Rams, 24-23 (LA)
1971—Cowboys, 28-21 (D)
1973—Rams, 37-31 (LA)
*Cowboys, 27-16 (D)
1975—Cowboys, 18-7 (D)
**Cowboys, 37-7 (LA)
1976—*Rams, 14-12 (D)
1978—Rams, 27-14 (LA)
**Cowboys, 28-0 (LA)
1979—Cowboys, 30-6 (D)
*Rams, 21-19 (D)
1980—Rams, 38-14 (LA)
***Cowboys, 34-13 (D)
1981—Cowboys, 29-17 (D)
1983—***Rams, 24-17 (D)
1984—Cowboys, 20-13 (LA)
1985—*Rams, 20-0 (LA)
1986—Rams, 29-10 (LA)
1987—Cowboys, 29-21 (LA)
(Points—Cowboys 473, Rams 445)
NFC Divisional Playoff
***NFC Championship*
****NFC First Round Playoff*

DALLAS vs. MIAMI
Dolphins lead series, 4-2
1971—*Cowboys, 24-3 (New Orleans)
1973—Dolphins, 14-7 (D)
1978—Dolphins, 23-16 (M)
1981—Cowboys, 28-27 (D)

1984—Dolphins, 28-21 (M)
1987—Dolphins, 20-14 (D)
(Points—Dolphins 115, Cowboys 110)
Super Bowl VI

DALLAS vs. MINNESOTA
Cowboys lead series, 10-6
1961—Cowboys, 21-7 (D)
Cowboys, 28-0 (M)
1966—Cowboys, 28-17 (D)
1968—Cowboys, 20-7 (M)
1970—Vikings, 54-13 (M)
1971—*Cowboys, 20-12 (M)
1973—**Vikings, 27-10 (D)
1974—Vikings, 23-21 (D)
1975—*Cowboys, 17-14 (M)
1977—Cowboys, 16-10 (M) OT
**Cowboys, 23-6 (D)
1978—Vikings, 21-10 (D)
1979—Cowboys, 36-20 (M)
1982—Vikings, 31-27 (M)
1983—Cowboys, 37-24 (M)
1987—Vikings, 44-38 (D) OT
(Points—Cowboys 365, Vikings 317)
**NFC Divisional Playoff*
***NFC Championship*

DALLAS vs. NEW ENGLAND
Cowboys lead series, 6-0
1971—Cowboys, 44-21 (D)
1975—Cowboys, 34-31 (NE)
1978—Cowboys, 17-10 (D)
1981—Cowboys, 35-21 (NE)
1984—Cowboys, 20-17 (D)
1987—Cowboys, 23-17 (NE) OT
(Points—Cowboys 173, Patriots 117)

DALLAS vs. NEW ORLEANS
Cowboys lead series, 11-1
1967—Cowboys, 14-10 (D)
Cowboys, 27-10 (NO)
1968—Cowboys, 17-3 (NO)
1969—Cowboys, 21-17 (NO)
Cowboys, 33-17 (D)
1971—Saints, 24-14 (NO)
1973—Cowboys, 40-3 (D)
1976—Cowboys, 24-6 (NO)
1978—Cowboys, 27-7 (D)
1982—Cowboys, 21-7 (D)
1983—Cowboys, 21-20 (D)
1984—Cowboys, 30-27 (D) OT
(Points—Cowboys 289, Saints 151)

DALLAS vs. N.Y. GIANTS
Cowboys lead series, 35-14-2
1960—Tie, 31-31 (NY)
1961—Giants, 31-10 (D)
Cowboys, 17-16 (NY)
1962—Giants, 41-10 (D)
Giants, 41-31 (NY)
1963—Giants, 37-21 (NY)
Giants, 34-27 (D)
1964—Tie, 13-13 (D)
Cowboys, 31-21 (NY)
1965—Cowboys, 31-2 (D)
Cowboys, 38-20 (NY)
1966—Cowboys, 52-7 (D)
Cowboys, 17-7 (NY)
1967—Cowboys, 38-24 (D)
1968—Giants, 27-21 (D)
Cowboys, 28-10 (NY)
1969—Cowboys, 25-3 (D)
1970—Cowboys, 28-10 (D)
Giants, 23-20 (NY)
1971—Cowboys, 20-13 (D)
Cowboys, 42-14 (NY)
1972—Cowboys, 23-14 (NY)
Giants, 23-3 (D)
1973—Cowboys, 45-28 (D)
Cowboys, 23-10 (New Haven)
1974—Giants, 14-6 (D)
Cowboys, 21-7 (New Haven)
1975—Cowboys, 13-7 (NY)
Cowboys, 14-3 (D)
1976—Cowboys, 24-14 (NY)
Cowboys, 9-3 (D)
1977—Cowboys, 41-21 (D)
Cowboys, 24-10 (NY)
1978—Cowboys, 34-24 (NY)
Cowboys, 24-3 (D)
1979—Cowboys, 16-14 (NY)
Cowboys, 28-7 (D)
1980—Cowboys, 24-3 (D)
Giants, 38-35 (NY)
1981—Cowboys, 18-10 (D)
Giants, 13-10 (NY) OT
1983—Cowboys, 28-13 (D)
Cowboys, 38-20 (NY)
1984—Giants, 28-7 (NY)
Giants, 19-7 (D)
1985—Cowboys, 30-29 (NY)
Cowboys, 28-21 (D)
1986—Cowboys, 31-28 (D)
Giants, 17-14 (NY)
1987—Cowboys, 16-14 (NY)
Cowboys, 33-24 (D)
(Points—Cowboys 1,218, Giants 904)

DALLAS vs. N.Y. JETS
Cowboys lead series, 4-0
1971—Cowboys, 52-10 (D)
1975—Cowboys, 31-21 (NY)
1978—Cowboys, 30-7 (NY)
1987—Cowboys, 38-24 (NY)
(Points—Cowboys 151, Jets 62)

DALLAS vs. PHILADELPHIA
Cowboys lead series, 36-19
1960—Eagles, 27-25 (D)
1961—Eagles, 43-7 (D)
Eagles, 35-13 (P)
1962—Cowboys, 41-19 (D)
Eagles, 28-14 (P)
1963—Eagles, 24-21 (P)
Cowboys, 27-20 (D)
1964—Eagles, 17-14 (D)
Eagles, 24-14 (P)
1965—Eagles, 35-24 (D)
Cowboys, 21-19 (P)
1966—Cowboys, 56-7 (D)
Eagles, 24-23 (P)
1967—Eagles, 21-14 (P)
Cowboys, 38-17 (D)
1968—Cowboys, 45-13 (P)
Cowboys, 34-14 (D)
1969—Cowboys, 38-7 (P)
Cowboys, 49-14 (D)
1970—Cowboys, 17-7 (P)
Cowboys, 21-17 (D)
1971—Cowboys, 42-7 (P)
Cowboys, 20-7 (D)
1972—Cowboys, 28-6 (D)
Cowboys, 28-7 (P)
1973—Eagles, 30-16 (P)
Cowboys, 31-10 (D)
1974—Eagles, 13-10 (P)
Cowboys, 31-24 (D)
1975—Cowboys, 20-17 (P)
Cowboys, 27-17 (D)
1976—Cowboys, 27-7 (D)
Cowboys, 26-7 (P)
1977—Cowboys, 16-10 (P)
Cowboys, 24-14 (D)
1978—Cowboys, 14-7 (D)
Cowboys, 31-13 (P)
1979—Eagles, 31-21 (D)
Cowboys, 24-17 (P)
1980—Eagles, 17-10 (P)
Cowboys, 35-27 (D)
*Eagles, 20-7 (P)
1981—Cowboys, 17-14 (P)
Cowboys, 21-10 (D)
1982—Eagles, 24-20 (D)
1983—Cowboys, 37-7 (D)
Cowboys, 27-20 (P)
1984—Cowboys, 23-17 (D)
Cowboys, 26-10 (P)
1985—Eagles, 16-14 (P)
Cowboys, 34-17 (D)
1986—Cowboys, 17-14 (P)
Eagles, 23-21 (D)
1987—Cowboys, 41-22 (D)
Eagles, 37-20 (P)
(Points—Cowboys 1,362, Eagles 971)
**NFC Championship*

DALLAS vs. PITTSBURGH
Steelers lead series, 12-11
1960—Steelers, 35-28 (D)
1961—Cowboys, 27-24 (D)
Steelers, 37-7 (P)
1962—Steelers, 30-28 (D)
Cowboys, 42-27 (P)
1963—Steelers, 27-21 (P)
Steelers, 24-19 (D)
1964—Steelers, 23-17 (P)
Cowboys, 17-14 (D)
1965—Steelers, 22-13 (P)
Cowboys, 24-17 (D)
1966—Cowboys, 52-21 (D)
Cowboys, 20-7 (P)
1967—Cowboys, 24-21 (P)
1968—Cowboys, 28-7 (D)
1969—Cowboys, 10-7 (P)
1972—Cowboys, 17-13 (D)
1975—*Steelers, 21-17 (Miami)
1977—Steelers, 28-13 (P)
1978—**Steelers, 35-31 (Miami)
1979—Steelers, 14-3 (P)
1982—Steelers, 36-28 (D)
1985—Cowboys, 27-13 (D)
(Points—Cowboys 513, Steelers 503)
**Super Bowl X*
***Super Bowl XIII*

DALLAS vs. ST. LOUIS
Cowboys lead series, 32-18-1
1960—Cardinals, 12-10 (StL)
1961—Cardinals, 31-17 (D)
Cardinals, 31-13 (StL)
1962—Cardinals, 28-24 (D)
Cardinals, 52-20 (StL)
1963—Cardinals, 34-7 (D)
Cowboys, 28-24 (StL)
1964—Cardinals, 16-6 (D)
Cowboys, 31-13 (StL)
1965—Cardinals, 20-13 (StL)
Cowboys, 27-13 (D)
1966—Tie, 10-10 (StL)
Cowboys, 31-17 (D)
1967—Cowboys, 46-21 (D)
1968—Cowboys, 27-10 (StL)
1969—Cowboys, 24-3 (D)
1970—Cardinals, 20-7 (StL)
Cardinals, 38-0 (D)
1971—Cowboys, 16-13 (StL)
Cowboys, 31-12 (D)
1972—Cowboys, 33-24 (D)
Cowboys, 27-6 (StL)
1973—Cowboys, 45-10 (D)
Cowboys, 30-3 (StL)
1974—Cardinals, 31-28 (StL)
Cowboys, 17-14 (D)
1975—Cowboys, 37-31 (D) OT
Cardinals, 31-17 (StL)
1976—Cardinals, 21-17 (StL)
Cowboys, 19-14 (D)
1977—Cowboys, 30-24 (StL)
Cardinals, 24-17 (D)
1978—Cowboys, 21-12 (D)
Cowboys, 24-21 (StL) OT
1979—Cowboys, 22-21 (StL)
Cowboys, 22-13 (D)
1980—Cowboys, 27-24 (StL)
Cowboys, 31-21 (D)
1981—Cowboys, 30-17 (D)
Cardinals, 20-17 (StL)
1982—Cowboys, 24-7 (StL)
1983—Cowboys, 34-17 (StL)
Cowboys, 35-17 (D)
1984—Cardinals, 31-20 (D)
Cowboys, 24-17 (StL)
1985—Cardinals, 21-10 (StL)
Cowboys, 35-17 (D)
1986—Cowboys, 31-7 (StL)
Cowboys, 37-6 (D)
1987—Cardinals, 24-13 (StL)
Cowboys, 21-16 (D)
(Points—Cowboys 1,183, Cardinals 980)

DALLAS vs. SAN DIEGO
Cowboys lead series, 3-1
1972—Cowboys, 34-28 (SD)
1980—Cowboys, 42-31 (D)
1983—Chargers, 24-23 (SD)
1986—Cowboys, 24-21 (SD)
(Points—Cowboys 123, Chargers 104)

DALLAS vs. SAN FRANCISCO
Series tied, 8-8-1
1960—49ers, 26-14 (D)
1963—49ers, 31-24 (SF)
1965—Cowboys, 39-31 (D)
1967—49ers, 24-16 (SF)
1969—Tie, 24-24 (D)
1970—*Cowboys, 17-10 (SF)
1971—*Cowboys, 14-3 (D)
1972—49ers, 31-10 (D)
**Cowboys, 30-28 (SF)
1974—Cowboys, 20-14 (D)
1977—Cowboys, 42-35 (SF)
1979—Cowboys, 21-13 (SF)
1980—Cowboys, 59-14 (D)
1981—49ers, 42-14 (SF)
*49ers, 28-27 (SF)
1983—49ers, 42-17 (SF)
1985—49ers, 31-16 (SF)
(Points—49ers 430, Cowboys 404)
**NFC Championship*
***NFC Divisional Playoff*

DALLAS vs. SEATTLE
Cowboys lead series, 3-1
1976—Cowboys, 28-13 (S)
1980—Cowboys, 51-7 (D)
1983—Cowboys, 35-10 (S)
1986—Seahawks, 31-14 (D)
(Points—Cowboys 128, Seahawks 61)

DALLAS vs. TAMPA BAY
Cowboys lead series, 6-0
1977—Cowboys, 23-7 (D)
1980—Cowboys, 28-17 (D)
1981—*Cowboys, 38-0 (D)
1982—Cowboys, 14-9 (D)
**Cowboys, 30-17 (D)
1983—Cowboys, 27-24 (D) OT
(Points—Cowboys 160, Buccaneers 74)
**NFC Divisional Playoff*
***NFC First Round Playoff*

DALLAS vs. WASHINGTON
Cowboys lead series, 31-23-2
1960—Redskins, 26-14 (W)
1961—Tie, 28-28 (D)
Redskins, 34-24 (W)
1962—Tie, 35-35 (D)
Cowboys, 38-10 (W)
1963—Redskins, 21-17 (W)
Cowboys, 35-20 (D)
1964—Cowboys, 24-18 (D)
Redskins, 28-16 (W)
1965—Cowboys, 27-7 (D)
Redskins, 34-31 (W)
1966—Cowboys, 31-30 (W)
Redskins, 34-31 (D)
1967—Cowboys, 17-14 (W)
Redskins, 27-20 (D)
1968—Cowboys, 44-24 (W)
Cowboys, 29-20 (D)
1969—Cowboys, 41-28 (W)
Cowboys, 20-10 (D)
1970—Cowboys, 45-21 (W)
Cowboys, 34-0 (D)
1971—Redskins, 20-16 (D)
Cowboys, 13-0 (W)
1972—Redskins, 24-20 (W)
Cowboys, 34-24 (D)
*Redskins, 26-3 (W)
1973—Redskins, 14-7 (W)
Cowboys, 27-7 (D)
1974—Redskins, 28-21 (W)
Cowboys, 24-23 (D)
1975—Redskins, 30-24 (W) OT
Cowboys, 31-10 (D)
1976—Cowboys, 20-7 (W)
Redskins, 27-14 (D)
1977—Cowboys, 34-16 (D)
Cowboys, 14-7 (W)
1978—Redskins, 9-5 (W)
Cowboys, 37-10 (D)
1979—Redskins, 34-20 (W)
Cowboys, 35-34 (D)
1980—Cowboys, 17-3 (W)
Cowboys, 14-10 (D)
1981—Cowboys, 26-10 (W)
Cowboys, 24-10 (D)
1982—Cowboys, 24-10 (W)
*Redskins, 31-17 (W)
1983—Cowboys, 31-30 (W)
Redskins, 31-10 (D)
1984—Redskins, 34-14 (W)
Redskins, 30-28 (D)
1985—Cowboys, 44-14 (D)
Cowboys, 13-7 (W)
1986—Cowboys, 30-6 (D)
Redskins, 41-14 (W)
1987—Redskins, 13-7 (D)
Redskins, 24-20 (W)
(Points—Cowboys 1,333, Redskins 1,123)
**NFC Championship*

DENVER vs. ATLANTA
Series tied, 3-3;
See Atlanta vs. Denver

DENVER vs. BUFFALO
Bills lead series, 14-9-1;
See Buffalo vs. Denver

DENVER vs. CHICAGO
Series tied, 4-4;
See Chicago vs. Denver

DENVER vs. CINCINNATI
Broncos lead series, 9-6;
See Cincinnati vs. Denver

DENVER vs. CLEVELAND
Broncos lead series, 10-3;
See Cleveland vs. Denver

DENVER vs. DALLAS
Cowboys lead series, 3-2;
See Dallas vs. Denver

DENVER vs. DETROIT
Broncos lead series, 4-2
1971—Lions, 24-20 (Den)
1974—Broncos, 31-27 (Det)
1978—Lions, 17-14 (Det)
1981—Broncos, 27-21 (Den)
1984—Broncos, 28-7 (Det)
1987—Broncos, 34-0 (Den)
(Points—Broncos 154, Lions 96)

DENVER vs. GREEN BAY
Broncos lead series, 3-1-1
1971—Packers, 34-13 (Mil)
1975—Broncos, 23-13 (D)
1978—Broncos, 16-3 (D)
1984—Broncos, 17-14 (D)
1987—Tie, 17-17 (Mil) OT
(Points—Broncos 86, Packers 81)

DENVER vs. HOUSTON
Oilers lead series, 19-11-1
1960—Oilers, 45-25 (D)
Oilers, 20-10 (H)
1961—Oilers, 55-14 (D)
Oilers, 45-14 (H)
1962—Broncos, 20-10 (D)
Oilers, 34-17 (H)
1963—Oilers, 20-14 (H)
Oilers, 33-24 (D)
1964—Oilers, 38-17 (D)
Oilers, 34-15 (H)
1965—Broncos, 28-17 (D)
Broncos, 31-21 (H)
1966—Oilers, 45-7 (H)
Broncos, 40-38 (D)
1967—Oilers, 10-6 (H)
Oilers, 20-18 (D)

1968—Oilers, 38-17 (H)
1969—Oilers, 24-21 (H)
Tie, 20-20 (D)
1970—Oilers, 31-21 (H)
1972—Broncos, 30-17 (D)
1973—Broncos, 48-20 (H)
1974—Broncos, 37-14 (D)
1976—Oilers, 17-3 (H)
1977—Broncos, 24-14 (H)
1979—*Oilers, 13-7 (H)
1980—Oilers, 20-16 (D)
1983—Broncos, 26-14 (H)
1985—Broncos, 31-20 (D)
1987—Oilers, 40-10 (D)
**Broncos, 34-10 (D)
(Points—Oilers 797, Broncos 645)
*AFC First Round Playoff
**AFC Divisional Playoff

DENVER vs. *INDIANAPOLIS
Broncos lead series, 6-1
1974—Broncos, 17-6 (B)
1977—Broncos, 27-13 (D)
1978—Colts, 7-6 (B)
1981—Broncos, 28-10 (D)
1983—Broncos, 17-10 (B)
Broncos, 21-19 (D)
1985—Broncos, 15-10 (I)
(Points—Broncos 131, Colts 75)
*Franchise in Baltimore prior to 1984

DENVER vs. *KANSAS CITY
Chiefs lead series, 34-21
1960—Texans, 17-14 (D)
Texans, 34-7 (Da)
1961—Texans, 19-12 (D)
Texans, 49-21 (Da)
1962—Texans, 24-3 (D)
Texans, 17-10 (Da)
1963—Chiefs, 59-7 (D)
Chiefs, 52-21 (KC)
1964—Broncos, 33-27 (D)
Chiefs, 49-39 (KC)
1965—Chiefs, 31-23 (D)
Chiefs, 45-35 (KC)
1966—Chiefs, 37-10 (KC)
Chiefs, 56-10 (D)
1967—Chiefs, 52-9 (KC)
Chiefs, 38-24 (D)
1968—Chiefs, 34-2 (KC)
Chiefs, 30-7 (D)
1969—Chiefs, 26-13 (D)
Chiefs, 31-17 (KC)
1970—Broncos, 26-13 (D)
Chiefs, 16-0 (KC)
1971—Chiefs, 16-3 (D)
Chiefs, 28-10 (KC)
1972—Chiefs, 45-24 (D)
Chiefs, 24-21 (KC)
1973—Chiefs, 16-14 (KC)
Broncos, 14-10 (D)
1974—Broncos, 17-14 (KC)
Chiefs, 42-34 (D)
1975—Broncos, 37-33 (D)
Chiefs, 26-13 (KC)
1976—Broncos, 35-26 (KC)
Broncos, 17-16 (D)
1977—Broncos, 23-7 (D)
Broncos, 14-7 (KC)
1978—Broncos, 23-17 (KC) OT
Broncos, 24-3 (D)
1979—Broncos, 24-10 (KC)
Broncos, 20-3 (D)
1980—Chiefs, 23-17 (D)
Chiefs, 31-14 (KC)
1981—Chiefs, 28-14 (KC)
Broncos, 16-13 (D)
1982—Chiefs, 37-16 (D)
1983—Broncos, 27-24 (D)
Chiefs, 48-17 (KC)
1984—Broncos, 21-0 (D)
Chiefs, 16-13 (KC)
1985—Broncos, 30-10 (KC)
Broncos, 14-13 (D)
1986—Broncos, 38-17 (D)
Chiefs, 37-10 (KC)
1987—Broncos, 26-17 (KC)
Broncos, 20-17 (D)
(Points—Chiefs 1,430, Broncos 1,003)
*Franchise in Dallas prior to 1963 and known as Texans

DENVER vs. *L.A. RAIDERS
Raiders lead series, 36-18-2
1960—Broncos, 31-14 (D)
Raiders, 48-10 (O)
1961—Raiders, 33-19 (O)
Broncos, 27-24 (D)
1962—Broncos, 44-7 (D)
Broncos, 23-6 (O)
1963—Raiders, 26-10 (D)
Raiders, 35-31 (O)
1964—Raiders, 40-7 (O)
Tie, 20-20 (D)
1965—Raiders, 28-20 (D)
Raiders, 24-13 (O)
1966—Raiders, 17-3 (D)
Raiders, 28-10 (O)
1967—Raiders, 51-0 (O)
Raiders, 21-17 (D)
1968—Raiders, 43-7 (D)
Raiders, 33-27 (O)
1969—Raiders, 24-14 (D)
Raiders, 41-10 (O)
1970—Raiders, 35-23 (O)
Raiders, 24-19 (D)
1971—Raiders, 27-16 (D)
Raiders, 21-13 (O)
1972—Broncos, 30-23 (O)
Raiders, 37-20 (D)
1973—Tie, 23-23 (D)
Raiders, 21-17 (O)
1974—Raiders, 28-17 (D)
Broncos, 20-17 (O)
1975—Raiders, 42-17 (D)
Raiders, 17-10 (O)
1976—Raiders, 17-10 (D)
Raiders, 19-6 (O)
1977—Broncos, 30-7 (O)
Raiders, 24-14 (D)
**Broncos, 20-17 (D)
1978—Broncos, 14-6 (D)
Broncos, 21-6 (O)
1979—Raiders, 27-3 (O)
Raiders, 14-10 (D)
1980—Raiders, 9-3 (O)
Raiders, 24-21 (D)
1981—Broncos, 9-7 (D)
Broncos, 17-0 (O)
1982—Raiders, 27-10 (LA)
1983—Raiders, 22-7 (D)
Raiders, 22-20 (LA)
1984—Broncos, 16-13 (D)
Broncos, 22-19 (LA) OT
1985—Raiders, 31-28 (LA) OT
Raiders, 17-14 (D) OT
1986—Broncos, 38-36 (D)
Broncos, 21-10 (LA)
1987—Broncos, 30-14 (D)
Broncos, 23-17 (LA)
(Points—Raiders 1,283, Broncos 975)
*Franchise in Oakland prior to 1982
**AFC Championship

DENVER vs. L.A. RAMS
Rams lead series, 3-2
1972—Broncos, 16-10 (LA)
1974—Rams, 17-10 (D)
1979—Rams, 13-9 (D)
1982—Broncos, 27-24 (LA)
1985—Rams, 20-16 (LA)
(Points—Rams 84, Broncos 78)

DENVER vs. MIAMI
Dolphins lead series, 5-2-1
1966—Dolphins, 24-7 (M)
Broncos, 17-7 (D)
1967—Dolphins, 35-21 (M)
1968—Broncos, 21-14 (D)
1969—Dolphins, 27-24 (M)
1971—Tie, 10-10 (D)
1975—Dolphins, 14-13 (M)
1985—Dolphins, 30-26 (D)
(Points—Dolphins 161, Broncos 139)

DENVER vs. MINNESOTA
Vikings lead series, 3-2
1972—Vikings, 23-20 (D)
1978—Vikings, 12-9 (M) OT
1981—Broncos, 19-17 (D)
1984—Broncos, 42-21 (D)
1987—Vikings, 34-27 (M)
(Points—Broncos 117, Vikings 107)

DENVER vs. *NEW ENGLAND
Broncos lead series, 14-12
1960—Broncos, 13-10 (B)
Broncos, 31-24 (D)
1961—Patriots, 45-17 (B)
Patriots, 28-24 (D)
1962—Patriots, 41-16 (B)
Patriots, 33-29 (D)
1963—Broncos, 14-10 (D)
Patriots, 40-21 (B)
1964—Patriots, 39-10 (D)
Patriots, 12-7 (B)
1965—Broncos, 27-10 (B)
Patriots, 28-20 (D)
1966—Patriots, 24-10 (D)
Broncos, 17-10 (B)
1967—Broncos, 26-21 (D)
1968—Patriots, 20-17 (D)
Broncos, 35-14 (B)
1969—Broncos, 35-7 (D)
1972—Broncos, 45-21 (D)
1976—Patriots, 38-14 (NE)
1979—Broncos, 45-10 (D)
1980—Patriots, 23-14 (NE)
1984—Broncos, 26-19 (D)
1986—Broncos, 27-20 (D)
**Broncos, 22-17 (D)
1987—Broncos, 31-20 (D)
(Points—Broncos 593, Patriots 584)
*Franchise in Boston prior to 1971
**AFC Divisional Playoff

DENVER vs. NEW ORLEANS
Broncos lead series, 4-0
1970—Broncos, 31-6 (NO)
1974—Broncos, 33-17 (D)
1979—Broncos, 10-3 (D)
1985—Broncos, 34-23 (D)
(Points—Broncos 108, Saints 49)

DENVER vs. N.Y. GIANTS
Giants lead series, 3-2
1972—Giants, 29-17 (NY)
1976—Broncos, 14-13 (D)
1980—Broncos, 14-9 (NY)
1986—Giants, 19-16 (NY)
*Giants, 39-20 (Pasadena)
(Points—Giants 109, Broncos 81)
*Super Bowl XXI

DENVER vs. *N.Y. JETS
Jets lead series, 11-10-1
1960—Titans, 28-24 (NY)
Titans, 30-27 (D)
1961—Titans, 35-28 (NY)
Broncos, 27-10 (D)
1962—Broncos, 32-10 (NY)
Titans, 46-45 (D)
1963—Tie, 35-35 (NY)
Jets, 14-9 (D)
1964—Jets, 30-6 (NY)
Broncos, 20-16 (D)
1965—Broncos, 16-13 (D)
Jets, 45-10 (NY)
1966—Jets, 16-7 (D)
1967—Jets, 38-24 (D)
Broncos, 33-24 (NY)
1968—Broncos, 21-13 (NY)
1969—Broncos, 21-19 (D)
1973—Broncos, 40-28 (NY)
1976—Broncos, 46-3 (D)
1978—Jets, 31-28 (D)
1980—Broncos, 31-24 (D)
1986—Jets, 22-10 (NY)
(Points—Broncos 540, Jets 530)
*Jets known as Titans prior to 1963

DENVER vs. PHILADELPHIA
Eagles lead series, 3-2
1971—Eagles, 17-16 (P)
1975—Broncos, 25-10 (D)
1980—Eagles, 27-6 (P)
1983—Eagles, 13-10 (D)
1986—Broncos, 33-7 (P)
(Points—Broncos 90, Eagles 74)

DENVER vs. PITTSBURGH
Broncos lead series, 8-5-1
1970—Broncos, 16-13 (D)
1971—Broncos, 22-10 (P)
1973—Broncos, 23-13 (P)
1974—Tie, 35-35 (D) OT
1975—Steelers, 20-9 (P)
1977—Broncos, 21-7 (D)
*Broncos, 34-21 (D)
1978—Steelers, 21-17 (D)
*Steelers, 33-10 (P)
1979—Steelers, 42-7 (P)
1983—Broncos, 14-10 (P)
1984—*Steelers, 24-17 (D)
1985—Broncos, 31-23 (P)
1986—Broncos, 21-10 (P)
(Points—Steelers 282, Broncos 277)
*AFC Divisional Playoff

DENVER vs. ST. LOUIS
Broncos lead series, 1-0-1
1973—Tie, 17-17 (StL)
1977—Broncos, 7-0 (D)
(Points—Broncos 24, Cardinals 17)

DENVER vs. *SAN DIEGO
Chargers lead series, 28-27-1
1960—Chargers, 23-19 (D)
Chargers, 41-33 (LA)
1961—Chargers, 37-0 (SD)
Chargers, 19-16 (D)
1962—Broncos, 30-21 (D)
Broncos, 23-20 (SD)
1963—Broncos, 50-34 (D)
Chargers, 58-20 (SD)
1964—Chargers, 42-14 (SD)
Chargers, 31-20 (D)
1965—Chargers, 34-31 (SD)
Chargers, 33-21 (D)
1966—Chargers, 24-17 (SD)
Broncos, 20-17 (D)
1967—Chargers, 38-21 (D)
Chargers, 24-20 (SD)
1968—Chargers, 55-24 (SD)
Chargers, 47-23 (D)
1969—Broncos, 13-0 (D)
Chargers, 45-24 (SD)
1970—Chargers, 24-21 (SD)
Tie, 17-17 (D)
1971—Broncos, 20-16 (D)
Chargers, 45-17 (SD)
1972—Chargers, 37-14 (SD)
Broncos, 38-13 (D)
1973—Broncos, 30-19 (D)
Broncos, 42-28 (SD)
1974—Broncos, 27-7 (D)
Chargers, 17-0 (SD)
1975—Broncos, 27-17 (SD)
Broncos, 13-10 (D) OT
1976—Broncos, 26-0 (D)
Broncos, 17-0 (SD)
1977—Broncos, 17-14 (SD)
Broncos, 17-9 (D)
1978—Broncos, 27-14 (D)
Chargers, 23-0 (SD)
1979—Broncos, 7-0 (D)
Chargers, 17-7 (SD)
1980—Chargers, 30-13 (D)
Broncos, 20-13 (SD)
1981—Broncos, 42-24 (D)
Chargers, 34-17 (SD)
1982—Chargers, 23-3 (D)
Chargers, 30-20 (SD)
1983—Broncos, 14-6 (D)
Chargers, 31-7 (SD)
1984—Broncos, 16-13 (SD)
Broncos, 16-13 (D)
1985—Chargers, 30-10 (SD)
Broncos, 30-24 (D) OT
1986—Broncos, 31-14 (SD)
Chargers, 9-3 (D)
1987—Broncos, 31-17 (SD)
Broncos, 24-0 (D)
(Points—Chargers 1,281, Broncos 1,120)
*Franchise in Los Angeles prior to 1961

DENVER vs. SAN FRANCISCO
Broncos lead series, 3-2
1970—49ers, 19-14 (SF)
1973—49ers, 36-34 (D)
1979—Broncos, 38-28 (SF)
1982—Broncos, 24-21 (D)
1985—Broncos, 17-16 (D)
(Points—Broncos 127, 49ers 120)

DENVER vs. SEATTLE
Broncos lead series, 13-9
1977—Broncos, 24-13 (S)
1978—Broncos, 28-7 (D)
Broncos, 20-17 (S) OT
1979—Broncos, 37-34 (D)
Seahawks, 28-23 (S)
1980—Broncos, 36-20 (D)
Broncos, 25-17 (S)
1981—Seahawks, 13-10 (S)
Broncos, 23-13 (D)
1982—Seahawks, 17-10 (D)
Seahawks, 13-11 (S)
1983—Seahawks, 27-19 (S)
Broncos, 38-27 (D)
*Seahawks, 31-7 (S)
1984—Seahawks, 27-24 (D)
Broncos, 31-14 (S)
1985—Broncos, 13-10 (D) OT
Broncos, 27-24 (S)
1986—Broncos, 20-13 (D)
Seahawks, 41-16 (S)
1987—Broncos, 40-17 (D)
Seahawks, 28-21 (S)
(Points—Broncos 503, Seahawks 451)
*AFC First Round Playoff

DENVER vs. TAMPA BAY
Broncos lead series, 2-0
1976—Broncos, 48-13 (D)
1981—Broncos, 24-7 (TB)
(Points—Broncos 72, Buccaneers 20)

DENVER vs. WASHINGTON
Redskins lead series, 3-2
1970—Redskins, 19-3 (D)
1974—Redskins, 30-3 (W)
1980—Broncos, 20-17 (D)
1986—Broncos, 31-30 (D)
1987—*Redskins, 42-10 (San Diego)
(Points—Redskins 138, Broncos 67)
*Super Bowl XXII

DETROIT vs. ATLANTA
Lions lead series, 13-5;
See Atlanta vs. Detroit

DETROIT vs. BUFFALO
Series tied, 1-1-1;
See Buffalo vs. Detroit

DETROIT vs. CHICAGO
Bears lead series, 67-44-5;
See Chicago vs. Detroit

DETROIT vs. CINCINNATI
Series tied, 2-2;
See Cincinnati vs. Detroit

DETROIT vs. CLEVELAND
Lions lead series, 12-4;
See Cleveland vs. Detroit

DETROIT vs. DALLAS
Cowboys lead series, 7-4;
See Dallas vs. Detroit

DETROIT vs. DENVER
Broncos lead series, 4-2;
See Denver vs. Detroit

***DETROIT vs. GREEN BAY**
Packers lead series, 59-49-7
1930—Packers, 47-13 (GB)
Tie, 6-6 (P)
1932—Packers, 15-10 (GB)
Spartans, 19-0 (P)
1933—Packers, 17-0 (GB)
Spartans, 7-0 (P)
1934—Lions, 3-0 (GB)
Packers, 3-0 (D)
1935—Packers, 13-9 (GB)
Packers, 31-7 (GB)
Lions, 20-10 (D)
1936—Packers, 20-18 (GB)
Packers, 26-17 (D)
1937—Packers, 26-6 (GB)
Packers, 14-13 (D)
1938—Lions, 17-7 (GB)
Packers, 28-7 (D)
1939—Packers, 26-7 (GB)
Packers, 12-7 (D)
1940—Lions, 23-14 (GB)
Packers, 50-7 (D)
1941—Packers, 23-0 (GB)
Packers, 24-7 (D)
1942—Packers, 38-7 (Mil)
Packers, 28-7 (D)
1943—Packers, 35-14 (GB)
Packers, 27-6 (D)
1944—Packers, 27-6 (GB)
Packers, 14-0 (D)
1945—Packers, 57-21 (Mil)
Lions, 14-3 (D)
1946—Packers, 10-7 (Mil)
Packers, 9-0 (D)
1947—Packers, 34-17 (GB)
Packers, 35-14 (D)
1948—Packers, 33-21 (GB)
Lions, 24-20 (D)
1949—Packers, 16-14 (GB)
Lions, 21-7 (D)
1950—Lions, 45-7 (GB)
Lions, 24-21 (D)
1951—Lions, 24-17 (GB)
Lions, 52-35 (D)
1952—Lions, 52-17 (GB)
Lions, 48-24 (D)
1953—Lions, 14-7 (GB)
Lions, 34-15 (D)
1954—Lions, 21-17 (GB)
Lions, 28-24 (D)
1955—Packers, 20-17 (GB)
Lions, 24-10 (D)
1956—Lions, 20-16 (GB)
Packers, 24-20 (D)
1957—Lions, 24-14 (GB)
Lions, 18-6 (D)
1958—Tie, 13-13 (GB)
Lions, 24-14 (D)
1959—Packers, 28-10 (GB)
Packers, 24-17 (D)
1960—Packers, 28-9 (GB)
Lions, 23-10 (D)
1961—Lions, 17-13 (Mil)
Packers, 17-9 (D)
1962—Packers, 9-7 (GB)
Lions, 26-14 (D)
1963—Packers, 31-10 (Mil)
Tie, 13-13 (D)
1964—Packers, 14-10 (D)
Packers, 30-7 (GB)
1965—Packers, 31-21 (D)
Lions, 12-7 (GB)
1966—Packers, 23-14 (GB)
Packers, 31-7 (D)
1967—Tie, 17-17 (GB)
Packers, 27-17 (D)
1968—Lions, 23-17 (GB)
Tie, 14-14 (D)
1969—Packers, 28-17 (D)
Lions, 16-10 (GB)
1970—Lions, 40-0 (GB)
Lions, 20-0 (D)
1971—Lions, 31-28 (D)
Tie, 14-14 (Mil)
1972—Packers, 24-23 (D)
Packers, 33-7 (GB)
1973—Tie, 13-13 (GB)
Lions, 34-0 (D)
1974—Packers, 21-19 (Mil)
Lions, 19-17 (D)
1975—Lions, 30-16 (Mil)
Lions, 13-10 (D)
1976—Packers, 24-14 (GB)
Lions, 27-6 (D)
1977—Lions, 10-6 (D)
Packers, 10-9 (GB)
1978—Packers, 13-7 (D)
Packers, 35-14 (Mil)
1979—Packers, 24-16 (Mil)
Packers, 18-13 (D)
1980—Lions, 29-7 (Mil)
Lions, 24-3 (D)
1981—Lions, 31-27 (D)
Packers, 31-17 (GB)
1982—Lions, 30-10 (GB)
Lions, 27-24 (D)
1983—Lions, 38-14 (D)
Lions, 23-20 (Mil) OT
1984—Packers, 41-9 (GB)
Lions, 31-28 (D)
1985—Packers, 43-10 (GB)
Packers, 26-23 (D)
1986—Lions, 21-14 (GB)
Packers, 44-40 (D)
1987—Lions, 19-16 (GB) OT
Packers, 34-33 (D)
(Points—Packers 2,236, Lions 2,012)
**Franchise in Portsmouth prior to 1934 and known as the Spartans*

DETROIT vs. HOUSTON
Series tied, 2-2
1971—Lions, 31-7 (H)
1975—Oilers, 24-8 (H)
1983—Oilers, 27-17 (H)
1986—Lions, 24-13 (D)
(Points—Lions 80, Oilers 71)

DETROIT vs. *INDIANAPOLIS
Colts lead series, 17-16-2
1953—Lions, 27-17 (B)
Lions, 17-7 (D)
1954—Lions, 35-0 (D)
Lions, 27-3 (B)
1955—Colts, 28-13 (B)
Lions, 24-14 (D)
1956—Lions, 31-14 (B)
Lions, 27-3 (D)
1957—Colts, 34-14 (B)
Lions, 31-27 (D)
1958—Colts, 28-15 (B)
Colts, 40-14 (D)
1959—Colts, 21-9 (B)
Colts, 31-24 (D)
1960—Lions, 30-17 (D)
Lions, 20-15 (B)
1961—Lions, 16-15 (B)
Colts, 17-14 (D)
1962—Lions, 29-20 (B)
Lions, 21-14 (D)
1963—Colts, 25-21 (D)
Colts, 24-21 (B)
1964—Colts, 34-0 (D)
Lions, 31-14 (B)
1965—Colts, 31-7 (B)
Tie, 24-24 (D)
1966—Colts, 45-14 (B)
Lions, 20-14 (D)
1967—Colts, 41-7 (B)
1968—Colts, 27-10 (D)
1969—Tie, 17-17 (B)
1973—Colts, 29-27 (D)
1977—Lions, 13-10 (B)
1980—Colts, 10-9 (D)
1985—Colts, 14-6 (I)
(Points—Colts 724, Lions 665)
**Franchise in Baltimore prior to 1984*

DETROIT vs. KANSAS CITY
Chiefs lead series, 3-2
1971—Lions, 32-21 (D)
1975—Chiefs, 24-21 (KC) OT
1980—Chiefs, 20-17 (KC)
1981—Lions, 27-10 (D)
1987—Chiefs, 27-20 (D)
(Points—Lions 117, Chiefs 102)

DETROIT vs. *L.A. RAIDERS
Raiders lead series, 4-2
1970—Lions, 28-14 (D)
1974—Raiders, 35-13 (O)
1978—Raiders, 29-17 (O)
1981—Lions, 16-0 (D)
1984—Raiders, 24-3 (D)
1987—Raiders, 27-7 (LA)
(Points—Raiders 129, Lions 84)
**Franchise in Oakland prior to 1982*

DETROIT vs. *L.A. RAMS
Rams lead series, 38-34-1
1937—Lions, 28-0 (C)
Lions, 27-7 (D)
1938—Rams, 21-17 (C)
Lions, 6-0 (D)
1939—Lions, 15-7 (D)
Rams, 14-3 (C)
1940—Lions, 6-0 (D)
Rams, 24-0 (C)
1941—Lions, 17-7 (D)
Lions, 14-0 (C)
1942—Rams, 14-0 (D)
Rams, 27-7 (C)
1944—Rams, 20-17 (D)
Lions, 26-14 (C)
1945—Rams, 28-21 (D)
1946—Rams, 35-14 (LA)
Rams, 41-20 (D)
1947—Rams, 27-13 (D)
Rams, 28-17 (LA)
1948—Rams, 44-7 (LA)
Rams, 34-27 (D)
1949—Rams, 27-24 (LA)
Rams, 21-10 (D)
1950—Rams, 30-28 (D)
Rams, 65-24 (LA)
1951—Rams, 27-21 (D)
Lions, 24-22 (LA)
1952—Lions, 17-14 (LA)
Lions, 24-16 (D)
**Lions, 31-21 (D)
1953—Rams, 31-19 (D)
Rams, 37-24 (LA)
1954—Lions, 21-3 (D)
Lions, 27-24 (LA)
1955—Rams, 17-10 (D)
Rams, 24-13 (LA)
1956—Lions, 24-21 (D)
Lions, 16-7 (LA)
1957—Lions, 10-7 (D)
Rams, 35-17 (LA)
1958—Rams, 42-28 (D)
Lions, 41-24 (LA)
1959—Lions, 17-7 (LA)
Lions, 23-17 (D)
1960—Rams, 48-35 (LA)
Lions, 12-10 (D)
1961—Lions, 14-13 (D)
Lions, 28-10 (LA)
1962—Lions, 13-10 (D)
Lions, 12-3 (LA)
1963—Lions, 23-2 (LA)
Rams, 28-21 (D)
1964—Tie, 17-17 (LA)
Lions, 37-17 (D)
1965—Lions, 20-0 (D)
Lions, 31-7 (LA)
1966—Rams, 14-7 (D)
Rams, 23-3 (LA)
1967—Rams, 31-7 (D)
1968—Rams, 10-7 (LA)
1969—Lions, 28-0 (D)
1970—Lions, 28-23 (LA)
1971—Rams, 21-13 (D)
1972—Lions, 34-17 (LA)
1974—Rams, 16-13 (LA)
1975—Rams, 20-0 (D)
1976—Rams, 20-17 (D)
1980—Lions, 41-20 (LA)
1981—Rams, 20-13 (LA)
1982—Lions, 19-14 (LA)
1983—Rams, 21-10 (LA)
1986—Rams, 14-10 (LA)
1987—Rams, 37-16 (D)
(Points—Rams 1,417, Lions 1,324)
**Franchise in Cleveland prior to 1946*
***Conference Playoff*

DETROIT vs. MIAMI
Dolphins lead series, 2-1
1973—Dolphins, 34-7 (M)
1979—Dolphins, 28-10 (D)
1985—Lions, 31-21 (D)
(Points—Dolphins 83, Lions 48)

DETROIT vs. MINNESOTA
Vikings lead series, 33-18-2
1961—Lions, 37-10 (M)
Lions, 13-7 (D)
1962—Lions, 17-6 (M)
Lions, 37-23 (D)
1963—Lions, 28-10 (D)
Vikings, 34-31 (M)
1964—Lions, 24-20 (M)
Tie, 23-23 (D)
1965—Lions, 31-29 (M)
Vikings, 29-7 (D)
1966—Lions, 32-31 (M)
Vikings, 28-16 (D)
1967—Tie, 10-10 (M)
Lions, 14-3 (D)
1968—Vikings, 24-10 (M)
Vikings, 13-6 (D)
1969—Vikings, 24-10 (M)
Vikings, 27-0 (D)
1970—Vikings, 30-17 (D)
Vikings, 24-20 (M)
1971—Vikings, 16-13 (D)
Vikings, 29-10 (M)
1972—Vikings, 34-10 (D)
Vikings, 16-14 (M)
1973—Vikings, 23-9 (D)
Vikings, 28-7 (M)
1974—Vikings, 7-6 (D)
Lions, 20-16 (M)
1975—Vikings, 25-19 (M)
Lions, 17-10 (D)
1976—Vikings, 10-9 (D)
Vikings, 31-23 (M)
1977—Vikings, 14-7 (M)
Vikings, 30-21 (D)
1978—Vikings, 17-7 (M)
Lions, 45-14 (D)
1979—Vikings, 13-10 (D)
Vikings, 14-7 (M)
1980—Lions, 27-7 (D)
Vikings, 34-0 (M)
1981—Vikings, 26-24 (M)
Lions, 45-7 (D)
1982—Vikings, 34-31 (D)
1983—Vikings, 20-17 (M)
Lions, 13-2 (D)
1984—Vikings, 29-28 (D)
Lions, 16-14 (M)
1985—Vikings, 16-13 (M)
Lions, 41-21 (D)
1986—Lions, 13-10 (M)
Vikings, 24-10 (D)
1987—Vikings, 34-19 (M)
Vikings, 17-14 (D)
(Points—Vikings, 1,047, Lions 948)

DETROIT vs. NEW ENGLAND
Series tied, 2-2
1971—Lions, 34-7 (NE)
1976—Lions, 30-10 (D)
1979—Patriots, 24-17 (NE)
1985—Patriots, 23-6 (NE)
(Points—Lions 87, Patriots 64)

DETROIT vs. NEW ORLEANS
Series tied, 4-4-1
1968—Tie, 20-20 (D)
1970—Saints, 19-17 (NO)
1972—Lions, 27-14 (D)
1973—Saints, 20-13 (NO)
1974—Lions, 19-14 (D)
1976—Saints, 17-16 (NO)
1977—Lions, 23-19 (D)
1979—Saints, 17-7 (NO)
1980—Lions, 24-13 (D)
(Points—Lions 166, Saints 153)

***DETROIT vs. N.Y. GIANTS**
Lions lead series, 18-11-1
1930—Giants, 19-6 (P)
1931—Spartans, 14-6 (P)
Giants, 14-0 (NY)
1932—Spartans, 7-0 (P)
Spartans, 6-0 (NY)
1933—Spartans, 17-7 (P)
Giants, 13-10 (NY)
1934—Lions, 9-0 (D)
1935—**Lions, 26-7 (D)
1936—Giants, 14-7 (NY)
Lions, 38-0 (D)
1937—Lions, 17-0 (NY)
1939—Lions, 18-14 (D)
1941—Giants, 20-13 (NY)
1943—Tie, 0-0 (D)
1945—Giants, 35-14 (NY)
1947—Lions, 35-7 (D)
1949—Lions, 45-21 (NY)
1953—Lions, 27-16 (NY)
1955—Giants, 24-19 (D)
1958—Giants, 19-17 (D)
1962—Giants, 17-14 (NY)
1964—Lions, 26-3 (D)
1967—Lions, 30-7 (NY)
1969—Lions, 24-0 (D)
1972—Lions, 30-16 (D)
1974—Lions, 20-19 (D)
1976—Giants, 24-10 (NY)
1982—Giants, 13-6 (D)
1983—Lions, 15-9 (D)
(Points—Lions 520, Giants 344)
**Franchise in Portsmouth prior to 1934 and known as the Spartans*
***NFL Championship*

DETROIT vs. N.Y. JETS
Series tied, 2-2
1972—Lions, 37-20 (D)
1979—Jets, 31-10 (NY)
1982—Jets, 28-13 (D)
1985—Lions, 31-20 (D)
(Points—Jets 99, Lions 91)

***DETROIT vs. PHILADELPHIA**
Lions lead series, 12-9-2
1933—Spartans, 25-0 (P)
1934—Lions, 10-0 (P)
1935—Lions, 35-0 (D)
1936—Lions, 23-0 (P)
1938—Eagles, 21-7 (D)
1940—Lions, 21-0 (P)
1941—Lions, 21-17 (D)
1945—Lions, 28-24 (D)
1948—Eagles, 45-21 (P)
1949—Eagles, 22-14 (D)
1951—Lions, 28-10 (P)
1954—Tie, 13-13 (D)
1957—Lions, 27-16 (P)
1960—Eagles, 28-10 (P)
1961—Eagles, 27-24 (D)
1965—Lions, 35-28 (P)
1968—Eagles, 12-0 (D)
1971—Eagles, 23-20 (D)
1974—Eagles, 28-17 (P)
1977—Lions, 17-13 (D)
1979—Eagles, 44-7 (P)
1984—Tie, 23-23 (D) OT
1986—Lions, 13-11 (P)
(Points—Lions 439, Eagles 405)

Franchise in Portsmouth prior to 1934 and known as the Spartans
DETROIT vs. *PITTSBURGH
Lions lead series, 13-9-1
1934—Lions, 40-7 (D)
1936—Lions, 28-3 (D)
1937—Lions, 7-3 (D)
1938—Lions, 16-7 (D)
1940—Pirates, 10-7 (D)
1942—Steelers, 35-7 (D)
1946—Lions, 17-7 (D)
1947—Steelers, 17-10 (P)
1948—Lions, 17-14 (D)
1949—Steelers, 14-7 (P)
1950—Lions, 10-7 (D)
1952—Lions, 31-6 (P)
1953—Lions, 38-21 (D)
1955—Lions, 31-28 (P)
1956—Lions, 45-7 (D)
1959—Tie, 10-10 (P)
1962—Lions, 45-7 (D)
1966—Steelers, 17-3 (P)
1967—Steelers, 24-14 (D)
1969—Steelers, 16-13 (P)
1973—Steelers, 24-10 (P)
1983—Lions, 45-3 (D)
1986—Steelers, 27-17 (P)
(Points—Lions 468, Steelers 314)
Steelers known as Pirates prior to 1941
***DETROIT vs. **ST. LOUIS**
Lions lead series, 25-15-5
1930—Tie, 0-0 (P)
Cardinals, 23-0 (C)
1931—Cardinals, 20-19 (C)
1932—Tie, 7-7 (P)
1933—Spartans, 7-6 (P)
1934—Lions, 6-0 (D)
Lions, 17-13 (C)
1935—Tie, 10-10 (D)
Lions, 7-6 (C)
1936—Lions, 39-0 (D)
Lions, 14-7 (C)
1937—Lions, 16-7 (C)
Lions, 16-7 (D)
1938—Lions, 10-0 (D)
Lions, 7-3 (C)
1939—Lions, 21-3 (D)
Lions, 17-3 (C)
1940—Tie, 0-0 (Buffalo)
Lions, 43-14 (C)
1941—Tie, 14-14 (C)
Lions, 21-3 (D)
1942—Cardinals, 13-0 (C)
Cardinals, 7-0 (D)
1943—Lions, 35-17 (D)
Lions, 7-0 (C)
1945—Lions, 10-0 (C)
Lions, 26-0 (D)
1946—Cardinals, 34-14 (C)
Cardinals, 36-14 (D)
1947—Cardinals, 45-21 (C)
Cardinals, 17-7 (D)
1948—Cardinals, 56-20 (C)
Cardinals, 28-14 (D)
1949—Lions, 24-7 (C)
Cardinals, 42-19 (D)
1959—Lions, 45-21 (D)
1961—Lions, 45-14 (StL)
1967—Cardinals, 38-28 (StL)
1969—Lions, 20-0 (D)
1970—Lions, 16-3 (D)
1973—Lions, 20-16 (StL)
1975—Cardinals, 24-13 (D)
1978—Cardinals, 21-14 (StL)
1980—Lions, 20-7 (D)
Cardinals, 24-23 (StL)
(Points—Lions 746, Cardinals 626)
Franchise in Portsmouth prior to 1934 and known as the Spartans
**Franchise in Chicago prior to 1960*
DETROIT vs. SAN DIEGO
Lions lead series, 3-2
1972—Lions, 34-20 (D)
1977—Lions, 20-0 (D)
1978—Lions, 31-14 (D)
1981—Chargers, 28-23 (SD)
1984—Chargers, 27-24 (SD)
(Points—Lions 132, Chargers 89)
DETROIT vs. SAN FRANCISCO
Lions lead series, 26-23-1
1950—Lions, 24-7 (D)
49ers, 28-27 (SF)
1951—49ers, 20-10 (D)
49ers, 21-17 (SF)
1952—49ers, 17-3 (SF)
49ers, 28-0 (D)
1953—Lions, 24-21 (D)
Lions, 14-10 (SF)
1954—49ers, 37-31 (SF)
Lions, 48-7 (D)
1955—49ers, 27-24 (D)
49ers, 38-21 (SF)
1956—Lions, 20-17 (D)
Lions, 17-13 (SF)
1957—49ers, 35-31 (SF)
Lions, 31-10 (D)
*Lions, 31-27 (SF)
1958—49ers, 24-21 (SF)
Lions, 35-21 (D)
1959—49ers, 34-13 (D)
49ers, 33-7 (SF)
1960—49ers, 14-10 (D)
Lions, 24-0 (SF)
1961—49ers, 49-0 (D)
Tie, 20-20 (SF)
1962—Lions, 45-24 (D)
Lions, 38-24 (SF)
1963—Lions, 26-3 (D)
Lions, 45-7 (SF)
1964—Lions, 26-17 (SF)
Lions, 24-7 (D)
1965—49ers, 27-21 (D)
49ers, 17-14 (SF)
1966—49ers, 27-24 (SF)
49ers, 41-14 (D)
1967—Lions, 45-3 (SF)
1968—49ers, 14-7 (D)
1969—Lions, 26-14 (SF)
1970—Lions, 28-7 (D)
1971—49ers, 31-27 (SF)
1973—Lions, 30-20 (D)
1974—Lions, 17-13 (D)
1975—Lions, 28-17 (SF)
1977—49ers, 28-7 (SF)
1978—Lions, 33-14 (D)
1980—Lions, 17-13 (D)
1981—Lions, 24-17 (D)
1983—**49ers, 24-23 (SF)
1984—49ers, 30-27 (D)
1985—Lions, 23-21 (D)
(Points—Lions 1,142, 49ers 1,018)
Conference Playoff
**NFC Divisional Playoff*
DETROIT vs. SEATTLE
Seahawks lead series, 3-1
1976—Lions, 41-14 (S)
1978—Seahawks, 28-16 (S)
1984—Seahawks, 38-17 (S)
1987—Seahawks, 37-14 (D)
(Points—Seahawks 117, Lions 88)
DETROIT vs. TAMPA BAY
Lions lead series, 11-9
1977—Lions, 16-7 (D)
1978—Lions, 15-7 (TB)
Lions, 34-23 (D)
1979—Buccaneers, 31-16 (TB)
Buccaneers, 16-14 (D)
1980—Lions, 24-10 (TB)
Lions, 27-14 (D)
1981—Buccaneers, 28-10 (TB)
Buccaneers, 20-17 (D)
1982—Buccaneers, 23-21 (TB)
1983—Lions, 11-0 (TB)
Lions, 23-20 (D)
1984—Buccaneers, 21-17 (TB)
Lions, 13-7 (D) OT
1985—Lions, 30-9 (D)
Buccaneers, 19-16 (TB) OT
1986—Buccaneers, 24-20 (D)
Lions, 38-17 (TB)
1987—Buccaneers, 31-27 (D)
Lions, 20-10 (TB)
(Points—Lions 409, Buccaneers 337)
***DETROIT vs. **WASHINGTON**
Redskins lead series, 20-8
1932—Spartans, 10-0 (P)
1933—Spartans, 13-0 (B)
1934—Lions, 24-0 (D)
1935—Lions, 17-7 (B)
Lions, 14-0 (D)
1938—Redskins, 7-5 (D)
1939—Redskins, 31-7 (W)
1940—Redskins, 20-14 (D)
1942—Redskins, 15-3 (D)
1943—Redskins, 42-20 (W)
1946—Redskins, 17-16 (W)
1947—Lions, 38-21 (D)
1948—Redskins, 46-21 (W)
1951—Lions, 35-17 (D)
1956—Redskins, 18-17 (W)
1965—Lions, 14-10 (D)
1968—Redskins, 14-3 (W)
1970—Redskins, 31-10 (W)
1973—Redskins, 20-0 (D)
1976—Redskins, 20-7 (W)
1978—Redskins, 21-19 (D)
1979—Redskins, 27-24 (D)
1981—Redskins, 33-31 (W)
1982—***Redskins, 31-7 (W)
1983—Redskins, 38-17 (W)
1984—Redskins, 28-14 (W)
1985—Redskins, 24-3 (W)
1987—Redskins, 20-13 (W)
(Points—Redskins 558, Lions 416)
Franchise in Portsmouth prior to 1934 and known as the Spartans.
**Franchise in Boston prior to 1937*
***NFC First Round Playoff*

GREEN BAY vs. ATLANTA
Packers lead series, 8-6;
See Atlanta vs. Green Bay
GREEN BAY vs. BUFFALO
Bills lead series, 2-1;
See Buffalo vs. Green Bay
GREEN BAY vs. CHICAGO
Bears lead series, 74-55-6;
See Chicago vs. Green Bay
GREEN BAY vs. CINCINNATI
Bengals lead series, 4-2;
See Cincinnati vs. Green Bay
GREEN BAY vs. CLEVELAND
Packers lead series, 8-5;
See Cleveland vs. Green Bay
GREEN BAY vs. DALLAS
Packers lead series, 8-5;
See Dallas vs. Green Bay
GREEN BAY vs. DENVER
Broncos lead series, 3-1-1;
See Denver vs. Green Bay
GREEN BAY vs. DETROIT
Packers lead series, 59-49-7;
See Detroit vs. Green Bay
GREEN BAY vs. HOUSTON
Oilers lead series, 3-2
1972—Packers, 23-10 (H)
1977—Oilers, 16-10 (GB)
1980—Oilers, 22-3 (GB)
1983—Packers, 41-38 (H) OT
1986—Oilers, 31-3 (GB)
(Points—Oilers 117, Packers 80)
GREEN BAY vs. *INDIANAPOLIS
Packers lead series, 18-17-1
1953—Packers, 37-14 (GB)
Packers, 35-24 (B)
1954—Packers, 7-6 (B)
Packers, 24-13 (Mil)
1955—Colts, 24-20 (Mil)
Colts, 14-10 (B)
1956—Packers, 38-33 (Mil)
Colts, 28-21 (B)
1957—Colts, 45-17 (Mil)
Packers, 24-21 (B)
1958—Colts, 24-17 (Mil)
Colts, 56-0 (B)
1959—Colts, 38-21 (B)
Colts, 28-24 (Mil)
1960—Packers, 35-21 (GB)
Colts, 38-24 (B)
1961—Packers, 45-7 (GB)
Colts, 45-21 (B)
1962—Packers, 17-6 (B)
Packers, 17-13 (GB)
1963—Packers, 31-20 (GB)
Packers, 34-20 (B)
1964—Colts, 21-20 (GB)
Colts, 24-21 (B)
1965—Packers, 20-17 (Mil)
Packers, 42-27 (B)
**Packers, 13-10 (GB) OT
1966—Packers, 24-3 (Mil)
Packers, 14-10 (B)
1967—Colts, 13-10 (B)
1968—Colts, 16-3 (GB)
1969—Colts, 14-6 (B)
1970—Colts, 13-10 (Mil)
1974—Packers, 20-13 (B)
1982—Tie, 20-20 (B) OT
1985—Colts, 37-10 (I)
(Points—Colts 776, Packers 752)
Franchise in Baltimore prior to 1984
**Conference Playoff*
GREEN BAY vs. KANSAS CITY
Packers lead series, 2-1-1
1966—*Packers, 35-10 (Los Angeles)
1973—Tie, 10-10 (Mil)
1977—Chiefs, 20-10 (KC)
1987—Packers, 23-3 (KC)
(Points—Packers 78, Chiefs 43)
Super Bowl I
GREEN BAY vs. *L.A. RAIDERS
Raiders lead series, 5-1
1967—**Packers, 33-14 (Miami)
1972—Raiders, 20-14 (GB)
1976—Raiders, 18-14 (O)
1978—Raiders, 28-3 (GB)
1984—Raiders, 28-7 (LA)
1987—Raiders, 20-0 (GB)
(Points—Raiders 128, Packers 71)
Franchise in Oakland prior to 1982
**Super Bowl II*
GREEN BAY vs. *L.A. RAMS
Rams lead series, 39-34-2
1937—Packers, 35-10 (C)
Packers, 35-7 (GB)
1938—Packers, 26-17 (GB)
Packers, 28-7 (C)
1939—Rams, 27-24 (GB)
Packers, 7-6 (C)
1940—Packers, 31-14 (GB)
Tie, 13-13 (C)
1941—Packers, 24-7 (Mil)
Packers, 17-14 (C)
1942—Packers, 45-28 (GB)
Packers, 30-12 (C)
1944—Packers, 30-21 (GB)
Packers, 42-7 (C)
1945—Rams, 27-14 (GB)
Rams, 20-7 (C)
1946—Rams, 21-17 (Mil)
Rams, 38-17 (LA)
1947—Packers, 17-14 (Mil)
Packers, 30-10 (LA)
1948—Packers, 16-0 (GB)
Rams, 24-10 (LA)
1949—Rams, 48-7 (GB)
Rams, 35-7 (LA)
1950—Rams, 45-14 (Mil)
Rams, 51-14 (LA)
1951—Rams, 28-0 (Mil)
Rams, 42-14 (LA)
1952—Rams, 30-28 (Mil)
Rams, 45-27 (LA)
1953—Rams, 38-20 (Mil)
Rams, 33-17 (LA)
1954—Packers, 35-17 (Mil)
Rams, 35-27 (LA)
1955—Packers, 30-28 (Mil)
Rams, 31-17 (LA)
1956—Packers, 42-17 (Mil)
Rams, 49-21 (LA)
1957—Rams, 31-27 (Mil)
Rams, 42-17 (LA)
1958—Rams, 20-7 (GB)
Rams, 34-20 (LA)
1959—Rams, 45-6 (Mil)
Packers, 38-20 (LA)
1960—Rams, 33-31 (Mil)
Packers, 35-2 (LA)
1961—Packers, 35-17 (GB)
Packers, 24-17 (LA)
1962—Packers, 41-10 (Mil)
Packers, 20-17 (LA)
1963—Packers, 42-10 (GB)
Packers, 31-14 (LA)
1964—Rams, 27-17 (Mil)
Tie, 24-24 (LA)
1965—Packers, 6-3 (Mil)
Rams, 21-10 (LA)
1966—Packers, 24-13 (GB)
Packers, 27-23 (LA)
1967—Rams, 27-24 (LA)
**Packers, 28-7 (Mil)
1968—Rams, 16-14 (Mil)
1969—Rams, 34-21 (LA)
1970—Rams, 31-21 (GB)
1971—Rams, 30-13 (LA)
1973—Rams, 24-7 (LA)
1974—Packers, 17-6 (Mil)
1975—Rams, 22-5 (LA)
1977—Rams, 24-6 (Mil)
1978—Rams, 31-14 (LA)
1980—Rams, 51-21 (LA)
1981—Rams, 35-23 (LA)
1982—Packers, 35-23 (Mil)
1983—Packers, 27-24 (Mil)
1984—Packers, 31-6 (Mil)
1985—Rams, 34-17 (LA)
(Points—Rams 1,783, Packers 1,641)
Franchise in Cleveland prior to 1946
**Conference Championship*
GREEN BAY vs. MIAMI
Dolphins lead series, 4-0
1971—Dolphins, 27-6 (Mia)
1975—Dolphins, 31-7 (GB)
1979—Dolphins, 27-7 (Mia)
1985—Dolphins, 34-24 (GB)
(Points—Dolphins 119, Packers 44)
GREEN BAY vs. MINNESOTA
Series tied, 26-26-1
1961—Packers, 33-7 (Minn)
Packers, 28-10 (Mil)
1962—Packers, 34-7 (GB)
Packers, 48-21 (Minn)
1963—Packers, 37-28 (Minn)
Packers, 28-7 (GB)
1964—Vikings, 24-23 (GB)
Packers, 42-13 (Minn)
1965—Packers, 38-13 (Minn)
Packers, 24-19 (GB)
1966—Vikings, 20-17 (GB)
Packers, 28-16 (Minn)
1967—Vikings, 10-7 (Mil)
Packers, 30-27 (Minn)
1968—Vikings, 26-13 (Mil)
Vikings, 14-10 (Minn)
1969—Vikings, 19-7 (Minn)
Vikings, 9-7 (Mil)
1970—Packers, 13-10 (Mil)
Vikings, 10-3 (Minn)
1971—Vikings, 24-13 (GB)
Vikings, 3-0 (Minn)

1972—Vikings, 27-13 (GB)
Packers, 23-7 (Minn)
1973—Vikings, 11-3 (Minn)
Vikings, 31-7 (GB)
1974—Vikings, 32-17 (GB)
Packers, 19-7 (Minn)
1975—Vikings, 28-17 (GB)
Vikings, 24-3 (Minn)
1976—Vikings, 17-10 (Mil)
Vikings, 20-9 (Minn)
1977—Vikings, 19-7 (Minn)
Vikings, 13-6 (GB)
1978—Vikings, 21-7 (Minn)
Tie, 10-10 (GB) OT
1979—Vikings, 27-21 (Minn) OT
Packers, 19-7 (Mil)
1980—Packers, 16-3 (GB)
Packers, 25-13 (Minn)
1981—Vikings, 30-13 (Mil)
Packers, 35-23 (Minn)
1982—Packers, 26-7 (Mil)
1983—Vikings, 20-17 (GB) OT
Packers, 29-21 (Minn)
1984—Packers, 45-17 (Mil)
Packers, 38-14 (Minn)
1985—Packers, 20-17 (Mil)
Packers, 27-17 (Minn)
1986—Vikings, 42-7 (Minn)
Vikings, 32-6 (GB)
1987—Packers, 23-16 (Minn)
Packers, 16-10 (Mil)
(Points—Packers 1,017, Vikings 920)

GREEN BAY vs. NEW ENGLAND
Patriots lead series, 2-1
1973—Patriots, 33-24 (NE)
1979—Packers, 27-14 (GB)
1985—Patriots, 26-20 (NE)
(Points—Patriots 73, Packers 71)

GREEN BAY vs. NEW ORLEANS
Packers lead series, 10-4
1968—Packers, 29-7 (Mil)
1971—Saints, 29-21 (Mil)
1972—Packers, 30-20 (NO)
1973—Packers, 30-10 (Mil)
1975—Saints, 20-19 (NO)
1976—Packers, 32-27 (Mil)
1977—Packers, 24-20 (NO)
1978—Packers, 28-17 (Mil)
1979—Packers, 28-19 (Mil)
1981—Packers, 35-7 (NO)
1984—Packers, 23-13 (NO)
1985—Packers, 38-14 (Mil)
1986—Saints, 24-10 (NO)
1987—Saints, 33-24 (NO)
(Points—Packers 371, Saints 260)

GREEN BAY vs. N.Y. GIANTS
Packers lead series, 25-20-2
1928—Giants, 6-0 (GB)
Packers, 7-0 (NY)
1929—Packers, 20-6 (NY)
1930—Packers, 14-7 (GB)
Giants, 13-6 (NY)
1931—Packers, 27-7 (GB)
Packers, 14-10 (NY)
1932—Packers, 13-0 (GB)
Giants, 6-0 (NY)
1933—Giants, 10-7 (Mil)
Giants, 17-6 (NY)
1934—Packers, 20-6 (Mil)
Giants, 17-3 (NY)
1935—Packers, 16-7 (GB)
1936—Packers, 26-14 (NY)
1937—Giants, 10-0 (NY)
1938—Giants, 15-3 (NY)
*Giants, 23-17 (NY)
1939—*Packers, 27-0 (Mil)
1940—Giants, 7-3 (NY)
1942—Tie, 21-21 (NY)
1943—Packers, 35-21 (NY)
1944—Giants, 24-0 (NY)
*Packers, 14-7 (NY)
1945—Packers, 23-14 (NY)
1947—Tie, 24-24 (NY)
1948—Giants, 49-3 (Mil)
1949—Giants, 30-10 (GB)
1952—Packers, 17-3 (NY)
1957—Giants, 31-17 (GB)
1959—Giants, 20-3 (NY)
1961—Packers, 20-17 (Mil)
*Packers, 37-0 (GB)
1962—*Packers, 16-7 (NY)
1967—Packers, 48-21 (NY)
1969—Packers, 20-10 (Mil)
1971—Giants, 42-40 (GB)
1973—Packers, 16-14 (New Haven)
1975—Packers, 40-14 (Mil)
1980—Giants, 27-21 (NY)
1981—Packers, 27-14 (NY)
Packers, 26-24 (Mil)
1982—Packers, 27-19 (NY)
1983—Giants, 27-3 (NY)
1985—Packers, 23-20 (GB)
1986—Giants, 55-24 (NY)
1987—Giants, 20-10 (NY)
(Points—Packers 794, Giants 756)
NFL Championship

GREEN BAY vs. N.Y. JETS
Jets lead series, 4-1
1973—Packers, 23-7 (Mil)
1979—Jets, 27-22 (GB)
1981—Jets, 28-3 (NY)
1982—Jets, 15-13 (NY)
1985—Jets, 24-3 (Mil)
(Points—Jets 101, Packers 64)

GREEN BAY vs. PHILADELPHIA
Packers lead series, 18-5
1933—Packers, 35-9 (GB)
Packers, 10-0 (P)
1934—Packers, 19-6 (GB)
1935—Packers, 13-6 (P)
1937—Packers, 37-7 (Mil)
1939—Packers, 23-16 (P)
1940—Packers, 27-20 (GB)
1942—Packers, 7-0 (P)
1946—Packers, 19-7 (P)
1947—Eagles, 28-14 (P)
1951—Packers, 37-24 (GB)
1952—Packers, 12-10 (Mil)
1954—Packers, 37-14 (P)
1958—Packers, 38-35 (GB)
1960—*Eagles, 17-13 (P)
1962—Packers, 49-0 (P)
1968—Packers, 30-13 (GB)
1970—Packers, 30-17 (Mil)
1974—Eagles, 36-14 (P)
1976—Packers, 28-13 (GB)
1978—Eagles, 10-3 (P)
1979—Eagles, 21-10 (GB)
1987—Packers, 16-10 (GB) OT
(Points—Packers 521, Eagles 319)
NFL Championship

GREEN BAY vs. *PITTSBURGH
Packers lead series, 16-11
1933—Packers, 47-0 (GB)
1935—Packers, 27-0 (GB)
Packers, 34-14 (P)
1936—Packers, 42-10 (Mil)
1938—Packers, 20-0 (GB)
1940—Packers, 24-3 (Mil)
1941—Packers, 54-7 (P)
1942—Packers, 24-21 (Mil)
1946—Packers, 17-7 (GB)
1947—Steelers, 18-17 (Mil)
1948—Steelers, 38-7 (P)
1949—Steelers, 30-7 (Mil)
1951—Packers, 35-33 (Mil)
Steelers, 28-7 (P)
1953—Steelers, 31-14 (P)
1954—Steelers, 21-20 (GB)
1957—Packers, 27-10 (P)
1960—Packers, 19-13 (P)
1963—Packers, 33-14 (Mil)
1965—Packers, 41-9 (P)
1967—Steelers, 24-17 (GB)
1969—Packers, 38-34 (P)
1970—Packers, 20-12 (P)
1975—Steelers, 16-13 (Mil)
1980—Steelers, 22-20 (P)
1983—Steelers, 25-21 (GB)
1986—Steelers, 27-3 (P)
(Points—Packers 648, Steelers 467)
Steelers known as Pirates prior to 1941

GREEN BAY vs. *ST. LOUIS
Packers lead series, 38-21-4
1921—Tie, 3-3 (C)
1922—Cardinals, 16-3 (C)
1924—Cardinals, 3-0 (C)
1925—Cardinals, 9-6 (C)
1926—Cardinals, 13-7 (GB)
Packers, 3-0 (C)
1927—Packers, 13-0 (GB)
Tie, 6-6 (C)
1928—Packers, 20-0 (GB)
1929—Packers, 9-2 (GB)
Packers, 7-6 (C)
Packers, 12-0 (C)
1930—Packers, 14-0 (GB)
Cardinals, 13-6 (C)
1931—Packers, 26-7 (GB)
Cardinals, 21-13 (C)
1932—Packers, 15-7 (GB)
Packers, 19-9 (C)
1933—Packers, 14-6 (C)
1934—Packers, 15-0 (GB)
Cardinals, 9-0 (Mil)
Cardinals, 6-0 (C)
1935—Cardinals, 7-6 (GB)
Cardinals, 3-0 (Mil)
Cardinals, 9-7 (C)
1936—Packers, 10-7 (GB)
Packers, 24-0 (Mil)
Tie, 0-0 (C)
1937—Cardinals, 14-7 (GB)
Packers, 34-13 (Mil)
1938—Packers, 28-7 (Mil)
Packers, 24-22 (Buffalo)
1939—Packers, 14-10 (GB)
Packers, 27-20 (Mil)
1940—Packers, 31-6 (Mil)
Packers, 28-7 (C)
1941—Packers, 14-13 (Mil)
Packers, 17-9 (GB)
1942—Packers, 17-13 (C)
Packers, 55-24 (GB)
1943—Packers, 28-7 (C)
Packers, 35-14 (Mil)
1945—Packers, 33-14 (GB)
1946—Packers, 19-7 (C)
Cardinals, 24-6 (GB)
1947—Cardinals, 14-10 (GB)
Cardinals, 21-20 (C)
1948—Cardinals, 17-7 (Mil)
Cardinals, 42-7 (C)
1949—Cardinals, 39-17 (Mil)
Cardinals, 41-21 (C)
1955—Packers, 31-14 (GB)
1956—Packers, 24-21 (C)
1962—Packers, 17-0 (Mil)
1963—Packers, 30-7 (StL)
1967—Packers, 31-23 (StL)
1969—Packers, 45-28 (GB)
1971—Tie, 16-16 (StL)
1973—Packers, 25-21 (GB)
1976—Cardinals, 29-0 (StL)
1982—**Packers, 41-16 (GB)
1984—Packers, 24-23 (GB)
1985—Cardinals, 43-28 (StL)
(Points—Packers 1,069, Cardinals 801)
Franchise in Chicago prior to 1960
***NFC First Round Playoff*

GREEN BAY vs. SAN DIEGO
Packers lead series, 3-1
1970—Packers, 22-20 (SD)
1974—Packers, 34-0 (GB)
1978—Packers, 24-3 (SD)
1984—Chargers, 34-28 (GB)
(Points—Packers 108, Chargers 57)

GREEN BAY vs. SAN FRANCISCO
49ers lead series, 24-20-1
1950—Packers, 25-21 (GB)
49ers, 30-14 (SF)
1951—49ers, 31-19 (SF)
1952—49ers, 24-14 (SF)
1953—49ers, 37-7 (Mil)
49ers, 48-14 (SF)
1954—49ers, 23-17 (Mil)
49ers, 35-0 (SF)
1955—Packers, 27-21 (Mil)
Packers, 28-7 (SF)
1956—49ers, 17-16 (GB)
49ers, 38-20 (SF)
1957—49ers, 24-14 (Mil)
49ers, 27-20 (SF)
1958—49ers, 33-12 (Mil)
49ers, 48-21 (SF)
1959—Packers, 21-20 (GB)
Packers, 36-14 (SF)
1960—Packers, 41-14 (Mil)
Packers, 13-0 (SF)
1961—Packers, 30-10 (GB)
49ers, 22-21 (SF)
1962—Packers, 31-13 (Mil)
Packers, 31-21 (SF)
1963—Packers, 28-10 (Mil)
Packers, 21-17 (SF)
1964—Packers, 24-14 (Mil)
49ers, 24-14 (SF)
1965—Packers, 27-10 (GB)
Tie, 24-24 (SF)
1966—49ers, 21-20 (SF)
Packers, 20-7 (Mil)
1967—Packers, 13-0 (GB)
1968—49ers, 27-20 (SF)
1969—Packers, 14-7 (Mil)
1970—49ers, 26-10 (SF)
1972—Packers, 34-24 (Mil)
1973—49ers, 20-6 (SF)
1974—49ers, 7-6 (SF)
1976—49ers, 26-14 (GB)
1977—Packers, 16-14 (Mil)
1980—Packers, 23-16 (Mil)
1981—49ers, 13-3 (Mil)
1986—49ers, 31-17 (Mil)
1987—49ers, 23-12 (GB)
(Points—49ers 939, Packers 858)

GREEN BAY vs. SEATTLE
Packers lead series, 3-2
1976—Packers, 27-20 (Mil)
1978—Packers, 45-28 (Mil)
1981—Packers, 34-24 (GB)
1984—Seahawks, 30-24 (Mil)
1987—Seahawks, 24-13 (S)
(Points—Packers 143, Seahawks 126)

GREEN BAY vs. TAMPA BAY
Packers lead series, 10-7-1
1977—Packers, 13-0 (TB)
1978—Packers, 9-7 (GB)
Packers, 17-7 (TB)
1979—Buccaneers, 21-10 (GB)
Buccaneers, 21-3 (TB)
1980—Tie, 14-14 (TB) OT
Buccaneers, 20-17 (Mil)
1981—Buccaneers, 21-10 (GB)
Buccaneers, 37-3 (TB)
1983—Packers, 55-14 (GB)
Packers, 12-9 (TB) OT
1984—Buccaneers, 30-27 (TB) OT
Packers, 27-14 (GB)
1985—Packers, 21-0 (GB)
Packers, 20-17 (TB)
1986—Packers, 31-7 (Mil)
Packers, 21-7 (TB)
1987—Buccaneers, 23-17 (Mil)
(Points—Packers 327, Buccaneers 269)

GREEN BAY vs. *WASHINGTON
Packers lead series, 14-12-1
1932—Packers, 21-0 (B)
1933—Tie, 7-7 (GB)
Redskins, 20-7 (B)
1934—Packers, 10-0 (B)
1936—Packers, 31-2 (GB)
Packers, 7-3 (B)
**Packers, 21-6 (New York)
1937—Redskins, 14-6 (W)
1939—Packers, 24-14 (Mil)
1941—Packers, 22-17 (W)
1943—Redskins, 33-7 (Mil)
1946—Packers, 20-7 (W)
1947—Packers, 27-10 (Mil)
1948—Redskins, 23-7 (Mil)
1949—Redskins, 30-0 (W)
1950—Packers, 35-21 (Mil)
1952—Packers, 35-20 (Mil)
1958—Redskins, 37-21 (W)
1959—Packers, 21-0 (GB)
1968—Packers, 27-7 (W)
1972—Redskins, 21-16 (W)
***Redskins, 16-3 (W)
1974—Redskins, 17-6 (GB)
1977—Redskins, 10-9 (W)
1979—Redskins, 38-21 (W)
1983—Packers, 48-47 (GB)
1986—Redskins, 16-7 (GB)
(Points—Packers 466, Redskins 436)
Franchise in Boston prior to 1937 and known as Braves prior to 1933
***NFL Championship*
****NFC Divisional Playoff*

HOUSTON vs. ATLANTA
Falcons lead series, 4-2;
See Atlanta vs. Houston

HOUSTON vs. BUFFALO
Oilers lead series, 18-10;
See Buffalo vs. Houston

HOUSTON vs. CHICAGO
Series tied, 2-2;
See Chicago vs. Houston

HOUSTON vs. CINCINNATI
Bengals lead series, 21-16-1;
See Cincinnati vs. Houston

HOUSTON vs. CLEVELAND
Browns lead series, 23-12;
See Cleveland vs. Houston

HOUSTON vs. DALLAS
Cowboys lead series, 4-1;
See Dallas vs. Houston

HOUSTON vs. DENVER
Oilers lead series, 19-11-1;
See Denver vs. Houston

HOUSTON vs. DETROIT
Series tied, 2-2;
See Detroit vs. Houston

HOUSTON vs. GREEN BAY
Oilers lead series, 3-2;
See Green Bay vs. Houston

HOUSTON vs. *INDIANAPOLIS
Colts lead series, 6-4
1970—Colts, 24-20 (H)
1973—Oilers, 31-27 (B)
1976—Colts, 38-14 (B)
1979—Oilers, 28-16 (B)
1980—Oilers, 21-16 (H)
1983—Colts, 20-10 (B)
1984—Colts, 35-21 (H)
1985—Colts, 34-16 (I)
1986—Oilers, 31-17 (H)
1987—Colts, 51-27 (I)
(Points—Colts 278, Oilers 219)
Franchise in Baltimore prior to 1984

HOUSTON vs. *KANSAS CITY
Chiefs lead series, 21-12
1960—Oilers, 20-10 (H)
Texans, 24-0 (D)
1961—Texans, 26-21 (D)
Oilers, 38-7 (H)
1962—Texans, 31-7 (H)
Oilers, 14-6 (D)
**Texans, 20-17 (H) OT
1963—Chiefs, 28-7 (KC)
Oilers, 28-7 (H)
1964—Chiefs, 28-7 (KC)

Chiefs, 28-19 (H)
1965—Chiefs, 52-21 (KC)
Oilers, 38-36 (H)
1966—Chiefs, 48-23 (KC)
1967—Chiefs, 25-20 (H)
Oilers, 24-19 (KC)
1968—Chiefs, 26-21 (H)
Chiefs, 24-10 (KC)
1969—Chiefs, 24-0 (KC)
1970—Chiefs, 24-9 (KC)
1971—Chiefs, 20-16 (H)
1973—Chiefs, 38-14 (KC)
1974—Chiefs, 17-7 (H)
1975—Oilers, 17-13 (KC)
1977—Oilers, 34-20 (H)
1978—Oilers, 20-17 (KC)
1979—Oilers, 20-6 (H)
1980—Chiefs, 21-20 (KC)
1981—Chiefs, 23-10 (KC)
1983—Chiefs, 13-10 (H) OT
1984—Oilers, 17-16 (KC)
1985—Oilers, 23-20 (H)
1986—Chiefs, 27-13 (KC)
(Points—Chiefs 744, Oilers 565)
Franchise in Dallas prior to 1963 and known as Texans
***AFL Championship*

HOUSTON vs. *L.A. RAIDERS
Raiders lead series, 22-10
1960—Oilers, 37-22 (O)
Raiders, 14-13 (H)
1961—Oilers, 55-0 (H)
Oilers, 47-16 (O)
1962—Oilers, 28-20 (O)
Oilers, 32-17 (H)
1963—Raiders, 24-13 (H)
Raiders, 52-49 (O)
1964—Oilers, 42-28 (H)
Raiders, 20-10 (O)
1965—Raiders, 21-17 (O)
Raiders, 33-21 (H)
1966—Oilers, 31-0 (H)
Raiders, 38-23 (O)
1967—Raiders, 19-7 (H)
**Raiders, 40-7 (O)
1968—Raiders, 24-15 (H)
1969—Raiders, 21-17 (O)
***Raiders, 56-7 (O)
1971—Raiders, 41-21 (O)
1972—Raiders, 34-0 (H)
1973—Raiders, 17-6 (H)
1975—Oilers, 27-26 (O)
1976—Raiders, 14-13 (H)
1977—Raiders, 34-29 (O)
1978—Raiders, 21-17 (O)
1979—Oilers, 31-17 (H)
1980—****Raiders, 27-7 (O)
1981—Oilers, 17-16 (H)
1983—Raiders, 20-6 (LA)
1984—Raiders, 24-14 (H)
1986—Raiders, 28-17 (H)
(Points—Raiders 784, Oilers 676)
**Franchise in Oakland prior to 1982*
***AFL Championship*
****Inter-Divisional Playoff*
*****AFC First Round Playoff*

HOUSTON vs. L.A. RAMS
Rams lead series, 3-2
1973—Rams, 31-26 (H)
1978—Rams, 10-6 (H)
1981—Oilers, 27-20 (LA)
1984—Rams, 27-16 (LA)
1987—Oilers, 20-16 (H)
(Points—Rams 104, Oilers 95)

HOUSTON vs. MIAMI
Series tied, 10-10
1966—Dolphins, 20-13 (H)
Dolphins, 29-28 (M)
1967—Oilers, 17-14 (H)
Oilers, 41-10 (M)
1968—Oilers, 24-10 (M)
Dolphins, 24-7 (H)
1969—Oilers, 22-10 (H)
Oilers, 32-7 (M)
1970—Dolphins, 20-10 (H)
1972—Dolphins, 34-13 (M)
1975—Oilers, 20-19 (H)
1977—Dolphins, 27-7 (M)
1978—Oilers, 35-30 (H)
*Oilers, 17-9 (M)
1979—Oilers, 9-6 (M)
1981—Dolphins, 16-10 (H)
1983—Dolphins, 24-17 (H)
1984—Dolphins, 28-10 (M)
1985—Oilers, 26-23 (H)
1986—Dolphins, 28-7 (M)
(Points—Dolphins 388, Oilers 365)
**AFC First Round Playoff*

HOUSTON vs. MINNESOTA
Series tied, 2-2
1974—Vikings, 51-10 (M)
1980—Oilers, 20-16 (H)
1983—Vikings, 34-14 (M)
1986—Oilers, 23-10 (H)
(Points—Vikings 111, Oilers 67)

HOUSTON vs. *NEW ENGLAND
Patriots lead series, 15-13-1
1960—Oilers, 24-10 (B)
Oilers, 37-21 (H)
1961—Tie, 31-31 (B)
Oilers, 27-15 (H)
1962—Patriots, 34-21 (B)
Oilers, 21-17 (H)
1963—Patriots, 45-3 (B)
Patriots, 46-28 (H)
1964—Patriots, 25-24 (B)
Patriots, 34-17 (H)
1965—Oilers, 31-10 (H)
Patriots, 42-14 (B)
1966—Patriots, 27-21 (B)
Patriots, 38-14 (H)
1967—Patriots, 18-7 (B)
Oilers, 27-6 (H)
1968—Oilers, 16-0 (B)
Oilers, 45-17 (H)
1969—Patriots, 24-0 (B)
Oilers, 27-23 (H)
1971—Patriots, 28-20 (NE)
1973—Patriots, 32-0 (H)
1975—Oilers, 7-0 (NE)
1978—Oilers, 26-23 (NE)
**Oilers, 31-14 (NE)
1980—Oilers, 38-34 (H)
1981—Patriots, 38-10 (NE)
1982—Patriots, 29-21 (NE)
1987—Patriots, 21-7 (H)
(Points—Patriots 702, Oilers 595)
**Franchise in Boston prior to 1971*
***AFC Divisional Playoff*

HOUSTON vs. NEW ORLEANS
Saints lead series, 3-2-1
1971—Tie, 13-13 (H)
1976—Oilers, 31-26 (NO)
1978—Oilers, 17-12 (NO)
1981—Saints, 27-24 (H)
1984—Saints, 27-10 (H)
1987—Saints, 24-10 (NO)
(Points—Saints 129, Oilers 105)

HOUSTON vs. N.Y. GIANTS
Giants lead series, 3-0
1973—Giants, 34-14 (NY)
1982—Giants, 17-14 (NY)
1985—Giants, 35-14 (H)
(Points—Giants 86, Oilers 42)

HOUSTON vs. *N.Y. JETS
Oilers lead series, 15-10-1
1960—Oilers, 27-21 (H)
Oilers, 42-28 (NY)
1961—Oilers, 49-13 (H)
Oilers, 48-21 (NY)
1962—Oilers, 56-17 (H)
Oilers, 44-10 (NY)
1963—Jets, 24-17 (NY)
Oilers, 31-27 (H)
1964—Jets, 24-21 (NY)
Oilers, 33-17 (H)
1965—Oilers, 27-21 (H)
Jets, 41-14 (NY)
1966—Jets, 52-13 (NY)
Oilers, 24-0 (H)
1967—Tie, 28-28 (NY)
1968—Jets, 20-14 (H)
Jets, 26-7 (NY)
1969—Jets, 26-17 (NY)
Jets, 34-26 (H)
1972—Oilers, 26-20 (H)
1974—Oilers, 27-22 (NY)
1977—Oilers, 20-0 (H)
1979—Oilers, 27-24 (H) OT
1980—Jets, 31-28 (NY) OT
1981—Jets, 33-17 (NY)
1984—Oilers, 31-20 (H)
(Points—Oilers 714, Jets 600)
**Jets known as Titans prior to 1963*

HOUSTON vs. PHILADELPHIA
Eagles lead series, 3-0
1972—Eagles, 18-17 (H)
1979—Eagles, 26-20 (H)
1982—Eagles, 35-14 (P)
(Points—Eagles 79, Oilers 51)

HOUSTON vs. PITTSBURGH
Steelers lead series, 26-11
1970—Oilers, 19-7 (P)
Steelers, 7-3 (H)
1971—Steelers, 23-16 (P)
Oilers, 29-3 (H)
1972—Steelers, 24-7 (P)
Steelers, 9-3 (H)
1973—Steelers, 36-7 (H)
Steelers, 33-7 (P)
1974—Steelers, 13-7 (H)
Oilers, 13-10 (P)
1975—Steelers, 24-17 (P)
Steelers, 32-9 (H)
1976—Steelers, 32-16 (P)
Steelers, 21-0 (H)
1977—Oilers, 27-10 (H)
Steelers, 27-10 (P)
1978—Oilers, 24-17 (P)
Steelers, 13-3 (H)
*Steelers, 34-5 (P)
1979—Steelers, 38-7 (P)
Oilers, 20-17 (H)
*Steelers, 27-13 (P)
1980—Steelers, 31-17 (P)
Oilers, 6-0 (H)
1981—Steelers, 26-13 (P)
Oilers, 21-20 (H)
1982—Steelers, 24-10 (H)
1983—Steelers, 40-28 (H)
Steelers, 17-10 (P)
1984—Steelers, 35-7 (P)
Oilers, 23-20 (H) OT
1985—Steelers, 20-0 (P)
Steelers, 30-7 (H)
1986—Steelers, 22-16 (H) OT
Steelers, 21-10 (P)
1987—Oilers, 23-3 (P)
Oilers, 24-16 (H)
(Points—Steelers 782, Oilers 477)
**AFC Championship*

HOUSTON vs. ST. LOUIS
Cardinals lead series, 3-1
1970—Cardinals, 44-0 (StL)
1974—Cardinals, 31-27 (H)
1979—Cardinals, 24-17 (H)
1985—Oilers, 20-10 (StL)
(Points—Cardinals 109, Oilers 64)

HOUSTON vs. *SAN DIEGO
Chargers lead series, 17-13-1
1960—Oilers, 38-28 (H)
Chargers, 24-21 (LA)
**Oilers, 24-16 (H)
1961—Chargers, 34-24 (SD)
Oilers, 33-13 (H)
**Oilers, 10-3 (SD)
1962—Oilers, 42-17 (SD)
Oilers, 33-27 (H)
1963—Chargers, 27-0 (SD)
Chargers 20-14 (H)
1964—Chargers, 27-21 (SD)
Chargers, 20-17 (H)
1965—Chargers, 31-14 (SD)
Chargers, 37-26 (H)
1966—Chargers, 28-22 (H)
1967—Chargers, 13-3 (SD)
Oilers, 24-17 (H)
1968—Chargers, 30-14 (SD)
1969—Chargers, 21-17 (H)
1970—Tie, 31-31 (SD)
1971—Oilers, 49-33 (H)
1972—Chargers, 34-20 (SD)
1974—Oilers, 21-14 (H)
1975—Oilers, 33-17 (H)
1976—Chargers, 30-27 (SD)
1978—Chargers, 45-24 (H)
1979—***Oilers, 17-14 (SD)
1984—Chargers, 31-14 (SD)
1985—Oilers, 37-35 (H)
1986—Chargers, 27-0 (SD)
1987—Oilers, 33-18 (H)
(Points—Chargers 762, Oilers 703)
**Franchise in Los Angeles prior to 1961*
***AFL Championship*
****AFC Divisional Playoff*

HOUSTON vs. SAN FRANCISCO
49ers lead series, 4-2
1970—49ers, 30-20 (H)
1975—Oilers, 27-13 (SF)
1978—Oilers, 20-19 (H)
1981—49ers, 28-6 (SF)
1984—49ers, 34-21 (H)
1987—49ers, 27-20 (SF)
(Points—49ers 151, Oilers 114)

HOUSTON vs. SEATTLE
Oilers lead series, 4-2
1977—Oilers, 22-10 (S)
1979—Seahawks, 34-14 (S)
1980—Seahawks, 26-7 (H)
1981—Oilers, 35-17 (H)
1982—Oilers, 23-21 (H)
1987—*Oilers, 23-20 (H) OT
(Points—Seahawks 128, Oilers 124)
*AFC First Round Playoffs

HOUSTON vs. TAMPA BAY
Oilers lead series, 2-1
1976—Oilers, 20-0 (H)
1980—Oilers, 20-14 (H)
1983—Buccaneers, 33-24 (TB)
(Points—Oilers 64, Buccaneers 47)

HOUSTON vs. WASHINGTON
Series tied, 2-2
1971—Redskins, 22-13 (W)
1975—Oilers, 13-10 (H)
1979—Oilers, 29-27 (W)
1985—Redskins, 16-13 (W)
(Points—Redskins 75, Oilers 68)

INDIANAPOLIS vs. ATLANTA
Colts lead series, 9-0;
See Atlanta vs. Indianapolis

INDIANAPOLIS vs. BUFFALO
Series tied, 17-17-1;
See Buffalo vs. Indianapolis

INDIANAPOLIS vs. CHICAGO
Colts lead series, 21-14;
See Chicago vs. Indianapolis

INDIANAPOLIS vs. CINCINNATI
Series tied, 5-5;
See Cincinnati vs. Indianapolis

INDIANAPOLIS vs. CLEVELAND
Browns lead series, 12-6;
See Cleveland vs. Indianapolis

INDIANAPOLIS vs. DALLAS
Cowboys lead series, 6-3;
See Dallas vs. Indianapolis

INDIANAPOLIS vs. DENVER
Broncos lead series, 6-1;
See Denver vs. Indianapolis

INDIANAPOLIS vs. DETROIT
Colts lead series, 17-16-2;
See Detroit vs. Indianapolis

INDIANAPOLIS vs. GREEN BAY
Packers lead series, 18-17-1;
See Green Bay vs. Indianapolis

INDIANAPOLIS vs. HOUSTON
Colts lead series, 6-4;
See Houston vs. Indianapolis

***INDIANAPOLIS vs. KANSAS CITY**
Chiefs lead series, 6-3
1970—Chiefs, 44-24 (B)
1972—Chiefs, 24-10 (KC)
1975—Colts, 28-14 (B)
1977—Colts, 17-6 (KC)
1979—Chiefs, 14-0 (KC)
Chiefs, 10-7 (B)
1980—Colts, 31-24 (KC)
Chiefs, 38-28 (B)
1985—Chiefs, 20-7 (KC)
(Points—Chiefs 194, Colts 152)
**Franchise in Baltimore prior to 1984*

***INDIANAPOLIS vs **L.A. RAIDERS**
Raiders lead series, 4-3
1970—***Colts, 27-17 (B)
1971—Colts, 37-14 (O)
1973—Raiders, 34-21 (B)
1975—Raiders, 31-20 (B)
1977—****Raiders, 37-31 (B) OT
1984—Raiders, 21-7 (LA)
1986—Colts, 30-24 (LA)
(Points—Raiders 178, Colts 173)
**Franchise in Baltimore prior to 1984*
***Franchise in Oakland prior to 1982*
****AFC Championship*
*****AFC Divisional Playoff*

***INDIANAPOLIS vs. L.A. RAMS**
Colts lead series, 20-15-2
1953—Rams, 21-13 (B)
Rams, 45-2 (LA)
1954—Rams, 48-0 (B)
Colts, 22-21 (LA)
1955—Tie, 17-17 (B)
Rams, 20-14 (LA)
1956—Colts, 56-21 (B)
Rams, 31-7 (LA)
1957—Colts, 31-14 (B)
Rams, 37-21 (LA)
1958—Colts, 34-7 (B)
Rams, 30-28 (LA)
1959—Colts, 35-21 (B)
Colts, 45-26 (LA)
1960—Colts, 31-17 (B)
Rams, 10-3 (LA)
1961—Colts, 27-24 (B)
Rams, 34-17 (LA)
1962—Colts, 30-27 (B)
Colts, 14-2 (LA)
1963—Rams, 17-16 (LA)
Colts, 19-16 (B)
1964—Colts, 35-20 (B)
Colts, 24-7 (LA)
1965—Colts, 35-20 (B)
Colts, 20-17 (LA)
1966—Colts, 17-3 (LA)
Rams, 23-7 (B)
1967—Tie, 24-24 (B)
Rams, 34-10 (LA)
1968—Colts, 27-10 (B)
Colts, 28-24 (LA)
1969—Rams, 27-20 (B)
Colts, 13-7 (LA)
1971—Colts, 24-17 (B)
1975—Rams, 24-13 (LA)
1986—Rams, 24-7 (I)
(Points—Rams 787, Colts 786)
**Franchise in Baltimore prior to 1984*

***INDIANAPOLIS vs. MIAMI**
Dolphins lead series, 27-10
1970—Colts, 35-0 (B)
Dolphins, 34-17 (M)
1971—Dolphins, 17-14 (M)

Colts, 14-3 (B)
**Dolphins, 21-0 (M)
1972—Dolphins, 23-0 (B)
Dolphins, 16-0 (M)
1973—Dolphins, 44-0 (M)
Colts, 16-3 (B)
1974—Dolphins, 17-7 (M)
Dolphins, 17-16 (B)
1975—Colts, 33-17 (M)
Colts, 10-7 (B) OT
1976—Colts, 28-14 (B)
Colts, 17-16 (M)
1977—Colts, 45-28 (B)
Dolphins, 17-6 (M)
1978—Dolphins, 42-0 (B)
Dolphins, 26-8 (M)
1979—Dolphins, 19-0 (M)
Dolphins, 28-24 (B)
1980—Colts, 30-17 (M)
Dolphins, 24-14 (B)
1981—Dolphins, 31-28 (B)
Dolphins, 27-10 (M)
1982—Dolphins, 24-20 (M)
Dolphins, 34-7 (B)
1983—Dolphins, 21-7 (B)
Dolphins, 37-0 (M)
1984—Dolphins, 44-7 (M)
Dolphins, 35-17 (I)
1985—Dolphins, 30-13 (M)
Dolphins, 34-20 (I)
1986—Dolphins, 30-10 (M)
Dolphins, 17-13 (I)
1987—Dolphins, 23-10 (I)
Colts, 40-21 (M)
(Points—Dolphins 858, Colts 536)
Franchise in Baltimore prior to 1984
***AFC Championship*

***INDIANAPOLIS vs. MINNESOTA**
Colts lead series, 12-5-1
1961—Colts, 34-33 (B)
Vikings, 28-20 (M)
1962—Colts, 34-7 (M)
Colts, 42-17 (B)
1963—Colts, 37-34 (M)
Colts, 41-10 (B)
1964—Vikings, 34-24 (M)
Colts, 17-14 (B)
1965—Colts, 35-16 (B)
Colts, 41-21 (M)
1966—Colts, 38-23 (M)
Colts, 20-17 (B)
1967—Tie, 20-20 (M)
1968—Colts, 21-9 (B)
**Colts, 24-14 (B)
1969—Vikings, 52-14 (M)
1971—Vikings, 10-3 (M)
1982—Vikings, 13-10 (M)
(Points—Colts 475, Vikings 372)
Franchise in Baltimore prior to 1984
Conference Championship

***INDIANAPOLIS vs. **NEW ENGLAND**
Patriots lead series, 19-16
1970—Colts, 14-6 (Bos)
Colts, 27-3 (Balt)
1971—Colts, 23-3 (NE)
Patriots, 21-17 (Balt)
1972—Colts, 24-17 (NE)
Colts, 31-0 (Balt)
1973—Patriots, 24-16 (NE)
Colts, 18-13 (Balt)
1974—Patriots, 42-3 (NE)
Patriots, 27-17 (Balt)
1975—Patriots, 21-10 (NE)
Colts, 34-21 (Balt)
1976—Colts, 27-13 (NE)
Patriots, 21-14 (Balt)
1977—Patriots, 17-3 (NE)
Colts, 30-24 (Balt)
1978—Colts, 34-27 (NE)
Patriots, 35-14 (Balt)
1979—Colts, 31-26 (Balt)
Patriots, 50-21 (NE)
1980—Patriots, 37-21 (Balt)
Patriots, 47-21 (NE)
1981—Colts, 29-28 (NE)
Colts, 23-21 (Balt)
1982—Patriots, 24-13 (Balt)
1983—Colts, 29-23 (NE) OT
Colts, 12-7 (B)
1984—Patriots, 50-17 (I)
Patriots, 16-10 (NE)
1985—Patriots, 34-15 (NE)
Patriots, 38-31 (I)
1986—Patriots, 33-3 (NE)
Patriots, 30-21 (I)
1987—Colts, 30-16 (I)
Patriots, 24-0 (NE)
(Points—Patriots 839, Colts 683)
Franchise in Baltimore prior to 1984
***Franchise in Boston prior to 1971*

***INDIANAPOLIS vs. NEW ORLEANS**
Colts lead series, 3-1
1967—Colts, 30-10 (B)
1969—Colts, 30-10 (NO)
1973—Colts, 14-10 (B)
1986—Saints, 17-14 (I)
(Points—Colts 88, Saints 47)
Franchise in Baltimore prior to 1984

***INDIANAPOLIS vs. N.Y. GIANTS**
Colts lead series, 7-3
1954—Colts, 20-14 (B)
1955—Giants, 17-7 (NY)
1958—Giants, 24-21 (NY)
**Colts, 23-17 (NY) OT
1959—**Colts, 31-16 (B)
1963—Giants, 37-28 (B)
1968—Colts, 26-0 (NY)
1971—Colts, 31-7 (NY)
1975—Colts, 21-0 (NY)
1979—Colts, 31-7 (NY)
(Points—Colts 239, Giants 139)
Franchise in Baltimore prior to 1984
***NFL Championship*

***INDIANAPOLIS vs. N.Y. JETS**
Series tied, 18-18
1968—**Jets 16-7 (Miami)
1970—Colts, 29-22 (NY)
Colts, 35-20 (B)
1971—Colts, 22-0 (B)
Colts, 14-13 (NY)
1972—Jets, 44-34 (B)
Jets, 24-20 (NY)
1973—Jets, 34-10 (B)
Jets, 20-17 (NY)
1974—Colts, 35-20 (NY)
Jets, 45-38 (B)
1975—Colts, 45-28 (NY)
Colts, 52-19 (B)
1976—Colts, 20-0 (NY)
Colts, 33-16 (B)
1977—Colts, 20-12 (NY)
Colts, 33-12 (B)
1978—Jets, 33-10 (B)
Jets, 24-16 (NY)
1979—Colts, 10-8 (B)
Jets, 30-17 (NY)
1980—Colts, 17-14 (NY)
Colts, 35-21 (B)
1981—Jets, 41-14 (B)
Jets, 25-0 (NY)
1982—Jets, 37-0 (NY)
1983—Colts, 17-14 (NY)
Jets, 10-6 (B)
1984—Jets, 23-14 (I)
Colts, 9-5 (NY)
1985—Jets, 25-20 (NY)
Jets, 35-17 (I)
1986—Jets, 26-7 (I)
Jets, 31-16 (NY)
1987—Colts, 6-0 (I)
Colts, 19-14 (NY)
(Points—Jets 761, Colts 714)
Franchise in Baltimore prior to 1984
***Super Bowl III*

***INDIANAPOLIS vs. PHILADELPHIA**
Series tied, 5-5
1953—Eagles, 45-14 (P)
1965—Colts, 34-24 (B)
1967—Colts, 38-6 (P)
1969—Colts, 24-20 (B)
1970—Colts, 29-10 (B)
1974—Eagles, 30-10 (P)
1978—Eagles, 17-14 (B)
1981—Eagles, 38-13 (P)
1983—Colts, 22-21 (P)
1984—Eagles, 16-7 (P)
(Points—Eagles 227, Colts 205)
Franchise in Baltimore prior to 1984

***INDIANAPOLIS vs. PITTSBURGH**
Steelers lead series, 10-4
1957—Steelers, 19-13 (B)
1968—Colts, 41-7 (P)
1971—Colts, 34-21 (B)
1974—Steelers, 30-0 (B)
1975—**Steelers, 28-10 (P)
1976—**Steelers, 40-14 (B)
1977—Colts, 31-21 (B)
1978—Steelers, 35-13 (P)
1979—Steelers, 17-13 (P)
1980—Steelers, 20-17 (B)
1983—Steelers, 24-13 (B)
1984—Colts, 17-16 (I)
1985—Steelers, 45-3 (P)
1987—Steelers, 21-7 (P)
(Points—Steelers 344, Colts 226)
Franchise in Baltimore prior to 1984
***AFC Divisional Playoff*

***INDIANAPOLIS vs. ST. LOUIS**
Cardinals lead series 5-4
1961—Colts, 16-0 (B)
1964—Colts, 47-27 (B)
1968—Colts, 27-0 (B)
1972—Cardinals, 10-3 (B)
1976—Cardinals, 24-17 (StL)
1978—Colts, 30-17 (StL)
1980—Cardinals, 17-10 (B)
1981—Cardinals, 35-24 (B)
1984—Cardinals, 34-33 (I)
(Points—Colts 207, Cardinals 164)
Franchise in Baltimore prior to 1984

***INDIANAPOLIS vs. SAN DIEGO**
Chargers lead series, 6-3
1970—Colts, 16-14 (SD)
1972—Chargers, 23-20 (B)
1976—Colts, 37-21 (SD)
1981—Chargers, 43-14 (B)
1982—Chargers, 44-26 (SD)
1984—Chargers, 38-10 (I)
1986—Chargers, 17-3 (I)
1987—Chargers, 16-13 (I)
Colts, 20-7 (SD)
(Points—Chargers 223, Colts 159)
Franchise in Baltimore prior to 1984

***INDIANAPOLIS vs. SAN FRANCISCO**
Colts lead series, 21-15
1953—49ers, 38-21 (B)
49ers, 45-14 (SF)
1954—Colts, 17-13 (B)
49ers, 10-7 (SF)
1955—Colts, 26-14 (B)
49ers, 35-24 (SF)
1956—49ers, 20-17 (B)
49ers, 30-17 (SF)
1957—Colts, 27-21 (B)
49ers, 17-13 (SF)
1958—Colts, 35-27 (B)
49ers, 21-12 (SF)
1959—Colts, 45-14 (B)
Colts, 34-14 (SF)
1960—49ers, 30-22 (B)
49ers, 34-10 (SF)
1961—Colts, 20-17 (B)
Colts, 27-24 (SF)
1962—49ers, 21-13 (B)
Colts, 22-3 (SF)
1963—Colts, 20-14 (SF)
Colts, 20-3 (B)
1964—Colts, 37-7 (B)
Colts, 14-3 (SF)
1965—Colts, 27-24 (B)
Colts, 34-28 (SF)
1966—Colts, 36-14 (B)
Colts, 30-14 (SF)
1967—Colts, 41-7 (B)
Colts, 26-9 (SF)
1968—Colts, 27-10 (B)
Colts, 42-14 (SF)
1969—49ers, 24-21 (B)
49ers, 20-17 (SF)
1972—49ers, 24-21 (SF)
1986—49ers, 35-14 (SF)
(Points—Colts 850, 49ers 698)
Franchise in Baltimore prior to 1984

***INDIANAPOLIS vs. SEATTLE**
Colts lead series, 2-0
1977—Colts, 29-14 (S)
1978—Colts, 17-14 (S)
(Points—Colts 46, Seahawks 28)
Franchise in Baltimore prior to 1984

***INDIANAPOLIS vs. TAMPA BAY**
Colts lead series, 3-1
1976—Colts, 42-17 (B)
1979—Buccaneers, 29-26 (B) OT
1985—Colts, 31-23 (TB)
1987—Colts, 24-6 (I)
(Points—Colts 123, Buccaneers 75)
Franchise in Baltimore prior to 1984

***INDIANAPOLIS vs. WASHINGTON**
Colts lead series, 15-6
1953—Colts, 27-17 (B)
1954—Redskins, 24-21 (W)
1955—Redskins, 14-13 (B)
1956—Colts, 19-17 (B)
1957—Colts, 21-17 (W)
1958—Colts, 35-10 (B)
1959—Redskins, 27-24 (W)
1960—Colts, 20-0 (B)
1961—Colts, 27-6 (W)
1962—Colts, 34-21 (B)
1963—Colts, 36-20 (W)
1964—Colts, 45-17 (B)
1965—Colts, 38-7 (W)
1966—Colts, 37-10 (B)
1967—Colts, 17-13 (W)
1969—Colts, 41-17 (B)
1973—Redskins, 22-14 (W)
1977—Colts, 10-3 (B)
1978—Colts, 21-17 (B)
1981—Redskins, 38-14 (W)
1984—Redskins, 35-7 (I)
(Points—Colts 521, Redskins 352)
Franchise in Baltimore prior to 1984

KANSAS CITY vs. ATLANTA
Chiefs lead series, 2-0;
See Atlanta vs. Kansas City

KANSAS CITY vs. BUFFALO
Bills lead series, 15-12-1;
See Buffalo vs. Kansas City

KANSAS CITY vs. CHICAGO
Bears lead series, 3-1;
See Chicago vs. Kansas City

KANSAS CITY vs. CINCINNATI
Chiefs lead series, 9-8;
See Cincinnati vs. Kansas City

KANSAS CITY vs. CLEVELAND
Series tied, 5-5-1;
See Cleveland vs. Kansas City

KANSAS CITY vs. DALLAS
Cowboys lead series, 2-1;
See Dallas vs. Kansas City

KANSAS CITY vs. DENVER
Chiefs lead series, 34-21;
See Denver vs. Kansas City

KANSAS CITY vs. DETROIT
Chiefs lead series, 3-2;
See Detroit vs. Kansas City

KANSAS CITY vs. GREEN BAY
Packers lead series, 2-1-1;
See Green Bay vs. Kansas City

KANSAS CITY vs. HOUSTON
Chiefs lead series, 21-12;
See Houston vs. Kansas City

KANSAS CITY vs. INDIANAPOLIS
Chiefs lead series, 6-3;
See Indianapolis vs. Kansas City

***KANSAS CITY vs. **L.A. RAIDERS**
Raiders lead series, 32-23-2
1960—Texans, 34-16 (O)
Raiders, 20-19 (D)
1961—Texans, 42-35 (O)
Texans, 43-11 (D)
1962—Texans, 26-16 (O)
Texans, 35-7 (D)
1963—Raiders, 10-7 (O)
Raiders, 22-7 (KC)
1964—Chiefs, 21-9 (O)
Chiefs, 42-7 (KC)
1965—Raiders, 37-10 (O)
Chiefs, 14-7 (KC)
1966—Chiefs, 32-10 (O)
Raiders, 34-13 (KC)
1967—Raiders, 23-21 (O)
Raiders, 44-22 (KC)
1968—Chiefs, 24-10 (KC)
Raiders, 38-21 (O)
***Raiders, 41-6 (O)
1969—Raiders, 27-24 (KC)
Raiders, 10-6 (O)
****Chiefs, 17-7 (O)
1970—Tie, 17-17 (KC)
Raiders, 20-6 (O)
1971—Tie, 20-20 (O)
Chiefs, 16-14 (KC)
1972—Chiefs, 27-14 (KC)
Raiders, 26-3 (O)
1973—Chiefs, 16-3 (KC)
Raiders, 37-7 (O)
1974—Raiders, 27-7 (O)
Raiders, 7-6 (KC)
1975—Chiefs, 42-10 (KC)
Raiders, 28-20 (O)
1976—Raiders, 24-21 (KC)
Raiders, 21-10 (O)
1977—Raiders, 37-28 (KC)
Raiders, 21-20 (O)
1978—Raiders, 28-6 (O)
Raiders, 20-10 (KC)
1979—Chiefs, 35-7 (KC)
Chiefs, 24-21 (O)
1980—Raiders, 27-14 (KC)
Chiefs, 31-17 (O)
1981—Chiefs, 27-0 (KC)
Chiefs, 28-17 (O)
1982—Raiders, 21-16 (KC)
1983—Raiders, 21-20 (LA)
Raiders, 28-20 (KC)
1984—Raiders, 22-20 (KC)
Raiders, 17-7 (LA)
1985—Chiefs, 36-20 (KC)
Raiders, 19-10 (LA)
1986—Raiders, 24-17 (KC)
Chiefs, 20-17 (LA)
1987—Raiders, 35-17 (LA)
Chiefs, 16-10 (KC)
(Points—Raiders 1,138, Chiefs 1,126)
Franchise in Dallas prior to 1963 and known as Texans
***Franchise in Oakland prior to 1982*
****Division Playoff*
*****AFL Championship*

KANSAS CITY vs. L.A. RAMS
Rams lead series, 3-0
1973—Rams, 23-13 (KC)
1982—Rams, 20-14 (LA)
1985—Rams, 16-0 (KC)
(Points—Rams 59, Chiefs 27)

KANSAS CITY vs. MIAMI
Series tied, 7-7
1966—Chiefs, 34-16 (KC)
Chiefs, 19-18 (M)
1967—Chiefs, 24-0 (M)

Chiefs, 41-0 (KC)
1968—Chiefs, 48-3 (M)
1969—Chiefs, 17-10 (KC)
1971—*Dolphins, 27-24 (KC) OT
1972—Dolphins, 20-10 (KC)
1974—Dolphins, 9-3 (M)
1976—Chiefs, 20-17 (M) OT
1981—Dolphins, 17-7 (KC)
1983—Dolphins, 14-6 (M)
1985—Dolphins, 31-0 (M)
1987—Dolphins, 42-0 (M)
(Points—Chiefs 253, Dolphins 224)
*AFC Divisional Playoff

KANSAS CITY vs. MINNESOTA
Series tied, 2-2
1969—*Chiefs, 23-7 (New Orleans)
1970—Vikings, 27-10 (M)
1974—Vikings, 35-15 (KC)
1981—Chiefs, 10-6 (M)
(Points—Vikings 75, Chiefs 58)
*Super Bowl IV

***KANSAS CITY vs. **NEW ENGLAND**
Chiefs lead series, 11-7-3
1960—Patriots, 42-14 (B)
Texans, 34-0 (D)
1961—Patriots, 18-17 (D)
Patriots, 28-21 (B)
1962—Texans, 42-28 (D)
Texans, 27-7 (B)
1963—Tie, 24-24 (B)
Chiefs, 35-3 (KC)
1964—Patriots, 24-7 (B)
Patriots, 31-24 (KC)
1965—Chiefs, 27-17 (KC)
Tie, 10-10 (B)
1966—Chiefs, 43-24 (B)
Tie, 27-27 (KC)
1967—Chiefs, 33-10 (B)
1968—Chiefs, 31-17 (KC)
1969—Chiefs, 31-0 (B)
1970—Chiefs, 23-10 (KC)
1973—Chiefs, 10-7 (NE)
1977—Patriots, 21-17 (NE)
1981—Patriots, 33-17 (NE)
(Points—Chiefs 514, Patriots 381)
*Franchise located in Dallas prior to 1963 and known as Texans
**Franchise in Boston prior to 1971

KANSAS CITY vs. NEW ORLEANS
Series tied, 2-2
1972—Chiefs, 20-17 (NO)
1976—Saints, 27-17 (KC)
1982—Saints, 27-17 (NO)
1985—Chiefs, 47-27 (NO)
(Points—Chiefs 101, Saints 98)

KANSAS CITY vs. N.Y. GIANTS
Giants lead series, 4-1
1974—Giants, 33-27 (KC)
1978—Giants, 26-10 (NY)
1979—Giants, 21-17 (KC)
1983—Chiefs, 38-17 (KC)
1984—Giants, 28-27 (NY)
(Points—Giants 125, Chiefs 119)

***KANSAS CITY vs. **N.Y. JETS**
Series tied, 13-13
1960—Titans, 37-35 (D)
Titans, 41-35 (NY)
1961—Titans, 28-7 (NY)
Texans, 35-24 (D)
1962—Texans, 20-17 (D)
Texans, 52-31 (NY)
1963—Jets, 17-0 (NY)
Chiefs, 48-0 (KC)
1964—Jets, 27-14 (NY)
Chiefs, 24-7 (KC)
1965—Chiefs, 14-10 (NY)
Jets, 13-10 (KC)
1966—Chiefs, 32-24 (NY)
1967—Chiefs, 42-18 (KC)
Chiefs, 21-7 (NY)
1968—Jets, 20-19 (KC)
1969—Chiefs, 34-16 (NY)
***Chiefs, 13-6 (NY)
1971—Jets, 13-10 (NY)
1974—Chiefs, 24-16 (KC)
1975—Jets, 30-24 (KC)
1982—Chiefs, 37-13 (KC)
1984—Jets, 17-16 (KC)
Jets, 28-7 (NY)
1986—****Jets, 35-15 (NY)
1987—Jets, 16-9 (KC)
(Points—Chiefs 597, Jets 511)
*Franchise in Dallas prior to 1963 and known as Texans
**Jets known as Titans prior to 1963
***Inter-Divisional Playoff
****AFC First Round Playoff

KANSAS CITY vs. PHILADELPHIA
Eagles lead series, 1-0
1972—Eagles, 21-20 (KC)

KANSAS CITY vs. PITTSBURGH
Steelers lead series, 10-5
1970—Chiefs, 31-14 (P)
1971—Chiefs, 38-16 (KC)
1972—Steelers, 16-7 (P)
1974—Steelers, 34-24 (KC)
1975—Steelers, 28-3 (P)
1976—Steelers, 45-0 (KC)
1978—Steelers, 27-24 (P)
1979—Steelers, 30-3 (KC)
1980—Steelers, 21-16 (P)
1981—Chiefs, 37-33 (P)
1982—Steelers, 35-14 (P)
1984—Chiefs, 37-27 (P)
1985—Steelers, 36-28 (KC)
1986—Chiefs, 24-19 (P)
1987—Steelers, 17-16 (KC)
(Points—Steelers 398, Chiefs 302)

KANSAS CITY vs. ST. LOUIS
Chiefs lead series, 3-1-1
1970—Tie, 6-6 (KC)
1974—Chiefs, 17-13 (StL)
1980—Chiefs, 21-13 (StL)
1983—Chiefs, 38-14 (KC)
1986—Cardinals, 23-14 (StL)
(Points—Chiefs 96, Cardinals 69)

***KANSAS CITY vs. **SAN DIEGO**
Series tied, 27-27-1
1960—Chargers, 21-20 (LA)
Texans, 17-0 (D)
1961—Chargers, 26-10 (D)
Chargers, 24-14 (SD)
1962—Chargers, 32-28 (SD)
Texans, 26-17 (D)
1963—Chargers, 24-10 (SD)
Chargers, 38-17 (KC)
1964—Chargers, 28-14 (KC)
Chiefs, 49-6 (SD)
1965—Tie, 10-10 (SD)
Chiefs, 31-7 (KC)
1966—Chiefs, 24-14 (KC)
Chiefs, 27-17 (SD)
1967—Chargers, 45-31 (SD)
Chargers, 17-16 (KC)
1968—Chiefs, 27-20 (KC)
Chiefs, 40-3 (SD)
1969—Chiefs, 27-9 (SD)
Chiefs, 27-3 (KC)
1970—Chiefs, 26-14 (KC)
Chargers, 31-13 (SD)
1971—Chargers, 21-14 (SD)
Chiefs, 31-10 (KC)
1972—Chiefs, 26-14 (SD)
Chargers, 27-17 (KC)
1973—Chiefs, 19-0 (SD)
Chiefs, 33-6 (KC)
1974—Chiefs, 24-14 (SD)
Chargers, 14-7 (KC)
1975—Chiefs, 12-10 (SD)
Chargers, 28-20 (KC)
1976—Chargers, 30-16 (KC)
Chiefs, 23-20 (SD)
1977—Chargers, 23-7 (KC)
Chiefs, 21-16 (SD)
1978—Chargers, 29-23 (SD) OT
Chiefs, 23-0 (KC)
1979—Chargers, 20-14 (KC)
Chargers, 28-7 (SD)
1980—Chargers, 24-7 (KC)
Chargers, 20-7 (SD)
1981—Chargers, 42-31 (KC)
Chargers, 22-20 (SD)
1982—Chiefs, 19-12 (KC)
1983—Chargers, 17-14 (KC)
Chargers, 41-38 (SD)
1984—Chiefs, 31-13 (KC)
Chiefs, 42-21 (SD)
1985—Chargers, 31-20 (SD)
Chiefs, 38-34 (KC)
1986—Chiefs, 42-41 (KC)
Chiefs, 24-23 (SD)
1987—Chiefs, 20-13 (KC)
Chargers, 42-21 (SD)
(Points—Chiefs 1,215, Chargers 1,112)
*Franchise in Dallas prior to 1963 and known as Texans
**Franchise in Los Angeles prior to 1961

KANSAS CITY vs. SAN FRANCISCO
49ers lead series, 3-1
1971—Chiefs, 26-17 (SF)
1975—49ers, 20-3 (KC)
1982—49ers, 26-13 (KC)
1985—49ers, 31-3 (SF)
(Points—49ers 94, Chiefs 45)

KANSAS CITY vs. SEATTLE
Chiefs lead series, 10-9
1977—Seahawks, 34-31 (KC)
1978—Seahawks, 13-10 (KC)
Seahawks, 23-19 (S)
1979—Chiefs, 24-6 (S)
Chiefs, 37-21 (KC)
1980—Seahawks, 17-16 (KC)
Chiefs, 31-30 (S)
1981—Chiefs, 20-14 (S)
Chiefs, 40-13 (KC)
1983—Chiefs, 17-13 (KC)
Seahawks, 51-48 (S) OT
1984—Seahawks, 45-0 (S)
Chiefs, 34-7 (KC)
1985—Chiefs, 28-7 (KC)
Seahawks, 24-6 (S)
1986—Seahawks, 23-17 (S)
Chiefs, 27-7 (KC)
1987—Seahawks, 43-14 (S)
Chiefs, 41-20 (KC)
(Points—Chiefs 460, Seahawks 411)

KANSAS CITY vs. TAMPA BAY
Chiefs lead series, 4-2
1976—Chiefs, 28-19 (TB)
1978—Buccaneers, 30-13 (KC)
1979—Buccaneers, 3-0 (TB)
1981—Chiefs, 19-10 (KC)
1984—Chiefs, 24-20 (KC)
1986—Chiefs, 27-20 (KC)
(Points—Chiefs 111, Buccaneers 102)

KANSAS CITY vs. WASHINGTON
Chiefs lead series, 2-1
1971—Chiefs, 27-20 (KC)
1976—Chiefs, 33-30 (W)
1983—Redskins, 27-12 (W)
(Points—Redskins 77, Chiefs 72)

L.A. RAIDERS vs. ATLANTA
Raiders lead series, 4-1;
See Atlanta vs. L.A. Raiders

L.A. RAIDERS vs. BUFFALO
Raiders lead series, 13-11;
See Buffalo vs. L.A. Raiders

L.A. RAIDERS vs. CHICAGO
Series tied, 3-3;
See Chicago vs. L.A. Raiders

L.A. RAIDERS vs. CINCINNATI
Raiders lead series, 12-4;
See Cincinnati vs. L.A. Raiders

L.A. RAIDERS vs. CLEVELAND
Raiders lead series, 10-2;
See Cleveland vs. L.A. Raiders

L.A. RAIDERS vs. DALLAS
Raiders lead series, 3-1;
See Dallas vs. L.A. Raiders

L.A. RAIDERS vs. DENVER
Raiders lead series, 36-18-2;
See Denver vs. L.A. Raiders

L.A. RAIDERS vs. DETROIT
Raiders lead series, 4-2;
See Detroit vs. L.A. Raiders

L.A. RAIDERS vs. GREEN BAY
Raiders lead series, 5-1;
See Green Bay vs. L.A. Raiders

L.A. RAIDERS vs. HOUSTON
Raiders lead series, 22-10;
See Houston vs. L.A. Raiders

L.A. RAIDERS vs. INDIANAPOLIS
Raiders lead series, 4-3;
See Indianapolis vs. L.A. Raiders

L.A. RAIDERS vs. KANSAS CITY
Raiders lead series, 32-23-2;
See Kansas City vs. L.A. Raiders

***L.A. RAIDERS vs. L.A. RAMS**
Raiders lead series, 4-1
1972—Raiders, 45-17 (O)
1977—Rams, 20-14 (LA)
1979—Raiders, 24-17 (LA)
1982—Raiders, 37-31 (LA Raiders)
1985—Raiders, 16-6 (LA Rams)
(Points—Raiders 136, Rams 91)
*Franchise in Oakland prior to 1982

***L.A. RAIDERS vs. MIAMI**
Raiders lead series, 15-3-1
1966—Raiders, 23-14 (M)
Raiders, 21-10 (O)
1967—Raiders, 31-17 (O)
1968—Raiders, 47-21 (M)
1969—Raiders, 20-17 (O)
Tie, 20-20 (M)
1970—Dolphins, 20-13 (M)
**Raiders, 21-14 (O)
1973—Raiders, 12-7 (O)
***Dolphins, 27-10 (M)
1974—**Raiders, 28-26 (O)
1975—Raiders, 31-21 (M)
1978—Dolphins, 23-6 (M)
1979—Raiders, 13-3 (O)
1980—Raiders, 16-10 (O)
1981—Raiders, 33-17 (M)
1983—Raiders, 27-14 (LA)
1984—Raiders, 45-34 (M)
1986—Raiders, 30-28 (M)
(Points—Raiders 447, Dolphins 343)
*Franchise in Oakland prior to 1982
**AFC Divisional Playoff
***AFC Championship

***L.A. RAIDERS vs. MINNESOTA**
Raiders lead series, 5-2
1973—Vikings, 24-16 (M)
1976—**Raiders, 32-14 (Pasadena)
1977—Raiders, 35-13 (O)
1978—Raiders, 27-20 (O)
1981—Raiders, 36-10 (M)
1984—Raiders, 23-20 (LA)
1987—Vikings, 31-20 (M)
(Points—Raiders 189, Vikings 132)
*Franchise in Oakland prior to 1982
**Super Bowl XI

***L.A. RAIDERS vs. **NEW ENGLAND**
Patriots lead series, 13-12-1
1960—Raiders, 27-14 (O)
Patriots, 34-28 (B)
1961—Patriots, 20-17 (B)
Patriots, 35-21 (O)
1962—Patriots, 26-16 (B)
Raiders, 20-0 (O)
1963—Patriots, 20-14 (O)
Patriots, 20-14 (B)
1964—Patriots, 17-14 (O)
Tie, 43-43 (B)
1965—Raiders, 24-10 (B)
Raiders, 30-21 (O)
1966—Patriots, 24-21 (B)
1967—Raiders, 35-7 (O)
Raiders, 48-14 (B)
1968—Raiders, 41-10 (O)
1969—Raiders, 38-23 (B)
1971—Patriots, 20-6 (NE)
1974—Raiders, 41-26 (O)
1976—Patriots, 48-17 (NE)
***Raiders, 24-21 (O)
1978—Patriots, 21-14 (O)
1981—Raiders, 27-17 (O)
1985—Raiders, 35-20 (NE)
***Patriots, 27-20 (LA)
1987—Patriots, 26-23 (NE)
(Points—Raiders 658, Patriots 564)
*Franchise in Oakland prior to 1982
**Franchise in Boston prior to 1971
***AFC Divisional Playoff

***L.A. RAIDERS vs. NEW ORLEANS**
Raiders lead series, 3-0-1
1971—Tie, 21-21 (NO)
1975—Raiders, 48-10 (O)
1979—Raiders, 42-35 (NO)
1985—Raiders, 23-13 (LA)
(Points—Raiders 134, Saints 79)
*Franchise in Oakland prior to 1982

***L.A. RAIDERS vs. N.Y. GIANTS**
Raiders lead series, 3-1
1973—Raiders, 42-0 (O)
1980—Raiders, 33-17 (NY)
1983—Raiders, 27-12 (LA)
1986—Giants, 14-9 (LA)
(Points—Raiders 111, Giants 43)
*Franchise in Oakland prior to 1982

***L.A. RAIDERS vs. **N.Y. JETS**
Raiders lead series, 12-11-2
1960—Raiders, 28-27 (NY)
Titans, 31-28 (O)
1961—Titans, 14-6 (O)
Titans, 23-12 (NY)
1962—Titans, 28-17 (O)
Titans, 31-21 (NY)
1963—Jets, 10-7 (NY)
Raiders, 49-26 (O)
1964—Jets, 35-13 (NY)
Raiders, 35-26 (O)
1965—Tie, 24-24 (NY)
Raiders, 24-14 (O)
1966—Raiders, 24-21 (NY)
Tie, 28-28 (O)
1967—Jets, 27-14 (NY)
Raiders, 38-29 (O)
1968—Raiders, 43-32 (O)
***Jets, 27-23 (NY)
1969—Raiders, 27-14 (NY)
1970—Raiders, 14-13 (NY)
1972—Raiders, 24-16 (O)
1977—Raiders, 28-27 (NY)
1979—Jets, 28-19 (NY)
1982—****Jets, 17-14 (LA)
1985—Raiders, 31-0 (LA)
(Points—Raiders 591, Jets 568)
*Franchise in Oakland prior to 1982
**Jets known as Titans prior to 1963
***AFL Championship
****AFC Second Round Playoff

***L.A. RAIDERS vs. PHILADELPHIA**
Raiders lead series, 3-2
1971—Raiders, 34-10 (O)
1976—Raiders, 26-7 (P)
1980—Eagles, 10-7 (P)
**Raiders, 27-10 (NO)
1986—Eagles, 33-27 (LA) OT
(Points—Raiders 121, Eagles 70)
*Franchise in Oakland prior to 1982
**Super Bowl XV

***L.A. RAIDERS vs. PITTSBURGH**
Raiders lead series, 9-6
1970—Raiders, 31-14 (O)
1972—Steelers, 34-28 (P)
**Steelers, 13-7 (P)
1973—Steelers, 17-9 (O)
**Raiders, 33-14 (O)
1974—Raiders, 17-0 (P)

***Steelers, 24-13 (O)
1975—***Steelers, 16-10 (P)
1976—Raiders, 31-28 (O)
***Raiders, 24-7 (O)
1977—Raiders, 16-7 (P)
1980—Raiders, 45-34 (P)
1981—Raiders, 30-27 (O)
1983—**Raiders, 38-10 (LA)
1984—Steelers, 13-7 (LA)
(Points—Raiders 339, Steelers 258)
Franchise in Oakland prior to 1982
***AFC Divisional Playoff*
****AFC Championship*

***L.A. RAIDERS vs. ST. LOUIS**
Series tied, 1-1
1973—Raiders, 17-10 (StL)
1983—Cardinals, 34-24 (LA)
(Points—Cardinals 44, Raiders 41)
Franchise in Oakland prior to 1982

***L.A. RAIDERS vs. **SAN DIEGO**
Raiders lead series, 35-20-2
1960—Chargers, 52-28 (LA)
Chargers, 41-17 (O)
1961—Chargers, 44-0 (SD)
Chargers, 41-10 (O)
1962—Chargers, 42-33 (O)
Chargers, 31-21 (SD)
1963—Raiders, 34-33 (SD)
Raiders, 41-27 (O)
1964—Chargers, 31-17 (O)
Raiders, 21-20 (SD)
1965—Chargers, 17-6 (O)
Chargers, 24-14 (SD)
1966—Chargers, 29-20 (O)
Raiders, 41-19 (SD)
1967—Raiders, 51-10 (O)
Raiders, 41-21 (SD)
1968—Chargers, 23-14 (O)
Raiders, 34-27 (SD)
1969—Raiders, 24-12 (SD)
Raiders, 21-16 (O)
1970—Tie, 27-27 (SD)
Raiders, 20-17 (O)
1971—Raiders, 34-0 (SD)
Raiders, 34-33 (O)
1972—Tie, 17-17 (O)
Raiders, 21-19 (SD)
1973—Raiders, 27-17 (SD)
Raiders, 31-3 (O)
1974—Raiders, 14-10 (SD)
Raiders, 17-10 (O)
1975—Raiders, 6-0 (SD)
Raiders, 25-0 (O)
1976—Raiders, 27-17 (SD)
Raiders, 24-0 (O)
1977—Raiders, 24-0 (O)
Chargers, 12-7 (SD)
1978—Raiders, 21-20 (SD)
Chargers, 27-23 (O)
1979—Chargers, 30-10 (SD)
Raiders, 45-22 (O)
1980—Chargers, 30-24 (SD) OT
Raiders, 38-24 (O)
***Raiders, 34-27 (SD)
1981—Chargers, 55-21 (O)
Chargers, 23-10 (SD)
1982—Raiders, 28-24 (LA)
Raiders, 41-34 (SD)
1983—Raiders, 42-10 (SD)
Raiders, 30-14 (LA)
1984—Raiders, 33-30 (LA)
Raiders, 44-37 (SD)
1985—Raiders, 34-21 (LA)
Chargers, 40-34 (SD) OT
1986—Raiders, 17-13 (LA)
Raiders, 37-31 (SD) OT
1987—Chargers, 23-17 (LA)
Chargers, 16-14 (SD)
(Points—Raiders 1,440, Chargers 1,293)
Franchise in Oakland prior to 1982
***Franchise in Los Angeles prior to 1961*
****AFC Championship*

***L.A. RAIDERS vs. SAN FRANCISCO**
Raiders lead series, 3-2
1970—49ers, 38-7 (O)
1974—Raiders, 35-24 (SF)
1979—Raiders, 23-10 (O)
1982—Raiders, 23-17 (SF)
1985—49ers, 34-10 (LA)
(Points—49ers 123, Raiders 98)
Franchise in Oakland prior to 1982

***L.A. RAIDERS vs. SEATTLE**
Series tied, 11-11
1977—Raiders, 44-7 (O)
1978—Seahawks, 27-7 (S)
Seahawks, 17-16 (O)
1979—Seahawks, 27-10 (S)
Seahawks, 29-24 (O)
1980—Raiders, 33-14 (O)
Raiders, 19-17 (S)
1981—Raiders, 20-10 (O)
Raiders, 32-31 (S)
1982—Raiders, 28-23 (LA)
1983—Seahawks, 38-36 (S)
Seahawks, 34-21 (LA)
**Raiders, 30-14 (LA)
1984—Raiders, 28-14 (LA)
Seahawks, 17-14 (S)
***Seahawks, 13-7 (S)
1985—Seahawks, 33-3 (S)
Raiders, 13-3 (LA)
1986—Raiders, 14-10 (LA)
Seahawks, 37-0 (S)
1987—Seahawks, 35-13 (LA)
Raiders, 37-14 (S)
(Points—Seahawks 464, Raiders 449)
Franchise in Oakland prior to 1982
***AFC Championship*
****AFC First Round Playoff*

***L.A. RAIDERS vs. TAMPA BAY**
Raiders lead series, 2-0
1976—Raiders, 49-16 (O)
1981—Raiders, 18-16 (O)
(Points—Raiders 67, Buccaneers 32)
Franchise in Oakland prior to 1982

***L.A. RAIDERS vs. WASHINGTON**
Raiders lead series, 4-2
1970—Raiders, 34-20 (O)
1975—Raiders, 26-23 (W) OT
1980—Raiders, 24-21 (O)
1983—Redskins, 37-35 (W)
**Raiders, 38-9 (Tampa)
1986—Redskins, 10-6 (W)
(Points—Raiders 163, Redskins 120)
Franchise in Oakland prior to 1982
***Super Bowl XVIII*

L.A. RAMS vs. ATLANTA
Rams lead series, 30-10-2;
See Atlanta vs. L.A. Rams

L.A. RAMS vs. BUFFALO
Rams lead series, 3-1;
See Buffalo vs. L.A. Rams

L.A. RAMS vs. CHICAGO
Bears lead series, 43-28-3;
See Chicago vs. L.A. Rams

L.A. RAMS vs. CINCINNATI
Bengals lead series, 3-2;
See Cincinnati vs. L.A. Rams

L.A. RAMS vs. CLEVELAND
Browns lead series, 9-7;
See Cleveland vs. L.A. Rams

L.A. RAMS vs. DALLAS
Series tied, 11-11;
See Dallas vs. L.A. Rams

L.A. RAMS vs. DENVER
Rams lead series, 3-2;
See Denver vs. L.A. Rams

L.A. RAMS vs. DETROIT
Rams lead series, 38-34-1;
See Detroit vs. L.A. Rams

L.A. RAMS vs. GREEN BAY
Rams lead series, 39-34-2;
See Green Bay vs. L.A. Rams

L.A. RAMS vs. HOUSTON
Rams lead series, 3-2;
See Houston vs. L.A. Rams

L.A. RAMS vs. INDIANAPOLIS
Colts lead series, 20-15-2;
See Indianapolis vs. L.A. Rams

L.A. RAMS vs. KANSAS CITY
Rams lead series, 3-0;
See Kansas City vs. L.A. Rams

L.A. RAMS VS. L.A. RAIDERS
Raiders lead series, 4-1;
See L.A. Raiders vs. L.A. Rams

L.A. RAMS vs. MIAMI
Dolphins lead series, 4-1
1971—Dolphins, 20-14 (LA)
1976—Rams, 31-28 (M)
1980—Dolphins, 35-14 (LA)
1983—Dolphins, 30-14 (M)
1986—Dolphins 37-31 (LA) OT
(Points—Dolphins 150, Rams 104)

L.A. RAMS vs. MINNESOTA
Vikings lead series, 16-12-2
1961—Rams, 31-17 (LA)
Vikings, 42-21 (M)
1962—Vikings, 38-14 (LA)
Tie, 24-24 (M)
1963—Rams, 27-24 (LA)
Vikings, 21-13 (M)
1964—Rams, 22-13 (LA)
Vikings, 34-13 (M)
1965—Vikings, 38-35 (LA)
Vikings, 24-13 (M)
1966—Vikings, 35-7 (M)
Rams, 21-6 (LA)
1967—Rams, 39-3 (LA)
1968—Rams, 31-3 (M)
1969—Vikings, 20-13 (LA)
*Vikings, 23-20 (M)
1970—Vikings, 13-3 (M)
1972—Vikings, 45-41 (LA)
1973—Vikings, 10-9 (M)
1974—Rams, 20-17 (LA)
**Vikings, 14-10 (M)
1976—Tie, 10-10 (M) OT
**Vikings, 24-13 (M)
1977—Rams, 35-3 (LA)
***Vikings, 14-7 (LA)
1978—Rams, 34-17 (M)
***Rams, 34-10 (LA)
1979—Rams, 27-21 (LA) OT
1985—Rams, 13-10 (LA)
1987—Vikings, 21-16 (LA)
(Points—Rams 616, Vikings 594)
Conference Championship
***NFC Championship*
****NFC Divisional Playoff*

L.A. RAMS vs. NEW ENGLAND
Patriots lead series, 3-1
1974—Patriots, 20-14 (NE)
1980—Rams, 17-14 (NE)
1983—Patriots, 21-7 (LA)
1986—Patriots, 30-28 (LA)
(Points—Patriots 85, Rams 66)

L.A. RAMS vs. NEW ORLEANS
Rams lead series, 24-12
1967—Rams, 27-13 (NO)
1969—Rams, 36-17 (LA)
1970—Rams, 30-17 (NO)
Rams, 34-16 (LA)
1971—Saints, 24-20 (NO)
Rams, 45-28 (LA)
1972—Rams, 34-14 (LA)
Saints, 19-16 (NO)
1973—Rams, 29-7 (LA)
Rams, 24-13 (NO)
1974—Rams, 24-0 (LA)
Saints, 20-7 (NO)
1975—Rams, 38-14 (LA)
Rams, 14-7 (NO)
1976—Rams, 16-10 (NO)
Rams, 33-14 (LA)
1977—Rams, 14-7 (LA)
Saints, 27-26 (NO)
1978—Rams, 26-20 (NO)
Saints, 10-3 (LA)
1979—Rams, 35-17 (NO)
Saints, 29-14 (LA)
1980—Rams, 45-31 (LA)
Rams, 27-7 (NO)
1981—Saints, 23-17 (NO)
Saints, 21-13 (LA)
1983—Rams, 30-27 (LA)
Rams, 26-24 (NO)
1984—Rams, 28-10 (NO)
Rams, 34-21 (LA)
1985—Rams, 28-10 (LA)
Saints, 29-3 (NO)
1986—Saints, 6-0 (NO)
Rams, 26-13 (LA)
1987—Saints, 37-10 (NO)
Saints, 31-14 (LA)
(Points—Rams 846, Saints 633)

***L.A. RAMS vs. N.Y. GIANTS**
Rams lead series, 16-8
1938—Giants, 28-0 (NY)
1940—Rams, 13-0 (NY)
1941—Giants, 49-14 (NY)
1945—Rams, 21-17 (NY)
1946—Rams, 31-21 (NY)
1947—Rams, 34-10 (LA)
1948—Rams, 52-37 (NY)
1953—Rams, 21-7 (LA)
1954—Rams, 17-16 (NY)
1959—Giants, 23-21 (LA)
1961—Giants, 24-14 (NY)
1966—Rams, 55-14 (LA)
1968—Rams, 24-21 (LA)
1970—Rams, 31-3 (NY)
1973—Rams, 40-6 (LA)
1976—Rams, 24-10 (LA)
1978—Rams, 20-17 (NY)
1979—Giants, 20-14 (LA)
1980—Rams, 28-7 (NY)
1981—Giants, 10-7 (NY)
1983—Rams, 16-6 (NY)
1984—Rams, 33-12 (LA)
**Giants, 16-13 (LA)
1985—Giants, 24-19 (NY)
(Points—Rams 562, Giants 398)
Franchise in Cleveland prior to 1946
***NFC First Round Playoff*

L.A. RAMS vs. N.Y. JETS
Rams lead series, 3-2
1970—Jets, 31-20 (LA)
1974—Rams, 20-13 (NY)
1980—Rams, 38-13 (LA)
1983—Jets, 27-24 (NY) OT
1986—Rams, 17-3 (NY)
(Points—Rams 119, Jets 87)

***L.A. RAMS vs. PHILADELPHIA**
Rams lead series, 15-10-1
1937—Rams, 21-3 (P)
1939—Rams, 35-13 (Colorado Springs)
1940—Rams, 21-13 (C)
1942—Rams, 24-14 (Akron)
1944—Eagles, 26-13 (P)
1945—Eagles, 28-14 (P)
1946—Eagles, 25-14 (LA)
1947—Eagles, 14-7 (P)
1948—Tie, 28-28 (LA)
1949—Eagles, 38-14 (P)
**Eagles, 14-0 (LA)
1950—Eagles, 56-20 (P)
1955—Rams, 23-21 (P)
1956—Rams, 27-7 (LA)
1957—Rams, 17-13 (LA)
1959—Eagles, 23-20 (P)
1964—Rams, 20-10 (LA)
1967—Rams, 33-17 (LA)
1969—Rams, 23-17 (P)
1972—Rams, 34-3 (P)
1975—Rams, 42-3 (P)
1977—Rams, 20-0 (LA)
1978—Rams, 16-14 (P)
1983—Eagles, 13-9 (P)
1985—Rams, 17-6 (P)
1986—Eagles, 34-20 (P)
(Points—Rams 532, Eagles 453)
Franchise in Cleveland prior to 1946
***NFL Championship*

***L.A. RAMS vs. **PITTSBURGH**
Rams lead series, 13-4-2
1938—Rams, 13-7 (New Orleans)
1939—Tie, 14-14 (C)
1941—Rams, 17-14 (Akron)
1947—Rams, 48-7 (P)
1948—Rams, 31-14 (LA)
1949—Tie, 7-7 (P)
1952—Rams, 28-14 (LA)
1955—Rams, 27-26 (LA)
1956—Steelers, 30-13 (P)
1961—Rams, 24-14 (LA)
1964—Rams, 26-14 (P)
1968—Rams, 45-10 (LA)
1971—Rams, 23-14 (P)
1975—Rams, 10-3 (LA)
1978—Rams, 10-7 (LA)
1979—***Steelers, 31-19 (Pasadena)
1981—Steelers, 24-0 (P)
1984—Steelers, 24-14 (P)
1987—Rams, 31-21 (LA)
(Points—Rams 400, Steelers 295)
Franchise in Cleveland prior to 1946
***Steelers known as Pirates prior to 1941*
****Super Bowl XIV*

***L.A. RAMS vs. **ST. LOUIS**
Rams lead series, 22-15-2
1937—Cardinals, 6-0 (Clev)
Cardinals, 13-7 (Chi)
1938—Cardinals, 7-6 (Clev)
Cardinals, 31-17 (Chi)
1939—Rams, 24-0 (Chi)
Rams, 14-0 (Clev)
1940—Rams, 26-14 (Clev)
Cardinals, 17-7 (Chi)
1941—Rams, 10-6 (Clev)
Cardinals, 7-0 (Chi)
1942—Cardinals, 7-0 (Chi)
Rams, 7-3 (Clev)
1945—Rams, 21-0 (Clev)
Rams, 35-21 (Chi)
1946—Cardinals, 34-10 (Chi)
Rams, 17-14 (LA)
1947—Rams, 27-7 (LA)
Cardinals, 17-10 (Chi)
1948—Cardinals, 27-22 (LA)
Cardinals, 27-24 (Chi)
1949—Tie, 28-28 (Chi)
Cardinals, 31-27 (LA)
1951—Rams, 45-21 (LA)
1953—Tie, 24-24 (Chi)
1954—Rams, 28-17 (LA)
1958—Rams, 20-14 (Chi)
1960—Cardinals, 43-21 (LA)
1965—Rams, 27-3 (StL)
1968—Rams, 24-13 (StL)
1970—Rams, 34-13 (LA)
1972—Cardinals, 24-14 (StL)
1975—***Rams, 35-23 (LA)
1976—Cardinals, 30-28 (LA)
1979—Rams, 21-0 (LA)
1980—Rams, 21-13 (StL)
1984—Rams, 16-13 (StL)
1985—Rams, 46-14 (LA)
1986—Rams, 16-10 (StL)
1987—Rams, 27-24 (StL)
(Points—Rams 786, Cardinals 616)
Franchise in Cleveland prior to 1946
***Franchise in Chicago prior to 1960*
****NFC Divisional Playoff*

L.A. RAMS vs. SAN DIEGO
Rams lead series, 2-1
1970—Rams, 37-10 (LA)
1975—Rams, 13-10 (SD) OT
1979—Chargers, 40-16 (LA)
(Points—Rams 66, Chargers 60)

L.A. RAMS vs. SAN FRANCISCO
Rams lead series, 45-29-2

1950—Rams, 35-14 (SF)
Rams, 28-21 (LA)
1951—49ers, 44-17 (SF)
Rams, 23-16 (LA)
1952—Rams, 35-9 (LA)
Rams, 34-21 (SF)
1953—49ers, 31-30 (SF)
49ers, 31-27 (LA)
1954—Tie, 24-24 (LA)
Rams, 42-34 (SF)
1955—Rams, 23-14 (SF)
Rams, 27-14 (LA)
1956—49ers, 33-30 (SF)
Rams, 30-6 (LA)
1957—49ers, 23-20 (SF)
Rams, 37-24 (LA)
1958—Rams, 33-3 (SF)
Rams, 56-7 (LA)
1959—49ers, 34-0 (SF)
49ers, 24-16 (LA)
1960—49ers, 13-9 (SF)
49ers, 23-7 (LA)
1961—49ers, 35-0 (SF)
Rams, 17-7 (LA)
1962—Rams, 28-14 (SF)
49ers, 24-17 (LA)
1963—Rams, 28-21 (LA)
Rams, 21-17 (SF)
1964—Rams, 42-14 (LA)
49ers, 28-7 (SF)
1965—49ers, 45-21 (LA)
49ers, 30-27 (SF)
1966—Rams, 34-3 (LA)
49ers, 21-13 (SF)
1967—49ers, 27-24 (LA)
Rams, 17-7 (SF)
1968—Rams, 24-10 (LA)
Tie, 20-20 (SF)
1969—Rams, 27-21 (SF)
Rams, 41-30 (LA)
1970—49ers, 20-6 (LA)
Rams, 30-13 (SF)
1971—Rams, 20-13 (SF)
Rams, 17-6 (LA)
1972—Rams, 31-7 (LA)
Rams, 26-16 (SF)
1973—Rams, 40-20 (SF)
Rams, 31-13 (LA)
1974—Rams, 37-14 (LA)
Rams, 15-13 (SF)
1975—Rams, 23-14 (SF)
49ers, 24-23 (LA)
1976—49ers, 16-0 (LA)
Rams, 23-3 (SF)
1977—Rams, 34-14 (LA)
Rams, 23-10 (SF)
1978—Rams, 27-10 (LA)
Rams, 31-28 (SF)
1979—Rams, 27-24 (LA)
Rams, 26-20 (SF)
1980—Rams, 48-26 (LA)
Rams, 31-17 (SF)
1981—49ers, 20-17 (SF)
49ers, 33-31 (LA)
1982—49ers, 30-24 (LA)
Rams, 21-20 (SF)
1983—Rams, 10-7 (SF)
49ers, 45-35 (LA)
1984—49ers, 33-0 (LA)
49ers, 19-16 (SF)
1985—49ers, 28-14 (LA)
Rams, 27-20 (SF)
1986—Rams, 16-13 (LA)
49ers, 24-14 (SF)
1987—49ers, 31-10 (LA)
49ers, 48-0 (SF)
(Points—Rams 1,795, 49ers 1,549)

L.A. RAMS vs. SEATTLE
Rams lead series, 3-0
1976—Rams, 45-6 (LA)
1979—Rams, 24-0 (S)
1985—Rams, 35-24 (S)
(Points—Rams 104, Seahawks 30)

L.A. RAMS vs. TAMPA BAY
Rams lead series, 7-2
1977—Rams, 31-0 (LA)
1978—Rams, 26-23 (LA)
1979—Buccaneers, 21-6 (TB)
*Rams, 9-0 (TB)
1980—Buccaneers, 10-9 (TB)
1984—Rams, 34-33 (TB)
1985—Rams, 31-27 (TB)
1986—Rams, 26-20 (LA) OT
1987—Rams, 35-3 (LA)
(Points—Rams 207, Buccaneers 137)
NFC Championship

***L.A. RAMS vs. WASHINGTON**
Redskins lead series, 15-6-1
1937—Redskins, 16-7 (C)
1938—Redskins, 37-13 (W)
1941—Redskins, 17-13 (W)
1942—Redskins, 33-14 (W)
1944—Redskins, 14-10 (W)
1945—**Rams, 15-14 (C)
1948—Rams, 41-13 (W)
1949—Rams, 53-27 (LA)
1951—Redskins, 31-21 (W)
1962—Redskins, 20-14 (W)
1963—Redskins, 37-14 (LA)
1967—Tie, 28-28 (LA)
1969—Rams, 24-13 (W)
1971—Redskins, 38-24 (LA)
1974—Redskins, 23-17 (LA)
***Rams, 19-10 (LA)
1977—Redskins, 17-14 (W)
1981—Redskins, 30-7 (LA)
1983—Redskins, 42-20 (LA)
***Redskins, 51-7 (W)
1986—****Redskins, 19-7 (W)
1987—Rams, 30-26 (W)
(Points—Redskins 556, Rams 412)
**Franchise in Cleveland prior to 1946*
***NFL Championship*
****NFC Divisional Playoff*
*****NFC First Round Playoff*

MIAMI vs. ATLANTA
Dolphins lead series, 4-1;
See Atlanta vs. Miami

MIAMI vs. BUFFALO
Dolphins lead series, 34-9-1;
See Buffalo vs. Miami

MIAMI vs. CHICAGO
Dolphins lead series, 4-0;
See Chicago vs. Miami

MIAMI vs. CINCINNATI
Dolphins lead series, 8-3;
See Cincinnati vs. Miami

MIAMI vs. CLEVELAND
Browns lead series, 4-3;
See Cleveland vs. Miami

MIAMI vs. DALLAS
Dolphins lead series, 4-2;
See Dallas vs. Miami

MIAMI vs. DENVER
Dolphins lead series, 5-2-1;
See Denver vs. Miami

MIAMI vs. DETROIT
Dolphins lead series, 2-1;
See Detroit vs. Miami

MIAMI vs. GREEN BAY
Dolphins lead series, 4-0;
See Green Bay vs. Miami

MIAMI vs. HOUSTON
Series tied, 10-10;
See Houston vs. Miami

MIAMI vs. INDIANAPOLIS
Dolphins lead series, 27-10;
See Indianapolis vs. Miami

MIAMI vs. KANSAS CITY
Series tied, 7-7;
See Kansas City vs. Miami

MIAMI vs. L.A. RAIDERS
Raiders lead series, 15-3-1;
See L.A. Raiders vs. Miami

MIAMI vs. L.A. RAMS
Dolphins lead series, 4-1;
See L.A. Rams vs. Miami

MIAMI vs. MINNESOTA
Dolphins lead series, 4-1
1972—Dolphins, 16-14 (Minn)
1973—*Dolphins, 24-7 (Houston)
1976—Vikings, 29-7 (Mia)
1979—Dolphins, 27-12 (Minn)
1982—Dolphins, 22-14 (Mia)
(Points—Dolphins 96, Vikings 76)
Super Bowl VIII

MIAMI vs. *NEW ENGLAND
Dolphins lead series, 25-19
1966—Patriots, 20-14 (M)
1967—Patriots, 41-10 (B)
Dolphins, 41-32 (M)
1968—Dolphins, 34-10 (B)
Dolphins, 38-7 (M)
1969—Dolphins, 17-16 (B)
Patriots, 38-23 (Tampa)
1970—Patriots, 27-14 (B)
Dolphins, 37-20 (M)
1971—Dolphins, 41-3 (M)
Patriots, 34-13 (NE)
1972—Dolphins, 52-0 (M)
Dolphins, 37-21 (NE)
1973—Dolphins, 44-23 (M)
Dolphins, 30-14 (NE)
1974—Patriots, 34-24 (NE)
Dolphins, 34-27 (M)
1975—Dolphins, 22-14 (NE)
Dolphins, 20-7 (M)
1976—Patriots, 30-14 (NE)
Dolphins, 10-3 (M)
1977—Dolphins, 17-5 (M)
Patriots, 14-10 (NE)
1978—Patriots, 33-24 (NE)
Dolphins, 23-3 (M)
1979—Patriots, 28-13 (NE)
Dolphins, 39-24 (M)
1980—Patriots, 34-0 (NE)
Dolphins, 16-13 (M) OT
1981—Dolphins, 30-27 (NE) OT
Dolphins, 24-14 (M)
1982—Patriots, 3-0 (NE)
**Dolphins, 28-13 (M)
1983—Dolphins, 34-24 (M)
Patriots, 17-6 (NE)
1984—Dolphins, 28-7 (M)
Dolphins, 44-24 (NE)
1985—Patriots, 17-13 (NE)
Dolphins, 30-27 (M)
***Patriots, 31-14 (M)
1986—Patriots, 34-7 (NE)
Patriots, 34-27 (M)
1987—Patriots, 28-21 (NE)
Patriots, 24-10 (M)
(Points—Dolphins 1,027, Patriots 899)
**Franchise in Boston prior to 1971*
***AFC First Round Playoff*
****AFC Championship*

MIAMI vs. NEW ORLEANS
Dolphins lead series, 4-1
1970—Dolphins, 21-10 (M)
1974—Dolphins, 21-0 (NO)
1980—Dolphins, 21-16 (M)
1983—Saints, 17-7 (NO)
1986—Dolphins, 31-27 (NO)
(Points—Dolphins 101, Saints 70)

MIAMI vs. N.Y. GIANTS
Dolphins lead series, 1-0
1972—Dolphins, 23-13 (NY)

MIAMI vs. N.Y. JETS
Dolphins lead series, 24-20-1
1966—Jets, 19-14 (M)
Jets, 30-13 (NY)
1967—Jets, 29-7 (NY)
Jets, 33-14 (M)
1968—Jets, 35-17 (NY)
Jets, 31-7 (M)
1969—Jets, 34-31 (NY)
Jets, 27-9 (M)
1970—Dolphins, 20-6 (NY)
Dolphins, 16-10 (M)
1971—Jets, 14-10 (M)
Dolphins, 30-14 (NY)
1972—Dolphins, 27-17 (NY)
Dolphins, 28-24 (M)
1973—Dolphins, 31-3 (M)
Dolphins, 24-14 (NY)
1974—Dolphins, 21-17 (M)
Jets, 17-14 (NY)
1975—Dolphins, 43-0 (NY)
Dolphins, 27-7 (M)
1976—Dolphins, 16-0 (M)
Dolphins, 27-7 (NY)
1977—Dolphins, 21-17 (M)
Dolphins, 14-10 (NY)
1978—Jets, 33-20 (NY)
Jets, 24-13 (M)
1979—Jets, 33-27 (NY)
Jets, 27-24 (M)
1980—Jets, 17-14 (NY)
Jets, 24-17 (M)
1981—Tie, 28-28 (M) OT
Jets, 16-15 (NY)
1982—Dolphins, 45-28 (NY)
Dolphins, 20-19 (M)
*Dolphins, 14-0 (M)
1983—Dolphins, 32-14 (NY)
Dolphins, 34-14 (M)
1984—Dolphins, 31-17 (NY)
Dolphins, 28-17 (M)
1985—Jets, 23-7 (NY)
Dolphins, 21-17 (M)
1986—Jets, 51-45 (NY) OT
Dolphins, 45-3 (M)
1987—Jets, 37-31 (NY) OT
Dolphins, 37-28 (M)
(Points—Dolphins 1,029, Jets 885)
AFC Championship

MIAMI vs. PHILADELPHIA
Dolphins lead series, 4-2
1970—Eagles, 24-17 (P)
1975—Dolphins, 24-16 (M)
1978—Eagles, 17-3 (P)
1981—Dolphins, 13-10 (M)
1984—Dolphins, 24-23 (M)
1987—Dolphins, 28-10 (P)
(Points—Dolphins 109, Eagles 100)

MIAMI vs. PITTSBURGH
Dolphins lead series, 8-3
1971—Dolphins, 24-21 (M)
1972—*Dolphins, 21-17 (P)
1973—Dolphins, 30-26 (M)
1976—Steelers, 14-3 (P)
1979—**Steelers, 34-14 (P)
1980—Steelers, 23-10 (P)
1981—Dolphins, 30-10 (M)
1984—Dolphins, 31-7 (P)
*Dolphins, 45-28 (M)
1985—Dolphins, 24-20 (M)
1987—Dolphins, 35-24 (M)
(Points—Dolphins 267, Steelers 224)
**AFC Championship*
***AFC Divisional Playoff*

MIAMI vs. ST. LOUIS
Dolphins lead series, 5-0
1972—Dolphins, 31-10 (M)
1977—Dolphins, 55-14 (StL)
1978—Dolphins, 24-10 (M)
1981—Dolphins, 20-7 (StL)
1984—Dolphins, 36-28 (StL)
(Points—Dolphins 166, Cardinals 69)

MIAMI vs. SAN DIEGO
Chargers lead series, 9-5
1966—Chargers, 44-10 (SD)
1967—Chargers, 24-0 (SD)
Dolphins, 41-24 (M)
1968—Chargers, 34-28 (SD)
1969—Chargers, 21-14 (M)
1972—Dolphins, 24-10 (M)
1974—Dolphins, 28-21 (SD)
1977—Chargers, 14-13 (M)
1978—Dolphins, 28-21 (SD)
1980—Chargers, 27-24 (M) OT
1981—*Chargers, 41-38 (M) OT
1982—**Dolphins, 34-13 (M)
1984—Chargers, 34-28 (SD) OT
1986—Chargers, 50-28 (SD)
(Points—Chargers 378, Dolphins 338)
**AFC Divisional Playoff*
***AFC Second Round Playoff*

MIAMI vs. SAN FRANCISCO
Dolphins lead series, 4-2
1973—Dolphins, 21-13 (M)
1977—Dolphins, 19-15 (SF)
1980—Dolphins, 17-13 (M)
1983—Dolphins, 20-17 (SF)
1984—*49ers, 38-16 (Stanford)
1986—49ers, 31-16 (M)
(Points—49ers 127, Dolphins 109)
Super Bowl XIX

MIAMI vs. SEATTLE
Dolphins lead series, 3-2
1977—Dolphins, 31-13 (M)
1979—Dolphins, 19-10 (M)
1983—*Seahawks, 27-20 (M)
1984—*Dolphins, 31-10 (M)
1987—Seahawks, 24-20 (S)
(Points—Dolphins 121, Seahawks 84)
AFC Divisional Playoff

MIAMI vs. TAMPA BAY
Dolphins lead series, 2-1
1976—Dolphins, 23-20 (TB)
1982—Buccaneers, 23-17 (TB)
1985—Dolphins, 41-38 (M)
(Points—Dolphins 81, Buccaneers 81)

MIAMI vs. WASHINGTON
Dolphins lead series, 5-2
1972—*Dolphins, 14-7 (Los Angeles)
1974—Redskins, 20-17 (W)
1978—Dolphins, 16-0 (W)
1981—Dolphins, 13-10 (M)
1982—**Redskins, 27-17 (Pasadena)
1984—Dolphins, 35-17 (W)
1987—Dolphins, 23-21 (M)
(Points—Dolphins 135, Redskins 102)
**Super Bowl VII*
***Super Bowl XVII*

MINNESOTA vs. ATLANTA
Vikings lead series, 10-6;
See Atlanta vs. Minnesota

MINNESOTA vs. BUFFALO
Vikings lead series, 4-1;
See Buffalo vs. Minnesota

MINNESOTA vs. CHICAGO
Vikings lead series, 26-25-2;
See Chicago vs. Minnesota

MINNESOTA vs. CINCINNATI
Bengals lead series, 3-2;
See Cincinnati vs. Minnesota

MINNESOTA vs. CLEVELAND
Vikings lead series, 7-2;
See Cleveland vs. Minnesota

MINNESOTA vs. DALLAS
Cowboys lead series, 10-6;
See Dallas vs. Minnesota

MINNESOTA vs. DENVER
Vikings lead series, 3-2;
See Denver vs. Minnesota

MINNESOTA vs. DETROIT
Vikings lead series, 33-18-2;
See Detroit vs. Minnesota

MINNESOTA vs. GREEN BAY
Series tied, 26-26-1;
See Green Bay vs. Minnesota

MINNESOTA vs. HOUSTON
Series tied, 2-2;
See Houston vs. Minnesota

MINNESOTA vs. INDIANAPOLIS
Colts lead series, 12-5-1;
See Indianapolis vs. Minnesota

MINNESOTA vs. KANSAS CITY
Series tied, 2-2;

See Kansas City vs. Minnesota
MINNESOTA vs. L.A. RAIDERS
Raiders lead series, 5-2;
See L.A. Raiders vs. Minnesota
MINNESOTA vs. L.A. RAMS
Vikings lead series, 16-12-2;
See L.A. Rams vs. Minnesota
MINNESOTA vs. MIAMI
Dolphins lead series, 4-1;
See Miami vs. Minnesota
MINNESOTA vs. *NEW ENGLAND
Patriots lead series, 2-1
1970—Vikings, 35-14 (B)
1974—Patriots, 17-14 (M)
1979—Patriots, 27-23 (NE)
(Points—Vikings 72, Patriots 58)
**Franchise in Boston prior to 1971*
MINNESOTA vs. NEW ORLEANS
Vikings lead series, 10-4
1968—Saints, 20-17 (NO)
1970—Vikings, 26-0 (M)
1971—Vikings, 23-10 (NO)
1972—Vikings, 37-6 (M)
1974—Vikings, 29-9 (M)
1975—Vikings, 20-7 (NO)
1976—Vikings, 40-9 (NO)
1978—Saints, 31-24 (NO)
1980—Vikings, 23-20 (NO)
1981—Vikings, 20-10 (M)
1983—Saints, 17-16 (NO)
1985—Saints, 30-23 (M)
1986—Vikings, 33-17 (M)
1987—*Vikings, 44-10 (NO)
(Points—Vikings 375, Saints 196)
*NFC First Round Playoff
MINNESOTA vs. N.Y. GIANTS
Vikings lead series, 6-2
1964—Vikings, 30-21 (NY)
1965—Vikings, 40-14 (M)
1967—Vikings, 27-24 (M)
1969—Giants, 24-23 (NY)
1971—Vikings, 17-10 (NY)
1973—Vikings, 31-7 (New Haven)
1976—Vikings, 24-7 (M)
1986—Giants, 22-20 (M)
(Points—Vikings 212, Giants 129)
MINNESOTA vs. N.Y. JETS
Jets lead series, 3-1
1970—Jets, 20-10 (NY)
1975—Vikings, 29-21 (M)
1979—Jets, 14-7 (NY)
1982—Jets 42-14 (M)
(Points—Jets 97, Vikings 60)
MINNESOTA vs. PHILADELPHIA
Vikings lead series, 9-4
1962—Vikings, 31-21 (M)
1963—Vikings, 34-13 (P)
1968—Vikings, 24-17 (P)
1971—Vikings, 13-0 (P)
1973—Vikings, 28-21 (M)
1976—Vikings, 31-12 (P)
1978—Vikings, 28-27 (M)
1980—Eagles, 42-7 (M)
*Eagles, 31-16 (P)
1981—Vikings, 35-23 (M)
1984—Eagles, 19-17 (P)
1985—Vikings, 28-23 (P)
Eagles, 37-35 (M)
(Points—Vikings 327, Eagles 286)
**NFC Divisional Playoff*
MINNESOTA vs. PITTSBURGH
Vikings lead series, 6-4
1962—Steelers, 39-31 (P)
1964—Vikings, 30-10 (M)
1967—Vikings, 41-27 (P)
1969—Vikings, 52-14 (M)
1972—Steelers, 23-10 (P)
1974—*Steelers, 16-6 (New Orleans)
1976—Vikings, 17-6 (M)
1980—Steelers, 23-17 (M)
1983—Vikings, 17-14 (P)
1986—Vikings, 31-7 (M)
(Points—Vikings 252, Steelers 179)
**Super Bowl IX*
MINNESOTA vs. ST. LOUIS
Cardinals lead series, 7-3
1963—Cardinals, 56-14 (M)
1967—Cardinals, 34-24 (M)
1969—Vikings, 27-10 (StL)
1972—Cardinals, 19-17 (M)
1974—Vikings, 28-24 (StL)
*Vikings, 30-14 (M)
1977—Cardinals, 27-7 (M)
1979—Cardinals, 37-7 (StL)
1981—Cardinals, 30-17 (StL)
1983—Cardinals, 41-31 (StL)
(Points—Cardinals 292, Vikings 202)
**NFC Divisional Playoff*
MINNESOTA vs. SAN DIEGO
Series tied, 3-3
1971—Chargers, 30-14 (SD)
1975—Vikings, 28-13 (M)
1978—Chargers, 13-7 (M)
1981—Vikings, 33-31 (SD)
1984—Chargers, 42-13 (M)
1985—Vikings, 21-17 (M)
(Points—Chargers 146, Vikings 116)
MINNESOTA vs. SAN FRANCISCO
Vikings lead series, 15-12-1
1961—49ers, 38-24 (M)
49ers, 38-28 (SF)
1962—49ers, 21-7 (SF)
49ers, 35-12 (M)
1963—Vikings, 24-20 (SF)
Vikings, 45-14 (M)
1964—Vikings, 27-22 (SF)
Vikings, 24-7 (M)
1965—Vikings, 42-41 (SF)
49ers, 45-24 (M)
1966—Tie, 20-20 (SF)
Vikings, 28-3 (SF)
1967—49ers, 27-21 (M)
1968—Vikings, 30-20 (SF)
1969—Vikings, 10-7 (M)
1970—*49ers, 17-14 (M)
1971—49ers, 13-9 (M)
1972—49ers, 20-17 (SF)
1973—Vikings, 17-13 (SF)
1975—Vikings, 27-17 (M)
1976—49ers, 20-16 (SF)
1977—Vikings, 28-27 (M)
1979—Vikings, 28-22 (M)
1983—49ers, 48-17 (M)
1984—49ers, 51-7 (SF)
1985—Vikings, 28-21 (M)
1986—Vikings, 27-24 (SF) OT
1987—*Vikings, 36-24 (SF)
(Points—49ers 675, Vikings 637)
**NFC Divisional Playoff*
MINNESOTA vs. SEATTLE
Seahawks lead series, 3-1
1976—Vikings, 27-21 (M)
1978—Seahawks, 29-28 (S)
1984—Seahawks, 20-12 (M)
1987—Seahawks, 28-17 (S)
(Points—Seahawks 98, Vikings 84)
MINNESOTA vs. TAMPA BAY
Vikings lead series, 14-6
1977—Vikings, 9-3 (TB)
1978—Buccaneers, 16-10 (M)
Vikings, 24-7 (TB)
1979—Buccaneers, 12-10 (M)
Vikings, 23-22 (TB)
1980—Vikings, 38-30 (M)
Vikings, 21-10 (TB)
1981—Buccaneers, 21-13 (TB)
Vikings, 25-10 (M)
1982—Vikings, 17-10 (M)
1983—Vikings, 19-16 (TB) OT
Buccaneers, 17-12 (M)
1984—Buccaneers, 35-31 (TB)
Vikings, 27-24 (M)
1985—Vikings, 31-16 (TB)
Vikings, 26-7 (M)
1986—Vikings, 23-10 (TB)
Vikings, 45-13 (M)
1987—Buccaneers, 20-10 (TB)
Vikings, 23-17 (M)
(Points—Vikings 437, Buccaneers 316)
MINNESOTA vs. WASHINGTON
Redskins lead series, 7-5
1968—Vikings, 27-14 (M)
1970—Vikings, 19-10 (W)
1972—Redskins, 24-21 (M)
1973—*Vikings, 27-20 (M)
1975—Redskins, 31-30 (W)
1976—*Vikings, 35-20 (M)
1980—Vikings, 39-14 (W)
1982—**Redskins, 21-7 (W)
1984—Redskins, 31-17 (M)
1986—Redskins, 44-38 (W) OT
1987—Redskins, 27-24 (M) OT
***Redskins, 17-10 (W)
(Points—Vikings 294, Redskins 273)
**NFC Divisional Playoff*
***NFC Second Round Playoff*
****NFC Championship*

NEW ENGLAND vs. ATLANTA
Patriots lead series, 3-2;
See Atlanta vs. New England
NEW ENGLAND vs. BUFFALO
Patriots lead series, 32-23-1;
See Buffalo vs. New England
NEW ENGLAND vs. CHICAGO
Bears lead series, 3-2;
See Chicago vs. New England
NEW ENGLAND vs. CINCINNATI
Patriots lead series, 6-4;
See Cincinnati vs. New England
NEW ENGLAND vs. CLEVELAND
Browns lead series, 7-2;
See Cleveland vs. New England
NEW ENGLAND vs. DALLAS
Cowboys lead series, 6-0;
See Dallas vs. New England
NEW ENGLAND vs. DENVER
Broncos lead series, 14-12;
See Denver vs. New England
NEW ENGLAND vs. DETROIT
Series tied, 2-2;
See Detroit vs. New England
NEW ENGLAND vs. GREEN BAY
Patriots lead series, 2-1;
See Green Bay vs. New England
NEW ENGLAND vs. HOUSTON
Patriots lead series, 15-13-1;
See Houston vs. New England
NEW ENGLAND vs. INDIANAPOLIS
Patriots lead series, 19-16;
See Indianapolis vs. New England
NEW ENGLAND vs. KANSAS CITY
Chiefs lead series, 11-7-3;
See Kansas City vs. New England
NEW ENGLAND vs. L.A. RAIDERS
Patriots lead series, 13-12-1;
See L.A. Raiders vs. New England
NEW ENGLAND vs. L.A. RAMS
Patriots lead series, 3-1;
See L.A. Rams vs. New England
NEW ENGLAND vs. MIAMI
Dolphins lead series, 25-19;
See Miami vs. New England
NEW ENGLAND vs. MINNESOTA
Patriots lead series, 2-1;
See Minnesota vs. New England
NEW ENGLAND vs. NEW ORLEANS
Patriots lead series, 5-0
1972—Patriots, 17-10 (NO)
1976—Patriots, 27-6 (NE)
1980—Patriots, 38-27 (NO)
1983—Patriots, 7-0 (NE)
1986—Patriots, 21-20 (NO)
(Points—Patriots 110, Saints 63)
***NEW ENGLAND vs. N.Y. GIANTS**
Giants lead series, 2-1
1970—Giants, 16-0 (B)
1974—Patriots, 28-20 (New Haven)
1987—Giants, 17-10 (NY)
(Points—Giants 53, Patriots 38)
**Franchise in Boston prior to 1971*
***NEW ENGLAND vs. **N.Y. JETS**
Jets lead series, 31-24-1
1960—Patriots, 28-24 (NY)
Patriots, 38-21 (B)
1961—Titans, 21-20 (B)
Titans, 37-30 (NY)
1962—Patriots, 43-14 (NY)
Patriots, 24-17 (B)
1963—Patriots, 38-14 (B)
Jets, 31-24 (NY)
1964—Patriots, 26-10 (B)
Jets, 35-14 (NY)
1965—Jets, 30-20 (B)
Patriots, 27-23 (NY)
1966—Tie, 24-24 (B)
Jets, 38-28 (NY)
1967—Jets, 30-23 (NY)
Jets, 29-24 (B)
1968—Jets, 47-31 (Birmingham)
Jets, 48-14 (NY)
1969—Jets, 23-14 (B)
Jets, 23-17 (NY)
1970—Jets, 31-21 (B)
Jets, 17-3 (NY)
1971—Patriots, 20-0 (NE)
Jets, 13-6 (NY)
1972—Jets, 41-13 (NE)
Jets, 34-10 (NY)
1973—Jets, 9-7 (NE)
Jets, 33-13 (NY)
1974—Patriots, 24-0 (NY)
Jets, 21-16 (NE)
1975—Jets, 36-7 (NY)
Jets, 30-28 (NE)
1976—Patriots, 41-7 (NE)
Patriots, 38-24 (NY)
1977—Jets, 30-27 (NY)
Patriots, 24-13 (NE)
1978—Patriots, 55-21 (NE)
Patriots, 19-17 (NY)
1979—Patriots, 56-3 (NE)
Jets, 27-26 (NY)
1980—Patriots, 21-11 (NY)
Patriots, 34-21 (NE)
1981—Jets, 28-24 (NY)
Jets, 17-6 (NE)
1982—Jets, 31-7 (NE)
1983—Patriots, 23-13 (NE)
Jets, 26-3 (NY)
1984—Patriots, 28-21 (NY)
Patriots, 30-20 (NE)
1985—Patriots, 20-13 (NE)
Jets, 16-13 (NY) OT
***Patriots, 26-14 (NY)
1986—Patriots, 20-6 (NY)
Jets, 31-24 (NE)
1987—Jets, 43-24 (NY)
Patriots, 42-20 (NE)
(Points—Patriots 1,306, Jets 1,277)
**Franchise in Boston prior to 1971*
***Jets known as Titans prior to 1963*
****AFC First Round Playoff*
NEW ENGLAND vs. PHILADELPHIA
Eagles lead series, 4-2
1973—Eagles, 24-23 (P)
1977—Patriots, 14-6 (NE)
1978—Patriots, 24-14 (NE)
1981—Eagles, 13-3 (P)
1984—Eagles, 27-17 (P)
1987—Eagles, 34-31 (NE) OT
(Points—Eagles 118, Patriots 112)
NEW ENGLAND vs. PITTSBURGH
Steelers lead series, 5-3
1972—Steelers, 33-3 (P)
1974—Steelers, 21-17 (NE)
1976—Patriots, 30-27 (P)
1979—Steelers, 16-13 (NE) OT
1981—Steelers, 27-21 (P) OT
1982—Steelers, 37-14 (P)
1983—Patriots, 28-23 (P)
1986—Patriots, 34-0 (P)
(Points—Steelers 184, Patriots 160)
***NEW ENGLAND vs. ST. LOUIS**
Cardinals lead series, 4-1
1970—Cardinals, 31-0 (StL)
1975—Cardinals, 24-17 (StL)
1978—Patriots, 16-6 (StL)
1981—Cardinals, 27-20 (NE)
1984—Cardinals, 33-10 (NE)
(Points—Cardinals 121, Patriots 63)
**Franchise in Boston prior to 1971*
***NEW ENGLAND vs. **SAN DIEGO**
Patriots lead series, 13-12-2
1960—Patriots, 35-0 (LA)
Chargers, 45-16 (B)
1961—Chargers, 38-27 (B)
Patriots, 41-0 (SD)
1962—Patriots, 24-20 (B)
Patriots, 20-14 (SD)
1963—Chargers, 17-13 (SD)
Chargers, 7-6 (B)
***Chargers, 51-10 (SD)
1964—Patriots, 33-28 (SD)
Chargers, 26-17 (B)
1965—Tie, 10-10 (B)
Patriots, 22-6 (SD)
1966—Chargers, 24-0 (SD)
Patriots, 35-17 (B)
1967—Chargers, 28-14 (SD)
Tie, 31-31 (SD)
1968—Chargers, 27-17 (B)
1969—Chargers, 13-10 (B)
Chargers, 28-18 (SD)
1970—Chargers, 16-14 (B)
1973—Patriots, 30-14 (NE)
1975—Patriots, 33-19 (SD)
1977—Patriots, 24-20 (SD)
1978—Patriots, 28-23 (NE)
1979—Patriots, 27-21 (NE)
1983—Patriots, 37-21 (NE)
(Points—Patriots 592, Chargers 564)
**Franchise in Boston prior to 1971*
***Franchise in Los Angeles prior to 1961*
****AFL Championship*
NEW ENGLAND vs. SAN FRANCISCO
49ers lead series, 4-1
1971—49ers, 27-10 (SF)
1975—Patriots, 24-16 (NE)
1980—49ers, 21-17 (SF)
1983—49ers, 33-13 (NE)
1986—49ers, 29-24 (NE)
(Points—49ers 126, Patriots 88)
NEW ENGLAND vs. SEATTLE
Patriots lead series, 5-2
1977—Patriots, 31-0 (NE)
1980—Patriots, 37-31 (S)
1982—Patriots, 16-0 (S)
1983—Seahawks, 24-6 (S)
1984—Patriots, 38-23 (NE)
1985—Patriots, 20-13 (S)
1986—Seahawks, 38-31 (NE)
(Points—Patriots 179, Seahawks 129)
NEW ENGLAND vs. TAMPA BAY
Patriots lead series, 2-0
1976—Patriots, 31-14 (TB)
1985—Patriots, 32-14 (TB)
(Points—Patriots 63, Buccaneers 28)
NEW ENGLAND vs. WASHINGTON
Redskins lead series, 3-1
1972—Patriots, 24-23 (NE)
1978—Redskins, 16-14 (NE)
1981—Redskins, 24-22 (W)
1984—Redskins, 26-10 (NE)
(Points—Redskins 89, Patriots 70)

NEW ORLEANS vs. ATLANTA
Falcons lead series, 24-13;
See Atlanta vs. New Orleans
NEW ORLEANS vs. BUFFALO
Bills lead series, 2-1;
See Buffalo vs. New Orleans

NEW ORLEANS vs. CHICAGO
Bears lead series, 7-5;
See Chicago vs. New Orleans
NEW ORLEANS vs. CINCINNATI
Series tied, 3-3;
See Cincinnati vs. New Orleans
NEW ORLEANS vs. CLEVELAND
Browns lead series, 8-2;
See Cleveland vs. New Orleans
NEW ORLEANS vs. DALLAS
Cowboys lead series, 11-1;
See Dallas vs. New Orleans
NEW ORLEANS vs. DENVER
Broncos lead series, 4-0;
See Denver vs. New Orleans
NEW ORLEANS vs. DETROIT
Series tied, 4-4-1;
See Detroit vs. New Orleans
NEW ORLEANS vs. GREEN BAY
Packers lead series, 10-4;
See Green Bay vs. New Orleans
NEW ORLEANS vs. HOUSTON
Saints lead series, 3-2-1;
See Houston vs. New Orleans
NEW ORLEANS vs. INDIANAPOLIS
Colts lead series, 3-1;
See Indianapolis vs. New Orleans
NEW ORLEANS vs. KANSAS CITY
Series tied, 2-2;
See Kansas City vs. New Orleans
NEW ORLEANS vs. L.A. RAIDERS
Raiders lead series, 3-0-1;
See L.A. Raiders vs. New Orleans
NEW ORLEANS vs. L.A. RAMS
Rams lead series, 24-12;
See L.A. Rams vs. New Orleans
NEW ORLEANS vs. MIAMI
Dolphins lead series, 4-1;
See Miami vs. New Orleans
NEW ORLEANS vs. MINNESOTA
Vikings lead series, 10-4;
See Minnesota vs. New Orleans
NEW ORLEANS vs. NEW ENGLAND
Patriots lead series, 5-0;
See New England vs. New Orleans
NEW ORLEANS vs. N.Y. GIANTS
Giants lead series, 7-6
1967—Giants, 27-21 (NY)
1968—Giants, 38-21 (NY)
1969—Saints, 25-24 (NY)
1970—Saints, 14-10 (NO)
1972—Giants, 45-21 (NY)
1975—Giants, 28-14 (NY)
1978—Saints, 28-17 (NO)
1979—Saints, 24-14 (NO)
1981—Giants, 20-7 (NY)
1984—Saints, 10-3 (NY)
1985—Giants, 21-13 (NO)
1986—Giants, 20-17 (NY)
1987—Saints, 23-14 (NO)
(Points—Giants 281, Saints 238)
NEW ORLEANS vs. N.Y. JETS
Jets lead series, 4-1
1972—Jets, 18-17 (NY)
1977—Jets, 16-13 (NO)
1980—Saints, 21-20 (NY)
1983—Jets, 31-28 (NO)
1986—Jets, 28-23 (NY)
(Points—Jets 113, Saints 102)
NEW ORLEANS vs. PHILADELPHIA
Eagles lead series, 9-6
1967—Saints, 31-24 (NO)
Eagles, 48-21 (P)
1968—Eagles, 29-17 (P)
1969—Eagles, 13-10 (P)
Saints, 26-17 (NO)
1972—Saints, 21-3 (NO)
1974—Saints, 14-10 (NO)
1977—Eagles, 28-7 (P)
1978—Eagles, 24-17 (NO)
1979—Eagles, 26-14 (NO)
1980—Eagles, 34-21 (NO)
1981—Eagles, 31-14 (NO)
1983—Saints, 20-17 (P) OT
1985—Saints, 23-21 (NO)
1987—Eagles, 27-17 (P)
(Points—Eagles 352, Saints 273)
NEW ORLEANS vs. PITTSBURGH
Saints lead series, 5-4
1967—Steelers, 14-10 (NO)
1968—Saints, 16-12 (P)
Saints, 24-14 (NO)
1969—Saints, 27-24 (NO)
1974—Steelers, 28-7 (NO)
1978—Steelers, 20-14 (P)
1981—Steelers, 20-6 (NO)
1984—Saints, 27-24 (NO)
1987—Saints, 20-16 (P)
(Points—Steelers 172, Saints 151)
NEW ORLEANS vs. ST. LOUIS
Cardinals lead series, 10-5
1967—Cardinals, 31-20 (StL)
1968—Cardinals, 21-20 (NO)
Cardinals, 31-17 (StL)
1969—Saints, 51-42 (StL)
1970—Cardinals, 24-17 (StL)
1974—Saints, 14-0 (NO)
1977—Cardinals, 49-31 (StL)
1980—Cardinals, 40-7 (NO)
1981—Cardinals, 30-3 (StL)
1982—Cardinals, 21-7 (NO)
1983—Saints, 28-17 (NO)
1984—Saints, 34-24 (NO)
1985—Cardinals, 28-16 (StL)
1986—Saints, 16-7 (StL)
1987—Cardinals, 24-19 (StL)
(Points—Cardinals 389, Saints 300)
NEW ORLEANS vs. SAN DIEGO
Chargers lead series, 3-0
1973—Chargers, 17-14 (SD)
1977—Chargers, 14-0 (NO)
1979—Chargers, 35-0 (NO)
(Points—Chargers 66, Saints 14)
NEW ORLEANS vs. SAN FRANCISCO
49ers lead series, 24-11-2
1967—49ers, 27-13 (SF)
1969—Saints, 43-38 (NO)
1970—Tie, 20-20 (SF)
49ers, 38-27 (NO)
1971—49ers, 38-20 (NO)
Saints, 26-20 (SF)
1972—49ers, 37-2 (NO)
Tie, 20-20 (SF)
1973—49ers, 40-0 (SF)
Saints, 16-10 (NO)
1974—49ers, 17-13 (NO)
49ers, 35-21 (SF)
1975—49ers, 35-21 (SF)
49ers, 16-6 (NO)
1976—49ers, 33-3 (SF)
49ers, 27-7 (NO)
1977—49ers, 10-7 (NO) OT
49ers, 20-17 (SF)
1978—Saints, 14-7 (SF)
Saints, 24-13 (NO)
1979—Saints, 30-21 (SF)
Saints, 31-20 (NO)
1980—49ers, 26-23 (NO)
49ers, 38-35 (SF) OT
1981—49ers, 21-14 (SF)
49ers, 21-17 (NO)
1982—Saints, 23-20 (SF)
1983—49ers, 32-13 (NO)
49ers, 27-0 (SF)
1984—49ers, 30-20 (SF)
49ers, 35-3 (NO)
1985—Saints, 20-17 (SF)
49ers, 31-19 (NO)
1986—49ers, 26-17 (SF)
Saints, 23-10 (NO)
1987—49ers, 24-22 (NO)
Saints, 26-24 (SF)
(Points—49ers 924, Saints 656)
NEW ORLEANS vs. SEATTLE
Seahawks lead series, 2-1
1976—Saints, 51-27 (S)
1979—Seahawks, 38-24 (S)
1985—Seahawks, 27-3 (NO)
(Points—Seahawks, 92, Saints 78)
NEW ORLEANS vs. TAMPA BAY
Saints lead series, 7-3
1977—Buccaneers, 33-14 (NO)
1978—Saints, 17-10 (TB)
1979—Saints, 42-14 (TB)
1981—Buccaneers, 31-14 (NO)
1982—Buccaneers, 13-10 (NO)
1983—Saints, 24-21 (TB)
1984—Saints, 17-13 (NO)
1985—Saints, 20-13 (NO)
1986—Saints, 38-7 (NO)
1987—Saints, 44-34 (NO)
(Points—Saints 240, Buccaneers 189)
NEW ORLEANS vs. WASHINGTON
Redskins lead series, 8-4
1967—Redskins, 30-10 (NO)
Saints, 30-14 (W)
1968—Saints, 37-17 (NO)
1969—Redskins, 26-20 (NO)
Redskins, 17-14 (W)
1971—Redskins, 24-14 (W)
1973—Saints, 19-3 (NO)
1975—Redskins, 41-3 (W)
1979—Saints, 14-10 (W)
1980—Redskins, 22-14 (W)
1982—Redskins, 27-10 (NO)
1986—Redskins, 14-6 (NO)
(Points—Redskins 245, Saints 191)

N.Y. GIANTS vs. ATLANTA
Falcons lead series, 6-5;
See Atlanta vs. N.Y. Giants
N.Y. GIANTS vs. BUFFALO
Series tied, 2-2;
See Buffalo vs. N.Y. Giants
N.Y. GIANTS vs. CHICAGO
Bears lead series, 28-16-2;
See Chicago vs. N.Y. Giants
N.Y. GIANTS vs. CINCINNATI
Bengals lead series, 3-0;
See Cincinnati vs. N.Y. Giants
N.Y. GIANTS vs. CLEVELAND
Browns lead series, 26-16-2;
See Cleveland vs. N.Y. Giants
N.Y. GIANTS vs. DALLAS
Cowboys lead series, 35-14-2;
See Dallas vs. N.Y. Giants
N.Y. GIANTS vs. DENVER
Giants lead series, 3-2;
See Denver vs. N.Y. Giants
N.Y. GIANTS vs. DETROIT
Lions lead series, 18-11-1;
See Detroit vs. N.Y. Giants
N.Y. GIANTS vs. GREEN BAY
Packers lead series, 25-20-2;
See Green Bay vs. N.Y. Giants
N.Y. GIANTS vs. HOUSTON
Giants lead series, 3-0;
See Houston vs. N.Y. Giants
N.Y. GIANTS vs. INDIANAPOLIS
Colts lead series, 7-3;
See Indianapolis vs. N.Y. Giants
N.Y. GIANTS vs. KANSAS CITY
Giants lead series, 4-1;
See Kansas City vs. N.Y. Giants
N.Y. GIANTS vs. L.A. RAIDERS
Raiders lead series, 3-1;
See L.A. Raiders vs. N.Y. Giants
N.Y. GIANTS vs. L.A. RAMS
Rams lead series, 16-8;
See L.A. Rams vs. N.Y. Giants
N.Y. GIANTS vs. MIAMI
Dolphins lead series, 1-0;
See Miami vs. N.Y. Giants
N.Y. GIANTS vs. MINNESOTA
Vikings lead series, 6-2;
See Minnesota vs. N.Y. Giants
N.Y. GIANTS vs. NEW ENGLAND
Giants lead series, 2-1;
See New England vs. N.Y. Giants
N.Y. GIANTS vs. NEW ORLEANS
Giants lead series, 7-6;
See New Orleans vs. N.Y. Giants
N.Y. GIANTS vs. N.Y. JETS
Giants lead series, 3-2
1970—Giants, 22-10 (NYJ)
1974—Jets, 26-20 (New Haven) OT
1981—Jets, 26-7 (NYG)
1984—Giants, 20-10 (NYJ)
1987—Giants, 20-7 (NYG)
(Points—Giants 89, Jets 79)
N.Y. GIANTS vs. PHILADELPHIA
Giants lead series, 60-45-2
1933—Giants, 56-0 (NY)
Giants, 20-14 (P)
1934—Giants, 17-0 (NY)
Eagles, 6-0 (P)
1935—Giants, 10-0 (NY)
Giants, 21-14 (P)
1936—Eagles, 10-7 (P)
Giants, 21-17 (NY)
1937—Giants, 16-7 (P)
Giants, 21-0 (NY)
1938—Eagles, 14-10 (P)
Giants, 17-7 (NY)
1939—Giants, 13-3 (P)
Giants, 27-10 (NY)
1940—Giants, 20-14 (P)
Giants, 17-7 (NY)
1941—Giants, 24-0 (P)
Giants, 16-0 (NY)
1942—Giants, 35-17 (NY)
Giants, 14-0 (P)
1944—Eagles, 24-17 (NY)
Tie, 21-21 (P)
1945—Eagles, 38-17 (P)
Giants, 28-21 (NY)
1946—Eagles, 24-14 (P)
Giants, 45-17 (NY)
1947—Eagles, 23-0 (P)
Eagles, 41-24 (NY)
1948—Eagles, 45-0 (P)
Eagles, 35-14 (NY)
1949—Eagles, 24-3 (NY)
Eagles, 17-3 (P)
1950—Giants, 7-3 (NY)
Giants, 9-7 (P)
1951—Giants, 26-24 (NY)
Giants, 23-7 (P)
1952—Giants, 31-7 (P)
Eagles, 14-10 (NY)
1953—Eagles, 30-7 (P)
Giants, 37-28 (NY)
1954—Giants, 27-14 (NY)
Eagles, 29-14 (P)
1955—Eagles, 27-17 (P)
Giants, 31-7 (NY)
1956—Giants, 20-3 (NY)
Giants, 21-7 (P)
1957—Giants, 24-20 (P)
Giants, 13-0 (NY)
1958—Eagles, 27-24 (P)
Giants, 24-10 (NY)
1959—Eagles, 49-21 (P)
Giants, 24-7 (NY)
1960—Eagles, 17-10 (NY)
Eagles, 31-23 (P)
1961—Giants, 38-21 (NY)
Giants, 28-24 (P)
1962—Giants, 29-13 (P)
Giants, 19-14 (NY)
1963—Giants, 37-14 (P)
Giants, 42-14 (NY)
1964—Eagles, 38-7 (P)
Eagles, 23-17 (NY)
1965—Giants, 16-14 (P)
Giants, 35-27 (NY)
1966—Eagles, 35-17 (P)
Eagles, 31-3 (NY)
1967—Giants, 44-7 (NY)
1968—Giants, 34-25 (P)
Giants, 7-6 (NY)
1969—Eagles, 23-20 (NY)
1970—Giants, 30-23 (NY)
Eagles, 23-20 (P)
1971—Eagles, 23-7 (P)
Eagles, 41-28 (NY)
1972—Giants, 27-12 (P)
Giants, 62-10 (NY)
1973—Tie, 23-23 (NY)
Eagles, 20-16 (P)
1974—Eagles, 35-7 (P)
Eagles, 20-7 (New Haven)
1975—Giants, 23-14 (P)
Eagles, 13-10 (NY)
1976—Eagles, 20-7 (P)
Eagles, 10-0 (NY)
1977—Eagles, 28-10 (NY)
Eagles, 17-14 (P)
1978—Eagles, 19-17 (NY)
Eagles, 20-3 (P)
1979—Eagles, 23-17 (P)
Eagles, 17-13 (NY)
1980—Eagles, 35-3 (P)
Eagles, 31-16 (NY)
1981—Eagles, 24-10 (NY)
Giants, 20-10 (P)
*Giants, 27-21 (P)
1982—Giants, 23-7 (NY)
Giants, 26-24 (P)
1983—Eagles, 17-13 (NY)
Giants, 23-0 (P)
1984—Giants, 28-27 (NY)
Eagles, 24-10 (P)
1985—Giants, 21-0 (NY)
Giants, 16-10 (P) OT
1986—Giants, 35-3 (NY)
Giants, 17-14 (P)
1987—Giants, 20-17 (P)
Giants, 23-20 (NY) OT
(Points—Giants 2,076, Eagles 1,862)
NFC First Round Playoff
N.Y. GIANTS vs. *PITTSBURGH
Giants lead series, 41-26-3
1933—Giants, 23-2 (P)
Giants, 27-3 (NY)
1934—Giants, 14-12 (P)
Giants, 17-7 (NY)
1935—Giants, 42-7 (P)
Giants, 13-0 (NY)
1936—Pirates, 10-7 (P)
1937—Giants, 10-7 (P)
Giants, 17-0 (NY)
1938—Giants, 27-14 (P)
Pirates, 13-10 (NY)
1939—Giants, 14-7 (P)
Giants, 23-7 (NY)
1940—Tie, 10-10 (P)
Giants, 12-0 (NY)
1941—Giants, 37-10 (P)
Giants, 28-7 (NY)
1942—Steelers, 13-10 (P)
Steelers, 17-9 (NY)
1945—Giants, 34-6 (P)
Steelers, 21-7 (NY)
1946—Giants, 17-14 (P)
Giants, 7-0 (NY)
1947—Steelers, 38-21 (NY)
Steelers, 24-7 (P)
1948—Giants, 34-27 (NY)
Steelers, 38-28 (P)
1949—Steelers, 28-7 (P)
Steelers, 21-17 (NY)
1950—Giants, 18-7 (P)
Steelers, 17-6 (NY)
1951—Tie, 13-13 (P)
Giants, 14-0 (NY)
1952—Steelers, 63-7 (P)
1953—Steelers, 24-14 (P)
Steelers, 14-10 (NY)
1954—Giants, 30-6 (P)
Giants, 24-3 (NY)
1955—Steelers, 30-23 (P)

Steelers, 19-17 (NY)
1956—Giants, 38-10 (NY)
Giants, 17-14 (P)
1957—Giants, 35-0 (NY)
Steelers, 21-10 (P)
1958—Giants, 17-6 (NY)
Steelers, 31-10 (P)
1959—Giants, 21-16 (P)
Steelers, 14-9 (NY)
1960—Giants, 19-17 (P)
Giants, 27-24 (NY)
1961—Giants, 17-14 (P)
Giants, 42-21 (NY)
1962—Giants, 31-27 (P)
Steelers, 20-17 (NY)
1963—Steelers, 31-0 (P)
Giants, 33-17 (NY)
1964—Steelers, 27-24 (P)
Steelers, 44-17 (NY)
1965—Giants, 23-13 (P)
Giants, 35-10 (NY)
1966—Tie, 34-34 (P)
Steelers, 47-28 (NY)
1967—Giants, 27-24 (P)
Giants, 28-20 (NY)
1968—Giants, 34-20 (P)
1969—Giants, 10-7 (NY)
Giants, 21-17 (P)
1971—Steelers, 17-13 (P)
1976—Steelers, 27-0 (NY)
1985—Giants, 28-10 (NY)
(Points—Giants 1,370, Steelers 1,159)
**Steelers known as Pirates prior to 1941*

N.Y. GIANTS vs. *ST. LOUIS
Giants lead series, 56-32-2
1926—Giants, 20-0 (NY)
1927—Giants, 28-7 (NY)
1929—Giants, 24-21 (NY)
1930—Giants, 25-12 (NY)
Giants, 13-7 (C)
1935—Cardinals, 14-13 (NY)
1936—Giants, 14-6 (NY)
1938—Giants, 6-0 (NY)
1939—Giants, 17-7 (NY)
1941—Cardinals, 10-7 (NY)
1942—Giants, 21-7 (NY)
1943—Giants, 24-13 (NY)
1946—Giants, 28-24 (NY)
1947—Giants, 35-31 (NY)
1948—Cardinals, 63-35 (NY)
1949—Giants, 41-38 (C)
1950—Cardinals, 17-3 (C)
Giants, 51-21 (NY)
1951—Giants, 28-17 (NY)
Giants, 10-0 (C)
1952—Cardinals, 24-23 (NY)
Giants, 28-6 (C)
1953—Giants, 21-7 (NY)
Giants, 23-20 (C)
1954—Giants, 41-10 (C)
Giants, 31-17 (NY)
1955—Cardinals, 28-17 (C)
Giants, 10-0 (NY)
1956—Cardinals, 35-27 (C)
Giants, 23-10 (NY)
1957—Giants, 27-14 (NY)
Giants, 28-21 (C)
1958—Giants, 37-7 (Buffalo)
Cardinals, 23-6 (NY)
1959—Giants, 9-3 (NY)
Giants, 30-20 (Minn)
1960—Giants, 35-14 (StL)
Cardinals, 20-13 (NY)
1961—Cardinals, 21-10 (NY)
Giants, 24-9 (StL)
1962—Giants, 31-14 (StL)
Giants, 31-28 (NY)
1963—Giants, 38-21 (StL)
Cardinals, 24-17 (NY)
1964—Giants, 34-17 (NY)
Tie, 10-10 (StL)
1965—Giants, 14-10 (NY)
Giants, 28-15 (StL)
1966—Cardinals, 24-19 (StL)
Cardinals, 20-17 (NY)
1967—Giants, 37-20 (StL)
Giants, 37-14 (NY)
1968—Cardinals, 28-21 (NY)
1969—Cardinals, 42-17 (StL)
Giants, 49-6 (NY)
1970—Giants, 35-17 (NY)
Giants, 34-17 (StL)
1971—Giants, 21-20 (StL)
Cardinals, 24-7 (NY)
1972—Giants, 27-21 (NY)
Giants, 13-7 (StL)
1973—Cardinals, 35-27 (StL)
Giants, 24-13 (New Haven)
1974—Cardinals, 23-21 (New Haven)
Cardinals, 26-14 (StL)
1975—Cardinals, 26-14 (StL)
Cardinals, 20-13 (NY)
1976—Cardinals, 27-21 (StL)
Cardinals, 17-14 (NY)
1977—Cardinals, 28-0 (StL)
Giants, 27-7 (NY)
1978—Cardinals, 20-10 (StL)
Giants, 17-0 (NY)
1979—Cardinals, 27-14 (NY)
Cardinals, 29-20 (StL)
1980—Giants, 41-35 (StL)
Cardinals, 23-7 (NY)
1981—Giants, 34-14 (NY)
Giants, 20-10 (StL)
1982—Cardinals, 24-21 (StL)
1983—Tie, 20-20 (StL) OT
Cardinals, 10-6 (NY)
1984—Giants, 16-10 (NY)
Cardinals, 31-21 (StL)
1985—Giants, 27-17 (NY)
Giants, 34-3 (StL)
1986—Giants, 13-6 (StL)
Giants, 27-7 (NY)
1987—Giants, 30-7 (NY)
Cardinals, 27-24 (StL)
(Points—Giants 2,020, Cardinals 1,565)
**Franchise in Chicago prior to 1960*

N.Y. GIANTS vs. SAN DIEGO
Giants lead series, 3-2
1971—Giants, 35-17 (NY)
1975—Giants, 35-24 (NY)
1980—Chargers, 44-7 (SD)
1983—Chargers, 41-34 (NY)
1986—Giants, 20-7 (NY)
(Points—Chargers 133, Giants 131)

N.Y. GIANTS vs. SAN FRANCISCO
Giants lead series, 12-8
1952—Giants, 23-14 (NY)
1956—Giants, 38-21 (SF)
1957—49ers, 27-17 (NY)
1960—Giants, 21-19 (SF)
1963—Giants, 48-14 (NY)
1968—49ers, 26-10 (NY)
1972—Giants, 23-17 (SF)
1975—Giants, 26-23 (SF)
1977—Giants, 20-17 (NY)
1978—Giants, 27-10 (NY)
1979—Giants, 32-16 (NY)
1980—49ers, 12-0 (SF)
1981—49ers, 17-10 (SF)
*49ers, 38-24 (SF)
1984—49ers, 31-10 (NY)
*49ers, 21-10 (SF)
1985—**Giants, 17-3 (NY)
1986—Giants, 21-17 (SF)
*Giants, 49-3 (NY)
1987—49ers, 41-21 (NY)
(Points—Giants 447, 49ers 387)
**NFC Divisional Playoff*
***NFC First Round Playoff*

N.Y. GIANTS vs. SEATTLE
Giants lead series, 3-2
1976—Giants, 28-16 (NY)
1980—Giants, 27-21 (S)
1981—Giants, 32-0 (S)
1983—Seahawks, 17-12 (NY)
1986—Seahawks, 17-12 (S)
(Points—Giants 111, Seahawks 71)

N.Y. GIANTS vs. TAMPA BAY
Giants lead series, 6-3
1977—Giants, 10-0 (TB)
1978—Giants, 19-13 (TB)
Giants, 17-14 (NY)
1979—Giants, 17-14 (NY)
Buccaneers, 31-3 (TB)
1980—Buccaneers, 30-13 (TB)
1984—Giants, 17-14 (NY)
Buccaneers, 20-17 (TB)
1985—Giants, 22-20 (NY)
(Points—Buccaneers 156, Giants 135)

N.Y. GIANTS vs. *WASHINGTON
Giants lead series, 61-48-3
1932—Braves, 14-6 (B)
Tie, 0-0 (NY)
1933—Redskins, 21-20 (B)
Giants, 7-0 (NY)
1934—Giants, 16-13 (B)
Giants, 3-0 (NY)
1935—Giants, 20-12 (B)
Giants, 17-6 (NY)
1936—Giants, 7-0 (B)
Redskins, 14-0 (NY)
1937—Redskins, 13-3 (W)
Redskins, 49-14 (NY)
1938—Giants, 10-7 (W)
Giants, 36-0 (NY)
1939—Tie, 0-0 (W)
Giants, 9-7 (NY)
1940—Redskins, 21-7 (W)
Giants, 21-7 (NY)
1941—Giants, 17-10 (W)
Giants, 20-13 (NY)
1942—Giants, 14-7 (W)
Redskins, 14-7 (NY)
1943—Giants, 14-10 (NY)
Giants, 31-7 (W)
**Redskins, 28-0 (NY)
1944—Giants, 16-13 (NY)
Giants, 31-0 (W)
1945—Redskins, 24-14 (NY)
Redskins, 17-0 (W)
1946—Redskins, 24-14 (W)
Giants, 31-0 (NY)
1947—Redskins, 28-20 (W)
Giants, 35-10 (NY)
1948—Redskins, 41-10 (W)
Redskins, 28-21 (NY)
1949—Giants, 45-35 (W)
Giants, 23-7 (NY)
1950—Giants, 21-17 (W)
Giants, 24-21 (NY)
1951—Giants, 35-14 (W)
Giants, 28-14 (NY)
1952—Giants, 14-10 (W)
Redskins, 27-17 (NY)
1953—Redskins, 13-9 (W)
Redskins, 24-21 (NY)
1954—Giants, 51-21 (W)
Giants, 24-7 (NY)
1955—Giants, 35-7 (NY)
Giants, 27-20 (W)
1956—Redskins, 33-7 (W)
Giants, 28-14 (NY)
1957—Giants, 24-20 (W)
Redskins, 31-14 (NY)
1958—Giants, 21-14 (W)
Giants, 30-0 (NY)
1959—Giants, 45-14 (NY)
Giants, 24-10 (W)
1960—Tie, 24-24 (NY)
Giants, 17-3 (W)
1961—Giants, 24-21 (W)
Giants, 53-0 (NY)
1962—Giants, 49-34 (NY)
Giants, 42-24 (NY)
1963—Giants, 24-14 (W)
Giants, 44-14 (NY)
1964—Giants, 13-10 (NY)
Redskins, 36-21 (W)
1965—Redskins, 23-7 (NY)
Giants, 27-10 (W)
1966—Giants, 13-10 (NY)
Redskins, 72-41 (W)
1967—Redskins, 38-34 (W)
1968—Giants, 48-21 (NY)
Giants, 13-10 (W)
1969—Redskins, 20-14 (W)
1970—Giants, 35-33 (NY)
Giants, 27-24 (W)
1971—Redskins, 30-3 (NY)
Redskins, 23-7 (W)
1972—Redskins, 23-16 (NY)
Redskins, 27-13 (W)
1973—Redskins, 21-3 (New Haven)
Redskins, 27-24 (W)
1974—Redskins, 13-10 (New Haven)
Redskins, 24-3 (W)
1975—Redskins, 49-13 (W)
Redskins, 21-13 (NY)
1976—Redskins, 19-17 (W)
Giants, 12-9 (NY)
1977—Giants, 20-17 (NY)
Giants, 17-6 (W)
1978—Giants, 17-6 (NY)
Redskins, 16-13 (W) OT
1979—Redskins, 27-0 (W)
Giants, 14-6 (NY)
1980—Redskins, 23-21 (NY)
Redskins, 16-13 (W)
1981—Giants, 17-7 (W)
Redskins, 30-27 (NY) OT
1982—Redskins, 27-17 (NY)
Redskins, 15-14 (W)
1983—Redskins, 33-17 (NY)
Redskins, 31-22 (W)
1984—Redskins, 30-14 (W)
Giants, 37-13 (NY)
1985—Giants, 17-3 (NY)
Redskins, 23-21 (W)
1986—Giants, 27-20 (NY)
Giants, 24-14 (W)
***Giants, 17-0 (NY)
1987—Redskins, 38-12 (NY)
Redskins, 23-19 (W)
(Points—Giants 2,179, Redskins 1,982)
**Franchise in Boston prior to 1937 and known as Braves prior to 1933*
***Division Playoff*
****NFC Championship*

N.Y. JETS vs. ATLANTA
Series tied, 2-2;
See Atlanta vs. N.Y. Jets

N.Y. JETS vs. BUFFALO
Jets lead series, 28-27;
See Buffalo vs. N.Y. Jets

N.Y. JETS vs. CHICAGO
Bears lead series, 2-1;
See Chicago vs. N.Y. Jets

N.Y. JETS vs. CINCINNATI
Jets lead series, 8-4;
See Cincinnati vs. N.Y. Jets

N.Y. JETS vs. CLEVELAND
Browns lead series, 8-3;
See Cleveland vs. N.Y. Jets

N.Y. JETS vs. DALLAS
Cowboys lead series, 4-0;
See Dallas vs. N.Y. Jets

N.Y. JETS vs. DENVER
Jets lead series, 11-10-1;
See Denver vs. N.Y. Jets

N.Y. JETS vs. DETROIT
Series tied, 2-2;
See Detroit vs. N.Y. Jets

N.Y. JETS vs. GREEN BAY
Jets lead series, 4-1;
See Green Bay vs. N.Y. Jets

N.Y. JETS vs. HOUSTON
Oilers lead series, 15-10-1;
See Houston vs. N.Y. Jets

N.Y. JETS vs. INDIANAPOLIS
Series tied, 18-18;
See Indianapolis vs. N.Y. Jets

N.Y. JETS vs. KANSAS CITY
Series tied, 13-13;
See Kansas City vs. N.Y. Jets

N.Y. JETS vs. L.A. RAIDERS
Raiders lead series, 12-11-2;
See L.A. Raiders vs. N.Y. Jets

N.Y. JETS vs. L.A. RAMS
Rams lead series, 3-2;
See L.A. Rams vs. N.Y. Jets

N.Y. JETS vs. MIAMI
Dolphins lead series, 24-20-1;
See Miami vs. N.Y. Jets

N.Y. JETS vs. MINNESOTA
Jets lead series, 3-1;
See Minnesota vs. N.Y. Jets

N.Y. JETS vs. NEW ENGLAND
Jets lead series, 31-24-1;
See New England vs. N.Y. Jets

N.Y. JETS vs. NEW ORLEANS
Jets lead series, 4-1;
See New Orleans vs. N.Y. Jets

N.Y. JETS vs. N.Y. GIANTS
Giants lead series, 3-2;
See N.Y. Giants vs. N.Y. Jets

N.Y. JETS vs. PHILADELPHIA
Eagles lead series, 4-0
1973—Eagles, 24-23 (P)
1977—Eagles, 27-0 (P)
1978—Eagles, 17-9 (P)
1987—Eagles, 38-27 (NY)
(Points—Eagles 106, Jets 59)

N.Y. JETS vs. PITTSBURGH
Steelers lead series, 9-0
1970—Steelers, 21-17 (P)
1973—Steelers, 26-14 (P)
1975—Steelers, 20-7 (NY)
1977—Steelers, 23-20 (NY)
1978—Steelers, 28-17 (NY)
1981—Steelers, 38-10 (P)
1983—Steelers, 34-7 (NY)
1984—Steelers, 23-17 (NY)
1986—Steelers, 45-24 (NY)
(Points—Steelers 258, Jets 133)

N.Y. JETS vs. ST. LOUIS
Cardinals lead series, 2-1
1971—Cardinals, 17-10 (StL)
1975—Cardinals 37-6 (NY)
1978—Jets, 23-10 (NY)
(Points—Cardinals 64, Jets 39)

***N.Y. JETS vs. **SAN DIEGO**
Chargers lead series, 14-7-1
1960—Chargers, 21-7 (NY)
Chargers, 50-43 (LA)
1961—Chargers, 25-10 (NY)
Chargers, 48-13 (SD)
1962—Chargers, 40-14 (SD)
Titans, 23-3 (NY)
1963—Chargers, 24-20 (SD)
Chargers, 53-7 (NY)
1964—Tie, 17-17 (NY)
Chargers, 38-3 (SD)
1965—Chargers, 34-9 (NY)
Chargers, 38-7 (SD)
1966—Jets, 17-16 (NY)
Chargers, 42-27 (SD)
1967—Jets, 42-31 (SD)
1968—Jets, 23-20 (NY)
Jets, 37-15 (SD)
1969—Chargers, 34-27 (SD)
1971—Chargers, 49-21 (SD)
1974—Jets, 27-14 (NY)
1975—Chargers, 24-16 (SD)
1983—Jets, 41-29 (SD)
(Points—Chargers 665, Jets 451)
**Jets known as Titans prior to 1963*
***Franchise in Los Angeles prior to 1961*

N.Y. JETS vs. SAN FRANCISCO
49ers lead series, 4-1
1971—49ers, 24-21 (NY)

1976—49ers, 17-6 (SF)
1980—49ers, 37-27 (NY)
1983—Jets, 27-13 (SF)
1986—49ers, 24-10 (SF)
(Points—49ers 115, Jets 91)

N.Y. JETS vs. SEATTLE
Seahawks lead series, 7-3
1977—Seahawks, 17-0 (NY)
1978—Seahawks, 24-17 (NY)
1979—Seahawks, 30-7 (S)
1980—Seahawks, 27-17 (NY)
1981—Seahawks, 19-3 (NY)
Seahawks, 27-23 (S)
1983—Seahawks, 17-10 (NY)
1985—Jets, 17-14 (NY)
1986—Jets, 38-7 (S)
1987—Jets, 30-14 (NY)
(Points—Seahawks 196, Jets 162)

N.Y. JETS vs. TAMPA BAY
Jets lead series, 3-1
1976—Jets, 34-0 (NY)
1982—Jets, 32-17 (NY)
1984—Buccaneers, 41-21 (TB)
1985—Jets, 62-28 (NY)
(Points—Jets 149, Buccaneers 86)

N.Y. JETS vs. WASHINGTON
Redskins lead series, 4-0
1972—Redskins, 35-17 (NY)
1976—Redskins, 37-16 (NY)
1978—Redskins, 23-3 (W)
1987—Redskins, 17-16 (W)
(Points—Redskins 112, Jets 52)

PHILADELPHIA vs. ATLANTA
Eagles lead series, 7-6-1;
See Atlanta vs. Philadelphia

PHILADELPHIA vs. BUFFALO
Eagles lead series, 4-1;
See Buffalo vs. Philadelphia

PHILADELPHIA vs. CHICAGO
Bears lead series, 21-4-1;
See Chicago vs. Philadelphia

PHILADELPHIA vs. CINCINNATI
Bengals lead series, 4-0;
See Cincinnati vs. Philadelphia

PHILADELPHIA vs. CLEVELAND
Browns lead series, 29-11-1;
See Cleveland vs. Philadelphia

PHILADELPHIA vs. DALLAS
Cowboys lead series, 36-19;
See Dallas vs. Philadelphia

PHILADELPHIA vs. DENVER
Eagles lead series, 3-2;
See Denver vs. Philadelphia

PHILADELPHIA vs. DETROIT
Lions lead series, 12-9-2;
See Detroit vs. Philadelphia

PHILADELPHIA vs. GREEN BAY
Packers lead series, 18-5;
See Green Bay vs. Philadelphia

PHILADELPHIA vs. HOUSTON
Eagles lead series, 3-0;
See Houston vs. Philadelphia

PHILADELPHIA vs. INDIANAPOLIS
Series tied, 5-5;
See Indianapolis vs. Philadelphia

PHILADELPHIA vs. KANSAS CITY
Eagles lead series, 1-0;
See Kansas City vs. Philadelphia

PHILADELPHIA vs. L.A. RAIDERS
Raiders lead series, 3-2;
See L.A. Raiders vs. Philadelphia

PHILADELPHIA vs. L.A. RAMS
Rams lead series, 15-10-1;
See L.A. Rams vs. Philadelphia

PHILADELPHIA vs. MIAMI
Dolphins lead series, 4-2;
See Miami vs. Philadelphia

PHILADELPHIA vs. MINNESOTA
Vikings lead series, 9-4;
See Minnesota vs. Philadelphia

PHILADELPHIA vs. NEW ENGLAND
Eagles lead series, 4-2;
See New England vs. Philadelphia

PHILADELPHIA vs. NEW ORLEANS
Eagles lead series, 9-6;
See New Orleans vs. Philadelphia

PHILADELPHIA vs. N.Y. GIANTS
Giants lead series, 60-45-2;
See N.Y. Giants vs. Philadelphia

PHILADELPHIA vs. N.Y. JETS
Eagles lead series, 4-0;
See N.Y. Jets vs. Philadelphia

PHILADELPHIA vs. *PITTSBURGH
Eagles lead series, 42-25-3
1933—Eagles, 25-6 (Phila)
1934—Eagles, 17-0 (Pitt)
Pirates, 9-7 (Phila)
1935—Pirates, 17-7 (Phila)
Eagles, 17-6 (Pitt)
1936—Pirates, 17-0 (Pitt)
Pirates, 6-0 (Johnstown, Pa.)
1937—Pirates, 27-14 (Pitt)
Pirates, 16-7 (Pitt)
1938—Eagles, 27-7 (Buffalo)
Eagles, 14-7 (Charleston, W. Va.)
1939—Eagles, 17-14 (Phila)
Pirates, 24-12 (Pitt)
1940—Pirates, 7-3 (Pitt)
Eagles, 7-0 (Phila)
1941—Eagles, 10-7 (Pitt)
Tie, 7-7 (Phila)
1942—Eagles, 24-14 (Pitt)
Steelers, 14-0 (Phila)
1945—Eagles, 45-3 (Pitt)
Eagles, 30-6 (Phila)
1946—Steelers, 10-7 (Pitt)
Eagles, 10-7 (Phila)
1947—Steelers, 35-24 (Pitt)
Eagles, 21-0 (Phila)
**Eagles, 21-0 (Pitt)
1948—Eagles, 34-7 (Pitt)
Eagles, 17-0 (Phila)
1949—Eagles, 38-7 (Pitt)
Eagles, 34-17 (Phila)
1950—Eagles, 17-10 (Pitt)
Steelers, 9-7 (Phila)
1951—Eagles, 34-13 (Pitt)
Steelers, 17-13 (Phila)
1952—Eagles, 31-25 (Pitt)
Eagles, 26-21 (Phila)
1953—Eagles, 23-17 (Phila)
Eagles, 35-7 (Pitt)
1954—Eagles, 24-22 (Phila)
Steelers, 17-7 (Pitt)
1955—Steelers, 13-7 (Pitt)
Eagles, 24-0 (Phila)
1956—Eagles, 35-21 (Pitt)
Eagles, 14-7 (Phila)
1957—Steelers, 6-0 (Pitt)
Eagles, 7-6 (Phila)
1958—Steelers, 24-3 (Pitt)
Steelers, 31-24 (Phila)
1959—Eagles, 28-24 (Phila)
Steelers, 31-0 (Pitt)
1960—Eagles, 34-7 (Phila)
Steelers, 27-21 (Pitt)
1961—Eagles, 21-16 (Phila)
Eagles, 35-24 (Pitt)
1962—Steelers, 13-7 (Pitt)
Steelers, 26-17 (Phila)
1963—Tie, 21-21 (Phila)
Tie, 20-20 (Pitt)
1964—Eagles, 21-7 (Phila)
Eagles, 34-10 (Pitt)
1965—Steelers, 20-14 (Phila)
Eagles, 47-13 (Pitt)
1966—Eagles, 31-14 (Pitt)
Eagles, 27-23 (Phila)
1967—Eagles, 34-24 (Phila)
1968—Steelers, 6-3 (Pitt)
1969—Eagles, 41-27 (Phila)
1970—Eagles, 30-20 (Phila)
1974—Steelers, 27-0 (Pitt)
1979—Eagles, 17-14 (Phila)
(Points—Eagles 1,330, Steelers 967)
**Steelers known as Pirates prior to 1941*
***Division Playoff*

PHILADELPHIA vs. *ST. LOUIS
Cardinals lead series, 42-35-5
1935—Cardinals, 12-3 (C)
1936—Cardinals, 13-0 (C)
1937—Tie, 6-6 (P)
1938—Eagles, 7-0 (Erie, Pa.)
1941—Eagles, 21-14 (P)
1945—Eagles, 21-6 (P)
1947—Cardinals, 45-21 (P)
**Cardinals, 28-21 (C)
1948—Cardinals, 21-14 (C)
**Eagles, 7-0 (P)
1949—Eagles, 28-3 (P)
1950—Eagles, 45-7 (C)
Cardinals, 14-10 (P)
1951—Eagles, 17-14 (C)
1952—Eagles, 10-7 (P)
Cardinals, 28-22 (C)
1953—Eagles, 56-17 (C)
Eagles, 38-0 (P)
1954—Eagles, 35-16 (C)
Eagles, 30-14 (P)
1955—Tie, 24-24 (C)
Eagles, 27-3 (P)
1956—Cardinals, 20-6 (P)
Cardinals, 28-17 (C)
1957—Eagles, 38-21 (C)
Cardinals, 31-27 (P)
1958—Tie, 21-21 (C)
Eagles, 49-21 (P)
1959—Eagles, 28-24 (Minn)
Eagles, 27-17 (P)
1960—Eagles, 31-27 (P)
Eagles, 20-6 (StL)
1961—Cardinals, 30-27 (P)
Eagles, 20-7 (StL)
1962—Cardinals, 27-21 (P)
Cardinals, 45-35 (StL)
1963—Cardinals, 28-24 (P)
Cardinals, 38-14 (StL)
1964—Cardinals, 38-13 (P)
Cardinals, 36-34 (StL)
1965—Eagles, 34-27 (P)
Eagles, 28-24 (StL)
1966—Cardinals, 16-13 (StL)
Cardinals, 41-10 (P)
1967—Cardinals, 48-14 (StL)
1968—Cardinals, 45-17 (P)
1969—Eagles, 34-30 (StL)
1970—Cardinals, 35-20 (P)
Cardinals, 23-14 (StL)
1971—Eagles, 37-20 (StL)
Eagles, 19-7 (P)
1972—Tie, 6-6 (P)
Cardinals, 24-23 (StL)
1973—Cardinals, 34-23 (P)
Eagles, 27-24 (StL)
1974—Cardinals, 7-3 (StL)
Cardinals, 13-3 (P)
1975—Cardinals, 31-20 (StL)
Cardinals, 24-23 (P)
1976—Cardinals, 33-14 (StL)
Cardinals, 17-14 (P)
1977—Cardinals, 21-17 (P)
Cardinals, 21-16 (StL)
1978—Cardinals, 16-10 (P)
Eagles, 14-10 (StL)
1979—Eagles, 24-20 (StL)
Eagles, 16-13 (P)
1980—Cardinals, 24-14 (StL)
Eagles, 17-3 (P)
1981—Eagles, 52-10 (StL)
Eagles, 38-0 (P)
1982—Cardinals, 23-20 (P)
1983—Cardinals, 14-11 (P)
Cardinals, 31-7 (StL)
1984—Cardinals, 34-14 (P)
Cardinals, 17-16 (StL)
1985—Eagles, 30-7 (P)
Eagles, 24-14 (StL)
1986—Cardinals, 13-10 (StL)
Tie, 10-10 (P) OT
1987—Eagles, 28-23 (StL)
Cardinals, 31-19 (P)
(Points—Eagles 1,718, Cardinals 1,641)
**Franchise in Chicago prior to 1960*
***NFL Championship*

PHILADELPHIA vs. SAN DIEGO
Series tied, 2-2
1974—Eagles, 13-7 (SD)
1980—Chargers, 22-21 (SD)
1985—Chargers, 20-14 (SD)
1986—Eagles, 23-7 (P)
(Points—Eagles 71, Chargers 56)

PHILADELPHIA vs. SAN FRANCISCO
49ers lead series, 10-4-1
1951—Eagles, 21-14 (P)
1953—49ers, 31-21 (SF)
1956—Tie, 10-10 (P)
1958—49ers, 30-24 (P)
1959—49ers, 24-14 (SF)
1964—49ers, 28-24 (P)
1966—Eagles, 35-34 (SF)
1967—49ers, 28-27 (P)
1969—49ers, 14-13 (SF)
1971—49ers, 31-3 (P)
1973—49ers, 38-28 (SF)
1975—Eagles, 27-17 (P)
1983—Eagles, 22-17 (SF)
1984—49ers, 21-9 (P)
1985—49ers, 24-13 (SF)
(Points—49ers 361, Eagles 291)

PHILADELPHIA vs. SEATTLE
Eagles lead series, 2-1
1976—Eagles, 27-10 (P)
1980—Eagles, 27-20 (S)
1986—Seahawks, 24-20 (S)
(Points—Eagles 74, Seahawks 54)

PHILADELPHIA vs. TAMPA BAY
Eagles lead series, 2-1
1977—Eagles, 13-3 (P)
1979—*Buccaneers, 24-17 (TB)
1981—Eagles, 20-10 (P)
(Points—Eagles 50, Buccaneers 37)
**NFC Divisional Playoff*

PHILADELPHIA vs. *WASHINGTON
Redskins lead series, 60-40-5
1934—Redskins, 6-0 (B)
Redskins, 14-7 (P)
1935—Eagles, 7-6 (B)
1936—Redskins, 26-3 (P)
Redskins, 17-7 (B)
1937—Eagles, 14-0 (W)
Redskins, 10-7 (P)
1938—Redskins, 26-23 (P)
Redskins, 20-14 (W)
1939—Redskins, 7-0 (P)
Redskins, 7-6 (W)
1940—Redskins, 34-17 (P)
Redskins, 13-6 (W)
1941—Redskins, 21-17 (P)
Redskins, 20-14 (W)
1942—Redskins, 14-10 (P)
Redskins, 30-27 (W)
1944—Tie, 31-31 (P)
Eagles, 37-7 (W)
1945—Redskins, 24-14 (W)
Eagles, 16-0 (P)
1946—Eagles, 28-24 (W)
Redskins, 27-10 (P)
1947—Eagles, 45-42 (P)
Eagles, 38-14 (W)
1948—Eagles, 45-0 (W)
Eagles, 42-21 (P)
1949—Eagles, 49-14 (P)
Eagles, 44-21 (W)
1950—Eagles, 35-3 (P)
Eagles, 33-0 (W)
1951—Redskins, 27-23 (P)
Eagles, 35-21 (W)
1952—Eagles, 38-20 (P)
Redskins, 27-21 (W)
1953—Tie, 21-21 (P)
Redskins, 10-0 (W)
1954—Eagles, 49-21 (W)
Eagles, 41-33 (P)
1955—Redskins, 31-30 (P)
Redskins, 34-21 (W)
1956—Eagles, 13-9 (P)
Redskins, 19-17 (W)
1957—Eagles, 21-12 (P)
Redskins, 42-7 (W)
1958—Redskins, 24-14 (P)
Redskins, 20-0 (W)
1959—Eagles, 30-23 (P)
Eagles, 34-14 (W)
1960—Eagles, 19-13 (P)
Eagles, 38-28 (W)
1961—Eagles, 14-7 (P)
Eagles, 27-24 (W)
1962—Redskins, 27-21 (P)
Eagles, 37-14 (W)
1963—Eagles, 37-24 (W)
Redskins, 13-10 (P)
1964—Redskins, 35-20 (W)
Redskins, 21-10 (P)
1965—Redskins, 23-21 (W)
Eagles, 21-14 (P)
1966—Redskins, 27-13 (P)
Eagles, 37-28 (W)
1967—Eagles, 35-24 (P)
Tie, 35-35 (W)
1968—Redskins, 17-14 (W)
Redskins, 16-10 (P)
1969—Tie, 28-28 (W)
Redskins, 34-29 (P)
1970—Redskins, 33-21 (P)
Redskins, 24-6 (W)
1971—Tie, 7-7 (W)
Redskins, 20-13 (P)
1972—Redskins, 14-0 (W)
Redskins, 23-7 (P)
1973—Redskins, 28-7 (P)
Redskins, 38-20 (W)
1974—Redskins, 27-20 (P)
Redskins, 26-7 (W)
1975—Eagles, 26-10 (P)
Eagles, 26-3 (W)
1976—Redskins, 20-17 (P) OT
Redskins, 24-0 (W)
1977—Redskins, 23-17 (W)
Redskins, 17-14 (P)
1978—Redskins, 35-30 (W)
Eagles, 17-10 (P)
1979—Eagles, 28-17 (P)
Redskins, 17-7 (W)
1980—Eagles, 24-14 (P)
Eagles, 24-0 (W)
1981—Eagles, 36-13 (P)
Redskins, 15-13 (W)
1982—Redskins, 37-34 (P) OT
Redskins, 13-9 (W)
1983—Redskins, 23-13 (P)
Redskins, 28-24 (W)
1984—Redskins, 20-0 (W)
Eagles, 16-10 (P)
1985—Eagles, 19-6 (W)
Redskins, 17-12 (P)
1986—Redskins, 41-14 (W)
Redskins, 21-14 (P)
1987—Redskins, 34-24 (W)
Eagles, 31-27 (P)
(Points—Eagles 2,134, Redskins 2,094)
**Franchise in Boston prior to 1937*

PITTSBURGH vs. ATLANTA
Steelers lead series, 7-1;
See Atlanta vs. Pittsburgh

PITTSBURGH vs. BUFFALO
Steelers lead series, 6-4;
See Buffalo vs. Pittsburgh

PITTSBURGH vs. CHICAGO
Bears lead series, 14-4-1;
See Chicago vs. Pittsburgh

PITTSBURGH vs. CINCINNATI
Steelers lead series, 20-15;
See Cincinnati vs. Pittsburgh
PITTSBURGH vs. CLEVELAND
Browns lead series, 45-31;
See Cleveland vs. Pittsburgh
PITTSBURGH vs. DALLAS
Steelers lead series, 12-11;
See Dallas vs. Pittsburgh
PITTSBURGH vs. DENVER
Broncos lead series, 8-5-1;
See Denver vs. Pittsburgh
PITTSBURGH vs. DETROIT
Lions lead series, 13-9-1;
See Detroit vs. Pittsburgh
PITTSBURGH vs. GREEN BAY
Packers lead series, 16-11;
See Green Bay vs. Pittsburgh
PITTSBURGH vs. HOUSTON
Steelers lead series, 26-11;
See Houston vs. Pittsburgh
PITTSBURGH vs. INDIANAPOLIS
Steelers lead series, 10-4;
See Indianapolis vs. Pittsburgh
PITTSBURGH vs. KANSAS CITY
Steelers lead series, 10-5;
See Kansas City vs. Pittsburgh
PITTSBURGH vs. L.A. RAIDERS
Raiders lead series, 9-6;
See L.A. Raiders vs. Pittsburgh
PITTSBURGH vs. L.A. RAMS
Rams lead series, 13-4-2;
See L.A. Rams vs. Pittsburgh
PITTSBURGH vs. MIAMI
Dolphins lead series, 8-3;
See Miami vs. Pittsburgh
PITTSBURGH vs. MINNESOTA
Vikings lead series, 6-4;
See Minnesota vs. Pittsburgh
PITTSBURGH vs. NEW ENGLAND
Steelers lead series, 5-3;
See New England vs. Pittsburgh
PITTSBURGH vs. NEW ORLEANS
Saints lead series, 5-4;
See New Orleans vs. Pittsburgh
PITTSBURGH vs. N.Y. GIANTS
Giants lead series, 41-26-3;
See N.Y. Giants vs. Pittsburgh
PITTSBURGH vs. N.Y. JETS
Steelers lead series, 9-0;
See N.Y. Jets vs. Pittsburgh
PITTSBURGH vs. PHILADELPHIA
Eagles lead series, 42-25-3;
See Philadelphia vs. Pittsburgh
***PITTSBURGH vs. **ST. LOUIS**
Steelers lead series, 29-20-3
1933—Pirates, 14-13 (C)
1935—Pirates, 17-13 (P)
1936—Cardinals, 14-6 (C)
1937—Cardinals, 13-7 (P)
1939—Cardinals, 10-0 (P)
1940—Tie, 7-7 (P)
1942—Steelers, 19-3 (P)
1945—Steelers, 23-0 (P)
1946—Steelers, 14-7 (P)
1948—Cardinals, 24-7 (P)
1950—Steelers, 28-17 (C)
Steelers, 28-7 (P)
1951—Steelers, 28-14 (C)
1952—Steelers, 34-28 (C)
Steelers, 17-14 (P)
1953—Steelers, 31-28 (P)
Steelers, 21-17 (C)
1954—Cardinals, 17-14 (C)
Steelers, 20-17 (P)
1955—Steelers, 14-7 (P)
Cardinals, 27-13 (C)
1956—Steelers, 14-7 (P)
Cardinals, 38-27 (C)
1957—Steelers, 29-20 (P)
Steelers, 27-2 (C)
1958—Steelers, 27-20 (C)
Steelers, 38-21 (P)
1959—Cardinals, 45-24 (C)
Steelers, 35-20 (P)
1960—Steelers, 27-14 (P)
Cardinals, 38-7 (StL)
1961—Steelers, 30-27 (P)
Cardinals, 20-0 (StL)
1962—Steelers, 26-17 (StL)
Steelers, 19-7 (P)
1963—Steelers, 23-10 (P)
Cardinals, 24-23 (StL)
1964—Cardinals, 34-30 (StL)
Cardinals, 21-20 (P)
1965—Cardinals, 20-7 (P)
Cardinals, 21-17 (P)
1966—Steelers, 30-9 (P)
Cardinals, 6-3 (StL)
1967—Cardinals, 28-14 (P)
Tie, 14-14 (StL)
1968—Tie, 28-28 (StL)
Cardinals, 20-10 (P)
1969—Cardinals, 27-14 (P)
Cardinals, 47-10 (StL)
1972—Steelers, 25-19 (StL)
1979—Steelers, 24-21 (StL)
1985—Steelers, 23-10 (P)
(Points—Steelers 1,007, Cardinals 952)
**Steelers known as Pirates prior to 1941*
***Franchise in Chicago prior to 1960*
PITTSBURGH vs. SAN DIEGO
Steelers lead series, 9-4
1971—Steelers, 21-17 (P)
1972—Steelers, 24-2 (SD)
1973—Steelers, 38-21 (P)
1975—Steelers, 37-0 (SD)
1976—Steelers, 23-0 (P)
1977—Steelers, 10-9 (SD)
1979—Chargers, 35-7 (SD)
1980—Chargers, 26-17 (SD)
1982—*Chargers, 31-28 (P)
1983—Steelers, 26-3 (P)
1984—Steelers, 52-24 (P)
1985—Chargers, 54-44 (SD)
1987—Steelers, 20-16 (SD)
(Points—Steelers 347, Chargers 238)
**AFC First Round Playoff*
PITTSBURGH vs. SAN FRANCISCO
Steelers lead series, 7-6
1951—49ers, 28-24 (P)
1952—Steelers, 24-7 (SF)
1954—49ers, 31-3 (SF)
1958—49ers, 23-20 (SF)
1961—Steelers, 20-10 (P)
1965—49ers, 27-17 (SF)
1968—49ers, 45-28 (P)
1973—Steelers, 37-14 (SF)
1977—Steelers, 27-0 (P)
1978—Steelers, 24-7 (SF)
1981—49ers, 17-14 (P)
1984—Steelers, 20-17 (SF)
1987—Steelers, 30-17 (P)
(Points—Steelers 288, 49ers 243)
PITTSBURGH vs. SEATTLE
Steelers lead series, 4-3
1977—Steelers, 30-20 (P)
1978—Steelers, 21-10 (P)
1981—Seahawks, 24-21 (S)
1982—Seahawks, 16-0 (S)
1983—Steelers, 27-21 (S)
1986—Seahawks, 30-0 (S)
1987—Steelers, 13-9 (P)
(Points—Seahawks 130, Steelers 112)
PITTSBURGH vs. TAMPA BAY
Steelers lead series, 3-0
1976—Steelers, 42-0 (P)
1980—Steelers, 24-21 (TB)
1983—Steelers, 17-12 (P)
(Points—Steelers 83, Buccaneers 33)
***PITTSBURGH vs. **WASHINGTON**
Redskins lead series, 40-27-3
1933—Redskins, 21-6 (P)
Pirates, 16-14 (B)
1934—Redskins, 7-0 (P)
Redskins, 39-0 (B)
1935—Pirates, 6-0 (P)
Redskins, 13-3 (B)
1936—Pirates, 10-0 (P)
Redskins, 30-0 (B)
1937—Redskins, 34-20 (W)
Pirates, 21-13 (P)
1938—Redskins, 7-0 (P)
Redskins, 15-0 (W)
1939—Redskins, 44-14 (W)
Redskins, 21-14 (P)
1940—Redskins, 40-10 (P)
Redskins, 37-10 (W)
1941—Redskins, 24-20 (P)
Redskins, 23-3 (W)
1942—Redskins, 28-14 (W)
Redskins, 14-0 (P)
1945—Redskins, 14-0 (P)
Redskins, 24-0 (W)
1946—Tie, 14-14 (W)
Steelers, 14-7 (P)
1947—Redskins, 27-26 (W)
Steelers, 21-14 (P)
1948—Redskins, 17-14 (W)
Steelers, 10-7 (P)
1949—Redskins, 27-14 (P)
Redskins, 27-14 (W)
1950—Steelers, 26-7 (W)
Redskins, 24-7 (P)
1951—Redskins, 22-7 (P)
Steelers, 20-10 (W)
1952—Redskins, 28-24 (P)
Steelers, 24-23 (W)
1953—Redskins, 17-9 (P)
Steelers, 14-13 (W)
1954—Steelers, 37-7 (P)
Redskins, 17-14 (W)
1955—Redskins, 23-14 (P)
Redskins, 28-17 (W)
1956—Steelers, 30-13 (P)
Steelers, 23-0 (W)
1957—Steelers, 28-7 (P)
Redskins, 10-3 (W)
1958—Steelers, 24-16 (P)
Tie, 14-14 (W)
1959—Redskins, 23-17 (P)
Steelers, 27-6 (W)
1960—Tie, 27-27 (W)
Steelers, 22-10 (P)
1961—Steelers, 20-0 (P)
Steelers, 30-14 (P)
1962—Steelers, 23-21 (P)
Steelers, 27-24 (W)
1963—Steelers, 38-27 (P)
Steelers, 34-28 (W)
1964—Redskins, 30-0 (P)
Steelers, 14-7 (W)
1965—Redskins, 31-3 (P)
Redskins, 35-14 (W)
1966—Redskins, 33-27 (P)
Redskins, 24-10 (W)
1967—Redskins, 15-10 (P)
1968—Redskins, 16-13 (W)
1969—Redskins, 14-7 (P)
1973—Steelers, 21-16 (P)
1979—Steelers, 38-7 (P)
1985—Redskins, 30-23 (P)
(Points—Redskins 1,319, Steelers 1,074)
**Steelers known as Pirates prior to 1941*
***Franchise in Boston prior to 1937*

ST. LOUIS vs. ATLANTA
Cardinals lead series, 7-4;
See Atlanta vs. St. Louis
ST. LOUIS vs. BUFFALO
Cardinals lead series, 3-2;
See Buffalo vs. St. Louis
ST. LOUIS vs. CHICAGO
Bears lead series, 50-25-6;
See Chicago vs. St. Louis
ST. LOUIS vs. CINCINNATI
Bengals lead series, 2-1;
See Cincinnati vs. St. Louis
ST. LOUIS vs. CLEVELAND
Browns lead series, 30-10-3;
See Cleveland vs. St. Louis
ST. LOUIS vs. DALLAS
Cowboys lead series, 32-18-1;
See Dallas vs. St. Louis
ST. LOUIS vs. DENVER
Broncos lead series, 1-0-1;
See Denver vs. St. Louis
ST. LOUIS vs. DETROIT
Lions lead series, 25-15-5;
See Detroit vs. St. Louis
ST. LOUIS vs. GREEN BAY
Packers lead series, 38-21-4;
See Green Bay vs. St. Louis
ST. LOUIS vs. HOUSTON
Cardinals lead series, 3-1;
See Houston vs. St. Louis
ST. LOUIS vs. INDIANAPOLIS
Cardinals lead series, 5-4;
See Indianapolis vs. St. Louis
ST. LOUIS vs. KANSAS CITY
Chiefs lead series, 3-1-1;
See Kansas City vs. St. Louis
ST. LOUIS vs. L.A. RAIDERS
Series tied, 1-1;
See L.A. Raiders vs. St. Louis
ST. LOUIS vs. L.A. RAMS
Rams lead series, 22-15-2;
See L.A. Rams vs. St. Louis
ST. LOUIS vs. MIAMI
Dolphins lead series, 5-0;
See Miami vs. St. Louis
ST. LOUIS vs. MINNESOTA
Cardinals lead series, 7-3;
See Minnesota vs. St. Louis
ST. LOUIS vs. NEW ENGLAND
Cardinals lead series, 4-1;
See New England vs. St. Louis
ST. LOUIS vs. NEW ORLEANS
Cardinals lead series, 10-5;
See New Orleans vs. St. Louis
ST. LOUIS vs. N.Y. GIANTS
Giants lead series, 56-32-2;
See N.Y. Giants vs. St. Louis
ST. LOUIS vs. N.Y. JETS
Cardinals lead series, 2-1;
See N.Y. Jets vs. St. Louis
ST. LOUIS vs. PHILADELPHIA
Cardinals lead series, 42-35-5;
See Philadelphia vs. St. Louis
ST. LOUIS vs. PITTSBURGH
Steelers lead series, 29-20-3;
See Pittsburgh vs. St. Louis
ST. LOUIS vs. SAN DIEGO
Chargers lead series, 3-1
1971—Chargers, 20-17 (SD)
1976—Chargers, 43-24 (SD)
1983—Cardinals, 44-14 (StL)
1987—Chargers, 28-24 (SD)
(Points—Cardinals 109, Chargers 105)
***ST. LOUIS vs. SAN FRANCISCO**
49ers lead series, 8-7
1951—Cardinals, 27-21 (SF)
1957—Cardinals, 20-10 (SF)
1962—49ers, 24-17 (StL)
1964—Cardinals, 23-13 (SF)
1968—49ers, 35-17 (SF)
1971—49ers, 26-14 (StL)
1974—Cardinals, 34-9 (SF)
1976—Cardinals, 23-20 (StL) OT
1978—Cardinals, 16-10 (SF)
1979—Cardinals, 13-10 (StL)
1980—49ers, 24-21 (SF) OT
1982—49ers, 31-20 (StL)
1983—49ers, 42-27 (StL)
1986—49ers, 43-17 (SF)
1987—49ers, 34-28 (SF)
(Points—49ers 352, Cardinals 317)
**Team in Chicago prior to 1960*
ST. LOUIS vs. SEATTLE
Cardinals lead series, 2-0
1976—Cardinals, 30-24 (S)
1983—Cardinals, 33-28 (StL)
(Points—Cardinals 63, Seahawks 52)
ST. LOUIS vs. TAMPA BAY
Cardinals lead series, 5-3
1977—Buccaneers, 17-7 (TB)
1981—Buccaneers, 20-10 (TB)
1983—Cardinals, 34-27 (TB)
1985—Buccaneers, 16-0 (TB)
1986—Cardinals, 30-19 (TB)
Cardinals, 21-17 (StL)
1987—Cardinals, 31-28 (StL)
Cardinals, 31-14 (TB)
(Points—Cardinals 164, Buccaneers 158)
***ST. LOUIS vs. **WASHINGTON**
Redskins lead series, 53-32-2
1932—Cardinals, 9-0 (B)
Braves, 8-6 (C)
1933—Redskins, 10-0 (C)
Tie, 0-0 (B)
1934—Redskins, 9-0 (B)
1935—Cardinals, 6-0 (B)
1936—Redskins, 13-10 (B)
1937—Cardinals, 21-14 (W)
1939—Redskins, 28-7 (W)
1940—Redskins, 28-21 (W)
1942—Redskins, 28-0 (W)
1943—Redskins, 13-7 (W)
1945—Redskins, 24-21 (W)
1947—Redskins, 45-21 (W)
1949—Cardinals, 38-7 (C)
1950—Cardinals, 38-28 (W)
1951—Redskins, 7-3 (C)
Redskins, 20-17 (W)
1952—Redskins, 23-7 (C)
Cardinals, 17-6 (W)
1953—Redskins, 24-13 (C)
Redskins, 28-17 (W)
1954—Cardinals, 38-16 (C)
Redskins, 37-20 (W)
1955—Cardinals, 24-10 (W)
Redskins, 31-0 (C)
1956—Cardinals, 31-3 (W)
Redskins, 17-14 (C)
1957—Redskins, 37-14 (C)
Cardinals, 44-14 (W)
1958—Cardinals, 37-10 (C)
Redskins, 45-31 (W)
1959—Cardinals, 49-21 (C)
Redskins, 23-14 (W)
1960—Cardinals, 44-7 (StL)
Cardinals, 26-14 (W)
1961—Cardinals, 24-0 (W)
Cardinals, 38-24 (StL)
1962—Redskins, 24-14 (W)
Tie, 17-17 (StL)
1963—Cardinals, 21-7 (W)
Cardinals, 24-20 (StL)
1964—Cardinals, 23-17 (W)
Cardinals, 38-24 (StL)
1965—Cardinals, 37-16 (W)
Redskins, 24-20 (StL)
1966—Cardinals, 23-7 (StL)
Redskins, 26-20 (W)
1967—Cardinals, 27-21 (W)
1968—Cardinals, 41-14 (StL)
1969—Redskins, 33-17 (W)
1970—Cardinals, 27-17 (StL)
Redskins, 28-27 (W)
1971—Redskins, 24-17 (StL)
Redskins, 20-0 (W)
1972—Redskins, 24-10 (W)
Redskins, 33-3 (StL)
1973—Cardinals, 34-27 (StL)
Redskins, 31-13 (W)
1974—Cardinals, 17-10 (W)
Cardinals, 23-20 (StL)
1975—Redskins, 27-17 (W)
Cardinals, 20-17 (StL) OT
1976—Redskins, 20-10 (W)
Redskins, 16-10 (StL)
1977—Redskins, 24-14 (W)

Redskins, 26-20 (StL)
1978—Redskins, 28-10 (StL)
Cardinals, 27-17 (W)
1979—Redskins, 17-7 (StL)
Redskins, 30-28 (W)
1980—Redskins, 23-0 (W)
Redskins, 31-7 (StL)
1981—Cardinals, 40-30 (StL)
Redskins, 42-21 (W)
1982—Redskins, 12-7 (StL)
Redskins, 28-0 (W)
1983—Redskins, 38-14 (StL)
Redskins, 45-7 (W)
1984—Cardinals, 26-24 (StL)
Redskins, 29-27 (W)
1985—Redskins, 27-10 (W)
Redskins, 27-16 (StL)
1986—Redskins, 28-21 (W)
Redskins, 20-17 (StL)
1987—Redskins, 28-21 (W)
Redskins, 34-17 (StL)
(Points—Redskins 1,844, Cardinals 1,634)
Team in Chicago prior to 1960
**Team in Boston prior to 1937 and known as Braves prior to 1933*

SAN DIEGO vs. ATLANTA
Falcons lead series, 2-0;
See Atlanta vs. San Diego
SAN DIEGO vs. BUFFALO
Chargers lead series, 17-9-2;
See Buffalo vs. San Diego
SAN DIEGO vs. CHICAGO
Chargers lead series, 4-1;
See Chicago vs. San Diego
SAN DIEGO vs. CINCINNATI
Chargers lead series, 11-7;
See Cincinnati vs. San Diego
SAN DIEGO vs. CLEVELAND
Chargers lead series, 6-5-1;
See Cleveland vs. San Diego
SAN DIEGO vs. DALLAS
Cowboys lead series, 3-1;
See Dallas vs. San Diego
SAN DIEGO vs. DENVER
Chargers lead series, 28-27-1;
See Denver vs. San Diego
SAN DIEGO vs. DETROIT
Lions lead series, 3-2;
See Detroit vs. San Diego
SAN DIEGO vs. GREEN BAY
Packers lead series, 3-1;
See Green Bay vs. San Diego
SAN DIEGO vs. HOUSTON
Chargers lead series, 17-13-1;
See Houston vs. San Diego
SAN DIEGO vs. INDIANAPOLIS
Chargers lead series, 6-3;
See Indianapolis vs. San Diego
SAN DIEGO vs. KANSAS CITY
Series tied, 27-27-1;
See Kansas City vs. San Diego
SAN DIEGO vs. L.A. RAIDERS
Raiders lead series, 35-20-2;
See L.A. Raiders vs. San Diego
SAN DIEGO vs. L.A. RAMS
Rams lead series, 2-1;
See L.A. Rams vs. San Diego
SAN DIEGO vs. MIAMI
Chargers lead series, 9-5;
See Miami vs. San Diego
SAN DIEGO vs. MINNESOTA
Series tied, 3-3;
See Minnesota vs. San Diego
SAN DIEGO vs. NEW ENGLAND
Patriots lead series, 13-12-2;
See New England vs. San Diego
SAN DIEGO vs. NEW ORLEANS
Chargers lead series, 3-0;
See New Orleans vs. San Diego
SAN DIEGO vs. N.Y. GIANTS
Giants lead series, 3-2;
See N.Y. Giants vs. San Diego
SAN DIEGO vs. N.Y. JETS
Chargers lead series, 14-7-1;
See N.Y. Jets vs. San Diego
SAN DIEGO vs. PHILADELPHIA
Series tied, 2-2;
See Philadelphia vs. San Diego
SAN DIEGO vs. PITTSBURGH
Steelers lead series, 9-4;
See Pittsburgh vs. San Diego
SAN DIEGO vs. ST. LOUIS
Chargers lead series, 3-1;
See St. Louis vs. San Diego
SAN DIEGO vs. SAN FRANCISCO
Chargers lead series, 3-1
1972—49ers, 34-3 (SF)
1976—Chargers, 13-7 (SD) OT
1979—Chargers, 31-9 (SD)
1982—Chargers, 41-37 (SF)
(Points—Chargers, 88, 49ers 87)
SAN DIEGO vs. SEATTLE
Series tied, 9-9
1977—Chargers, 30-28 (S)
1978—Chargers, 24-20 (S)
Chargers, 37-10 (SD)
1979—Chargers, 33-16 (S)
Chargers, 20-10 (SD)
1980—Chargers, 34-13 (S)
Chargers, 21-14 (SD)
1981—Chargers, 24-10 (SD)
Seahawks, 44-23 (S)
1983—Seahawks, 34-31 (S)
Chargers, 28-21 (SD)
1984—Seahawks, 31-17 (S)
Seahawks, 24-0 (SD)
1985—Seahawks, 49-35 (SD)
Seahawks, 26-21 (S)
1986—Seahawks, 33-7 (S)
Seahawks, 34-24 (SD)
1987—Seahawks, 34-3 (S)
(Points—Seahawks 451, Chargers 412)
SAN DIEGO vs. TAMPA BAY
Chargers lead series, 3-0
1976—Chargers, 23-0 (TB)
1981—Chargers, 24-23 (TB)
1987—Chargers, 17-13 (TB)
(Points—Chargers 64, Buccaneers 36)
SAN DIEGO vs. WASHINGTON
Redskins lead series, 4-0
1973—Redskins, 38-0 (W)
1980—Redskins, 40-17 (W)
1983—Redskins, 27-24 (SD)
1986—Redskins, 30-27 (SD)
(Points—Redskins 135, Chargers 68)

SAN FRANCISCO vs. ATLANTA
49ers lead series, 24-17-1;
See Atlanta vs. San Francisco
SAN FRANCISCO vs. BUFFALO
Bills lead series, 2-1;
See Buffalo vs. San Francisco
SAN FRANCISCO vs. CHICAGO
Series tied, 24-24-1;
See Chicago vs. San Francisco
SAN FRANCISCO vs. CINCINNATI
49ers lead series, 5-1;
See Cincinnati vs. San Francisco
SAN FRANCISCO vs. CLEVELAND
Browns lead series, 8-5;
See Cleveland vs. San Francisco
SAN FRANCISCO vs. DALLAS
Series tied, 8-8-1;
See Dallas vs. San Francisco
SAN FRANCISCO vs. DENVER
Broncos lead series, 3-2;
See Denver vs. San Francisco
SAN FRANCISCO vs. DETROIT
Lions lead series, 26-23-1;
See Detroit vs. San Francisco
SAN FRANCISCO vs. GREEN BAY
49ers lead series, 24-20-1;
See Green Bay vs. San Francisco
SAN FRANCISCO vs. HOUSTON
49ers lead series, 4-2;
See Houston vs. San Francisco
SAN FRANCISCO vs. INDIANAPOLIS
Colts lead series, 21-15;
See Indianapolis vs. San Francisco
SAN FRANCISCO vs. KANSAS CITY
49ers lead series, 3-1;
See Kansas City vs. San Francisco
SAN FRANCISCO vs. L.A RAIDERS
Raiders lead series, 3-2;
See L.A. Raiders vs. San Francisco
SAN FRANCISCO vs. L.A. RAMS
Rams lead series, 45-29-2;
See L.A. Rams vs. San Francisco
SAN FRANCISCO vs. MIAMI
Dolphins lead series, 4-2;
See Miami vs. San Francisco
SAN FRANCISCO vs. MINNESOTA
Vikings lead series, 15-12-1;
See Minnesota vs. San Francisco
SAN FRANCISCO vs. NEW ENGLAND
49ers lead series, 4-1;
See New England vs. San Francisco
SAN FRANCISCO vs. NEW ORLEANS
49ers lead series, 24-11-2;
See New Orleans vs. San Francisco
SAN FRANCISCO vs. N.Y. GIANTS
Giants lead series, 12-8;
See N.Y. Giants vs. San Francisco
SAN FRANCISCO vs. N.Y. JETS
49ers lead series, 4-1;
See N.Y. Jets vs. San Francisco
SAN FRANCISCO vs. PHILADELPHIA
49ers lead series, 10-4-1;
See Philadelphia vs. San Francisco
SAN FRANCISCO vs. PITTSBURGH
Steelers lead series, 7-6;
See Pittsburgh vs. San Francisco
SAN FRANCISCO vs. ST. LOUIS
49ers lead series, 8-7;
See St. Louis vs. San Francisco
SAN FRANCISCO vs. SAN DIEGO
Chargers lead series, 3-1;
See San Diego vs. San Francisco
SAN FRANCISCO vs. SEATTLE
49ers lead series, 2-1
1976—49ers, 37-21 (S)
1979—Seahawks, 35-24 (SF)
1985—49ers, 19-6 (SF)
(Points—49ers 80, Seahawks 62)
SAN FRANCISCO vs. TAMPA BAY
49ers lead series, 7-1
1977—49ers, 20-10 (SF)
1978—49ers, 6-3 (SF)
1979—49ers, 23-7 (SF)
1980—Buccaneers, 24-23 (SF)
1983—49ers, 35-21 (SF)
1984—49ers, 24-17 (SF)
1986—49ers, 31-7 (TB)
1987—49ers, 24-10 (TB)
(Points—49ers 186, Buccaneers 99)
SAN FRANCISCO vs. WASHINGTON
49ers lead series, 8-7-1
1952—49ers, 23-17 (W)
1954—49ers, 41-7 (SF)
1955—Redskins, 7-0 (W)
1961—49ers, 35-3 (SF)
1967—Redskins, 31-28 (W)
1969—Tie, 17-17 (SF)
1970—49ers, 26-17 (SF)
1971—*49ers, 24-20 (SF)
1973—Redskins, 33-9 (W)
1976—Redskins, 24-21 (SF)
1978—Redskins, 38-20 (W)
1981—49ers, 30-17 (W)
1983—**Redskins, 24-21 (W)
1984—49ers, 37-31 (SF)
1985—49ers, 35-8 (W)
1986—Redskins, 14-6 (W)
(Points—49ers 373, Redskins 308)
NFC Divisional Playoff
***NFC Championship*

SEATTLE vs. ATLANTA
Seahawks lead series, 3-0;
See Atlanta vs. Seattle
SEATTLE vs. BUFFALO
Seahawks lead series, 2-0;
See Buffalo vs. Seattle
SEATTLE vs. CHICAGO
Seahawks lead series, 4-1;
See Chicago vs. Seattle
SEATTLE vs. CINCINNATI
Bengals lead series, 5-2;
See Cincinnati vs. Seattle
SEATTLE vs. CLEVELAND
Seahawks lead series, 7-2;
See Cleveland vs. Seattle
SEATTLE vs. DALLAS
Cowboys lead series, 3-1;
See Dallas vs. Seattle
SEATTLE vs. DENVER
Broncos lead series, 13-9;
See Denver vs. Seattle
SEATTLE vs. DETROIT
Seahawks lead series, 3-1;
See Detroit vs. Seattle
SEATTLE vs. GREEN BAY
Packers lead series, 3-2;
See Green Bay vs. Seattle
SEATTLE vs. HOUSTON
Oilers lead series, 4-2;
See Houston vs. Seattle
SEATTLE vs. INDIANAPOLIS
Colts lead series, 2-0;
See Indianapolis vs. Seattle
SEATTLE vs. KANSAS CITY
Chiefs lead series, 10-9;
See Kansas City vs. Seattle
SEATTLE vs. L.A. RAIDERS
Series tied, 11-11;
See L.A. Raiders vs. Seattle
SEATTLE vs. L.A. RAMS
Rams lead series, 3-0;
See L.A. Rams vs. Seattle
SEATTLE vs. MIAMI
Dolphins lead series, 3-2;
See Miami vs. Seattle
SEATTLE vs. MINNESOTA
Seahawks lead series, 3-1;
See Minnesota vs. Seattle
SEATTLE vs. NEW ENGLAND
Patriots lead series, 5-2;
See New England vs. Seattle
SEATTLE vs. NEW ORLEANS
Seahawks lead series, 2-1;
See New Orleans vs. Seattle
SEATTLE vs. N.Y. GIANTS
Giants lead series, 3-2;
See N.Y. Giants vs. Seattle
SEATTLE vs. N.Y. JETS
Seahawks lead series, 7-3;
See N.Y. Jets vs. Seattle
SEATTLE vs. PHILADELPHIA
Eagles lead series, 2-1;
See Philadelphia vs. Seattle
SEATTLE vs. PITTSBURGH
Steelers lead series, 4-3;
See Pittsburgh vs. Seattle
SEATTLE vs. ST. LOUIS
Cardinals lead series, 2-0;
See St. Louis vs. Seattle
SEATTLE vs. SAN DIEGO
Series tied, 9-9;
See San Diego vs. Seattle
SEATTLE vs. SAN FRANCISCO
49ers lead series, 2-1;
See San Francisco vs. Seattle
SEATTLE vs. TAMPA BAY
Seahawks lead series, 2-0
1976—Seahawks, 13-10 (TB)
1977—Seahawks, 30-23 (S)
(Points—Seahawks 43, Buccaneers 33)
SEATTLE vs. WASHINGTON
Redskins lead series, 3-1
1976—Redskins, 31-7 (W)
1980—Seahawks, 14-0 (W)
1983—Redskins, 27-17 (S)
1986—Redskins, 19-14 (W)
(Points—Redskins 77, Seahawks 52)

TAMPA BAY vs. ATLANTA
Buccaneers lead series, 4-3;
See Atlanta vs. Tampa Bay
TAMPA BAY vs. BUFFALO
Buccaneers lead series, 3-1;
See Buffalo vs. Tampa Bay
TAMPA BAY vs. CHICAGO
Bears lead series, 16-4;
See Chicago vs. Tampa Bay
TAMPA BAY vs. CINCINNATI
Bengals lead series, 2-1;
See Cincinnati vs. Tampa Bay
TAMPA BAY vs. CLEVELAND
Browns lead series, 3-0;
See Cleveland vs. Tampa Bay
TAMPA BAY vs. DALLAS
Cowboys lead series, 6-0;
See Dallas vs. Tampa Bay
TAMPA BAY vs. DENVER
Broncos lead series, 2-0;
See Denver vs. Tampa Bay
TAMPA BAY vs. DETROIT
Lions lead series, 11-9;
See Detroit vs. Tampa Bay
TAMPA BAY vs. GREEN BAY
Packers lead series, 10-7-1;
See Green Bay vs. Tampa Bay
TAMPA BAY vs. HOUSTON
Oilers lead series, 2-1;
See Houston vs. Tampa Bay
TAMPA BAY vs. INDIANAPOLIS
Colts lead series, 3-1;
See Indianapolis vs. Tampa Bay
TAMPA BAY vs. KANSAS CITY
Chiefs lead series, 4-2;
See Kansas City vs. Tampa Bay
TAMPA BAY vs. L.A RAIDERS
Raiders lead series, 2-0;
See L.A. Raiders vs. Tampa Bay
TAMPA BAY vs. L.A. RAMS
Rams lead series, 7-2;
See L.A. Rams vs. Tampa Bay
TAMPA BAY vs. MIAMI
Dolphins lead series, 2-1;
See Miami vs. Tampa Bay
TAMPA BAY vs. MINNESOTA
Vikings lead series, 14-6;
See Minnesota vs. Tampa Bay
TAMPA BAY vs. NEW ENGLAND
Patriots lead series, 2-0;
See New England vs. Tampa Bay
TAMPA BAY vs. NEW ORLEANS
Saints lead series, 7-3;
See New Orleans vs. Tampa Bay
TAMPA BAY vs. N.Y. GIANTS
Giants lead series, 6-3;
See N.Y. Giants vs. Tampa Bay
TAMPA BAY vs. N.Y. JETS
Jets lead series, 3-1;
See N.Y. Jets vs. Tampa Bay
TAMPA BAY vs. PHILADELPHIA
Eagles lead series, 2-1;
See Philadelphia vs. Tampa Bay
TAMPA BAY vs. PITTSBURGH
Steelers lead series, 3-0;
See Pittsburgh vs. Tampa Bay
TAMPA BAY vs. ST. LOUIS
Cardinals lead series, 5-3;
See St. Louis vs. Tampa Bay
TAMPA BAY vs. SAN DIEGO
Chargers lead series, 3-0;
See San Diego vs. Tampa Bay
TAMPA BAY vs. SAN FRANCISCO
49ers lead series, 7-1;
See San Francisco vs. Tampa Bay

TAMPA BAY vs. SEATTLE
Seahawks lead series, 2-0;
See Seattle vs. Tampa Bay
TAMPA BAY vs. WASHINGTON
Redskins lead series, 2-0
1977—Redskins, 10-0 (TB)
1982—Redskins, 21-13 (TB)
(Points—Redskins 31, Buccaneers 13)

WASHINGTON vs. ATLANTA
Redskins lead series, 9-3-1;
See Atlanta vs. Washington
WASHINGTON vs. BUFFALO
Redskins lead series, 3-2;
See Buffalo vs. Washington
WASHINGTON vs. CHICAGO
Bears lead series, 20-13-1;
See Chicago vs. Washington
WASHINGTON vs. CINCINNATI
Redskins lead series, 3-1;
See Cincinnati vs. Washington
WASHINGTON vs. CLEVELAND
Browns lead series, 31-8-1;
See Cleveland vs. Washington
WASHINGTON vs. DALLAS
Cowboys lead series, 31-23-2;
See Dallas vs. Washington
WASHINGTON vs. DENVER
Redskins lead series, 3-2;
See Denver vs. Washington
WASHINGTON vs. DETROIT
Redskins lead series, 20-8;
See Detroit vs. Washington
WASHINGTON vs. GREEN BAY
Packers lead series, 14-12-1;
See Green Bay vs. Washington
WASHINGTON vs. HOUSTON
Series tied, 2-2;
See Houston vs. Washington
WASHINGTON vs. INDIANAPOLIS
Colts lead series, 15-6;
See Indianapolis vs. Washington
WASHINGTON vs. KANSAS CITY
Chiefs lead series, 2-1;
See Kansas City vs. Washington
WASHINGTON vs. L.A. RAIDERS
Raiders lead series, 4-2;
See L.A. Raiders vs. Washington
WASHINGTON vs. L.A. RAMS
Redskins lead series, 15-6-1;
See L.A. Rams vs. Washington
WASHINGTON vs. MIAMI
Dolphins lead series, 5-2;
See Miami vs. Washington
WASHINGTON vs. MINNESOTA
Redskins lead series, 7-5;
See Minnesota vs. Washington
WASHINGTON vs. NEW ENGLAND
Redskins lead series, 3-1;
See New England vs. Washington
WASHINGTON vs. NEW ORLEANS
Redskins lead series, 8-4;
See New Orleans vs. Washington
WASHINGTON vs. N.Y. GIANTS
Giants lead series, 61-48-3;
See N.Y. Giants vs. Washington
WASHINGTON vs. N.Y. JETS
Redskins lead series, 4-0;
See N.Y. Jets vs. Washington
WASHINGTON vs. PHILADELPHIA
Redskins lead series, 60-40-5;
See Philadelphia vs. Washington
WASHINGTON vs. PITTSBURGH
Redskins lead series, 40-27-3;
See Pittsburgh vs. Washington
WASHINGTON vs. ST. LOUIS
Redskins lead series, 53-32-2;
See St. Louis vs. Washington
WASHINGTON vs. SAN DIEGO
Redskins lead series, 4-0;
See San Diego vs. Washington
WASHINGTON vs. SAN FRANCISCO
49ers lead series, 8-7-1;
See San Francisco vs. Washington
WASHINGTON vs. SEATTLE
Redskins lead series, 3-1;
See Seattle vs. Washington
WASHINGTON vs. TAMPA BAY
Redskins lead series, 2-0;
See Tampa Bay vs. Washington

Results

Season	Date	Winner (Share)	Loser (Share)	Score	Site	Attendance
XXII	1-31-88	Washington ($36,000)	Denver ($18,000)	42-10	San Diego	73,302
XXI	1-25-87	N.Y. Giants ($36,000)	Denver ($18,000)	39-20	Pasadena	101,063
XX	1-26-86	Chicago ($36,000)	New England ($18,000)	46-10	New Orleans	73,818
XIX	1-20-85	San Francisco ($36,000)	Miami ($18,000)	38-16	Stanford	84,059
XVIII	1-22-84	L.A. Raiders ($36,000)	Washington ($18,000)	38-9	Tampa	72,920
XVII	1-30-83	Washington ($36,000)	Miami ($18,000)	27-17	Pasadena	103,667
XVI	1-24-82	San Francisco ($18,000)	Cincinnati ($9,000)	26-21	Pontiac	81,270
XV	1-25-81	Oakland ($18,000)	Philadelphia ($9,000)	27-10	New Orleans	76,135
XIV	1-20-80	Pittsburgh ($18,000)	Los Angeles ($9,000)	31-19	Pasadena	103,985
XIII	1-21-79	Pittsburgh ($18,000)	Dallas ($9,000)	35-31	Miami	79,484
XII	1-15-78	Dallas ($18,000)	Denver ($9,000)	27-10	New Orleans	75,583
XI	1-9-77	Oakland ($15,000)	Minnesota ($7,500)	32-14	Pasadena	103,438
X	1-18-76	Pittsburgh ($15,000)	Dallas ($7,500)	21-17	Miami	80,187
IX	1-12-75	Pittsburgh ($15,000)	Minnesota ($7,500)	16-6	New Orleans	80,997
VIII	1-13-74	Miami ($15,000)	Minnesota ($7,500)	24-7	Houston	71,882
VII	1-14-73	Miami ($15,000)	Washington ($7,500)	14-7	Los Angeles	90,182
VI	1-16-72	Dallas ($15,000)	Miami ($7,500)	24-3	New Orleans	81,023
V	1-17-71	Baltimore ($15,000)	Miami ($7,500)	16-13	Miami	79,204
IV	1-11-70	Kansas City ($15,000)	Miami ($7,500)	23-7	New Orleans	80,562
III	1-12-69	N.Y. Jets ($15,000)	Baltimore ($7,500)	16-7	Miami	75,389
II	1-14-68	Green Bay ($15,000)	Oakland ($7,500)	33-14	Miami	75,546
I	1-15-67	Green Bay ($15,000)	Kansas City ($7,500)	35-10	Los Angeles	61,946

Super Bowl Composite Standings

	W	L	Pct.	Pts.	OP
Pittsburgh Steelers	4	0	1.000	103	73
Green Bay Packers	2	0	1.000	68	24
San Francisco 49ers	2	0	1.000	64	37
Chicago Bears	1	0	1.000	46	10
New York Giants	1	0	1.000	39	20
New York Jets	1	0	1.000	16	7
Oakland/L.A. Raiders	3	1	.750	111	66
Washington Redskins	2	2	.500	85	79
Baltimore Colts	1	1	.500	23	29
Kansas City Chiefs	1	1	.500	33	42
Dallas Cowboys	2	3	.400	112	85
Miami Dolphins	2	3	.400	74	103
Cincinnati Bengals	0	1	.000	21	26
Los Angeles Rams	0	1	.000	19	31
New England Patriots	0	1	.000	10	46
Philadelphia Eagles	0	1	.000	10	27
Denver Broncos	0	3	.000	40	108
Minnesota Vikings	0	4	.000	34	95

Past Super Bowl Most Valuable Players

(Selected by Sport Magazine)

Super Bowl I — QB Bart Starr, Green Bay
Super Bowl II — QB Bart Starr, Green Bay
Super Bowl III — QB Joe Namath, New York Jets
Super Bowl IV — QB Len Dawson, Kansas City
Super Bowl V — LB Chuck Howley, Dallas
Super Bowl VI — QB Roger Staubach, Dallas
Super Bowl VII — S Jake Scott, Miami
Super Bowl VIII — RB Larry Csonka, Miami
Super Bowl IX — RB Franco Harris, Pittsburgh
Super Bowl X — WR Lynn Swann, Pittsburgh
Super Bowl XI — WR Fred Biletnikoff, Oakland
Super Bowl XII — DT Randy White and DE Harvey Martin, Dallas
Super Bowl XIII — QB Terry Bradshaw, Pittsburgh
Super Bowl XIV — QB Terry Bradshaw, Pittsburgh
Super Bowl XV — QB Jim Plunkett, Oakland
Super Bowl XVI — QB Joe Montana, San Francisco
Super Bowl XVII — RB John Riggins, Washington
Super Bowl XVIII — RB Marcus Allen, Los Angeles Raiders
Super Bowl XIX — QB Joe Montana, San Francisco
Super Bowl XX — DE Richard Dent, Chicago
Super Bowl XXI — QB Phil Simms, New York Giants
Super Bowl XXII — QB Doug Williams, Washington

Super Bowl XXII

San Diego Jack Murphy Stadium, San Diego, California January 31, 1988
Attendance: 73,302

WASHINGTON 42, DENVER 10—NFC champion Washington won Super Bowl XXII and its second NFL championship of the 1980s with a 42-10 decision over AFC champion Denver. The Redskins, who also won Super Bowl XVII, enjoyed a record-setting second quarter en route to the victory. The Broncos broke in front 10-0 when quarterback John Elway threw a 56-yard touchdown pass to wide receiver Ricky Nattiel on the Broncos' first play from scrimmage. Following a Washington punt, Denver's Rich Karlis kicked a 24-yard field goal to cap a seven-play, 61-yard scoring drive. The Redskins then erupted for 35 points on five straight possessions in the second period and coasted thereafter. The 35 points established an NFL postseason mark for most points scored in a period, bettering the previous total of 21 by San Francisco in Super Bowl XIX and Chicago in Super Bowl XX. Redskins quarterback Doug Williams led the second-period explosion by throwing a Super Bowl record-tying four touchdown passes, including 80- and 50-yarders to wide receiver Ricky Sanders, a 27-yarder to wide receiver Gary Clark, and an 8-yarder to tight end Clint Didier. Washington scored five touchdowns in 18 plays with total time of possession of only 5:47. Overall, Williams completed 18 of 29 passes for 340 yards and was named the game's most valuable player. His pass-yardage total eclipsed the previous Super Bowl record of 331 yards by Joe Montana of San Francisco in Super Bowl XIX. Sanders ended with 193 yards on eight catches, breaking the previous Super Bowl yardage record of 161 yards by Lynn Swann of Pittsburgh in Game X. Rookie running back Timmy Smith was the game's leading rusher with 22 carries for a Super Bowl record 204 yards, breaking the previous mark of 191 yards by Marcus Allen of the Raiders in Game XVIII. Smith also scored twice on runs of 58 and 5 yards. Washington's six touchdowns and 602 total yards gained also set Super Bowl records. Redskins cornerback Barry Wilburn had two of the team's three interceptions, and free safety Alvin Walton had two of Washington's five sacks.

Washington (42)	Offense	Denver (10)
Gary Clark	WR	Mark Jackson
Joe Jacoby	LT	Dave Studdard
Raleigh McKenzie	LG	Keith Bishop
Jeff Bostic	C	Mike Freeman
R.C. Thielemann	RG	Stefan Humphries
Mark May	RT	Ken Lanier
Clint Didier	TE	Clarence Kay
Don Warren	TE-WR	Ricky Nattiel
Doug Williams	QB	John Elway
Timmy Smith	RB	Sammy Winder
Ricky Sanders	WR-RB	Gene Lang
	Defense	
Charles Mann	LE	Andre Townsend
Dave Butz	LT-NT	Greg Kragen
Darryl Grant	RT-RE	Rulon Jones
Dexter Manley	RE-LOLB	Simon Fletcher
Mel Kaufman	LLB-LILB	Karl Mecklenburg
Neal Olkewicz	MLB-RILB	Ricky Hunley
Monte Coleman	RLB-ROLB	Jim Ryan
Darrell Green	LCB	Mark Haynes
Todd Bowles	RCB	Steve Wilson
Barry Wilburn	SS	Dennis Smith
Alvin Walton	FS	Tony Lilly

Substitutions

Washington—Offense: K—Ali Haji-Sheikh. P—Steve Cox. QB—Jay Schroeder. RB—Reggie Branch, Kelvin Bryant, Keith Griffin, George Rogers. WR—Art Monk, Eric Yarber. TE—Terry Orr, Anthony Jones. G—Rick Kehr. T—Russ Grimm. Defense: E—Markus Koch, Steve Hamilton. T—Dean Hamel. LB—Ravin Caldwell, Kurt Gouviea, Rich Milot. CB—Brian Davis, Clarence Vaughn, Dennis Woodberry. S—Vernon Dean.

Denver—Offense: K—Rich Karlis. P—Mike Horan. QB—Gary Kubiak. RB—Ken Bell, Tony Boddie, Steve Sewell. WR—Vance Johnson, Steve Watson. TE—Bobby Micho, Orson Mobley. T—Keith Kartz. Defense: E—Walt Bowyer, Freddie Gilbert. LB—Mike Brooks, Rick Dennison, Bruce Klostermann, Tim Lucas. CB—Kevin Clark, Bruce Plummer. S—Tyrone Braxton, Jeremiah Castille, Randy Robbins. DNP: C—Larry Lee.

Officials

Referee—Bob McElwee. Umpire—Al Conway. Line Judge—Jack Fette. Head Linesman—Dale Hamer. Back Judge—Al Jury. Field Judge—Johnny Grier. Side Judge—Don Wedge.

Scoring

Washington (NFC)	0	35	0	7	— 42
Denver (AFC)	10	0	0	0	— 10

Den —Nattiel 56 pass from Elway (Karlis kick)
Den —FG Karlis 24
Wash—Sanders 80 pass from Williams (Haji-Sheikh kick)
Wash—Clark 27 pass from Williams (Haji-Sheikh kick)
Wash—Smith 58 run (Haji-Sheikh kick)
Wash—Sanders 50 pass from Williams (Haji-Sheikh kick)
Wash—Didier 8 pass from Williams (Haji-Sheikh kick)
Wash—Smith 4 run (Haji-Sheikh kick)

Team Statistics

	Washington	Denver
Total First Downs	25	18
First Downs Rushing	13	6
First Downs Passing	11	10
First Downs Penalty	1	2
Total Net Yardage	602	327
Total Offensive Plays	72	61
Average Gain per Offensive Play	8.4	5.4
Rushes	40	17
Yards Gained Rushing (net)	280	97
Average Yards per Rush	7.0	5.7
Passes Attempted	30	39
Passes Completed	18	15
Had Intercepted	1	3
Tackled Attempting to Pass	2	5
Yards Lost Attempting to Pass	18	50
Yards Gained Passing (net)	322	230
Punts	4	7
Average Distance	37.5	36.1
Punt Returns	1	2
Punt Return Yardage	0	18
Kickoff Returns	3	5
Kickoff Return Yardage	46	88
Interception Return Yardage	11	0
Total Return Yardage	57	106
Fumbles	1	0
Own Fumbles Recovered	1	0
Opponents Fumbles Recovered	0	0
Penalties	6	5
Yards Penalized	65	26
Total Points Scored	42	10
Touchdowns	6	1
Touchdowns Rushing	2	0
Touchdowns Passing	4	1
Touchdowns Returns	0	0
Extra Points	6	1
Field Goals	0	1
Field Goals Attempted	1	2
Safeties	0	0
Third Down Efficiency	9/15	2/12
Fourth Down Efficiency	0/0	0/0
Time of Possession	35:15	24:45

Individual Statistics

Rushing

Washington	No.	Yds.	LG	TD
Smith	22	204	58t	2
Bryant	8	38	15	0
Clark	1	25	25	0
Rogers	5	17	5	0
Griffin	1	2	2	0
Williams	2	−2	−1	0
Sanders	1	−4	−4	0
Denver	**No.**	**Yds.**	**LG**	**TD**
Lang	5	38	13	0
Elway	3	32	21	0
Winder	8	30	13	0
Sewell	1	−3	−3	0

Passing

Wash.	Att.	Comp.	Yds.	TD	Int.
Williams	29	18	340	4	1
Schroeder	1	0	0	0	0
Denver	**Att.**	**Comp.**	**Yds.**	**TD**	**Int.**
Elway	38	14	257	1	3
Sewell	1	1	23	0	0

Receiving

Washington	No.	Yds.	LG	TD
Sanders	9	193	80t	2
Clark	3	55	27t	1
Warren	2	15	9	0
Monk	1	40	40	0
Bryant	1	20	20	0
Smith	1	9	9	0
Didier	1	8	8t	1
Denver	**No.**	**Yds.**	**LG**	**TD**
Jackson	4	76	32	0
Sewell	4	41	18	0
Nattiel	2	69	56t	1
Kay	2	38	27	0
Winder	1	26	26	0
Elway	1	23	23	0
Lang	1	7	7	0

Interceptions

Washington	No.	Yds.	LG	TD
Wilburn	2	11	11	0
Davis	1	0	0	0
Denver	**No.**	**Yds.**	**LG**	**TD**
Castille	1	0	0	0

Punting

Washington	No.	Avg.	LG	Blk.
Cox	4	37.5	42	0
Denver	**No.**	**Avg.**	**LG**	**Blk.**
Horan	7	36.1	43	0

Punt Returns

Washington	No.	FC	Yds.	LG	TD
Green	1	1	0	0	0
Yarber	0	1	0	0	0
Denver	**No.**	**FC**	**Yds.**	**LG**	**TD**
Clark	2	0	18	9	0

Kickoff Returns

Washington	No.	Yds.	LG	TD
Sanders	3	46	16	0
Denver	**No.**	**Yds.**	**LG**	**TD**
Bell	5	88	21	0

Super Bowl XXI

Rose Bowl, Pasadena, California — January 25, 1987
Attendance: 101,063

NEW YORK GIANTS 39, DENVER 20—The NFC champion New York Giants captured their first NFL title since 1956 when they downed the AFC champion Denver Broncos, 39-20, in Super Bowl XXI. The victory marked the NFC's fifth NFL title in the past six seasons. The Broncos, behind the passing of quarterback John Elway, who was 13 of 20 for 187 yards in the first half, held a 10-9 lead at intermission, the narrowest halftime margin in Super Bowl history. Denver's Rich Karlis opened the scoring with a Super Bowl record-tying 48-yard field goal. New York drove 78 yards in nine plays on the next series to take a 7-3 lead on quarterback Phil Simms's six-yard touchdown pass to tight end Zeke Mowatt. The Broncos came right back with a 58-yard scoring drive on six plays capped by Elway's four-yard touchdown run. The only scoring in the second period was the sack of Elway in the end zone by defensive end George Martin for a New York safety. The Giants produced a key defensive stand early in the second quarter when the Broncos had a first down at the New York one-yard line, but failed to score on three running plays and Karlis's 23-yard missed field-goal attempt. The Giants took command of the game in the third period en route to a 30-point second half, the most ever scored in one half of Super Bowl play. New York took the lead for good on tight end Mark Bavaro's 13-yard touchdown catch 4:52 into the third period. The nine-play, 63-yard scoring drive included the successful conversion of a fourth down and one play on the New York 46-yard line. Denver was limited to only two net yards on 10 offensive plays in the third period. Simms set Super Bowl records for most consecutive completions (10) and highest completion percentage (88 percent on 22 completions in 25 attempts). He also passed for 268 yards and three touchdowns and was named the game's most valuable player. New York running back Joe Morris was the game's leading rusher with 20 carries for 67 yards. Denver wide receiver Vance Johnson led all receivers with five catches for 121 yards. The Giants defeated their three playoff opponents by a cumulative total of 82 points (New York 105, opponents 23), the largest such margin by a Super Bowl winner.

Denver (AFC)	10	0	0	10	— 20
N.Y. Giants (NFC)	7	2	17	13	— 39

Den —FG Karlis 48
NYG—Mowatt 6 pass from Simms (Allegre kick)
Den —Elway 4 run (Karlis kick)
NYG—Safety, Martin tackled Elway in end zone
NYG—Bavaro 13 pass from Simms (Allegre kick)
NYG—Morris 1 run (Allegre kick)
NYG—McConkey 6 pass from Simms (Allegre kick)
Den —FG Karlis 28
NYG—Anderson 2 run (kick failed)
Den —V. Johnson 47 pass from Elway (Karlis kick)

Super Bowl XX

Louisiana Superdome, New Orleans, Louisiana — January 26, 1986
Attendance: 73,818

CHICAGO 46, NEW ENGLAND 10—The NFC champion Chicago Bears, seeking their first NFL title since 1963, scored a Super Bowl-record 46 points in downing AFC champion New England 46-10 in Super Bowl XX. The previous record for most points in a Super Bowl was 38, shared by San Francisco in XIX and the Los Angeles Raiders in XVIII. The Bears' league-leading defense tied the Super Bowl record for sacks (7) and limited the Patriots to a record-low seven yards rushing. New England took the quickest lead in Super Bowl history when Tony Franklin kicked a 36-yard field goal with 1:19 elapsed in the first period. The score came about because of Larry McGrew's fumble recovery at the Chicago 19-yard line. However, the Bears rebounded for a 23-3 first-half lead, while building a yardage advantage of 236 total yards to New England's minus 19. Running back Matt Suhey rushed eight times for 37 yards, including an 11-yard touchdown run, and caught one pass for 24 yards in the first half. After the Patriots first drive of the second half ended with a punt to the Bears' 4-yard line, Chicago marched 96 yards in nine plays with quarterback Jim McMahon's one-yard scoring run capping the drive. McMahon became the first quarterback in Super Bowl history to rush for a pair of touchdowns. The Bears completed their scoring via a 28-yard interception return by reserve cornerback Reggie Phillips, a one-yard run by defensive tackle/fullback William Perry, and a safety when defensive end Henry Waechter tackled Patriots quarterback Steve Grogan in the end zone. Bears defensive end Richard Dent became the fourth defender to be named the game's most valuable player after contributing 1½ sacks. The Bears' victory margin of 36 points was the largest in Super Bowl history, bettering the previous mark of 29 by the Los Angeles Raiders when they topped Washington 38-9 in Game XVIII. McMahon completed 12 of 20 passes for 256 yards before leaving the game in the fourth period with a wrist injury. The NFL's all-time leading rusher, Bears running back Walter Payton, carried 22 times for 61 yards. Wide receiver Willie Gault caught four passes for 129 yards, the fourth-most receiving yards in a Super Bowl. Chicago coach Mike Ditka became the second man (Tom Flores of Raiders was the other) who played in a Super Bowl and coached a team to a victory in the game.

Chicago (NFC)	13	10	21	2	— 46
New England (AFC)	3	0	0	7	— 10

NE—FG Franklin 36
Chi—FG Butler 28
Chi—FG Butler 24
Chi—Suhey 11 run (Butler kick)
Chi—McMahon 2 run (Butler kick)
Chi—FG Butler 24
Chi—McMahon 1 run (Butler kick)
Chi—Phillips 28 interception return (Butler kick)

Chi—Perry 1 run (Butler kick)
NE—Fryar 8 pass from Grogan (Franklin kick)
Chi—Safety, Waechter tackled Grogan in end zone

Super Bowl XIX

Stanford Stadium, Stanford, California January 20, 1985
Attendance: 84,059

SAN FRANCISCO 38, MIAMI 16—The San Francisco 49ers captured their second Super Bowl title with a dominating offense and a defense that tamed Miami's explosive passing attack. The Dolphins held a 10-7 lead at the end of the first period, which represented the most points scored by two teams in an opening quarter of a Super Bowl. However, the 49ers used excellent field position in the second period to build a 28-16 halftime lead. Running back Roger Craig set a Super Bowl record by scoring three touchdowns on pass receptions of 8 and 16 yards and a run of 2 yards. San Francisco's Joe Montana was voted the game's most valuable player. He joined Green Bay's Bart Starr and Pittsburgh's Terry Bradshaw as the only two-time Super Bowl most valuable players. Montana completed 24 of 35 passes for a Super Bowl-record 331 yards and three touchdowns, and rushed five times for 59 yards, including a six-yard touchdown. Craig had 58 yards on 15 carries and caught seven passes for 77 yards. Wendell Tyler rushed 13 times for 65 yards and had four catches for 70 yards. Dwight Clark had six receptions for 77 yards, while Russ Francis had five for 60. San Francisco's 537 total net yards bettered the previous Super Bowl record of 429 yards by Oakland in Super Bowl XI. The 49ers also held a time of possession advantage over the Dolphins of 37:11 to 22:49.

Miami (AFC)	10	6	0	0	— 16
San Francisco (NFC)	7	21	10	0	— 38

Mia—FG von Schamann 37
SF—Monroe 33 pass from Montana (Wersching kick)
Mia—D. Johnson 2 pass from Marino (von Schamann kick)
SF—Craig 8 pass from Montana (Wersching kick)
SF—Montana 6 run (Wersching kick)
SF—Craig 2 run (Wersching kick)
Mia—FG von Schamann 31
Mia—FG von Schamann 30
SF—FG Wersching 27
SF—Craig 16 pass from Montana (Wersching kick)

Super Bowl XVIII

Tampa Stadium, Tampa, Florida January 22, 1984
Attendance: 72,920

LOS ANGELES RAIDERS 38, WASHINGTON 9—The Los Angeles Raiders dominated the Washington Redskins from the beginning in Super Bowl XVIII and achieved the most lopsided victory in Super Bowl history, surpassing Green Bay's 35-10 win over Kansas City in Super Bowl I. The Raiders took a 7-0 lead 4:52 into the game when Derrick Jensen blocked a Jeff Hayes punt and recovered it in the end zone for a touchdown. With 9:14 remaining in the first half, Raiders quarterback Jim Plunkett threw a 12-yard touchdown pass to wide receiver Cliff Branch to complete a three-play, 65-yard drive. Washington cut the Raiders' lead to 14-3 on a 24-yard field goal by Mark Moseley. With seven seconds left in the first half, Raiders linebacker Jack Squirek intercepted a Joe Theismann pass at the Redskins' 5-yard line and ran it in for a touchdown to give Los Angeles a 21-3 halftime lead. In the third period, running back Marcus Allen, who rushed for a Super Bowl record 191 yards on 20 carries, increased the Raiders' lead to 35-3 on touchdown runs of 5 and 74 yards, the latter erasing the previous Super Bowl record of 58 yards set by Baltimore's Tom Matte in Game III. Allen was named the game's most valuable player. The victory over Washington raised Raiders coach Tom Flores' playoff record to 8-1, including a 27-10 win against Philadelphia in Super Bowl XV. The 38 points scored by the Raiders was the highest total by a Super Bowl team. The previous high was 35 points by Green Bay in Game I.

Washington (NFC)	0	3	6	0	— 9
L.A. Raiders (AFC)	7	14	14	3	— 38

Raiders—Jensen recovered blocked punt in end zone (Bahr kick)
Raiders—Branch 12 pass from Plunkett (Bahr kick)
Wash—FG Moseley 24
Raiders—Squirek 5 interception return (Bahr kick)
Wash—Riggins 1 run (kick blocked)
Raiders—Allen 5 run (Bahr kick)
Raiders—Allen 74 run (Bahr kick)
Raiders—FG Bahr 21

Super Bowl XVII

Rose Bowl, Pasadena, California January 30, 1983
Attendance: 103,667

WASHINGTON 27, MIAMI 17—Fullback John Riggins's Super Bowl record 166 yards on 38 carries sparked Washington to a 27-17 victory over AFC champion Miami. It was Riggins's fourth straight 100-yard rushing game during the playoffs, also a record. The win marked Washington's first NFL title since 1942, and was only the second time in Super Bowl history NFC teams scored consecutive victories (Green Bay did it in Super Bowls I and II and San Francisco won Super Bowl XVI). The Redskins, under second-year head coach Joe Gibbs, used a balanced offense that accounted for 400 total yards (a Super Bowl record 276 yards rushing and 124 passing), second in Super Bowl history to 429 yards by Oakland in Super Bowl XI. The Dolphins built a 17-10 halftime lead on a 76-yard touchdown pass from quarterback David Woodley to wide receiver Jimmy Cefalo 6:49 into the first period, a 20-yard field goal by Uwe von Schamann with 6:00 left in the half, and a Super Bowl record 98-yard kickoff return by Fulton Walker with 1:38 remaining. Washington had tied the score at 10-10 with 1:51 left on a four-yard touchdown pass from Joe Theismann to wide receiver Alvin Garrett. Mark Moseley started the Redskins' scoring with a 31-yard field goal late in the first period, and added a 20-yarder midway through the third period to cut the Dolphins' lead to 17-13. Riggins, who was voted the game's most valuable player, gave Washington its first lead of the game with 10:01 left when he ran 43 yards off left tackle for a touchdown on a fourth-and-one situation. Wide receiver Charlie Brown caught a six-yard scoring pass from Theismann with 1:55 left to complete the scoring. The Dolphins managed only 176 yards (142 in first half). Theismann completed 15 of 23 passes for 143 yards, two touchdowns, and had two interceptions. For Miami, Woodley was 4 of 14 for 97 yards, with one touchdown, and one interception. Don Strock was 0 for 3 in relief.

Miami (AFC)	7	10	0	0	— 17
Washington (NFC)	0	10	3	14	— 27

Mia—Cefalo 76 pass from Woodley (von Schamann kick)
Wash—FG Moseley 31
Mia—FG von Schamann 20
Wash—Garrett 4 pass from Theismann (Moseley kick)
Mia—Walker 98 kickoff return (von Schamann kick)
Wash—FG Moseley 20
Wash—Riggins 43 run (Moseley kick)
Wash—Brown 6 pass from Theismann (Moseley kick)

Super Bowl XVI

Pontiac Silverdome, Pontiac, Michigan January 24, 1982
Attendance: 81,270

SAN FRANCISCO 26, CINCINNATI 21—Ray Wersching's Super Bowl record-tying four field goals and Joe Montana's controlled passing helped lift the San Francisco 49ers to their first NFL championship with a 26-21 victory over Cincinnati. The 49ers built a game-record 20-0 halftime lead via Montana's one-yard touchdown run, which capped an 11-play, 68-yard drive; fullback Earl Cooper's 11-yard scoring pass from Montana, which climaxed a Super Bowl record 92-yard drive on 12 plays; and Wersching's 22- and 26-yard field goals. The Bengals rebounded in the second half, closing the gap to 20-14 on quarterback Ken Anderson's five-yard run and Dan Ross's four-yard reception from Anderson, who established Super Bowl passing records for completions (25) and completion percentage (73.5 percent on 25 of 34). Wersching added early fourth-period field goals of 40 and 23 yards to increase the 49ers' lead to 26-14. The Bengals managed to score on an Anderson-to-Ross three-yard pass with only 16 seconds remaining. Ross set a Super Bowl record with 11 receptions for 104 yards. Montana, the game's most valuable player, completed 14 of 22 passes for 157 yards. Cincinnati compiled 356 yards to San Francisco's 275, which marked the first time in Super Bowl history that the team that gained the most yards from scrimmage lost the game.

San Francisco (NFC)	7	13	0	6	— 26
Cincinnati (AFC)	0	0	7	14	— 21

SF—Montana 1 run (Wersching kick)
SF—Cooper 11 pass from Montana (Wersching kick)
SF—FG Wersching 22
SF—FG Wersching 26
Cin—Anderson 5 run (Breech kick)
Cin—Ross 4 pass from Anderson (Breech kick)
SF—FG Wersching 40
SF—FG Wersching 23
Cin—Ross 3 pass from Anderson (Breech kick)

Super Bowl XV

Louisiana Superdome, New Orleans, Louisiana January 25, 1981
Attendance: 76,135

OAKLAND 27, PHILADELPHIA 10—Jim Plunkett threw three touchdown passes, including an 80-yarder to Kenny King, as the Raiders became the first wild card team to win the Super Bowl. Plunkett's touchdown bomb to King—the longest play in Super Bowl history—gave Oakland a decisive 14-0 lead with nine seconds left in the first period. Linebacker Rod Martin had set up Oakland's first touchdown, a two-yard reception by Cliff Branch, with a 16-yard interception return to the Eagles' 32 yard line. The Eagles never recovered from that early deficit, managing only a Tony Franklin field goal (30 yards) and an eight-yard touchdown pass from Ron Jaworski to Keith Krepfle the rest of the game. Plunkett, who became a starter in the sixth game of the season, completed 13 of 21 for 261 yards and was named the game's most valuable player. Oakland won 9 of 11 games with Plunkett starting, but that was good enough only for second place in the AFC West, although they tied division winner San Diego with an 11-5 record. The Raiders, who had previously won Super Bowl XI over Minnesota, had to win three playoff games to get to the championship game. Oakland defeated Houston 27-7 at home followed by road victories over Cleveland, 14-12 and San Diego, 34-27. Oakland's Mark van Eeghen was the game's leading rusher with 80 yards on 19 carries. Philadelphia's Wilbert Montgomery led all receivers with six receptions for 91 yards. Branch had five for 67 and Harold Carmichael of Philadelphia five for 83. Martin finished the game with three interceptions, a Super Bowl record.

Oakland (AFC)	14	0	10	3	— 27
Philadelphia (NFC)	0	3	0	7	— 10

Oak—Branch 2 pass from Plunkett (Bahr kick)
Oak—King 80 pass from Plunkett (Bahr kick)
Phil—FG Franklin 30
Oak—Branch 29 pass from Plunkett (Bahr kick)
Oak—FG Bahr 46
Phil—Krepfle 8 pass from Jaworski (Franklin kick)
Oak—FG Bahr 35

Super Bowl XIV

Rose Bowl, Pasadena, California January 20, 1980

Attendance: 103,985

PITTSBURGH 31, LOS ANGELES 19—Terry Bradshaw completed 14 of 21 passes for 309 yards and set two passing records as the Steelers became the first team to win four Super Bowls. Despite three interceptions by the Rams, Bradshaw kept his poise and brought the Steelers from behind twice in the second half. Trailing 13-10 at halftime, Pittsburgh went ahead 17-13 when Bradshaw hit Lynn Swann with a 47-yard touchdown pass after 2:48 of the third quarter. On the Rams' next possession Vince Ferragamo, who completed 15 of 25 passes for 212 yards, responded with a 50-yard pass to Billy Waddy that moved Los Angeles from its own 26 to the Steelers' 24. On the following play, Lawrence McCutcheon connected with Ron Smith on a halfback option pass that gave the Rams a 19-17 lead. On Pittsburgh's initial possession of the final period, Bradshaw lofted a 73-yard scoring pass to John Stallworth to put the Steelers in front to stay, 24-19. Franco Harris scored on a one-yard run later in the quarter to seal the verdict. A 45-yard pass from Bradshaw to Stallworth was the key play in the drive to Harris's score. Bradshaw, the game's most valuable player for the second straight year, set career Super Bowl records for most touchdown passes (nine) and most passing yards (932). Larry Anderson gave the Steelers excellent field position throughout the game with five kickoff returns for a record 162 yards.

Los Angeles (NFC)	7	6	6	0 — 19
Pittsburgh (AFC)	3	7	7	14 — 31

Pitt—FG Bahr 41
LA—Bryant 1 run (Corral kick)
Pitt—Harris 1 run (Bahr kick)
LA—FG Corral 31
LA—FG Corral 45
Pitt—Swann 47 pass from Bradshaw (Bahr kick)
LA—Smith 24 pass from McCutcheon (kick failed)
Pitt—Stallworth 73 pass from Bradshaw (Bahr kick)
Pitt—Harris 1 run (Bahr kick)

Super Bowl XIII

Orange Bowl, Miami, Florida January 21, 1979

Attendance: 79,484

PITTSBURGH 35, DALLAS 31—Terry Bradshaw threw a record four touchdown passes to lead the Steelers to victory. The Steelers became the first team to win three Super Bowls, mostly because of Bradshaw's accurate arm. Bradshaw, voted the game's most valuable player, completed 17 of 30 passes for 318 yards, a personal high. Three of those passes went for touchdowns—two to John Stallworth and the third, with 26 seconds remaining in the second period, to Rocky Bleier. The Cowboys scored twice before intermission on Roger Staubach's 39-yard pass to Tony Hill and a 37-yard run by linebacker Mike Hegman, who stole the ball from Bradshaw. The Steelers broke open the contest with two touchdowns in a span of 19 seconds midway through the final period. Franco Harris rambled 22 yards up the middle to give the Steelers a 28-17 lead with 7:10 left. Pittsburgh got the ball right back when Randy White fumbled the kickoff and Dennis Winston recovered for the Steelers. On first down, Bradshaw hit Lynn Swann with an 18-yard scoring pass to boost the Steelers' lead to 35-17 with 6:51 to play. The Cowboys refused to let the Steelers run away with the contest. Staubach connected with Billy Joe DuPree on a seven-yard scoring pass with 2:23 left. Then the Cowboys recovered an onside kick and Staubach took them in for another score, passing four yards to Butch Johnson with 22 seconds remaining. Bleier recovered another onside kick with 17 seconds left to seal the victory for the Steelers.

Pittsburgh (AFC)	7	14	0	14 — 35
Dallas (NFC)	7	7	3	14 — 31

Pitt—Stallworth 28 pass from Bradshaw (Gerela kick)
Dall—Hill 39 pass from Staubach (Septien kick)
Dall—Hegman 37 fumble recovery return (Septien kick)
Pitt—Stallworth 75 pass from Bradshaw (Gerela kick)
Pitt—Bleier 7 pass from Bradshaw (Gerela kick)
Dall—FG Septien 27
Pitt—Harris 22 run (Gerela kick)
Pitt—Swann 18 pass from Bradshaw (Gerela kick)
Dall—DuPree 7 pass from Staubach (Septien kick)
Dall—B. Johnson 4 pass from Staubach (Septien kick)

Super Bowl XII

Louisiana Superdome, New Orleans, Louisiana January 15, 1978

Attendance: 75,583

DALLAS 27, DENVER 10—The Cowboys evened their Super Bowl record at 2-2 by defeating Denver before a sellout crowd of 75,583, plus 102,010,000 television viewers, the largest audience ever to watch a sporting event. Dallas converted two interceptions into 10 points and Efren Herrera added a 35-yard field goal for a 13-0 halftime advantage. In the third period Craig Morton engineered a drive to the Cowboys' 30 and Jim Turner's 47-yard field goal made the score 13-3. After an exchange of punts, Butch Johnson made a spectacular diving catch in the end zone to complete a 45-yard pass from Roger Staubach and put the Cowboys ahead 20-3. Following Rick Upchurch's 67-yard kickoff return, Norris Weese guided the Broncos to a touchdown to cut the Dallas lead to 20-10. Dallas clinched the victory when running back Robert Newhouse threw a 29-yard touchdown pass to Golden Richards with 7:04 remaining in the game. It was the first pass thrown by Newhouse since 1975. Harvey Martin and Randy White, who were named co-most valuable players, led the Cowboys' defense, which recovered four fumbles and intercepted four passes.

Dallas (NFC)	10	3	7	7 — 27
Denver (AFC)	0	0	10	0 — 10

Dall—Dorsett 3 run (Herrera kick)
Dall—FG Herrera 35
Dall—FG Herrera 43
Den—FG Turner 47
Dall—Johnson 45 pass from Staubach (Herrera kick)
Den—Lytle 1 run (Turner kick)
Dall—Richards 29 pass from Newhouse (Herrera kick)

Super Bowl XI

Rose Bowl, Pasadena, California January 9, 1977

Attendance: 103,438

OAKLAND 32, MINNESOTA 14—The Raiders won their first NFL championship before a record Super Bowl crowd plus 81 million television viewers, the largest audience ever to watch a sporting event. The Raiders gained a record-breaking 429 yards, including running back Clarence Davis's 137 yards rushing. Wide receiver Fred Biletnikoff made four key receptions, which earned him the game's most valuable player trophy. Oakland scored on three successive possessions in the second quarter to build a 16-0 halftime lead. Errol Mann's 24-yard field goal opened the scoring, then the AFC champions put together drives of 64 and 35 yards, scoring on a one-yard pass from Ken Stabler to Dave Casper and a one-yard run by Pete Banaszak. The Raiders increased their lead to 19-0 on a 40-yard field goal in the third quarter, but Minnesota responded with a 12-play, 58-yard drive late in the period, with Fran Tarkenton passing eight yards to wide receiver Sammy White to cut the deficit to 19-7. Two fourth-quarter interceptions clinched the title for the Raiders. One set up Banaszak's second touchdown run, the other resulted in cornerback Willie Brown's Super Bowl record 75-yard interception return.

Oakland (AFC)	0	16	3	13 — 32
Minnesota (NFC)	0	0	7	7 — 14

Oak—FG Mann 24
Oak—Casper 1 pass from Stabler (Mann kick)
Oak—Banaszak 1 run (kick failed)
Oak—FG Mann 40
Minn—S. White 8 pass from Tarkenton (Cox kick)
Oak—Banaszak 2 run (Mann kick)
Oak—Brown 75 interception return (kick failed)
Minn—Voigt 13 pass from Lee (Cox kick)

Super Bowl X

Orange Bowl, Miami, Florida January 18, 1976

Attendance: 80,187

PITTSBURGH 21, DALLAS 17—The Steelers won the Super Bowl for the second year in a row on Terry Bradshaw's 64-yard touchdown pass to Lynn Swann and an aggressive defense that snuffed out a late rally by the Cowboys with an end-zone interception on the final play of the game. In the fourth quarter, Pittsburgh ran on fourth down and gave up the ball on the Cowboys' 39 with 1:22 to play. Roger Staubach ran and passed for two first downs but his last desperation pass was picked off by Glen Edwards. Dallas's scoring was the result of two touchdown passes by Staubach, one to Drew Pearson for 29 yards and the other to Percy Howard for 34 yards. Toni Fritsch had a 36-yard field goal. The Steelers scored on two touchdown passes by Bradshaw, one to Randy Grossman for seven yards and the long bomb to Swann. Roy Gerela had 36- and 18-yard field goals. Reggie Harrison blocked a punt through the end zone for a safety. Swann set a Super Bowl record by gaining 161 yards on his four receptions.

Dallas (NFC)	7	3	0	7 — 17
Pittsburgh (AFC)	7	0	0	14 — 21

Dall—D. Pearson 29 pass from Staubach (Fritsch kick)
Pitt—Grossman 7 pass from Bradshaw (Gerela kick)
Dall—FG Fritsch 36
Pitt—Safety, Harrison blocked Hoopes's punt through end zone
Pitt—FG Gerela 36
Pitt—FG Gerela 18
Pitt—Swann 64 pass from Bradshaw (kick failed)
Dall—P. Howard 34 pass from Staubach (Fritsch kick)

Super Bowl IX

Tulane Stadium, New Orleans, Louisiana January 12, 1975

Attendance: 80,997

PITTSBURGH 16, MINNESOTA 6—AFC champion Pittsburgh, in its initial Super Bowl appearance, and NFC champion Minnesota, making a third bid for its first Super Bowl title, struggled through a first half in which the only score was produced by the Steelers' defense when Dwight White downed Vikings' quarterback Fran Tarkenton in the end zone for a safety 7:49 into the second period. The Steelers forced another break and took advantage on the second half kickoff when Minnesota's Bill Brown fumbled and Marv Kellum recovered for Pittsburgh on the Vikings' 30. After Rocky Bleier failed to gain on first down, Franco Harris carried three consecutive times for 24 yards, a loss of 3, and a 12-yard touchdown and a 9-0 lead. Though its offense was completely stymied by Pittsburgh's defense, Minnesota managed to move into a threatening position after 4:27 of the final period when Matt Blair blocked Bobby Walden's punt and Terry Brown recovered the ball in the end zone for a touchdown. Fred Cox's kick failed and the Steelers led 9-6. Pittsburgh wasted no time putting the victory away. The Steelers took the ensuing kickoff and marched 66 yards in 11 plays, climaxed by Terry Bradshaw's four-yard scoring pass to Larry Brown with 3:31 left. Pittsburgh's defense permitted Minnesota only 119 yards total offense, including a Super Bowl low of 17 yards rushing. The Steelers, meanwhile, gained 333 yards, including Harris's record 158 yards on 34 carries.

Pittsburgh (AFC)	0	2	7	7	— 16
Minnesota (NFC)	0	0	0	6	— 6

Pitt —Safety, White downed Tarkenton in end zone
Pitt —Harris 12 run (Gerela kick)
Minn—T. Brown recovered blocked punt in end zone (kick failed)
Pitt —L. Brown 4 pass from Bradshaw (Gerela kick)

Super Bowl VIII

Rice Stadium, Houston, Texas — January 13, 1974
Attendance: 71,882

MIAMI 24, MINNESOTA 7—The defending NFL champion Dolphins, representing the AFC for the third straight year, scored the first two times they had possession on marches of 62 and 56 yards in the first period while the Miami defense limited the Vikings to only seven plays. Larry Csonka climaxed the initial 10-play drive with a five-yard touchdown bolt through right guard after 5:27 had elapsed. Four plays later, Miami began another 10-play scoring drive, which ended with Jim Kiick bursting one yard through the middle for another touchdown after 13:38 of the period. Garo Yepremian added a 28-yard field goal midway in the second period for a 17-0 Miami lead. Minnesota then drove from its 20 to a second-and-two situation on the Miami 7 yard line with 1:18 left in the half. But on two plays, Miami limited Oscar Reed to one yard. On fourth-and-one from the 6, Reed went over right tackle, but Dolphins middle linebacker Nick Buoniconti jarred the ball loose and Jake Scott recovered for Miami to halt the Minnesota threat. The Vikings were unable to muster enough offense in the second half to threaten the Dolphins. Csonka rushed 33 times for a Super Bowl record 145 yards. Bob Griese of Miami completed six of seven passes for 73 yards.

Minnesota (NFC)	0	0	0	7	— 7
Miami (AFC)	14	3	7	0	— 24

Mia —Csonka 5 run (Yepremian kick)
Mia —Kiick 1 run (Yepremian kick)
Mia —FG Yepremian 28
Mia —Csonka 2 run (Yepremian kick)
Minn—Tarkenton 4 run (Cox kick)

Super Bowl VII

Memorial Coliseum, Los Angeles, California — January 14, 1973
Attendance: 90,182

MIAMI 14, WASHINGTON 7—The Dolphins played virtually perfect football in the first half as their defense permitted the Redskins to cross midfield only once and their offense turned good field position into two touchdowns. On its third possession, Miami opened its first scoring drive from the Dolphins' 37 yard line. An 18-yard pass from Bob Griese to Paul Warfield preceded by three plays Griese's 28-yard touchdown pass to Howard Twilley. After Washington moved from its 17 to the Miami 48 with two minutes remaining in the first half, Dolphins linebacker Nick Buoniconti intercepted a Billy Kilmer pass at the Miami 41 and returned it to the Washington 27. Jim Kiick ran for three yards, Larry Csonka for three, Griese passed to Jim Mandich for 19, and Kiick gained one to the 1 yard line. With 18 seconds left until intermission, Kiick scored from the 1. Washington's only touchdown came with 7:07 left in the game and resulted from a misplayed field goal attempt and fumble by Garo Yepremian, with the Redskins' Mike Bass picking the ball out of the air and running 49 yards for the score.

Miami (AFC)	7	7	0	0	— 14
Washington (NFC)	0	0	0	7	— 7

Mia —Twilley 28 pass from Griese (Yepremian kick)
Mia —Kiick 1 run (Yepremian kick)
Wash—Bass 49 fumble recovery return (Knight kick)

Super Bowl VI

Tulane Stadium, New Orleans, Louisiana — January 16, 1972
Attendance: 81,023

DALLAS 24, MIAMI 3—The Cowboys rushed for a record 252 yards and their defense limited the Dolphins to a low of 185 yards while not permitting a touchdown for the first time in Super Bowl history. Dallas converted Chuck Howley's recovery of Larry Csonka's first fumble of the season into a 3-0 advantage and led at halftime 10-3. After Dallas received the second-half kickoff, Duane Thomas led a 71-yard march in eight plays for a 17-3 margin. Howley intercepted Bob Griese's pass at the 50 and returned it to the Miami 9 early in the fourth period, and three plays later Roger Staubach passed seven yards to Mike Ditka for the final touchdown. Thomas rushed for 95 yards and Walt Garrison gained 74. Staubach, voted the game's most valuable player, completed 12 of 19 passes for 119 yards and two touchdowns.

Dallas (NFC)	3	7	7	7	— 24
Miami (AFC)	0	3	0	0	— 3

Dall—FG Clark 9
Dall—Alworth 7 pass from Staubach (Clark kick)
Mia—FG Yepremian 31
Dall—D. Thomas 3 run (Clark kick)
Dall—Ditka 7 pass from Staubach (Clark kick)

Super Bowl V

Orange Bowl, Miami, Florida — January 17, 1971
Attendance: 79,204

BALTIMORE 16, DALLAS 13—A 32-yard field goal by first-year kicker Jim O'Brien brought the Baltimore Colts a victory over the Dallas Cowboys in the final five seconds of Super Bowl V. The game between the champions of the AFC and NFC was played on artificial turf for the first time. Dallas led 13-6 at the half but interceptions by Rick Volk and Mike Curtis set up a Baltimore touchdown and O'Brien's decisive kick in the fourth period. Earl Morrall relieved an injured Johnny Unitas late in the first half, although Unitas completed the Colts' only scoring pass. It caromed off receiver Eddie Hinton's fingertips, off Dallas defensive back Mel Renfro, and finally settled into the grasp of John Mackey, who went 45 yards to score on a 75-yard play.

Baltimore (AFC)	0	6	0	10	— 16
Dallas (NFC)	3	10	0	0	— 13

Dall—FG Clark 14
Dall—FG Clark 30
Balt—Mackey 75 pass from Unitas (kick blocked)
Dall—Thomas 7 pass from Morton (Clark kick)
Balt—Nowatzke 2 run (O'Brien kick)
Balt—FG O'Brien 32

Super Bowl IV

Tulane Stadium, New Orleans, Louisiana — January 11, 1970
Attendance: 80,562

KANSAS CITY 23, MINNESOTA 7—The AFL squared the Super Bowl at two games apiece with the NFL, building a 16-0 halftime lead behind Len Dawson's superb quarterbacking and a powerful defense. Dawson, the fourth consecutive quarterback to be chosen the Super Bowl's top player, called an almost flawless game, completing 12 of 17 passes and hitting Otis Taylor on a 46-yard play for the final Chiefs touchdown. The Kansas City defense limited Minnesota's strong rushing game to 67 yards and had three interceptions and two fumble recoveries. The crowd of 80,562 set a Super Bowl record, as did the gross receipts of $3,817,872.69.

Minnesota (NFL)	0	0	7	0	— 7
Kansas City (AFL)	3	13	7	0	— 23

KC —FG Stenerud 48
KC —FG Stenerud 32
KC —FG Stenerud 25
KC —Garrett 5 run (Stenerud kick)
Minn—Osborn 4 run (Cox kick)
KC —Taylor 46 pass from Dawson (Stenerud kick)

Super Bowl III

Orange Bowl, Miami, Florida — January 12, 1969
Attendance: 75,389

NEW YORK JETS 16, BALTIMORE 7—Jets quarterback Joe Namath "guaranteed" victory on the Thursday before the game, then went out and led the AFL to its first Super Bowl victory over a Baltimore team that had lost only once in 16 games all season. Namath, chosen the outstanding player, completed 17 of 28 passes for 206 yards and directed a steady attack that dominated the NFL champions after the Jets' defense had intercepted Colts quarterback Earl Morrall three times in the first half. The Jets had 337 total yards, including 121 yards rushing by Matt Snell. Johnny Unitas, who had missed most of the season with a sore elbow, came off the bench and led Baltimore to its only touchdown late in the fourth quarter after New York led 16-0.

New York Jets (AFL)	0	7	6	3	— 16
Baltimore (NFL)	0	0	0	7	— 7

NYJ—Snell 4 run (Turner kick)
NYJ—FG Turner 32
NYJ—FG Turner 30
NYJ—FG Turner 9
Balt—Hill 1 run (Michaels kick)

Super Bowl II

Orange Bowl, Miami, Florida — January 14, 1968
Attendance: 75,546

GREEN BAY 33, OAKLAND 14—Green Bay, after winning its third consecutive NFL championship, won the Super Bowl title for the second straight year 33-14 over the AFL champion Raiders in a game that drew the first $3-million gate in football history. Bart Starr again was chosen the game's most valuable player as he completed 13 of 24 passes for 202 yards and one touchdown and directed a Packers attack that was in control all the way after building a 16-7 halftime lead. Don Chandler kicked four field goals and all-pro cornerback Herb Adderley capped the Green Bay scoring with a 60-yard run with an interception. The game marked the last for Vince Lombardi as Packers coach, ending nine years at Green Bay in which he won six Western Conference championships, five NFL championships, and two Super Bowls.

Green Bay (NFL)	3	13	10	7	— 33
Oakland (AFL)	0	7	0	7	— 14

GB —FG Chandler 39
GB —FG Chandler 20
GB —Dowler 62 pass from Starr (Chandler kick)
Oak—Miller 23 pass from Lamonica (Blanda kick)
GB —FG Chandler 43
GB —Anderson 2 run (Chandler kick)
GB —FG Chandler 31
GB —Adderley 60 interception return (Chandler kick)
Oak—Miller 23 pass from Lamonica (Blanda kick)

Super Bowl I

Memorial Coliseum, Los Angeles, California — January 15, 1967
Attendance: 61,946

GREEN BAY 35, KANSAS CITY 10—The Green Bay Packers opened the Super Bowl series by defeating Kansas City's American Football League champions 35-10 behind the passing of Bart Starr, the receiving of Max

McGee, and a key interception by all-pro safety Willie Wood. Green Bay broke open the game with three second-half touchdowns, the first of which was set up by Wood's 40-yard return of an interception to the Chiefs' 5 yard line. McGee, filling in for ailing Boyd Dowler after having caught only three passes all season, caught seven from Starr for 138 yards and two touchdowns. Elijah Pitts ran for two other scores. The Chiefs' 10 points came in the second quarter, the only touchdown on a seven-yard pass from Len Dawson to Curtis McClinton. Starr completed 16 of 23 passes for 250 yards and two touchdowns and was chosen the most valuable player. The Packers collected $15,000 per man and the Chiefs $7,500—the largest single-game shares in the history of team sports.

Kansas City (AFL)	0	10	0	0	— 10
Green Bay (NFL)	7	7	14	7	— 35

GB—McGee 37 pass from Starr (Chandler kick)
KC—McClinton 7 pass from Dawson (Mercer kick)
GB—Taylor 14 run (Chandler kick)
KC—FG Mercer 31
GB—Pitts 5 run (Chandler kick)
GB—McGee 13 pass from Starr (Chandler kick)
GB—Pitts 1 run (Chandler kick)

AFC Championship Game

Includes AFL Championship Games (1960-69)

Results

Season	Date	Winner (Share)	Loser (Share)	Score	Site	Attendance
1987	Jan. 17	Denver ($18,000)	Cleveland ($18,000)	38-33	Denver	76,197
1986	Jan. 11	Denver ($18,000)	Cleveland ($18,000)	23-20*	Cleveland	79,973
1985	Jan. 12	New England ($18,000)	Miami ($18,000)	31-14	Miami	75,662
1984	Jan. 6	Miami ($18,000)	Pittsburgh ($18,000)	45-28	Miami	76,029
1983	Jan. 8	L.A. Raiders ($18,000)	Seattle ($18,000)	30-14	Los Angeles	91,445
1982	Jan. 23	Miami ($18,000)	N.Y. Jets ($18,000)	14-0	Miami	67,396
1981	Jan. 10	Cincinnati ($9,000)	San Diego ($9,000)	27-7	Cincinnati	46,302
1980	Jan. 11	Oakland ($9,000)	San Diego ($9,000)	34-27	San Diego	52,675
1979	Jan. 6	Pittsburgh ($9,000)	Houston ($9,000)	27-13	Pittsburgh	50,475
1978	Jan. 7	Pittsburgh ($9,000)	Houston ($9,000)	34-5	Pittsburgh	50,725
1977	Jan. 1	Denver ($9,000)	Oakland ($9,000)	20-17	Denver	75,044
1976	Dec. 26	Oakland ($8,500)	Pittsburgh ($5,500)	24-7	Oakland	53,821
1975	Jan. 4	Pittsburgh ($8,500)	Oakland ($5,500)	16-10	Pittsburgh	50,609
1974	Dec. 29	Pittsburgh ($8,500)	Oakland ($5,500)	24-13	Oakland	53,800
1973	Dec. 30	Miami ($8,500)	Oakland ($5,500)	27-10	Miami	79,325
1972	Dec. 31	Miami ($8,500)	Pittsburgh ($5,500)	21-17	Pittsburgh	50,845
1971	Jan. 2	Miami ($8,500)	Baltimore ($5,500)	21-0	Miami	76,622
1970	Jan. 3	Baltimore ($8,500)	Oakland ($5,500)	27-17	Baltimore	54,799
1969	Jan. 4	Kansas City ($7,755)	Oakland ($6,252)	17-7	Oakland	53,564
1968	Dec. 29	N.Y. Jets ($7,007)	Oakland ($5,349)	27-23	New York	62,627
1967	Dec. 31	Oakland ($6,321)	Houston ($4,996)	40-7	Oakland	53,330
1966	Jan. 1	Kansas City ($5,309)	Buffalo ($3,799)	31-7	Buffalo	42,080
1965	Dec. 26	Buffalo ($5,189)	San Diego ($3,447)	23-0	San Diego	30,361
1964	Dec. 26	Buffalo ($2,668)	San Diego ($1,738)	20-7	Buffalo	40,242
1963	Jan. 5	San Diego ($2,498)	Boston ($1,596)	51-10	San Diego	30,127
1962	Dec. 23	Dallas ($2,206)	Houston ($1,471)	20-17*	Houston	37,981
1961	Dec. 24	Houston ($1,792)	San Diego ($1,111)	10-3	San Diego	29,556
1960	Jan. 1	Houston ($1,025)	L.A. Chargers ($718)	24-16	Houston	32,183

**Sudden death overtime.*

AFC Championship Game Composite Standings

	W	L	Pct.	Pts.	OP
Denver Broncos	3	0	1.000	81	70
Kansas City Chiefs*	3	0	1.000	68	31
Cincinnati Bengals	1	0	1.000	27	7
Miami Dolphins	5	1	.833	142	86
Buffalo Bills	2	1	.667	50	38
Pittsburgh Steelers	4	3	.571	153	131
Baltimore Colts	1	1	.500	27	38
New England Patriots**	1	1	.500	41	65
New York Jets	1	1	.500	27	37
Oakland/L.A. Raiders	4	7	.364	225	213
Houston Oilers	2	4	.333	76	140
San Diego Chargers***	1	6	.143	111	148
Seattle Seahawks	0	1	.000	14	30
Cleveland Browns	0	2	.000	53	61

**One game played when franchise was in Dallas (Texans). (Won 20-17)*
***One game played when franchise was in Boston. (Lost 51-10)*
****One game played when franchise was in Los Angeles. (Lost 24-16)*

1987 American Football Conference Championship Game

Mile High Stadium, Denver, Colorado January 17, 1988

Attendance: 76,197

Denver 38, Cleveland 33—AFC West champion Denver became the first team to win back-to-back AFC titles since Pittsburgh in 1978-79 by defeating Cleveland for the second straight year, 38-33. Reserve cornerback Jeremiah Castille forced and then recovered a fumble by Cleveland running back Earnest Byner at the Broncos' 3-yard line with 65 seconds to play to insure Denver's third Super Bowl appearance. Denver jumped to a 21-3 halftime lead. Defensive end Freddie Gilbert halted Cleveland's first drive of the game by intercepting Bernie Kosar's pass. That set up John Elway's eight-yard touchdown pass to wide receiver Ricky Nattiel. Running backs Steve Sewell and Gene Lang each scored on one-yard runs to give Denver its lead. The Browns roared back in the second half by scoring 28 points in the first 19:22. Kosar fired scoring passes to wide receiver Reggie Langhorne (18 yards) and Byner (32), who also scored on a four-yard run. Kosar's four-yard strike to wide receiver Webster Slaughter on the Browns' opening drive of the fourth quarter tied the score 31-31 with 10:38 to play. But Elway, who completed 14 of 26 passes for 281 yards and three touchdowns, finished off a 75-yard drive with a 20-yard touchdown pass to running back Sammy Winder with 4:01 remaining for the decisive score. Kosar completed an AFC Championship Game record 26 of 41 passes for 356 yards and three touchdowns. Byner caught seven passes for 120 yards and a touchdown. Denver wide receiver Mark Jackson had four receptions for 134 yards, including a club postseason record 80-yard scoring catch.

Cleveland (33)	Offense	Denver (38)
Reggie Langhorne	WR	Ricky Nattiel
Paul Farren	LT	Dave Studdard
Gregg Rakoczy	LG	Keith Bishop
Mike Babb	C	Mike Freeman
Dan Fike	RG	Stefan Humphries
Cody Risien	RT	Ken Lanier
Ozzie Newsome	TE	Clarence Kay
Webster Slaughter	WR	Mark Jackson
Bernie Kosar	QB	John Elway
Derek Tennell	TE-RB	Sammy Winder
Kevin Mack	RB	Gene Lang
	Defense	
Sam Clancy	LE	Andre Townsend
Dave Puzzuoli	NT	Greg Kragen
Carl Hairston	RE	Rulon Jones
Lucius Sanford	LOLB	Simon Fletcher
Eddie Johnson	LILB	Karl Mecklenburg
Mike Johnson	RILB	Ricky Hunley
Clay Matthews	ROLB	Jim Ryan
Frank Minnifield	LCB	Mark Haynes
Hanford Dixon	RCB	Steve Wilson
Ray Ellis	SS	Dennis Smith
Felix Wright	FS	Tony Lilly

Substitutions

Cleveland—Offense: K—Matt Bahr. P—Lee Johnson. QB—Mike Pagel. RB—Earnest Byner, Herman Fontenot, Tim Manoa. WR—Brian Brennan, Gerald McNeil, Clarence Weathers. C—Frank Winters. G—Larry Williams. T—Darryl Haley. Defense: E—Al Baker, Reggie Camp, Darryl Sims. LB—David Grayson, Anthony Griggs, Nick Miller. CB—Stephen Braggs, Mark Harper, D.D. Hoggard. S—Chris Rockins. DNP: QB—Gary Danielson.
Denver—Offense: K—Rich Karlis. P—Mike Horan. QB—Gary Kubiak. RB—Ken Bell, Tony Boddie, Steve Sewell. WR—Steve Watson. TE—Mitch Andrews, Bobby Micho, Orson Mobley. T—Keith Kartz. Defense: E—Walt Bowyer, Freddie Gilbert. LB—Mike Brooks, Rick Dennison, Bruce Klostermann, Tim Lucas. CB—Kevin Clark, Bruce Plummer. S—Tyrone Braxton, Jeremiah Castille, Randy Robbins. DNP: C—Larry Lee.

Officials

Referee—Jim Tunney. Umpire—Ben Montgomery. Line Judge—Ron Blum. Head Linesman—Sid Semon. Back Judge—Roy Clymer. Field Judge—Dick Dolak. Side Judge—Bill Quinby.

Scoring

Cleveland	0	3	21	9 — 33
Denver	14	7	10	7 — 38

Den —Nattiel 8 pass from Elway (Karlis kick)
Den —Sewell 1 run (Karlis kick)
Clev—FG Bahr 24
Den —Lang 1 run (Karlis kick)
Clev—Langhorne 18 pass from Kosar (Bahr kick)
Den —Jackson 80 pass from Elway (Karlis kick)
Clev—Byner 32 pass from Kosar (Bahr kick)
Clev—Byner 4 run (Bahr kick)
Den —FG Karlis 38
Clev—Slaughter 4 pass from Kosar (Bahr kick)
Den —Winder 20 pass from Elway (Karlis kick)
Clev—Safety Horan ran out of the end zone

Team Statistics

	Cleveland	Denver
Total First Downs	25	24
First Downs Rushing	8	10
First Downs Passing	15	11
First Downs Penalty	2	3
Total Net Yardage	464	412
Total Offensive Plays	70	67
Average Gain per Offensive Play	6.6	6.1
Rushes	27	39
Yards Gained Rushing (net)	128	156
Average Yards per Rush	4.7	4.0
Passes Attempted	41	26
Passes Completed	26	14
Had Intercepted	1	1
Times Tackled Attempting to Pass	2	2
Yards Lost Attempting to Pass	20	25
Yards Gained Passing (net)	336	256
Punts	2	3
Average Distance	48.0	33.7
Punt Returns	2	2
Punt Return Yardage	24	13
Kickoff Returns	5	3
Kickoff Return Yardage	94	43
Interception Return Yardage	13	0
Total Return Yardage	131	56
Fumbles	3	2
Own Fumbles Recovered	0	2
Opponents Fumbles Recovered	0	3
Penalties	7	7
Yards Penalized	59	44
Total Points Scored	33	38
Touchdowns Rushing	1	2
Touchdowns Passing	3	3
Touchdowns Returns	0	0
Extra Points	4	5
Field Goals	1	1
Field Goals Attempted	2	2
Safeties	1	0
Third Down Efficiency	8/14	7/14
Fourth Down Efficiency	1/1	0/1
Time of Possession	31:37	28:23

Individual Statistics

Rushing

Cleveland	**No.**	**Yds.**	**LG**	**TD**
Byner	15	67	16	1
Mack	12	61	14	0
Denver	**No.**	**Yds.**	**LG**	**TD**
Winder	20	72	10	0
Lang	5	51	42	1
Elway	11	36	11	0
Boddie	1	8	8	0
Sewell	1	1	1t	1
Horan	1	−12	−12	0

Passing

Cleveland	**Att.**	**Comp.**	**Yds.**	**TD**	**Int.**
Kosar	41	26	356	3	1
Denver	**Att.**	**Comp.**	**Yds.**	**TD**	**Int.**
Elway	26	14	281	3	1

Receiving

Cleveland	**No.**	**Yds.**	**LG**	**TD**
Byner	7	120	53	1
Slaughter	4	53	24	1
Brennan	4	48	19	0
Mack	4	28	9	0
Newsome	3	35	25	0
Langhorne	2	48	30	1
Weathers	1	19	19	0
Tennell	1	5	5	0
Denver	**No.**	**Yds.**	**LG**	**TD**
Nattiel	5	95	26	1
M. Jackson	4	134	80t	1
Winder	3	34	20t	1
Sewell	1	10	10	0
Mobley	1	8	8	0

Interceptions

Cleveland	**No.**	**Yds.**	**LG**	**TD**
Wright	1	13	13	0
Denver	**No.**	**Yds.**	**LG**	**TD**
Gilbert	1	0	0	0

Punting

Cleveland	**No.**	**Avg.**	**LG**	**Blk.**
L. Johnson	2	48.0	59	0
Denver	**No.**	**Avg.**	**LG**	**Blk.**
Horan	2	41.5	44	0
Elway	1	18.0	18	0

Punt Returns

Cleveland	**No.**	**FC**	**Yds.**	**LG**	**TD**
McNeil	2	0	24	17	0
Denver	**No.**	**FC**	**Yds.**	**LG**	**TD**
Clark	2	0	13	10	0

Kickoff Returns

Cleveland	**No.**	**FC**	**Yds.**	**LG**	**TD**
McNeil	5	1	94	28	0
Denver	**No.**	**FC**	**Yds.**	**LG**	**TD**
Bell	3	0	43	23	0

NFC Championship Game

Includes NFL Championship Games (1932-69)

Results

Season	Date	Winner (Share)	Loser (Share)	Score	Site	Attendance
1987	Jan. 17	Washington ($18,000)	Minnesota ($18,000)	17-10	Washington	55,212
1986	Jan. 11	New York Giants ($18,000)	Washington ($18,000)	17-0	New York	76,891
1985	Jan. 12	Chicago ($18,000)	L.A. Rams ($18,000)	24-0	Chicago	66,030
1984	Jan. 6	San Francisco ($18,000)	Chicago ($18,000)	23-0	San Francisco	61,336
1983	Jan. 8	Washington ($18,000)	San Francisco ($18,000)	24-21	Washington	55,363
1982	Jan. 22	Washington ($18,000)	Dallas ($18,000)	31-17	Washington	55,045
1981	Jan. 10	San Francisco ($9,000)	Dallas ($9,000)	28-27	San Francisco	60,525
1980	Jan. 11	Philadelphia ($9,000)	Dallas ($9,000)	20-7	Philadelphia	71,522
1979	Jan. 6	Los Angeles ($9,000)	Tampa Bay ($9,000)	9-0	Tampa Bay	72,033
1978	Jan. 7	Dallas ($9,000)	Los Angeles ($9,000)	28-0	Los Angeles	71,086
1977	Jan. 1	Dallas ($9,000)	Minnesota ($9,000)	23-6	Dallas	64,293
1976	Dec. 26	Minnesota ($8,500)	Los Angeles ($5,500)	24-13	Minnesota	48,379
1975	Jan. 4	Dallas ($8,500)	Los Angeles ($5,500)	37-7	Los Angeles	88,919
1974	Dec. 29	Minnesota ($8,500)	Los Angeles ($5,500)	14-10	Minnesota	48,444
1973	Dec. 30	Minnesota ($8,500)	Dallas ($5,500)	27-10	Dallas	64,422
1972	Dec. 31	Washington ($8,500)	Dallas ($5,500)	26-3	Washington	53,129
1971	Jan. 2	Dallas ($8,500)	San Francisco ($5,500)	14-3	Dallas	63,409
1970	Jan. 3	Dallas ($8,500)	San Francisco ($5,500)	17-10	San Francisco	59,364
1969	Jan. 4	Minnesota ($7,930)	Cleveland ($5,118)	27-7	Minnesota	46,503
1968	Dec. 29	Baltimore ($9,306)	Cleveland ($5,963)	34-0	Cleveland	78,410
1967	Dec. 31	Green Bay ($7,950)	Dallas ($5,299)	21-17	Green Bay	50,861
1966	Jan. 1	Green Bay ($9,813)	Dallas ($6,527)	34-27	Dallas	74,152
1965	Jan. 2	Green Bay ($7,819)	Cleveland ($5,288)	23-12	Green Bay	50,777
1964	Dec. 27	Cleveland ($8,052)	Baltimore ($5,571)	27-0	Cleveland	79,544
1963	Dec. 29	Chicago ($5,899)	New York ($4,218)	14-10	Chicago	45,801
1962	Dec. 30	Green Bay ($5,888)	New York ($4,166)	16-7	New York	64,892
1961	Dec. 31	Green Bay ($5,195)	New York ($3,339)	37-0	Green Bay	39,029
1960	Dec. 26	Philadelphia ($5,116)	Green Bay ($3,105)	17-13	Philadelphia	67,325
1959	Dec. 27	Baltimore ($4,674)	New York ($3,083)	31-16	Baltimore	57,545
1958	Dec. 28	Baltimore ($4,718)	New York ($3,111)	23-17*	New York	64,185
1957	Dec. 29	Detroit ($4,295)	Cleveland ($2,750)	59-14	Detroit	55,263
1956	Dec. 30	New York ($3,779)	Chi. Bears ($2,485)	47-7	New York	56,836
1955	Dec. 26	Cleveland ($3,508)	Los Angeles ($2,316)	38-14	Los Angeles	85,693
1954	Dec. 26	Cleveland ($2,478)	Detroit ($1,585)	56-10	Cleveland	43,827
1953	Dec. 27	Detroit ($2,424)	Cleveland ($1,654)	17-16	Detroit	54,577
1952	Dec. 28	Detroit ($2,274)	Cleveland ($1,712)	17-7	Cleveland	50,934
1951	Dec. 23	Los Angeles ($2,108)	Cleveland ($1,483)	24-17	Los Angeles	57,522

1950	Dec. 24	Cleveland ($1,113)	Los Angeles ($686)	30-28	Cleveland	29,751
1949	Dec. 18	Philadelphia ($1,094)	Los Angeles ($739)	14-0	Los Angeles	27,980
1948	Dec. 19	Philadelphia ($1,540)	Chi. Cardinals ($874)	7-0	Philadelphia	36,309
1947	Dec. 28	Chi. Cardinals ($1,132)	Philadelphia ($754)	28-21	Chicago	30,759
1946	Dec. 15	Chi. Bears ($1,975)	New York ($1,295)	24-14	New York	58,346
1945	Dec. 16	Cleveland ($1,469)	Washington ($902)	15-14	Cleveland	32,178
1944	Dec. 17	Green Bay ($1,449)	New York ($814)	14-7	New York	46,016
1943	Dec. 26	Chi. Bears ($1,146)	Washington ($765)	41-21	Chicago	34,320
1942	Dec. 13	Washington ($965)	Chi. Bears ($637)	14-6	Washington	36,006
1941	Dec. 21	Chi. Bears ($430)	New York ($288)	37-9	Chicago	13,341
1940	Dec. 8	Chi. Bears ($873)	Washington ($606)	73-0	Washington	36,034
1939	Dec. 10	Green Bay ($703.97)	New York ($455.57)	27-0	Milwaukee	32,279
1938	Dec. 11	New York ($504.45)	Green Bay ($368.81)	23-17	New York	48,120
1937	Dec. 12	Washington ($225.90)	Chi. Bears ($127.78)	28-21	Chicago	15,870
1936	Dec. 13	Green Bay ($250)	Boston ($180)	21-6	New York	29,545
1935	Dec. 15	Detroit ($313.35)	New York ($200.20)	26-7	Detroit	15,000
1934	Dec. 9	New York ($621)	Chi. Bears ($414.02)	30-13	New York	35,059
1933	Dec. 17	Chi. Bears ($210.34)	New York ($140.22)	23-21	Chicago	26,000
1932	Dec. 18	Chi. Bears	Portsmouth	9-0	Chicago	11,198

**Sudden death overtime.*

NFC Championship Game Composite Standings

	W	L	Pct.	Pts.	OP
Green Bay Packers	8	2	.800	223	116
Philadelphia Eagles	4	1	.800	79	48
Baltimore Colts	3	1	.750	88	60
Detroit Lions*	4	2	.667	129	109
Minnesota Vikings	4	2	.667	108	80
Chicago Bears	8	5	.615	292	217
Washington Redskins**	6	5	.545	181	245
St. Louis Cardinals***	1	1	.500	28	28
Dallas Cowboys	5	7	.417	227	213
San Francisco 49ers	2	3	.400	85	82
Cleveland Browns	4	7	.364	224	253
Los Angeles Rams****	3	8	.273	120	240
New York Giants	4	11	.267	225	309
Tampa Bay Buccaneers	0	1	.000	0	9

**One game played when franchise was in Portsmouth. (Lost 9-0)*
***One game played when franchise was in Boston. (Lost 21-6)*
****Both games played when franchise was in Chicago. (Won 28-21, lost 7-0)*
*****One game played when franchise was in Cleveland. (Won 15-14)*

1987 National Football Conference Championship Game

Robert F. Kennedy Stadium, Washington, D.C. January 17, 1988
Attendance: 55,212

Washington 17, Minnesota 10 —NFC Eastern Division champion Washington advanced to its third Super Bowl in the past six seasons by downing Minnesota 17-10. The Redskins consistently applied pressure to Vikings quarterback Wade Wilson and accumulated eight sacks, one off the NFL playoff record of nine. Defensive tackle Dave Butz, with two sacks, and defensive end Dexter Manley, with one-and-a-half sacks, led the charge. Washington's defense limited Minnesota to 259 yards. Washington scored first when quarterback Doug Williams threw a 42-yard touchdown pass to Kelvin Bryant to complete an eight-play, 98-yard drive. Redskins linebacker Mel Kaufman had an interception in the third quarter and returned it to the Vikings' 17-yard line to set up a 28-yard field goal by Ali Haji-Sheikh that gave Washington a 10-7 lead. Early in the final period, the Vikings' Anthony Carter returned a punt 26 yards to midfield, that set up Chuck Nelson's 18-yard field goal. The Redskins responded with an 18-play, 70-yard drive that concluded with wide receiver Gary Clark's seven-yard touchdown catch with 5:06 remaining. Minnesota drove to the Washington 6-yard line but had an incomplete pass on fourth down with 52 seconds left.

Minnesota (10)	Offense	Washington (17)
Anthony Carter	WR	Gary Clark
Gary Zimmerman	LT	Joe Jacoby
David Huffman	LG	Raleigh McKenzie
Kirk Lowdermilk	C	Jeff Bostic
Greg Koch	RG	R.C. Thielemann
Tim Irwin	RT	Mark May
Steve Jordan	TE	Anthony Jones
Leo Lewis	WR-TE	Don Warren
Wade Wilson	QB	Doug Williams
Darrin Nelson	RB	George Rogers
Alfred Anderson	RB-WR	Ricky Sanders
	Defense	
Doug Martin	LE	Charles Mann
Henry Thomas	LT	Dave Butz
Keith Millard	RT	Darryl Grant
Chris Doleman	RE	Dexter Manley
David Howard	LLB	Mel Kaufman
Scott Studwell	MLB	Neal Olkewicz
Jesse Solomon	RLB	Monte Coleman
Issiac Holt	LCB	Darrell Green
Carl Lee	RCB	Barry Wilburn
Joey Browner	SS	Alvin Walton
John Harris	FS	Todd Bowles

Substitutions

Minnesota—Offense: K—Chuck Nelson. P—Bucky Scribner. RB—D.J. Dozier, Rick Fenney, Allen Rice. WR—Jim Gustafson, Hassan Jones. TE—Carl Hilton. C—Chris Foote. G—Mark MacDonald, Randy Rasmussen. Defense: E—Stafford Mays. T—Tim Newton. LB—Sam Anno, Walker Lee Ashley, Ray Berry, Chris Martin. CB—Wymon Henderson, Reggie Rutland. S—Steve Freeman, Neal Guggemos. DNP: QB—Rich Gannon, Tommy Kramer.
Washington—Offense: K—Ali Haji-Sheikh. P—Steve Cox. QB—Jay Schroeder. RB—Reggie Branch, Kelvin Bryant, Timmy Smith. WR—Anthony Allen, Eric Yarber. TE—Clint Didier, Terry Orr. C—David Jones. G—Rick Kehr. T—Russ Grimm. Defense: E—Markus Koch, Steve Hamilton. T—Dean Hamel. LB—Ravin Caldwell, Kurt Gouviea. CB—Brian Davis, Tim Morrison, Clarence Vaughn, Dennis Woodberry. S—Vernon Dean.

Officials

Referee—Ben Dreith. Umpire—Ron Botchan. Line Judge—Dick McKenzie. Head Linesman—Earnie Frantz. Back Judge—Jim Poole. Field Judge—Pat Mallette. Side Judge—Dave Parry.

Scoring

Minnesota	0	7	0	3	— 10
Washington	7	0	3	7	— 17

Wash —Bryant 42 pass from Williams (Haji-Sheikh kick)
Minn —Lewis 23 pass from Wilson (C. Nelson kick)
Wash —FG Haji-Sheikh 28
Minn —FG C. Nelson 18
Wash —Clark 7 pass from Williams (Haji-Sheikh kick)

Team Statistics

	Minnesota	Washington
Total First Downs	16	11
First Downs Rushing	5	7
First Downs Passing	10	4
First Downs Penalty	1	0
Total Net Yardage	259	280
Total Offensive Plays	68	60
Average Gain per Offensive Play	3.8	4.7
Rushes	21	34
Yards Gained Rushing (net)	76	161
Average Yards per Rush	3.6	4.7
Passes Attempted	39	26
Passes Completed	19	9
Had Intercepted	1	0
Times Tackled Attempting to Pass	8	0
Yards Lost Attempting to Pass	60	0
Yards Gained Passing (net)	183	119
Punts	10	8
Average Distance	33.2	39.1
Punt Returns	4	4
Punt Return Yardage	57	10
Kickoff Returns	3	3
Kickoff Return Yardage	58	54
Interception Return Yardage	0	10

Total Return Yardage	115	74
Fumbles	0	1
Own Fumbles Recovered	0	1
Opponents Fumbles Recovered	0	0
Penalties	2	3
Yards Penalized	10	18
Total Points Scored	10	17
Touchdowns Rushing	0	0
Touchdowns Passing	1	2
Touchdowns Returns	0	0
Extra Points	1	2
Field Goals	1	1
Field Goals Attempted	1	3
Safeties	0	0
Third Down Efficiency	3/15	5/16
Fourth Down Efficiency	0/1	0/0
Time of Possession	33:02	26:58

Individual Statistics

Rushing

Minnesota	No.	Yds.	LG	TD
Wilson	4	28	11	0
Anderson	4	25	9	0
D. Nelson	8	15	9	0
Rice	1	8	8	0
Fenney	2	2	2	0
Dozier	2	−2	0	0

Washington	No.	Yds.	LG	TD
Smith	13	72	34	0
Rogers	12	46	9	0
Sanders	1	28	28	0
Williams	4	7	10	0
Clark	1	5	5	0
Bryant	3	3	6	0

Passing

Minn.	Att.	Comp.	Yds.	TD	Int.
Wilson	39	19	243	1	1

Wash.	Att.	Comp.	Yds.	TD	Int.
Williams	26	9	119	2	0

Receiving

Minnesota	No.	Yds.	LG	TD
Carter	7	85	23	0
Lewis	4	54	23t	1
Jordan	3	56	36	0
D. Nelson	3	25	10	0
Rice	1	15	15	0
Anderson	1	8	8	0

Washington	No.	Yds.	LG	TD
Bryant	4	47	42t	1
Clark	3	57	43	1
Allen	1	9	9	0
Warren	1	6	6	0

Interceptions

Minnesota	No.	Yds.	LG	TD
None				

Washington	No.	Yds.	LG	TD
Kaufman	1	10	10	0

Punting

Minnesota	No.	Avg.	LG	Blk.
Scribner	10	33.2	40	0

Washington	No.	Avg.	LG	Blk.
Cox	8	39.1	48	0

Punt Returns

Minnesota	No.	FC	Yds.	LG	TD
Carter	4	2	57	26	0

Washington	No.	FC	Yds.	LG	TD
Green	2	1	1	1	0
Yarber	1	0	9	9	0
Dean	1	0	0	0	0

Kickoff Returns

Minnesota	No.	Yds.	LG	TD
D. Nelson	2	43	28	0
Rice	1	15	15	0

Washington	No.	Yds.	LG	TD
Sanders	2	30	26	0
Smith	1	24	24	0

AFC Divisional Playoffs

Includes Second-Round Playoff Games (1982), AFC Inter-Divisional Games (1969), and special playoff games to break ties for AFL Division Championships (1963, 1968)

Results

Season	Date	Winner (Share)	Loser (Share)	Score	Site	Attendance
1987	Jan. 10	Denver ($10,000)	Houston ($10,000)	34-10	Denver	75,440
	Jan. 9	Cleveland ($10,000)	Indianapolis ($10,000)	38-21	Cleveland	79,372
1986	Jan. 4	Denver ($10,000)	New England ($10,000)	22-17	Denver	75,262
	Jan. 3	Cleveland ($10,000)	N.Y. Jets ($10,000)	23-20*	Cleveland	79,720
1985	Jan. 5	New England ($10,000)	L.A. Raiders ($10,000)	27-20	Los Angeles	87,163
	Jan. 4	Miami ($10,000)	Cleveland ($10,000)	24-21	Miami	74,667
1984	Dec. 30	Pittsburgh ($10,000)	Denver ($10,000)	24-17	Denver	74,981
	Dec. 29	Miami ($10,000)	Seattle ($10,000)	31-10	Miami	73,469
1983	Jan. 1	L.A. Raiders ($10,000)	Pittsburgh ($10,000)	38-10	Los Angeles	90,380
	Dec. 31	Seattle ($10,000)	Miami ($10,000)	27-20	Miami	74,136
1982	Jan. 16	Miami ($10,000)	San Diego ($10,000)	34-13	Miami	71,383
	Jan. 15	N.Y. Jets ($10,000)	L.A. Raiders ($10,000)	17-14	Los Angeles	90,038
1981	Jan. 3	Cincinnati ($5,000)	Buffalo ($5,000)	28-21	Cincinnati	55,420
	Jan. 2	San Diego ($5,000)	Miami ($5,000)	41-38*	Miami	73,735
1980	Jan. 4	Oakland ($5,000)	Cleveland ($5,000)	14-12	Cleveland	78,245
	Jan. 3	San Diego ($5,000)	Buffalo ($5,000)	20-14	San Diego	52,253
1979	Dec. 30	Pittsburgh ($5,000)	Miami ($5,000)	34-14	Pittsburgh	50,214
	Dec. 29	Houston ($5,000)	San Diego ($5,000)	17-14	San Diego	51,192
1978	Dec. 31	Houston ($5,000)	New England ($5,000)	31-14	New England	60,735
	Dec. 30	Pittsburgh ($5,000)	Denver ($5,000)	33-10	Pittsburgh	50,230
1977	Dec. 24	Oakland ($5,000)	Baltimore ($5,000)	37-31	Baltimore	59,925
	Dec. 24	Denver ($5,000)	Pittsburgh ($5,000)	34-21	Denver	75,059
1976	Dec. 19	Pittsburgh ($)	Baltimore ($)	40-14	Baltimore	59,296
	Dec. 18	Oakland ($)	New England ($)	24-21	Oakland	53,050
1975	Dec. 28	Oakland ($)	Cincinnati ($)	31-28	Oakland	53,030
	Dec. 27	Pittsburgh ($)	Baltimore ($)	28-10	Pittsburgh	49,557
1974	Dec. 22	Pittsburgh ($)	Buffalo ($)	32-14	Pittsburgh	49,841
	Dec. 21	Oakland ($)	Miami ($)	28-26	Oakland	53,023
1973	Dec. 23	Miami ($)	Cincinnati ($)	34-16	Miami	78,928
	Dec. 22	Oakland ($)	Pittsburgh ($)	33-14	Oakland	52,646
1972	Dec. 24	Miami ($)	Cleveland ($)	20-14	Miami	78,916
	Dec. 23	Pittsburgh ($)	Oakland ($)	13-7	Pittsburgh	50,327
1971	Dec. 26	Baltimore ($)	Cleveland ($)	20-3	Cleveland	70,734
	Dec. 25	Miami ($)	Kansas City ($)	27-24*	Kansas City	45,822
1970	Dec. 27	Oakland ($)	Miami ($)	21-14	Oakland	52,594
	Dec. 26	Baltimore ($)	Cincinnati ($)	17-0	Baltimore	49,694
1969	Dec. 21	Oakland ($)	Houston ($)	56-7	Oakland	53,539
	Dec. 20	Kansas City ($)	N.Y. Jets ($)	13-6	New York	62,977
1968	Dec. 22	Oakland ($)	Kansas City ($)	41-6	Oakland	53,605
1963	Dec. 28	Boston ($)	Buffalo ($)	26-8	Buffalo	33,044

**Sudden Death Overtime.*
$ Players received 1/14 of annual salary for playoff appearances.

1987 AFC Divisional Playoffs

Cleveland Stadium, Cleveland, Ohio January 9, 1988
Attendance: 79,372

Cleveland 38, Indianapolis 21—Quarterback Bernie Kosar threw for three touchdowns, and running back Earnest Byner rushed 122 yards and scored two touchdowns, as the Browns advanced to their second straight AFC Championship Game with a 38-21 triumph over the Colts. Cleveland took the opening kickoff and drove 86 yards for a touchdown. Kosar capped the 15-play drive with a 10-yard scoring pass to Byner. After Indianapolis tied the score 7-7, Kosar hit wide receiver Reggie Langhorne on a 39-yard scoring pass with 1:51 to go in the first half. But Jack Trudeau's 19-yard touchdown pass to Eric Dickerson, 42 seconds before intermission, tied the score 14-14. The turning point in the game came midway through the third quarter when safety Felix Wright intercepted a Trudeau pass at the Cleveland 14-yard line. The Browns then concluded another 86-yard drive on Byner's two-yard run. Kosar (20 of 31 passes for 229 yards) threw three touchdown passes for the first time in his four postseason games. Cornerback Frank Minnifield returned an interception 48 yards for the game's final touchdown with 39 seconds left. The Browns averaged 6.2 yards per play in gaining 404 yards. Cleveland converted 11 of 14 third-down plays.

Indianapolis	7	7	0	7	—21
Cleveland	7	7	7	17	—38

Clev—Byner 10 pass from Kosar (Bahr kick)
Ind —Beach 2 pass from Trudeau (Biasucci kick)
Clev—Langhorne 39 pass from Kosar (Bahr kick)
Ind —Dickerson 19 pass from Trudeau (Biasucci kick)
Clev—Byner 2 run (Bahr kick)
Clev—FG Bahr 22
Clev—Brennan 2 pass from Kosar (Bahr kick)
Ind —Bentley 1 run (Biasucci kick)
Clev—Minnifield 48 interception return (Bahr kick)

Mile High Stadium, Denver, Colorado January 10, 1988
Attendance: 75,440

Denver 34, Houston 10—Denver quarterback John Elway passed for two touchdowns and ran for a third as the Broncos defeated the Oilers 34-10 to become the first AFC West team since the San Diego Chargers of 1980 and 1981 to play in consecutive AFC Championship Games. Denver capitalized on two Houston turnovers to take a 14-0 first-quarter lead. Safety Steve Wilson recovered Warren Moon's lateral to Mike Rozier at the Oilers' 1-yard line to set up Gene Lang's one-yard touchdown run. Karl Mecklenburg's interception on Houston's next possession led to Elway's first touchdown pass, a 27-yarder to Clarence Kay. Kay also caught a one-yarder in the second quarter for the first two-touchdown game of his four-year career. Elway, who completed 14 of 25 for 259 yards, scored on a three-yard run with 4:23 remaining to seal the win. Wide receiver Vance Johnson caught four passes for 105 yards, including a 55-yarder to set up Kay's second score. The Broncos held the Oilers to 73 rushing yards.

Houston	0	3	0	7	—10
Denver	14	10	3	7	—34

Den—Lang 1 run (Karlis kick)
Den—Kay 27 pass from Elway (Karlis kick)
Den—FG Karlis 43
Hou—FG Zendejas 46
Den—Kay 1 pass from Elway (Karlis kick)
Den—FG Karlis 23
Hou—Givins 19 pass from Moon (Zendejas kick)
Den—Elway 3 run (Karlis kick)

NFC Divisional Playoffs

Includes Second-Round Playoff Games (1982), NFL Conference Championship Games (1967-69), and special playoff games to break ties for NFL Division or Conference Championships (1941, 1943, 1947, 1950, 1952, 1957, 1958, 1965)

Results

Season	Date	Winner (Share)	Loser (Share)	Score	Site	Attendance
1987	Jan. 10	Washington ($10,000)	Chicago ($10,000)	21-17	Chicago	65,268
	Jan. 9	Minnesota ($10,000)	San Francisco ($10,000)	36-24	San Francisco	63,008
1986	Jan. 4	N.Y. Giants ($10,000)	San Francisco ($10,000)	49-3	East Rutherford	75,691
	Jan. 3	Washington ($10,000)	Chicago ($10,000)	27-13	Chicago	65,524
1985	Jan. 5	Chicago ($10,000)	N.Y. Giants ($10,000)	21-0	Chicago	65,670
	Jan. 4	L.A. Rams ($10,000)	Dallas ($10,000)	20-0	Anaheim	66,581
1984	Dec. 30	Chicago ($10,000)	Washington ($10,000)	23-19	Washington	55,431
	Dec. 29	San Francisco ($10,000)	N.Y. Giants ($10,000)	21-10	San Francisco	60,303
1983	Jan. 1	Washington ($10,000)	L.A. Rams ($10,000)	51-7	Washington	54,440
	Dec. 31	San Francisco ($10,000)	Detroit ($10,000)	24-23	San Francisco	59,979
1982	Jan. 16	Dallas ($10,000)	Green Bay ($10,000)	37-26	Dallas	63,972
	Jan. 15	Washington ($10,000)	Minnesota ($10,000)	21-7	Washington	54,593
1981	Jan. 3	San Francisco ($5,000)	N.Y. Giants ($5,000)	38-24	San Francisco	58,360
	Jan. 2	Dallas ($5,000)	Tampa Bay ($5,000)	38-0	Dallas	64,848
1980	Jan. 4	Dallas ($5,000)	Atlanta ($5,000)	30-27	Atlanta	59,793
	Jan. 3	Philadelphia ($5,000)	Minnesota ($5,000)	31-16	Philadelphia	70,178
1979	Dec. 30	Los Angeles ($5,000)	Dallas ($5,000)	21-19	Dallas	64,792
	Dec. 29	Tampa Bay ($5,000)	Philadelphia ($5,000)	24-17	Tampa Bay	71,402
1978	Dec. 31	Los Angeles ($5,000)	Minnesota ($5,000)	34-10	Los Angeles	70,436
	Dec. 30	Dallas ($5,000)	Atlanta ($5,000)	27-20	Dallas	63,406
1977	Dec. 26	Dallas ($5,000)	Chicago ($5,000)	37-7	Dallas	63,260
	Dec. 26	Minnesota ($5,000)	Los Angeles ($5,000)	14-7	Los Angeles	70,203
1976	Dec. 19	Los Angeles ($)	Dallas ($)	14-12	Dallas	63,283
	Dec. 18	Minnesota ($)	Washington ($)	35-20	Minnesota	47,466
1975	Dec. 28	Dallas ($)	Minnesota ($)	17-14	Minnesota	48,050
	Dec. 27	Los Angeles ($)	St. Louis ($)	35-23	Los Angeles	73,459
1974	Dec. 22	Los Angeles ($)	Washington ($)	19-10	Los Angeles	77,925
	Dec. 21	Minnesota ($)	St. Louis ($)	30-14	Minnesota	48,150
1973	Dec. 23	Dallas ($)	Los Angeles ($)	27-16	Dallas	63,272
	Dec. 22	Minnesota ($)	Washington ($)	27-20	Minnesota	48,040
1972	Dec. 24	Washington ($)	Green Bay ($)	16-3	Washington	52,321
	Dec. 23	Dallas ($)	San Francisco ($)	30-28	San Francisco	59,746
1971	Dec. 26	San Francisco ($)	Washington ($)	24-20	San Francisco	45,327
	Dec. 25	Dallas ($)	Minnesota ($)	20-12	Minnesota	47,307
1970	Dec. 27	San Francisco ($)	Minnesota ($)	17-14	Minnesota	45,103
	Dec. 26	Dallas ($)	Detroit ($)	5-0	Dallas	69,613
1969	Dec. 28	Cleveland ($)	Dallas ($)	38-14	Dallas	69,321
	Dec. 27	Minnesota ($)	Los Angeles ($)	23-20	Minnesota	47,900
1968	Dec. 22	Baltimore ($)	Minnesota ($)	24-14	Baltimore	60,238
	Dec. 21	Cleveland ($)	Dallas ($)	31-20	Cleveland	81,497
1967	Dec. 24	Dallas ($)	Cleveland ($)	52-14	Dallas	70,786
	Dec. 23	Green Bay ($)	Los Angeles ($)	28-7	Milwaukee	49,861
1965	Dec. 26	Green Bay ($)	Baltimore ($)	13-10*	Green Bay	50,484
1958	Dec. 21	N.Y. Giants (#)	Cleveland (#)	10-0	New York	61,274
1957	Dec. 22	Detroit (#)	San Francisco (#)	31-27	San Francisco	60,118
1952	Dec. 21	Detroit (#)	Los Angeles (#)	31-21	Detroit	47,645
1950	Dec. 17	Los Angeles (#)	Chicago Bears (#)	24-14	Los Angeles	83,501
	Dec. 17	Cleveland (#)	N.Y. Giants (#)	8-3	Cleveland	33,054
1947	Dec. 21	Philadelphia (#)	Pittsburgh (#)	21-0	Pittsburgh	35,729
1943	Dec. 19	Washington (+)	N.Y. Giants (+)	28-0	New York	42,800
1941	Dec. 14	Chicago Bears (+)	Green Bay (+)	33-14	Chicago	43,425

**Sudden Death Overtime.*
$ Players received 1/14 of annual salary for playoff appearances.
 # Players received 1/12 of annual salary for playoff appearances.
+ Players received 1/10 of annual salary for playoff appearances.

1987 NFC Divisional Playoffs

Candlestick Park, San Francisco, California January 9, 1988
Attendance: 63,008

Minnesota 36, San Francisco 24—Minnesota advanced to its first NFC Championship Game since 1977 by defeating San Francisco 36-24. Wide receiver Anthony Carter established an NFL playoff record with 227 receiving yards on 10 receptions. The old record of 198 yards was set by Tom Fears of the Los Angeles Rams in 1950. Quarterback Wade Wilson played the entire game for the Vikings, completing 20 of 34 passes for 298 yards. Kicker Chuck Nelson made all five of his field-goal attempts. (21, 23, 40, 46, and 23 yards). Rookie cornerback Reggie Rutland added a 45-yard interception return for a touchdown. The Vikings' defense had four sacks and two interceptions.

Minnesota	3	17	10	6 — 36
San Francisco	3	0	14	7 — 24

Minn — FG C. Nelson 21
SF — FG Wersching 43
Minn — Hilton 7 pass from Wilson (C. Nelson kick)
Minn — FG C. Nelson 23
Minn — Rutland 45 interception return (C. Nelson kick)
SF — Fuller 48 interception return (Wersching kick)
Minn — Jones 5 pass from Wilson (C. Nelson kick)
SF — Young 5 run (Wersching kick)
Minn — FG C. Nelson 40
Minn — FG C. Nelson 46
SF — Frank 16 pass from Young (Wersching kick)
Minn — FG C. Nelson 23

Soldier Field, Chicago, Illinois January 10, 1988
Attendance: 65,268

Washington 21, Chicago 17—NFC East champion Washington qualified for its fourth NFC Championship Game in the past six seasons by coming from behind to edge NFC Central titlist Chicago 21-17. The Bears jumped to a 14-0 lead midway through the second quarter. However, the Redskins rallied to tie the game by halftime on running back George Rogers's three-yard touchdown run and tight end Clint Didier's 18-yard touchdown reception from quarterback Doug Williams. The deciding score came with 3:20 elapsed in the third quarter when cornerback Darrell Green returned a Bears punt 52 yards for a touchdown. Williams completed 14 of 29 passes for 207 yards and one touchdown. Wide receiver Ricky Sanders, starting for the injured Art Monk, caught six passes for 92 yards.

Washington	0	14	7	0 — 21
Chicago	7	7	3	0 — 17

Chi – Thomas 2 run (Butler kick)
Chi – Morris 14 pass from McMahon (Butler kick)
Wash – Rogers 3 run (Haji-Sheikh kick)
Wash – Didier 18 pass from Williams (Haji-Sheikh kick)
Wash – Green 52 punt return (Haji-Sheikh kick)
Chi – FG Butler 25

AFC First-Round Playoff Games

Results

Season	Date	Winner (Share)	Loser (Share)	Score	Site	Attendance
1987	Jan. 3	Houston ($6,000)	Seattle ($6,000)	23-20*	Houston	50,519
1986	Dec. 28	N.Y. Jets ($6,000)	Kansas City ($6,000)	35-15	East Rutherford	75,210
1985	Dec. 28	New England ($6,000)	N.Y. Jets ($6,000)	26-14	East Rutherford	75,945
1984	Dec. 22	Seattle ($6,000)	L.A. Raiders ($6,000)	13-7	Seattle	62,049
1983	Dec. 24	Seattle ($6,000)	Denver ($6,000)	31-7	Seattle	64,275
1982	Jan. 9	N.Y. Jets ($6,000)	Cincinnati ($6,000)	44-17	Cincinnati	57,560
	Jan. 9	San Diego ($6,000)	Pittsburgh ($6,000)	31-28	Pittsburgh	53,546
	Jan. 8	L.A. Raiders ($6,000)	Cleveland ($6,000)	27-10	Los Angeles	56,555
	Jan. 8	Miami ($6,000)	New England ($6,000)	28-13	Miami	68,842
1981	Dec. 27	Buffalo ($3,000)	N.Y. Jets ($3,000)	31-27	New York	57,050
1980	Dec. 28	Oakland ($3,000)	Houston ($3,000)	27-7	Oakland	53,333
1979	Dec. 23	Houston ($3,000)	Denver ($3,000)	13-7	Houston	48,776
1978	Dec. 24	Houston ($3,000)	Miami ($3,000)	17-9	Miami	72,445

**Sudden death overtime.*

1987 AFC First-Round Playoff Game

Astrodome, Houston, Texas January 3, 1988
Attendance: 50,519

Houston 23, Seattle 20—Oilers kicker Tony Zendejas atoned for a fourth-quarter 29-yard field goal miss by converting a 42-yarder 8:05 into overtime to help Houston advance to the divisional playoffs for the first time since 1980. Quarterback Warren Moon completed 21 of 32 passes for 273 yards and one touchdown in his initial NFL playoff game. Drew Hill and Ernest Givins combined for 13 catches for 173 yards, including six for 71 on third downs. Wide receiver Willie Drewrey's first NFL touchdown catch, a 29-yarder, gave the Oilers a 20-13 lead in the third quarter. However, Seattle quarterback Dave Krieg hit wide receiver Steve Largent on a 12-yard scoring pass in the final 1:47 to tie the score and send the game into overtime. Houston held a 47:44 to 20:21 time-of-possession advantage over Seattle and outgained the Seahawks 437 yards to 250.

Seattle	7	3	3	7	0 — 20
Houston	3	10	7	0	3 — 23

Sea—Largent 20 pass from Krieg (Johnson kick)
Hou—FG Zendejas 47
Hou—Rozier 1 run (Zendejas kick)
Hou—FG Zendejas 49
Sea—FG Johnson 33
Sea—FG Johnson 41
Hou—Drewrey 29 pass from Moon (Zendejas kick)
Sea—Largent 12 pass from Krieg (Johnson kick)
Hou—FG Zendejas 42

NFC First-Round Playoff Games

Results

Season	Date	Winner (Share)	Loser (Share)	Score	Site	Attendance
1987	Jan. 3	Minnesota ($6,000)	New Orleans ($6,000)	44-10	New Orleans	68,546
1986	Dec. 28	Washington ($6,000)	L.A. Rams ($6,000)	19-7	Washington	54,567
1985	Dec. 29	N.Y. Giants ($6,000)	San Francisco ($6,000)	17-3	East Rutherford	75,131
1984	Dec. 23	N.Y. Giants ($6,000)	L.A. Rams ($6,000)	16-3	Anaheim	67,037
1983	Dec. 26	L.A. Rams ($6,000)	Dallas ($6,000)	24-17	Dallas	62,118
1982	Jan. 9	Dallas ($6,000)	Tampa Bay ($6,000)	30-17	Dallas	65,042
	Jan. 9	Minnesota ($6,000)	Atlanta ($6,000)	30-24	Minnesota	60,560
	Jan. 8	Green Bay ($6,000)	St. Louis ($6,000)	41-16	Green Bay	54,282
	Jan. 8	Washington ($6,000)	Detroit ($6,000)	31-7	Washington	55,045
1981	Dec. 27	N.Y. Giants ($3,000)	Philadelphia ($3,000)	27-21	Philadelphia	71,611
1980	Dec. 28	Dallas ($3,000)	Los Angeles ($3,000)	34-13	Dallas	63,052
1979	Dec. 23	Philadelphia ($3,000)	Chicago ($3,000)	27-17	Philadelphia	69,397
1978	Dec. 24	Atlanta ($3,000)	Philadelphia ($3,000)	14-13	Atlanta	59,403

1987 NFC First-Round Playoff Game

Louisiana Superdome, New Orleans, Louisiana — January 3, 1988
Attendance: 68,546

Minnesota 44, New Orleans 10—Minnesota scored the most points ever in a Wild Card game in downing host New Orleans. The Vikings compiled 417 yards and yielded only 149 in advancing to the divisional playoffs. Minnesota held a time-of-possession advantage of 41:18 to 18:42. In addition, the defense had four interceptions, two fumble recoveries, and two sacks. Vikings wide receiver Anthony Carter caught six passes for 79 yards, including a 10-yard touchdown. His 84-yard punt return touchdown broke the previous NFL playoff record of 81 yards by the Bears' Hugh Gallarneau in 1941. Darrin Nelson carried 17 times for 73 yards for Minnesota.

Minnesota	10	21	3	10	— 44
New Orleans	7	3	0	0	— 10

NO —Martin 10 pass from Hebert (Andersen kick)
Minn—FG C. Nelson 42
Minn—Carter 84 punt return (C. Nelson kick)
Minn—Jordan 5 pass from Wilson (C. Nelson kick)
Minn—Carter 10 pass from Rice (C. Nelson kick)
NO —FG Andersen 40
Minn—Jones 44 pass from Wilson (C. Nelson kick)
Minn—FG C. Nelson 32
Minn—FG C. Nelson 19
Minn—Dozier 8 run (C. Nelson kick)

AFC-NFC PRO BOWL SUMMARIES

AFC-NFC Pro Bowl At A Glance (1971-1988)

NFC leads series, 10-8

Results

Year	Date	Winner (Share)	Loser (Share)	Score	Site	Attendance
1988	Feb. 7	AFC ($10,000)	NFC ($5,000)	15-6	Honolulu	50,113
1987	Feb. 1	AFC ($10,000)	NFC ($5,000)	10-6	Honolulu	50,101
1986	Feb. 2	NFC ($10,000)	AFC ($5,000)	28-24	Honolulu	50,101
1985	Jan. 27	AFC ($10,000)	NFC ($5,000)	22-14	Honolulu	50,385
1984	Jan. 29	NFC ($10,000)	AFC ($5,000)	45-3	Honolulu	50,445
1983	Feb. 6	NFC ($10,000)	AFC ($5,000)	20-19	Honolulu	49,583
1982	Jan. 31	AFC ($5,000)	NFC ($2,500)	16-13	Honolulu	50,402
1981	Feb. 1	NFC ($5,000)	AFC ($2,500)	21-7	Honolulu	50,360
1980	Jan. 27	NFC ($5,000)	AFC ($2,500)	37-27	Honolulu	49,800
1979	Jan. 29	NFC ($5,000)	AFC ($2,500)	13-7	Los Angeles	46,281
1978	Jan. 23	NFC ($5,000)	AFC ($2,500)	14-13	Tampa	51,337
1977	Jan. 17	AFC ($2,000)	NFC ($1,500)	24-14	Seattle	64,752
1976	Jan. 26	NFC ($2,000)	AFC ($1,500)	23-20	New Orleans	30,546
1975	Jan. 20	NFC ($2,000)	AFC ($1,500)	17-10	Miami	26,484
1974	Jan. 20	AFC ($2,000)	NFC ($1,500)	15-13	Kansas City	66,918
1973	Jan. 21	AFC ($2,000)	NFC ($1,500)	33-28	Irving	37,091
1972	Jan. 23	AFC ($2,000)	NFC ($1,500)	26-13	Los Angeles	53,647
1971	Jan. 24	NFC ($2,000)	AFC ($1,500)	27-6	Los Angeles	48,222

1988 AFC-NFC Pro Bowl

Aloha Stadium, Honolulu, Hawaii February 7, 1988
Attendance: 50,113

AFC 15, NFC 6—Led by a tenacious pass rush, the AFC defeated the NFC for the second consecutive year, 15-6, before the fifth straight sellout crowd in Honolulu's Aloha Stadium. Buffalo quarterback Jim Kelly scored the game's lone touchdown on a one-yard run for a 7-6 halftime lead. Colts kicker Dean Biasucci added field goals from 37 and 30 yards to complete the AFC's scoring. Saints kicker Morten Andersen had 25- and 36-yard field goals to account for the NFC's points. AFC defenders held the NFC to 213 yards and recorded eight sacks. Bills defensive end Bruce Smith, who had five tackles and two sacks, was voted the game's outstanding player. Oilers running back Mike Rozier led all rushers with 49 yards on nine carries. Jets wide receiver Al Toon had five receptions for 75 yards. The AFC generated 341 yards total offense and held a time-of-possession advantage of 34:14 to 25:46. By winning, the AFC cut the NFC's lead in the Pro Bowl series to 10-8.

NFC (6)	Offense	AFC (15)
Jerry Rice (San Francisco)	WR	Al Toon (N.Y. Jets)
Gary Zimmerman (Minnesota)	LT	Cody Risien (Cleveland)
Dennis Harrah (L.A. Rams)	LG	Keith Bishop (Denver)
Jay Hilgenberg (Chicago)	C	Ray Donaldson (Indianapolis)
Bill Fralic (Atlanta)	RG	Mike Munchak (Houston)
Jackie Slater (L.A. Rams)	RT	Chris Hinton (Indianapolis)
Steve Jordan (Minnesota)	TE	Kellen Winslow (San Diego)
Mike Quick (Philadelphia)	WR	Carlos Carson (Kansas City)
Joe Montana (San Francisco)	QB	John Elway (Denver)
Gerald Riggs (Atlanta)	RB	Marcus Allen (L.A. Raiders)
Charles White (L.A. Rams)	RB	Kevin Mack (Cleveland)
	Defense	
Reggie White (Philadelphia)	LE	Howie Long (L.A. Raiders)
Michael Carter (San Francisco)	NT	Bill Maas (Kansas City)
Chris Doleman (Minnesota)	RE	Bruce Smith (Buffalo)
Carl Banks (N.Y. Giants)	LOLB	Andre Tippett (New England)
Mike Singletary (Chicago)	LILB	Karl Mecklenburg (Denver)
Harry Carson (N.Y. Giants)	RILB	Fredd Young (Seattle)
Wilber Marshall (Chicago)	ROLB	Duane Bickett (Indianapolis)
Darrell Green (Washington)	LCB	Frank Minnifield (Cleveland)
Jerry Gray (L.A. Rams)	RCB	Hanford Dixon (Cleveland)
Joey Browner (Minnesota)	SS	Kenny Easley (Seattle)
Ronnie Lott (San Francisco)	FS	Deron Cherry (Kansas City)

Substitutions

NFC—Offense: K—Morten Andersen (New Orleans). P—Jim Arnold (Detroit). QB—Neil Lomax (St. Louis). RB—Roger Craig (San Francisco), Herschel Walker (Dallas). WR—Anthony Carter (Minnesota), Gary Clark (Washington). TE—Hoby Brenner (New Orleans). C—Doug Smith (L.A. Rams). G—Brad Edelman (New Orleans). T—Luis Sharpe (St. Louis). Defense: E—Charles Mann (Washington). NT—Steve McMichael (Chicago). LB—Sam Mills (New Orleans), Scott Studwell (Minnesota), Lawrence Taylor (N.Y. Giants). CB—Dave Waymer (New Orleans). S—Dave Duerson (Chicago). KR—Vai Sikahema (St. Louis). ST—Ron Wolfley (St. Louis).

AFC—Offense: K—Dean Biasucci (Indianapolis). P—Ralf Mojsiejenko (San Diego). QB—Jim Kelly (Buffalo), Bernie Kosar (Cleveland). RB—Eric Dickerson (Indianapolis), Mike Rozier (Houston). WR—Steve Largent (Seattle), Stanley Morgan (New England). TE—Todd Christensen (L.A. Raiders). C—Mike Webster (Pittsburgh). G—Ron Solt (Indianapolis). T—Jim Lachey (San Diego). Defense: E—Jacob Green (Seattle). NT—Tim Krumrie (Cincinnati). LB—Clay Matthews (Cleveland), John Offerdahl (Miami). CB—Albert Lewis (Kansas City). S—Keith Bostic (Houston). KR—Gerald McNeil (Cleveland). ST—Steve Tasker (Buffalo).

Head Coaches

NFC—Jerry Burns (Minnesota)
AFC—Marty Schottenheimer (Cleveland)

Officials

Referee—Dick Hantak. Umpire—Neil Gereb. Line Judge—Boyce Smith. Head Linesman—Frank Glover. Back Judge—Tom Kelleher. Field Judge—Bill Stanley. Side Judge—Gary Lane.

Scoring

NFC	0	6	0	0	— 6
AFC	0	7	6	2	— 15

NFC—FG Andersen 25
AFC—Kelly 1 run (Biasucci kick)
NFC—FG Andersen 36
AFC—FG Biasucci 37
AFC—FG Biasucci 30
AFC—Safety, Montana forced out of end zone

Team Statistics

	NFC	AFC
Total First Downs	13	21
First Downs Rushing	4	10
First Downs Passing	9	9
First Downs Penalty	0	2
Total Net Yardage	213	341
Total Offensive Plays	61	82
Average Gain per Offensive Play	3.5	4.2
Rushes	19	39
Yards Gained Rushing (net)	85	134
Average Yards per Rush	4.5	3.4
Passes Attempted	34	42
Passes Completed	15	21
Passes Had Intercepted	4	1
Times Tackled Attempting to Pass	8	1
Yards Lost Attempting to Pass	37	9
Yards Gained Passing (net)	128	207
Punts	7	6
Average Distance	49.6	41.2
Punt Returns	4	6
Punt Return Yardage	20	82
Kickoff Returns	4	1
Kickoff Return Yardage	92	15
Interception Return Yardage	7	58
Total Return Yardage	119	155
Fumbles	4	6
Own Fumbles Recovered	3	2
Opponents Fumbles Recovered	4	1
Penalties	13	1
Yards Penalized	86	5
Total Points Scored	6	15
Touchdowns	0	1
Touchdowns Rushing	0	1
Touchdowns Passing	0	0
Touchdowns Returns	0	0
Extra Points	0	1
Field Goals	2	2
Field Goals Attempted	3	3
Safeties	0	1
Third Down Efficiency	3/14	7/18
Fourth Down Efficiency	0/0	1/1
Time of Possession	25:46	34:14

Individual Statistics

Rushing

NFC	No.	Yds.	LG	TD
Walker	5	26	13	0
Riggs	2	16	13	0
White, C.	6	14	4	0
Craig	3	8	7	0
Carter, A.	1	8	8	0
Montana	1	8	8	0
Lomax	1	5	5	0
AFC	**No.**	**Yds.**	**LG**	**TD**
Rozier	9	49	13	0
Allen	11	46	22	0
Mack	4	16	6	0
Dickerson	10	13	8	0
Kelly	4	10	12	1
Kosar	1	0	0	0

Passing

NFC	Att.	Comp.	Yds.	TD	Int.
Montana	19	8	96	0	2
Lomax	15	7	69	0	2
AFC	**Att.**	**Comp.**	**Yds.**	**TD**	**Int.**
Kosar	17	10	124	0	1
Kelly	16	10	83	0	0
Elway	8	1	9	0	0
Allen	1	0	0	0	0

Receiving

NFC	No.	Yds.	LG	TD
Quick	3	44	18	0
Riggs	3	29	16	0
Clark	3	26	16	0
Walker	2	20	10	0
Craig	2	13	7	0
Rice	1	17	17	0
Jordan	1	16	16	0
AFC	**No.**	**Yds.**	**LG**	**TD**
Toon	5	75	31	0
Christensen	4	33	10	0
Allen	4	19	10	0
Mack	3	14	9	0
Morgan	2	41	27	0
Largent	1	17	17	0
Winslow	1	15	15	0
Rozier	1	2	2	0

Interceptions

NFC	No.	Yds.	LG	TD
Lott	1	7	7	0
Green	0	0	0	0
AFC	**No.**	**Yds.**	**LG**	**TD**
Easley	1	38	38	0
Lewis	1	12	12	0
Dixon	1	8	8	0
Young	1	0	0	0

Punting

NFC	No.	Avg.	LG	Blk.
Arnold	7	49.6	57	0
AFC	**No.**	**Avg.**	**LG**	**Blk.**
Mojsiejenko	6	41.2	49	0

Punt Returns

NFC	No.	FC	Yds.	LG	TD
Sikahema	4	0	20	12	0
AFC	**No.**	**FC**	**Yds.**	**LG**	**TD**
McNeil	6	0	82	19	0

Kickoff Returns

NFC	No.	Yds.	LG	TD
Sikahema	4	92	32	0
AFC	**No.**	**Yds.**	**LG**	**TD**
McNeil	1	15	15	0

1987 AFC-NFC Pro Bowl

Aloha Stadium, Honolulu, Hawaii February 1, 1987

Attendance: 50,101

AFC 10, NFC 6—The AFC defeated the NFC, 10-6, in the lowest-scoring game in AFC-NFC Pro Bowl history. The AFC took a 10-0 halftime lead on Broncos quarterback John Elway's 10-yard touchdown pass to Raiders tight end Todd Christensen and Patriots kicker Tony Franklin's 26-yard field goal. The AFC defense made the lead stand up by forcing the NFC to settle for a pair of field goals from 38 and 19 yards by Saints kicker Morten Andersen after the NFC had first downs at the AFC 31-, 7-, 16-, 15-, 5-, and 7-yard lines. Both AFC scores were set up by fumble recoveries by Seahawks linebacker Fredd Young and Dolphins linebacker John Offerdahl, respectively. Eagles defensive end Reggie White, who tied a Pro Bowl record with four sacks and also contributed seven solo tackles, was voted the game's outstanding player. The AFC victory cut the NFC's lead in the Pro Bowl series to 10-7.

AFC	7	3	0	0	— 10
NFC	0	0	3	3	— 6

AFC—Christensen 10 pass from Elway (Franklin kick)
AFC—FG Franklin 26
NFC—FG Andersen 38
NFC—FG Andersen 19

1986 AFC-NFC Pro Bowl

Aloha Stadium, Honolulu, Hawaii February 2, 1986

Attendance: 50,101

NFC 28, AFC 24—New York Giants quarterback Phil Simms brought the NFC back from a 24-7 halftime deficit to a 28-24 win over the AFC. Simms, who completed 15 of 27 passes for 212 yards and three touchdowns, was named the most valuable player of the game. The AFC had taken its first-half lead behind a two-yard run by Los Angeles Raiders running back Marcus Allen, who also threw a 51-yard scoring pass to San Diego wide receiver Wes Chandler, an 11-yard touchdown catch by Pittsburgh wide receiver Louis Lipps, and a 34-yard field goal by Steelers kicker Gary Anderson. Minnesota's Joey Browner accounted for the NFC's only score before halftime with a 48-yard touchdown interception return. After intermission, the NFC blanked the AFC while scoring three touchdowns via a 15-yard catch by Washington wide receiver Art Monk, a 2-yard reception by Dallas tight end Doug Cosbie, and a 15-yard catch by Tampa Bay tight end Jimmie Giles with 2:47 remaining in the game. The victory gave the NFC a 10-6 Pro Bowl record vs. the AFC.

NFC	0	7	7	14	— 28
AFC	7	17	0	0	— 24

AFC—Allen 2 run (Anderson kick)
NFC—Browner 48 interception return (Andersen kick)
AFC—Chandler 51 pass from Allen (Anderson kick)
AFC—FG Anderson 34
AFC—Lipps 11 pass from O'Brien (Anderson kick)
NFC—Monk 15 pass from Simms (Andersen kick)
NFC—Cosbie 2 pass from Simms (Andersen kick)
NFC—Giles 15 pass from Simms (Andersen kick)

1985 AFC-NFC Pro Bowl

Aloha Stadium, Honolulu, Hawaii January 27, 1985

Attendance: 50,385

AFC 22, NFC 14—Defensive end Art Still of the Kansas City Chiefs recovered a fumble and returned it 83 yards for a touchdown to clinch the AFC's victory over the NFC. Still's touchdown came in the fourth period with the AFC trailing 14-12 and was one of several outstanding defensive plays in a Pro Bowl dominated by two record-breaking defenses. Both teams combined for a Pro Bowl-record 17 sacks, including four by New York Jets defensive end Mark Gastineau, who was named the game's outstanding player. The AFC's first score came on a safety when Gastineau tackled running back Eric Dickerson of the Los Angeles Rams in the end zone. The AFC's second score, a six-yard pass from Miami's Dan Marino to Los Angeles Raiders running back Marcus Allen, was set up by a partial block of a punt by Seahawks linebacker Fredd Young. The NFC led the series 9-6, since it started in 1971.

AFC	0	9	0	13	— 22
NFC	0	0	7	7	— 14

AFC—Safety, Gastineau tackled Dickerson in end zone
AFC—Allen 6 pass from Marino (Johnson kick)
NFC—Lofton 13 pass from Montana (Stenerud kick)
NFC—Payton 1 run (Stenerud kick)
AFC—FG Johnson 33
AFC—Still 83 fumble recovery return (Johnson kick)
AFC—FG Johnson 22

1984 AFC-NFC Pro Bowl

Aloha Stadium, Honolulu, Hawaii January 29, 1984

Attendance: 50,445

NFC 45, AFC 3—The NFC won its sixth Pro Bowl in the last seven seasons, 45-3 over the AFC. The NFC was led by the passing of most valuable player Joe Theismann of Washington, who completed 21 of 27 passes for 242 yards and three touchdowns. Theismann set Pro Bowl records for completions and touchdown passes. The NFC established Pro Bowl marks for most points scored and fewest points allowed. Running back William Andrews of Atlanta had six carries for 43 yards and caught four passes for 49 yards, including scoring receptions of 16 and 2 yards. Los Angeles Rams rookie Eric Dickerson gained 46 yards on 11 carries, including a 14-yard touchdown run, and had 45 yards on five catches. Rams safety Nolan Cromwell had a 44-yard interception return for a touchdown early in the third period to give the NFC a commanding 24-3 lead. Green Bay wide receiver James Lofton caught an eight-yard touchdown pass, while tight end teammate Paul Coffman had a six-yard scoring catch.

NFC	3	14	14	14	— 45
AFC	0	3	0	0	— 3

NFC—FG Haji-Sheikh 23
NFC—Andrews 16 pass from Theismann (Haji-Sheikh kick)
NFC—Andrews 2 pass from Montana (Haji-Sheikh kick)
AFC—FG Anderson 43
NFC—Cromwell 44 interception return (Haji-Sheikh kick)
NFC—Lofton 8 pass from Theismann (Haji-Sheikh kick)
NFC—Coffman 6 pass from Theismann (Haji-Sheikh kick)
NFC—Dickerson 14 run (Haji-Sheikh kick)

1983 AFC-NFC Pro Bowl

Aloha Stadium, Honolulu, Hawaii Sunday, February 6, 1983

Attendance: 49,883

NFC 20, AFC 19—Danny White threw an 11-yard touchdown pass to John Jefferson with 35 seconds remaining to give the NFC a 20-19 victory over the AFC. White, who completed 14 of 26 passes for 162 yards, kept the winning 65-yard drive alive with a 14-yard completion to Jefferson on a fourth-and-seven play at the AFC 25. The AFC was ahead 12-10 at halftime and increased the lead to 19-10 in the third period, when Marcus Allen scored on a one-yard run. Dan Fouts, who attempted 30 passes, set Pro Bowl records for most completions (17) and yards (274). John Stallworth was the AFC's leading receiver with seven catches for 67 yards. William Andrews topped the NFC with five receptions for 48 yards. Fouts and Jefferson were voted co-winners of the player of the game award.

AFC	9	3	7	0	— 19
NFC	0	10	0	10	— 20

AFC—Walker 34 pass from Fouts (Benirschke kick)
AFC—Safety, Still tackled Theismann in end zone
NFC—Andrews 3 run (Moseley kick)
NFC—FG Moseley 35
AFC—FG Benirschke 29
AFC—Allen 1 run (Benirschke kick)
NFC—FG Moseley 41
NFC—Jefferson 11 pass from D. White (Moseley kick)

1982 AFC-NFC Pro Bowl

Aloha Stadium, Honolulu, Hawaii — Sunday, January 31, 1982

Attendance: 50,402

AFC 16, NFC 13—Nick Lowery kicked a 23-yard field goal with three seconds remaining to give the AFC a 16-13 victory over the NFC. Lowery's kick climaxed a 69-yard drive directed by quarterback Dan Fouts. The NFC gained a 13-13 tie with 2:43 to go when Tony Dorsett ran four yards for a touchdown. In the drive to the game-winning field goal, Fouts completed three passes, including a 23-yarder to San Diego teammate Kellen Winslow that put the ball on the NFC's 5-yard line. Two plays later, Lowery kicked the field goal. Winslow, who caught six passes for 86 yards, was named co-player of the game along with NFC defensive end Lee Roy Selmon.

NFC	0	6	0	7	— 13
AFC	0	0	13	3	— 16

NFC—Giles 4 pass from Montana (kick blocked)
AFC—Muncie 2 run (kick failed)
AFC—Campbell 1 run (Lowery kick)
NFC—Dorsett 4 run (Septien kick)
AFC—FG Lowery 23

1981 AFC-NFC Pro Bowl

Aloha Stadium, Honolulu, Hawaii — February 1, 1981

Attendance: 50,360

NFC 21, AFC 7—Ed Murray kicked four field goals and Steve Bartkowski fired a 55-yard scoring pass to Alfred Jenkins to lead the NFC to its fourth straight victory over the AFC and a 7-4 edge in the series. Murray was named the game's most valuable player and missed tying Garo Yepremian's Pro Bowl record of five field goals when a 37-yard attempt hit the crossbar with 22 seconds remaining. The AFC's only score came on a nine-yard pass from Brian Sipe to Stanley Morgan in the second period. Bartkowski completed 9 of 21 passes for 173 yards, while Sipe connected on 10 of 15 for 142 yards. Ottis Anderson led all rushers with 70 yards on 10 carries. Earl Campbell, the NFL's leading rusher in 1980, was limited to 24 yards on eight attempts.

AFC	0	7	0	0	— 7
NFC	3	6	0	12	— 21

NFC—FG Murray 31
AFC—Morgan 9 pass from Sipe (J. Smith kick)
NFC—FG Murray 31
NFC—FG Murray 34
NFC—Jenkins 55 pass from Bartkowski (Murray kick)
NFC—FG Murray 36
NFC—Safety (Team)

1980 AFC-NFC Pro Bowl

Aloha Stadium, Honolulu, Hawaii — January 27, 1980

Attendance: 49,800

NFC 37, AFC 27—Running back Chuck Muncie ran for two touchdowns and threw a 25-yard option pass for another score to give the NFC its third consecutive victory over the AFC. Muncie, who was selected the game's most valuable player, snapped a 3-3 tie on a one-yard touchdown run at 1:41 of the second quarter, then scored on an 11-yard run in the fourth quarter for the NFC's final touchdown. Two scoring records were set in the game—37 points by the NFC, eclipsing the 33 by the AFC in 1973, and the 64 points by both teams, surpassing the 61 scored in 1973.

NFC	3	20	7	7	— 37
AFC	3	7	10	7	— 27

NFC—FG Moseley 37
AFC—FG Fritsch 19
NFC—Muncie 1 run (Moseley kick)
AFC—Pruitt 1 pass from Bradshaw (Fritsch kick)
NFC—D. Hill 13 pass from Manning (kick failed)
NFC—T. Hill 25 pass from Muncie (Moseley kick)
NFC—Henry 86 punt return (Moseley kick)
AFC—Campbell 2 run (Fritsch kick)
AFC—FG Fritsch 29
NFC—Muncie 11 run (Moseley kick)
AFC—Campbell 1 run (Fritsch kick)

1979 AFC-NFC Pro Bowl

Memorial Coliseum, Los Angeles, California — January 29, 1979

Attendance: 46,281

NFC 13, AFC 7—Roger Staubach completed 9 of 15 passes for 125 yards, including the winning touchdown on a 19-yard strike to Dallas Cowboys teammate Tony Hill in the third period. The winning drive began at the AFC's 45 yard line after a shanked punt. Staubach hit Ahmad Rashad with passes of 15 and 17 yards to set up Hill's decisive catch. The victory gave the NFC a 5-4 advantage in Pro Bowl games. Rashad, who accounted for 89 yards on five receptions, was named the player of the game. The AFC led 7-6 at halftime on Bob Griese's eight-yard scoring toss to Steve Largent late in the second quarter. Largent finished the game with five receptions for 75 yards. The NFC scored first as Archie Manning marched his team 70 yards in 11 plays, capped by Wilbert Montgomery's two-yard touchdown run. The AFC's Earl Campbell was the game's leading rusher with 66 yards on 12 carries.

AFC	0	7	0	0	— 7
NFC	0	6	7	0	— 13

NFC—Montgomery 2 run (kick failed)
AFC—Largent 8 pass from Griese (Yepremian kick)
NFC—T. Hill 19 pass from Staubach (Corral kick)

1978 AFC-NFC Pro Bowl

Tampa Stadium, Tampa, Florida — January 23, 1978

Attendance: 51,337

NFC 14, AFC 13—Walter Payton, the NFL's leading rusher in 1977, sparked a second-half comeback to give the NFC a 14-13 win and tie the series between the two conferences at four victories each. Payton, who was the game's most valuable player, gained 77 yards on 13 carries and scored the tying touchdown on a one-yard burst with 7:37 left in the game. Efren Herrera kicked the winning extra point. The AFC dominated the first half of the game, taking a 13-0 lead on field goals of 21 and 39 yards by Toni Linhart and a 10-yard touchdown pass from Ken Stabler to Oakland teammate Cliff Branch. On the NFC's first possession of the second half, Pat Haden put together the first touchdown drive after Eddie Brown returned Ray Guy's punt to the AFC 46-yard line. Haden connected on all four of his passes on that drive, finally hitting Terry Metcalf with a four-yard scoring toss. The NFC continued to rally and, with Jim Hart at quarterback, moved 63 yards in 12 plays for the go-ahead score. During the winning drive, Hart completed five of six passes for 38 yards and Payton picked up 20 more on the ground.

AFC	3	10	0	0	— 13
NFC	0	0	7	7	— 14

AFC—FG Linhart 21
AFC—Branch 10 pass from Stabler (Linhart kick)
AFC—FG Linhart 39
NFC—Metcalf 4 pass from Haden (Herrera kick)
NFC—Payton 1 run (Herrera kick)

1977 AFC-NFC Pro Bowl

Kingdome, Seattle, Washington — January 17, 1977

Attendance: 64,752

AFC 24, NFC 14—O. J. Simpson's three-yard touchdown burst at 7:03 of the first quarter gave the AFC a lead it would not surrender, the victory breaking a two-game NFC win streak and giving the American Conference stars a 4-3 series lead. The AFC took a 17-7 lead midway through the second period on the first of two Ken Anderson touchdown passes, a 12-yarder to Charlie Joiner. But the NFC mounted a 73-yard drive capped by Lawrence McCutcheon's one-yard touchdown plunge to pull within three of the AFC, 17-14, at the half. Following a scoreless third quarter, player of the game Mel Blount thwarted a possible NFC score when he intercepted Jim Hart's pass in the end zone. Less than three minutes later, Blount again picked off a Hart pass, returning it 16 yards to the NFC 27. That set up Anderson's 27-yard touchdown strike to Cliff Branch for the final score.

NFC	0	14	0	0	— 14
AFC	10	7	0	7	— 24

AFC—Simpson 3 run (Linhart kick)
AFC—FG Linhart 31
NFC—Thomas 15 run (Bakken kick)
AFC—Joiner 12 pass from Anderson (Linhart kick)
NFC—McCutcheon 1 run (Bakken kick)
AFC—Branch 27 pass from Anderson (Linhart kick)

1976 AFC-NFC Pro Bowl

Superdome, New Orleans, Louisiana — January 26, 1976

Attendance: 30,546

NFC 23, AFC 20—Mike Boryla, a late substitute who did not enter the game until 5:39 remained, lifted the National Football Conference to a 23-20 victory over the American Football Conference with two touchdown passes in the final minutes. It was the second straight NFC win, squaring the series at 3-3. Until Boryla started firing the ball the AFC was in control, leading 13-0 at the half. Boryla entered the game after Billy Johnson had raced 90 yards with a punt to make the score 20-9 in favor of the AFC. He floated a 14-yard pass to Terry Metcalf and later fired an eight-yarder to Mel Gray for the winner.

AFC	0	13	0	7	— 20
NFC	0	0	9	14	— 23

AFC—FG Stenerud 20
AFC—FG Stenerud 35
AFC—Burrough 64 pass from Pastorini (Stenerud kick)
NFC—FG Bakken 42
NFC—Foreman 4 pass from Hart (kick blocked)
AFC—Johnson 90 punt return (Stenerud kick)
NFC—Metcalf 14 pass from Boryla (Bakken kick)
NFC—Gray 8 pass from Boryla (Bakken kick)

1975 AFC-NFC Pro Bowl

Orange Bowl, Miami, Florida — January 20, 1975

Attendance: 26,484

NFC 17, AFC 10—Los Angeles quarterback James Harris, who took over the NFC offense after Jim Hart of St. Louis suffered a laceration above his right eye in the second period, threw a pair of touchdown passes early in the fourth period to pace the NFC to its second victory in the five-game Pro Bowl series. The NFC win snapped a three-game AFC victory string. Harris, who was named the player of the game, connected with St. Louis's Mel Gray for an eight-yard touchdown 2:03 into the final period. One minute and 24 seconds later, following a recovery by Washington's Ken Houston of a fumble by Franco Harris of Pittsburgh, Harris tossed another eight-yard scoring pass to Washington's Charley Taylor for the decisive points.

NFC	0	3	0	14	— 17
AFC	0	0	10	0	— 10

NFC—FG Marcol 33
AFC—Warfield 32 pass from Griese (Gerela kick)
AFC—FG Gerela 33
NFC—Gray 8 pass from J. Harris (Marcol kick)
NFC—Taylor 8 pass from J. Harris (Marcol kick)

1974 AFC-NFC Pro Bowl

Arrowhead Stadium, Kansas City, Missouri — January 20, 1974

Attendance: 66,918

AFC 15, NFC 13—Miami's Garo Yepremian kicked his fifth consecutive field goal without a miss from the 42-yard line with 21 seconds remaining to give the AFC its third straight victory since the NFC won the inaugural game following the 1970 season. The field goal by Yepremian, who was voted the game's outstanding player, offset a 21-yard field goal by Atlanta's Nick Mike-Mayer that had given the NFC a 13-12 advantage with 1:41 remaining. The only touchdown in the game was scored by the NFC on a 14-yard pass from Philadelphia's Roman Gabriel to Lawrence McCutcheon of the Los Angeles Rams.

NFC	0	10	0	3	— 13
AFC	3	3	3	6	— 15

AFC—FG Yepremian 16
NFC—FG Mike-Mayer 27
NFC—McCutcheon 14 pass from Gabriel (Mike-Mayer kick)
AFC—FG Yepremian 37
AFC—FG Yepremian 27
AFC—FG Yepremian 41
NFC—FG Mike-Mayer 21
AFC—FG Yepremian 42

1973 AFC-NFC Pro Bowl

Texas Stadium, Irving, Texas — January 21, 1973

Attendance: 37,091

AFC 33, NFC 28—Paced by the rushing and receiving of player of the game O.J. Simpson, the AFC erased a 14-0 first period deficit and built a commanding 33-14 lead midway through the fourth period before the NFC managed two touchdowns in the final minute of play. Simpson rushed for 112 yards and caught three passes for 58 more to gain unanimous recognition in the balloting for player of the game. John Brockington scored three touchdowns for the NFC.

AFC	0	10	10	13	— 33
NFC	14	0	0	14	— 28

NFC—Brockington 1 run (Marcol kick)
NFC—Brockington 3 pass from Kilmer (Marcol kick)
AFC—Simpson 7 run (Gerela kick)
AFC—FG Gerela 18
AFC—FG Gerela 22
AFC—Hubbard 11 run (Gerela kick)
AFC—O. Taylor 5 pass from Lamonica (kick failed)
AFC—Bell 12 interception return (Gerela kick)
NFC—Brockington 1 run (Marcol kick)
NFC—Kwalick 12 pass from Snead (Marcol kick)

1972 AFC-NFC Pro Bowl

Memorial Coliseum, Los Angeles, California — January 23, 1972

Attendance: 53,647

AFC 26, NFC 13—Four field goals by Jan Stenerud of Kansas City, including a 6-6 tie-breaker from 48 yards, helped lift the AFC from a 6-0 deficit to a 19-6 advantage early in the fourth period. The AFC defense picked off three interceptions. Stenerud was selected as the outstanding offensive player and his Kansas City teammate, linebacker Willie Lanier, was the game's outstanding defensive player.

AFC	0	3	13	10	— 26
NFC	0	6	0	7	— 13

NFC—Grim 50 pass from Landry (kick failed)
AFC—FG Stenerud 25
AFC—FG Stenerud 23
AFC—FG Stenerud 48
AFC—Morin 5 pass from Dawson (Stenerud kick)
AFC—FG Stenerud 42
NFC—V. Washington 2 run (Knight kick)
AFC—F. Little 6 run (Stenerud kick)

1971 AFC-NFC Pro Bowl

Memorial Coliseum, Los Angeles, California — January 24, 1971

Attendance: 48,222

NFC 27, AFC 6—Mel Renfro of Dallas broke open the first meeting between the American Football Conference and National Football Conference all-star teams as he returned a pair of punts 82 and 56 yards for touchdowns in the final period to provide the NFC with a 27-6 victory over the AFC. Renfro was voted the game's outstanding back and linebacker Fred Carr of Green Bay the outstanding lineman.

AFC	0	3	3	0	— 6
NFC	0	3	10	14	— 27

AFC—FG Stenerud 37
NFC—FG Cox 13
NFC—Osborn 23 pass from Brodie (Cox kick)
NFC—FG Cox 35
AFC—FG Stenerud 16
NFC—Renfro 82 punt return (Cox kick)
NFC—Renfro 56 punt return (Cox kick)

Pro Bowl All-Time Results

Date	Result	Site (attendance)	Honored players
Jan. 15, 1939	New York Giants 13, Pro All-Stars 10	Wrigley Field, Los Angeles (20,000)	
Jan. 14, 1940	Green Bay 16, NFL All-Stars 7	Gilmore Stadium, Los Angeles (18,000)	
Dec. 29, 1940	Chicago Bears 28, NFL All-Stars 14	Gilmore Stadium, Los Angeles (21,624)	
Jan. 4, 1942	Chicago Bears 35, NFL All-Stars 24	Polo Grounds, New York (17,725)	
Dec. 27, 1942	NFL All-Stars 17, Washington 14	Shibe Park, Philadelphia (18,671)	
Jan. 14, 1951	American Conf. 28, National Conf. 27	Los Angeles Memorial Coliseum (53,676)	Otto Graham, Cleveland, player of the game
Jan. 12, 1952	National Conf. 30, American Conf. 13	Los Angeles Memorial Coliseum (19,400)	Dan Towler, Los Angeles, player of the game
Jan. 10, 1953	National Conf. 27, American Conf. 7	Los Angeles Memorial Coliseum (34,208)	Don Doll, Detroit, player of the game
Jan. 17, 1954	East 20, West 9	Los Angeles Memorial Coliseum (44,214)	Chuck Bednarik, Philadelphia, player of the game
Jan. 16, 1955	West 26, East 19	Los Angeles Memorial Coliseum (43,972)	Billy Wilson, San Francisco, player of the game
Jan. 15, 1956	East 31, West 30	Los Angeles Memorial Coliseum (37,867)	Ollie Matson, Chi. Cardinals, player of the game
Jan. 13, 1957	West 19, East 10	Los Angeles Memorial Coliseum (44,177)	Bert Rechichar, Baltimore, outstanding back Ernie Stautner, Pittsburgh, outstanding lineman
Jan. 12, 1958	West 26, East 7	Los Angeles Memorial Coliseum (66,634)	Hugh McElhenny, San Francisco, outstanding back Gene Brito, Washington, outstanding lineman
Jan. 11, 1959	East 28, West 21	Los Angeles Memorial Coliseum (72,250)	Frank Gifford, N.Y. Giants, outstanding back Doug Atkins, Chi. Bears, outstanding lineman
Jan. 17, 1960	West 38, East 21	Los Angeles Memorial Coliseum (56,876)	Johnny Unitas, Baltimore, outstanding back Gene (Big Daddy) Lipscomb, Baltimore, outstanding lineman
Jan. 15, 1961	West 35, East 31	Los Angeles Memorial Coliseum (62,971)	Johnny Unitas, Baltimore, outstanding back Sam Huff, N.Y. Giants, outstanding lineman
Jan. 7, 1962	AFL West 47, East 27	Balboa Stadium, San Diego (20,973)	Cotton Davidson, Dallas Texans, player of the game
Jan. 14, 1962	NFL West 31, East 30	Los Angeles Memorial Coliseum (57,409)	Jim Brown, Cleveland, outstanding back Henry Jordan, Green Bay, outstanding lineman
Jan. 13, 1963	AFL West 21, East 14	Balboa Stadium, San Diego (27,641)	Curtis McClinton, Dallas Texans, outstanding offensive player Earl Faison, San Diego, outstanding defensive player
Jan. 13, 1963	NFL East 30, West 20	Los Angeles Memorial Coliseum (61,374)	Jim Brown, Cleveland, player of the game Gene (Big Daddy) Lipscomb, Pittsburgh, outstanding lineman
Jan. 12, 1964	NFL West 31, East 17	Los Angeles Memorial Coliseum (67,242)	Johnny Unitas, Baltimore, player of the game Gino Marchetti, Baltimore, outstanding lineman
Jan. 19, 1964	AFL West 27, East 24	Balboa Stadium, San Diego (20,016)	Keith Lincoln, San Diego, outstanding offensive player Archie Matsos, Oakland, outstanding defensive player
Jan. 10, 1965	NFL West 34, East 14	Los Angeles Memorial Coliseum (60,598)	Fran Tarkenton, Minnesota, outstanding back Terry Barr, Detroit, outstanding lineman
Jan. 16, 1965	AFL West 38, East 14	Jeppesen Stadium, Houston (15,446)	Keith Lincoln, San Diego, outstanding offensive player Willie Brown, Denver, outstanding defensive player
Jan. 15, 1966	AFL All-Stars 30, Buffalo 19	Rice Stadium, Houston (35,572)	Joe Namath, N.Y. Jets, most valuable player, offense Frank Buncom, San Diego, most valuable player, defense
Jan. 15, 1966	NFL East 36, West 7	Los Angeles Memorial Coliseum (60,124)	Jim Brown, Cleveland, outstanding back Dale Meinert, St. Louis, outstanding lineman
Jan. 21, 1967	AFL East 30, West 23	Oakland-Alameda County Coliseum (18,876)	Babe Parilli, Boston, outstanding offensive player Verlon Biggs, N.Y. Jets, outstanding defensive player
Jan. 22, 1967	NFL East 20, West 10	Los Angeles Memorial Coliseum (15,062)	Gale Sayers, Chicago, outstanding back Floyd Peters, Philadelphia, outstanding lineman
Jan. 21, 1968	AFL East 25, West 24	Gator Bowl, Jacksonville, Fla. (40,103)	Joe Namath and Don Maynard, N.Y. Jets, out. off. players Leslie (Speedy) Duncan, San Diego, out. def. player
Jan. 21, 1968	NFL West 38, East 20	Los Angeles Memorial Coliseum (53,289)	Gale Sayers, Chicago, outstanding back Dave Robinson, Green Bay, outstanding lineman
Jan. 19, 1969	AFL West 38, East 25	Gator Bowl, Jacksonville, Fla. (41,058)	Len Dawson, Kansas City, outstanding offensive player George Webster, Houston, outstanding defensive player
Jan. 19, 1969	NFL West 10, East 7	Los Angeles Memorial Coliseum (32,050)	Roman Gabriel, Los Angeles, outstanding back Merlin Olsen, Los Angeles, outstanding lineman
Jan. 17, 1970	AFL West 26, East 3	Astrodome, Houston (30,170)	John Hadl, San Diego, player of the game
Jan. 18, 1970	NFL West 16, East 13	Los Angeles Memorial Coliseum (57,486)	Gale Sayers, Chicago, outstanding back George Andrie, Dallas, outstanding lineman
Jan. 24, 1971	NFC 27, AFC 6	Los Angeles Memorial Coliseum (48,222)	Mel Renfro, Dallas, outstanding back Fred Carr, Green Bay, outstanding lineman
Jan. 23, 1972	AFC 26, NFC 13	Los Angeles Memorial Coliseum (53,647)	Jan Stenerud, Kansas City, outstanding offensive player Willie Lanier, Kansas City, outstanding defensive player
Jan. 21, 1973	AFC 33, NFC 28	Texas Stadium, Irving (47,879)	O.J. Simpson, Buffalo, player of the game
Jan. 20, 1974	AFC 15, NFC 13	Arrowhead Stadium, Kansas City (51,484)	Garo Yepremian, Miami, player of the game
Jan. 20, 1975	NFC 17, AFC 10	Orange Bowl, Miami (26,484)	James Harris, Los Angeles, player of the game
Jan. 26, 1976	NFC 23, AFC 20	Louisiana Superdome, New Orleans (32,108)	Billy Johnson, Houston, player of the game
Jan. 17, 1977	AFC 24, NFC 14	Kingdome, Seattle (63,214)	Mel Blount, Pittsburgh, player of the game
Jan. 23, 1978	NFC 14, AFC 13	Tampa Stadium (51,337)	Walter Payton, Chicago, player of the game
Jan. 29, 1979	NFC 13, AFC 7	Los Angeles Memorial Coliseum (46,281)	Ahmad Rashad, Minnesota, player of the game
Jan. 27, 1980	NFC 37, AFC 27	Aloha Stadium, Honolulu (48,060)	Chuck Muncie, New Orleans, player of the game
Feb. 1, 1981	NFC 21, AFC 7	Aloha Stadium, Honolulu (50,360)	Eddie Murray, Detroit, player of the game
Jan. 31, 1982	AFC 16, NFC 13	Aloha Stadium, Honolulu (50,402)	Kellen Winslow, San Diego, and Lee Roy Selmon, Tampa Bay, players of the game
Feb. 6, 1983	NFC 20, AFC 19	Aloha Stadium, Honolulu (49,883)	Dan Fouts, San Diego, and John Jefferson, Green Bay, players of the game
Jan. 29, 1984	NFC 45, AFC 3	Aloha Stadium, Honolulu (50,445)	Joe Theismann, Washington, player of the game
Jan. 27, 1985	AFC 22, NFC 14	Aloha Stadium, Honolulu (50,385)	Mark Gastineau, N.Y. Jets, player of the game
Feb. 2, 1986	NFC 28, AFC 24	Aloha Stadium, Honolulu (50,101)	Phil Simms, N.Y. Giants, player of the game
Feb. 1, 1987	AFC 10, NFC 6	Aloha Stadium, Honolulu (50,101)	Reggie White, Philadelphia, player of the game
Feb. 7, 1988	AFC 15, NFC 6	Aloha Stadium, Honolulu (50,113)	Bruce Smith, Buffalo, player of the game

Regular Season Interconference Records, 1970-1987

American Football Conference

Eastern Division	W	L	T	Pct.
Miami	48	11	0	.814
New England	26	32	0	.448
Indianapolis	22	28	1	.441
New York Jets	24	34	0	.414
Buffalo	20	33	1	.382
Central Division				
Pittsburgh	38	21	0	.644
Cincinnati	35	24	0	.593
Cleveland	30	31	0	.492
Houston	22	38	1	.369
Western Division				
Los Angeles Raiders	43	18	1	.702
Seattle	23	13	0	.639
Denver	35	27	2	.563
San Diego	27	28	0	.491
Kansas City	21	27	2	.440

National Football Conference

Eastern Division	W	L	T	Pct.
Dallas	41	19	0	.683
Washington	34	23	0	.596
Philadelphia	33	24	0	.579
St. Louis	24	25	2	.490
New York Giants	23	27	0	.460
Central Division				
Minnesota	30	30	0	.500
Chicago	25	34	0	.424
Detroit	23	34	1	.405
Green Bay	19	38	3	.342
Tampa Bay	10	20	0	.333
Western Division				
Los Angeles Rams	34	27	0	.557
San Francisco	33	30	0	.524
Atlanta	20	41	0	.328
New Orleans	16	42	2	.283

Interconference Victories, 1970-1987

Regular Season	AFC	NFC	Tie
1970	12	27	1
1971	15	23	2
1972	20	19	1
1973	19	19	2
1974	23	17	0
1975	23	17	0
1976	16	12	0
1977	19	9	0
1978	31	21	0
1979	36	16	0
1980	33	19	0
1981	24	28	0
1982	15	14	1
1983	26	26	0
1984	26	26	0
1985	27	25	0
1986	26	26	0
1987	23	22	1
Total	414	366	8

Preseason	AFC	NFC	Tie
1970	21	28	1
1971	28	28	3
1972	27	25	4
1973	23	35	2
1974	35	25	0
1975	30	26	1
1976	30	31	0
1977	38	25	0
1978	20	19	0
1979	25	18	0
1980	22	20	1
1981	18	19	0
1982	25	16	0
1983	15	24	0
1984	16	19	0
1985	10	22	1
1986	22	17	0
1987	22	22	0
Total	427	419	13

AFC VS. NFC (REGULAR SEASON), 1970-1987

	1970	1971	1972	1973	1974	1975	1976	1977	1978	1979	1980	1981	1982	1983	1984	1985	1986	1987	Totals
Miami	2-1	3-0	3-0	3-0	2-1	3-0	0-2	2-0	3-1	4-0	4-0	3-1	1-1	3-1	4-0	3-1	2-2	3-0	48-11
L.A. Raiders	1-2	1-1-1	3-0	2-1	3-0	3-0	3-0	1-1	4-0	4-0	2-2	2-2	3-0	2-2	3-1	3-1	1-3	2-2	43-18-1
Pittsburgh	0-3	1-2	2-1	3-0	3-0	2-1	1-1	2-0	3-1	3-1	4-0	3-1	1-0	2-2	3-1	1-3	2-2	2-2	38-21
Denver	2-2	1-3	1-3	0-3-1	2-2	2-1	2-0	1-1	2-2	3-1	3-1	3-1	2-1	0-2	3-1	3-1	3-1	2-1-1	35-27-2
Cincinnati	1-2	1-2	2-1	2-1	2-1	3-0	2-0	2-1	2-2	2-2	2-2	2-2	1-0	3-1	2-2	2-2	3-1	1-2	35-24
Cleveland	0-3	2-1	1-2	1-2	1-2	1-3	2-0	1-1	4-0	3-1	3-1	3-1	0-2	2-2	1-3	1-3	2-2	2-2	30-31
San Diego	1-2	2-1	0-3	1-2	1-2	0-3	2-0	1-1	2-2	3-1	2-2	2-2	1-0	2-2	4-0	1-1	0-4	2-0	27-28
New England	0-3	0-3	3-0	2-1	3-0	1-2	1-1	2-0	2-2	3-1	1-3	0-4	0-1	2-2	0-4	3-1	3-1	0-3	26-32
N.Y. Jets	2-1	0-3	1-2	0-3	2-1	0-3	0-2	1-1	1-3	3-1	1-3	2-0	4-0	3-1	0-2	2-2	2-2	0-4	24-34
Seattle								1-0	3-1	3-1	1-3	0-2	1-0	1-3	4-0	2-2	3-1	4-0	23-13
Houston	0-3	0-2-1	0-3	0-3	0-3	3-0	2-0	2-0	2-2	2-2	4-0	1-3	0-3	1-3	0-4	1-3	2-2	2-2	22-38-1
Indianapolis	3-0	2-1	0-3	2-1	1-2	2-1	0-2	1-1	2-2	1-1	1-1	0-4	0-1-1	2-0	0-4	3-1	1-3	1-0	22-28-1
Kansas City	0-2-1	2-1	2-1	1-1-1	1-2	2-1	1-1	1-1	0-2	0-2	2-0	2-2	0-3	2-2	1-1	2-2	1-1	1-2	21-27-2
Buffalo	0-3	0-3	2-0-1	2-1	2-1	1-2	0-2	1-1	1-1	2-2	3-1	1-3	1-2	1-3	1-3	0-2	1-1	1-2	20-33-1
Tampa Bay							0-1												0-1
TOTALS	12-27-1	15-23-2	20-19-1	19-19-2	23-17	23-17	16-12	19-9	31-21	36-16	33-19	24-28	15-14-1	26-26	26-26	27-25	26-26	23-22-1	414-366-8

NFC VS. AFC (REGULAR SEASON), 1970-1987

	1970	1971	1972	1973	1974	1975	1976	1977	1978	1979	1980	1981	1982	1983	1984	1985	1986	1987	Totals
Dallas	3-0	3-0	3-0	2-1	2-1	2-1	2-0	1-1	3-1	1-3	3-1	4-0	2-1	2-2	2-2	3-1	1-3	2-1	41-19
L.A. Rams	2-1	1-2	1-2	3-0	3-1	3-0	1-1	2-0	2-2	2-2	2-2	1-3	1-2	1-3	3-1	3-1	2-2	1-2	34-27
Washington	2-1	1-2	1-2	2-1	2-1	1-2	1-1	1-1	2-2	2-2	1-3	2-2		4-0	3-1	4-0	3-1	2-1	34-23
Philadelphia	2-1	1-2	2-1	2-1	2-1	0-3	0-2	1-1	3-1	2-2	3-1	3-1	2-1	1-1	3-1	1-1	2-2	3-1	33-24
San Francisco	4-0	2-1	2-1	1-2	0-3	1-2	1-1	0-2	1-3	0-4	2-2	3-1	1-3	2-2	3-1	3-1	4-0	3-1	33-30
Minnesota	2-1	2-1	1-2	2-1	2-1	4-0	2-0	1-1	1-3	1-3	1-3	1-3	1-3	4-0	0-4	2-0	1-3	2-1	30-30
Chicago	1-2	1-2	1-2	2-2	0-3	0-3	0-2	1-1	0-4	2-2	0-4	4-0	1-1	1-1	2-2	3-1	4-0	2-2	25-34
St. Louis	2-0-1	2-1	1-2	0-2-1	2-1	2-1	1-1	0-2	0-4	1-3	1-1	3-1		3-1	3-1	2-2	1-1	0-1	24-25-2
Detroit	3-0	4-0	2-0-1	0-3	1-2	1-2	2-0	2-0	2-2	0-4	0-2	2-2	0-1	1-3	0-4	2-2	1-3	0-4	23-34-1
N.Y. Giants	3-0	1-2	1-2	1-2	1-2	2-1	0-2	0-2	1-1	1-1	1-3	1-1	1-0	0-4	2-0	2-2	3-1	2-1	23-27
Atlanta	1-2	3-0	2-2	2-1	0-3	1-2	0-2	0-2	1-3	1-3	2-2	1-3	1-1	3-1	1-3	0-4	1-3	0-4	20-41
Green Bay	2-1	2-1	2-1	1-1-1	2-1	0-3	0-2	0-3	2-2	1-3	1-3	1-1	1-1-1	2-2	0-4	0-4	1-3	1-2-1	19-38-3
New Orleans	0-3	0-1-2	0-3	1-2	0-3	0-3	1-2	0-2	1-3	0-4	1-3	2-2	1-0	1-3	3-1	0-4	1-3	4-0	16-42-2
Tampa Bay								0-1	2-0	2-0	1-3	0-4	2-1	1-3	1-1	0-4	1-1	0-2	10-20
Seattle							1-0												1-0
TOTALS	27-12-1	23-15-2	19-20-1	19-19-2	17-23	17-23	12-16	9-19	21-31	16-36	19-33	28-24	14-15-1	26-26	26-26	25-27	26-26	22-23-1	366-414-8

1987 Interconference Games

(Home Team in capital letters)

AFC 23, NFC 22, 1 Tie

AFC Victories

Los Angeles Raiders 20, GREEN BAY 0
HOUSTON 20, Los Angeles Rams 16
PITTSBURGH 30, San Francisco 17
LOS ANGELES RAIDERS 27, Detroit 7
SAN DIEGO 28, St. Louis 24
Pittsburgh 28, ATLANTA 12
San Diego 17, TAMPA BAY 13
BUFFALO 6, New York Giants 3 (OT)
Seattle 37, DETROIT 14
HOUSTON 37, Atlanta 33
CLEVELAND 30, Los Angeles Rams 17
DENVER 34, Detroit 0
SEATTLE 28, Minnesota 17
CLEVELAND 38, Atlanta 3
Cincinnati 16, ATLANTA 10
SEATTLE 24, Green Bay 13
DENVER 31, Chicago 29
Miami 20, DALLAS 14
Kansas City 27, DETROIT 20
Miami 28, PHILADELPHIA 10
Seattle 34, CHICAGO 21
MIAMI 23, Washington 21
INDIANAPOLIS 24, Tampa Bay 6

NFC Victories

NEW ORLEANS 28, Cleveland 21
San Francisco 27, CINCINNATI 26
Dallas 38, NEW YORK JETS 24
LOS ANGELES RAMS 31, Pittsburgh 21
MINNESOTA 34, Denver 27
WASHINGTON 17, New York Jets 16
CHICAGO 31, Kansas City 28
Washington 27, BUFFALO 7
SAN FRANCISCO 27, Houston 20
MINNESOTA 31, Los Angeles Raiders 20
NEW YORK GIANTS 17, New England 10
Dallas 23, NEW ENGLAND 17 (OT)
Green Bay 23, KANSAS CITY 3
New Orleans 20, PITTSBURGH 16
Philadelphia 34, NEW ENGLAND 31 (OT)
SAN FRANCISCO 38, Cleveland 24
NEW ORLEANS 24, Houston 10
New Orleans 41, CINCINNATI 24
Philadelphia 38, NEW YORK JETS 27
PHILADELPHIA 17, Buffalo 7
Chicago 6, LOS ANGELES RAIDERS 3
NEW YORK GIANTS 20, New York Jets 7

Tie: GREEN BAY 17, Denver 17

Monday Night Football, 1970–1987

(Home Team in capitals, games listed in chronological order.)

1987
CHICAGO 34, New York Giants 19
NEW YORK JETS 43, New England 24
San Francisco 41, NEW YORK GIANTS 21
DENVER 30, Los Angeles Raiders 14
Washington 13, DALLAS 7
CLEVELAND 30, Los Angeles Rams 17
MINNESOTA 34, Denver 27
DALLAS 33, New York Giants 24
NEW YORK JETS 30, Seattle 14
DENVER 31, Chicago 29
Los Angeles Rams 30, WASHINGTON 26
Los Angeles Raiders 37, SEATTLE 14
MIAMI 37, New York Jets 28
SAN FRANCISCO 41, Chicago 0
Dallas 29, LOS ANGELES RAMS 21
New England 24, MIAMI 10

1986
DALLAS 31, New York Giants 28
Denver 21, PITTSBURGH 10
Chicago 25, GREEN BAY 12
Dallas 31, ST. LOUIS 7
SEATTLE 33, San Diego 7
CINCINNATI 24, Pittsburgh 22
NEW YORK JETS 22, Denver 10
NEW YORK GIANTS 27, Washington 20
Los Angeles Rams 20, CHICAGO 17
CLEVELAND 26, Miami 16
WASHINGTON 14, San Francisco 6
MIAMI 45, New York Jets 3
New York Giants 21, SAN FRANCISCO 17
SEATTLE 37, Los Angeles Raiders 0
Chicago 16, DETROIT 13
New England 34, MIAMI 27

1985
DALLAS 44, Washington 14
CLEVELAND 17, Pittsburgh 7
Los Angeles Rams 35, SEATTLE 24
Cincinnati 37, PITTSBURGH 24
WASHINGTON 27, St. Louis 10
NEW YORK JETS 23, Miami 7
CHICAGO 23, Green Bay 7
LOS ANGELES RAIDERS 34, San Diego 21
ST. LOUIS 21, Dallas 10
DENVER 17, San Francisco 16
WASHINGTON 23, New York Giants 21
SAN FRANCISCO 19, Seattle 6
MIAMI 38, Chicago 24
Los Angeles Rams 27, SAN FRANCISCO 20
MIAMI 30, New England 27
L.A. Raiders 16, L.A. RAMS 6

1984
Dallas 20, LOS ANGELES RAMS 13
SAN FRANCISCO 37, Washington 31
Miami 21, BUFFALO 17
LOS ANGELES RAIDERS 33, San Diego 30
PITTSBURGH 38, Cincinnati 17
San Francisco 31, NEW YORK GIANTS 10
DENVER 17, Green Bay 14
Los Angeles Rams 24, ATLANTA 10
Seattle 24, SAN DIEGO 0
WASHINGTON 27, Atlanta 14
SEATTLE 17, Los Angeles Raiders 14
NEW ORLEANS 27, Pittsburgh 24
MIAMI 28, New York Jets 17
SAN DIEGO 20, Chicago 7
Los Angeles Raiders 24, DETROIT 3
MIAMI 28, Dallas 21

1983
Dallas 31, WASHINGTON 30
San Diego 17, KANSAS CITY 14
LOS ANGELES RAIDERS 27, Miami 14
NEW YORK GIANTS 27, Green Bay 3
New York Jets 34, BUFFALO 10
Pittsburgh 24, CINCINNATI 14
GREEN BAY 48, Washington 47
ST. LOUIS 20, New York Giants 20 (OT)
Washington 27, SAN DIEGO 24
DETROIT 15, New York Giants 9
Los Angeles Rams 36, ATLANTA 13
New York Jets 31, NEW ORLEANS 28
MIAMI 38, Cincinnati 14
DETROIT 13, Minnesota 2
Green Bay 12, TAMPA BAY 9 (OT)
SAN FRANCISCO 42, Dallas 17

1982
Pittsburgh 36, DALLAS 28
Green Bay 27, NEW YORK GIANTS 19
LOS ANGELES RAIDERS 28, San Diego 24
TAMPA BAY 23, Miami 17
New York Jets 28, DETROIT 13
Dallas 37, HOUSTON 7
SAN DIEGO 50, Cincinnati 34
MIAMI 27, Buffalo 10
MINNESOTA 31, Dallas 27

1981
San Diego 44, CLEVELAND 14
Oakland 36, MINNESOTA 10
Dallas 35, NEW ENGLAND 21
Los Angeles 24, CHICAGO 7
PHILADELPHIA 16, Atlanta 13
BUFFALO 31, Miami 21
DETROIT 48, Chicago 17
PITTSBURGH 26, Houston 13
DENVER 19, Minnesota 17
DALLAS 27, Buffalo 14
SEATTLE 44, San Diego 23
ATLANTA 31, Minnesota 30
MIAMI 13, Philadelphia 10
OAKLAND 30, Pittsburgh 27
LOS ANGELES 21, Atlanta 16
SAN DIEGO 23, Oakland 10

1980
Dallas 17, WASHINGTON 3
Houston 16, CLEVELAND 7
PHILADELPHIA 35, New York Giants 3
NEW ENGLAND 23, Denver 14
CHICAGO 23, Tampa Bay 0
DENVER 20, Washington 17
Oakland 45, PITTSBURGH 34
NEW YORK JETS 17, Miami 14
CLEVELAND 27, Chicago 21
HOUSTON 38, New England 34
Oakland 19, SEATTLE 17
Los Angeles 27, NEW ORLEANS 7
OAKLAND 9, Denver 3
MIAMI 16, New England 13 (OT)
LOS ANGELES 38, Dallas 14
SAN DIEGO 26, Pittsburgh 17

1979
Pittsburgh 16, NEW ENGLAND 13 (OT)
Atlanta 14, PHILADELPHIA 10
WASHINGTON 27, New York Giants 0
CLEVELAND 26, Dallas 7
GREEN BAY 27, New England 14
OAKLAND 13, Miami 3
NEW YORK JETS 14, Minnesota 7
PITTSBURGH 42, Denver 7
Seattle 31, ATLANTA 28
Houston 9, MIAMI 6
Philadelphia 31, DALLAS 21
LOS ANGELES 20, Atlanta 14
SEATTLE 30, New York Jets 7
Oakland 42, NEW ORLEANS 35
HOUSTON 20, Pittsburgh 17
SAN DIEGO 17, Denver 7

1978
DALLAS 38, Baltimore 0
MINNESOTA 12, Denver 9 (OT)
Baltimore 34, NEW ENGLAND 27
Minnesota 24, CHICAGO 20
WASHINGTON 9, Dallas 5
MIAMI 21, Cincinnati 0
DENVER 16, Chicago 7
Houston 24, PITTSBURGH 17
ATLANTA 15, Los Angeles 7
BALTIMORE 21, Washington 17
Oakland 34, CINCINNATI 21
HOUSTON 35, Miami 30
Pittsburgh 24, SAN FRANCISCO 7
SAN DIEGO 40, Chicago 7
Cincinnati 20, LOS ANGELES 19
MIAMI 23, New England 3

1977
PITTSBURGH 27, San Francisco 0
CLEVELAND 30, New England 27 (OT)
Oakland 37, KANSAS CITY 28
CHICAGO 24, Los Angeles 23
PITTSBURGH 20, Cincinnati 14
LOS ANGELES 35, Minnesota 3
ST. LOUIS 28, New York Giants 0
BALTIMORE 10, Washington 3
St. Louis 24, DALLAS 17
WASHINGTON 10, Green Bay 9
OAKLAND 34, Buffalo 13
MIAMI 17, Baltimore 6
Dallas 42, SAN FRANCISCO 35

1976
Miami 30, BUFFALO 21
Oakland 24, KANSAS CITY 21
Washington 20, PHILADELPHIA 17 (OT)
MINNESOTA 17, Pittsburgh 6
San Francisco 16, LOS ANGELES 0
NEW ENGLAND 41, New York Jets 7
WASHINGTON 20, St. Louis 10
BALTIMORE 38, Houston 14
CINCINNATI 20, Los Angeles 12
DALLAS 17, Buffalo 10
Baltimore 17, MIAMI 16
SAN FRANCISCO 20, Minnesota 16
OAKLAND 35, Cincinnati 20

1975
Oakland 31, MIAMI 21
DENVER 23, Green Bay 13
Dallas 36, DETROIT 10
WASHINGTON 27, St. Louis 17
New York Giants 17, BUFFALO 14
Minnesota 13, CHICAGO 9
Los Angeles 42, PHILADELPHIA 3
Kansas City 34, DALLAS 31
CINCINNATI 33, Buffalo 24
Pittsburgh 32, HOUSTON 9
MIAMI 20, New England 7
OAKLAND 17, Denver 10
SAN DIEGO 24, New York Jets 16

1974
BUFFALO 21, Oakland 20
PHILADELPHIA 13, Dallas 10
WASHINGTON 30, Denver 3
MIAMI 21, New York Jets 17
DETROIT 17, San Francisco 13
CHICAGO 10, Green Bay 9
PITTSBURGH 24, Atlanta 17
Los Angeles 15, SAN FRANCISCO 13
Minnesota 28, ST. LOUIS 24
Kansas City 42, DENVER 34
Pittsburgh 28, NEW ORLEANS 7
MIAMI 24, Cincinnati 3
Washington 23, LOS ANGELES 17

1973
GREEN BAY 23, New York Jets 7
DALLAS 40, New Orleans 3
DETROIT 31, Atlanta 6
WASHINGTON 14, Dallas 7
Miami 17, CLEVELAND 9
DENVER 23, Oakland 23
BUFFALO 23, Kansas City 14
PITTSBURGH 21, Washington 16
KANSAS CITY 19, Chicago 7
ATLANTA 20, Minnesota 14
SAN FRANCISCO 20, Green Bay 6
MIAMI 30, Pittsburgh 26
LOS ANGELES 40, New York Giants 6

1972
Washington 24, MINNESOTA 21
Kansas City 20, NEW ORLEANS 17
New York Giants 27, PHILADELPHIA 12
Oakland 34, HOUSTON 0
Green Bay 24, DETROIT 23
CHICAGO 13, Minnesota 10
DALLAS 28, Detroit 24
Baltimore 24, NEW ENGLAND 17
Cleveland 21, SAN DIEGO 17
WASHINGTON 24, Atlanta 13
MIAMI 31, St. Louis 10
Los Angeles 26, SAN FRANCISCO 16
OAKLAND 24, New York Jets 16

1971
Minnesota 16, DETROIT 13
ST. LOUIS 17, New York Jets 10
Oakland 34, CLEVELAND 20
DALLAS 20, New York Giants 13
KANSAS CITY 38, Pittsburgh 16
MINNESOTA 10, Baltimore 3
GREEN BAY 14, Detroit 14
BALTIMORE 24, Los Angeles 17
SAN DIEGO 20, St. Louis 17
ATLANTA 28, Green Bay 21
MIAMI 34, Chicago 3
Kansas City 26, SAN FRANCISCO 17
Washington 38, LOS ANGELES 24

1970
CLEVELAND 31, New York Jets 21
Kansas City 44, BALTIMORE 24
DETROIT 28, Chicago 14
Green Bay 22, SAN DIEGO 20
OAKLAND 34, Washington 20
MINNESOTA 13, Los Angeles 3
PITTSBURGH 21, Cincinnati 10
Baltimore 13, GREEN BAY 10
St. Louis 38, DALLAS 0
PHILADELPHIA 23, New York Giants 20
Miami 20, ATLANTA 7
Cleveland 21, HOUSTON 10
Detroit 28, LOS ANGELES 23

Monday Night Won-Loss Records, 1970-1987

	Total	1987	1986	1985	1984	1983	1982	1981	1980	1979	1978	1977	1976	1975	1974	1973	1972	1971	1970
Buffalo	3-9				0-1	0-1	0-1	1-1				0-1	0-2	0-2	1-0	1-0			
Cincinnati	5-10		1-0	1-0	0-1	0-2	0-1				1-2	0-1	1-1	1-0	0-1				0-1
Cleveland	9-4	1-0	1-0	1-0				0-1	1-1	1-0		1-0				0-1	1-0	0-1	2-0
Denver	9-10-1	2-1	1-1	1-0	1-0			1-0	1-2	0-2	1-1			1-1	0-2	0-0-1			
Houston	6-6						0-1	0-1	2-0	2-0	2-0		0-1	0-1			0-1		0-1
Indianapolis	8-4										2-1	1-1	2-0				1-0	1-1	1-1
Kansas City	7-4					0-1						0-1	0-1	1-0	1-0	1-1	1-0	2-0	1-0
L.A. Raiders	25-5-1	1-1	0-1	2-0	2-1	1-0	1-0	2-1	3-0	2-0	1-0	2-0	2-0	2-0	0-1	0-0-1	2-0	1-0	1-0
Miami	23-13	1-1	1-2	2-1	3-0	1-1	1-1	1-1	1-1	0-2	2-1	1-0	1-1	1-1	2-0	2-0	1-0	1-0	1-0
New England	4-12	1-1	1-0	0-1				0-1	1-2	0-2	0-2	0-1	1-0	0-1			0-1		
New York Jets	9-11	2-1	1-1	1-0	0-1	2-0	1-0		1-0	1-1			0-1	0-1	0-1	0-1	0-1	0-1	0-1
Pittsburgh	14-13		0-2	0-2	1-1	1-0	1-0	1-1	0-2	2-1	1-1	2-0	0-1	1-0	2-0	1-1		0-1	1-0
San Diego	10-9		0-1	0-1	1-2	1-1	1-1	2-1	1-0	1-0	1-0			1-0			0-1	1-0	0-1
Seattle	7-5	0-2	2-0	0-2	2-0			1-0	0-1	2-0									
Atlanta	5-11				0-2	0-1		1-2		1-2	1-0				0-1	1-1	0-1	1-0	0-1
Chicago	8-15	1-2	2-1	1-1	0-1			0-2	1-1		0-3	1-0		0-1	1-0	0-1	1-0	0-1	0-1
Dallas	18-15	2-1	2-0	1-1	1-1	1-1	1-2	2-0	1-1	0-2	1-1	1-1	1-0	1-1	0-1	1-1	1-0	1-0	0-1
Detroit	7-7-1		0-1		0-1	2-0	0-1	1-0						0-1	1-0	1-0	0-2	0-1-1	2-0
Green Bay	7-10-1		0-1	0-1	0-1	2-1	1-0			1-0		0-1		0-1	0-1	1-1	1-0	0-1-1	1-1
L.A. Rams	16-14	1-2	1-0	2-1	1-1	1-0		2-0	2-0	1-0	0-2	1-1	0-2	1-0	1-1	1-0	1-0	0-2	0-2
Minnesota	10-10	1-0				0-1	1-0	0-3		0-1	2-0	0-1	1-1	1-0	1-0	0-1	0-2	2-0	1-0
New Orleans	1-6				1-0	0-1			0-1	0-1					0-1	0-1	0-1		
New York Giants	5-14-1	0-3	2-1	0-1	0-1	1-1-1	0-1		0-1	0-1		0-1		1-0		0-1	1-0	0-1	0-1
Philadelphia	5-5							1-1	1-0	1-1			0-1	0-1	1-0		0-1		1-0
St. Louis	5-7-1		0-1	1-1		0-0-1						2-0	0-1	0-1	0-1		0-1	1-1	1-0
San Francisco	9-11	2-0	0-2	1-2	2-0	1-0					0-1	0-2	2-0		0-2	1-0	0-1	0-1	
Tampa Bay	1-2					0-1	1-0		0-1										
Washington	18-12	1-1	1-1	2-1	1-1	1-2			0-2	1-0	1-1	1-1	2-0	1-0	2-0	1-1	2-0	1-0	0-1

Monday Night Syndrome

1987

Of the 15 winning teams:	11 won the next week 4 lost the next week 0 tied the next week	Of the 30 NFL teams:	16 won the next week 14 lost the next week 0 tied the next week
Of the 15 losing teams:	5 won the next week 10 lost the next week 0 tied the next week		

1970-87

Of the 244 winning teams:	139 won the next week 102 lost the next week 3 tied the next week	Of the 494 NFL teams:	270 won the next week 220 lost the next week 4 tied the next week
Of the 244 losing teams:	126 won the next week 117 lost the next week 1 tied the next week		
Of the 6 tying teams:	5 won the next week 1 lost the next week 0 tied the next week		

Thursday-Sunday Night Football, 1974-1987

(Home Team in capitals, games listed in chronological order.)

1987
NEW YORK GIANTS 17, New England 10 (Sun.)
SAN DIEGO 16, Los Angeles Raiders 14 (Sun.)
Miami 20, DALLAS 14 (Sun.)
SAN FRANCISCO 38, Cleveland 24 (Sun.)
Chicago 30, MINNESOTA 24 (Sun.)
SEATTLE 28, Denver 21 (Sun.)
MIAMI 23, Washington 21 (Sun.)
SAN FRANCISCO 48, Los Angeles Rams 0 (Sun.)

1986
New England 20, NEW YORK JETS 6 (Thur.)
Cincinnati 30, CLEVELAND 13 (Thur.)
Los Angeles Raiders 37, SAN DIEGO 31 (OT) (Thur.)
LOS ANGELES RAMS 29, Dallas 10 (Sun.)
SAN FRANCISCO 24, Los Angeles Rams 14 (Fri.)

1985
KANSAS CITY 36, Los Angeles Raiders 20 (Thur.)
Chicago 33, MINNESOTA 24 (Thur.)
Dallas 30, NEW YORK GIANTS 29 (Sun.)
SAN DIEGO 54, Pittsburgh 44 (Sun.)
Denver 27, SEATTLE 24 (Fri.)

1984
Pittsburgh 23, NEW YORK JETS 17 (Thur.)
Denver 24, CLEVELAND 14 (Sun.)
DALLAS 30, New Orleans 27 (Sun.)
Washington 31, MINNESOTA 17 (Thur.)
SAN FRANCISCO 19, Los Angeles Rams 16 (Fri.)

1983
San Francisco 48, MINNESOTA 17 (Thur.)
CLEVELAND 17, Cincinnati 7 (Thur.)
Los Angeles Raiders 40, DALLAS 38 (Sun.)
Los Angeles Raiders 42, SAN DIEGO 10 (Thur.)
MIAMI 34, New York Jets 14 (Fri.)

1982
BUFFALO 23, Minnesota 22 (Thur.)
SAN FRANCISCO 30, Los Angeles Rams 24 (Thur.)
ATLANTA 17, San Francisco 7 (Sun.)

1981
MIAMI 30, Pittsburgh 10 (Thur.)
Philadelphia 20, BUFFALO 14 (Thur.)
DALLAS 29, Los Angeles 17 (Sun.)
HOUSTON 17, Cleveland 13 (Thur.)

1980
TAMPA BAY 10, Los Angeles 9 (Thur.)
DALLAS 42, San Diego 31 (Sun.)
San Diego 27, MIAMI 24 (OT) (Thur.)
HOUSTON 6, Pittsburgh 0 (Thur.)

1979
Los Angeles 13, DENVER 9 (Thur.)
DALLAS 30, Los Angeles 6 (Sun.)
OAKLAND 45, San Diego 22 (Thur.)
MIAMI 39, New England 24 (Thur.)

1978
New England 21, OAKLAND 14 (Sun.)
Minnesota 21, DALLAS 10 (Thur.)
LOS ANGELES 10, Pittsburgh 7 (Sun.)
Denver 21, OAKLAND 6 (Sun.)

1977
Minnesota 30, DETROIT 21 (Sat.)

1976
Los Angeles 20, DETROIT 17 (Sat.)

1975
LOS ANGELES 10, Pittsburgh 3 (Sat.)

1974
OAKLAND 27, Dallas 23 (Sat.)

History of Overtime Games

Preseason

Aug. 28, 1955	Los Angeles 23, New York Giants 17, at Portland, Oregon
Aug. 24, 1962	Denver 27, Dallas Texans 24, at Fort Worth, Texas
Aug. 10, 1974	San Diego 20, New York Jets 14, at San Diego
Aug. 17, 1974	Pittsburgh 33, Philadelphia 30, at Philadelphia
Aug. 17, 1974	Dallas 19, Houston 13, at Dallas
Aug. 17, 1974	Cincinnati 13, Atlanta 7, at Atlanta
Sept. 6, 1974	Buffalo 23, New York Giants 17, at Buffalo
Aug. 9, 1975	Baltimore 23, Denver 20, at Denver
Aug. 30, 1975	New England 20, Green Bay 17, at Milwaukee
Sept. 13, 1975	Minnesota 14, San Diego 14, at San Diego
Aug. 1, 1976	New England 13, New York Giants 7, at New England
Aug. 2, 1976	Kansas City 9, Houston 3, at Kansas City
Aug. 20, 1976	New Orleans 26, Baltimore 20, at Baltimore
Sept. 4, 1976	Dallas 26, Houston 20, at Dallas
Aug. 13, 1977	Seattle 23, Dallas 17, at Seattle
Aug. 28, 1977	New England 13, Pittsburgh 10, at New England
Aug. 28, 1977	New York Giants 24, Buffalo 21, at East Rutherford, N.J.
Aug. 2, 1979	Seattle 12, Minnesota 9, at Minnesota
Aug. 4, 1979	Los Angeles 20, Oakland 14, at Los Angeles
Aug. 24, 1979	Denver 20, New England 17, at Denver
Aug. 23, 1980	Tampa Bay 20, Cincinnati 14, at Tampa Bay
Aug. 5, 1981	San Francisco 27, Seattle 24, at Seattle
Aug. 29, 1981	New Orleans 20, Detroit 17, at New Orleans
Aug. 28, 1982	Miami 17, Kansas City 17, at Kansas City
Sept. 3, 1982	Miami 16, New York Giants 13, at Miami
Aug. 6, 1983	L.A. Raiders 26, San Francisco 23, at Los Angeles
Aug. 6, 1983	Atlanta 13, Washington 10, at Atlanta
Aug. 13, 1983	St. Louis 27, Chicago 24, at St. Louis
Aug. 18, 1983	New York Jets 20, Cincinnati 17, at Cincinnati
Aug. 27, 1983	Chicago 20, Kansas City 17, at Chicago
Aug. 11, 1984	Pittsburgh 20, Philadelphia 17, at Pittsburgh
Aug. 9, 1985	Buffalo 10, Detroit 10, at Pontiac, Mich.
Aug. 10, 1985	Minnesota 16, Miami 13, at Miami
Aug. 17, 1985	Dallas 27, San Diego 24, at San Diego
Aug. 24, 1985	N.Y. Giants 34, N.Y. Jets 31, at East Rutherford, N.J.
Aug. 15, 1986	Washington 27, Pittsburgh 24, at Washington
Aug. 15, 1986	Detroit 30, Seattle 27, at Detroit
Aug. 23, 1986	Los Angeles Rams 20, San Diego 17, at Anaheim
Aug. 30, 1986	Minnesota 23, Indianapolis 20, at Indianapolis
Aug. 23, 1987	Philadelphia 19, New England 13, at New England
Sept. 5, 1987	Cleveland 30, Green Bay 24, at Milwaukee
Sept. 6, 1987	Kansas City 13, St. Louis 10, at Memphis, Tenn.

Regular Season

Sept. 22, 1974—Pittsburgh 35, Denver 35, at Denver; Steelers win toss. Gilliam's pass intercepted and returned by Rowser to Denver's 42. Turner misses 41-yard field goal. Walden punts and Greer returns to Broncos' 39. Van Heusen punts and Edwards returns to Steelers' 16. Game ends with Steelers on own 26.

Nov. 10, 1974—New York Jets 26, New York Giants 20, at New Haven, Conn.; Giants win toss. Gogolak misses 42-yard field goal. Namath passes to Boozer for five yards and touchdown at 6:53.

Sept. 28, 1975—Dallas 37, St. Louis 31, at Dallas; Cardinals win toss. Hart's pass intercepted and returned by Jordan to Cardinals' 37. Staubach passes to DuPree for three yards and touchdown at 7:53.

Oct. 12, 1975—Los Angeles 13, San Diego 10, at San Diego; Chargers win toss. Partee punts to Rams' 14. Dempsey kicks 22-yard field goal at 9:27.

Nov. 2, 1975—Washington 30, Dallas 24, at Washington; Cowboys win toss. Staubach's pass intercepted and returned by Houston to Cowboys' 35. Kilmer runs one yard for touchdown at 6:34.

Nov. 16, 1975—St. Louis 20, Washington 17, at St. Louis; Cardinals win toss. Bakken kicks 37-yard field goal at 7:00.

Nov. 23, 1975—Kansas City 24, Detroit 21, at Kansas City; Lions win toss. Chiefs take over on downs at own 38. Stenerud kicks 26-yard field goal at 6:44.

Nov. 23, 1975—Oakland 26, Washington 23, at Washington; Redskins win toss. Bragg punts to Raiders' 42. Blanda kicks 27-yard field goal at 7:13.

Nov. 30, 1975—Denver 13, San Diego 10, at Denver; Broncos win toss. Turner kicks 25-yard field goal at 4:13.

Nov. 30, 1975—Oakland 37, Atlanta 34, at Oakland; Falcons win toss. James punts to Raiders' 16. Guy punts and Herron returns to Falcons' 41. Nick Mike-Mayer misses 45-yard field goal. Guy punts into Falcons' end zone. James punts to Raiders' 39. Blanda kicks 36-yard field goal at 15:00.

Dec. 14, 1975—Baltimore 10, Miami 7, at Baltimore; Dolphins win toss. Seiple punts to Colts' 4. Linhart kicks 31-yard field goal at 12:44.

Sept. 19, 1976—Minnesota 10, Los Angeles 10, at Minnesota; Vikings win toss. Tarkenton's pass intercepted by Monte Jackson and returned to Minnesota 16. Allen blocks Dempsey's 30-yard field goal attempt, ball rolls into end zone for touchback. Clabo punts and Scribner returns to Rams' 20. Rusty Jackson punts to Vikings' 35. Tarkenton's pass intercepted by Kay at Rams' 1, no return. Game ends with Rams on own 3.

*__Sept. 27, 1976—Washington 20, Philadelphia 17,__ at Philadelphia; Eagles win toss. Jones punts and E. Brown loses one yard on return to Redskins' 40. Bragg punts 51 yards into end zone for touchback. Jones punts and E. Brown returns to Redskins' 42. Bragg punts and Marshall returns to Eagles' 41. Boryla's pass intercepted by Dusek at Redskins' 37, no return. Bragg punts and Bradley returns. Philadelphia holding penalty moves ball back to Eagles' 8. Boryla pass intercepted by E. Brown and returned to Eagles' 22. Moseley kicks 29-yard field goal at 12:49.

Oct. 17, 1976—Kansas City 20, Miami 17, at Miami; Chiefs win toss. Wilson punts into end zone for touchback. Bulaich fumbles into Kansas City end zone, Collier recovers for touchback. Stenerud kicks 34-yard field goal at 14:48.

Oct. 31, 1976—St. Louis 23, San Francisco 20, at St. Louis; Cardinals win toss. Joyce punts and Leonard fumbles on return, Jones recovers at 49ers' 43. Bakken kicks 21-yard field goal at 6:42.

Dec. 5, 1976—San Diego 13, San Francisco 7, at San Diego; Chargers win toss. Morris runs 13 yards for touchdown at 5:12.

Sept. 18, 1977—Dallas 16, Minnesota 10, at Minnesota; Vikings win toss. Dallas starts on Vikings' 47 after a punt early in the overtime period. Staubach scores seven plays later on a four-yard run at 6:14.

*__Sept. 26, 1977—Cleveland 30, New England 27,__ at Cleveland; Browns win toss. Sipe throws a 22-yard pass to Logan at Patriots' 19. Cockroft kicks 35-yard field goal at 4:45.

Oct. 16, 1977—Minnesota 22, Chicago 16, at Minnesota; Bears win toss. Parsons punts 53 yards to Vikings' 18. Minnesota drives to Bears' 11. On a first-and-10, Vikings fake a field goal and holder Krause hits Voigt with a touchdown pass at 6:45.

Oct. 30, 1977—Cincinnati 13, Houston 10, at Cincinnati; Bengals win toss. Bahr kicks a 22-yard field goal at 5:51.

Nov. 13, 1977—San Francisco 10, New Orleans 7, at New Orleans; Saints win toss. Saints fail to move ball and Blanchard punts to 49ers' 41. Wersching kicks a 33-yard field goal at 6:33.

Dec. 18, 1977—Chicago 12, New York Giants 9, at East Rutherford, N.J.; Giants win toss. The ball changes hands eight times before Thomas kicks a 28-yard field goal at 14:51.

Sept. 10, 1978—Cleveland 13, Cincinnati 10, at Cleveland; Browns win toss. Collins returns kickoff 41 yards to Browns' 47. Cockroft kicks 27-yard field goal at 4:30.

*__Sept. 11, 1978—Minnesota 12, Denver 9,__ at Minnesota; Vikings win toss. Danmeier kicks 44-yard field goal at 2:56.

Sept. 24, 1978—Pittsburgh 15, Cleveland 9, at Pittsburgh; Steelers win toss. Cunningham scores on a 37-yard "gadget" pass from Bradshaw at 3:43. Steelers start winning drive on their 21.

Sept. 24, 1978—Denver 23, Kansas City 17, at Kansas City; Broncos win toss. Dilts punts to Kansas City. Chiefs advance to Broncos' 40 where Reed fails to make first down on fourth-and-one situation. Broncos march downfield. Preston scores two-yard touchdown at 10:28.

Oct. 1, 1978—Oakland 25, Chicago 19, at Chicago; Bears win toss. Both teams punt on first possession. On Chicago's second offensive series, Colzie intercepts Avellini's pass and returns it to Bears' 3. Three plays later, Whittington runs two yards for a touchdown at 5:19.

Oct. 15, 1978—Dallas 24, St. Louis 21, at St. Louis; Cowboys win toss. Dallas drives from its 23 into field goal range. Septien kicks 27-yard field goal at 3:28.

Oct. 29, 1978—Denver 20, Seattle 17, at Seattle; Broncos win toss. Ball changes hands four times before Turner kicks 18-yard field goal at 12:59.

Nov. 12, 1978—San Diego 29, Kansas City 23, at San Diego; Chiefs win toss. Fouts hits Jefferson for decisive 14-yard touchdown pass on the last play (15:00) of overtime period.

Nov. 12, 1978—Washington 16, New York Giants 13, at Washington; Redskins win toss. Moseley kicks winning 45-yard field goal at 8:32 after missing first down field goal attempt of 35 yards at 4:50.

Nov. 26, 1978—Green Bay 10, Minnesota 10, at Green Bay; Packers win toss. Both teams have possession of the ball four times.

Dec. 9, 1978—Cleveland 37, New York Jets 34, at Cleveland; Browns win toss. Cockroft kicks 22-yard field goal at 3:07.

Sept. 2, 1979—Atlanta 40, New Orleans 34, at New Orleans; Falcons win toss. Bartkowski's pass intercepted by Myers and returned to Falcons' 46. Erxleben punts to Falcons' 4. James punts to Chandler on Saints' 43. Erxleben punts and Ryckman returns to Falcons' 28. James punts and Chandler returns to Saints' 36. Erxleben retrieves punt snap on Saints' 1 and attempts pass. Mayberry intercepts and returns six yards for touchdown at 8:22.

Sept. 2, 1979—Cleveland 25, New York Jets 22, at New York; Jets win toss. Leahy's 43-yard field goal attempt goes wide right at 4:41. Evans's punt blocked by Dykes is recovered by Newton. Ramsey punts into end zone for touchback. Evans punts and Harper returns to Jets' 24. Robinson's pass intercepted by Davis and returned 33 yards to Jets' 31. Cockroft kicks 27-yard field goal at 14:45.

*__Sept. 3, 1979—Pittsburgh 16, New England 13,__ at Foxboro; Patriots win toss. Hare punts to Swann at Steelers' 31. Bahr kicks 41-yard field goal at 5:10.

Sept. 9, 1979—Tampa Bay 29, Baltimore 26, at Baltimore; Colts win toss. Landry fumbles, recovered by Kollar at Colts' 14. O'Donoghue kicks 31-yard, first-down field goal at 1:41.

Sept. 16, 1979—Denver 20, Atlanta 17, at Atlanta; Broncos win toss. Broncos march 65 yards to Falcons' 7. Turner kicks 24-yard field goal at 6:15.

Sept. 23, 1979—Houston 30, Cincinnati 27, at Cincinnati; Oilers win toss. Parsley punts and Lusby returns to Bengals' 33. Bahr's 32-yard field goal attempt is wide right at 8:05. Parsley's punt downed on Bengals' 5. McInally punts and Ellender returns to Bengals' 42. Fritsch's third down, 29-yard field goal attempt hits left upright and bounces through at 14:28.

Sept. 23, 1979—Minnesota 27, Green Bay 21, at Minnesota; Vikings win toss. Kramer throws 50-yard touchdown pass to Rashad at 3:18.

Oct. 28, 1979—Houston 27, New York Jets 24, at Houston; Oilers win toss. Oilers march 58 yards to Jets' 18. Fritsch kicks 35-yard field goal at 5:10.

Nov. 18, 1979—Cleveland 30, Miami 24, at Cleveland; Browns win toss. Sipe passes 39 yards to Rucker for touchdown at 1:59.

Nov. 25, 1979—Pittsburgh 33, Cleveland 30, at Pittsburgh; Browns win toss. Sipe's pass intercepted by Blount on Steelers' 4. Bradshaw pass intercepted by Bolton on Browns' 12. Evans punts and Bell returns to Steelers' 17. Bahr kicks 37-yard field goal at 14:51.

Nov. 25, 1979—Buffalo 16, New England 13, at Foxboro; Patriots win toss. Hare's punt downed on Bills' 38. Jackson punts and Morgan returns to Patriots' 20. Grogan's pass intercepted by Haslett and returned to Bills' 42. Ferguson's 51-yard pass to Butler sets up N. Mike-Mayer's 29-yard field goal at 9:15.

*indicates Monday night game
#indicates Thursday night game

Dec. 2, 1979—Los Angeles 27, Minnesota 21, at Los Angeles; Rams win toss. Clark punts and Miller returns to Vikings' 25. Kramer's pass intercepted by Brown and returned to Rams' 40. Cromwell, holding for 22-yard field goal attempt, runs around left end untouched for winning score at 6:53.

Sept. 7, 1980—Green Bay 12, Chicago 6, at Green Bay; Bears win toss. Parsons punts and Nixon returns 16 yards. Five plays later, Marcol returns own blocked field goal attempt 24 yards for touchdown at 6:00.

Sept. 14, 1980—San Diego 30, Oakland 24, at San Diego; Raiders win toss. Pastorini's first-down pass intercepted by Edwards. Millen intercepts Fouts' first-down pass and returns to San Diego 46. Bahr's 50-yard field goal attempt partially blocked by Williams and recovered on Chargers' 32. Eight plays later, Fouts throws 24-yard touchdown pass to Jefferson at 8:09.

Sept. 14, 1980—San Francisco 24, St. Louis 21, at San Francisco; Cardinals win toss. Swider punts and Robinson returns to 49ers' 32. San Francisco drives 52 yards to St. Louis 16, where Wersching kicks 33-yard field goal at 4:12.

Oct. 12, 1980—Green Bay 14, Tampa Bay 14, at Tampa Bay; Packers win toss. Teams trade punts twice. Lee returns second Tampa Bay punt to Green Bay 42. Dickey completes three passes to Buccaneers' 18, where Birney's 36-yard field goal attempt is wide right as time expires.

Nov. 9, 1980—Atlanta 33, St. Louis 27, at St. Louis; Falcons win toss. Strong runs 21 yards for touchdown at 4:20.

#Nov. 20, 1980—San Diego 27, Miami 24, at Miami; Chargers win toss. Partridge punts into end zone, Dolphins take over on their own 20. Woodley's pass for Nathan intercepted by Lowe and returned 28 yards to Dolphins' 12. Benirschke kicks 28-yard field goal at 7:14.

Nov. 23, 1980—New York Jets 31, Houston 28, at New York; Jets win toss. Leahy kicks 38-yard field goal at 3:58.

Nov. 27, 1980—Chicago 23, Detroit 17, at Detroit; Bears win toss. Williams returns kickoff 95 yards for touchdown at 0:21.

Dec. 7, 1980—Buffalo 10, Los Angeles 7, at Buffalo; Rams win toss. Corral punts and Hooks returns to Bills' 34. Ferguson's 30-yard pass to Lewis sets up N. Mike-Mayer's 30-yard field goal at 5:14.

Dec. 7, 1980—San Francisco 38, New Orleans 35, at San Francisco; Saints win toss. Erxleben's punt downed by Hardy on 49ers' 27. Wersching kicks 36-yard field goal at 7:40.

***Dec. 8, 1980—Miami 16, New England 13,** at Miami; Dolphins win toss. Von Schamann kicks 23-yard field goal at 3:20.

Dec. 14, 1980—Cincinnati 17, Chicago 14, at Chicago; Bengals win toss. Breech kicks 28-yard field goal at 4:23.

Dec. 21, 1980—Los Angeles 20, Atlanta 17, at Los Angeles; Rams win toss. Corral's punt downed at Rams' 37. James punts into end zone for touchback. Corral's punt downed on Falcons' 17. Bartkowski fumbles when hit by Harris, recovered by Delaney. Corral kicks 23-yard field goal on first play of possession at 7:00.

Sept. 27, 1981—Cincinnati 27, Buffalo 24, at Cincinnati; Bills win toss. Cater punts into end zone for touchback. Bengals drive to the Bills' 10 where Breech kicks 28-yard field goal at 9:33.

Sept. 27, 1981—Pittsburgh 27, New England 21, at Pittsburgh; Patriots win toss. Hubach punts and Smith returns five yards to midfield. Four plays later Bradshaw throws 24-yard touchdown pass to Swann at 3:19.

Oct. 4, 1981—Miami 28, New York Jets 28, at Miami; Jets win toss. Teams trade punts twice. Leahy's 48-yard field goal attempt is wide right as time expires.

Oct. 25, 1981—New York Giants 27, Atlanta 24, at Atlanta; Giants win toss. Jennings' punt goes out of bounds at New York 47. Bright returns Atlanta punt to Giants' 14. Woerner fair catches punt at own 28. Andrews fumbles on first play, recovered by Van Pelt. Danelo kicks 40-yard field goal four plays later at 9:20.

Oct. 25, 1981—Chicago 20, San Diego 17, at Chicago; Bears win toss. Teams trade punts. Bears' second punt returned by Brooks to Chargers' 33. Fouts pass intercepted by Fencik and returned 32 yards to San Diego 27. Roveto kicks 27-yard field goal seven plays later at 9:30.

Nov. 8, 1981—Chicago 16, Kansas City 13, at Kansas City; Bears win toss. Teams trade punts. Kansas City takes over on downs on its own 38. Fuller's fumble recovered by Harris on Chicago 36. Roveto's 37-yard field goal wide, but Chiefs penalized for leverage. Roveto's 22-yard field goal attempt three plays later is good at 13:07.

Nov. 8, 1981—Denver 23, Cleveland 20, at Denver; Browns win toss. D. Smith recovers Hill's fumble at Denver 48. Morton's 33-yard pass to Upchurch and six-yard run by Preston set up Steinfort's 30-yard field goal at 4:10.

Nov. 8, 1981—Miami 30, New England 27, at New England; Dolphins win toss. Orosz punts and Morgan returns six yards to New England 26. Grogan's pass intercepted by Brudzinski who returns 19 yards to Patriots' 26. Von Schamann kicks 30-yard field goal on first down at 7:09.

Nov. 15, 1981—Washington 30, New York Giants 27, at New York; Giants win toss. Nelms returns Giants' punt 26 yards to New York 47. Five plays later Moseley kicks 48-yard field goal at 3:44.

Dec. 20, 1981—New York Giants 13, Dallas 10, at New York; Cowboys win toss and kick off. Jennings punts to Dallas 40. Taylor recovers Dorsett's fumble on second down. Danelo's 33-yard field goal attempt hits right upright and bounces back. White's pass for Pearson intercepted by Hunt and returned seven yards to Dallas 24. Four plays later Danelo kicks 35-yard field goal at 6:19.

Sept. 12, 1982—Washington 37, Philadelphia 34, at Philadelphia; Redskins win toss. Theismann completes five passes for 63 yards to set up Moseley's 26-yard field goal at 4:47.

Sept. 19, 1982—Pittsburgh 26, Cincinnati 20, at Pittsburgh; Bengals win toss. Anderson's pass intended for Kreider intercepted by Woodruff and returned 30 yards to Cincinnati 2. Bradshaw completes two-yard touchdown pass to Stallworth on first down at 1:08.

Dec. 19, 1982—Baltimore 20, Green Bay 20, at Baltimore; Packers win toss. K. Anderson intercepts Dickey's first-down pass and returns to Packers' 42. Miller's 44-yard field goal attempt blocked by G. Lewis. Teams trade punts before Stenerud's 47-yard field goal attempt is wide right. Teams trade punts again before time expires in Colts possession.

Jan. 2, 1983—Tampa Bay 26, Chicago 23, at Tampa Bay; Bears win toss. Parsons punts to T. Bell at Buccaneers' 40. Capece kicks 33-yard field goal at 3:14.

Sept. 4, 1983—Baltimore 29, New England 23, at New England; Patriots win toss. Cooks runs 52 yards with fumble recovery three plays into overtime at 0:30.

Sept. 4, 1983—Green Bay 41, Houston 38, at Houston; Packers win toss. Stenerud kicks 42-yard field goal at 5:55.

Sept. 11, 1983—New York Giants 16, Atlanta 13, at Atlanta; Giants win toss. Dennis returns kickoff 54 yards to Atlanta 41. Haji-Sheikh kicks 30-yard field goal at 3:38.

Sept. 18, 1983—New Orleans 34, Chicago 31, at New Orleans; Bears win toss. Parsons punts and Groth returns five yards to New Orleans 34. Stabler pass intercepted by Schmidt at Chicago 47. Parsons punt downed by Gentry at New Orleans 2. Stabler gains 36 yards in four passes; Wilson 38 in six carries. Andersen kicks 41-yard field goal at 10:57.

Sept. 18, 1983—Minnesota 19, Tampa Bay 16, at Tampa; Vikings win toss. Coleman punts and Bell returns eight yards to Tampa Bay 47. Capece's 33-yard field goal attempt sails wide at 7:26. Dils and Young combine for 48-yard gain to Tampa Bay 27. Ricardo kicks 42-yard field goal at 9:27.

Sept. 25, 1983—Baltimore 22, Chicago 19, at Baltimore; Colts win toss. Allegre kicks 33-yard field goal nine plays later at 4:51.

Sept. 25, 1983—Cleveland 30, San Diego 24, at San Diego; Browns win toss. Walker returns kickoff 33 yards to Cleveland 37. Sipe completes 48-yard touchdown pass to Holt four plays later at 1:53.

Sept. 25, 1983—New York Jets 27, Los Angeles Rams 24, at New York; Jets win toss. Ramsey punts to Irvin who returns to 25 but penalty puts Rams on own 13. Holmes 30-yard interception return sets up Leahy's 26-yard field goal at 3:22.

Oct. 9, 1983—Buffalo 38, Miami 35, at Miami; Dolphins win toss. Von Schamann's 52-yard field goal attempt goes wide at 12:36. Cater punts to Clayton who loses 11 to own 13. Von Schamann's 43-yard field goal attempt sails wide at 5:15. Danelo kicks 36-yard field goal nine plays later at 13:58.

Oct. 9, 1983—Dallas 27, Tampa Bay 24, at Dallas; Cowboys win toss. Septien's 51-yard field goal attempt goes wide but Buccaneers penalized for roughing kicker. Septien kicks 42-yard field goal at 4:38.

Oct. 23, 1983—Kansas City 13, Houston 10, at Houston; Chiefs win toss. Lowery kicks 41-yard field goal 13 plays later at 7:41.

Oct. 23, 1983—Minnesota 20, Green Bay 17, at Green Bay; Packers win toss. Scribner's punt downed on Vikings' 42. Ricardo kicks 32-yard field goal eight plays later at 5:05.

***Oct. 24, 1983—New York Giants 20, St. Louis 20,** at St. Louis; Cardinals win toss. Teams trade punts before O'Donoghue's 44-yard field goal attempt is wide left. Jennings' punt returned by Bird to St. Louis 21. Lomax pass intercepted by Haynes who loses six yards to New York 33. Jennings' punt downed on St. Louis 17. O'Donoghue's 19-yard field goal attempt is wide right. Rutledge's pass intercepted by L. Washington who returns 25 yards to New York 25. O'Donoghue's 42-yard field goal attempt is wide right. Rutledge's pass intercepted by W. Smith at St. Louis 33 to end game.

Oct. 30, 1983—Cleveland 25, Houston 19, at Cleveland; Oilers win toss. Teams trade punts. Nielsen's pass intercepted by Whitwell who returns to Houston 20. Green runs 20 yards for touchdown on first down at 6:34.

Nov. 20, 1983—Detroit 23, Green Bay 20, at Milwaukee; Packers win toss. Scribner punts and Jenkins returns 14 yards to Green Bay 45. Murray's 33-yard field goal attempt is wide left at 9:32. Whitehurst's pass intercepted by Watkins and returned to Green Bay 27. Murray kicks 37-yard field goal four plays later at 8:30.

Nov. 27, 1983—Atlanta 47, Green Bay 41, at Atlanta; Packers win toss. K. Johnson returns interception 31 yards for touchdown at 2:13.

Nov. 27, 1983—Seattle 51, Kansas City 48, at Seattle; Seahawks win toss. Dixon's 47-yard kickoff return sets up N. Johnson's 42-yard field goal at 1:36.

Dec. 11, 1983—New Orleans 20, Philadelphia 17, at Philadelphia; Eagles win toss. Runager punts to Groth who fair catches on New Orleans 32. Stabler completes two passes for 36 yards to Goodlow to set up Andersen's 50-yard field goal at 5:30.

***Dec. 12, 1983—Green Bay 12, Tampa Bay 9,** at Tampa; Packers win toss. Stenerud kicks 23-yard field goal 11 plays later at 4:07.

Sept. 9, 1984—Detroit 27, Atlanta 24, at Atlanta; Lions win toss. Murray kicks 48-yard field goal nine plays later at 5:06.

Sept. 30, 1984—Tampa Bay 30, Green Bay 27, at Tampa; Packers win toss. Scribner punts 44 yards to Tampa Bay 2. Epps returns Garcia's punt three yards to Green Bay 27. Scribner's punt downed on Buccaneers' 33. Ariri kicks 46-yard field goal 11 plays later at 10:32.

Oct. 14, 1984—Detroit 13, Tampa Bay 7, at Detroit; Buccaneers win toss. Tampa Bay drives to Lions' 39 before Wilder fumbles. Five plays later Danielson hits Thompson with 37-yard touchdown pass at 4:34.

Oct. 21, 1984—Dallas 30, New Orleans 27, at Dallas; Cowboys win toss. Septien kicks 41-yard field goal eight plays later at 3:42.

Oct. 28, 1984—Denver 22, Los Angeles Raiders 19, at Los Angeles; Raiders win toss. Hawkins fumble recovered by Foley at Denver 7. Teams trade punts. Karlis' 42-yard field goal attempt is wide left. Teams trade punts. Wilson pass intercepted by R. Jackson at Los Angeles 45, returned 23 yards to Los Angeles 22. Karlis kicks 35-yard field goal two plays later at 15:00.

Nov. 4, 1984—Philadelphia 23, Detroit 23, at Detroit; Lions win toss. Lions drive to Eagles' 3 in eight plays. Murray's 21-yard field goal attempt hits right upright and bounces back. Jaworski's pass intercepted by Watkins at Detroit 5. Teams trade punts. Cooper returns Black's punt five yards to Eagles' 14. Time expires four plays later with Eagles on own 21.

*indicates Monday night game
#indicates Thursday night game

Nov. 18, 1984—San Diego 34, Miami 28, at San Diego; Chargers win toss. McGee scores eight plays later on a 25-yard run at 3:17.

Dec. 2, 1984—Cincinnati 20, Cleveland 17, at Cleveland; Browns win toss. Simmons returns Cox's punt 30 yards to Cleveland 35. Breech kicks 35-yard field goal seven plays later at 4:34.

Dec. 2, 1984—Houston 23, Pittsburgh 20, at Houston; Oilers win toss. Cooper kicks 30-yard field goal 16 plays later at 5:53.

Sept. 8, 1985—St. Louis 27, Cleveland 24, at Cleveland; Cardinals win toss. O'Donoghue kicks 35-yard field goal nine plays later at 5:27.

Sept. 29, 1985—New York Giants 16, Philadelphia 10, at Philadelphia; Eagles win toss. Jaworski's pass tipped by Quick and intercepted by Patterson who returns 29 yards for touchdown at 0:55.

Oct. 20, 1985—Denver 13, Seattle 10, at Denver; Seahawks win toss. Teams trade punts twice. Krieg's pass intercepted by Hunter and returned to Seahawks' 15. Karlis kicks 24-yard field goal four plays later at 9:19.

Nov. 10, 1985—Philadelphia 23, Atlanta 17, at Philadelphia; Falcons win toss. Donnelly's 62-yard punt goes out of bounds at Eagles' 1. Jaworski completes 99-yard touchdown pass to Quick two plays later at 1:49.

Nov. 10, 1985—San Diego 40, Los Angeles Raiders 34, at San Diego; Chargers win toss. James scores on 17-yard run seven plays later at 3:44.

Nov. 17, 1985—Denver 30, San Diego 24, at Denver; Chargers win toss. Thomas' 40-yard field goal attempt blocked by Smith and returned 60 yards by Wright for touchdown at 4:45.

Nov. 24, 1985—New York Jets 16, New England 13, at New York; Jets win toss. Teams trade punts twice. Patriots' second punt returned 46 yards by Sohn to Patriots' 15. Leahy kicks 32-yard field goal one play later at 10:05.

Nov. 24, 1985—Tampa Bay 19, Detroit 16, at Tampa; Lions win toss. Teams trade punts. Lions' punt downed on Buccaneers' 38. Igwebuike kicks 24-yard field goal 11 plays later at 12:31.

Nov. 24, 1985—Los Angeles Raiders 31, Denver 28, at Los Angeles; Raiders win toss. Bahr kicks 32-yard field goal six plays later at 2:42.

Dec. 8, 1985—Los Angeles Raiders 17, Denver 14, at Denver; Broncos win toss. Teams trade punts twice. Elway's fumble recovered by Townsend at Broncos' 8. Bahr kicks 26-yard field goal one play later at 4:55.

Sept. 14, 1986—Chicago 13, Philadelphia 10, at Chicago; Eagles win toss. Crawford's fumble of kickoff recovered by Jackson at Eagles' 35. Butler kicks 23-yard field goal 10 plays later at 5:56.

Sept. 14, 1986—Cincinnati 36, Buffalo 33, at Cincinnati; Bills win toss. Zander intercepts Kelly's first-down pass and returns it to Bills' 17. Breech kicks 20-yard field goal two plays later at 0:56.

Sept. 21, 1986—New York Jets 51, Miami 45, at New York; Jets win toss. O'Brien completes 43-yard touchdown pass to Walker five plays later at 2:35.

Sept. 28, 1986—Pittsburgh 22, Houston 16, at Houston; Oilers win toss. Johnson's punt returned 41 yards by Woods to Oilers' 15. Abercrombie scores on three-yard run three plays later at 2:35.

Sept. 28, 1986—Atlanta 23, Tampa Bay 20, at Tampa; Falcons win toss. Teams trade punts. Luckhurst kicks 34-yard field goal 10 plays later at 12:35.

Oct. 5, 1986—Los Angeles Rams 26, Tampa Bay 20, at Anaheim; Rams win toss. Dickerson scores four plays later on 42-yard run at 2:16.

Oct. 12, 1986—Minnesota 27, San Francisco 24, at San Francisco; Vikings win toss. C. Nelson kicks 28-yard field goal nine plays later at 4:27.

Oct. 19, 1986—San Francisco 10, Atlanta 10, at Atlanta; Falcons win toss. Teams trade punts twice. Donnelly punts to 49ers' 27. The following play Wilson recovers Rice's fumble at 49ers' 46 as time expires.

Nov. 2, 1986—Washington 44, Minnesota 38, at Washington; Redskins win toss. Schroeder completes 38-yard touchdown pass to Clark four plays later at 1:46.

Nov. 20, 1986—Los Angeles Raiders 37, San Diego 31, at San Diego; Raiders win toss. Teams trade punts. Allen scores five plays later on 28-yard run at 8:33.

Nov. 23, 1986—Cleveland 37, Pittsburgh 31, at Cleveland; Browns win toss. Teams trade punts. Six plays later Kosar hits Slaughter with 36-yard touchdown pass at 6:37.

Nov. 30, 1986—Chicago 13, Pittsburgh 10, at Chicago; Bears win toss and kick off. Newsome's punt returned by Barnes to Chicago 49. Butler kicks 42-yard field goal five plays later at 3:55.

Nov. 30, 1986—Philadelphia 33, Los Angeles Raiders 27, at Los Angeles; Eagles win toss. Teams trade punts. Long recovers Cunningham's fumble at Philadelphia 42. Waters returns Allen's fumble 81 yards to Los Angeles 4. Cunningham scores on one-yard run two plays later at 6:53.

Nov. 30, 1986—Cleveland 13, Houston 10, at Cleveland; Oilers win toss and kick off. Gossett punts to Houston 39. Luck's pass intercepted by Minnifield at Cleveland 21. Gossett punts to Houston 34. Luck's pass intercepted by Minnifield at Cleveland 43 who returns 20 yards to Houston 37. Moseley kicks 29-yard field goal nine plays later at 14:44.

Dec. 7, 1986—St. Louis 10, Philadelphia 10, at Philadelphia; Cardinals win toss. White blocks Schubert's 40-yard field goal attempt. Teams trade punts. McFadden's 43-yard field goal attempt is wide left. Schubert's 37-yard field goal attempt is wide right. Cavanaugh's pass intercepted by Carter and returned to Eagles' 48 to end game.

Dec. 14, 1986—Miami 37, Los Angeles Rams 31, at Anaheim; Dolphins win toss. Marino completes 20-yard touchdown pass to Duper six plays later at 3:04.

Sept. 20, 1987—Denver 17, Green Bay 17, at Green Bay; Packers win toss. Del Greco's 47-yard field goal attempt is short. Teams trade punts. Elway intercepted by Noble who returns 10 yards to Green Bay 34. Davis fumbles on next play and Smith recovers. Two plays later, Karlis's 40-yard field goal attempt is wide left. Time expires two plays later with Packers on own 23.

Oct. 11, 1987—Detroit 19, Green Bay 16, at Green Bay; Lions win toss. Prindle's 42-yard field goal attempt is wide left. Packers punt downed on Detroit 17. Prindle kicks 31-yard field goal 16 plays later at 12:26.

Oct. 18, 1987—New York Jets 37, Miami 31, at New York; Jets win toss. Teams trade punts. Ryan intercepted by Hooper at Jets' 47 who returns 11 yards. Mackey intercepted by Haslett at Jets' 37 who returns 9 yards. Jets punt. Mackey intercepted by Radachowsky who returns 45 yards to Miami 24. Ryan completes eight-yard touchdown pass to Hunter five plays later at 14:26.

Oct. 18, 1987—Green Bay 16, Philadelphia 10, at Green Bay; Packers win toss. Hargrove scores on seven-yard run 10 plays later at 5:04.

Oct. 18, 1987—Buffalo 6, New York Giants 3, at Buffalo; Bills win toss. Schlopy's 28-yard field goal attempt is wide left. Teams trade punts. Rutledge intercepted by Clark who returns 23 yards to Buffalo 40. Schlopy kicks 27-yard field goal nine plays later at 14:41.

Oct. 25, 1987—Buffalo 34, Miami 31, at Miami; Bills win toss. Norwood kicks 27-yard field goal seven plays later at 4:12.

Nov. 1, 1987—San Diego 27, Cleveland 24, at San Diego; Browns win toss. Kosar intercepted by Glenn who returns 20 yards to Browns' 25. Abbott kicks 33-yard field goal three plays later at 2:16.

Nov. 15, 1987—Dallas 23, New England 17, at New England; Cowboys win toss. Walker scores on 60-yard run four plays later at 1:50.

Nov. 26, 1987—Minnesota 44, Dallas 38, at Dallas; Vikings win toss. Coleman's punt downed by Hilton at Cowboys' 37. White intercepted by Studwell who returns 12 yards to Vikings' 37. D. Nelson scores on 24-yard run seven plays later at 7:51.

Nov. 29, 1987—Philadelphia 34, New England 31, at New England; Patriots win toss. Ramsey intercepted by Joyner who returns 29 yards to Eagles' 32. Fryar fair catches Teltschik's punt at Patriots' 13. Franklin's 46-yard field goal attempt is short. McFadden's 39-yard field goal attempt is wide left. Tatupu fumbles on next play and Cobb recovers. McFadden kicks 38-yard field goal four plays later at 12:16.

Dec. 6, 1987—New York Giants 23, Philadelphia 20, at New York; Giants win toss and kick off. Teams trade punts twice. Teltschik's punt is returned 16 yards by McConkey to Eagles' 33. Three plays later, Allegre's 50-yard field goal attempt is blocked by Joyner and returned 25 yards by Hoage to Eagles' 30. McConkey returns Teltschik's punt four yards to Giants' 44. Allegre kicks 28-yard field goal four plays later at 10:42.

Dec. 6, 1987—Cincinnati 30, Kansas City 27, at Cincinnati; Bengals win toss. Teams trade punts. Breech kicks 32-yard field goal 16 plays later at 9:44.

Dec. 26, 1987—Washington 27, Minnesota 24, at Minnesota; Redskins win toss. Haji-Sheikh kicks 26-yard field goal six plays later at 2:09.

*indicates Monday night game
#indicates Thursday night game

Postseason

Dec. 28, 1958—Baltimore 23, New York Giants 17, at New York; Giants win toss. Maynard returns kickoff to Giants' 20. Chandler punts and Taseff returns one yard to Colts' 20. Colts win at 8:15 on a one-yard run by Ameche.

Dec. 23, 1962—Dallas Texans 20, Houston Oilers 17, at Houston; Texans win toss and kick off. Jancik returns kickoff to Oilers' 33. Norton punts and Jackson makes fair catch on Texans' 22. Wilson punts and Jancik makes fair catch on Oilers' 45. Robinson intercepts Blanda's pass and returns 13 yards to Oilers' 47. Wilson's punt rolls dead at Oilers' 12. Hull intercepts Blanda's pass and returns 23 yards to midfield. Texans win at 17:54 on a 25-yard field goal by Brooker.

Dec. 26, 1965—Green Bay 13, Baltimore 10, at Green Bay; Packers win toss. Moore returns kickoff to Packers' 22. Chandler punts and Haymond returns nine yards to Colts' 41. Gilburg punts and Wood makes fair catch at Packers' 21. Chandler punts and Haymond returns one yard to Colts' 41. Michaels misses 47-yard field goal. Packers win at 13:39 on 25-yard field goal by Chandler.

Dec. 25, 1971—Miami 27, Kansas City 24, at Kansas City; Chiefs win toss. Podolak, after a lateral from Buchanan, returns kickoff to Chiefs' 46. Stenerud's 42-yard field goal is blocked. Seiple punts and Podolak makes fair catch at Chiefs' 17. Wilson punts and Scott returns 18 yards to Dolphins' 39. Yepremian misses 62-yard field goal. Scott intercepts Dawson's pass and returns 13 yards to Dolphins' 46. Seiple punts and Podolak loses one yard to Chiefs' 15. Wilson punts and Scott makes fair catch on Dolphins' 30. Dolphins win at 22:40 on a 37-yard field goal by Yepremian.

Dec. 24, 1977—Oakland 37, Baltimore 31, at Baltimore; Colts win toss. Raiders start on own 42 following a punt late in the first overtime. Oakland works way into a threatening position on Stabler's 19-yard pass to Branch at Colts' 26. Four plays later, on the second play of the second overtime, Stabler hits Casper with a 10-yard touchdown pass at 15:43.

Jan. 2, 1982—San Diego 41, Miami 38, at Miami; Chargers win toss. San Diego drives from its 13 to Miami 8. On second-and-goal, Benirschke misses 27-yard field goal attempt wide left at 9:15. Miami has the ball twice and San Diego twice more before the Dolphins get their third possession. Miami drives from the San Diego 46 to Chargers' 17 and on fourth-and-two, von Schamann's 34-yard field goal attempt is blocked by San Diego's Winslow after 11:27. Fouts then completes four of five passes, including a 29-yarder to Joiner that puts the ball on Dolphins' 10. On first down, Benirschke kicks a 20-yard field goal at 13:52. San Diego's winning drive covered 74 yards in six plays.

Jan. 3, 1987—Cleveland 23, New York Jets 20, at Cleveland; Jets win toss. Jets' punt downed at Browns' 26. Moseley's 23-yard field goal attempt is wide right. Teams trade punts. Jets' second punt downed at Browns' 31. First overtime period expires eight plays later with Browns in possession at Jets' 42. Moseley kicks 27-yard field goal four plays into second overtime at 17:02.

Jan. 11, 1987—Denver 23, Cleveland 20, at Cleveland; Browns win toss. Broncos hold Browns on four downs. Browns' punt returned four yards to Denver's 25. Elway completes 22- and 28-yard passes to set up Karlis's 33-yard field goal nine plays into drive at 5:38.

Jan. 3, 1988—Houston 23, Seattle 20, at Houston. Seahawks win toss. Rodriguez punts to K. Johnson who returns one yard to Houston 15. Zendejas kicks 32-yard field goal 12 plays later at 8:05.

NFL Postseason Overtime Games (By Length of Game)

Dec. 25, 1971	Miami 27, KANSAS CITY 24	82:40
Dec. 23, 1962	Dallas Texans 20, HOUSTON 17	77:54
Jan. 3, 1987	CLEVELAND 23, New York Jets 20	77:02
Dec. 24, 1977	Oakland 37, BALTIMORE 31	75:43
Jan. 2, 1982	San Diego 41, MIAMI 38	73:52
Dec. 26, 1965	GREEN BAY 13, Baltimore 10	73:39
Dec. 28, 1958	Baltimore 23, N.Y. GIANTS 17	68:15
Jan. 3, 1988	HOUSTON 23, Seattle 20	68:05
Jan. 11, 1987	Denver 23, CLEVELAND 20	65:38

Home team in CAPS

Overtime Won-Lost Records, 1974-1987 (Regular Season)

	W	L	T
Atlanta	4	7	1
Buffalo	5	2	0
Chicago	6	7	0
Cincinnati	6	3	0
Cleveland	9	6	0
Dallas	6	3	0
Denver	8	3	2
Detroit	4	3	1
Green Bay	4	6	4
Houston	3	7	0
Indianapolis	3	1	1
Kansas City	3	5	0
Los Angeles Raiders	6	4	0
Los Angeles Rams	4	3	1
Miami	3	9	1
Minnesota	7	4	2
New England	0	10	0
New Orleans	2	4	0
New York Giants	5	5	1
New York Jets	6	3	1
Philadelphia	3	7	2
Pittsburgh	6	3	1
St. Louis	3	4	2
San Diego	7	6	0
San Francisco	3	3	1
Seattle	1	2	0
Tampa Bay	4	6	1
Washington	7	2	0

Overtime Games By Year (Regular Season)

1987-13	1980-13
1986-16	1979-12
1985-10	1978-11
1984- 9	1977- 6
1983-19	1976- 5
1982- 4	1975- 9
1981-10	1974- 2

Overtime Game Summary—1974-1987

There have been 139 overtime games in regular-season play since the rule was adopted in 1974. The breakdown follows:

95 times both teams had at least one possession (68%)

44 times the team which won the coin toss drove for winning score (29 FG, 15 TD) (32%)

72 times the team which won the coin toss won the game (52%)

56 times the team which lost the coin toss won the game (40%)

86 games were decided by a field goal (62%)

42 games were decided by a touchdown (30%)

11 games ended tied (8%). Last time: Denver 17, Green Bay 17; 9/20/87

70 times the home team won the game (50%)

58 times the visiting team won the game (42%)

Most Overtime Games, Season

5 Green Bay Packers, 1983

4 Denver Broncos, 1985

3 By many teams, last time: Green Bay Packers, New England Patriots, Philadelphia Eagles, 1987

Longest Consecutive Game Streaks Without Overtime (current)

75 games Indianapolis Colts (last OT game, 9/25/83 vs. Chicago)

55 games New Orleans Saints (last OT game, 10/21/84 vs. Dallas)

40 games Seattle Seahawks (last OT game, 10/25/85 vs. Denver)

Shortest Overtime Games

0:21 Chicago 23, Detroit 17; 11/27/80—Initial overtime kickoff return for a touchdown.

0:30 Baltimore 29, New England 23; 9/4/83

0:55 New York Giants 16, Philadelphia 10; 9/29/85

Longest Overtime Games (All Postseason Games)

22:40 Miami 27, Kansas City 24; 12/25/71

17:54 Dallas Texans 20, Houston 17; 12/23/62

17:02 Cleveland 23, New York Jets 20; 1/3/87

There have been eight postseason overtime games dating back to 1958. In all cases, both teams had at least one possession. Last postseason overtime: Houston 23, Seattle 20; 1/3/88.

Overtime Scoring Summary

86 were decided by a field goal

17 were decided by a touchdown pass

16 were decided by a touchdown run

3 were decided by interceptions (Atlanta 40, New Orleans 34, 9/2/79; Atlanta 47, Green Bay 41, 11/27/83; New York Giants 16, Philadelphia 10; 9/29/85)

1 was decided by a kickoff return (Chicago 23, Detroit 17; 11/27/80)

1 was decided by a fumble recovery (Baltimore 29, New England 23; 9/4/83)

1 was decided on a fake field goal/touchdown run (Los Angeles Rams 27, Minnesota 21; 12/2/79)

1 was decided on a fake field goal/touchdown pass (Minnesota 22, Chicago 16; 10/16/77)

1 was decided on a blocked field goal (Denver 30, San Diego 24; 11/17/85)

1 was decided on a blocked field goal/recovery by kicker (Green Bay 12, Chicago 6; 9/7/80)

11 ended tied

Overtime Records

Longest Touchdown Pass

99 Yards—Ron Jaworski to Mike Quick, Philadelphia 23, Atlanta 17 (11/10/85)

50 Yards—Tommy Kramer to Ahmad Rashad, Minnesota 27, Green Bay 21 (9/23/79)

48 Yards—Brian Sipe to Harry Holt, Cleveland 30, San Diego 24 (9/23/83)

Longest Touchdown Run

60 Yards—Herschel Walker, Dallas 23, New England 17 (11/15/87)

42 Yards—Eric Dickerson, Los Angeles Rams 26, Tampa Bay 20 (10/5/86)

28 Yards—Marcus Allen, Los Angeles Raiders 37, San Diego 31 (11/20/86)

Longest Field Goal

50 Yards—Morten Andersen, New Orleans 20, Philadelphia 17 (12/11/83)

48 Yards—Eddie Murray, Detroit 27, Atlanta 24 (9/9/84);
Mark Moseley, Washington 30, New York Giants 27 (11/15/81)

46 Yards—Obed Ariri, Tampa Bay 30, Green Bay 27 (9/30/84)

Longest Touchdown Plays

99 Yards—(Pass) Ron Jaworski to Mike Quick, Philadelphia 23, Atlanta 17 (11/10/85)

60 Yards—(Blocked field goal return) Louis Wright, Denver 30, San Diego 24 (11/17/85)
(Run) Herschel Walker, Dallas 23, New England 17 (11/15/87)

52 Yards—(Fumble recovery) Johnie Cooks, Baltimore 29, New England 23 (9/4/83)

Chicago All-Star Game

Pro teams won 31, lost 19, and tied 2. The game was discontinued after 1976.

Year	Date	Winner	Loser	Attendance
1976	July 23	Pittsburgh 24	All-Stars 0	52,895
1975	Aug. 1	Pittsburgh 21	All-Stars 14	54,103
1974		No game was played		
1973	July 27	Miami 14	All-Stars 3	54,103
1972	July 28	Dallas 20	All-Stars 7	54,162
1971	July 30	Baltimore 24	All-Stars 17	52,289
1970	July 31	Kansas City 24	All-Stars 3	69,940
1969	Aug. 1	N.Y. Jets 26	All-Stars 24	74,208
1968	Aug. 2	Green Bay 34	All-Stars 17	69,917
1967	Aug. 4	Green Bay 27	All-Stars 0	70,934
1966	Aug. 5	Green Bay 38	All-Stars 0	72,000
1965	Aug. 6	Cleveland 24	All-Stars 16	68,000
1964	Aug. 7	Chicago 28	All-Stars 17	65,000
1963	Aug. 2	All-Stars 20	Green Bay 17	65,000
1962	Aug. 3	Green Bay 42	All-Stars 20	65,000
1961	Aug. 4	Philadelphia 28	All-Stars 14	66,000
1960	Aug. 12	Baltimore 32	All-Stars 7	70,000
1959	Aug. 14	Baltimore 29	All-Stars 0	70,000
1958	Aug. 15	All-Stars 35	Detroit 19	70,000
1957	Aug. 9	N.Y. Giants 22	All-Stars 12	75,000
1956	Aug. 10	Cleveland 26	All-Stars 0	75,000
1955	Aug. 12	All-Stars 30	Cleveland 27	75,000
1954	Aug. 13	Detroit 31	All-Stars 6	93,470
1953	Aug. 14	Detroit 24	All-Stars 10	93,818
1952	Aug. 15	Los Angeles 10	All-Stars 7	88,316
1951	Aug. 17	Cleveland 33	All-Stars 0	92,180
1950	Aug. 11	All-Stars 17	Philadelphia 7	88,885
1949	Aug. 12	Philadelphia 38	All-Stars 0	93,780
1948	Aug. 20	Chi. Cardinals 28	All-Stars 0	101,220
1947	Aug. 22	All-Stars 16	Chi. Bears 0	105,840
1946	Aug. 23	All-Stars 16	Los Angeles 0	97,380
1945	Aug. 30	Green Bay 19	All-Stars 7	92,753
1944	Aug. 30	Chi. Bears 24	All-Stars 21	48,769
1943	Aug. 25	All-Stars 27	Washington 7	48,471
1942	Aug. 28	Chi. Bears 21	All-Stars 0	101,100
1941	Aug. 28	Chi. Bears 37	All-Stars 13	98,203
1940	Aug. 29	Green Bay 45	All-Stars 28	84,567
1939	Aug. 30	N.Y. Giants 9	All-Stars 0	81,456
1938	Aug. 31	All-Stars 28	Washington 16	74,250
1937	Sept. 1	All-Stars 6	Green Bay 0	84,560
1936	Sept. 3	All-Stars 7	Detroit 7 (tie)	76,000
1935	Aug. 29	Chi. Bears 5	All-Stars 0	77,450
1934	Aug. 31	Chi. Bears 0	All-Stars 0 (tie)	79,432

NFL Playoff Bowl

Western Conference won 8, Eastern Conference won 2. All games played at Miami's Orange Bowl.

1970	Los Angeles Rams 31, Dallas Cowboys 0
1969	Dallas Cowboys 17, Minnesota Vikings 13
1968	Los Angeles Rams 30, Cleveland Browns 6
1967	Baltimore Colts 20, Philadelphia Eagles 14
1966	Baltimore Colts 35, Dallas Cowboys 3
1965	St. Louis Cardinals 24, Green Bay Packers 17
1964	Green Bay Packers 40, Cleveland Browns 23
1963	Detroit Lions 17, Pittsburgh Steelers 10
1962	Detroit Lions 28, Philadelphia Eagles 10
1961	Detroit Lions 17, Cleveland Browns 16

Pro Football Hall of Fame Game

1962	New York Giants 21, St. Louis Cardinals 21
1963	Pittsburgh Steelers 16, Cleveland Browns 7
1964	Baltimore Colts 48, Pittsburgh Steelers 17
1965	Washington Redskins 20, Detroit Lions 3
1966	No game
1967	Philadelphia Eagles 28, Cleveland Browns 13
1968	Chicago Bears 30, Dallas Cowboys 24
1969	Green Bay Packers 38, Atlanta Falcons 24
1970	New Orleans Saints 14, Minnesota Vikings 13
1971	Los Angeles Rams (NFC) 17, Houston Oilers (AFC) 6
1972	Kansas City Chiefs (AFC) 23, New York Giants (NFC) 17
1973	San Francisco 49ers (NFC) 20, New England Patriots (AFC) 7
1974	St. Louis Cardinals (NFC) 21, Buffalo Bills (AFC) 13
1975	Washington Redskins (NFC) 17, Cincinnati Bengals (AFC) 9
1976	Denver Broncos (AFC) 10, Detroit Lions (NFC) 7
1977	Chicago Bears (NFC) 20, New York Jets (AFC) 6
1978	Philadelphia Eagles (NFC) 17, Miami Dolphins (AFC) 3
1979	Oakland Raiders (AFC) 20, Dallas Cowboys (NFC) 13
1980	San Diego Chargers (AFC) 0, Green Bay Packers (NFC) 0
1981	Cleveland Browns (AFC) 24, Atlanta Falcons (NFC) 10
1982	Minnesota Vikings (NFC) 30, Baltimore Colts (AFC) 14
1983	Pittsburgh Steelers (AFC) 27, New Orleans Saints (NFC) 14
1984	Seattle Seahawks (AFC) 38, Tampa Bay Buccaneers (NFC) 0
1985	New York Giants (NFC) 21, Houston Oilers (AFC) 20
1986	New England Patriots (AFC) 21, St. Louis Cardinals (NFC) 16
1987	San Francisco 49ers (NFC) 20, Kansas City Chiefs (AFC) 7

NFL International Games

Date	Site	Teams
Aug. 12, 1950	Ottawa, Canada	N.Y. Giants vs. Ottawa Rough Riders
Aug. 15, 1960	Toronto, Canada	N.Y. Giants vs. Chicago Bears
Aug. 8, 1961	Hamilton, Canada	Buffalo Bills vs. Hamilton Tiger-Cats
Aug. 25, 1969	Montreal, Canada	Boston Patriots vs. Detroit Lions
Sept. 11, 1969	Montreal, Canada	N.Y. Giants vs. Pittsburgh Steelers
Aug. 16, 1976	Tokyo, Japan	St. Louis Cardinals vs. San Diego
Aug. 5, 1978	Mexico City, Mexico	New Orleans vs. Philadelphia
Aug. 6, 1983	London, England	St. Louis vs. Minnesota
Aug. 3, 1986	London, England	Chicago vs. Dallas
Aug. 9, 1987	London, England	Denver vs. Los Angeles Rams

NFL Paid Attendance

Year	Regular Season		Average	Postseason	Super Bowl
1987*	11,406,166 (210 games)		54,315	656,977 (10)	73,302
1986	13,588,551 (224 games)		60,663	734,002 (10)	101,063
1985	13,345,047 (224 games)		59,567	710,768 (10)	73,818
1984	13,398,112 (224 games)		59,813	665,194 (10)	84,059
1983	13,277,222 (224 games)		59,273	675,513 (10)	72,932
1982**	7,367,438 (126 games)		58,472	1,033,153 (16)	103,667
1981	13,606,990 (224 games)		60,745	637,763 (10)	81,270
1980	13,392,230 (224 games)		59,787	624,430 (10)	75,500
1979	13,182,039 (224 games)		58,848	630,326 (10)	103,985
1978	12,771,800 (224 games)		57,017	624,388 (10)	79,641
1977	11,018,632 (196 games)		56,218	534,925 (8)	75,804
1976	11,070,543 (196 games)		56,482	492,884 (8)	103,438
1975	10,213,193 (182 games)		56,116	475,919 (8)	80,187
1974	10,236,322 (182 games)		56,244	438,664 (8)	80,997
1973	10,730,933 (182 games)		58,961	525,433 (8)	71,882
1972	10,445,827 (182 games)		57,395	483,345 (8)	90,182
1971	10,076,035 (182 games)		55,363	483,891 (8)	81,023
1970	9,533,333 (182 games)		52,381	458,493 (8)	79,204
1969	6,096,127 (112 games)	NFL	54,430	162,279 (3)	80,562
	2,843,373 (70 games)	AFL	40,620	167,088 (3)	
1968	5,882,313 (112 games)	NFL	52,521	215,902 (3)	75,377
	2,635,004 (70 games)	AFL	37,643	114,438 (2)	
1967	5,938,924 (112 games)	NFL	53,026	166,208 (3)	75,546
	2,295,697 (63 games)	AFL	36,439	53,330 (1)	
1966	5,337,044 (105 games)	NFL	50,829	74,152 (1)	61,946†
	2,160,369 (63 games)	AFL	34,291	42,080 (1)	
1965	4,634,021 (98 games)	NFL	47,286	100,304 (2)	
	1,782,384 (56 games)	AFL	31,828	30,361 (1)	
1964	4,563,049 (98 games)	NFL	46,562	79,544 (1)	
	1,447,875 (56 games)	AFL	25,855	40,242 (1)	
1963	4,163,643 (98 games)	NFL	42,486	45,801 (1)	
	1,208,697 (56 games)	AFL	21,584	63,171 (2)	
1962	4,003,421 (98 games)	NFL	40,851	64,892 (1)	
	1,147,302 (56 games)	AFL	20,487	37,981 (1)	
1961	3,986,159 (98 games)	NFL	40,675	39,029 (1)	
	1,002,657 (56 games)	AFL	17,904	29,556 (1)	
1960	3,128,296 (78 games)	NFL	40,106	67,325 (1)	
	926,156 (56 games)	AFL	16,538	32,183 (1)	
1959	3,140,000 (72 games)		43,617	57,545 (1)	
1958	3,006,124 (72 games)		41,752	123,659 (2)	
1957	2,836,318 (72 games)		39,393	119,579 (2)	
1956	2,551,263 (72 games)		35,434	56,836 (1)	
1955	2,521,836 (72 games)		35,026	85,693 (1)	
1954	2,190,571 (72 games)		30,425	43,827 (1)	
1953	2,164,585 (72 games)		30,064	54,577 (1)	
1952	2,052,126 (72 games)		28,502	97,507 (2)	
1951	1,913,019 (72 games)		26,570	57,522 (1)	
1950	1,977,753 (78 games)		25,356	136,647 (3)	
1949	1,391,735 (60 games)		23,196	27,980 (1)	
1948	1,525,243 (60 games)		25,421	36,309 (1)	
1947	1,837,437 (60 games)		30,624	66,268 (2)	
1946	1,732,135 (55 games)		31,493	58,346 (1)	
1945	1,270,401 (50 games)		25,408	32,178 (1)	
1944	1,019,649 (50 games)		20,393	46,016 (1)	
1943	969,128 (40 games)		24,228	71,315 (2)	
1942	887,920 (55 games)		16,144	36,006 (1)	
1941	1,108,615 (55 games)		20,157	55,870 (2)	
1940	1,063,025 (55 games)		19,328	36,034 (1)	
1939	1,071,200 (55 games)		19,476	32,279 (1)	
1938	937,197 (55 games)		17,040	48,120 (1)	
1937	963,039 (55 games)		17,510	15,878 (1)	
1936	816,007 (54 games)		15,111	29,545 (1)	
1935	638,178 (53 games)		12,041	15,000 (1)	
1934	492,684 (60 games)		8,211	35,059 (1)	

*Players 24-day strike reduced 224-game schedule to 210 games.
**Players 57-day strike reduced 224-game schedule to 126 games.
†Only Super Bowl that did not sell out.

NFL's 10 Biggest Attendance Weekends

(Paid Count)

Weekend	Games	Attendance
October 27-28, 1985	14	902,128
October 12-13, 1980	14	898,223
September 23-24, 1984	14	894,402
November 11-12, 1979	14	890,972
September 16, 19-20, 1983	14	886,323
November 20, 23-24, 1980	14	885,601
November 9-10, 1986	14	882,762
September 12-13, 1982	14	882,042
November 15-16, 1981	14	881,486
September 5-6-7, 1981	14	881,439

NFL's 10 Highest Scoring Weekends

Point Total	Date	Weekend
761	October 16-17, 1983	7th
736	October 25-26, 1987	7th
732	November 9-10, 1980	10th
725	November 24, 27-28, 1983	13th
711	November 26, 29-30, 1987	12th
710	November 28, December 1-2, 1985	13th
696	October 2-3, 1983	5th
676	September 21-22, 1980	3rd
675	October 23-24, 1983	8th
675	December 19-22, 1986	16th

Top 10 Televised Sports Events

(Based on A.C. Nielsen Figures)

Program	Date	Network	Share	Rating
Super Bowl XVI	1/24/82	CBS	73.0	49.1
Super Bowl XVII	1/30/83	NBC	69.0	48.6
Super Bowl XX	1/26/86	NBC	70.0	48.3
Super Bowl XII	1/15/78	CBS	67.0	47.2
Super Bowl XIII	1/21/79	NBC	74.0	47.1
Super Bowl XVIII	1/22/84	CBS	71.0	46.4
Super Bowl XIX	1/20/85	ABC	63.0	46.4
Super Bowl XIV	1/20/80	CBS	67.0	46.3
Super Bowl XXI	1/25/87	CBS	66.0	45.8
Super Bowl XI	1/9/77	NBC	73.0	44.4

Ten Most Watched TV Programs & Estimated Total Number of Viewers

(Based on A.C. Nielsen Figures)

Program	Date	Network	*Total Viewers
Super Bowl XX	Jan. 26, 1986	NBC	127,000,000
Super Bowl XXI	Jan. 25, 1987	CBS	122,640,000
M*A*S*H (Special)	Feb. 28, 1983	CBS	121,624,000
Super Bowl XIX	Jan. 20, 1985	ABC	115,936,000
Super Bowl XXII	Jan. 31, 1988	ABC	115,000,000
Super Bowl XVI	Jan. 24, 1982	CBS	110,230,000
Super Bowl XVII	Jan. 30, 1983	NBC	109,040,000
Super Bowl XII	Jan. 15, 1978	CBS	102,010,000
Roots, Part 8	Jan. 30, 1977	ABC	98,706,000
Super Bowl XIV	Jan. 20, 1980	CBS	97,800,000

*Watched some portion of the broadcast

NUMBER-ONE DRAFT CHOICES

Season	Team	Player	Position	College
1988	Atlanta	Aundray Bruce	LB	Auburn
1987	Tampa Bay	Vinny Testaverde	QB	Miami
1986	Tampa Bay	Bo Jackson	RB	Auburn
1985	Buffalo	Bruce Smith	DE	Virginia Tech
1984	New England	Irving Fryar	WR	Nebraska
1983	Baltimore	John Elway	QB	Stanford
1982	New England	Kenneth Sims	DT	Texas
1981	New Orleans	George Rogers	RB	South Carolina
1980	Detroit	Billy Sims	RB	Oklahoma
1979	Buffalo	Tom Cousineau	LB	Ohio State
1978	Houston	Earl Campbell	RB	Texas
1977	Tampa Bay	Ricky Bell	RB	Southern California
1976	Tampa Bay	Lee Roy Selmon	DE	Oklahoma
1975	Atlanta	Steve Bartkowski	QB	California
1974	Dallas	Ed Jones	DE	Tennessee State
1973	Houston	John Matuszak	DE	Tampa
1972	Buffalo	Walt Patulski	DE	Notre Dame
1971	New England	Jim Plunkett	QB	Stanford
1970	Pittsburgh	Terry Bradshaw	QB	Louisiana Tech
1969	Buffalo (AFL)	O.J. Simpson	RB	Southern California
1968	Minnesota	Ron Yary	T	Southern California
1967	Baltimore	Bubba Smith	DT	Michigan State
1966	Atlanta	Tommy Nobis	LB	Texas
	Miami (AFL)	Jim Grabowski	RB	Illinois
1965	New York Giants	Tucker Frederickson	RB	Auburn
	Houston (AFL)	Lawrence Elkins	E	Baylor
1964	San Francisco	Dave Parks	E	Texas Tech
	Boston (AFL)	Jack Concannon	QB	Boston College
1963	Los Angeles	Terry Baker	QB	Oregon State
	Kansas City (AFL)	Buck Buchanan	DT	Grambling
1962	Washington	Ernie Davis	RB	Syracuse
	Oakland (AFL)	Roman Gabriel	QB	North Carolina State
1961	Minnesota	Tommy Mason	RB	Tulane
	Buffalo (AFL)	Ken Rice	G	Auburn
1960	Los Angeles	Billy Cannon	RB	Louisiana State
	(AFL had no formal first pick)			
1959	Green Bay	Randy Duncan	QB	Iowa
1958	Chicago Cardinals	King Hill	QB	Rice
1957	Green Bay	Paul Hornung	HB	Notre Dame
1956	Pittsburgh	Gary Glick	DB	Colorado A&M
1955	Baltimore	George Shaw	QB	Oregon
1954	Cleveland	Bobby Garrett	QB	Stanford
1953	San Francisco	Harry Babcock	E	Georgia
1952	Los Angeles	Bill Wade	QB	Vanderbilt
1951	New York Giants	Kyle Rote	HB	Southern Methodist
1950	Detroit	Leon Hart	E	Notre Dame
1949	Philadelphia	Chuck Bednarik	C	Pennsylvania
1948	Washington	Harry Gilmer	QB	Alabama
1947	Chicago Bears	Bob Fenimore	HB	Oklahoma A&M
1946	Boston	Frank Dancewicz	QB	Notre Dame
1945	Chicago Cardinals	Charley Trippi	HB	Georgia
1944	Boston	Angelo Bertelli	QB	Notre Dame
1943	Detroit	Frank Sinkwich	HB	Georgia
1942	Pittsburgh	Bill Dudley	HB	Virginia
1941	Chicago Bears	Tom Harmon	HB	Michigan
1940	Chicago Cardinals	George Cafego	HB	Tennessee
1939	Chicago Cardinals	Ki Aldrich	C	Texas Christian
1938	Cleveland	Corbett Davis	FB	Indiana
1937	Philadelphia	Sam Francis	FB	Nebraska
1936	Philadelphia	Jay Berwanger	HB	Chicago

Note: From 1947 through 1958, the first selection in the draft was a Bonus pick, awarded to the winner of a random draw. That club, in turn, forfeited its last-round draft choice. The winner of the Bonus choice was eliminated from future draws. The system was abolished after 1958, by which time all clubs had received a Bonus choice.

If club had no first-round selection, first player drafted is listed with round in parentheses.

Atlanta Falcons

Year	Player, College, Position
1966	Tommy Nobis, Texas, LB
	Randy Johnson, Texas A&I, QB
1967	Leo Carroll, San Diego State, DE (2)
1968	Claude Humphrey, Tennessee State, DE
1969	George Kunz, Notre Dame, T
1970	John Small, Citadel, LB
1971	Joe Profit, Northeast Louisiana, RB
1972	Clarence Ellis, Notre Dame, DB
1973	Greg Marx, Notre Dame, DT (2)
1974	Gerald Tinker, Kent State, WR (2)
1975	Steve Bartkowski, California, QB
1976	Bubba Bean, Texas A&M, RB
1977	Warren Bryant, Kentucky, T
	Wilson Faumuina, San Jose State, DT
1978	Mike Kenn, Michigan, T
1979	Don Smith, Miami, DE
1980	Junior Miller, Nebraska, TE
1981	Bobby Butler, Florida State, DB
1982	Gerald Riggs, Arizona State, RB
1983	Mike Pitts, Alabama, DE
1984	Rick Bryan, Oklahoma, DT
1985	Bill Fralic, Pittsburgh, T
1986	Tony Casillas, Oklahoma, NT
	Tim Green, Syracuse, LB
1987	Chris Miller, Oregon, QB
1988	Aundray Bruce, Auburn, LB

Buffalo Bills

Year	Player, College, Position
1960	Richie Lucas, Penn State, QB
1961	Ken Rice, Auburn, T
1962	Ernie Davis, Syracuse, RB
1963	Dave Behrman, Michigan State, C
1964	Carl Eller, Minnesota, DE
1965	Jim Davidson, Ohio State, T
1966	Mike Dennis, Mississippi, RB
1967	John Pitts, Arizona State, S
1968	Haven Moses, San Diego State, WR
1969	O.J. Simpson, Southern California, RB
1970	Al Cowlings, Southern California, DE
1971	J. D. Hill, Arizona State, WR
1972	Walt Patulski, Notre Dame, DE
1973	Paul Seymour, Michigan, TE
	Joe DeLamielleure, Michigan State, G
1974	Reuben Gant, Oklahoma State, TE
1975	Tom Ruud, Nebraska, LB
1976	Mario Clark, Oregon, DB
1977	Phil Dokes, Oklahoma State, DT
1978	Terry Miller, Oklahoma State, RB
1979	Tom Cousineau, Ohio State, LB
	Jerry Butler, Clemson, WR
1980	Jim Ritcher, North Carolina State, C
1981	Booker Moore, Penn State, RB
1982	Perry Tuttle, Clemson, WR
1983	Tony Hunter, Notre Dame, TE
	Jim Kelly, Miami, QB
1984	Greg Bell, Notre Dame, RB
1985	Bruce Smith, Virginia Tech, DE
	Derrick Burroughs, Memphis State, DB
1986	Ronnie Harmon, Iowa, RB
	Will Wolford, Vanderbilt, T
1987	Shane Conlan, Penn State, LB
1988	Thurman Thomas, Oklahoma State, RB (2)

Chicago Bears

Year	Player, College, Position
1936	Joe Stydahar, West Virginia, T
1937	Les McDonald, Nebraska, E
1938	Joe Gray, Oregon State, B
1939	Sid Luckman, Columbia, QB
	Bill Osmanski, Holy Cross, B
1940	Clyde (Bulldog) Turner, Hardin-Simmons, C
1941	Tom Harmon, Michigan, B
1942	Frankie Albert, Stanford, B
1943	Bob Steber, Missouri, B
1944	Ray Evans, Kansas, B
1945	Don Lund, Michigan, B
1946	Johnny Lujack, Notre Dame, QB
1947	Bob Fenimore, Oklahoma State, B
	Don Kindt, Wisconsin, B
1948	Bobby Layne, Texas, QB
	Max Bumgardner, Texas, E
1949	Dick Harris, Texas, C
1950	Chuck Hunsinger, Florida, B
	Fred Morrison, Ohio State, B
1951	Bob Williams, Notre Dame, B
	Billy Stone, Bradley, B
	Gene Schroeder, Virginia, E
1952	Jim Dooley, Miami, B
1953	Billy Anderson, Compton (Calif.) J.C., B
1954	Stan Wallace, Illinois, B
1955	Ron Drzewiecki, Marquette, B
1956	Menan (Tex) Schriewer, Texas, E
1957	Earl Leggett, Louisiana State, T
1958	Chuck Howley, West Virginia, G
1959	Don Clark, Ohio State, B
1960	Roger Davis, Syracuse, G
1961	Mike Ditka, Pittsburgh, E
1962	Ronnie Bull, Baylor, RB
1963	Dave Behrman, Michigan State, C
1964	Dick Evey, Tennessee, DT
1965	Dick Butkus, Illinois, LB
	Gale Sayers, Kansas, RB
	Steve DeLong, Tennessee, T
1966	George Rice, Louisiana State, DT
1967	Loyd Phillips, Arkansas, DE
1968	Mike Hull, Southern California, RB
1969	Rufus Mayes, Ohio State, T
1970	George Farmer, UCLA, WR (3)
1971	Joe Moore, Missouri, RB
1972	Lionel Antoine, Southern Illinois, T
	Craig Clemons, Iowa, DB
1973	Wally Chambers, Eastern Kentucky, DE
1974	Waymond Bryant, Tennessee State, LB
	Dave Gallagher, Michigan, DT
1975	Walter Payton, Jackson State, RB
1976	Dennis Lick, Wisconsin, T
1977	Ted Albrecht, California, T
1978	Brad Shearer, Texas, DT (3)
1979	Dan Hampton, Arkansas, DT
	Al Harris, Arizona State, DE
1980	Otis Wilson, Louisville, LB
1981	Keith Van Horne, Southern California, T
1982	Jim McMahon, Brigham Young, QB
1983	Jim Covert, Pittsburgh, T
	Willie Gault, Tennessee, WR
1984	Wilber Marshall, Florida, LB
1985	William Perry, Clemson, DT
1986	Neal Anderson, Florida, RB
1987	Jim Harbaugh, Michigan, QB
1988	Brad Muster, Stanford, RB
	Wendell Davis, Louisiana State, WR

Cincinnati Bengals

Year	Player, College, Position
1968	Bob Johnson, Tennessee, C
1969	Greg Cook, Cincinnati, QB
1970	Mike Reid, Penn State, DT
1971	Vernon Holland, Tennessee State, T
1972	Sherman White, California, DE
1973	Isaac Curtis, San Diego State, WR
1974	Bill Kollar, Montana State, DT
1975	Glenn Cameron, Florida, LB
1976	Billy Brooks, Oklahoma, WR
	Archie Griffin, Ohio State, RB
1977	Eddie Edwards, Miami, DT
	Wilson Whitley, Houston, DT
	Mike Cobb, Michigan State, TE
1978	Ross Browner, Notre Dame, DT
	Blair Bush, Washington, C
1979	Jack Thompson, Washington State, QB
	Charles Alexander, Louisiana State, RB
1980	Anthony Muñoz, Southern California, T
1981	David Verser, Kansas, WR
1982	Glen Collins, Mississippi State, DE
1983	Dave Rimington, Nebraska, C
1984	Ricky Hunley, Arizona, LB
	Pete Koch, Maryland, DE
	Brian Blados, North Carolina, T
1985	Eddie Brown, Miami, WR
	Emanuel King, Alabama, LB
1986	Joe Kelly, Washington, LB
	Tim McGee, Tennessee, WR
1987	Jason Buck, Brigham Young, DE
1988	Rickey Dixon, Oklahoma, DB

Cleveland Browns

Year	Player, College, Position
1950	Ken Carpenter, Oregon State, B
1951	Ken Konz, Louisiana State, B
1952	Bert Rechichar, Tennessee, DB
	Harry Agganis, Boston U., QB
1953	Doug Atkins, Tennessee, DE
1954	Bobby Garrett, Stanford, QB
	John Bauer, Illinois, G
1955	Kurt Burris, Oklahoma, C
1956	Preston Carpenter, Arkansas, B
1957	Jim Brown, Syracuse, RB
1958	Jim Shofner, Texas Christian, DB
1959	Rich Kreitling, Illinois, DE
1960	Jim Houston, Ohio State, DE
1961	Bobby Crespino, Mississippi, TE
1962	Gary Collins, Maryland, WR
	Leroy Jackson, Western Illinois, RB
1963	Tom Hutchinson, Kentucky, WR
1964	Paul Warfield, Ohio State, WR
1965	James Garcia, Purdue, T (2)
1966	Milt Morin, Massachusetts, TE
1967	Bob Matheson, Duke, LB
1968	Marvin Upshaw, Trinity, Tex., DT-DE
1969	Ron Johnson, Michigan, RB
1970	Mike Phipps, Purdue, QB
	Bob McKay, Texas, T
1971	Clarence Scott, Kansas State, CB
1972	Thom Darden, Michigan, DB
1973	Steve Holden, Arizona State, WR
	Pete Adams, Southern California, T
1974	Billy Corbett, Johnson C. Smith, T (2)
1975	Mack Mitchell, Houston, DE
1976	Mike Pruitt, Purdue, RB
1977	Robert Jackson, Texas A&M, LB
1978	Clay Matthews, Southern California, LB
	Ozzie Newsome, Alabama, TE
1979	Willis Adams, Houston, WR
1980	Charles White, Southern California, RB
1981	Hanford Dixon, Southern Mississippi, DB
1982	Chip Banks, Southern California, LB
1983	Ron Brown, Arizona State, WR (2)
1984	Don Rogers, UCLA, DB
1985	Greg Allen, Florida State, RB (2)
1986	Webster Slaughter, San Diego State, WR (2)
1987	Mike Junkin, Duke, LB
1988	Clifford Charlton, Florida, LB

Dallas Cowboys

Year	Player, College, Position
1960	None
1961	Bob Lilly, Texas Christian, DT
1962	Sonny Gibbs, Texas Christian, QB (2)
1963	Lee Roy Jordan, Alabama, LB
1964	Scott Appleton, Texas, DT
1965	Craig Morton, California, QB
1966	John Niland, Iowa, G
1967	Phil Clark, Northwestern, DB (3)
1968	Dennis Homan, Alabama, WR
1969	Calvin Hill, Yale, RB
1970	Duane Thomas, West Texas State, RB
1971	Tody Smith, Southern California, DE
1972	Bill Thomas, Boston College, RB
1973	Billy Joe DuPree, Michigan State, TE
1974	Ed (Too Tall) Jones, Tennessee State, DE
	Charley Young, North Carolina State, RB
1975	Randy White, Maryland, LB
	Thomas Henderson, Langston, LB
1976	Aaron Kyle, Wyoming, DB
1977	Tony Dorsett, Pittsburgh, RB
1978	Larry Bethea, Michigan State, DE
1979	Robert Shaw, Tennessee, C
1980	Bill Roe, Colorado, LB (3)
1981	Howard Richards, Missouri, T
1982	Rod Hill, Kentucky State, DB
1983	Jim Jeffcoat, Arizona State, DE
1984	Billy Cannon, Jr., Texas A&M, LB
1985	Kevin Brooks, Michigan, DE
1986	Mike Sherrard, UCLA, WR
1987	Danny Noonan, Nebraska, DT
1988	Michael Irvin, Miami, WR

Denver Broncos

Year	Player, College, Position
1960	Roger LeClerc, Trinity, Conn., C
1961	Bob Gaiters, New Mexico State, RB
1962	Merlin Olsen, Utah State, DT
1963	Kermit Alexander, UCLA, CB
1964	Bob Brown, Nebraska, T
1965	Dick Butkus, Illinois, LB (2)
1966	Jerry Shay, Purdue, DT
1967	Floyd Little, Syracuse, RB
1968	Curley Culp, Arizona State, DE (2)
1969	Grady Cavness, Texas-El Paso, DB (2)
1970	Bob Anderson, Colorado, RB
1971	Marv Montgomery, Southern California, T
1972	Riley Odoms, Houston, TE
1973	Otis Armstrong, Purdue, RB
1974	Randy Gradishar, Ohio State, LB
1975	Louis Wright, San Jose State, DB
1976	Tom Glassic, Virginia, G
1977	Steve Schindler, Boston College, G
1978	Don Latimer, Miami, DT
1979	Kelvin Clark, Nebraska, T
1980	Rulon Jones, Utah State, DE (2)
1981	Dennis Smith, Southern California, DB
1982	Gerald Willhite, San Jose State, RB
1983	Chris Hinton, Northwestern, G
1984	Andre Townsend, Mississippi, DE (2)
1985	Steve Sewell, Oklahoma, RB
1986	Jim Juriga, Illinois, T (4)
1987	Ricky Nattiel, Florida, WR
1988	Ted Gregory, Syracuse, NT

Detroit Lions

Year	Player, College, Position
1936	Sid Wagner, Michigan State, G
1937	Lloyd Cardwell, Nebraska, B
1938	Alex Wojciechowicz, Fordham, C
1939	John Pingel, Michigan State, B
1940	Doyle Nave, Southern California, B
1941	Jim Thomason, Texas A&M, B
1942	Bob Westfall, Michigan, B
1943	Frank Sinkwich, Georgia, B
1944	Otto Graham, Northwestern, B
1945	Frank Szymanski, Notre Dame, C
1946	Bill Dellastatious, Missouri, B
1947	Glenn Davis, Army, B
1948	Y.A. Tittle, Louisiana State, B
1949	John Rauch, Georgia, B
1950	Leon Hart, Notre Dame, E
	Joe Watson, Rice, C
1951	Dick Stanfel, San Francisco, G (2)
1952	Yale Lary, Texas A&M, B (3)
1953	Harley Sewell, Texas, G
1954	Dick Chapman, Rice, T
1955	Dave Middleton, Auburn, B
1956	Hopalong Cassady, Ohio State, B
1957	Bill Glass, Baylor, G
1958	Alex Karras, Iowa, T
1959	Nick Pietrosante, Notre Dame, B
1960	John Robinson, Louisiana State, S
1961	Danny LaRose, Missouri, T (2)
1962	John Hadl, Kansas, QB
1963	Daryl Sanders, Ohio State, T
1964	Pete Beathard, Southern California, QB
1965	Tom Nowatzke, Indiana, RB
1966	Nick Eddy, Notre Dame, RB (2)
1967	Mel Farr, UCLA, RB
1968	Greg Landry, Massachusetts, QB
	Earl McCullouch, Southern California, WR
1969	Altie Taylor, Utah State, RB (2)
1970	Steve Owens, Oklahoma, RB
1971	Bob Bell, Cincinnati, DT
1972	Herb Orvis, Colorado, DE
1973	Ernie Price, Texas A&I, DE
1974	Ed O'Neil, Penn State, LB
1975	Lynn Boden, South Dakota State, G
1976	James Hunter, Grambling, DB
	Lawrence Gaines, Wyoming, RB
1977	Walt Williams, New Mexico State, DB (2)
1978	Luther Bradley, Notre Dame, DB
1979	Keith Dorney, Penn State, T
1980	Billy Sims, Oklahoma, RB
1981	Mark Nichols, San Jose State, WR
1982	Jimmy Williams, Nebraska, LB
1983	James Jones, Florida, RB
1984	David Lewis, California, TE
1985	Lomas Brown, Florida, T
1986	Chuck Long, Iowa, QB
1987	Reggie Rogers, Washington, DE
1988	Bennie Blades, Miami, DB

Green Bay Packers

Year	Player, College, Position
1936	Russ Letlow, San Francisco, G
1937	Eddie Jankowski, Wisconsin, B
1938	Cecil Isbell, Purdue, B
1939	Larry Buhler, Minnesota, B
1940	Harold Van Every, Minnesota, B
1941	George Paskvan, Wisconsin, B
1942	Urban Odson, Minnesota, T
1943	Dick Wildung, Minnesota, T
1944	Merv Pregulman, Michigan, G
1945	Walt Schlinkman, Texas Tech, B
1946	Johnny (Strike) Strzykalski, Marquette, B
1947	Ernie Case, UCLA, B
1948	Earl (Jug) Girard, Wisconsin, B
1949	Stan Heath, Nevada, B
1950	Clayton Tonnemaker, Minnesota, C
1951	Bob Gain, Kentucky, T
1952	Babe Parilli, Kentucky, QB
1953	Al Carmichael, Southern California, B
1954	Art Hunter, Notre Dame, T
	Veryl Switzer, Kansas State, B
1955	Tom Bettis, Purdue, G
1956	Jack Losch, Miami, B
1957	Paul Hornung, Notre Dame, B
	Ron Kramer, Michigan, E
1958	Dan Currie, Michigan State, C
1959	Randy Duncan, Iowa, B
1960	Tom Moore, Vanderbilt, RB
1961	Herb Adderley, Michigan State, CB
1962	Earl Gros, Louisiana State, RB
1963	Dave Robinson, Penn State, LB
1964	Lloyd Voss, Nebraska, DT
1965	Donny Anderson, Texas Tech, RB
	Lawrence Elkins, Baylor, E
1966	Jim Grabowski, Illinois, RB
	Gale Gillingham, Minnesota, T
1967	Bob Hyland, Boston College, C
	Don Horn, San Diego State, QB
1968	Fred Carr, Texas-El Paso, LB
	Bill Lueck, Arizona, G
1969	Rich Moore, Villanova, DT
1970	Mike McCoy, Notre Dame, DT
	Rich McGeorge, Elon, TE
1971	John Brockington, Ohio State, RB
1972	Willie Buchanon, San Diego State, DB
	Jerry Tagge, Nebraska, QB
1973	Barry Smith, Florida State, WR
1974	Barty Smith, Richmond, RB
1975	Bill Bain, Southern California, G (2)
1976	Mark Koncar, Colorado, T
1977	Mike Butler, Kansas, DE
	Ezra Johnson, Morris Brown, DE
1978	James Lofton, Stanford, WR
	John Anderson, Michigan, LB
1979	Eddie Lee Ivery, Georgia Tech, RB
1980	Bruce Clark, Penn State, DE
	George Cumby, Oklahoma, LB
1981	Rich Campbell, California, QB
1982	Ron Hallstrom, Iowa, G
1983	Tim Lewis, Pittsburgh, DB
1984	Alphonso Carreker, Florida State, DE
1985	Ken Ruettgers, Southern California, T
1986	Kenneth Davis, Texas Christian, RB (2)
1987	Brent Fullwood, Auburn, RB
1988	Sterling Sharpe, South Carolina, WR

Houston Oilers

Year	Player, College, Position
1960	Billy Cannon, Louisiana State, RB
1961	Mike Ditka, Pittsburgh, E
1962	Ray Jacobs, Howard Payne, DT
1963	Danny Brabham, Arkansas, LB
1964	Scott Appleton, Texas, DT
1965	Lawrence Elkins, Baylor, WR
1966	Tommy Nobis, Texas, LB
1967	George Webster, Michigan State, LB
	Tom Regner, Notre Dame, G
1968	Mac Haik, Mississippi, WR (2)
1969	Ron Pritchard, Arizona State, LB
1970	Doug Wilkerson, N. Carolina Central, G
1971	Dan Pastorini, Santa Clara, QB
1972	Greg Sampson, Stanford, DE
1973	John Matuszak, Tampa, DE
	George Amundson, Iowa State, RB
1974	Steve Manstedt, Nebraska, LB (4)
1975	Robert Brazile, Jackson State, LB
	Don Hardeman, Texas A&I, RB
1976	Mike Barber, Louisiana Tech, TE (2)
1977	Morris Towns, Missouri, T
1978	Earl Campbell, Texas, RB
1979	Mike Stensrud, Iowa State, DE (2)
1980	Angelo Fields, Michigan State, T (2)
1981	Michael Holston, Morgan State, WR (3)
1982	Mike Munchak, Penn State, G
1983	Bruce Matthews, Southern California, T
1984	Dean Steinkuhler, Nebraska, T
1985	Ray Childress, Texas A&M, DE
	Richard Johnson, Wisconsin, DB
1986	Jim Everett, Purdue, QB
1987	Alonzo Highsmith, Miami, RB
	Haywood Jeffires, North Carolina St., WR
1988	Lorenzo White, Michigan State, RB

Indianapolis Colts

Year	Player, College, Position
1953	Billy Vessels, Oklahoma, B
1954	Cotton Davidson, Baylor, B
1955	George Shaw, Oregon, B
	Alan Ameche, Wisconsin, FB
1956	Lenny Moore, Penn State, B
1957	Jim Parker, Ohio State, G
1958	Lenny Lyles, Louisville, B
1959	Jackie Burkett, Auburn, C
1960	Ron Mix, Southern California, T
1961	Tom Matte, Ohio State, RB
1962	Wendell Harris, Louisiana State, S
1963	Bob Vogel, Ohio State, T
1964	Marv Woodson, Indiana, CB
1965	Mike Curtis, Duke, LB
1966	Sam Ball, Kentucky, T
1967	Bubba Smith, Michigan State, DT
	Jim Detwiler, Michigan, RB
1968	John Williams, Minnesota, G
1969	Eddie Hinton, Oklahoma, WR
1970	Norman Bulaich, Texas Christian, RB
1971	Don McCauley, North Carolina, RB
	Leonard Dunlap, North Texas State, DB
1972	Tom Drougas, Oregon, T
1973	Bert Jones, Louisiana State, QB
	Joe Ehrmann, DT, Syracuse
1974	John Dutton, Nebraska, DE
	Roger Carr, Louisiana Tech, WR
1975	Ken Huff, North Carolina, G
1976	Ken Novak, Purdue, DT
1977	Randy Burke, Kentucky, WR
1978	Reese McCall, Auburn, TE
1979	Barry Krauss, Alabama, LB
1980	Curtis Dickey, Texas A&M, RB
	Derrick Hatchett, Texas, DB
1981	Randy McMillan, Pittsburgh, RB
	Donnell Thompson, North Carolina, DT
1982	Johnie Cooks, Mississippi State, LB
	Art Schlichter, Ohio State, QB
1983	John Elway, Stanford, QB
1984	Leonard Coleman, Vanderbilt, DB
	Ron Solt, Maryland, G
1985	Duane Bickett, Southern California, LB
1986	Jon Hand, Alabama, DE
1987	Cornelius Bennett, Alabama, LB
1988	Chris Chandler, Washington, QB (3)

Kansas City Chiefs

Year	Player, College, Position
1960	Don Meredith, Southern Methodist, QB
1961	E.J. Holub, Texas Tech, C
1962	Ronnie Bull, Baylor, RB
1963	Buck Buchanan, Grambling, DT
	Ed Budde, Michigan State, G
1964	Pete Beathard, Southern California, QB
1965	Gale Sayers, Kansas, RB
1966	Aaron Brown, Minnesota, DE
1967	Gene Trosch, Miami, DE-DT
1968	Mo Moorman, Texas A&M, G
	George Daney, Texas-El Paso, G
1969	Jim Marsalis, Tennessee State, CB
1970	Sid Smith, Southern California, T
1971	Elmo Wright, Houston, WR
1972	Jeff Kinney, Nebraska, RB
1973	Gary Butler, Rice, TE (2)

1974 Woody Green, Arizona State, RB
1975 Elmore Stephens, Kentucky, TE (2)
1976 Rod Walters, Iowa, G
1977 Gary Green, Baylor, DB
1978 Art Still, Kentucky, DE
1979 Mike Bell, Colorado State, DE
Steve Fuller, Clemson, QB
1980 Brad Budde, Southern California, G
1981 Willie Scott, South Carolina, TE
1982 Anthony Hancock, Tennessee, WR
1983 Todd Blackledge, Penn State, QB
1984 Bill Maas, Pittsburgh, DT
John Alt, Iowa, T
1985 Ethan Horton, North Carolina, RB
1986 Brian Jozwiak, West Virginia, T
1987 Paul Palmer, Temple, RB
1988 Neil Smith, Nebraska, DE

Los Angeles Raiders

Year Player, College, Position

1960 Dale Hackbart, Wisconsin, CB
1961 Joe Rutgens, Illinois, DT
1962 Roman Gabriel, North Carolina State, QB
1963 George Wilson, Alabama, RB (6)
1964 Tony Lorick, Arizona State, RB
1965 Harry Schuh, Memphis State, T
1966 Rodger Bird, Kentucky, S
1967 Gene Upshaw, Texas A&I, G
1968 Eldridge Dickey, Tennessee State, QB
1969 Art Thoms, Syracuse, DT
1970 Raymond Chester, Morgan State, TE
1971 Jack Tatum, Ohio State, S
1972 Mike Siani, Villanova, WR
1973 Ray Guy, Southern Mississippi, K-P
1974 Henry Lawrence, Florida A&M, T
1975 Neal Colzie, Ohio State, DB
1976 Charles Philyaw, Texas Southern, DT (2)
1977 Mike Davis, Colorado, DB (2)
1978 Dave Browning, Washington, DE (2)
1979 Willie Jones, Florida State, DE (2)
1980 Marc Wilson, Brigham Young, QB
1981 Ted Watts, Texas Tech, DB
Curt Marsh, Washington, T
1982 Marcus Allen, Southern California, RB
1983 Don Mosebar, Southern California, T
1984 Sean Jones, Northeastern, DE (2)
1985 Jessie Hester, Florida State, WR
1986 Bob Buczkowski, Pittsburgh, DE
1987 John Clay, Missouri, T
1988 Tim Brown, Notre Dame, WR
Terry McDaniel, Tennessee, DB
Scott Davis, Illinois, DE

Los Angeles Rams

Year Player, College, Position

1937 Johnny Drake, Purdue, B
1938 Corbett Davis, Indiana, B
1939 Parker Hall, Mississippi, B
1940 Ollie Cordill, Rice, B
1941 Rudy Mucha, Washington, C
1942 Jack Wilson, Baylor, B
1943 Mike Holovak, Boston College, B
1944 Tony Butkovich, Illinois, B
1945 Elroy (Crazylegs) Hirsch, Wisconsin, B
1946 Emil Sitko, Notre Dame, B
1947 Herman Wedemeyer, St. Mary's, Calif., B
1948 Tom Keane, West Virginia, B (2)
1949 Bobby Thomason, Virginia Military, B
1950 Ralph Pasquariello, Villanova, B
Stan West, Oklahoma, G
1951 Bud McFadin, Texas, G
1952 Bill Wade, Vanderbilt, QB
Bob Carey, Michigan State, E
1953 Donn Moomaw, UCLA, C
Ed Barker, Washington State, E
1954 Ed Beatty, Cincinnati, C
1955 Larry Morris, Georgia Tech, C
1956 Joe Marconi, West Virginia, B
Charles Horton, Vanderbilt, B
1957 Jon Arnett, Southern California, B
Del Shofner, Baylor, E
1958 Lou Michaels, Kentucky, T
Jim Phillips, Auburn, E
1959 Dick Bass, Pacific, B
Paul Dickson, Baylor, T
1960 Billy Cannon, Louisiana State, RB
1961 Marlin McKeever, Southern California, E-LB
1962 Roman Gabriel, North Carolina State, QB
Merlin Olsen, Utah State, DT
1963 Terry Baker, Oregon State, QB
Rufus Guthrie, Georgia Tech, G
1964 Bill Munson, Utah State, QB
1965 Clancy Williams, Washington State, CB
1966 Tom Mack, Michigan, G
1967 Willie Ellison, Texas Southern, RB (2)
1968 Gary Beban, UCLA, QB (2)
1969 Larry Smith, Florida, RB
Jim Seymour, Notre Dame, WR
Bob Klein, Southern California, TE
1970 Jack Reynolds, Tennessee, LB
1971 Isiah Robertson, Southern, LB
Jack Youngblood, Florida, DE
1972 Jim Bertelsen, Texas, RB (2)
1973 Cullen Bryant, Colorado, DB (2)
1974 John Cappelletti, Penn State, RB
1975 Mike Fanning, Notre Dame, DT
Dennis Harrah, Miami, T
Doug France, Ohio State, T
1976 Kevin McLain, Colorado State, LB
1977 Bob Brudzinski, Ohio State, LB
1978 Elvis Peacock, Oklahoma, RB
1979 George Andrews, Nebraska, LB
Kent Hill, Georgia Tech, T
1980 Johnnie Johnson, Texas, DB
1981 Mel Owens, Michigan, LB
1982 Barry Redden, Richmond, RB
1983 Eric Dickerson, Southern Methodist, RB
1984 Hal Stephens, East Carolina, DE (5)
1985 Jerry Gray, Texas, DB
1986 Mike Schad, Queen's University, Canada, T
1987 Donald Evans, Winston-Salem, DE (2)
1988 Gaston Green, UCLA, RB
Aaron Cox, Arizona State, WR

Miami Dolphins

Year Player, College, Position

1966 Jim Grabowski, Illinois, RB
Rick Norton, Kentucky, QB
1967 Bob Griese, Purdue, QB
1968 Larry Csonka, Syracuse, RB
Doug Crusan, Indiana, T
1969 Bill Stanfill, Georgia, DE
1970 Jim Mandich, Michigan, TE (2)
1971 Otto Stowe, Iowa State, WR (2)
1972 Mike Kadish, Notre Dame, DT
1973 Chuck Bradley, Oregon, C (2)
1974 Donald Reese, Jackson State, DE
1975 Darryl Carlton, Tampa, T
1976 Larry Gordon, Arizona State, LB
Kim Bokamper, San Jose State, LB
1977 A.J. Duhe, Louisiana State, DT
1978 Guy Benjamin, Stanford, QB (2)
1979 Jon Giesler, Michigan, T
1980 Don McNeal, Alabama, DB
1981 David Overstreet, Oklahoma, RB
1982 Roy Foster, Southern California, G
1983 Dan Marino, Pittsburgh, QB
1984 Jackie Shipp, Oklahoma, LB
1985 Lorenzo Hampton, Florida, RB
1986 John Offerdahl, Western Michigan, LB (2)
1987 John Bosa, Boston College, DE
1988 Eric Kumerow, Ohio State, DE

Minnesota Vikings

Year Player, College, Position

1961 Tommy Mason, Tulane, RB
1962 Bill Miller, Miami, WR (3)
1963 Jim Dunaway, Mississippi, T
1964 Carl Eller, Minnesota, DE
1965 Jack Snow, Notre Dame, WR
1966 Jerry Shay, Purdue, DT
1967 Clint Jones, Michigan State, RB
Gene Washington, Michigan State, WR
Alan Page, Notre Dame, DT
1968 Ron Yary, Southern California, T
1969 Ed White, California, G (2)
1970 John Ward, Oklahoma State, DT
1971 Leo Hayden, Ohio State, RB
1972 Jeff Siemon, Stanford, LB
1973 Chuck Foreman, Miami, RB
1974 Fred McNeill, UCLA, LB
Steve Riley, Southern California, T
1975 Mark Mullaney, Colorado State, DE
1976 James White, Oklahoma State, DT
1977 Tommy Kramer, Rice, QB
1978 Randy Holloway, Pittsburgh, DE
1979 Ted Brown, North Carolina State, RB
1980 Doug Martin, Washington, DT
1981 Mardye McDole, Mississippi State, WR (2)
1982 Darrin Nelson, Stanford, RB
1983 Joey Browner, Southern California, DB
1984 Keith Millard, Washington State, DE
1985 Chris Doleman, Pittsburgh, LB
1986 Gerald Robinson, Auburn, DE
1987 D.J. Dozier, Penn State, RB
1988 Randall McDaniel, Arizona State, G

New England Patriots

Year Player, College, Position

1960 Ron Burton, Northwestern, RB
1961 Tommy Mason, Tulane, RB
1962 Gary Collins, Maryland, WR
1963 Art Graham, Boston College, WR
1964 Jack Concannon, Boston College, QB
1965 Jerry Rush, Michigan State, DE
1966 Karl Singer, Purdue, T
1967 John Charles, Purdue, S
1968 Dennis Byrd, North Carolina State, DE
1969 Ron Sellers, Florida State, WR
1970 Phil Olsen, Utah State, DE
1971 Jim Plunkett, Stanford, QB
1972 Tom Reynolds, San Diego State, WR (2)
1973 John Hannah, Alabama, G
Sam Cunningham, Southern California, RB
Darryl Stingley, Purdue, WR
1974 Steve Corbett, Boston College, G (2)
1975 Russ Francis, Oregon, TE
1976 Mike Haynes, Arizona State, DB
Pete Brock, Colorado, C
Tim Fox, Ohio State, DB
1977 Raymond Clayborn, Texas, DB
Stanley Morgan, Tennessee, WR
1978 Bob Cryder, Alabama, G
1979 Rick Sanford, South Carolina, DB
1980 Roland James, Tennessee, DB
Vagas Ferguson, Notre Dame, RB
1981 Brian Holloway, Stanford, T
1982 Kenneth Sims, Texas, DT
Lester Williams, Miami, DT
1983 Tony Eason, Illinois, QB
1984 Irving Fryar, Nebraska, WR
1985 Trevor Matich, Brigham Young, C
1986 Reggie Dupard, Southern Methodist, RB
1987 Bruce Armstrong, Louisville, T
1988 John Stephens, Northwestern St., La., RB

New Orleans Saints

Year Player, College, Position

1967 Les Kelley, Alabama, RB
1968 Kevin Hardy, Notre Dame, DE
1969 John Shinners, Xavier, G
1970 Ken Burrough, Texas Southern, WR
1971 Archie Manning, Mississippi, QB
1972 Royce Smith, Georgia, G
1973 Derland Moore, Oklahoma, DE (2)
1974 Rick Middleton, Ohio State, LB
1975 Larry Burton, Purdue, WR
Kurt Schumacher, Ohio State, T
1976 Chuck Muncie, California, RB
1977 Joe Campbell, Maryland, DE
1978 Wes Chandler, Florida, WR
1979 Russell Erxleben, Texas, P-K
1980 Stan Brock, Colorado, T
1981 George Rogers, South Carolina, RB
1982 Lindsay Scott, Georgia, WR
1983 Steve Korte, Arkansas, G (2)
1984 James Geathers, Wichita State, DE
1985 Alvin Toles, Tennessee, LB
1986 Jim Dombrowski, Virginia, T
1987 Shawn Knight, Brigham Young, DT
1988 Craig Heyward, Pittsburgh, RB

New York Giants

Year Player, College, Position

1936 Art Lewis, Ohio U., T
1937 Ed Widseth, Minnesota, T
1938 George Karamatic, Gonzaga, B
1939 Walt Neilson, Arizona, B
1940 Grenville Lansdell, Southern California, B
1941 George Franck, Minnesota, B

1942 Merle Hapes, Mississippi, B
1943 Steve Filipowicz, Fordham, B
1944 Billy Hillenbrand, Indiana, B
1945 Elmer Barbour, Wake Forest, B
1946 George Connor, Notre Dame, T
1947 Vic Schwall, Northwestern, B
1948 Tony Minisi, Pennsylvania, B
1949 Paul Page, Southern Methodist, B
1950 Travis Tidwell, Auburn, B
1951 Kyle Rote, Southern Methodist, B
Jim Spavital, Oklahoma A&M, B
1952 Frank Gifford, Southern California, B
1953 Bobby Marlow, Alabama, B
1954 Ken Buck, Pacific, C (2)
1955 Joe Heap, Notre Dame, B
1956 Henry Moore, Arkansas, B (2)
1957 Sam DeLuca, South Carolina, T (2)
1958 Phil King, Vanderbilt, B
1959 Lee Grosscup, Utah, B
1960 Lou Cordileone, Clemson, G
1961 Bruce Tarbox, Syracuse, G (2)
1962 Jerry Hillebrand, Colorado, LB
1963 Frank Lasky, Florida, T (2)
1964 Joe Don Looney, Oklahoma, RB
1965 Tucker Frederickson, Auburn, RB
1966 Francis Peay, Missouri, T
1967 Louis Thompson, Alabama, DT (4)
1968 Dick Buzin, Penn State, T (2)
1969 Fred Dryer, San Diego State, DE
1970 Jim Files, Oklahoma, LB
1971 Rocky Thompson, West Texas State, WR
1972 Eldridge Small, Texas A&I, DB
Larry Jacobson, Nebraska, DE
1973 Brad Van Pelt, Michigan State, LB (2)
1974 John Hicks, Ohio State, G
1975 Al Simpson, Colorado State, T (2)
1976 Troy Archer, Colorado, DE
1977 Gary Jeter, Southern California, DT
1978 Gordon King, Stanford, T
1979 Phil Simms, Morehead State, QB
1980 Mark Haynes, Colorado, DB
1981 Lawrence Taylor, North Carolina, LB
1982 Butch Woolfolk, Michigan, RB
1983 Terry Kinard, Clemson, DB
1984 Carl Banks, Michigan State, LB
William Roberts, Ohio State, T
1985 George Adams, Kentucky, RB
1986 Eric Dorsey, Notre Dame, DE
1987 Mark Ingram, Michigan State, WR
1988 Eric Moore, Indiana, T

New York Jets

Year Player, College, Position

1960 George Izo, Notre Dame, QB
1961 Tom Brown, Minnesota, G
1962 Sandy Stephens, Minnesota, QB
1963 Jerry Stovall, Louisiana State, S
1964 Matt Snell, Ohio State, RB
1965 Joe Namath, Alabama, QB
Tom Nowatzke, Indiana, RB
1966 Bill Yearby, Michigan, DT
1967 Paul Seiler, Notre Dame, T
1968 Lee White, Weber State, RB
1969 Dave Foley, Ohio State, T
1970 Steve Tannen, Florida, CB
1971 John Riggins, Kansas, RB
1972 Jerome Barkum, Jackson State, WR
Mike Taylor, Michigan, LB
1973 Burgess Owens, Miami, DB
1974 Carl Barzilauskas, Indiana, DT
1975 Anthony Davis, Southern California, RB (2)
1976 Richard Todd, Alabama, QB
1977 Marvin Powell, Southern California, T
1978 Chris Ward, Ohio State, T
1979 Marty Lyons, Alabama, DE
1980 Johnny (Lam) Jones, Texas, WR
1981 Freeman McNeil, UCLA, RB
1982 Bob Crable, Notre Dame, LB
1983 Ken O'Brien, Cal-Davis, QB
1984 Russell Carter, Southern Methodist, DB
Ron Faurot, Arkansas, DE
1985 Al Toon, Wisconsin, WR
1986 Mike Haight, Iowa, T
1987 Roger Vick, Texas A&M, RB
1988 Dave Cadigan, Southern California, T

Philadelphia Eagles

Year Player, College, Position

1936 Jay Berwanger, Chicago, B
1937 Sam Francis, Nebraska, B
1938 Jim McDonald, Ohio State, B
1939 Davey O'Brien, Texas Christian, B
1940 George McAfee, Duke, B
1941 Art Jones, Richmond, B (2)
1942 Pete Kmetovic, Stanford, B
1943 Joe Muha, Virginia Military, B
1944 Steve Van Buren, Louisiana State, B
1945 John Yonaker, Notre Dame, E
1946 Leo Riggs, Southern California, B
1947 Neill Armstrong, Oklahoma A&M, E
1948 Clyde (Smackover) Scott, Arkansas, B
1949 Chuck Bednarik, Pennsylvania, C
Frank Tripucka, Notre Dame, B
1950 Harry (Bud) Grant, Minnesota, E
1951 Ebert Van Buren, Louisiana State, B
Chet Mutryn, Xavier, B
1952 Johnny Bright, Drake, B
1953 Al Conway, Army, B (2)
1954 Neil Worden, Notre Dame, B
1955 Dick Bielski, Maryland, B
1956 Bob Pellegrini, Maryland, C
1957 Clarence Peaks, Michigan State, B
1958 Walt Kowalczyk, Michigan State, B
1959 J.D. Smith, Rice, T (2)
1960 Ron Burton, Northwestern, RB
1961 Art Baker, Syracuse, RB
1962 Pete Case, Georgia, G (2)
1963 Ed Budde, Michigan State, G
1964 Bob Brown, Nebraska, T
1965 Ray Rissmiller, Georgia, T (2)
1966 Randy Beisler, Indiana, DE
1967 Harry Jones, Arkansas, RB
1968 Tim Rossovich, Southern California, DE
1969 Leroy Keyes, Purdue, RB
1970 Steve Zabel, Oklahoma, TE
1971 Richard Harris, Grambling, DE
1972 John Reaves, Florida, QB
1973 Jerry Sisemore, Texas, T
Charle Young, Southern California, TE
1974 Mitch Sutton, Kansas, DT (3)
1975 Bill Capraun, Miami, T (7)
1976 Mike Smith, Florida, DE (4)
1977 Skip Sharp, Kansas, DB (5)
1978 Reggie Wilkes, Georgia Tech, LB (3)
1979 Jerry Robinson, UCLA, LB
1980 Roynell Young, Alcorn State, DB
1981 Leonard Mitchell, Houston, DE
1982 Mike Quick, North Carolina State, WR
1983 Michael Haddix, Mississippi State, RB
1984 Kenny Jackson, Penn State, WR
1985 Kevin Allen, Indiana, T
1986 Keith Byars, Ohio State, RB
1987 Jerome Brown, Miami, DT
1988 Keith Jackson, Oklahoma, TE

Phoenix Cardinals

Year Player, College, Position

1936 Jim Lawrence, Texas Christian, B
1937 Ray Buivid, Marquette, B
1938 Jack Robbins, Arkansas, B
1939 Charles (Ki) Aldrich, Texas Christian, C
1940 George Cafego, Tennessee, B
1941 John Kimbrough, Texas A&M, B
1942 Steve Lach, Duke, B
1943 Glenn Dobbs, Tulsa, B
1944 Pat Harder, Wisconsin, B
1945 Charley Trippi, Georgia, B
1946 Dub Jones, Louisiana State, B
1947 DeWitt (Tex) Coulter, Army, T
1948 Jim Spavital, Oklahoma A&M, B
1949 Bill Fischer, Notre Dame, G
1950 Jack Jennings, Ohio State, T (2)
1951 Jerry Groom, Notre Dame, C
1952 Ollie Matson, San Francisco, B
1953 Johnny Olszewski, California, B
1954 Lamar McHan, Arkansas, B
1955 Max Boydston, Oklahoma, E
1956 Joe Childress, Auburn, B
1957 Jerry Tubbs, Oklahoma, C
1958 King Hill, Rice, B
John David Crow, Texas A&M, B
1959 Bill Stacy, Mississippi State, B
1960 George Izo, Notre Dame, QB
1961 Ken Rice, Auburn, T
1962 Fate Echols, Northwestern, DT
Irv Goode, Kentucky, C
1963 Jerry Stovall, Louisiana State, S
Don Brumm, Purdue, DE
1964 Ken Kortas, Louisville, DT
1965 Joe Namath, Alabama, QB
1966 Carl McAdams, Oklahoma, LB
1967 Dave Williams, Washington, WR
1968 MacArthur Lane, Utah State, RB
1969 Roger Wehrli, Missouri, DB
1970 Larry Stegent, Texas A&M, RB
1971 Norm Thompson, Utah, CB
1972 Bobby Moore, Oregon, RB-WR
1973 Dave Butz, Purdue, DT
1974 J.V. Cain, Colorado, TE
1975 Tim Gray, Texas A&M, DB
1976 Mike Dawson, Arizona, DT
1977 Steve Pisarkiewicz, Missouri, QB
1978 Steve Little, Arkansas, K
Ken Greene, Washington State, DB
1979 Ottis Anderson, Miami, RB
1980 Curtis Greer, Michigan, DE
1981 E. J. Junior, Alabama, LB
1982 Luis Sharpe, UCLA, T
1983 Leonard Smith, McNeese State, DB
1984 Clyde Duncan, Tennessee, WR
1985 Freddie Joe Nunn, Mississippi, LB
1986 Anthony Bell, Michigan State, LB
1987 Kelly Stouffer, Colorado State, QB
1988 Ken Harvey, California, LB

Pittsburgh Steelers

Year Player, College, Position

1936 Bill Shakespeare, Notre Dame, B
1937 Mike Basrak, Duquesne, C
1938 Byron (Whizzer) White, Colorado, B
1939 Bill Patterson, Baylor, B (3)
1940 Kay Eakin, Arkansas, B
1941 Chet Gladchuk, Boston College, C (2)
1942 Bill Dudley, Virginia, B
1943 Bill Daley, Minnesota, B
1944 Johnny Podesto, St. Mary's, Calif., B
1945 Paul Duhart, Florida, B
1946 Felix (Doc) Blanchard, Army, B
1947 Hub Bechtol, Texas, E
1948 Dan Edwards, Georgia, E
1949 Bobby Gage, Clemson, B
1950 Lynn Chandnois, Michigan State, B
1951 Butch Avinger, Alabama, B
1952 Ed Modzelewski, Maryland, B
1953 Ted Marchibroda, St. Bonaventure, B
1954 Johnny Lattner, Notre Dame, B
1955 Frank Varrichione, Notre Dame, T
1956 Gary Glick, Colorado A&M, B
Art Davis, Mississippi State, B
1957 Len Dawson, Purdue, B
1958 Larry Krutko, West Virginia, B (2)
1959 Tom Barnett, Purdue, B (8)
1960 Jack Spikes, Texas Christian, RB
1961 Myron Pottios, Notre Dame, LB (2)
1962 Bob Ferguson, Ohio State, RB
1963 Frank Atkinson, Stanford, T (8)
1964 Paul Martha, Pittsburgh, S
1965 Roy Jefferson, Utah, WR (2)
1966 Dick Leftridge, West Virginia, RB
1967 Don Shy, San Diego State, RB (2)
1968 Mike Taylor, Southern California, T
1969 Joe Greene, North Texas State, DT
1970 Terry Bradshaw, Louisiana Tech, QB
1971 Frank Lewis, Grambling, WR
1972 Franco Harris, Penn State, RB
1973 J.T. Thomas, Florida State, DB
1974 Lynn Swann, Southern California, WR
1975 Dave Brown, Michigan, DB
1976 Bennie Cunningham, Clemson, TE
1977 Robin Cole, New Mexico, LB
1978 Ron Johnson, Eastern Michigan, DB
1979 Greg Hawthorne, Baylor, RB
1980 Mark Malone, Arizona State, QB
1981 Keith Gary, Oklahoma, DE
1982 Walter Abercrombie, Baylor, RB
1983 Gabriel Rivera, Texas Tech, DT
1984 Louis Lipps, Southern Mississippi, WR
1985 Darryl Sims, Wisconsin, DE
1986 John Rienstra, Temple, G
1987 Rod Woodson, Purdue, DB
1988 Aaron Jones, Eastern Kentucky, DE

San Diego Chargers

Year	Player, College, Position
1960	Monty Stickles, Notre Dame, E
1961	Earl Faison, Indiana, DE
1962	Bob Ferguson, Ohio State, RB
1963	Walt Sweeney, Syracuse, G
1964	Ted Davis, Georgia Tech, LB
1965	Steve DeLong, Tennessee, DE
1966	Don Davis, Cal State-Los Angeles, DT
1967	Ron Billingsley, Wyoming, DE
1968	Russ Washington, Missouri, DT
	Jimmy Hill, Texas A&I, DB
1969	Marty Domres, Columbia, QB
	Bob Babich, Miami, Ohio, LB
1970	Walker Gillette, Richmond, WR
1971	Leon Burns, Long Beach State, RB
1972	Pete Lazetich, Stanford, DE (2)
1973	Johnny Rodgers, Nebraska, WR
1974	Bo Matthews, Colorado, RB
	Don Goode, Kansas, LB
1975	Gary Johnson, Grambling, DT
	Mike Williams, Louisiana State, DB
1976	Joe Washington, Oklahoma, RB
1977	Bob Rush, Memphis State, C
1978	John Jefferson, Arizona State, WR
1979	Kellen Winslow, Missouri, TE
1980	Ed Luther, San Jose State, QB (4)
1981	James Brooks, Auburn, RB
1982	Hollis Hall, Clemson, DB (7)
1983	Billy Ray Smith, Arkansas, LB
	Gary Anderson, Arkansas, WR
	Gill Byrd, San Jose State, DB
1984	Mossy Cade, Texas, DB
1985	Jim Lachey, Ohio State, G
1986	Leslie O'Neal, Oklahoma State, DE
	James FitzPatrick, Southern California, T
1987	Rod Bernstine, Texas A&M, TE
1988	Anthony Miller, Tennessee, WR

San Francisco 49ers

Year	Player, College, Position
1950	Leo Nomellini, Minnesota, T
1951	Y.A. Tittle, Louisiana State, B
1952	Hugh McElhenny, Washington, B
1953	Harry Babcock, Georgia, E
	Tom Stolhandske, Texas, E
1954	Bernie Faloney, Maryland, B
1955	Dickie Moegle, Rice, B
1956	Earl Morrall, Michigan State, B
1957	John Brodie, Stanford, B
1958	Jim Pace, Michigan, B
	Charlie Krueger, Texas A&M, T
1959	Dave Baker, Oklahoma, B
	Dan James, Ohio State, C
1960	Monty Stickles, Notre Dame, E
1961	Jimmy Johnson, UCLA, CB
	Bernie Casey, Bowling Green, WR
	Bill Kilmer, UCLA, QB
1962	Lance Alworth, Arkansas, WR
1963	Kermit Alexander, UCLA, CB
1964	Dave Parks, Texas Tech, WR
1965	Ken Willard, North Carolina, RB
	George Donnelly, Illinois, DB
1966	Stan Hindman, Mississippi, DE
1967	Steve Spurrier, Florida, QB
	Cas Banaszek, Northwestern, T
1968	Forrest Blue, Auburn, C
1969	Ted Kwalick, Penn State, TE
	Gene Washington, Stanford, WR
1970	Cedrick Hardman, North Texas State, DE
	Bruce Taylor, Boston U., DB
1971	Tim Anderson, Ohio State, DB
1972	Terry Beasley, Auburn, WR
1973	Mike Holmes, Texas Southern, DB
1974	Wilbur Jackson, Alabama, RB
	Bill Sandifer, UCLA, DT
1975	Jimmy Webb, Mississippi State, DT
1976	Randy Cross, UCLA, C (2)
1977	Elmo Boyd, Eastern Kentucky, WR (3)
1978	Ken MacAfee, Notre Dame, TE
	Dan Bunz, Cal State-Long Beach, LB
1979	James Owens, UCLA, WR (2)
1980	Earl Cooper, Rice, RB
	Jim Stuckey, Clemson, DT
1981	Ronnie Lott, Southern California, DB
1982	Bubba Paris, Michigan, T (2)
1983	Roger Craig, Nebraska, RB (2)
1984	Todd Shell, Brigham Young, LB
1985	Jerry Rice, Mississippi Valley State, WR
1986	Larry Roberts, Alabama, DE (2)
1987	Harris Barton, North Carolina, T
	Terrence Flagler, Clemson, RB
1988	Danny Stubbs, Miami, DE (2)

Seattle Seahawks

Year	Player, College, Position
1976	Steve Niehaus, Notre Dame, DT
1977	Steve August, Tulsa, G
1978	Keith Simpson, Memphis State, DB
1979	Manu Tuiasosopo, UCLA, DT
1980	Jacob Green, Texas A&M, DE
1981	Ken Easley, UCLA, DB
1982	Jeff Bryant, Clemson, DE
1983	Curt Warner, Penn State, RB
1984	Terry Taylor, Southern Illinois, DB
1985	Owen Gill, Iowa, RB (2)
1986	John L. Williams, Florida, RB
1987	Tony Woods, Pittsburgh, LB
1988	Brian Blades, Miami, WR (2)

Tampa Bay Buccaneers

Year	Player, College, Position
1976	Lee Roy Selmon, Oklahoma, DT
1977	Ricky Bell, Southern California, RB
1978	Doug Williams, Grambling, QB
1979	Greg Roberts, Oklahoma, G (2)
1980	Ray Snell, Wisconsin, G
1981	Hugh Green, Pittsburgh, LB
1982	Sean Farrell, Penn State, G
1983	Randy Grimes, Baylor, C (2)
1984	Keith Browner, Southern California, LB (2)
1985	Ron Holmes, Washington, DE
1986	Bo Jackson, Auburn, RB
	Roderick Jones, Southern Methodist, DB
1987	Vinny Testaverde, Miami, QB
1988	Paul Gruber, Wisconsin, T

Washington Redskins

Year	Player, College, Position
1936	Riley Smith, Alabama, B
1937	Sammy Baugh, Texas Christian, B
1938	Andy Farkas, Detroit, B
1939	I.B. Hale, Texas Christian, T
1940	Ed Boell, New York U., B
1941	Forest Evashevski, Michigan, B
1942	Orban (Spec) Sanders, Texas, B
1943	Jack Jenkins, Missouri, B
1944	Mike Micka, Colgate, B
1945	Jim Hardy, Southern California, B
1946	Cal Rossi, UCLA, B*
1947	Cal Rossi, UCLA, B
1948	Harry Gilmer, Alabama, B
	Lowell Tew, Alabama, B
1949	Rob Goode, Texas A&M, B
1950	George Thomas, Oklahoma, B
1951	Leon Heath, Oklahoma, B
1952	Larry Isbell, Baylor, B
1953	Jack Scarbath, Maryland, B
1954	Steve Meilinger, Kentucky, E
1955	Ralph Guglielmi, Notre Dame, B
1956	Ed Vereb, Maryland, B
1957	Don Bosseler, Miami, B
1958	Mike Sommer, George Washington, B (2)
1959	Don Allard, Boston College, B
1960	Richie Lucas, Penn State, QB
1961	Norman Snead, Wake Forest, QB
	Joe Rutgens, Illinois, DT
1962	Ernie Davis, Syracuse, RB
1963	Pat Richter, Wisconsin, TE
1964	Charley Taylor, Arizona State, RB-WR
1965	Bob Breitenstein, Tulsa, T (2)
1966	Charlie Gogolak, Princeton, K
1967	Ray McDonald, Idaho, RB
1968	Jim Smith, Oregon, DB
1969	Eugene Epps, Texas-El Paso, DB (2)
1970	Bill Brundige, Colorado, DT (2)
1971	Cotton Speyrer, Texas, WR (2)
1972	Moses Denson, Maryland State, RB (8)
1973	Charles Cantrell, Lamar, G (5)
1974	Jon Keyworth, Colorado, TE (6)
1975	Mike Thomas, Nevada-Las Vegas, RB (6)
1976	Mike Hughes, Baylor, G (5)
1977	Duncan McColl, Stanford, DE (4)
1978	Tony Green, Florida, RB (6)
1979	Don Warren, San Diego State, TE (4)
1980	Art Monk, Syracuse, WR
1981	Mark May, Pittsburgh, T
1982	Vernon Dean, San Diego State, DB (2)
1983	Darrell Green, Texas A&I, DB
1984	Bob Slater, Oklahoma, DT (2)
1985	Tory Nixon, San Diego State, DB (2)
1986	Markus Koch, Boise State, DE (2)
1987	Brian Davis, Nebraska, DB (2)
1988	Chip Lohmiller, Minnesota, K (2)

**Choice lost due to ineligibility.*

RECORDS

All-Time Records 304
Outstanding Performers 324
Yearly Statistical Leaders 329
Super Bowl Records 335
Postseason Game Records 342
AFC-NFC Pro Bowl Game Records 351

ALL-TIME RECORDS

Compiled by Elias Sports Bureau

The following records reflect all available official information on the National Football League from its formation in 1920 to date. Also included are all applicable records from the American Football League, 1960-69.

Individual Records

Service

Most Seasons

26 George Blanda, Chi. Bears, 1949, 1950-58; Baltimore, 1950; Houston, 1960-66; Oakland, 1967-75
21 Earl Morrall, San Francisco, 1956; Pittsburgh, 1957-58; Detroit, 1958-64; N.Y. Giants, 1965-67; Baltimore, 1968-71; Miami, 1972-76
20 Jim Marshall, Cleveland, 1960; Minnesota, 1961-79

Most Seasons, One Club

19 Jim Marshall, Minnesota, 1961-79
18 Jim Hart, St. Louis, 1966-83
Jeff Van Note, Atlanta, 1969-86
17 Lou Groza, Cleveland, 1950-59, 1961-67
Johnny Unitas, Baltimore, 1956-72
John Brodie, San Francisco, 1957-73
Jim Bakken, St. Louis, 1962-78
Mick Tingelhoff, Minnesota, 1962-78

Most Games Played, Career

340 George Blanda, Chi. Bears, 1949, 1950-58; Baltimore, 1950; Houston, 1960-66; Oakland, 1967-75
282 Jim Marshall, Cleveland, 1960; Minnesota, 1961-79
263 Jan Stenerud, Kansas City, 1967-79; Green Bay, 1980-83; Minnesota, 1984-85

Most Consecutive Games Played, Career

282 Jim Marshall, Cleveland, 1960; Minnesota, 1961-79
240 Mick Tingelhoff, Minnesota, 1962-78
234 Jim Bakken, St. Louis, 1962-78

Most Seasons, Coach

40 George Halas, Chi. Bears, 1920-29, 1933-42, 1946-55, 1958-67
33 Earl (Curly) Lambeau, Green Bay, 1921-49; Chi. Cardinals, 1950-51; Washington, 1952-53
28 Tom Landry, Dallas, 1960-87 (current)

Scoring

Most Seasons Leading League

5 Don Hutson, Green Bay, 1940-44
Gino Cappelletti, Boston, 1961, 1963-66
3 Earl (Dutch) Clark, Portsmouth, 1932; Detroit, 1935-36
Pat Harder, Chi. Cardinals, 1947-49
Paul Hornung, Green Bay, 1959-61
2 Jack Manders, Chi. Bears, 1934, 1937
Gordy Soltau, San Francisco, 1952-53
Doak Walker, Detroit, 1950, 1955
Gene Mingo, Denver, 1960, 1962
Jim Turner, N.Y. Jets, 1968-69
Fred Cox, Minnesota, 1969-70
Chester Marcol, Green Bay, 1972, 1974
John Smith, New England, 1979-80

Most Consecutive Seasons Leading League

5 Don Hutson, Green Bay, 1940-44
4 Gino Cappelletti, Boston, 1963-66
3 Pat Harder, Chi. Cardinals, 1947-49
Paul Hornung, Green Bay, 1959-61

Points

Most Points, Career

2,002 George Blanda, Chi. Bears, 1949, 1950-58; Baltimore, 1950; Houston, 1960-66; Oakland, 1967-75 (9-td, 943-pat, 335-fg)
1,699 Jan Stenerud, Kansas City, 1967-79; Green Bay, 1980-83; Minnesota, 1984-85 (580-pat, 373-fg)
1,439 Jim Turner, N.Y. Jets, 1964-70; Denver, 1971-79 (1-td, 521-pat, 304-fg)

Most Points, Season

176 Paul Hornung, Green Bay, 1960 (15-td, 41-pat, 15-fg)
161 Mark Moseley, Washington, 1983 (62-pat, 33-fg)
155 Gino Cappelletti, Boston, 1964 (7-td, 38-pat, 25-fg)

Most Points, No Touchdowns, Season

161 Mark Moseley, Washington, 1983 (62-pat, 33-fg)
145 Jim Turner, N.Y. Jets, 1968 (43-pat, 34-fg)
144 Kevin Butler, Chicago, 1985 (51-pat, 31-fg)

Most Seasons, 100 or More Points

7 Jan Stenerud, Kansas City, 1967-71; Green Bay, 1981, 1983
6 Gino Cappelletti, Boston, 1961-66
George Blanda, Houston, 1960-61; Oakland, 1967-69, 1973
Bruce Gossett, Los Angeles, 1966-67, 1969; San Francisco, 1970-71, 1973
5 Lou Michaels, Pittsburgh, 1962; Baltimore, 1964-65, 1967-68
Tony Franklin, Philadelphia, 1979, 1981; New England, 1984-86
Nick Lowery, Kansas City, 1981, 1983-86

Most Points, Rookie, Season

144 Kevin Butler, Chicago, 1985 (51-pat, 31-fg)
132 Gale Sayers, Chicago, 1965 (22-td)
128 Doak Walker, Detroit, 1950 (11-td, 38-pat, 8-fg)
Cookie Gilchrist, Buffalo, 1962 (15-td, 14-pat, 8-fg)
Chester Marcol, Green Bay, 1972 (29-pat, 33-fg)

Most Points, Game

40 Ernie Nevers, Chi. Cardinals vs. Chi. Bears, Nov. 28, 1929 (6-td, 4-pat)
36 Dub Jones, Cleveland vs. Chi. Bears, Nov. 25, 1951 (6-td)
Gale Sayers, Chicago vs. San Francisco, Dec. 12, 1965 (6-td)
33 Paul Hornung, Green Bay vs. Baltimore, Oct. 8, 1961 (4-td, 6-pat, 1-fg)

Most Consecutive Games Scoring

151 Fred Cox, Minnesota, 1963-73
133 Garo Yepremian, Miami, 1970-78; New Orleans, 1979
128 Rafael Septien, Los Angeles, 1977; Dallas, 1978-85

Touchdowns

Most Seasons Leading League

8 Don Hutson, Green Bay, 1935-38, 1941-44
3 Jim Brown, Cleveland, 1958-59, 1963
Lance Alworth, San Diego, 1964-66
2 By many players

Most Consecutive Seasons Leading League

4 Don Hutson, Green Bay, 1935-38, 1941-44
3 Lance Alworth, San Diego, 1964-66
2 By many players

Most Touchdowns, Career

126 Jim Brown, Cleveland, 1957-65 (106-r, 20-p)
125 Walter Payton, Chicago, 1975-87 (110-r, 15-p)
116 John Riggins, N.Y. Jets, 1971-75; Washington, 1976-79, 1981-85 (104-r, 12-p)

Most Touchdowns, Season

24 John Riggins, Washington, 1983 (24-r)
23 O.J. Simpson, Buffalo, 1975 (16-r, 7-p)
Jerry Rice, San Francisco, 1987 (1-r, 22-p)
22 Gale Sayers, Chicago, 1965 (14-r, 6-p, 2-ret)
Chuck Foreman, Minnesota, 1975 (13-r, 9-p)

Most Touchdowns, Rookie, Season

22 Gale Sayers, Chicago, 1965 (14-r, 6-p, 2-ret)
20 Eric Dickerson, L.A. Rams, 1983 (18-r, 2-p)
16 Billy Sims, Detroit, 1980 (13-r, 3-p)

Most Touchdowns, Game

6 Ernie Nevers, Chi. Cardinals vs. Chi. Bears, Nov. 28, 1929 (6-r)
Dub Jones, Cleveland vs. Chi. Bears, Nov. 25, 1951 (4-r, 2-p)
Gale Sayers, Chicago vs. San Francisco, Dec. 12, 1965 (4-r, 1-p, 1-ret)
5 Bob Shaw, Chi. Cardinals vs. Baltimore, Oct. 2, 1950 (5-p)
Jim Brown, Cleveland vs. Baltimore, Nov. 1, 1959 (5-r)
Abner Haynes, Dall. Texans vs. Oakland, Nov. 26, 1961 (4-r, 1-p)
Billy Cannon, Houston vs. N.Y. Titans, Dec. 10, 1961 (3-r, 2-p)
Cookie Gilchrist, Buffalo vs. N.Y. Jets, Dec. 8, 1963 (5-r)
Paul Hornung, Green Bay vs. Baltimore, Dec. 12, 1965 (3-r, 2-p)
Kellen Winslow, San Diego vs. Oakland, Nov. 22, 1981 (5-p)
4 By many players

Most Consecutive Games Scoring Touchdowns

18 Lenny Moore, Baltimore, 1963-65
14 O.J. Simpson, Buffalo, 1975
13 John Riggins, Washington, 1982-83
Jerry Rice, San Francisco, 1986-87 (current)

Points After Touchdown

Most Seasons Leading League

8 George Blanda, Chi. Bears, 1956; Houston, 1961-62; Oakland, 1967-69, 1972, 1974
4 Bob Waterfield, Cleveland, 1945; Los Angeles, 1946, 1950, 1952
3 Earl (Dutch) Clark, Portsmouth, 1932; Detroit, 1935-36
Jack Manders, Chi. Bears, 1933-35
Don Hutson, Green Bay, 1941-42, 1945

Most Points After Touchdown Attempted, Career

959 George Blanda, Chi. Bears, 1949, 1950-58; Baltimore, 1950; Houston, 1960-66; Oakland, 1967-75
657 Lou Groza, Cleveland, 1950-59, 1961-67
601 Jan Stenerud, Kansas City, 1967-79; Green Bay, 1980-83; Minnesota, 1984-85

Most Points After Touchdown Attempted, Season

70 Uwe von Schamann, Miami, 1984
65 George Blanda, Houston, 1961
63 Mark Moseley, Washington, 1983

Most Points After Touchdown Attempted, Game

10 Charlie Gogolak, Washington vs. N.Y. Giants, Nov. 27, 1966
9 Pat Harder, Chi. Cardinals vs. N.Y. Giants, Oct. 17, 1948; vs. N.Y. Bulldogs, Nov. 13, 1949
Bob Waterfield, Los Angeles vs. Baltimore, Oct. 22, 1950
Bob Thomas, Chicago vs. Green Bay, Dec. 7, 1980
8 By many players

Most Points After Touchdown, Career

943 George Blanda, Chi. Bears, 1949, 1950-58; Baltimore, 1950; Houston, 1960-66; Oakland, 1967-75
641 Lou Groza, Cleveland, 1950-59, 1961-67
580 Jan Stenerud, Kansas City, 1967-79; Green Bay, 1980-83; Minnesota, 1984-85

Most Points After Touchdown, Season

66 Uwe von Schamann, Miami, 1984
64 George Blanda, Houston, 1961
62 Mark Moseley, Washington, 1983

Most Points After Touchdown, Game

9 Pat Harder, Chi. Cardinals vs. N.Y. Giants, Oct. 17, 1948
Bob Waterfield, Los Angeles vs. Baltimore, Oct. 22, 1950
Charlie Gogolak, Washington vs. N.Y. Giants, Nov. 27, 1966
8 By many players

Most Consecutive Points After Touchdown

234 Tommy Davis, San Francisco, 1959-65
221 Jim Turner, N.Y. Jets, 1967-70; Denver, 1971-74
201 George Blanda, Oakland, 1967-71

Highest Points After Touchdown Percentage, Career (200 points after touchdown)

99.43 Tommy Davis, San Francisco, 1959-69 (350-348)
99.29 Nick Lowery, New England, 1978; Kansas City, 1980-87 (283-281)
98.33 George Blanda, Chi. Bears, 1949, 1950-58; Baltimore, 1950; Houston, 1960-66; Oakland, 1967-75 (959-943)

Most Points After Touchdown, No Misses, Season

56 Danny Villanueva, Dallas, 1966
Ray Wersching, San Francisco, 1984
54 Mike Clark, Dallas, 1968
George Blanda, Oakland, 1968
53 Pat Harder, Chi. Cardinals, 1948

Most Points After Touchdown, No Misses, Game
9 Pat Harder, Chi. Cardinals vs. N.Y. Giants, Oct. 17, 1948
Bob Waterfield, Los Angeles vs. Baltimore, Oct. 22, 1950
8 By many players

Field Goals

Most Seasons Leading League
5 Lou Groza, Cleveland, 1950, 1952-54, 1957
4 Jack Manders, Chi. Bears, 1933-34, 1936-37
Ward Cuff, N.Y. Giants, 1938-39, 1943; Green Bay, 1947
Mark Moseley, Washington, 1976-77, 1979, 1982
3 Bob Waterfield, Los Angeles, 1947, 1949, 1951
Gino Cappelletti, Boston, 1961, 1963-64
Fred Cox, Minnesota, 1965, 1969-70
Jan Stenerud, Kansas City, 1967, 1970, 1975

Most Consecutive Seasons Leading League
3 Lou Groza, Cleveland, 1952-54
2 By many players

Most Field Goals Attempted, Career
638 George Blanda, Chi. Bears, 1949, 1950-58; Baltimore, 1950; Houston, 1960-66; Oakland, 1967-75
558 Jan Stenerud, Kansas City, 1967-79; Green Bay, 1980-83; Minnesota, 1984-85
488 Jim Turner, N.Y. Jets, 1964-70; Denver, 1971-79

Most Field Goals Attempted, Season
49 Bruce Gossett, Los Angeles, 1966
Curt Knight, Washington, 1971
48 Chester Marcol, Green Bay, 1972
47 Jim Turner, N.Y. Jets, 1969
David Ray, Los Angeles, 1973
Mark Moseley, Washington, 1983

Most Field Goals Attempted, Game
9 Jim Bakken, St. Louis vs. Pittsburgh, Sept. 24, 1967
8 Lou Michaels, Pittsburgh vs. St. Louis, Dec. 2, 1962
Garo Yepremian, Detroit vs. Minnesota, Nov. 13, 1966
Jim Turner, N.Y. Jets vs. Buffalo, Nov. 3, 1968
7 By many players

Most Field Goals, Career
373 Jan Stenerud, Kansas City, 1967-79; Green Bay, 1980-83; Minnesota, 1984-85
335 George Blanda, Chi. Bears, 1949, 1950-58; Baltimore, 1950; Houston, 1960-66; Oakland, 1967-75
304 Jim Turner, N.Y. Jets, 1964-70; Denver, 1971-79

Most Field Goals, Season
35 Ali Haji-Sheikh, N.Y. Giants, 1983
34 Jim Turner, N.Y. Jets, 1968
33 Chester Marcol, Green Bay, 1972
Mark Moseley, Washington, 1983
Gary Anderson, Pittsburgh, 1985

Most Field Goals, Rookie, Season
35 Ali Haji-Sheikh, N.Y. Giants, 1983
33 Chester Marcol, Green Bay, 1972
31 Kevin Butler, Chicago, 1985

Most Field Goals, Game
7 Jim Bakken, St. Louis vs. Pittsburgh, Sept. 24, 1967
6 Gino Cappelletti, Boston vs. Denver, Oct. 4, 1964
Garo Yepremian, Detroit vs. Minnesota, Nov. 13, 1966
Jim Turner, N.Y. Jets vs. Buffalo, Nov. 3, 1968
Tom Dempsey, Philadelphia vs. Houston, Nov. 12, 1972
Bobby Howfield, N.Y. Jets vs. New Orleans, Dec. 3, 1972
Jim Bakken, St. Louis vs. Atlanta, Dec. 9, 1973
Joe Danelo, N.Y. Giants vs. Seattle, Oct. 18, 1981
Ray Wersching, San Francisco vs. New Orleans, Oct. 16, 1983
5 By many players

Most Field Goals, One Quarter
4 Garo Yepremian, Detroit vs. Minnesota, Nov. 13, 1966 (second quarter)
Curt Knight, Washington vs. N.Y. Giants, Nov. 15, 1970 (second quarter)
Roger Ruzek, Dallas vs. N.Y. Giants, Nov. 2, 1987 (fourth quarter)
3 By many players

Most Consecutive Games Scoring Field Goals
31 Fred Cox, Minnesota, 1968-70
28 Jim Turner, N.Y. Jets, 1970; Denver, 1971-72
21 Bruce Gossett, San Francisco, 1970-72
Ray Wersching, San Francisco, 1986-87

Most Consecutive Field Goals
23 Mark Moseley, Washington, 1981-82
22 Pat Leahy, N.Y. Jets, 1985-86
20 Garo Yepremian, Miami, 1978; New Orleans, 1979
Morten Andersen, New Orleans, 1985-86

Longest Field Goal
63 Tom Dempsey, New Orleans vs. Detroit, Nov. 8, 1970
60 Steve Cox, Cleveland vs. Cincinnati, Oct. 21, 1984
59 Tony Franklin, Philadelphia vs. Dallas, Nov. 12, 1979

Highest Field Goal Percentage, Career (100 field goals)
79.62 Morten Andersen, New Orleans, 1982-87 (157-125)
77.84 Gary Anderson, Pittsburgh, 1982-87 (176-137)
76.99 Nick Lowery, New England, 1978; Kansas City, 1980-87 (226-174)

Highest Field Goal Percentage, Season (Qualifiers)
95.24 Mark Moseley, Washington, 1982 (21-20)
91.67 Jan Stenerud, Green Bay, 1981 (24-22)
88.89 Nick Lowery, Kansas City, 1985 (27-24)
Dean Biasucci, Indianapolis, 1987 (27-24)

Most Field Goals, No Misses, Game
6 Gino Cappelletti, Boston vs. Denver, Oct. 4, 1964
Joe Danelo, N.Y. Giants vs. Seattle, Oct. 18, 1981
Ray Wersching, San Francisco vs. New Orleans, Oct. 16, 1983
5 Roger LeClerc, Chicago vs. Detroit, Dec. 3, 1961
Lou Michaels, Baltimore vs. San Francisco, Sept. 25, 1966
Mac Percival, Chicago vs. Philadelphia, Oct. 20, 1968
Roy Gerela, Houston vs. Miami, Sept. 28, 1969
Jan Stenerud, Kansas City vs. Buffalo, Nov. 2, 1969; vs. Buffalo, Dec. 7, 1969; Minnesota vs. Detroit, Sept. 23, 1984
Horst Muhlmann, Cincinnati vs. Buffalo, Nov. 8, 1970; vs. Pittsburgh, Sept. 24, 1972
Bruce Gossett, San Francisco vs. Denver, Sept. 23, 1973
Nick Mike-Mayer, Atlanta vs. Los Angeles, Nov. 4, 1973
Curt Knight, Washington vs. Baltimore, Nov. 18, 1973
Tim Mazzetti, Atlanta vs. Los Angeles, Oct. 30, 1978
Ed Murray, Detroit vs. Green Bay, Sept. 14, 1980
Rich Karlis, Denver vs. Seattle, Nov. 20, 1983
Pat Leahy, N.Y. Jets vs. Cincinnati, Sept. 16, 1984
Nick Lowery, Kansas City vs. L.A. Raiders, Sept. 12, 1985
Eric Schubert, N.Y. Giants vs. Tampa Bay, Nov. 3, 1985
Gary Anderson, Pittsburgh vs. Kansas City, Nov. 10, 1985
Morten Andersen, New Orleans vs. L.A. Rams, Dec. 1, 1985
Roger Ruzek, Dallas vs. L.A. Rams, Dec. 21, 1987

Most Field Goals, 50 or More Yards, Career
17 Jan Stenerud, Kansas City, 1967-79; Green Bay, 1980-83; Minnesota, 1984-85
14 Nick Lowery, New England, 1978; Kansas City, 1980-87
13 Ed Murray, Detroit, 1980-87

Most Field Goals, 50 or More Yards, Season
5 Fred Steinfort, Denver, 1980
Norm Johnson, Seattle, 1986
4 Horst Muhlmann, Cincinnati, 1970
Mark Moseley, Washington, 1977
Nick Lowery, Kansas City, 1980
Raul Allegre, Baltimore, 1983
3 By many players

Most Field Goals, 50 or More Yards, Game
2 Jim Martin, Detroit vs. Baltimore, Oct. 23, 1960
Tom Dempsey, New Orleans vs. Los Angeles, Dec. 6, 1970
Chris Bahr, Cincinnati vs. Houston, Sept. 23, 1979
Nick Lowery, Kansas City vs. Seattle, Sept. 14, 1980; vs. New Orleans, Sept. 8, 1985; vs. Detroit, Nov. 26, 1987
Mark Moseley, Washington vs. New Orleans, Oct. 26, 1980
Fred Steinfort, Denver vs. Seattle, Dec. 21, 1980
Mick Luckhurst, Atlanta vs. Denver, Dec. 5, 1982; vs. L.A. Rams, Oct. 7, 1984
Morten Andersen, New Orleans vs. Philadelphia, Dec. 11, 1983
Paul McFadden, Philadelphia vs. Detroit, Nov. 4, 1984
Pat Leahy, N.Y. Jets vs. New England, Oct. 20, 1985
Tony Zendejas, Houston vs. San Diego, Nov. 24, 1985
Norm Johnson, Seattle vs. L.A. Raiders, Dec. 8, 1986
Raul Allegre, N.Y. Giants vs. Philadelphia, Nov. 15, 1987

Safeties

Most Safeties, Career
4 Ted Hendricks, Baltimore, 1969-73; Green Bay, 1974; Oakland, 1975-81; L.A. Raiders, 1982-83
Doug English, Detroit, 1975-79, 1981-85
3 Bill McPeak, Pittsburgh, 1949-57
Charlie Krueger, San Francisco, 1959-73
Ernie Stautner, Pittsburgh, 1950-63
Jim Katcavage, N.Y. Giants, 1956-68
Roger Brown, Detroit, 1960-66; Los Angeles, 1967-69
Bruce Maher, Detroit, 1960-67; N.Y. Giants, 1968-69
Ron McDole, St. Louis, 1961; Houston, 1962; Buffalo, 1963-70; Washington, 1971-78
Alan Page, Minnesota, 1967-78; Chicago, 1979-81
Rulon Jones, Denver, 1980-87
2 By many players

Most Safeties, Season
2 Tom Nash, Green Bay, 1932
Roger Brown, Detroit, 1962
Ron McDole, Buffalo, 1964
Alan Page, Minnesota, 1971
Fred Dryer, Los Angeles, 1973
Benny Barnes, Dallas, 1973
James Young, Houston, 1977
Tom Hannon, Minnesota, 1981
Doug English, Detroit, 1983
Don Blackmon, New England, 1985

Most Safeties, Game
2 Fred Dryer, Los Angeles vs. Green Bay, Oct. 21, 1973

Rushing

Most Seasons Leading League
8 Jim Brown, Cleveland, 1957-61, 1963-65
4 Steve Van Buren, Philadelphia, 1945, 1947-49
O.J. Simpson, Buffalo, 1972-73, 1975-76
3 Earl Campbell, Houston, 1978-80
Eric Dickerson, L.A. Rams, 1983-84, 1986

Most Consecutive Seasons Leading League
5 Jim Brown, Cleveland, 1957-61
3 Steve Van Buren, Philadelphia, 1947-49
Jim Brown, Cleveland, 1963-65
Earl Campbell, Houston, 1978-80
2 Bill Paschal, N.Y. Giants, 1943-44
Joe Perry, San Francisco, 1953-54
Jim Nance, Boston, 1966-67
Leroy Kelly, Cleveland, 1967-68
O.J. Simpson, Buffalo, 1972-73; 1975-76
Eric Dickerson, L.A. Rams, 1983-84

Attempts

Most Seasons Leading League
6 Jim Brown, Cleveland, 1958-59, 1961, 1963-65
4 Steve Van Buren, Philadelphia, 1947-50
Walter Payton, Chicago, 1976-79
3 Cookie Gilchrist, Buffalo, 1963-64; Denver, 1965
Jim Nance, Boston, 1966-67, 1969
O. J. Simpson, Buffalo, 1973-75

Most Consecutive Seasons Leading League
4 Steve Van Buren, Philadelphia, 1947-50
Walter Payton, Chicago, 1976-79
3 Jim Brown, Cleveland, 1963-65
Cookie Gilchrist, Buffalo, 1963-64; Denver, 1965
O.J. Simpson, Buffalo, 1973-75
2 By many players

Most Attempts, Career
3,838 Walter Payton, Chicago, 1975-87
2,949 Franco Harris, Pittsburgh, 1972-83; Seattle, 1984
2,916 John Riggins, N.Y. Jets, 1971-75; Washington, 1976-79, 1981-85
Most Attempts, Season
407 James Wilder, Tampa Bay, 1984
404 Eric Dickerson, L.A. Rams, 1986
397 Gerald Riggs, Atlanta, 1985
Most Attempts, Rookie, Season
390 Eric Dickerson, L.A. Rams, 1983
378 George Rogers, New Orleans, 1981
335 Curt Warner, Seattle, 1983
Most Attempts, Game
43 Butch Woolfolk, N.Y. Giants vs. Philadelphia, Nov. 20, 1983
James Wilder, Tampa Bay vs. Green Bay, Sept. 30, 1984 (OT)
42 James Wilder, Tampa Bay vs. Pittsburgh, Oct. 30, 1983
41 Franco Harris, Pittsburgh vs. Cincinnati, Oct. 17, 1976
Gerald Riggs, Atlanta vs. L.A. Rams, Nov. 17, 1985

Yards Gained
Most Yards Gained, Career
16,726 Walter Payton, Chicago, 1975-87
12,312 Jim Brown, Cleveland, 1957-65
12,120 Franco Harris, Pittsburgh, 1972-83; Seattle, 1984
Most Seasons, 1,000 or More Yards Rushing
10 Walter Payton, Chicago, 1976-81, 1983-86
8 Franco Harris, Pittsburgh, 1972, 1974-79, 1983
Tony Dorsett, Dallas, 1977-81, 1983-85
7 Jim Brown, Cleveland, 1958-61, 1963-65
Most Consecutive Seasons, 1,000 or More Yards Rushing
6 Franco Harris, Pittsburgh, 1974-79
Walter Payton, Chicago, 1976-81
5 Jim Taylor, Green Bay, 1960-64
O.J. Simpson, Buffalo, 1972-76
Tony Dorsett, Dallas, 1977-81
Eric Dickerson, L.A. Rams, 1983-86; L.A. Rams-Indianapolis, 1987
4 Jim Brown, Cleveland, 1958-61
Earl Campbell, Houston, 1978-81
Walter Payton, Chicago, 1983-86
Most Yards Gained, Season
2,105 Eric Dickerson, L.A. Rams, 1984
2,003 O.J. Simpson, Buffalo, 1973
1,934 Earl Campbell, Houston, 1980
Most Yards Gained, Rookie, Season
1,808 Eric Dickerson, L.A. Rams, 1983
1,674 George Rogers, New Orleans, 1981
1,605 Ottis Anderson, St. Louis, 1979
Most Yards Gained, Game
275 Walter Payton, Chicago vs. Minnesota, Nov. 20, 1977
273 O.J. Simpson, Buffalo vs. Detroit, Nov. 25, 1976
250 O.J. Simpson, Buffalo vs. New England, Sept. 16, 1973
Most Games, 200 or More Yards Rushing, Career
6 O.J. Simpson, Buffalo, 1969-77; San Francisco, 1978-79
4 Jim Brown, Cleveland, 1957-65
Earl Campbell, Houston, 1978-84; New Orleans, 1984-85
3 Eric Dickerson, L.A. Rams, 1983-87; Indianapolis, 1987
Most Games, 200 or More Yards Rushing, Season
4 Earl Campbell, Houston, 1980
3 O.J. Simpson, Buffalo, 1973
2 Jim Brown, Cleveland, 1963
O.J. Simpson, Buffalo, 1976
Walter Payton, Chicago, 1977
Eric Dickerson, L.A. Rams, 1984
Most Consecutive Games, 200 or More Yards Rushing
2 O.J. Simpson, Buffalo, 1973, 1976
Earl Campbell, Houston, 1980
Most Games, 100 or More Yards Rushing, Career
77 Walter Payton, Chicago, 1975-87
58 Jim Brown, Cleveland, 1957-65
47 Franco Harris, Pittsburgh, 1972-83; Seattle, 1984
Most Games, 100 or More Yards Rushing, Season
12 Eric Dickerson, L.A. Rams, 1984
11 O.J. Simpson, Buffalo, 1973
Earl Campbell, Houston, 1979
Marcus Allen, L.A. Raiders, 1985
Eric Dickerson, L.A. Rams, 1986
10 Walter Payton, Chicago, 1977, 1985
Earl Campbell, Houston, 1980
Most Consecutive Games, 100 or More Yards Rushing
11 Marcus Allen, L.A. Raiders, 1985-86
9 Walter Payton, Chicago, 1985
7 O.J. Simpson, Buffalo, 1972-73
Earl Campbell, Houston, 1979
Longest Run From Scrimmage
99 Tony Dorsett, Dallas vs. Minnesota, Jan. 3, 1983 (TD)
97 Andy Uram, Green Bay vs. Chi. Cardinals, Oct. 8, 1939 (TD)
Bob Gage, Pittsburgh vs. Chi. Bears, Dec. 4, 1949 (TD)
96 Jim Spavital, Baltimore vs. Green Bay, Nov. 5, 1950 (TD)
Bob Hoernschemeyer, Detroit vs. N.Y. Yanks, Nov. 23, 1950 (TD)

Average Gain
Highest Average Gain, Career (700 attempts)
5.22 Jim Brown, Cleveland, 1957-65 (2,359-12,312)
5.14 Eugene (Mercury) Morris, Miami, 1969-75; San Diego, 1976 (804-4,133)
5.00 Gale Sayers, Chicago, 1965-71 (991-4,956)
Highest Average Gain, Season (Qualifiers)
9.94 Beattie Feathers, Chi. Bears, 1934 (101-1,004)
6.87 Bobby Douglass, Chicago, 1972 (141-968)
6.78 Dan Towler, Los Angeles, 1951 (126-854)
Highest Average Gain, Game (10 attempts)
17.09 Marion Motley, Cleveland vs. Pittsburgh, Oct. 29, 1950 (11-188)
16.70 Bill Grimes, Green Bay vs. N.Y. Yanks, Oct. 8, 1950 (10-167)
16.57 Bobby Mitchell, Cleveland vs. Washington, Nov. 15, 1959 (14-232)

Touchdowns
Most Seasons Leading League
5 Jim Brown, Cleveland, 1957-59, 1963, 1965
4 Steve Van Buren, Philadelphia, 1945, 1947-49
3 Abner Haynes, Dall. Texans, 1960-62
Cookie Gilchrist, Buffalo, 1962-64
Paul Lowe, L.A. Chargers, 1960; San Diego, 1961, 1965
Leroy Kelly, Cleveland, 1966-68
Most Consecutive Seasons Leading League
3 Steve Van Buren, Philadelphia, 1947-49
Jim Brown, Cleveland, 1957-59
Abner Haynes, Dall. Texans, 1960-62
Cookie Gilchrist, Buffalo, 1962-64
Leroy Kelly, Cleveland, 1966-68
Most Touchdowns, Career
110 Walter Payton, Chicago, 1975-87
106 Jim Brown, Cleveland, 1957-65
104 John Riggins, N.Y. Jets, 1971-75; Washington, 1976-79, 1981-85
Most Touchdowns, Season
24 John Riggins, Washington, 1983
21 Joe Morris, N.Y. Giants, 1985
19 Jim Taylor, Green Bay, 1962
Earl Campbell, Houston, 1979
Chuck Muncie, San Diego, 1981
Most Touchdowns, Rookie, Season
18 Eric Dickerson, L.A. Rams, 1983
14 Gale Sayers, Chicago, 1965
13 Earl Campbell, Houston, 1978
Billy Sims, Detroit, 1980
George Rogers, New Orleans, 1981
Curt Warner, Seattle, 1983
Most Touchdowns, Game
6 Ernie Nevers, Chi. Cardinals vs. Chi. Bears, Nov. 28, 1929
5 Jim Brown, Cleveland vs. Baltimore, Nov. 1, 1959
Cookie Gilchrist, Buffalo vs. N.Y. Jets, Dec. 8, 1963
4 By many players
Most Consecutive Games Rushing for Touchdowns
13 John Riggins, Washington, 1982-83
George Rogers, Washington, 1985-86
11 Lenny Moore, Baltimore, 1963-64
9 Leroy Kelly, Cleveland, 1968

Passing
Most Seasons Leading League
6 Sammy Baugh, Washington, 1937, 1940, 1943, 1945, 1947, 1949
4 Len Dawson, Dall. Texans; 1962; Kansas City, 1964, 1966, 1968
Roger Staubach, Dallas, 1971, 1973, 1978-79
Ken Anderson, Cincinnati, 1974-75, 1981-82
3 Arnie Herber, Green Bay, 1932, 1934, 1936
Norm Van Brocklin, Los Angeles, 1950, 1952, 1954
Bart Starr, Green Bay, 1962, 1964, 1966
Most Consecutive Seasons Leading League
2 Cecil Isbell, Green Bay, 1941-42
Milt Plum, Cleveland, 1960-61
Ken Anderson, Cincinnati, 1974-75, 1981-82
Roger Staubach, Dallas, 1978-79

Pass Rating
Highest Pass Rating, Career (1,500 attempts)
94.1 Dan Marino, Miami, 1983-87
92.5 Joe Montana, San Francisco, 1979-87
86.8 Ken O'Brien, N.Y. Jets, 1984-87
Highest Pass Rating, Season (Qualifiers)
110.4 Milt Plum, Cleveland, 1960
109.9 Sammy Baugh, Washington, 1945
108.9 Dan Marino, Miami, 1984
Highest Pass Rating, Rookie, Season (Qualifiers)
96.0 Dan Marino, Miami, 1983
88.2 Greg Cook, Cincinnati, 1969
84.0 Charlie Conerly, N.Y. Giants, 1948

Attempts
Most Seasons Leading League
4 Sammy Baugh, Washington, 1937, 1943, 1947-48
Johnny Unitas, Baltimore, 1957, 1959-61
George Blanda, Chi. Bears, 1953; Houston, 1963-65
3 Arnie Herber, Green Bay, 1932, 1934, 1936
Sonny Jurgensen, Washington, 1966-67, 1969
2 By many players
Most Consecutive Seasons Leading League
3 Johnny Unitas, Baltimore, 1959-61
George Blanda, Houston, 1963-65
2 By many players
Most Passes Attempted, Career
6,467 Fran Tarkenton, Minnesota, 1961-66, 1972-78; N.Y. Giants, 1967-71
5,604 Dan Fouts, San Diego, 1973-87
5,186 Johnny Unitas, Baltimore, 1956-72; San Diego, 1973
Most Passes Attempted, Season
623 Dan Marino, Miami, 1986
609 Dan Fouts, San Diego, 1981
605 John Elway, Denver, 1985
Most Passes Attempted, Rookie, Season
439 Jim Zorn, Seattle, 1976
417 Jack Trudeau, Indianapolis, 1986
375 Norm Snead, Washington, 1961
Most Passes Attempted, Game
68 George Blanda, Houston vs. Buffalo, Nov. 1, 1964
62 Joe Namath, N.Y. Jets vs. Baltimore, Oct. 18, 1970
Steve Dils, Minnesota vs. Tampa Bay, Sept. 5, 1981
Phil Simms, N.Y. Giants vs. Cincinnati, Oct. 13, 1985
61 Tommy Kramer, Minnesota vs. New England, Dec. 16, 1979
Neil Lomax, St. Louis vs. San Diego, Sept. 20, 1987

Completions

Most Seasons Leading League

5 Sammy Baugh, Washington, 1937, 1943, 1945, 1947-48
4 George Blanda, Chi. Bears, 1953; Houston, 1963-65
Sonny Jurgensen, Philadelphia, 1961; Washington, 1966-67, 1969
3 Arnie Herber, Green Bay, 1932, 1934, 1936
Johnny Unitas, Baltimore, 1959-60, 1963
John Brodie, San Francisco, 1965, 1968, 1970
Fran Tarkenton, Minnesota, 1975-76, 1978
Dan Marino, Miami, 1984-86

Most Consecutive Seasons Leading League

3 George Blanda, Houston, 1963-65
Dan Marino, Miami, 1984-86
2 By many players

Most Passes Completed, Career

3,686 Fran Tarkenton, Minnesota, 1961-66, 1972-78; N.Y. Giants, 1967-71
3,297 Dan Fouts, San Diego, 1973-87
2,830 Johnny Unitas, Baltimore, 1956-72; San Diego, 1973

Most Passes Completed, Season

378 Dan Marino, Miami, 1986
362 Dan Marino, Miami, 1984
360 Dan Fouts, San Diego, 1981

Most Passes Completed, Rookie, Season

208 Jim Zorn, Seattle, 1976
204 Jack Trudeau, Indianapolis, 1986
183 Jeff Komlo, Detroit, 1979

Most Passes Completed, Game

42 Richard Todd, N.Y. Jets vs. San Francisco, Sept. 21, 1980
40 Ken Anderson, Cincinnati vs. San Diego, Dec. 20, 1982
Phil Simms, N.Y. Giants vs. Cincinnati, Oct. 13, 1985
39 Dan Marino, Miami vs. Buffalo, Nov. 16, 1986

Most Consecutive Passes Completed

22 Joe Montana, San Francisco vs. Cleveland (5), Nov. 29, 1987; vs. Green Bay (17), Dec. 6, 1987
20 Ken Anderson, Cincinnati vs. Houston, Jan. 2, 1983
18 Steve DeBerg, Denver vs. L.A. Rams (17), Dec. 12, 1982; vs. Kansas City (1), Dec. 19, 1982
Lynn Dickey, Green Bay vs. Houston, Sept. 4, 1983
Joe Montana, San Francisco vs. L.A. Rams (13), Oct. 28, 1984; vs. Cincinnati (5), Nov. 4, 1984

Completion Percentage

Most Seasons Leading League

8 Len Dawson, Dall. Texans, 1962; Kansas City, 1964-69, 1975
7 Sammy Baugh, Washington, 1940, 1942-43, 1945, 1947-49
4 Bart Starr, Green Bay, 1962, 1966, 1968-69
Joe Montana, San Francisco, 1980-81, 1985, 1987

Most Consecutive Seasons Leading League

6 Len Dawson, Kansas City, 1964-69
3 Sammy Baugh, Washington, 1947-49
Otto Graham, Cleveland, 1953-55
Milt Plum, Cleveland, 1959-61
2 By many players

Highest Completion Percentage, Career (1,500 attempts)

63.61 Joe Montana, San Francisco, 1979-87 (3,276-2,084)
60.63 Dan Marino, Miami, 1983-87 (2,494-1,512)
60.47 Ken O'Brien, N.Y. Jets, 1984-87 (1,566-947)

Highest Completion Percentage, Season (Qualifiers)

70.55 Ken Anderson, Cincinnati, 1982 (309-218)
70.33 Sammy Baugh, Washington, 1945 (182-128)
67.29 Steve Bartkowski, Atlanta, 1984 (269-181)

Highest Completion Percentage, Rookie, Season (Qualifiers)

58.45 Dan Marino, Miami, 1983 (296-173)
57.14 Jim McMahon, Chicago, 1982 (269-181)
56.07 Fran Tarkenton, Minnesota, 1961 (280-157)

Highest Completion Percentage, Game (20 attempts)

90.91 Ken Anderson, Cincinnati vs. Pittsburgh, Nov. 10, 1974 (22-20)
90.48 Lynn Dickey, Green Bay vs. New Orleans, Dec. 13, 1981 (21-19)
87.50 Danny White, Dallas vs. Philadelphia, Nov. 6, 1983 (24-21)

Yards Gained

Most Seasons Leading League

5 Sonny Jurgensen, Philadelphia, 1961-62; Washington, 1966-67, 1969
4 Sammy Baugh, Washington, 1937, 1940, 1947-48
Johnny Unitas, Baltimore, 1957, 1959-60, 1963
Dan Fouts, San Diego, 1979-82
3 Arnie Herber, Green Bay, 1932, 1934, 1936
Sid Luckman, Chi. Bears, 1943, 1945-46
John Brodie, San Francisco, 1965, 1968, 1970
John Hadl, San Diego, 1965, 1968, 1971
Joe Namath, N.Y. Jets, 1966-67, 1972
Dan Marino, Miami, 1984-86

Most Consecutive Seasons Leading League

4 Dan Fouts, San Diego, 1979-82
3 Dan Marino, Miami, 1984-86
2 By many players

Most Yards Gained, Career

47,003 Fran Tarkenton, Minnesota, 1961-66, 1972-78; N.Y. Giants, 1967-71
43,040 Dan Fouts, San Diego, 1973-87
40,239 Johnny Unitas, Baltimore, 1956-72; San Diego, 1973

Most Seasons, 3,000 or More Yards Passing

6 Dan Fouts, San Diego, 1979-81, 1984-86
5 Sonny Jurgensen, Philadelphia, 1961-62; Washington, 1966-67, 1969
Tommy Kramer, Minnesota, 1979-81, 1985-86
Joe Montana, San Francisco, 1981, 1983-85, 1987
4 Brian Sipe, Cleveland, 1979-81, 1983
Ron Jaworski, Philadelphia, 1980-81, 1983, 1985
Danny White, Dallas, 1980-81, 1983, 1985
Dan Marino, Miami, 1984-87

Most Yards Gained, Season

5,084 Dan Marino, Miami, 1984
4,802 Dan Fouts, San Diego, 1981
4,746 Dan Marino, Miami, 1986

Most Yards Gained, Rookie, Season

2,571 Jim Zorn, Seattle, 1976
2,507 Dennis Shaw, Buffalo, 1970
2,337 Norm Snead, Washington, 1961

Most Yards Gained, Game

554 Norm Van Brocklin, Los Angeles vs. N.Y. Yanks, Sept. 28, 1951
513 Phil Simms, N.Y. Giants vs. Cincinnati, Oct. 13, 1985
509 Vince Ferragamo, L.A. Rams vs. Chicago, Dec. 26, 1982

Most Games, 400 or More Yards Passing, Career

7 Dan Marino, Miami, 1983-87
6 Dan Fouts, San Diego, 1973-87
5 Sonny Jurgensen, Philadelphia, 1957-63; Washington, 1964-74

Most Games, 400 or More Yards Passing, Season

4 Dan Marino, Miami, 1984
3 Dan Marino, Miami, 1986
2 George Blanda, Houston, 1961
Sonny Jurgensen, Philadelphia, 1961
Joe Namath, N.Y. Jets, 1972
Dan Fouts, San Diego, 1982, 1985
Phil Simms, N.Y. Giants, 1985
Ken O'Brien, N.Y. Jets, 1986
Bernie Kosar, Cleveland, 1986

Most Consecutive Games, 400 or More Yards Passing

2 Dan Fouts, San Diego, 1982
Dan Marino, Miami, 1984
Phil Simms, N.Y. Giants, 1985

Most Games, 300 or More Yards Passing, Career

51 Dan Fouts, San Diego, 1973-87
26 Johnny Unitas, Baltimore, 1956-72; San Diego, 1973
Dan Marino, Miami, 1983-87
25 Sonny Jurgensen, Philadelphia, 1957-63; Washington, 1964-74

Most Games, 300 or More Yards Passing, Season

9 Dan Marino, Miami, 1984
8 Dan Fouts, San Diego, 1980
7 Dan Fouts, San Diego, 1981, 1985
Bill Kenney, Kansas City, 1983
Neil Lomax, St. Louis, 1984

Most Consecutive Games, 300 or More Yards Passing, Season

5 Joe Montana, San Francisco, 1982
4 Dan Fouts, San Diego, 1979
Bill Kenney, Kansas City, 1983
3 By many players

Longest Pass Completion (All TDs except as noted)

99 Frank Filchock (to Farkas), Washington vs. Pittsburgh, Oct. 15, 1939
George Izo (to Mitchell), Washington vs. Cleveland, Sept. 15, 1963
Karl Sweetan (to Studstill), Detroit vs. Baltimore, Oct. 16, 1966
Sonny Jurgensen (to Allen), Washington vs. Chicago, Sept. 15, 1968
Jim Plunkett (to Branch), L.A. Raiders vs. Washington, Oct. 2, 1983
Ron Jaworski (to Quick), Philadelphia vs. Atlanta, Nov. 10, 1985
98 Doug Russell (to Tinsley), Chi. Cardinals vs. Cleveland, Nov. 27, 1938
Ogden Compton (to Lane), Chi. Cardinals vs. Green Bay, Nov. 13, 1955
Bill Wade (to Farrington), Chicago Bears vs. Detroit, Oct. 8, 1961
Jacky Lee (to Dewveall), Houston vs. San Diego, Nov. 25, 1962
Earl Morrall (to Jones), N.Y. Giants vs. Pittsburgh, Sept. 11, 1966
Jim Hart (to Moore), St. Louis vs. Los Angeles, Dec. 10, 1972 (no TD)
97 Pat Coffee (to Tinsley), Chi. Cardinals vs. Chi. Bears, Dec. 5, 1937
Bobby Layne (to Box), Detroit vs. Green Bay, Nov. 26, 1953
George Shaw (to Tarr), Denver vs. Boston, Sept. 21, 1962

Average Gain

Most Seasons Leading League

7 Sid Luckman, Chi. Bears, 1939-43, 1946-47
3 Arnie Herber, Green Bay, 1932, 1934, 1936
Norm Van Brocklin, Los Angeles, 1950, 1952, 1954
Len Dawson, Dall. Texans, 1962; Kansas City, 1966, 1968
Bart Starr, Green Bay, 1966-68

Most Consecutive Seasons Leading League

5 Sid Luckman, Chi. Bears, 1939-43
3 Bart Starr, Green Bay, 1966-68
2 Bernie Masterson, Chi. Bears, 1937-38
Sid Luckman, Chi. Bears, 1946-47
Johnny Unitas, Baltimore, 1964-65
Terry Bradshaw, Pittsburgh, 1977-78
Steve Grogan, New England, 1980-81

Highest Average Gain, Career (1,500 attempts)

8.63 Otto Graham, Cleveland, 1950-55 (1,565-13,499)
8.42 Sid Luckman, Chi. Bears, 1939-50 (1,744-14,686)
8.16 Norm Van Brocklin, Los Angeles, 1949-57; Philadelphia, 1958-60 (2,895-23,611)

Highest Average Gain, Season (Qualifiers)

11.17 Tommy O'Connell, Cleveland, 1957 (110-1,229)
10.86 Sid Luckman, Chi. Bears, 1943 (202-2,194)
10.55 Otto Graham, Cleveland, 1953 (258-2,722)

Highest Average Gain, Rookie, Season (Qualifiers)

9.411 Greg Cook, Cincinnati, 1969 (197-1,854)
9.409 Bob Waterfield, Cleveland, 1945 (171-1,609)
8.36 Zeke Bratkowski, Chi. Bears, 1954 (130-1,087)

Highest Average Gain, Game (20 attempts)

18.58 Sammy Baugh, Washington vs. Boston, Oct. 31, 1948 (24-446)
18.50 Johnny Unitas, Baltimore vs. Atlanta, Nov. 12, 1967 (20-370)
17.71 Joe Namath, N.Y. Jets vs. Baltimore, Sept. 24, 1972 (28-496)

Touchdowns

Most Seasons Leading League

4 Johnny Unitas, Baltimore, 1957-60
Len Dawson, Dall. Texans, 1962; Kansas City, 1963, 1965-66
3 Arnie Herber, Green Bay, 1932, 1934, 1936
Sid Luckman, Chi. Bears, 1943, 1945-46
Y.A. Tittle, San Francisco, 1955; N.Y. Giants, 1962-63
Dan Marino, Miami, 1984-86
2 By many players

Most Consecutive Seasons Leading League
4 Johnny Unitas, Baltimore, 1957-60
3 Dan Marino, Miami, 1984-86
2 By many players

Most Touchdown Passes, Career
342 Fran Tarkenton, Minnesota, 1961-66, 1972-78; N.Y. Giants, 1967-71
290 Johnny Unitas, Baltimore, 1956-72: San Diego, 1973
255 Sonny Jurgensen, Philadelphia, 1957-63; Washington, 1964-74

Most Touchdown Passes, Season
48 Dan Marino, Miami, 1984
44 Dan Marino, Miami, 1986
36 George Blanda, Houston, 1961
Y.A. Tittle, N.Y. Giants, 1963

Most Touchdown Passes, Rookie, Season
22 Charlie Conerly, N.Y. Giants, 1948
20 Dan Marino, Miami, 1983
19 Jim Plunkett, New England, 1971

Most Touchdown Passes, Game
7 Sid Luckman, Chi. Bears vs. N.Y. Giants, Nov. 14, 1943
Adrian Burk, Philadelphia vs. Washington, Oct. 17, 1954
George Blanda, Houston vs. N.Y. Titans, Nov. 19, 1961
Y.A. Tittle, N.Y. Giants vs. Washington, Oct. 28, 1962
Joe Kapp, Minnesota vs. Baltimore, Sept. 28, 1969
6 By many players. Last time: Tommy Kramer, Minnesota vs. Green Bay, Sept. 28, 1986

Most Games, Four or More Touchdown Passes, Career
17 Johnny Unitas, Baltimore, 1956-72; San Diego, 1973
14 Dan Marino, Miami, 1983-87
13 George Blanda, Chi. Bears, 1949, 1950-58; Baltimore, 1950; Houston, 1960-66; Oakland, 1967-75

Most Games, Four or More Touchdown Passes, Season
6 Dan Marino, Miami, 1984
5 Dan Marino, Miami, 1986
4 George Blanda, Houston, 1961
Vince Ferragamo, Los Angeles, 1980

Most Consecutive Games, Four or More Touchdown Passes
4 Dan Marino, Miami, 1984
2 By many players

Most Consecutive Games, Touchdown Passes
47 Johnny Unitas, Baltimore, 1956-60
30 Dan Marino, Miami, 1985-87
28 Dave Krieg, Seattle, 1983-85

Had Intercepted

Most Consecutive Passes Attempted, None Intercepted
294 Bart Starr, Green Bay, 1964-65
208 Milt Plum, Cleveland, 1959-60
206 Roman Gabriel, Los Angeles, 1968-69

Most Passes Had Intercepted, Career
277 George Blanda, Chi. Bears, 1949, 1950-58; Baltimore, 1950; Houston, 1960-66; Oakland, 1967-75
268 John Hadl, San Diego, 1962-72; Los Angeles, 1973-74; Green Bay, 1974-75; Houston, 1976-77
266 Fran Tarkenton, Minnesota, 1961-66, 1972-78; N.Y. Giants, 1967-71

Most Passes Had Intercepted, Season
42 George Blanda, Houston, 1962
34 Frank Tripucka, Denver, 1960
32 John Hadl, San Diego, 1968
Fran Tarkenton, Minnesota, 1978

Most Passes Had Intercepted, Game
8 Jim Hardy, Chi. Cardinals vs. Philadelphia, Sept. 24, 1950
7 Parker Hall, Cleveland vs. Green Bay, Nov. 8, 1942
Frank Sinkwich, Detroit vs. Green Bay, Oct. 24, 1943
Bob Waterfield, Los Angeles vs. Green Bay, Oct. 17, 1948
Zeke Bratkowski, Chicago vs. Baltimore, Oct. 2, 1960
Tommy Wade, Pittsburgh vs. Philadelphia, Dec. 12, 1965
Ken Stabler, Oakland vs. Denver, Oct. 16, 1977
Steve DeBerg, Tampa Bay vs. San Francisco, Sept. 7, 1986
6 By many players

Most Attempts, No Interceptions, Game
57 Joe Montana, San Francisco vs. Atlanta, Oct. 6, 1985
54 Dan Marino, Miami vs. Buffalo, Nov. 16, 1986
51 Scott Brunner, N.Y. Giants vs. St. Louis, Dec. 26, 1982

Lowest Percentage, Passes Had Intercepted

Most Seasons Leading League, Lowest Percentage, Passes Had Intercepted
5 Sammy Baugh, Washington, 1940, 1942, 1944-45, 1947
3 Charlie Conerly, N.Y. Giants, 1950, 1956, 1959
Bart Starr, Green Bay, 1962, 1964, 1966
Roger Staubach, Dallas, 1971, 1977, 1979
Ken Anderson, Cincinnati, 1972, 1981-82
2 By many players

Lowest Percentage, Passes Had Intercepted, Career (1,500 attempts)
2.72 Joe Montana, San Francisco, 1979-87 (3,276-89)
2.75 Ken O'Brien, N.Y. Jets, 1984-87 (1,566-43)
2.92 Neil Lomax, St. Louis, 1981-87 (2,710-79)

Lowest Percentage, Passes Had Intercepted, Season (Qualifiers)
0.66 Joe Ferguson, Buffalo, 1976 (151-1)
1.16 Steve Bartkowski, Atlanta, 1983 (432-5)
1.20 Bart Starr, Green Bay, 1966 (251-3)

Lowest Percentage, Passes Had Intercepted, Rookie, Season (Qualifiers)
2.03 Dan Marino, Miami, 1983 (296-6)
2.10 Gary Wood, N.Y. Giants, 1964 (143-3)
2.82 Bernie Kosar, Cleveland, 1985 (248-7)

Times Sacked

Times Sacked has been compiled since 1963.

Most Times Sacked, Career
483 Fran Tarkenton, Minnesota, 1961-66, 1972-78; N.Y. Giants, 1967-71
405 Craig Morton, Dallas, 1965-74; N.Y. Giants, 1974-76; Denver, 1977-82
398 Ken Anderson, Cincinnati, 1971-86

Most Times Sacked, Season
72 Randall Cunningham, Philadelphia, 1986
62 Ken O'Brien, N.Y. Jets, 1985
61 Neil Lomax, St. Louis, 1985

Most Times Sacked, Game
12 Bert Jones, Baltimore vs. St. Louis, Oct. 26, 1980
Warren Moon, Houston vs. Dallas, Sept. 29, 1985
11 Charley Johnson, St. Louis vs. N.Y. Giants, Nov. 1, 1964
Bart Starr, Green Bay vs. Detroit, Nov. 7, 1965
Jack Kemp, Buffalo vs. Oakland, Oct. 15, 1967
Bob Berry, Atlanta vs. St. Louis, Nov. 24, 1968
Greg Landry, Detroit vs. Dallas, Oct. 6, 1975
Ron Jaworski, Philadelphia vs. St. Louis, Dec. 18, 1983
Paul McDonald, Cleveland vs. Kansas City, Sept. 30, 1984
Archie Manning, Minnesota vs. Chicago, Oct. 28, 1984
Steve Pelluer, Dallas vs. San Diego, Nov. 16, 1986
Randall Cunningham, Philadelphia vs. L.A. Raiders, Nov. 30, 1986 (OT)
David Norrie, N.Y. Jets vs. Dallas, Oct. 4, 1987
10 By many players

Pass Receiving

Most Seasons Leading League
8 Don Hutson, Green Bay, 1936-37, 1939, 1941-45
5 Lionel Taylor, Denver, 1960-63, 1965
3 Tom Fears, Los Angeles, 1948-50
Pete Pihos, Philadelphia, 1953-55
Billy Wilson, San Francisco, 1954, 1956-57
Raymond Berry, Baltimore, 1958-60
Lance Alworth, San Diego, 1966, 1968-69

Most Consecutive Seasons Leading League
5 Don Hutson, Green Bay, 1941-45
4 Lionel Taylor, Denver, 1960-63
3 Tom Fears, Los Angeles, 1948-50
Pete Pihos, Philadelphia, 1953-55
Raymond Berry, Baltimore, 1958-60

Most Pass Receptions, Career
752 Steve Largent, Seattle, 1976-87
750 Charlie Joiner, Houston, 1969-72; Cincinnati, 1972-75; San Diego, 1976-86
649 Charley Taylor, Washington, 1964-75, 1977

Most Seasons, 50 or More Pass Receptions
10 Steve Largent, Seattle, 1976, 1978-81, 1983-87
7 Raymond Berry, Baltimore, 1958-62, 1965-66
Art Powell, N.Y. Titans, 1960-62; Oakland, 1963-66
Lance Alworth, San Diego, 1963-69
Charley Taylor, Washington, 1964, 1966-67, 1969, 1973-75
Charlie Joiner, San Diego, 1976, 1979-81, 1983-85
Wes Chandler, New Orleans, 1979-80; New Orleans-San Diego, 1981; San Diego, 1983-86
Dwight Clark, San Francisco, 1980-86
James Lofton, Green Bay, 1979-81, 1983-86
Kellen Winslow, San Diego, 1980-84, 1986-87
6 Lionel Taylor, Denver, 1960-65
Bobby Mitchell, Washington, 1962-67
Ahmad Rashad, Minnesota, 1976-81
Ozzie Newsome, Cleveland, 1979-81, 1983-85

Most Pass Receptions, Season
106 Art Monk, Washington, 1984
101 Charley Hennigan, Houston, 1964
100 Lionel Taylor, Denver, 1961

Most Pass Receptions, Rookie, Season
83 Earl Cooper, San Francisco, 1980
72 Bill Groman, Houston, 1960
67 Jack Clancy, Miami, 1967
Cris Collinsworth, Cincinnati, 1981

Most Pass Receptions, Game
18 Tom Fears, Los Angeles vs. Green Bay, Dec. 3, 1950
17 Clark Gaines, N.Y. Jets vs. San Francisco, Sept. 21, 1980
16 Sonny Randle, St. Louis vs. N.Y. Giants, Nov. 4, 1962

Most Consecutive Games, Pass Receptions
152 Steve Largent, Seattle, 1977-87 (current)
127 Harold Carmichael, Philadelphia, 1972-80
Ozzie Newsome, Cleveland, 1979-87 (current)
121 Mel Gray, St. Louis, 1973-82

Yards Gained

Most Seasons Leading League
7 Don Hutson, Green Bay, 1936, 1938-39, 1941-44
3 Raymond Berry, Baltimore, 1957, 1959-60
Lance Alworth, San Diego, 1965-66, 1968
2 By many players

Most Consecutive Seasons Leading League
4 Don Hutson, Green Bay, 1941-44
2 By many players

Most Yards Gained, Career
12,146 Charlie Joiner, Houston, 1969-72; Cincinnati, 1972-75; San Diego, 1976-86
12,041 Steve Largent, Seattle, 1976-87
11,834 Don Maynard, N.Y. Giants, 1958; N.Y. Jets, 1960-72; St. Louis, 1973

Most Seasons, 1,000 or More Yards, Pass Receiving
8 Steve Largent, Seattle, 1978-81, 1983-86
7 Lance Alworth, San Diego, 1963-69
5 Art Powell, N.Y. Titans, 1960, 1962; Oakland, 1963-64, 1966
Don Maynard, N.Y. Jets, 1960, 1962, 1965, 1967-68
James Lofton, Green Bay, 1980-81, 1983-85

Most Yards Gained, Season
1,746 Charley Hennigan, Houston, 1961
1,602 Lance Alworth, San Diego, 1965
1,570 Jerry Rice, San Francisco, 1986

Most Yards Gained, Rookie, Season
1,473 Bill Groman, Houston, 1960
1,231 Bill Howton, Green Bay, 1952
1,131 Bill Brooks, Indianapolis, 1986

Most Yards Gained, Game
309 Stephone Paige, Kansas City vs. San Diego, Dec. 22, 1985

303 Jim Benton, Cleveland vs. Detroit, Nov. 22, 1945
302 Cloyce Box, Detroit vs. Baltimore, Dec. 3, 1950

Most Games, 200 or More Yards Pass Receiving, Career
5 Lance Alworth, San Diego, 1962-70; Dallas, 1971-72
4 Don Hutson, Green Bay, 1935-45
Charley Hennigan, Houston, 1960-66
3 Don Maynard, N.Y. Giants, 1958; N.Y. Jets, 1960-72; St. Louis, 1973
Wes Chandler, New Orleans, 1978-81; San Diego, 1981-87

Most Games, 200 or More Yards Pass Receiving, Season
3 Charley Hennigan, Houston, 1961
2 Don Hutson, Green Bay, 1942
Gene Roberts, N.Y. Giants, 1949
Lance Alworth, San Diego, 1963
Don Maynard, N.Y. Jets, 1968

Most Games, 100 or More Yards Pass Receiving, Career
50 Don Maynard, N.Y. Giants, 1958; N.Y. Jets, 1960-72; St. Louis, 1973
41 Lance Alworth, San Diego, 1962-70; Dallas, 1971-72
40 Steve Largent, Seattle, 1976-87

Most Games, 100 or More Yards Pass Receiving, Season
10 Charley Hennigan, Houston, 1961
9 Elroy (Crazylegs) Hirsch, Los Angeles, 1951
Bill Groman, Houston, 1960
Lance Alworth, San Diego, 1965
Don Maynard, N.Y. Jets, 1967
Stanley Morgan, New England, 1986
8 Charley Hennigan, Houston, 1964
Lance Alworth, San Diego, 1967
Mark Duper, Miami, 1986

Most Consecutive Games, 100 or More Yards Pass Receiving
7 Charley Hennigan, Houston, 1961
Bill Groman, Houston, 1961
6 Raymond Berry, Baltimore, 1960
Pat Studstill, Detroit, 1966
5 Elroy (Crazylegs) Hirsch, Los Angeles, 1951
Bob Boyd, Los Angeles, 1954
Terry Barr, Detroit, 1963
Lance Alworth, San Diego, 1966

Longest Pass Reception (All TDs except as noted)
99 Andy Farkas (from Filchock), Washington vs. Pittsburgh, Oct. 15, 1939
Bobby Mitchell (from Izo), Washington vs. Cleveland, Sept. 15, 1963
Pat Studstill (from Sweetan), Detroit vs. Baltimore, Oct. 16, 1966
Gerry Allen (from Jurgensen), Washington vs. Chicago, Sept. 15, 1968
Cliff Branch (from Plunkett), L.A. Raiders vs. Washington, Oct. 2, 1983
Mike Quick (from Jaworski), Philadelphia vs. Atlanta, Nov. 10, 1985
98 Gaynell Tinsley (from Russell), Chi. Cardinals vs. Cleveland, Nov. 17, 1938
Dick (Night Train) Lane (from Compton), Chi. Cardinals vs. Green Bay, Nov. 13, 1955
John Farrington (from Wade), Chicago vs. Detroit, Oct. 8, 1961
Willard Dewveall (from Lee), Houston vs. San Diego, Nov. 25, 1962
Homer Jones (from Morrall), N.Y. Giants vs. Pittsburgh, Sept. 11, 1966
Bobby Moore (from Hart), St. Louis vs. Los Angeles, Dec. 10, 1972 (no TD)
97 Gaynell Tinsley (from Coffee), Chi. Cardinals vs. Chi. Bears, Dec. 5, 1937
Cloyce Box (from Layne), Detroit vs. Green Bay, Nov. 26, 1953
Jerry Tarr (from Shaw), Denver vs. Boston, Sept. 21, 1962

Average Gain

Highest Average Gain, Career (200 receptions)
22.26 Homer Jones, N.Y. Giants, 1964-69; Cleveland, 1970 (224-4,986)
20.82 Buddy Dial, Pittsburgh, 1959-63; Dallas, 1964-66 (261-5,436)
20.24 Harlon Hill, Chi. Bears, 1954-61; Pittsburgh, 1962; Detroit, 1962 (233-4,717)

Highest Average Gain, Season (24 receptions)
32.58 Don Currivan, Boston, 1947 (24-782)
31.44 Bucky Pope, Los Angeles, 1964 (25-786)
28.60 Bobby Duckworth, San Diego, 1984 (25-715)

Highest Average Gain, Game (3 receptions)
60.67 Bill Groman, Houston vs. Denver, Nov. 20, 1960 (3-182)
Homer Jones, N.Y. Giants vs. Washington, Dec. 12, 1965 (3-182)
60.33 Don Currivan, Boston vs. Washington, Nov. 30, 1947 (3-181)
59.67 Bobby Duckworth, San Diego vs. Chicago, Dec. 3, 1984 (3-179)

Touchdowns

Most Seasons Leading League
9 Don Hutson, Green Bay, 1935-38, 1940-44
3 Lance Alworth, San Diego, 1964-66
2 By many players

Most Consecutive Seasons Leading League
5 Don Hutson, Green Bay, 1940-44
4 Don Hutson, Green Bay, 1935-38
3 Lance Alworth, San Diego, 1964-66

Most Touchdowns, Career
99 Don Hutson, Green Bay, 1935-45
95 Steve Largent, Seattle, 1976-87
88 Don Maynard, N.Y. Giants, 1958; N.Y. Jets, 1960-72; St. Louis, 1973

Most Touchdowns, Season
22 Jerry Rice, San Francisco, 1987
18 Mark Clayton, Miami, 1984
17 Don Hutson, Green Bay, 1942
Elroy (Crazylegs) Hirsch, Los Angeles, 1951
Bill Groman, Houston, 1961

Most Touchdowns, Rookie, Season
13 Bill Howton, Green Bay, 1952
John Jefferson, San Diego, 1979
12 Harlon Hill, Chi. Bears, 1954
Bill Groman, Houston, 1960
Mike Ditka, Chicago, 1961
Bob Hayes, Dallas, 1965
10 Bill Swiacki, N.Y. Giants, 1948
Bucky Pope, Los Angeles, 1964
Sammy White, Minnesota, 1976
Daryl Turner, Seattle, 1984

Most Touchdowns, Game
5 Bob Shaw, Chi. Cardinals vs. Baltimore, Oct. 2, 1950
Kellen Winslow, San Diego vs. Oakland, Nov. 22, 1981
4 By many players. Last time: Wesley Walker, N.Y. Jets vs. Miami, Sept. 21, 1986 (OT)

Most Consecutive Games, Touchdowns
13 Jerry Rice, San Francisco, 1986-87 (current)
11 Elroy (Crazylegs) Hirsch, Los Angeles, 1950-51
Buddy Dial, Pittsburgh, 1959-60
9 Lance Alworth, San Diego, 1963

Interceptions By

Most Seasons Leading League
3 Everson Walls, Dallas, 1981-82, 1985
2 Dick (Night Train) Lane, Los Angeles, 1952; Chi. Cardinals, 1954
Jack Christiansen, Detroit, 1953, 1957
Milt Davis, Baltimore, 1957, 1959
Dick Lynch, N.Y. Giants, 1961, 1963
Johnny Robinson, Kansas City, 1966, 1970
Bill Bradley, Philadelphia, 1971-72
Emmitt Thomas, Kansas City, 1969, 1974

Most Interceptions By, Career
81 Paul Krause, Washington, 1964-67; Minnesota, 1968-79
79 Emlen Tunnell, N.Y. Giants, 1948-58; Green Bay, 1959-61
68 Dick (Night Train) Lane, Los Angeles, 1952-53; Chi. Cardinals, 1954-59; Detroit, 1960-65

Most Interceptions By, Season
14 Dick (Night Train) Lane, Los Angeles, 1952
13 Dan Sandifer, Washington, 1948
Orban (Spec) Sanders, N.Y. Yanks, 1950
Lester Hayes, Oakland, 1980
12 By nine players

Most Interceptions By, Rookie, Season
14 Dick (Night Train) Lane, Los Angeles, 1952
13 Dan Sandifer, Washington, 1948
12 Woodley Lewis, Los Angeles, 1950
Paul Krause, Washington, 1964

Most Interceptions By, Game
4 Sammy Baugh, Washington vs. Detroit, Nov. 14, 1943
Dan Sandifer, Washington vs. Boston, Oct. 31, 1948
Don Doll, Detroit vs. Chi. Cardinals, Oct. 23, 1949
Bob Nussbaumer, Chi. Cardinals vs. N.Y. Bulldogs, Nov. 13, 1949
Russ Craft, Philadelphia vs. Chi. Cardinals, Sept. 24, 1950
Bobby Dillon, Green Bay vs. Detroit, Nov. 26, 1953
Jack Butler, Pittsburgh vs. Washington, Dec. 13, 1953
Austin (Goose) Gonsoulin, Denver vs. Buffalo, Sept. 18, 1960
Jerry Norton, St. Louis vs. Washington, Nov. 20, 1960; vs. Pittsburgh, Nov. 26, 1961
Dave Baker, San Francisco vs. L.A. Rams, Dec. 4, 1960
Bobby Ply, Dall. Texans vs. San Diego, Dec. 16, 1962
Bobby Hunt, Kansas City vs. Houston, Oct. 4, 1964
Willie Brown, Denver vs. N.Y. Jets, Nov. 15, 1964
Dick Anderson, Miami vs. Pittsburgh, Dec. 3, 1973
Willie Buchanon, Green Bay vs. San Diego, Sept. 24, 1978
Deron Cherry, Kansas City vs. Seattle, Sept. 29, 1985

Most Consecutive Games, Passes Intercepted By
8 Tom Morrow, Oakland, 1962-63
7 Paul Krause, Washington, 1964
Larry Wilson, St. Louis, 1966
Ben Davis, Cleveland, 1968
6 Dick (Night Train) Lane, Chi. Cardinals, 1954-55
Will Sherman, Los Angeles, 1954-55
Jim Shofner, Cleveland, 1960
Paul Krause, Minnesota, 1968
Willie Williams, N.Y. Giants, 1968
Kermit Alexander, San Francisco, 1968-69
Mel Blount, Pittsburgh, 1975
Eric Harris, Kansas City, 1980
Lester Hayes, Oakland, 1980
Barry Wilburn, Washington, 1987

Yards Gained

Most Seasons Leading League
2 Dick (Night Train) Lane, Los Angeles, 1952; Chi. Cardinals, 1954
Herb Adderley, Green Bay, 1965, 1969
Dick Anderson, Miami, 1968, 1970

Most Yards Gained, Career
1,282 Emlen Tunnell, N.Y. Giants, 1948-58; Green Bay, 1959-61
1,207 Dick (Night Train) Lane, Los Angeles, 1952-53; Chi. Cardinals, 1954-59; Detroit, 1960-65
1,185 Paul Krause, Washington, 1964-67; Minnesota, 1968-79

Most Yards Gained, Season
349 Charlie McNeil, San Diego, 1961
301 Don Doll, Detroit, 1949
298 Dick (Night Train) Lane, Los Angeles, 1952

Most Yards Gained, Rookie, Season
301 Don Doll, Detroit, 1949
298 Dick (Night Train) Lane, Los Angeles, 1952
275 Woodley Lewis, Los Angeles, 1950

Most Yards Gained, Game
177 Charlie McNeil, San Diego vs. Houston, Sept. 24, 1961
167 Dick Jauron, Detroit vs. Chicago, Nov. 18, 1973
151 Tom Myers, New Orleans vs. Minnesota, Sept. 3, 1978
Mike Haynes, L.A. Raiders vs. Miami, Dec. 2, 1984

Longest Return (All TDs)
103 Vencie Glenn, San Diego vs. Denver, Nov. 29, 1987
102 Bob Smith, Detroit vs. Chi. Bears, Nov. 24, 1949
Erich Barnes, N.Y. Giants vs. Dall. Cowboys, Oct. 15, 1961
Gary Barbaro, Kansas City vs. Seattle, Dec. 11, 1977
Louis Breeden, Cincinnati vs. San Diego, Nov. 8, 1981
101 Richie Petitbon, Chicago vs Los Angeles, Dec. 9, 1962
Henry Carr, N.Y. Giants vs. Los Angeles, Nov. 13, 1966
Tony Greene, Buffalo vs. Kansas City, Oct. 3, 1976
Tom Pridemore, Atlanta vs. San Francisco, Sept. 20, 1981

Touchdowns

Most Touchdowns, Career

9 Ken Houston, Houston, 1967-72; Washington, 1973-80
7 Herb Adderley, Green Bay, 1961-69; Dallas, 1970-72
Erich Barnes, Chi. Bears, 1958-60; N.Y. Giants, 1961-64; Cleveland, 1965-70
Lem Barney, Detroit, 1967-77
6 Tom Janik, Denver, 1963-64; Buffalo, 1965-68; Boston, 1969-70; New England, 1971
Miller Farr, Denver, 1965; San Diego, 1965-66; Houston, 1967-69; St. Louis, 1970-72; Detroit, 1973
Bobby Bell, Kansas City, 1963-74

Most Touchdowns, Season

4 Ken Houston, Houston, 1971
Jim Kearney, Kansas City, 1972
3 Dick Harris, San Diego, 1961
Dick Lynch, N.Y. Giants, 1963
Herb Adderley, Green Bay, 1965
Lem Barney, Detroit, 1967
Miller Farr, Houston, 1967
Monte Jackson, Los Angeles, 1976
Rod Perry, Los Angeles, 1978
Ronnie Lott, San Francisco, 1981
Lloyd Burruss, Kansas City, 1986
2 By many players

Most Touchdowns, Rookie, Season

3 Lem Barney, Detroit, 1967
Ronnie Lott, San Francisco, 1981
2 By many players

Most Touchdowns, Game

2 Bill Blackburn, Chi. Cardinals vs. Boston, Oct. 24, 1948
Dan Sandifer, Washington vs. Boston, Oct. 31, 1948
Bob Franklin, Cleveland vs. Chicago, Dec. 11, 1960
Bill Stacy, St. Louis vs. Dall. Cowboys, Nov. 5, 1961
Jerry Norton, St. Louis vs. Pittsburgh, Nov. 26, 1961
Miller Farr, Houston vs. Buffalo, Dec. 7, 1968
Ken Houston, Houston vs. San Diego, Dec. 19, 1971
Jim Kearney, Kansas City vs. Denver, Oct. 1, 1972
Lemar Parrish, Cincinnati vs. Houston, Dec. 17, 1972
Dick Anderson, Miami vs. Pittsburgh, Dec. 3, 1973
Prentice McCray, New England vs. N.Y. Jets, Nov. 21, 1976
Kenny Johnson, Atlanta vs. Green Bay, Nov. 27, 1983 (OT)
Mike Kozlowski, Miami vs. N.Y. Jets, Dec. 16, 1983
Dave Brown, Seattle vs. Kansas City, Nov. 4, 1984
Lloyd Burruss, Kansas City vs. San Diego, Oct. 19, 1986

Punting

Most Seasons Leading League

4 Sammy Baugh, Washington, 1940-43
Jerrel Wilson, Kansas City, 1965, 1968, 1972-73
3 Yale Lary, Detroit, 1959, 1961, 1963
Jim Fraser, Denver, 1962-64
Ray Guy, Oakland, 1974-75, 1977
Rohn Stark, Baltimore, 1983; Indianapolis, 1985-86
2 By many players

Most Consecutive Seasons Leading League

4 Sammy Baugh, Washington, 1940-43
3 Jim Fraser, Denver, 1962-64
2 By many players

Punts

Most Punts, Career

1,154 Dave Jennings, N.Y. Giants, 1974-84; N.Y. Jets, 1985-87
1,083 John James, Atlanta, 1972-81; Detroit, 1982, Houston, 1982-84
1,072 Jerrel Wilson, Kansas City, 1963-77; New England, 1978

Most Punts, Season

114 Bob Parsons, Chicago, 1981
109 John James, Atlanta, 1978
108 John Teltschik, Philadelphia, 1986

Most Punts, Rookie, Season

108 John Teltschik, Philadelphia, 1986
99 Lewis Colbert, Kansas City, 1986
96 Mike Connell, San Francisco, 1978
Chris Norman, Denver, 1984

Most Punts, Game

15 John Teltschik, Philadelphia vs. N.Y. Giants, Dec. 6, 1987 (OT)
14 Dick Nesbitt, Chi. Cardinals vs. Chi. Bears, Nov. 30, 1933
Keith Molesworth, Chi. Bears vs. Green Bay, Dec. 10, 1933
Sammy Baugh, Washington vs. Philadelphia, Nov. 5, 1939
Carl Kinscherf, N.Y. Giants vs. Detroit, Nov. 7, 1943
George Taliaferro, N.Y. Yanks vs. Los Angeles, Sept. 28, 1951
12 Parker Hall, Cleveland vs. Green Bay, Nov. 26, 1939
Beryl Clark, Chi. Cardinals vs. Detroit, Sept. 15, 1940
Len Barnum, Philadelphia vs. Washington, Oct. 4, 1942
Horace Gillom, Cleveland vs. Philadelphia, Dec. 3, 1950
Adrian Burk, Philadelphia vs. Green Bay, Nov. 2, 1952; vs. N.Y. Giants, Dec. 12, 1954
Bob Scarpitto, Denver vs. Oakland, Sept. 10, 1967
Bill Van Heusen, Denver vs. Cincinnati, Oct. 6, 1968
Tom Blanchard, New Orleans vs. Minnesota, Nov. 16, 1975
Rusty Jackson, Los Angeles vs. San Francisco, Nov. 21, 1976
Wilbur Summers, Detroit vs. San Francisco, Oct. 23, 1977
John James, Atlanta vs. Washington, Dec. 10, 1978
Luke Prestridge, Denver vs. Buffalo, Oct. 25, 1981
Greg Coleman, Minnesota vs. Green Bay, Nov. 21, 1982

Longest Punt

98 Steve O'Neal, N.Y. Jets vs. Denver, Sept. 21, 1969
94 Joe Lintzenich, Chi. Bears vs. N.Y. Giants, Nov. 16, 1931
90 Don Chandler, Green Bay vs. San Francisco, Oct. 10, 1965

Average Yardage

Highest Average, Punting, Career (300 punts)

45.10 Sammy Baugh, Washington, 1937-52 (338-15,245)
44.68 Tommy Davis, San Francisco, 1959-69 (511-22,833)
44.46 Rohn Stark, Baltimore, 1982-83; Indianapolis, 1984-87 (450-20,007)

Highest Average, Punting, Season (Qualifiers)

51.40 Sammy Baugh, Washington, 1940 (35-1,799)
48.94 Yale Lary, Detroit, 1963 (35-1,713)
48.73 Sammy Baugh, Washington, 1941 (30-1,462)

Highest Average, Punting, Rookie, Season (Qualifiers)

46.40 Bobby Walden, Minnesota, 1964 (72-3,341)
46.22 Dave Lewis, Cincinnati, 1970 (79-3,651)
45.92 Frank Sinkwich, Detroit, 1943 (12-551)

Highest Average, Punting, Game (4 punts)

61.75 Bob Cifers, Detroit vs. Chi. Bears, Nov. 24, 1946 (4-247)
61.60 Roy McKay, Green Bay vs. Chi. Cardinals, Oct. 28, 1945 (5-308)
59.40 Sammy Baugh, Washington vs. Detroit, Oct. 27, 1940 (5-297)

Punts Had Blocked

Most Consecutive Punts, None Blocked

623 Dave Jennings, N.Y. Giants, 1976-83
619 Ray Guy, Oakland, 1979-81; L.A. Raiders, 1982-86
578 Bobby Walden, Minnesota, 1964-67; Pittsburgh, 1968-72

Most Punts Had Blocked, Career

14 Herman Weaver, Detroit, 1970-76; Seattle, 1977-80
12 Jerrel Wilson, Kansas City, 1963-77; New England, 1978
Tom Blanchard, N.Y. Giants, 1971-73; New Orleans, 1974-78; Tampa Bay, 1979-81
11 David Lee, Baltimore, 1966-78

Punt Returns

Most Seasons Leading League

3 Les (Speedy) Duncan, San Diego, 1965-66; Washington, 1971
Rick Upchurch, Denver, 1976, 1978, 1982
2 Dick Christy, N.Y. Titans, 1961-62
Claude Gibson, Oakland, 1963-64
Billy Johnson, Houston, 1975, 1977

Punt Returns

Most Punt Returns, Career

279 Billy Johnson, Houston, 1974-80; Atlanta, 1982-87
258 Emlen Tunnell, N.Y. Giants, 1948-58; Green Bay, 1959-61
253 Alvin Haymond, Baltimore, 1964-67; Philadelphia, 1968; Los Angeles, 1969-71; Washington, 1972; Houston, 1973

Most Punt Returns, Season

70 Danny Reece, Tampa Bay, 1979
62 Fulton Walker, Miami-L.A. Raiders, 1985
58 J. T. Smith, Kansas City, 1979
Greg Pruitt, L.A. Raiders, 1983

Most Punt Returns, Rookie, Season

57 Lew Barnes, Chicago, 1986
54 James Jones, Dallas, 1980
53 Louis Lipps, Pittsburgh, 1984

Most Punt Returns, Game

11 Eddie Brown, Washington vs. Tampa Bay, Oct. 9, 1977
10 Theo Bell, Pittsburgh vs. Buffalo, Dec. 16, 1979
Mike Nelms, Washington vs. New Orleans, Dec. 26, 1982
9 Rodger Bird, Oakland vs. Denver, Sept. 10, 1967
Ralph McGill, San Francisco vs. Atlanta, Oct. 29, 1972
Ed Podolak, Kansas City vs. San Diego, Nov. 10, 1974
Anthony Leonard, San Francisco vs. New Orleans, Oct. 17, 1976
Butch Johnson, Dallas vs. Buffalo, Nov. 15, 1976
Larry Marshall, Philadelphia vs. Tampa Bay, Sept. 18, 1977
Nesby Glasgow, Baltimore vs. Kansas City, Sept. 2, 1979
Mike Nelms, Washington vs. St. Louis, Dec. 21, 1980
Leon Bright, N.Y. Giants vs. Philadelphia, Dec. 11, 1982
Pete Shaw, N.Y. Giants vs. Philadelphia, Nov. 20, 1983
Cleotha Montgomery, L.A. Raiders vs. Detroit, Dec. 10, 1984
Phil McConkey, N.Y. Giants vs. Philadelphia, Dec. 6, 1987 (OT)

Fair Catches

Most Fair Catches, Season

24 Ken Graham, San Diego, 1969
22 Lem Barney, Detroit, 1976
21 Ed Podolak, Kansas City, 1970
Steve Schubert, Chicago, 1978
Stanley Morgan, New England, 1979

Most Fair Catches, Game

7 Lem Barney, Detroit vs. Chicago, Nov. 21, 1976
Bobby Morse, Philadelphia vs. Buffalo, Dec. 27, 1987
6 Jake Scott, Miami vs. Buffalo, Dec. 20, 1970
Greg Pruitt, L.A. Raiders vs. Seattle, Oct. 7, 1984
5 By many players

Yards Gained

Most Seasons Leading League

3 Alvin Haymond, Baltimore, 1965-66; Los Angeles, 1969
2 Bill Dudley, Pittsburgh, 1942, 1946
Emlen Tunnell, N.Y. Giants, 1951-52
Dick Christy, N.Y. Titans, 1961-62
Claude Gibson, Oakland, 1963-64
Rodger Bird, Oakland, 1966-67
J. T. Smith, Kansas City, 1979-80
Vai Sikahema, St. Louis, 1986-87

Most Yards Gained, Career

3,291 Billy Johnson, Houston, 1974-80; Atlanta, 1982-87
3,008 Rick Upchurch, Denver, 1975-83
2,660 Mike Fuller, San Diego, 1975-80; Cincinnati, 1981-82

Most Yards Gained, Season

692 Fulton Walker, Miami-L.A. Raiders, 1985
666 Greg Pruitt, L.A. Raiders, 1983
656 Louis Lipps, Pittsburgh, 1984

Most Yards Gained, Rookie, Season

656 Louis Lipps, Pittsburgh, 1984
655 Neal Colzie, Oakland, 1975
608 Mike Haynes, New England, 1976

Most Yards Gained, Game
207 LeRoy Irvin, Los Angeles vs. Atlanta, Oct. 11, 1981
205 George Atkinson, Oakland vs. Buffalo, Sept. 15, 1968
184 Tom Watkins, Detroit vs. San Francisco, Oct. 6, 1963

Longest Punt Return (All TDs)
98 Gil LeFebvre, Cincinnati vs. Brooklyn, Dec. 3, 1933
Charlie West, Minnesota vs. Washington, Nov. 3, 1968
Dennis Morgan, Dallas vs. St. Louis, Oct. 13, 1974
97 Greg Pruitt, L.A. Raiders vs. Washington, Oct. 2, 1983
96 Bill Dudley, Washington vs. Pittsburgh, Dec. 3, 1950

Average Yardage

Highest Average, Career (75 returns)
12.78 George McAfee, Chi. Bears, 1940-41, 1945-50 (112-1,431)
12.75 Jack Christiansen, Detroit, 1951-58 (85-1,084)
12.55 Claude Gibson, San Diego, 1961-62; Oakland, 1963-65 (110-1,381)

Highest Average, Season (Qualifiers)
23.00 Herb Rich, Baltimore, 1950 (12-276)
21.47 Jack Christiansen, Detroit, 1952 (15-322)
21.28 Dick Christy, N.Y. Titans, 1961 (18-383)

Highest Average, Rookie, Season (Qualifiers)
23.00 Herb Rich, Baltimore, 1950 (12-276)
20.88 Jerry Davis, Chi. Cardinals, 1948 (16-334)
20.73 Frank Sinkwich, Detroit, 1943 (11-228)

Highest Average, Game (3 returns)
47.67 Chuck Latourette, St. Louis vs. New Orleans, Sept. 29, 1968 (3-143)
47.33 Johnny Roland, St. Louis vs. Philadelphia, Oct. 2, 1966 (3-142)
45.67 Dick Christy, N.Y. Titans vs. Denver, Sept. 24, 1961 (3-137)

Touchdowns

Most Touchdowns, Career
8 Jack Christiansen, Detroit, 1951-58
Rick Upchurch, Denver, 1975-83
6 Billy Johnson, Houston, 1974-80; Atlanta, 1982-87
5 Emlen Tunnell, N.Y. Giants, 1948-58; Green Bay, 1959-61

Most Touchdowns, Season
4 Jack Christiansen, Detroit, 1951
Rick Upchurch, Denver, 1976
3 Emlen Tunnell, N.Y. Giants, 1951
Billy Johnson, Houston, 1975
LeRoy Irvin, Los Angeles, 1981
2 By many players

Most Touchdowns, Rookie, Season
4 Jack Christiansen, Detroit, 1951
2 By six players

Most Touchdowns, Game
2 Jack Christiansen, Detroit vs. Los Angeles, Oct. 14, 1951; vs. Green Bay, Nov. 22, 1951
Dick Christy, N.Y. Titans vs. Denver, Sept. 24, 1961
Rick Upchurch, Denver vs. Cleveland, Sept. 26, 1976
LeRoy Irvin, Los Angeles vs. Atlanta, Oct. 11, 1981
Vai Sikahema, St. Louis vs. Tampa Bay, Dec. 21, 1986

Kickoff Returns

Most Seasons Leading League
3 Abe Woodson, San Francisco, 1959, 1962-63
2 Lynn Chandnois, Pittsburgh, 1951-52
Bobby Jancik, Houston, 1962-63
Travis Williams, Green Bay, 1967; Los Angeles, 1971

Kickoff Returns

Most Kickoff Returns, Career
275 Ron Smith, Chicago, 1965, 1970-72; Atlanta, 1966-67; Los Angeles, 1968-69; San Diego, 1973; Oakland, 1974
243 Bruce Harper, N.Y. Jets, 1977-84
194 Steve Odom, Green Bay, 1974-79; N.Y. Giants, 1979

Most Kickoff Returns, Season
60 Drew Hill, Los Angeles, 1981
55 Bruce Harper, N.Y. Jets, 1978, 1979
David Turner, Cincinnati, 1979
Stump Mitchell, St. Louis, 1981
53 Eddie Payton, Minnesota, 1980
Buster Rhymes, Minnesota, 1985

Most Kickoff Returns, Rookie, Season
55 Stump Mitchell, St. Louis, 1981
53 Buster Rhymes, Minnesota, 1985
50 Nesby Glasgow, Baltimore, 1979
Dino Hall, Cleveland, 1979

Most Kickoff Returns, Game
9 Noland Smith, Kansas City vs. Oakland, Nov. 23, 1967
Dino Hall, Cleveland vs. Pittsburgh, Oct. 7, 1979
Paul Palmer, Kansas City vs. Seattle, Sept. 20, 1987
8 George Taliaferro, N.Y. Yanks vs. N.Y. Giants, Dec. 3, 1950
Bobby Jancik, Houston vs. Boston, Dec. 8, 1963; vs. Oakland, Dec. 22, 1963
Mel Renfro, Dallas vs. Green Bay, Nov. 29, 1964
Willie Porter, Boston vs. N.Y. Jets, Sept. 22, 1968
Keith Moody, Buffalo vs. Seattle, Oct. 30, 1977
Brian Baschnagel, Chicago vs. Houston, Nov. 6, 1977
Bruce Harper, N.Y. Jets vs. New England, Oct. 29, 1978; vs. New England, Sept. 9, 1979
Dino Hall, Cleveland vs. Pittsburgh, Nov. 25, 1979
Terry Metcalf, Washington vs. St. Louis, Sept. 20, 1981
Harlan Huckleby, Green Bay vs. Washington, Oct. 17, 1983
Gary Ellerson, Green Bay vs. St. Louis, Sept. 29, 1985
Bobby Humphery, N.Y. Jets vs. Cincinnati, Dec. 21, 1986
Bobby Joe Edmonds, Seattle vs. L.A. Raiders, Nov. 30, 1987
7 By many players

Yards Gained

Most Seasons Leading League
3 Bruce Harper, N.Y. Jets, 1977-79
2 Marshall Goldberg, Chi. Cardinals, 1941-42
Woodley Lewis, Los Angeles, 1953-54
Al Carmichael, Green Bay, 1956-57
Timmy Brown, Philadelphia, 1961, 1963
Bobby Jancik, Houston, 1963, 1966
Ron Smith, Atlanta, 1966-67

Most Yards Gained, Career
6,922 Ron Smith, Chicago, 1965, 1970-72; Atlanta, 1966-67; Los Angeles, 1968-69; San Diego, 1973; Oakland, 1974
5,538 Abe Woodson, San Francisco, 1958-64; St. Louis, 1965-66
5,407 Bruce Harper, N.Y. Jets, 1977-84

Most Yards Gained, Season
1,345 Buster Rhymes, Minnesota, 1985
1,317 Bobby Jancik, Houston, 1963
1,314 Dave Hampton, Green Bay, 1971

Most Yards Gained, Rookie, Season
1,345 Buster Rhymes, Minnesota, 1985
1,292 Stump Mitchell, St. Louis, 1981
1,245 Odell Barry, Denver, 1964

Most Yards Gained, Game
294 Wally Triplett, Detroit vs. Los Angeles, Oct. 29, 1950
247 Timmy Brown, Philadelphia vs. Dallas, Nov. 6, 1966
244 Noland Smith, Kansas City vs. San Diego, Oct. 15, 1967

Longest Kickoff Return (All TDs)
106 Al Carmichael, Green Bay vs. Chi. Bears, Oct. 7, 1956
Noland Smith, Kansas City vs. Denver, Dec. 17, 1967
Roy Green, St. Louis vs. Dallas, Oct. 21, 1979
105 Frank Seno, Chi. Cardinals vs. N.Y. Giants, Oct. 20, 1946
Ollie Matson, Chi. Cardinals vs. Washington, Oct. 14, 1956
Abe Woodson, San Francisco vs. Los Angeles, Nov. 8, 1959
Timmy Brown, Philadelphia vs. Cleveland, Sept. 17, 1961
Jon Arnett, Los Angeles vs. Detroit, Oct. 29, 1961
Eugene (Mercury) Morris, Miami vs. Cincinnati, Sept. 14, 1969
Travis Williams, Los Angeles vs. New Orleans, Dec. 5, 1971
104 By many players

Average Yardage

Highest Average, Career (75 returns)
30.56 Gale Sayers, Chicago, 1965-71 (91-2,781)
29.57 Lynn Chandnois, Pittsburgh, 1950-56 (92-2,720)
28.69 Abe Woodson, San Francisco, 1958-64; St. Louis, 1965-66 (193-5,538)

Highest Average, Season (Qualifiers)
41.06 Travis Williams, Green Bay, 1967 (18-739)
37.69 Gale Sayers, Chicago, 1967 (16-603)
35.50 Ollie Matson, Chi. Cardinals, 1958 (14-497)

Highest Average, Rookie, Season (Qualifiers)
41.06 Travis Williams, Green Bay, 1967 (18-739)
33.08 Tom Moore, Green Bay, 1960 (12-397)
32.88 Duriel Harris, Miami, 1976 (17-559)

Highest Average, Game (3 returns)
73.50 Wally Triplett, Detroit vs. Los Angeles, Oct. 29, 1950 (4-294)
67.33 Lenny Lyles, San Francisco vs. Baltimore, Dec. 18, 1960 (3-202)
65.33 Ken Hall, Houston vs. N.Y. Titans, Oct. 23, 1960 (3-196)

Touchdowns

Most Touchdowns, Career
6 Ollie Matson, Chi. Cardinals, 1952, 1954-58; L.A. Rams, 1959-62; Detroit, 1963; Philadelphia, 1964
Gale Sayers, Chicago, 1965-71
Travis Williams, Green Bay, 1967-70; Los Angeles, 1971
5 Bobby Mitchell, Cleveland, 1958-61; Washington, 1962-68
Abe Woodson, San Francisco, 1958-64; St. Louis, 1965-66
Timmy Brown, Green Bay, 1959; Philadelphia, 1960-67; Baltimore, 1968
4 Cecil Turner, Chicago, 1968-73
Ron Brown, L.A. Rams, 1984-87

Most Touchdowns, Season
4 Travis Williams, Green Bay, 1967
Cecil Turner, Chicago, 1970
3 Verda (Vitamin T) Smith, Los Angeles, 1950
Abe Woodson, San Francisco, 1963
Gale Sayers, Chicago, 1967
Raymond Clayborn, New England, 1977
Ron Brown, L.A. Rams, 1985
2 By many players

Most Touchdowns, Rookie, Season
4 Travis Williams, Green Bay, 1967
3 Raymond Clayborn, New England, 1977
2 By seven players

Most Touchdowns, Game
2 Timmy Brown, Philadelphia vs. Dallas, Nov. 6, 1966
Travis Williams, Green Bay vs. Cleveland, Nov. 12, 1967
Ron Brown, L.A. Rams vs. Green Bay, Nov. 24, 1985

Combined Kick Returns

Most Combined Kick Returns, Career
510 Ron Smith, Chicago, 1965, 1970-72; Atlanta, 1966-67; Los Angeles, 1968-69; San Diego, 1973; Oakland, 1974 (p-235, k-275)
426 Bruce Harper, N.Y. Jets, 1977-84 (p-183, k-243)
423 Alvin Haymond, Baltimore, 1964-67; Philadelphia, 1968; Los Angeles, 1969-71; Washington, 1972; Houston, 1973 (p-253, k-170)

Most Combined Kick Returns, Season
100 Larry Jones, Washington, 1975 (p-53, k-47)
97 Stump Mitchell, St. Louis, 1981 (p-42, k-55)
94 Nesby Glasgow, Baltimore, 1979 (p-44, k-50)

Most Combined Kick Returns, Game
13 Stump Mitchell, St. Louis vs. Atlanta, Oct. 18, 1981 (p-6, k-7)
12 Mel Renfro, Dallas vs. Green Bay, Nov. 29, 1964 (p-4, k-8)
Larry Jones, Washington vs. Dallas, Dec. 13, 1975 (p-6, k-6)
Eddie Brown, Washington vs. Tampa Bay, Oct. 9, 1977 (p-11, k-1)
Nesby Glasgow, Baltimore vs. Denver, Sept. 2, 1979 (p-9, k-3)
11 By many players

Yards Gained

Most Yards Returned, Career

8,710 Ron Smith, Chicago, 1965, 1970-72; Atlanta, 1966-67; Los Angeles, 1968-69; San Diego, 1973; Oakland, 1974 (p-1,788, k-6,922)
7,191 Bruce Harper, N.Y. Jets, 1977-84 (p-1,784, k-5,407)
6,740 Les (Speedy) Duncan, San Diego, 1964-70; Washington, 1971-74 (p-2,201, k-4,539)

Most Yards Returned, Season

1,737 Stump Mitchell, St. Louis, 1981 (p-445, k-1,292)
1,658 Bruce Harper, N.Y. Jets, 1978 (p-378, k-1,280)
1,591 Mike Nelms, Washington, 1981 (p-492, k-1,099)

Most Yards Returned, Game

294 Wally Triplett, Detroit vs. Los Angeles, Oct. 29, 1950 (k-294)
Woodley Lewis, Los Angeles vs. Detroit, Oct. 18, 1953 (p-120, k-174)
289 Eddie Payton, Detroit vs. Minnesota, Dec. 17, 1977 (p-105, k-184)
282 Les (Speedy) Duncan, San Diego vs. N.Y. Jets, Nov. 24, 1968 (p-102, k-180)

Touchdowns

Most Touchdowns, Career

9 Ollie Matson, Chi. Cardinals, 1952, 1954-58; Los Angeles, 1959-62; Detroit, 1963; Philadelphia, 1964-66 (p-3, k-6)
8 Jack Christiansen, Detroit, 1951-58 (p-8)
Bobby Mitchell, Cleveland, 1958-61; Washington, 1962-68 (p-3, k-5)
Gale Sayers, Chicago, 1965-71 (p-2, k-6)
Rick Upchurch, Denver, 1975-83 (p-8)
Billy Johnson, Houston, 1974-80; Atlanta, 1982-87 (p-6, k-2)
7 Abe Woodson, San Francisco, 1958-64; St. Louis, 1965-66 (p-2, k-5)

Most Touchdowns, Season

4 Jack Christiansen, Detroit, 1951 (p-4)
Emlen Tunnell, N.Y. Giants, 1951 (p-3, k-1)
Gale Sayers, Chicago, 1967 (p-1, k-3)
Travis Williams, Green Bay, 1967 (k-4)
Cecil Turner, Chicago, 1970 (k-4)
Billy Johnson, Houston, 1975 (p-3, k-1)
Rick Upchurch, Denver, 1976 (p-4)
3 Verda (Vitamin T) Smith, Los Angeles, 1950 (k-3)
Abe Woodson, San Francisco, 1963 (k-3)
Raymond Clayborn, New England, 1977 (k-3)
Billy Johnson, Houston, 1977 (p-2, k-1)
LeRoy Irvin, Los Angeles, 1981 (p-3)
Ron Brown, L.A. Rams, 1985 (k-3)
2 By many players

Most Touchdowns, Game

2 Jack Christiansen, Detroit vs. Los Angeles, Oct. 14, 1951 (p-2); vs. Green Bay, Nov. 22, 1951 (p-2)
Jim Patton, N.Y. Giants vs. Washington, Oct. 30, 1955 (p-1, k-1)
Bobby Mitchell, Cleveland vs. Philadelphia, Nov. 23, 1958 (p-1, k-1)
Dick Christy, N.Y. Titans vs. Denver, Sept. 24, 1961 (p-2)
Al Frazier, Denver vs. Boston, Dec. 3, 1961 (p-1, k-1)
Timmy Brown, Philadelphia vs. Dallas, Nov. 6, 1966 (k-2)
Travis Williams, Green Bay vs. Cleveland, Nov. 12, 1967 (k-2); vs. Pittsburgh, Nov. 2, 1969 (p-1, k-1)
Gale Sayers, Chicago vs. San Francisco, Dec. 3, 1967 (p-1, k-1)
Rick Upchurch, Denver vs. Cleveland, Sept. 26, 1976 (p-2)
Eddie Payton, Detroit vs. Minnesota, Dec. 17, 1977 (p-1, k-1)
LeRoy Irvin, Los Angeles vs. Atlanta, Oct. 11, 1981 (p-2)
Ron Brown, L.A. Rams vs. Green Bay, Nov. 24, 1985 (k-2)
Vai Sikahema, St. Louis vs. Tampa Bay, Dec. 21, 1986 (p-2)

Fumbles

Most Fumbles, Career

106 Dan Fouts, San Diego, 1973-87
105 Roman Gabriel, Los Angeles, 1962-72; Philadelphia, 1973-77
95 Johnny Unitas, Baltimore, 1956-72; San Diego, 1973

Most Fumbles, Season

17 Dan Pastorini, Houston, 1973
Warren Moon, Houston, 1984
16 Don Meredith, Dallas, 1964
Joe Cribbs, Buffalo, 1980
Steve Fuller, Kansas City, 1980
Paul McDonald, Cleveland, 1984
Phil Simms, N.Y. Giants, 1985
15 Paul Christman, Chi. Cardinals, 1946
Sammy Baugh, Washington, 1947
Sam Etcheverry, St. Louis, 1961
Len Dawson, Kansas City, 1964
Terry Metcalf, St. Louis, 1976
Steve DeBerg, Tampa Bay, 1984

Most Fumbles, Game

7 Len Dawson, Kansas City vs. San Diego, Nov. 15, 1964
6 Sam Etcheverry, St. Louis vs. N.Y. Giants, Sept. 17, 1961
5 Paul Christman, Chi. Cardinals vs. Green Bay, Nov. 10, 1946
Charlie Conerly, N.Y. Giants vs. San Francisco, Dec. 1, 1957
Jack Kemp, Buffalo vs. Houston, Oct. 29, 1967
Roman Gabriel, Philadelphia vs. Oakland, Nov. 21, 1976
Randall Cunningham, Philadelphia vs. L.A. Raiders, Nov. 30, 1986 (OT)
Willie Totten, Buffalo vs. Indianapolis, Oct. 4, 1987
Dave Walter, Cincinnati vs. Seattle, Oct. 11, 1987

Fumbles Recovered

Most Fumbles Recovered, Career, Own and Opponents'

43 Fran Tarkenton, Minnesota, 1961-66, 1972-78; N.Y. Giants, 1967-71 (43 own)
38 Jack Kemp, Pittsburgh, 1957; L.A. Chargers, 1960; San Diego, 1961-62; Buffalo, 1962-67, 1969 (38 own)
Dan Fouts, San Diego, 1973-87 (37 own, 1 opp)
37 Roman Gabriel, Los Angeles, 1962-72; Philadelphia, 1973-77 (37 own)

Most Fumbles Recovered, Season, Own and Opponents'

9 Don Hultz, Minnesota, 1963 (9 opp)
8 Paul Christman, Chi. Cardinals, 1945 (8 own)
Joe Schmidt, Detroit, 1955 (8 opp)
Bill Butler, Minnesota, 1963 (8 own)
Kermit Alexander, San Francisco, 1965 (4 own, 4 opp)
Jack Lambert, Pittsburgh, 1976 (1 own, 7 opp)
Danny White, Dallas, 1981 (8 own)
7 By many players

Most Fumbles Recovered, Game, Own and Opponents'

4 Otto Graham, Cleveland vs. N.Y. Giants, Oct. 25, 1953 (4 own)
Sam Etcheverry, St. Louis vs. N.Y. Giants, Sept. 17, 1961 (4 own)
Roman Gabriel, Los Angeles vs. San Francisco, Oct. 12, 1969 (4 own)
Joe Ferguson, Buffalo vs. Miami, Sept. 18, 1977 (4 own)
Randall Cunningham, Philadelphia vs. L.A. Raiders, Nov. 30, 1986 (OT) (4 own)
3 By many players

Own Fumbles Recovered

Most Own Fumbles Recovered, Career

43 Fran Tarkenton, Minnesota, 1961-66, 1972-78; N.Y. Giants, 1967-71
38 Jack Kemp, Pittsburgh, 1957; L.A. Chargers, 1960; San Diego, 1961-62; Buffalo, 1962-67, 1969
37 Roman Gabriel, Los Angeles, 1962-72; Philadelphia, 1973-77
Dan Fouts, San Diego, 1973-87

Most Own Fumbles Recovered, Season

8 Paul Christman, Chi. Cardinals, 1945
Bill Butler, Minnesota, 1963
Danny White, Dallas, 1981
7 Sammy Baugh, Washington, 1947
Tommy Thompson, Philadelphia, 1947
John Roach, St. Louis, 1960
Jack Larscheid, Oakland, 1960
Gary Huff, Chicago, 1974
Terry Metcalf, St. Louis, 1974
Joe Ferguson, Buffalo, 1977
Fran Tarkenton, Minnesota, 1978
Greg Pruitt, L.A. Raiders, 1983
Warren Moon, Houston, 1984
6 By many players

Most Own Fumbles Recovered, Game

4 Otto Graham, Cleveland vs. N.Y. Giants, Oct. 25, 1953
Sam Etcheverry, St. Louis vs. N.Y. Giants, Sept. 17, 1961
Roman Gabriel, Los Angeles vs. San Francisco, Oct. 12, 1969
Joe Ferguson, Buffalo vs. Miami, Sept. 18, 1977
Randall Cunningham, Philadelphia vs. L.A. Raiders, Nov. 30, 1986 (OT)
3 By many players

Opponents' Fumbles Recovered

Most Opponents' Fumbles Recovered, Career

29 Jim Marshall, Cleveland, 1960; Minnesota, 1961-79
25 Dick Butkus, Chicago, 1965-73
23 Carl Eller, Minnesota, 1964-78; Seattle, 1979
Reggie Williams, Cincinnati, 1976-87

Most Opponents' Fumbles Recovered, Season

9 Don Hultz, Minnesota, 1963
8 Joe Schmidt, Detroit, 1955
7 Alan Page, Minnesota, 1970
Jack Lambert, Pittsburgh, 1976

Most Opponents' Fumbles Recovered, Game

3 Corwin Clatt, Chi. Cardinals vs. Detroit, Nov. 6, 1949
Vic Sears, Philadelphia vs. Green Bay, Nov. 2, 1952
Ed Beatty, San Francisco vs. Los Angeles, Oct. 7, 1956
Ron Carroll, Houston vs. Cincinnati, Oct. 27, 1974
Maurice Spencer, New Orleans vs. Atlanta, Oct. 10, 1976
Steve Nelson, New England vs. Philadelphia, Oct. 8, 1978
Charles Jackson, Kansas City vs. Pittsburgh, Sept. 6, 1981
Willie Buchanon, San Diego vs. Denver, Sept. 27, 1981
Joey Browner, Minnesota vs. San Francisco, Sept. 8, 1985
2 By many players

Yards Returning Fumbles

Longest Fumble Run (All TDs)

104 Jack Tatum, Oakland vs. Green Bay, Sept. 24, 1972 (opp)
98 George Halas, Chi. Bears vs. Oorang Indians, Marion, Ohio, Nov. 4, 1923 (opp)
97 Chuck Howley, Dallas vs. Atlanta, Oct. 2, 1966 (opp)

Touchdowns

Most Touchdowns, Career (Total)

4 Bill Thompson, Denver, 1969-81
3 Ralph Heywood, Detroit, 1947-48; Boston, 1948; N.Y. Bulldogs, 1949
Leo Sugar, Chi. Cardinals, 1954-59; St. Louis, 1960; Philadelphia, 1961; Detroit, 1962
Bud McFadin, Los Angeles, 1952-56; Denver, 1960-63; Houston, 1964-65
Doug Cline, Houston, 1960-66; San Diego, 1966
Bob Lilly, Dall. Cowboys, 1961-74
Chris Hanburger, Washington, 1965-78
Lemar Parrish, Cincinnati, 1970-77; Washington, 1978-81; Buffalo, 1982
Paul Krause, Washington, 1964-67; Minnesota, 1968-79
Brad Dusek, Washington, 1974-81
David Logan, Tampa Bay, 1979-86; Green Bay, 1987
Thomas Howard, Kansas City, 1977-83; St. Louis, 1984-85
2 By many players

Most Touchdowns, Season (Total)

2 Harold McPhail, Boston, 1934
Harry Ebding, Detroit, 1937
John Morelli, Boston, 1944
Frank Maznicki, Boston, 1947
Fred (Dippy) Evans, Chi. Bears, 1948
Ralph Heywood, Boston, 1948
Art Tait, N.Y. Yanks, 1951
John Dwyer, Los Angeles, 1952
Leo Sugar, Chi. Cardinals, 1957
Doug Cline, Houston, 1961
Jim Bradshaw, Pittsburgh, 1964
Royce Berry, Cincinnati, 1970
Ahmad Rashad, Buffalo, 1974
Tim Gray, Kansas City, 1977
Charles Phillips, Oakland, 1978
Kenny Johnson, Atlanta, 1981

George Martin, N.Y. Giants, 1981
Del Rodgers, Green Bay, 1982
Mike Douglass, Green Bay, 1983
Shelton Robinson, Seattle, 1983

Most Touchdowns, Career (Own recovered)
2 Ken Kavanaugh, Chi. Bears, 1940-41, 1945-50
Mike Ditka, Chicago, 1961-66; Philadelphia, 1967-68; Dallas, 1969-72
Gail Cogdill, Detroit, 1960-68; Baltimore, 1968; Atlanta, 1969-70
Ahmad Rashad, St. Louis, 1972-73; Buffalo, 1974; Minnesota, 1976-82
Jim Mitchell, Atlanta, 1969-79
Drew Pearson, Dallas, 1973-83
Del Rodgers, Green Bay, 1982, 1984; San Francisco, 1987

Most Touchdowns, Season (Own recovered)
2 Ahmad Rashad, Buffalo, 1974
Del Rodgers, Green Bay, 1982
1 By many players

Most Touchdowns, Career (Opponents' recovered)
3 Leo Sugar, Chi. Cardinals, 1954-59; St. Louis, 1960; Philadelphia, 1961; Detroit, 1962
Doug Cline, Houston, 1960-66; San Diego, 1966
Bud McFadin, Los Angeles, 1952-56; Denver, 1960-63; Houston, 1964-65
Bob Lilly, Dall. Cowboys, 1961-74
Chris Hanburger, Washington, 1965-78
Paul Krause, Washington, 1964-67; Minnesota, 1968-79
Lemar Parrish, Cincinnati, 1970-77; Washington, 1978-81; Buffalo, 1982
Bill Thompson, Denver, 1969-81
Brad Dusek, Washington, 1974-81
David Logan, Tampa Bay, 1979-86; Green Bay, 1987
Thomas Howard, Kansas City, 1977-83; St. Louis, 1984-85
2 By many players

Most Touchdowns, Season (Opponents' recovered)
2 Harold McPhail, Boston, 1934
Harry Ebding, Detroit, 1937
John Morelli, Boston, 1944
Frank Maznicki, Boston, 1947
Fred (Dippy) Evans, Chi. Bears, 1948
Ralph Heywood, Boston, 1948
Art Tait, N.Y. Yanks, 1951
John Dwyer, Los Angeles, 1952
Leo Sugar, Chi. Cardinals, 1957
Doug Cline, Houston, 1961
Jim Bradshaw, Pittsburgh, 1964
Royce Berry, Cincinnati, 1970
Tim Gray, Kansas City, 1977
Charles Phillips, Oakland, 1978
Kenny Johnson, Atlanta, 1981
George Martin, N.Y. Giants, 1981
Mike Douglass, Green Bay, 1983
Shelton Robinson, Seattle, 1983

Most Touchdowns, Game (Opponents' recovered)
2 Fred (Dippy) Evans, Chi. Bears vs. Washington, Nov. 28, 1948

Combined Net Yards Gained

Rushing, receiving, interception returns, punt returns, kickoff returns, and fumble returns

Most Seasons Leading League
5 Jim Brown, Cleveland, 1958-61, 1964
3 Cliff Battles, Boston, 1932-33; Washington, 1937
Gale Sayers, Chicago, 1965-67
Eric Dickerson, L.A. Rams, 1983-84, 1986
2 By many players

Most Consecutive Seasons Leading League
4 Jim Brown, Cleveland, 1958-61
3 Gale Sayers, Chicago, 1965-67
2 Cliff Battles, Boston, 1932-33
Charley Trippi, Chi. Cardinals, 1948-49
Timmy Brown, Philadelphia, 1962-63
Floyd Little, Denver, 1967-68
James Brooks, San Diego, 1981-82
Eric Dickerson, L.A. Rams, 1983-84

Attempts

Most Attempts, Career
4,368 Walter Payton, Chicago, 1975-87
3,281 Franco Harris, Pittsburgh, 1972-83; Seattle, 1984
3,174 John Riggins, N.Y. Jets, 1971-75; Washington, 1976-79, 1981-85

Most Attempts, Season
496 James Wilder, Tampa Bay, 1984
449 Marcus Allen, L.A. Raiders, 1985
442 Eric Dickerson, L.A. Rams, 1983

Most Attempts, Rookie, Season
442 Eric Dickerson, L.A. Rams, 1983
395 George Rogers, New Orleans, 1981
390 Joe Cribbs, Buffalo, 1980

Most Attempts, Game
48 James Wilder, Tampa Bay vs. Pittsburgh, Oct. 30, 1983
47 James Wilder, Tampa Bay vs. Green Bay, Sept. 30, 1984 (OT)
46 Gerald Riggs, Atlanta vs. L.A. Rams, Nov. 17, 1985

Yards Gained

Most Yards Gained, Career
21,803 Walter Payton, Chicago, 1975-87
15,501 Tony Dorsett, Dallas, 1977-87
15,459 Jim Brown, Cleveland, 1957-65

Most Yards Gained, Season
2,535 Lionel James, San Diego, 1985
2,462 Terry Metcalf, St. Louis, 1975
2,444 Mack Herron, New England, 1974

Most Yards Gained, Rookie, Season
2,272 Gale Sayers, Chicago, 1965
2,212 Eric Dickerson, L.A. Rams, 1983
2,100 Abner Haynes, Dall. Texans, 1960

Most Yards Gained, Game
373 Billy Cannon, Houston vs. N.Y. Titans, Dec. 10, 1961
345 Lionel James, San Diego vs. L.A. Raiders, Nov. 10, 1985 (OT)
341 Timmy Brown, Philadelphia vs. St. Louis, Dec. 16, 1962

Sacks

Sacks have been compiled since 1982.

Most Sacks, Career
73.5 Lawrence Taylor, N.Y. Giants, 1982-87
73 Dexter Manley, Washington, 1982-87
67 Mark Gastineau, N.Y. Jets, 1982-87
Jacob Green, Seattle, 1982-87

Most Sacks, Season
22 Mark Gastineau, N.Y. Jets, 1984
21 Reggie White, Philadelphia, 1987
20.5 Lawrence Taylor, N.Y. Giants, 1986

Most Sacks, Game
6 Fred Dean, San Francisco vs. New Orleans, Nov. 13, 1983
5.5 William Gay, Detroit vs. Tampa Bay, Sept. 4, 1983
5 Howie Long, L.A. Raiders vs. Washington, Oct. 2, 1983
Randy Holloway, Minnesota vs. Atlanta, Sept. 16, 1984
Jim Jeffcoat, Dallas vs. Washington, Nov. 10, 1985
Leslie O'Neal, San Diego vs. Dallas, Nov. 16, 1986

Miscellaneous

Longest Return of Missed Field Goal (All TDs)
101 Al Nelson, Philadelphia vs. Dallas, Sept. 26, 1971
100 Al Nelson, Philadelphia vs. Cleveland, Dec. 11, 1966
Ken Ellis, Green Bay vs. N.Y. Giants, Sept. 19, 1971
99 Jerry Williams, Los Angeles vs. Green Bay, Dec. 16, 1951
Carl Taseff, Baltimore vs. Los Angeles, Dec. 12, 1959
Timmy Brown, Philadelphia vs. St. Louis, Sept. 16, 1962

Team Records

Championships

Most Seasons League Champion
11 Green Bay, 1929-31, 1936, 1939, 1944, 1961-62, 1965-67
9 Chi. Bears, 1921, 1932-33, 1940-41, 1943, 1946, 1963, 1985
5 N.Y. Giants, 1927, 1934, 1938, 1956, 1986

Most Consecutive Seasons League Champion
3 Green Bay, 1929-31, 1965-67
2 Canton, 1922-23
Chi. Bears, 1932-33, 1940-41
Philadelphia, 1948-49
Detroit, 1952-53
Cleveland, 1954-55
Baltimore, 1958-59
Houston, 1960-61
Green Bay, 1961-62
Buffalo, 1964-65
Miami, 1972-73
Pittsburgh, 1974-75, 1978-79

Most Times Finishing First, Regular Season (Since 1933)
17 Clev. Browns, 1950-55, 1957, 1964-65, 1967-69, 1971, 1980, 1985-87
15 Clev./L.A. Rams, 1945, 1949-51, 1955, 1967, 1969, 1973-79, 1985
N.Y. Giants, 1933-35, 1938-39, 1941, 1944, 1946, 1956, 1958-59, 1961-63, 1986
14 Chi. Bears, 1933-34, 1937, 1940-43, 1946, 1956, 1963, 1984-87

Most Consecutive Times Finishing First, Regular Season (Since 1933)
7 Los Angeles, 1973-79
6 Cleveland, 1950-55
Dallas, 1966-71
Minnesota, 1973-78
Pittsburgh, 1974-79
5 Oakland, 1972-76

Games Won

Most Consecutive Games Won (Incl. postseason games)
18 Chi. Bears, 1933-34, 1941-42
Miami, 1972-73
17 Oakland, 1976-77
14 Washington, 1942-43

Most Consecutive Games Won (Regular season)
17 Chi. Bears, 1933-34
16 Chi. Bears, 1941-42
Miami, 1971-73; 1983-84
15 L.A. Chargers/San Diego, 1960-61

Most Consecutive Games Without Defeat (Incl. postseason games)
25 Canton, 1921-23 (won 22, tied 3)
23 Green Bay, 1928-30 (won 21, tied 2)
18 Chi. Bears, 1933-34 (won 18); 1941-42 (won 18)
Miami, 1972-73 (won 18)

Most Consecutive Games Without Defeat (Regular season)
25 Canton, 1921-23 (won 22, tied 3)
24 Chi. Bears, 1941-43 (won 23, tied 1)
23 Green Bay, 1928-30 (won 21, tied 2)

Most Games Won, Season (Incl. postseason games)
18 San Francisco, 1984
Chicago, 1985
17 Miami, 1972
Pittsburgh, 1978
N.Y. Giants, 1986
16 Oakland, 1976
San Francisco, 1981
Washington, 1983
Miami, 1984

Most Games Won, Season (Since 1932)
15 San Francisco, 1984
Chicago, 1985

14 Miami, 1972, 1984
Pittsburgh, 1978
Washington, 1983
Chicago, 1986
N.Y. Giants, 1986
13 Chi. Bears, 1934
Green Bay, 1962
Oakland, 1967, 1976
Baltimore, 1968
San Francisco, 1981, 1987
Denver, 1984

Most Consecutive Games Won, Season (Incl. postseason games)
17 Miami, 1972
13 Chi. Bears, 1934
Oakland, 1976
12 Minnesota, 1969
San Francisco, 1984
Chicago, 1985
N.Y. Giants, 1986

Most Consecutive Games Won, Season
14 Miami, 1972
13 Chi. Bears, 1934
12 Minnesota, 1969
Chicago, 1985

Most Consecutive Games Won, Start of Season
14 Miami, 1972, entire season
13 Chi. Bears, 1934, entire season
12 Chicago, 1985

Most Consecutive Games Won, End of Season
14 Miami, 1972, entire season
13 Chi. Bears, 1934, entire season
11 Chi. Bears, 1942, entire season
Cleveland, 1951

Most Consecutive Games Without Defeat, Season (Incl. postseason games)
17 Miami, 1972
13 Chi. Bears, 1926, 1934
Green Bay, 1929
Baltimore, 1967
Oakland, 1976
12 Canton, 1922, 1923
Minnesota, 1969
San Francisco, 1984
Chicago, 1985
N.Y. Giants, 1986

Most Consecutive Games Without Defeat, Season
14 Miami, 1972
13 Chi. Bears, 1926, 1934
Green Bay, 1929
Baltimore, 1967
12 Canton, 1922, 1923
Minnesota, 1969
Chicago, 1985

Most Consecutive Games Without Defeat, Start of Season
14 Miami, 1972, entire season
13 Chi. Bears, 1926, 1934, entire seasons
Green Bay, 1929, entire season
Baltimore, 1967
12 Canton, 1922, 1923, entire seasons
Chicago, 1985

Most Consecutive Games Without Defeat, End of Season
14 Miami, 1972, entire season
13 Green Bay, 1929, entire season
Chi. Bears, 1934, entire season
12 Canton, 1922, 1923, entire seasons

Most Consecutive Home Games Won
27 Miami, 1971-74
20 Green Bay, 1929-32
18 Oakland, 1968-70
Dallas, 1979-81

Most Consecutive Home Games Without Defeat
30 Green Bay, 1928-33 (won 27, tied 3)
27 Miami, 1971-74 (won 27)
18 Chi. Bears, 1932-35 (won 17, tied 1); 1941-44 (won 17, tied 1)
Oakland, 1968-70 (won 18)
Dallas, 1979-81 (won 18)

Most Consecutive Road Games Won
11 L.A. Chargers/San Diego, 1960-61
10 Chi. Bears, 1941-42
Dallas, 1968-69
9 Chi. Bears, 1933-34
Kansas City, 1966-67
Oakland, 1967-68, 1974-75, 1976-77
Pittsburgh, 1974-75
Washington, 1981-83
San Francisco, 1983-84

Most Consecutive Road Games Without Defeat
13 Chi. Bears, 1941-43 (won 12, tied 1)
12 Green Bay, 1928-30 (won 10, tied 2)
11 L.A. Chargers/San Diego, 1960-61 (won 11)
Los Angeles, 1966-68 (won 10, tied 1)

Most Shutout Games Won or Tied, Season (Since 1932)
7 Chi. Bears, 1932 (won 4, tied 3)
Green Bay, 1932 (won 6, tied 1)
Detroit, 1934 (won 7)
5 Chi. Cardinals, 1934 (won 5)
N.Y. Giants, 1944 (won 5)
Pittsburgh, 1976 (won 5)
4 By many teams

Most Consecutive Shutout Games Won or Tied (Since 1932)
7 Detroit, 1934 (won 7)
3 Chi. Bears, 1932 (tied 3)
Green Bay, 1932 (won 3)
New York, 1935 (won 3)
St. Louis, 1970 (won 3)
Pittsburgh, 1976 (won 3)
2 By many teams

Games Lost

Most Consecutive Games Lost
26 Tampa Bay, 1976-77
19 Chi. Cardinals, 1942-43, 1945
Oakland, 1961-62
18 Houston, 1972-73

Most Consecutive Games Without Victory
26 Tampa Bay, 1976-77 (lost 26)
23 Washington, 1960-61 (lost 20, tied 3)

Most Games Lost, Season (Since 1932)
15 New Orleans, 1980
14 Tampa Bay, 1976, 1983, 1985, 1986
San Francisco, 1978, 1979
Detroit, 1979
Baltimore, 1981
New England, 1981
Houston, 1983
Buffalo, 1984, 1985
13 Oakland, 1962
Chicago, 1969
Pittsburgh, 1969
Buffalo, 1971
Houston, 1972, 1973, 1984
Minnesota, 1984
Indianapolis, 1986

Most Consecutive Games Lost, Season
14 Tampa Bay, 1976
New Orleans, 1980
Baltimore, 1981
13 Oakland, 1962
Indianapolis, 1986
12 Tampa Bay, 1977

Most Consecutive Games Lost, Start of Season
14 Tampa Bay, 1976, entire season
New Orleans, 1980
13 Oakland, 1962
Indianapolis, 1986
12 Tampa Bay, 1977

Most Consecutive Games Lost, End of Season
14 Tampa Bay, 1976, entire season
13 Pittsburgh, 1969
11 Philadelphia, 1936
Detroit, 1942, entire season
Houston, 1972

Most Consecutive Games Without Victory, Season
14 Tampa Bay, 1976, entire season
New Orleans, 1980
Baltimore, 1981
13 Washington, 1961
Oakland, 1962
Indianapolis, 1986
12 Dall. Cowboys, 1960, entire season
Tampa Bay, 1977

Most Consecutive Games Without Victory, Start of Season
14 Tampa Bay, 1976, entire season
New Orleans, 1980
13 Washington, 1961
Oakland, 1962
Indianapolis, 1986
12 Dall. Cowboys, 1960, entire season
Tampa Bay, 1977

Most Consecutive Games Without Victory, End of Season
14 Tampa Bay, 1976, entire season
13 Pittsburgh, 1969
12 Dall. Cowboys, 1960, entire season

Most Consecutive Home Games Lost
13 Houston, 1972-73
Tampa Bay, 1976-77
11 Oakland, 1961-62
Los Angeles, 1961-63
10 Pittsburgh, 1937-39
Washington, 1960-61
N.Y. Giants, 1973-75
New Orleans, 1979-80

Most Consecutive Home Games Without Victory
13 Houston, 1972-73 (lost 13)
Tampa Bay, 1976-77 (lost 13)
12 Philadelphia, 1936-38 (lost 11, tied 1)
11 Washington, 1960-61 (lost 10, tied 1)
Oakland, 1961-62 (lost 11)
Los Angeles, 1961-63 (lost 11)

Most Consecutive Road Games Lost
23 Houston, 1981-84
22 Buffalo, 1983-86
19 Tampa Bay, 1983-85

Most Consecutive Road Games Without Victory
23 Houston, 1981-84 (lost 23)
22 Buffalo, 1983-86 (lost 22)
19 Tampa Bay, 1983-85 (lost 19)

Most Shutout Games Lost or Tied, Season (Since 1932)
6 Cincinnati, 1934 (lost 6)
Pittsburgh, 1934 (lost 6)
Philadelphia, 1936 (lost 6)
Tampa Bay, 1977 (lost 6)
5 Boston, 1932 (lost 4, tied 1), 1933 (lost 4, tied 1)
N.Y. Giants, 1932 (lost 4, tied 1)
Cincinnati, 1933 (lost 4, tied 1)
Brooklyn, 1934 (lost 5), 1942 (lost 5)

Detroit, 1942 (lost 5)
Tampa Bay, 1976 (lost 5)
4 By many teams

Most Consecutive Shutout Games Lost or Tied (Since 1932)
6 Brooklyn, 1942-43 (lost 6)
4 Chi. Bears, 1932 (lost 1, tied 3)
Philadelphia, 1936 (lost 4)
3 Chi. Cardinals, 1934 (lost 3), 1938 (lost 3)
Brooklyn, 1935 (lost 3), 1937 (lost 3)
Oakland, 1981 (lost 3)

Tie Games

Most Tie Games, Season
6 Chi. Bears, 1932
5 Frankford, 1929
4 Chi. Bears, 1924
Orange, 1929
Portsmouth, 1932

Most Consecutive Tie Games
3 Chi. Bears, 1932
2 By many teams

Scoring

Most Seasons Leading League
9 Chi. Bears, 1934-35, 1939, 1941-43, 1946-47, 1956
6 Green Bay, 1932, 1936-38, 1961-62
L.A. Rams, 1950-52, 1957, 1967, 1973
5 Oakland, 1967-69, 1974, 1977
Dall. Cowboys, 1966, 1968, 1971, 1978, 1980
San Diego, 1963, 1965, 1981-82, 1985

Most Consecutive Seasons Leading League
3 Green Bay, 1936-38
Chi. Bears, 1941-43
Los Angeles, 1950-52
Oakland, 1967-69

Points

Most Points, Season
541 Washington, 1983
513 Houston, 1961
Miami, 1984
479 Dallas, 1983

Fewest Points, Season (Since 1932)
37 Cincinnati/St. Louis, 1934
38 Cincinnati, 1933
Detroit, 1942
51 Pittsburgh, 1934
Philadelphia, 1936

Most Points, Game
72 Washington vs. N.Y. Giants, Nov. 27, 1966
70 Los Angeles vs. Baltimore, Oct. 22, 1950
65 Chi. Cardinals vs. N.Y. Bulldogs, Nov. 13, 1949
Los Angeles vs. Detroit, Oct. 29, 1950

Most Points, Both Teams, Game
113 Washington (72) vs. N.Y. Giants (41), Nov. 27, 1966
101 Oakland (52) vs. Houston (49), Dec. 22, 1963
99 Seattle (51) vs. Kansas City (48), Nov. 27, 1983 (OT)

Fewest Points, Both Teams, Game
0 In many games. Last time: N.Y. Giants vs. Detroit, Nov. 7, 1943

Most Points, Shutout Victory, Game
64 Philadelphia vs. Cincinnati, Nov. 6, 1934
62 Akron vs. Oorang, Oct. 29, 1922
60 Rock Island vs. Evansville, Oct. 15, 1922
Chi. Cardinals vs. Rochester, Oct. 7, 1923

Fewest Points, Shutout Victory, Game
2 Green Bay vs. Chi. Bears, Oct. 16, 1932
Chi. Bears vs. Green Bay, Sept. 18, 1938

Most Points Overcome to Win Game
28 San Francisco vs. New Orleans, Dec. 7, 1980 (OT) (trailed 7-35, won 38-35)
25 St. Louis vs. Tampa Bay, Nov. 8, 1987 (trailed 3-28, won 31-28)
24 Philadelphia vs. Washington, Oct. 27, 1946 (trailed 0-24, won 28-24)
Detroit vs. Baltimore, Oct. 20, 1957 (trailed 3-27, won 31-27)
Philadelphia vs. Chi. Cardinals, Oct. 25, 1959 (trailed 0-24, won 28-24)
Denver vs. Boston, Oct. 23, 1960 (trailed 0-24, won 31-24)
Miami vs. New England, Dec. 15, 1974 (trailed 0-24, won 34-27)
Minnesota vs. San Francisco, Dec. 4, 1977 (trailed 0-24, won 28-27)
Denver vs. Seattle, Sept. 23, 1979 (trailed 10-34, won 37-34)
Houston vs. Cincinnati, Sept. 23, 1979 (OT) (trailed 0-24, won 30-27)
L.A. Raiders vs. San Diego, Nov. 22, 1982 (trailed 0-24, won 28-24)

Most Points Overcome to Tie Game
31 Denver vs. Buffalo, Nov. 27, 1960 (trailed 7-38, tied 38-38)
28 Los Angeles vs. Philadelphia, Oct. 3, 1948 (trailed 0-28, tied 28-28)

Most Points, Each Half
1st: 49 Green Bay vs. Tampa Bay, Oct. 2, 1983
45 Green Bay vs. Cleveland, Nov. 12, 1967
2nd: 49 Chi. Bears vs. Philadelphia, Nov. 30, 1941
48 Chi. Cardinals vs. Baltimore, Oct. 2, 1950
N.Y. Giants vs. Baltimore, Nov. 19, 1950

Most Points, Both Teams, Each Half
1st: 70 Houston (35) vs. Oakland (35), Dec. 22, 1963
2nd: 65 Washington (38) vs. N.Y. Giants (27), Nov. 27, 1966

Most Points, One Quarter
41 Green Bay vs. Detroit, Oct. 7, 1945 (second quarter)
Los Angeles vs. Detroit, Oct. 29, 1950 (third quarter)
37 Los Angeles vs. Green Bay, Sept. 21, 1980 (second quarter)
35 Chi. Cardinals vs. Boston, Oct. 24, 1948 (third quarter)
Green Bay vs. Cleveland, Nov. 12, 1967 (first quarter); vs. Tampa Bay, Oct. 2, 1983 (second quarter)

Most Points, Both Teams, One Quarter
49 Oakland (28) vs. Houston (21), Dec. 22, 1963 (second quarter)
48 Green Bay (41) vs. Detroit (7), Oct. 7, 1945 (second quarter)
Los Angeles (41) vs. Detroit (7), Oct. 29, 1950 (third quarter)
47 St. Louis (27) vs. Philadelphia (20), Dec. 13, 1964 (second quarter)

Most Points, Each Quarter
1st: 35 Green Bay vs. Cleveland, Nov. 12, 1967
2nd: 41 Green Bay vs. Detroit, Oct. 7, 1945
3rd: 41 Los Angeles vs. Detroit, Oct. 29, 1950
4th: 31 Oakland vs. Denver, Dec. 17, 1960; vs. San Diego, Dec. 8, 1963
Atlanta vs. Green Bay, Sept. 13, 1981

Most Points, Both Teams, Each Quarter
1st: 42 Green Bay (35) vs. Cleveland (7), Nov. 12, 1967
2nd: 49 Oakland (28) vs. Houston (21), Dec. 22, 1963
3rd: 48 Los Angeles (41) vs. Detroit (7), Oct. 29, 1950
4th: 42 Chi. Cardinals (28) vs. Philadelphia (14), Dec. 7, 1947
Green Bay (28) vs. Chi. Bears (14), Nov. 6, 1955
N.Y. Jets (28) vs. Boston (14), Oct. 27, 1968
Pittsburgh (21) vs. Cleveland (21), Oct. 18, 1969

Most Consecutive Games Scoring
274 Cleveland, 1950-71
218 Dallas, 1970-85
217 Oakland, 1966-81

Touchdowns

Most Seasons Leading League, Touchdowns
13 Chi. Bears, 1932, 1934-35, 1939, 1941-44, 1946-48, 1956, 1965
7 Dall. Cowboys, 1966, 1968, 1971, 1973, 1977-78, 1980
6 Oakland, 1967-69, 1972, 1974, 1977
San Diego, 1963, 1965, 1979, 1981-82, 1985

Most Consecutive Seasons Leading League, Touchdowns
4 Chi. Bears, 1941-44
Los Angeles, 1949-52
3 Chi. Bears, 1946-48
Baltimore, 1957-59
Oakland, 1967-69
2 By many teams

Most Touchdowns, Season
70 Miami, 1984
66 Houston, 1961
64 Los Angeles, 1950

Fewest Touchdowns, Season (Since 1932)
3 Cincinnati, 1933
4 Cincinnati/St. Louis, 1934
5 Detroit, 1942

Most Touchdowns, Game
10 Philadelphia vs. Cincinnati, Nov. 6, 1934
Los Angeles vs. Baltimore, Oct. 22, 1950
Washington vs. N.Y. Giants, Nov. 27, 1966
9 Chi. Cardinals vs. Rochester, Oct. 7, 1923; vs. N.Y. Giants, Oct. 17, 1948; vs. N.Y. Bulldogs, Nov. 13, 1949
Los Angeles vs. Detroit, Oct. 29, 1950
Pittsburgh vs. N.Y. Giants, Nov. 30, 1952
Chicago vs. San Francisco, Dec. 12, 1965; vs. Green Bay, Dec. 7, 1980
8 By many teams.

Most Touchdowns, Both Teams, Game
16 Washington (10) vs. N.Y. Giants (6), Nov. 27, 1966
14 Chi. Cardinals (9) vs. N.Y. Giants (5), Oct. 17, 1948
Los Angeles (10) vs. Baltimore (4), Oct. 22, 1950
Houston (7) vs. Oakland (7), Dec. 22, 1963
13 New Orleans (7) vs. St. Louis (6), Nov. 2, 1969
Kansas City (7) vs. Seattle (6), Nov. 27, 1983 (OT)
San Diego (8) vs. Pittsburgh (5), Dec. 8, 1985
N.Y. Jets (7) vs. Miami (6), Sept. 21, 1986 (OT)

Most Consecutive Games Scoring Touchdowns
166 Cleveland, 1957-69
97 Oakland, 1966-73
96 Kansas City, 1963-70

Points After Touchdown

Most Points After Touchdown, Season
66 Miami, 1984
65 Houston, 1961
62 Washington, 1983

Fewest Points After Touchdown, Season
2 Chi. Cardinals, 1933
3 Cincinnati, 1933
Pittsburgh, 1934
4 Cincinnati/St. Louis, 1934

Most Points After Touchdown, Game
10 Los Angeles vs. Baltimore, Oct. 22, 1950
9 Chi. Cardinals vs. N.Y. Giants, Oct. 17, 1948
Pittsburgh vs. N.Y. Giants, Nov. 30, 1952
Washington vs. N.Y. Giants, Nov. 27, 1966
8 By many teams

Most Points After Touchdown, Both Teams, Game
14 Chi. Cardinals (9) vs. N.Y. Giants (5), Oct. 17, 1948
Houston (7) vs. Oakland (7), Dec. 22, 1963
Washington (9) vs. N.Y. Giants (5), Nov. 27, 1966
13 Los Angeles (10) vs. Baltimore (3), Oct. 22, 1950
12 In many games

Field Goals

Most Seasons Leading League, Field Goals
11 Green Bay, 1935-36, 1940-43, 1946-47, 1955, 1972, 1974
7 Washington, 1945, 1956, 1971, 1976-77, 1979, 1982
N.Y. Giants, 1933, 1937, 1939, 1941, 1944, 1959, 1983
5 Portsmouth/Detroit, 1932-33, 1937-38, 1980

Most Consecutive Seasons Leading League, Field Goals
4 Green Bay, 1940-43
3 Cleveland, 1952-54
2 By many teams

Most Field Goals Attempted, Season
49 Los Angeles, 1966
Washington, 1971
48 Green Bay, 1972

47 N.Y. Jets, 1969
Los Angeles, 1973
Washington, 1983

Fewest Field Goals Attempted, Season (Since 1938)
0 Chi. Bears, 1944
2 Cleveland, 1939
Card-Pitt, 1944
Boston, 1946
Chi. Bears, 1947
3 Chi. Bears, 1945
Cleveland, 1945

Most Field Goals Attempted, Game
9 St. Louis vs. Pittsburgh, Sept. 24, 1967
8 Pittsburgh vs. St. Louis, Dec. 2, 1962
Detroit vs. Minnesota, Nov. 13, 1966
N.Y. Jets vs. Buffalo, Nov. 3, 1968
7 By many teams

Most Field Goals Attempted, Both Teams, Game
11 St. Louis (6) vs. Pittsburgh (5), Nov. 13, 1966
Washington (6) vs. Chicago (5), Nov. 14, 1971
Green Bay (6) vs. Detroit (5), Sept. 29, 1974
Washington (6) vs. N.Y. Giants (5), Nov. 14, 1976
10 Denver (5) vs. Boston (5), Nov. 11, 1962
Boston (7) vs. San Diego (3), Sept. 20, 1964
Buffalo (7) vs. Houston (3), Dec. 5, 1965
St. Louis (7) vs. Atlanta (3), Dec. 11, 1966
Boston (7) vs. Buffalo (3), Sept. 24, 1967
Detroit (7) vs. Minnesota (3), Sept. 20, 1971
Washington (7) vs. Houston (3), Oct. 10, 1971
Green Bay (5) vs. St. Louis (5), Dec. 5, 1971
Kansas City (7) vs. Buffalo (3), Dec. 19, 1971
Kansas City (5) vs. San Diego (5), Oct. 29, 1972
Minnesota (6) vs. Chicago (4), Sept. 23, 1973
Cleveland (7) vs. Denver (3), Oct. 19, 1975
Cleveland (5) vs. Denver (5), Oct. 5, 1980
9 In many games

Most Field Goals, Season
35 N.Y. Giants, 1983
34 N.Y. Jets, 1968
33 Green Bay, 1972
Washington, 1983
Pittsburgh, 1985
New Orleans, 1987

Fewest Field Goals, Season (Since 1932)
0 Boston, 1932, 1935
Chi. Cardinals, 1932, 1945
Green Bay, 1932, 1944
N.Y. Giants, 1932
Brooklyn, 1944
Card-Pitt, 1944
Chi. Bears, 1944, 1947
Boston, 1946
Baltimore, 1950
Dallas, 1952

Most Field Goals, Game
7 St. Louis vs. Pittsburgh, Sept. 24, 1967
6 Boston vs. Denver, Oct. 4, 1964
Detroit vs. Minnesota, Nov. 13, 1966
N.Y. Jets vs. Buffalo, Nov. 3, 1968; vs. New Orleans, Dec. 3, 1972
Philadelphia vs. Houston, Nov. 12, 1972
St. Louis vs. Atlanta, Dec. 9, 1973
N.Y. Giants vs. Seattle, Oct. 18, 1981
San Francisco vs. New Orleans, Oct. 16, 1983
5 By many teams

Most Field Goals, Both Teams, Game
8 Cleveland (4) vs. St. Louis (4), Sept. 20, 1964
Chicago (5) vs. Philadelphia (3), Oct. 20, 1968
Washington (5) vs. Chicago (3), Nov. 14, 1971
Kansas City (5) vs. Buffalo (3), Dec. 19, 1971
Detroit (4) vs. Green Bay (4), Sept. 29, 1974
Cleveland (5) vs. Denver (3), Oct. 19, 1975
New England (4) vs. San Diego (4), Nov. 9, 1975
San Francisco (6) vs. New Orleans (2), Oct. 16, 1983
7 In many games

Most Consecutive Games Scoring Field Goals
31 Minnesota, 1968-70
21 San Francisco, 1970-72
20 Los Angeles, 1970-71
Miami, 1970-72

Safeties

Most Safeties, Season
4 Detroit, 1962
3 Green Bay, 1932, 1975
Pittsburgh, 1947
N.Y. Yanks, 1950
Detroit, 1960
St. Louis, 1960
Buffalo, 1964
Minnesota, 1965, 1981
Cleveland, 1970
L.A. Rams, 1973, 1984
Houston, 1977
Dallas, 1981
Oakland, 1981
Chicago, 1985
2 By many teams

Most Safeties, Game
3 L.A. Rams vs. N.Y. Giants, Sept. 30, 1984
2 Cincinnati vs. Chi. Cardinals, Nov. 19, 1933
Detroit vs. Brooklyn, Dec. 1, 1935
N.Y. Giants vs. Pittsburgh, Sept. 17, 1950; vs. Washington, Nov. 5, 1961
Chicago vs. Pittsburgh, Nov. 9, 1969
Dallas vs. Philadelphia, Nov. 19, 1972
Los Angeles vs. Green Bay, Oct. 21, 1973
Oakland vs. San Diego, Oct. 26, 1975
Denver vs. Seattle, Jan. 2, 1983
New Orleans vs. Cleveland, Sept. 13, 1987
Buffalo vs. Denver, Nov. 8, 1987

Most Safeties, Both Teams, Game
3 L.A. Rams (3) vs. N.Y. Giants (0), Sept. 30, 1984
2 Chi. Bears (1) vs. San Francisco (1), Oct. 19, 1952
Cincinnati (1) vs. Los Angeles (1), Oct. 22, 1972
Atlanta (1) vs. Detroit (1), Oct. 5, 1980
(Also see previous record)

First Downs

Most Seasons Leading League
9 Chi. Bears, 1935, 1939, 1941, 1943, 1945, 1947-49, 1955
7 San Diego, 1965, 1969, 1980-83, 1985
6 L.A. Rams, 1946, 1950-51, 1954, 1957, 1973

Most Consecutive Seasons Leading League
4 San Diego, 1980-83
3 Chi. Bears, 1947-49
2 By many teams

Most First Downs, Season
387 Miami, 1984
380 San Diego, 1985
379 San Diego, 1981

Fewest First Downs, Season
51 Cincinnati, 1933
64 Pittsburgh, 1935
67 Philadelphia, 1937

Most First Downs, Game
38 Los Angeles vs. N.Y. Giants, Nov. 13, 1966
37 Green Bay vs. Philadelphia, Nov. 11, 1962
36 Pittsburgh vs. Cleveland, Nov. 25, 1979 (OT)

Fewest First Downs, Game
0 N.Y. Giants vs. Green Bay, Oct. 1, 1933; vs. Washington, Sept. 27, 1942
Pittsburgh vs. Boston, Oct. 29, 1933
Philadelphia vs. Detroit, Sept. 20, 1935
Denver vs. Houston, Sept. 3, 1966

Most First Downs, Both Teams, Game
62 San Diego (32) vs. Seattle (30), Sept. 15, 1985
59 Miami (31) vs. Buffalo (28), Oct. 9, 1983 (OT)
Seattle (33) vs. Kansas City (26), Nov. 27, 1983 (OT)
N.Y. Jets (32) vs. Miami (27), Sept. 21, 1986 (OT)
58 Los Angeles (30) vs. Chi. Bears (28), Oct. 24, 1954
Denver (34) vs. Kansas City (24), Nov. 18, 1974
Atlanta (35) vs. New Orleans (23), Sept. 2, 1979 (OT)
Pittsburgh (36) vs. Cleveland (22), Nov. 25, 1979 (OT)
San Diego (34) vs. Miami (24), Nov. 18, 1984 (OT)
Cincinnati (32) vs. San Diego (26), Sept. 22, 1985

Fewest First Downs, Both Teams, Game
5 N.Y. Giants (0) vs. Green Bay (5), Oct. 1, 1933

Most First Downs, Rushing, Season
181 New England, 1978
177 Los Angeles, 1973
176 Chicago, 1985

Fewest First Downs, Rushing, Season
36 Cleveland, 1942
Boston, 1944
39 Brooklyn, 1943
40 Philadelphia, 1940
Detroit, 1945

Most First Downs, Rushing, Game
25 Philadelphia vs. Washington, Dec. 2, 1951
21 Cleveland vs. Philadelphia, Dec. 13, 1959
Los Angeles vs. New Orleans, Nov. 25, 1973
Pittsburgh vs. Kansas City, Nov. 7, 1976
New England vs. Denver, Nov. 28, 1976
Oakland vs. Green Bay, Sept. 17, 1978
20 By eight teams

Fewest First Downs, Rushing, Game
0 By many teams. Last time: New England vs. New Orleans, Nov. 30, 1986

Most First Downs, Passing, Season
259 San Diego, 1985
250 Miami, 1986
244 San Diego, 1980

Fewest First Downs, Passing, Season
18 Pittsburgh, 1941
23 Brooklyn, 1942
N.Y. Giants, 1944
24 N.Y. Giants, 1943

Most First Downs, Passing, Game
29 N.Y. Giants vs. Cincinnati, Oct. 13, 1985
27 San Diego vs. Seattle, Sept. 15, 1985
25 Denver vs. Kansas City, Nov. 18, 1974
N.Y Jets vs. San Francisco, Sept. 21, 1980

Fewest First Downs, Passing, Game
0 By many teams. Last time: St. Louis vs. New Orleans, Oct. 11, 1987

Most First Downs, Penalty, Season
42 Chicago, 1987
41 Denver, 1986
39 Seattle, 1978

Fewest First Downs, Penalty, Season
2 Brooklyn, 1940
4 Chi. Cardinals, 1940
N.Y. Giants, 1942, 1944
Washington, 1944
Cleveland, 1952
Kansas City, 1969

5 Brooklyn, 1939
Chi. Bears, 1939
Detroit, 1953
Los Angeles, 1953
Houston, 1982

Most First Downs, Penalty, Game
11 Denver vs. Houston, Oct. 6, 1985
9 Chi. Bears vs. Cleveland, Nov. 25, 1951
Baltimore vs. Pittsburgh, Oct. 30, 1977
8 Philadelphia vs. Detroit, Dec. 2, 1979
Cincinnati vs. N.Y. Jets, Oct. 6, 1985
Buffalo vs. Houston, Sept. 20, 1987

Fewest First Downs, Penalty, Game
0 By many teams

Net Yards Gained Rushing and Passing

Most Seasons Leading League
12 Chi. Bears, 1932, 1934-35, 1939, 1941-44, 1947, 1949, 1955-56
7 San Diego, 1963, 1965, 1980-83, 1985
6 L.A. Rams, 1946, 1950-51, 1954, 1957, 1973
Baltimore, 1958-60, 1964, 1967, 1976
Dall. Cowboys, 1966, 1968-69, 1971, 1974, 1977

Most Consecutive Seasons Leading League
4 Chi. Bears, 1941-44
San Diego, 1980-83
3 Baltimore, 1958-60
Houston, 1960-62
Oakland, 1968-70
2 By many teams

Most Yards Gained, Season
6,936 Miami, 1984
6,744 San Diego, 1981
6,535 San Diego, 1985

Fewest Yards Gained, Season
1,150 Cincinnati, 1933
1,443 Chi. Cardinals, 1934
1,486 Chi. Cardinals, 1933

Most Yards Gained, Game
735 Los Angeles vs. N.Y. Yanks, Sept. 28, 1951
683 Pittsburgh vs. Chi. Cardinals, Dec. 13, 1958
682 Chi. Bears vs. N.Y. Giants, Nov. 14, 1943

Fewest Yards Gained, Game
−7 Seattle vs. Los Angeles, Nov. 4, 1979
−5 Denver vs. Oakland, Sept. 10, 1967
14 Chi. Cardinals vs. Detroit, Sept. 15, 1940

Most Yards Gained, Both Teams, Game
1,133 Los Angeles (636) vs. N.Y. Yanks (497), Nov. 19, 1950
1,102 San Diego (661) vs. Cincinnati (441), Dec. 20, 1982
1,087 St. Louis (589) vs. Philadelphia (498), Dec. 16, 1962

Fewest Yards Gained, Both Teams, Game
30 Chi. Cardinals (14) vs. Detroit (16), Sept. 15, 1940

Most Consecutive Games, 400 or More Yards Gained
11 San Diego, 1982-83
6 Houston, 1961-62
San Diego, 1981
San Francisco, 1987
5 Chi. Bears, 1947, 1955
Los Angeles, 1950
Philadelphia, 1953
Oakland, 1968
New England, 1981
Cincinnati, 1986

Most Consecutive Games, 300 or More Yards Gained
29 Los Angeles, 1949-51
26 Miami, 1983-85
20 Chi. Bears, 1948-50

Rushing

Most Seasons Leading League
16 Chi. Bears, 1932, 1934-35, 1939-42, 1951, 1955-56, 1968, 1977, 1983-86
6 Cleveland, 1958-59, 1963, 1965-67
5 Buffalo, 1962, 1964, 1973, 1975, 1982

Most Consecutive Seasons Leading League
4 Chi. Bears, 1939-42, 1983-86
3 Detroit, 1936-38
San Francisco, 1952-54
Cleveland, 1965-67
2 By many teams

Most Rushing Attempts, Season
681 Oakland, 1977
674 Chicago, 1984
671 New England, 1978

Fewest Rushing Attempts, Season
211 Philadelphia, 1982
219 San Francisco, 1982
225 Houston, 1982

Most Rushing Attempts, Game
72 Chi. Bears vs. Brooklyn, Oct. 20, 1935
70 Chi. Cardinals vs. Green Bay, Dec. 5, 1948
69 Chi. Cardinals vs. Green Bay, Dec. 6, 1936
Kansas City vs. Cincinnati, Sept. 3, 1978

Fewest Rushing Attempts, Game
6 Chi. Cardinals vs. Boston, Oct. 29, 1933
7 Oakland vs. Buffalo, Oct. 15, 1963
Houston vs. N.Y. Giants, Dec. 8, 1985
8 Denver vs. Oakland, Dec. 17, 1960
Buffalo vs. St. Louis, Sept. 9, 1984

Most Rushing Attempts, Both Teams, Game
108 Chi. Cardinals (70) vs. Green Bay (38), Dec. 5, 1948
105 Oakland (62) vs. Atlanta (43), Nov. 30, 1975 (OT)
103 Kansas City (53) vs. San Diego (50), Nov. 12, 1978 (OT)

Fewest Rushing Attempts, Both Teams, Game
36 Cincinnati (16) vs. Chi. Bears (20), Sept. 30, 1934
37 Atlanta (18) vs. San Francisco (19), Oct. 6, 1985
38 N.Y. Jets (13) vs. Buffalo (25), Nov. 8, 1964

Yards Gained

Most Yards Gained Rushing, Season
3,165 New England, 1978
3,088 Buffalo, 1973
2,986 Kansas City, 1978

Fewest Yards Gained Rushing, Season
298 Philadelphia, 1940
467 Detroit, 1946
471 Boston, 1944

Most Yards Gained Rushing, Game
426 Detroit vs. Pittsburgh, Nov. 4, 1934
423 N.Y. Giants vs. Baltimore, Nov. 19, 1950
420 Boston vs. N.Y. Giants, Oct. 8, 1933

Fewest Yards Gained Rushing, Game
−53 Detroit vs. Chi. Cardinals, Oct. 17, 1943
−36 Philadelphia vs. Chi. Bears, Nov. 19, 1939
−33 Phil-Pitt vs. Brooklyn, Oct. 2, 1943

Most Yards Gained Rushing, Both Teams, Game
595 Los Angeles (371) vs. N.Y. Yanks (224), Nov. 18, 1951
574 Chi. Bears (396) vs. Pittsburgh (178), Oct. 10, 1934
557 Chi. Bears (406) vs. Green Bay (151), Nov. 6, 1955

Fewest Yards Gained Rushing, Both Teams, Game
−15 Detroit (−53) vs. Chi. Cardinals (38), Oct. 17, 1943
4 Detroit (−10) vs. Chi. Cardinals (14), Sept. 15, 1940
63 Chi. Cardinals (−1) vs. N.Y. Giants (64), Oct. 18, 1953

Average Gain

Highest Average Gain, Rushing, Season
5.74 Cleveland, 1963
5.65 San Francisco, 1954
5.56 San Diego, 1963

Lowest Average Gain, Rushing, Season
0.94 Philadelphia, 1940
1.45 Boston, 1944
1.55 Pittsburgh, 1935

Touchdowns

Most Touchdowns, Rushing, Season
36 Green Bay, 1962
33 Pittsburgh, 1976
30 Chi. Bears, 1941
New England, 1978
Washington, 1983

Fewest Touchdowns, Rushing, Season
1 Brooklyn, 1934
2 Chi. Cardinals, 1933
Cincinnati, 1933
Pittsburgh, 1934, 1940
Philadelphia, 1935, 1936, 1937, 1938, 1972
3 By many teams

Most Touchdowns, Rushing, Game
7 Los Angeles vs. Atlanta, Dec. 4, 1976
6 By many teams

Most Touchdowns, Rushing, Both Teams, Game
8 Los Angeles (6) vs. N.Y. Yanks (2), Nov. 18, 1951
Cleveland (6) vs. Los Angeles (2), Nov. 24, 1957
7 In many games

Passing

Attempts

Most Passes Attempted, Season
709 Minnesota, 1981
662 San Diego, 1984
645 Miami, 1986

Fewest Passes Attempted, Season
102 Cincinnati, 1933
106 Boston, 1933
120 Detroit, 1937

Most Passes Attempted, Game
68 Houston vs. Buffalo, Nov 1, 1964
65 San Diego vs. Kansas City, Oct. 19, 1986
63 Minnesota vs. Tampa Bay, Sept. 5, 1981

Fewest Passes Attempted, Game
0 Green Bay vs. Portsmouth, Oct. 8, 1933
Detroit vs. Cleveland, Sept. 10, 1937
Pittsburgh vs. Brooklyn, Nov. 16, 1941; vs. Los Angeles, Nov. 13, 1949
Cleveland vs. Philadelphia, Dec. 3, 1950

Most Passes Attempted, Both Teams, Game
104 Miami (55) vs. N.Y. Jets (49), Oct. 18, 1987 (OT)
102 San Francisco (57) vs. Atlanta (45), Oct. 6, 1985
100 Tampa Bay (54) vs. Kansas City (46), Oct. 28, 1984
San Francisco (60) vs. Washington (40), Nov. 17, 1986

Fewest Passes Attempted, Both Teams, Game
4 Chi. Cardinals (1) vs. Detroit (3), Nov. 3, 1935
Detroit (0) vs. Cleveland (4), Sept. 10, 1937
6 Chi. Cardinals (2) vs. Detroit (4), Sept. 15, 1940
8 Brooklyn (2) vs. Philadelphia (6), Oct. 1, 1939

Completions

Most Passes Completed, Season
401 San Diego, 1984
392 Miami, 1986
386 San Diego, 1985

Fewest Passes Completed, Season
25 Cincinnati, 1933
33 Boston, 1933
34 Chi. Cardinals, 1934
Detroit, 1934

Most Passes Completed, Game
42 N.Y. Jets vs. San Francisco, Sept. 21, 1980
40 Cincinnati vs. San Diego, Dec. 20, 1982
Dallas vs. Detroit, Sept. 15, 1985
N.Y. Giants vs. Cincinnati, Oct. 13, 1985
39 Miami vs. Buffalo, Nov. 16, 1986
Fewest Passes Completed, Game
0 By many teams. Last time: Buffalo vs. N.Y. Jets, Sept. 29, 1974
Most Passes Completed, Both Teams, Game
68 San Francisco (37) vs. Atlanta (31), Oct. 6, 1985
66 Cincinnati (40) vs. San Diego (26), Dec. 20, 1982
65 San Diego (33) vs. San Francisco (32), Dec. 11, 1982
San Diego (37) vs. Miami (28), Nov. 18, 1984 (OT)
Fewest Passes Completed, Both Teams, Game
1 Chi. Cardinals (0) vs. Philadelphia (1), Nov. 8, 1936
Detroit (0) vs. Cleveland (1), Sept. 10, 1937
Chi. Cardinals (0) vs. Detroit (1), Sept. 15, 1940
Brooklyn (0) vs. Pittsburgh (1), Nov. 29, 1942
2 Chi. Cardinals (0) vs. Detroit (2), Nov. 3, 1935
Buffalo (0) vs. N.Y. Jets (2), Sept. 29, 1974
3 Brooklyn (1) vs. Philadelphia (2), Oct. 1, 1939

Yards Gained
Most Seasons Leading League, Passing Yardage
10 San Diego, 1965, 1968, 1971, 1978-83, 1985
8 Chi. Bears, 1932, 1939, 1941, 1943, 1945, 1949, 1954, 1964
7 Washington, 1938, 1940, 1944, 1947-48, 1967, 1974
Most Consecutive Seasons Leading League, Passing Yardage
6 San Diego, 1978-83
4 Green Bay, 1934-37
2 By many teams
Most Yards Gained, Passing, Season
5,018 Miami, 1984
4,870 San Diego, 1985
4,779 Miami, 1986
Fewest Yards Gained, Passing, Season
302 Chi. Cardinals, 1934
357 Cincinnati, 1933
459 Boston, 1934
Most Yards Gained, Passing, Game
554 Los Angeles vs. N.Y. Yanks, Sept. 28, 1951
530 Minnesota vs. Baltimore, Sept. 28, 1969
506 L.A. Rams vs. Chicago, Dec. 26, 1982
Fewest Yards Gained, Passing, Game
−53 Denver vs. Oakland, Sept. 10, 1967
−52 Cincinnati vs. Houston, Oct. 31, 1971
−39 Atlanta vs. San Francisco, Oct. 23, 1976
Most Yards Gained, Passing, Both Teams, Game
884 N.Y. Jets (449) vs. Miami (435), Sept. 21, 1986 (OT)
883 San Diego (486) vs. Cincinnati (397), Dec. 20, 1982
849 Minnesota (471) vs. Washington (378), Nov. 2, 1986 (OT)
Fewest Yards Gained, Passing, Both Teams, Game
−11 Green Bay (−10) vs. Dallas (−1), Oct. 24, 1965
1 Chi. Cardinals (0) vs. Philadelphia (1), Nov. 8, 1936
7 Brooklyn (0) vs. Pittsburgh (7), Nov. 29, 1942

Times Sacked
Most Seasons Leading League, Fewest Times Sacked
7 Miami, 1973, 1982-87
4 San Diego, 1963-64, 1967-68
San Francisco, 1964-65, 1970-71
3 N.Y. Jets, 1965-66, 1968
Houston, 1961-62, 1978
St. Louis, 1974-76
Most Consecutive Seasons Leading League, Fewest Times Sacked
6 Miami, 1982-87
3 St. Louis, 1974-76
2 By many teams
Most Times Sacked, Season
104 Philadelphia, 1986
72 Philadelphia, 1987
70 Atlanta, 1968
Fewest Times Sacked, Season
8 San Francisco, 1970
St. Louis, 1975
9 N.Y. Jets, 1966
10 N.Y. Giants, 1972
Most Times Sacked, Game
12 Pittsburgh vs. Dallas, Nov. 20, 1966
Baltimore vs. St. Louis, Oct. 26, 1980
Detroit vs. Chicago, Dec. 16, 1984
Houston vs. Dallas, Sept. 29, 1985
11 St. Louis vs. N.Y. Giants, Nov. 1, 1964
Los Angeles vs. Baltimore, Nov. 22, 1964
Denver vs. Buffalo, Dec. 13, 1964; vs. Oakland, Nov. 5, 1967
Green Bay vs. Detroit, Nov. 7, 1965
Buffalo vs. Oakland, Oct. 15, 1967
Atlanta vs. St. Louis, Nov. 24, 1968; vs. Cleveland, Nov. 18, 1984
Detroit vs. Dallas, Oct. 6, 1975
Philadelphia vs. St. Louis, Dec. 18, 1983; vs. Detroit, Nov. 16, 1986; vs. L.A. Raiders, Nov. 30, 1986 (OT); vs. Chicago, Oct. 4, 1987
Cleveland vs. Kansas City, Sept. 30, 1984
Minnesota vs. Chicago, Oct. 28, 1984
Dallas vs. San Diego, Nov. 16, 1986
L.A. Raiders vs. Seattle, Dec. 8, 1986
N.Y. Jets vs. Dallas, Oct. 4, 1987
10 By many teams
Most Times Sacked, Both Teams, Game
18 Green Bay (10) vs. San Diego (8), Sept. 24, 1978
17 Buffalo (10) vs. N.Y. Titans (7), Nov. 23, 1961
Pittsburgh (12) vs. Dallas (5), Nov. 20, 1966
Atlanta (9) vs. Philadelphia (8), Dec. 16, 1984
Philadelphia (11) vs. L.A. Raiders (6), Nov. 30, 1986 (OT)
16 Los Angeles (11) vs. Baltimore (5), Nov. 22, 1964
Buffalo (11) vs. Oakland (5), Oct. 15, 1967

Completion Percentage
Most Seasons Leading League, Completion Percentage
11 Washington, 1937, 1939-40, 1942-45, 1947-48, 1969-70
7 Green Bay, 1936, 1941, 1961-62, 1964, 1966, 1968
San Francisco, 1952, 1957-58, 1965, 1981, 1983, 1987
6 Cleveland, 1951, 1953-55, 1959-60
Dall. Texans/Kansas City, 1962, 1964, 1966-69
Most Consecutive Seasons Leading League, Completion Percentage
4 Washington, 1942-45
Kansas City, 1966-69
3 Cleveland, 1953-55
2 By many teams
Highest Completion Percentage, Season
70.645 Cincinnati, 1982 (310-219)
64.271 San Francisco, 1987 (501-322)
64.266 Oakland, 1976 (361-232)
Lowest Completion Percentage, Season
22.9 Philadelphia, 1936 (170-39)
24.5 Cincinnati, 1933 (102-25)
25.0 Pittsburgh, 1941 (168-42)

Touchdowns
Most Touchdowns, Passing, Season
49 Miami, 1984
48 Houston, 1961
46 Miami, 1986
Fewest Touchdowns, Passing, Season
0 Cincinnati, 1933
Pittsburgh, 1945
1 Boston, 1932, 1933
Chi. Cardinals, 1934
Cincinnati/St. Louis, 1934
Detroit, 1942
2 Chi. Cardinals, 1932, 1935
Stapleton, 1932
Brooklyn, 1936
Pittsburgh, 1942
Most Touchdowns, Passing, Game
7 Chi. Bears vs. N.Y. Giants, Nov. 14, 1943
Philadelphia vs. Washington, Oct. 17, 1954
Houston vs. N.Y. Titans, Nov. 19, 1961; vs. N.Y. Titans, Oct. 14, 1962
N.Y. Giants vs. Washington, Oct. 28, 1962
Minnesota vs. Baltimore, Sept. 28, 1969
San Diego vs. Oakland, Nov. 22, 1981
6 By many teams.
Most Touchdowns, Passing, Both Teams, Game
12 New Orleans (6) vs. St. Louis (6), Nov. 2, 1969
11 N.Y. Giants (7) vs. Washington (4), Oct. 28, 1962
Oakland (6) vs. Houston (5), Dec. 22, 1963
10 Miami (6) vs. N.Y. Jets (4), Sept. 21, 1986 (OT)

Passes Had Intercepted
Most Passes Had Intercepted, Season
48 Houston, 1962
45 Denver, 1961
41 Card-Pitt, 1944
Fewest Passes Had Intercepted, Season
5 Cleveland, 1960
Green Bay, 1966
6 Green Bay, 1964
St. Louis, 1982
7 Los Angeles, 1969
Most Passes Had Intercepted, Game
9 Detroit vs. Green Bay, Oct. 24, 1943
Pittsburgh vs. Philadelphia, Dec. 12, 1965
8 Green Bay vs. N.Y. Giants, Nov. 21, 1948
Chi. Cardinals vs. Philadelphia, Sept. 24, 1950
N.Y. Yanks vs. N.Y. Giants, Dec. 16, 1951
Denver vs. Houston, Dec. 2, 1962
Chi. Bears vs. Detroit, Sept. 22, 1968
Baltimore vs. N.Y. Jets, Sept. 23, 1973
7 By many teams. Last time: Green Bay vs. New Orleans, Sept. 14, 1986
Most Passes Had Intercepted, Both Teams, Game
13 Denver (8) vs. Houston (5), Dec. 2, 1962
11 Philadelphia (7) vs. Boston (4), Nov. 3, 1935
Boston (6) vs. Pittsburgh (5), Dec. 1, 1935
Cleveland (7) vs. Green Bay (4), Oct. 30, 1938
Green Bay (7) vs. Detroit (4), Oct. 20, 1940
Detroit (7) vs. Chi. Bears (4), Nov. 22, 1942
Detroit (7) vs. Cleveland (4), Nov. 26, 1944
Chi. Cardinals (8) vs. Philadelphia (3), Sept. 24, 1950
Washington (7) vs. N.Y. Giants (4), Dec. 8, 1963
Pittsburgh (9) vs. Philadelphia (2), Dec 12, 1965
10 In many games

Punting
Most Seasons Leading League (Average Distance)
6 Washington, 1940-43, 1945, 1958
Denver, 1962-64, 1966-67, 1982
Kansas City, 1968, 1971-73, 1979, 1984
4 L.A. Rams, 1946, 1949, 1955-56
Baltimore/Indianapolis, 1966, 1969, 1983, 1985
3 Cleveland, 1950-52
San Francisco, 1957, 1962, 1965
N.Y. Giants, 1959, 1980, 1986
Cincinnati, 1970, 1978, 1981
Oakland, 1974, 1975, 1977
L.A. Chargers/San Diego, 1960, 1969, 1987

Most Consecutive Seasons Leading League (Average Distance)
4 Washington, 1940-43
3 Cleveland, 1950-52
Denver, 1962-64
Kansas City, 1971-73

Most Punts, Season
114 Chicago, 1981
113 Boston, 1934
Brooklyn, 1934
112 Boston, 1935

Fewest Punts, Season
23 San Diego, 1982
31 Cincinnati, 1982
32 Chi. Bears, 1941

Most Punts, Game
17 Chi. Bears vs. Green Bay, Oct. 22, 1933
Cincinnati vs. Pittsburgh, Oct. 22, 1933
16 Cincinnati vs. Portsmouth, Sept. 17, 1933
Chi. Cardinals vs. Chi. Bears, Nov. 30, 1933; vs. Detroit, Sept. 15, 1940

Fewest Punts, Game
0 By many teams. Last time: Cleveland vs. New Orleans, Sept. 13, 1987

Most Punts, Both Teams, Game
31 Chi. Bears (17) vs. Green Bay (14), Oct. 22, 1933
Cincinnati (17), vs. Pittsburgh (14), Oct. 22, 1933
29 Chi. Cardinals (15) vs. Cincinnati (14), Nov. 12, 1933
Chi. Cardinals (16) vs. Chi. Bears (13), Nov. 30, 1933
Chi. Cardinals (16) vs. Detroit (13), Sept. 15, 1940

Fewest Punts, Both Teams, Game
1 Dall. Cowboys (0) vs. Cleveland (1), Dec. 3, 1961
Chicago (0) vs. Detroit (1), Oct. 1, 1972
San Francisco (0) vs. N.Y. Giants (1), Oct. 15, 1972
Green Bay (0) vs. Buffalo (1), Dec. 5, 1982
Miami (0) vs. Buffalo (1), Oct. 12, 1986
2 In many games

Average Yardage

Highest Average Distance, Punting, Season
47.6 Detroit, 1961 (56-2,664)
47.0 Pittsburgh, 1961 (73-3,431)
46.9 Pittsburgh, 1953 (80-3,752)

Lowest Average Distance, Punting, Season
32.7 Card-Pitt, 1944 (60-1,964)
33.8 Cincinnati, 1986 (59-1,996)
33.9 Detroit, 1969 (74-2,510)

Punt Returns

Most Seasons Leading League (Average Return)
8 Detroit, 1943-45, 1951-52, 1962, 1966, 1969
7 Chi. Cardinals/St. Louis, 1948-49, 1955-56, 1959, 1986-87
5 Cleveland, 1958, 1960, 1964-65, 1967
Green Bay, 1950, 1953-54, 1961, 1972
Dall. Texans/Kansas City, 1960, 1968, 1970, 1979-80

Most Consecutive Seasons Leading League (Average Return)
3 Detroit, 1943-45
2 By many teams

Most Punt Returns, Season
71 Pittsburgh, 1976
Tampa Bay, 1979
L.A. Raiders, 1985
67 Pittsburgh, 1974
Los Angeles, 1978
L.A. Raiders, 1984
65 San Francisco, 1976

Fewest Punt Returns, Season
12 Baltimore, 1981
San Diego, 1982
14 Los Angeles, 1961
Philadelphia, 1962
Baltimore, 1982
15 Houston, 1960
Washington, 1960
Oakland, 1961
N.Y. Giants, 1969
Philadelphia, 1973
Kansas City, 1982

Most Punt Returns, Game
12 Philadelphia vs. Cleveland, Dec. 3, 1950
11 Chi. Bears vs. Chi. Cardinals, Oct. 8, 1950
Washington vs. Tampa Bay, Oct. 9, 1977
10 Philadelphia vs. N.Y. Giants, Nov. 26, 1950
Philadelphia vs. Tampa Bay, Sept. 18, 1977
Pittsburgh vs. Buffalo, Dec. 16, 1979
Washington vs. New Orleans, Dec. 26, 1982

Most Punt Returns, Both Teams, Game
17 Philadelphia (12) vs. Cleveland (5), Dec. 3, 1950
16 N.Y. Giants (9) vs. Philadelphia (7), Dec. 12, 1954
Washington (11) vs. Tampa Bay (5), Oct. 9, 1977
15 Detroit (8) vs. Cleveland (7), Sept. 27, 1942
Los Angeles (8) vs. Baltimore (7), Nov. 27, 1966
Pittsburgh (8) vs. Houston (7), Dec. 1, 1974
Philadelphia (10) vs. Tampa Bay (5), Sept. 18, 1977
Baltimore (9) vs. Kansas City (6), Sept. 2, 1979
Washington (10) vs. New Orleans (5), Dec. 26, 1982
L.A. Raiders (8) vs. Cleveland (7), Nov. 16, 1986

Fair Catches

Most Fair Catches, Season
34 Baltimore, 1971
32 San Diego, 1969
30 St. Louis, 1967
Minnesota, 1971

Fewest Fair Catches, Season
0 San Diego, 1975
New England, 1976
Tampa Bay, 1976
Pittsburgh, 1977
Dallas, 1982
1 Cleveland, 1974
San Francisco, 1975
Kansas City, 1976
St. Louis, 1976, 1982
San Diego, 1976
L.A. Rams, 1982
Tampa Bay, 1982
2 By many teams

Most Fair Catches, Game
7 Minnesota vs. Dallas, Sept. 25, 1966
Detroit vs. Chicago, Nov. 21, 1976
Philadelphia vs. Buffalo, Dec. 27, 1987
6 By many teams

Yards Gained

Most Yards, Punt Returns, Season
785 L.A. Raiders, 1985
781 Chi. Bears, 1948
774 Pittsburgh, 1974

Fewest Yards, Punt Returns, Season
27 St. Louis, 1965
35 N.Y. Giants, 1965
37 New England, 1972

Most Yards, Punt Returns, Game
231 Detroit vs. San Francisco, Oct. 6, 1963
225 Oakland vs. Buffalo, Sept. 15, 1968
219 Los Angeles vs. Atlanta, Oct. 11, 1981

Most Yards, Punt Returns, Both Teams, Game
282 Los Angeles (219) vs. Atlanta (63), Oct. 11, 1981
245 Detroit (231) vs. San Francisco (14), Oct. 6, 1963
244 Oakland (225) vs. Buffalo (19), Sept. 15, 1968

Average Yards Returning Punts

Highest Average, Punt Returns, Season
20.2 Chi. Bears, 1941 (27-546)
19.1 Chi. Cardinals, 1948 (35-669)
18.2 Chi. Cardinals, 1949 (30-546)

Lowest Average, Punt Returns, Season
1.2 St. Louis, 1965 (23-27)
1.5 N.Y. Giants, 1965 (24-35)
1.7 Washington, 1970 (27-45)

Touchdowns Returning Punts

Most Touchdowns, Punt Returns, Season
5 Chi. Cardinals, 1959
4 Chi. Cardinals, 1948
Detroit, 1951
N.Y. Giants, 1951
Denver, 1976
3 Washington, 1941
Detroit, 1952
Pittsburgh, 1952
Houston, 1975
Los Angeles, 1981

Most Touchdowns, Punt Returns, Game
2 Detroit vs. Los Angeles, Oct. 14, 1951; vs. Green Bay, Nov. 22, 1951
Chi. Cardinals vs. Pittsburgh, Nov. 1, 1959; vs. N.Y. Giants, Nov. 22, 1959
N.Y. Titans vs. Denver, Sept. 24, 1961
Denver vs. Cleveland, Sept. 26, 1976
Los Angeles vs. Atlanta, Oct. 11, 1981
St. Louis vs. Tampa Bay, Dec. 21, 1986

Most Touchdowns, Punt Returns, Both Teams, Game
2 Philadelphia (1) vs. Washington (1), Nov. 9, 1952
Kansas City (1) vs. Buffalo (1), Sept. 11, 1966
Baltimore (1) vs. New England (1), Nov. 18, 1979
L.A. Raiders (1) vs. Philadelphia (1), Nov. 30, 1986 (OT)
(Also see previous record)

Kickoff Returns

Most Seasons Leading League (Average Return)
7 Washington, 1942, 1947, 1962-63, 1973-74, 1981
6 Chicago Bears, 1943, 1948, 1958, 1966, 1972, 1985
5 N.Y. Giants, 1944, 1946, 1949, 1951, 1953

Most Consecutive Seasons Leading League (Average Return)
3 Denver, 1965-67
2 By many teams

Most Kickoff Returns, Season
88 New Orleans, 1980
86 Minnesota, 1984
84 Baltimore, 1981

Fewest Kickoff Returns, Season
17 N.Y. Giants, 1944
20 N.Y. Giants, 1941, 1943
Chi. Bears, 1942
23 Washington, 1942

Most Kickoff Returns, Game
12 N.Y. Giants vs. Washington, Nov. 27, 1966
10 By many teams

Most Kickoff Returns, Both Teams, Game
19 N.Y. Giants (12) vs. Washington (7), Nov. 27, 1966
18 Houston (10) vs. Oakland (8), Dec. 22, 1963
17 Washington (9) vs. Green Bay (8), Oct. 17, 1983
San Diego (9) vs. Pittsburgh (8), Dec. 8, 1985
Detroit (9) vs. Green Bay (8), Nov. 27, 1986

Yards Gained

Most Yards, Kickoff Returns, Season

1,973 New Orleans, 1980
1,824 Houston, 1963
1,801 Denver, 1963

Fewest Yards, Kickoff Returns, Season

282 N.Y. Giants, 1940
381 Green Bay, 1940
424 Chicago, 1963

Most Yards, Kickoff Returns, Game

362 Detroit vs. Los Angeles, Oct. 29, 1950
304 Chi. Bears vs. Green Bay, Nov. 9, 1952
295 Denver vs. Boston, Oct. 4, 1964

Most Yards, Kickoff Returns, Both Teams, Game

560 Detroit (362) vs. Los Angeles (198), Oct. 29, 1950
453 Washington (236) vs. Philadelphia (217), Sept. 28, 1947
447 N.Y. Giants (236) vs. Cleveland (211), Dec. 4, 1966

Average Yardage

Highest Average, Kickoff Returns, Season

29.4 Chicago, 1972 (52-1,528)
28.9 Pittsburgh, 1952 (39-1,128)
28.2 Washington, 1962 (61-1,720)

Lowest Average, Kickoff Returns, Season

16.3 Chicago, 1963 (26-424)
16.4 Chicago, 1983 (58-953)
16.5 San Diego, 1961 (51-642)

Touchdowns

Most Touchdowns, Kickoff Returns, Season

4 Green Bay, 1967
Chicago, 1970
3 L.A. Rams, 1950, 1985
Chi. Cardinals, 1954
San Francisco, 1963
Denver, 1966
Chicago, 1967
New England, 1977
2 By many teams

Most Touchdowns, Kickoff Returns, Game

2 Chi. Bears vs. Green Bay, Sept. 22, 1940; vs. Green Bay, Nov. 9, 1952
Philadelphia vs. Dallas, Nov. 6, 1966
Green Bay vs. Cleveland, Nov. 12, 1967
L.A. Rams vs. Green Bay, Nov. 24, 1985

Most Touchdowns, Kickoff Returns, Both Teams, Game

2 Washington (1) vs. Philadelphia (1), Nov. 1, 1942
Washington (1) vs. Philadelphia (1), Sept. 28, 1947
Los Angeles (1) vs. Detroit (1), Oct. 29, 1950
N.Y. Yanks (1) vs. N.Y. Giants (1), Nov. 4, 1951 (consecutive)
Baltimore (1) vs. Chi. Bears (1), Oct. 4, 1958
Buffalo (1) vs. Boston (1), Nov. 3, 1962
Pittsburgh (1) vs. Dallas (1), Oct. 30, 1966
St. Louis (1) vs. Washington (1), Sept. 23, 1973 (consecutive)
Atlanta (1) vs. San Francisco (1), Dec. 20, 1987 (consecutive)
(Also see previous record)

Fumbles

Most Fumbles, Season

56 Chi. Bears, 1938
San Francisco, 1978
54 Philadelphia, 1946
51 New England, 1973

Fewest Fumbles, Season

8 Cleveland, 1959
11 Green Bay, 1944
12 Brooklyn, 1934
Detroit, 1943
Cincinnati, 1982
Minnesota, 1982

Most Fumbles, Game

10 Phil-Pitt vs. New York, Oct. 9, 1943
Detroit vs. Minnesota, Nov. 12, 1967
Kansas City vs. Houston, Oct. 12, 1969
San Francisco vs. Detroit, Dec. 17, 1978
9 Philadelphia vs. Green Bay, Oct. 13, 1946
Kansas City vs. San Diego, Nov. 15, 1964
N.Y. Giants vs. Buffalo, Oct. 20, 1975
St. Louis vs. Washington, Oct. 25, 1976
San Diego vs. Green Bay, Sept. 24, 1978
Pittsburgh vs. Cincinnati, Oct. 14, 1979
Cleveland vs. Seattle, Dec. 20, 1981
8 By many teams. Last time: Tampa Bay vs. New York Jets, Dec. 12, 1982

Most Fumbles, Both Teams, Game

14 Chi. Bears (7) vs. Cleveland (7), Nov. 24, 1940
St. Louis (8) vs. N.Y. Giants (6), Sept. 17, 1961
Kansas City (10) vs. Houston (4), Oct. 12, 1969
13 Washington (8) vs. Pittsburgh (5), Nov. 14, 1937
Philadelphia (7) vs. Boston (6), Dec. 8, 1946
N.Y. Giants (7) vs. Washington (6), Nov. 5, 1950
Kansas City (9) vs. San Diego (4), Nov. 15, 1964
Buffalo (7) vs. Denver (6), Dec. 13, 1964
N.Y. Jets (7) vs. Houston (6), Sept. 12, 1965
Houston (8) vs. Pittsburgh (5), Dec. 9, 1973
St. Louis (9) vs. Washington (4), Oct. 25, 1976
Cleveland (9) vs. Seattle (4), Dec. 20, 1981
Green Bay (7) vs. Detroit (6), Oct. 6, 1985
12 In many games

Fumbles Lost

Most Fumbles Lost, Season

36 Chi. Cardinals, 1959
31 Green Bay, 1952
29 Chi. Cardinals, 1946
Pittsburgh, 1950

Fewest Fumbles Lost, Season

3 Philadelphia, 1938
Minnesota, 1980
4 San Francisco, 1960
Kansas City, 1982
5 Chi. Cardinals, 1943
Detroit, 1943
N.Y. Giants, 1943
Cleveland, 1959
Minnesota, 1982

Most Fumbles Lost, Game

8 St. Louis vs. Washington, Oct. 25, 1976
7 Cincinnati vs. Buffalo, Nov. 30, 1969
Cleveland vs. Seattle, Dec. 20, 1981
6 By many teams. Last time: L.A. Rams vs. New England, Dec. 11, 1983

Fumbles Recovered

Most Fumbles Recovered, Season, Own and Opponents'

58 Minnesota, 1963 (27 own, 31 opp)
51 Chi. Bears, 1938 (37 own, 14 opp)
San Francisco, 1978 (24 own, 27 opp)
50 Philadelphia, 1987 (23 own, 27 opp)

Fewest Fumbles Recovered, Season, Own and Opponents'

9 San Francisco, 1982 (5 own, 4 opp)
11 Cincinnati, 1982 (5 own, 6 opp)
13 Baltimore, 1967 (5 own, 8 opp)
N.Y. Jets, 1967 (7 own, 6 opp)
Philadelphia, 1968 (6 own, 7 opp)
Miami, 1973 (5 own, 8 opp)
Chicago, 1982 (6 own, 7 opp)
Denver, 1982 (6 own, 7 opp)
Miami, 1982 (5 own, 8 opp)
N.Y. Giants, 1982 (7 own, 6 opp)

Most Fumbles Recovered, Game, Own and Opponents'

10 Denver vs. Buffalo, Dec. 13, 1964 (5 own, 5 opp)
Pittsburgh vs. Houston, Dec. 9, 1973 (5 own, 5 opp)
Washington vs. St. Louis, Oct. 25, 1976 (2 own, 8 opp)
9 St. Louis vs. N.Y. Giants, Sept. 17, 1961 (6 own, 3 opp)
Houston vs. Cincinnati, Oct. 27, 1974 (4 own, 5 opp)
Kansas City vs. Dallas, Nov. 10, 1975 (4 own, 5 opp)
Green Bay vs. Detroit, Oct. 6, 1985 (5 own, 4 opp)
8 By many teams

Most Own Fumbles Recovered, Season

37 Chi. Bears, 1938
28 Pittsburgh, 1987
27 Philadelphia, 1946
Minnesota, 1963

Fewest Own Fumbles Recovered, Season

2 Washington, 1958
3 Detroit, 1956
Cleveland, 1959
Houston, 1982
4 By many teams

Most Opponents' Fumbles Recovered, Season

31 Minnesota, 1963
29 Cleveland, 1951
28 Green Bay, 1946
Houston, 1977
Seattle, 1983

Fewest Opponents' Fumbles Recovered, Season

3 Los Angeles, 1974
4 Philadelphia, 1944
San Francisco, 1982
5 Baltimore, 1982

Most Opponents' Fumbles Recovered, Game

8 Washington vs. St. Louis, Oct. 25, 1976
7 Buffalo vs. Cincinnati, Nov. 30, 1969
Seattle vs. Cleveland, Dec. 20, 1981
6 By many teams. Last time: New England vs. L.A. Rams, Dec. 11, 1983

Touchdowns

Most Touchdowns, Fumbles Recovered, Season, Own and Opponents'

5 Chi. Bears, 1942 (1 own, 4 opp)
Los Angeles, 1952 (1 own, 4 opp)
San Francisco, 1965 (1 own, 4 opp)
Oakland, 1978 (2 own, 3 opp)
4 Chi. Bears, 1948 (1 own, 3 opp)
Boston, 1948 (4 opp)
Denver, 1979 (1 own, 3 opp), 1984 (4 opp)
Atlanta, 1981 (1 own, 3 opp)
St. Louis, 1987 (4 opp)
3 By many teams

Most Touchdowns, Own Fumbles Recovered, Season

2 Chi. Bears, 1953
New England, 1973
Buffalo, 1974
Denver, 1975
Oakland, 1978
Green Bay, 1982
New Orleans, 1983
Cleveland, 1986

Most Touchdowns, Opponents' Fumbles Recovered, Season

4 Detroit, 1937
Chi. Bears, 1942
Boston, 1948
Los Angeles, 1952
San Francisco, 1965
Denver, 1984
St. Louis, 1987
3 By many teams

Most Touchdowns, Fumbles Recovered, Game, Own and Opponents'
2 Detroit vs. Cleveland, Nov. 7, 1937 (2 opp); vs. Green Bay, Sept. 17, 1950 (1 own, 1 opp); vs. Chi. Cardinals, Dec. 6, 1959 (1 own, 1 opp); vs. Minnesota, Dec. 9, 1962 (1 own, 1 opp)
Philadelphia vs. New York, Sept. 25, 1938 (2 opp); vs. St. Louis, Nov. 21, 1971 (1 own, 1 opp)
Chi. Bears vs. Washington, Nov. 28, 1948 (2 opp)
N.Y. Giants vs. Pittsburgh, Sept. 17, 1950 (2 opp); vs. Green Bay, Sept. 19, 1971 (2 opp)
Cleveland vs. Dall. Cowboys, Dec. 3, 1961 (2 opp); vs. N.Y. Giants, Oct. 25, 1964 (2 opp)
Green Bay vs. Dallas, Nov. 26, 1964 (2 opp)
San Francisco vs. Detroit, Nov. 14, 1965 (2 opp)
Oakland vs. Buffalo, Dec. 24, 1967 (2 opp)
Washington vs. San Diego, Sept. 16, 1973 (2 opp); vs. Minnesota, Nov. 29, 1984 (1 own, 1 opp)
New Orleans vs. San Francisco, Oct. 19, 1975 (2 opp)
Cincinnati vs. Pittsburgh, Oct. 14, 1979 (2 opp)
Atlanta vs. Detroit, Oct. 5, 1980 (2 opp)
Kansas City vs. Oakland, Oct. 5, 1980 (2 opp)
New England vs. Baltimore, Nov. 23, 1980 (2 opp)
Denver vs. Green Bay, Oct. 15, 1984 (2 opp)
Miami vs. Kansas City, Oct. 11, 1987 (2 opp)
St. Louis vs. New Orleans, Oct. 11, 1987 (2 opp)

Most Touchdowns, Own Fumbles Recovered, Game
1 By many teams

Most Touchdowns, Opponents' Fumbles Recovered, Game
2 Detroit vs. Cleveland, Nov. 7, 1937
Philadelphia vs. N.Y. Giants, Sept. 25, 1938
Chi. Bears vs. Washington, Nov. 28, 1948
N.Y. Giants vs. Pittsburgh, Sept. 17, 1950; vs. Green Bay, Sept. 19, 1971
Cleveland vs. Dall. Cowboys, Dec. 3, 1961; vs. N.Y. Giants, Oct. 25, 1964
Green Bay vs. Dallas, Nov. 26, 1964
San Francisco vs. Detroit, Nov. 14, 1965
Oakland vs. Buffalo, Dec. 24, 1967
Washington vs. San Diego, Sept. 16, 1973
New Orleans vs. San Francisco, Oct. 19, 1975
Cincinnati vs. Pittsburgh, Oct. 14, 1979
Atlanta vs. Detroit, Oct. 5, 1980
Kansas City vs. Oakland, Oct. 5, 1980
New England vs. Baltimore, Nov. 23, 1980
Denver vs. Green Bay, Oct. 15, 1984
Miami vs. Kansas City, Oct. 11, 1987
St. Louis vs. New Orleans, Oct. 11, 1987

Turnovers

(Number of times losing the ball on interceptions and fumbles.)

Most Turnovers, Season
63 San Francisco, 1978
58 Chi. Bears, 1947
Pittsburgh, 1950
N.Y. Giants, 1983
57 Green Bay, 1950
Houston, 1962, 1963
Pittsburgh, 1965

Fewest Turnovers, Season
12 Kansas City, 1982
14 N.Y. Giants, 1943
Cleveland, 1959
16 San Francisco, 1960
Cincinnati, 1982
St. Louis, 1982
Washington, 1982

Most Turnovers, Game
12 Detroit vs. Chi. Bears, Nov. 22, 1942
Chi. Cardinals vs. Philadelphia, Sept. 24, 1950
Pittsburgh vs. Philadelphia, Dec. 12, 1965
11 San Diego vs. Green Bay, Sept. 24, 1978
10 Washington vs. N.Y. Giants, Dec. 4, 1938; vs. N.Y. Giants, Dec. 8, 1963
Pittsburgh vs. Green Bay, Nov. 23, 1941
Detroit vs. Green Bay, Oct. 24, 1943; vs. Denver, Oct. 7, 1984
Chi. Cardinals vs. Green Bay, Nov. 10, 1946; vs. N.Y. Giants, Nov. 2, 1952
Minnesota vs. Detroit, Dec. 9, 1962
Houston vs. Oakland, Sept. 7, 1963
Chicago vs. Detroit, Sept. 22, 1968
St. Louis vs. Washington, Oct. 25, 1976
N.Y. Jets vs. New England, Nov. 21, 1976
San Francisco vs. Dallas, Oct. 12, 1980
Cleveland vs. Seattle, Dec. 20, 1981

Most Turnovers, Both Teams, Game
17 Detroit (12) vs. Chi. Bears (5), Nov. 22, 1942
Boston (9) vs. Philadelphia (8), Dec. 8, 1946
16 Chi. Cardinals (12) vs. Philadelphia (4), Sept. 24, 1950
Chi. Cardinals (8) vs. Chi. Bears (8), Dec. 7, 1958
Minnesota (10) vs. Detroit (6), Dec. 9, 1962
Houston (9) vs. Kansas City (7), Oct. 12, 1969
15 Philadelphia (8) vs. Chi. Cardinals (7), Oct. 3, 1954
Denver (9) vs. Houston (6), Dec. 2, 1962
Washington (10) vs. N.Y. Giants (5), Dec. 8, 1963
St. Louis (9) vs. Kansas City (6), Oct. 2, 1983

Penalties

Most Seasons Leading League, Fewest Penalties
11 Miami, 1968, 1976-84, 1986
9 Pittsburgh, 1946-47, 1950-52, 1954, 1963, 1965, 1968
5 Green Bay, 1955-56, 1966-67, 1974
Boston/New England, 1962, 1964-65, 1973, 1987

Most Consecutive Seasons Leading League, Fewest Penalties
9 Miami, 1976-84
3 Pittsburgh, 1950-52
2 By many teams

Most Seasons Leading League, Most Penalties
16 Chi. Bears, 1941-44, 1946-49, 1951, 1959-61, 1963, 1965, 1968, 1976
7 Oakland/L.A. Raiders, 1963, 1966, 1968-69, 1975, 1982, 1984
6 L.A. Rams, 1950, 1952, 1962, 1969, 1978, 1980

Most Consecutive Seasons Leading League, Most Penalties
4 Chi. Bears, 1941-44, 1946-49
3 Chi. Cardinals, 1954-56
Chi. Bears, 1959-61

Fewest Penalties, Season
19 Detroit, 1937
21 Boston, 1935
24 Philadelphia, 1936

Most Penalties, Season
144 Buffalo, 1983
143 L.A. Raiders, 1984
138 Detroit, 1984

Fewest Penalties, Game
0 By many teams. Last time: Seattle vs. Pittsburgh, Dec. 6, 1987

Most Penalties, Game
22 Brooklyn vs. Green Bay, Sept. 17, 1944
Chi. Bears vs. Philadelphia, Nov. 26, 1944
21 Cleveland vs. Chi. Bears, Nov. 25, 1951
20 Tampa Bay vs. Seattle, Oct. 17, 1976

Fewest Penalties, Both Teams, Game
0 Brooklyn vs. Pittsburgh, Oct. 28, 1934
Brooklyn vs. Boston, Sept. 28, 1936
Cleveland vs. Chi. Bears, Oct. 9, 1938
Pittsburgh vs. Philadelphia, Nov. 10, 1940

Most Penalties, Both Teams, Game
37 Cleveland (21) vs. Chi. Bears (16), Nov. 25, 1951
35 Tampa Bay (20) vs. Seattle (15), Oct. 17, 1976
33 Brooklyn (22) vs. Green Bay (11), Sept. 17, 1944

Yards Penalized

Most Seasons Leading League, Fewest Yards Penalized
11 Miami, 1967-68, 1973, 1977-84
8 Boston/Washington, 1935, 1953-54, 1956-58, 1970, 1985
7 Pittsburgh, 1946-47, 1950, 1952, 1962, 1965, 1968

Most Consecutive Seasons Leading League, Fewest Yards Penalized
8 Miami, 1977-84
3 Washington, 1956-58
Boston, 1964-66
2 By many teams

Most Seasons Leading League, Most Yards Penalized
15 Chi. Bears, 1935, 1937, 1939-44, 1946-47, 1949, 1951, 1961-62, 1968
7 Oakland/L.A. Raiders, 1963-64, 1968-69, 1975, 1982, 1984
6 Buffalo, 1962, 1967, 1970, 1972, 1981, 1983

Most Consecutive Seasons Leading League, Most Yards Penalized
6 Chi. Bears, 1939-44
3 Cleveland, 1976-78
2 By many teams

Fewest Yards Penalized, Season
139 Detroit, 1937
146 Philadelphia, 1937
159 Philadelphia, 1936

Most Yards Penalized, Season
1,274 Oakland, 1969
1,239 Baltimore, 1979
1,209 L.A. Raiders, 1984

Fewest Yards Penalized, Game
0 By many teams. Last time: Seattle vs. Pittsburgh, Dec. 6, 1987

Most Yards Penalized, Game
209 Cleveland vs. Chi. Bears, Nov. 25, 1951
190 Tampa Bay vs. Seattle, Oct. 17, 1976
189 Houston vs. Buffalo, Oct. 31, 1965

Fewest Yards Penalized, Both Teams, Game
0 Brooklyn vs. Pittsburgh, Oct. 28, 1934
Brooklyn vs. Boston, Sept. 28, 1936
Cleveland vs. Chi. Bears, Oct. 9, 1938
Pittsburgh vs. Philadelphia, Nov. 10, 1940

Most Yards Penalized, Both Teams, Game
374 Cleveland (209) vs. Chi. Bears (165), Nov. 25, 1951
310 Tampa Bay (190) vs. Seattle (120), Oct. 17, 1976
309 Green Bay (184) vs. Boston (125), Oct. 21, 1945

Defense

Scoring

Most Seasons Leading League, Fewest Points Allowed
8 N.Y. Giants, 1935, 1938-39, 1941, 1944, 1958-59, 1961
Chi. Bears, 1932, 1936-37, 1942, 1948, 1963, 1985-86
6 Cleveland, 1951, 1953-57
5 Green Bay, 1935, 1947, 1962, 1965-66

Most Consecutive Seasons Leading League, Fewest Points Allowed
5 Cleveland, 1953-57
3 Buffalo, 1964-66
Minnesota, 1969-71
2 By many teams

Fewest Points Allowed, Season (Since 1932)
44 Chi. Bears, 1932
54 Brooklyn, 1933
59 Detroit, 1934

Most Points Allowed, Season
533 Baltimore, 1981
501 N.Y. Giants, 1966
487 New Orleans, 1980

Fewest Touchdowns Allowed, Season (Since 1932)
6 Chi. Bears, 1932
Brooklyn, 1933
7 Detroit, 1934
8 Green Bay, 1932

Most Touchdowns Allowed, Season
68 Baltimore, 1981
66 N.Y. Giants, 1966
63 Baltimore, 1950

First Downs
Fewest First Downs Allowed Season
77 Detroit, 1935
79 Boston, 1935
82 Washington, 1937
Most First Downs Allowed, Season
406 Baltimore, 1981
371 Seattle, 1981
366 Green Bay, 1983
Fewest First Downs Allowed, Rushing, Season
35 Chi. Bears, 1942
40 Green Bay, 1939
41 Brooklyn, 1944
Most First Downs Allowed, Rushing, Season
179 Detroit, 1985
178 New Orleans, 1980
175 Seattle, 1981
Fewest First Downs Allowed, Passing, Season
33 Chi. Bears, 1943
34 Pittsburgh, 1941
Washington, 1943
35 Detroit, 1940
Philadelphia, 1940, 1944
Most First Downs Allowed, Passing, Season
218 San Diego, 1985
216 San Diego, 1981
N.Y. Jets, 1986
214 Baltimore, 1981
Fewest First Downs Allowed, Penalty, Season
1 Boston, 1944
3 Philadelphia, 1940
Pittsburgh, 1945
Washington, 1957
4 Cleveland, 1940
Green Bay, 1943
N.Y. Giants, 1943
Most First Downs Allowed, Penalty, Season
48 Houston, 1985
46 Houston, 1986
43 L.A. Raiders, 1984

Net Yards Allowed Rushing and Passing
Most Seasons Leading League, Fewest Yards Allowed
8 Chi. Bears, 1942-43, 1948, 1958, 1963, 1984-86
6 N.Y. Giants, 1938, 1940-41, 1951, 1956, 1959
5 Boston/Washington, 1935-37, 1939, 1946
Philadelphia, 1944-45, 1949, 1953, 1981
Most Consecutive Seasons Leading League, Fewest Yards Allowed
3 Boston/Washington, 1935-37
Chicago, 1984-86
2 By many teams
Fewest Yards Allowed, Season
1,539 Chi. Cardinals, 1934
1,703 Chi. Bears, 1942
1,789 Brooklyn, 1933
Most Yards Allowed, Season
6,793 Baltimore, 1981
6,403 Green Bay, 1983
6,352 Minnesota, 1984

Rushing
Most Seasons Leading League, Fewest Yards Allowed
9 Chi. Bears, 1937, 1939, 1942, 1946, 1949, 1963, 1984-85, 1987
7 Detroit, 1938, 1950, 1952, 1962, 1970, 1980-81
6 Dallas, 1966-69, 1972, 1978
Most Consecutive Seasons Leading League, Fewest Yards Allowed
4 Dallas, 1966-69
2 By many teams
Fewest Yards Allowed, Rushing, Season
519 Chi. Bears, 1942
558 Philadelphia, 1944
762 Pittsburgh, 1982
Most Yards Allowed, Rushing, Season
3,228 Buffalo, 1978
3,106 New Orleans, 1980
3,010 Baltimore, 1978
Fewest Touchdowns Allowed, Rushing, Season
2 Detroit, 1934
Dallas, 1968
Minnesota, 1971
3 By many teams
Most Touchdowns Allowed, Rushing, Season
36 Oakland, 1961
31 N.Y. Giants, 1980
Tampa Bay, 1986
30 Baltimore, 1981

Passing
Most Seasons Leading League, Fewest Yards Allowed
8 Green Bay, 1947-48, 1962, 1964-68
7 Washington, 1939, 1942, 1945, 1952-53, 1980, 1985
6 Chi. Bears, 1938, 1943-44, 1958, 1960, 1963
Most Consecutive Seasons Leading League, Fewest Yards Allowed
5 Green Bay, 1964-68
2 By many teams

Fewest Yards Allowed, Passing, Season
545 Philadelphia, 1934
558 Portsmouth, 1933
585 Chi. Cardinals, 1934
Most Yards Allowed, Passing, Season
4,389 N.Y. Jets, 1986
4,311 San Diego, 1981
4,293 San Diego, 1985
Fewest Touchdowns Allowed, Passing, Season
1 Portsmouth, 1932
Philadelphia, 1934
2 Brooklyn, 1933
Chi. Bears, 1934
3 Chi. Bears, 1932, 1936
Green Bay, 1932, 1934
N.Y. Giants, 1939, 1944
Most Touchdowns Allowed, Passing, Season
40 Denver, 1963
38 St. Louis, 1969
37 Washington, 1961
Baltimore, 1981

Sacks
Most Seasons Leading League
5 Oakland/L.A. Raiders, 1966-68, 1982, 1986
4 Boston/New England, 1961, 1963, 1977, 1979
Dallas, 1966, 1968-69, 1978
3 Dallas/Kansas City, 1960, 1965, 1969
San Francisco, 1967, 1972, 1976
Most Consecutive Seasons Leading League
3 Oakland, 1966-68
2 Dallas, 1968-69
Most Sacks, Season
72 Chicago, 1984
70 Chicago, 1987
68 N.Y. Giants, 1985
Fewest Sacks, Season
11 Baltimore, 1982
12 Buffalo, 1982
13 Baltimore, 1981
Most Sacks, Game
12 Dallas vs. Pittsburgh, Nov. 20, 1966; vs. Houston, Sept. 29, 1985
St. Louis vs. Baltimore, Oct. 26, 1980
Chicago vs. Detroit, Dec. 16, 1984
11 N.Y. Giants vs. St. Louis, Nov. 1, 1964
Baltimore vs. Los Angeles, Nov. 22, 1964
Buffalo vs. Denver, Dec. 13, 1964
Detroit vs. Green Bay, Nov. 7, 1965; vs. Philadelphia, Nov. 16, 1986
Oakland vs. Buffalo, Oct. 15, 1967; vs. Denver, Nov. 5, 1967
St. Louis vs. Atlanta, Nov. 24, 1968; vs. Philadelphia, Dec. 18, 1983
Dallas vs. Detroit, Oct. 6, 1975; vs. N.Y. Jets, Oct. 4, 1987
Kansas City vs. Cleveland, Sept. 30, 1984
Chicago vs. Minnesota, Oct. 28, 1984; vs. Philadelphia, Oct. 4, 1987
Cleveland vs. Atlanta, Nov. 18, 1984
San Diego vs. Dallas, Nov. 16, 1986
L.A. Raiders vs. Philadelphia, Nov. 30, 1986 (OT)
Seattle vs. L.A. Raiders, Dec. 8, 1986
10 By many teams
Most Opponents Yards Lost Attempting to Pass, Season
666 Oakland, 1967
583 Chicago, 1984
573 San Francisco, 1976
Fewest Opponents Yards Lost Attempting to Pass, Season
75 Green Bay, 1956
77 N.Y. Bulldogs, 1949
78 Green Bay, 1958

Interceptions By
Most Seasons Leading League
9 N.Y. Giants, 1933, 1937-39, 1944, 1948, 1951, 1954, 1961
8 Green Bay, 1940, 1942-43, 1947, 1955, 1957, 1962, 1965
7 Chi. Bears, 1935-36, 1941-42, 1946, 1963, 1985
Most Consecutive Seasons Leading League
5 Kansas City, 1966-70
3 N.Y. Giants, 1937-39
2 By many teams
Most Passes Intercepted By, Season
49 San Diego, 1961
42 Green Bay, 1943
41 N.Y. Giants, 1951
Fewest Passes Intercepted By, Season
3 Houston, 1982
5 Baltimore, 1982
6 Houston, 1972
St. Louis, 1982
Most Passes Intercepted By, Game
9 Green Bay vs. Detroit, Oct. 24, 1943
Philadelphia vs. Pittsburgh, Dec. 12, 1965
8 N.Y. Giants vs. Green Bay, Nov. 21, 1948; vs. N.Y. Yanks, Dec. 16, 1951
Philadelphia vs. Chi. Cardinals, Sept. 24, 1950
Houston vs. Denver, Dec. 2, 1962
Detroit vs. Chicago, Sept. 22, 1968
N.Y. Jets vs. Baltimore, Sept. 23, 1973
7 By many teams. Last time: New Orleans vs. Green Bay, Sept. 14, 1986
Most Consecutive Games, One or More Interceptions By
46 L.A. Chargers/San Diego, 1960-63
37 Detroit, 1960-63
36 Boston, 1944-47
Washington, 1962-65
Most Yards Returning Interceptions, Season
929 San Diego, 1961
712 Los Angeles, 1952
697 Seattle, 1984

Fewest Yards Returning Interceptions, Season
5 Los Angeles, 1959
42 Philadelphia, 1982
47 Houston, 1982
Most Yards Returning Interceptions, Game
325 Seattle vs. Kansas City, Nov. 4, 1984
314 Los Angeles vs. San Francisco, Oct. 18, 1964
245 Houston vs. N.Y. Jets, Oct. 15, 1967
Most Touchdowns, Returning Interceptions, Season
9 San Diego, 1961
7 Seattle, 1984
6 Cleveland, 1960
Green Bay, 1966
Detroit, 1967
Houston, 1967
Most Touchdowns Returning Interceptions, Game
4 Seattle vs. Kansas City, Nov. 4, 1984
3 Baltimore vs. Green Bay, Nov. 5, 1950
Cleveland vs. Chicago, Dec. 11, 1960
Philadelphia vs. Pittsburgh, Dec. 12, 1965
Baltimore vs. Pittsburgh, Sept. 29, 1968
Buffalo vs. N.Y. Jets, Sept. 29, 1968
Houston vs. San Diego, Dec. 19, 1971
Cincinnati vs. Houston, Dec. 17, 1972
Tampa Bay vs. New Orleans, Dec. 11, 1977
2 By many teams
Most Touchdowns Returning Interceptions, Both Teams, Game
4 Philadelphia (3) vs. Pittsburgh (1), Dec. 12, 1965
Seattle (4) vs. Kansas City (0), Nov. 4, 1984
3 Los Angeles (2) vs. Detroit (1), Nov. 1, 1953
Cleveland (2) vs. N.Y. Giants (1), Dec. 18, 1960
Pittsburgh (2) vs. Cincinnati (1), Oct. 10, 1983
Kansas City (2) vs. San Diego (1), Oct. 19, 1986
(Also see previous record)

Punt Returns
Fewest Opponents Punt Returns, Season
7 Washington, 1962
San Diego, 1982
10 Buffalo, 1982
11 Boston, 1962
Most Opponents Punt Returns, Season
71 Tampa Bay, 1976, 1977
69 N.Y. Giants, 1953
68 Cleveland, 1974
Fewest Yards Allowed, Punt Returns, Season
22 Green Bay, 1967
34 Washington, 1962
39 Cleveland, 1959
Washington, 1972
Most Yards Allowed, Punt Returns, Season
932 Green Bay, 1949
913 Boston, 1947
906 New Orleans, 1974
Lowest Average Allowed, Punt Returns, Season
1.20 Chi. Cardinals, 1954 (46-55)
1.22 Cleveland, 1959 (32-39)
1.55 Chi. Cardinals, 1953 (44-68)
Highest Average Allowed, Punt Returns, Season
18.6 Green Bay, 1949 (50-932)
18.0 Cleveland, 1977 (31-558)
17.9 Boston, 1960 (20-357)
Most Touchdowns Allowed, Punt Returns, Season
4 New York, 1959
3 Green Bay, 1949
Chi. Cardinals, 1951
Los Angeles, 1951
Washington, 1952
Dallas, 1952
Pittsburgh, 1959
N.Y. Jets, 1968
Cleveland, 1977
Atlanta, 1986
Tampa Bay, 1986
2 By many teams

Kickoff Returns
Fewest Opponents Kickoff Returns, Season
10 Brooklyn, 1943
15 Detroit, 1942
Brooklyn, 1944
18 Cleveland, 1941
Boston, 1944
Most Opponents Kickoff Returns, Season
91 Washington, 1983
89 New England, 1980
88 San Diego, 1981
Fewest Yards Allowed, Kickoff Returns, Season
225 Brooklyn, 1943
293 Brooklyn, 1944
361 Seattle, 1982
Most Yards Allowed, Kickoff Returns, Season
2,045 Kansas City, 1966
1,827 Chicago, 1985
1,816 N.Y. Giants, 1963
Lowest Average Allowed, Kickoff Returns, Season
14.3 Cleveland, 1980 (71-1,018)
15.0 Seattle, 1982 (24-361)
15.8 Buffalo, 1987 (43-679)
Highest Average Allowed, Kickoff Returns, Season
29.5 N.Y. Jets, 1972 (47-1,386)
29.4 Los Angeles, 1950 (48-1,411)
29.1 New England, 1971 (49-1,427)
Most Touchdowns Allowed, Kickoff Returns, Season
3 Minnesota, 1963, 1970
Dallas, 1966
Detroit, 1980
Pittsburgh, 1986
2 By many teams

Fumbles
Fewest Opponents Fumbles, Season
11 Cleveland, 1956
Baltimore, 1982
13 Los Angeles, 1956
Chicago, 1960
Cleveland, 1963, 1965
Detroit, 1967
San Diego, 1969
14 Baltimore, 1970
Oakland, 1975
Buffalo, 1982
St. Louis, 1982
San Francisco, 1982
Most Opponents Fumbles, Season
50 Minnesota, 1963
San Francisco, 1978
48 N.Y. Giants, 1980
N.Y. Jets, 1986
47 N.Y. Giants, 1977
Seattle, 1984

Turnovers
(Number of times losing the ball on interceptions and fumbles.)
Fewest Opponents Turnovers, Season
11 Baltimore, 1982
13 San Francisco, 1982
15 St. Louis, 1982
Most Opponents Turnovers, Season
66 San Diego, 1961
63 Seattle, 1984
61 Washington, 1983
Most Opponents Turnovers, Game
12 Chi. Bears vs. Detroit, Nov. 22, 1942
Philadelphia vs. Chi. Cardinals, Sept. 24, 1950; vs. Pittsburgh, Dec. 12, 1965
11 Green Bay vs. San Diego, Sept. 24, 1978
10 N.Y. Giants vs. Washington, Dec. 4, 1938; vs. Chi. Cardinals, Nov. 2, 1952; vs. Washington, Dec. 8, 1963
Green Bay vs. Pittsburgh, Nov. 23, 1941; vs. Detroit, Oct. 24, 1943; vs. Chi. Cardinals, Nov. 10, 1946
Detroit vs. Minnesota, Dec. 9, 1962; vs. Chicago, Sept. 22, 1968
Oakland vs. Houston, Sept. 7, 1963
Washington vs. St. Louis, Oct. 25, 1976
New England vs. N.Y. Jets, Nov. 21, 1976
Dallas vs. San Francisco, Oct. 12, 1980
Seattle vs. Cleveland, Dec. 20, 1981
Denver vs. Detroit, Oct. 7, 1984

OUTSTANDING PERFORMERS

1,000 Yards Rushing in a Season

Year	Player, Team	Att.	Yards	Avg.	Long	TD
1987	Charles White, L.A. Rams	324	1,374	4.2	58	11
	Eric Dickerson, L.A. Rams-Indianapolis[5]	283	1,288	4.6	57	6
1986	Eric Dickerson, L.A. Rams[4]	404	1,821	4.5	42	11
	Joe Morris, N.Y. Giants[2]	341	1,516	4.4	54	14
	Curt Warner, Seattle[3]	319	1,481	4.6	60	13
	*Rueben Mayes, New Orleans	286	1,353	4.7	50	8
	Walter Payton, Chicago[10]	321	1,333	4.2	41	8
	Gerald Riggs, Atlanta[3]	343	1,327	3.9	31	9
	George Rogers, Washington[4]	303	1,203	4.0	42	18
	James Brooks, Cincinnati	205	1,087	5.3	56	5
1985	Marcus Allen, L.A. Raiders[3]	390	1,759	4.6	61	11
	Gerald Riggs, Atlanta[2]	397	1,719	4.3	50	10
	Walter Payton, Chicago[9]	324	1,551	4.8	40	9
	Joe Morris, N.Y. Giants	294	1,336	4.5	65	21
	Freeman McNeil, N.Y. Jets[2]	294	1,331	4.5	69	3
	Tony Dorsett, Dallas[8]	305	1,307	4.3	60	7
	James Wilder, Tampa Bay[2]	365	1,300	3.6	28	10
	Eric Dickerson, L.A. Rams[3]	292	1,234	4.2	43	12
	Craig James, New England	263	1,227	4.7	65	5
	*Kevin Mack, Cleveland	222	1,104	5.0	61	7
	Curt Warner, Seattle[2]	291	1,094	3.8	38	8
	George Rogers, Washington[3]	231	1,093	4.7	35	7
	Roger Craig, San Francisco	214	1,050	4.9	62	9
	Earnest Jackson, Philadelphia[2]	282	1,028	3.6	59	5
	Stump Mitchell, St. Louis	183	1,006	5.5	64	7
	Earnest Byner, Cleveland	244	1,002	4.1	36	8
1984	Eric Dickerson, L.A. Rams[2]	379	2,105	5.6	66	14
	Walter Payton, Chicago[8]	381	1,684	4.4	72	11
	James Wilder, Tampa Bay	407	1,544	3.8	37	13
	Gerald Riggs, Atlanta	353	1,486	4.2	57	13
	Wendell Tyler, San Francisco[3]	246	1,262	5.1	40	7
	John Riggins, Washington[5]	327	1,239	3.8	24	14
	Tony Dorsett, Dallas[7]	302	1,189	3.9	31	6
	Earnest Jackson, San Diego	296	1,179	4.0	32	8
	Ottis Anderson, St. Louis[5]	289	1,174	4.1	24	6
	Marcus Allen, L.A. Raiders[2]	275	1,168	4.2	52	13
	Sammy Winder, Denver	296	1,153	3.9	24	4
	*Greg Bell, Buffalo	262	1,100	4.2	85	7
	Freeman McNeil, N.Y. Jets	229	1,070	4.7	53	5
1983	*Eric Dickerson, L.A. Rams	390	1,808	4.6	85	18
	William Andrews, Atlanta[4]	331	1,567	4.7	27	7
	*Curt Warner, Seattle	335	1,449	4.3	60	13
	Walter Payton, Chicago[7]	314	1,421	4.5	49	6
	John Riggins, Washington[4]	375	1,347	3.6	44	24
	Tony Dorsett, Dallas[6]	289	1,321	4.6	77	8
	Earl Campbell, Houston[5]	322	1,301	4.0	42	12
	Ottis Anderson, St. Louis[4]	296	1,270	4.3	43	5
	Mike Pruitt, Cleveland[4]	293	1,184	4.0	27	10
	George Rogers, New Orleans[2]	256	1,144	4.5	76	5
	Joe Cribbs, Buffalo[3]	263	1,131	4.3	45	3
	Curtis Dickey, Baltimore	254	1,122	4.4	56	4
	Tony Collins, New England	219	1,049	4.8	50	10
	Billy Sims, Detroit[3]	220	1,040	4.7	41	7
	Marcus Allen, L.A. Raiders	266	1,014	3.8	19	9
	Franco Harris, Pittsburgh[8]	279	1,007	3.6	19	5
1981	*George Rogers, New Orleans	378	1,674	4.4	79	13
	Tony Dorsett, Dallas[5]	342	1,646	4.8	75	4
	Billy Sims, Detroit[2]	296	1,437	4.9	51	13
	Wilbert Montgomery, Philadelphia[3]	286	1,402	4.9	41	8
	Ottis Anderson, St. Louis[3]	328	1,376	4.2	28	9
	Earl Campbell, Houston[4]	361	1,376	3.8	43	10
	William Andrews, Atlanta[3]	289	1,301	4.5	29	10
	Walter Payton, Chicago[6]	339	1,222	3.6	39	6
	Chuck Muncie, San Diego[2]	251	1,144	4.6	73	19
	*Joe Delaney, Kansas City	234	1,121	4.8	82	3
	Mike Pruitt, Cleveland[3]	247	1,103	4.5	21	7
	Joe Cribbs, Buffalo[2]	257	1,097	4.3	35	3
	Pete Johnson, Cincinnati	274	1,077	3.9	39	12
	Wendell Tyler, Los Angeles[2]	260	1,074	4.1	69	12
	Ted Brown, Minnesota	274	1,063	3.9	34	6
1980	Earl Campbell, Houston[3]	373	1,934	5.2	55	13
	Walter Payton, Chicago[5]	317	1,460	4.6	69	6
	Ottis Anderson, St. Louis[2]	301	1,352	4.5	52	9
	William Andrews, Atlanta[2]	265	1,308	4.9	33	4
	*Billy Sims, Detroit	313	1,303	4.2	52	13
	Tony Dorsett, Dallas[4]	278	1,185	4.3	56	11
	*Joe Cribbs, Buffalo	306	1,185	3.9	48	11
	Mike Pruitt, Cleveland[2]	249	1,034	4.2	56	6
1979	Earl Campbell, Houston[2]	368	1,697	4.6	61	19
	Walter Payton, Chicago[4]	369	1,610	4.4	43	14
	*Ottis Anderson, St. Louis	331	1,605	4.8	76	8
	Wilbert Montgomery, Philadelphia[2]	338	1,512	4.5	62	9
	Mike Pruitt, Cleveland	264	1,294	4.9	77	9
	Ricky Bell, Tampa Bay	283	1,263	4.5	49	7
	Chuck Muncie, New Orleans	238	1,198	5.0	69	11
	Franco Harris, Pittsburgh[7]	267	1,186	4.4	71	11
	John Riggins, Washington[3]	260	1,153	4.4	66	9
	Wendell Tyler, Los Angeles	218	1,109	5.1	63	9
	Tony Dorsett, Dallas[3]	250	1,107	4.4	41	6
	*William Andrews, Atlanta	239	1,023	4.3	23	3
1978	*Earl Campbell, Houston	302	1,450	4.8	81	13
	Walter Payton, Chicago[3]	333	1,395	4.2	76	11
	Tony Dorsett, Dallas[2]	290	1,325	4.6	63	7
	Delvin Williams, Miami[2]	272	1,258	4.6	58	8
	Wilbert Montgomery, Philadelphia	259	1,220	4.7	47	9
	Terdell Middleton, Green Bay	284	1,116	3.9	76	11
	Franco Harris, Pittsburgh[6]	310	1,082	3.5	37	8
	Mark van Eeghen, Oakland[3]	270	1,080	4.0	34	9
	*Terry Miller, Buffalo	238	1,060	4.5	60	7
	Tony Reed, Kansas City	206	1,053	5.1	62	5
	John Riggins, Washington[2]	248	1,014	4.1	31	5
1977	Walter Payton, Chicago[2]	339	1,852	5.5	73	14
	Mark van Eeghen, Oakland[2]	324	1,273	3.9	27	7
	Lawrence McCutcheon, Los Angeles[4]	294	1,238	4.2	48	7
	Franco Harris, Pittsburgh[5]	300	1,162	3.9	61	11
	Lydell Mitchell, Baltimore[3]	301	1,159	3.9	64	3
	Chuck Foreman, Minnesota[3]	270	1,112	4.1	51	6
	Greg Pruitt, Cleveland[3]	236	1,086	4.6	78	3
	Sam Cunningham, New England	270	1,015	3.8	31	4
	*Tony Dorsett, Dallas	208	1,007	4.8	84	12
1976	O.J. Simpson, Buffalo[5]	290	1,503	5.2	75	8
	Walter Payton, Chicago	311	1,390	4.5	60	13
	Delvin Williams, San Francisco	248	1,203	4.9	80	7
	Lydell Mitchell, Baltimore[2]	289	1,200	4.2	43	5
	Lawrence McCutcheon, Los Angeles[3]	291	1,168	4.0	40	9
	Chuck Foreman, Minnesota[2]	278	1,155	4.2	46	13
	Franco Harris, Pittsburgh[4]	289	1,128	3.9	30	14
	Mike Thomas, Washington	254	1,101	4.3	28	5
	Rocky Bleier, Pittsburgh	220	1,036	4.7	28	5
	Mark van Eeghen, Oakland	233	1,012	4.3	21	3
	Otis Armstrong, Denver[2]	247	1,008	4.1	31	5
	Greg Pruitt, Cleveland[2]	209	1,000	4.8	64	4
1975	O.J. Simpson, Buffalo[4]	329	1,817	5.5	88	16
	Franco Harris, Pittsburgh[3]	262	1,246	4.8	36	10
	Lydell Mitchell, Baltimore	289	1,193	4.1	70	11
	Jim Otis, St. Louis	269	1,076	4.0	30	5
	Chuck Foreman, Minnesota	280	1,070	3.8	31	13
	Greg Pruitt, Cleveland	217	1,067	4.9	50	8
	John Riggins, N.Y. Jets	238	1,005	4.2	42	8
	Dave Hampton, Atlanta	250	1,002	4.0	22	5
1974	Otis Armstrong, Denver	263	1,407	5.3	43	9
	*Don Woods, San Diego	227	1,162	5.1	56	7
	O.J. Simpson, Buffalo[3]	270	1,125	4.2	41	3
	Lawrence McCutcheon, Los Angeles[2]	236	1,109	4.7	23	3
	Franco Harris, Pittsburgh[2]	208	1,006	4.8	54	5
1973	O.J. Simpson, Buffalo[2]	332	2,003	6.0	80	12
	John Brockington, Green Bay[3]	265	1,144	4.3	53	3
	Calvin Hill, Dallas[2]	273	1,142	4.2	21	6
	Lawrence McCutcheon, Los Angeles	210	1,097	5.2	37	2
	Larry Csonka, Miami[3]	219	1,003	4.6	25	5
1972	O.J. Simpson, Buffalo	292	1,251	4.3	94	6
	Larry Brown, Washington[2]	285	1,216	4.3	38	8
	Ron Johnson, N.Y. Giants[2]	298	1,182	4.0	35	9
	Larry Csonka, Miami[2]	213	1,117	5.2	45	6
	Marv Hubbard, Oakland	219	1,100	5.0	39	4
	*Franco Harris, Pittsburgh	188	1,055	5.6	75	10
	Calvin Hill, Dallas	245	1,036	4.2	26	6
	Mike Garrett, San Diego[2]	272	1,031	3.8	41	6
	John Brockington, Green Bay[2]	274	1,027	3.7	30	8
	Eugene (Mercury) Morris, Miami	190	1,000	5.3	33	12
1971	Floyd Little, Denver	284	1,133	4.0	40	6
	*John Brockington, Green Bay	216	1,105	5.1	52	4
	Larry Csonka, Miami	195	1,051	5.4	28	7
	Steve Owens, Detroit	246	1,035	4.2	23	8
	Willie Ellison, Los Angeles	211	1,000	4.7	80	4
1970	Larry Brown, Washington	237	1,125	4.7	75	5
	Ron Johnson, N.Y. Giants	263	1,027	3.9	68	8
1969	Gale Sayers, Chicago[2]	236	1,032	4.4	28	8
1968	Leroy Kelly, Cleveland[3]	248	1,239	5.0	65	16
	*Paul Robinson, Cincinnati	238	1,023	4.3	87	8
1967	Jim Nance, Boston[2]	269	1,216	4.5	53	7
	Leroy Kelly, Cleveland[2]	235	1,205	5.1	42	11
	Hoyle Granger, Houston	236	1,194	5.1	67	6
	Mike Garrett, Kansas City	236	1,087	4.6	58	9
1966	Jim Nance, Boston	299	1,458	4.9	65	11
	Gale Sayers, Chicago	229	1,231	5.4	58	8
	Leroy Kelly, Cleveland	209	1,141	5.5	70	15
	Dick Bass, Los Angeles[2]	248	1,090	4.4	50	8
1965	Jim Brown, Cleveland[7]	289	1,544	5.3	67	17
	Paul Lowe, San Diego[2]	222	1,121	5.0	59	7
1964	Jim Brown, Cleveland[6]	280	1,446	5.2	71	7
	Jim Taylor, Green Bay[5]	235	1,169	5.0	84	12
	John Henry Johnson, Pittsburgh[2]	235	1,048	4.5	45	7
1963	Jim Brown, Cleveland[5]	291	1,863	6.4	80	12
	Clem Daniels, Oakland	215	1,099	5.1	74	3
	Jim Taylor, Green Bay[4]	248	1,018	4.1	40	9
	Paul Lowe, San Diego	177	1,010	5.7	66	8
1962	Jim Taylor, Green Bay[3]	272	1,474	5.4	51	19
	John Henry Johnson, Pittsburgh	251	1,141	4.5	40	7
	*Cookie Gilchrist, Buffalo	214	1,096	5.1	44	13
	Abner Haynes, Dall. Texans	221	1,049	4.7	71	13
	Dick Bass, Los Angeles	196	1,033	5.3	57	6
	Charlie Tolar, Houston	244	1,012	4.1	25	7
1961	Jim Brown, Cleveland[4]	305	1,408	4.6	38	8
	Jim Taylor, Green Bay[2]	243	1,307	5.4	53	15
1960	Jim Brown, Cleveland[3]	215	1,257	5.8	71	9
	Jim Taylor, Green Bay	230	1,101	4.8	32	11
	John David Crow, St. Louis	183	1,071	5.9	57	6
1959	Jim Brown, Cleveland[2]	290	1,329	4.6	70	14
	J. D. Smith, San Francisco	207	1,036	5.0	73	10
1958	Jim Brown, Cleveland	257	1,527	5.9	65	17
1956	Rick Casares, Chi. Bears	234	1,126	4.8	68	12
1954	Joe Perry, San Francisco[2]	173	1,049	6.1	58	8
1953	Joe Perry, San Francisco	192	1,018	5.3	51	10

1949	Steve Van Buren, Philadelphia[2]	263	1,146	4.4	41	11
	Tony Canadeo, Green Bay	208	1,052	5.1	54	4
1947	Steve Van Buren, Philadelphia	217	1,008	4.6	45	13
1934	*Beattie Feathers, Chi. Bears	101	1,004	9.9	82	8

**First year in the league.*

200 Yards Rushing in a Game

Date	Player, Team, Opponent	Att.	Yards	TD
Nov. 30, 1987	*Bo Jackson, L.A. Raiders vs. Seattle	18	221	2
Nov. 15, 1987	Charles White, L.A. Rams vs. St. Louis	34	213	1
Dec. 7, 1986	Rueben Mayes, New Orleans vs. Miami	28	203	2
Oct. 5, 1986	Eric Dickerson, L.A. Rams vs. Tampa Bay (OT)	30	207	2
Dec. 21, 1985	George Rogers, Washington vs. St. Louis	34	206	1
Dec. 21, 1985	Joe Morris, N.Y. Giants vs. Pittsburgh	36	202	3
Dec. 9, 1984	Eric Dickerson, L.A. Rams vs. Houston	27	215	2
Nov. 18, 1984	*Greg Bell, Buffalo vs. Dallas	27	206	1
Nov. 4, 1984	Eric Dickerson, L.A. Rams vs. St. Louis	21	208	0
Sept. 2, 1984	Gerald Riggs, Atlanta vs. New Orleans	35	202	2
Nov. 27, 1983	*Curt Warner, Seattle vs. Kansas City (OT)	32	207	3
Nov. 6, 1983	James Wilder, Tampa Bay vs. Minnesota	31	219	1
Sept. 18, 1983	Tony Collins, New England vs. N.Y. Jets	23	212	3
Sept. 4, 1983	George Rogers, New Orleans vs. St. Louis	24	206	2
Dec. 21, 1980	Earl Campbell, Houston vs. Minnesota	29	203	1
Nov. 16, 1980	Earl Campbell, Houston vs. Chicago	31	206	0
Oct. 26, 1980	Earl Campbell, Houston vs. Cincinnati	27	202	2
Oct. 19, 1980	Earl Campbell, Houston vs. Tampa Bay	33	203	0
Nov. 26, 1978	*Terry Miller, Buffalo vs. N.Y. Giants	21	208	2
Dec. 4, 1977	*Tony Dorsett, Dallas vs. Philadelphia	23	206	2
Nov. 20, 1977	Walter Payton, Chicago vs. Minnesota	40	275	1
Oct. 30, 1977	Walter Payton, Chicago vs. Green Bay	23	205	2
Dec. 5, 1976	O.J. Simpson, Buffalo vs. Miami	24	203	1
Nov. 25, 1976	O.J. Simpson, Buffalo vs. Detroit	29	273	2
Oct. 24, 1976	Chuck Foreman, Minnesota vs. Philadelphia	28	200	2
Dec. 14, 1975	Greg Pruitt, Cleveland vs. Kansas City	26	214	3
Sept. 28, 1975	O.J. Simpson, Buffalo vs. Pittsburgh	28	227	1
Dec. 16, 1973	O.J. Simpson, Buffalo vs. N.Y. Jets	34	200	1
Dec. 9, 1973	O.J. Simpson, Buffalo vs. New England	22	219	1
Sept. 16, 1973	O.J. Simpson, Buffalo vs. New England	29	250	2
Dec. 5, 1971	Willie Ellison, Los Angeles vs. New Orleans	26	247	1
Dec. 20, 1970	John (Frenchy) Fuqua, Pittsburgh vs. Philadelphia	20	218	2
Nov. 3, 1968	Gale Sayers, Chicago vs. Green Bay	24	205	0
Oct. 30, 1966	Jim Nance, Boston vs. Oakland	38	208	2
Oct. 10, 1964	John Henry Johnson, Pittsburgh vs. Cleveland	30	200	3
Dec. 8, 1963	Cookie Gilchrist, Buffalo vs. N.Y. Jets	36	243	5
Nov. 3, 1963	Jim Brown, Cleveland vs. Philadelphia	28	223	1
Oct. 20, 1963	Clem Daniels, Oakland vs. N.Y. Jets	27	200	2
Sept. 22, 1963	Jim Brown, Cleveland vs. Dallas	20	232	2
Dec. 10, 1961	Billy Cannon, Houston vs. N.Y. Titans	25	216	3
Nov. 19, 1961	Jim Brown, Cleveland vs. Philadelphia	34	237	4
Dec. 18, 1960	John David Crow, St. Louis vs. Pittsburgh	24	203	0
Nov. 15, 1959	Bobby Mitchell, Cleveland vs. Washington	14	232	3
Nov. 24, 1957	*Jim Brown, Cleveland vs. Los Angeles	31	237	4
Dec. 16, 1956	*Tom Wilson, Los Angeles vs. Green Bay	23	223	0
Nov. 22, 1953	Dan Towler, Los Angeles vs. Baltimore	14	205	1
Nov. 12, 1950	Gene Roberts, N.Y. Giants vs. Chi. Cardinals	26	218	2
Nov. 27, 1949	Steve Van Buren, Philadelphia vs. Pittsburgh	27	205	0
Oct. 8, 1933	Cliff Battles, Boston vs. N.Y. Giants	16	215	1

**First year in the league.*

Times 200 or More

49 times by 34 players . . . Simpson 6; Brown, Campbell 4; Dickerson 3; Payton, Rogers 2.

4,000 Yards Passing in a Season

Year	Player, Team	Att.	Comp.	Pct.	Yards	TD	Int.
1986	Dan Marino, Miami[3]	623	378	60.7	4,746	44	23
	Jay Schroeder, Washington	541	276	51.0	4,109	22	22
1985	Dan Marino, Miami[2]	567	336	59.3	4,137	30	21
1984	Dan Marino, Miami	564	362	64.2	5,084	48	17
	Neil Lomax, St. Louis	560	345	61.6	4,614	28	16
	Phil Simms, N.Y. Giants	533	286	53.7	4,044	22	18
1983	Lynn Dickey, Green Bay	484	289	59.7	4,458	32	29
	Bill Kenney, Kansas City	603	346	57.4	4,348	24	18
1981	Dan Fouts, San Diego[3]	609	360	59.1	4,802	33	17
1980	Dan Fouts, San Diego[2]	589	348	59.1	4,715	30	24
	Brian Sipe, Cleveland	554	337	60.8	4,132	30	14
1979	Dan Fouts, San Diego	530	332	62.6	4,082	24	24
1967	Joe Namath, N.Y. Jets	491	258	52.5	4,007	26	28

400 Yards Passing in a Game

Date	Player, Team, Opponent	Att.	Comp.	Yards	TD
Nov. 29, 1987	Tom Ramsey, New England vs. Philadelphia	53	34	402	3
Nov. 22, 1987	Boomer Esiason, Cincinnati vs. Pittsburgh	53	30	409	0
Sept. 20, 1987	Neil Lomax, St. Louis vs. San Diego	61	32	457	3
Dec. 21, 1986	Boomer Esiason, Cincinnati vs. N.Y. Jets	30	23	425	5
Dec. 14, 1986	Dan Marino, Miami vs. L.A. Rams (OT)	46	29	403	5
Nov. 23, 1986	Bernie Kosar, Cleveland vs. Pittsburgh (OT)	46	28	414	2
Nov. 17, 1986	Joe Montana, San Francisco vs. Washington	60	33	441	0
Nov. 16, 1986	Dan Marino, Miami vs. Buffalo	54	39	404	4
Nov. 10, 1986	Bernie Kosar, Cleveland vs. Miami	50	32	401	0
Nov. 2, 1986	Tommy Kramer, Minnesota vs. Washington (OT)	35	20	490	4
Nov. 2, 1986	Ken O'Brien, N.Y. Jets vs. Seattle	32	26	431	4
Oct. 27, 1986	Jay Schroeder, Washington vs. N.Y. Giants	40	22	420	1
Oct. 12, 1986	Steve Grogan, New England vs. N.Y. Jets	42	23	401	3
Sept. 21, 1986	Ken O'Brien, N.Y. Jets vs. Miami (OT)	43	29	479	4
Sept. 21, 1986	Dan Marino, Miami vs. N.Y. Jets (OT)	50	30	448	6
Sept. 21, 1986	Tony Eason, New England vs. Seattle	45	26	414	3
Dec. 20, 1985	John Elway, Denver vs. Seattle	42	24	432	1
Nov. 10, 1985	Dan Fouts, San Diego vs. L.A. Raiders (OT)	41	26	436	4
Oct. 13, 1985	Phil Simms, N.Y. Giants vs. Cincinnati	62	40	513	1
Oct. 13, 1985	Dave Krieg, Seattle vs. Atlanta	51	33	405	4
Oct. 6, 1985	Phil Simms, N.Y. Giants vs. Dallas	36	18	432	3
Oct. 6, 1985	Joe Montana, San Francisco vs. Atlanta	57	37	429	5
Sept. 19, 1985	Tommy Kramer, Minnesota vs. Chicago	55	28	436	3
Sept. 15, 1985	Dan Fouts, San Diego vs. Seattle	43	29	440	4
Dec. 16, 1984	Neil Lomax, St. Louis vs. Washington	46	37	468	2
Dec. 9, 1984	Dan Marino, Miami vs. Indianapolis	41	29	404	4
Dec. 2, 1984	Dan Marino, Miami vs. L.A. Raiders	57	35	470	4
Nov. 25, 1984	Dave Krieg, Seattle vs. Denver	44	30	406	3
Nov. 4, 1984	Dan Marino, Miami vs. N.Y. Jets	42	23	422	2
Oct. 21, 1984	Dan Fouts, San Diego vs. L.A. Raiders	45	24	410	3
Sept. 30, 1984	Dan Marino, Miami vs. St. Louis	36	24	429	3
Sept. 2, 1984	Phil Simms, N.Y. Giants vs. Philadelphia	30	23	409	4
Dec. 11, 1983	Bill Kenney, Kansas City vs. San Diego	41	31	411	4
Nov. 20, 1983	Dave Krieg, Seattle vs. Denver	42	31	418	3
Oct. 9, 1983	Joe Ferguson, Buffalo vs. Miami (OT)	55	38	419	5
Oct. 2, 1983	Joe Theismann, Washington vs. L.A. Raiders	39	23	417	3
Sept. 25, 1983	Richard Todd, N.Y. Jets vs. L.A. Rams (OT)	50	37	446	2
Dec. 26, 1982	Vince Ferragamo, L.A. Rams vs. Chicago	46	30	509	3
Dec. 20, 1982	Dan Fouts, San Diego vs. Cincinnati	40	25	435	1
Dec. 20, 1982	Ken Anderson, Cincinnati vs. San Diego	56	40	416	2
Dec. 11, 1982	Dan Fouts, San Diego vs. San Francisco	48	33	444	5
Nov. 21, 1982	Joe Montana, San Francisco vs. St. Louis	39	26	408	3
Nov. 15, 1981	Steve Bartkowski, Atlanta vs. Pittsburgh	50	33	416	2
Oct. 25, 1981	Brian Sipe, Cleveland vs. Baltimore	41	30	444	4
Oct. 25, 1981	David Woodley, Miami vs. Dallas	37	21	408	3
Oct. 11, 1981	Tommy Kramer, Minnesota vs. San Diego	43	27	444	4
Dec. 14, 1980	Tommy Kramer, Minnesota vs. Cleveland	49	38	456	4
Nov. 16, 1980	Doug Williams, Tampa Bay vs. Minnesota	55	30	486	4
Oct. 19, 1980	Dan Fouts, San Diego vs. N.Y. Giants	41	26	444	3
Oct. 12, 1980	Lynn Dickey, Green Bay vs. Tampa Bay (OT)	51	35	418	1
Sept. 21, 1980	Richard Todd, N.Y. Jets vs. San Francisco	60	42	447	3
Oct. 3, 1976	James Harris, Los Angeles vs. Miami	29	17	436	2
Nov. 17, 1975	Ken Anderson, Cincinnati vs. Buffalo	46	30	447	2
Nov. 18, 1974	Charley Johnson, Denver vs. Kansas City	42	28	445	2
Dec. 11, 1972	Joe Namath, N.Y. Jets vs. Oakland	46	25	403	1
Sept. 24, 1972	Joe Namath, N.Y. Jets vs. Baltimore	28	15	496	6
Dec. 21, 1969	Don Horn, Green Bay vs. St. Louis	31	22	410	5
Sept. 28, 1969	Joe Kapp, Minnesota vs. Baltimore	43	28	449	7
Sept. 9, 1968	Pete Beathard, Houston vs. Kansas City	48	23	413	2
Nov. 26, 1967	Sonny Jurgensen, Washington vs. Cleveland	50	32	418	3
Oct. 1, 1967	Joe Namath, N.Y. Jets vs. Miami	39	23	415	3
Sept. 17, 1967	Johnny Unitas, Baltimore vs. Atlanta	32	22	401	2
Nov. 13, 1966	Don Meredith, Dallas vs. Washington	29	21	406	2
Nov. 28, 1965	Sonny Jurgensen, Washington vs. Dallas	43	26	411	3
Oct. 24, 1965	Fran Tarkenton, Minnesota vs. San Francisco	35	21	407	3
Nov. 1, 1964	Len Dawson, Kansas City vs. Denver	38	23	435	6
Oct. 25, 1964	Cotton Davidson, Oakland vs. Denver	36	23	427	5
Oct. 16, 1964	Babe Parilli, Boston vs. Oakland	47	25	422	4
Dec. 22, 1963	Tom Flores, Oakland vs. Houston	29	17	407	6
Nov. 17, 1963	Norm Snead, Washington vs. Pittsburgh	40	23	424	2
Nov. 10, 1963	Don Meredith, Dallas vs. San Francisco	48	30	460	3
Oct. 13, 1963	Charley Johnson, St. Louis vs. Pittsburgh	41	20	428	2
Dec. 16, 1962	Sonny Jurgensen, Philadelphia vs. St. Louis	34	15	419	5
Nov. 18, 1962	Bill Wade, Chicago vs. Dall. Cowboys	46	28	466	2
Oct. 28, 1962	Y.A. Tittle, N.Y. Giants vs. Washington	39	27	505	7
Sept. 15, 1962	Frank Tripucka, Denver vs. Buffalo	56	29	447	2
Dec. 17, 1961	Sonny Jurgensen, Philadelphia vs. Detroit	42	27	403	3
Nov. 19, 1961	George Blanda, Houston vs. N.Y. Titans	32	20	418	7
Oct. 29, 1961	George Blanda, Houston vs. Buffalo	32	18	464	4
Oct. 29, 1961	Sonny Jurgensen, Philadelphia vs. Washington	41	27	436	3
Oct. 13, 1961	Jacky Lee, Houston vs. Boston	41	27	457	2
Dec. 13, 1958	Bobby Layne, Pittsburgh vs. Chi. Cardinals	49	23	409	2
Nov. 8, 1953	Bobby Thomason, Philadelphia vs. N.Y. Giants	44	22	437	4
Oct. 4, 1952	Otto Graham, Cleveland vs. Pittsburgh	49	21	401	3
Sept. 28, 1951	Norm Van Brocklin, Los Angeles vs. N.Y. Yanks	41	27	554	5
Dec. 11, 1949	Johnny Lujack, Chi. Bears vs. Chi. Cardinals	39	24	468	6
Oct. 31, 1948	Sammy Baugh, Washington vs. Boston	24	17	446	4
Oct. 31, 1948	Jim Hardy, Los Angeles vs. Chi. Cardinals	53	28	406	3
Nov. 14, 1943	Sid Luckman, Chi. Bears vs. N.Y. Giants	32	21	433	7

Times 400 or More

89 times by 54 players . . . Marino 7; Fouts 6; Jurgensen 5; Kramer 4; Krieg, Montana, Namath, Simms 3; Anderson, Blanda, Esiason, Johnson, Kosar, Lomax, Meredith, O'Brien, Todd 2.

1,000 Yards Pass Receiving in a Season

Year	Player, Team	No.	Yards	Avg.	Long	TD
1987	J. T. Smith, St. Louis[2]	91	1,117	12.3	38	8
	Jerry Rice, San Francisco[2]	65	1,078	16.6	57	22
	Gary Clark, Washington[2]	56	1,066	19.0	84	7
	Carlos Carson, Kansas City[3]	55	1,044	19.0	81	7
1986	Jerry Rice, San Francisco	86	1,570	18.3	66	15
	Stanley Morgan, New England[3]	84	1,491	17.8	44	10
	Mark Duper, Miami[3]	67	1,313	19.6	85	11
	Gary Clark, Washington	74	1,265	17.1	55	7
	Al Toon, N.Y. Jets	85	1,176	13.8	62	8
	Todd Christensen, L.A. Raiders[3]	95	1,153	12.1	35	8
	Mark Clayton, Miami[2]	60	1,150	19.2	68	10
	*Bill Brooks, Indianapolis	65	1,131	17.4	84	8
	Drew Hill, Houston[2]	65	1,112	17.1	81	5
	Steve Largent, Seattle[8]	70	1,070	15.3	38	9
	Art Monk, Washington[3]	73	1,068	14.6	69	4
	*Earnest Givens, Houston	61	1,062	17.4	60	3
	Cris Collinsworth, Cincinnati[4]	62	1,024	16.5	46	10
	Wesley Walker, N.Y. Jets[2]	49	1,016	20.7	83	12

	J.T. Smith, St. Louis	80	1,014	12.7	45	6
	Mark Bavaro, N.Y. Giants	66	1,001	15.2	41	4
1985	Steve Largent, Seattle[7]	79	1,287	16.3	43	6
	Mike Quick, Philadelphia[3]	73	1,247	17.1	99	11
	Art Monk, Washington[2]	91	1,226	13.5	53	2
	Wes Chandler, San Diego[4]	67	1,199	17.9	75	10
	Drew Hill, Houston	64	1,169	18.3	57	9
	James Lofton, Green Bay[5]	69	1,153	16.7	56	4
	Louis Lipps, Pittsburgh	59	1,134	19.2	51	12
	Cris Collinsworth, Cincinnati[3]	65	1,125	17.3	71	5
	Tony Hill, Dallas[3]	74	1,113	15.0	53	7
	Lionel James, San Diego	86	1,027	11.9	67	6
	Roger Craig, San Francisco	92	1,016	11.0	73	6
1984	Roy Green, St. Louis[2]	78	1,555	19.9	83	12
	John Stallworth, Pittsburgh[3]	80	1,395	17.4	51	11
	Mark Clayton, Miami	73	1,389	19.0	65	18
	Art Monk, Washington	106	1,372	12.9	72	7
	James Lofton, Green Bay[4]	62	1,361	22.0	79	7
	Mark Duper, Miami[2]	71	1,306	18.4	80	8
	Steve Watson, Denver[3]	69	1,170	17.0	73	7
	Steve Largent, Seattle[6]	74	1,164	15.7	65	12
	Tim Smith, Houston[2]	69	1,141	16.5	75	4
	Stacey Bailey, Atlanta	67	1,138	17.0	61	6
	Carlos Carson, Kansas City[2]	57	1,078	18.9	57	4
	Mike Quick, Philadelphia[2]	61	1,052	17.2	90	9
	Todd Christensen, L.A. Raiders[2]	80	1,007	12.6	38	7
	Kevin House, Tampa Bay[2]	76	1,005	13.2	55	5
	Ozzie Newsome, Cleveland[2]	89	1,001	11.2	52	5
1983	Mike Quick, Philadelphia	69	1,409	20.4	83	13
	Carlos Carson, Kansas City	80	1,351	16.9	50	7
	James Lofton, Green Bay[3]	58	1,300	22.4	74	8
	Todd Christensen, L.A. Raiders	92	1,247	13.6	45	12
	Roy Green, St. Louis	78	1,227	15.7	71	14
	Charlie Brown, Washington	78	1,225	15.7	75	8
	Tim Smith, Houston	83	1,176	14.2	47	6
	Kellen Winslow, San Diego[3]	88	1,172	13.3	46	8
	Earnest Gray, N.Y. Giants	78	1,139	14.6	62	5
	Steve Watson, Denver[2]	59	1,133	19.2	78	5
	Cris Collinsworth, Cincinnati[2]	66	1,130	17.1	63	5
	Steve Largent, Seattle[5]	72	1,074	14.9	46	11
	Mark Duper, Miami	51	1,003	19.7	85	10
1982	Wes Chandler, San Diego[3]	49	1,032	21.1	66	9
1981	Alfred Jenkins, Atlanta[2]	70	1,358	19.4	67	13
	James Lofton, Green Bay[2]	71	1,294	18.2	75	8
	Frank Lewis, Buffalo[2]	70	1,244	17.8	33	4
	Steve Watson, Denver	60	1,244	20.7	95	13
	Steve Largent, Seattle[4]	75	1,224	16.3	57	9
	Charlie Joiner, San Diego[4]	70	1,188	17.0	57	7
	Kevin House, Tampa Bay	56	1,176	21.0	84	9
	Wes Chandler, N.O.-San Diego[2]	69	1,142	16.6	51	6
	Dwight Clark, San Francisco	85	1,105	13.0	78	4
	John Stallworth, Pittsburgh[2]	63	1,098	17.4	55	5
	Kellen Winslow, San Diego[2]	88	1,075	12.2	67	10
	Pat Tilley, St. Louis	66	1,040	15.8	75	3
	Stanley Morgan, New England[2]	44	1,029	23.4	76	6
	Harold Carmichael, Philadelphia[3]	61	1,028	16.9	85	6
	Freddie Scott, Detroit	53	1,022	19.3	48	5
	*Cris Collinsworth, Cincinnati	67	1,009	15.1	74	8
	Joe Senser, Minnesota	79	1,004	12.7	53	8
	Ozzie Newsome, Cleveland	69	1,002	14.5	62	6
	Sammy White, Minnesota	66	1,001	15.2	53	3
1980	John Jefferson, San Diego[3]	82	1,340	16.3	58	13
	Kellen Winslow, San Diego	89	1,290	14.5	65	9
	James Lofton, Green Bay	71	1,226	17.3	47	4
	Charlie Joiner, San Diego[3]	71	1,132	15.9	51	4
	Ahmad Rashad, Minnesota[2]	69	1,095	15.9	76	5
	Steve Largent, Seattle[3]	66	1,064	16.1	67	6
	Tony Hill, Dallas[2]	60	1,055	17.6	58	8
	Alfred Jenkins, Atlanta	57	1,026	18.0	57	6
1979	Steve Largent, Seattle[2]	66	1,237	18.7	55	9
	John Stallworth, Pittsburgh	70	1,183	16.9	65	8
	Ahmad Rashad, Minnesota	80	1,156	14.5	52	9
	John Jefferson, San Diego[2]	61	1,090	17.9	65	10
	Frank Lewis, Buffalo	54	1,082	20.0	55	2
	Wes Chandler, New Orleans	65	1,069	16.4	85	6
	Tony Hill, Dallas	60	1,062	17.7	75	10
	Drew Pearson, Dallas[2]	55	1,026	18.7	56	8
	Wallace Francis, Atlanta	74	1,013	13.7	42	8
	Harold Jackson, New England[3]	45	1,013	22.5	59	7
	Charlie Joiner, San Diego[2]	72	1,008	14.0	39	4
	Stanley Morgan, New England	44	1,002	22.8	63	12
1978	Wesley Walker, N.Y. Jets	48	1,169	24.4	77	8
	Steve Largent, Seattle	71	1,168	16.5	57	8
	Harold Carmichael, Philadelphia[2]	55	1,072	19.5	56	8
	*John Jefferson, San Diego	56	1,001	17.9	46	13
1976	Roger Carr, Baltimore	43	1,112	25.9	79	11
	Cliff Branch, Oakland[2]	46	1,111	24.2	88	12
	Charlie Joiner, San Diego	50	1,056	21.1	81	7
1975	Ken Burrough, Houston	53	1,063	20.1	77	8
1974	Cliff Branch, Oakland	60	1,092	18.2	67	13
	Drew Pearson, Dallas	62	1,087	17.5	50	2
1973	Harold Carmichael, Philadelphia	67	1,116	16.7	73	9
1972	Harold Jackson, Philadelphia[2]	62	1,048	16.9	77	4
	John Gilliam, Minnesota	47	1,035	22.0	66	7
1971	Otis Taylor, Kansas City[2]	57	1,110	19.5	82	7
1970	Gene Washington, San Francisco	53	1,100	20.8	79	12
	Marlin Briscoe, Buffalo	57	1,036	18.2	48	8
	Dick Gordon, Chicago	71	1,026	14.5	69	13
	Gary Garrison, San Diego[2]	44	1,006	22.9	67	12
1969	Warren Wells, Oakland[2]	47	1,260	26.8	80	14
	Harold Jackson, Philadelphia	65	1,116	17.2	65	9
	Roy Jefferson, Pittsburgh[2]	67	1,079	16.1	63	9
	Dan Abramowicz, New Orleans	73	1,015	13.9	49	7
	Lance Alworth, San Diego[7]	64	1,003	15.7	76	4
1968	Lance Alworth, San Diego[6]	68	1,312	19.3	80	10
	Don Maynard, N.Y. Jets[5]	57	1,297	22.8	87	10
	George Sauer, N.Y. Jets[3]	66	1,141	17.3	43	3
	Warren Wells, Oakland	53	1,137	21.5	94	11
	Gary Garrison, San Diego	52	1,103	21.2	84	10
	Roy Jefferson, Pittsburgh	58	1,074	18.5	62	11
	Paul Warfield, Cleveland	50	1,067	21.3	65	12
	Homer Jones, N.Y. Giants[3]	45	1,057	23.5	84	7
	Fred Biletnikoff, Oakland	61	1,037	17.0	82	6
	Lance Rentzel, Dallas	54	1,009	18.7	65	6
1967	Don Maynard, N.Y. Jets[4]	71	1,434	20.2	75	10
	Ben Hawkins, Philadelphia	59	1,265	21.4	87	10
	Homer Jones, N.Y. Giants[2]	49	1,209	24.7	70	13
	Jackie Smith, St. Louis	56	1,205	21.5	76	9
	George Sauer, N.Y. Jets[2]	75	1,189	15.9	61	6
	Lance Alworth, San Diego[5]	52	1,010	19.4	71	9
1966	Lance Alworth, San Diego[4]	73	1,383	18.9	78	13
	Otis Taylor, Kansas City	58	1,297	22.4	89	8
	Pat Studstill, Detroit	67	1,266	18.9	99	5
	Bob Hayes, Dallas[2]	64	1,232	19.3	95	13
	Charlie Frazier, Houston	57	1,129	19.8	79	12
	Charley Taylor, Washington	72	1,119	15.5	86	12
	George Sauer, N.Y. Jets	63	1,081	17.2	77	5
	Homer Jones, N.Y. Giants	48	1,044	21.8	98	8
	Art Powell, Oakland[5]	53	1,026	19.4	46	11
1965	Lance Alworth, San Diego[3]	69	1,602	23.2	85	14
	Dave Parks, San Francisco	80	1,344	16.8	53	12
	Don Maynard, N.Y. Jets[3]	68	1,218	17.9	56	14
	Pete Retzlaff, Philadelphia	66	1,190	18.0	78	10
	Lionel Taylor, Denver[4]	85	1,131	13.3	63	6
	Tommy McDonald, Los Angeles[3]	67	1,036	15.5	51	9
	*Bob Hayes, Dallas	46	1,003	21.8	82	12
1964	Charley Hennigan, Houston[3]	101	1,546	15.3	53	8
	Art Powell, Oakland[4]	76	1,361	17.9	77	11
	Lance Alworth, San Diego[2]	61	1,235	20.2	82	13
	Johnny Morris, Chicago	93	1,200	12.9	63	10
	Elbert Dubenion, Buffalo	42	1,139	27.1	72	10
	Terry Barr, Detroit[2]	57	1,030	18.1	58	9
1963	Bobby Mitchell, Washington[2]	69	1,436	20.8	99	7
	Art Powell, Oakland[3]	73	1,304	17.9	85	16
	Buddy Dial, Pittsburgh[2]	60	1,295	21.6	83	9
	Lance Alworth, San Diego	61	1,205	19.8	85	11
	Del Shofner, N.Y. Giants[4]	64	1,181	18.5	70	9
	Lionel Taylor, Denver[3]	78	1,101	14.1	72	10
	Terry Barr, Detroit	66	1,086	16.5	75	13
	Charley Hennigan, Houston[2]	61	1,051	17.2	83	10
	Sonny Randle, St. Louis[2]	51	1,014	19.9	68	12
	Bake Turner, N.Y. Jets	71	1,009	14.2	53	6
1962	Bobby Mitchell, Washington	72	1,384	19.2	81	11
	Sonny Randle, St. Louis	63	1,158	18.4	86	7
	Tommy McDonald, Philadelphia[2]	58	1,146	19.8	60	10
	Del Shofner, N.Y. Giants[3]	53	1,133	21.4	69	12
	Art Powell, N.Y. Titans[2]	64	1,130	17.7	80	8
	Frank Clarke, Dall. Cowboys	47	1,043	22.2	66	14
	Don Maynard, N.Y. Titans[2]	56	1,041	18.6	86	8
1961	Charley Hennigan, Houston	82	1,746	21.3	80	12
	Lionel Taylor, Denver[2]	100	1,176	11.8	52	4
	Bill Groman, Houston[2]	50	1,175	23.5	80	17
	Tommy McDonald, Philadelphia	64	1,144	17.9	66	13
	Del Shofner, N.Y. Giants[2]	68	1,125	16.5	46	11
	Jim Phillips, Los Angeles	78	1,092	14.0	69	5
	*Mike Ditka, Chicago	56	1,076	19.2	76	12
	Dave Kocourek, San Diego	55	1,055	19.2	76	4
	Buddy Dial, Pittsburgh	53	1,047	19.8	88	12
	R.C. Owens, San Francisco	55	1,032	18.8	54	5
1960	*Bill Groman, Houston	72	1,473	20.5	92	12
	Raymond Berry, Baltimore	74	1,298	17.5	70	10
	Don Maynard, N.Y. Titans	72	1,265	17.6	65	6
	Lionel Taylor, Denver	92	1,235	13.4	80	12
	Art Powell, N.Y. Titans	69	1,167	16.9	76	14
1958	Del Shofner, Los Angeles	51	1,097	21.5	92	8
1956	Bill Howton, Green Bay[2]	55	1,188	21.6	66	12
	Harlon Hill, Chi. Bears[2]	47	1,128	24.0	79	11
1954	Bob Boyd, Los Angeles	53	1,212	22.9	80	6
	*Harlon Hill, Chi. Bears	45	1,124	25.0	76	12
1953	Pete Pihos, Philadelphia	63	1,049	16.7	59	10
1952	*Bill Howton, Green Bay	53	1,231	23.2	90	13
1951	Elroy (Crazylegs) Hirsch, Los Angeles	66	1,495	22.7	91	17
1950	Tom Fears, Los Angeles[2]	84	1,116	13.3	53	7
	Cloyce Box, Detroit	50	1,009	20.2	82	11
1949	Bob Mann, Detroit	66	1,014	15.4	64	4
	Tom Fears, Los Angeles	77	1,013	13.2	51	9
1945	Jim Benton, Cleveland	45	1,067	23.7	84	8
1942	Don Hutson, Green Bay	74	1,211	16.4	73	17

**First year in the league.*

250 Yards Pass Receiving in a Game

Date	Player, Team, Opponent	No.	Yards	TD
Oct. 18, 1987	Steve Largent, Seattle vs. Detroit	15	261	3
Oct. 4, 1987	*Anthony Allen, Washington vs. St. Louis	7	255	3
Dec. 22, 1985	Stephone Paige, Kansas City vs. San Diego	8	309	2
Dec. 20, 1982	Wes Chandler, San Diego vs. Cincinnati	10	260	2
Sept. 23, 1979	*Jerry Butler, Buffalo vs. N.Y. Jets	10	255	4
Nov. 4, 1962	Sonny Randle, St. Louis vs. N.Y. Giants	16	256	1
Oct. 28, 1962	Del Shofner, N.Y. Giants vs. Washington	11	269	1
Oct. 13, 1961	Charley Hennigan, Houston vs. Boston	13	272	1
Oct. 21, 1956	Billy Howton, Green Bay vs. Los Angeles	7	257	2
Dec. 3, 1950	Cloyce Box, Detroit vs. Baltimore	12	302	4
Nov. 22, 1945	Jim Benton, Cleveland vs. Detroit	10	303	1

**First year in the league.*

2,000 Combined Net Yards Gained in a Season

Year	Player, Team	Rushing Att.-Yds.	Pass Rec.	Punt Ret.	Kickoff Ret.	Fum. Runs	Total Yds.
1986	Eric Dickerson, L.A. Rams	404-1,821	26-205	0-0	0-0	2-0	432-2,026
	Gary Anderson, San Diego	127-442	80-871	25-227	24-482	2-0	258-2,022
1985	Lionel James, San Diego	105-516	86-1,027	25-213	36-779	1-0	253-2,535
	Marcus Allen, L.A. Raiders	380-1,759	67-555	0-0	0-0	2-(−6)	449-2,308
	Roger Craig, San Fran.	214-1,050	92-1,016	0-0	0-0	0-0	306-2,066
	Walter Payton, Chicago	324-1,551	49-483	0-0	0-0	1-0	374-2,034
1984	Eric Dickerson, L.A. Rams	379-2,105	21-139	0-0	0-0	4-15	404-2,259
	James Wilder, Tampa Bay	407-1,544	85-685	0-0	0-0	4-0	496-2,229
	Walter Payton, Chicago	381-1,684	45-368	0-0	0-0	1-0	427-2,052
1983*	Eric Dickerson, L.A. Rams	390-1,808	51-404	0-0	0-0	1-0	442-2,212
	William Andrews, Atlanta	331-1,567	59-609	0-0	0-0	2-0	392-2,176
	Walter Payton, Chicago	314-1,421	53-607	0-0	0-0	2-0	369-2,028
1981*	James Brooks, San Diego	109-525	46-329	22-290	40-949	2-0	219-2,093
	William Andrews, Atlanta	289-1,301	81-735	0-0	0-0	0-0	370-2,036
1980	Bruce Harper, N.Y. Jets	45-126	50-634	28-242	49-1,070	3-0	175-2,072
1979	Wilbert Montgomery, Phil.	338-1,512	41-494	0-0	1-6	2-0	382-2,012
1978	Bruce Harper, N.Y. Jets	58-303	13-196	30-378	55-1,280	1-0	157-2,157
1977	Walter Payton, Chicago	339-1,852	27-269	0-0	2-95	5-0	373-2,216
	Terry Metcalf, St. Louis	149-739	34-403	14-108	32-772	1-0	230-2,022
1975	Terry Metcalf, St. Louis	165-816	43-378	23-285	35-960	2-23	268-2,462
	O.J. Simpson, Buffalo	329-1,817	28-426	0-0	0-0	1-0	358-2,243
1974	Mack Herron, New England	231-824	38-474	35-517	28-629	3-0	335-2,444
	Otis Armstrong, Denver	263-1,407	38-405	0-0	16-386	1-0	318-2,198
	Terry Metcalf, St. Louis	152-718	50-377	26-340	20-623	7-0	255-2,058
1973	O.J. Simpson, Buffalo	332-2,003	6-70	0-0	0-0	0-0	338-2,073
1966	Gale Sayers, Chicago	229-1,231	34-447	6-44	23-718	3-0	295-2,440
	Leroy Kelly, Cleveland	209-1,141	32-366	13-104	19-403	0-0	273-2,014
1965*	Gale Sayers, Chicago	166-867	29-507	16-238	21-660	4-0	236-2,272
1963	Timmy Brown, Philadelphia	192-841	36-487	16-152	33-945	2-3	279-2,428
	Jim Brown, Cleveland	291-1,863	24-268	0-0	0-0	0-0	315-2,131
1962	Timmy Brown, Philadelphia	137-545	52-849	6-81	30-831	4-0	229-2,306
	Dick Christy, N.Y. Titans	114-535	62-538	15-250	38-824	2-0	231-2,147
1961	Billy Cannon, Houston	200-948	43-586	9-70	18-439	2-0	272-2,043
1960*	Abner Haynes, Dall. Texans	156-875	55-576	14-215	19-434	4-0	248-2,100

**First year in the league.*

300 Combined Net Yards Gained in a Game

Date	Player, Team, Opponent	No.	Yards	TD
Dec. 22, 1985	Stephone Paige, Kansas City vs. San Diego	8	309	2
Nov. 10, 1985	Lionel James, San Diego vs. L.A. Raiders (OT)	23	345	0
Sept. 22, 1985	Lionel James, San Diego vs. Cincinnati	20	316	2
Dec. 21, 1975	Walter Payton, Chicago vs. New Orleans	32	300	1
Nov. 23, 1975	Greg Pruitt, Cleveland vs. Cincinnati	28	304	2
Nov. 1, 1970	Eugene (Mercury) Morris, Miami vs. Baltimore	17	302	0
Oct. 4, 1970	O. J. Simpson, Buffalo vs. N.Y. Jets	26	303	2
Dec. 6, 1969	Jerry LeVias, Houston vs. N.Y. Jets	18	329	1
Nov. 2, 1969	Travis Williams, Green Bay vs. Pittsburgh	11	314	3
Dec. 18, 1966	Gale Sayers, Chicago vs. Minnesota	20	339	2
Dec. 12, 1965	Gale Sayers, Chicago vs. San Francisco	17	336	6
Nov. 17, 1963	Gary Ballman, Pittsburgh vs. Washington	12	320	2
Dec. 16, 1962	Timmy Brown, Philadelphia vs. St. Louis	19	341	2
Dec. 10, 1961	Billy Cannon, Houston vs. N.Y. Titans	32	373	5
Nov 19, 1961	Jim Brown, Cleveland vs. Philadelphia	38	313	4
Dec. 3, 1950	Cloyce Box, Detroit vs. Baltimore	13	302	4
Oct. 29, 1950	Wally Triplett, Detroit vs. Los Angeles	11	331	1
Nov. 22, 1945	Jim Benton, Cleveland vs. Detroit	10	303	1

Top 20 Scorers

Player	Years	TD	FG	PAT	TP
George Blanda	26	9	335	943	2,002
Jan Stenerud	19	0	373	580	1,699
Jim Turner	16	1	304	521	1,439
Mark Moseley	16	0	300	482	1,382
Jim Bakken	17	0	282	534	1,380
Fred Cox	15	0	282	519	1,365
Lou Groza	17	1	234	641	1,349
Gino Cappelletti	11	42	176	350	1,130
Ray Wersching	15	0	222	456	1,122
Don Cockroft	13	0	216	432	1,080
Pat Leahy	14	0	218	424	1,078
Garo Yepremian	14	0	210	444	1,074
Chris Bahr	12	0	206	424	1,042
Bruce Gossett	11	0	219	374	1,031
Sam Baker	15	2	179	428	977
Rafael Septien	10	0	180	420	960
Lou Michaels	13	1	187	386	955
Roy Gerela	11	0	184	351	903
Bobby Walston	12	46	80	365	881
Pete Gogolak	11	0	173	344	863

Cappelletti's total includes four two-point conversions. Michaels's total includes one safety.

Top 20 Touchdown Scorers

Player	Years	Rush	Pass Rec.	Returns	Total TD
Jim Brown	9	106	20	0	126
Walter Payton	13	110	15	0	125
John Riggins	14	104	12	0	116
Lenny Moore	12	63	48	2	113
Don Hutson	11	3	99	3	105
Franco Harris	13	91	9	0	100
Steve Largent	12	1	95	0	96
Jim Taylor	10	83	10	0	93
Bobby Mitchell	11	18	65	8	91
Leroy Kelly	10	74	13	3	90
Charley Taylor	13	11	79	0	90
Don Maynard	15	0	88	0	88
Lance Alworth	11	2	85	0	87
Tony Dorsett	11	72	13	1	86
Paul Warfield	13	1	85	0	86
Tommy McDonald	12	0	84	1	85
Pete Johnson	8	76	6	0	82
Art Powell	10	0	81	1	82
Harold Carmichael	14	0	79	0	79
Frank Gifford	12	34	43	1	78

Top 20 Rushers

Player	Years	Att.	Yards	Avg.	Long	TD
Walter Payton	13	3,838	16,726	4.4	76	110
Jim Brown	9	2,359	12,312	5.2	80	106
Franco Harris	13	2,949	12,120	4.1	75	91
Tony Dorsett	11	2,755	12,036	4.4	99	72
John Riggins	14	2,916	11,352	3.9	66	104
O.J. Simpson	11	2,404	11,236	4.7	94	61
Earl Campbell	8	2,187	9,407	4.3	81	74
Jim Taylor	10	1,941	8,597	4.4	84	83
Joe Perry	14	1,737	8,378	4.8	78	53
Eric Dickerson	5	1,748	8,256	4.7	85	61
Ottis Anderson	9	1,884	8,086	4.3	76	47
Larry Csonka	11	1,891	8,081	4.3	54	64
Mike Pruitt	11	1,844	7,378	4.0	77	51
Leroy Kelly	10	1,727	7,274	4.2	70	74
George Rogers	7	1,692	7,176	4.2	79	54
John Henry Johnson	13	1,571	6,803	4.3	87	48
Wilbert Montgomery	9	1,540	6,789	4.4	90	45
Chuck Muncie	9	1,561	6,702	4.3	73	71
Mark van Eeghen	10	1,652	6,650	4.0	34	37
Lawrence McCutcheon	10	1,521	6,578	4.3	48	26

Top 20 Passers

Player	Years	Att.	Comp.	Pct. Comp.	Yards	TD	Pct. TD	Int.	Pct. Int.	Avg. Gain	Rating
Dan Marino	5	2,494	1,512	60.6	19,422	168	6.7	80	3.2	7.79	94.1
Joe Montana	9	3,276	2,084	63.6	24,552	172	5.3	89	2.7	7.49	92.5
Ken O'Brien	4	1,566	947	60.5	11,676	69	4.4	43	2.7	7.46	86.8
Dave Krieg	8	2,116	1,224	57.8	15,808	130	6.1	88	4.2	7.47	84.6
Roger Staubach	11	2,958	1,685	57.0	22,700	153	5.2	109	3.7	7.67	83.4
Sonny Jurgensen	18	4,262	2,433	57.1	32,224	255	6.0	189	4.4	7.56	82.6
Len Dawson	19	3,741	2,136	57.1	28,711	239	6.4	183	4.9	7.67	82.6
Neil Lomax	7	2,710	1,562	57.6	19,376	116	4.3	79	2.9	7.15	82.0
Danny White	12	2,908	1,732	59.6	21,685	154	5.3	129	4.4	7.46	82.0
Ken Anderson	16	4,475	2,654	59.3	32,838	197	4.4	160	3.6	7.34	81.9
Bart Starr	16	3,149	1,808	57.4	24,718	152	4.8	138	4.4	7.85	80.5
Fran Tarkenton	18	6,467	3,686	57.0	47,003	342	5.3	266	4.1	7.27	80.4
Dan Fouts	15	5,604	3,297	58.8	43,040	254	4.5	242	4.3	7.68	80.2
Bill Kenney	8	2,316	1,272	54.9	16,728	105	4.5	81	3.5	7.22	78.5
Bert Jones	10	2,551	1,430	56.1	18,190	124	4.9	101	4.0	7.13	78.2
Johnny Unitas	18	5,186	2,830	54.6	40,239	290	5.6	253	4.9	7.76	78.2
Otto Graham	6	1,565	872	55.7	13,499	88	5.6	94	6.0	8.63	78.2
Frank Ryan	13	2,133	1,090	51.1	16,042	149	7.0	111	5.2	7.52	77.6
Joe Theismann	12	3,602	2,044	56.7	25,206	160	4.4	138	3.8	7.00	77.4
Bob Griese	14	3,429	1,926	56.2	25,092	192	5.6	172	5.0	7.32	77.1

1,500 or more attempts. The passing ratings are based on performance standards established for completion percentage, interception percentage, touchdown percentage, and average gain. Passers are allocated points according to how their marks compare with those standards.

Top 20 Pass Receivers

Player	Years	No.	Yards	Avg.	Long	TD
Steve Largent	12	752	12,041	16.0	74	95
Charlie Joiner	18	750	12,146	16.2	87	65
Charley Taylor	13	649	9,110	14.0	88	79
Don Maynard	15	633	11,834	18.7	87	88
Raymond Berry	13	631	9,275	14.7	70	68
Harold Carmichael	14	590	8,985	15.2	85	79
Fred Biletnikoff	14	589	8,974	15.2	82	76
Harold Jackson	16	579	10,372	17.9	79	76
Ozzie Newsome	10	575	7,073	12.3	74	42
James Lofton	10	571	10,536	18.5	80	54
Lionel Taylor	10	567	7,195	12.7	80	45
Wes Chandler	10	555	8,933	16.1	85	56
Lance Alworth	11	542	10,266	18.9	85	85
Kellen Winslow	9	541	6,741	12.5	67	45
John Stallworth	14	537	8,723	16.2	74	63
Bobby Mitchell	11	521	7,954	15.3	99	65
Nat Moore	13	510	7,546	14.8	79	74
Dwight Clark	9	506	6,750	13.3	80	48
Art Monk	8	504	7,033	14.0	79	34
Bill Howton	12	503	8,459	16.8	90	61

Top 20 Interceptors

Player	Years	No.	Yards	Avg.	Long	TD
Paul Krause	16	81	1,185	14.6	81	3
Emlen Tunnell	14	79	1,282	16.2	55	4
Dick (Night Train) Lane	14	68	1,207	17.8	80	5
Ken Riley	15	65	596	9.2	66	5
Dick LeBeau	13	62	762	12.3	70	3
Emmitt Thomas	13	58	937	16.2	73	5
Bobby Boyd	9	57	994	17.4	74	4
Johnny Robinson	12	57	741	13.0	57	1
Mel Blount	14	57	736	12.9	52	2
Lem Barney	11	56	1,077	19.2	71	7
Pat Fischer	17	56	941	16.8	69	4
Willie Brown	16	54	472	8.7	45	2
Dave Brown	13	53	659	12.4	90	5
Bobby Dillon	8	52	976	18.8	61	5
Jack Butler	9	52	826	15.9	52	4
Larry Wilson	13	52	800	15.4	96	5

Jim Patton	12	52	712	13.7	51	2
Mel Renfro	14	52	626	12.0	90	3
Bobby Bryant	13	51	749	14.7	56	3
Donnie Shell	14	51	490	9.6	67	2

Top 20 Punters

Player	Years	No.	Yards	Avg.	Long	Blk.
Sammy Baugh	16	338	15,245	45.1	85	9
Tommy Davis	11	511	22,833	44.7	82	2
Rohn Stark	6	450	20,007	44.5	72	4
Yale Lary	11	503	22,279	44.3	74	4
Horace Gillom	7	385	16,872	43.8	80	5
Jerry Norton	11	358	15,671	43.8	78	2
Don Chandler	12	660	28,678	43.5	90	4
Jerrel Wilson	16	1,072	46,139	43.0	72	12
Norm Van Brocklin	12	523	22,413	42.9	72	3
Danny Villanueva	8	488	20,862	42.8	68	2
Bobby Joe Green	14	970	41,317	42.6	75	3
Sam Baker	15	703	29,938	42.6	72	2
Rich Camarillo	7	468	19,922	42.6	76	4
Ray Guy	14	1,049	44,493	42.4	74	3
Bob Waterfield	8	315	13,367	42.4	88	5
Curley Johnson	10	559	23,651	42.3	73	6
Jim Arnold	5	366	15,474	42.3	64	3
Jim Norton	9	522	21,961	42.1	79	7
Steve Cox	7	380	15,991	42.1	77	6
George Roberts	5	306	12,544	42.0	71	4

300 or more punts.

Top 20 Punt Returners

Player	Years	No.	Yards	Avg.	Long	TD
George McAfee	8	112	1,431	12.8	74	2
Jack Christiansen	8	85	1,084	12.8	89	8
Claude Gibson	5	110	1,381	12.6	85	3
Vai Sikahema	2	87	1,072	12.3	76	3
Bill Dudley	9	124	1,515	12.2	96	3
Rick Upchurch	9	248	3,008	12.1	92	8
Henry Ellard	5	112	1,355	12.1	83	4
Billy Johnson	13	279	3,291	11.8	87	6
Louis Lipps	4	99	1,155	11.7	76	3
Mack Herron	3	84	982	11.7	66	0
Bill Thompson	13	157	1,814	11.6	60	0
Bosh Pritchard	6	95	1,072	11.3	81	2
Rodger Bird	3	94	1,063	11.3	78	0
Irving Fryar	4	126	1,407	11.2	85	3
Bob Hayes	11	104	1,158	11.1	90	3
Terry Metcalf	6	84	936	11.1	69	1
Floyd Little	9	81	893	11.0	72	2
Les (Speedy) Duncan	11	202	2,201	10.9	95	4
Verda (Vitamin T) Smith	5	75	814	10.9	85	1
J.T. Smith	10	247	2,611	10.6	88	4

75 or more returns.

Top 20 Kickoff Returners

Player	Years	No.	Yards	Avg.	Long	TD
Gale Sayers	7	91	2,781	30.6	103	6
Lynn Chandnois	7	92	2,720	29.6	93	3
Abe Woodson	9	193	5,538	28.7	105	5
Claude (Buddy) Young	6	90	2,514	27.9	104	2
Travis Williams	5	102	2,801	27.5	105	6
Joe Arenas	7	139	3,798	27.3	96	1
Clarence Davis	8	79	2,140	27.1	76	0
Lenny Lyles	12	81	2,161	26.7	103	3
Steve Van Buren	8	76	2,030	26.7	98	3
Bobby Jancik	6	158	4,185	26.5	61	0
Eugene (Mercury) Morris	8	111	2,947	26.5	105	3
Bobby Mitchell	11	102	2,690	26.4	98	5
Mel Renfro	14	85	2,246	26.4	100	2
Ollie Matson	14	143	3,746	26.2	105	6
Alvin Haymond	10	170	4,438	26.1	98	2
Noland Smith	3	82	2,137	26.1	106	1
Tim Brown	10	184	4,781	26.0	105	5
Al Nelson	9	101	2,625	26.0	78	0
Vic Washington	6	129	3,341	25.9	98	1
Dave Hampton	8	113	2,923	25.9	101	3

75 or more returns.

Top 20 Combined Yards Gained

	Years	Tot.	Rush.	Rec.	Int. Ret.	Punt Ret.	Kickoff Ret.	Fumble Ret.
Walter Payton	13	21,803	16,726	4,538	0	0	539	0
Tony Dorsett	11	15,501	12,036	3,432	0	0	0	33
Jim Brown	9	15,459	12,312	2,499	0	0	648	0
Franco Harris	13	14,622	12,120	2,287	0	0	233	−18
O.J. Simpson	11	14,368	11,236	2,142	0	0	990	0
Bobby Mitchell	11	14,078	2,735	7,954	0	699	2,690	0
John Riggins	14	13,435	11,352	2,090	0	0	0	−7
Greg Pruitt	12	13,262	5,672	3,069	0	2,007	2,514	0
Ollie Matson	14	12,884	5,173	3,285	51	595	3,746	34
Tim Brown	10	12,684	3,862	3,399	0	639	4,781	3
Lenny Moore	12	12,451	5,174	6,039	0	56	1,180	2
Don Maynard	15	12,379	70	11,834	0	132	343	0
Charlie Joiner	18	12,367	22	12,146	0	0	194	5
Steve Largent	12	12,351	86	12,041	0	68	156	0
Leroy Kelly	10	12,330	7,274	2,281	0	990	1,784	1
Floyd Little	9	12,173	6,323	2,418	0	893	2,523	16
Abner Haynes	8	12,065	4,630	3,535	0	875	3,025	0
Bruce Harper	8	11,429	1,829	2,409	0	1,784	5,407	0
Hugh McElhenny	13	11,375	5,281	3,247	0	920	1,921	6
Lance Alworth	11	10,920	129	10,266	0	309	216	0

YEARLY STATISTICAL LEADERS

Annual Scoring Leaders

Year	Player, Team	TD	FG	PAT	TP
1987	Jerry Rice, San Francisco, NFC	23	0	0	138
	Jim Breech, Cincinnati, AFC	0	24	25	97
1986	Tony Franklin, New England, AFC	0	32	44	140
	Kevin Butler, Chicago, NFC	0	28	36	120
1985	*Kevin Butler, Chicago, NFC	0	31	51	144
	Gary Anderson, Pittsburgh, AFC	0	33	40	139
1984	Ray Wersching, San Francisco, NFC	0	25	56	131
	Gary Anderson, Pittsburgh, AFC	0	24	45	117
1983	Mark Moseley, Washington, NFC	0	33	62	161
	Gary Anderson, Pittsburgh, AFC	0	27	38	119
1982	*Marcus Allen, L.A. Raiders, AFC	14	0	0	84
	Wendell Tyler, L.A. Rams, NFC	13	0	0	78
1981	Ed Murray, Detroit, NFC	0	25	46	121
	Rafael Septien, Dallas, NFC	0	27	40	121
	Jim Breech, Cincinnati, AFC	0	22	49	115
	Nick Lowery, Kansas City, AFC	0	26	37	115
1980	John Smith, New England, AFC	0	26	51	129
	*Ed Murray, Detroit, NFC	0	27	35	116
1979	John Smith, New England, AFC	0	23	46	115
	Mark Moseley, Washington, NFC	0	25	39	114
1978	*Frank Corral, Los Angeles, NFC	0	29	31	118
	Pat Leahy, N.Y. Jets, AFC	0	22	41	107
1977	Errol Mann, Oakland, AFC	0	20	39	99
	Walter Payton, Chicago, NFC	16	0	0	96
1976	Toni Linhart, Baltimore, AFC	0	20	49	109
	Mark Moseley, Washington, NFC	0	22	31	97
1975	O.J. Simpson, Buffalo, AFC	23	0	0	138
	Chuck Foreman, Minnesota, NFC	22	0	0	132
1974	Chester Marcol, Green Bay, NFC	0	25	19	94
	Roy Gerela, Pittsburgh, AFC	0	20	33	93
1973	David Ray, Los Angeles, NFC	0	30	40	130
	Roy Gerela, Pittsburgh, AFC	0	29	36	123
1972	*Chester Marcol, Green Bay, NFC	0	33	29	128
	Bobby Howfield, N.Y. Jets, AFC	0	27	40	121
1971	Garo Yepremian, Miami, AFC	0	28	33	117
	Curt Knight, Washington, NFC	0	29	27	114
1970	Fred Cox, Minnesota, NFC	0	30	35	125
	Jan Stenerud, Kansas City, AFC	0	30	26	116
1969	Jim Turner, N.Y. Jets, AFL	0	32	33	129
	Fred Cox, Minnesota, NFL	0	26	43	121
1968	Jim Turner, N.Y. Jets, AFL	0	34	43	145
	Leroy Kelly, Cleveland, NFL	20	0	0	120
1967	Jim Bakken, St. Louis, NFL	0	27	36	117
	George Blanda, Oakland, AFL	0	20	56	116
1966	Gino Cappelletti, Boston, AFL	6	16	35	119
	Bruce Gossett, Los Angeles, NFL	0	28	29	113
1965	*Gale Sayers, Chicago, NFL	22	0	0	132
	Gino Cappelletti, Boston, AFL	9	17	27	132
1964	Gino Cappelletti, Boston, AFL	7	25	36	#155
	Lenny Moore, Baltimore, NFL	20	0	0	120
1963	Gino Cappelletti, Boston, AFL	2	22	35	113
	Don Chandler, N.Y. Giants, NFL	0	18	52	106
1962	Gene Mingo, Denver, AFL	4	27	32	137
	Jim Taylor, Green Bay, NFL	19	0	0	114
1961	Gino Cappelletti, Boston, AFL	8	17	48	147
	Paul Hornung, Green Bay, NFL	10	15	41	146
1960	Paul Hornung, Green Bay, NFL	15	15	41	176
	*Gene Mingo, Denver, AFL	6	18	33	123
1959	Paul Hornung, Green Bay	7	7	31	94
1958	Jim Brown, Cleveland	18	0	0	108
1957	Sam Baker, Washington	1	14	29	77
	Lou Groza, Cleveland	0	15	32	77
1956	Bobby Layne, Detroit	5	12	33	99
1955	Doak Walker, Detroit	7	9	27	96
1954	Bobby Walston, Philadelphia	11	4	36	114
1953	Gordy Soltau, San Francisco	6	10	48	114
1952	Gordy Soltau, San Francisco	7	6	34	94
1951	Elroy (Crazylegs) Hirsch, Los Angeles	17	0	0	102
1950	*Doak Walker, Detroit	11	8	38	128
1949	Pat Harder, Chi. Cardinals	8	3	45	102
	Gene Roberts, N.Y. Giants	17	0	0	102
1948	Pat Harder, Chi. Cardinals	6	7	53	110
1947	Pat Harder, Chi. Cardinals	7	7	39	102
1946	Ted Fritsch, Green Bay	10	9	13	100
1945	Steve Van Buren, Philadelphia	18	0	2	110
1944	Don Hutson, Green Bay	9	0	31	85
1943	Don Hutson, Green Bay	12	3	36	117
1942	Don Hutson, Green Bay	17	1	33	138
1941	Don Hutson, Green Bay	12	1	20	95
1940	Don Hutson, Green Bay	7	0	15	57
1939	Andy Farkas, Washington	11	0	2	68
1938	Clarke Hinkle, Green Bay	7	3	7	58
1937	Jack Manders, Chi. Bears	5	8	15	69
1936	Earl (Dutch) Clark, Detroit	7	4	19	73
1935	Earl (Dutch) Clark, Detroit	6	1	16	55
1934	Jack Manders, Chi. Bears	3	10	31	79
1933	Ken Strong, N.Y. Giants	6	5	13	64
	Glenn Presnell, Portsmouth	6	6	10	64
1932	Earl (Dutch) Clark, Portsmouth	6	3	10	55

First year in the league.
#Cappelletti's total includes a two-point conversion.

Annual Leaders—Most Field Goals Made

Year	Player, Team	Att.	Made	Pct.
1987	Morten Andersen, New Orleans, NFC	36	28	77.8
	Dean Biasucci, Indianapolis, AFC	27	24	88.9
	Jim Breech, Cincinnati, AFC	30	24	80.0
1986	Tony Franklin, New England, AFC	41	32	78.0
	Kevin Butler, Chicago, NFC	41	28	68.3
1985	Gary Anderson, Pittsburgh, AFC	42	33	78.6
	Morten Andersen, New Orleans, NFC	35	31	88.6
	*Kevin Butler, Chicago, NFC	37	31	83.8
1984	*Paul McFadden, Philadelphia, NFC	37	30	81.1
	Gary Anderson, Pittsburgh, AFC	32	24	75.0
	Matt Bahr, Cleveland, AFC	32	24	75.0
1983	*Ali Haji-Sheikh, N.Y. Giants, NFC	42	35	83.3
	*Raul Allegre, Baltimore, AFC	35	30	85.7
1982	Mark Moseley, Washington, NFC	21	20	95.2
	Nick Lowery, Kansas City, AFC	24	19	79.2
1981	Rafael Septien, Dallas, NFC	35	27	77.1
	Nick Lowery, Kansas City, AFC	36	26	72.2
1980	*Ed Murray, Detroit, NFC	42	27	64.3
	John Smith, New England, AFC	34	26	76.5
	Fred Steinfort, Denver, AFC	34	26	76.5
1979	Mark Moseley, Washington, NFC	33	25	75.8
	John Smith, New England, AFC	33	23	69.7
1978	*Frank Corral, Los Angeles, NFC	43	29	67.4
	Pat Leahy, N.Y. Jets, AFC	30	22	73.3
1977	Mark Moseley, Washington, NFC	37	21	56.8
	Errol Mann, Oakland, AFC	28	20	71.4
1976	Mark Moseley, Washington, NFC	34	22	64.7
	Jan Stenerud, Kansas City, AFC	38	21	55.3
1975	Jan Stenerud, Kansas City, AFC	32	22	68.8
	Toni Fritsch, Dallas, NFC	35	22	62.9
1974	Chester Marcol, Green Bay, NFC	39	25	64.1
	Roy Gerela, Pittsburgh, AFC	29	20	69.0
1973	David Ray, Los Angeles, NFC	47	30	63.8
	Roy Gerela, Pittsburgh, AFC	43	29	67.4
1972	*Chester Marcol, Green Bay, NFC	48	33	68.8
	Roy Gerela, Pittsburgh, AFC	41	28	68.3
1971	Curt Knight, Washington, NFC	49	29	59.2
	Garo Yepremian, Miami, AFC	40	28	70.0
1970	Jan Stenerud, Kansas City, AFC	42	30	71.4
	Fred Cox, Minnesota, NFC	46	30	65.2
1969	Jim Turner, N.Y. Jets, AFL	47	32	68.1
	Fred Cox, Minnesota, NFL	37	26	70.3
1968	Jim Turner, N.Y. Jets, AFL	46	34	73.9
	Mac Percival, Chicago, NFL	36	25	69.4
1967	Jim Bakken, St. Louis, NFL	39	27	69.2
	Jan Stenerud, Kansas City, AFL	36	21	58.3
1966	Bruce Gossett, Los Angeles, NFL	49	28	57.1
	Mike Mercer, Oakland-Kansas City, AFL	30	21	70.0
1965	Pete Gogolak, Buffalo, AFL	46	28	60.9
	Fred Cox, Minnesota, NFL	35	23	65.7
1964	Jim Bakken, St. Louis, NFL	38	25	65.8
	Gino Cappelletti, Boston, AFL	39	25	64.1
1963	Jim Martin, Baltimore, NFL	39	24	61.5
	Gino Cappelletti, Boston, AFL	38	22	57.9
1962	Gene Mingo, Denver, AFL	39	27	69.2
	Lou Michaels, Pittsburgh, NFL	42	26	61.9
1961	Steve Myhra, Baltimore, NFL	39	21	53.8
	Gino Cappelletti, Boston, AFL	32	17	53.1
1960	Tommy Davis, San Francisco, NFL	32	19	59.4
	*Gene Mingo, Denver, AFL	28	18	64.3
1959	Pat Summerall, New York Giants	29	20	69.0
1958	Paige Cothren, Los Angeles	25	14	56.0
	*Tom Miner, Pittsburgh	28	14	50.0
1957	Lou Groza, Cleveland	22	15	68.2
1956	Sam Baker, Washington	25	17	68.0
1955	Fred Cone, Green Bay	24	16	66.7
1954	Lou Groza, Cleveland	24	16	66.7
1953	Lou Groza, Cleveland	26	23	88.5
1952	Lou Groza, Cleveland	33	19	57.6
1951	Bob Waterfield, Los Angeles	23	13	56.5
1950	*Lou Groza, Cleveland	19	13	68.4
1949	Cliff Patton, Philadelphia	18	9	50.0
	Bob Waterfield, Los Angeles	16	9	56.3
1948	Cliff Patton, Philadelphia	12	8	66.7
1947	Ward Cuff, Green Bay	16	7	43.8
	Pat Harder, Chi. Cardinals	10	7	70.0
	Bob Waterfield, Los Angeles	16	7	43.8
1946	Ted Fritsch, Green Bay	17	9	52.9
1945	Joe Aguirre, Washington	13	7	53.8
1944	Ken Strong, N.Y. Giants	12	6	50.0
1943	Ward Cuff, N.Y. Giants	9	3	33.3
	Don Hutson, Green Bay	5	3	60.0
1942	Bill Daddio, Chi. Cardinals	10	5	50.0
1941	Clarke Hinkle, Green Bay	14	6	42.9
1940	Clarke Hinkle, Green Bay	14	9	64.3
1939	Ward Cuff, N.Y. Giants	16	7	43.8
1938	Ward Cuff, N.Y. Giants	9	5	55.6
	Ralph Kercheval, Brooklyn	13	5	38.5
1937	Jack Manders, Chi. Bears		8	
1936	Jack Manders, Chi. Bears		7	
	Armand Niccolai, Pittsburgh		7	
1935	Armand Niccolai, Pittsburgh		6	
	Bill Smith, Chi. Cardinals		6	
1934	Jack Manders, Chi. Bears		10	
1933	*Jack Manders, Chi. Bears		6	
	Glenn Presnell, Portsmouth		6	
1932	Earl (Dutch) Clark, Portsmouth		3	

First year in the league.

Annual Rushing Leaders

Year	Player, Team	Att.	Yards	Avg.	TD
1987	Charles White, L.A. Rams, NFC	324	1,374	4.2	11
	Eric Dickerson, Indianapolis, AFC	223	1,011	4.5	5
1986	Eric Dickerson, L.A. Rams, NFC	404	1,821	4.5	11
	Curt Warner, Seattle, AFC	319	1,481	4.6	13
1985	Marcus Allen, L.A. Raiders, AFC	380	1,759	4.6	11
	Gerald Riggs, Atlanta, NFC	397	1,719	4.3	10
1984	Eric Dickerson, L.A. Rams, NFC	379	2,105	5.6	14
	Earnest Jackson, San Diego, AFC	296	1,179	4.0	8
1983	*Eric Dickerson, L.A. Rams, NFC	390	1,808	4.6	18
	*Curt Warner, Seattle, AFC	335	1,449	4.3	13
1982	Freeman McNeil, N.Y. Jets, AFC	151	786	5.2	6
	Tony Dorsett, Dallas, NFC	177	745	4.2	5
1981	*George Rogers, New Orleans, NFC	378	1,674	4.4	13
	Earl Campbell, Houston, AFC	361	1,376	3.8	10
1980	Earl Campbell, Houston, AFC	373	1,934	5.2	13
	Walter Payton, Chicago, NFC	317	1,460	4.6	6
1979	Earl Campbell, Houston, AFC	368	1,697	4.6	19
	Walter Payton, Chicago, NFC	369	1,610	4.4	14
1978	*Earl Campbell, Houston, AFC	302	1,450	4.8	13
	Walter Payton, Chicago, NFC	333	1,395	4.2	11
1977	Walter Payton, Chicago, NFC	339	1,852	5.5	14
	Mark van Eeghen, Oakland, AFC	324	1,273	3.9	7
1976	O.J. Simpson, Buffalo, AFC	290	1,503	5.2	8
	Walter Payton, Chicago, NFC	311	1,390	4.5	13
1975	O.J. Simpson, Buffalo, AFC	329	1,817	5.5	16
	Jim Otis, St. Louis, NFC	269	1,076	4.0	5
1974	Otis Armstrong, Denver, AFC	263	1,407	5.3	9
	Lawrence McCutcheon, Los Angeles, NFC	236	1,109	4.7	3
1973	O.J. Simpson, Buffalo, AFC	332	2,003	6.0	12
	John Brockington, Green Bay, NFC	265	1,144	4.3	3
1972	O.J. Simpson, Buffalo, AFC	292	1,251	4.3	6
	Larry Brown, Washington, NFC	285	1,216	4.3	8
1971	Floyd Little, Denver, AFC	284	1,133	4.0	6
	*John Brockington, Green Bay, NFC	216	1,105	5.1	4
1970	Larry Brown, Washington, NFC	237	1,125	4.7	5
	Floyd Little, Denver, AFC	209	901	4.3	3
1969	Gale Sayers, Chicago, NFL	236	1,032	4.4	8
	Dickie Post, San Diego, AFL	182	873	4.8	6
1968	Leroy Kelly, Cleveland, NFL	248	1,239	5.0	16
	*Paul Robinson, Cincinnati, AFL	238	1,023	4.3	8
1967	Jim Nance, Boston, AFL	269	1,216	4.5	7
	Leroy Kelly, Cleveland, NFL	235	1,205	5.1	11
1966	Jim Nance, Boston, AFL	299	1,458	4.9	11
	Gale Sayers, Chicago, NFL	229	1,231	5.4	8
1965	Jim Brown, Cleveland, NFL	289	1,544	5.3	17
	Paul Lowe, San Diego, AFL	222	1,121	5.0	7
1964	Jim Brown, Cleveland, NFL	280	1,446	5.2	7
	Cookie Gilchrist, Buffalo, AFL	230	981	4.3	6
1963	Jim Brown, Cleveland, NFL	291	1,863	6.4	12
	Clem Daniels, Oakland, AFL	215	1,099	5.1	3
1962	Jim Taylor, Green Bay, NFL	272	1,474	5.4	19
	*Cookie Gilchrist, Buffalo, AFL	214	1,096	5.1	13
1961	Jim Brown, Cleveland, NFL	305	1,408	4.6	8
	Billy Cannon, Houston, AFL	200	948	4.7	6
1960	Jim Brown, Cleveland, NFL	215	1,257	5.8	9
	*Abner Haynes, Dall. Texans, AFL	156	875	5.6	9
1959	Jim Brown, Cleveland	290	1,329	4.6	14
1958	Jim Brown, Cleveland	257	1,527	5.9	17
1957	*Jim Brown, Cleveland	202	942	4.7	9
1956	Rick Casares, Chi. Bears	234	1,126	4.8	12
1955	*Alan Ameche, Baltimore	213	961	4.5	9
1954	Joe Perry, San Francisco	173	1,049	6.1	8
1953	Joe Perry, San Francisco	192	1,018	5.3	10
1952	Dan Towler, Los Angeles	156	894	5.7	10
1951	Eddie Price, N.Y. Giants	271	971	3.6	7
1950	*Marion Motley, Cleveland	140	810	5.8	3
1949	Steve Van Buren, Philadelphia	263	1,146	4.4	11
1948	Steve Van Buren, Philadelphia	201	945	4.7	10
1947	Steve Van Buren, Philadelphia	217	1,008	4.6	13
1946	Bill Dudley, Pittsburgh	146	604	4.1	3
1945	Steve Van Buren, Philadelphia	143	832	5.8	15
1944	Bill Paschal, N.Y. Giants	196	737	3.8	9
1943	*Bill Paschal, N.Y. Giants	147	572	3.9	10
1942	*Bill Dudley, Pittsburgh	162	696	4.3	5
1941	Clarence (Pug) Manders, Brooklyn	111	486	4.4	5
1940	Byron (Whizzer) White, Detroit	146	514	3.5	5
1939	*Bill Osmanski, Chicago	121	699	5.8	7
1938	*Byron (Whizzer) White, Pittsburgh	152	567	3.7	4
1937	Cliff Battles, Washington	216	874	4.0	5
1936	*Alphonse (Tuffy) Leemans, N.Y. Giants	206	830	4.0	2
1935	Doug Russell, Chi. Cardinals	140	499	3.6	0
1934	*Beattie Feathers, Chi. Bears	101	1,004	9.9	8
1933	Jim Musick, Boston	173	809	4.7	5
1932	*Cliff Battles, Boston	148	576	3.9	3

**First year in the league.*

Annual Passing Leaders

Year	Player, Team	Att.	Comp.	Yards	TD	Int.
1987	Joe Montana, San Francisco, NFC	398	266	3,054	31	13
	Bernie Kosar, Cleveland, AFC	389	241	3,033	22	9
1986	Tommy Kramer, Minnesota, NFC	372	208	3,000	24	10
	Dan Marino, Miami, AFC	623	378	4,746	44	23
1985	Ken O'Brien, N.Y. Jets, AFC	488	297	3,888	25	8
	Joe Montana, San Francisco, NFC	494	303	3,653	27	13
1984	Dan Marino, Miami, AFC	564	362	5,084	48	17
	Joe Montana, San Francisco, NFC	432	279	3,630	28	10
1983	Steve Bartkowski, Atlanta, NFC	432	274	3,167	22	5
	*Dan Marino, Miami, AFC	296	173	2,210	20	6
1982	Ken Anderson, Cincinnati, AFC	309	218	2,495	12	9
	Joe Theismann, Washington, NFC	252	161	2,033	13	9
1981	Ken Anderson, Cincinnati, AFC	479	300	3,754	29	10
	Joe Montana, San Francisco, NFC	488	311	3,565	19	12
1980	Brian Sipe, Cleveland, AFC	554	337	4,132	30	14
	Ron Jaworski, Philadelphia, NFC	451	257	3,529	27	12
1979	Roger Staubach, Dallas, NFC	461	267	3,586	27	11
	Dan Fouts, San Diego, AFC	530	332	4,082	24	24
1978	Roger Staubach, Dallas, NFC	413	231	3,190	25	16
	Terry Bradshaw, Pittsburgh, AFC	368	207	2,915	28	20
1977	Bob Griese, Miami, AFC	307	180	2,252	22	13
	Roger Staubach, Dallas, NFC	361	210	2,620	18	9
1976	Ken Stabler, Oakland, AFC	291	194	2,737	27	17
	James Harris, Los Angeles, NFC	158	91	1,460	8	6
1975	Ken Anderson, Cincinnati, AFC	377	228	3,169	21	11
	Fran Tarkenton, Minnesota, NFC	425	273	2,994	25	13
1974	Ken Anderson, Cincinnati, AFC	328	213	2,667	18	10
	Sonny Jurgensen, Washington, NFC	167	107	1,185	11	5
1973	Roger Staubach, Dallas, NFC	286	179	2,428	23	15
	Ken Stabler, Oakland, AFC	260	163	1,997	14	10
1972	Norm Snead, N.Y. Giants, NFC	325	196	2,307	17	12
	Earl Morrall, Miami, AFC	150	83	1,360	11	7
1971	Roger Staubach, Dallas, NFC	211	126	1,882	15	4
	Bob Griese, Miami, AFC	263	145	2,089	19	9
1970	John Brodie, San Francisco, NFC	378	223	2,941	24	10
	Daryle Lamonica, Oakland, AFC	356	179	2,516	22	15
1969	Sonny Jurgensen, Washington, NFL	442	274	3,102	22	15
	*Greg Cook, Cincinnati, AFL	197	106	1,854	15	11
1968	Len Dawson, Kansas City, AFL	224	131	2,109	17	9
	Earl Morrall, Baltimore, NFL	317	182	2,909	26	17
1967	Sonny Jurgensen, Washington, NFL	508	288	3,747	31	16
	Daryle Lamonica, Oakland, AFL	425	220	3,228	30	20
1966	Bart Starr, Green Bay, NFL	251	156	2,257	14	3
	Len Dawson, Kansas City, AFL	284	159	2,527	26	10
1965	Rudy Bukich, Chicago, NFL	312	176	2,641	20	9
	John Hadl, San Diego, AFL	348	174	2,798	20	21
1964	Len Dawson, Kansas City, AFL	354	199	2,879	30	18
	Bart Starr, Green Bay, NFL	272	163	2,144	15	4
1963	Y.A. Tittle, N.Y. Giants, NFL	367	221	3,145	36	14
	Tobin Rote, San Diego, AFL	286	170	2,510	20	17
1962	Len Dawson, Dall. Texans, AFL	310	189	2,759	29	17
	Bart Starr, Green Bay, NFL	285	178	2,438	12	9
1961	George Blanda, Houston, AFL	362	187	3,330	36	22
	Milt Plum, Cleveland, NFL	302	177	2,416	18	10
1960	Milt Plum, Cleveland, NFL	250	151	2,297	21	5
	Jack Kemp, L.A. Chargers, AFL	406	211	3,018	20	25
1959	Charlie Conerly, N.Y. Giants	194	113	1,706	14	4
1958	Eddie LeBaron, Washington	145	79	1,365	11	10
1957	Tommy O'Connell, Cleveland	110	63	1,229	9	8
1956	Ed Brown, Chi. Bears	168	96	1,667	11	12
1955	Otto Graham, Cleveland	185	98	1,721	15	8
1954	Norm Van Brocklin, Los Angeles	260	139	2,637	13	21
1953	Otto Graham, Cleveland	258	167	2,722	11	9
1952	Norm Van Brocklin, Los Angeles	205	113	1,736	14	17
1951	Bob Waterfield, Los Angeles	176	88	1,566	13	10
1950	Norm Van Brocklin, Los Angeles	233	127	2,061	18	14
1949	Sammy Baugh, Washington	255	145	1,903	18	14
1948	Tommy Thompson, Philadelphia	246	141	1,965	25	11
1947	Sammy Baugh, Washington	354	210	2,938	25	15
1946	Bob Waterfield, Los Angeles	251	127	1,747	18	17
1945	Sammy Baugh, Washington	182	128	1,669	11	4
	Sid Luckman, Chi. Bears	217	117	1,725	14	10
1944	Frank Filchock, Washington	147	84	1,139	13	9
1943	Sammy Baugh, Washington	239	133	1,754	23	19
1942	Cecil Isbell, Green Bay	268	146	2,021	24	14
1941	Cecil Isbell, Green Bay	206	117	1,479	15	11
1940	Sammy Baugh, Washington	177	111	1,367	12	10
1939	*Parker Hall, Cleveland	208	106	1,227	9	13
1938	Ed Danowski, N.Y. Giants	129	70	848	7	8
1937	*Sammy Baugh, Washington	171	81	1,127	8	14
1936	Arnie Herber, Green Bay	173	77	1,239	11	13
1935	Ed Danowski, N.Y. Giants	113	57	794	10	9
1934	Arnie Herber, Green Bay	115	42	799	8	12
1933	*Harry Newman, N.Y. Giants	136	53	973	11	17
1932	Arnie Herber, Green Bay	101	37	639	9	9

**First year in the league.*

Annual Pass Receiving Leaders

Year	Player, Team	No.	Yards	Avg.	TD
1987	J.T. Smith, St. Louis, NFC	91	1,117	12.3	8
	Al Toon, N.Y. Jets, AFC	68	976	14.4	5
1986	Todd Christensen, L.A. Raiders, AFC	95	1,153	12.1	8
	Jerry Rice, San Francisco, NFC	86	1,570	18.3	15
1985	Roger Craig, San Francisco, NFC	92	1,016	11.0	6
	Lionel James, San Diego, AFC	86	1,027	11.9	6
1984	Art Monk, Washington, NFC	106	1,372	12.9	7
	Ozzie Newsome, Cleveland, AFC	89	1,001	11.2	5
1983	Todd Christensen, L.A. Raiders, AFC	92	1,247	13.6	12
	Roy Green, St. Louis, NFC	78	1,227	15.7	14
	Charlie Brown, Washington, NFC	78	1,225	15.7	8
	Earnest Gray, N.Y. Giants, NFC	78	1,139	14.6	5
1982	Dwight Clark, San Francisco, NFC	60	913	15.2	5
	Kellen Winslow, San Diego, AFC	54	721	13.4	6
1981	Kellen Winslow, San Diego, AFC	88	1,075	12.2	10
	Dwight Clark, San Francisco, NFC	85	1,105	13.0	4
1980	Kellen Winslow, San Diego, AFC	89	1,290	14.5	9
	*Earl Cooper, San Francisco, NFC	83	567	6.8	4
1979	Joe Washington, Baltimore, AFC	82	750	9.1	3
	Ahmad Rashad, Minnesota, NFC	80	1,156	14.5	9
1978	Rickey Young, Minnesota, NFC	88	704	8.0	5
	Steve Largent, Seattle, AFC	71	1,168	16.5	8
1977	Lydell Mitchell, Baltimore, AFC	71	620	8.7	4
	Ahmad Rashad, Minnesota, NFC	51	681	13.4	2
1976	MacArthur Lane, Kansas City, AFC	66	686	10.4	1
	Drew Pearson, Dallas, NFC	58	806	13.9	6
1975	Chuck Foreman, Minnesota, NFC	73	691	9.5	9

Year	Player, Team	No.	Yards	Avg.	TD
	Reggie Rucker, Cleveland, AFC	60	770	12.8	3
	Lydell Mitchell, Baltimore, AFC	60	544	9.1	4
1974	Lydell Mitchell, Baltimore, AFC	72	544	7.6	2
	Charles Young, Philadelphia, NFC	63	696	11.0	3
1973	Harold Carmichael, Philadelphia, NFC	67	1,116	16.7	9
	Fred Willis, Houston, AFC	57	371	6.5	1
1972	Harold Jackson, Philadelphia, NFC	62	1,048	16.9	4
	Fred Biletnikoff, Oakland, AFC	58	802	13.8	7
1971	Fred Biletnikoff, Oakland, AFC	61	929	15.2	9
	Bob Tucker, N.Y. Giants, NFC	59	791	13.4	4
1970	Dick Gordon, Chicago, NFC	71	1,026	14.5	13
	Marlin Briscoe, Buffalo, AFC	57	1,036	18.2	8
1969	Dan Abramowicz, New Orleans, NFL	73	1,015	13.9	7
	Lance Alworth, San Diego, AFL	64	1,003	15.7	4
1968	Clifton McNeil, San Francisco, NFL	71	994	14.0	7
	Lance Alworth, San Diego, AFL	68	1,312	19.3	10
1967	George Sauer, N.Y. Jets, AFL	75	1,189	15.9	6
	Charley Taylor, Washington, NFL	70	990	14.1	9
1966	Lance Alworth, San Diego, AFL	73	1,383	18.9	13
	Charley Taylor, Washington, NFL	72	1,119	15.5	12
1965	Lionel Taylor, Denver, AFL	85	1,131	13.3	6
	Dave Parks, San Francisco, NFL	80	1,344	16.8	12
1964	Charley Hennigan, Houston, AFL	101	1,546	15.3	8
	Johnny Morris, Chicago, NFL	93	1,200	12.9	10
1963	Lionel Taylor, Denver, AFL	78	1,101	14.1	10
	Bobby Joe Conrad, St. Louis, NFL	73	967	13.2	10
1962	Lionel Taylor, Denver, AFL	77	908	11.8	4
	Bobby Mitchell, Washington, NFL	72	1,384	19.2	11
1961	Lionel Taylor, Denver, AFL	100	1,176	11.8	4
	Jim (Red) Phillips, Los Angeles, NFL	78	1,092	14.0	5
1960	Lionel Taylor, Denver, AFL	92	1,235	13.4	12
	Raymond Berry, Baltimore, NFL	74	1,298	17.5	10
1959	Raymond Berry, Baltimore	66	959	14.5	14
1958	Raymond Berry, Baltimore	56	794	14.2	9
	Pete Retzlaff, Philadelphia	56	766	13.7	2
1957	Billy Wilson, San Francisco	52	757	14.6	6
1956	Billy Wilson, San Francisco	60	889	14.8	5
1955	Pete Pihos, Philadelphia	62	864	13.9	7
1954	Pete Pihos, Philadelphia	60	872	14.5	10
	Billy Wilson, San Francisco	60	830	13.8	5
1953	Pete Pihos, Philadelphia	63	1,049	16.7	10
1952	Mac Speedie, Cleveland	62	911	14.7	5
1951	Elroy (Crazylegs) Hirsch, Los Angeles	66	1,495	22.7	17
1950	Tom Fears, Los Angeles	84	1,116	13.3	7
1949	Tom Fears, Los Angeles	77	1,013	13.2	9
1948	*Tom Fears, Los Angeles	51	698	13.7	4
1947	Jim Keane, Chi. Bears	64	910	14.2	10
1946	Jim Benton, Los Angeles	63	981	15.6	6
1945	Don Hutson, Green Bay	47	834	17.7	9
1944	Don Hutson, Green Bay	58	866	14.9	9
1943	Don Hutson, Green Bay	47	776	16.5	11
1942	Don Hutson, Green Bay	74	1,211	16.4	17
1941	Don Hutson, Green Bay	58	738	12.7	10
1940	*Don Looney, Philadelphia	58	707	12.2	4
1939	Don Hutson, Green Bay	34	846	24.9	6
1938	Gaynell Tinsley, Chi. Cardinals	41	516	12.6	1
1937	Don Hutson, Green Bay	41	552	13.5	7
1936	Don Hutson, Green Bay	34	536	15.8	8
1935	*Tod Goodwin, N.Y. Giants	26	432	16.6	4
1934	Joe Carter, Philadelphia	16	238	14.9	4
	Morris (Red) Badgro, N.Y. Giants	16	206	12.9	1
1933	John (Shipwreck) Kelly, Brooklyn	22	246	11.2	3
1932	Ray Flaherty, N.Y. Giants	21	350	16.7	3

**First year in the league.*

Annual Interception Leaders

Year	Player, Team	No.	Yards	TD
1987	Barry Wilburn, Washington, NFC	9	135	1
	Mike Prior, Indianapolis, AFC	6	57	0
	Mark Kelso, Buffalo, AFC	6	25	0
	Keith Bostic, Houston, AFC	6	−14	0
1986	Ronnie Lott, San Francisco, NFC	10	134	1
	Deron Cherry, Kansas City, AFC	9	150	0
1985	Everson Walls, Dallas, NFC	9	31	0
	Albert Lewis, Kansas City, AFC	8	59	0
	Eugene Daniel, Indianapolis, AFC	8	53	0
1984	Ken Easley, Seattle, AFC	10	126	2
	*Tom Flynn, Green Bay, NFC	9	106	0
1983	Mark Murphy, Washington, NFC	9	127	0
	Ken Riley, Cincinnati, AFC	8	89	2
	Vann McElroy, L.A. Raiders, AFC	8	68	0
1982	Everson Walls, Dallas, NFC	7	61	0
	Ken Riley, Cincinnati, AFC	5	88	1
	Bobby Jackson, N.Y. Jets, AFC	5	84	1
	Dwayne Woodruff, Pittsburgh, AFC	5	53	0
	Donnie Shell, Pittsburgh, AFC	5	27	0
1981	*Everson Walls, Dallas, NFC	11	133	0
	John Harris, Seattle, AFC	10	155	2
1980	Lester Hayes, Oakland, AFC	13	273	1
	Nolan Cromwell, Los Angeles, NFC	8	140	1
1979	Mike Reinfeldt, Houston, AFC	12	205	0
	Lemar Parrish, Washington, NFC	9	65	0
1978	Thom Darden, Cleveland, AFC	10	200	0
	Ken Stone, St. Louis, NFC	9	139	0
	Willie Buchanon, Green Bay, NFC	9	93	1
1977	Lyle Blackwood, Baltimore, AFC	10	163	0
	Rolland Lawrence, Atlanta, NFC	7	138	0
1976	Monte Jackson, Los Angeles, NFC	10	173	3
	Ken Riley, Cincinnati, AFC	9	141	1
1975	Mel Blount, Pittsburgh, AFC	11	121	0
	Paul Krause, Minnesota, NFC	10	201	0
1974	Emmitt Thomas, Kansas City, AFC	12	214	2
	Ray Brown, Atlanta, NFC	8	164	1
1973	Dick Anderson, Miami, AFC	8	163	2
	Mike Wagner, Pittsburgh, AFC	8	134	0
	Bobby Bryant, Minnesota, NFC	7	105	1
1972	Bill Bradley, Philadelphia, NFC	9	73	0
	Mike Sensibaugh, Kansas City, AFC	8	65	0
1971	Bill Bradley, Philadelphia, NFC	11	248	0
	Ken Houston, Houston, AFC	9	220	4
1970	Johnny Robinson, Kansas City, AFC	10	155	0
	Dick LeBeau, Detroit, NFC	9	96	0
1969	Mel Renfro, Dallas, NFL	10	118	0
	Emmitt Thomas, Kansas City, AFL	9	146	1
1968	Dave Grayson, Oakland, AFL	10	195	1
	Willie Williams, N.Y. Giants, NFL	10	103	0
1967	Miller Farr, Houston, AFL	10	264	3
	*Lem Barney, Detroit, NFL	10	232	3
	Tom Janik, Buffalo, AFL	10	222	2
	Dave Whitsell, New Orleans, NFL	10	178	2
	Dick Westmoreland, Miami, AFL	10	127	1
1966	Larry Wilson, St. Louis, NFL	10	180	2
	Johnny Robinson, Kansas City, AFL	10	136	1
	Bobby Hunt, Kansas City, AFL	10	113	0
1965	W.K. Hicks, Houston, AFL	9	156	0
	Bobby Boyd, Baltimore, NFL	9	78	1
1964	Dainard Paulson, N.Y. Jets, AFL	12	157	1
	*Paul Krause, Washington, NFL	12	140	1
1963	Fred Glick, Houston, AFL	12	180	1
	Dick Lynch, N.Y. Giants, NFL	9	251	3
	Roosevelt Taylor, Chicago, NFL	9	172	1
1962	Lee Riley, N.Y. Titans, AFL	11	122	0
	Willie Wood, Green Bay, NFL	9	132	0
1961	Billy Atkins, Buffalo, AFL	10	158	0
	Dick Lynch, N.Y. Giants, NFL	9	60	0
1960	*Austin (Goose) Gonsoulin, Denver, AFL	11	98	0
	Dave Baker, San Francisco, NFL	10	96	0
	Jerry Norton, St. Louis, NFL	10	96	0
1959	Dean Derby, Pittsburgh	7	127	0
	Milt Davis, Baltimore	7	119	1
	Don Shinnick, Baltimore	7	70	0
1958	Jim Patton, N.Y. Giants	11	183	0
1957	*Milt Davis, Baltimore	10	219	2
	Jack Christiansen, Detroit	10	137	1
	Jack Butler, Pittsburgh	10	85	0
1956	Lindon Crow, Chi. Cardinals	11	170	0
1955	Will Sherman, Los Angeles	11	101	0
1954	Dick (Night Train) Lane, Chi. Cardinals	10	181	0
1953	Jack Christiansen, Detroit	12	238	1
1952	*Dick (Night Train) Lane, Los Angeles	14	298	2
1951	Otto Schnellbacher, N.Y. Giants	11	194	2
1950	*Orban (Spec) Sanders, N.Y. Yanks	13	199	0
1949	Bob Nussbaumer, Chi. Cardinals	12	157	0
1948	*Dan Sandifer, Washington	13	258	2
1947	Frank Reagan, N.Y. Giants	10	203	0
	Frank Seno, Boston	10	100	0
1946	Bill Dudley, Pittsburgh	10	242	1
1945	Roy Zimmerman, Philadelphia	7	90	0
1944	*Howard Livingston, N.Y. Giants	9	172	1
1943	Sammy Baugh, Washington	11	112	0
1942	Clyde (Bulldog) Turner, Chi. Bears	8	96	1
1941	Marshall Goldberg, Chi. Cardinals	7	54	0
	*Art Jones, Pittsburgh	7	35	0
1940	Clarence (Ace) Parker, Brooklyn	6	146	1
	Kent Ryan, Detroit	6	65	0
	Don Hutson, Green Bay	6	24	0

**First year in the league.*

Annual Punting Leaders

Year	Player, Team	No.	Avg.	Long
1987	Rick Donnelly, Atlanta, NFC	61	44.0	62
	Ralf Mojsiejenko, San Diego, AFC	67	42.9	57
1986	Rohn Stark, Indianapolis, AFC	76	45.2	63
	Sean Landeta, N.Y. Giants, NFC	79	44.8	61
1985	Rohn Stark, Indianapolis, AFC	78	45.9	68
	*Rick Donnelly, Atlanta, NFC	59	43.6	68
1984	Jim Arnold, Kansas City, AFC	98	44.9	63
	*Brian Hansen, New Orleans, NFC	69	43.8	66
1983	Rohn Stark, Baltimore, AFC	91	45.3	68
	*Frank Garcia, Tampa Bay, NFC	95	42.2	64
1982	Luke Prestridge, Denver, AFC	45	45.0	65
	Carl Birdsong, St. Louis, NFC	54	43.8	65
1981	Pat McInally, Cincinnati, AFC	72	45.4	62
	Tom Skladany, Detroit, NFC	64	43.5	74
1980	Dave Jennings, N.Y. Giants, NFC	94	44.8	63
	Luke Prestridge, Denver, AFC	70	43.9	57
1979	*Bob Grupp, Kansas City, AFC	89	43.6	74
	Dave Jennings, N.Y. Giants, NFC	104	42.7	72
1978	Pat McInally, Cincinnati, AFC	91	43.1	65
	*Tom Skladany, Detroit, NFC	86	42.5	63
1977	Ray Guy, Oakland, AFC	59	43.3	74
	Tom Blanchard, New Orleans, NFC	82	42.4	66
1976	Marv Bateman, Buffalo, AFC	86	42.8	78
	John James, Atlanta, NFC	101	42.1	67
1975	Ray Guy, Oakland, AFC	68	43.8	64
	Herman Weaver, Detroit, NFC	80	42.0	61
1974	Ray Guy, Oakland, AFC	74	42.2	66
	Tom Blanchard, New Orleans, NFC	88	42.1	71
1973	Jerrel Wilson, Kansas City, AFC	80	45.5	68
	*Tom Wittum, San Francisco, NFC	79	43.7	62
1972	Jerrel Wilson, Kansas City, AFC	66	44.8	69
	Dave Chapple, Los Angeles, NFC	53	44.2	70
1971	Dave Lewis, Cincinnati, AFC	72	44.8	56
	Tom McNeill, Philadelphia, NFC	73	42.0	64
1970	*Dave Lewis, Cincinnati, AFC	79	46.2	63

Year	Player, Team	No.	Avg.	Long
	*Julian Fagan, New Orleans, NFC	77	42.5	64
1969	David Lee, Baltimore, NFL	57	45.3	66
	Dennis Partee, San Diego, AFL	71	44.6	62
1968	Jerrel Wilson, Kansas City, AFL	63	45.1	70
	Billy Lothridge, Atlanta, NFL	75	44.3	70
1967	Bob Scarpitto, Denver, AFL	105	44.9	73
	Billy Lothridge, Atlanta, NFL	87	43.7	62
1966	Bob Scarpitto, Denver, AFL	76	45.8	70
	*David Lee, Baltimore, NFL	49	45.6	64
1965	Gary Collins, Cleveland, NFL	65	46.7	71
	Jerrel Wilson, Kansas City, AFL	69	45.4	64
1964	*Bobby Walden, Minnesota, NFL	72	46.4	73
	Jim Fraser, Denver, AFL	73	44.2	67
1963	Yale Lary, Detroit, NFL	35	48.9	73
	Jim Fraser, Denver, AFL	81	44.4	66
1962	Tommy Davis, San Francisco, NFL	48	45.6	82
	Jim Fraser, Denver, AFL	55	43.6	75
1961	Yale Lary, Detroit, NFL	52	48.4	71
	Billy Atkins, Buffalo, AFL	85	44.5	70
1960	Jerry Norton, St. Louis, NFL	39	45.6	62
	*Paul Maguire, L.A. Chargers, AFL	43	40.5	61
1959	Yale Lary, Detroit	45	47.1	67
1958	Sam Baker, Washington	48	45.4	64
1957	Don Chandler, N.Y. Giants	60	44.6	61
1956	Norm Van Brocklin, Los Angeles	48	43.1	72
1955	Norm Van Brocklin, Los Angeles	60	44.6	61
1954	Pat Brady, Pittsburgh	66	43.2	72
1953	Pat Brady, Pittsburgh	80	46.9	64
1952	Horace Gillom, Cleveland	61	45.7	73
1951	Horace Gillom, Cleveland	73	45.5	66
1950	*Fred (Curly) Morrison, Chi. Bears	57	43.3	65
1949	*Mike Boyda, N.Y. Bulldogs	56	44.2	61
1948	Joe Muha, Philadelphia	57	47.3	82
1947	Jack Jacobs, Green Bay	57	43.5	74
1946	Roy McKay, Green Bay	64	42.7	64
1945	Roy McKay, Green Bay	44	41.2	73
1944	Frank Sinkwich, Detroit	45	41.0	73
1943	Sammy Baugh, Washington	50	45.9	81
1942	Sammy Baugh, Washington	37	48.2	74
1941	Sammy Baugh, Washington	30	48.7	75
1940	Sammy Baugh, Washington	35	51.4	85
1939	*Parker Hall, Cleveland	58	40.8	80

**First year in the league.*

Annual Punt Return Leaders

Year	Player, Team	No.	Yards	Avg.	Long	TD
1987	Mel Gray, New Orleans, NFC	24	352	14.7	80	0
	Bobby Joe Edmonds, Seattle, AFC	20	251	12.6	40	0
1986	*Bobby Joe Edmonds, Seattle, AFC	34	419	12.3	75	1
	*Vai Sikahema, St. Louis, NFC	43	522	12.1	71	2
1985	Irving Fryar, New England, AFC	37	520	14.1	85	2
	Henry Ellard, L.A. Rams, NFC	37	501	13.5	80	1
1984	Mike Martin, Cincinnati, AFC	24	376	15.7	55	0
	Henry Ellard, L.A. Rams, NFC	30	403	13.4	83	2
1983	*Henry Ellard, L.A. Rams, NFC	16	217	13.6	72	1
	Kirk Springs, N.Y. Jets, AFC	23	287	12.5	76	1
1982	Rick Upchurch, Denver, AFC	15	242	16.1	78	2
	Billy Johnson, Atlanta, NFC	24	273	11.4	71	0
1981	LeRoy Irvin, Los Angeles, NFC	46	615	13.4	84	3
	*James Brooks, San Diego, AFC	22	290	13.2	42	0
1980	J. T. Smith, Kansas City, AFC	40	581	14.5	75	2
	*Kenny Johnson, Atlanta, NFC	23	281	12.2	56	0
1979	John Sciarra, Philadelphia, NFC	16	182	11.4	38	0
	*Tony Nathan, Miami, AFC	28	306	10.9	86	1
1978	Rick Upchurch, Denver, AFC	36	493	13.7	75	1
	Jackie Wallace, Los Angeles, NFC	52	618	11.9	58	0
1977	Billy Johnson, Houston, AFC	35	539	15.4	87	2
	Larry Marshall, Philadelphia, NFC	46	489	10.6	48	0
1976	Rick Upchurch, Denver, AFC	39	536	13.7	92	4
	Eddie Brown, Washington, NFC	48	646	13.5	71	1
1975	Billy Johnson, Houston, AFC	40	612	15.3	83	3
	Terry Metcalf, St. Louis, NFC	23	285	12.4	69	1
1974	Lemar Parrish, Cincinnati, AFC	18	338	18.8	90	2
	Dick Jauron, Detroit, NFC	17	286	16.8	58	0
1973	Bruce Taylor, San Francisco, NFC	15	207	13.8	61	0
	Ron Smith, San Diego, AFC	27	352	13.0	84	2
1972	*Ken Ellis, Green Bay, NFC	14	215	15.4	80	1
	Chris Farasopoulos, N.Y. Jets, AFC	17	179	10.5	65	1
1971	Les (Speedy) Duncan, Washington, NFC	22	233	10.6	33	0
	Leroy Kelly, Cleveland, AFC	30	292	9.7	74	0
1970	Ed Podolak, Kansas City, AFC	23	311	13.5	60	0
	*Bruce Taylor, San Francisco, NFC	43	516	12.0	76	0
1969	Alvin Haymond, Los Angeles, NFL	33	435	13.2	52	0
	*Bill Thompson, Denver, AFL	25	288	11.5	40	0
1968	Bob Hayes, Dallas, NFL	15	312	20.8	90	2
	Noland Smith, Kansas City, AFL	18	270	15.0	80	1
1967	Floyd Little, Denver, AFL	16	270	16.9	72	1
	Ben Davis, Cleveland, NFL	18	229	12.7	52	1
1966	Les (Speedy) Duncan, San Diego, AFL	18	238	13.2	81	1
	Johnny Roland, St. Louis, NFL	20	221	11.1	86	1
1965	Leroy Kelly, Cleveland, NFL	17	265	15.6	67	2
	Les (Speedy) Duncan, San Diego, AFL	30	464	15.5	66	2
1964	Bobby Jancik, Houston, AFL	12	220	18.3	82	1
	Tommy Watkins, Detroit, NFL	16	238	14.9	68	2
1963	Dick James, Washington, NFL	16	214	13.4	39	0
	Claude (Hoot) Gibson, Oakland, AFL	26	307	11.8	85	2
1962	Dick Christy, N.Y. Titans, AFL	15	250	16.7	73	2
	Pat Studstill, Detroit, NFL	29	457	15.8	44	0
1961	Dick Christy, N.Y. Titans, AFL	18	383	21.3	70	2
	Willie Wood, Green Bay, NFL	14	225	16.1	72	2
1960	*Abner Haynes, Dall. Texans, AFL	14	215	15.4	46	0
	Abe Woodson, San Francisco, NFL	13	174	13.4	48	0
1959	Johnny Morris, Chi. Bears	14	171	12.2	78	1
1958	Jon Arnett, Los Angeles	18	223	12.4	58	0
1957	Bert Zagers, Washington	14	217	15.5	76	2
1956	Ken Konz, Cleveland	13	187	14.4	65	1
1955	Ollie Matson, Chi. Cardinals	13	245	18.8	78	2
1954	*Veryl Switzer, Green Bay	24	306	12.8	93	1
1953	Charley Trippi, Chi. Cardinals	21	239	11.4	38	0
1952	Jack Christiansen, Detroit	15	322	21.5	79	2
1951	Claude (Buddy) Young, N.Y. Yanks	12	231	19.3	79	1
1950	*Herb Rich, Baltimore	12	276	23.0	86	1
1949	Verda (Vitamin T) Smith, Los Angeles	27	427	15.8	85	1
1948	George McAfee, Chi. Bears	30	417	13.9	60	1
1947	*Walt Slater, Pittsburgh	28	435	15.5	33	0
1946	Bill Dudley, Pittsburgh	27	385	14.3	52	0
1945	*Dave Ryan, Detroit	15	220	14.7	56	0
1944	*Steve Van Buren, Philadelphia	15	230	15.3	55	1
1943	Andy Farkas, Washington	15	168	11.2	33	0
1942	Merlyn Condit, Brooklyn	21	210	10.0	23	0
1941	Byron (Whizzer) White, Detroit	19	262	13.8	64	0

**First year in the league.*

Annual Kickoff Return Leaders

Year	Player, Team	No.	Yards	Avg.	Long	TD
1987	Sylvester Stamps, Atlanta, NFC	24	660	27.5	97	1
	Paul Palmer, Kansas City, AFC	38	923	24.3	95	2
1986	Dennis Gentry, Chicago, NFC	20	576	28.8	91	1
	*Lupe Sanchez, Pittsburgh, AFC	25	591	23.6	64	0
1985	Ron Brown, L.A. Rams, NFC	28	918	32.8	98	3
	Glen Young, Cleveland, AFC	35	898	25.7	63	0
1984	*Bobby Humphery, N.Y. Jets, AFC	22	675	30.7	97	1
	Barry Redden, L.A. Rams, NFC	23	530	23.0	40	0
1983	Fulton Walker, Miami, AFC	36	962	26.7	78	0
	Darrin Nelson, Minnesota, NFC	18	445	24.7	50	0
1982	*Mike Mosley, Buffalo, AFC	18	487	27.1	66	0
	Alvin Hall, Detroit, NFC	16	426	26.6	96	1
1981	Mike Nelms, Washington, NFC	37	1,099	29.7	84	0
	Carl Roaches, Houston, AFC	28	769	27.5	96	1
1980	Horace Ivory, New England, AFC	36	992	27.6	98	1
	Rich Mauti, New Orleans, NFC	31	798	25.7	52	0
1979	Larry Brunson, Oakland, AFC	17	441	25.9	89	0
	*Jimmy Edwards, Minnesota, NFC	44	1,103	25.1	83	0
1978	Steve Odom, Green Bay, NFC	25	677	27.1	95	1
	*Keith Wright, Cleveland, AFC	30	789	26.3	86	0
1977	*Raymond Clayborn, New England, AFC	28	869	31.0	101	3
	*Wilbert Montgomery, Philadelphia, NFC	23	619	26.9	99	1
1976	*Duriel Harris, Miami, AFC	17	559	32.9	69	0
	Cullen Bryant, Los Angeles, NFC	16	459	28.7	90	1
1975	*Walter Payton, Chicago, NFC	14	444	31.7	70	0
	Harold Hart, Oakland, AFC	17	518	30.5	102	1
1974	Terry Metcalf, St. Louis, NFC	20	623	31.2	94	1
	Greg Pruitt, Cleveland, AFC	22	606	27.5	88	1
1973	Carl Garrett, Chicago, NFC	16	486	30.4	67	0
	*Wallace Francis, Buffalo, AFC	23	687	29.9	101	2
1972	Ron Smith, Chicago, NFC	30	924	30.8	94	1
	*Bruce Laird, Baltimore, AFC	29	843	29.1	73	0
1971	Travis Williams, Los Angeles, NFC	25	743	29.7	105	1
	Eugene (Mercury) Morris, Miami, AFC	15	423	28.2	94	1
1970	Jim Duncan, Baltimore, AFC	20	707	35.4	99	1
	Cecil Turner, Chicago, NFC	23	752	32.7	96	4
1969	Bobby Williams, Detroit, NFL	17	563	33.1	96	1
	*Bill Thompson, Denver, AFL	18	513	28.5	63	0
1968	Preston Pearson, Baltimore, NFL	15	527	35.1	102	2
	*George Atkinson, Oakland, AFL	32	802	25.1	60	0
1967	*Travis Williams, Green Bay, NFL	18	739	41.1	104	4
	*Zeke Moore, Houston, AFL	14	405	28.9	92	1
1966	Gale Sayers, Chicago, NFL	23	718	31.2	93	2
	*Goldie Sellers, Denver, AFL	19	541	28.5	100	2
1965	Tommy Watkins, Detroit, NFL	17	584	34.4	94	0
	Abner Haynes, Denver, AFL	34	901	26.5	60	0
1964	*Clarence Childs, N.Y. Giants, NFL	34	987	29.0	100	1
	Bo Roberson, Oakland, AFL	36	975	27.1	59	0
1963	Abe Woodson, San Francisco, NFL	29	935	32.2	103	3
	Bobby Jancik, Houston, AFL	45	1,317	29.3	53	0
1962	Abe Woodson, San Francisco, NFL	37	1,157	31.3	79	0
	*Bobby Jancik, Houston, AFL	24	826	30.3	61	0
1961	Dick Bass, Los Angeles, NFL	23	698	30.3	64	0
	*Dave Grayson, Dall. Texans, AFL	16	453	28.3	73	0
1960	*Tom Moore, Green Bay, NFL	12	397	33.1	84	0
	Ken Hall, Houston, AFL	19	594	31.3	104	1
1959	Abe Woodson, San Francisco	13	382	29.4	105	1
1958	Ollie Matson, Chi. Cardinals	14	497	35.5	101	2
1957	*Jon Arnett, Los Angeles	18	504	28.0	98	1
1956	*Tom Wilson, Los Angeles	15	477	31.8	103	1
1955	Al Carmichael, Green Bay	14	418	29.9	100	1
1954	Billy Reynolds, Cleveland	14	413	29.5	51	0
1953	Joe Arenas, San Francisco	16	551	34.4	82	0
1952	Lynn Chandnois, Pittsburgh	17	599	35.2	93	2
1951	Lynn Chandnois, Pittsburgh	12	390	32.5	55	0
1950	Verda (Vitamin T) Smith, Los Angeles	22	742	33.7	97	3
1949	*Don Doll, Detroit	21	536	25.5	56	0
1948	*Joe Scott, N.Y. Giants	20	569	28.5	99	1
1947	Eddie Saenz, Washington	29	797	27.5	94	2
1946	Abe Karnofsky, Boston	21	599	28.5	97	1
1945	Steve Van Buren, Philadelphia	13	373	28.7	98	1
1944	Bob Thurbon, Card.-Pitt.	12	291	24.3	55	0
1943	Ken Heineman, Brooklyn	16	444	27.8	69	0
1942	Marshall Goldberg, Chi. Cardinals	15	393	26.2	95	1
1941	Marshall Goldberg, Chi. Cardinals	12	290	24.2	41	0

**First year in the league.*

Points Scored

Year	Team	Points
1987	San Francisco, NFC	459
	Cleveland, AFC	390
1986	Miami, AFC	430
	Minnesota, NFC	398
1985	San Diego, AFC	467
	Chicago, NFC	456
1984	Miami, AFC	513
	San Francisco, NFC	475
1983	Washington, NFC	541
	L.A. Raiders, AFC	442
1982	San Diego, AFC	288
	Dallas, NFC	226
	Green Bay, NFC	226
1981	San Diego, AFC	478
	Atlanta, NFC	426
1980	Dallas, NFC	454
	New England, AFC	441
1979	Pittsburgh, AFC	416
	Dallas, NFC	371
1978	Dallas, NFC	384
	Miami, AFC	372
1977	Oakland, AFC	351
	Dallas, NFC	345
1976	Baltimore, AFC	417
	Los Angeles, NFC	351
1975	Buffalo, AFC	420
	Minnesota, NFC	377
1974	Oakland, AFC	355
	Washington, NFC	320
1973	Los Angeles, NFC	388
	Denver, AFC	354
1972	Miami, AFC	385
	San Francisco, NFC	353
1971	Dallas, NFC	406
	Oakland, AFC	344
1970	San Francisco, NFC	352
	Baltimore, AFC	321
1969	Minnesota, NFL	379
	Oakland, AFL	377
1968	Oakland, AFL	453
	Dallas, NFL	431
1967	Oakland, AFL	468
	Los Angeles, NFL	398
1966	Kansas City, AFL	448
	Dallas, NFL	445
1965	San Francisco, NFL	421
	San Diego, AFL	340
1964	Baltimore, NFL	428
	Buffalo, AFL	400
1963	N.Y. Giants, NFL	448
	San Diego, AFL	399
1962	Green Bay, NFL	415
	Dall. Texans, AFL	389
1961	Houston, AFL	513
	Green Bay, NFL	391
1960	N.Y. Titans, AFL	382
	Cleveland, NFL	362
1959	Baltimore	374
1958	Baltimore	381
1957	Los Angeles	307
1956	Chi. Bears	363
1955	Cleveland	349
1954	Detroit	337
1953	San Francisco	372
1952	Los Angeles	349
1951	Los Angeles	392
1950	Los Angeles	466
1949	Philadelphia	364
1948	Chi. Cardinals	395
1947	Chi. Bears	363
1946	Chi. Bears	289
1945	Philadelphia	272
1944	Philadelphia	267
1943	Chi. Bears	303
1942	Chi. Bears	376
1941	Chi. Bears	396
1940	Washington	245
1939	Chi. Bears	298
1938	Green Bay	223
1937	Green Bay	220
1936	Green Bay	248
1935	Chi. Bears	192
1934	Chi. Bears	286
1933	N.Y. Giants	244
1932	Green Bay	152

Total Yards Gained

Year	Team	Yards
1987	San Francisco, NFC	5,987
	Denver, AFC	5,624
1986	Cincinnati, AFC	6,490
	San Francisco, NFC	6,082
1985	San Diego, AFC	6,535
	San Francisco, NFC	5,920
1984	Miami, AFC	6,936
	San Francisco, NFC	6,366
1983	San Diego, AFC	6,197
	Green Bay, NFC	6,172
1982	San Diego, AFC	4,048
	San Francisco, NFC	3,242
1981	San Diego, AFC	6,744
	Detroit, NFC	5,933
1980	San Diego, AFC	6,410
	Los Angeles, NFC	6,006
1979	Pittsburgh, AFC	6,258
	Dallas, NFC	5,968
1978	New England, AFC	5,965
	Dallas, NFC	5,959
1977	Dallas, NFC	4,812
	Oakland, AFC	4,736
1976	Baltimore, AFC	5,236
	St. Louis, NFC	5,136
1975	Buffalo, AFC	5,467
	Dallas, NFC	5,025
1974	Dallas, NFC	4,983
	Oakland, AFC	4,718
1973	Los Angeles, NFC	4,906
	Oakland, AFC	4,773
1972	Miami, AFC	5,036
	N.Y. Giants, NFC	4,483
1971	Dallas, NFC	5,035
	San Diego, AFC	4,738
1970	Oakland, AFC	4,829
	San Francisco, NFC	4,503
1969	Dallas, NFL	5,122
	Oakland, AFL	5,036
1968	Oakland, AFL	5,696
	Dallas, NFL	5,117
1967	N.Y. Jets, AFL	5,152
	Baltimore, NFL	5,008
1966	Dallas, NFL	5,145
	Kansas City, AFL	5,114
1965	San Francisco, NFL	5,270
	San Diego, AFL	5,188
1964	Buffalo, AFL	5,206
	Baltimore, NFL	4,779
1963	San Diego, AFL	5,153
	N.Y. Giants, NFL	5,024
1962	N.Y. Giants, NFL	5,005
	Houston, AFL	4,971
1961	Houston, AFL	6,288
	Philadelphia, NFL	5,112
1960	Houston, AFL	4,936
	Baltimore, NFL	4,245
1959	Baltimore	4,458
1958	Baltimore	4,539
1957	Los Angeles	4,143
1956	Chi. Bears	4,537
1955	Chi. Bears	4,316
1954	Los Angeles	5,187
1953	Philadelphia	4,811
1952	Cleveland	4,352
1951	Los Angeles	5,506
1950	Los Angeles	5,420
1949	Chi. Bears	4,873
1948	Chi. Cardinals	4,705
1947	Chi. Bears	5,053
1946	Los Angeles	3,793
1945	Washington	3,549
1944	Chi. Bears	3,239
1943	Chi. Bears	4,045
1942	Chi. Bears	3,900
1941	Chi. Bears	4,265
1940	Green Bay	3,400
1939	Chi. Bears	3,988
1938	Green Bay	3,037
1937	Green Bay	3,201
1936	Detroit	3,703
1935	Chi. Bears	3,454
1934	Chi. Bears	3,900
1933	N.Y. Giants	2,973
1932	Chi. Bears	2,755

Yards Rushing

Year	Team	Yards
1987	San Francisco, NFC	2,237
	L.A. Raiders, AFC	2,197
1986	Chicago, NFC	2,700
	Cincinnati, AFC	2,533
1985	Chicago, NFC	2,761
	Indianapolis, AFC	2,439
1984	Chicago, NFC	2,974
	N.Y. Jets, AFC	2,189
1983	Chicago, NFC	2,727
	Baltimore, AFC	2,695
1982	Buffalo, AFC	1,371
	Dallas, NFC	1,313
1981	Detroit, NFC	2,795
	Kansas City, AFC	2,633
1980	Los Angeles, NFC	2,799
	Houston, AFC	2,635
1979	N.Y. Jets, AFC	2,646
	St. Louis, NFC	2,582
1978	New England, AFC	3,165
	Dallas, NFC	2,783
1977	Chicago, NFC	2,811
	Oakland, AFC	2,627
1976	Pittsburgh, AFC	2,971
	Los Angeles, NFC	2,528
1975	Buffalo, AFC	2,974
	Dallas, NFC	2,432
1974	Dallas, NFC	2,454
	Pittsburgh, AFC	2,417
1973	Buffalo, AFC	3,088
	Los Angeles, NFC	2,925
1972	Miami, AFC	2,960
	Chicago, NFC	2,360
1971	Miami, AFC	2,429
	Detroit, NFC	2,376
1970	Dallas, NFC	2,300
	Miami, AFC	2,082
1969	Dallas, NFL	2,276
	Kansas City, AFL	2,220
1968	Chicago, NFL	2,377
	Kansas City, AFL	2,227
1967	Cleveland, NFL	2,139
	Houston, AFL	2,122
1966	Kansas City, AFL	2,274
	Cleveland, NFL	2,166
1965	Cleveland, NFL	2,331
	San Diego, AFL	2,085
1964	Green Bay, NFL	2,276
	Buffalo, AFL	2,040
1963	Cleveland, NFL	2,639
	San Diego, AFL	2,203
1962	Buffalo, AFL	2,480
	Green Bay, NFL	2,460
1961	Green Bay, NFL	2,350
	Dall. Texans, AFL	2,189
1960	St. Louis, NFL	2,356
	Oakland, AFL	2,056
1959	Cleveland	2,149
1958	Cleveland	2,526
1957	Los Angeles	2,142
1956	Chi. Bears	2,468
1955	Chi. Bears	2,388
1954	San Francisco	2,498
1953	San Francisco	2,230
1952	San Francisco	1,905
1951	Chi. Bears	2,408
1950	N.Y. Giants	2,336
1949	Philadelphia	2,607
1948	Chi. Cardinals	2,560
1947	Los Angeles	2,171
1946	Green Bay	1,765
1945	Cleveland	1,714
1944	Philadelphia	1,661
1943	Phil-Pitt	1,730
1942	Chi. Bears	1,881
1941	Chi. Bears	2,263
1940	Chi. Bears	1,818
1939	Chi. Bears	2,043
1938	Detroit	1,893
1937	Detroit	2,074
1936	Detroit	2,885
1935	Chi. Bears	2,096
1934	Chi. Bears	2,847
1933	Boston	2,260
1932	Chi. Bears	1,770

Yards Passing

Leadership in this category has been based on net yards since 1952.

Year	Team	Yards
1987	Miami, AFC	3,876
	San Francisco, NFC	3,750
1986	Miami, AFC	4,779
	San Francisco, NFC	4,096
1985	San Diego, AFC	4,870
	Dallas, NFC	3,861
1984	Miami, AFC	5,018
	St. Louis, NFC	4,257
1983	San Diego, AFC	4,661
	Green Bay, NFC	4,365
1982	San Diego, AFC	2,927
	San Francisco, NFC	2,502
1981	San Diego, AFC	4,739
	Minnesota, NFC	4,333
1980	San Diego, AFC	4,531
	Minnesota, NFC	3,688
1979	San Diego, AFC	3,915
	San Francisco, NFC	3,641
1978	San Diego, AFC	3,375
	Minnesota, NFC	3,243
1977	Buffalo, AFC	2,530
	St. Louis, NFC	2,499
1976	Baltimore, AFC	2,933
	Minnesota, NFC	2,855
1975	Cincinnati, AFC	3,241
	Washington, NFC	2,917
1974	Washington, NFC	2,978
	Cincinnati, AFC	2,804
1973	Philadelphia, NFC	2,998
	Denver, AFC	2,519
1972	N.Y. Jets, AFC	2,777
	San Francisco, NFC	2,735
1971	San Diego, AFC	3,134
	Dallas, NFC	2,786
1970	San Francisco, NFC	2,923
	Oakland, AFC	2,865
1969	Oakland, AFL	3,271
	San Francisco, NFL	3,158
1968	San Diego, AFL	3,623
	Dallas, NFL	3,026
1967	N.Y. Jets, AFL	3,845
	Washington, NFL	3,730
1966	N.Y. Jets, AFL	3,464
	Dallas, NFL	3,023
1965	San Francisco, NFL	3,487
	San Diego, AFL	3,103
1964	Houston, AFL	3,527
	Chicago, NFL	2,841
1963	Baltimore, NFL	3,296
	Houston, AFL	3,222
1962	Denver, AFL	3,404
	Philadelphia, NFL	3,385
1961	Houston, AFL	4,392
	Philadelphia, NFL	3,605
1960	Houston, AFL	3,203
	Baltimore, NFL	2,956
1959	Baltimore	2,753
1958	Pittsburgh	2,752
1957	Baltimore	2,388
1956	Los Angeles	2,419
1955	Philadelphia	2,472
1954	Chi. Bears	3,104
1953	Philadelphia	3,089
1952	Cleveland	2,566
1951	Los Angeles	3,296
1950	Los Angeles	3,709
1949	Chi. Bears	3,055
1948	Washington	2,861
1947	Washington	3,336
1946	Los Angeles	2,080
1945	Chi. Bears	1,857
1944	Washington	2,021
1943	Chi. Bears	2,310
1942	Green Bay	2,407
1941	Chi. Bears	2,002
1940	Washington	1,887
1939	Chi. Bears	1,965
1938	Washington	1,536
1937	Green Bay	1,398
1936	Green Bay	1,629
1935	Green Bay	1,449
1934	Green Bay	1,165
1933	N.Y. Giants	1,348
1932	Chi. Bears	1,013

Fewest Points Allowed

Year	Team	Points
1987	Indianapolis, AFC	238
	San Francisco, NFC	253
1986	Chicago, NFC	187
	Seattle, AFC	293
1985	Chicago, NFC	198
	N.Y. Jets, AFC	264
1984	San Francisco, NFC	227
	Denver, AFC	241
1983	Miami, AFC	250
	Detroit, NFC	286
1982	Washington, NFC	128
	Miami, AFC	131
1981	Philadelphia, NFC	221
	Miami, AFC	275
1980	Philadelphia, NFC	222
	Houston, AFC	251
1979	Tampa Bay, NFC	237
	San Diego, AFC	246
1978	Pittsburgh, AFC	195
	Dallas, NFC	208
1977	Atlanta, NFC	129
	Denver, AFC	148
1976	Pittsburgh, AFC	138
	Minnesota, NFC	176
1975	Los Angeles, NFC	135
	Pittsburgh, AFC	162
1974	Los Angeles, NFC	181
	Pittsburgh, AFC	189
1973	Miami, AFC	150
	Minnesota, NFC	168
1972	Miami, AFC	171
	Washington, NFC	218
1971	Minnesota, NFC	139
	Baltimore, AFC	140
1970	Minnesota, NFC	143
	Miami, AFC	228
1969	Minnesota, NFL	133
	Kansas City, AFL	177
1968	Baltimore, NFL	144
	Kansas City, AFL	170
1967	Los Angeles, NFL	196
	Houston, AFL	199
1966	Green Bay, NFL	163
	Buffalo, AFL	255
1965	Green B!y, NFL	224
	Buffalo, AFL	226
1964	Baltimore, NFL	225
	Buffalo, AFL	242
1963	Chicago, NFL	144
	San Diego, AFL	255
1962	Green Bay, NFL	148
	Dall. Texans, AFL	233
1961	San Diego, AFL	219
	N.Y. Giants, NFL	220
1960	San Francisco, NFL	205
	Dall. Texans, AFL	253
1959	N.Y. Giants	170

1958	N.Y. Giants	183
1957	Cleveland	172
1956	Cleveland	177
1955	Cleveland	218
1954	Cleveland	162
1953	Cleveland	162
1952	Detroit	192
1951	Cleveland	152
1950	Philadelphia	141
1949	Philadelphia	134
1948	Chi. Bears	151
1947	Green Bay	210
1946	Pittsburgh	117
1945	Washington	121
1944	N.Y. Giants	75
1943	Washington	137
1942	Chi. Bears	84
1941	N.Y. Giants	114
1940	Brooklyn	120
1939	N.Y. Giants	85
1938	N.Y. Giants	79
1937	Chi. Bears	100
1936	Chi. Bears	94
1935	Green Bay	96
	N.Y. Giants	96
1934	Detroit	59
1933	Brooklyn	54
1932	Chi. Bears	44

Fewest Total Yards Allowed

Year	Team	Yards
1987	San Francisco, NFC	4,095
	Cleveland, AFC	4,264
1986	Chicago, NFC	4,130
	L.A. Raiders, AFC	4,804
1985	Chicago, NFC	4,135
	L.A. Raiders, AFC	4,603
1984	Chicago, NFC	3,863
	Cleveland, AFC	4,641
1983	Cincinnati, AFC	4,327
	New Orleans, NFC	4,691
1982	Miami, AFC	2,312
	Tampa Bay, NFC	2,442
1981	Philadelphia, NFC	4,447
	N.Y. Jets, AFC	4,871
1980	Buffalo, AFC	4,101
	Philadelphia, NFC	4,443
1979	Tampa Bay, NFC	3,949
	Pittsburgh, AFC	4,270
1978	Los Angeles, NFC	3,893
	Pittsburgh, AFC	4,168
1977	Dallas, NFC	3,213
	New England, AFC	3,638
1976	Pittsburgh, AFC	3,323
	San Francisco, NFC	3,562
1975	Minnesota, NFC	3,153
	Oakland, AFC	3,629
1974	Pittsburgh, AFC	3,074
	Washington, NFC	3,285
1973	Los Angeles, NFC	2,951
	Oakland, AFC	3,160
1972	Miami, AFC	3,297
	Green Bay, NFC	3,474
1971	Baltimore, AFC	2,852
	Minnesota, NFC	3,406
1970	Minnesota, NFC	2,803
	N.Y. Jets, AFC	3,655
1969	Minnesota, NFL	2,720
	Kansas City, AFL	3,163
1968	Los Angeles, NFL	3,118
	N.Y. Jets, AFL	3,363
1967	Oakland, AFL	3,294
	Green Bay, NFL	3,300
1966	St. Louis, NFL	3,492
	Oakland, AFL	3,910
1965	San Diego, AFL	3,262
	Detroit, NFL	3,557
1964	Green Bay, NFL	3,179
	Buffalo, AFL	3,878
1963	Chicago, NFL	3,176
	Boston, AFL	3,834
1962	Detroit, NFL	3,217
	Dall. Texans, AFL	3,951
1961	San Diego, AFL	3,726
	Baltimore, NFL	3,782
1960	St. Louis, NFL	3,029
	Buffalo, AFL	3,866
1959	N.Y. Giants	2,843
1958	Chi. Bears	3,066
1957	Pittsburgh	2,791
1956	N.Y. Giants	3,081
1955	Cleveland	2,841
1954	Cleveland	2,658
1953	Philadelphia	2,998
1952	Cleveland	3,075
1951	N.Y. Giants	3,250
1950	Cleveland	3,154
1949	Philadelphia	2,831
1948	Chi. Bears	2,931
1947	Green Bay	3,396
1946	Washington	2,451
1945	Philadelphia	2,073
1944	Philadelphia	1,943
1943	Chi. Bears	2,262
1942	Chi. Bears	1,703
1941	N.Y. Giants	2,368
1940	N.Y. Giants	2,219
1939	Washington	2,116
1938	N.Y. Giants	2,029
1937	Washington	2,123
1936	Boston	2,181
1935	Boston	1,996
1934	Chi. Cardinals	1,539
1933	Brooklyn	1,789

Fewest Yards Rushing Allowed

Year	Team	Yards
1987	Chicago, NFC	1,413
	Cleveland, AFC	1,433
1986	N.Y. Giants, NFC	1,284
	Denver, AFC	1,651
1985	Chicago, NFC	1,319
	N.Y. Jets, AFC	1,516
1984	Chicago, NFC	1,377
	Pittsburgh, AFC	1,617
1983	Washington, NFC	1,289
	Cincinnati, AFC	1,499
1982	Pittsburgh, AFC	762
	Detroit, NFC	854
1981	Detroit, NFC	1,623
	Kansas City, AFC	1,747
1980	Detroit, NFC	1,599
	Cincinnati, AFC	1,680
1979	Denver, AFC	1,693
	Tampa Bay, NFC	1,873
1978	Dallas, NFC	1,721
	Pittsburgh, AFC	1,774
1977	Denver, AFC	1,531
	Dallas, NFC	1,651
1976	Pittsburgh, AFC	1,457
	Los Angeles, NFC	1,564
1975	Minnesota, NFC	1,532
	Houston, AFC	1,680
1974	Los Angeles, NFC	1,302
	New England, AFC	1,587
1973	Los Angeles, NFC	1,270
	Oakland, AFC	1,470
1972	Dallas, NFC	1,515
	Miami, AFC	1,548
1971	Baltimore, AFC	1,113
	Dallas, NFC	1,144
1970	Detroit, NFC	1,152
	N.Y. Jets, AFC	1,283
1969	Dallas, NFL	1,050
	Kansas City, AFL	1,091
1968	Dallas, NFL	1,195
	N.Y. Jets, AFL	1,195
1967	Dallas, NFL	1,081
	Oakland, AFL	1,129
1966	Buffalo, AFL	1,051
	Dallas, NFL	1,176
1965	San Diego, AFL	1,094
	Los Angeles, NFL	1,409
1964	Buffalo, AFL	913
	Los Angeles, NFL	1,501
1963	Boston, AFL	1,107
	Chicago, NFL	1,442
1962	Detroit, NFL	1,231
	Dall. Texans, AFL	1,250
1961	Boston, AFL	1,041
	Pittsburgh, NFL	1,463
1960	St. Louis, NFL	1,212
	Dall. Texans, AFL	1,338
1959	N.Y. Giants	1,261
1958	Baltimore	1,291
1957	Baltimore	1,174
1956	N.Y. Giants	1,443
1955	Cleveland	1,189
1954	Cleveland	1,050
1953	Philadelphia	1,117
1952	Detroit	1,145
1951	N.Y. Giants	913
1950	Detroit	1,367
1949	Chi. Bears	1,196
1948	Philadelphia	1,209
1947	Philadelphia	1,329
1946	Chi. Bears	1,060
1945	Philadelphia	817
1944	Philadelphia	558
1943	Phil-Pitt	793
1942	Chi. Bears	519
1941	Washington	1,042
1940	N.Y. Giants	977
1939	Chi. Bears	812
1938	Detroit	1,081
1937	Chi. Bears	933
1936	Boston	1,148
1935	Boston	998
1934	Chi. Cardinals	954
1933	Brooklyn	964

Fewest Yards Passing Allowed

Leadership in this category has been based on net yards since 1952.

Year	Team	Yards
1987	San Francisco, NFC	2,484
	L.A. Raiders, AFC	2,727
1986	St. Louis, NFC	2,637
	New England, AFC	2,978
1985	Washington, NFC	2,746
	Pittsburgh, AFC	2,783
1984	New Orleans, NFC	2,453
	Cleveland, AFC	2,696
1983	New Orleans, NFC	2,691
	Cincinnati, AFC	2,828
1982	Miami, AFC	1,027
	Tampa Bay, NFC	1,384
1981	Philadelphia, NFC	2,696
	Buffalo, AFC	2,870
1980	Washington, NFC	2,171
	Buffalo, AFC	2,282
1979	Tampa Bay, NFC	2,076
	Buffalo, AFC	2,530
1978	Buffalo, AFC	1,960
	Los Angeles, NFC	2,048
1977	Atlanta, NFC	1,384
	San Diego, AFC	1,725
1976	Minnesota, NFC	1,575
	Cincinnati, AFC	1,758
1975	Minnesota, NFC	1,621
	Cincinnati, AFC	1,729
1974	Pittsburgh, AFC	1,466
	Atlanta, NFC	1,572
1973	Miami, AFC	1,290
	Atlanta, NFC	1,430
1972	Minnesota, NFC	1,699
	Cleveland, AFC	1,736
1971	Atlanta, NFC	1,638
	Baltimore, AFC	1,739
1970	Minnesota, NFC	1,438
	Kansas City, AFC	2,010
1969	Minnesota, NFL	1,631
	Kansas City, AFL	2,072
1968	Houston, AFL	1,671
	Green Bay, NFL	1,796
1967	Green Bay, NFL	1,377
	Buffalo, AFL	1,825
1966	Green Bay, NFL	1,959
	Oakland, AFL	2,118
1965	Green Bay, NFL	1,981
	San Diego, AFL	2,168
1964	Green Bay, NFL	1,647
	San Diego, AFL	2,518
1963	Chicago, NFL	1,734
	Oakland, AFL	2,589
1962	Green Bay, NFL	1,746
	Oakland, AFL	2,306
1961	Baltimore, NFL	1,913
	San Diego, AFL	2,363
1960	Chicago, NFL	1,388
	Buffalo, AFL	2,124
1959	N.Y. Giants	1,582
1958	Chi. Bears	1,769
1957	Cleveland	1,300
1956	Cleveland	1,103
1955	Pittsburgh	1,295
1954	Cleveland	1,608
1953	Washington	1,751
1952	Washington	1,580
1951	Pittsburgh	1,687
1950	Cleveland	1,581
1949	Philadelphia	1,607
1948	Green Bay	1,626
1947	Green Bay	1,790
1946	Pittsburgh	939
1945	Washington	1,121
1944	Chi. Bears	1,052
1943	Chi. Bears	980
1942	Washington	1,093
1941	Pittsburgh	1,168
1940	Philadelphia	1,012
1939	Washington	1,116
1938	Chi. Bears	897
1937	Detroit	804
1936	Philadelphia	853
1935	Chi. Cardinals	793
1934	Philadelphia	545
1933	Portsmouth	558

SUPER BOWL RECORDS

Compiled by Elias Sports Bureau

1967: Super Bowl I
1968: Super Bowl II
1969: Super Bowl III
1970: Super Bowl IV
1971: Super Bowl V
1972: Super Bowl VI
1973: Super Bowl VII
1974: Super Bowl VIII
1975: Super Bowl IX
1976: Super Bowl X
1977: Super Bowl XI
1978: Super Bowl XII
1979: Super Bowl XIII
1980: Super Bowl XIV
1981: Super Bowl XV
1982: Super Bowl XVI
1983: Super Bowl XVII
1984: Super Bowl XVIII
1985: Super Bowl XIX
1986: Super Bowl XX
1987: Super Bowl XXI
1988: Super Bowl XXII

Individual Records

Service

Most Games

5 Marv Fleming, Green Bay, 1967-68; Miami, 1972-74
Larry Cole, Dallas, 1971-72, 1976, 1978-79
Cliff Harris, Dallas, 1971-72, 1976, 1978-79
D.D. Lewis, Dallas, 1971-72, 1976, 1978-79
Preston Pearson, Baltimore, 1969; Pittsburgh, 1975; Dallas, 1976, 1978-79
Charlie Waters, Dallas, 1971-72, 1976, 1978-79
Rayfield Wright, Dallas, 1971-72, 1976, 1978-79
4 By many players

Most Games, Winning Team

4 By many players

Most Games, Coach

6 Don Shula, Baltimore, 1969; Miami, 1972-74, 1983, 1985
5 Tom Landry, Dallas, 1971-72, 1976, 1978-79
4 Bud Grant, Minnesota, 1970, 1974-75, 1977
Chuck Noll, Pittsburgh, 1975-76, 1979-80

Most Games, Winning Team, Coach

4 Chuck Noll, Pittsburgh, 1975-76, 1979-80
2 Vince Lombardi, Green Bay, 1967-68
Tom Landry, Dallas, 1972, 1978
Don Shula, Miami, 1973-74
Tom Flores, Oakland, 1981; L.A. Raiders, 1984
Bill Walsh, San Francisco, 1982, 1985
Joe Gibbs, Washington, 1983, 1988

Most Games, Losing Team, Coach

4 Bud Grant, Minnesota, 1970, 1974-75, 1977
Don Shula, Baltimore, 1969; Miami, 1972, 1983, 1985
3 Tom Landry, Dallas, 1971, 1976, 1979
2 Dan Reeves, Denver, 1987-88

Scoring

Points

Most Points, Career

24 Franco Harris, Pittsburgh, 4 games (4-td)
22 Ray Wersching, San Francisco, 2 games (7-pat, 5-fg)
20 Don Chandler, Green Bay, 2 games (8-pat, 4-fg)

Most Points, Game

18 Roger Craig, San Francisco vs. Miami, 1985 (3-td)
15 Don Chandler, Green Bay vs. Oakland, 1968 (3-pat, 4-fg)
14 Ray Wersching, San Francisco vs. Cincinnati, 1982 (2-pat, 4-fg)
Kevin Butler, Chicago vs. New England, 1986 (5-pat, 3-fg)

Touchdowns

Most Touchdowns, Career

4 Franco Harris, Pittsburgh, 4 games (4-r)
3 John Stallworth, Pittsburgh, 4 games (3-p)
Lynn Swann, Pittsburgh, 4 games (3-p)
Cliff Branch, Oakland-L.A. Raiders, 3 games (3-p)
Roger Craig, San Francisco, 1 game (1-r, 2-p)
2 By many players

Most Touchdowns, Game

3 Roger Craig, San Francisco vs. Miami, 1985 (1-r, 2-p)
2 Max McGee, Green Bay vs. Kansas City, 1967 (2-p)
Elijah Pitts, Green Bay vs. Kansas City, 1967 (2-r)
Bill Miller, Oakland vs. Green Bay, 1968 (2-p)
Larry Csonka, Miami vs. Minnesota, 1974 (2-r)
Pete Banaszak, Oakland vs. Minnesota, 1977 (2-r)
John Stallworth, Pittsburgh vs. Dallas, 1979 (2-p)
Franco Harris, Pittsburgh vs. Los Angeles, 1980 (2-r)
Cliff Branch, Oakland vs. Philadelphia, 1981 (2-p)
Dan Ross, Cincinnati vs. San Francisco, 1982 (2-p)
Marcus Allen, L.A. Raiders vs. Washington, 1984 (2-r)
Jim McMahon, Chicago vs. New England, 1986 (2-r)
Ricky Sanders, Washington vs. Denver, 1988 (2-p)
Timmy Smith, Washington vs. Denver, 1988 (2-r)

Points After Touchdown

Most Points After Touchdown, Career

8 Don Chandler, Green Bay, 2 games (8 att)
Roy Gerela, Pittsburgh, 3 games (9 att)
Chris Bahr, Oakland-L.A. Raiders, 2 games (8 att)
7 Ray Wersching, San Francisco, 2 games (7 att)
6 Ali Haji-Sheikh, Washington, 1 game (6 att)

Most Points After Touchdown, Game

6 Ali Haji-Sheikh, Washington vs. Denver, 1988 (6 att)
5 Don Chandler, Green Bay vs. Kansas City, 1967 (5 att)
Roy Gerela, Pittsburgh vs. Dallas, 1979 (5 att)
Chris Bahr, L.A. Raiders vs. Washington, 1984 (5 att)
Ray Wersching, San Francisco vs. Miami, 1985 (5 att)
Kevin Butler, Chicago vs. New England, 1986 (5 att)
4 Rafael Septien, Dallas vs. Pittsburgh, 1979 (4 att)
Matt Bahr, Pittsburgh vs. Los Angeles, 1980 (4 att)
Raul Allegre, N.Y. Giants vs. Denver, 1987 (5 att)

Field Goals

Field Goals Attempted, Career

7 Roy Gerela, Pittsburgh, 3 games
6 Jim Turner, N.Y. Jets-Denver, 2 games
Rich Karlis, Denver, 2 games
5 Efren Herrera, Dallas, 1 game
Ray Wersching, San Francisco, 2 games

Most Field Goals Attempted, Game

5 Jim Turner, N.Y. Jets vs. Baltimore, 1969
Efren Herrera, Dallas vs. Denver, 1978
4 Don Chandler, Green Bay vs. Oakland, 1968
Roy Gerela, Pittsburgh vs. Dallas, 1976
Ray Wersching, San Francisco vs. Cincinnati, 1982
Rich Karlis, Denver vs. N.Y. Giants, 1987

Most Field Goals, Career

5 Ray Wersching, San Francisco, 2 games (5 att)
4 Don Chandler, Green Bay, 2 games (4 att)
Jim Turner, N.Y. Jets-Denver, 2 games (6 att)
Uwe von Schamann, Miami, 2 games (4 att)
3 Mike Clark, Dallas, 2 games (3 att)
Jan Stenerud, Kansas City, 1 game (3 att)
Chris Bahr, Oakland-L.A. Raiders, 2 games (4 att)
Mark Moseley, Washington, 2 games (4 att)
Kevin Butler, Chicago, 1 game (3 att)
Rich Karlis, Denver, 2 games (6 att)

Most Field Goals, Game

4 Don Chandler, Green Bay vs. Oakland, 1968
Ray Wersching, San Francisco vs. Cincinnati, 1982
3 Jim Turner, N.Y. Jets vs. Baltimore, 1969
Jan Stenerud, Kansas City vs. Minnesota, 1970
Uwe von Schamann, Miami vs. San Francisco, 1985
Kevin Butler, Chicago vs. New England, 1986

Longest Field Goal

48 Jan Stenerud, Kansas City vs. Minnesota, 1970
Rich Karlis, Denver vs. N.Y. Giants, 1987
47 Jim Turner, Denver vs. Dallas, 1978
46 Chris Bahr, Oakland vs. Philadelphia, 1981

Safeties

Most Safeties, Game

1 Dwight White, Pittsburgh vs. Minnesota, 1975
Reggie Harrison, Pittsburgh vs. Dallas, 1976
Henry Waechter, Chicago vs. New England, 1986
George Martin, N.Y. Giants vs. Denver, 1987

Rushing

Attempts

Most Attempts, Career

101 Franco Harris, Pittsburgh, 4 games
64 John Riggins, Washington, 2 games
57 Larry Csonka, Miami, 3 games

Most Attempts, Game

38 John Riggins, Washington vs. Miami, 1983
34 Franco Harris, Pittsburgh vs. Minnesota, 1975
33 Larry Csonka, Miami vs. Minnesota, 1974

Yards Gained

Most Yards Gained, Career

354 Franco Harris, Pittsburgh, 4 games
297 Larry Csonka, Miami, 3 games
230 John Riggins, Washington, 2 games

Most Yards Gained, Game

204 Timmy Smith, Washington vs. Denver, 1988
191 Marcus Allen, L.A. Raiders vs. Washington, 1984
166 John Riggins, Washington vs. Miami, 1983

Longest Run From Scrimmage

74 Marcus Allen, L.A. Raiders vs. Washington, 1984 (TD)
58 Tom Matte, Baltimore vs. N.Y. Jets, 1969
Timmy Smith, Washington vs. Denver, 1988 (TD)
49 Larry Csonka, Miami vs. Washington, 1973

Average Gain

Highest Average Gain, Career (20 attempts)

9.6 Marcus Allen, L.A. Raiders, 1 game (20-191)
9.3 Timmy Smith, Washington, 1 game (22-204)
5.3 Walt Garrison, Dallas, 2 games (26-139)

Highest Average Gain, Game (10 attempts)

10.5 Tom Matte, Baltimore vs. N.Y. Jets, 1969 (11-116)
9.6 Marcus Allen, L.A. Raiders vs. Washington, 1984 (20-191)
9.3 Timmy Smith, Washington vs. Denver, 1988 (22-204)

Touchdowns

Most Touchdowns, Career

4 Franco Harris, Pittsburgh, 4 games
2 Elijah Pitts, Green Bay, 1 game
Jim Kiick, Miami, 3 games
Larry Csonka, Miami, 3 games
Pete Banaszak, Oakland, 2 games
Marcus Allen, L.A. Raiders, 1 game
John Riggins, Washington, 2 games
Jim McMahon, Chicago, 1 game
Timmy Smith, Washington, 1 game

Most Touchdowns, Game

2 Elijah Pitts, Green Bay vs. Kansas City, 1967
Larry Csonka, Miami vs. Minnesota, 1974
Pete Banaszak, Oakland vs. Minnesota, 1977
Franco Harris, Pittsburgh vs. Los Angeles, 1980
Marcus Allen, L.A. Raiders vs. Washington, 1984
Jim McMahon, Chicago vs. New England, 1986
Timmy Smith, Washington vs. Denver, 1988

Passing
Attempts
Most Passes Attempted, Career
98 Roger Staubach, Dallas, 4 games
89 Fran Tarkenton, Minnesota, 3 games
84 Terry Bradshaw, Pittsburgh, 4 games
Most Passes Attempted, Game
50 Dan Marino, Miami vs. San Francisco, 1985
38 Ron Jaworski, Philadelphia vs. Oakland, 1981
John Elway, Denver vs. Washington, 1988
37 John Elway, Denver vs. N.Y. Giants, 1987

Completions
Most Passes Completed, Career
61 Roger Staubach, Dallas, 4 games
49 Terry Bradshaw, Pittsburgh, 4 games
46 Fran Tarkenton, Minnesota, 3 games
Most Passes Completed, Game
29 Dan Marino, Miami vs. San Francisco, 1985
25 Ken Anderson, Cincinnati vs. San Francisco, 1982
24 Joe Montana, San Francisco vs. Miami, 1985
Most Consecutive Completions, Game
10 Phil Simms, N.Y. Giants vs. Denver, 1987
8 Len Dawson, Kansas City vs. Green Bay, 1967
Joe Theismann, Washington vs. Miami, 1983

Completion Percentage
Highest Completion Percentage, Career (40 attempts)
66.7 Joe Montana, San Francisco, 2 games (57-38)
63.6 Len Dawson, Kansas City, 2 games (44-28)
63.4 Bob Griese, Miami, 3 games (41-26)
Highest Completion Percentage, Game (20 attempts)
88.0 Phil Simms, N.Y. Giants vs. Denver, 1987 (25-22)
73.5 Ken Anderson, Cincinnati vs. San Francisco, 1982 (34-25)
69.6 Bart Starr, Green Bay vs. Kansas City, 1967 (23-16)

Yards Gained
Most Yards Gained, Career
932 Terry Bradshaw, Pittsburgh, 4 games
734 Roger Staubach, Dallas, 4 games
561 John Elway, Denver, 2 games
Most Yards Gained, Game
340 Doug Williams, Washington vs. Denver, 1988
331 Joe Montana, San Francisco vs. Miami, 1985
318 Terry Bradshaw, Pittsburgh vs. Dallas, 1979
Dan Marino, Miami vs. San Francisco, 1985
Longest Pass Completion
80 Jim Plunkett (to King), Oakland vs. Philadelphia, 1981 (TD)
Doug Williams (to Sanders), Washington vs. Denver, 1988 (TD)
76 David Woodley (to Cefalo), Miami vs. Washington, 1983 (TD)
75 Johnny Unitas (to Mackey), Baltimore vs. Dallas, 1971 (TD)
Terry Bradshaw (to Stallworth), Pittsburgh vs. Dallas, 1979 (TD)

Average Gain
Highest Average Gain, Career (40 attempts)
11.10 Terry Bradshaw, Pittsburgh, 4 games (84-932)
9.62 Bart Starr, Green Bay, 2 games (47-452)
9.41 Jim Plunkett, Oakland-L.A. Raiders, 2 games (46-433)
Highest Average Gain, Game (20 attempts)
14.71 Terry Bradshaw, Pittsburgh vs. Los Angeles, 1980 (21-309)
12.80 Jim McMahon, Chicago vs. New England, 1986 (20-256)
12.43 Jim Plunkett, Oakland vs. Philadelphia, 1981 (21-261)

Touchdowns
Most Touchdown Passes, Career
9 Terry Bradshaw, Pittsburgh, 4 games
8 Roger Staubach, Dallas, 4 games
4 Jim Plunkett, Oakland-L.A. Raiders, 2 games
Joe Montana, San Francisco, 2 games
Doug Williams, Washington, 1 game
Most Touchdown Passes, Game
4 Terry Bradshaw, Pittsburgh vs. Dallas, 1979
Doug Williams, Washington vs. Denver, 1988
3 Roger Staubach, Dallas vs. Pittsburgh, 1979
Jim Plunkett, Oakland vs. Philadelphia, 1981
Joe Montana, San Francisco vs. Miami, 1985
Phil Simms, N.Y. Giants vs. Denver, 1987
2 By many players

Had Intercepted
Lowest Percentage, Passes Had Intercepted, Career (40 attempts)
0.00 Jim Plunkett, Oakland-L.A. Raiders, 2 games (46-0)
Joe Montana, San Francisco, 2 games (57-0)
2.13 Bart Starr, Green Bay, 2 games (47-1)
4.08 Roger Staubach, Dallas, 4 games (98-4)
Most Attempts, Without Interception, Game
35 Joe Montana, San Francisco vs. Miami, 1985
28 Joe Namath, N.Y. Jets vs. Baltimore, 1969
25 Roger Staubach, Dallas vs. Denver, 1978
Jim Plunkett, L.A. Raiders vs. Washington, 1984
Phil Simms, N.Y. Giants vs. Denver, 1987
Most Passes Had Intercepted, Career
7 Craig Morton, Dallas-Denver, 2 games
6 Fran Tarkenton, Minnesota, 3 games
4 Earl Morrall, Baltimore-Miami, 4 games
Roger Staubach, Dallas, 4 games
Terry Bradshaw, Pittsburgh, 4 games
Joe Theismann, Washington, 2 games
John Elway, Denver, 2 games
Most Passes Had Intercepted, Game
4 Craig Morton, Denver vs. Dallas, 1978
3 By eight players

Pass Receiving
Receptions
Most Receptions, Career
16 Lynn Swann, Pittsburgh, 4 games
15 Chuck Foreman, Minnesota, 3 games
14 Cliff Branch, Oakland-L.A. Raiders, 3 games
Most Receptions, Game
11 Dan Ross, Cincinnati vs. San Francisco, 1982
10 Tony Nathan, Miami vs. San Francisco, 1985
9 Ricky Sanders, Washington vs. Denver, 1988

Yards Gained
Most Yards Gained, Career
364 Lynn Swann, Pittsburgh, 4 games
268 John Stallworth, Pittsburgh, 4 games
193 Ricky Sanders, Washington, 1 game
Most Yards Gained, Game
193 Ricky Sanders, Washington vs. Denver, 1988
161 Lynn Swann, Pittsburgh vs. Dallas, 1976
138 Max McGee, Green Bay vs. Kansas City, 1967
Longest Reception
80 Kenny King (from Plunkett), Oakland vs. Philadelphia, 1981 (TD)
Ricky Sanders (from Williams), Washington vs. Denver, 1988 (TD)
76 Jimmy Cefalo (from Woodley), Miami vs. Washington, 1983 (TD)
75 John Mackey (from Unitas), Baltimore vs. Dallas, 1971 (TD)
John Stallworth (from Bradshaw), Pittsburgh vs. Dallas, 1979 (TD)

Average Gain
Highest Average Gain, Career (8 receptions)
24.4 John Stallworth, Pittsburgh, 4 games (11-268)
22.8 Lynn Swann, Pittsburgh, 4 games (16-364)
21.4 Ricky Sanders, Washington, 1 game (9-193)
Highest Average Gain, Game (3 receptions)
40.33 John Stallworth, Pittsburgh vs. Los Angeles, 1980 (3-121)
40.25 Lynn Swann, Pittsburgh vs. Dallas, 1979 (4-161)
38.33 John Stallworth, Pittsburgh vs. Dallas, 1979 (3-115)

Touchdowns
Most Touchdowns, Career
3 John Stallworth, Pittsburgh, 4 games
Lynn Swann, Pittsburgh, 4 games
Cliff Branch, Oakland-L.A. Raiders, 3 games
2 Max McGee, Green Bay, 2 games
Bill Miller, Oakland, 1 game
Butch Johnson, Dallas, 2 games
Dan Ross, Cincinnati, 1 game
Roger Craig, San Francisco, 1 game
Ricky Sanders, Washington, 1 game
Most Touchdowns, Game
2 Max McGee, Green Bay vs. Kansas City, 1967
Bill Miller, Oakland vs. Green Bay, 1968
John Stallworth, Pittsburgh vs. Dallas, 1979
Cliff Branch, Oakland vs. Philadelphia, 1981
Dan Ross, Cincinnati vs. San Francisco, 1982
Roger Craig, San Francisco vs. Miami, 1985
Ricky Sanders, Washington vs. Denver, 1988

Interceptions By
Most Interceptions By, Career
3 Chuck Howley, Dallas, 2 games
Rod Martin, Oakland-L.A. Raiders, 2 games
2 Randy Beverly, N.Y. Jets, 1 game
Jake Scott, Miami, 3 games
Mike Wagner, Pittsburgh, 3 games
Mel Blount, Pittsburgh, 4 games
Eric Wright, San Francisco, 2 games
Barry Wilburn, Washington, 1 game
Most Interceptions By, Game
3 Rod Martin, Oakland vs. Philadelphia, 1981
2 Randy Beverly, N.Y. Jets vs. Baltimore, 1969
Chuck Howley, Dallas vs. Baltimore, 1971
Jake Scott, Miami vs. Washington, 1973
Barry Wilburn, Washington vs. Denver, 1988

Yards Gained
Most Yards Gained, Career
75 Willie Brown, Oakland, 2 games
63 Chuck Howley, Dallas, 2 games
Jake Scott, Miami, 3 games
60 Herb Adderley, Green Bay-Dallas, 4 games
Most Yards Gained, Game
75 Willie Brown, Oakland vs. Minnesota, 1977
63 Jake Scott, Miami vs. Washington, 1973
60 Herb Adderley, Green Bay vs. Oakland, 1968
Longest Return
75 Willie Brown, Oakland vs. Minnesota, 1977 (TD)
60 Herb Adderley, Green Bay vs. Oakland, 1968 (TD)
55 Jake Scott, Miami vs. Washington, 1973

Touchdowns
Most Touchdowns, Game
1 Herb Adderley, Green Bay vs. Oakland, 1968
Willie Brown, Oakland vs. Minnesota, 1977
Jack Squirek, L.A. Raiders vs. Washington, 1984
Reggie Phillips, Chicago vs. New England, 1986

Punting
Most Punts, Career
17 Mike Eischeid, Oakland-Minnesota, 3 games
15 Larry Seiple, Miami, 3 games
14 Ron Widby, Dallas, 2 games
Ray Guy, Oakland-L.A. Raiders, 3 games

Most Punts, Game
9 Ron Widby, Dallas vs. Baltimore, 1971
7 By eight players

Longest Punt
62 Rich Camarillo, New England vs. Chicago, 1986
61 Jerrel Wilson, Kansas City vs. Green Bay, 1967
59 Jerrel Wilson, Kansas City vs. Minnesota, 1970
Bobby Walden, Pittsburgh vs. Dallas, 1976
Ken Clark, Los Angeles vs. Pittsburgh, 1980
Sean Landeta, N.Y. Giants vs. Denver, 1987

Average Yardage
Highest Average, Punting, Career (10 punts)
46.5 Jerrel Wilson, Kansas City, 2 games (11-511)
41.9 Ray Guy, Oakland-L.A. Raiders, 3 games (14-587)
41.3 Larry Seiple, Miami, 3 games (15-620)

Highest Average, Punting, Game (4 punts)
48.5 Jerrel Wilson, Kansas City vs. Minnesota, 1970 (4-194)
46.3 Jim Miller, San Francisco vs. Cincinnati, 1982 (4-185)
45.3 Jerrel Wilson, Kansas City vs. Green Bay, 1967 (7-317)

Punt Returns
Most Punt Returns, Career
6 Willie Wood, Green Bay, 2 games
Jake Scott, Miami, 3 games
Theo Bell, Pittsburgh, 2 games
Mike Nelms, Washington, 1 game
5 Dana McLemore, San Francisco, 1 game
4 By seven players

Most Punt Returns, Game
6 Mike Nelms, Washington vs. Miami, 1983
5 Willie Wood, Green Bay vs. Oakland, 1968
Dana McLemore, San Francisco vs. Miami, 1985
4 By six players

Most Fair Catches, Game
3 Ron Gardin, Baltimore vs. Dallas, 1971
Golden Richards, Dallas vs. Pittsburgh, 1976
Greg Pruitt, L.A. Raiders vs. Washington, 1984

Yards Gained
Most Yards Gained, Career
52 Mike Nelms, Washington, 1 game
51 Dana McLemore, San Francisco, 1 game
45 Jake Scott, Miami, 3 games

Most Yards Gained, Game
52 Mike Nelms, Washington vs. Miami, 1983
51 Dana McLemore, San Francisco vs. Miami, 1985
43 Neal Colzie, Oakland vs. Minnesota, 1977

Longest Return
34 Darrell Green, Washington vs. L.A. Raiders, 1984
31 Willie Wood, Green Bay vs. Oakland, 1968
28 Dana McLemore, San Francisco vs. Miami, 1985

Average Yardage
Highest Average, Career (4 returns)
10.8 Neal Colzie, Oakland, 1 game (4-43)
10.2 Dana McLemore, San Francisco, 1 game (5-51)
8.8 Mike Fuller, Cincinnati, 1 game (4-35)

Highest Average, Game (3 returns)
11.3 Lynn Swann, Pittsburgh vs. Minnesota, 1975 (3-34)
10.8 Neal Colzie, Oakland vs. Minnesota, 1977 (4-43)
10.2 Dana McLemore, San Francisco vs. Miami, 1985 (5-51)

Touchdowns
Most Touchdowns, Game
None

Kickoff Returns
Most Kickoff Returns, Career
8 Larry Anderson, Pittsburgh, 2 games
Fulton Walker, Miami, 2 games
Ken Bell, Denver, 2 games
7 Preston Pearson, Baltimore-Pittsburgh-Dallas, 5 games
Stephen Starring, New England, 1 game
6 Eugene (Mercury) Morris, Miami, 3 games

Most Kickoff Returns, Game
7 Stephen Starring, New England vs. Chicago, 1986
5 Larry Anderson, Pittsburgh vs. Los Angeles, 1980
Billy Campfield, Philadelphia vs. Oakland, 1981
David Verser, Cincinnati vs. San Francisco, 1982
Alvin Garrett, Washington vs. L.A. Raiders, 1984
Ken Bell, Denver vs. Washington, 1988

Yards Gained
Most Yards Gained, Career
283 Fulton Walker, Miami, 2 games
207 Larry Anderson, Pittsburgh, 2 games
153 Stephen Starring, New England, 1 game

Most Yards Gained, Game
190 Fulton Walker, Miami vs. Washington, 1983
162 Larry Anderson, Pittsburgh vs. Los Angeles, 1980
153 Stephen Starring, New England vs. Chicago, 1986

Longest Return
98 Fulton Walker, Miami vs. Washington, 1983 (TD)
67 Rick Upchurch, Denver vs. Dallas, 1978
48 Thomas Henderson, Dallas vs. Pittsburgh, 1976 (lateral)

Average Yardage
Highest Average, Career (4 returns)
35.4 Fulton Walker, Miami, 2 games (8-283)
25.9 Larry Anderson, Pittsburgh, 2 games (8-207)
22.5 Jim Duncan, Baltimore, 1 game (4-90)

Highest Average, Game (3 returns)
47.5 Fulton Walker, Miami vs. Washington, 1983 (4-190)
32.4 Larry Anderson, Pittsburgh vs. Los Angeles, 1980 (5-162)
31.3 Rick Upchurch, Denver vs. Dallas, 1978 (3-94)

Touchdowns
Most Touchdowns, Game
1 Fulton Walker, Miami vs. Washington, 1983

Fumbles
Most Fumbles, Career
5 Roger Staubach, Dallas, 4 games
3 Franco Harris, Pittsburgh, 4 games
Terry Bradshaw, Pittsburgh, 4 games
2 By five players

Most Fumbles, Game
3 Roger Staubach, Dallas vs. Pittsburgh, 1976
2 Franco Harris, Pittsburgh vs. Minnesota, 1975
Butch Johnson, Dallas vs. Denver, 1978
Terry Bradshaw, Pittsburgh vs. Dallas, 1979

Recoveries
Most Fumbles Recovered, Career
2 Jake Scott, Miami, 3 games (1 own, 1 opp)
Fran Tarkenton, Minnesota, 3 games (2 own)
Franco Harris, Pittsburgh, 4 games (2 own)
Roger Staubach, Dallas, 4 games (2 own)
Bobby Walden, Pittsburgh, 2 games (2 own)
John Fitzgerald, Dallas, 4 games (2 own)
Randy Hughes, Dallas, 3 games (2 opp)
Butch Johnson, Dallas, 2 games (2 own)
Mike Singletary, Chicago, 1 game (2 opp)

Most Fumbles Recovered, Game
2 Jake Scott, Miami vs. Minnesota, 1974 (1 own, 1 opp)
Roger Staubach, Dallas vs. Pittsburgh, 1976 (2 own)
Randy Hughes, Dallas vs. Denver, 1978 (2 opp)
Butch Johnson, Dallas vs. Denver, 1978 (2 own)
Mike Singletary, Chicago vs. New England, 1986 (2 opp)

Yards Gained
Most Yards Gained, Game
49 Mike Bass, Washington vs. Miami, 1973 (opp)
37 Mike Hegman, Dallas vs. Pittsburgh, 1979 (opp)
21 Randy Hughes, Dallas vs. Denver, 1978 (opp)

Longest Return
49 Mike Bass, Washington vs. Miami, 1973 (TD)
37 Mike Hegman, Dallas vs. Pittsburgh, 1979 (TD)
19 Randy Hughes, Dallas vs. Denver, 1978

Touchdowns
Most Touchdowns, Game
1 Mike Bass, Washington vs. Miami, 1973 (opp 49 yds)
Mike Hegman, Dallas vs. Pittsburgh, 1979 (opp 37 yds)

Combined Net Yards Gained
Attempts
Most Attempts, Career
108 Franco Harris, Pittsburgh, 4 games
66 John Riggins, Washington, 2 games
60 Larry Csonka, Miami, 3 games

Most Attempts, Game
39 John Riggins, Washington vs. Miami, 1983
35 Franco Harris, Pittsburgh vs. Minnesota, 1975
34 Matt Snell, N.Y. Jets vs. Baltimore, 1969

Yards Gained
Most Yards Gained, Career
468 Franco Harris, Pittsburgh, 4 games
391 Lynn Swann, Pittsburgh, 4 games
314 Larry Csonka, Miami, 3 games

Most Yards Gained, Game
239 Ricky Sanders, Washington vs. Denver, 1988
213 Timmy Smith, Washington vs. Denver, 1988
209 Marcus Allen, L.A. Raiders vs. Washington, 1984

Sacks
Sacks have been compiled since 1983.

Most Sacks, Game
2 Dwaine Board, San Francisco vs. Miami, 1985
Dennis Owens, New England vs. Chicago, 1986
Otis Wilson, Chicago vs. New England, 1986
Leonard Marshall, N.Y. Giants vs. Denver, 1987
Alvin Walton, Washington vs. Denver, 1988

Team Records

Games, Victories, Defeats
Most Games
5 Dallas, 1971-72, 1976, 1978-79
Miami, 1972-74, 1983, 1985
4 Minnesota, 1970, 1974-75, 1977
Pittsburgh, 1975-76, 1979-80
Oakland/L.A. Raiders, 1968, 1977, 1981, 1984
Washington, 1973, 1983-84, 1988
3 Denver, 1978, 1987-88

Most Consecutive Games
3 Miami, 1972-74
2 Green Bay, 1967-68
Dallas, 1971-72
Minnesota, 1974-75
Pittsburgh, 1975-76, 1979-80

Washington, 1983-84
Denver, 1987-88

Most Games Won
4 Pittsburgh, 1975-76, 1979-80
3 Oakland/L.A. Raiders, 1977, 1981, 1984
2 Green Bay, 1967-68
Miami, 1973-74
Dallas, 1972, 1978
San Francisco, 1982, 1985
Washington, 1983, 1988

Most Consecutive Games Won
2 Green Bay, 1967-68
Miami, 1973-74
Pittsburgh, 1975-76, 1979-80

Most Games Lost
4 Minnesota, 1970, 1974-75, 1977
3 Dallas, 1971, 1976, 1979
Miami, 1972, 1983, 1985
Denver, 1978, 1987-88
2 Washington, 1973, 1984

Most Consecutive Games Lost
2 Minnesota, 1974-75
Denver, 1987-88

Scoring

Most Points, Game
46 Chicago vs. New England, 1986
42 Washington vs. Denver, 1988
39 N.Y. Giants vs. Denver, 1987

Fewest Points, Game
3 Miami vs. Dallas, 1972
6 Minnesota vs. Pittsburgh, 1975
7 By four teams

Most Points, Both Teams, Game
66 Pittsburgh (35) vs. Dallas (31), 1979
59 N.Y. Giants (39) vs. Denver (20), 1987
56 Chicago (46) vs. New England (10), 1986

Fewest Points, Both Teams, Game
21 Washington (7) vs. Miami (14), 1973
22 Minnesota (6) vs. Pittsburgh (16), 1975
23 Baltimore (7) vs. N.Y. Jets (16), 1969

Largest Margin of Victory, Game
36 Chicago vs. New England, 1986 (46-10)
32 Washington vs. Denver, 1988 (42-10)
29 L.A. Raiders vs. Washington, 1984 (38-9)

Most Points, Each Half
1st: 35 Washington vs. Denver, 1988
2nd: 30 N.Y. Giants vs. Denver, 1987

Most Points, Each Quarter
1st: 14 Miami vs. Minnesota, 1974
Oakland vs. Philadelphia, 1981
2nd: 35 Washington vs. Denver, 1988
3rd: 21 Chicago vs. New England, 1986
4th: 14 Pittsburgh vs. Dallas, 1976; vs. Dallas, 1979; vs. Los Angeles, 1980
Dallas vs. Pittsburgh, 1979
Cincinnati vs. San Francisco, 1982
Washington vs. Miami, 1983

Most Points, Both Teams, Each Half
1st: 45 Washington (35) vs. Denver (10), 1988
2nd: 40 N.Y. Giants (30) vs. Denver (10), 1987

Fewest Points, Both Teams, Each Half
1st: 2 Minnesota (0) vs. Pittsburgh (2), 1975
2nd: 7 Miami (0) vs. Washington (7), 1973
Denver (0) vs. Washington (7), 1988

Most Points, Both Teams, Each Quarter
1st: 17 Miami (10) vs. San Francisco (7), 1985
Denver (10) vs. N.Y. Giants (7), 1987
2nd: 35 Washington (35) vs. Denver (0), 1988
3rd: 21 Chicago (21) vs. New England (0), 1986
4th: 28 Dallas (14) vs. Pittsburgh (14), 1979

Touchdowns

Most Touchdowns, Game
6 Washington vs. Denver, 1988
5 Green Bay vs. Kansas City, 1967
Pittsburgh vs. Dallas, 1979
L.A. Raiders vs. Washington, 1984
San Francisco vs. Miami, 1985
Chicago vs. New England, 1986
N.Y. Giants vs. Denver, 1987
4 Oakland vs. Minnesota, 1977
Dallas vs. Pittsburgh, 1979
Pittsburgh vs. Los Angeles, 1980

Fewest Touchdowns, Game
0 Miami vs. Dallas, 1972
1 By 14 teams

Most Touchdowns, Both Teams, Game
9 Pittsburgh (5) vs. Dallas (4), 1979
7 N.Y. Giants (5) vs. Denver (2), 1987
Washington (6) vs. Denver (1), 1988
6 Green Bay (5) vs. Kansas City (1), 1967
Oakland (4) vs. Minnesota (2), 1977
Pittsburgh (4) vs. Los Angeles (2), 1980
L.A. Raiders (5) vs. Washington (1), 1984
San Francisco (5) vs. Miami (1), 1985
Chicago (5) vs. New England (1), 1986

Fewest Touchdowns, Both Teams, Game
2 Baltimore (1) vs. N.Y. Jets (1), 1969
3 In five games

Points After Touchdown

Most Points After Touchdown, Game
6 Washington vs. Denver, 1988
5 Green Bay vs. Kansas City, 1967
Pittsburgh vs. Dallas, 1979
L.A. Raiders vs. Washington, 1984
San Francisco vs. Miami, 1985
Chicago vs. New England, 1986
4 Dallas vs. Pittsburgh, 1979
Pittsburgh vs. Los Angeles, 1980
N.Y. Giants vs. Denver, 1987

Most Points After Touchdown, Both Teams, Game
9 Pittsburgh (5) vs. Dallas (4), 1979
7 Washington (6) vs. Denver (1), 1988
6 Green Bay (5) vs. Kansas City (1), 1967
San Francisco (5) vs. Miami (1), 1985
Chicago (5) vs. New England (1), 1986
N.Y. Giants (4) vs. Denver (2), 1987

Fewest Points After Touchdown, Both Teams, Game
2 Baltimore (1) vs. N.Y. Jets (1), 1969
Baltimore (1) vs. Dallas (1), 1971
Minnesota (0) vs. Pittsburgh (2), 1975

Field Goals

Most Field Goals Attempted, Game
5 N.Y. Jets vs. Baltimore, 1969
Dallas vs. Denver, 1978
4 Green Bay vs. Oakland, 1968
Pittsburgh vs. Dallas, 1976
San Francisco vs. Cincinnati, 1982
Denver vs. N.Y. Giants, 1987

Most Field Goals Attempted, Both Teams, Game
7 N.Y. Jets (5) vs. Baltimore (2), 1969
6 Dallas (5) vs. Denver (1), 1978
5 Green Bay (4) vs. Oakland (1), 1968
Pittsburgh (4) vs. Dallas (1), 1976
Oakland (3) vs. Philadelphia (2), 1981
Denver (4) vs. N.Y. Giants (1), 1987

Fewest Field Goals Attempted, Both Teams, Game
1 Minnesota (0) vs. Miami (1), 1974
2 Green Bay (0) vs. Kansas City (2), 1967
Miami (1) vs. Washington (1), 1973
Dallas (1) vs. Pittsburgh (1), 1979

Most Field Goals, Game
4 Green Bay vs. Oakland, 1968
San Francisco vs. Cincinnati, 1982
3 N.Y. Jets vs. Baltimore, 1969
Kansas City vs. Minnesota, 1970
Miami vs. San Francisco, 1985
Chicago vs. New England, 1986

Most Field Goals, Both Teams, Game
4 Green Bay (4) vs. Oakland (0), 1968
San Francisco (4) vs. Cincinnati (0), 1982
Miami (3) vs. San Francisco (1), 1985
Chicago (3) vs. New England (1), 1986
3 In eight games

Fewest Field Goals, Both Teams, Game
0 Miami vs. Washington, 1973
Pittsburgh vs. Minnesota, 1975
1 Green Bay (0) vs. Kansas City (1), 1967
Minnesota (0) vs. Miami (1), 1974
Pittsburgh (0) vs. Dallas (1), 1979
Washington (0) vs. Denver (1), 1988

Safeties

Most Safeties, Game
1 Pittsburgh vs. Minnesota, 1975; vs. Dallas, 1976
Chicago vs. New England, 1986
N.Y. Giants vs. Denver, 1987

First Downs

Most First Downs, Game
31 San Francisco vs. Miami, 1985
25 Washington vs. Denver, 1988
24 Cincinnati vs. San Francisco, 1982
Washington vs. Miami, 1983
N.Y. Giants vs. Denver, 1987

Fewest First Downs, Game
9 Minnesota vs. Pittsburgh, 1975
Miami vs. Washington, 1983
10 Dallas vs. Baltimore, 1971
Miami vs. Dallas, 1972
11 Denver vs. Dallas, 1978

Most First Downs, Both Teams, Game
50 San Francisco (31) vs. Miami (19), 1985
47 N.Y. Giants (24) vs. Denver (23), 1987
44 Cincinnati (24) vs. San Francisco (20), 1982

Fewest First Downs, Both Teams, Game
24 Dallas (10) vs. Baltimore (14), 1971
26 Minnesota (9) vs. Pittsburgh (17), 1975
27 Pittsburgh (13) vs. Dallas (14), 1976

Rushing

Most First Downs, Rushing, Game
16 San Francisco vs. Miami, 1985
15 Dallas vs. Miami, 1972
14 Washington vs. Miami, 1983

Fewest First Downs, Rushing, Game
1 New England vs. Chicago, 1986
2 Minnesota vs. Kansas City, 1970; vs. Pittsburgh, 1975; vs. Oakland, 1977
Pittsburgh vs. Dallas, 1979
Miami vs. San Francisco, 1985
3 Miami vs. Dallas, 1972
Philadelphia vs. Oakland, 1981

Most First Downs, Rushing, Both Teams, Game
21 Washington (14) vs. Miami (7), 1983
19 Washington (13) vs. Denver (6), 1988
18 Dallas (15) vs. Miami (3), 1972
Miami (13) vs. Minnesota (5), 1974
San Francisco (16) vs. Miami (2), 1985

Fewest First Downs, Rushing, Both Teams, Game
8 Baltimore (4) vs. Dallas (4), 1971
Pittsburgh (2) vs. Dallas (6), 1979
9 Philadelphia (3) vs. Oakland (6), 1981
10 Minnesota (2) vs. Kansas City (8), 1970

Passing

Most First Downs, Passing, Game
17 Miami vs. San Francisco, 1985
16 Denver vs. N.Y. Giants, 1987
15 Minnesota vs. Oakland, 1977
Pittsburgh vs. Dallas, 1979
San Francisco vs. Miami, 1985

Fewest First Downs, Passing, Game
1 Denver vs. Dallas, 1978
2 Miami vs. Washington, 1983
4 Miami vs. Minnesota, 1974

Most First Downs, Passing, Both Teams, Game
32 Miami (17) vs. San Francisco (15), 1985
29 Denver (16) vs. N.Y. Giants (13), 1987
28 Pittsburgh (15) vs. Dallas (13), 1979

Fewest First Downs, Passing, Both Teams, Game
9 Denver (1) vs. Dallas (8), 1978
10 Minnesota (5) vs. Pittsburgh (5), 1975
11 Dallas (5) vs. Baltimore (6), 1971
Miami (2) vs. Washington (9), 1983

Penalty

Most First Downs, Penalty, Game
4 Baltimore vs. Dallas, 1971
Miami vs. Minnesota, 1974
Cincinnati vs. San Francisco, 1982
3 Kansas City vs. Minnesota, 1970
Minnesota vs. Oakland, 1977

Most First Downs, Penalty, Both Teams, Game
6 Cincinnati (4) vs. San Francisco (2), 1982
5 Baltimore (4) vs. Dallas (1), 1971
Miami (4) vs. Minnesota (1), 1974
4 Kansas City (3) vs. Minnesota (1), 1970

Fewest First Downs, Penalty, Both Teams, Game
0 Dallas vs. Miami, 1972
Miami vs. Washington, 1973
Dallas vs. Pittsburgh, 1976
Miami vs. San Francisco, 1985
1 Green Bay (0) vs. Kansas City (1), 1967
Miami (0) vs. Washington (1), 1983

Net Yards Gained Rushing and Passing

Most Yards Gained, Game
602 Washington vs. Denver, 1988
537 San Francisco vs. Miami, 1985
429 Oakland vs. Minnesota, 1977

Fewest Yards Gained, Game
119 Minnesota vs. Pittsburgh, 1975
123 New England vs. Chicago, 1986
156 Denver vs. Dallas, 1978

Most Yards Gained, Both Teams, Game
929 Washington (602) vs. Denver (327), 1988
851 San Francisco (537) vs. Miami (314), 1985
782 Oakland (429) vs. Minnesota (353), 1977

Fewest Yards Gained, Both Teams, Game
452 Minnesota (119) vs. Pittsburgh (333), 1975
481 Washington (228) vs. Miami (253), 1973
Denver (156) vs. Dallas (325), 1978
497 Minnesota (238) vs. Miami (259), 1974

Rushing

Attempts

Most Attempts, Game
57 Pittsburgh vs. Minnesota, 1975
53 Miami vs. Minnesota, 1974
52 Oakland vs. Minnesota, 1977
Washington vs. Miami, 1983

Fewest Attempts, Game
9 Miami vs. San Francisco, 1985
11 New England vs. Chicago, 1986
17 Denver vs. Washington, 1988

Most Attempts, Both Teams, Game
81 Washington (52) vs. Miami (29), 1983
78 Pittsburgh (57) vs. Minnesota (21), 1975
Oakland (52) vs. Minnesota (26), 1977
77 Miami (53) vs. Minnesota (24), 1974
Pittsburgh (46) vs. Dallas (31), 1976

Fewest Attempts, Both Teams, Game
49 Miami (9) vs. San Francisco (40), 1985
52 Kansas City (19) vs. Green Bay (33), 1967
56 Pittsburgh (24) vs. Dallas (32), 1979

Yards Gained

Most Yards Gained, Game
280 Washington vs. Denver, 1988
276 Washington vs. Miami, 1983
266 Oakland vs. Minnesota, 1977

Fewest Yards Gained, Game
7 New England vs. Chicago, 1986
17 Minnesota vs. Pittsburgh, 1975
25 Miami vs. San Francisco, 1985

Most Yards Gained, Both Teams, Game
377 Washington (280) vs. Denver (97), 1988
372 Washington (276) vs. Miami (96), 1983
337 Oakland (266) vs. Minnesota (71), 1977

Fewest Yards Gained, Both Teams, Game
171 Baltimore (69) vs. Dallas (102), 1971
174 New England (7) vs. Chicago (167), 1986
186 Philadelphia (69) vs. Oakland (117), 1981

Average Gain

Highest Average Gain, Game
7.00 L.A. Raiders vs. Washington, 1984 (33-231)
Washington vs. Denver, 1988 (40-280)
6.22 Baltimore vs. N.Y. Jets, 1969 (23-143)
5.71 Denver vs. Washington, 1988 (17-97)

Lowest Average Gain, Game
0.64 New England vs. Chicago, 1986 (11-7)
0.81 Minnesota vs. Pittsburgh, 1975 (21-17)
2.23 Baltimore vs. Dallas, 1971 (31-69)

Touchdowns

Most Touchdowns, Game
4 Chicago vs. New England, 1986
3 Green Bay vs. Kansas City, 1967
Miami vs. Minnesota, 1974
2 Oakland vs. Minnesota, 1977
Pittsburgh vs. Los Angeles, 1980
L.A. Raiders vs. Washington, 1984
San Francisco vs. Miami, 1985
N.Y. Giants vs. Denver, 1987
Washington vs. Denver, 1988

Fewest Touchdowns, Game
0 By 15 teams

Most Touchdowns, Both Teams, Game
4 Miami (3) vs. Minnesota (1), 1974
Chicago (4) vs. New England (0), 1986
3 Green Bay (3) vs. Kansas City (0), 1967
Pittsburgh (2) vs. Los Angeles (1), 1980
L.A. Raiders (2) vs. Washington (1), 1984
N.Y. Giants (2) vs. Denver (1), 1987

Fewest Touchdowns, Both Teams, Game
0 Pittsburgh vs. Dallas, 1976
Oakland vs. Philadelphia, 1981
1 In seven games

Passing

Attempts

Most Passes Attempted, Game
50 Miami vs. San Francisco, 1985
44 Minnesota vs. Oakland, 1977
41 Baltimore vs. N.Y. Jets, 1969
Denver vs. N.Y. Giants, 1987

Fewest Passes Attempted, Game
7 Miami vs. Minnesota, 1974
11 Miami vs. Washington, 1973
14 Pittsburgh vs. Minnesota, 1975

Most Passes Attempted, Both Teams, Game
85 Miami (50) vs. San Francisco (35), 1985
70 Baltimore (41) vs. N.Y. Jets (29), 1969
69 Denver (39) vs. Washington (30), 1988

Fewest Passes Attempted, Both Teams, Game
35 Miami (7) vs. Minnesota (28), 1974
39 Miami (11) vs. Washington (28), 1973
40 Pittsburgh (14) vs. Minnesota (26), 1975
Miami (17) vs. Washington (23), 1983

Completions

Most Passes Completed, Game
29 Miami vs. San Francisco, 1985
26 Denver vs. N.Y. Giants, 1987
25 Cincinnati vs. San Francisco, 1982

Fewest Passes Completed, Game
4 Miami vs. Washington, 1983
6 Miami vs. Minnesota, 1974
8 Miami vs. Washington, 1973
Denver vs. Dallas, 1978

Most Passes Completed, Both Teams, Game
53 Miami (29) vs. San Francisco (24), 1985
48 Denver (26) vs. N.Y. Giants (22), 1987
39 Cincinnati (25) vs. San Francisco (14), 1982

Fewest Passes Completed, Both Teams, Game
19 Miami (4) vs. Washington (15), 1983
20 Pittsburgh (9) vs. Minnesota (11), 1975
22 Miami (8) vs. Washington (14), 1973

Completion Percentage

Highest Completion Percentage, Game (20 attempts)
88.0 N.Y. Giants vs. Denver, 1987 (25-22)
73.5 Cincinnati vs. San Francisco, 1982 (34-25)
68.6 San Francisco vs. Miami, 1985 (35-24)

Lowest Completion Percentage, Game (20 attempts)
32.0 Denver vs. Dallas, 1978 (25-8)
38.5 Denver vs. Washington, 1988 (39-15)
41.5 Baltimore vs. N.Y. Jets, 1969 (41-17)

Yards Gained

Most Yards Gained, Game
326 San Francisco vs. Miami, 1985

322 Washington vs. Denver, 1988
320 Denver vs. N.Y. Giants, 1987

Fewest Yards Gained, Game
35 Denver vs. Dallas, 1978
63 Miami vs. Minnesota, 1974
69 Miami vs. Washington, 1973

Most Yards Gained, Both Teams, Game
615 San Francisco (326) vs. Miami (289), 1985
583 Denver (320) vs. N.Y. Giants (263), 1987
552 Washington (322) vs. Denver (230), 1988

Fewest Yards Gained, Both Teams, Game
156 Miami (69) vs. Washington (87), 1973
186 Pittsburgh (84) vs. Minnesota (102), 1975
205 Dallas (100) vs. Miami (105), 1972

Times Sacked

Most Times Sacked, Game
7 Dallas vs. Pittsburgh, 1976
New England vs. Chicago, 1986
6 Kansas City vs. Green Bay, 1967
Washington vs. L.A. Raiders, 1984
5 Dallas vs. Denver, 1978; vs. Pittsburgh, 1979
Cincinnati vs. San Francisco, 1982
Denver vs. Washington, 1988

Fewest Times Sacked, Game
0 Baltimore vs. N.Y. Jets, 1969; vs. Dallas, 1971
Minnesota vs. Pittsburgh, 1975
Pittsburgh vs. Los Angeles, 1980
Philadelphia vs. Oakland, 1981
1 By eight teams

Most Times Sacked, Both Teams, Game
10 New England (7) vs. Chicago (3), 1986
9 Kansas City (6) vs. Green Bay (3), 1967
Dallas (7) vs. Pittsburgh (2), 1976
Dallas (5) vs. Denver (4), 1978
Dallas (5) vs. Pittsburgh (4), 1979
8 Washington (6) vs. L.A. Raiders (2), 1984

Fewest Times Sacked, Both Teams, Game
1 Philadelphia (0) vs. Oakland (1), 1981
2 Baltimore (0) vs. N.Y. Jets (2), 1969
Baltimore (0) vs. Dallas (2), 1971
Minnesota (0) vs. Pittsburgh (2), 1975
3 In three games

Touchdowns

Most Touchdowns, Game
4 Pittsburgh vs. Dallas, 1979
Washington vs. Denver, 1988
3 Dallas vs. Pittsburgh, 1979
Oakland vs. Philadelphia, 1981
San Francisco vs. Miami, 1985
N.Y. Giants vs. Denver, 1987
2 By 10 teams

Fewest Touchdowns, Game
0 By 11 teams

Most Touchdowns, Both Teams, Game
7 Pittsburgh (4) vs. Dallas (3), 1979
5 Washington (4) vs. Denver (1), 1988
4 Dallas (2) vs. Pittsburgh (2), 1976
Oakland (3) vs. Philadelphia (1), 1981
San Francisco (3) vs. Miami (1), 1985
N.Y. Giants (3) vs. Denver (1), 1987

Fewest Touchdowns, Both Teams, Game
0 N.Y. Jets vs. Baltimore, 1969
Miami vs. Minnesota, 1974
1 In five games

Interceptions By

Most Interceptions By, Game
4 N.Y. Jets vs. Baltimore, 1969
Dallas vs. Denver, 1978
3 By nine teams

Most Interceptions By, Both Teams, Game
6 Baltimore (3) vs. Dallas (3), 1971
4 In six games

Fewest Interceptions By, Both Teams, Game
1 Oakland (0) vs. Green Bay (1), 1968
Miami (0) vs. Dallas (1), 1972
Minnesota (0) vs. Miami (1), 1974
N.Y. Giants (0) vs. Denver (1), 1987

Yards Gained

Most Yards Gained, Game
95 Miami vs. Washington, 1973
91 Oakland vs. Minnesota, 1977
89 Pittsburgh vs. Dallas, 1976

Most Yards Gained, Both Teams, Game
95 Miami (95) vs. Washington (0), 1973
91 Oakland (91) vs. Minnesota (0), 1977
89 Pittsburgh (89) vs. Dallas (0), 1976

Touchdowns

Most Touchdowns, Game
1 Green Bay vs. Oakland, 1968
Oakland vs. Minnesota, 1977
L.A. Raiders vs. Washington, 1984
Chicago vs. New England, 1986

Punting

Most Punts, Game
9 Dallas vs. Baltimore, 1971
8 Washington vs. L.A. Raiders, 1984
7 By seven teams

Fewest Punts, Game
2 Pittsburgh vs. Los Angeles, 1980
Denver vs. N.Y. Giants, 1987
3 By nine teams

Most Punts, Both Teams, Game
15 Washington (8) vs. L.A. Raiders (7), 1984
13 Dallas (9) vs. Baltimore (4), 1971
Pittsburgh (7) vs. Minnesota (6), 1975
12 In three games

Fewest Punts, Both Teams, Game
5 Denver (2) vs. N.Y. Giants (3), 1987
6 Oakland (3) vs. Philadelphia (3), 1981
7 In four games

Average Yardage

Highest Average, Game (4 punts)
48.50 Kansas City vs. Minnesota, 1970 (4-194)
46.25 San Francisco vs. Cincinnati, 1982 (4-185)
45.29 Kansas City vs. Green Bay, 1967 (7-317)

Lowest Average, Game (4 punts)
31.20 Washington vs. Miami, 1973 (5-156)
32.38 Washington vs. L.A. Raiders, 1984 (8-259)
32.40 Oakland vs. Minnesota, 1977 (5-162)

Punt Returns

Most Punt Returns, Game
6 Washington vs. Miami, 1983
5 By five teams

Fewest Punt Returns, Game
0 Minnesota vs. Miami, 1974
1 By 11 teams

Most Punt Returns, Both Teams, Game
9 Pittsburgh (5) vs. Minnesota (4), 1975
8 Green Bay (5) vs. Oakland (3), 1968
Baltimore (5) vs. Dallas (3), 1971
Washington (6) vs. Miami (2), 1983
7 Green Bay (4) vs. Kansas City (3), 1967
Oakland (4) vs. Minnesota (3), 1977
San Francisco (5) vs. Miami (2), 1985

Fewest Punt Returns, Both Teams, Game
2 Dallas (1) vs. Miami (1), 1972
Denver (1) vs. N.Y. Giants (1), 1987
3 Kansas City (1) vs. Minnesota (2), 1970
Minnesota (0) vs. Miami (3), 1974
Washington (1) vs. Denver (2), 1988
4 L.A. Raiders (2) vs. Washington (2), 1984
Chicago (2) vs. New England (2), 1986

Yards Gained

Most Yards Gained, Game
52 Washington vs. Miami, 1983
51 San Francisco vs. Miami, 1985
43 Oakland vs. Minnesota, 1977

Fewest Yards Gained, Game
−1 Dallas vs. Miami, 1972
0 By five teams

Most Yards Gained, Both Teams, Game
74 Washington (52) vs. Miami (22), 1983
66 San Francisco (51) vs. Miami (15), 1985
60 Dallas (33) vs. Pittsburgh (27), 1979

Fewest Yards Gained, Both Teams, Game
13 Miami (4) vs. Washington (9), 1973
18 Kansas City (0) vs. Minnesota (18), 1970
Washington (0) vs. Denver (18), 1988
20 Dallas (−1) vs. Miami (21), 1972
Minnesota (0) vs. Miami (20), 1974

Average Return

Highest Average, Game (3 returns)
10.8 Oakland vs. Minnesota, 1977 (4-43)
10.2 San Francisco vs. Miami, 1985 (5-51)
8.8 Cincinnati vs. San Francisco, 1982 (4-35)

Touchdowns

Most Touchdowns, Game
None

Kickoff Returns

Most Kickoff Returns, Game
7 Oakland vs. Green Bay, 1968
Minnesota vs. Oakland, 1977
Cincinnati vs. San Francisco, 1982
Washington vs. L.A. Raiders, 1984
Miami vs. San Francisco, 1985
New England vs. Chicago, 1986
6 By six teams

Fewest Kickoff Returns, Game
1 N.Y. Jets vs. Baltimore, 1969
L.A. Raiders vs. Washington, 1984
2 By six teams

Most Kickoff Returns, Both Teams, Game
11 Los Angeles (6) vs. Pittsburgh (5), 1980
Miami (7) vs. San Francisco (4), 1985
New England (7) vs. Chicago (4), 1986
10 Oakland (7) vs. Green Bay (3), 1968
9 In eight games

Fewest Kickoff Returns, Both Teams, Game
5 N.Y. Jets (1) vs. Baltimore (4), 1969
Miami (2) vs. Washington (3), 1973
6 In three games

Yards Gained

Most Yards Gained, Game

222 Miami vs. Washington, 1983
173 Denver vs. Dallas, 1978
162 Pittsburgh vs. Los Angeles, 1980

Fewest Yards Gained, Game

17 L.A. Raiders vs. Washington, 1984
25 N.Y. Jets vs. Baltimore, 1969
32 Pittsburgh vs. Minnesota, 1975

Most Yards Gained, Both Teams, Game

279 Miami (222) vs. Washington (57), 1983
231 Pittsburgh (162) vs. Los Angeles (79), 1980
224 Denver (173) vs. Dallas (51), 1978

Fewest Yards Gained, Both Teams, Game

78 Miami (33) vs. Washington (45), 1973
82 Pittsburgh (32) vs. Minnesota (50), 1975
92 San Francisco (40) vs. Cincinnati (52), 1982

Average Gain

Highest Average, Game (3 returns)

37.0 Miami vs. Washington, 1983 (6-222)
32.4 Pittsburgh vs. Los Angeles, 1980 (5-162)
28.8 Denver vs. Dallas, 1978 (6-173)

Touchdowns

Most Touchdowns, Game

1 Miami vs. Washington, 1983

Penalties

Most Penalties, Game

12 Dallas vs. Denver, 1978
10 Dallas vs. Baltimore, 1971
9 Dallas vs. Pittsburgh, 1979

Fewest Penalties, Game

0 Miami vs. Dallas, 1972
Pittsburgh vs. Dallas, 1976
1 Green Bay vs. Oakland, 1968
Miami vs. Minnesota, 1974; vs. San Francisco, 1985
2 By four teams

Most Penalties, Both Teams, Game

20 Dallas (12) vs. Denver (8), 1978
16 Cincinnati (8) vs. San Francisco (8), 1982
14 Dallas (10) vs. Baltimore (4), 1971
Dallas (9) vs. Pittsburgh (5), 1979

Fewest Penalties, Both Teams, Game

2 Pittsburgh (0) vs. Dallas (2), 1976
3 Miami (0) vs. Dallas (3), 1972
Miami (1) vs. San Francisco (2), 1985
5 Green Bay (1) vs. Oakland (4), 1968

Yards Penalized

Most Yards Penalized, Game

133 Dallas vs. Baltimore, 1971
122 Pittsburgh vs. Minnesota, 1975
94 Dallas vs. Denver, 1978

Fewest Yards Penalized, Game

0 Miami vs. Dallas, 1972
Pittsburgh vs. Dallas, 1976
4 Miami vs. Minnesota, 1974
10 Miami vs. San Francisco, 1985
San Francisco vs. Miami, 1985

Most Yards Penalized, Both Teams, Game

164 Dallas (133) vs. Baltimore (31), 1971
154 Dallas (94) vs. Denver (60), 1978
140 Pittsburgh (122) vs. Minnesota (18), 1975

Fewest Yards Penalized, Both Teams, Game

15 Miami (0) vs. Dallas (15), 1972
20 Pittsburgh (0) vs. Dallas (20), 1976
Miami (10) vs. San Francisco (10), 1985
43 Green Bay (12) vs. Oakland (31), 1968

Fumbles

Most Fumbles, Game

6 Dallas vs. Denver, 1978
5 Baltimore vs. Dallas, 1971
4 In four games

Fewest Fumbles, Game

0 By eight teams

Most Fumbles, Both Teams, Game

10 Dallas (6) vs. Denver (4), 1978
8 Dallas (4) vs. Pittsburgh (4), 1976
7 Pittsburgh (4) vs. Minnesota (3), 1975
New England (4) vs. Chicago (3), 1986

Fewest Fumbles, Both Teams, Game

0 Los Angeles vs. Pittsburgh, 1980
1 Oakland (0) vs. Minnesota (1), 1977
Oakland (0) vs. Philadelphia (1), 1981
Denver (0) vs. Washington (1), 1988
2 In four games

Most Fumbles Lost, Game

4 Baltimore vs. Dallas, 1971
Denver vs. Dallas, 1978
New England vs. Chicago, 1986
2 In many games

Most Fumbles Lost, Both Teams, Game

6 Denver (4) vs. Dallas (2), 1978
New England (4) vs. Chicago (2), 1986
5 Baltimore (4) vs. Dallas (1), 1971
4 Minnesota (2) vs. Pittsburgh (2), 1975
Dallas (2) vs. Pittsburgh (2), 1979

Fewest Fumbles Lost, Both Teams, Game

0 Green Bay vs. Kansas City, 1967
Dallas vs. Pittsburgh, 1976
Los Angeles vs. Pittsburgh, 1980
Denver vs. N.Y. Giants, 1987
Denver vs. Washington, 1988
1 Washington (0) vs. Miami (1), 1973
Miami (0) vs. Minnesota (1), 1974
Oakland (0) vs. Minnesota (1), 1977
Oakland (0) vs. Philadelphia (1), 1981
Washington (0) vs. Miami (1), 1983
2 In four games

Most Fumbles Recovered, Game

8 Dallas vs. Denver, 1978 (4 own, 4 opp)
5 Chicago vs. New England, 1986 (1 own, 4 opp)
4 Pittsburgh vs. Minnesota, 1975 (2 own, 2 opp)
Dallas vs. Pittsburgh, 1976 (4 own)

Turnovers

(Number of times losing the ball on interceptions and fumbles.)

Most Turnovers, Game

8 Denver vs. Dallas, 1978
7 Baltimore vs. Dallas, 1971
6 New England vs. Chicago, 1986

Fewest Turnovers, Game

0 Green Bay vs. Oakland, 1968
Miami vs. Minnesota, 1974
Pittsburgh vs. Dallas, 1976
Oakland vs. Minnesota, 1977; vs. Philadelphia, 1981
N.Y. Giants vs. Denver, 1987
1 By many teams

Most Turnovers, Both Teams, Game

11 Baltimore (7) vs. Dallas (4), 1971
10 Denver (8) vs. Dallas (2), 1978
8 New England (6) vs. Chicago (2), 1986

Fewest Turnovers, Both Teams, Game

1 N.Y. Giants (0) vs. Denver (1), 1987
2 Green Bay (1) vs. Kansas City (1), 1967
Miami (0) vs. Minnesota (2), 1974
3 Green Bay (0) vs. Oakland (3), 1968
Pittsburgh (0) vs. Dallas (3), 1976
Oakland (0) vs. Minnesota (3), 1977

POSTSEASON GAME RECORDS

Compiled by Elias Sports Bureau

Throughout this all-time postseason record section, the following abbreviations are used to indicate various levels of postseason games:

SB Super Bowl (1966 to date)
AFC AFC Championship Game (1970 to date) or AFL Championship Game (1960-69)
NFC NFC Championship Game (1970 to date) or NFL Championship Game (1933-69)
AFC-D AFC Divisional Playoff Game (1970 to date), AFC Second-Round Playoff Game (1982), AFL Inter-Divisional Playoff Game (1969), or special playoff game to break tie for AFL Division Championship (1963, 1968)
NFC-D NFC Divisional Playoff Game (1970 to date), NFC Second-Round Playoff Game (1982), NFL Conference Championship Game (1967-69), or special playoff game to break tie for NFL Division or Conference Championship (1941, 1943, 1947, 1950, 1952, 1957, 1958, 1965)
AFC-FR AFC First-Round Playoff Game (1978 to date)
NFC-FR NFC First-Round Playoff Game (1978 to date)

Year references are to the season following which the postseason game occurred, even if the game was played in the next calendar year.

Postseason Game Composite Standings

	W	L	Pct.	Pts.	OP
Green Bay Packers	13	5	.722	416	259
Pittsburgh Steelers	15	8	.652	533	447
Los Angeles Raiders*	19	12	.613	761	535
Detroit Lions	6	4	.600	221	208
Miami Dolphins	14	10	.583	535	468
Philadelphia Eagles	7	5	.583	219	173
Washington Redskins**	16	12	.571	569	523
Dallas Cowboys	20	16	.556	805	640
Kansas City Chiefs***	5	4	.556	159	182
San Francisco 49ers	9	8	.529	358	373
Chicago Bears	11	10	.524	474	396
Indianapolis Colts****	8	8	.500	285	300
Houston Oilers	7	7	.500	201	321
New York Jets	5	5	.500	206	183
Seattle Seahawks	3	3	.500	115	118
Minnesota Vikings	12	13	.480	468	478
Denver Broncos	6	7	.462	252	327
New England Patriots†	4	6	.400	195	258
New York Giants	10	16	.385	430	485
Los Angeles Rams††	11	18	.379	441	619
Buffalo Bills	3	5	.375	138	171
Cleveland Browns	9	16	.360	489	559
San Diego Chargers†††	4	8	.333	230	279
Cincinnati Bengals	2	5	.286	137	180
Atlanta Falcons	1	3	.250	85	100
Tampa Bay Buccaneers	1	3	.250	41	94
St. Louis Cardinals††††	1	4	.200	81	134
New Orleans Saints	0	1	.000	10	44

**24 games played when franchise was in Oakland. (Won 15, lost 9, 587 points scored, 435 points allowed)*
***One game played when franchise was in Boston. (Lost 21-6)*
****One game played when franchise was Dallas Texans. (Lost 20-17)*
*****15 games played when franchise was in Baltimore. (Won 8, lost 7, 264 points scored, 262 points allowed)*
†Two games played when franchise was in Boston. (Won 26-8, lost 51-10)
††One game played when franchise was in Cleveland. (Won 15-14)
†††One game played when franchise was in Los Angeles. (Lost 24-16)
††††Two games played when franchise was in Chicago. (Won 28-21, lost 7-0)

Individual Records

Service

Most Games, Career
27 D. D. Lewis, Dallas (SB-5, NFC-9, NFC-D 12, NFC-FR 1)
26 Larry Cole, Dallas (SB-5, NFC-8, NFC-D-12, NFC-FR 1)
25 Charlie Waters, Dallas (SB-5, NFC-9, NFC-D 10, NFC-FR 1)

Scoring

Points

Most Points, Career
115 George Blanda, Chi. Bears-Houston-Oakland, 19 games (49-pat, 22-fg)
102 Franco Harris, Pittsburgh, 19 games (17-td)
95 Rafael Septien, L.A. Rams-Dallas, 15 games (41-pat, 18-fg)

Most Points, Game
19 Pat Harder, NFC-D: Detroit vs. Los Angeles, 1952 (2-td, 4-pat, 1-fg)
Paul Hornung, NFC: Green Bay vs. N.Y. Giants, 1961 (1-td, 4-pat, 3-fg)
18 By 15 players

Touchdowns

Most Touchdowns, Career
17 Franco Harris, Pittsburgh, 19 games (16-r, 1-p)
12 John Riggins, Washington, 9 games (12-r)
John Stallworth, Pittsburgh, 18 games (12-p)
10 Fred Biletnikoff, Oakland, 19 games (10-p)
Larry Csonka, Miami, 12 games (9-r, 1-p)
Tony Dorsett, Dallas, 17 games (9-r, 1-p)
Marcus Allen, L.A. Raiders, 7 games (8-r, 2-p)

Most Touchdowns, Game
3 Andy Farkas, NFC-D: Washington vs. N.Y. Giants, 1943 (3-r)
Tom Fears, NFC-D: Los Angeles vs. Chi. Bears, 1950 (3-p)
Otto Graham, NFC: Cleveland vs. Detroit, 1954 (3-r)
Gary Collins, NFC: Cleveland vs. Baltimore, 1964 (3-p)
Craig Baynham, NFC-D: Dallas vs. Cleveland, 1967 (2-r, 1-p)
Fred Biletnikoff, AFC-D: Oakland vs. Kansas City, 1968 (3-p)
Tom Matte, NFC: Baltimore vs. Cleveland, 1968 (3-r)
Larry Schreiber, NFC-D: San Francisco vs. Dallas, 1972 (3-r)
Larry Csonka, AFC: Miami vs. Oakland, 1973 (3-r)
Franco Harris, AFC-D: Pittsburgh vs. Buffalo, 1974 (3-r)
Preston Pearson, NFC: Dallas vs. Los Angeles, 1975 (3-p)
Dave Casper, AFC-D: Oakland vs. Baltimore, 1977 (OT) (3-p)
Alvin Garrett, NFC-FR: Washington vs. Detroit, 1982 (3-p)
John Riggins, NFC-D: Washington vs. L.A. Rams, 1983 (3-r)
Roger Craig, SB: San Francisco vs. Miami, 1984 (1-r, 2-p)

Most Consecutive Games Scoring Touchdowns
8 John Stallworth, Pittsburgh, 1978-83
7 John Riggins, Washington, 1982-84
Marcus Allen, L.A. Raiders, 1982-85 (current)
5 Duane Thomas, Dallas, 1970-71
Franco Harris, Pittsburgh, 1974-75
Franco Harris, Pittsburgh, 1977-79

Points After Touchdown

Most Points After Touchdown, Career
49 George Blanda, Chi. Bears-Houston-Oakland, 19 games (49 att)
41 Rafael Septien, L.A. Rams-Dallas, 15 games (41 att)
38 Fred Cox, Minnesota, 18 games (40 att)

Most Points After Touchdown, Game
8 Lou Groza, NFC: Cleveland vs. Detroit, 1954 (8 att)
Jim Martin, NFC: Detroit vs. Cleveland, 1957 (8 att)
George Blanda, AFC-D: Oakland vs. Houston, 1969 (8 att)
7 Danny Villanueva, NFC-D: Dallas vs. Cleveland, 1967 (7 att)
Raul Allegre, NFC-D: N.Y. Giants vs. San Francisco, 1986
6 George Blair, AFC: San Diego vs. Boston, 1963 (6 att)
Mark Moseley, NFC-D: Washington vs. L.A. Rams, 1983 (6 att)
Uwe von Schamann, AFC: Miami vs. Pittsburgh, 1984 (6 att)
Ali Haji-Sheikh, SB: Washington vs. Denver, 1987 (6 att)

Most Points After Touchdown, No Misses, Career
49 George Blanda, Chi. Bears-Houston-Oakland, 19 games
41 Rafael Septien, L.A. Rams-Dallas, 14 games
33 Chris Bahr, Oakland-L.A. Raiders, 11 games

Field Goals

Most Field Goals Attempted, Career
39 George Blanda, Chi. Bears-Houston-Oakland, 19 games
31 Mark Moseley, Washington-Cleveland, 11 games
27 Roy Gerela, Houston-Pittsburgh, 15 games

Most Field Goals Attempted, Game
6 George Blanda, AFC: Oakland vs. Houston, 1967
David Ray, NFC-D: Los Angeles vs. Dallas, 1973
Mark Moseley, AFC-D: Cleveland vs. N.Y. Jets, 1986 (OT)
5 Jerry Kramer, NFC: Green Bay vs. N.Y. Giants, 1962
Gino Cappelletti, AFC-D: Boston vs. Buffalo, 1963
Pete Gogolak, AFC: Buffalo vs. San Diego, 1965
Jan Stenerud, AFC-D: Kansas City vs. N.Y. Jets, 1969
George Blanda, AFC-D: Oakland vs. Pittsburgh, 1973
Ed Murray, NFC-D: Detroit vs. San Francisco, 1983
Mark Moseley, NFC: Washington vs. San Francisco, 1983
Tony Franklin, AFC-FR: New England vs. N.Y. Jets, 1985
Tony Zendejas, AFC-FR: Houston vs. Seattle, 1987 (OT)
Chuck Nelson, NFC-D: Minnesota vs. San Francisco, 1987
4 By many players

Most Field Goals, Career
22 George Blanda, Chi. Bears-Houston-Oakland, 19 games
20 Toni Fritsch, Dallas-Houston, 14 games
18 Rafael Septien, L.A. Rams-Dallas, 15 games

Most Field Goals, Game
5 Chuck Nelson, NFC-D: Minnesota vs. San Francisco, 1987
4 Gino Cappelletti, AFC-D: Boston vs. Buffalo, 1963
George Blanda, AFC: Oakland vs. Houston, 1967
Don Chandler, SB: Green Bay vs. Oakland, 1967
Curt Knight, NFC: Washington vs. Dallas, 1972
George Blanda, AFC-D: Oakland vs. Pittsburgh, 1973
Ray Wersching, SB: San Francisco vs. Cincinnati, 1981
Tony Franklin, AFC-FR: New England vs. N.Y. Jets, 1985
Jess Atkinson, NFC-FR: Washington vs. L.A. Rams, 1986
3 By many players

Most Consecutive Field Goals
15 Rafael Septien, Dallas, 1978-82
9 Chuck Nelson, Minnesota, 1987 (current)
8 Tony Fritsch, Houston, 1978-79

Longest Field Goal
54 Ed Murray, NFC-D: Detroit vs. San Francisco, 1983
52 Lou Groza, NFC: Cleveland vs. Los Angeles, 1951
Curt Knight, NFC-D: Washington vs. Minnesota, 1973
Matt Bahr, AFC-FR: Cleveland vs. L.A. Raiders, 1982
51 Fuad Reveiz, AFC-D: Miami vs. Cleveland, 1985

Highest Field Goal Percentage, Career (10 field goals)
85.7 Rafael Septien, L.A. Rams-Dallas, 15 games (21-18)
80.0 Toni Fritsch, Dallas-Houston, 14 games (25-20)
78.9 Chris Bahr, Oakland-L.A. Raiders, 11 games (19-15)

Safeties

Most Safeties, Game
1 Bill Willis, NFC-D: Cleveland vs. N.Y. Giants, 1950
Carl Eller, NFC-D: Minnesota vs. Los Angeles, 1969

George Andrie, NFC-D: Dallas vs. Detroit, 1970
Alan Page, NFC-D: Minnesota vs. Dallas, 1971
Dwight White, SB: Pittsburgh vs. Minnesota, 1974
Reggie Harrison, SB: Pittsburgh vs. Dallas, 1975
Jim Jensen, NFC-D: Dallas vs. Los Angeles, 1976
Ted Washington, AFC: Houston vs. Pittsburgh, 1978
Randy White, NFC-D: Dallas vs. Los Angeles, 1979
Henry Waechter, SB: Chicago vs. New England, 1985
Rulon Jones, AFC-FR: Denver vs. New England, 1986
George Martin, SB: N.Y. Giants vs. Denver, 1986
D.D. Hoggard, AFC: Cleveland vs. Denver, 1987

Rushing

Attempts

Most Attempts, Career
400 Franco Harris, Pittsburgh, 19 games
302 Tony Dorsett, Dallas, 17 games
251 John Riggins, Washington, 9 games

Most Attempts, Game
38 Ricky Bell, NFC-D: Tampa Bay vs. Philadelphia, 1979
John Riggins, SB: Washington vs. Miami, 1982
37 Lawrence McCutcheon, NFC-D: Los Angeles vs. St. Louis, 1975
John Riggins, NFC-D: Washington vs. Minnesota, 1982
36 John Riggins, NFC: Washington vs. Dallas, 1982
John Riggins, NFC: Washington vs. San Francisco, 1983

Yards Gained

Most Yards Gained, Career
1,556 Franco Harris, Pittsburgh, 19 games
1,383 Tony Dorsett, Dallas, 17 games
996 John Riggins, Washington, 9 games

Most Yards Gained, Game
248 Eric Dickerson, NFC-D: L.A. Rams vs. Dallas, 1985
206 Keith Lincoln, AFC: San Diego vs. Boston, 1963
204 Timmy Smith, SB: Washington vs. Denver, 1987

Most Games, 100 or More Yards Rushing, Career
6 John Riggins, Washington, 9 games
5 Franco Harris, Pittsburgh, 19 games
4 Larry Csonka, Miami, 12 games
Chuck Foreman, Minnesota, 13 games
Marcus Allen, L.A. Raiders, 7 games

Most Consecutive Games, 100 or More Yards Rushing
6 John Riggins, Washington, 1982-83
3 Larry Csonka, Miami, 1973-74
Franco Harris, Pittsburgh, 1974-75
Marcus Allen, L.A. Raiders, 1983

Longest Run From Scrimmage
74 Marcus Allen, SB: L.A. Raiders vs. Washington, 1983 (TD)
71 Hugh McElhenny, NFC-D: San Francisco vs. Detroit, 1957
James Lofton, NFC-D: Green Bay vs. Dallas, 1982 (TD)
70 Elmer Angsman, NFC: Chi. Cardinals vs. Philadelphia, 1947 (twice, 2 TDs)

Average Gain

Highest Average Gain, Career (50 attempts)
6.71 Timmy Smith, Washington, 3 games (51-342)
6.67 Paul Lowe, L.A. Chargers-San Diego, 5 games (57-380)
6.48 Earnest Byner, Cleveland, 4 games (54-350)

Highest Average Gain, Game (10 attempts)
15.90 Elmer Angsman, NFC: Chi. Cardinals vs. Philadelphia, 1947 (10-159)
15.85 Keith Lincoln, AFC: San Diego vs. Boston, 1963 (13-206)
10.90 Bill Osmanski, NFC: Chi. Bears vs. Washington, 1940 (10-109)

Touchdowns

Most Touchdowns, Career
16 Franco Harris, Pittsburgh, 19 games
12 John Riggins, Washington, 9 games
9 Larry Csonka, Miami, 12 games
Tony Dorsett, Dallas, 17 games

Most Touchdowns, Game
3 Andy Farkas, NFC-D: Washington vs. N.Y. Giants, 1943
Otto Graham, NFC: Cleveland vs. Detroit, 1954
Tom Matte, NFC: Baltimore vs. Cleveland, 1968
Larry Schreiber, NFC-D: San Francisco vs. Dallas, 1972
Larry Csonka, AFC: Miami vs. Oakland, 1973
Franco Harris, AFC-D: Pittsburgh vs. Buffalo, 1974
John Riggins, NFC-D: Washington vs. L.A. Rams, 1983

Most Consecutive Games Rushing for Touchdowns
7 John Riggins, Washington, 1982-84
5 Franco Harris, Pittsburgh, 1974-75
Franco Harris, Pittsburgh, 1977-79
3 By many players

Passing

Pass Rating

Highest Pass Rating, Career (100 attempts)
104.8 Bart Starr, Green Bay, 10 games
93.3 Ken Anderson, Cincinnati, 6 games
91.4 Joe Theismann, Washington, 10 games

Attempts

Most Passes Attempted, Career
456 Terry Bradshaw, Pittsburgh, 19 games
410 Roger Staubach, Dallas, 20 games
363 Joe Montana, San Francisco, 11 games

Most Passes Attempted, Game
64 Bernie Kosar, AFC-D: Cleveland vs. N.Y. Jets, 1986 (OT)
53 Dan Fouts, AFC-D: San Diego vs. Miami, 1981 (OT)
Danny White, NFC-FR: Dallas vs. L.A. Rams, 1983
51 Richard Todd, AFC-FR: N.Y. Jets vs. Buffalo, 1981
Neil Lomax, NFC-FR: St. Louis vs. Green Bay, 1982

Completions

Most Passes Completed, Career
261 Terry Bradshaw, Pittsburgh, 19 games
223 Roger Staubach, Dallas, 20 games
214 Joe Montana, San Francisco, 11 games

Most Passes Completed, Game
33 Dan Fouts, AFC-D: San Diego vs. Miami, 1981 (OT)
Bernie Kosar, AFC-D: Cleveland vs. N.Y. Jets, 1986 (OT)
32 Neil Lomax, NFC-FR: St. Louis vs. Green Bay, 1982
Danny White, NFC-FR: Dallas vs. L.A. Rams, 1983
29 Don Strock, AFC-D: Miami vs. San Diego, 1981 (OT)
Dan Marino, SB: Miami vs. San Francisco, 1984

Completion Percentage

Highest Completion Percentage, Career (100 attempts)
66.3 Ken Anderson, Cincinnati, 6 games (166-110)
61.2 Dan Pastorini, Houston, 5 games (116-71)
61.0 Bart Starr, Green Bay, 10 games (213-130)

Highest Completion Percentage, Game (15 completions)
88.0 Phil Simms, SB: N.Y. Giants vs. Denver, 1986 (25-22)
84.2 David Woodley, AFC-FR: Miami vs. New England, 1982 (19-16)
78.9 Norm Van Brocklin, NFC-D: Los Angeles vs. Detroit, 1952 (19-15)

Yards Gained

Most Yards Gained, Career
3,833 Terry Bradshaw, Pittsburgh, 19 games
2,791 Roger Staubach, Dallas, 20 games
2,671 Joe Montana, San Francisco, 11 games

Most Yards Gained, Game
489 Bernie Kosar, AFC-D: Cleveland vs. N.Y. Jets, 1986 (OT)
433 Dan Fouts, AFC-D: San Diego vs. Miami, 1981 (OT)
421 Dan Marino, AFC: Miami vs. Pittsburgh, 1984

Most Games, 300 or More Yards Passing, Career
5 Dan Fouts, San Diego, 7 games
4 Joe Montana, San Francisco, 10 games
3 Terry Bradshaw, Pittsburgh, 19 games
Danny White, Dallas, 17 games
Dan Marino, Miami, 4 games

Most Consecutive Games, 300 or More Yards Passing
4 Dan Fouts, San Diego, 1979-81
2 Daryle Lamonica, Oakland, 1968
Ken Anderson, Cincinnati, 1981-82
Terry Bradshaw, Pittsburgh, 1979-82
Joe Montana, San Francisco, 1983-84
Dan Marino, Miami, 1984

Longest Pass Completion
93 Daryle Lamonica (to Dubenion), AFC-D: Buffalo vs. Boston, 1963 (TD)
88 George Blanda (to Cannon), AFC: Houston vs. L.A. Chargers, 1960 (TD)
86 Don Meredith (to Hayes), NFC-D: Dallas vs. Cleveland, 1967 (TD)

Average Gain

Highest Average Gain, Career (100 attempts)
8.45 Joe Theismann, Washington, 10 games (211-1,782)
8.43 Jim Plunkett, Oakland-L.A. Raiders, 10 games (272-2,293)
8.41 Terry Bradshaw, Pittsburgh, 19 games (456-3,833)

Highest Average Gain, Game (20 attempts)
14.71 Terry Bradshaw, SB: Pittsburgh vs. Los Angeles, 1979 (21-309)
13.33 Bob Waterfield, NFC-D: Los Angeles vs. Chi. Bears, 1950 (21-280)
13.16 Dan Marino, AFC: Miami vs. Pittsburgh, 1984 (32-421)

Touchdowns

Most Touchdown Passes, Career
30 Terry Bradshaw, Pittsburgh, 19 games
24 Roger Staubach, Dallas, 20 games
19 Daryle Lamonica, Buffalo-Oakland, 13 games
Ken Stabler, Oakland-Houston, 13 games

Most Touchdown Passes, Game
6 Daryle Lamonica, AFC-D: Oakland vs. Houston, 1969
5 Sid Luckman, NFC: Chi. Bears vs. Washington, 1943
Daryle Lamonica, AFC-D: Oakland vs. Kansas City, 1968
4 Otto Graham, NFC: Cleveland vs. Los Angeles, 1950
Tobin Rote, NFC: Detroit vs. Cleveland, 1957
Bart Starr, NFC: Green Bay vs. Dallas, 1966
Ken Stabler, AFC-D: Oakland vs. Miami, 1974
Roger Staubach, NFC: Dallas vs. Los Angeles, 1975
Terry Bradshaw, SB: Pittsburgh vs. Dallas, 1978
Don Strock, AFC-D: Miami vs. San Diego, 1981 (OT)
Lynn Dickey, NFC-FR: Green Bay vs. St. Louis, 1982
Dan Marino, AFC: Miami vs. Pittsburgh, 1984
Doug Williams, SB: Washington vs. Denver, 1987

Most Consecutive Games, Touchdown Passes
10 Ken Stabler, Oakland, 1973-77
8 Terry Bradshaw, Pittsburgh, 1977-82
Joe Montana, San Francisco, 1981-84
7 John Elway, Denver, 1984-87 (current)

Had Intercepted

Lowest Percentage, Passes Had Intercepted, Career (100 attempts)
1.41 Bart Starr, Green Bay, 10 games (213-3)
1.51 Phil Simms, N.Y. Giants, 7 games (199-3)
1.89 Jay Schroeder, Washington, 6 games (106-2)

Most Attempts Without Interception, Game
47 Daryle Lamonica, AFC: Oakland vs. N.Y. Jets, 1968
42 Dan Fouts, AFC-FR: San Diego vs. Pittsburgh, 1982
39 Daryle Lamonica, AFC-D: Oakland vs. Kansas City, 1968
Ron Jaworski, NFC-D: Philadelphia vs. Tampa Bay, 1979
Tommy Kramer, NFC-D: Minnesota vs. Washington, 1982

Most Passes Had Intercepted, Career
26 Terry Bradshaw, Pittsburgh, 19 games
19 Roger Staubach, Dallas, 20 games
17 George Blanda, Chi. Bears-Houston-Oakland, 19 games
Fran Tarkenton, Minnesota, 11 games

Most Passes Had Intercepted, Game
6 Frank Filchock, NFC: N.Y. Giants vs. Chi. Bears, 1946
Bobby Layne, NFC: Detroit vs. Cleveland, 1954
Norm Van Brocklin, NFC: Los Angeles vs. Cleveland, 1955

5 Frank Filchock, NFC: Washington vs. Chi. Bears, 1940
George Blanda, AFC: Houston vs. San Diego, 1961
George Blanda, AFC: Houston vs. Dall. Texans, 1962 (OT)
Y.A. Tittle, NFC: N.Y. Giants vs. Chicago, 1963
Mike Phipps, AFC-D: Cleveland vs. Miami, 1972
Dan Pastorini, AFC: Houston vs. Pittsburgh, 1978
Dan Fouts, AFC-D: San Diego vs. Houston, 1979
Tommy Kramer, NFC-D: Minnesota vs. Philadelphia, 1980
Dan Fouts, AFC-D: San Diego vs. Miami, 1982
Richard Todd, AFC: N.Y. Jets vs Miami, 1982
Gary Danielson, NFC-D: Detroit vs. San Francisco, 1983
4 By many players

Pass Receiving

Receptions

Most Receptions, Career
73 Cliff Branch, Oakland-L.A. Raiders, 22 games
70 Fred Biletnikoff, Oakland, 19 games
67 Drew Pearson, Dallas, 22 games

Most Receptions, Game
13 Kellen Winslow, AFC-D: San Diego vs. Miami, 1981 (OT)
12 Raymond Berry, NFC: Baltimore vs. N.Y. Giants, 1958
11 Dante Lavelli, NFC: Cleveland vs. Los Angeles, 1950
Dan Ross, SB: Cincinnati vs. San Francisco, 1981
Franco Harris, AFC-FR: Pittsburgh vs. San Diego, 1982
Steve Watson, AFC-D: Denver vs. Pittsburgh, 1984

Most Consecutive Games, Pass Receptions
22 Drew Pearson, Dallas, 1973-83
18 Paul Warfield, Cleveland-Miami, 1964-74
Cliff Branch, Oakland-L.A. Raiders, 1974-83
17 John Stallworth, Pittsburgh, 1974-84

Yards Gained

Most Yards Gained, Career
1,289 Cliff Branch, Oakland-L.A. Raiders, 22 games
1,167 Fred Biletnikoff, Oakland, 19 games
1,121 Paul Warfield, Cleveland-Miami, 18 games

Most Yards Gained, Game
227 Anthony Carter, NFC-D: Minnesota vs. San Francisco, 1987
198 Tom Fears, NFC-D: Los Angeles vs. Chi. Bears, 1950
193 Ricky Sanders, SB: Washington vs. Denver, 1987

Most Games, 100 or More Yards Receiving, Career
5 John Stallworth, Pittsburgh, 18 games
4 Fred Biletnikoff, Oakland, 19 games
Dwight Clark, San Francisco, 7 games
3 Tom Fears, L.A. Rams, 6 games
Cliff Branch, Oakland-L.A. Raiders, 22 games
Tony Nathan, Miami, 10 games

Most Consecutive Games, 100 or More Yards Receiving, Career
3 Tom Fears, Los Angeles, 1950-51
2 Lenny Moore, Baltimore, 1958-59
Fred Biletnikoff, Oakland, 1968
Paul Warfield, Miami, 1971
Charlie Joiner, San Diego, 1981
Dwight Clark, San Francisco, 1981
Cris Collinsworth, Cincinnati, 1981-82
John Stallworth, Pittsburgh, 1979-82
Wesley Walker, N.Y. Jets, 1982
Charlie Brown, Washington, 1983
Steve Largent, Seattle, 1984-87 (current)

Longest Reception
93 Elbert Dubenion (from Lamonica), AFC-D: Buffalo vs. Boston, 1963 (TD)
88 Billy Cannon (from Blanda), AFC: Houston vs. L.A. Chargers, 1960 (TD)
86 Bob Hayes (from Meredith), NFC: Dallas vs. Cleveland, 1967 (TD)

Average Gain

Highest Average Gain, Career (20 receptions)
22.8 Harold Jackson, L.A. Rams-New England-Minnesota-Seattle, 14 games (24-548)
20.7 Charlie Brown, Washington, 8 games (31-643)
20.5 Frank Lewis, Pittsburgh-Buffalo, 12 games (27-553)

Highest Average Gain, Game (3 receptions)
46.3 Harold Jackson, NFC: Los Angeles vs. Minnesota, 1974 (3-139)
42.7 Billy Cannon, AFC: Houston vs. L.A. Chargers, 1960 (3-128)
42.0 Lenny Moore, NFC: Baltimore vs. N.Y. Giants, 1959 (3-126)

Touchdowns

Most Touchdowns, Career
12 John Stallworth, Pittsburgh, 18 games
10 Fred Biletnikoff, Oakland, 19 games
9 Lynn Swann, Pittsburgh, 16 games

Most Touchdowns, Game
3 Tom Fears, NFC-D: Los Angeles vs. Chi. Bears, 1950
Gary Collins, NFC: Cleveland vs. Baltimore, 1964
Fred Biletnikoff, AFC-D: Oakland vs. Kansas City, 1968
Preston Pearson, NFC: Dallas vs. Los Angeles, 1975
Dave Casper, AFC-D: Oakland vs. Baltimore, 1977 (OT)
Alvin Garrett, NFC-FR: Washington vs. Detroit, 1982

Most Consecutive Games, Touchdown Passes Caught
8 John Stallworth, Pittsburgh, 1978-83
4 Lynn Swann, Pittsburgh, 1978-79
Harold Carmichael, Philadelphia, 1978-80
Fred Solomon, San Francisco, 1983-84
3 By many players

Interceptions By

Most Interceptions, Career
9 Charlie Waters, Dallas, 25 games
Bill Simpson, Los Angeles-Buffalo, 11 games
8 Lester Hayes, Oakland-L.A. Raiders, 13 games
7 Willie Brown, Oakland, 17 games
Dennis Thurman, Dallas, 14 games

Most Interceptions, Game
4 Vernon Perry, AFC-D: Houston vs. San Diego, 1979
3 Joe Laws, NFC: Green Bay vs. N.Y. Giants, 1944
Charlie Waters, NFC-D: Dallas vs. Chicago, 1977
Rod Martin, SB: Oakland vs. Philadelphia, 1980
Dennis Thurman, NFC-D: Dallas vs. Green Bay, 1982
A.J. Duhe, AFC: Miami vs. N.Y. Jets, 1982
2 By many players

Most Consecutive Games, Interceptions
3 Warren Lahr, Cleveland, 1950-51
Ken Gorgal, Cleveland, 1950-53
Joe Schmidt, Detroit, 1954-57
Emmitt Thomas, Kansas City, 1969
Mel Renfro, Dallas, 1970
Rick Volk, Baltimore, 1970-71
Mike Wagner, Pittsburgh, 1975-76
Randy Hughes, Dallas, 1977-78
Vernon Perry, Houston, 1979-80
Lester Hayes, Oakland, 1980
Gerald Small, Miami, 1982
Lester Hayes, L.A. Raiders, 1982-83
Fred Marion, New England, 1985
John Harris, Seattle-Minnesota, 1984-87

Yards Gained

Most Yards Gained, Career
196 Willie Brown, Oakland, 17 games
151 Glen Edwards, Pittsburgh-San Diego, 17 games
149 Bill Simpson, Los Angeles-Buffalo, 11 games
LeRoy Irvin, L.A. Rams, 7 games

Most Yards Gained, Game
98 Darrol Ray, AFC-FR: N.Y. Jets vs. Cincinnati, 1982
94 LeRoy Irvin, NFC-FR: L.A. Rams vs. Dallas, 1983
88 Walt Sumner, NFC-D: Cleveland vs. Dallas, 1969

Longest Return
98 Darrol Ray, AFC-FR: N.Y. Jets vs. Cincinnati, 1982 (TD)
94 LeRoy Irvin, NFC-FR: L.A. Rams vs. Dallas, 1983
88 Walt Sumner, NFC-D: Cleveland vs. Dallas, 1969 (TD)

Touchdowns

Most Touchdowns, Career
3 Willie Brown, Oakland, 17 games
2 Lester Hayes, Oakland-L.A. Raiders, 13 games

Most Touchdowns, Game
1 By 43 players

Punting

Most Punts, Career
111 Ray Guy, Oakland-L.A. Raiders, 22 games
84 Danny White, Dallas, 18 games
73 Mike Eischeid, Oakland-Minnesota, 14 games

Most Punts, Game
14 Dave Jennings, AFC-D: N.Y. Jets vs. Cleveland, 1986 (OT)
12 David Lee, AFC-D: Baltimore vs. Oakland, 1977 (OT)
11 Ken Strong, NFC: N.Y. Giants vs. Chi. Bears, 1933
Jim Norton, AFC: Houston vs. Oakland, 1967
Dale Hatcher, NFC: L.A. Rams vs. Chicago, 1985

Longest Punt
76 Ed Danowski, NFC: N.Y. Giants vs. Detroit, 1935
72 Charlie Conerly, NFC-D: N.Y. Giants vs. Cleveland, 1950
71 Ray Guy, AFC: Oakland vs. San Diego, 1980

Average Yardage

Highest Average, Career (20 punts)
44.5 Rich Camarillo, New England, 6 games (35-1,559)
43.4 Jerrel Wilson, Kansas City-New England, 8 games (43-1,866)
43.1 Don Chandler, N.Y. Giants-Green Bay, 14 games (53-2,282)

Highest Average, Game (4 punts)
56.0 Ray Guy, AFC: Oakland vs. San Diego, 1980 (4-224)
52.5 Sammy Baugh, NFC: Washington vs. Chi. Bears, 1942 (6-315)
51.4 John Hadl, AFC: San Diego vs. Buffalo, 1965 (5-257)

Punt Returns

Most Punt Returns, Career
25 Theo Bell, Pittsburgh-Tampa Bay, 10 games
19 Willie Wood, Green Bay, 10 games
Butch Johnson, Dallas-Denver, 18 games
Phil McConkey, N.Y. Giants, 5 games
18 Neal Colzie, Oakland-Miami-Tampa Bay, 10 games

Most Punt Returns, Game
7 Ron Gardin, AFC-D: Baltimore vs. Cincinnati, 1970
Carl Roaches, AFC-FR: Houston vs. Oakland, 1980
Gerald McNeil, AFC-D: Cleveland vs. N.Y. Jets, 1986 (OT)
Phil McConkey, NFC-D: N.Y. Giants vs. San Francisco, 1986
6 George McAfee, NFC-D: Chi. Bears vs. Los Angeles, 1950
Eddie Brown, NFC-D: Washington vs. Minnesota, 1976
Theo Bell, AFC: Pittsburgh vs. Houston, 1978
Eddie Brown, NFC: Los Angeles vs. Tampa Bay, 1979
John Sciarra, NFC: Philadelphia vs. Dallas, 1980
Kurt Sohn, AFC: N.Y. Jets vs. Miami, 1982
Mike Nelms, SB: Washington vs. Miami, 1982
Anthony Carter, NFC-FR: Minnesota vs. New Orleans, 1987
5 By many players

Yards Gained

Most Yards Gained, Career
221 Neal Colzie, Oakland-Miami-Tampa Bay, 10 games
Anthony Carter, Minnesota, 3 games
208 Butch Johnson, Dallas-Denver, 18 games
204 Theo Bell, Pittsburgh-Tampa Bay, 10 games

Most Yards Gained, Game
143 Anthony Carter, NFC-FR: Minnesota vs. New Orleans, 1987

141 Bob Hayes, NFC-D: Dallas vs. Cleveland, 1967
102 Charley Trippi, NFC: Chi. Cardinals vs. Philadelphia, 1947

Longest Return
84 Anthony Carter, NFC-FR: Minnesota vs. New Orleans, 1987 (TD)
81 Hugh Gallarneau, NFC-D: Chi. Bears vs. Green Bay, 1941 (TD)
79 Bosh Pritchard, NFC-D: Philadelphia vs. Pittsburgh, 1947 (TD)

Average Yardage
Highest Average, Career (10 returns)
18.4 Anthony Carter, Minnesota, 3 games (12-221)
12.6 Bob Hayes, Dallas, 15 games (12-151)
12.4 Mike Fuller, San Diego-Cincinnati, 7 games (13-161)

Highest Average Gain, Game (3 returns)
47.0 Bob Hayes, NFC-D: Dallas vs. Cleveland, 1967 (3-141)
29.0 George (Butch) Byrd, AFC: Buffalo vs. San Diego, 1965 (3-87)
25.3 Bosh Pritchard, NFC-D: Philadelphia vs. Pittsburgh, 1947 (4-101)

Touchdowns
Most Touchdowns
1 Hugh Gallarneau, NFC-D: Chicago Bears vs. Green Bay, 1941
Bosh Pritchard, NFC-D: Philadelphia vs. Pittsburgh, 1947
Charley Trippi, NFC: Chicago Cardinals vs. Philadelphia, 1947
Verda (Vitamin T) Smith, NFC-D: Los Angeles vs. Detroit, 1952
George (Butch) Byrd, AFC: Buffalo vs. San Diego, 1965
Golden Richards, NFC: Dallas vs. Minnesota, 1973
Wes Chandler, AFC-D: San Diego vs. Miami, 1981 (OT)
Shaun Gayle, NFC-D: Chicago vs. N.Y. Giants, 1985
Anthony Carter, NFC-FR: Minnesota vs. New Orleans, 1987
Darrell Green, NFC-D: Washington vs. Chicago, 1987

Kickoff Returns
Most Kickoff Returns, Career
29 Fulton Walker, Miami-L.A. Raiders, 10 games
19 Preston Pearson, Baltimore-Pittsburgh-Dallas, 22 games
18 Charlie West, Minnesota, 9 games

Most Kickoff Returns, Game
7 Don Bingham, NFC: Chi. Bears vs. N.Y. Giants, 1956
Reggie Brown, NFC-FR: Atlanta vs. Minnesota, 1982
David Verser, AFC-FR: Cincinnati vs. N.Y. Jets, 1982
Del Rodgers, NFC-D: Green Bay vs. Dallas, 1982
Henry Ellard, NFC-D: L.A. Rams vs. Washington, 1983
Stephen Starring, SB: New England vs. Chicago, 1985
6 Wallace Francis, AFC-D: Buffalo vs. Pittsburgh, 1974
Eddie Brown, NFC-D: Washington vs. Minnesota, 1976
Eddie Payton, NFC-D: Minnesota vs. Philadelphia, 1980
Alvin Hall, NFC-FR: Detroit vs. Washington, 1982
Fulton Walker, AFC-D: Miami vs. Seattle, 1983
Johnny Hector, AFC-FR: N.Y. Jets vs. New England, 1985
Lorenzo Hampton, AFC: Miami vs. New England, 1985
Albert Bentley, AFC-D: Indianapolis vs. Cleveland, 1987
5 By many players

Yards Gained
Most Yards Gained, Career
677 Fulton Walker, Miami-L.A. Raiders, 10 games
481 Carl Garrett, Oakland, 5 games
458 Cullen Bryant, L.A. Rams-Seattle, 19 games

Most Yards Gained, Game
190 Fulton Walker, SB: Miami vs. Washington, 1982
170 Les (Speedy) Duncan, NFC-D: Washington vs. San Francisco, 1971
169 Carl Garrett, AFC-D: Oakland vs. Baltimore, 1977 (OT)

Longest Return
98 Fulton Walker, SB: Miami vs. Washington, 1982 (TD)
97 Vic Washington, NFC-D: San Francisco vs. Dallas, 1972 (TD)
89 Nat Moore, AFC-D: Miami vs. Oakland, 1974 (TD)
Rod Hill, NFC-D: Dallas vs. Green Bay, 1982

Average Yardage
Highest Average, Career (10 returns)
30.1 Carl Garrett, Oakland, 5 games (16-481)
27.9 George Atkinson, Oakland, 16 games (12-335)
24.2 Larry Anderson, Pittsburgh, 6 games (16-387)

Highest Average, Game (3 returns)
56.7 Les (Speedy) Duncan, NFC-D: Washington vs. San Francisco, 1971 (3-170)
51.3 Ed Podolak, AFC-D: Kansas City vs. Miami, 1971 (OT) (3-154)
49.0 Les (Speedy) Duncan, AFC: San Diego vs. Buffalo, 1964 (3-147)

Touchdowns
Most Touchdowns
1 Vic Washington, NFC-D: San Francisco vs. Dallas, 1972
Nat Moore, AFC-D: Miami vs. Oakland, 1974
Marshall Johnson, AFC-D: Baltimore vs. Oakland, 1977 (OT)
Fulton Walker, SB: Miami vs. Washington, 1982

Fumbles
Most Fumbles, Career
13 Tony Dorsett, Dallas, 17 games
10 Franco Harris, Pittsburgh, 19 games
Terry Bradshaw, Pittsburgh, 19 games
Roger Staubach, Dallas, 20 games
9 Chuck Foreman, Minnesota, 13 games

Most Fumbles, Game
4 Brian Sipe, AFC-D: Cleveland vs. Oakland, 1980
3 Y.A. Tittle, NFC-D: San Francisco vs. Detroit, 1957
Bill Nelsen, AFC-D: Cleveland vs. Baltimore, 1972
Chuck Foreman, NFC: Minnesota vs. Los Angeles, 1974
Lawrence McCutcheon, NFC-D: Los Angeles vs. St. Louis, 1975
Roger Staubach, SB: Dallas vs. Pittsburgh, 1975
Terry Bradshaw, AFC: Pittsburgh vs. Houston, 1978
Earl Campbell, AFC: Houston vs. Pittsburgh, 1978
Franco Harris, AFC: Pittsburgh vs. Houston, 1978
Chuck Muncie, AFC: San Diego vs. Cincinnati, 1981
Andra Franklin, AFC-FR: Miami vs. New England, 1982
Eric Dickerson, NFC-FR: L.A. Rams vs. Washington, 1986
2 By many players

Recoveries
Most Own Fumbles Recovered, Career
5 Roger Staubach, Dallas, 20 games
4 Fran Tarkenton, Minnesota, 11 games
3 Alex Webster, N.Y. Giants, 7 games
Don Meredith, Dallas, 4 games
Franco Harris, Pittsburgh, 19 games
Gerry Mullins, Pittsburgh, 18 games
Ron Jaworski, Los Angeles-Philadelphia, 10 games
Lyle Blackwood, Cincinnati-Baltimore-Miami, 14 games

Most Opponents' Fumbles Recovered, Career
4 Cliff Harris, Dallas, 21 games
Harvey Martin, Dallas, 22 games
Ted Hendricks, Baltimore-Oakland-L.A. Raiders, 21 games
3 Paul Krause, Minnesota, 19 games
Jack Lambert, Pittsburgh, 18 games
Fred Dryer, Los Angeles, 14 games
Charlie Waters, Dallas, 25 games
Jack Ham, Pittsburgh, 16 games
Mike Hegman, Dallas, 16 games
Tom Jackson, Denver, 10 games
Mike Singletary, Chicago, 7 games
Monte Coleman, Washington, 14 games
Darryl Grant, Washington, 14 games
Alvin Walton, Washington, 6 games
2 By many players

Most Fumbles Recovered, Game, Own and Opponents'
3 Jack Lambert, AFC: Pittsburgh vs. Oakland, 1975 (3 opp)
Ron Jaworski, NFC-FR: Philadelphia vs. N.Y. Giants, 1981 (3 own)
2 By many players

Yards Gained
Longest Return
93 Andy Russell, AFC-D: Pittsburgh vs. Baltimore, 1975 (opp, TD)
60 Mike Curtis, NFC-D: Baltimore vs. Minnesota, 1968 (opp, TD)
Hugh Green, NFC-FR: Tampa Bay vs. Dallas, 1982 (opp, TD)
52 Wilber Marshall, NFC: Chicago vs. L.A. Rams, 1985 (opp, TD)

Touchdowns
Most Touchdowns
1 By 22 players

Combined Net Yards Gained
Rushing, receiving, interception returns, punt returns, kickoff returns, and fumble returns.

Attempts
Most Attempts, Career
454 Franco Harris, Pittsburgh, 19 games
350 Tony Dorsett, Dallas, 17 games
275 Chuck Foreman, Minnesota, 13 games

Most Attempts, Game
40 Lawrence McCutcheon, NFC-D: Los Angeles vs. St. Louis, 1975
39 John Riggins, SB: Washington vs. Miami, 1982
38 Ricky Bell, NFC-D: Tampa Bay vs. Philadelphia, 1979
Rob Carpenter, NFC-FR: N.Y. Giants vs. Philadelphia, 1981

Yards Gained
Most Yards Gained, Career
2,060 Franco Harris, Pittsburgh, 19 games
1,786 Tony Dorsett, Dallas, 17 games
1,307 Chuck Foreman, Minnesota, 13 games

Most Yards Gained, Game
350 Ed Podolak, AFC-D: Kansas City vs. Miami, 1971 (OT)
329 Keith Lincoln, AFC: San Diego vs. Boston, 1963
285 Bob Hayes, NFC-D: Dallas vs. Cleveland, 1967

Sacks
Sacks have been compiled since 1982

Most Sacks, Career
10.5 Richard Dent, Chicago, 7 games
8 Dexter Manley, Washington, 14 games
7.5 Mark Gastineau, N.Y. Jets, 6 games

Most Sacks, Game
3.5 Rich Milot, NFC-D: Washington vs. Chicago, 1984
Richard Dent, NFC-D: Chicago vs. N.Y. Giants, 1985
3 Richard Dent, NFC-D: Chicago vs. Washington, 1984
Garin Veris, AFC-FR: New England vs. N.Y. Jets, 1985
Gary Jeter, NFC-D: L.A. Rams vs. Dallas, 1985
Carl Hairston, AFC-D: Cleveland vs. N.Y. Jets, 1986 (OT)
Charles Mann, NFC-D: Washington vs. Chicago, 1987
2.5 Lyle Alzado, AFC-D: L.A. Raiders vs. Pittsburgh, 1983
Jacob Green, AFC-FR: Seattle vs. L.A. Raiders, 1984

Team Records

Games, Victories, Defeats
Most Consecutive Seasons Participating in Postseason Games
9 Dallas, 1975-83
8 Dallas, 1966-73
Pittsburgh, 1972-79
Los Angeles, 1973-80
6 Cleveland, 1950-55
Oakland, 1972-77
Minnesota, 1973-78

Most Games
36 Dallas, 1966-73, 1975-83, 1985
31 Oakland/L. A. Raiders, 1967-70, 1973-77, 1980, 1982-85
29 Cleveland/L. A. Rams, 1945, 1949-52, 1955, 1967, 1969, 1973-80, 1983-86

Most Games Won
20 Dallas, 1967, 1970-73, 1975, 1977-78, 1980-82
19 Oakland/L. A. Raiders, 1967-70, 1973-77, 1980, 1982-83
16 Washington, 1937, 1942-43, 1972, 1982-83, 1986-87

Most Consecutive Games Won
9 Green Bay, 1961-62, 1965-67
7 Pittsburgh, 1974-76
6 Miami, 1972-73
Pittsburgh, 1978-79
Washington, 1982-83

Most Games Lost
18 L.A. Rams, 1949-50, 1952, 1955, 1967, 1969, 1973-80, 1983-86
16 Dallas, 1966-70, 1972-73, 1975-76, 1978-83, 1985
N. Y. Giants, 1933, 1935, 1939, 1941, 1943-44, 1946, 1950, 1958-59, 1961-63, 1981, 1984-85
Cleveland, 1951-53, 1957-58, 1965, 1967-69, 1971-72, 1980, 1982, 1985-87
13 Minnesota, 1968-71, 1973-78, 1980, 1982, 1987

Most Consecutive Games Lost
6 N. Y. Giants, 1939, 1941, 1943-44, 1946, 1950
Cleveland, 1969, 1971-72, 1980, 1982, 1985
5 N. Y. Giants, 1958-59, 1961-63
Los Angeles, 1952, 1955, 1967, 1969, 1973
Denver, 1977-79, 1983-84
Baltimore/Indianapolis, 1971, 1975-77, 1987 (current)
4 Washington, 1972-74, 1976
Miami, 1974, 1978-79, 1981
Chi. Cardinals/St. Louis, 1948, 1974-75, 1982 (current)
Boston/New England, 1963, 1976, 1978, 1982

Scoring

Most Points, Game
73 NFC: Chi. Bears vs. Washington, 1940
59 NFC: Detroit vs. Cleveland, 1957
56 NFC: Cleveland vs. Detroit, 1954
AFC-D: Oakland vs. Houston, 1969

Most Points, Both Teams, Game
79 AFC-D: San Diego (41) vs. Miami (38), 1981 (OT)
73 NFC: Chi. Bears (73) vs. Washington (0), 1940
NFC: Detroit (59) vs. Cleveland (14), 1957
AFC: Miami (45) vs. Pittsburgh (28), 1984
71 AFC: Denver (38) vs. Cleveland (33), 1987

Fewest Points, Both Teams, Game
5 NFC-D: Detroit (0) vs. Dallas (5), 1970
7 NFC: Chi. Cardinals (0) vs. Philadelphia (7), 1948
9 NFC: Tampa Bay (0) vs. Los Angeles (9), 1979

Largest Margin of Victory, Game
73 NFC: Chi. Bears vs. Washington, 1940 (73-0)
49 AFC-D: Oakland vs. Houston, 1969 (56-7)
46 NFC: Cleveland vs. Detroit, 1954 (56-10)
NFC-D: N.Y. Giants vs. San Francisco, 1986 (49-3)

Most Points, Shutout Victory, Game
73 NFC: Chi. Bears vs. Washington, 1940
38 NFC-D: Dallas vs. Tampa Bay, 1981
37 NFC: Green Bay vs. N.Y. Giants, 1961

Most Points Overcome to Win Game
20 NFC-D: Detroit vs. San Francisco, 1957 (trailed 7-27, won 31-27)
18 NFC-D: Dallas vs. San Francisco, 1972 (trailed 3-21, won 30-28)
AFC-D: Miami vs. Cleveland, 1985 (trailed 3-21, won 24-21)
14 NFC-D: Philadelphia vs. Minnesota, 1980 (trailed 0-14, won 31-16)
NFC-D: Dallas vs. Atlanta, 1980 (trailed 10-24, won 30-27)
NFC-D: Washington vs. Chicago, 1987 (trailed 0-14, won 21-17)

Most Points, Each Half
1st: 38 NFC-D: Washington vs. L.A. Rams, 1983
35 NFC: Cleveland vs. Detroit, 1954
AFC-D: Oakland vs. Houston, 1969
SB: Washington vs. Denver, 1987
34 NFC: N. Y. Giants vs. Chi. Bears, 1956
2nd: 45 NFC: Chi. Bears vs. Washington, 1940
30 SB: N.Y. Giants vs. Denver, 1986
AFC: Cleveland vs. Denver, 1987
28 NFC: Chi. Bears vs. N. Y. Giants, 1941
NFC: Detroit vs. Cleveland, 1957
NFC-D: Dallas vs. Cleveland, 1967
NFC-D: Dallas vs. Tampa Bay, 1981

Most Points, Each Quarter
1st: 28 AFC-D: Oakland vs. Houston, 1969
24 AFC-D: San Diego vs. Miami, 1981 (OT)
21 NFC: Chi. Bears vs. Washington, 1940
AFC: San Diego vs. Boston, 1963
AFC-D: Oakland vs. Kansas City, 1968
AFC: Oakland vs. San Diego, 1980
2nd: 35 SB: Washington vs. Denver, 1987
26 AFC-D: Pittsburgh vs. Buffalo, 1974
24 NFC-D: Chi. Bears vs. Green Bay, 1941
NFC: Green Bay vs. N. Y. Giants, 1961
3rd: 26 NFC: Chi. Bears vs. Washington, 1940
21 NFC-D: Dallas vs. Cleveland, 1967
NFC-D: Dallas vs. Tampa Bay, 1981
AFC-D: L.A. Raiders vs. Pittsburgh, 1983
SB: Chicago vs. New England, 1985
NFC-D: N.Y. Giants vs. San Francisco, 1986
AFC: Cleveland vs. Denver, 1987
17 NFC: Cleveland vs. Baltimore, 1964
NFC-D: Dallas vs. Chicago, 1977
SB: N.Y. Giants vs. Denver, 1986
4th 27 NFC: N.Y. Giants vs. Chi. Bears, 1934
24 NFC: Baltimore vs. N. Y. Giants, 1959
21 AFC: Pittsburgh vs. Oakland, 1974
NFC: Dallas vs. Los Angeles, 1978
AFC-FR: N. Y. Jets vs. Cincinnati, 1982
NFC: San Francisco vs. Washington, 1983
OT: 6 NFC: Baltimore vs. N.Y. Giants, 1958
AFC-D: Oakland vs. Baltimore, 1977

Touchdowns

Most Touchdowns, Game
11 NFC: Chi. Bears vs. Washington, 1940
8 NFC: Cleveland vs. Detroit, 1954
NFC: Detroit vs. Cleveland, 1957
AFC-D: Oakland vs. Houston, 1969
7 AFC: San Diego vs. Boston, 1963
NFC-D: Dallas vs. Cleveland, 1967
NFC-D: N.Y. Giants vs. San Francisco, 1986

Most Touchdowns, Both Teams, Game
11 NFC: Chi. Bears (11) vs. Washington (0), 1940
10 NFC: Detroit (8) vs. Cleveland (2), 1957
AFC-D: Miami (5) vs. San Diego (5), 1981 (OT)
AFC: Miami (6) vs. Pittsburgh (4), 1984
9 NFC: Chi. Bears (6) vs. Washington (3), 1943
NFC: Cleveland (8) vs. Detroit (1), 1954
NFC-D: Dallas (7) vs. Cleveland (2), 1967
AFC-D: Oakland (8) vs. Houston (1), 1969
AFC-D: Oakland (5) vs. Baltimore (4), 1977 (OT)
SB: Pittsburgh (5) vs. Dallas (4), 1978
AFC: Denver (5) vs. Cleveland (4), 1987

Fewest Touchdowns, Both Teams, Game
0 NFC-D: N.Y. Giants vs. Cleveland, 1950
NFC-D: Dallas vs. Detroit, 1970
NFC: Los Angeles vs. Tampa Bay, 1979
1 NFC: Chi. Cardinals (0) vs. Philadelphia (1), 1948
AFC: San Diego (0) vs. Houston (1), 1961
AFC-D: N. Y. Jets (0) vs. Kansas City (1), 1969
NFC-D: Green Bay (0) vs. Washington (1), 1972
2 In many games

Points After Touchdown

Most Points After Touchdown, Game
8 NFC: Cleveland vs. Detroit, 1954
NFC: Detroit vs. Cleveland, 1957
AFC-D: Oakland vs. Houston, 1969
7 NFC: Chi. Bears vs. Washington, 1940
NFC-D: Dallas vs. Cleveland, 1967
NFC-D: N.Y. Giants vs. San Francisco, 1986
6 AFC: San Diego vs. Boston, 1963
NFC-D: Washington vs. L.A. Rams, 1983
AFC: Miami vs. Pittsburgh, 1984

Most Points After Touchdown, Both Teams, Game
10 NFC: Detroit (8) vs. Cleveland (2), 1957
AFC-D: Miami (5) vs. San Diego (5), 1981 (OT)
AFC: Miami (6) vs. Pittsburgh (4), 1984
9 NFC: Cleveland (8) vs. Detroit (1), 1954
NFC-D: Dallas (7) vs. Cleveland (2), 1967
AFC-D: Oakland (8) vs. Houston (1), 1969
AFC: Denver (5) vs. Cleveland (4), 1987
8 In many games

Fewest Points After Touchdown, Both Teams, Game
0 NFC-D: N.Y. Giants vs. Cleveland, 1950
NFC-D: Dallas vs. Detroit, 1970
NFC: Los Angeles vs. Tampa Bay, 1979

Field Goals

Most Field Goals, Game
5 NFC-D: Minnesota vs. San Francisco, 1987
4 AFC-D: Boston vs. Buffalo, 1963
AFC: Oakland vs. Houston, 1967
SB: Green Bay vs. Oakland, 1967
NFC: Washington vs. Dallas, 1972
AFC-D: Oakland vs. Pittsburgh, 1973
SB: San Francisco vs. Cincinnati, 1981
AFC-FR: New England vs. N.Y. Jets, 1985
NFC-FR: Washington vs. L.A. Rams, 1986
3 By many teams

Most Field Goals, Both Teams, Game
6 NFC-D: Minnesota (5) vs. San Francisco (1), 1987
5 NFC: Green Bay (3) vs. Cleveland (2), 1965
AFC: Oakland (3) vs. N.Y. Jets (2), 1968
NFC: Washington (4) vs. Dallas (1), 1972
AFC-D: Cincinnati (3) vs. Miami (2), 1973
NFC-D: Los Angeles (3) vs. Dallas (2), 1973
NFC-D: Dallas (3) vs. Green Bay (2), 1982
NFC-FR: N.Y. Giants (3) vs. L.A. Rams (2), 1984
AFC-D: Cleveland (3) vs. N.Y. Jets (2), 1986 (OT)
AFC: Denver (3) vs. Cleveland (2), 1986 (OT)
AFC-FR: Houston (3) vs. Seattle (2), 1987 (OT)
4 In many games

Most Field Goals Attempted, Game
6 AFC: Oakland vs. Houston, 1967
NFC-D: Los Angeles vs. Dallas, 1973
AFC-D: Cleveland vs. N.Y. Jets, 1986 (OT)
5 By many teams

Most Field Goals Attempted, Both Teams, Game
8 NFC-D: Los Angeles (6) vs. Dallas (2), 1973
NFC-D: Detroit (5) vs. San Francisco (3), 1983
AFC-D: Cleveland (6) vs. N.Y. Jets (2), 1986 (OT)
NFC-D: Minnesota (5) vs. San Francisco (3), 1987
7 In many games

Safeties

Most Safeties, Game
1 By 17 teams

First Downs

Most First Downs, Game
34 AFC-D: San Diego vs. Miami, 1981 (OT)
33 AFC-D: Cleveland vs. N.Y. Jets, 1986 (OT)
31 SB: San Francisco vs. Miami, 1984

Fewest First Downs, Game
6 NFC: N.Y. Giants vs. Green Bay, 1961
7 NFC: Green Bay vs. Boston, 1936
NFC-D: Pittsburgh vs. Philadelphia, 1947
NFC: Chi. Cardinals vs. Philadelphia, 1948
NFC: Los Angeles vs. Philadelphia, 1949
NFC-D: Cleveland vs. N. Y. Giants, 1958
AFC-D: Cincinnati vs. Baltimore, 1970
NFC-D: Detroit vs. Dallas, 1970
8 By many teams

Most First Downs, Both Teams, Game
59 AFC-D: San Diego (34) vs. Miami (25), 1981 (OT)
55 AFC-FR: San Diego (29) vs. Pittsburgh (26), 1982
50 AFC: Oakland (28) vs. Baltimore (22), 1977 (OT)
NFC-FR: St. Louis (28) vs. Green Bay (22), 1982
AFC-FR: N. Y. Jets (27) vs. Cincinnati (23), 1982
AFC: Miami (28) vs. Pittsburgh (22), 1984
SB: San Francisco (31) vs. Miami (19), 1984

Fewest First Downs, Both Teams, Game
15 NFC: Green Bay (7) vs. Boston (8), 1936
19 NFC: N. Y. Giants (9) vs. Green Bay (10), 1939
NFC: Washington (9) vs. Chi. Bears (10), 1942
20 NFC-D: Cleveland (9) vs. N. Y. Giants (11), 1950

Rushing

Most First Downs, Rushing, Game
19 NFC-FR: Dallas vs. Los Angeles, 1980
18 AFC-D: Miami vs. Cincinnati, 1973
AFC-D: Pittsburgh vs. Buffalo, 1974
16 NFC: Philadelphia vs. Chi. Cardinals, 1948
NFC: Dallas vs. San Francisco, 1970

Fewest First Downs, Rushing, Game
0 NFC: Los Angeles vs. Philadelphia, 1949
AFC-D: Buffalo vs. Boston, 1963
AFC: Oakland vs. Pittsburgh, 1974
NFC-FR: New Orleans vs. Minnesota, 1987
1 NFC: N. Y. Giants vs. Green Bay, 1961
AFC-D: Houston vs. Oakland, 1969
NFC: Los Angeles vs. Dallas, 1975
AFC-FR: Cleveland vs. L. A. Raiders, 1982
NFC-D: N.Y. Giants vs. Chicago, 1985
SB: New England vs. Chicago, 1985
AFC-FR: Seattle vs. Houston, 1987 (OT)
2 By many teams

Most First Downs, Rushing, Both Teams, Game
25 NFC-FR: Dallas (19) vs. Los Angeles (6), 1980
23 NFC: Cleveland (15) vs. Detroit (8), 1952
AFC-D: Miami (18) vs. Cincinnati (5), 1973
AFC-D: Pittsburgh (18) vs. Buffalo (5), 1974
22 AFC: Miami (18) vs. Oakland (4), 1973
AFC-D: Buffalo (11) vs. Cincinnati (11), 1981
AFC-D: L.A. Raiders (13) vs. Pittsburgh (9), 1983

Fewest First Downs, Rushing, Both Teams, Game
5 AFC-D: Buffalo (0) vs. Boston (5), 1963
6 NFC: Green Bay (2) vs. Boston (4), 1936
NFC-D: Baltimore (2) vs. Minnesota (4), 1968
AFC-D: Houston (1) vs. Oakland (5), 1969
7 NFC-D: Washington (2) vs. N. Y. Giants (5), 1943
NFC: Baltimore (3) vs. N. Y. Giants (4), 1959
NFC: Washington (3) vs. Dallas (4), 1972
AFC-FR: N. Y. Jets (3) vs. Buffalo (4), 1981

Passing

Most First Downs, Passing, Game
21 AFC-D: Miami vs. San Diego, 1981 (OT)
AFC-D: San Diego vs. Miami, 1981 (OT)
AFC-D: Cleveland vs. N.Y. Jets, 1986 (OT)
20 NFC-FR: Dallas vs. L.A. Rams, 1983
19 NFC-FR: St. Louis vs. Green Bay, 1982
NFC-FR: Dallas vs. Tampa Bay, 1982
AFC-FR: Pittsburgh vs. San Diego, 1982
AFC-FR: San Diego vs. Pittsburgh, 1982
NFC: Dallas vs. Washington, 1982

Fewest First Downs, Passing, Game
0 NFC: Philadelphia vs. Chi. Cardinals, 1948
1 NFC-D: N. Y. Giants vs. Washington, 1943
NFC: Cleveland vs. Detroit, 1953
SB: Denver vs. Dallas, 1977
2 By many teams

Most First Downs, Passing, Both Teams, Game
42 AFC-D: Miami (21) vs. San Diego (21), 1981 (OT)
38 AFC-FR: Pittsburgh (19) vs. San Diego (19), 1982
32 NFC-FR: St. Louis (19) vs. Green Bay (13), 1982
AFC: Miami (18) vs. Pittsburgh (14), 1984
SB: Miami (17) vs. San Francisco (15), 1984

Fewest First Downs, Passing, Both Teams, Game
2 NFC: Philadelphia (0) vs. Chi. Cardinals (2), 1948
4 NFC-D: Cleveland (2) vs. N. Y. Giants (2), 1950
5 NFC: Detroit (2) vs. N. Y. Giants (3), 1935
NFC: Green Bay (2) vs. N. Y. Giants (3), 1939

Penalty

Most First Downs, Penalty, Game
7 AFC-D: New England vs. Oakland, 1976
6 AFC-D: Cleveland vs. N.Y. Jets, 1986 (OT)
5 AFC-FR: Cleveland vs. L. A. Raiders, 1982

Most First Downs, Penalty, Both Teams, Game
9 AFC-D: New England (7) vs. Oakland (2), 1976
8 NFC-FR: Atlanta (4) vs. Minnesota (4), 1982
7 AFC-D: Baltimore (4) vs. Oakland (3), 1977 (OT)

Net Yards Gained Rushing and Passing

Most Yards Gained, Game
610 AFC: San Diego vs. Boston, 1963
602 SB: Washington vs. Denver, 1987
569 AFC: Miami vs. Pittsburgh, 1984

Fewest Yards Gained, Game
86 NFC-D: Cleveland vs. N.Y. Giants, 1958
99 NFC: Chi. Cardinals vs. Philadelphia, 1948
114 NFC-D: N.Y. Giants vs. Washington, 1943

Most Yards Gained, Both Teams, Game
1,036 AFC-D: San Diego (564) vs. Miami (472), 1981 (OT)
1,024 AFC: Miami (569) vs. Pittsburgh (455), 1984
929 SB: Washington (602) vs. Denver (327), 1987

Fewest Yards Gained, Both Teams, Game
331 NFC: Chi. Cardinals (99) vs. Philadelphia (232), 1948
332 NFC-D: N.Y. Giants (150) vs. Cleveland (182), 1950
336 NFC: Boston (116) vs. Green Bay (220), 1936

Rushing

Attempts

Most Attempts, Game
65 NFC: Detroit vs. N.Y. Giants, 1935
61 NFC: Philadelphia vs. Los Angeles, 1949
59 AFC: New England vs. Miami, 1985

Fewest Attempts, Game
9 SB: Miami vs. San Francisco, 1984
11 SB: New England vs. Chicago, 1985
AFC-FR: Seattle vs. Houston, 1987 (OT)
12 AFC-D: Buffalo vs. Boston, 1963

Most Attempts, Both Teams, Game
109 NFC: Detroit (65) vs. N.Y. Giants (44), 1935
97 AFC-D: Baltimore (50) vs. Oakland (47), 1977 (OT)
91 NFC: Philadelphia (57) vs. Chi. Cardinals (34), 1948

Fewest Attempts, Both Teams, Game
45 AFC-FR: N.Y. Jets (22) vs. Buffalo (23), 1981
46 AFC: Buffalo (13) vs. Kansas City (33), 1966
48 AFC-D: Buffalo (12) vs. Boston (36), 1963
AFC: Boston (16) vs. San Diego (32), 1963

Yards Gained

Most Yards Gained, Game
382 NFC: Chi. Bears vs. Washington, 1940
338 NFC-FR: Dallas vs. Los Angeles, 1980
318 AFC: San Diego vs. Boston, 1963

Fewest Yards Gained, Game
7 AFC-D: Buffalo vs. Boston, 1963
SB: New England vs. Chicago, 1985
17 SB: Minnesota vs. Pittsburgh, 1974
21 NFC: Los Angeles vs. Philadelphia, 1949

Most Yards Gained, Both Teams, Game
430 NFC-FR: Dallas (338) vs. Los Angeles (92), 1980
426 NFC: Cleveland (227) vs. Detroit (199), 1952
404 NFC: Chi. Bears (382) vs. Washington (22), 1940

Fewest Yards Gained, Both Teams, Game
90 AFC-D: Buffalo (7) vs. Boston (83), 1963
106 NFC: Boston (39) vs. Green Bay (67), 1936
128 NFC-FR: Philadelphia (53) vs. Atlanta (75), 1978

Average Gain

Highest Average Gain, Game
9.94 AFC: San Diego vs. Boston, 1963 (32-318)
9.29 NFC-D: Green Bay vs. Dallas, 1982 (17-158)
7.35 NFC-FR: Dallas vs. Los Angeles, 1980 (46-338)

Lowest Average Gain, Game
0.58 AFC-D: Buffalo vs. Boston, 1963 (12-7)
0.64 SB: New England vs. Chicago, 1985 (11-7)
0.81 SB: Minnesota vs. Pittsburgh, 1974 (21-17)

Touchdowns

Most Touchdowns, Game
7 NFC: Chi. Bears vs. Washington, 1940
5 NFC: Cleveland vs. Detroit, 1954
4 NFC: Detroit vs. N.Y. Giants, 1935
AFC: San Diego vs. Boston, 1963
NFC-D: Dallas vs. Cleveland, 1967
NFC: Baltimore vs. Cleveland, 1968
NFC-FR: Dallas vs. Los Angeles, 1980
AFC-D: L.A. Raiders vs. Pittsburgh, 1983
SB: Chicago vs. New England, 1985

Most Touchdowns, Both Teams, Game
7 NFC: Chi. Bears (7) vs. Washington (0), 1940
6 NFC: Cleveland (5) vs. Detroit (1), 1954
5 NFC: Chi. Cardinals (3) vs. Philadelphia (2), 1947
AFC: San Diego (4) vs. Boston (1), 1963
AFC-D: Cincinnati (3) vs. Buffalo (2), 1981

Passing

Attempts

Most Attempts, Game
65 AFC-D: Cleveland vs. N.Y. Jets, 1986 (OT)
54 AFC-D: San Diego vs. Miami, 1981 (OT)
53 NFC-FR: Dallas vs. L.A. Rams, 1983

Fewest Attempts, Game
5 NFC: Detroit vs. N.Y. Giants, 1935
6 AFC: Miami vs. Oakland, 1973
7 SB: Miami vs. Minnesota, 1973

Most Attempts, Both Teams, Game
102 AFC-D: San Diego (54) vs. Miami (48), 1981 (OT)
96 AFC: N.Y. Jets (49) vs. Oakland (47), 1968
95 AFC-D: Cleveland (65) vs. N.Y. Jets (30), 1986 (OT)

Completions

Most Completions, Game

34 AFC-D: Cleveland vs. N.Y. Jets, 1986 (OT)
33 AFC-D: San Diego vs. Miami, 1981 (OT)
32 NFC-FR: St. Louis vs. Green Bay, 1982
NFC-FR: Dallas vs. L.A. Rams, 1983

Fewest Completions, Game

2 NFC: Detroit vs. N.Y. Giants, 1935
NFC: Philadelphia vs. Chi. Cardinals, 1948
3 NFC: N.Y. Giants vs. Chi. Bears, 1941
NFC: Green Bay vs. N.Y. Giants, 1944
NFC: Chi. Cardinals vs. Philadelphia, 1947
NFC: Chi. Cardinals vs. Philadelphia, 1948
NFC-D: Cleveland vs. N.Y. Giants, 1950
NFC-D: N.Y. Giants vs. Cleveland, 1950
NFC: Cleveland vs. Detroit, 1953
AFC: Miami vs. Oakland, 1973
4 NFC-D: Dallas vs. Detroit, 1970
AFC: Miami vs. Baltimore, 1971
SB: Miami vs. Washington, 1982
AFC-FR: Seattle vs. L.A. Raiders, 1984

Most Completions, Both Teams, Game

64 AFC-D: San Diego (33) vs. Miami (31), 1981 (OT)
55 AFC-FR: Pittsburgh (28) vs. San Diego (27), 1982
53 SB: Miami (29) vs. San Francisco (24), 1984

Fewest Completions, Both Teams, Game

5 NFC: Philadelphia (2) vs. Chi. Cardinals (3), 1948
6 NFC: Detroit (2) vs. N.Y. Giants (4), 1935
NFC-D: Cleveland (3) vs. N.Y. Giants (3), 1950
11 NFC: Green Bay (3) vs. N.Y. Giants (8), 1944
NFC-D: Dallas (4) vs. Detroit (7), 1970

Completion Percentage

Highest Completion Percentage, Game (20 attempts)

88.0 SB: N.Y. Giants vs. Denver, 1986 (25-22)
80.0 NFC-D: Washington vs. L.A. Rams, 1983 (25-20)
79.2 AFC-D: Pittsburgh vs. Baltimore, 1976 (24-19)

Lowest Completion Percentage, Game (20 attempts)

18.5 NFC: Tampa Bay vs. Los Angeles, 1979 (27-5)
20.0 NFC-D: N.Y. Giants vs. Washington, 1943 (20-4)
25.8 NFC: Chi. Bears vs. Washington, 1937 (31-8)

Yards Gained

Most Yards Gained, Game

483 AFC-D: Cleveland vs. N.Y. Jets, 1986 (OT)
435 AFC: Miami vs. Pittsburgh, 1984
415 AFC-D: San Diego vs. Miami, 1981 (OT)

Fewest Yards Gained, Game

3 NFC: Chi. Cardinals vs. Philadelphia, 1948
7 NFC: Philadelphia vs. Chi. Cardinals, 1948
9 NFC-D: N.Y. Giants vs. Cleveland, 1950
NFC: Cleveland vs. Detroit, 1953

Most Yards Gained, Both Teams, Game

809 AFC-D: San Diego (415) vs. Miami (394), 1981 (OT)
747 AFC: Miami (435) vs. Pittsburgh (312), 1984
666 AFC-D: Cleveland (483) vs. N.Y. Jets (183), 1986 (OT)

Fewest Yards Gained, Both Teams, Game

10 NFC: Chi. Cardinals (3) vs. Philadelphia (7), 1948
38 NFC-D: N.Y. Giants (9) vs. Cleveland (29), 1950
102 NFC-D: Dallas (22) vs. Detroit (80), 1970

Times Sacked

Most Times Sacked, Game

9 AFC: Kansas City vs. Buffalo, 1966
NFC: Chicago vs. San Francisco, 1984
AFC-D: N.Y. Jets vs. Cleveland, 1986 (OT)
8 NFC: Green Bay vs. Dallas, 1967
NFC: Minnesota vs. Washington, 1987
7 NFC-D: Dallas vs. Los Angeles, 1973
SB: Dallas vs. Pittsburgh, 1975
AFC-FR: Houston vs. Oakland, 1980
NFC-D: Washington vs. Chicago, 1984
SB: New England vs. Chicago, 1985

Most Times Sacked, Both Teams, Game

13 AFC: Kansas City (9) vs. Buffalo (4), 1966
AFC-D: N.Y. Jets (9) vs. Cleveland (4), 1986 (OT)
12 NFC-D: Dallas (7) vs. Los Angeles (5), 1973
NFC-D: Washington (7) vs. Chicago (5), 1984
NFC: Chicago (9) vs. San Francisco (3), 1984
10 AFC-FR: Houston (7) vs. Oakland (3), 1980
NFC-D: N.Y. Giants (6) vs. San Francisco (4), 1984
SB: New England (7) vs. Chicago (3), 1985

Fewest Times Sacked, Both Teams, Game

0 AFC-D: Buffalo vs. Pittsburgh, 1974
AFC-FR: Pittsburgh vs. San Diego, 1982
1 In many games

Touchdowns

Most Touchdowns, Game

6 AFC-D: Oakland vs. Houston, 1969
5 NFC: Chi. Bears vs. Washington, 1943
NFC: Detroit vs. Cleveland, 1957
AFC-D: Oakland vs. Kansas City, 1968
4 NFC: Cleveland vs. Los Angeles, 1950
NFC: Green Bay vs. Dallas, 1966
AFC-D: Oakland vs. Miami, 1974
NFC: Dallas vs. Los Angeles, 1975
SB: Pittsburgh vs. Dallas, 1978
AFC-D: Miami vs. San Diego, 1981 (OT)
NFC-FR: Green Bay vs. St. Louis, 1982
AFC: Miami vs. Pittsburgh, 1984
NFC-D: N.Y. Giants vs. San Francisco, 1986
SB: Washington vs. Denver, 1987

Most Touchdowns, Both Teams, Game

7 NFC: Chi. Bears (5) vs. Washington (2), 1943
AFC-D: Oakland (6) vs. Houston (1), 1969
SB: Pittsburgh (4) vs. Dallas (3), 1978
AFC-D: Miami (4) vs. San Diego (3), 1981 (OT)
AFC: Miami (4) vs. Pittsburgh (3), 1984
6 NFC-FR: Green Bay (4) vs. St. Louis (2), 1982
AFC: Cleveland (3) vs. Denver (3), 1987
5 In many games

Interceptions By

Most Interceptions By, Game

8 NFC: Chi. Bears vs. Washington, 1940
7 NFC: Cleveland vs. Los Angeles, 1955
6 NFC: Green Bay vs. N.Y. Giants, 1939
NFC: Chi. Bears vs. N.Y. Giants, 1946
NFC: Cleveland vs. Detroit, 1954
AFC: San Diego vs. Houston, 1961

Most Interceptions By, Both Teams, Game

10 NFC: Cleveland (7) vs. Los Angeles (3), 1955
AFC: San Diego (6) vs. Houston (4), 1961
9 NFC: Green Bay (6) vs. N.Y. Giants (3), 1939
8 NFC: Chi. Bears (8) vs. Washington (0), 1940
NFC: Chi. Bears (6) vs. N.Y. Giants (2), 1946
NFC: Cleveland (6) vs. Detroit (2), 1954
AFC-FR: Buffalo (4) vs. N.Y. Jets (4), 1981
AFC: Miami (5) vs. N.Y. Jets (3), 1982

Yards Gained

Most Yards Gained, Game

138 AFC-FR: N.Y. Jets vs. Cincinnati, 1982
136 AFC: Dall. Texans vs. Houston, 1962 (OT)
130 NFC-D: Los Angeles vs. St. Louis, 1975

Most Yards Gained, Both Teams, Game

156 NFC: Green Bay (123) vs. N.Y. Giants (33), 1939
149 NFC: Cleveland (103) vs. Los Angeles (46), 1955
141 AFC-FR: Buffalo (79) vs. N.Y. Jets (62), 1981

Touchdowns

Most Touchdowns, Game

3 NFC: Chi. Bears vs. Washington, 1940
2 NFC-D: Los Angeles vs. St. Louis, 1975
1 In many games

Punting

Most Punts, Game

14 AFC-D: N.Y. Jets vs. Cleveland, 1986 (OT)
13 NFC: N.Y. Giants vs. Chi. Bears, 1933
AFC-D: Baltimore vs. Oakland, 1977 (OT)
11 AFC: Houston vs. Oakland, 1967
AFC-D: Houston vs. Oakland, 1969
NFC: L.A. Rams vs. Chicago, 1985

Fewest Punts, Game

0 NFC-FR: St. Louis vs. Green Bay, 1982
AFC-FR: N.Y. Jets vs. Cincinnati, 1982
1 NFC-D: Cleveland vs. Dallas, 1969
AFC: Miami vs. Oakland, 1973
AFC-D: Oakland vs. Cincinnati, 1975
AFC-D: Pittsburgh vs. Baltimore, 1976
AFC: Pittsburgh vs. Houston, 1978
NFC-FR: Green Bay vs. St. Louis, 1982
AFC-FR: Miami vs. New England, 1982
AFC-FR: San Diego vs. Pittsburgh, 1982
AFC-D: Cleveland vs. Indianapolis, 1987
2 In many games

Most Punts, Both Teams, Game

23 NFC: N.Y. Giants (13) vs. Chi. Bears (10), 1933
22 AFC-D: N.Y. Jets (14) vs. Cleveland (8), 1986 (OT)
21 AFC-D: Baltimore (13) vs. Oakland (8), 1977 (OT)
NFC: L.A. Rams (11) vs. Chicago (10), 1985

Fewest Punts, Both Teams, Game

1 NFC-FR: St. Louis (0) vs. Green Bay (1), 1982
2 AFC-FR: N.Y. Jets (0) vs. Cincinnati (2), 1982
3 AFC: Miami (1) vs. Oakland (2), 1973
AFC-FR: San Diego (1) vs. Pittsburgh (2), 1982

Average Yardage

Highest Average, Punting, Game (4 punts)

56.0 AFC: Oakland vs. San Diego, 1980
52.5 NFC: Washington vs. Chi. Bears, 1942
51.3 AFC: Pittsburgh vs. Miami, 1972

Lowest Average, Punting, Game (4 punts)

24.9 NFC: Washington vs. Chi. Bears, 1937
25.5 NFC: Green Bay vs. N.Y. Giants, 1962
27.8 AFC-D: San Diego vs. Buffalo, 1980

Punt Returns

Most Punt Returns, Game

8 NFC: Green Bay vs. N.Y. Giants, 1944
7 By eight teams

Most Punt Returns, Both Teams, Game

13 AFC-FR: Houston (7) vs. Oakland (6), 1980
11 NFC: Green Bay (8) vs. N.Y. Giants (3), 1944
NFC-D: Green Bay (6) vs. Baltimore (5), 1965
10 In many games

Fewest Punt Returns, Both Teams, Game

0 NFC: Chi. Bears vs. N.Y. Giants, 1941
AFC: Boston vs. San Diego, 1963
NFC-FR: Green Bay vs. St. Louis, 1982
1 AFC: Miami (0) vs. Pittsburgh (1), 1972
AFC: Cincinnati (0) vs. San Diego (1), 1981
AFC-FR: Cincinnati (0) vs. N.Y. Jets (1), 1982

Fewest Attempts, Both Teams, Game
18 NFC: Detroit (5) vs. N.Y. Giants (13), 1935
21 NFC: Chi. Bears (7) vs. N.Y. Giants (14), 1933
23 NFC: Chi. Cardinals (11) vs. Philadelphia (12), 1948
AFC-FR: San Diego (0) vs. Pittsburgh (1), 1982
NFC-D: Minnesota (0) vs. Washington (1), 1982
AFC: Seattle (0) vs. L.A. Raiders (1), 1983
2 In many games

Yards Gained
Most Yards Gained, Game
155 NFC-D: Dallas vs. Cleveland, 1967
150 NFC: Chi. Cardinals vs. Philadelphia, 1947
143 NFC-FR: Minnesota vs. New Orleans, 1987
Fewest Yards Gained, Game
−10 NFC: Green Bay vs. Cleveland, 1965
−9 NFC: Dallas vs. Green Bay, 1966
AFC-D: Kansas City vs. Oakland, 1968
−5 AFC-D: Miami vs. Oakland, 1970
NFC-D: San Francisco vs. Dallas, 1972
NFC: Dallas vs. Washington, 1972
Most Yards Gained, Both Teams, Game
166 NFC-D: Dallas (155) vs. Cleveland (11), 1967
160 NFC: Chi. Cardinals (150) vs. Philadelphia (10), 1947
146 NFC-D: Philadelphia (112) vs. Pittsburgh (34), 1947
Fewest Yards Gained, Both Teams, Game
−9 NFC: Dallas (−9) vs. Green Bay (0), 1966
−6 AFC-D: Miami (−5) vs. Oakland (−1), 1970
−3 NFC-D: San Francisco (−5) vs. Dallas (2), 1972

Touchdowns
Most Touchdowns, Game
1 By 10 teams

Kickoff Returns
Most Kickoff Returns, Game
10 NFC-D: L.A. Rams vs. Washington, 1983
9 NFC: Chi. Bears vs. N.Y. Giants, 1956
AFC: Boston vs. San Diego, 1963
AFC: Houston vs. Oakland, 1967
8 By many teams
Most Kickoff Returns, Both Teams, Game
13 NFC-D: Green Bay (7) vs. Dallas (6), 1982
12 AFC: Boston (9) vs. San Diego (3), 1963
NFC: Dallas (6) vs. Green Bay (6), 1966
AFC-D: Baltimore (6) vs. Oakland (6), 1977 (OT)
AFC: Oakland (6) vs. San Diego (6), 1980
AFC-D: Miami (6) vs. San Diego (6), 1981 (OT)
NFC-D: N.Y. Giants (7) vs. San Francisco (5), 1981
AFC-FR: Cincinnati (8) vs. N.Y. Jets (4), 1982
NFC-D: L.A. Rams (10) vs. Washington (2), 1983
11 In many games
Fewest Kickoff Returns, Both Teams, Game
1 NFC: Green Bay (0) vs. Boston (1), 1936
2 NFC-D: Los Angeles (0) vs. Chi. Bears (2), 1950
AFC: Houston (0) vs. San Diego (2), 1961
AFC-D: Oakland (1) vs. Pittsburgh (1), 1972
AFC-D: N.Y. Jets (0) vs. L.A. Raiders (2), 1982
AFC: Miami (1) vs. N.Y. Jets (1), 1982
NFC: N.Y. Giants (0) vs. Washington (2), 1986
3 In many games

Yards Gained
Most Yards Gained, Game
225 NFC: Washington vs. Chi. Bears, 1940
222 SB: Miami vs. Washington, 1982
215 AFC: Houston vs. Oakland, 1967
Most Yards Gained, Both Teams, Game
379 AFC-D: Baltimore (193) vs. Oakland (186), 1977 (OT)
321 NFC-D: Dallas (173) vs. Green Bay (148), 1982
318 AFC-D: Miami (183) vs. Oakland (135), 1974
Fewest Yards Gained, Both Teams, Game
15 NFC: N.Y. Giants (0) vs. Washington (15), 1986
31 NFC-D: Los Angeles (0) vs. Chi. Bears (31), 1950
32 NFC: Green Bay (0) vs. Boston (32), 1936

Touchdowns
Most Touchdowns, Game
1 NFC-D: San Francisco vs. Dallas, 1972
AFC-D: Miami vs. Oakland, 1974
AFC-D: Baltimore vs. Oakland, 1977 (OT)
SB: Miami vs. Washington, 1982

Penalties
Most Penalties, Game
14 AFC-FR: Oakland vs. Houston, 1980
NFC-D: San Francisco vs. N.Y. Giants, 1981
12 NFC-D: Chi. Bears vs. Green Bay, 1941
AFC-D: Pittsburgh vs. Baltimore, 1976
SB: Dallas vs. Denver, 1977
AFC-FR: N.Y. Jets vs. Cincinnati, 1982
11 NFC: N.Y. Giants vs. Green Bay, 1944
AFC-D: Oakland vs. New England, 1976
AFC-D: Pittsburgh vs. Denver, 1978
NFC-FR: Dallas vs. Los Angeles, 1980
NFC-D: San Francisco vs. N.Y. Giants, 1986
Fewest Penalties, Game
0 NFC: Philadelphia vs. Green Bay, 1960
NFC-D: Detroit vs. Dallas, 1970
AFC-D: Miami vs. Oakland, 1970
SB: Miami vs. Dallas, 1971
NFC-D: Washington vs. Minnesota, 1973
SB: Pittsburgh vs. Dallas, 1975
1 By many teams
Most Penalties, Both Teams, Game
22 AFC-FR: Oakland (14) vs. Houston (8), 1980
NFC-D: San Francisco (14) vs. N.Y. Giants (8), 1981
21 AFC-D: Oakland (11) vs. New England (10), 1976
20 SB: Dallas (12) vs. Denver (8), 1977
Fewest Penalties, Both Teams, Game
2 NFC: Washington (1) vs. Chi. Bears (1), 1937
NFC-D: Washington (0) vs. Minnesota (2), 1973
SB: Pittsburgh (0) vs. Dallas (2), 1975
3 AFC: Miami (1) vs. Baltimore (2), 1971
NFC: San Francisco (1) vs. Dallas (2), 1971
SB: Miami (0) vs. Dallas (3), 1971
AFC-D: Pittsburgh (1) vs. Oakland (2), 1972
AFC-D: Miami (1) vs. Cincinnati (2), 1973
SB: Miami (1) vs. San Francisco (2), 1984
4 NFC-D: Cleveland (2) vs. Dallas (2), 1967
NFC-D: Minnesota (1) vs. San Francisco (3), 1970
AFC-D: Miami (0) vs. Oakland (4), 1970
NFC-D: Dallas (2) vs. Minnesota (2), 1971

Yards Penalized
Most Yards Penalized, Game
145 NFC-D: San Francisco vs. N.Y. Giants, 1981
133 SB: Dallas vs. Baltimore, 1970
128 NFC-D: Chi. Bears vs. Green Bay, 1941
Fewest Yards Penalized, Game
0 By six teams
Most Yards Penalized, Both Teams, Game
206 NFC-D: San Francisco (145) vs. N.Y. Giants (61), 1981
192 AFC-D: Denver (104) vs. Pittsburgh (88), 1978
182 NFC-FR: Atlanta (98) vs. Minnesota (84), 1982
Fewest Yards Penalized, Both Teams, Game
9 NFC-D: Washington (0) vs. Minnesota (9), 1973
15 SB: Miami (0) vs. Dallas (15), 1971
20 NFC: Washington (5) vs. Chi. Bears (15), 1937
AFC-D: Pittsburgh (5) vs. Oakland (15), 1972
SB: Pittsburgh (0) vs. Dallas (20), 1975
Miami (10) vs. San Francisco (10), 1984

Fumbles
Most Fumbles, Game
6 By nine teams
Most Fumbles, Both Teams, Game
12 AFC: Houston (6) vs. Pittsburgh (6), 1978
10 NFC: Chi. Bears (5) vs. N.Y. Giants (5), 1934
SB: Dallas (6) vs. Denver (4), 1977
9 NFC-D: San Francisco (6) vs. Detroit (3), 1957
NFC-D: San Francisco (5) vs. Dallas (4), 1972
NFC: Dallas (5) vs. Philadelphia (4), 1980
Most Fumbles Lost, Game
4 NFC: N.Y. Giants vs. Baltimore, 1958 (OT)
AFC: Kansas City vs. Oakland, 1969
SB: Baltimore vs. Dallas, 1970
AFC: Pittsburgh vs. Oakland, 1975
SB: Denver vs. Dallas, 1977
AFC: Houston vs. Pittsburgh, 1978
AFC: Miami vs. New England, 1985
SB: New England vs. Chicago, 1985
NFC-FR: L.A. Rams vs. Washington, 1986
3 By many teams
Fewest Fumbles, Both Teams, Game
0 NFC: Green Bay vs. Cleveland, 1965
AFC: Buffalo vs. San Diego, 1965
AFC-D: Oakland vs. Miami, 1974
AFC-D: Houston vs. San Diego, 1979
NFC-D: Dallas vs. Los Angeles, 1979
SB: Los Angeles vs. Pittsburgh, 1979
AFC-D: Buffalo vs. Cincinnati, 1981
AFC-D: Cleveland vs. N.Y. Jets, 1986 (OT)
AFC-D: Denver vs. New England, 1986
SB: Denver vs. N.Y. Giants, 1986
1 In many games

Recoveries
Most Total Fumbles Recovered, Game
8 SB: Dallas vs. Denver, 1977 (4 own, 4 opp)
7 NFC: Chi. Bears vs. N.Y. Giants, 1934 (5 own, 2 opp)
NFC-D: San Francisco vs. Detroit, 1957 (4 own, 3 opp)
NFC-D: San Francisco vs. Dallas, 1972 (4 own, 3 opp)
AFC: Pittsburgh vs. Houston, 1978 (3 own, 4 opp)
6 AFC: Houston vs. San Diego, 1961 (4 own, 2 opp)
AFC-D: Cleveland vs. Baltimore, 1971 (4 own, 2 opp)
AFC-D: Cleveland vs. Oakland, 1980 (5 own, 1 opp)
NFC: Philadelphia vs. Dallas, 1980 (3 own, 3 opp)
Most Own Fumbles Recovered, Game
5 NFC: Chi. Bears vs. N.Y. Giants, 1934
AFC-D: Cleveland vs. Oakland, 1980
4 By many teams

Turnovers
(Numbers of times losing the ball on interceptions and fumbles.)
Most Turnovers, Game
9 NFC: Washington vs. Chi. Bears, 1940
NFC: Detroit vs. Cleveland, 1954
AFC: Houston vs. Pittsburgh, 1978
8 NFC: N.Y. Giants vs. Chi. Bears, 1946
NFC: Los Angeles vs. Cleveland, 1955
NFC: Cleveland vs. Detroit, 1957
SB: Denver vs. Dallas, 1977
NFC-D: Minnesota vs. Philadelphia, 1980

7 AFC: Houston vs. San Diego, 1961
SB: Baltimore vs. Dallas, 1970
AFC: Pittsburgh vs. Oakland, 1975
NFC-D: Chicago vs. Dallas, 1977
NFC: Los Angeles vs. Dallas, 1978
AFC-D: San Diego vs. Miami, 1982

Fewest Turnovers, Game

0 By many teams

Most Turnovers, Both Teams, Game

14 AFC: Houston (9) vs. Pittsburgh (5), 1978
13 NFC: Detroit (9) vs. Cleveland (4), 1954
AFC: Houston (7) vs. San Diego (6), 1961
12 AFC: Pittsburgh (7) vs. Oakland (5), 1975

Fewest Turnovers, Both Teams, Game

1 AFC-D: Baltimore (0) vs. Cincinnati (1), 1970
AFC-D: Pittsburgh (0) vs. Buffalo (1), 1974
AFC: Oakland (0) vs. Pittsburgh (1), 1976
NFC-D: Minnesota (0) vs. Washington (1), 1982
NFC-D: Chicago (0) vs. N.Y. Giants (1), 1985
SB: N.Y. Giants (0) vs. Denver (1), 1986
NFC: Washington (0) vs. Minnesota (1), 1987
2 In many games

AFC-NFC PRO BOWL RECORDS

Compiled by Elias Sports Bureau

Individual Records

Service

Most Games

9 *Ken Houston, Houston, 1971-73; Washington, 1974-79
Joe Greene, Pittsburgh, 1971-77, 1979-80
Jack Lambert, Pittsburgh, 1976-84
Walter Payton, Chicago, 1977-81, 1984-87
Harry Carson, N.Y. Giants, 1979-80, 1982-88
Mike Webster, Pittsburgh, 1979-86, 1988
8 Tom Mack, Los Angeles, 1971-76, 1978-79
*Franco Harris, Pittsburgh, 1973-76, 1978-81
Lemar Parrish, Cincinnati, 1971-72, 1975-77; Washington, 1978, 1980-81
Art Shell, Oakland, 1973-79, 1981
Ted Hendricks, Baltimore, 1972-74; Green Bay, 1975; Oakland, 1981-82; L.A. Raiders, 1983-84
*John Hannah, New England, 1977, 1979-83, 1985-86
*Randy White, Dallas, 1978, 1980-86
*Mike Haynes, New England, 1978-81, 1983; L.A. Raiders, 1985-87
7 Ron Yary, Minnesota, 1972-78
Elvin Bethea, Houston, 1972-76, 1979-80
Roger Wehrli, St. Louis, 1971-72, 1975-78, 1980
Jack Youngblood, Los Angeles, 1974-80
Ray Guy, Oakland, 1974-79, 1981
Robert Brazile, Houston, 1977-83
Randy Gradishar, Denver, 1976, 1978-80, 1982-84
James Lofton, Green Bay, 1979, 1981-86
Lawrence Taylor, N.Y. Giants, 1982-88
*Also selected, but did not play, in one additional game

Scoring

Points

Most Points, Career

30 Jan Stenerud, Kansas City, 1971-72, 1976; Green Bay, 1985 (6-pat, 8-fg)
18 John Brockington, Green Bay, 1972-74 (3-td)
Earl Campbell, Houston, 1979-82, 1984 (3-td)
Chuck Muncie, New Orleans, 1980; San Diego, 1982-83 (3-td)
William Andrews, Atlanta, 1981-84 (3-td)
Marcus Allen, L.A. Raiders, 1983, 1985-86, 1988 (3-td)
16 Garo Yepremian, Miami, 1974, 1979 (1-pat, 5-fg)
Morten Andersen, New Orleans, 1986-88 (4-pat, 4-fg)

Most Points, Game

18 John Brockington, Green Bay, 1973 (3-td)
15 Garo Yepremian, Miami, 1974 (5-fg)
14 Jan Stenerud, Kansas City, 1972 (2-pat, 4-fg)

Touchdowns

Most Touchdowns, Career

3 John Brockington, Green Bay, 1972-74 (2-r, 1-p)
Earl Campbell, Houston, 1979-82, 1984 (3-r)
Chuck Muncie, New Orleans, 1980; San Diego, 1982-83 (3-r)
William Andrews, Atlanta, 1981-84 (1-r, 2-p)
Marcus Allen, L.A. Raiders, 1983, 1985-86, 1988 (2-r, 1-p)
2 By 10 players

Most Touchdowns, Game

3 John Brockington, Green Bay, 1973 (2-r, 1-p)
2 Mel Renfro, Dallas, 1971 (2-ret)
Earl Campbell, Houston, 1980 (2-r)
Chuck Muncie, New Orleans, 1980 (2-r)
William Andrews, Atlanta, 1984 (2-p)

Points After Touchdown

Most Points After Touchdown, Career

6 Chester Marcol, Green Bay, 1973, 1975 (6 att)
Mark Moseley, Washington, 1980, 1983 (7 att)
Ali Haji-Sheikh, N.Y. Giants, 1984 (6 att)
Jan Stenerud, Kansas City, 1971-72, 1976; Green Bay, 1985 (6 att)

Most Points After Touchdown, Game

6 Ali Haji-Sheikh, N.Y. Giants, 1984 (6 att)
4 Chester Marcol, Green Bay, 1973 (4 att)
Mark Moseley, Washington, 1980 (5 att)
Morten Andersen, New Orleans, 1986 (4 att)

Field Goals

Most Field Goals Attempted, Career

15 Jan Stenerud, Kansas City, 1971-72, 1976; Green Bay, 1985
7 Garo Yepremian, Miami, 1974, 1979
Mark Moseley, Washington, 1980, 1983
6 Ed Murray, Detroit, 1981
Morten Andersen, New Orleans, 1986-88

Most Field Goals Attempted, Game

6 Jan Stenerud, Kansas City, 1972
Ed Murray, Detroit, 1981
Mark Moseley, Washington, 1983
5 Garo Yepremian, Miami, 1974
4 Jan Stenerud, Kansas City, 1976

Most Field Goals, Career

8 Jan Stenerud, Kansas City, 1971-72, 1976; Green Bay, 1985
5 Garo Yepremian, Miami, 1974, 1979
4 Ed Murray, Detroit, 1981
Morten Andersen, New Orleans, 1986-88

Most Field Goals, Game

5 Garo Yepremian, Miami, 1974 (5 att)
4 Jan Stenerud, Kansas City, 1972 (6 att)
Ed Murray, Detroit, 1981 (6 att)
2 By many players

Longest Field Goal

48 Jan Stenerud, Kansas City, 1972
43 Gary Anderson, Pittsburgh, 1984
42 Jim Bakken, St. Louis, 1976

Safeties

Most Safeties, Game

1 Art Still, Kansas City, 1983
Mark Gastineau, N.Y. Jets, 1985

Rushing

Attempts

Most Attempts, Career

81 Walter Payton, Chicago, 1977-81, 1984-87
68 O.J. Simpson, Buffalo, 1973-77
46 Franco Harris, Pittsburgh, 1973-76, 1978-81
Earl Campbell, Houston, 1979-82, 1984

Most Attempts, Game

19 O.J. Simpson, Buffalo, 1974
17 Marv Hubbard, Oakland, 1974
16 O.J. Simpson, Buffalo, 1973
Marcus Allen, L.A. Raiders, 1986

Yards Gained

Most Yards Gained, Career

368 Walter Payton, Chicago, 1977-81, 1984-87
356 O.J. Simpson, Buffalo, 1973-77
220 Earl Campbell, Houston, 1979-82, 1984

Most Yards Gained, Game

112 O. J. Simpson, Buffalo, 1973
104 Marv Hubbard, Oakland, 1974
77 Walter Payton, Chicago, 1978

Longest Run From Scrimmage

41 Lawrence McCutcheon, Los Angeles, 1976
30 O.J. Simpson, Buffalo, 1975
29 Franco Harris, Pittsburgh, 1973

Average Gain

Highest Average Gain, Career (20 attempts)

5.81 Marv Hubbard, Oakland, 1972-74 (36-209)
5.71 Wilbert Montgomery, Philadelphia, 1979-80 (21-120)
5.36 Larry Csonka, Miami, 1971-72, 1975 (22-118)

Highest Average Gain, Game (10 attempts)

7.00 O.J. Simpson, Buffalo, 1973 (16-112)
Ottis Anderson, St. Louis, 1981 (10-70)
6.91 Walter Payton, Chicago, 1985 (11-76)
6.90 Earl Campbell, Houston, 1980 (10-69)

Touchdowns

Most Touchdowns, Career

3 Earl Campbell, Houston, 1979-82, 1984
Chuck Muncie, New Orleans, 1980; San Diego, 1982-83
2 John Brockington, Green Bay, 1972-74
O.J. Simpson, Buffalo, 1973-77
Walter Payton, Chicago, 1977-81, 1984-87
Marcus Allen, L.A. Raiders, 1983, 1985-86, 1988

Most Touchdowns, Game

2 John Brockington, Green Bay, 1973
Earl Campbell, Houston, 1980
Chuck Muncie, New Orleans, 1980

Passing

Attempts

Most Attempts, Career

120 Dan Fouts, San Diego, 1980-84, 1986
88 Bob Griese, Miami, 1971-72, 1974-75, 1977, 1979
57 Joe Montana, San Francisco, 1982, 1984-85, 1988

Most Attempts, Game

32 Bill Kenney, Kansas City, 1984
30 Dan Fouts, San Diego, 1983
28 Jim Hart, St. Louis, 1976

Completions

Most Completions, Career

63 Dan Fouts, San Diego, 1980-84, 1986
44 Bob Griese, Miami, 1971-72, 1974-75, 1977, 1979
33 Ken Anderson, Cincinnati, 1976-77, 1982-83

Most Completions, Game

21 Joe Theismann, Washington, 1984
17 Dan Fouts, San Diego, 1983
16 Dan Fouts, San Diego, 1986

Completion Percentage

Highest Completion Percentage, Career (40 attempts)

68.9 Joe Theismann, Washington, 1983-84 (45-31)
58.9 Ken Anderson, Cincinnati, 1976-77, 1982-83 (56-33)
52.5 Dan Fouts, San Diego, 1980-84, 1986 (120-63)

Highest Completion Percentage, Game (10 attempts)

90.0 Archie Manning, New Orleans, 1980 (10-9)
77.8 Joe Theismann, Washington, 1984 (27-21)
71.4 Joe Montana, San Francisco, 1985 (14-10)

Yards Gained

Most Yards Gained, Career

890 Dan Fouts, San Diego, 1980-84, 1986
554 Bob Griese, Miami, 1971-72, 1974-75, 1977, 1979
398 Ken Anderson, Cincinnati, 1976-77, 1982-83

Most Yards Gained, Game
274 Dan Fouts, San Diego, 1983
242 Joe Theismann, Washington, 1984
212 Phil Simms, N.Y. Giants, 1986
Longest Completion
64 Dan Pastorini, Houston (to Burrough, Houston), 1976 (TD)
57 James Harris, Los Angeles (to Gray, St. Louis), 1975
Ken Anderson, Cincinnati (to G. Pruitt, Cleveland), 1977
56 Dan Marino, Miami (to Allen, L.A. Raiders), 1985

Average Gain
Highest Average Gain, Career (40 attempts)
7.64 Joe Theismann, Washington, 1983-84 (45-344)
7.42 Dan Fouts, San Diego, 1980-84, 1986 (120-890)
7.11 Ken Anderson, Cincinnati, 1976-77, 1982-83 (56-398)
Highest Average Gain, Game (10 attempts)
11.40 Ken Anderson, Cincinnati, 1977 (10-114)
11.20 Archie Manning, New Orleans, 1980 (10-112)
11.09 Greg Landry, Detroit, 1972 (11-122)

Touchdowns
Most Touchdowns, Career
3 Joe Theismann, Washington, 1983-84
Joe Montana, San Francisco, 1982, 1984-85, 1988
Phil Simms, N.Y. Giants, 1986
2 James Harris, Los Angeles, 1975
Mike Boryla, Philadelphia, 1976
Ken Anderson, Cincinnati, 1976-77, 1982-83
Most Touchdowns, Game
3 Joe Theismann, Washington, 1984
Phil Simms, N.Y. Giants, 1986
2 James Harris, Los Angeles, 1975
Mike Boryla, Philadelphia, 1976
Ken Anderson, Cincinnati, 1977

Had Intercepted
Most Passes Had Intercepted, Career
8 Dan Fouts, San Diego, 1980-84, 1986
6 Jim Hart, St. Louis, 1975-78
5 Ken Stabler, Oakland, 1974-75, 1978
Most Passes Had Intercepted, Game
5 Jim Hart, St. Louis, 1977
4 Ken Stabler, Oakland, 1974
3 Dan Fouts, San Diego, 1986
Most Attempts, Without Interception, Game
27 Joe Theismann, Washington, 1984
Phil Simms, N.Y. Giants, 1986
26 John Brodie, San Francisco, 1971
Danny White, Dallas, 1983
21 Roman Gabriel, Philadelphia, 1974
Dan Marino, Miami, 1985

Percentage, Passes Had Intercepted
Lowest Percentage, Passes Had Intercepted, Career (40 attempts)
0.00 Joe Theismann, Washington, 1983-84 (45-0)
3.41 Bob Griese, Miami, 1971-72, 1974-75, 1977, 1979 (88-3)
5.36 Ken Anderson, Cincinnati, 1976-77, 1982-83 (56-3)

Pass Receiving
Receptions
Most Receptions, Career
18 Walter Payton, Chicago, 1977-81, 1984-87
17 Steve Largent, Seattle, 1979, 1982, 1985-88
14 John Stallworth, Pittsburgh, 1980, 1983, 1985
James Lofton, Green Bay, 1979, 1981-86
Marcus Allen, L.A. Raiders, 1983, 1985-86, 1988
Most Receptions, Game
8 Steve Largent, Seattle, 1986
7 John Stallworth, Pittsburgh, 1983
6 John Stallworth, Pittsburgh, 1980
Kellen Winslow, San Diego, 1982

Yards Gained
Most Yards Gained, Career
236 Steve Largent, Seattle, 1979, 1982, 1985-88
226 Wes Chandler, New Orleans, 1980; San Diego, 1983-84, 1986
206 James Lofton, Green Bay, 1979, 1981-86
Most Yards Gained, Game
114 Wes Chandler, San Diego, 1986
96 Ken Burrough, Houston, 1976
91 Alfred Jenkins, Atlanta, 1981
Longest Reception
64 Ken Burrough, Houston (from Pastorini, Houston), 1976 (TD)
57 Mel Gray, St. Louis (from Harris, Los Angeles), 1975
Greg Pruitt, Cleveland (from Anderson, Cincinnati), 1977
56 Marcus Allen, L.A. Raiders (from Marino, Miami), 1985

Touchdowns
Most Touchdowns, Career
2 Mel Gray, St. Louis, 1975-78
Cliff Branch, Oakland, 1975-78
Terry Metcalf, St. Louis, 1975-76, 1978
Tony Hill, Dallas, 1979-80, 1986
William Andrews, Atlanta, 1981-84
James Lofton, Green Bay, 1979, 1981-86
Jimmie Giles, Tampa Bay, 1981-83, 1986
Most Touchdowns, Game
2 William Andrews, Atlanta, 1984

Interceptions By
Most Interceptions, Career
4 Everson Walls, Dallas, 1982-84, 1986
3 Ken Houston, Houston, 1971-73; Washington, 1974-79
Jack Lambert, Pittsburgh, 1976-84
Ted Hendricks, Baltimore, 1972-74; Green Bay, 1975; Oakland, 1981-82; L.A. Raiders, 1983-84
Mike Haynes, New England, 1978-81, 1983; L.A. Raiders, 1985-87
2 By five players
Most Interceptions By, Game
2 Mel Blount, Pittsburgh, 1977
Everson Walls, Dallas, 1982, 1983
LeRoy Irvin, L.A. Rams, 1986

Yards Gained
Most Yards Gained, Career
77 Ted Hendricks, Baltimore, 1972-74; Green Bay, 1975; Oakland, 1981-82; L.A. Raiders, 1983-84
48 Joey Browner, Minnesota, 1986-88
44 Nolan Cromwell, L.A. Rams, 1981-84
Most Yards Gained, Game
65 Ted Hendricks, Baltimore, 1973
48 Joey Browner, Minnesota, 1986
44 Nolan Cromwell, L.A. Rams, 1984
Longest Gain
65 Ted Hendricks, Baltimore, 1973
48 Joey Browner, Minnesota, 1986 (TD)
44 Nolan Cromwell, L.A. Rams, 1984 (TD)

Touchdowns
Most Touchdowns, Game
1 Bobby Bell, Kansas City, 1973
Nolan Cromwell, L.A. Rams, 1984
Joey Browner, Minnesota, 1986

Punting
Most Punts, Career
33 Ray Guy, Oakland, 1974-79, 1981
19 Dave Jennings, N.Y. Giants, 1979-81, 1983
16 Jerrel Wilson, Kansas City, 1971-73
Tom Wittum, San Francisco, 1974-75
Most Punts, Game
10 Reggie Roby, Miami, 1985
9 Tom Wittum, San Francisco, 1974
Rohn Stark, Indianapolis, 1987
8 Jerrel Wilson, Kansas City, 1971
Tom Skladany, Detroit, 1982
Longest Punt
64 Tom Wittum, San Francisco, 1974
61 Reggie Roby, Miami, 1985
60 Ron Widby, Dallas, 1972

Average Yardage
Highest Average, Career (10 punts)
45.25 Jerrel Wilson, Kansas City, 1971-73 (16-724)
44.64 Ray Guy, Oakland, 1974-79, 1981 (33-1,473)
44.63 Tom Wittum, San Francisco, 1974-75 (16-714)
Highest Average, Game (4 punts)
49.57 Jim Arnold, Detroit, 1988 (7-347)
49.00 Ray Guy, Oakland, 1974 (4-196)
47.75 Bob Grupp, Kansas City, 1980 (4-191)

Punt Returns
Most Punt Returns, Career
13 Rick Upchurch, Denver, 1977, 1979-80, 1983
11 Vai Sikahema, St. Louis, 1987-88
10 Mike Nelms, Washington, 1981-83
Most Punt Returns, Game
7 Vai Sikahema, St. Louis, 1987
6 Henry Ellard, L.A. Rams, 1985
Gerald McNeil, Cleveland, 1988
5 Rick Upchurch, Denver, 1980
Mike Nelms, Washington, 1981
Carl Roaches, Houston, 1982
Most Fair Catches, Game
2 Jerry Logan, Baltimore, 1971
Dick Anderson, Miami, 1974
Henry Ellard, L.A. Rams, 1985

Yards Gained
Most Yards Gained, Career
183 Billy Johnson, Houston, 1976, 1978; Atlanta, 1984
138 Rick Upchurch, Denver, 1977, 1979-80, 1983
119 Mike Nelms, Washington, 1981-83
Most Yards Gained, Game
159 Billy Johnson, Houston, 1976
138 Mel Renfro, Dallas, 1971
117 Wally Henry, Philadelphia, 1980
Longest Punt Return
90 Billy Johnson, Houston, 1976 (TD)
86 Wally Henry, Philadelphia, 1980 (TD)
82 Mel Renfro, Dallas, 1971 (TD)

Touchdowns
Most Touchdowns, Game
2 Mel Renfro, Dallas, 1971
1 Billy Johnson, Houston, 1976
Wally Henry, Philadelphia, 1980

Kickoff Returns
Most Kickoff Returns, Career
10 Rick Upchurch, Denver, 1977, 1979-80, 1983
Greg Pruitt, Cleveland, 1974-75, 1977-78; L.A. Raiders, 1984
8 Mike Nelms, Washington, 1981-83
6 Terry Metcalf, St. Louis, 1975-76, 1978
Vai Sikahema, St. Louis, 1987-88

Most Kickoff Returns, Game
6 Greg Pruitt, L.A. Raiders, 1984
5 Les (Speedy) Duncan, Washington, 1972
Ron Smith, Chicago, 1973
Herb Mul-Key, Washington, 1974
4 By six players

Yards Gained
Most Yards Gained, Career
309 Greg Pruitt, Cleveland, 1974-75, 1977-78; L.A. Raiders, 1984
222 Rick Upchurch, Denver, 1977, 1979-80, 1983
175 Les (Speedy) Duncan, Washington, 1972
Most Yards Gained, Game
192 Greg Pruitt, L.A. Raiders, 1984
175 Les (Speedy) Duncan, Washington, 1972
152 Ron Smith, Chicago, 1973
Longest Kickoff Return
62 Greg Pruitt, L.A. Raiders, 1984
61 Eugene (Mercury) Morris, Miami, 1972
55 Ron Smith, Chicago, 1973

Touchdowns
Most Touchdowns, Game
None

Fumbles
Most Fumbles, Career
6 Dan Fouts, San Diego, 1980-84, 1986
4 Lawrence McCutcheon, Los Angeles, 1974-78
Franco Harris, Pittsburgh, 1973-76, 1978-81
Jay Schroeder, Washington, 1987
Vai Sikahema, St. Louis, 1987-88
3 O.J. Simpson, Buffalo, 1973-77
William Andrews, Atlanta, 1981-84
Joe Montana, San Francisco, 1982, 1984-85, 1988
Walter Payton, Chicago, 1977-81, 1984-87
Neil Lomax, St. Louis, 1985, 1988
Most Fumbles, Game
4 Jay Schroeder, Washington, 1987
3 Dan Fouts, San Diego, 1982
Vai Sikahema, St. Louis, 1987
2 By 11 players

Recoveries
Most Fumbles Recovered, Career
3 Harold Jackson, Philadelphia, 1973; Los Angeles, 1974, 1976, 1978 (3-own)
Dan Fouts, San Diego, 1980-84, 1986 (3-own)
Randy White, Dallas, 1978, 1980-86 (3-opp)
2 By many players
Most Fumbles Recovered, Game
2 Dick Anderson, Miami, 1974 (1-own, 1-opp)
Harold Jackson, Los Angeles, 1974 (2-own)
Dan Fouts, San Diego, 1982 (2-own)

Yardage
Longest Fumble Return
83 Art Still, Kansas City, 1985 (TD, opp)
51 Phil Villapiano, Oakland, 1974 (opp)
37 Sam Mills, New Orleans, 1988 (opp)

Touchdowns
Most Touchdowns, Game
1 Art Still, Kansas City, 1985

Sacks
Sacks have been compiled since 1983.
Most Sacks, Career
7 Mark Gastineau, N.Y. Jets, 1983-86
6 Howie Long, L.A. Raiders, 1984-88
5 Reggie White, Philadelphia, 1987-88
Most Sacks, Game
4 Mark Gastineau, N.Y. Jets, 1985
Reggie White, Philadelphia, 1987
3 Richard Dent, Chicago, 1985
2 By many players

Team Records

Scoring
Most Points, Game
45 NFC, 1984
Fewest Points, Game
3 AFC, 1984
Most Points, Both Teams, Game
64 NFC (37) vs. AFC (27), 1980
Fewest Points, Both Teams, Game
16 NFC (6) vs. AFC (10), 1987

Touchdowns
Most Touchdowns, Game
6 NFC, 1984
Fewest Touchdowns, Game
0 AFC, 1971, 1974, 1984
NFC, 1987, 1988
Most Touchdowns, Both Teams, Game
8 AFC (4) vs. NFC (4), 1973
NFC (5) vs. AFC (3), 1980
Fewest Touchdowns, Both Teams, Game
1 AFC (0) vs. NFC (1), 1974
NFC (0) vs. AFC (1), 1987
NFC (0) vs. AFC (1), 1988

Points After Touchdown
Most Points After Touchdown, Game
6 NFC, 1984
Most Points After Touchdown, Both Teams, Game
7 NFC (4) vs. AFC (3), 1973
NFC (4) vs. AFC (3), 1980
NFC (4) vs. AFC (3), 1986

Field Goals
Most Field Goals Attempted, Game
6 AFC, 1972
NFC, 1981, 1983
Most Field Goals Attempted, Both Teams, Game
9 NFC (6) vs. AFC (3), 1983
Most Field Goals, Game
5 AFC, 1974
Most Field Goals, Both Teams, Game
7 AFC (5) vs. NFC (2), 1974

Net Yards Gained Rushing And Passing
Most Yards Gained, Game
466 AFC, 1983
Fewest Yards Gained, Game
146 AFC, 1971
Most Yards Gained, Both Teams, Game
811 AFC (466) vs. NFC (345), 1983
Fewest Yards Gained, Both Teams, Game
424 AFC (202) vs. NFC (222), 1987

Rushing
Attempts
Most Attempts, Game
50 AFC, 1974
Fewest Attempts, Game
18 AFC, 1984
Most Attempts, Both Teams, Game
80 AFC (50) vs. NFC (30), 1974
Fewest Attempts, Both Teams, Game
54 AFC (27) vs. NFC (27), 1983
AFC (18) vs. NFC (36), 1984

Yards Gained
Most Yards Gained, Game
224 NFC, 1976
Fewest Yards Gained, Game
64 NFC, 1974
Most Yards Gained, Both Teams, Game
425 NFC (224) vs. AFC (201), 1976
Fewest Yards Gained, Both Teams, Game
178 AFC (66) vs. NFC (112), 1971

Touchdowns
Most Touchdowns, Game
2 AFC, 1973, 1980, 1982
NFC, 1973, 1977, 1980
Most Touchdowns, Both Teams, Game
4 AFC (2) vs. NFC (2), 1973
AFC (2) vs. NFC (2), 1980

Passing
Attempts
Most Attempts, Game
50 AFC, 1983
Fewest Attempts, Game
17 NFC, 1972
Most Attempts, Both Teams, Game
94 AFC (50) vs. NFC (44), 1983
Fewest Attempts, Both Teams, Game
42 NFC (17) vs. AFC (25), 1972

Completions
Most Completions, Game
31 AFC, 1983
Fewest Completions, Game
7 NFC, 1972, 1982
Most Completions, Both Teams, Game
55 AFC (31) vs. NFC (24), 1983
Fewest Completions, Both Teams, Game
18 NFC (7) vs. AFC (11), 1972

Yards Gained
Most Yards Gained, Game
387 AFC, 1983
Fewest Yards Gained, Game
42 NFC, 1982
Most Yards Gained, Both Teams, Game
608 AFC (387) vs. NFC (221), 1983
Fewest Yards Gained, Both Teams, Game
215 NFC (89) vs. AFC (126), 1972

Times Sacked
Most Times Sacked, Game
9 NFC, 1985
Fewest Times Sacked, Game
0 NFC, 1971
Most Times Sacked, Both Teams, Game
17 NFC (9) vs. AFC (8), 1985
Fewest Times Sacked, Both Teams, Game
4 AFC (2) vs. NFC (2), 1978

Touchdowns
Most Touchdowns, Game
4 NFC, 1984
Most Touchdowns, Both Teams, Game
5 NFC (3) vs. AFC (2), 1986

Interceptions By
Most Interceptions By, Game
6 AFC, 1977
Most Interceptions By, Both Teams, Game
7 AFC (6) vs. NFC (1), 1977

Yards Gained
Most Yards Gained, Game
78 NFC, 1986
Most Yards Gained, Both Teams, Game
99 NFC (64) vs. AFC (35), 1975

Touchdowns
Most Touchdowns, Game
1 AFC, 1973
NFC, 1984, 1986

Punting
Most Punts, Game
10 AFC, 1985
Fewest Punts, Game
2 NFC, 1984
Most Punts, Both Teams, Game
16 AFC (10) vs. NFC (6), 1985
Fewest Punts, Both Teams, Game
6 NFC (2) vs. AFC (4), 1984

Average Yardage
Highest Average, Game
49.57 NFC, 1988 (7-347)

Punt Returns
Most Punt Returns, Game
7 NFC, 1985, 1987
Fewest Punt Returns, Game
0 AFC, 1984
Most Punt Returns, Both Teams, Game
11 NFC (7) vs. AFC (4), 1985
Fewest Punt Returns, Both Teams, Game
3 AFC (0) vs. NFC (3), 1984

Yards Gained
Most Yards Gained, Game
177 AFC, 1976
Fewest Yards Gained, Game
0 AFC, 1984
Most Yards Gained, Both Teams, Game
263 AFC (177) vs. NFC (86), 1976
Fewest Yards Gained, Both Teams, Game
16 AFC (0) vs. NFC (16), 1984

Touchdowns
Most Touchdowns, Game
2 NFC, 1971

Kickoff Returns
Most Kickoff Returns, Game
7 AFC, 1984
Fewest Kickoff Returns, Game
1 NFC, 1971, 1984
AFC, 1988
Most Kickoff Returns, Both Teams, Game
10 AFC (5) vs. NFC (5), 1976
AFC (5) vs. NFC (5), 1986
Fewest Kickoff Returns, Both Teams, Game
5 NFC (2) vs. AFC (3), 1979
AFC (1) vs. NFC (4), 1988

Yards Gained
Most Yards Gained, Game
215 AFC, 1984
Fewest Yards Gained, Game
6 NFC, 1971
Most Yards Gained, Both Teams, Game
293 NFC (200) vs. AFC (93), 1972
Fewest Yards Gained, Both Teams, Game
99 NFC (48) vs. AFC (51), 1987

Touchdowns
Most Touchdowns, Game
None

Fumbles
Most Fumbles, Game
10 NFC, 1974
Most Fumbles, Both Teams, Game
15 NFC (10) vs. AFC (5), 1974

Recoveries
Most Fumbles Recovered, Game
10 NFC, 1974 (6 own, 4 opp)
Most Fumbles Lost, Game
4 AFC, 1974, 1988

Yards Gained
Most Yards Gained, Game
87 AFC, 1985

Touchdowns
Most Touchdowns, Game
1 AFC, 1985

Turnovers
(Number of times losing the ball on interceptions and fumbles.)
Most Turnovers, Game
8 AFC, 1974
Fewest Turnovers, Game
1 AFC, 1972, 1976, 1978, 1979, 1985, 1987
NFC, 1976, 1980, 1983
Most Turnovers, Both Teams, Game
12 AFC (8) vs. NFC (4), 1974
Fewest Turnovers, Both Teams, Game
2 AFC (1) vs. NFC (1), 1976

RULES

1988 NFL Roster of Officials 356
Official Signals 358
Digest of Rules 362

1988 NFL Roster of Officials

Art McNally, Supervisor of Officials
Jack Reader, Assistant Supervisor of Officials
Joe Gardi, Assistant Supervisor of Officials
Tony Veteri, Assistant Supervisor of Officials

No.	Name	Position	College
115	Ancich, Hendi	Umpire	Harbor College
81	Anderson, Dave	Head Linesman	Salem College
34	Austin, Gerald	Side Judge	Western Carolina
22	Baetz, Paul	Back Judge	Heidelberg
116	Baker, Bob	Line Judge	East Texas State
55	Barnes, Tom	Head Linesman	Minnesota
14	Barth, Gene	Referee	St. Louis
56	Baynes, Ron	Line Judge	Auburn
59	Beeks, Bob	Line Judge	Lincoln
17	Bergman, Jerry	Head Linesman	Duquesne
83	Blum, Ron	Line Judge	Marin College
110	Botchan, Ron	Umpire	Occidental
101	Boylston, Bob	Umpire	Alabama
43	Cashion, Red	Referee	Texas A&M
24	Clymer, Roy	Back Judge	New Mexico State
27	Conway, Al	Umpire	Army
61	Creed, Dick	Side Judge	Louisville
78	Demmas, Art	Umpire	Vanderbilt
45	DeSouza, Ron	Line Judge	Morgan State
74	Dodez, Ray	Line Judge	Wooster
31	Dolack, Dick	Field Judge	Ferris State
6	Dooley, Tom	Referee	VMI
113	Dorkowski, Don	Field Judge	Cal State-L.A.
102	Douglas, Merrill	Side Judge	Utah
12	Dreith, Ben	Referee	Colorado State
57	Fiffick, Ed	Umpire	Marquette
47	Fincken, Tom	Side Judge	Kansas St. Teachers
111	Frantz, Earnie	Head Linesman	No College
62	Gandy, Duwayne	Side Judge	Tulsa
50	Gereb, Neil	Umpire	California
72	Gierke, Terry	Head Linesman	Portland State
15	Glass, Bama	Line Judge	Colorado
85	Glover, Frank	Head Linesman	Morris Brown
23	Grier, Johnny	Referee	D.C. Teachers
40	Haggerty, Pat	Referee	Colorado State
96	Hakes, Don	Field Judge	Bradley
104	Hamer, Dale	Head Linesman	Calif. Univ., Pa.
42	Hamilton, Dave	Umpire	Utah
44	Hampton, Donnie	Field Judge	Georgia
105	Hantak, Dick	Referee	Southeast Missouri
66	Hawk, Dave	Side Judge	Southern Methodist
112	Haynes, Joe	Line Judge	Alcorn State
16	Jackson, Doyle	Side Judge	Central Arkansas
54	Johnson, Jack	Line Judge	Pacific Lutheran
114	Johnson, Tom	Head Linesman	Miami, Ohio
97	Jones, Nathan	Side Judge	Lewis & Clark
60	Jorgensen, Dick	Referee	Wisconsin
106	Jury, Al	Back Judge	San Bernardino Valley
107	Kearney, Jim	Back Judge	Pennsylvania
67	Keck, John	Umpire	Cornell College
108	Kemp, Stan	Side Judge	Michigan
86	Kukar, Bernie	Field Judge	St. John's
120	Lane, Gary	Side Judge	Missouri
18	Lewis, Bob	Field Judge	No College
21	Liske, Pete	Back Judge	Penn State
49	Look, Dean	Back Judge	Michigan State
90	Mace, Gil	Side Judge	Westminster
82	Mallette, Pat	Field Judge	Nebraska
9	Markbreit, Jerry	Referee	Illinois
94	Marshall, Vern	Line Judge	Linfield
38	Maurer, Bruce	Back Judge	Ohio State
48	McCarter, Gordon	Referee	Western Reserve
95	McElwee, Bob	Referee	Navy
41	McKenzie, Dick	Line Judge	Ashland
76	Merrifield, Ed	Field Judge	Missouri
35	Miles, Leo	Head Linesman	Virginia State
117	Montgomery, Ben	Umpire	Morehouse
36	Moore, Bob	Back Judge	Dayton
88	Moss, Dave	Umpire	Dartmouth
20	Nemmers, Larry	Side Judge	Upper Iowa
51	Orem, Dale	Line Judge	Louisville
77	Orr, Don	Field Judge	Vanderbilt
64	Parry, Dave	Side Judge	Wabash
10	Phares, Ron	Head Linesman	Virginia Tech
79	Pointer, Aaron	Head Linesman	Pacific Lutheran
92	Poole, Jim	Back Judge	San Diego State
58	Quinby, Bill	Side Judge	Iowa State
5	Quirk, Jim	Line Judge	Delaware
53	Reynolds, Bill	Line Judge	West Chester State
68	Richard, Louis	Back Judge	Southwest Louisiana
30	Riggs, Dennis	Umpire	Louisville
46	Robison, John	Field Judge	Utah
33	Roe, Howard	Line Judge	Wichita State
98	Rosser, Jimmy	Back Judge	Auburn
70	Seeman, Jerry	Referee	Winona State
109	Semon, Sid	Head Linesman	So. California
118	Sifferman, Tom	Back Judge	Seattle
7	Silva, Fred	Referee	San Jose State
73	Skelton, Bobby	Field Judge	Alabama
29	Slavin, Howard	Side Judge	So. California
3	Smith, Boyce	Line Judge	Vanderbilt
119	Spitler, Ron	Field Judge	Panhandle State
91	Stanley, Bill	Field Judge	Redlands
103	Stuart, Rex	Umpire	Appalachian State
37	Toler, Burl	Head Linesman	San Francisco
52	Tompkins, Ben	Back Judge	Texas
4	Toole, Doug	Back Judge	Utah State
32	Tunney, Jim	Referee	Occidental
93	Vaughan, Jack	Field Judge	Mississippi State
100	Wagner, Bob	Umpire	Penn State
28	Wedge, Don	Back Judge	Ohio Wesleyan
87	Weidner, Paul	Head Linesman	Cincinnati
89	Wells, Gordon	Umpire	Occidental
99	Williams, Banks	Back Judge	Houston
8	Williams, Dale	Head Linesman	Cal St.-Northridge
84	Wortman, Bob	Field Judge	Findlay
11	Wyant, Fred	Referee	West Virginia

Numerical Roster

No.	Name	Position
3	Boyce Smith	LJ
4	Doug Toole	BJ
5	Jim Quirk	LJ
6	Tom Dooley	R
7	Fred Silva	R
8	Dale Williams	HL
9	Jerry Markbreit	R
10	Ron Phares	HL
11	Fred Wyant	R
12	Ben Dreith	R
14	Gene Barth	R
15	Bama Glass	LJ
16	Doyle Jackson	SJ
17	Jerry Bergman	HL
18	Bob Lewis	FJ
20	Larry Nemmers	SJ
21	Pete Liske	BJ
22	Paul Baetz	BJ
23	Johnny Grier	R
24	Roy Clymer	BJ
27	Al Conway	U
28	Don Wedge	BJ
29	Howard Slavin	SJ
30	Dennis Riggs	U
31	Dick Dolack	FJ
32	Jim Tunney	R
33	Howard Roe	LJ
34	Gerald Austin	SJ
35	Leo Miles	HL
36	Bob Moore	BJ
37	Burl Toler	HL
38	Bruce Maurer	BJ
40	Pat Haggerty	R
41	Dick McKenzie	LJ
42	Dave Hamilton	U
43	Red Cashion	R
44	Donnie Hampton	FJ
45	Ron DeSouza	LJ
46	John Robison	FJ
47	Tom Fincken	SJ
48	Gordon McCarter	R
49	Dean Look	BJ
50	Neil Gereb	U
51	Dale Orem	LJ
52	Ben Tompkins	BJ
53	Bill Reynolds	LJ
54	Jack Johnson	LJ
55	Tom Barnes	HL
56	Ron Baynes	LJ
57	Ed Fiffick	U
58	Bill Quinby	SJ
59	Bob Beeks	LJ
60	Dick Jorgensen	R
61	Dick Creed	SJ
62	Duwayne Gandy	SJ
64	Dave Parry	SJ
66	Dave Hawk	SJ
67	John Keck	U
68	Louis Richard	BJ
70	Jerry Seeman	R
72	Terry Gierke	HL
73	Bobby Skelton	FJ
74	Ray Dodez	LJ
76	Ed Merrifield	FJ
77	Don Orr	FJ
78	Art Demmas	U
79	Aaron Pointer	HL
81	Dave Anderson	HL
82	Pat Mallette	FJ
83	Ron Blum	LJ
84	Bob Wortman	FJ
85	Frank Glover	HL
86	Bernie Kukar	FJ
87	Paul Weidner	HL
88	Dave Moss	U
89	Gordon Wells	U
90	Gil Mace	SJ
91	Bill Stanley	FJ
92	Jim Poole	BJ
93	Jack Vaughan	FJ
94	Vern Marshall	LJ
95	Bob McElwee	R
96	Don Hakes	FJ
97	Nathan Jones	SJ
98	Jimmy Rosser	BJ
99	Banks Williams	BJ
100	Bob Wagner	U
101	Bob Boylston	U
102	Merrill Douglas	SJ
103	Rex Stuart	U
104	Dale Hamer	HL
105	Dick Hantak	R
106	Al Jury	BJ
107	Jim Kearney	BJ
108	Stan Kemp	SJ
109	Sid Semon	HL
110	Ron Botchan	U
111	Earnie Frantz	HL
112	Joe Haynes	LJ
113	Don Dorkowski	FJ
114	Tom Johnson	HL
115	Hendi Ancich	U
116	Bob Baker	LJ
117	Ben Montgomery	U
118	Tom Sifferman	BJ
119	Ron Spitler	FJ
120	Gary Lane	SJ

1988 Officials at a Glance

Referees

Gene Barth, No. **14,** St. Louis, president, oil company, 18th year.

Red Cashion, No. **43,** Texas A&M, chairman of the board, insurance company, 17th year.

Tom Dooley, No. **6,** VMI, general contractor, 11th year.

Ben Dreith, No. **12,** Colorado State, teacher-counselor, 29th year.

Johnny Grier, No. **23,** D.C. Teachers, planning engineer, telephone company, 8th year.

Pat Haggerty, No. **40,** Colorado State, teacher, 24th year.

Dick Hantak, No. **105,** S.E. Missouri, high school department chairman, 11th year.

Dick Jorgensen, No. **60,** Wisconsin, bank president, 21st year.

Jerry Markbreit, No. **9,** Illinois, trade and barter manager, 13th year.

Gordon McCarter, No. **48,** Western Reserve, regional sales manager, 22nd year.

Bob McElwee, No. **95,** U.S. Naval Academy, owner, construction company, 13th year.

Jerry Seeman, No. **70,** Winona State, district school administrator, 14th year.

Fred Silva, No. **7,** San Jose State, consultant, 22nd year.

Jim Tunney, No. **32,** Occidental, president of motivation company and professional speaker, 29th year.

Fred Wyant, No. **11,** West Virginia, executive sales director, life insurance company, former NFL player, 23rd year.

Umpires

Hendi Ancich, No. **115,** Harbor, longshoreman, 7th year.

Ron Botchan, No. **110,** Occidental, college professor, former AFL player, 9th year.

Bob Boylston, No. **101,** Alabama, stockbroker, 11th year.

Al Conway, No. **27,** Army, vice-president, manufacturing, 20th year.

Art Demmas, No. **78,** Vanderbilt, investments and financial planning, insurance company, 21st year.

Ed Fiffick, No. **57,** Marquette, podiatric physician, 10th year.

Neil Gereb, No. **50,** California, project manager, aircraft company, 8th year.

Dave Hamilton, No. **42,** Utah, assistant executive director, 14th year.

John Keck, No. **67,** Cornell, petroleum distributor, 17th year.

Ben Montgomery, No. **117,** Morehouse, school administrator, 7th year.

Dave Moss, No. **88,** Dartmouth, financial counselor, 9th year.

Dennis Riggs, No. **30,** Bellarmine, vice-president, development and public affairs, 1st year.

Rex Stuart, No. **103,** Appalachian State, insurance agent, 5th year.

Bob Wagner, No. **100,** Penn State, executive director, 4th year.

Gordon Wells, No. **89,** Occidental, chairman, college physical education department, 17th year.

Head Linesman

Dave Anderson, No. **81,** Salem, insurance executive, 5th year.

Tom Barnes, No. **55,** Minnesota, president, manufacturer's representative, 3rd year.

Jerry Bergman, No. **17,** Duquesne, executive director, pension fund, 23rd year.

Earnie Frantz, No. **111,** vice-president and manager, land title company, 8th year.

Terry Gierke, No. **72,** Portland State, real estate broker, 8th year.

Frank Glover, No. **85,** Morris Brown, assistant superintendent, public schools, 17th year.

Dale Hamer, No. **104,** California (Pa.) University, vice-president, equipment finance, 11th year.

Tom Johnson, No. **114,** Miami, Ohio, teacher, 7th year.

Leo Miles, No. **35,** Virginia State, retired university athletic director, former NFL player, 20th year.

Ron Phares, No. **10,** Virginia Tech, vice-president, general contracting firm, 4th year.

Aaron Pointer, No. **79,** Pacific Lutheran, recreation specialist, 2nd year.

Sid Semon, No. **109,** Southern California, chairman, physical education department, 11th year.

Burl Toler, No. **37,** San Francisco, director of personnel, San Francisco Community College District, 24th year.

Paul Weidner, No. **87,** Cincinnati, marketing manager, 3rd year.

Dale Williams, No. **8,** California State-Northridge, coordinator of athletic officials, 9th year.

Line Judges

Bob Baker, No. **116,** East Texas State, educator, 2nd year.

Ron Baynes, No. **56,** Auburn, teacher, counselor, coach, 2nd year.

Bob Beeks, No. **59,** Lincoln, retired law enforcement officer, 21st year.

Ron Blum, No. **83,** Marin College, P.G.A. golf professional, 4th year.

Ron DeSouza, No. **45,** Morgan State, vice-president, administration, 9th year.

Ray Dodez, No. **74,** Wooster, communications consultant, 21st year.

Bama Glass, No. **15,** Colorado, manager, retail sales, 10th year.

Joe Haynes, No. **112,** Alcorn State, deputy superintendent, public schools, 5th year.

Jack Johnson, No. **54,** Pacific Lutheran, president, sports promotions, 13th year.

Vern Marshall, No. **94,** Linfield College, counselor, 15th year.

Dick McKenzie, No. **41,** Ashland, school treasurer, 11th year.

Dale Orem, No. **51,** Louisville, mayor, 9th year.

Jim Quirk, No. **5,** Delaware, vice-president, international sales, 1st year.

Bill Reynolds, No. **53,** West Chester State, teacher and athletic director, 14th year.

Howard Roe, No. **33,** Wichita State, director of administration, 5th year.

Boyce Smith, No. **3,** Vanderbilt, sales, employee benefits, and insurance, 8th year.

Back Judges

Paul Baetz, No. **22,** Heidelberg, financial consultant, 11th year.

Roy Clymer, No. **24,** New Mexico State, district manager, gas company, 9th year.

Al Jury, No. **106,** San Bernardino Valley, state traffic officer, 11th year.

Jim Kearney, No. **107,** Pennsylvania, marketing manager, 11th year.

Pete Liske, No. **21,** Penn State, athletic administrator, former NFL player, 6th year.

Dean Look, No. **49,** Michigan State, vice-president, medical equipment, former AFL player, 16th year.

Bruce Maurer, No. **38,** Ohio State, administrator, collegiate sports, 2nd year.

Bob Moore, No. **36,** Dayton, attorney, 5th year.

Jim Poole, No. **92,** San Diego State, college physical education professor, 14th year.

Louis Richard, No. **68,** S.W. Louisiana, sales representative, 3rd year.

Jimmy Rosser, No. **98,** Auburn, vice-president, temporary service, 12th year.

Tom Sifferman, No. **118,** Seattle, manufacturer's representative, 3rd year.

Ben Tompkins, No. **52,** Texas, attorney, 18th year.

Doug Toole, No. **4,** Utah State, physical therapist, orthopedic and sports medicine, 1st year.

Don Wedge, No. **28,** Ohio Wesleyan, business consultant, 17th year.

Banks Williams, No. **99,** Houston, vice-president sales, concrete company, 11th year.

Side Judges

Gerald Austin, No. **34,** Western Carolina, associate superintendent, county schools, 7th year.

Richard Creed, No. **61,** Louisville, real estate manager, 11th year.

Merrill Douglas, No. **102,** Utah, deputy sheriff, former NFL player, 8th year.

Tom Fincken, No. **47,** Emporia State, educator, 5th year.

Duwayne Gandy, No. **62,** Tulsa, regional sales manager, educational publishing, 8th year.

Dave Hawk, No. **66,** Southern Methodist, owner, warehousing company, 17th year.

Doyle Jackson, No. **16,** Central Arkansas, high school teacher and department head, 1st year.

Nate Jones, No. **97,** Lewis and Clark, high school principal, 12th year.

Stan Kemp, No. **108,** Michigan, vice-president, commercial insurance, 3rd year.

Gary Lane, No. **120,** Missouri, divisional sales manufacturer, former NFL player, 7th year.

Gil Mace, No. **90,** Westminster, national account manager, 15th year.

Larry Nemmers, No. **20,** Upper Iowa, high school principal, 4th year.

Dave Parry, No. **64,** Wabash, high school athletic director, 14th year.

Howard Slavin, No. **29,** Southern California, attorney, 2nd year.

Bill Quinby, No. **58,** Iowa, director, career counseling, 11th year.

Field Judges

Dick Dolack, No. **31,** Ferris State, pharmacist, 23rd year.

Don Dorkowski, No. **113,** Los Angeles State, department head, teacher, 3rd year.

Don Hakes, No. **96,** Bradley, high school dean of students, 12th year.

Donnie Hampton, No. **44,** Georgia, president, mortgage company, 1st year.

Bernie Kukar, No. **86,** St. John's, owner/director, summer camp for boys, 5th year.

Bob Lewis, No. **18,** retired U.S. government specialist, 13th year.

Pat Mallette, No. **82,** Nebraska, real estate broker, 20th year.

Ed Merrifield, No. **76,** Missouri, sales representative, 14th year.

Don Orr, No. **77,** Vanderbilt, mechanical contractor, 18th year.

John Robison, No. **46,** Utah, high school counselor and coach, 1st year.

Bobby Skelton, No. **73,** Alabama, industrial representative, 4th year.

Ron Spitler, No. **119,** Panhandle State, owner, service center, 7th year.

Bill Stanley, No. **91,** Redlands, college dean, athletic director, 15th year.

Jack Vaughan, No. **93,** Mississippi State, financial services, 13th year.

Bob Wortman, No. **84,** Findlay, supervisor, college basketball officials, 23rd year.

1

TOUCHDOWN, FIELD GOAL, or SUCCESSFUL TRY
Both arms extended above head.

2

SAFETY
Palms together above head.

3

FIRST DOWN
Arm pointed toward defensive team's goal.

4

DEAD BALL or NEUTRAL ZONE ESTABLISHED
One arm above head with an open hand.
With fist closed: **Fourth Down.**

5

BALL ILLEGALLY TOUCHED, KICKED, OR BATTED
Fingertips tap both shoulders.

6

TIME OUT
Hands crisscrossed above head.
Same signal followed by placing one hand on top of cap: **Referee's Time Out.**
Same signal followed by arm swung at side: **Touchback.**

7

NO TIME OUT or TIME IN WITH WHISTLE
Full arm circled to simulate moving clock.

8

DELAY OF GAME, ILLEGAL SUBSTITUTION, or EXCESS TIME OUT
Folded arms.

9

FALSE START, ILLEGAL SHIFT, ILLEGAL PROCEDURE, ILLEGAL FORMATION, or KICKOFF OR SAFETY KICK OUT OF BOUNDS
Forearms rotated over and over in front of body.

10

PERSONAL FOUL
One wrist striking the other above head.

Same signal followed by swinging leg: **Running Into or Roughing Kicker.**

Same signal followed by raised arm swinging forward: **Running Into or Roughing Passer.**

Same signal followed by hand striking back of calf: **Clipping**

11

HOLDING
Grasping one wrist, the fist clenched, in front of chest.

12

ILLEGAL USE OF HANDS, ARMS, OR BODY
Grasping one wrist, the hand open and facing forward, in front of chest.

13

PENALTY REFUSED, INCOMPLETE PASS, PLAY OVER, or MISSED GOAL
Hands shifted in horizontal plane.

14

PASS JUGGLED INBOUNDS AND CAUGHT OUT OF BOUNDS
Hands up and down in front of chest (following incomplete pass signal).

15

ILLEGAL FORWARD PASS
One hand waved behind back followed by loss of down signal (23).

16

INTENTIONAL GROUNDING OF PASS
Parallel arms waved in a diagonal plane across body. Followed by loss of down signal (23).

17

INTERFERENCE WITH FORWARD PASS or FAIR CATCH
Hands open and extended forward from shoulders with hands vertical.

18

INVALID FAIR CATCH SIGNAL
One hand waved above head.

19

INELIGIBLE RECEIVER OR INELIGIBLE MEMBER OF KICKING TEAM DOWNFIELD
Right hand touching top of cap.

20

ILLEGAL CONTACT
One open hand extended forward.

21

OFFSIDE or ENCROACHING
Hands on hips.

22

ILLEGAL MOTION AT SNAP
Horizontal arc with one hand.

23

LOSS OF DOWN
Both hands held behind head.

24

CRAWLING, INTERLOCKING INTERFERENCE, PUSHING, or HELPING RUNNER
Pushing movement of hands to front with arms downward.

25

TOUCHING A FORWARD PASS OR SCRIMMAGE KICK
Diagonal motion of one hand across another.

26

UNSPORTSMANLIKE CONDUCT
Arms outstretched, palms down. (Same signal means continuous action fouls are disregarded.) Chop block.

27

ILLEGAL CUT or BLOCKING BELOW THE WAIST
Hand striking front of thigh preceded by personal foul signal (10).

28

ILLEGAL CRACKBACK
Strike of an open right hand against the right mid thigh preceded by personal foul signal (10).

29

PLAYER DISQUALIFIED
Ejection signal.

30

TRIPPING
Repeated action of right foot in back of left heel.

31

UNCATCHABLE FORWARD PASS
Palm of right hand held parallel to ground above head and moved back and forth.

NFL Digest of Rules

This Digest of Rules of the National Football League has been prepared to aid players, fans, and members of the press, radio, and television media in their understanding of the game.

It is not meant to be a substitute for the official rule book. In any case of conflict between these explanations and the official rules, the rules always have precedence.

In order to make it easier to coordinate the information in this digest the topics discussed generally follow the order of the rule book.

Officials' Jurisdictions, Positions, and Duties

Referee—General oversight and control of game. Gives signals for all fouls and is final authority for rule interpretations. Takes a position in backfield 10 to 12 yards behind line of scrimmage, favors right side (if quarterback is right-handed passer). Determines legality of snap, observes deep back(s) for legal motion. On running play, observes quarterback during and after handoff, remains with him until action has cleared away, then proceeds downfield, checking on runner and contact behind him. When runner is downed, Referee determines forward progress from wing official and if necessary, adjusts final position of ball.

On pass plays, drops back as quarterback begins to fade back, picks up legality of blocks by near linemen. Changes to complete concentration on quarterback as defenders approach. Primarily responsible to rule on possible roughing action on passer and if ball becomes loose, rules whether ball is free on a fumble or dead on an incomplete pass.

During kicking situations, Referee has primary responsibility to rule on kicker's actions and whether or not any subsequent contact by a defender is legal.

Umpire—Primary responsibility to rule on players' equipment, as well as their conduct and actions on scrimmage line. Lines up approximately four to five yards downfield, varying position from in front of weakside tackle to strongside guard. Looks for possible false start by offensive linemen. Observes legality of contact by both offensive linemen while blocking and by defensive players while they attempt to ward off blockers. Is prepared to call rule infractions if they occur on offense or defense. Moves forward to line of scrimmage when pass play develops in order to insure that interior linemen do not move illegally downfield. If offensive linemen indicate screen pass is to be attempted, Umpire shifts his attention toward screen side, picks up potential receiver in order to insure that he will legally be permitted to run his pattern and continues to rule on action of blockers. Umpire is to assist in ruling on incomplete or trapped passes when ball is thrown overhead or short.

Head Linesman—Primarily responsible for ruling on offside, encroachment, and actions pertaining to scrimmage line prior to or at snap. Keys on closest setback on his side of the field. On pass plays, Linesman is responsible to clear this receiver approximately seven yards downfield as he moves to a point five yards beyond the line. Linesman's secondary responsibility is to rule on any illegal action taken by defenders on any delay receiver moving downfield. Has full responsibility for ruling on sideline plays on his side, e.g., pass receiver or runner in or out of bounds. Together with Referee, Linesman is responsible for keeping track of number of downs and is in charge of mechanics of his chain crew in connection with its duties.

Linesman must be prepared to assist in determining forward progress by a runner on play directed toward middle or into his side zone. He, in turn, is to signal Referee or Umpire what forward point ball has reached. Linesman is also responsible to rule on legality of action involving any receiver who approaches his side zone. He is to call pass interference when the infraction occurs and is to rule on legality of blockers and defenders on plays involving ball carriers, whether it is entirely a running play, a combination pass and run, or a play involving a kick.

Line Judge—Straddles line of scrimmage on side of field opposite Linesman. Keeps time of game as a backup for clock operator. Along with Linesman is responsible for offside, encroachment, and actions pertaining to scrimmage line prior to or at snap. Line Judge keys on closest setback on his side of field. Line Judge is to observe his receiver until he moves at least seven yards downfield. He then moves toward backfield side, being especially alert to rule on any back in motion and on flight of ball when pass is made (he must rule whether forward or backward). Line Judge has primary responsibility to rule whether or not passer is behind or beyond line of scrimmage when pass is made. He also assists in observing actions by blockers and defenders who are on his side of field. After pass is thrown, Line Judge directs attention toward activities that occur in back of Umpire. During punting situations, Line Judge remains at line of scrimmage to be sure that only the end men move downfield until kick has been made. He also rules whether or not the kick crossed line and then observes action by members of the kicking team who are moving downfield to cover the kick.

Back Judge—Operates on same side of field as Line Judge, 17 yards deep. Keys on wide receiver on his side. Concentrates on path of end or back, observing legality of his potential block(s) or of actions taken against him. Is prepared to rule from <u>deep</u> position on holding or illegal use of hands by end or back or on defensive infractions committed by player guarding him. Has primary responsibility to make decisions involving sideline on his side of field, e.g., pass receiver or runner in or out of bounds.

Back Judge makes decisions involving catching, recovery, or illegal touching of a loose ball beyond line of scrimmage; rules on plays involving pass receiver, including legality of catch or pass interference; assists in covering actions of runner, including blocks by teammates and that of defenders; calls clipping on punt returns; and, together with Field Judge, rules whether or not field goal attempts are successful.

Side Judge—Operates on same side of field as Linesman, 17 yards deep. Keys on wide receiver on his side. Concentrates on path of end or back, observing legality of his potential block(s) or of actions taken against him. Is prepared to rule from <u>deep</u> position on holding or illegal use of hands by end or back or on defensive infractions committed by player guarding him. Has primary responsibility to make decisions involving sideline on his side of field, e.g., pass receiver or runner in or out of bounds.

Side Judge makes decisions involving catching, recovery, or illegal touching of a loose ball beyond line of scrimmage; rules on plays involving pass receiver, including legality of catch or pass interference; assists in covering actions of runner, including blocks by teammates and that of defenders; and calls clipping on punt returns.

Field Judge—Takes a position 25 yards downfield. In general, favors the tight end's side of field. Keys on tight end, concentrates on his path and observes legality of tight end's potential block(s) or of actions taken against him. Is prepared to rule from <u>deep</u> position on holding or illegal use of hands by end or back or on defensive infractions committed by player guarding him.

Field Judge times interval between plays on 30-second clock plus intermission between two periods of each half; makes decisions involving catching, recovery, or illegal touching of a loose ball beyond line of scrimmage; is responsible to rule on plays involving end line; calls pass interference, fair catch infractions, and clipping on kick returns; and, together with Back Judge, rules whether or not field goals and conversions are successful.

Definitions

1. **Chucking:** Warding off an opponent who is in front of a defender by contacting him with a quick extension of arm or arms, followed by the return of arm(s) to a flexed position, thereby breaking the original contact.
2. **Clipping:** Throwing the body across the back of an opponent's leg or hitting him from the back below the waist while moving up from behind unless the opponent is a runner or the action is in close line play.
3. **Close Line Play:** The area between the positions normally occupied by the offensive tackles, extending three yards on each side of the line of scrimmage.
4. **Crackback:** Eligible receivers who take or move to a position more than two yards outside the tackle may not block an opponent below the waist if they then move back inside to block.
5. **Dead Ball:** Ball not in play.
6. **Double Foul:** A foul by each team during the same down.
7. **Down:** The period of action that starts when the ball is put in play and ends when it is dead.
8. **Encroachment:** When a player enters the neutral zone and makes contact with an opponent before the ball is snapped.
9. **Fair Catch:** An unhindered catch of a kick by a member of the receiving team who must raise one arm a full length above his head while the kick is in flight.
10. **Foul:** Any violation of a playing rule.
11. **Free Kick:** A kickoff, kick after a safety, or kick after a fair catch. It may be a placekick, dropkick, or punt, except a punt may <u>not</u> be used on a kickoff.
12. **Fumble:** The loss of possession of the ball.
13. **Impetus:** The action of a player that gives momentum to the ball.
14. **Live Ball:** A ball legally free kicked or snapped. It continues in play until the down ends.
15. **Loose Ball:** A live ball not in possession of any player.
16. **Muff:** The touching of a loose ball by a player in an <u>unsuccessful</u> attempt to obtain possession.
17. **Neutral Zone:** The space the length of a ball between the two scrimmage lines. The offensive team and defensive team must remain behind their end of the ball.
    Exception: The offensive player who snaps the ball.
18. **Offside:** A player is offside when any part of his body is beyond his scrimmage or free kick line <u>when the ball is snapped</u>.
19. **Own Goal:** The goal <u>a team is guarding</u>.
20. **Pocket Area:** Applies from a point two yards outside of either offensive tackle and includes the tight end if he drops off the line of scrimmage to pass protect. Pocket extends longitudinally behind the line back to offensive team's own end line.
21. **Possession:** When a player controls the ball throughout the act of <u>clearly</u> touching both feet, or any other part of his body other than his <u>hand(s), to</u> the ground inbounds.
22. **Punt:** A kick made when a player drops the ball and kicks it while it is in flight.
23. **Safety:** The situation in which the ball is dead on or behind a team's own goal if the <u>impetus</u> comes from a player on that team. Two points are scored for the <u>opposing</u> team.
24. **Shift:** The movement of two or more offensive players at the same time before the snap.
25. **Striking:** The act of swinging, clubbing, or propelling the arm or forearm in contacting an opponent.
26. **Sudden Death:** The continuation of a tied game into sudden death overtime in which the team scoring first (by safety, field goal, or touchdown) wins.
27. **Touchback:** When a ball is dead on or behind a team's own goal line, provided the impetus came from an opponent and provided it is not a touchdown or a missed field goal.
28. **Touchdown:** When any part of the ball, legally in possession of a player inbounds, is on, above, or over the opponent's goal line, provided it is not a touchback.
29. **Unsportsmanlike Conduct:** Any act contrary to the generally understood principles of sportsmanship.

Summary of Penalties

Automatic First Down

1. Awarded to offensive team on all defensive fouls with these exceptions:
   (a) Offside.
   (b) Encroachment.
   (c) Delay of game.
   (d) Illegal substitution.
   (e) Excessive time out(s).
   (f) Incidental grasp of facemask.
   (g) Prolonged, excessive or premeditated celebrations by individual players or groups of players.
   (h) Running into the kicker.

Loss of Down (No yardage)

1. Second forward pass behind the line.
2. Forward pass strikes ground, goal post, or crossbar.
3. Forward pass goes out of bounds.
4. Forward pass is first touched by eligible receiver who has gone out of bounds and returned.
5. Forward pass touches or is caught by an ineligible receiver on or behind line.
6. Forward pass thrown from behind line of scrimmage after ball once crossed the line.

Five Yards

1. Crawling.
2. Defensive holding or illegal use of hands (automatic first down).
3. Delay of game.
4. Encroachment.
5. Too many time outs.
6. False start.
7. Illegal formation.
8. Illegal shift.
9. Illegal motion.
10. Illegal substitution.
11. First onside kickoff out of bounds between goal lines and not touched.
12. Invalid fair catch signal.
13. More than 11 players on the field at snap for either team.
14. Less than seven men on offensive line at snap.
15. Offside.
16. Failure to pause one second after shift or huddle.
17. Running into kicker (automatic first down).
18. More than one man in motion at snap.
19. Grasping facemask of opponent.
20. Player out of bounds at snap.
21. Ineligible member(s) of kicking team going beyond line of scrimmage before ball is kicked.
22. Illegal return.
23. Failure to report change of eligibility.
24. Prolonged, excessive or premeditated celebrations by individual players or groups of players.

10 Yards

1. Offensive pass interference.
2. Ineligible player downfield during passing down.
3. Holding, illegal use of hands, arms or body by offense.
4. Tripping by a member of either team.
5. Helping the runner.
6. Illegal batting or punching a loose ball.
7. Deliberately kicking a loose ball.

15 Yards

1. Chop block.
2. Clipping below the waist.
3. Fair catch interference.
4. Illegal crackback block by offense.
5. Piling on (automatic first down).
6. Roughing the kicker (automatic first down).
7. Roughing the passer (automatic first down).
8. Twisting, turning, or pulling an opponent by the facemask.
9. Unnecessary roughness.
10. Unsportsmanlike conduct.
11. Delay of game at start of either half.
12. Illegal blocking below the waist.
13. A tackler using his helmet to butt, spear, or ram an opponent.
14. Any player who uses the top of his helmet unnecessarily.
15. A punter, placekicker or holder who simulates being roughed by a defensive player.
16. A defender who takes a running start from beyond the line of scrimmage in an attempt to block a field goal or point after touchdown.

Five Yards and Loss of Down

1. Forward pass thrown from beyond line of scrimmage.

10 Yards and Loss of Down

1. Intentional grounding of forward pass (safety if passer is in own end zone). If foul occurs more than 10 yards behind line, play results in loss of down at spot of foul.

15 Yards and Loss of Coin Toss Option

1. Team's late arrival on the field prior to scheduled kickoff.

15 Yards (and disqualification if flagrant)

1. Striking opponent with fist.
2. Kicking or kneeing opponent.
3. Striking opponent on head or neck with forearm, elbow, or hands whether or not the initial contact is made below the neck area.
4. Roughing kicker.
5. Roughing passer.
6. Malicious unnecessary roughness.
7. Unsportsmanlike conduct.
8. Palpably unfair act. (Distance penalty determined by the Referee after consultation with other officials.)

15 Yards and Automatic Disqualification

1. Using a helmet that is not worn as a weapon.

Suspension From Game

1. Illegal equipment. (Player may return after one down when legally equipped.)

Touchdown

1. When Referee determines a palpably unfair act deprived a team of a touchdown. (Example: Player comes off bench and tackles runner apparently en route to touchdown.)

Field

1. Sidelines and end lines are out of bounds. The goal line is actually in the end zone. A player with the ball in his possession scores when the ball is on, above, or over the goal line.
2. The field is rimmed by a white border, a minimum six feet wide, along the sidelines. All of this is out of bounds.
3. The hashmarks (inbound lines) are 70 feet, 9 inches from each sideline.
4. Goal posts must be single-standard type, offset from the end line and painted bright gold. The goal posts must be 18 feet, 6 inches wide and the top face of the crossbar must be 10 feet above the ground. Vertical posts extend at least 30 feet above the crossbar. A ribbon 4 inches by 42 inches long is to be attached to the top of each post. The actual goal is the plane extending indefinitely above the crossbar and between the outer edges of the posts.
5. The field is 360 feet long and 160 feet wide. The end zones are 30 feet deep. The line used in try-for-point plays is two yards out from the goal line.
6. Chain crew members and ball boys must be uniformly identifiable.
7. All clubs must use standardized sideline markers. Pylons must be used for goal line and end line markings.
8. End zone markings and club identification at 50 yard line must be approved by the Commissioner to avoid any confusion as to delineation of goal lines, sidelines, and end lines.

Ball

1. The home club must have 24 balls available for testing by the Referee one hour before game time. In case of bad weather, a playable ball is to be substituted on request of the offensive team captain.

Coin Toss

1. The toss of coin will take place within three minutes of kickoff in center of field. The toss will be called by the visiting captain. The winner may choose one of two privileges and the loser gets the other:
   (a) Receive or kick
   (b) Goal his team will defend
2. Immediately prior to the start of the second half, the captains of both teams must inform the officials of their respective choices. The loser of the original coin toss gets first choice.

Timing

1. The stadium clock is official. In case it stops or is operating incorrectly, the Line Judge takes over the official timing on the field.
2. Each period is 15 minutes. The intermission between the periods is two minutes. Halftime is 15 minutes, unless otherwise specified.
3. On charged team time outs, the Field Judge starts watch and blows whistle after 1 minute 50 seconds, unless television does not utilize the time for commercial. In this case the length of the time out is reduced to 40 seconds.
4. Referee may allow two minutes for injured player and three minutes for equipment repair.
5. Each team is allowed three time outs each half.
6. Time between plays will be 45 seconds from the end of a given play until the snap of the ball for the next play, or a 30-second interval after certain administrative stoppages and game delays.
7. Clock will start running when ball is snapped following all changes of team possession.
8. Consecutive team time outs can be taken by opposing teams but the length of the second time out will be reduced to 40 seconds.

Sudden Death

1. The sudden death system of determining the winner shall prevail when score is tied at the end of the regulation playing time of all NFL games. The team scoring first during overtime play shall be the winner and the game automatically ends upon any score (by safety, field goal, or touchdown) or when a score is awarded by Referee for a palpably unfair act.
2. At the end of regulation time the Referee will immediately toss coin at center of field in accordance with rules pertaining to the usual pregame toss. The captain of the visiting team will call the toss.
3. Following a three-minute intermission after the end of the regulation game, play will be continued in 15-minute periods or until there is a score. There is a two-minute intermission between subsequent periods. The teams change goals at the start of each period. Each team has three time outs and general provisions for play in the last two minutes of a half shall prevail. Disqualified players are not allowed to return.
   Exception: In preseason and regular season games there shall be a maximum of 15 minutes of sudden death with two time outs instead of three. General provisions for play in the last two minutes of a half will be in force.

Timing in Final Two Minutes of Each Half

1. On kickoff, clock does not start until the ball has been legally touched by player of either team in the field of play. (In all other cases, clock starts with kickoff.)
2. A team cannot "buy" an excess time out for a penalty. However, a fourth time out is allowed without penalty for an injured player, who must be removed immediately. A fifth time out or more is allowed for an injury and a five-yard penalty is assessed if the clock was running. Additionally, if the clock was running and the score is tied or the team in possession is losing, the ball cannot be put in play for at least 10 seconds on the fourth or more time out. The half or game can end while those 10 seconds are run off on the clock.
3. If the defensive team is behind in the score and commits a foul when it has no time outs left in the final 30 seconds of either half, the offensive team can decline the penalty for the foul and have the time on the clock expire.

Try-for-Point

1. After a touchdown, the scoring team is allowed a try-for-point during one scrimmage down. The ball may be spotted anywhere between the inbounds lines, two or more yards from the goal line. The successful conversion counts one point, whether by run, kick, or pass.
2. The defensive team never can score on a try-for-point. As soon as defense gets possession, or kick is blocked, ball is dead.
3. Any distance penalty for fouls committed by the defense that prevent the try from being attempted can be enforced on the succeeding kickoff. Any foul committed on a successful try will result in a distance penalty being assessed on the ensuing kickoff.
4. Only the fumbling player may advance a fumble during a try-for-point.

Players-Substitutions

1. Each team is permitted 11 men on the field at the snap.
2. Unlimited substitution is permitted. However, players may enter the field only when the ball is dead. Players who have been substituted for are not permitted to linger on the field. Such lingering will be interpreted as unsportsmanlike conduct.
3. Players leaving the game must be out of bounds on their own side, clearing the field between the end lines, before a snap or free kick. If player crosses end line leaving field, it is delay of game (five-yard penalty).

Kickoff

1. The kickoff shall be from the kicking team's 35 yard line at the start of each half and after a field goal and try-for-point. A kickoff is one type of free kick.
2. Either a one-, two-, or three-inch tee may be used (no tee permitted for field goal or try-for-point plays). The ball is put in play by a placekick or dropkick.
3. If kickoff clears the opponent's goal posts it is not a field goal.
4. A kickoff is illegal unless it travels 10 yards OR is touched by the receiving team. Once the ball is touched by the receiving team it is a free ball. Receivers may recover and advance. Kicking team may recover but NOT advance UNLESS receiver had possession and lost the ball.
5. When a kickoff goes out of bounds between the goal lines without being touched by the receiving team, the ball belongs to the receivers 30 yards from the spot of the kick or at the out-of-bounds spot unless the ball went out-of-bounds the first time an onside kick was attempted. In this case the kicking team is to be penalized five yards and the ball must be kicked again.
6. When a kickoff goes out of bounds between the goal lines and is touched last by receiving team, it is receiver's ball at out-of-bounds spot.

Free Kick

1. In addition to a kickoff, the other free kicks are a kick after a safety and a kick after a fair catch. In both cases, a dropkick, placekick, or punt may be used (a punt may not be used on a kickoff).
2. On a free kick after a fair catch, captain of receiving team has the option to put ball in play by punt, dropkick, or placekick without a tee, or by snap. If the placekick or dropkick goes between the uprights a field goal is scored.
3. On a free kick after a safety, the team scored upon puts ball in play by a punt, dropkick, or placekick without tee. No score can be made on a free kick following a safety, even if a series of penalties places team in position. (A field goal can be scored only on a play from scrimmage or a free kick after a fair catch.)

Field Goal

1. All field goals attempted and missed from scrimmage line beyond the 20 yard line will result in the defensive team taking possession of the ball at the scrimmage line. On any field goal attempted and missed from scrimmage line inside the 20 yard line, ball will revert to defensive team at the 20 yard line.

Safety

1. The important factor in a safety is impetus. Two points are scored for the opposing team when the ball is dead on or behind a team's own goal line if the impetus came from a player on that team.

Examples of Safety:

(a) Blocked punt goes out of kicking team's end zone. Impetus was provided by punting team. The block only changes direction of ball, not impetus.
(b) Ball carrier retreats from field of play into his own end zone and is downed. Ball carrier provides impetus.
(c) Offensive team commits a foul and spot of enforcement is behind its own goal line.
(d) Player on receiving team muffs punt and, trying to get ball, forces or illegally kicks it into end zone where he or a teammate recovers. He has given new impetus to the ball.

Examples of Non-Safety:

(a) Player intercepts a pass and his momentum carries him into his own end zone. Ball is put in play at spot of interception.
(b) Player intercepts a pass in his own end zone and is downed. Impetus came from passing team, not from defense. (Touchback)
(c) Player passes from behind his own goal line. Opponent bats down ball in end zone. (Incomplete pass)

Measuring

1. The forward point of the ball is used when measuring.

Position of Players at Snap

1. Offensive team must have at least seven players on line.
2. Offensive players, not on line, must be at least one yard back at snap. (**Exception:** player who takes snap.)
3. No interior lineman may move after taking or simulating a three-point stance.
4. No player of either team may invade neutral zone before snap.
5. No player of offensive team may charge or move, after assuming set position, in such manner as to lead defense to believe snap has started.
6. If a player changes his eligibility, the Referee must alert the defensive captain after player has reported to him.
7. All players of offensive team must be stationary at snap, except one back who may be in motion parallel to scrimmage line or backward (not forward).
8. After a shift or huddle all players on offensive team must come to an absolute stop for at least one second with no movement of hands, feet, head, or swaying of body.
9. Quarterbacks can be called for a false start penalty (five yards) if their actions are judged to be an obvious attempt to draw an opponent offside.

Use of Hands, Arms, and Body

1. No player on offense may assist a runner except by blocking for him. There shall be no interlocking interference.
2. A runner may ward off opponents with his hands and arms but no other player on offense may use hands or arms to obstruct an opponent by grasping with hands, pushing, or encircling any part of his body during a block.
3. Blocking:
   (a) During a legal block, contact can be made with the head, shoulders, hands and/or outer surface of the forearm, or any other part of the body.
   (b) Hands (open or closed) must be inside the blocker's elbows and can be thrust forward to contact an opponent as long as the contact is inside the opponent's frame. Hands cannot be thrust forward above the frame to contact an opponent on the neck, face or head. **Note:** The frame is defined as that part of the opponent's body below the neck that is presented to the blocker. Hands with extended arms can be thrust forward to contact an opponent within the opponent's frame anywhere on the field.
   (c) As the play develops, a blocker is permitted to work for and maintain position on an opponent as long as he does not push from behind or clip (outside legal clip zone). A blocker lined up more than two yards outside the tackle is subject, also, to the crackback rule and cannot move into the clip zone and push or clip from behind.
   (d) Blocker cannot use his hands or arms to push from behind, hang onto, or encircle an opponent in a manner that restricts his movement as the play develops.
   (e) By use of up and down action of the arm(s), the blocker is permitted to ward off the opponent's attempt to grasp his jersey or arms.
4. A defensive player may not tackle or hold an opponent other than a runner. Otherwise, he may use his hands, arms, or body only:
   (a) To defend or protect himself against an obstructing opponent.
   Exception: An eligible receiver is considered to be an obstructing opponent ONLY to a point five yards beyond the line of scrimmage unless the player who receives the snap clearly demonstrates no further intention to pass the ball. Within this five-yard zone, a defensive player may make contact with an eligible receiver that may be maintained as long as it is continuous and unbroken. The defensive player cannot use his hands or arms to push from behind, hang onto, or encircle an eligible receiver in a manner that restricts movement as the play develops. Beyond this five-yard limitation, a defender may use his hands or arms ONLY to defend or protect himself against impending contact caused by a receiver. In such reaction, the defender may not contact a receiver who attempts to take a path to evade him.
   (b) To push or pull opponent out of the way on line of scrimmage.
   (c) In actual attempt to get at or tackle runner.
   (d) To push or pull opponent out of the way in a legal attempt to recover a loose ball.
   (e) During a legal block on an opponent who is not an eligible pass receiver.
   (f) When legally blocking an eligible pass receiver above the waist.
   Exception: Eligible receivers lined up within two yards of the tackle, whether on or immediately behind the line, may be blocked below the waist at or behind the line of scrimmage. NO eligible receiver may be blocked below the waist after he goes beyond the line.
   Note: Once the quarterback hands off or pitches the ball to a back, or if the quarterback leaves the pocket area, the restrictions on the defensive team relative to the offensive receivers will end, provided the ball is not in the air.

5. A defensive player must not contact an opponent above the shoulders with the palm of his hand except to ward him off on the line. This exception is permitted only if it is not a repeated act against the same opponent during any one contact. In all other cases the palms may be used on head, neck, or face only to ward off or push an opponent in legal attempt to get at the ball.
6. Any offensive player who pretends to possess the ball or to whom a teammate pretends to give the ball may be tackled provided he is crossing his scrimmage line between the ends of a normal tight offensive line.
7. An offensive player who lines up more than two yards outside his own tackle or a player who, at the snap, is in a backfield position and subsequently takes a position more than two yards outside a tackle may not clip an opponent anywhere nor may he contact an opponent below the waist if the blocker is moving toward the ball and if contact is made within an area five yards on either side of the line.
8. A player of either team may block at any time provided it is not pass interference, fair catch interference, or unnecessary roughness.
9. A player may not bat or punch:
   (a) A loose ball (in field of play) toward his opponent's goal line or in any direction in either end zone.
   (b) A ball in player possession or attempt to get possession.
   Exception: A forward or backward pass may be batted, tipped, or deflected in any direction at any time by either the offense or the defense.
   Note: A pass in flight that is controlled or caught may only be thrown backward.
10. No player may deliberately kick any ball except as a punt, dropkick, or placekick.

Forward Pass

1. A forward pass may be touched or caught by any eligible receiver. All members of the defensive team are eligible. Eligible receivers on the offensive team are players on either end of line (other than center, guard, or tackle) or players at least one yard behind the line at the snap. A T-formation quarterback is not eligible to receive a forward pass during a play from scrimmage. **Exception:** T-formation quarterback becomes eligible if pass is previously touched by an eligible receiver.
2. An offensive team may make only one forward pass during each play from scrimmage (Loss of down).
3. The passer must be behind his line of scrimmage (Loss of down and five yards, enforced from the spot of pass).
4. Any eligible offensive player may catch a forward pass. If a pass is touched by one offensive player and touched or caught by a second eligible offensive player, pass completion is legal. Further, all offensive players become eligible once a pass is touched by an eligible receiver or any defensive player.
5. The rules concerning a forward pass and ineligible receivers:
   (a) If ball is touched accidentally by an ineligible receiver on or behind his line: loss of down.
   (b) If ineligible receiver is illegally downfield: loss of 10 yards.
   (c) If touched or caught (intentionally or accidentally) by ineligible receiver beyond the line: loss of 10 yards or loss of down.
6. If a forward pass is caught simultaneously by eligible players on opposing teams, possession goes to passing team.
7. Any forward pass becomes incomplete and ball is dead if:
   (a) Pass hits the ground or goes out of bounds.
   (b) Hits the goal post or the crossbar of either team.
   (c) Is caught by offensive player after touching ineligible receiver.
   (d) An illegal pass is caught by the passer.
8. A forward pass is complete when a receiver clearly touches the ground with both feet inbounds while in possession of the ball. If a receiver would have landed inbounds with both feet but is carried or pushed out of bounds while maintaining possession of the ball, pass is complete at the out-of-bounds spot.
9. If an eligible receiver goes out of bounds accidentally or is forced out by a defender and returns to catch a pass, the play is regarded as a pass caught out of bounds. (Loss of down, no yardage.)
10. On a fourth down pass—when the offensive team is inside the opposition's 20 yard line—an incomplete pass results in a loss of down at the line of scrimmage.
11. If a personal foul is committed by the defense prior to the completion of a pass, the penalty is 15 yards from the spot where ball becomes dead.
12. If a personal foul is committed by the offense prior to the completion of a pass, the penalty is 15 yards from the previous line of scrimmage.

Intentional Grounding of Forward Pass

1. Intentional grounding of a forward pass is a foul: loss of down and 10 yards from previous spot if passer is in the field of play or loss of down at the spot of the foul if it occurs more than 10 yards behind the line or safety if passer is in his own end zone when ball is released.
2. It is considered intentional grounding of a forward pass when the ball strikes the ground after the passer throws, tosses, or lobs the ball to prevent a loss of yards by his team.
3. It is not intentional grounding when the defensive rushers have not put sufficient pressure on the passer to prevent him, for strategic purposes, from throwing the ball away in a natural and effective motion even though there is no apparent chance of completion.

Protection of Passer

1. By interpretation, a pass begins when the passer—with possession of ball—starts to bring his hand forward. If ball strikes ground after this action has begun, play is ruled an incomplete pass. If passer loses control of ball prior to his bringing his hand forward, play is ruled a fumble.
2. No defensive player may run into a passer of a legal forward pass after the ball has left his hand (15 yards). The Referee must determine whether opponent had a reasonable chance to stop his momentum during an attempt to block the pass or tackle the passer while he still had the ball.
3. Officials are to blow the play dead as soon as the quarterback is clearly in the grasp of any tackler.

Pass Interference

1. There shall be no interference with a forward pass thrown from behind the line. The restriction for the passing team starts with the snap. The restriction on the defensive team starts when the ball leaves the passer's hand. Both restrictions end when the ball is touched by anyone.
2. The penalty for defensive pass interference is an automatic first down at the spot of the foul. If interference is in the end zone, it is first down for the offense on the defense's 1 yard line. If previous spot was inside the defense's 2 yard line, penalty is half the distance to the goal line.
3. The penalty for offensive pass interference is 10 yards from the previous spot.
4. It is pass interference by either team when any player movement beyond the offensive line significantly hinders the progress of an eligible player or such player's opportunity to catch the ball during a legal forward pass. When players are competing for position to make a play on the ball, any contact by hands, arms or body shall be considered incidental unless prohibited. Prohibited conduct shall be when a player physically restricts or impedes the opponent in such a manner that is visually evident and materially affects the opponent's opportunity to gain position or retain his position to catch the ball. If a player has gained position, he shall not be considered to have impeded or restricted his opponent in a prohibited manner if all of his actions are a bona fide effort to go to and catch the ball. Provided an eligible player is not interfered with in such a manner, the following exceptions to pass interference will prevail:
   (a) If neither player is looking for the ball and there is incidental contact in the act of moving to the ball that does not materially affect the route of an eligible player, there is no interference. If there is any question whether the incidental contact materially affects the route, the ruling shall be no interference.
   Note: Inadvertent tripping is not a foul in this situation.
   (b) Any eligible player looking for and intent on playing the ball who initiates contact, however severe, while attempting to move to the spot of completion or interception will not be called for interference.
   (c) Any eligible player who makes contact, however severe, with one or more eligible players while looking for and making a genuine attempt to catch or bat a reachable ball, will not be called for interference.
   (d) It must be remembered that defensive players have as much right to the ball as offensive eligible receivers.
   (e) Pass interference by the defense is not to be called when the forward pass is clearly uncatchable.
   (f) Note: There is no defensive pass interference behind the line.

Backward Pass

1. Any pass not forward is regarded as a backward pass or lateral. A pass parallel to the line is a backward pass. A runner may pass backward at any time. Any player on either team may catch the pass or recover the ball after it touches the ground.
2. A backward pass that strikes the ground can be recovered and advanced by offensive team.
3. A backward pass that strikes the ground can be recovered but cannot be advanced by the defensive team.
4. A backward pass caught in the air can be advanced by the defensive team.

Fumble

1. The distinction between a fumble and a muff should be kept in mind in considering rules about fumbles. A fumble is the loss of possession of the ball. A muff is the touching of a loose ball by a player in an unsuccessful attempt to obtain possession.
2. A fumble may be advanced by any player on either team regardless of whether recovered before or after ball hits the ground.
3. A fumble that goes forward and out of bounds will return to the fumbling team at the spot of the fumble unless the ball goes out of bounds in the opponent's end zone. In this case, the defensive team is to take possession at the spot of the fumble.
4. If an offensive player fumbles anywhere on the field during a fourth down play, or if a player fumbles on any down after the two-minute warning in a half, only the fumbling player is permitted to recover and/or advance the ball. If recovered by any other offensive player, the ball is dead at the spot of the fumble unless it is recovered behind the spot of the fumble. In that case, ball is dead at spot of recovery. Any defensive player may recover and/or advance any fumble.
   Exception: The fourth-down fumble rule does not apply if a player touches, but does not possess, a direct snap from center, i.e., a snap in flight as opposed to a hand-to-hand exchange.

Kicks From Scrimmage

1. Any punt or missed field goal that touches a goal post is dead.
2. During a kick from scrimmage, only the end men, as eligible receivers on the line of scrimmage at the time of the snap, are permitted to go beyond the line before the ball is kicked.
   Exception: An eligible receiver who, at the snap, is aligned or in motion behind the line and more than one yard outside the end man on his side of the line, clearly making him the outside receiver, REPLACES that end man as the player eligible to go downfield after the snap. All other members of the kicking team must remain at the line of scrimmage until the ball has been kicked.

3. Any punt that is blocked and does not cross the line of scrimmage can be recovered and advanced by either team. However, if offensive team recovers it must make the yardage necessary for its first down to retain possession if punt was on fourth down.
4. The kicking team may never advance its own kick even though legal recovery is made beyond the line of scrimmage. Possession only.
5. A member of the receiving team may not run into or rough a kicker who kicks from behind his line unless contact is:
   (a) Incidental to and after he had touched ball in flight.
   (b) Caused by kicker's own motions.
   (c) Occurs during a quick kick, or a kick made after a run, or after kicker recovers a loose ball. Ball is loose when kicker muffs snap or snap hits ground.
   (d) Defender is blocked into kicker.
   The penalty for running into the kicker is 5 yards. For roughing the kicker: 15 yards, an automatic first down and disqualification if flagrant.
6. If a member of the kicking team attempting to down the ball on or inside opponent's 5 yard line carries the ball into the end zone, it is a touchback.
7. Fouls during a punt are enforced from the previous spot (line of scrimmage). **Exception:** Illegal touching, illegal fair catch, invalid fair catch signal, and fouls by the receiving team during loose ball after ball is kicked.
8. While the ball is in the air or rolling on the ground following a punt or field goal attempt and receiving team commits a foul before gaining possession, receiving team will retain possession and will be penalized for its foul.
9. It will be illegal for a defensive player to jump or stand on any player, or be picked up by a teammate or to use a hand or hands on a teammate to gain additional height in an attempt to block a kick (Penalty 15 yards, unsportsmanlike conduct).
10. A punted ball remains a kicked ball until it is declared dead or in possession of either team.
11. Any member of the punting team may down the ball anywhere in the field of play. However, it is illegal touching (Official's time out and receiver's ball at spot of illegal touching). This foul does not offset any foul by receivers during the down.
12. Defensive team may advance all kicks from scrimmage (including unsuccessful field goal) whether or not ball crosses defensive team's goal line. Rules pertaining to kicks from scrimmage apply until defensive team gains possession.

Fair Catch

1. The member of the receiving team must raise one arm a full length above his head and wave it from side to side while kick is in flight. (Failure to give proper sign: receivers' ball five yards behind spot of signal.) **Note:** It is legal for the receiver to shield his eyes from the sun by raising one hand no higher than the helmet.
2. No opponent may interfere with the fair catcher, the ball, or his path to the ball. Penalty: 15 yards from spot of foul and fair catch is awarded.
3. A player who signals for a fair catch is not required to catch the ball. However, if a player signals for a fair catch, he may not block or initiate contact with any player on the kicking team until the ball touches a player. Penalty: snap 15 yards behind spot of foul.
4. If ball hits ground or is touched by member of kicking team in flight, fair catch signal is off and all rules for a kicked ball apply.
5. Any undue advance by a fair catch receiver is delay of game. No specific distance is specified for "undue advance" as ball is dead at spot of catch. If player comes to a reasonable stop, no penalty. For violation, five yards.
6. If time expires while ball is in play and a fair catch is awarded, receiving team may choose to extend the period with one free kick down. However, placekicker may not use tee.

Foul on Last Play of Half or Game

1. On a foul by defense on last play of half or game, the down is replayed if penalty is accepted.
2. On a foul by the offense on last play of half or game, the down is not replayed and the play in which the foul is committed is nullified.
   Exception: Fair catch interference, foul following change of possession, illegal touching. No score by offense counts.
3. On double foul on last play of half or game, down is replayed.

Spot of Enforcement of Foul

1. There are four basic spots at which a penalty for a foul is enforced:
   (a) Spot of foul: The spot where the foul is committed.
   (b) Previous spot: The spot where the ball was put in play.
   (c) Spot of snap, pass, fumble, return kick, or free kick: The spot where the act connected with the foul occurred.
   (d) Succeeding spot: The spot where the ball next would be put in play if no distance penalty were to be enforced.
   Exception: If foul occurs after a touchdown and before the whistle for a try-for-point, succeeding spot is spot of next kickoff.
2. All fouls committed by offensive team behind the line of scrimmage and in the field of play shall be penalized from the previous spot.
3. When spot of enforcement for fouls involving defensive holding or illegal use of hands by the defense is behind the line of scrimmage, any penalty yardage to be assessed on that play shall be measured from the line if the foul occurred beyond the line.

Double Foul

1. If there is a double foul during a down in which there is a change of possession, the team last gaining possession may keep the ball unless its foul was committed prior to the change of possession.
2. If double foul occurs after a change of possession, the defensive team retains the ball at the spot of its foul or dead ball spot.
3. If one of the fouls of a double foul involves disqualification, that player must be removed, but no penalty yardage is to be assessed.
4. If the kickers foul during a punt before possession changes and the receivers foul after possession changes, penalties will be offset and the down is replayed.

Penalty Enforced on Following Kickoff

1. When a team scores by touchdown, field goal, extra point, or safety and either team commits a personal foul, unsportsmanlike conduct, or obvious unfair act during the down, the penalty will be assessed on the following kickoff.

NOTES

NOTES